AFRICA

The Traveler's Africa

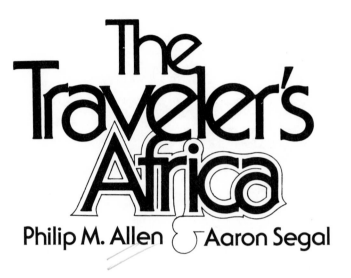

The Traveler's Africa

Philip M. Allen & Aaron Segal

A GUIDE TO THE ENTIRE CONTINENT

HOPKINSON AND BLAKE, PUBLISHERS • NEW YORK

DT
2
A45

64056

To Barbara, Catherine, Jamey, Marcus and Shelby
and all other Africa travelers

Africke hath ewer beene the least knowen and haunted parte in the world, chiefly by reason of the situation thereof under the torride Zone; which the ancients thought to be unhabitable. Whose opinion, although in verie deede it is not true, bicause we knowe that betweene the two Tropickes there are most fruitefull countries.

John Pory, 1600

Foreword

This is a travel book for every kind of traveler—the rich, the budget-conscious and the backpacker; the tour-buyer and the adventurer; the scholar, the sportsman, the curious, and the seeker of beauty and truth. It is a big book, for this reason, and it is not likely to be read through from first page to last, nor is it meant to be. The casual traveler can skim its contents and still get more advice about transportation, hotels, restaurants and places to visit than is available in any other source. The serious traveler—the one who is truly interested in Africa and its people—will find, if he digs in, a depth of background information and insights uncommon in guide books.

This is the first comprehensive guide to the entire African continent, and it is written with an authority and a candor that bespeak the special qualifications of its authors.

Philip Allen and Aaron Segal know Africa from having lived and worked there. They are Africa professionals—part of that circle of writers, social scientists and technicians who have made this continent the focus of their careers.

It took Allen and Segal 18 months to sift and organize the material for this book and to write it, but the intelligence that went into it—the thousands upon thousands of details and observations—was drawn from years of a close (and affectionate) relationship with Africa.

Philip Allen first came to Africa in 1962 when he was appointed American consul in Madagascar (with wide responsibilities around the Indian Ocean). Some special things happened in Madagascar: his son was born there, he learned the difficult Malagasy language (the beginning of an acquaintanceship with many African cultures), and he fell in love with Africa. He and his family later moved to Lagos, in Nigeria, and then to Abidjan, in the Ivory Coast. In Lagos he began a long association with the African-American Institute as director of its technical training and education programs, a job that kept him traveling almost constantly among 24 countries. He came to know intimately every airport, market-place and hotel bar on half the continent. Even on his occasional holidays he traveled, taking off on jaunts around the continent with his wife and children to see a festival he hadn't seen or simply to get to know still another place and another people. (Out of this has come a considerable amount of sensitive writing on African society and culture and materials for the Third World courses he now teaches in Vermont.)

Aaron Segal succumbed to the lure of Africa when he was a 19-year-old student and he has returned many times for long periods, much of the time working as a correspondent for American, English and African publications. As a journalist, Segal has been better known in Africa for his persistence than his tact. A large, shaggy man with extraordinary vitality, he became a familiar figure in the volatile 1960's when he went careering through the continent from one trouble spot to the next, reporting his findings with hard-edged language that endeared him not at all to some nervous governments. Such was his reputation in these years that during the 1964 upheaval in Rwanda a hapless British correspondent was detained at a military roadblock because the lock on his valise bore the name "Segal." Readers of The Traveler's Africa will encounter Segal's crisp impressions in all his chapters. Sample: "Don't get sick in Burundi. Medical facilities in the capital are poor and elsewhere in the country they are awful or non-existent."

Despite some differences in the personalities of the authors (the analytic reader will detect them), the collaboration on this book went smoothly. Having known each other as professional Africa-watchers, Allen and Segal came to the project with mutual respect. On the basic premise of the book there was instant agreement: this would not be a compendium of tourist office euphemisms but an honest picture of Africa, warthogs and all. It would curry no one's favor, no handouts would be sought or accepted, and indeed if the sensitivities of governments and travel operators had to be pinched, so be it.

Above all, appraisals of places and conditions were to be made on the basis of personal experience. And recognizing that even two such seasoned travelers as they could not meet this standard for a continent so vast, they went to work organizing a network of correspondents and checkers they could trust. Allen made a final three-month swing around the continent and returned with a carton of notes to his farm in Vermont. Segal took another look at 18 countries before settling in at Cornell (where he has a visiting professorship) to write.

Soon the wires between Danby and Ithaca warmed up with almost daily phone conferences. All copy written by one was verified by the other, and often by a third person who had special knowledge of a particular country. When disputes couldn't be settled on the phone, the authors met in New York. After a year and a half of writing, checking and rewriting, the job was done.

Done, that is, to the limits imposed by the vicissitudes of life, normal and otherwise. Considering the sheer volume of facts and figures packed into these pages and the length of time required to transform a manuscript into the book you hold in your hand, it must be understood that total accuracy is impossible. Even as you read this a president may topple, a new bridge may go up, a poor restaurant may undergo a salutary change of ownership and menu, a clean hotel may go to seed, and a seedy hotel may burn to the ground. We invite travelers to inform us of changes and to tell us of their own experiences to help us in updating the next edition.

Len Karlin, President
Hopkinson and Blake

The Authors

Philip M. Allen

Dr. Allen began his deep involvement with Africa in 1962 when he was transferred from the American Embassy in Bonn to a new post as American consul in Tananarive, Madagascar. In 1966 he left the Foreign Service to join the African-American Institute as administrator of its educational programs in 24 countries in West, North and Central Africa. Two years later he became the Institute's director of training and research at its headquarters in New York.

Dr. Allen now lives on a farm in Danby, Vermont, with his wife and two children. In addition to tending his goats, he teaches African civilization on several campuses in the state, is a consultant on Africa for several organizations, and writes on African affairs for many publications in this country and abroad. His published works include a Carnegie Endowment monograph on "Self-Determination in the Western Indian Ocean." Now he intends to buckle down to a novel dealing with Africa.

Dr. Allen is 41 years old and a native of Philadelphia. He was graduated from Swarthmore College summa cum laude and received his doctorate in the liberal arts from Emory University.

Aaron Segal

Dr. Segal first went to Africa as part of a student exchange program in 1957, when he was 19. He returned often while completing his education and later covered the continent as a correspondent for the London *Spectator* and the *Kenya Weekly News*. In 1971 he became editor of the magazine *Africa Report*.

Currently a visiting associate professor of government at Cornell, he has also taught at the University of California at Berkeley, the University of East Africa and the University of Puerto Rico and was a Fulbright lecturer in Argentina. He is the author of two books on the Caribbean and has written many articles—mainly on Africa—for such publications as the *Atlantic Monthly, Economist, Nation, New Republic* and *New Statesman*.

Dr. Segal, now 35, was born and raised in California. After graduating from Occidental College, he was awarded a Rhodes Scholarship to Oxford, where he received the B. Phil. degree. He later earned the Ph.D. in political science at Berkeley. He is married and has a son.

Contributors

Andrew Gilboy (Backpacking). Mr. Gilboy spent four years in Africa as a teacher of English in Senegal and has traveled through 22 countries.

Kristin W. Henry (Egypt). Mrs. Henry has been living in Egypt for five years. She has taught at the American University in Cairo and is now working on translations of modern Arabic literature.

Louise E. Jefferson (maps). Artist, writer and photographer, Miss Jefferson has traversed Africa in five lengthy trips. She is a member of the executive committee of the Women's Africa Committee.

David Laitin (Somalia). Mr. Laitin taught in Somalia as a Peace Corps Volunteer and is now studying for a doctorate in political science at the University of California at Berkeley.

Lynn K. Mytelka (Congo-Brazzaville). Dr. Mytelka, who did research in Central Africa in connection with her work for a doctorate in political science at Johns Hopkins, now is a member of the faculty of Carleton University in Ottawa.

Ivar Nelson (Botswana, Lesotho, Swaziland). Mr. Nelson spent two years in Kenya as a Peace Corps Volunteer and two years in Swaziland in the diplomatic service.

Bette Saunders (Africa by Air). Miss Saunders is an airlines executive and a frequent traveler to Africa.

Morgan Towne (Ethiopia). Miss Towne is a free-lance writer who has lived in Ethiopia and Kenya for the past four years.

Important: Changing Costs

Two devaluations of the US dollar and a world in which currency exchange rates go up and down like yo-yos complicate life for travelers. Prices for hotel rooms, restaurants, car rentals and other travel facilities are also going up and down, sometimes at a daily or weekly pace. This means that the prices quoted in this book, and in any other travel book for that matter, are not necessarily current.

Yet travel in Africa remains, devaluations and all, generally less expensive than elsewhere—once you get there, that is. Labor costs, for instance, are still very low—keeping down the cost of services. In addition, many African currencies are directly or indirectly tied to the US dollar and were devalued accordingly. Thus the purchasing power of the US dollar in East Africa and some other countries is at least what it was before devaluation. The major exceptions are those countries where currencies are tied to the French franc and the dollar now buys less. Some African countries have currencies that are tied to little or nothing. Here US dollars, or any other convertible currency, are highly prized and can go a very long way.

Africans, like the rest of us, are living with inflation. It is safe to expect continuing price increases across the board. Most prices in this book prevailed in 1972-1973. These prices and exchange rates precede the 1973 US devaluation. You can assume that because of devaluation and inflation prices have risen by at least 5 or 10 per cent.

Another caveat: Nomenclature, while not as mercurial as prices, also is subject to change. A number of independent African countries are in the process of substituting African or Africanized names for European designations.

Contents

North Africa

Northeast Africa

East Africa

Central Africa

West Africa

Southern Africa

Indian Ocean

Authors of country chapters—*By Philip M. Allen:* Angola, Canary Islands, Central African Republic, Chad, Comoro Islands, Dahomey, Gabon, the Gambia, Ghana, Guinea, Ivory Coast, Liberia, Madagascar, Mali, Mauritania, Mauritius, Namibia, Niger, Nigeria, Reunion, Sao Tomé and Principe, Senegal, Seychelles, Sierra Leone, South Africa, Togo, Upper Volta, Zaïre. *By Aaron Segal:* Algeria, Burundi, Cameroon, Cape Verde Islands, Ceuta and Melilla, Equatorial Guinea, Kenya, Libya, Malawi, Morocco, Mozambique, Portuguese Guinea, Rhodesia, Rwanda, Spanish Sahara, Sudan, Tanzania, Territory of the Afars and Issas, Tunisia, Uganda, Zambia, Zanzibar. *By Kristin W. Henry:* Egypt. *By David Laitin:* Somalia. *By Lynn K. Mytelka* (with Aaron Segal): the Congo. *By Ivar Nelson:* Botswana, Lesotho, Swaziland. *By Morgan Towne:* Ethiopia.

Maps *(by Louise E. Jefferson)*—Continent: end leafs. Regions: North, 72; Northeast, 154; East, 240; Central, 348; West, 446; Southern, 684; Indian Ocean, 832. Countries: Algeria, 76; Angola, 688; Botswana, 700; Burundi, 243; Cameroon, 352; Central African Republic, 367; Chad, 378; Congo, 393; Dahomey, 456; Egypt, 158; Equatorial Guinea, 401; Ethiopia, 181; Gabon, 406; the Gambia, 470; Ghana, 484; Guinea, 502; Ivory Coast, 516; Kenya, 252; Lesotho, 712; Liberia, 540; Libya, 201; Madagascar, 846; Malawi, 720; Mali, 552; Mauritania, 566; Mauritius, 870; Morocco, 107; Mozambique, 733; Namibia, 748; Niger, 578; Nigeria, 594; Portuguese Guinea, 622; Rhodesia, 760; Rwanda, 282; Senegal, 630; Sierra Leone, 650; Somalia, 211; South Africa, 778; Spanish Sahara, 126; Sudan, 221; Swaziland, 806; Tanzania, 292; Territory of the Afars and Issas, 232; Togo, 662; Tunisia, 132; Uganda, 317; Upper Volta, 672; Zaïre, 425; Zambia, 818.

Introduction

A dozen big reasons and a hundred others bring travelers to Africa. They come to explore new worlds and to understand the old, to enjoy sun and open skies, to mix with people of color and movement, to do business, and to watch some of the earth's last remaining herds of free animals in majestic physical settings. Above all, they come for discovery—of something quiet and grand in a ravaged past, something hopeful in a clouded and difficult future.

Man and his society began in Africa, and great civilizations lie buried in its earth. After centuries of exploitation, Africans are coming into control of their own destinies, and their long-scorned history is now being told. Modern nations superimposed haphazardly across the frontiers of the resurrected old kingdoms claim their right to transform heritage and technology, dream and reality, into new societies.

Never so sinister as we'd painted it, Africa has been less a dark than a lost continent—lost to us and lost for a time to its own heirs. Approached with a will to discovery, the continent that is one-sixth of the earth's surface is sufficiently exciting and comfortable to satisfy almost anyone's expectations of adventure, holiday, study or residence.

People go to Africa just to see things: the pyramids of the Nile and the monuments of Timbuktu and Zimbabwe; the magnificence of Victoria Falls, the Great Rift Valley, the Congo forest and the Mountains of the Moon; evolution's traces at Olduvai Gorge and history's degradation in the Gold Coast slave castles; the realms of animals and the vitality of people living on their changing, tormented and still-beloved earth. They also come to swim, fish, climb mountains, play or watch games, to gamble in elegance, shop in abundance, dance the long night through, live in luxury and hunt with some certainty of a kill. Others come in search of economic triumphs and ideological eldorados, of cultural renaissance and "tribal" or pre-industrial innocence.

1

An incomparable diversity inhabits Africa's towns, forests and grass-lands, its rapidly changing economies and durable cultures. The con-tinent grows some of the world's biggest people and some of the smallest, packs them into ineffably dynamic cities and spreads them over unfath-omably lonely countryside; it promotes the natural interdependence of the rhino and tick-bird, the young and the aged; it displays mighty rivers that dwindle to sand in times of drought and lowly peanuts that pyramid into mountains after harvests. Its dancers cleave to the pulsing earth, while bards soar to the heavens in praise-songs and epic poetry.

Less than a tenth of Africa is rain forest dense enough to be called "jungle," and less than a fifth is occupied by the Sahara, Kalahari and Namib deserts. Most of the remaining land stretches from temperate coastal and mountain ranges in the north and south over a vast central plateau covered with woods and grasslands. Toward the eastern rim of this plateau, mountains overshadow splendid valleys and lakes. To the west and south, the land undulates between great river basins—the Congo-Zaïre, the Zambezi and the Niger—dropping off sharply into green coastal forests and the sea. Much of this continent enjoys constant sum-mertime, but its rains are irregular and humidity assaults the coasts. Breezes are all the more welcome, air-conditioning a pervasive luxury, but as you go inland the world dries off.

Africa's politics seldom get in the traveler's way. Forty of the 57 territo-ries discussed in this book are independent African states, all but Ethiopia and Liberia the recent products of the "winds of change." White minor-ities rule in Rhodesia and South Africa, Portugal in its vestigial empire, and France, England and Spain in small enclaves and islands. Exploita-tion clashes with the right of self-determination in these minority-gov-erned places. Everywhere the urge to prosperity encounters poverty, hunger and disease. Yet there is little of the depressing squalor or hope-lessness that elsewhere impose on the sensibilities. Most of newly inde-pendent Africa invites visitors to share its experiences of trading and building, its passionate memories and its natural heritage, its originality in communal life, and its polyrhythmic powers of expression.

The power, the joy and the great music of Africa beat unevenly across a vast human landscape on a huge and ungainly continent. They coexist with elements of poverty, corruption, unmerited privilege, ugly racism in the south, and social fragility everywhere. If you demand unadulterated comfort, fail-safe sightseeing, unambiguous nation-building, bucolic pu-rity, happy peasants, Zen yens, drug scenes or scrupulous officials, you'll be better off touring other, more beaten, tracks. But if you can be patient with diversity, tolerant of a capricious travel industry, ready for perpetual change, you can regain much in Africa that was lost, and discover much that is new. Here 300 million people confute the generations of myth that presumed them to be inferior, incompetent, primitive. You meet them, not as new myths, but as realities, admirably creative, tragically destructive, hospitable and bitter, beautiful and not beautiful, immensely human.

Nobody need feel mentally, physically or racially blocked from Africa. Whether you are black or white, wealthy or ragged, young or old, Africa knows how to treat you with respect. Children enjoy the life it brings them, young people grasp its vitality; adults appreciate its concentration on the values of survival under duress, and the elderly its habit of honoring those who have done their work and are ready for ancestorhood.

You can either plot your Africa trajectory to catch the things that interest you most, or pass in pilgrimage through a kaleidescope of sensation. Approached with goodwill, gusto and grace, the traveler's Africa offers a super-abundance of experiences, especially the joy of discovery.

PMA

Planning the Trip

Accent on Time

With money, energy and good planning, a traveler can do almost everything he likes in Africa, except see it all—not in one lifetime. An Africa trip inevitably covers great distances and devours masses of time. Of course some visitors have special preoccupations which can take them anywhere for a few days—a business deal in Nigeria or Zaïre, a philatelic convention in Ethiopia, a festival in Ghana or independence day in Swaziland, a hit-and-run shopper's jaunt across the Mediterranean or a winter world cruise when sun and sea outrank the appeal of any continent.

But if you are going to Africa for the first time and want to enjoy the experience, allow as many weeks as you can afford, choose an itinerary with sufficient flexibility for detours and digressions, and pay healthy respect to the breadth of the Atlantic Ocean, the distances across the African landscape and the wearying succession of time zones between continents. Or choose a tour with balanced emphases on the places that interest you most. Be reconciled to missing some things, for you get far more out of a realistically selective African trip than any butterfly sequence of one-night stands across the continent.

Given no more than a week, you can fly economically and pleasurably for a holiday in Morocco, Tunisia, Egypt or the Canary Islands. That's about all you can do unless you're on a larger European swing with the chance for a week's side trip into the Mediterranean margins of North Africa. If you leave from North America, two weeks is a minimum for concentration on one or two favored countries south of the Sahara—Ethiopia, Kenya, Tanzania, South Africa, Ghana, Senegal, Ivory Coast or Mauritius, for instance.

Visiting several countries within a geographical region requires a solid three-week period. The more likely combinations include Egypt and Ethiopia in Northeast Africa; Morocco and Tunisia in North Africa; Ghana, Togo and the Ivory Coast in West Africa; Kenya, Tanzania and

4

Zanzibar in East Africa; Botswana and South Africa in the Southern region; Cameroon and Zaïre in the center; Madagascar and Mauritius in the Indian Ocean. A month will permit the thorough exploration of a region or two contiguous regions, but count on spending a full day in transit between them.

Taking a month or more, you can travel comfortably in a couple of regions, combining, for example, the abundance of East or Southern African wildlife with the peaks of historical and cultural interest in West, North or Northeast Africa. If you have more than two months, you can begin thinking of a full swing around the continent, or a deeper penetration of place, using a steady base of operations.

If you have less than a month, your time is more efficiently spent with a few compromises. You can settle for less exciting game parks in Central or West Africa, for instance, in deference to the pre-eminently human and social appeal of those regions; or, accept a weaker cultural impression and inferior cuisine in favor of East Africa's natural grandeur. North, Southern and East Africa excel in accommodations, climate and facility in English, while the Indian Ocean places offer unique blends of Asian, African and European assets. The Sudanic interior (Mauritania, Mali, Upper Volta, Niger, Chad, the Sudan) redeems its absence of comfort and travel facility by the thrill of discovery in old yet unfamiliar lands.

When to Travel

Go to Africa at any time you please and don't let the climate figure seriously in your plans. Our summer period from June to September finds much of Africa enjoying gentle, semi-tropical weather, comparable to springtime in California or Florida. There are exceptions: the Sahara Desert is unbearably hot at that season and some of West Africa doesn't cool off until a little later in the year. From November to March, Southern African and Indian Ocean shores are at their sunniest and the Sahara is tolerable; but North African coasts become wet and chilly, West and Central Africa grow increasingly arid.

Scheduled events in Africa should exert little influence on the timing of your trip. There's almost always something going on somewhere in the continent, and you can seldom plot a trajectory to strike any distant rendezvous on an African calendar with any guarantee of success. Unless you have overriding interest in specific ceremonies, high seasons for hunting and fishing, or low tide in tourist traffic, you are better off choosing the places or experiences that appeal most strongly to you, verifying in appropriate country chapters their accessibility during your chosen season for travel.

Where to Go

How does one begin to choose among 57 territories, millions of square miles and more than 300 million people? You might start with comparative ratings of major travel qualities in the seven geographic regions of Africa—like those in the following chart, which summarizes the authors' personal evaluations. For a fuller explanation of regional and national attractions, consult the introductions to each region and the country chapters that succeed them.

Regional Attractions	North	North-east	East	Central	West	South	Indian Ocean
Historical Interest	4	5	3	2	4	3	3
Political-Economic Interest	2	2	3	3	4	4	2
Traditional Arts	4	4	2	3	5	2	3
Entertainment and Nightlife	2	2	2	3	4	2	1
Religious and Ceremonial Interest	4	4	2	4	5	2	3
Wildlife, Hunting, Scenery	3	2	5	3	2	4	3
Climate, Beaches, Water Sports	4	1	4	2	2	4	5
Shopping	5	4	3	2	4	2	3
Tourist Facilities	4	2	4	2	3	4	3
Accessibility	4	2	3	1	3	3	1

Scale: 1—poor 2—fair 3—good 4—excellent 5—superb

Who's Going Where

Travel from Europe and America to Africa has been expanding by 15 to 20 per cent annually for the past decade. American travelers manifest large-scale preferences for Kenya, Morocco, Ethiopia, South Africa, Ghana, Tanzania, Egypt, the Canary Islands and Liberia. You are likely to find a few Americans wherever you go, except in Congo-Brazzaville and Equatorial Guinea, where they are unwanted, and Burundi and Uganda where, at this writing, no foreign visitors are welcome.

British tourists appear to favor Egypt, South Africa, Rhodesia, Kenya, Tanzania and, in increasing numbers, the Seychelles and Mauritius, as well as their long-familiar haunts in the Canaries. The French have a penchant for Morocco, Algeria, Tunisia, the Ivory Coast, Senegal, Madagascar and the Comoro Islands. Substantial numbers of Germans, Italians and Swiss have discovered the attractions of the Kenyan and Tanzanian coasts, as well as East Africa's interior wildlife. The Scandanavians also go to East Africa, the Canary Islands, Morocco, Tunisia and Egypt, and their own West African "find," the Gambia.

November through February are the high seasons for European travelers to East and Southern Africa, June to September for Americans. North and Northeast Africa have two seasons for Europeans and Americans: June to September along the warm coasts, and November to March when the interior enjoys temperate spring weather. West Africa has also developed a two-season travel year; you will need to book popular spots well in advance during the summer and winter. The Indian Ocean region—an established favorite for cruise ships—is attracting a growing clientele on air package tours from Western Europe. Central Africa mainly draws visitors on business or study tours.

How to Travel: Tours

Organized tours booked in the United States or Europe can save time, money and worry, especially on a first visit. But if you pick the wrong tour it can be an ordeal. Standard formulas emphasize wildlife, birdlife, beach life, night life, university life, and so on. The appendix identifies North American travel agencies specializing in Africa, major airlines and shipping companies that serve Africa, and educational and adventure travel groups.

Before paying your deposit, inquire about the size of the contemplated tour group, the ages, sex, occupations, nationalities and languages of your fellow travelers, and the qualifications of the guides. Moving large distances around Africa in a cluster of more than 20 people is usually asking for trouble. Morocco, Tunisia, the Canaries and the countries of East and Southern Africa are accustomed to handling large groups, but this is not the case in West, Central and Northeast Africa or the Indian Ocean, where special arrangements must be made to assure adequate accommodations, transportation and other services. In any case, there should be at least one staff person for every 10 group members.

When selecting a tour, try to determine how much time you will have on your own. Some tours permit only the briefest visits to museums, parks, markets and villages; the rest of the day is consumed in transit. Ship "turn-around" and port clearances consume from two to four hours of any cruise visit—more in Nigeria, South Africa, Morocco and Tanzania. Airport-to-town transfers take at least an hour each way.

Make sure you are getting what you pay for when you choose a tour. Do the contracted tour prices include breakfast, lunches on all-day excursions, porterage of luggage, air-conditioning, laundry and tips? Do they give you a choice between single and double rooms? Do you stay in acceptable hotels?

On Your Own, On the Spot

Taking Africa on your own invites risks along with rewards. You can encounter mishaps over hotel reservations, planes and trains that don't run on time, guides who don't guide, or buses and taxis that break down. You will have to deal with these problems yourself, perhaps in a language other than English. But this is the way to meet Africans, guarantee excitement and perhaps save money in the bargain.

Some travelers prefer to make their own arrangements for transportation to and from Africa, booking or improvising local tours on arrival. You can economize by using the charters or non-scheduled flights discussed in the section "Africa by Air." Attractive and reasonably-priced tours—arranged by local travel agencies or government bureaus—are available in Kenya, Tanzania, Zanzibar, South Africa, Mozambique, Morocco, Tunisia, the Canary Islands, Ethiopia, the Gambia, Senegal, the Ivory Coast and a few other countries. The names and addresses of these agencies are given in the country chapters.

You can also improvise a tour group—with the help of hotel personnel or a local travel agency (or friendships made in a bar)—whenever you need companions to fill a game park minibus, arrange an audience with some local dignitary or visit a museum outside regular business hours. Such groups also can share the cost for certain festivals or special performances by local troupes.

A convenient combination of group package tour and free-lance travel is the tailored itinerary known in the travel industry as F.I.T. (Foreign Inclusive Tour). Most of the travel agents listed in the appendix can arrange F.I.T.'s to suit individual preferences. Where schedules are tight, flights rarely available, and good hotels scarce, it makes sense to book in advance through an agent with reliable local correspondents or affiliates. Indeed, whether on a tour or alone, reserve all the big places well in advance and try to get written confirmations.

Preparing To Go

Visitors to most of Africa need weeks of planning, visa-hunting and vaccinations. Tropical climates and imperfect sanitation impose certain precautionary health measures, discussed in Section B of this chapter; suggestions for further acquisition of information about Africa appear in Section C, and tips on what to pack in Section D. The chapter concludes with a checklist for documents, medical kits and baggage.

But first, your portfolio of formalities—or what's needed to keep on the sunny side of bureaucracy.

A / GETTING YOURSELF IN ORDER

Africa's immigration, customs and public health officials tend to take a solemn view of international formality, although they probably waive more formalities than their counterparts in the United States. Countries vary widely in this respect, and the human temper, even on official business, fluctuates beyond predictability. Hence, it's best to expect pettiness from bureaucracy, and to keep yourself "in order."

Passports

A valid passport and an International Certificate of Vaccination are the two documents without which nobody lets you travel. The latter, commonly known as the "yellow health card," is easily stapled inside the back cover of your passport. A United States passport certifies your identity and citizenship, provides space for foreign visas and entry-exit stamps, officially requests decent treatment for you from authorities abroad, and implicitly guarantees to accept you back in the United States if you get into trouble elsewhere.

9

You may apply in person for a passport at (1) Department of State passport offices in Boston, Chicago, Honolulu, Los Angeles, Miami, New Orleans, New York, Philadelphia, San Francisco, Seattle and Washington, D.C.; (2) any Federal or State Court authorized by law to naturalize aliens; (3) US post offices in certain cities; and (4) US consulates (or consular sections of embassies) abroad. You must provide proof of American citizenship. Spouses and children may be included in a single passport or travel with their own, but in either case all must appear in person to file application. It's usually worth the extra expense to obtain separate passports for any family member likely to be traveling alone (or left alone while others travel) within the five-year period of the passport's validity. Passports are not renewable.

In addition to proof of citizenship, you must furnish two recent identical photographs, in color or black and white, not larger than 3″ x 3″ nor smaller than 2½″ x 2½″, full face (not profile), smiling or stern. Get at least 20 extra prints for visas and retain the negative.

Passports cost $12. Once your application is complete, you can have the passport by mail in 10 days to two weeks (four or five days if you plead urgency). A regular passport has 15 blank pages for visas and entry-exit stamps. These can get filled up rapidly en route, especially since most governments refuse to stamp their visas on a page that already has something on it, however unobtrusive. Hence, if you are traveling to 10 or more visa-issuing countries, ask at the outset for extra pages in your passport. And as you accumulate rubber-stamp mementos of your journey, get additional "accordion pleats" of pages free of charge at passport offices or at American consulates abroad.

When the new passport arrives, make a record of your passport number, date of issuance and expiration, and place of issuance. Always carry the passport on your person, not in your luggage. The signature you use on your passport will often be compared with the way you sign checks and travelers checks, visa applications and the like. It's best to keep the signature legible and invariable.

Visas

Americans must obtain visas (in effect, entry authorizations) before seeking to enter all African countries except Botswana, Central African Republic, Canary Islands, Ceuta and Melilla, Djibouti, Lesotho, Malawi, Morocco, Reunion, Rhodesia, Seychelles, Swaziland and Tunisia. Cameroon, Egypt, Ethiopia and Senegal will "sell" visas to you on arrival, and several other countries issue sufficiently liberal "transit visas" at points of entry to cover the duration of most tourist visits. (See the country chapters for discussions of African visa idiosyncrasies.) Otherwise, obtaining visas is a time-consuming, aggravating and totally anachronistic process imposed on us as a reflex action by sovereign states.

Apply for visas in person if you can spare the time. They are issued by consulates, consular sections of embassies and (in New York) missions to the UN, a few official travel offices, or consulates of other governments accredited to represent the country wherever it does not itself have diplomatic representation. The country profiles of this book provide pertinent information. Bring your passport with you; also bring your yellow vaccination certificate, several passport photographs, and cash—$2 to $5 in most cases, although some visas are issued gratis. (Burundi charges $7 and Gabon $10.) In cases where a consul must obtain home government approval for the visa, you may expedite the process by paying for an exchange of cables.

Unless you are going to reside or do business in the country, you should ask for a visitor's (tourist) visa. In the case of very brief visits, a transit visa may suffice. Some visitors' visas are valid for only short periods after issuance, or for visits of 30 days or less; be sure that yours will cover your anticipated arrival. You can usually extend the life of your visa, or transfer to a longer-term type, at the Interior Ministry once you are in the capital city.

If you expect to enter and leave a country more than once, ask for a multiple-entry visa.

Some governments (Zaïre and South Africa, for instance) require proof of financial solvency and moral rectitude before they will grant a visa, and most consulates request proof of passage out of the country. A round trip air or ocean ticket, confirmation of bookings from a tour group or travel agency, or a reference from a bank or employer usually suffices for these purposes.

If you're traveling on behalf of a company or other organization, get multiple copies of a letterhead statement identifying you as its agent, describing your itinerary, asking for "normal courtesies," and, if possible, guaranteeing your expenses. If your visa application asks for a "reference" and/or "residence" in the country of destination, write in "United States Ambassador," even if you don't happen to know his name, and either "United States Embassy" or the name of a major hotel as your address (whether you intend to stay there or not). You need not go into detail about prospective business deals or professional work.

And try on your first visit to get the visa stamped in your passport while you wait. Some politically nervous nations require authorization from their capitals. Others insist as a matter of principle or bureaucratic dignity on keeping your passport overnight, obliging you to return.

Thus, you can seldom count on getting more than one or two visas a day, even shunting by taxi between offices in Washington or jumping from office to office in New York.

If you are unable to visit consular offices, you can obtain most visas by mail. The process usually requires writing to obtain forms, returning them (by registered mail) with your passport, photographs and fees, and waiting several weeks to get the passport back. Obviously, you can do only one or two countries a month this way, at best. And you may find yourself taking time to hunt for additional visas once you have already started traveling.

Visa Procurement Services

If you travel in a tour group or book an itinerary through a travel agent, or are representing an organization or business, you might have others make the telephone calls, write the letters of introduction, fill out the forms, do the legwork and pay the visa fees for you. They will need your passport, health certificate, passport photographs and prospective itinerary. Or you can do what many travelers do—turn to professional visa procurement firms in New York or Washington. They charge a fee, of course. Since fees vary, especially for groups, you can shop among the following agencies: Travel Agenda Inc., 119 W. 57th Street, New York, N.Y. 10019 (tel. 212/265-7887); Foreign Visa Service, 475 Fifth Avenue, New York 10017 (686-0934); Visa Center Inc., 507 Fifth Avenue, New York 10017 (986-0924); Visa and Passport Service, 1010 Vermont Avenue NW, Washington, D.C. 20005 (202/783-6290).

Financial Formalities

Usually, it's best to carry your funds in a combination of media. These include: (1) Travelers checks in $10, $20 and a few $50 denominations; the smaller the better in order to make change efficiently and reduce the quantity of local currencies in your pocket. Checks from virtually all banks with international affiliations are recognized throughout Africa, but at present only Barclays Bank issues them free of charge. (2) For large sums and/or long trips, a cashier's check, letter of credit or bank draft addressed to you or to a specified bank in a country of destination. (3) Several dozen one-dollar bills to use for tips, airport and in-flight consumption, airport taxes and other minor expenses when you don't want to change a travelers check into quantities of local currency. (4) The aforementioned letter of introduction from your employer or sponsoring organization, especially if it guarantees your expenses.

(5) American Express or Diners Club credit cards, the only widely acceptable examples of their breed in Africa; you can get them with international directories listing the (usually expensive) places that honor them. An Air Travel Card (ATC), usually issued by airlines to organizations, can be used in lieu of deposits on rented vehicles.

Miscellaneous Documents

There's no end to the number of cards and letters of introduction you can carry to facilitate travel or help you out of a jam. One of the authors once got across a difficult border by flashing an expired library card. These are the more useful items to obtain in advance:

International Driving. Some governments in English-speaking countries recognize your American driver's license if it bears your photo. But for $3, and two of those ubiquitous passport photos, licensed drivers can obtain an International Driving Permit through any automobile club in the United States. The permit, valid for one year, is recognized by most African countries. It's also helpful for identification if you lose your passport. If you belong to an automobile club, take advantage of its foreign travel services, and carry your membership card with you; it not only facilitates service from "partner" clubs abroad, but also sometimes qualifies you for discounts on hotel accommodations and other arrangements. Ask for lists and addresses of associated clubs abroad. If you don't understand international road symbols, get an explanatory chart from your club.

Business Bona Fides. When traveling for business or professional reasons, it makes sense to carry abundant calling cards, letters of introduction and other tools of the trade. It's a good idea to write in advance, announcing your visit to the American ambassador in the appropriate African capital, and to the African country's ambassador in the United States, no matter how modestly you assess your own importance in the world of statesmen. If you get replies from government contacts, the exchange of correspondence might also help with visa offices, immigration police, customs officials, car rental agencies and other sometimes truculent services.

Student Identity Cards. To establish eligibility for charter flights, special rates on trains and buses and access to hostels, dormitories and other facilities, students might make the following collection: an identity card from your own college or school, preferably bearing your photo; an international student identity card obtainable from campus representatives of the National Student Association or from the Council on

International Educational Exchange, 777 United Nations Plaza, New York, N.Y. 10017 (tel. 212/661-0310); a Youth Hostel Card, available for $5 from the American Youth Hostels Association, 535 West End Avenue, New York, N.Y. 10024 (tel. 212/799-8510) and applicable at youth hostels in Egypt, Kenya, Morocco, South Africa and a few other countries. Letters of introduction from scouting organizations, or the YMCA or YWCA, Four-H clubs and other groups can be helpful.

Firearms. All countries require special licenses for the importation of guns and ammunition, and most will oblige you to purchase a hunting license as well. The consulate that issues your visa should be asked to help with such documentation before you leave on your trip.

Animals. A certificate of immunization against rabies and a veterinarian's confirmation of good health must accompany your pets. Some countries have additional requirements; ask at the consulates here.

Insurance

Check your health plan before going abroad to ensure medical coverage outside the United States. All-inclusive medical-travel-baggage insurance policies are available to cover accidents, medical expenses and losses while away from home. Or you can select specific policies on baggage, valuables and the like. Baggage insurance is useful in Africa—not because baggage handling is less efficient there or the personnel more corrupt than anywhere else, but because the enormous distances and paucity of flights reduce the chances of recovering lost items promptly, if at all.

Keeping in Touch

Leave your itinerary and a list of forwarding addresses with at least one friend at home. If you don't know where you'll be staying in Africa, give the Consular Section, US Embassy, as your mail drop in capital cities, and have your correspondents mark their envelopes "Hold for arrival on/about . . . (date)." Cables can be addressed to you c/o AMEMBASSY (name of capital city and country) or AMCONSUL (name of country and city other than capital, assuming there is a US consulate there).

B / GETTING BODY AND SOUL READY

Before you go have a thorough physical examination, preferably by a physician with some experience in tropical medicine. Your pre-trip physical should include a tuberculin skin test, chest X-ray, electrocardiogram and blood count. Take a written report of the exam with you, noting particularly any items that might assist diagnosis or treatment when abroad. After you return, have a thorough post-trip physical as soon as possible, including stool analysis for ova and parasites.

Immunizations

Shots rank with visas as the most onerous and time-consuming preparation for an African trip, but they're far more practical. Begin your series six weeks to two months before departure—longer if you react with unusual sensitivity to certain injections.

All immunizations should be noted by the physician on the International Certificate of Vaccination (yellow card) issued free by the US Public Health Service (PHS) under the approval of the UN's World Health Organization.

Blank yellow cards are available from PHS officials as well as most travel agents and many medical facilities. Staple the card to the back of your passport. The doctor signs each immunization and a PHS office or authorized institute, laboratory or hospital should stamp an endorsement on it. Make sure that the doctor writes the dates of immunization in international style: 11 March 1973, rather than 3/11/73, which could be read as November 3.

For last-minute injections, the Life Extension Institute, 11 East 44th Street, New York, N.Y. 10016 (tel. 212/687-2560) gives all the major shots except yellow fever without appointments from 9 am to 4 pm Monday through Friday at $5 per shot. It is authorized to validate smallpox vaccinations in health certificates.

The following immunizations are *generally required* for all travelers seeking to enter African countries, or to re-enter the US from Africa:

Smallpox. A vaccination at least 10 days old but no older than three years, confirmed by the physician to have "taken" (re-vaccinations are usually considered valid at the moment they are administered). The certification must indicate the manufacturer and lot number of the vaccine used.

Yellow Fever. Required for travelers to sub-Sahara Africa and most other tropical zones. Since only PHS installations can administer this perishable live vaccine, inoculations are usually given only on scheduled days and hours at specified sites. The accepted validity of a single immunization is 10 years.

Cholera. Required periodically for countries where outbreaks of the disease have occurred or are feared. Two shots are given at a week's interval, followed by single-shot boosters every six months.

The following immunizations are *strongly recommended* by medical authorities for most persons traveling to Africa:

Malaria Preventive. Usually chloroquine phosphate, needed for most areas of the continent. Pill swallowing should begin on the day of arrival and repeated every seven days on the same day of the week; it should continue for four weeks after return from a potentially malarial area.

Typhoid Fever. Two shots two weeks apart, followed by an annual booster. Paratyphoid injections are no longer advised.

Polio. Either injected (Salk) or orally taken (Sabin); if you have already taken the basic round, a booster is recommended.

Gamma Globulin. A single intra-muscular shot can be helpful in warding off infections like hepatitis; immunization is only partially effective, however, and lasts for four months only.

Tetanus and Diphtheria. Usually given in a combined inoculation.

Measles. For people who have never had the disease or developed immunity to it.

Besides immunizations, medical precautions should include a regular first aid kit (see check list) and the Red Cross first aid manual. Also recommended is the brief, non-technical *Medical Advice for the Traveler* (Popular Library, 1972, 95¢) by Dr. Kevin M. Cahill, an experienced Africa traveler. Some other considerations:

Antihistamines. Especially if you have allergies to grasses, pollens, dust or other common irritants; also helpful for relief from bites, skin rashes and other discomforts.

Paregoric (by prescription only). Probably the most effective and safest way to control diarrhea and other problems of adaptation to strange food, water, stresses of travel, changes of time and the like. Water purification tablets are useful when you are unable to boil and/or filter suspicious drinking water.

Further Suggestions for Health and Comfort. In town or bush it's a good idea to have insect repellent for the uncovered skin (remember that the more you sweat the less you repel), but repellents and insecticides are available in Africa. You won't need a snake-bite kit unless you go looking for snakes, but wear leather shoes on your strolls in rural areas. Sunglasses, suntan lotion, lip ice and salt tablets are useful items.

Your yellow immunization card and physical examination report should include an indication of your blood type and RH factor. Persons with special health problems (allergies, adverse reactions to antibiotics, diabetes, epilepsy, heart conditions and the like) may purchase a lifetime membership for $7 in the non-profit Medic Alert system, Turlock, Cal.

95380. Members can wear or carry an engraved Medic Alert emblem identifying their particular medical problem and providing the world-wide, toll-free telephone number (209/634-4917) that physicians and others may call for medical history and other emergency information. If you wear glasses, carry an extra pair safely in your baggage and bring along the prescription in case you break or lose both pairs.

C / GETTING THE SPIRIT READY

Whenever you start and whatever your tastes, you'll have no trouble keeping busy in preparation for your African experience. The following suggestions may help.

Courses. If you have enough time, you might enroll in a course on Africa at an accessible college or adult education program. There is a directory of college-level courses maintained by the Secretariat of the African Studies Association (ASA), 218 Shiffman Center, Brandeis University, Waltham, Mass. 02154.

African Students. You can profitably spend a few hours talking with African students in your vicinity. There are nearly 10,000 on American campuses. Call the Foreign Student Adviser of any college for the names of student groups, schedules of social events or individuals who might welcome an invitation.

Government Information. African government information services are sometimes very good, sometimes non-existent, usually in between those poles. Addresses of recommended information sources appear in the profiles of this book's country chapters. Our own survey while preparing this book revealed the following New York/Washington diplomatic missions or tourist offices as most helpful: Ghana, the Ivory Coast, Kenya, Lesotho, Mauritius, Morocco, Niger, Portugal, Rhodesia, Rwanda, Sierra Leone, South Africa, Spain, Swaziland, Togo, Uganda and Zambia. Most other missions responded only after repeated telephone calls and letters, and usually with inadequate information. Some government ministries replied to inquiries that their US-based representatives ignored. A few provided no response whatever: Burundi, the Central African Republic, Congo (Brazzaville), Equatorial Guinea, Republic of Guinea, Mali, Nigeria, Senegal.

Museums. Some museums and galleries in the United States have particularly interesting permanent collections of African art, and occasional temporary exhibits. (See appendix.)

Films. It's not especially useful to seek out movie or picture-book imagery of Africa—not before you go there to see things for yourself, anyway. The great Bogart movies and the French and British adventure films are primarily vehicles for the dramas of Americans and Europeans against a passive African setting. Your African setting will be more active, even if your drama proves less romantic. If, however, a good African-made feature film comes your way—anything of Ousmane Sembène's, for instance, or one of several recent Algerian productions—you will find meat for thought, interpretation and planning there.

Some documentary films on Africa are stimulating, many are informative, others are just time-consuming. In any case, they are probably better saved until your return, when local schools, clubs or other audiences may be clamoring for an illustrated program on your voyage. A catalog of documentary films on Africa can be obtained from the African Studies Center, University of Indiana, Bloomington, Ind. 47401. Some documentaries are rented through public libraries and the Visual Aids Service, University of Illinois, Champaign, Ill. 61820.

Music. You can prepare all you want for the extraordinary experience of African music without spoiling the immediacy of its impact. Folkways Records' Ethnic Library has a number of expertly recorded LP's. There are other good albums of traditional and urban African music on Columbia, EMI-Pathé, Reprise and other labels. But don't go overboard in record purchases before you travel. You'll inevitably begin to prefer some styles, instruments and musicians, whether in rural traditions or city high-life settings, and you may want to compose your own collection of recordings or direct tapings once you're there. Watch for appearances of African performers in this country.

Books. An annotated list of general books and periodicals on Africa appears in the appendix. In addition, each country chapter contains recommended reading. Most of these titles are available in paperback editions at good bookstores, or otherwise at larger public or university libraries. If you plan to travel in any of the 25 countries that use French as an official language pick up a pocket dictionary or phrase book.

Maps. The most accurate, exhaustive and compact of the available maps of Africa are published in the Michelin Tire Company's "red" series: No. 153 for North and West Africa, 154 for Northeast Africa and the Red Sea and 155 for Central, East and Southern Africa (including Madagascar). The maps contain details on distances (in kilometers and miles), road surfaces and seasonal road conditions, up-country accommodations, rainfall and temperature and other basic matters. Our appendix has tables of metric conversions for distances, temperature, weight and volume, and clothing sizes.

D / GETTING YOUR LUGGAGE READY

To stay within airline weight allowances (44 pounds in tourist and economy classes, 66 in first class) and minimize delays at customs, try traveling with just two bags: one large suitcase and one sizable, tough overnight case or airline flight bag that will fit underneath the airplane seat in front of you. The smaller bag should be suitable for jaunts to the beach or hotel swimming pool, or for overnight excursions. You might carry a canvas ditty-bag or a flat briefcase inside the big suitcase. Label each bag on the outside and the inside and carry two keys for your big suitcase—one in your pocket, the other in the second bag. If your suitcase isn't immediately recognizable, put tape or some other marker on it so that you can spot it emerging from the baggage limbo of arrival terminals, buses and elevators.

Clothing. Most travelers going to a strange place tend to overload their baggage. They eventually regret both the superfluous burden and the absence of space for acquisitions en route. For Africa, carry minimal but washable clothing and accessories. Light cottons still are best; one suffers in close-knit nylons and "miracle" fibers. Once you're there, if you find the circumstances too hot, too cold, too formal or too informal for your wardrobe, take advantage of the continent's own ample stocks. If your sturdy shoes are presentable, wear them for normal walking and for cocktailing both; nobody will notice the difference. And then rely on sneakers and a pair of sandals (bought in Africa and left behind) for the rest of your footgear, unless you are a mountain climber, ballroom dancer or trout fisherman. A single foldable hat or scarf should suffice for both rain and sun; only movie colonialists wear pith helmets and only mobsters appear in fedoras.

At least one set of informal clothing should cover your arms and legs without binding wrists or ankles: you may need to defend against mosquitoes, but you'll have to perspire some, too. Shorts are indispensable for relaxation (in French-speaking hotels you can even wear them at dinner), but white shorts, like pith helmets, may recall the wrong experiences in Africa. Khaki and other neutral colors are best for game parks, and indeed for laundering. Bush jackets and safari suits, made in Africa, are increasingly popular for both sexes.

A sweater is useful in every country of Africa; where the chill doesn't warrant it, the air-conditioning will. A raincoat can perhaps double as a bathrobe, but otherwise coats make sense only in a few winter highland cities. Umbrellas seldom justify the nuisance of carrying them on the road and in the air; you can buy cheap ones in the first African town you come to during a rainy spell.

Never but never bring clothing that must be dry-cleaned—it's disastrous for your garment and your purse.

A Few Packing Suggestions. Put your small heavies (books, electric razor, cameras, binoculars, bottles of whatever liquid) and all valuables in your hand baggage, which is usually not weighed at airline check-in counters—although the clerks are entitled to weigh it whenever the spirit moves them. If they insist on so doing, stuff everything in your pockets or string it around your neck and look very fierce. Never put the following items in your suitcase: passport, yellow immunization card, travelers checks or cash, credit cards, addresses, letters of introduction or of confirmation, cameras and other valuable equipment, travel guides like this one, or anything that might spoil in the sub-zero temperatures of airplane baggage holds. Detergents, alcohol, perfumed stuff, medicines and other spillables should be packed in tight containers with tape around the top. Don't bring your furs, perishable lace, heirloom jewelry or evening dress unless you can't do without them.

Cameras and Film. A 35-mm camera with an 80-mm lens is ideal for black and white or color. A 150- to 300-mm telephoto lens is most effective for animal photography. Bring a haze filter, lens guard and dustproof case or bag. You can also have fun with a cheap, simple camera or an instant-developing Polaroid. A hand-held 8-mm film camera with a zoom lens can provide an admirable trip record.

Bring with you the motion picture and still film that you expect to need. Weaker-sensitivity emulsions make the best color slides. Standard still film is available in color and black and white in Africa if you run out, but it is expensive except at duty-free shops. It is hard to find 16-mm motion picture film, and 8-mm is costly and not always available.

Binoculars. The ideal safari binoculars are 7-by-50 or 8-by-40 strength, but you can probably be happy with less power.

Electrical Appliances. Cyclage and voltage vary widely within and between countries. Many cities use 220-240 volt AC current at 50 cycles. Battery operated appliances are advisable—bring along a few extra batteries and tapes for your transistor radios and recorders (although you can get replacements, you seldom run out at just the right moment). Carry with you an adapter plug for the wider European-type sockets. If your electric razor fails you, you can pick up a safety razor.

Registration of Equipment. If you are carrying a relatively new foreign-manufactured camera, tape recorder, set of binoculars, watch or other expensive appliance, have the manufacturer's serial number registered by the US Customs Service before you leave. The customs certificate will help avoid currency complications in Africa as well as quarrels with American customs.

Pets. Unless you absolutely can't live without them, leave your pets at home with a sympathetic caretaker. They do not thrive on long rides inside crates, or changes of climate and food. If you take them, you will have no end of problems with quarantines, hotels, parks, markets and transportation.

CHECKLIST

Documents. Valid passport, tickets, International Certificates of Vaccination (smallpox, yellow fever), unexpired visas, extra passport photos and negative, travelers checks, some dollar bills, credit cards, letters of credit, air travel card, International Drivers Permit, personal calling cards, letters of introduction, student identity card, Youth Hostel Card, club or other membership cards, Medic Alert emblem, addresses of personal doctor, lawyer, insurance agent, bank, travel insurance, report of pre-trip physical exam, record of blood type and RH factor, eyeglass prescription, US Customs certificate for foreign-manufactured valuable items, serial numbers for air tickets, credit cards, camera lens and case.

Luggage. Washable changes of clothes, comfortable walking shoes, sneakers, sandals, swimsuit and bag, foldable hat, sunglasses, handkerchiefs, extra pair of eyeglasses, needle and thread, matches, candle, penknife with bottle opener, cork and plastic bottle caps, scissors, spoon, safety pins, adhesive tape, cosmetic and toilet kit, soap and container, detergent, washcloth and/or pre-moistened towelettes, plastic or aluminum hanger, clothes brush, clothesline, shoelaces, several plastic bags, ballpoint pens or pen with refill cartridges, writing paper and envelopes, paper clips, rubber bands, pocket flashlight, transistor radio, electric or safety razor, tape recorder and tape, typewriter, adapter plug, batteries, camera and film, binoculars.

Medical Kit. Aspirins in plastic bottle, iodine, anti-bacterial ointment (Neosporin), Band-aids, gauze, adhesive tape, malaria preventives, insect repellent, paregoric, Red Cross first aid booklet, sleeping pills, codeine or other analgesic, antibiotic for severe infections, vaseline jelly, salt tablets, antihistamines, suntan lotion, lip ice, water purification tablets, nose spray or inhaler, eye-wash, thermometer and motion sickness pills.

PMA and AS

Africa by Air

By Bette Saunders

Most of us have a limited time to spend on vacation, so flying is the best way to cover the long distances between the United States and Africa. In the same time it takes to get to Paris, it's possible to get from New York to Dakar on a non-stop flight. This Pan Am/Air Afrique service from North America continues across the African continent, calling at almost every major city along the way on alternate days. It is one of the few scheduled direct services from the US to Africa and is a marvelously time-saving ride as far as Monrovia, Liberia.

If you are going beyond Robertsfield Airport (Monrovia) in one hop, the time saved is not worth the stress of airport-jumping all the way across Africa just for the convenience of staying on the same plane. Flying non-stop from New York to Western Europe and changing planes will certainly be more pleasant than a string of chicken dinners and airport lounges to Kinshasa or beyond.

The direct services to Africa all leave from New York. If you are starting from any other US city you can fly to Africa with a change of planes either in New York or Europe, or both places. If you fly to Africa from the West Coast, the Midwest or the South there is little difference in travel time between a European or a New York routing. Making your connections in Europe and thus bypassing New York will not affect the price of your ticket.

Fares are determined by class of service (first class or economy), time of year, length of stay, number of people traveling together or age of passengers. These variables are grouped into elaborate sets of rules governing the price of your ticket. It's possible to buy round trip air transportation on a scheduled airline from New York to Casablanca for $242—a special fare with restrictions on length of stay, time of year and stopovers. You could also pay $956 for a round trip between the same cities on the same plane—first class and without time restrictions.

It's up to you to decide whether extra comfort, wider seats and a ticket valid for a year are worth the difference in price. Make yourself familiar with what's available, but consult your travel agent (his services are generally free to you) to be sure you're getting the best buy.

Individual Fares

Nairobi is 8,841 miles from New York by air. A better statement is that one pays for 8,841 miles when buying a ticket to Nairobi. For a round trip cost of $1,104 a traveler can go to Nairobi, stay as long as he likes (up to a year), fly economy class on all stretches and make a few stops on the way and a few stops returning—as long as the distance flown in either direction does not exceed 8,841 miles. Many variations in routing are possible without extra cost.

This fare is available all year, every day of the week, provided you don't fly the Atlantic stretch eastbound during June, July or August, or westbound during July, August or September. (Flying during these high-traffic periods costs about $90 extra each way.) Staying longer than one year doesn't mean you can't come home; it simply means that one year after the date of your first flight, you should return the unused portion of your ticket and apply the refunded amount against the price of a new ticket homeward—a price which may be higher one year later.

Most of us are not lucky enough to have a year to spend seeing Africa, so the airlines have a special "14-45 excursion" fare for individual travelers who stay at least 14 days, but who are homebound not more than 45 days after leaving. These prices are a lot more reasonable. New York to Nairobi round trip is $808. (If you start your trip in June, July or August, it's $63 more.) This "14-45 excursion" to Africa allows five other stopovers besides Nairobi. A word of advice, however, for those who use an excursion ticket—try to keep your stops in a fairly straight line going and coming to your farthest point. Backtracking (changing direction) causes extra expense.

If you decide to go via Europe, you should know that your presence there for a few hours does not count as a stopover if you leave within 24 hours of your arrival. And by not stopping (staying 24 hours) in Europe, you can fly on weekends (Friday and Saturday eastbound and Saturday and Sunday westbound) without paying the $15 additional charge that travelers to European destinations may be paying to fly on weekends.

When planning stopovers, the trick is to try to keep them in order. This means that the farthest point should be near the middle of the itinerary. A few suggestions for an $808, low season, excursion fare:

1. New York/Addis Ababa/Entebbe/Nairobi/Mombasa/Dar es Salaam/Casablanca/New York; or

2. New York/Algiers/Khartoum/Addis Ababa/Nairobi/Mombasa/ Dar es Salaam/New York; or

3. New York/Dakar/Abidjan/Cotonou/Douala/Kinshasa/Casablanca /New York; or

4. New York/Accra/Lagos/Kinshasa/Douala/Bamako/Dakar/New York; or

5. New York/Rio de Janeiro/Johannesburg/Salisbury/Nairobi/Entebbe/Addis Ababa/New York. (This one is different. Most people don't consider going to Africa via South America.)

These plans will also work in reverse, but your fare may change if you switch a city or two from one itinerary to another. On the New York/ Algiers or the New York/Addis plan, you can use an airline which flies via Europe and still pay $808.

If you'd like to spend some time in Europe as well as in Africa, you can substitute a European stop for an African city at the same $808 fare. In fact, you can substitute up to four European stops, but they must be taken two on the way out, two on return. For example: New York/ Amsterdam/Rome/Cairo/Nairobi/Mombasa/Addis/New York; or New York/Paris/Geneva/Addis/Nairobi/Athens/Rome/New York.

European connections on plans 1–5 may not work out at this fare because of the elaborate manner by which airlines figure their prices.

The secret of the fare structure with the scheduled lines is that you're actually being charged by the mile. Here's a brief explanation of the way it works. Every pair of cities is assigned a number of miles and a price for the pair. The assigned mileage is the measured distance increased by 20 per cent. This 20 per cent enables some airlines to participate in routes on which they would not normally be competitive. The effect for the customer is free stopovers between points of origin and destination.

Except when special rules prevent it, you may make as many stops as you like outbound and inbound within the permitted mileage, which is usually generous enough to allow a variety of routings. If you travel more than the allowed mileage you pay for the extra distance. On the other hand, there's no refund for unused mileage as long as you still arrive at your destination by air. You generally won't save money by covering part of the distance by other means of transportation and then continuing from there to your destination.

Caveat Emptor

An editorial aside is appropriate here, concerning price per mile. First, we need to be equipped with a few figures:

from	to	miles	price	cost per mile
New York	Paris	4,353	$226	$.0519
New York	Casablanca	4,428	254	.0573
New York	Dakar	4,574	382	.0835
New York	Accra	6,228	451	.0724
New York	Nairobi	8,841	583	.0659

The price per mile to Africa is higher than that to Europe. A comparison of New York/Paris and New York/Casablanca shows that the difference of 75 miles costs an extra $28; and to Dakar, 146 miles farther, it's an additional $128. That's a very expensive piece of air.

The problem is compounded when you try to fly the most direct route in order to save money, only to find that it's almost impossible to accomplish this because most of the trans-Atlantic services go to Europe first.

There are—for as long as they last—special fares on the scheduled carriers on the Atlantic run for the under-23 age group (30, in some cases). The youth fare scheme can be combined successfully with other low fares to get you to Africa inexpensively. A youth fare to Rome is $229 (round trip, economy class), except in high season—June, July and August going east, July, August and September going west—when the price becomes $280. Rome is almost half the distance between New York and East Africa but $229 and $280 are considerably less than half the price of a ticket to East Africa.

And finally, no discussion of inexpensive travel would be complete without mentioning Icelandic Airlines. They have the lowest fares for scheduled service on the North Atlantic route.

Group Fares

Groups are magic cost reducers. Travel agencies save money by booking blocks of plane seats or hotel rooms. The savings are passed on in the form of special group air fares.

Some group air fares to Africa come as packages with prepaid ground arrangements. There are two types of these group fares with prepaid land: the 14- to 21-day, year-round fare for 15 passengers, and the 10-passenger, winter-only fare. In each instance you do not have to find the other people. The airline or the tour operator will do it for you.

To go to Nairobi from New York on a "group inclusive tour" for 15 people costs $640 for the round trip air fare; the land prices start at $100 for 14 days and 13 nights. The land arrangements are minimal: hotel (second class), breakfast, one sightseeing tour and transfers (between airport and hotel). Any stopovers will be planned into the tour before you leave. Your activities are not organized hour by hour as they are on the escorted tours. There's lots of time to do what you want.

Since departures on this plan are not firm until 30 days before the selected date, it's advisable to pick a time when you're sure other people are traveling (during school breaks or before a holiday, for instance); your chances of leaving as scheduled increase.

Watch the 30-day mark carefully. After the departure date is confirmed, cancellation within 30 days may result in forfeiture of 25 per cent of the air fare, and, in some cases, all of the costs for the ground portion. Read all the fine print. Of course, nobody buys one of these packages with cancellation in mind, but emergencies do arise.

Winter 1972-73 has brought Senegal and the Ivory Coast into a new $325 and $393 air fare range, respectively. This is the other type of group inclusive tour fare: 10 passengers, nine days minimum on the ground, 16 days maximum. The land arrangements must also be paid in advance (a minimum of $10 per day, but this is an unrealistic figure—you'll probably have to spend more). So nine days in Dakar in the winter *could* cost as little as $415, with no frills—about the same as two weeks in Barbados. At this writing the fares are available only to Dakar and Abidjan, but if they prove profitable to the airlines we can look forward to more of these special fares to new winter vacation spots in Africa.

The airlines involved will round up the people in the same way as for the other group. Sign up for a pre-organized jaunt and fly when the group goes. But remember, you really are committed to fly with the group. With most of these tours, your ticket is forfeited if you miss your flight for any reason. It pays to have travelers insurance.

Don't plan to split too far off from these tours. Fares within Africa are expensive. Round trip Dakar/Accra is $301. It becomes very costly to throw away the prepaid ground arrangements. Long side trips quickly use up what you save by buying into this type of group.

If you're a clever traveler, you can arrange a group tour for yourself and 9 or 14 friends. There's no discount on the air fare to the organizer but the land accommodations and tours are virtually free to a wheeler-dealer who is willing to take on the job of organizing the group.

Children's Fares

Children will enjoy Africa immensely. Those from 2 through 12 years of age can fly for half the adult fare (unless the parent has a youth ticket). Infants or children under 2 travel for less than 10 per cent on the air portion. Ground arrangements are another matter; the price for children is pre-set by the tour operator.

Tickets

An airline ticket is really only a receipt for monies paid. On the day the first portion is flown it becomes a contract between you and the airline to which you've paid the money and between you and each carrier listed on the ticket.

The contract is for air transportation between the two airports listed in the origin and destination boxes on the tickets. It means that the airlines named must fly you via the route specified in the body of the ticket (or a comparable route), making stops as indicated on the coupons (pages) of the ticket, on the day, date and time noted on each coupon. If there's an extended delay or a missed flight resulting from weather conditions or mechanical difficulties, or for other technical reasons, the airline will provide you with meals or refreshment coupons and hotel space where necessary. No additional expenses en route will be paid by the carriers for passengers traveling on special fares, excursions or group tickets. These are the people who can't afford to get sick and miss their flights—even with a doctor's note there's no extension at this fare level.

Passengers with one-year tickets are not quite as restricted. They get occasional free hotel rooms and meals when flying long distances, like New York/Nairobi. If there's a plane change in Frankfurt, for instance, and a few hours to wait for connections, they'll be put up at a hotel free of charge. If you're traveling at this fare, you can also afford to get sick. Your ticket will be extended if you present a medical certificate.

You may change your itinerary at any time unless you have a group ticket. (As explained previously, with a group ticket any change must be made by all the passengers; splitting away means you pay the extra costs.) When you do need to make changes, it's best not to do it at airports— use the city ticketing facilities where possible. Airport personnel cannot devote enough time to making the best judgments affecting the price of your trip, and mistakes can be costly. Always save your ticket-backs. You can submit them for a refund even after the route has been flown.

Protect your cash investment by writing the ticket numbers somewhere (on your travelers check receipts, for instance). Write down the date and place of issue as well—you'll find them in the box in the upper right-hand corner. If you lose your tickets, this information may help you get new tickets without extra expense. With these details and an IOU, an airline—at the discretion of the station manager—can reissue a ticket.

Baggage

First class passengers are allowed up to 66 pounds of luggage; those flying economy class or at special fares are limited to 44 pounds. Charges for overweight baggage are computed at one-half of one per cent of the first class fare per pound. The excess baggage rate for a New York to Casablanca flight is $2.39 per pound; from New York to Cape Town it's $4.72 per pound. You may carry on board a coat, a camera and accessories, reading material, an umbrella and a woman's handbag without having to weigh these items. Other unchecked (carry-on) luggage, such as flight bags, cosmetic cases and under-the-seat valises, may be counted as part of the weight allowance at the option of the airline.

If you're coming home with accumulated purchases and additional luggage, ask the carrier if you'd save money by sending it at air cargo rates instead of paying the overweight charges. As air cargo, it may even leave on the same plane as you do. Unfortunately, it may not arrive with you if you have connections to make to your destination. And it should be noted that unaccompanied baggage is not included as part of your $100 duty-free allowance.

Charters: Organizing Your Own

It is advantageous these days to belong to a group or club classified as eligible to charter aircraft. Any existing group that is formed for a purpose other than travel may, provided it has existed for two years and has the required number of members, rent a plane and its crew. A member of the group and his immediate family (spouse and dependents) can buy tickets at an inexpensive rate on this charter flight.

The spokesman for the group gets a flat price for the plane; the services (food, drinks, cabin stewards and crew) are all included. This total is divided by the number of seats, and the resultant seat price is offered to the group members. There's no fancy bookkeeping. Each seat is the same price for child, youth, spouse or group member.

A charter to Monrovia, for example—this one flown direct from New York and return on an aircraft rented from a scheduled airline—costs $71,000. (It's all economy class, an 11-day round trip.) With 150 seats, the round trip is $353 per person (compared with $662 scheduled).

There are three things that the charter organizer should know and do to make sure that his group gets the best deal: (a) start early, (b) shop and (c) negotiate.

The Africa charters are the most difficult for the scheduled airlines to arrange. The reasons for this are loads, permits, embargoes and lots of technical things. Starting six months to a year ahead puts you in a good position to get the dates you want, especially if you're planning a summer trip. There are also high seasons in the charter business. Flying between June 11 and August 10 outbound could raise the seat price by about $60. When you contact the airline, it helps to have alternate dates for out and back trips. Ask questions. Play around with the number of seats (or the "configuration," as it's called). Different configurations produce different prices per seat. The length of stay of a charter group will not affect the price.

Shopping among several airlines will produce the best results. One airline may have a plane available, the other may not. One may leave from a convenient place, the other may have to charge a ferrying fee—a price for moving an empty plane from where it is to where you want it. But at a cost of two to seven dollars a mile it adds only a few pennies to the cost per seat. If a group is leaving from Shreveport, Louisiana, it adds immeasurably to their convenience and relatively little to their costs when the passengers can leave together from their hometown airport rather than each having to get to New York on his own.

Airlines have varying amounts of influence. This becomes important when they must deal with the political problems of embargoes; that is, when they apply for landing permits in the countries you want to visit. It helps to choose a carrier which flies regularly to those places.

When all these details have been cleared, copies of the completed contracts are mailed to your group to be signed by its representative. When the contract is signed (or 90 days before flight departure) 10 per cent of the total price is due. An additional 40 per cent must be paid 60 days in advance, and the 50 per cent balance is payable 30 days before the flight. The payment dates are negotiable, however, and the airlines are very amenable to your preferences. Surprisingly, using a travel agent to help with the arrangements does not affect the price, so if you want to apply for a charter for your group and don't feel equipped for the task, get a reliable agent to help out. He gets a nice commission from the airline plus a chance to make money on the land arrangements as well.

Charter rates are based on cost per mile but there are many variables, including the type of aircraft—707, DC-8, Stretch 8 or 747 (which began flying to Nairobi in 1973). It's also possible to cut out some of the frills and get a better price per seat. An open bar or complimentary flight bags or a choice of menus add to operating expenses and can be eliminated to cut down the cost per seat.

I negotiated a charter flight to Nairobi just to get a sample price. For a 186-seat Stretch DC-8, flown New York to Nairobi, leaving in June 1972 and returning in September, I was offered a round trip price per seat of $400, which included flight bags, open bar, choice of menu and a stop in Europe.

All airlines will try to sell a charter, even if they don't have scheduled service to Africa. Reputation, reliability of schedule, service, extra comforts, fancy ground service and lots of in-flight extras are what you get when you negotiate with the scheduled airlines for charters.

Supplementals

If you have a group you can also buy space on a supplemental airline. Some of the larger supplementals are Trans International Airlines (350 Fifth Avenue, New York, N.Y. 10001, tel. 212/563-7725), World (666 Fifth Avenue, New York 10019, tel. 757-4207) and Saturn (516 Fifth Avenue, New York 10036, tel. 661-6996).

Unlike the scheduled carriers, supplementals will split their charters. Splitting means that if you're unable to fill the whole plane, the charterer can sell the other seats to another group going to the same place. According to the rules, a charter can be split into blocks of 40 seats. It would obviously be easier for a small club or group to fill 40 seats on a supplemental charter than 150 or more on a full charter with a scheduled line. Remember also that the same guidelines for shopping around and rules governing deposits and payments apply here as for the other types of charters.

Supplementals are the most economical, most maligned and misunderstood of all types of air transportation. Supplementals, or non-skeds, as they're also called, are a very important part of passenger air traffic. These airlines offer additional seats for high density routes at lower prices. Most of the supplementals have properly maintained jet equipment. So we're dealing with safe, modern airplanes.

The difference is in the style. I think of it as the plain pipe-rack theory. The startling result of this no-frills approach to travel is the price to you—$135 round trip New York/Frankfurt in low season and $190 round trip in high season. High season for supplementals is June, July and August eastbound and July, August and September westbound. Leave in May; return in August; split the two and pay $162.50. Once in Frankfurt, London or other transfer point, you can purchase other "supplemental" transportation to Africa.

But flying supplementals means you won't be pampered in flight or on the ground. These lines don't have staffs of uniformed ticket sales agents or 24-hour telephone service to solve your problems. For that matter, neither do they provide a glamorous place for your arrival and departure.

In New York, for instance, the North Passenger Terminal of the Kennedy International Airport is used for supplemental departures. This is a hangar out in the boondocks with a few benches. And you may have to sit there for some time if there's a delay. Since these companies usually have only three to five aircraft on the whole system, a delay at takeoff or in flight for one group can mushroom from a few hours into two days for the next groups which are booked to use the same plane.

On the other hand, you may have no difficulty. And the savings (10 per cent and up per seat) make it worthwhile for many travelers to put up with the inconveniences.

If it's so inexpensive, why doesn't everyone ride the non-skeds? One reason is that not everybody is aware that they exist. Another is the tag "non-sked." When they first began to do business, supplemental carriers would not take off until the planes were full. This meant that passengers could not be sure until the last minute when they would leave, and other arrangements could not be finalized without this assurance.

Charter Organizers

Several organizations are now in the North America-to-Africa charter business, with groups usually departing in December, June and July. Theoretically, one must have been a member of the organization for at least six months in order to buy a seat on one of its charters. Memberships are easily available. Educators to Africa Association (African-American Institute, 866 United Nations Plaza, New York, N.Y. 10017, tel. 212/421-2500) charges an annual fee of $15 for teachers, $20 for general members and $10 for students. Its December 1972–January 1973 round trip fare to members for New York to Accra flights was $315 per person, half-fare for children. Summer rates from New York to West Africa are similar, with a $500 round trip to Nairobi.

Other charter flights from North America to Africa are organized in and around university communities, sometimes by alumni or student groups. The University of California at Berkeley and the University of California at Los Angeles have operated summer charter flights to West Africa in recent years at about $400 round trip. UCLA, Wesleyan and other alumni groups have arranged East African charters. Watch student newspapers and bulletin boards for leads on these flights. University Travel (44 Brattle Street, Cambridge, Mass., tel. 617/864-7800) is a good source for East Coast charters to Africa.

Non-academic organizations have also begun to promote their own charter flights. CORE runs flights to East and West Africa (contact Cyril Boynes, Director of Cultural Affairs, CORE, 200 West 135th Street, New York, N. Y. 10030, tel. 212/368-3723). The Heritage Foundation (94 Bergen Street, New Brunswick, N.J., tel. 201/247-2501) arranges charters to East Africa. Another West African charter is organized by the Africa Study Group (49 Rutland Square, Boston, Mass. 02118, tel. 617/266-4449).

Inexpensive Flights: Europe to Africa

Reduced fares from Europe to Africa are by no means confined to groups, students or youths. Each government has its own eligibility rules, with the British, Swiss and West Germans imposing the fewest restrictions.

Information and bookings on student flights are available through the Council on International Educational Exchange (777 United Nations Plaza, New York, N.Y. 10017, tel. 212/661-0310). The Council publishes a useful booklet on Student Air Travel Association flights, and issues the International Student Identity Card. The card is proof of your eligibility for these flights as well as for hostels and other privileges. Cards cost $2 and are issued only to full-time high school and college or university students. During the summer of 1972 there were student flights from major European cities to Tangier, Tunis and Nairobi (the last a $344 round trip from London).

There are Europe-to-Africa charters open to the general public as well as to students. Ask at the British Student Travel Center in New York (80 Fifth Avenue, tel. 212/243-9114), or in London (44 Goodge Street, tel. 01-580-8182). Few charters to Africa operate out of France or Italy, and those from Denmark and Sweden are generally confined to nationals of those countries and combined with package tours.

Travelers have also put together summer charter flights from New York to Tel Aviv, Israel, and from there to Addis Ababa or Nairobi, at special El Al student rates—total round trip fares of $500. Check with El Al Airlines or with the Israeli Students' Organization (515 Park Avenue, New York, N.Y., tel 212/753-3920).

London is a major departure point for charter and supplemental flights to Africa. Loxlines Safaris (119 Oxford Street, tel. 01-734-5788) has five or more monthly flights between London and Nairobi in June, July, August and September (about $300 round trip). Nilestar Tours (623 Grand Building, Trafalgar Square, tel. 01-930-1895) also has frequent flights to East Africa. (In the US, Nilestar has offices in New York, Chicago and Los Angeles). GT Travel (Murray House, 3-5 Vandon Street, Westminster, tel. 01-222-2013) has flights to East, West and Southern Africa. (GT's New York office is at 104 East 40th Street, tel. 212/725-1458.) Each of these firms also operates package tours which they will try to sell you in addition to the air transportation. If your money is short, buy only the flight and rely on this book for less expensive lodgings.

Luxavia is a private South African supplemental and charter carrier that flies between Luxembourg and Johannesburg. Luxavia's North American representative is the Icelandic Airlines office in New York.

Other offices are in London (Grand Building, Trafalgar Square) and in Johannesburg (Mobile House, 8 Plissik Street).

From Frankfurt, Atlantis Airways flies weekly to Nairobi for round trip fares of approximately $220, including one week of simple bed-and-breakfast accommodations. Arrangements can be made through the travel department of the Kaufhof-Hertie department stores in Cologne and other West German cities.

Charter flights and inexpensive package tours from Switzerland to North and East Africa are available from Kuoni International Travel (Bahnhofplatz 1, Zurich, tel. 441261).

Touropa Austria (Karlsplatz 20, Vienna 1, Austria) has a weekly charter from Vienna to Nairobi between December and March.

Airline prices change each year—like their planes, they go up. By the time you read this, the fares quoted will no longer be in effect. But if you shop carefully you'll get the maximum benefit for your transportation dollars.

AFRICA BY SEA

If you have a lot of time and a fondness for sea air and the relaxed atmosphere of deck life, you can make your trip to Africa by luxury cruise ship or passenger-freighter. Ships leave several major North American ports on a direct route to Africa. Many more ships, of course, leave from European ports—if you've a mind to combine Europe and Africa. See the appendix for names and addresses of ship lines.

AFRICA BY LAND

From Western Europe you can drive a car, take a bus or train, or even hitchhike to Africa. There are quick, convenient and inexpensive car-ferries crossing the Mediterranean from Gibraltar, Lisbon and several Spanish ports to Morocco. You can also take a ferry from Marseille, Genoa or Naples to Algeria and Tunisia. See the appendix for details.

You can buy or rent a car in Western Europe, drive it through North Africa, and return. Or you can combine hitchhiking and bus-riding for this Mediterranean route. The Sud-Express train ride from Paris's Gare d'Austerlitz to Casablanca takes 48 hours, crossing the Straits of Gibraltar by ferry.

Traveling in Africa

Here are some observations and suggestions that apply generally to travel on the African continent. They are arranged according to the sequence found in the country chapters—beginning with Money Matters, and proceeding to advice on Getting In and Out, Getting Around Within the Country, Where to Stay, Where and What to Eat, What to See and Do, What to Buy, Local Attitudes, Weather and What to Wear and How Long to Stay, Communication and Emergencies.

MONEY MATTERS

Only Liberia uses the US dollar as a medium of exchange. Elsewhere, you must trade dollars for ngwees, silys, zaïres or other local currency. Persistent trade deficits and shortages of reserves keep most national currencies inconvertible. Hence they are worthless outside their country of issue, or at best can be exchanged elsewhere only at painful discounts. Where such strictures apply, wise travelers exchange only what they need in small denominations on a day-to-day basis, avoiding an accumulation of colorful but otherwise worthless paper at the end of the visit. Whatever excess currency you have on departure will be of use only for tips and airport-shop purchases and flight departure taxes.

Convertible Currencies

CFA francs, South African rands and Spanish pesetas are the only convertible African currencies. One or another version of the CFA franc circulates in 13 former French colonies and two French territories. ("CFA" is the French abbreviation of African Financial Community.)

Its convertibility and exchange rates are pegged to the French franc. The Equatorial CFA franc is used in Cameroon, Chad, the Central African Republic, Gabon and the People's Republic of the Congo (Brazzaville). It has the same value as, and can be exchanged for, the West African CFA franc used in Dahomey, Ivory Coast, Mauritania, Niger, Senegal, Togo and Upper Volta (but not in Mali or Guinea, which have inconvertible national currencies). Reunion and the Comoros in the Indian Ocean have their own CFA francs. The Territory of the Afars and Issas in Northeast Africa uses a special Djibouti franc. Madagascar's French-supported Malagasy franc (FMG) has been inconvertible since late 1972.

The CFA system is controlled in Paris and has recently come under criticism by several member governments. Mauritania intends to replace it with a new national currency and other countries may follow suit. While the system stands, however, you can convert between dollars and CFA francs without compunction; the Bank of France is committed to pay French francs or dollars on demand in exchange for your CFA's.

The South African rand is a hard currency exchangeable for dollars in South Africa, Namibia (South West Africa), Botswana, Lesotho and Swaziland, where it circulates as legal tender, and at hotels in Mozambique and Rhodesia.

The Spanish peseta is used in the Canary Islands, Spanish Sahara, Ceuta and Melilla.

Where to Exchange Currencies

Most airports have banking offices where you can change enough money for the first few days of your visit, provided that you arrive at a time when banks are open (see country profiles for national holidays). Seaports and overland borders rarely have such facilities in Africa: if you are traveling by surface, you must either use dollars or other convertible currency until you get to a bank or hotel.

Generally, leading hotels will exchange currency or travelers checks, although sometimes only for their own guests. They tend, however, to offer slightly less favorable rates of exchange than banks. In Egypt and Tunisia certain government-owned shops and other businesses offer discounts for dollars used in conjunction with a purchase.

Coins

Metal money cannot be converted anywhere. Coins should be used up in the country of issue or brought home for your nephew's collection. Excess foreign coins (US or other) can be spent outside their homeland only to tip a waiter or taxi driver at an airport, or somebody at an international hotel in the country next door; such recipients have a fighting chance of trading these coins to a patron going in the opposite direction. But a Kenyan hotel porter has no more use for Ghanaian pesewas than a taxi driver in Philadelphia.

Currency Declaration Forms

All countries with inconvertible currencies, and some others, issue currency declaration forms on arrival. You are to declare how much foreign currency you are bringing in and subsequently to record each exchange transaction you make, whether at banks, hotels or shops. The forms have to be presented to customs officials on departure. Even if you use a credit card, be sure to record your transactions, lest you be suspected of acquiring local currency illegally. Black markets frequently accompany inconvertible currencies. The returns on patronizing them rarely justify the risks of severe penalty involved, or the harm done the African economy.

Transferring Funds

Should the need arise, ask your home bank to cable a transfer in your name to a designated bank in Africa. All major American banks have lists of African correspondents. Unless you are in a convertible currency zone, the funds transferred will probably be in national currency rather than dollars.

GETTING IN AND OUT

You will save time and trouble by obtaining your visas before getting to Africa. If you need to get them while traveling, be sure to carry extra passport pages, photographs and cash. British or French embassies in Africa can sometimes issue visas for several former colonies on a single visit to their offices.

Entry and Departure Forms

Each time you enter or leave a country, you must fill out at least one form. Some airlines carry stocks of blank forms, enabling you to complete paperwork on the plane. It helps to memorize your passport number and date of issue. Replies to questions should be short, simple and non-provocative. For instance, under "occupation" call yourself teacher, businessman, housewife or student rather than anthropologist, television executive, social worker or research consultant on prison reform. If you aren't certain where you will be staying, give the name of any decent hotel or the US embassy. Once handed in to immigration, the form is likely not to be seen again.

Health Controls

If your yellow International Certificates of Vaccination are in order, you will usually have no trouble with health formalities on arrival. Should you need a vaccination during your travels, ask at the point of entry to have it provided by a qualified medical person.

Customs Formalities

Customs controls are generally perfunctory for visitors with tourist visas. Customs inspectors usually take oral declarations at face value except in Libya, South Africa, Nigeria and Zaïre, where baggage inspections are frequent. Make your declarations simple, honest and dead-pan.

Most African governments allow tourists to bring in reasonable amounts of personal effects without paying duty. These may include clothing, toilet articles, jewelry, reading material, a carton of cigarettes or a box of cigars or a half-pound of tobacco, one bottle of liquor, a tape recorder, a transistor radio, a typewriter and writing materials, a phonograph and records, sporting equipment, cameras and film. Items that are packaged as if they might be resold may draw questions. Untailored cloth bought in another country sometimes poses a problem—in Nigeria, for instance; send your textile purchases home.

Customs and Cars

If you cross borders by car you will need (1) a triptyque or carnet de passage en douane to avoid posting a customs bond, (2) a green international insurance card or some other proof of insurance covering the country you are entering, (3) license plates with a national symbol (e.g., EAK for East Africa Kenya), (4) an international, national or US state driver's license. American automobile clubs and national automobile associations in Africa can help with these arrangements. If you cross a border in a taxi or chauffered car, make sure that the driver and vehicle are properly documented.

Arrival and Departure Taxes

Some African governments impose arrival taxes, usually tagging them onto hotel bills. Many more require an airport departure tax (see country profiles). Try to retain enough local currency to cover these taxes on your way out. In general, you should not have to pay the departure tax if you are in transit, have not left the airport, or (in most cases) simply spent less than 24 hours in the country.

Bribes and Dashes

On arrival or departure in some countries you may be approached by an official, or someone purporting to be an official, asking for a bribe—commonly known in English-speaking West Africa as "dash" and in French-speaking countries as a "cadeau" (gift) or "biche." Such approaches are generally made with a hint that your documents or luggage may not be in order. Zaïre and Nigeria are among the worst offenders in this respect. If you fall prey to a bribe-seeker ask to see the director of customs or immigration—even if you know you've broken the rules. Chances are his office will have a poster reading "Help Stamp Out Corruption."

Airport to Town

Most international airports have bus, limousine or taxi service to town. Major airlines and hotels often provide their own bus service. A few airports—including those at Kinshasa, Douala, Lagos and Addis Ababa—expose travelers to hordes of importuning taxi drivers and random hustlers. Once past customs, count and lock your bags. If there is no public or hotel bus, take a taxi, but negotiate the price before you get in. (Use the fares in our country profiles as a guide.)

GETTING AROUND IN AFRICA

For better or worse, African roads, airways and other transportation conditions are part of the travel experience, not a transition between experiences. If you can take time to enjoy the ride—or the wait—the transportation systems aren't all that bad or the confusion that irritating.

Africa on Foot

Walking offers extraordinary pleasures throughout the continent. The largest African cities are safe by day or night (except Johannesburg, where high crime rates prevail, and Cairo, where women should be escorted at night) and some have good city maps. Don't be afraid to walk into crowded markets, bazaars or congested business and residential areas. Walking is a way of life, and people everywhere are ready to help you if you lose your way.

Bicycles, Motorscooters, Motorcycles

Bicycles are Africa's most popular vehicles; visitors can rent them cheaply through hotels or shops. Cycling is safe and fun, except in rush-hour city traffic. Bikes can be put aboard buses and used in rural areas. Motorscooters and motorcycles are much more expensive, harder to rent and dangerous in traffic and on bad roads.

Taxis

Most African cities have two types of taxis, private and collective.

Private taxis: A few of these are metered, but the meters do not always work. In any case, negotiate a price before entering; tipping is not customary. Private taxis can be found cruising or parked outside major hotels and transport depots. In some cities you can summon them by telephone. Drivers usually speak a smattering of English or French, depending on the country, and often are knowledgeable guides. Where language is a problem, it's helpful to have someone on the hotel staff write out your destination in the local language.

Fares often go up for trips at night, out of town, over rough roads or during bad weather. If you find a driver you like, negotiate a price for extended periods. If his documents are in order you can hire him to go from one country to another, especially in West Africa where short trips often cross several borders.

Collective taxis: These are station wagons or small buses that carry as many passengers as they can hold. They run on regular routes, at more or less fixed fares, within and between cities. In rare instances they cross national borders. They are less expensive than private taxis and faster than buses. In some cities, like Accra, they also operate as town taxis, taking individual passengers to their destinations.

Collective taxis usually leave only after acquiring a full load, departing from bus and taxi stations called "motor parks" in English-speaking West Africa and "parcs routiers" or "taxi-gares" in French-speaking countries. You can often take a collective taxi up to the border, walk across, and catch another on the other side.

Buses (City, Inter-City, International)

Most big cities have inexpensive buses that run city routes, but they are slow and usually very crowded. In smaller towns buses are likely to be dilapidated and their schedules haphazard.

You can travel between major cities comfortably and inexpensively by bus in Morocco, Tunisia, Nigeria, Sierra Leone, Zaïre, South Africa, Malawi, Zambia and East Africa. Elsewhere the inter-city buses are usually aged and crowded (with animals and merchandise as well as people). They depart only when full and travel at unsafe speeds.

Bus service between countries is limited but improving. The best bus lines are those connecting South Africa and its neighbors; Kenya, Tanzania, Uganda and Zambia; Ghana and Upper Volta; and Senegal, Mauritania and the Gambia.

Perhaps the most exciting international bus trip in Africa is the eight-day journey from Addis Ababa to Nairobi, with changes of buses at Dilla in Ethiopia and Moyale in Kenya. If you take long bus trips, bring along some canned food, a sleeping bag and plenty of insecticide.

Mammy-wagons

A West African speciality, but found in one form or another everywhere in Africa, is the truck chassis made over into a rude passenger bus. Known as "mammy-wagons" in Ghana and Nigeria, where they are often owned by women market traders, they provide a cheap, unforgettable, unsafe and irregular way of getting around. Proverbs, prophecies and slogans decorate their panels—such as "God is Able," "Anything You Do," "Safe Journey," "John Wayne" and "The Beautyful Ones Are Not Yet Born." Mammy-wagons run between cities, to smaller towns and villages, and, in West Africa, across some of the national borders.

Auto Rentals

Rates and makes of cars vary widely. Our country chapters provide the names of rental agencies, but check with hotel personnel about their reliability. Also, inspect your car thoroughly before you accept it—for spare tires (two if you're to be driving on rough roads), tire changing equipment, proper documents, tool kits, safety belts and jerricans. Ask for maps and guide-books, and inquire about service stations out of town. (This information is also often available from national automobile associations, especially in East and South Africa.) Check the rental contract for responsibility for cost of repairs (especially broken windshields), accidents, break-downs and towing, and get forfeit of responsibility agreements in writing.

If you're planning a long trip over unfamiliar roads, you probably should hire a driver. The cost is normally quite low. But make sure he has a driver's license and that he speaks the language of the area to which you're heading.

An international license and a credit card are all you usually need to rent a car if you are 18 or older. Sometimes cash deposits are required. Nowhere in Africa can you rent a car in one country and leave it in another; in fact, no agencies let you drop a rented car off in another city, even within the same country, without paying for a return run.

Peugeot station wagons and Volkswagen bugs are the most durable for trips on all-weather roads and the most easily serviced. For very rough roads, however, you may need four-wheel-drive, at much higher rates.

Fly and Drive

Increasingly popular is the round-trip air ticket, purchased in North America or Europe, that includes the rental of a car in Africa. For example, BOAC and Swissair are associated with Avis in fly-drive arrangements in Kenya and South Africa; Royal Air Maroc has a fly-drive fare between London and Casablanca. Such combinations may be particularly attractive for two, three or four persons willing to share a rented car.

Buying a Car

Unless you are planning an extended stay, purchasing a car in Africa, new or used, makes little sense. Although used-car dealers exist in most cities, and newspapers carry ads for private sales, buyers run into a barrage of tax and registration quandaries. The safest procedure is to buy a well-known make from an authorized dealer—with a written guarantee that he will buy it back.

Driving Conditions

Driving is a good way to see much of Africa but it has its problems. There are few freeways or even divided highways, distances are great, rural gas stations are few and far between, gasoline is expensive, pedestrian and cyclist traffic is erratic, and elderly trucks thunder along the roads at precarious speeds. Take your time, avoid night driving outside cities, study maps and touring guides, and hire a driver when in doubt. If you have an accident, especially one involving a pedestrian, it's best in most countries to go straight to the nearest police post. If you need repairs, establish the price with the mechanic before work begins. Traffic moves on the left in East Africa, Rhodesia, South Africa, Mozambique, Mauritius and the Gambia.

Driving conditions vary greatly from place to place and from season to season. Potholes, ruts, mud and dust are frequent hazards. Accident rates on African roads are high. Use your horn on bends and narrow grades, in traversing village market areas and when passing another vehicle.

Asphalt or cement roads are often referred to as "tarmac" in English or "goudron" in French. For every paved African mile there are hundreds of unpaved miles, often of a reddish laterite clay which turns to goo when wet. Unpaved roads in East and Southern Africa are of murram, a black clay surface that becomes slithery after a rain and at other times emits clouds of dust.

Driving Between Countries

Road travel around the continent can be both delightful and frustrating. Some border posts and international ferry crossings close for weekends. On weekdays they may close at 5 pm, during lunch hours, or at other odd moments. Border officials will often ask for handouts, especially between Zaïre and East African countries, between Sierra Leone and Guinea and between Nigeria and its neighbors. They may bluff, refusing passage unless you pay, but remember—help stamp out corruption.

Trains

Africa has some of the world's last remaining steam passenger trains. It also has luxurious diesel and electric expresses (in Algeria, Kenya and South Africa).

Cecil Rhodes's dream of a Cape-to-Cairo railway was never realized, and you cannot (for political reasons) follow the only east-west transcontinental rail link (Angola to the Indian Ocean), but you can travel long distances comfortably by train. There's good rail service in Morocco, Algeria, Egypt, South Africa, Rhodesia, Angola, Senegal, Ivory Coast, Kenya, Uganda, Tanzania and Madagascar. Traveling first class (with sleepers and dining car) can be quite elegant. Second class is pleasant and tidy; third class is inexpensive but uncomfortable.

For traveling between countries, there's train service linking Algeria and Morocco, Egypt and the Sudan, Djibouti and Ethiopia, Kenya and Uganda, Senegal and Mali, Ivory Coast and Upper Volta, and throughout Southern Africa.

Boats

Some of Africa's lakes and rivers offer superb boat trips, usually on small steamers carrying passengers and freight to numerous ports. The boats are relaxing, convivial and inexpensive. The lakes: Victoria, Malawi, Tanganyika and Kivu; the rivers: the Nile, Niger, Senegal, Congo (Zaïre), Gambia, Zambezi and Ubangi.

Lake and river steamers link Egypt and the Sudan; Senegal, Mauritania and Mali; Kenya, Tanzania and Uganda; and Burundi, Zaïre and Tanzania. There will soon be Niger River boats connecting Mali, Niger and Nigeria.

Along the coast, cruise ships and passenger-freighters put in at many ports, but this is a slow and uncertain way of getting around.

Planes

Aircraft networks thoroughly cover the distances between major points in Africa, although traffic volume seldom warrants frequent scheduling. Most countries have national airlines, with propeller and turbo-prop equipment (the venerable but reliable DC-3, the Hawker-Siddley and the Viscount) for domestic flights, and jets for inter-African journeys. These planes can often be chartered for special group flights, but virtually every country has a number of private air charter firms and aero-clubs as well.

Veteran African travelers have their favorite airplane stories. Joseph Spieler of The New York Times News Service recalls a trip north on an Ethiopian Airlines DC-3 from Addis Ababa to Gondar, the ancient Ethiopian capital: "At Gondar I do the sights and reboard a DC-3 that afternoon to go to Asmara. Plane lands on grass pasture decorated with a windsock and attendant calls out, '15 minutes rest stop.' This is Axum, another ancient Ethiopian city. I get off to say goodbye to friends who are staying overnight there. As we exchange addresses there is a roar. Plane is moving. Rest stop only two minutes old. I run and manage to pull alongside the plane's door. 'Wait! Stop!' Jacket, wallet, cameras all on the plane. 'Stop!' Face looks out from window and smiles. Lungs and heart give 'ten seconds to self-destruct' warning. I fall behind, cabin door opens, hands reach out and voice suggests, 'Jump!' I pick up speed, move close to door, summon strength of numerous tubercular ancestors, and jump. Feet lift four inches off the ground. Arms grab mine. More arms, finally many arms. I am pulled into plane to the sound of cheering."

While it is unlikely that you will ever have to jump into a moving plane, you can expect to come home with your own African flight stories —particularly if you stray from the jets that cruise the popular routes.

Even if you're flying, allow a full day to travel from one country to another, including the chance of delays and the time consumed in arrival and departure formalities. Where scheduled flights between countries occur less than daily, book well in advance and confirm your bookings. This is especially important if you're flying between East and West or Central Africa. If you charter a flight between countries make sure the pilot has landing rights and clearances at the airport of destination.

WHERE TO STAY

Some of Africa's major hotels—like the Mamounia in Marrakesh, the Ivoire Intercontinental in Abidjan and the Mount Nelson in Cape Town —rank among the world's best in every respect. As tourism grows, modern highrise hotels and broad, luxurious motels are springing up, but for the present only Morocco, Tunisia, the Canary Islands, Egypt, Kenya and South Africa offer a full range of accommodations according to European scales.

Excellent luxury lodgings exist in capital cities, mountain resorts and beach areas throughout the continent—particularly in Senegal, the Ivory Coast, Ethiopia, Malawi, Rhodesia, Angola and Mauritius. But most of these countries suffer from a scarcity of acceptable moderately priced establishments ($8-$15, single with bath) and offer a scanty choice in their less frequented areas. Most countries have at least one or two international class hotels (comparable to official first-class or three-star ratings in Europe). The exceptions are the Sudan, Libya, Burundi, Zanzibar, Equatorial Guinea and Cape Verde Islands; even there, however, you can find decent lodgings, albeit sometimes at luxury prices.

In many countries the traveler with ample funds can choose between a gleaming new hotel suitable for Miami Beach or Omaha, and an older establishment with a sense of space and old world decor. The authors gravitate toward some of the latter type, even if the plumbing is noisier and the switchboard slower: for example, the Norfolk in Nairobi, Ryall's in Blantyre, the Park in Mauritius, the Plage in Cotonou and the Tunisia Palace in Tunis.

British and French styles have left their respective marks on Africa's hotels. In British-influenced places, morning tea is brought to your room at 6 am unless you succeed in impressing the management with your preference for sleep. There are substantial four-course breakfasts and afternoon tea, of course, and lots of boiled vegetables on the menu. Service tends to be mannered and bars observe rigid opening and closing hours. The French have bequeathed continental breakfasts of café au lait and rolls, hard-stuffed wedges for pillows, bidets, late leisurely dinner hours, and an appreciation for wine, mineral water and sauces.

The traveler with a modest budget will find a slender selection of medium-priced hotels, pensions, and government or university guest houses all over Africa. The ratio of small hotels is higher in former French territories, whereas the English-speaking countries tend to make more government and other non-commercial facilities available to travelers. Low-budget visitors have abundant opportunities for camping, as well as some cheap hotels, cabins, hostels and school dormitories.

In addition to campsites, the great national parks usually offer a choice between well-equipped and often quite sumptuous lodges, and thatched-roof bungalows (with kitchens and showers) known as "bandas" in East Africa, "rondavels" in Southern Africa and "paillottes" in French. West and Central African park accommodations are less impressive in range and convenience.

Resourceful travelers in rural areas and small towns will often be able to bed down at boarding schools, government travel quarters (rest-houses), mission stations and private homes. Accommodating residents include teachers, tradesmen and local officials, as well as volunteers of the US Peace Corps, the Canadian Universities Service Overseas (CUSO) and their counterparts in British, French, West German, Israeli, Scandinavian, and United Nations programs. In return for free lodging, it's customary to bring something from town (cigarettes, books, periodicals, rare canned goods, liquor—except for missionaries), or at least to lend a hand with chores.

Prices, Service, Tipping

A few African governments (Morocco, Tunisia, Angola, South Africa) classify their hotels strictly, thus regulating prices according to criteria of accommodations and service. Usually, however, rates are determined by local conditions of demand and competition. Where there are few first-class hotels in a busy place (like Kinshasa, Fort Lamy, Lagos, Freetown, Accra and Tananarive) they can often charge the sky's limit for room rent and supplementaries. In these cases, the price gap ($10 to $20 a day) between international class and more modest acceptable lodgings is often worth exploiting—provided you can tolerate shabbier structures, cut-rate services and wheezing facilities. Most new hotels (post-1965) have rooms with private baths and central air-conditioning—not true of many older places where you often share plumbing facilities and pay a surcharge for use of the air-conditioner.

Annexes to the new hotels, often called "cabañas" or "bungalows," are usually more private, luxurious and closer to the swimming pool than the main building, and more expensive, whereas the reverse applies to older establishments. Thus, in small towns and the outskirts of cities, you can often sleep in rough but cheap circumstances at an otherwise first-class hotel.

It helps to ask before you book whether taxes and service charges are included in quoted hotel prices. If not, you may discover a 10 to 20 per cent difference between the eventual bill and what you expected to pay. An increasing number of hostelries, old and new, are charging extra for breakfast, as they have always done for room television and laundry.

Laundry is a notorious money-maker for the establishment, not for the laundress, so that you aren't exactly denying bread to the hungry if you do your own washing (ignore signs in your room prohibiting this unless there's a genuine water shortage), or if you find a private launderer through a local resident. Shoes left outside your door at night will be shined free of charge—although some international places ask you to notify the hall porter. At least they won't be thrown out, as at some posh American hotels.

Service charges, like laundry fees, don't go directly or entirely to the service personnel. Hence, although tipping is rare among the regular European and African clientele of most hotels, the occasional visitor can often improve the service he gets, and the humor of the people around him, by offering an extra 10 to 25 cents at the appropriate time. A 25 to 50 cent tip to the baggage porter on arrival, and an early gratuity to the porter, waiter and chambermaid, identify you as a worthy guest. Bartenders, receptionists and maîtres d'hôtel usually get tipped only on special occasions.

Most major hotels have or can recommend excellent (and expensive) men's and women's hairdressing salons. Generally there are good and much less expensive shops nearby. In Abidjan or Ouagadougou, for instance, a man can get a razor-cut and shampoo at the hotel for five dollars and a normal haircut in town for two dollars. Near the markets are African barbers who offer a variety of hair styles for 25 cents (you do the shampooing when you get back to the hotel).

WHERE AND WHAT TO EAT

Best of the national cuisines are those of Morocco, Tunisia, Egypt, Ethiopia, Madagascar, Senegal and Ghana, but each country has its own specialties. Restaurant prices and value compare favorably with Western European and North American standards. The kitchens of major hotels almost exclusively produce an international fare, with a few diluted African recipes.

Dining room terminology requires some clarification: in East and West Africa, a "European menu" usually means British pulp food and isn't worth trying. A "Continental menu" refers to Swiss or Austrian versions of everybody else's cuisine. An "international menu" generally is what is found with French names in Lebanese restaurants, where the kebabs are still your best bet. "Chinese" food in French-speaking Africa is usually Vietnamese, while in Portuguese territories it means Cantonese (from Macão). Ethiopia, Kenya, Mauritius, Nigeria and South Africa have authentically Chinese places. Generally, "French" means French.

Indian and Pakistani restaurants are excellent in Kenya, Tanzania and Malawi. Inexpensive restaurants and canteens catering primarily to Africans usually can be found near bus and railroad stations, markets and bazaars; the skewered meat and dumplings are good.

Health Rules

Wherever you eat, a few simple health rules are in order. Avoid cold plates, buffets, custards, pastries or other foods that have been prepared in advance and left standing. Also avoid raw fish and meats cooked rare. Freshly cooked vegetables are safe, as are fresh fruits with unbroken skins. Skip the salad unless you've seen it washed. What matters most is how food is prepared and not where you eat it or what price you pay.

City tap water usually needs to be boiled, filtered or avoided, but a swig generally can be taken for rinsing toothpaste. Cautious travelers will avoid ice-cubes and request that bottled mineral water, wine or other beverages be opened in their presence.

Bottled beer and fruit juices are safest.

African Foods

Many delicious fruits are available in Africa—including guavas, papayas, dates, coconuts, tamarinds, oranges, mangoes, bananas, pineapples, melons and avocados. African staple foods include maize (corn), millet, sorghum, rice, plantain banana, cassava (manioc) and yams, all prepared in varieties of soups, stews, dumplings, sauces and porridges. Chicken, beef, lamb, veal, goat and game meat, such as boar or venison, may also go in the pot. Also fresh seafood near the coasts and river and lake fish inland. On your first effort, you might try African dishes with spices and seasonings on the side, leaving you free to modify flavors and bite.

Desserts, pastries and appetizers are based on groundnuts (peanuts), cashew nuts, almonds, chocolate, honey, fruits and, in West Africa, the stimulating kola nut.

Drinkables

Most countries produce good, inexpensive, locally bottled beers and fruit juices. Bottled soft drinks are sometimes less hygienic. Algeria, Tunisia, Morocco, Egypt, Ethiopia, South Africa, Tanzania and Madagascar have their own wines. Imported mineral water is expensive but good local mineral waters are available in Ethiopia, Morocco, Madagascar, Algeria and elsewhere. Fresh coffee, cocoa and tea—African grown—are generally excellent. Pasteurized milk is available in Kenya, Rhodesia and South Africa. Elsewhere, you can get powdered milk, or local milk that needs to be boiled, or goat's milk, which is safe.

Imported liquor is very expensive unless purchased duty free; gin, scotch and brandy cost from $6 to $30 for a fifth. Egypt, Ghana, Kenya, Nigeria, South Africa and Uganda have less expensive domestic liquor. Everywhere there are fermented concoctions produced from ingredients such as bananas, maize and palm sap. Stick to the legally bottled stuff unless you have a yen for moonshine.

WHAT TO SEE AND DO

To make the most of an African visit you must deal with a continent of sights and sounds, a millennium of history, the world's greatest concentrations of wildlife, a multitude of languages and traditions, intricacies of rural community and the vigor of surging cities. Music is a way of life for Africans, dance a mode of comprehending all the world, and the earth a good place to work.

Cities

Capital cities monopolize the communications and conveniences of most African countries. Your visit is likely to start and end in town, and even your forays into game parks, forests and mountains usually conclude in air-conditioned lodgings, with a bath and a good meal at the end of the day. An African city is a mixed bag of styles and influences. An African crowd invariably justifies a pause in your day—whether at festivals and sporting matches, ebullient markets, family ceremonies or political rallies. People in as many sizes, skills and preoccupations as anywhere on earth combine into rhythmic, complex communities, both in town and beyond.

The Rural Scene

Eight out of 10 Africans live outside population centers (10,000 and above) and the urbanites return to their rural sources with regularity. The countryside, where the animals are, remains the natural setting for most of the great sculpture, dance and music. Out there, masks are still sacred, drums speak, ancestors remain in power, dance focuses the world's body and spirit, and itinerant troubadors (griots) celebrate the history of Africans inside the communal circle. It may mean some dusty travel, but you haven't really been to Africa unless you've seen a bit of rural life.

The Cultural Scene

Back in town, the most authentic environment for traditional art is established at museum compounds in Niamey, Lagos, Oshogbo, Abomey, Rabat and Dar es Salaam. Excellent collections exists in museums and galleries in Dakar, Nairobi, Cairo, Addis Ababa, Tunis and Algiers. Artists and craftsmen cluster at work in and around the great museums, marketplaces and artisans' quarters of the towns. Western styles in painting, sculpture and architecture are on exhibit in North and Southern Africa, and in other cosmopolitan centers like Nairobi, Abidjan, Dakar, Accra and Lagos. National museums in most capitals have collections of history and natural history, technology and local lore.

The ruined past is on display at Roman and Punic sites in North Africa, the ancient Nile cities of Egypt and the Sudan, the slave forts and castles of Gorée Island (Senegal), Ghana and Dahomey; great civilizations are recalled throughout Ethiopia and the Sudan, at Timbuktu and Gao in Mali, and at Zimbabwe's stone ruins (Rhodesia), Kilwa, Gedi and other East African sites. Archaeological remains and rock paintings bear witness to ancient societies in the arid areas of Tanzania, Algeria, Mauritania, Chad, Namibia and South Africa.

The so-called "tribal" dancing included in package tours usually represents a stagey and often pallid version of African dance. The real thing can be seen if you are lucky enough to come upon a community festival or family celebration. National, local and student dance groups are often highly imaginative. Some of the best can be found (when not on foreign tour) in the cities of Algeria, Ghana, Guinea, Mali, Morocco, Sierra Leone and Tunisia.

Audacious blends of traditional and modern theater appear in the Yoruba operas of Nigeria, the universities of Ghana and Dar es Salaam and the strolling players of Madagascar. Amateur and professional theater thrives in many capitals.

Talented filmmakers work in Algeria, Nigeria, Senegal and Egypt. Cinema clubs, especially in French-speaking countries, are good places to see their work. Elsewhere film-going is more of a social than an aesthetic experience—best for watching African audiences respond to hoary westerns, muscle melodramas and Egyptian or Indian musical comedies.

Night Life

Africans enjoy uninhibited, affable night life, often at outdoor dance pavilions with minimum cover charges and lots of high-life, Congo jazz, soul and other city music. The best joints, open from 10 or 11 pm until dawn, are found in Accra, Lagos, Dakar and Kinshasa. Saturday nights are particularly lively. Women come with or without escorts and anyone may dance with anyone. You can nurse a beer all night if you want to.

This nocturnal life goes on alongside European fashions in discotheques, cocktail, dinner and dance parties, private clubs, hotel dance bands and floorshows. Tourists, resident whites and affluent Africans mix in these settings. International entertainers sometimes make appearances in the North African cities, Nairobi, Accra, Dakar and Abidjan. On occasion they perform in smaller cities on tours sponsored by the British, Chinese, Soviet, French, German, Israeli, American and other official cultural programs.

Meeting People

The African family, a community that often includes hundreds of persons, is an auspicious forum for meeting people. Bringing greetings from a member of the family who is abroad—perhaps a student—can serve as an introduction. International clubs like Rotary, Lions and Masonic orders are useful in Liberia, Nigeria and a few other countries where Africans have joined them. Many church and professional associations in Africa, including physicians, lawyers and teachers, have international affiliations and their members enjoy meeting visiting counterparts. But even a chance acquaintance in a hotel, bar, taxi or on a campus may draw you into the family circle.

Schools and Projects

For a dramatic introduction to Africa's hopes and problems, consider visiting a number of schools, in and out of town. Half the continent's population is under 20 years of age; families and government make extraordinary efforts for education, with both success and disenchantment.

Africa has many modern, handsome universities that are worth a visit. Among the most attractive are those in Nairobi, Ibadan, Dakar, Dar es Salaam, Kinshasa, Abidjan and Legon. Accompanying a student back to his rural home can provide insights into the changes and contrasts of African society.

A proliferation of social and economic development projects, many of them under the auspices of international organizations, offer opportunities to learn about modern Africa. Some projects succeed and others don't, but many are of interest—including experimental farms, community development programs, artisans' cooperatives and public health projects in rural areas, especially in Tanzania, Ivory Coast and Botswana.

Business and Trade

Those interested in economic life may want to visit stock and commodity exchanges in Lagos, Nairobi, Johannesburg and elsewhere. Chambers of commerce and industry and US embassy commercial attaches and economic officers can help with visits to factories, plantations, hydroelectric projects and the like.

Government and Courts

Most African states are dominated by their executive governments, but where national parliaments exist, even when powerless, their debates can be lively. This is particularly the case in Kenya, Tanzania, Liberia, Mauritius and South Africa. Elsewhere political life warms up in university settings, in bars and sidewalk cafes, at rallies and demonstrations.

Urban and rural courtrooms are stages for the changing panorama of African society. Generally open to the public, judicial proceedings are often conducted in English or French, with a mixture of traditional, colonial and post-independence law. A day in the courts of South Africa is particularly recommended for those who wish to know how its racial laws affect the lives of ordinary people.

Religion

Religion, both traditional and adopted, plays a vital part in African life. Where blends of cultures have occurred, Catholic and Protestant liturgy uses African music. Independent and "separatist" churches number in the thousands, especially in West, Central and Southern Africa. They have absorbed Christian elements into traditional "animist" doctrine. A few, like the Kimbanguists in Zaïre, have grown large and gained international recognition. Their services are often fascinating and they usually welcome visitors.

Islam, too, has become Africanized in the West African interior and on the East African coast, while retaining its predominantly Arab character in Northern Africa and the Indian Ocean. Even where mosques are open to visitors, permission to enter should be requested. Most mosques are closed to non-Moslems in Morocco, Egypt and Libya.

The major Islamic holidays have varying dates according to the Islamic calendar. Ramadan is a holy month of daytime fasting and the pace of business slows. Its termination, Idd al Fitr, like Lent for Christians, is celebrated with joyous feasting and thanksgiving. Moulod, marking the birth of the prophet Mohammed in 570 AD, is an austere, religious occasion. Minor Islamic religious holidays include the festive Idd al Idha (Tabaski), celebrating the consent of Abraham to sacrifice his son Isaac, and Idd al Hegira, commemorating the flight of Mohammed from Mecca in 622 AD.

Friday is the Moslem day of rest and prayer; offices and shops are often closed.

Animist beliefs are held by most Africans, some of them members of Moslem or Christian sects as well. Visitors may sometimes attend cult ceremonies by invitation; these include initiations, harvest celebrations, mask dances and divination rituals.

Wildlife

The major national parks and animal concentrations are in Kenya, Tanzania, Uganda, Zaïre, Zambia, Rhodesia, Botswana, South Africa and Mozambique. A short drive or a brief flight over the sparsely populated "bush" country outside towns in Niger, Chad, Gabon and Cameroon affords glimpses of animals.

Visits to the parks require a vehicle, booked through an overseas or local tour, or rented on the spot. Park rangers can be hired at reasonable cost to help locate the animals. Comfortable overnight accommodations are available in most parks. Park rules require visitors to remain inside their vehicles with the windows rolled up, to refrain from feeding the animals, and to give the elephants right of way. Our favorite parks are Serengeti, Arusha and Ngorongoro in Tanzania, Aberdare, Amboseli, Tsavo and Samburu in Kenya, Virunga (ex-Albert) in Zaïre, Murchison and Queen Elizabeth in Uganda, Luangwa Valley in Zambia and Wankie in Rhodesia.

Each has superb scenery, outstanding concentrations of wild life and excellent accommodations.

You are free to photograph wildlife at will in parks. Any camera will do but a zoom or telephoto lens is best, with an ultraviolet filter in front of the lens to soften the tones. Professional firms specialize in photographic safaris for the connoisseur. Respect the strong sunlight, always unload your camera in the shade, and keep in mind the contrast between the bright light or brilliant haze and the darker animals. Watch out for underexposure and take your light meter readings by pointing down to exclude the sky.

Most Africans, incidentally, lack access to the game parks and hence have never seen the animals that draw the tourists.

The Sporting Life

If you want to hunt the "big five"—lion, elephant, rhino, leopard or buffalo—you will need several thousand dollars and the services of a licensed professional hunter. Even antelope and deer hunting is expensive. The chapters on Botswana, the Central African Republic, Chad, Gabon, Kenya, Mozambique, Tanzania, Uganda, Rhodesia, South Africa and Zambia list addresses for operators of hunting trips. If you are content to hunt smaller game and birds, there are private clubs in many countries that can be of assistance. Big game hunting is a well-organized industry in East Africa; it is less regulated and somewhat less expensive in Botswana, Central Africa and Mozambique.

Ocean sport-fishing is popular in Angola, Mauritius, Mozambique, Namibia, Senegal, Seychelles, South Africa and Tanzania. Arrangements can be made locally or from abroad. In West Africa coastal fishermen will often take travelers out in their canoes and trawlers for a small fee. Lake and river fishing is organized through anglers' clubs in Malawi, Kenya, Ethiopia and Zambia, but there are many opportunities to go fishing on your own throughout Africa.

The Indian Ocean coast and islands are superb for skindiving and seashell collecting around magnificent coral reefs. There is also good underwater sport along the Mediterranean coasts of Algeria, Morocco and Tunisia, the Red Sea coasts of Ethiopia, Djibouti and Somalia, and some Atlantic Ocean areas like the Canary Islands, Senegal, Mauritania and Angola. Snorkeling and other equipment can usually be rented locally.

Water skiing is popular off the Indian Ocean coasts, the Atlantic coasts near large cities and on some of the larger inland lakes and lagoons. Swimming should be confined to oceans and artificial pools since many rivers and lakes are likely to be contaminated with bilharzia. The Atlantic beaches are pounded by a heavy surf most of the year, but they are relatively shark-free compared to some Indian Ocean coasts.

Africa has slopes and peaks to challenge the most experienced skier or alpinist. You can ski at resorts in Algeria, Lesotho, Morocco and South Africa. Mountain climbing is best in East Africa, where you can choose a pleasant ascent up the 20,000-foot Mt. Kilimanjaro or undertake the rigors of Mt. Kenya and the Ruwenzori Mountains of the Moon. Cameroon, Morocco, Ethiopia, the Indian Ocean islands, Lesotho and South Africa also offer mountaineering.

Soccer football is the universal African sport, played on weekends before enthusiastic crowds in large stadiums and on countless open patches of ground. Traditional forms of wrestling are staged in West Africa, Madagascar and Uganda. Amateur boxing pleases crowds in Nigeria, East and Southern Africa. Horse racing draws fans in Egypt, Kenya, Madagascar, Mauritius, Nigeria and South Africa; polo is a traditional sport in Nigeria. Kenya, with its Olympic champions, is the leader in track and field, popular also in Ethiopia, Uganda and Madagascar. Basketball, field hockey, table tennis and volleyball are catching on in the cities.

There are horse shows in North Africa, Southern Africa, Madagascar and Mauritius.

Luxury hotels and private clubs in most countries offer golf, horseback riding, tennis, yachting and sometimes cricket, rugby and other sports. Visitors are often admitted for a fee as temporary club members.

Tours and Guides

City travel agencies—especially in East, Southern and North Africa—can program your ventures into game parks, lake and mountain country and hunting-fishing grounds. Their tours of cities and environs provide welcome orientation, but only if you lack the time and/or transportation to make your own surveys. The most professional tour guides tend to be the least sympathetic—to their clients and to the African subject. A local student, taxi driver, friend of a hotel clerk or other amateur escort can usually do as well and for less expense. Through such city acquaintances you can also arrange to visit families and schools up country and to keep abreast of harvest and initiation festivals where community life is at its most vivid—especially in Ghana, Mali, Nigeria, most other West African countries and Madagascar.

Ministries of Education and USIS cultural officers can also set up visits. Government ministries and foreign missions (including UN agencies) should facilitate a look at the development process. University personnel, chambers of commerce, syndicats d'initiative in French-speaking countries and local officials are frequently helpful.

WHAT TO BUY

There are no Hong Kongs or Singapores in Africa, but there is an abundance of sculpture, metal work, ivory, jewelry, leather goods, ceramics, embroidery, weaving, printed cloth, carpets and tapestries and much else. Film, medicines, cosmetics and other items of utility to the traveler can be picked up virtually anywhere en route, but imported goods are likely to be expensive and European labels and sizes can be confusing. (See the appendix for size conversions.)

Art

Contemporary African art often consists of traditional materials, influences and styles mixed with Western ideas and techniques. At its worst, in so-called airport art, it panders to popular distortions of African "primitivism" with thousands of glossy items that look mass-produced and sometimes are. At its best—as in the work of the Oshogbo artists in Nigeria, many of the painters and weavers in Ethiopia, and the sculptors and painters in North Africa, Ghana, the Ivory Coast and Mozambique— modern African art is passionate and exciting.

Traditional sculpture (masks and statues primarily) survives among the communities it still serves in West Africa, Zaïre, Ethiopia and Madagascar. You will have difficulty finding genuine "antiquities" these days, and will pay the price of rarity—as well as meeting government export license requirements for significant works. When you purchase gold jewelry, ivory, rugs and other expensive items look for government seals or stamps endorsing the quality.

Clothing

Variety, flair and audacity have made African styles fashionable outside the continent. While you're there, you can choose between ready-made local garments or inexpensive custom tailoring from exquisite patterns. Many visitors bring back prints, tie-dyes and batiks for curtains and room decorations. Clothing styles include the long, flowing and often brocaded West African men's and women's robes known as booboos, togas of golden kente cloth in Ghana, North African jellabas and kaftans modified into fashionable gowns and suits for casual wear, and the colorful and inexpensive kitenge cloth of East Africa, easily fashioned into comfortable dashikis or other sportswear. Hats, women's head-ties and caps come woven, beaded or knitted. They are made from straw, wool, cotton, raffia palm, seashells, hides and skins.

Stamps and Coins

African post offices carry first-day covers and other stamps of particular interest to collectors. Coin collecting friends will also appreciate attractive commemorative coins and medals issued by some governments.

Animals, Hides, Skins

Live animals may be imported from Africa (parrots and monkeys are favorites) but you will need government export permits, veterinarian's certificates and US Customs approval. For the free leaflet "So You Want to Import a Pet," write to the US Commissioner of Customs, Washington, D.C. 20226. There are no restrictions on hides and skins of domesticated animals or abundant wildlife like gazelles and zebras. However, both the African and US governments bar the export-import of hides and skins of endangered species such as leopard and cheetah.

Where and How to Buy

Making purchases directly from a craftsman or artist is the best way to buy things. Shopping in the outdoor markets—and bargaining for your goods —is second best. Those who lack time or patience, however, may prefer dealing with the regular shops, where prices are higher but fixed, and where merchants will arrange to ship items home. Some shops, especially those that are government owned or operated, will allow discounts for purchases made with travelers checks or other foreign exchange.

Some travelers detest bargaining as a demeaning, time-consuming ritual that always ends to their disadvantage. But most visitors get the habit fairly soon and begin to enjoy it—as Africans do. A good rule of thumb is to check the fixed prices on items in the expensive shops (starting with those that are government owned) and then expect to do 25 to 50 per cent better by bargaining in markets and bazaars or with street traders. Your starting price should be half what you are willing to pay. Always bargain with a sense of humor, never when in a hurry.

Many things can be shipped by air or sea freight before you start back. Larger shops will do this for you. If you use the post, send valuable items by registered mail.

US Customs

A traveler who has been outside the US more than 48 hours is allowed to bring back $100 worth of goods duty-free. Families may file joint declarations, pooling each member's allowance. Should you exceed the $100 ceiling, don't fret. US tariffs on most African items are very low. Works of art, if they're intended for your home and not for sale, are duty-free.

Separate gifts valued at $10 or less which are shipped to persons in the US are not subject to duty or counted in your $100 allowance. Hotels will usually help to wrap and mail small packages. Label them "unsolicited gift, value under $10." The US Customs Service has free brochures explaining this and other procedures.

Film Processing

Black and white still film can be competently processed in most African cities, but color can be handled only in Johannesburg and Nairobi. If you mail exposed film, send it in the pouch provided by the manufacturer or in a package marked "Undeveloped photographic film of US manufacture —examine with care." Send movie film to the manufacturer.

LOCAL ATTITUDES

Travelers, especially off the main tourist paths, often are objects of curiosity. It helps to say hello and exchange greetings—in the most appropriate language you can muster. The tone matters more than the words. Brash children may tag along, at a safe distance, eager to chat, gape or be amused. Don't be upset if they call at you, using the local term for "European" or "white"—sometimes even if you are black or brown.

Andrew Gilboy, who wrote this book's chapter on backpacking, says: "Curiosity and questions directed at you reflect a thirst for information about other people and places and not rudeness. Try not to be affronted if asked about your family, why you are traveling, where you are staying and how much it costs." Everywhere students will be eager to exchange addresses and become pen pals.

Dignity is a cardinal quality of African personal relations. No matter what other travelers or residents do, it is highly offensive to use first names for elders and to address servants or waiters as "boy."

Gilboy offers these observations about social contacts: "In many parts of Africa rising is often optional, but you must shake hands with all the people in a room whether you know them or not. There are various ways to do it. In some places just before separating hands, both people snap their thumb and third finger together, breaking the handshake with a crack of friendship. There are many variations of 'soul' handshakes and plenty of opportunities to learn them. Women participate in handshaking, especially among themselves, but older men or Moslem religious dignitaries may bypass outstretched female hands."

Taking Photos

It is always appropriate to ask permission before taking close-up photographs of people. Some Africans, especially Moslems, may have religious objections. Others may be sensitive about their poverty. The donation of an instant photo from a Polaroid camera can often overcome reluctance. At times you may be asked for a small fee by your subject. This is especially true of Pygmies and Masai people in East Africa who are besieged by foreign photographers. Pay up or put the camera away.

It is prudent everywhere to avoid photographing military vehicles and installations or soldiers; some countries such as Egypt and Zanzibar make it illegal. Photos of animals, scenery and festivals are totally unrestricted.

Beggars

Travelers will be dogged by beggars in the cities of Morocco, Egypt, the Sudan, Somalia, Djibouti, Senegal and Nigeria, among others. Algeria, Tanzania and Guinea have eliminated begging, and many governments seek from time to time to eradicate the nuisance. Begging is an hereditary, sometimes honorable, profession in Moslem-influenced places, particularly among the physically handicapped, and alms-giving an obligation of the faithful. The practice should not be confused with bribe-seeking by petty officials or unsolicited offers of "guide" service encountered throughout the Mediterranean world.

Hospitality and Courtesy

Most Africans are poor by our standards. Hospitality is important, however, and reciprocity in gifts a treasured ritual. If you're invited to a home or village bring along a token item—bottled drinks or cigarettes for the elders and perhaps candy, chewing gum or fruit for the children. It is the gesture rather than the value of the gift that counts. At home many Africans eat with their right hand, but they will usually provide utensils for their non-African guests.

Punctuality

Outside the cities people rise and go to bed early, relying on natural divisions of the day. In Swahili the first hour of the day is 6 am. Everywhere time is treated casually and punctuality is no consuming passion. Try not to organize your trip around rigid schedules.

Sex and Sexuality

Many things in Africa will seem strange to Americans just as what we take for granted often bewilders others. Sexual matters are no exception. Because thighs are considered erogenous zones, many governments prohibit miniskirts and shorts. Female breasts are sometimes not regarded in the same way. Family and childbearing are what matter for most Africans. Extramarital sex is neither approved nor taken seriously. Attitudes toward sex are stricter in Islamic countries where women are often still secluded. In all the rapidly growing cities and towns men far outnumber women; urban prostitution, promiscuity and veneral disease are widespread.

Friendship is often expressed in totally non-sexual physical contact between persons of the same sex, as, for instance, when African men stroll along holding hands. Overt homosexuality is rare.

Africans and Americans

Ethnic community often transcends national, class or racial identity among Africans. That abused term "tribe" may refer to a cultural and linguistic group numbering hundreds, or hundreds of thousands or millions of people who share a common history. Others, whatever their appearance or manners, are strangers. Their interest in African customs and values is appreciated but their opinions on the merits of "tribalism" are irrelevant.

Americans are little known in many parts of Africa, and not readily distinguished from nationals of the former European colonial powers. Interest in the United States often focuses on politics, racial problems, rock and soul music and, for students, the chances of obtaining scholarships. It is most unwise to respond to student appeals with unrealistic hopes of university admissions, scholarships or jobs—unless you are actually prepared to help. To many Africans desperate for further education, a casual remark may be taken seriously and lead to misunderstandings.

Africans familiar with tourists generally see Americans as sociable, inclined to ask friendly questions, free with information about themselves and their own society, highly sensitive to dirt and unsanitary conditions but ready to tolerate discomfort when the goal is worth the trouble. Americans are also known for being critical of the elitist attitudes copied or continued from colonial models, and especially of officiousness on the part of government and hotel employees.

It helps to be flexible about small matters—to use local currencies rather than expecting dollars to be accepted everywhere, to endure the absence of *Time* and *Newsweek*, or ignorance of the dry martini.

COMMUNICATION

Although linguists identify something like 700 languages in Africa, a knowledge of English and/or some French will get you around the cities and many rural areas.

The British taught Africans English terms so expect to hear "shed-yool" for schedule, "lorry" for truck, "tarmac" for asphalt, "school-leaver" for elementary school graduate and "GCE" or "Cambridge" for high school graduating exams. Spelling similarly follows British rules, except in Liberia where American English is written and spoken with a southern drawl.

A working knowledge of French helps wherever it is the official language. It is almost essential in Burundi, the Central African Republic, the Comoro Islands and Chad, where English is scarcely known—unless you're traveling in a guided tour group.

African Languages

Arabic, English and French are probably the three most widely spoken languages in Africa. Hausa in West Africa and Swahili in East Africa are first languages for many millions, and second or third languages for tens of millions. Each has a written literature going back hundred of years. Wherever you are, using a few simple greetings in the local language will be appreciated.

Communications Media

Radio, television and the press in most of Africa are government owned or controlled. Listening or reading can be interesting if less than informative. Government radio stations are strong on African pop music, and government press releases weak on news. There are a few private radio stations. Television is mostly confined to the cities and tends to rely on programs imported from Europe and the United States.

National film industries are emerging in Algeria, Egypt, Senegal and Nigeria, and a small number of talented cinematographers are at work in Tunisia, Niger, Ghana and the Ivory Coast. African publishing is growing rapidly, particularly in schoolbook production, but also in fiction. Enterprising publishing firms thrive in Algeria, Cameroon, Ghana, Kenya, Nigeria, South Africa and Tunisia.

The best way to stay abreast of world events while traveling in Africa is to listen to shortwave BBC and Voice of America broadcasts, heard on any good transistor radio. Selected American and European periodicals are available at airports, hotels and bookshops.

Mail

African postal service is not nearly as beautiful as African stamps. The mails are erratic and letters are frequently lost. Domestic rates are low, sometimes one-third to one-half of US rates. Airmail letters take three to seven days between most African cities and North America. Postcards and oversized envelopes can be delayed. Airmail packages may take one to two weeks; surface mail one to four months. Send important items by registered mail. Sometimes urgent letters can be sent through airlines offices with direct flights to Europe or the US.

General delivery (poste restante) services at post offices are notoriously unreliable. It's best to have your correspondence addressed to hotels or travel agents on your itinerary or, when in doubt, to US embassies or consulates (c/o Visitors' Mail); these offices will hold or forward your mail on request.

Telecommunications

Internal telephone service is poor almost everywhere in Africa, although improving in some places. Local calls require patience. Public phones are usually found only in post offices. Telephone directories may be hopelessly out of date or inaccurate. It is sometimes easier, and less expensive, to make a call to Europe than to another African country—a legacy of the colonial communications systems. Inter-African or overseas radio-telephone service is operated through central post offices. Ground stations for communications satellites in Abidjan, Nairobi, Kinshasa, Casablanca, Lagos, Tananarive and Las Palmas have improved the quality of calls from those cities to the United States.

Airlines, major hotels and travel agencies have telex services. Night letters (LT's) carry 22 words for the same price as 11-word regular cables. Night letters and cables, like mail, are delivered to post office boxes in most African countries rather than to homes or offices.

Time Zones

The African continent and the Indian Ocean Islands are divided into five time zones based on Greenwich Mean Time (GMT). Traveling eastward across Africa from the extreme west, you begin in Dakar one hour behind GMT (US Eastern Standard Time is five hours behind) and end in the Western Indian Ocean, three hours ahead of GMT. Thus, any place in Africa is four to eight hours later than New York City. For instance, when it is noon in Nairobi (1200) it is 1 pm (1300) in Tananarive, 11 am in Cairo and Johannesburg, 10 am in Kinshasa, Tunis and Rome, 9 am in Accra, Lagos, Paris and London (GMT time), 8 am in Dakar and Monrovia and 4 am in New York.

EMERGENCIES

If you're going to spend at least a few days in a country, it is a good idea to register at American embassies or consulates. Those offices can provide the names of physicians and dentists, as well as explanations of local laws. Larger posts have marine guards and 24-hour telephone service.

There are adequate hospital facilities in most larger cities. Watch out for unsterilized needles—a good way to get hepatitis. Some African governments have low-cost or free medical services but they are not always available to non-citizens. Travel insurance is safer.

Although thievery in the cities is increasing, most of Africa is considerably freer of violent crime than the United States. Protect passports and wallets from pickpockets. If your passport is lost or stolen, report your loss to the local police and the US embassy or consulate.

Political disruptions occur with some frequency in Africa, but rarely do they affect the traveler. Coups are seldom accompanied by violence. Still, if there are signs that trouble is brewing, check in at the American embassy for advice. But don't travel in the expectation that Africa will be thrusting political adventures in your path: law, order and public tranquility are the rule.

PMA and AS

Backpacking in Africa

By Andrew Gilboy

The rewards of backpacking in Africa are great and the discomforts depend mostly on your own attitude and flexibility. By traveling into the interior of these colorful countries rather than limiting yourself to their more Westernized capitals, you will live, eat and communicate with African people, visit the places where Africa's dramatic history unfolded before foreigners arrived and see Africans dancing not for tourists but for themselves. In short, you can experience Africa as it really exists for most of its people.

This chapter seeks to answer some questions you may have about inexpensive travel through Africa's interior: what kind of transportation to take, where to eat and sleep and what to bring. I have avoided listing cheap hotels, bargain restaurants or the places "not to be missed."

Most Africans welcome guests, appreciate the sincere interest of foreigners in their way of life and reciprocate with a fresh curiosity of their own. These qualities are expressed in African terms and may not correspond with our Western ways. Some behavior may even appear rude when quite the opposite is intended.

Tourism is increasing but so far is confined primarily to capital cities and game parks. People of the interior areas have had relatively little contact with travelers and are especially curious and genuinely open. While traveling among them you must be very sensitive to local traditions and customs. African countries have their share of flies, mosquitoes, heat and dust—about as much as the southern part of the US or Italy.

Going by Land

If you are in a hurry don't travel by land. Fly to the different capitals and see Africa as a tourist. You will see the seats of newly independent countries, get an idea of Africa's urban problems and perhaps visit a market. But traditional life styles are found in the interior where 80 per cent of Africans still work the land. With a minimum of three weeks in a country or region, you can escape the capital and bridge the gulf separating urban and rural Africa. Land travel inland is slow and irregular, but somehow everyone seems to reach his destination.

Most public transports wait in the taxi garage until full before leaving. This means you wait, and wait, and count each entering passenger, and watch the luggage being loaded on top, and wait. It can take minutes, hours, days or occasionally weeks to get enough people in one transport, depending on the country, season and destination.

But once on the trail, it can be a lot of fun. There is a very real leveling between the rich and poor, old and young, visitor and host when all are crammed into the back of an open bus. Only senior government officials and the wealthy fly. Everyone else goes by land. Even though a broken spring, a washed-out bridge, or a nasty customs official can delay you for days, the experience is exciting and brings you in close contact with African life. It is in these situations that you may feel the warmth of African hospitality.

Types of Transportation

Public land transportation in Africa is by train, boat, "bush taxi," small and large bus or open truck. Trains are slow but friendly, especially in third class, and are comfortable in first or second. River travel is often possible depending on the season. There are steam or diesel river boats on the Senegal, Gambia, Niger, Benue, Cross and Zaïre (Congo) rivers as well as on the great East African lakes. There are also barges, smaller locally made boats hauling goods and people, canoes and dhows.

The most expensive common transport is the bush taxi, a seven- to nine-passenger European station wagon. It is fairly comfortable and is restricted to paved or reasonably good roads. The cost for 100 miles might be between $2 and $3. The smaller buses hold from 15 to 25 passengers and resemble pick-up trucks fitted in the back with seats and a roof. The larger 80-passenger buses are usually the slowest, least roomy and most prone to breakdowns. They also have the highest ratio of chickens and goats. Exceptions are the state-controlled bus companies in Niger, Sierra Leone, Ghana and East Africa, which provide reliable service.

There are also the good but relatively expensive Midwest or Greyhound Bus Lines in Nigeria (about $3.30 one way for a 95-mile trip between Lagos and Ibadan). The large open trucks are only for the adventurous off to hard-to-reach places; for example, Kayes to Nioro du

Sahel in Mali, parts of northeastern Zaïre, or Tambacounda to Kédougou in Senegal.

You can find out about land travel by inquiring at the taxi garage, bus depot, gare populaire, police station or police checkpoint on the road. To get accurate information ask several people the same questions and verify ticket prices by asking other passengers what they paid.

Areas of Travel

Land travel in East Africa (Tanzania, Kenya and Uganda) is much easier and cheaper than in Central and most of West Africa. For example, the 400-mile trip from Nairobi to Kampala takes from 10 to 12 hours in a scheduled bus and costs under $5. In West Africa, although the going is slower, you can travel by land from the westernmost point of the continent (Senegal) to Central Africa (Cameroon)—an enormous expanse of over 3,000 miles—by using several sub-Saharan routes. Here are some possibilities:

Dakar (Senegal) to Bamako (Mali): Twice weekly "express" train, 30 hours.

Bamako to Ouagadougou (Upper Volta): Scheduled bus ("Trans-Africaine") to Bobo-Dioulasso through Sikasso. Bobo-Dioulasso to Ouagadougou by train. Two to three days.

Bamako to Gao (Mali): By Niger River boat August to December stopping at Segou, Mopti and Timbuktu. Six days.

Gao to Niamey (Niger): Twice weekly scheduled bus (SNTN- Société Nationale de Transport Nigérien, still called the "Trans-Africaine" locally).

Ouagadougou to Niamey: Scheduled bus, lorries available.

Niamey to Zinder (Niger): Four SNTN buses a week for the two-day trip.

Niamey to Kano (Nigeria): Same as above. Leave bus the first night at Birni-Nkonni to go through Sokoto, or change at Maradi the second day to go through Katsina. Two to four days.

Zinder to Agadès (Niger): Weekly scheduled bus, lorries available. (See desert routes.)

Kano to Ibadan and Lagos (Nigeria): Scheduled bus, train (very slow), small truck and lorries. Twenty-four hours minimum.

The coastal route, with a number of interesting detours into interior forest territory, starts in Freetown (Sierra Leone). Go southeast to Abidjan, capital of the Ivory Coast, then take the less traveled road along the Gulf of Guinea coast, entering Ghana at Half Assini. Continuing toward Takoradi and Accra, this road passes by several historic forts and castles (at Elmina and Cape Coast) built at the beginning of European influence in Africa. After Accra you can continue to follow the coast through Togo and Dahomey to Lagos. Cross lower Nigeria just above the great Niger River delta, enter Cameroon at Ekok and continue on through Mamfé to Douala.

It is impossible to travel directly south from Senegal through Guinea-Bissau and into the Republic of Guinea (Conakry). The borders are closed to travelers because the Guineans of Bissau are engaged in a war of liberation from centuries of Portuguese colonial rule. Even if the borders were not closed to travelers, the way would be extremely difficult.

Only three routes—open most of the year—cross the vast Sahara desert between Arab North Africa (Morocco, Algeria, Tunisia) and Black West Africa.

Western route: Casablanca (Morocco) to Agadir, Tiznit, Aaiún (Spanish Sahara), Bir-Moghrein (Mauritania), Atar, Nouakchott, St. Louis (Senegal) and Dakar.

Middle route: Oujda (Morocco) or Oran (Algeria) to Béchar, Adrar, Gao (Mali) and Niamey (Niger).

Eastern route: Algiers (Algeria) to El-Golea, In Salah, Tamanrasset, Agadès (Niger) and Zinder.

Travel with experienced people and plan to spend a week or more finding a ride. Driving is usually at night and can take from four to 14 days.

In much of Central Africa movement is best by river—Zaïre (Congo), Ubangi, Kasai—since the roads are extremely bad and Americans cannot get visas to cross the People's Republic of Congo (Brazzaville). To travel from Yaoundé (Cameroon) to Kinshasa (Zaïre), go overland by bus or truck to Bangui, capital of the Central African Republic, and take a boat to Kinshasa. You can continue on to Zambia and Southern Africa by taking a boat to Ilebo (formerly Port Francqui), train and road combination to Lubumbashi and road thereafter. Or you can get to Kisangani and East Africa from Kinshasa (by boat) and from Bangui (by boat and truck).

Hitchhiking is difficult in the interiors of all West African countries except Nigeria—and there, as in East Africa, you may be asked to pay. If you have lots of time and patience it is possible to find free rides. Ask around at the market, local factories, transport companies, repair garages, petrol stations or wherever you see lorries.

Renting a car or taxi is expensive. Buying a car is possible but is worthwhile only in East or Southern Africa. Car ownership minimizes your contact with people and presents new problems: breakdowns, insurance, accidents, crossing borders and reselling the car. You cannot buy your way out of a broken axle 360 miles northwest of Ouagadougou.

Lodging

There is at least one cheap, decent place to stay in every capital (YMCA, student lodge, university dormitory, Peace Corps hostel). In the interior there are often rest-houses with the basics, or cheap African-owned hotels. Wherever possible I recommend patronizing African rather than foreign-owned establishments to give impetus to the growth of indigenous businesses. Generally there are far more facilities for backpackers in East Africa than elsewhere.

If you are friendly and sincerely interested in Africans, you are likely to be invited to sleep and eat in someone's home.

Food

If you are not hung up on meat and potatoes, the different tastes and textures of African food can be a fascinating side adventure. Try a mouth-watering bowl of Senegalese thiébou diéné (pronounced "cheboodjin"): fluffy rice, pieces of fresh fish, cooked carrots, cabbage, tomatoes, potatoes and eggplant, all neatly spiced with red pepper. Or sample Moroccan couscous, Nigerian gari, fried bananas from the Ivory Coast, and the most pan-African dish of all—groundnut (peanut) sauce over rice.

Eating is a family affair, usually around a bowl on the floor or in the compound courtyard, without utensils. Take cues on exactly how to eat from those around you. Africans always wash their hands before and after meals, and eat only with the right hand. Never use the left hand for eating, handing things to people or sticking in your mouth. This is a custom you will understand better after a few weeks in Africa. Eat heartily—it's the highest compliment a guest can pay a host.

There are good cheap African restaurants in every town, often near the taxi depots, where women cook food especially for travelers. If you are in a transport that doesn't stop for long periods, or in a remote area, all you really need are a can of sardines, a jar of peanut butter, some bread or biscuits, a few cans of fruit juice, some candy and water.

When you tire of iodized water, try each country's line of soft drinks and beer, although they are often more expensive than locally made palm wine or rice beer. In Mali drown yourself in the most delicious pure tamarind and guava juice sold cold at the state supply stores. Also try cold milk in Ghana, beer made from millet in Niger and semi-sweet chocolate in Cameroon. If the right ingredients are available, well-prepared African food is nutritious, spicy (red pepper is an easily acquired habit—or ask for less of it in the cooking) and a good change from fries, burgers and shakes.

What to Bring

Follow the traveler's golden rule in packing: if in doubt, leave it out. You do not need a rechargeable shaver, 20 pairs of underwear or a wrist watch. You will walk a lot and will want room in your luggage for purchases of African crafts, clothes and works of art. With little more than basic hiking equipment you can travel comfortably.

Whether you carry a backpack (recommended), a small suitcase or a durable bag, the following items are necessary: blanket or sleeping bag, small flashlight, simple can opener, pocket knife with bottle opener, towel, extra pair of eye glasses, plastic water bottle or canteen, plastic bag of medicine (malaria and diarrhea pills, water purification tablets, aspirin, penicillin ointment for minor wounds, a few Band-aids), toilet paper, extra passport pictures, a hat, a candle, matches, a pen and tablet, and the accurate and comprehensive Michelin "red" maps of Africa (numbers 153, 154, 155). Plus something for passport, papers and cash which you can keep on your person. Most of these things are easily available in any African capital.

The following items may be useful and, again, can be bought in Africa: collapsible umbrella, mosquito net and string, soap dish, sun glasses, a small mirror, a tiny bottled-gas burner and pan to cook coffee and soup, a spoon and a small piece of foam rubber to sit or sleep on.

Unless you play the cocktail circuit in the capitals, you will never need a suit, tie or good dress. Nor will you need a bathrobe (a large piece of African cloth draped around you is acceptable) or shorts. Men and women should take: blue jeans, a pair or two of wash-and-wear pants, a light sweater and jacket, one long-sleeved and some short-sleeved shirts (all washable cottons), and a pair of shoes for the city. Sandals (available everywhere) are ideal for traveling. Women may want in addition (particularly in excessive heat or when mosquitoes are not bothersome) one or two wash-and-wear cotton dresses.

Bring US currency in travelers checks, but have some cash on hand to change on the spot for local currency. There is a black market demand for the US dollar, British pound, French franc, etc., in Nigeria, Ghana, East Africa, Ethiopia, Zaïre, Egypt and some other areas. Exchange rates vary enormously from one dealer to the next and even officially from bank to bank. Other travelers are the best source of information.

What to Do

Living or traveling by land in Africa forces a change in your concept of time. The tempo is slow and the rhythm uneven. You might have to wait hours in a taxi in a state of seemingly infinite immobility, and then find yourself careening down the road at frightening speed. You will wonder why the driver waited hours to get only two more passengers instead of leaving and arriving earlier. Because of high unemployment and a scarcity of cash, an African's time is not worth very much money in his own society. You will have to realize this while waiting. Stretch your patience to—and sometimes beyond—its current limits, and above all keep your sense of humor.

Since there are few castles, cathedrals or cafes in Africa, you may wonder what to do with your time when not on the road. If you take an interest in Africa, there are famous places, mosques, palaces, an occasional ruin and some museums to visit. Or you may want to get involved in archaeological work (always in progress in different parts of the continent). Try a museum, university or foreign embassy in Africa for more information. Take along a few paperbacks on African history, art, politics and people. You will learn most by engaging with Africans in one of their favorite pastimes, conversation.

Most travelers find the market the most exciting place in any city. Here all the colors of Africa merge, and new sounds and smells leap at you faster than you can react. Whether you are interested in leather goods, straw baskets, silver and gold jewelry, pottery, handwoven tapestries and blankets, African cloth, seeing what people eat and wear, smelling spices and incense, watching tailors embroider, or simply meeting people, the market is the place. Everyone goes there—to buy, sell or exchange goods, to meet and chat with friends and to browse. It is the center of all daytime activity.

People from every ethnic group in a given area can be found in the market with their distinctive goods. Since the smaller markets in the interior are usually weekly or biweekly affairs, be at your destination on the right day. Bargaining is the law of the market, so be aware of what others pay or be able to negotiate well.

Keep alert for national holidays, tribal fetes and local dances. These are always colorful and exciting, but rarely publicized by newspapers. Information is spread by word of mouth or by radio in the local language. The arrival of a visiting president or dignitary is also an occasion for dancing and pageantry. Nearly all events of this type are public or informal, so enjoy them with everyone else.

Precautions

You are safer in any African city than in New York or Chicago. Violence against foreigners is very rare anywhere and especially rare in the interior.

The crime rate is probably highest in Nigeria and East Africa, but it is insignificant compared to America. Petty robbery is the most frequent crime. No matter how little money you take, you will have more than most Africans earn in a year. Thieves are daring and look for cash, watches, cameras, tape recorders, jewelry, shoes and fancy clothes. Be sure to carry your cash, passport and record of your travelers check numbers on you at all times. If robbed, notify police first, then look for your belongings in the market. Spread the word around town with friends and above all—especially in Moslem Africa—have a charm made (called a "gris-gris" in French or "juju" in English) against future misfortune.

Two women traveling alone need not fear sexual abuse, although modesty is a good idea and miniskirts or hot pants outside the cities are not recommended. Women should take their cue on wearing pants from the local school girls and professional women, especially in rural areas. Be aware of dress length and the amount of body exposed in Moslem countries where it can be offending. Since Africans are personally clean and modest, a dirty traveler in messy clothes is an insult to them: they can interpret slovenliness as a mockery of their poverty. I am convinced that some African countries hassle certain travelers because of their insensitivity to local customs, not because of beards and beads.

Consider backpacking through Africa if you are up to a few discomforts and, more important, if you have enough time. If you do go and hit it off well with Africans, your trip will be enjoyable; it is the African people, rather than distant monuments or remains of past glory, that make travel there so exciting.

North Africa

Algeria
Canary Islands
Ceuta and Melilla
Morocco
Spanish Sahara
Tunisia

THE REGION AT A GLANCE

Three millennia of commerce and conquest have defined modern North Africa, a broad corridor of land between the Mediterranean Sea and the Sahara Desert. The indigenous population of Berber people welcomed, sometimes resisted, and usually retreated from waves of Phoenicians, Romans, Arabs, Spanish and French. Berber tribes still dwell in the mountains and desert areas of Morocco and Algeria.

Spain prevails at the region's westernmost points—the lovely Canary Islands and the desolate Spanish Sahara, as well as in the ancient coastal city-states of Ceuta and Melilla. France still calls much of the tune in Morocco, Algeria and Tunisia, the three independent states of the Maghreb (western zone of Islam).

Yet for all the remaining strength of Europe in political and economic affairs, the Maghreb remains Arab in language, religion and social organization. Arab invasions began in the 7th century, and for a thousand years Arab merchants, scholars and governments dealt regularly with the Berbers and the Sudanic African civilizations across the Sahara. Warfare and slave trading beginning in the early 17th century turned the Sahara from a traveled ocean of sand into a desert barrier, separating North Africa from the rest of the continent.

Tunisia and Morocco recovered their independence in 1956, after more than a century as "protectorates" of France and Spain, whereas Algeria, settled by a million Europeans, had to win its sovereignty in 1962

71

NORTH AFRICA

after eight years of war against France. The Algerian republic continues militant and nationalist, dedicated to agrarian reform, international neutrality and an Islamic socialist order. Tunisia lives in closer harmony with the European spirit of the northern Mediterranean, Adriatic and Aegean seas; crowds of European visitors flock to her sunny, cosmopolitan and exhilarating shores. Morocco, the ancient monarchy, bounded by sea and mountain, receives its own abundance of tourists dazzled by a host of natural and man-made splendors; but the Moroccan social order has become increasingly disturbed as new aspirations confront traditions of hierarchy and privilege dating from centuries of Moroccan rule over the Iberian peninsula and the entire western Sahara.

North Africa's several seas, rich deposits of civilization, fertile hillsides, broad plains and national dramas are all relatively accessible to one another. Travelers can move easily east and west by combinations of air, road, rail and Sahara track. The Canaries stand well within ship and air routes from Europe and the Maghreb. Ceuta, Melilla and Moroccan Tangier

North African souk

Bus

Beach, Rabat

are touched by immense numbers of transient visitors from Spain. In the booming tourist atmosphere of splendid Morocco, open-armed Tunisia and the spring-like Canaries, it takes diligence to find corners not yet demeaned by the ubiquitous picture postcards, the European mass-tour migrations and the commercialism of the tourist industry. But such places exist and are worth the search.

From the Canary Islands to Tunisia, this is the region of closest proximity for Western travelers. It offers extraordinary beauty, art and pageantry, a contrast of climates, superb opportunities for shopping and relaxation, an unsurpassed alternation of cities, countryside, beaches and mountains, and a varied amalgam of East and West on Africa's continent.

PMA

Algeria

(République Algérienne)

Profile

STATUS: Independent republic since July 3, 1962. Formerly part of Metropolitan France.

SIZE: 919,595 square miles (about one-fourth the size of the US). Population—14,000,000.

GEOGRAPHY: Seven-eighths desert; 640 miles of coastal plains along Mediterranean Sea; Atlas mountains running from east to west. Principal cities—Algiers (capital, 1,000,000), Oran (440,000), Constantine (280,000).

CLIMATE: Temperate climate along the coast; temperatures may reach the 90's in summer and drop to the 40's in winter. Sahara very hot (especially June to September) but temperatures drop 40 degrees at night.

LANGUAGES: Arabic and French.

CURRENCY: Algerian dinar, divided into 100 centimes. 1 dinar = 23 cents; $1.00 = 4.35 dinars.

VISAS: Required. Available from Algerian Interests Section, Embassy of Guinea, Washington. Fee $3.07 (up to three-months stay). Four passport photos needed. Allow two to three weeks for processing. Also available at Algerian embassies in Paris, Tunis, Rabat.

AIRPORT: Dar El Beida (ALG), 13 miles from Algiers. Frequent flights to Lyon, Marseille, Paris, Rome, Geneva, Tripoli, Tunis, Casablanca, Middle East and Eastern Europe. Airport departure taxes—domestic, 5 dinars; within Africa, 10 dinars; outside Africa, 15 dinars.

NATIONAL HOLIDAYS: May 1, Labor Day; July 3, Independence Day; November 1, anniversary of 1965 coup; Moslem holidays.

INFORMATION SOURCES: *In US*—Algerian Interests Section, Embassy of Guinea, 2118 Kalorama Road NW, Washington, D.C. 20008 (tel. 202/234-7246). *In Algiers*—Office National Algérien du Tourisme, 25 Rue Khelifa Boukhalfa (tel. 64-68-65).

By Aaron Segal

A visit to this young and fiercely proud republic can be both frustrating and rewarding. The Algerian Government does not discourage tourism, but neither does it go out of its way to provide comforts. Travelers who accept these terms will encounter a combination of Arab, Berber and French civilizations and a striking contrast of geographic zones—a fertile and beautiful 640-mile Mediterranean coast protected by rugged mountain ranges from the immense, harsh Saharan interior.

The colonization of Algeria by France began about 1830 when French troops staked out a piece of the coast. Not far behind were the French commercial interests, which ultimately extended their influence over most of the country. In 1870–71, during the Franco-German war, French settlers arrived in large numbers for the first time, many from Alsace and Lorraine fleeing German rule. The settlers, known as "pieds noirs" (literally, black feet), dominated a prosperous economy based on citrus fruits, wine and grains.

By the time Algerians began their bloody seven-year war for independence in 1954 there were a million French settlers in Algeria's towns and farms. They regarded Algeria as their birthright, and vigorously opposed Arab-Berber majority rule. The war ended in 1962 with the nationalist movement triumphant at a cost of hundreds of thousands killed or wounded. Although the settlers were repatriated, the economy was still tied to France by a number of preferential agreements.

Since independence Algeria has concentrated on economic development to provide its extremely youthful population of 14 million with the promised fruits of the revolution. The government has assumed control of the bountiful petroleum and natural gas resources, as well as other industries, and made clear its intention to achieve economic as well as political independence. It maintains a love-hate relationship with France, cooperates closely with most of the socialist nations, and expresses an extremely militant attitude against Israel. An eminent example of successful revolution, Algeria has welcomed representatives of nationalist movements from white-ruled Africa and elsewhere.

The country is headed by the taciturn President Houari Boumedienne, a veteran guerrilla leader of the Algerian war who ousted the more flamboyant Ahmed Ben Bella in a 1965 coup. Boumedienne's leadership depends largely on Western-educated technologists, army officers who led the guerrilla struggle, and traditionalists seeking expanded influence for the Arabic language and Islamic faith.

The Algerian revolution is graphically portrayed in the film *Battle of Algiers*. Post-independence developments are analyzed in David and

Marina Ottaway's *Algeria: The Politics of a Socialist Revolution* (University of California Press, 1970) and William B. Quandt's *Revolution and Political Leadership: Algeria, 1954–1968* (MIT Press, 1969).

Money Matters

The Algerian dinar is not convertible and not exportable. Exchange controls are rigorous and any temptation to operate on the black market should be resisted. Exchange your foreign currency at the Banque Centrale d'Algérie or the Banque Nationale d'Algérie, which are open from 8 to 11:30 am and 2:15 to 4:30 pm during the week. The banks are closed on Saturdays and during summer afternoons. The Algerians have inherited the French passion for bureaucracy; queues are likely to be long and service inefficient. The bank office at the Algiers airport is often closed. It is advisable to have French francs on hand; they are accepted by taxi drivers and others. Major hotels accept travelers checks and a few will take credit cards. Convert into Algerian currency only what you will need during your visit—and not a dinar more.

Getting In and Out

If you arrive without a visa you will not be allowed in (you may have to spend a night in jail if there is not an immediate flight out). Algeria broke diplomatic relations with the United States during the 1967 Arab-Israeli war but a handful of Algerian diplomats remain in Washington at the Embassy of Guinea (Conakry). A visa application and passport may be sent to Washington by registered mail with a self-addressed stamped envelope. Allow two to three weeks if you use this somewhat risky procedure. If you apply in person in Washington, Paris, Tunis or Rabat you may get a visa in two or three days, but don't count on it.

Algiers, Constantine and Oran are linked by numerous Air France and Air Algérie flights to Marseille and Paris; Swissair has excellent connections with Geneva. All these airlines offer special 10- to 14-day excursion fares. The three North African airlines—Air Algérie, Air Tunis and Royal Air Maroc—have regular flights covering Casablanca, Algiers and Tunis. Reservations should be booked well in advance and reconfirmed, especially during peak summer travel months.

There are good flight connections to Libya, Egypt and the Middle East. The only direct flights to sub-Saharan Africa are twice a week on Soviet and East German airlines from Algiers to Conakry (Guinean visa required). Other connections between Algeria and West Africa can be made in Casablanca, Marseille or Paris.

There is regular bus service between Algeria and border towns in

Morocco and Tunisia. But it is still not possible to rent a car in Tunisia or Morocco and leave it in Algeria or vice versa. Border customs officials are meticulous about documents for private cars and you will be turned back if everything is not in order. Hitchhiking from Morocco or Tunisia to Algeria is possible. There are excellent paved coastal roads, but traffic often consists of trucks, and payment from riders is expected. You can also enter Algeria via a slow daily train from the Moroccan border town of Oujda to Oran. The train ride provides an opportunity to get a glimpse of peasant life along the way.

You can also come by boat. The three North African countries operate a combined coastal freighter service with an itinerary that encompasses Casablanca, Oran, Algiers, Constantine and Tunis. The freighters take a few passengers. The CGTM Line (61 boulevard des Dames, Marseille) operates two-class passenger and car ferry service from Marseille to the Algerian ports of Algiers, Oran and Annaba. So, if you like, you can bring a car across the Mediterranean.

Some intrepid travelers make a trans-Saharan trip along the caravan trails that link Arab and Black Africa. All major trans-Saharan routes pass through Algeria but the traveler must know what he's doing. You'll need a four-wheel-drive vehicle, supplies of fuel, oil, food and water, spare parts, sand gear and some mechanical skills. Regular air patrols to spot stranded travelers no longer exist; if you get stuck, and are alone, good luck. Beyond the Algerian Sahara oil towns there are tracks (known in French as "pistes") marked by oil drums. They tend to get covered by sand and woe to you if you take the wrong turn. The heat and sand-storms make travel especially poor from early June to mid-September.

None of this means that trans-Saharan travel is impossible. Hundreds of travelers make the trip each year; thousands of Tuareg tribesmen thrive on these routes, crossing in six months in caravans of 50 to 150 camels. One way to travel is in a convoy with an experienced organization like Lindblad Travel of New York or Mini-Trek, Siafu and Encounter Overland Tours of London. All organize regular trans-Saharan trips at prices ranging from $400 to $2,000 per person depending on the number in the party, length of stay, etc.

But, if you insist on making the trip alone, be sure to inform the Algerian authorities of your plans. They are your main hope in case of trouble. Notify the Department of Saharan Affairs in Algiers and get the required permit from the municipality or sous-préfecture in the town you are departing from. In acquiring the permit you will be asked for detailed travel plans with estimated arrival times. This may prompt the Algerians to look for you if you fail to arrive. Here's a note of comfort:

It's illegal to refuse help to travelers who are stranded on the pistes.

The trans-Saharan trip is still one of the greatest and most challenging adventures available on this continent. There are three north-south routes —one good, one not so good and one bad. The best route starts in Algiers and goes via Tamanrasset to Agadès in northern Niger. You will need four-wheel drive when the asphalt gives out at El Goléa (340 miles south of Algiers) for the next 450-mile stretch to Tamanrasset, which has a small military base, a few shops and fresh water. About 565 tortuous miles follow before you reach the town of Agadès. Shovels, sand mats, flashlight, goggles and firewood for the sometimes freezing Saharan nights are all needed for this stretch.

If you want to try hitchhiking, you can reach Tamanrasset by heavy-duty trucks serving the oil towns. Be prepared to wait at Tamanrasset for a truck going through to Agadès, and to pay $5 to $10 for the thrill of a lifetime. Trucks roll at night, so you will probably have to sleep beneath the truck during the heat of day. Hitchhikers can go part of the way by bus. There's a weekly bus from Algiers to Tamanrasset operated by the Société Algérienne des Transports Sahariens.

The second route, tolerable but less traveled and longer, stretches from Algiers or Oran via Colomb-Béchar (once the site of French atomic testing in the Sahara) to Gao in Mali. If you drive you must carry supplies for a 1,331-mile run along endless stretches of track. Trucks also take passengers on the five-day run from Adrar to Gao for $40 including food.

Avoid the bad and dangerous third route from Tindouf through northern Mauritania to its capitol of Nouakchott; sand has eroded the tracks and an American diplomat died attempting to make the crossing in 1971.

Physically easier is an east-west cross-Saharan trip between Algeria and Tunisia. Roads are usually good and some of them are paved. You can drive from the southern Tunisian city of Gafsa to the border oasis of Nefta (Tunisia) which has a hotel straight out of a Rudolf Valentino film. If you have proper visas, papers and Algerian or French currency, the border can be crossed here by a good road to El Oued, Touggourt, and the Algerian Sahara. Be sure to inquire before starting out whether any of your prospective roads or border crossings happens to be closed. The roads are much worse and the borders more frequently closed along the Sahara between Morocco and Algeria.

Getting Around Within Algeria

Fortunately, trips within Algeria are less rigorous. Major roads are mostly paved and well maintained, there is safe and reliable bus service within and between major cities, and there's inexpensive coastal train service. The National Tourist Office has guided tours in microbuses and chauffeur-driven cars. Automobile rentals are available in Algiers and Oran. You can also fly to many places. Air Algérie schedules flights throughout the country, including Saharan oases.

On arriving at the Algiers airport you may find the airport disorganized and confusing. Taxis charge $5 for the 10-mile trip to town. Wait for the bus (no announcements) and pay 50 cents for the ride to the Air Algérie terminus downtown, which is within walking distance of most hotels. Same set-up in Oran.

In town buses are crowded at rush hours but rides are cheap (5 cents). The central city bus depot in Algiers is next to the Grande Poste (post office building). Taxis are hard to find and their meters are unreliable.

The Société des Transports has regular, inexpensive bus service between cities. Inter-city buses are crowded too and you may have to stand on shorter runs, but they provide a chance to meet Algerians and see the countryside. There is also crack overnight train service between Algiers and Oran, and slower daily trains from Algiers to Constantine and Oran to Oujda, Morocco.

Hitchhiking is surprisingly good considering the scarcity of traffic on main highways, but be prepared to pay some small amount for the lift. Women are advised that it's not a good idea to travel this way without a male companion.

Hertz and Avis have car rental agencies in Algiers but not at the airport. Auto rentals require a deposit of $100 or more in Algerian currency (which you may have to spend in a hurry before departure since it can neither be taken out legally nor converted). In Algiers, Hertz is at 5 rue Curtillet (tel. 65-89-08); Avis at 109 rue Didouche Mourad (tel. 33-15-75). In Oran, autos may be rented from Afric Car, 9 boulevard Zirout Youcef (tel. 34-32-37) and Auto Parc, 6 rue du Commandant Faradj (tel. 33-15-75).

Guided tours, especially of the Sahara, are available through the National Tourist Office in Algiers (ONAT, 25-27 rue Khelifa Boukhalfa (tel. 64-68-65). Tours cost $15 to $30 per day depending on the size of the party and type of accommodations desired (these prices do not include air fares). The costs are low because the government wants to show travelers what the Sahara has to offer.

Travel agencies in Algiers offering tours include the Agence de Tourisme Algérien, 2 place Sheikh Ben Badis (tel. 62-26-00), the Touring Club d'Algérie, 1 rue Lacépède (tel. 63-30-08) and Wagons-Lits/Cook, 61 rue Ben Mehidi Larbi (tel. 63-20-12).

Where to Stay

Since independence, hotel construction and maintenance have lagged in favor of education and other priorities.

In ALGIERS hotels are crowded, expensive, run-down, with poor service and a reluctance to accept or acknowledge reservations. In the center of the city, the once elegant *Hôtel Aletti* has 140 rooms at $20 to $30. The *Hôtel St. Georges*, with gardens and harbor view, has similar rates but more atmosphere. The *Albert I* charges $10 to $20 for rather shabby rooms. More moderately priced but decent, although without private baths, are the *Moderne* on Avenue de la Liberté, the *Angleterre* and *Regina* on Boulevard Ben Boulaid ($3 to $4 per night, single). Also reasonably priced and recommended is the *Hôtel Oasis* on Avenue de la République near the port and the Casbah. Although there are no youth hostels in Algeria, a bed or cot may be found (especially during holidays) at the residential facilities of the National University in Algiers, which has branches in Constantine and Oran, and at lycées.

Outside Algiers the traveler has fewer choices. In CONSTANTINE the *Transatlantique* was once the luxury hotel but has declined to the level of the *Cirta* and *Panoramique*. The Cirta is clean and has a touch of faded elegance. In ORAN the *Grand, Martinez* and *Royal* hotels offer comparable nondescript facilities for $10 to $20.

Things get better rather than worse in the interior. The government runs a chain of modern and attractive hotels and provides tent facilities for those who prefer the outdoors. Among the better hotels are *Le Caïd* in BOU SAADA (with nightly belly dancing in the air-conditioned bar) and the *Transatlantique* ($10 per person, all-inclusive) in the charming date-growing oasis of GHARDAIA. In several of the oases, Bedouin tourist camps offer tents, minimal sleeping and washing facilities, but good food for $9 a day. They are run by the Tourist Office and move with the seasons. The mountain towns of TIZI OUZOU, AIN TEMOUCHANT and TLEMCEN have simple, rustic hotels, often operated by the municipality.

Algerians themselves take their holidays at the beaches, especially during summer months. Here the government has provided holiday camps for low-income workers and students that offer a good opportunity for foreigners to feel the pulse of this dynamic young society. Near Algiers, the beach towns of MORETTI and ZERALDA have modern hotels, and TIPASA has the added attraction of fine Roman ruins. Inquire at the Tourist Office about staying at a workers' or students' holiday camp. More ample and expensive beach facilities, including villas and camping, are operated by the Touring Club d'Algérie at LARHAT (80 miles from Algiers), ANNABA and AIN EL TURK, the resort beach for Oran.

Where and What to Eat

Aiming at agricultural self-sufficiency, the government has restricted all but essential food imports. A few restaurants cater to businessmen and diplomats but dining out is not an Algerian custom. Major hotels have restaurants offering French and Algerian dishes with delicious fresh peaches, pears and, during the summer, watermelon. Algerian wines are a good buy at $1 to $2 per bottle. Vin ordinaire is strong and rough; the better red wines (Mascara, Sahel and Medea) are only slightly more expensive and savory. Local beers tend to be gassy and light and the local mineral water is drinkable (as is the tap water).

Recommended restaurants in ALGIERS include the *Sinbad* near the fishing port in the Place des Martyrs. The fish and wine are excellent and the setting simple and picturesque. *El Bacour* offers Algerian food for about $5 per person. More moderately priced are the *Café d'Angleterre* and *Le Berry*, both near the Hôtel d'Angleterre. *Le Grand Maghreb* has a ritzy atmosphere and genuine Algerian food. The *Colombo* serves French and Italian dishes. Try the restaurants on the Corniche along the seafront. *Le Corsaire*, outside town, provides fine food and dancing. Also on the outskirts of town is the rather expensive but excellent *Auberge du Moulin* in Cheragas. The university neighborhood has sidewalk cafes and student restaurants.

In ORAN, standard French and Algerian cuisine is available at the leading hotels, and Algerian specialties are served at *Nahawand, El Djazair* and *Nuits du Liban*.

CONSTANTINE hotels are also the principal places for dining. *Bendjelloul, Victoire* and *Dounyazad* specialize in Algerian fare.

The staple of Algerian cuisine is couscous, made from steamed semolina flour and vegetables such as chick peas, often served with a fish or meat sauce or mechoui (braised mutton or lamb). Tajines are stews made of lamb, beef, chicken or fish. A real treat is pastilla, a layered, pastry-wrapped concoction of eggs, pigeon or chicken, onions, almonds, spices and sugar. For dessert or a sidewalk snack try the almond-based pastries known as "cornes de gazelle" (gazelle's horns). Food fanciers with a knowledge of French will enjoy *Les Grandes Recettes de la Cuisine Algérienne* ($5), a beautiful and excellent cookbook published by SNED, the Algerian state publishing house.

What to See and Do

ALGIERS, with a population of one million, is a fascinating but difficult city to explore. Built on steep hills descending to the port, it is not easy to navigate on foot although that is the best way to see its teeming Casbah—a warren of homes, courtyards and shops. Try the local bakeries for pastries and sweets. There is a lively morning fish and vegetable market. Several distinguished mosques date from the Ottoman era. Also worth visiting are the National Museum of Moslem and Classic Antiquities and the university, which is now open throughout the year. A bus from the Grande Poste takes you to the chic residential suburb of El Biar, past the palace of the president, and provides superb views of the harbor and city. A city map is useful and can be purchased for $1 at kiosks and bookstores. It lists both the former French and the new Arabic names of streets; in asking directions it often helps to give the former, which may still be used.

During the first week of September the annual Algiers trade fair is held at the fairgrounds near the airport (reached from the city by special buses). Thirty-five or more countries, including China, North Korea, Britain, the Soviet Union and France (but not the United States), exhibit each year. The real attractions are the nightly performances of Algerian folk dances and theater, the displays of Algeria's young industries—and the throngs of Algerian school children at the exhibits.

Night life in Algeria is limited to hotel bars and cabarets catering to foreigners and a few tame hangouts for civil servants. Algiers has the Blue Note and Le Corsaire; Oran, the Nuits du Liban and the Scotch Club; and Constantine, Le Manoir. The women of Algeria are significantly less emancipated than those of Tunisia, despite their participation in the revolution, and are more likely to patronize theatrical performances than clubs. The Théâtre National Algérien performs in Algiers, Constantine and Oran and is well worth seeing, especially if you can arrange for a university student to translate the Arabic into French. There are performances also by university and other student theater groups.

Algeria has a budding film industry that makes one or two feature-length films a year, several documentaries, and occasional co-productions (such as Z and Battle of Algiers) with foreign directors. There is a Cinémathèque in downtown Algiers which has daily screenings of film classics and sometimes an Algerian production, as well as post-film discussions. It's a good place to meet students and young artists.

Algiers is flanked by fine Mediterranean beaches, good for swimming and skindiving from March through October. All are reached by bus from the center of town and are likely to be crowded on weekends. Djemila has seafood restaurants, El Djemila nightclub and good beaches 10 miles from town. Sidi Ferruch is farther out among cool pine forests, with white sand beaches and historical monuments marking the arrival of French troops in 1830 and Allied forces in 1942. The Club des Pins was developed as a conference center for a 1965 meeting of Afro-Asian states which was canceled on short notice by the coup that toppled Ben Bella. Perhaps the most interesting of the beach resorts is Tipasa, 45 miles west of Algiers, where you can see a well-preserved Roman forum, theater and temple, take a swim and sample the local seafood. Twenty miles west of Tipasa is the town of Cherchell with an excellent beach, good restaurants and interesting Roman ruins and artifacts.

Algiers and its environs also offer tennis, horseback riding and racing, yachting, golf and rowing. Most of these activities require temporary membership in the appropriate local club, arranged through the Tourist Office. Skiing is possible in January and February at the resort of Chrea, 40 miles south in the Aurès Mountains, and at Tikjda, 100 miles away. Facilities are poor, however, and the light snowfall makes Algerian skiing uninteresting.

East of Algiers lies the land of the Kabyls, Algeria's mountain people of Berber origin, whose industry and independent spirit can best be experienced in their picturesque mountain villages. By car from Algiers you can tour the mountains, stop at a beach or two, and return the same night. Regular bus service makes this a good two- to three-day trip. The Kabylia is a land of steep mountains, hidden valleys, fortified villages, fine crafts (especially embroidery), and a rugged, remarkable people. Its coast, not yet discovered by tourists, has sand beaches and rocky stretches for underwater fishermen. Its camping sites make it ideal for those who enjoy outdoor life. Inland is the Kabyls' chief town of Tizi Ouzou, a crafts center, and the nearby village of Sidi Belloua, with a spectacular mountain view and the shrine of a local Moslem marabout (a holy man credited with supernatural power).

Continuing east along the mountain road connecting Tizi Ouzou to Constantine, Algeria's third largest city, there are numerous splendid lookout points. Worth a stop is *Djemila*, one of the best-preserved Roman sites in North Africa.

CONSTANTINE, at the top of a steep rock, is divided from its suburbs by a massive ravine that can be crossed by foot bridge. The downward view into the canyons is unforgettable. For conventional sightseeing, the excellent Gustave Mercier Museum houses Roman, early Christian and Moslem relics. The Ahmed Bey Palace is an ornate monument in Arabic tradition. The Casbah, with its walls still bearing Roman inscriptions, is picturesque, especially the Djezerine butchers' quarter. The world's largest mosque is under construction in Constantine. It makes an interesting contrast to the government-built steel rolling mill in El Hadjar, a new town between Constantine and the port of Annaba. Visits to both enable foreigners to appreciate the marriage of Islam and technology to which the Algerian leadership aspires.

The Aurès Mountains are 100 miles south of Constantine, an easy trip by car or bus. The drive is scenic, and you can stop at the Roman and Byzantine ruins of *Timgad*, the charming gardens of Rhoufi, and the lunar-like craters near the village of Menaa.

A trip to the Sahara is one of the real treats for any traveler to Algeria. It is a world apart, with extraordinary landscapes of dunes, oases, mountains, and natural gas and oil rigs. Saharan craftsmanship is also unique. The area is easily and inexpensively reached by domestic Air Algérie flights, regular bus service to the major towns, rented car, or package tours operated by the Tourist Office. Nor need the traveler experience discomfort, since Saharan hotels are modern and attractive. But it is best to visit during the winter.

One of the most attractive oasis towns is GHARDAIA, 389 miles south of Algiers, with date palms, gold- and silversmiths, and the miracle of life in the Sahara. Its population of 25,000 consists largely of Moazabites, followers of an 8th century puritanical Islamic sect, who are noted for their artistic and trading skills. There's a lively marketplace, a classic mosque and a panoramic view from the Mahakma administrative building. The road to Ghardaia from Algiers passes through Lagouat, the Saharan oasis closest to the coast, which is interesting for its mosque and the religious shrine to its own marabout.

Beyond Ghardaia lie the great trans-Saharan routes including the six- to 10-day road crossing to Agadès in Niger via Tamanrasset. Along the route lies the oasis of El Goléa, with its gardens and ksar (traditional fortress) on the edge of the Grand Eastern Erg, the monumental sand dunes that have solidified into craggy, rocky, windswept mountains. South of El Goléa is the date palm oasis of In Salah with its mosque and gardens. Two hundred miles farther south are the Arak Gorges, great rifts cut into the sand and desert.

TAMANRASSET is a modern administrative and military center, the last Algerian outpost in the Sahara. From there you can proceed south across the Sahara or northeast to the 10,000-foot Hoggar Mountains and the plateau of Assekren. Another rugged but splendid side trip is to the Tassili N'Ajjer Mountains where recently-discovered Tassili cave paintings gracefully depict hunters, dancers and family groups of a Saharan people who flourished there 6,000 years ago. Flights from Algiers, as well as package tours, connect Tamanrasset with the tiny village of Djanet, from which guides lead travelers on foot to Tassili.

From Oran, a less-traveled road descends into the western Sahara to

Gao in Mali. Known as the Tanezrouft route, after a medieval Saharan imperial dynasty, this road passes the former French nuclear testing center at Reggane, a chain of date palm oases between Adrar and Reggane, and, near Gourara, a series of ksars and fortified villages.

Algeria is a country where social and economic processes are sufficiently interesting to help compensate for the frustrations of generally poor hotels and inferior service. A visit to one or more of the nearly 100 state-owned industries, particularly the steel mill or gas liquefaction facilities, conveys how much industrialization means to Algeria. Agricultural co-operatives show the achievements and difficulties of land reform. Combine these with a visit to the technical institutes, in which the government has made the most of its educational investment. You can arrange these visits through the Tourist Office (you'll need a little patience in dealing with this agency).

You might consider combining a Saharan trip with a glimpse at Algeria's booming petrochemical industry, which may soon be piping Saharan natural gas to the coast for liquefaction and shipment across the Atlantic to the United States. Ask at Sonatrach (the Algerian state petroleum corporation) offices in Algiers to visit a Saharan oil or natural gas rig, perhaps at Hassi Messaoud, the world's third largest natural gas deposit. The gas liquefaction plants and coastal shipping terminals can also be seen at Arzew near Oran, or at Skida near Constantine.

ORAN, with a population of almost half a million, is Algeria's second largest city and the center of its western region. The site of several novels by its native son, Albert Camus, it was given its character by Spanish and Corsican settlers who built a city of stone with terraces and verandas. The old town has the palm-lined Municipal Gardens with a miniature zoo, and romantic place names like the Street of Bitterness and the Street of God's Love. The city has several mosques dating from Turkish times and the Demaeght Museum, with prehistoric, cultural and art objects. Oran has excellent, easily-reached beaches, a pleasant port and a growing petrochemical industry nearby.

A good two-day trip from Oran by road, rail or bus covers fertile wine-growing plains and the farming town of Ain Temouchant with its attractive mosque, the former French Legion base of Sidi bel Abbès, and the historic Atlas Mountain stronghold of Tlemcen, the country's most important religious center, where the Algerian revolution was nurtured. Tlemcen has an historic museum, several Moslem shrines to which the faithful make pilgrimages, and a classic 13th century mosque. Worth seeing in and near Tlemcen are the Great Mosque; the Mosque of Sidi Halloui, named for a 13th century mystic; the Mosque and mausoleum (koubba) of Sidi Bou Meddine, a 12th century holy man, and the 13th century minaret of Mansourah, a fine example of Moorish architecture.

What to Buy

Algerian handicrafts are more expensive and lower in quality than those of Morocco and Tunisia. An exception is jewelry from the Sahara. The government is encouraging the production of leather goods, ceramics, rugs, silver and gold filigree work, and other traditional items. These can be seen and purchased at the Maison de l'Artisanat (House of Crafts) in Algiers and Oran. You can also buy good pottery in the Kabylia region and fine woven wool in the souks of the Algiers Casbah. Bookstores are packed with Third World revolutionary literature.

Local Attitudes

Algerians are proud of their revolution, and identify with what they consider to be similar struggles elsewhere, whether in Cuba, Vietnam or the Middle East. Visitors may be sharply questioned about American involvement in Vietnam, Israel and South Africa, although the government is anxious to sell its gas and oil to the US, partly to reduce its dependence on France.

While representatives of Angolan, South African, Mozambican and other nationalist movements are welcome in Algiers, there is no tolerance for counter-culture adherents, particularly those flaunting sexual or drug freedom. Like other militant countries, Algeria has both a pragmatic and a puritanical cast. No servility here, and fewer beggars on the street. Waiting on tourists is far from the national pastime and as long as the petroleum and natural gas flow, the government will give tourism low priority. It prefers to invest in simple holiday camps rather than hotels (except in the Sahara).

Weather, What to Wear, How Long to Stay

The climate is temperate throughout much of the year along the coast, resembling that of Southern California without the smog. During the summer, an afternoon at the beach is customary, as is casual attire for the towns. Miniskirts are permitted and even worn by an occasional daring Algerian girl, but they will bring stares and remarks. Stick to slacks. The mountains are cool throughout the year; sweaters are called for in spring and summer, overcoats in winter. The Sahara blazes during the day but its temperature drops 40 degrees at night; you'll need sunglasses, a sweater, shorts, walking shoes, suntan lotion and a hat—also face protection from chafing sand.

A trip to Algeria is difficult to combine with other African countries, except Morocco and Tunisia. Yet its recent history and political and economic stance give it an important role in pan-African affairs. A two- to three-day visit to Algiers might be squeezed in at the beginning or end of an all-African trip. Otherwise a week is needed to see Algiers and to fly to one or two Saharan sites. A two-week stay would allow for the Sahara, Algiers, the Kabylia, one or more beach resorts (preferably Tipasa) and either Constantine or Oran.

Communication

Some Algerians have university degrees from the US, Canada or England, but most of the estimated 25,000 technologists have been educated in France or in French-oriented Algerian schools. French is indispensable for traveling outside Algiers. Travelers familiar with classical Arabic will find the Algerian dialect difficult at first.

Postal service is slow, inefficient and unreliable for surface packages. Phone service is good within Algiers, between cities, and from Algiers to Paris.

The Algerian press, radio and television all parrot the government line in French and Arabic. The French-language daily newspaper, *El Moujahid*, is deadly dull. Weekly news magazines like *Algérie Actualité* and *Révolution Africaine* are more informative. The latter is the organ of the moribund official FLN political party. Educated Algerians prefer *Le Monde* or other Parisian papers which arrive by air on the day of publication. Attractive, inexpensive books are produced in French and Arabic by the government publishing house, SNED. These include a highly popular series of paperback novels in French featuring Mourad Saber, Algeria's super-spy who bests the Israelis, the CIA and the Mafia.

Emergencies

Although diplomatic relations were broken in 1967, the United States retains a small mission in Algiers, located in a villa in El Biar. The address is 4 chemin Cheikh Bachir Brahmi (tel. 60-14-25). Officially, Switzerland represents the United States. There are excellent hospitals and physicians in Algiers, and the army is occasionally helpful outside the main towns.

Canary Islands

(Islas Canarías)

Profile

STATUS: Provinces of Spain with resident governors responsible to Madrid.

SIZE: 2,808 square miles. Population—1,300,000, primarily Spanish.

GEOGRAPHY: Seven principal islands (Tenerife, Gran Canaria, Fuerteventura, La Palma, Lanzarote, Hierro and Gomera) plus six smaller islands, 75 miles off northwest African coast. Varied vegetation and volcanic topography. Principal towns—Las Palmas (port, 260,000) on the island of Gran Canaria; Santa Cruz de Tenerife (capital, port, 200,000).

CLIMATE: Year-round temperatures in the 70's. Rainy season during November and December.

LANGUAGE: Spanish.

CURRENCY: Spanish peseta, divided into 100 centimos. 1 peseta = $0.016 (1.6 US cents); $1.00 = 62.5 pesetas.

VISAS: Not required.

AIRPORT: Gando (LPA), 16 miles from Las Palmas. Regular connections with Spain, frequent flights to and from West Africa, European capitals and New York.

NATIONAL HOLIDAYS: July 18, Spanish National Day; Catholic holidays.

INFORMATION SOURCES: *In US*—Spanish Consulate General, 964 Third Avenue, New York, N.Y. 10022 (tel. 212/355-4080). *In Las Palmas*—Tourist Information Office, Casa del Turismo, Parque Santa Catalina (tel. 264623). *In Santa Cruz de Tenerife*—Tourist Information Office, Palacio Insular (tel. 242227). *In Madrid*—Ministry of Information and Tourism, Avenida del Generalisimo 39 (tel. 279-62-00).

By Philip M. Allen

Oldest and most durable of Europe's African settlements, the Canaries are prospering today by drawing multitudes of tourists to their soft beaches and quick-changing landscapes, their easy climate and considerate costs.

Phoenician sea lore and Greek legend contributed many romantic identities to this Atlantic archipelago—the Hesperides Gardens, the Elysian Fields, Atlas' rock, the final summits of Atlantis, the Fortunate Isles and the hotbed of Gorgons. But the sweet name that stuck came from a story told to gullible Romans by a wily king of Mauritania to keep them out of his domain. The story he related was of ferocious tiger-sized dogs ("canes") roaming the islands. The islands later lent their canine title to the small songbird that lives there.

The dog story permitted several medieval centuries of peaceful isolation for the Guanche (Moorish-Berber) population of the islands. But pirate marauding followed, and the incursion of Renaissance powers led to a creeping occupation by Spain from 1402. The Guanche resisted throughout the 15th century but they were absorbed finally into the conquering Spanish Christian society. The population today has only a rare blue-eyed Guanche, and even fewer of Black African or Arab stock. Africa, only 75 miles away, has little presence on the Spanish Canaries. And self-determination has no conspicuous appeal despite the existence of a Canarian nationalist movement, which is based in Algiers.

Now constituting two provinces of metropolitan Spain, the archipelago of Tenerife, Gran Canaria, Fuerteventura, La Palma, Lanzarote, Hierro and Gomera have entertained foreigners aplenty. The first "Spanish" king of the eastern islands was Jehan de Bethancourt, a Norman. Columbus paused at this final outpost of the known world before setting out into the void. Admiral "Trafalgar" Nelson lost his right arm in a futile attempt to storm Santa Cruz de Tenerife, the Canaries' capital, in 1797. Nelson has a street named after him in Santa Cruz, chivalrous symbol of the intimacy between the sunny Canaries and the Britons. Englishmen have long enjoyed the islands' wines and bananas, and occasionally retired to tranquil villa-keeping in their eternal springtime.

Each island displays its own luxurious vegetation, bleak lava beds, desert scrub, golden sands and black beach, pine forests, mountain peaks, craters and grottos. All this is contained within so narrow a compass that the "all-around traveler" can take a Grand Tour from zone to zone, experience to experience, almost while staying at the same hotel. In the straits between the Canaries and the African coast there is a wealth of marine life to delight the skindiver and sport fisherman.

These advantages, now sprung open to legions of European and North American visitors the year round, constitute one of the world's major tourist booms. Prices for accommodations, meals, transportation, amusements and souvenirs rank with the lowest in Europe. The modern ports of Las Palmas and Santa Cruz de Tenerife thrive on duty-free import and export. Their bunkering facilities have also become popular among Atlantic Ocean fishing operations and, since the closing of the Suez Canal, for ships using the long circle route around Africa.

Little literature is available in English about the Canaries beyond the ephemeral reminiscences of gentle travelers and burly sea warriors. The Union Castle Company has issued the helpful *Madeira and the Canary Islands, A Concise Guide for the Visitor* (London, 1966) and there is a study of the Guanches by E. A. Hooton entitled *The Ancient Inhabitants of the Canary Islands* (Harvard, 1925).

Money Matters

Controls on money exchanges, customs and banking are suitably loose for the purposes of free trading and fashionable consumption. The Banco Hispaño Americano, the Banco de Canarías, and other establishments maintain branches on several islands and keep convenient hours. Everybody in the main towns and resorts deals in dollars and travelers checks; major credit cards are welcomed in the ports and hotels. Metropolitan Spanish pesetas are the Canarian currency.

Getting In and Out

Gando Airport, 16 miles outside Las Palmas, connects Gran Canaria with Europe and New York (six and a half hours). The frequency of flights increases during the winter season. Cheap charter rates are available from most major European and other western hemisphere capitals. Each of the other main islands is equipped with airfield and seaport. With monolingual agents, casual and confused business practices and primitive communications, Gando's services seem provincial for so popular a place. Still, visas are not needed and police and customs are quite liberal. Charter agencies which bring in the bulk of European tourists provide their own ground services.

Las Palmas also has the world's third largest bunkering port, lying three days out of Southampton by Union Castle liner and other vessels, and 48 hours by fast ship from Spain. British agencies now offer winter cruise packages between Las Palmas, Dakar (Senegal) and Bathurst (the Gambia), thus adding a touch of Africa to the vacation. The Paquet Lines sail two or three times each month out of Marseille, with three classes ranging from $65 to $200 one way. The Norwegian Concordia Lines have monthly sailings from New York to the Canaries for about $270. Some ships go to Santa Cruz de Tenerife as well as (or instead of) Las Palmas; steaming into the capital affords a fine view of Pico del Tiede's snowy cap, a classic beacon for discoverers, conquerors, exiles and tourists.

Getting Around Within the Canaries

The seven major islands and six islets lie within a skein of sea routes. Gomera can be visited between night boats from Santa Cruz de Tenerife, for instance, and Las Palmas is only 52 miles from Tenerife. La Palma island is 150 miles and Lanzarote 130 miles from Las Palmas. Air Iberia connects the seven airfields, and there are good roads even over the broken contours of Gran Canaria and the pocks and piles of Lanzarote. New Mercedes taxis are everywhere. Tour agencies command spanking clean buses and competent guides for group excursions.

Every island has adequate bus links between its major points for those who want to avoid the expense of taxis or rented cars and who shun group tours. Cycling poses something of a challenge because the terrain is generally hilly. Hitchhiking is not uncommon, especially during European vacation seasons. Tenerife's 12,560-foot Mt. Tiede and other peaks are easily conquered by amateur alpinists; there is also a 15-minute cable lift to El Tiede's summit.

Tourism is a developed industry in the Canaries: coordination and regulation of services are entrusted to the Ministry of Information and Tourism in Madrid with tourist offices and branch delegates in each island capital. Insular, the semi-official travel agency, serves all the islands with an impressive variety of programmed tours (headquarters at Léon y Castillo 372-74, Las Palmas; tel. 242845-9). The Touring Club de España (Triana 120, Las Palmas; tel. 223921) can help plot excursions for automobile club members. The Ministry issues official brochures in several languages on the islands, obtainable from Spanish consulates and from Air Iberia. Guide books on Spain usually include the Canaries. Pick up your travel literature before setting off for the islands because tourist flocks may have devoured everything available on the newsstands there.

Where to Stay

The Canaries possess luxury palaces, Edwardian hotels, paradors (government inns), pensions and rooming houses, beach bungalows, apartments and seamen's hostels. Winter visitors should write for reservations, since this is the season for chartering large-scale escapes from Europe. Tourist Information Offices have unofficial lists of hotels. Price quotations usually include a 15 per cent service charge.

GRAN CANARIA. On this island innumerable hostelries thrust their balconies over the two beaches (Canteras and Alcaravañeras) of Las Palmas, but for luxury and convenience in town choose the *Reina Isabel* (singles from $7.50 to $10; doubles from $12 to $17.50). The *Hotel Metropole* offers proximity to the Alcaravañeras Beach as well as a swimming pool (singles $5 to $7; doubles $9 to $11). The *Hotel Imperial Playa* overlooks Canteras Beach (singles $5 to $8; doubles $12 to $17). The beautiful old *Santa Catalina* sits back in Doramas Park surrounded by dragon trees near the municipal zoo and the traditional village cluster of the Pueblo Canario (singles from $7.50; doubles from $12.30 to $20). Pensions and cheap rooming houses without meals flourish near both the beaches and the city center.

Accommodations outside Las Palmas include the inexpensive *Guayarmina Hotel* in the Berrazales Valley, with thermal bathing and salubrious waters; the elaborate archways and tiled roofs of the government's *Parador de la Cruz de Tejeda* in the lofty center of the island (singles from $2.50 to $3; doubles from $3.50 to $4), and the *Hotel Santa Brigida* in the El Monte wine country, a favorite of the British (singles from $3.20 to $5; doubles from $5 to $7.50). Maspalomas's several new hotels, all moderate in price, with beach clubs and golf courses, include the enormous *Maspalomas Oasis* (the most luxurious) with singles from $5 to $10, doubles from $7.70 to $15.70.

TENERIFE. Santa Cruz, the capital, has excellent hotels in reasonable price categories. The best include the handsome *Mencey*, the *Brujas*, the *Parque*, and the *Anaje*. Las Cañadas National Park has the *Parador Cañadas del Tiede* at the foot of the mountain. Golden Medano Beach contains the fashionable *Hotel Medano* as well as more modest lodgings for bathers. Bajamar offers the *Nautilus*, the *Neptuno*, and the *Delfin*. Playa Santiago boasts a new first class *Hotel de Los Gigantes* by the Acantilado de los Gigantes. At Puerto de la Cruz, across the island from the capital, there are these luxury hotels: the *Hotel Taoro*, in a park overlooking the beach, the enormous *Las Vegas, San Felipe* and the *Orotava Gardens*. In the $5 (single) to $8 (double) class, there are the *Tigaiga, El Tope, Martianez* and *Tenerife Playa*, all with proximity to black sands, saltwater pool, boutiques, fine cafes and night life.

OTHER ISLANDS. The tall *Arrecife Gran Hotel* on LANZAROTE ISLAND, with its splendid gardens, pool and water sports facilities, has recently been supplemented by the smaller *Lancelot Playa* and the luxurious *San Antonio* at Playa de los Pocillos. Cheaper Arrecife accommodations are offered by the *Hotel España*. Bungalows, apartments, a shopping center and hotel complex of *Los Fariones* are 10 miles south of Arrecife on a fine beach with craggy red rock. FUERTEVENTURA ISLAND has its *Parador*, built into basalt rock, and LA PALMA the *Parador Santa Cruz de la Palma* one-half mile from the little harbor. The places to come for hiking, backpacking and inexpensive pension or hostel lodgings are the less well-known islands—FUERTEVENTURA, GOMERA and HIERRO. Ask about accommodations at Tourist Information Offices.

Where and What to Eat

The cuisine of the Spanish coasts is duplicated here. TENERIFE leads with several good restaurants and cafes at Santa Cruz (Santa Catalina Square), La Laguna, Bajamar, Puerto de la Cruz (try *El Cortigo* and *Patio Canario*), Medano and Tenbel. Las Palmas has elegant dining at the *Reina Isabel* and the Basque *Restaurant Ikea*. Idiomatic Canarian food rewards the visitor who goes out of his way to vary the standard fare, in the tascas (bistros) of villages, in valley inns like the one at Hermoso on GOMERA, at fishermen's nests like those at Puerto de las Nievas near Agaete on GRAN CANARIA; in the Timanfaya at Yaiza on LANZAROTE, and the nearby Islote de Hilario on the Montaña del Fuego where fish and chicken are baked in nature's volcanic ovens. A 10 per cent tip is customary.

At such places, for eminently reasonable prices ($1.50 up for a full meal with table wine), the lucky forager can taste not only the paella, fish soup and wines of the mainland, but also salt-baked sardines (sancochos), small crustaceans (bogavantes), catfish (viejas cocidas), watercress and herb soup (potaje de berros y jaramajos), stews (pucheros), a special mackerel "caviar" of Gomera, and the traditional Guanche staple, gofio—roasted flour of corn, wheat or oats, eaten in dumplings, porridges, in aromatic couscous or sprinkled like grated cheese over other dishes.

Often served with these platters are delicious, wrinkled, marinated potatoes eaten in their jackets (papas arrugadas), the tomatoes and bananas that grow in abundance throughout the archipelago, and hot sauces (mojo picon) taken straight or mixed with tomatoes and peppers (mojo colorado) or with parsley instead of peppers (mojo verde). Goat and rabbit meat augment the roster of steaks, stew, chops and chicken.

Every island has its fruit desserts, including watermelon (sandia), as well as pastries of almonds, honey and figs. Local wines like Lanzarote's dry mauve Malvasias (malmsey to the British), the Tintos de Monte of Tenerife, the Gran Canarios, and the Hierros adorn the more elegant Canarian tables. Most beverages are inexpensive everywhere.

What to See and Do

Not all the Canaries have yet become tourist maelstroms. Fuerteventura, Gomera, Hierro and (for the time being) Lanzarote remain underattended by the Spanish, British and Northern European sunseekers deposited by the thousands on the jet runways of Las Palmas and Santa Cruz de Tenerife.

On the island of TENERIFE, the town of Santa Cruz still retains a Spanish Creole flavor and a relatively unspoiled hinterland despite the lures of its free port, Tiede Mountain, and the eight-mile-wide Cañadas crater (one of the broadest on earth). The town has a handsome residential quarter with well-designed plazas and gardens, an interesting market, an archaeological museum behind the big port, a bull ring and the busy shops of the harbor district.

A few miles above Santa Cruz stands La Laguna, once capital of the archipelago and still seat of the university, the Church of the Conception and the Rubicon Diocese. Its old streets with their balustraded buildings warrant a half-day's stroll. Then come the roadsides bright with flowers, banana plantations, the beaches at Medano and Los Cristianos, and the elegant but crowded tourist complex of Puerto de la Cruz. Forests of pines and palms set off a bleak landscape at Los Azulejos. Botanical gardens in Cañadas National Park and Montaña Blanca stand near the start of the ascent to Tiede's summit.

On the smaller, circular central island of GRAN CANARIA, Las Palmas has a booming port and two municipal beaches. It also has a few admirable cultural monuments: the Museo Canario, shrine of the Guanche epoch; the Columbus Museum, in a fine old mansion where the Genoan stayed, and 16th and 17th century residences of the Vegueta quarter with carved ceilings and doors, teakwood balconies in Moorish and Andalusian styles. The basalt Cathedral of Santa Ana is remarkable mainly for its collection of religious artifacts and for the view from its tower. The Museo de Nestor de la Torre honors a protean son of Las Palmas, genius of design and decor. Nestor's Pueblo Canario complex in Doramas Park preserves a sense of Canarian village style between the business district and the Old City; it is animated by folk music and dancing on Thursdays and Sundays at noon. Las Palmas also has a fine arts gallery, a theater, castle, several other parks and a golf course.

Drier and less green than Tenerife, the Gran Canarian countryside is cut by steep ravines running from a rock jumble at the center summit down to the sea. It is ringed by white beaches like Maspalomas, in a sudden palm oasis surrounded by dunes; this is a full-scale resort, with good hotels and bars, parks, gardens, water sports and boutiques. Near Maspalomas is a NASA satellite tracking station. Good pottery is made in the cave village of Atalaya near Santa Brigida. There are admirable old churches and finely balustraded residences everywhere, especially those at Teror, Telde and Arucas. Outside Agaete, the countryside becomes wild and rocky, with frequent changes of vegetation.

LANZAROTE, surely destined to become the next favorite of Riviera refugees, should be savored as soon as possible, and approached with a suspension of disbelief. The island surges upward from several fine beaches through a lava wasteland west of Arrecife to nature's own grave-yard in the Montaña del Fuego. Already discovered by movie camera crews and bus tours, this landscape dramatizes the elemental victories of fire and air: the earth of Lanzarote is crusted, desiccated and choked; rain and dew are trapped in lava concavities with lattice-like sides which cup roots and shield stems of grapevines, fig bushes, onion, tomato and tobacco plants; sea water is captured in lava beds and allowed to evaporate leaving behind salt for fish processing. There are 300 volcanic craters in the south of Lanzarote. Several had their final devastating moment in 1824, and one, El Golfo, now contains a salt lake.

Camels plow Lanzarote's black fields and jiggle tourists up crater sides to breathtaking views. The restaurant Islote de Hilario on the Montaña del Fuego serves as a starting point of the "lunar route" bus tour for those who spurn the camel caravan. As the bus labors over the desolate Timanfaya region, a tape recording emits information in discreet British accents punctuated by appropriate samples of Last Judgment music from three centuries. Guides at the Islote restaurant demonstrate the powers of their Fire Mountain's subsoil, where food cooks itself, steam explodes from tubes, and bushes burst into flame after brief contact with the un-comfortable spirit of the crater.

Moving northward, Lanzarote begins to green again, but only slightly. Trees and gardens adorn pretty white villas around Guatiza and nearby Teguise with its monastery and its mandolin (timple) makers. The northern coastal cliffs hold strange caves and staggering views. The Cueva de los Verdes is a four-mile-long volcanic tunnel. Arrecife town is a pleasant port of 20,000 people flanked by fishing villages, two minor castles and an esplanade.

Pièce de résistance of Lanzarote is a puzzling merger of natural gran-deur and human embellishment called Jameos del Agua. This is a sub-terranean lake disposed in a poem of rock and light, water and space, Malagueña music and wine. The caverns have a good restaurant, several bars and a nightclub patronized by chic tribes of privileged youth. Mirac-ulously escaping garish grandiosity, the Jameos are the realization of

César Manrique, resident genius of Lanzarote. Manrique also sculpted the huge, exuberant post-cubist Peasants Monument that rises out of the fields near Guatiza.

Nothing is quite the same after an experience of Lanzarote, but the other small islands of the Canaries have fewer people to share their merits. LA PALMA is green around its central Taburiente crater; its beaches are of black sand and its peak, craters and woods surround the visitor with a mood of their own. Santa Cruz de la Palma, small and business-like, is a pleasant place for walkers. Silk weavers work at the little mountain town of El Paso.

Remote HIERRO ISLAND is a tiny pastorale of rocks and grazing land, the source of a first-rate goat cheese and a fragrant wine.

GOMERA, where Columbus heard Mass and is said to have fallen in love with Countess Beatrice de Bobadilla, now sleeps among its forests and ravines. Small boats take passengers under the cliffs, and the fortunate hill comber can still hear Gomera's strange mountain whistle language, called Silbo.

FUERTEVENTURA remains underpopulated and undiscovered—a rough, partly laterite mass, larger than Gran Canaria or Lanzarote, ringed by beaches with opportunities for solitary hiking, deep-sea fishing and diving. Try Jandia Beach at the foot of a desolate mountain range on the southern end of the island. Inland from Puerto del Rosario, Fuerteventura's capital, Betancuria has a gruff old square-towered cathedral and a recollection of the 15th century suzerainty of Jehan de Bethancourt. Like Lanzarote and Hierro, Fuerteventura suffers from a scarcity of rainfall. It is occasionally visited by a sandy harmattan wind from the Sahara.

Throughout the archipelago, the traveler finds music: Canarian adaptations of Andalusia, Castille and North Africa emerge in a more reflective, languid mood—the music of the isas and folias, saltonas, arroros and tajarestes. The Malagueña is danced without castanets in the slow swaying of a conservative, insular people capable of considerable pathos.

Other tempers may seek tennis and pelota (jai alai), golf and trap-shooting. Garrocha, a form of pole-vaulting, is popular with the well-built Canarians whose girls frequently cop beauty prizes and whose wrestlers grapple in teams under particularly austere rules. Cockfighting has been brought in from Spain. Tourists at Las Palmas, Santa Cruz de Tenerife and the beach resorts go to flamenco bars, discotheques and bistros, mingling with other tourists and with sailors, stevedores and hustlers.

Festivals come in swift succession in this fervently Catholic land. A pilgrimage for San Isidro at Orotava on Tenerife the Sunday following Corpus Christi in March is especially interesting. San Gines is honored at

Arrecife on Lanzarote every August 24–29. The week before Carnival Sunday, visitors come to the festival of the Virgin of the Pines at Teror on Gran Canaria. There are many more that can be identified by the local Tourist Information Offices.

What to Buy

The entire archipelago is a free port. The port shops of Las Palmas and Santa Cruz, many of them managed by Indian merchants, swarm with electrical and optical goods, beverages, cigarettes, imported clothing and other international articles at discount (albeit not sensationally low) prices. Prices can be knocked down further with astute bargaining. Shops close between 1 and 4 pm, and on Saturday afternoon.

Canarian women produce several handsome styles of embroidery including the Calado silks of Tenerife and La Palma, the Roseta of Lanzarote, and colorful table settings from Ingenio on Gran Canaria. Canarian artisanry is best represented by the timple (mandolin), made in Teguise on Lanzarote; pottery, especially of Tenerife; nicely carved boxes and chests; decorative knives; palm, reed and osier (willow) straw products, and a prized brand of cigar tobacco. Recordings of Canarian songs (those of Mary Sánchez, for instance) make prized possessions and gifts. "Peasant" merchants, like their city counterparts, are used to selling to tourists; their prices are reasonable but don't expect to surprise any of them with shrewd haggling. Guatiza on Lanzarote has a new artisans village around César Manrique's Peasants Monument.

Local Attitudes

Despite the conservatism of Canarians, their tourist economy requires accommodation to bikinis, minis, sport shirts, longer hair and informality. Unlike most of Africa, they are also used to numerous tourists of their own nationality and culture. Americans are still relatively rare (except on Gran Canaria), and their reputation benefits from a traditional Canarian fondness for Englishmen.

Weather, What to Wear, How Long to Stay

Bathed by a branch of the Gulf Stream and cooled by tradewinds, the Canaries invite year-round arrivals. Temperatures, excluding the mountaintops and a few desert plains, remain perpetually in the 70's. November and December bring rain to the more mountainous islands, sometimes in stormy southwesters; nowhere does rain make much impression between May and September. Late spring and early summer find the flowers of the Orotava Valley of Tenerife at their peak, and the contrast between Lanzarote's bleak southland and its more fertile north is most poignant then.

Residents dress conservatively and some of the older British hotels encourage a change of attire for dinner and evening. Tourists dress like tourists. Brighter night spots like the Jameos del Agua of Lanzarote, the clubs at Puerto de la Cruz and the Las Palmas riviera bring out the most elaborate fashions of our "casual" epoch.

Travel in the Canaries usually follows one of three standard formulas: (1) a two-day dip into Las Palmas or Santa Cruz en route to or from a continent; (2) a two-month season in a rented villa, apartment or bungalow, which gives the visitor a chance to cover all the terrain, or (3) the vacation fortnight which should allow two days in Santa Cruz and La Laguna, two more for the interior and the beaches of Tenerife, three days for the center, north and south of Gran Canaria, and at least two days for Lanzarote. Air Iberia and many other companies offer inexpensive fortnight package plans from the United States and Europe.

Communication

Hotel personnel, port merchants and an occasional taxi driver speak English well, and the Insular agency employs several British guides. There are substantial colonies of British and Germans, Scandinavians on chartered vacations, a growing number of Americans abandoning the Caribbean, and a small contingent of Americans with the NASA tracking station at Maspalomas on Gran Canaria. The Spanish spoken in the Canaries emerges in a clear, southerly sing-song with a few local oddities of vocabulary.

Telephone, telegraph and postal links are adequate throughout the archipelago and with mainland Spain, but equipment is archaic and overseas links faulty. Hotels, banks and major businesses use Telex. Have your packages mailed by the dealer.

Emergencies

Medical services in the Canaries are satisfactory. Las Palmas has a British-American clinic and many English-speaking doctors. When in doubt fly to Madrid. The US consulate is located at Léon y Castillo, Las Palmas.

Ceuta and Melilla

Profile

STATUS: Under Spanish sovereignty.

SIZE: Ceuta, about 7 square miles; Melilla, about 4.5 square miles. Both cities have populations of 100,000.

GEOGRAPHY: Ceuta, a port on Moroccan coast of Mediterranean Sea, separated by 25 miles of straits from Algeciras, Spain and Rock of Gibraltar; Melilla, a port 300 miles east on same coast, 120 miles by sea south of Málaga, Spain.

CLIMATE: Sunny and pleasant. Average temperatures 70 to 80 degrees; coolest in December and January (50 to 60 degrees).

LANGUAGES: Spanish (official), Arabic and French.

CURRENCY: Spanish peseta. 10 pesetas = 16 cents; $1.00 = 62.5 pesetas.

VISAS: Not required.

AIRPORTS: Melilla Airport (MLN), has flights daily except Sunday to and from Málaga, Spain. Ceuta relies on Tétouan Airport (TTU) and Tangier Airport (TNG); latter is linked with Casablanca, Gibraltar, London, Paris, Barcelona, Málaga, Madrid.

NATIONAL HOLIDAYS: May 1; July 18; Catholic holidays.

INFORMATION SOURCES: *In US*—Spanish Consulate General, 964 Third Avenue, New York, N.Y. 10022 (tel. 212/355-4080); Spanish National Tourist Office, 989 Fifth Avenue, New York, N.Y. 10017 (tel. 212/759-3842). *In Ceuta*—Information Bureau of the Undersecretary of Tourism, Jardines de la Argentina (tel. 1379). *In Melilla*—Tourist Office, General Macias 1 (tel. 1494).

By Aaron Segal

These small enclaves, Spain's last possessions on the Mediterranean coast of North Africa, are physically and culturally closer to Andalusia than to Morocco, which surrounds and separates them. Visitors can explore their beaches, shops, historic churches and forts, and savor their panoramic views. The climate is wonderful, prices are reasonable and tourism is well organized. Travelers to Ceuta and Melilla will find an African extension of Spain in these tranquil, prosperous ports, yet these two pleasant places are not quite as attractive or as interesting as their Moroccan neighbors, Tangier and Tétouan, where the atmosphere is more exotic and the sights more diversified.

Probably founded by the Phoenicians, the cities blossomed under later Roman rule. They were partly destroyed in subsequent invasions by barbarians and Moors but were restored with the arrival of Christianity and the Byzantine Empire. Their colorful past is reflected in their architecture—vestiges of Roman, Moorish, Portuguese and Spanish occupation.

The majority of the population is Spanish, and the economy of both cities is tied to that of Spain despite their proximity to Morocco, which still hopes to absorb these two Hispanic territorial units. Morocco claims sovereignty but so far has made no effort to oust the Spanish. Ceuta and Melilla remain politically and temperamentally part of Spain, as they have since the 17th century. Unlike Spanish Sahara, on the southern Moroccan border, there are no plans here for eventual independence.

Money Matters

The fully convertible Spanish peseta is the legal currency, exchanged at 62.5 pesetas to US$1. Travelers checks are accepted at banks, hotels and leading shops. Moroccan currency is also accepted, but at a slightly lower rate than the official Moroccan valuation. This means that you can obtain more Moroccan money for your dollar in Ceuta and Melilla, but it is illegal to enter Morocco with currency purchased in this manner.

Getting In and Out

There is no airport in Ceuta. The closest is in Morocco, at Tétouan, 25 miles away. The larger Tangier Airport is 58 miles distant. You can reach Ceuta easily from either airport by bus or rented car.

If you're coming from Spain, you can cross from Algeciras via the daily car-and-passenger ferry to Ceuta. The crossing takes an hour and a half. One-way passenger fares are $2 first class and $1 second class. The fares for autos range from $9 to $18, depending on the size of the vehicle.

You can fly directly to Melilla. Iberia Airlines has planes from Málaga, Spain, daily except Sundays (about an hour). Melilla is nearly 300 miles from Tangier. There's an inexpensive bus that covers the distance.

From Spain, Compania Transmediterranea runs eight-hour car-and-passenger ferries from Málaga. The cost is $3 to $7 per passenger (second or first class) and $14 to $25 per vehicle.

Where to Stay

Each city has several comfortable, moderately priced hotels, boarding houses (pensions) and hostels. The *Gran Hotel Ulisses* in CEUTA has 126 rooms, a pool and a good restaurant. Cheaper and more modest are the *Miramar*, *Alhambra* and *Atlante* pensions. The Tourist Information Bureau will help with maps and reservations and may even be able to provide addresses of families who accept low-budget travelers.

MELILLA has eight hotels and pensions. The best hotel is the 33-room *Rusadir*. The *España* and *Nacional* are decent, inexpensive pensions. The Melilla Tourist Office assists with reservations and maps and in placing travelers with families.

Where and What to Eat

The hotels and pensions have the best restaurants. A highlight of any menu is fresh seafood, especially prawns, crayfish and lobsters. The cuisine is generally Andalusian—saffron rice and seafood paellas are delicious, especially accompanied by Moroccan or Spanish wines. Also available are Moroccan meat specialties, including pinchitos and shish kebab, adapted to Spanish tastes.

What to See and Do

CEUTA has a fine Mediterranean climate, pleasantly warm during the summer and rarely below 50 degrees in the winter. This permits the pleasures of strolling, swimming, boating, fishing or sheer idleness. Like other Spaniards, locals take an early evening "paseo." The most popular place for this promenade is the spacious Plaza de Africa. On other agreeable walks you can see the modern Ayuntamiento (town hall), the shrine of Nuestra Señora de Africa (Our Lady of Africa), the 15th century Foso (moat) de San Felipe and the Andalusian cathedral dating from the same period. You can climb (or take a taxi) up 600-foot Mt. Hacho, outside the town, for a magnificent view across the Straits of Gibraltar.

Ceuta is built on an isthmus jutting into the Mediterranean. Its shorefront offers broad beaches and sheltered coves only a short distance from town. Buses from the city go to the more distant resorts, including Tarajal, near the Moroccan border. Equipment can be rented for angling and underwater spear fishing. The Club Nautico has boats for hire. Trawlers and other craft in the picturesque port make daily fishing trips.

Ceuta residents are great sports enthusiasts. There are private clubs for soccer football, water sports and horseback riding. The Tourist Office can arrange temporary admission to these clubs.

Ceuta also takes pride in its festivals and fairs. There is an impressive parade of floats during Easter Week. On June 13, the people make a colorful pilgrimage to the shrine of San Antonio on Mt. Hacho, where they give a show of folklore characteristic of southern Spain. July 16 is the feast of the Virgen del Carmen, celebrated at the harbor with a water-borne procession of gaily decorated fishing boats. A trade fair is held during the first two weeks of July. Festivals of Our Lady of Africa begin in late July and end on August 5.

MELILLA is slightly smaller than Ceuta but about equal in population. The majority of its inhabitants are Spanish; about 10 per cent are Moroccan Arabs and Jews. The modern section of the city is broad and spacious, featuring the Montelete shopping area, the Plaza de España, the Palacio Municipal (town hall), and the main Avenida del General-isimo, leading off the central plaza. More interesting is the higher, older part of the city known as "El Pueblo" (The Village). Here you can see the massive medieval city walls, the fortress with its carved stone entrances, the Foso de Hornabeque, the lovely Plaza de los Algibes, and the church of La Purísma Concepción with its shrine to the patroness of the city. Near the church is the Museo Municipal, which has a collection of artifacts from Roman and medieval times.

Like Ceuta, Melilla can easily be seen on foot, although there are frequent city buses and moderately priced taxis. You can take a bus or taxi to the large public beach east of the town and to the Cape of Three Forks, which has rugged cliffs jutting into the Mediterranean.

For sports, the Club Nautico and the Military Equestrian Club are both open to visitors. December and January are chilly but you can swim the rest of the year.

Melilla attracts fewer tourists than Ceuta. Its festivals are a bit less colorful but are more authentically Spanish. Throughout Easter Week there are processions and floats. In July there is music and dancing by visiting Spanish groups in the outdoor theater in Lobera Park. Early in September the city honors its patron saint, Our Lady of Victory, with a fiesta that includes bullfights, cultural exhibits and parades.

What to Buy

Ceuta is a free port and has many shops specializing in imported goods. Make sure that manufactured items come with a warranty, since some manufacturers refuse to honor claims on items purchased in free ports. Moroccan and Spanish handicrafts are also available, but at higher prices than you would pay elsewhere. Melilla has more local craftsmen, especially in the tiny leather goods boutiques and other shops in the Montelete section. Merchants in both cities will expect you to bargain.

Local Attitudes

Geared to tourism, the people are tolerant and cosmopolitan. However, Spanish law is harsh for drug offenses. Relations with Morocco are cordial, but there is always a touch of political uncertainty in the air. Loyalty to Spain is strong.

Weather, What to Wear, How Long to Stay

With 300 sunny days a year and Mediterranean breezes reducing the heat, the climate is a dream except for a chilly, damp December and January and a hot August. Clothing is casual although miniskirts and abbreviated shorts are worn only at the beach. Bikinis here are okay.

A day in each city is enough to see the major sights. You might want to stay longer just to relax. Ceuta and Melilla are convenient to Spain and tourist routes, and villas can be rented more economically in either of these towns than on the Costa Azul.

Communication

Spanish is the official language, but French and Moroccan Arabic are also widely spoken. In tourist offices, major hotels and leading shops you can usually find someone who speaks English.

Postal service is reliable for shipping packages home. Telephone rates are reasonable and there are good connections to Málaga and Madrid.

Emergencies

There is no US diplomatic representation in either city. The nearest American consulate is at Tangier, on the Chemin des Amoureux (tel. 159-04). There are modest local hospitals in both cities, but for a serious illness it would be better to go to Málaga or Madrid.

Morocco

(Royaume du Maroc)

Profile

STATUS: Monarchy, independent since March, 1956. Formerly protectorate divided between France and Spain.

SIZE: 172,415 square miles (slightly larger than California). Population—15,300,000 (Arabs and Berbers).

GEOGRAPHY: Fertile coastal plains. Rif mountain range in north, Atlas and Anti-Atlas mountains screening center and south from Sahara desert. Principal cities—Rabat (capital, 450,000), Casablanca (port and commercial center, 1,400,000), Fez (300,000), Tangier, Marrakesh, Meknès, Agadir, Oujda, Tetouan.

CLIMATE: Generally sunny and temperate, with rainy fall and winter on northern coast. Tangier temperatures in the high 70's in summer; damp and chilly in winter (50's). Casablanca temperatures are in the 60's in winter (40's at night) and 80's in summer. Saharan heat in the south.

LANGUAGES: Arabic and French, Spanish in the north.

CURRENCY: Moroccan dirham, divided into 100 Moroccan francs. 1 dirham = 20 cents; $1.00 = 5 dirhams.

VISAS: Not required (up to three-months' stay).

AIRPORTS: Casablanca Airport (CAS), four miles from city. Frequent flights to and from Western Europe, North Africa and New York. Airport bus to Casablanca bus station, 5 dirhams ($1.00). Rabat Airport (RBA), five miles from city. Frequent flights to and from France. Tangier Airport (TNG), eight miles from city. Frequent flights to and from Europe. International departure tax, all airports—8 dirhams ($1.60).

NATIONAL HOLIDAYS: March 3, Independence Day; Moslem holidays.

INFORMATION SOURCES: *In US*—Moroccan National Tourist Office, 597 Fifth Avenue, New York, N.Y. 10017 (tel. 212/421-5771); Embassy of Morocco, 1601 21st Street NW, Washington, D.C. 20009 (tel. 202/462-7979); Permanent Mission of the Kingdom of Morocco to the UN, 757 Third Avenue, New York, N.Y. 10017 (tel. 212/421-1580). *In Rabat*— Office National Marocain du Tourisme, 22 avenue d'Alger, P.O. Box 19 (tel. 212-52).

By Aaron Segal

Morocco provides the richest combination of travel experience and travel bargain in Africa. It is the country most easily and economically reached from Europe and North America, its internal transportation is reliable, and it has an extensive and attractive range of accommodations. Best of all, it is full of fine art, crafts and food, splendid traditional cities, and lovely beaches and mountain resorts. Travelers find a full range of comforts here at reasonable prices, with excellent service, in a setting reminiscent of medieval Islam and the splendor of the Almoravids. These charms attract nearly one million visitors annually, although many are merely day-trippers who cross the Straits of Gibraltar for a quick look at Tangier, which is not nearly as interesting as Morocco's major cities.

Berber and Arab traditions in architecture, art and social life still flourish in Morocco, and the influences of recent French and Spanish rule are also apparent. But sensitive travelers may be deterred by social injustice, corruption, economic stagnation and the resultant popular discontent under the present government. There is little evidence that even the benefits derived from tourism trickle down to the people.

Despite its proximity to Europe, Morocco has evolved its own distinctive heritage. In the south live descendants of the Moors, whose architecture ultimately dominated Spain and Portugal. But another part of Morocco's cultural integrity derives from the sequestered position of part of its population in the 10,000-foot Atlas and Anti-Atlas mountain chains that stretch across the country. The indigenous Berber inhabitants and their Rifian counterparts in the north had been colonized by the Phoenicians of Carthage before the rise of Christianity. These invaders were replaced in turn by Roman legions, Arab cavalry and Christian Crusaders. However, the mountain villagers were never fully conquered and were only partly assimilated, continuing to tend their herds and clinging to their ancient customs.

Arab and Berber dynasties controlled Morocco from the 7th until the late 19th century, when European powers, extending across the Mediterranean, eventually agreed to let France and, later, Spain divide the country into protectorates. France had the larger share, controlling the central and southern portions. The sultan was allowed to remain as religious leader and figurehead. Spain annexed a smaller area in the north under a similar arrangement.

France used divide-and-rule tactics to stir Arab-Berber rivalries while increasing the economic value of their newly-acquired territory. Production of wine and citrus fruits was stepped up, and Casablanca was developed into a major modern port.

In contrast, the city of Tangier, facing Gibraltar, was declared an international zone and governed by a committee of consuls from nine nations including the US. As a free port and currency zone, it remained until after World War II a boisterous international center of intrigue and vice, becoming part of Morocco again when the country gained its independence. It has kept some of its cosmopolitan flavor.

The partitioning of Morocco and the introduction of alien ways by an influx of French and Spanish settlers sparked a bloody nationalist revival that reached its climax in the 1950's. It was led by the scion of a centuries-old Fez dynasty (descended from Sherif, brother of the Prophet Mohammed), Sultan Mohammed Ben Yussuf. Exiled to Madagascar by the French but recalled in the face of mounting unrest, he was enthroned as King Mohammed V in 1955. In March, 1956, France granted Morocco its sovereignty and Spain followed suit. Only the towns of Ceuta and Melilla and a Saharan desert enclave are still under Spanish control.

When King Mohammed V died in 1961 his 31-year-old son, Hassan II, brought a playboy reputation to the throne. Now very much a serious monarch, Hassan has struggled to reconcile an articulate and organized Left composed of students and urban workers, a status-conscious Right comprising landowners, wealthy merchants and long-standing French commercial interests, a volatile but confused military and bureaucratic Center, and a profoundly traditional peasantry. To keep the monarchy and its extensive powers intact, he has used carrot-and-stick measures to divide the opposition. Although he has begun to broaden the base of his regime and seeks to revive the lagging economy, his reign has been marked by violence. His most serious challenger from the Left, Mehdi Ben Barka, was mysteriously assassinated in France in 1965. The king himself survived a bloody palace revolt in July, 1971, and a theatrical assassination attempt aboard an airplane in mid-flight in August, 1972, both led by military officers.

An excellent account of Morocco's passionate politics is John Waterbury's *The Commander of the Faithful* (Columbia University Press, 1970). E. W. Bovill's *The Golden Trade of the Moors* (Oxford University Press, 1958) recounts Moroccan history and contacts with Black Africa. The Tourist Office has free brochures.

Money Matters

The Moroccan dirham is loosely tied to the French franc and is usually valued at 20 US cents. Taking Moroccan currency in or out of the country is illegal and foreign exchange controls exist at all customs points. There is a black market because the dirham is generally available in

Gibraltar and southern Spain at a five to 10 per cent discount. But even with currency exchanged at the legal rate Morocco is relatively inexpensive, with prices well below Spanish tourist areas.

Foreign banks include First National City, which has branches in Rabat and Casablanca. American Express is represented in Casablanca, Agadir, Rabat and Tangier. Credit cards and travelers checks are accepted at major hotels. Banks are open weekdays from 8 to 11:30 am and 2 to 6 pm. Foreign currency can be exchanged legally only for dirhams, except at the airport upon leaving the country. As in Algeria and Tunisia, you are presented on arrival with a slip of paper to record your foreign exchange transactions. It should be shown to customs when you leave.

Getting In and Out

Pan American Airways operates several flights a week from New York to Casablanca, with tempting excursion fares. Royal Air Maroc offers a $160 round trip "Air-Car" fare from London, including auto rental. There are daily flights from Madrid, Lisbon, Paris, Frankfurt, Marseille and Geneva. Frequent charter flights also operate from virtually all points in Western Europe. There are four weekly flights from Algiers and Tunis and occasional flights from Dakar, Accra, Lagos and other points east and south. The airports at Rabat and Tangier are also well connected to many Western European cities.

Scores of Mediterranean and African luxury cruises call at Casablanca and Tangier but permit only one- or two-day stopovers.

Morocco is most often approached from Spain and France. You can rent or purchase a car in Paris, drive it 1,200 miles on paved roads along the coast of Spain, take the ferry at Algeciras, Málaga or Gibraltar, visit Morocco and return to Europe by a variety of routes. The Algeciras-Tangier ferry costs $4 per person one way; about $15 per vehicle, depending on size. The ferry between Ceuta (a Spanish city east of Tangier) and Algeciras is even cheaper. There are also car ferries from Marseille and Southampton, and regular passenger ship service from Marseille.

One of the most leisurely ways to reach Morocco is by train, connecting with the ferry that crosses the Straits of Gibraltar. Elegant first class coach service one way from Paris to Casablanca costs $60 for the two-day trip ($42 second class without sleeping car). A Eurailpass (bought in North America before your departure; special rates for students between the ages of 14 and 26) gives you unlimited rail travel in 13 European countries for three weeks to three months. The Eurailpass can be used to reach Málaga or Algeciras for the inexpensive ferry crossing.

Getting Around Within Morocco

Traveling in Morocco is easy and fun. The best means of transportation is a car. International car insurance and a valid driver's license are all you need for Morocco—plus mandatory yellow headlamps for night driving. Major roads are paved and well maintained, and auto rental is relatively inexpensive. Hertz, Avis and other firms have agencies in major cities. To help you avoid paying the national gas tax, discount gasoline coupons are available at the Banque Marocaine du Commerce Extérieur. Hitch-hiking is good on major roads, but you may wish to carry a national flag or sticker since motorists favor foreigners.

The Compagnie des Transports Marocains (CTM) has regular and rapid bus service to all parts of the country. Fares are low, buses are comfortable and there is no better way to meet Moroccans. Fares and schedules are available at CTM bus depots in the towns.

The railway is slightly less expensive but slower. The daily train from Casablanca to Tangier leaves at 8 am and arrives at 2 pm to connect with the car ferry to Spain. There are also daily trains from Casablanca to Marrakesh, Rabat, Fez, Meknès and on to Oujda and the Algerian border. The trains are slow and cheap, but comfortable.

Near the bus depots collective taxis—usually Peugeot station wagons—shuttle between the cities. They depart as soon as they are filled and provide faster but somewhat more expensive (and more dangerous) service than buses or trains. Within the city there are two kinds of metered taxis. "Petits" taxis, usually painted red, are cheaper but, unlike the larger cabs, do not carry baggage.

English-speaking travelers who prefer a more organized visit can choose from an abundance of package tours offered by more than 20 travel agencies in the United States and Canada. Most include Spain and Portugal in the itinerary. The Moroccan National Tourist Office in New York has information, including a useful packet of travel literature, lists of available tours and a guide to Moroccan hotels with current prices. The American Youth Hostel Association in New York operates a summer minibus tour for teenagers, called the Marrakesh Express, between Spain and Morocco.

Government tourist offices in the cities can provide licensed guides and a wide choice of local tours.

Michelin map #169 of Morocco is available for $1.40. If you can read French get Hachette's comprehensive *Guide Bleu*. There are also a $7.95 Fodor *Guide to Morocco* and a $6.95 *Travelers Guide to Morocco* by Christopher Kininmonth (Bobbs-Merrill). The Fodor guide is better on hotels, Kininmonth on history and sightseeing.

Where to Stay

Morocco has accommodations to suit virtually every pocketbook and taste. Hotels are classified by the government in five price-fixed categories. Reservations are never a problem except at the most expensive establishments. With full board (pension complète) you will save money but will deny yourself the pleasure of sampling the fare offered by the fine restaurants in the cities.

Camping sites abound on the Atlantic and Mediterranean coasts. The country also has the best network of youth hostels in Africa. There are hostels—known in French as "auberges de jeunesse"—in Casablanca, Agadir, Tangier and Meknès; the best are at Ifrane and Azrou in the Atlas mountains. Hostelers will need a US national card ($5 to age 18, $10 above 18) from the American Youth Hostel Association, 535 West End Avenue, New York, N.Y. 10024, or a less expensive Moroccan card that cannot be used outside the country. The hostels are sometimes crowded and dirty and the food less than hygienic, but their managements are not fussy about accommodating travelers over the age limit of 25 or about enforcing the 10 pm closing hour.

Travelers must guard their passports against thieves, especially in hostels and in Tangier.

CASABLANCA has two outstanding luxury hotels, El Mansour and Marhaba, both $20 a day per person for demi-pension (breakfast and one other meal). Good bets in the $10 to $15 range for demi-pension are the Majestic, Windsor and Excelsior. The 43-bed Hôtel Suisse, clean and comfortable, is $5 to $10 per person, demi-pension.

Along the coast at MOHAMMEDIA, near Casablanca, the splendid Hôtel Miramar supplies full board at $15 a person. The resort of OUALIDIA, south of Casablanca, has two charming and rustic hotels: L'Hyppocampe, with 20 rooms at $6 a person, full board, and L'Auberge de la Lagune, with nine beds at $5.50 a person, full board.

RABAT has the deluxe 259-room Rabat Hilton at $22 a day per person for demi-pension. In the same price range, the American-managed Hôtel de la Tour Hassan is a lovely place in Moroccan style with 150 beds. A centrally located and entirely satisfactory hotel is the Royal, offering very pleasant bathless rooms with breakfast at $3 or less.

MARRAKESH is where Winston Churchill used to bask in the winter sun. Its Hôtel Mamounia is deservedly world famous. Huge, old-fashioned rooms open onto orange groves. Take a look even if you cannot afford the rates, which begin at $20 a person, demi-pension. Others in the luxury range are the 180-bed Hôtel es Saadi, Les Almoravides and the new Holiday and Ramada inns (also in Casablanca and Agadir).

Good values are the *Hôtel Koutoubia* and the *Grand Hôtel Tazi* near the splendid Djemaa el Fna square, at $8 to $9 a person for full board. The centrally located *Hôtel CTM* is the best buy for low-budget travelers.

In AGADIR recommended hotels include the *Marhaba* at $20 a day per person for full board, $15.50 for demi-pension; the 60-bed *Salam*, with a fine Moroccan restaurant, at $13 a person, full board, and the small (14 rooms) low-budget *Petite Suède* at $7 full board, $5 demi-pension. The *Royal*, in the same price range, is also good.

At ESSAOUIRA, north of Agadir, the *Hôtel des Iles* has a magnificent location and splendid service in the luxury price range. South of Agadir in the Sahara are two fine hotels. The 62-room *Grand Hôtel du Sud* in TAFRAOUT charges $12 a person for full board. The exclusive and exquisite *Gazelle d'Or* in TAROUDANT has 20 rooms at $32 a person, full board. More modest is the 26-bed *Hôtel Taroudant* with $5 to $10 rates.

FEZ has the magnificent *Les Merinides Hôtel* in the luxury class, and the *Grand Hôtel* and *Hôtel CTM* in the $5 to $10 demi-pension range. Also recommended is the *Hôtel Zalagh*, located in the new city (demi-pension at $10 a person). In neighboring MEKNÈS the five-star *Hôtel Transatlantique* costs $21 a day per person for full board, and the convenient *Hôtel de Nice*, $5 a day for demi-pension. In the mountains, AZROU has the simple and cheap *Hôtel des Cèdres*, IFRANE the excellent *Grand Hôtel* ($8 a day, full board) or the slightly less expensive *Hôtel des Lilas*.

TANGIER has at least two luxury hotels, *Les Almohades* and the *Intercontinental*, with rates about $20 a day for full board. The 40-bed *Miramar* charges $10 a day, full board. The *Résidence Andaloucia*, *Hôtel Olid* and *Hôtel Becerra* are modest, inexpensive ($3 to $5) and centrally located. The modern 80-bed *Hôtel Rembrandt* is also conveniently situated and has a cheerful family atmosphere and moderate prices.

In the mountain town of CHECHAOUEN, 77 miles southeast of Tangier, is the good *Hôtel de Chaouen*, $8 per person, demi-pension. Farther south in coastal LARACHE, the hotels *España* and *Cervantes* provide modest and quiet accommodations.

The chain of government-operated *Grand* hotels in ERFOUD, TINEGHIR, OUARZAZATE, ZAGOR, TAROUDANT and TAFRAOUT all charge $10 to $20 for fine service and accommodations.

Along the coasts there are many holiday camps offering a wide range of sports and pleasures at reasonable rates. Some must be booked in advance through package tours but others are open to casual visitors. Many cater primarily to holidaying Frenchmen and are virtually separated from the real Morocco.

Villas can be rented in Tangier and Tetouan for $150 to $250 per month. There are fewer available in summer. Prices are lower in Marrakesh, but it is harder to find a home there with fully modern facilities.

Where and What to Eat

Morocco's cuisine is exquisite. The national dish is couscous, a combination of boiled chicken or lamb with semolina, vegetables and sauce. Other national favorites are mechoui (roasted lamb), pastilla (a flaky pigeon pie) and various sorts of tajine (stews with a lamb or poultry base). Everything is washed down with tasty and inexpensive Moroccan wine (red or white), excellent locally bottled mineral water, refreshing green mint tea or coffee. Beware of the Moroccan wine dealer's tendency to adulterate his product. Cafes and street vendors offer good soups, chicken with almonds or lemon, skewered meat brochettes of beef, mutton and veal, and lovely almond, honey, cinnamon and sugar pastries.

Good restaurants are everywhere—in the leading hotels and also tucked away in the side streets and bustling alleys of the medinas (the traditional walled cities). Because Moroccan Moslems don't consume alcohol many smaller restaurants serve only non-alcoholic beverages. At the more elaborate places, service includes repeated ceremonial hand-washing in silver basins followed by a spray of rose water.

Among the best restaurants are those in the *Marhaba* and *Mansour* hotels in CASABLANCA, and the less expensive ($3 per person) *Etoile Marocaine* nearby. There are several excellent seafood restaurants along the city's shore, among them the gorgeous *La Mer*. *Ma Bretagne* is noted for its seafood while *La Lombardie* and *La Normande* serve creditable Italian and French food respectively. *Al Mounia* has Moroccan dishes. The *Tournebroche* is another excellent French restaurant.

Recommended in RABAT are the intimate *Oasis* (about $4), the *Diffa Room* in the Tour Hassan Hotel ($5), and the sumptuous *Palais Kabbaj*. Less expensive are the French *Père Louis* and *Jour et Nuit*, and in TETOUAN the *Restaurant Central*.

Le Sanglier Qui Fume (The Steaming Wild Boar) is a charming rustic inn in the hills at OUIRGANE above Marrakesh. It has fine food, a delightful bar and a little outdoor zoo. At the *Palais de Fès* in the Boutawil section of FEZ you can dine reclining on brocade couches. Price: only $5 a person. Phone 347-07 in Fez to order in advance since there are no regular hours. The *Tour d'Argent* and *Hôtel Palais Jamai* restaurants are also excellent.

One of the best restaurants in all of Morocco is the *Maison Arabe* in the medina of MARRAKESH. No flim-flam or dancers, just great food. Reserve the day before (226-04). No menu; you take what's offered, and with no regret. If you want dancing with your food, Marrakesh has plenty of places for you. For snacks try the stall in the Djemaa square. The *Taverne*, *Dar es Salaam* and *Ksar el Hamra* are also worth trying.

The best dining of all is in Moroccan homes. You sit at a table, or lounge on a rug and cushions, and are served from ornate platters. Help yourself with the right hand (only) to generous portions. You'll be given fresh, often scented, water for washing. At the end, there's mint tea. Belching is a Moroccan expression of appreciation.

Moroccan city tap water is drinkable, but bottled mineral water and beer, or the excellent local wines, are preferable. Cabernet, Doumi and Valpierre are good Moroccan red wines; Judor is an orange drink, and Oulmes is a good mineral water.

What to See and Do

The National Tourist Office provides guides, maps and information in each major city. It will tell you about special traditional events on national holidays. Spring celebrations include Idd el Kebir, a feast of pilgrimage preceding Ramadan; the Feast of the Throne on March 3, the Moslem New Year; Idd el Fitr, celebrating the end of Ramadan, and Idd Mouloud, the feast of the Prophet's nativity. Most of these holidays occur on different dates each year in accordance with the Islamic calendar.

There are also scores of local holidays and festivals, including the 10-day May National Folklore Festival in Marrakesh, the glorious May rose festival in M'Gouna and the June cherry festival in Sefrou. Inquire about the "fantasia," a spectacular display of horsemanship, and jump at the chance to attend one. Most frequent in the south, they involve hundreds of costumed horsemen charging as if in battle, singing war songs and firing muskets. Ask about Moslem saints' days, "Moussems."

In Morocco, just looking can be enjoyable—at the flowing jellaba robes of men, the kaftans of women, the sights and sounds of the great marketplaces and medinas, the acrobats, jugglers and musicians in public squares, the faithful praying on Fridays. The best way of looking is on foot, wending one's way through the noisy crowds and savoring the exuberance of the traditional quarters of Moroccan cities. The medina passages are too narrow and crowded for bicycles but you might want to rent one through your hotel to use in other parts of the cities.

CASABLANCA is the principal port and commercial center. Its downtown boulevards and office buildings have a Mediterranean quality. The outskirts of the city are ringed by massive bidonvilles, new shantytowns of urban dwellers eking out a precarious existence. Their ragged children seek out tourists downtown for small handouts. Street con men are among the slickest in Africa.

Casablanca's Corniche (coast road), reached by public bus, has several good but crowded beaches. Most of the night life is found along the Corniche, at discotheques such as the Lido, Acapulco and Miami, which cater primarily to tourists at the Ain Diab and Anfa beaches.

The city has a few pleasant public parks and gardens, an interesting Ecole des Beaux Arts training artists and craftsmen, two public golf courses and several sports clubs (tennis and riding) in which temporary membership is available (Union Sportive Marocaine). It also is the home of most of Morocco's 40,000 Jews, mainly older business people.

RABAT, the national capital, is one hour by rail or road from Casablanca. Its medina has many fine old homes and a lively souk with excellent crafts on sale—especially rugs and leather. The lofty Tour Hassan dominates the town with a magnificent view of elegant white villas and gardens, the old quarters, the river and Rabat's sister town, Salé. Begun in the 12th century as the world's largest mosque, the tower is a monument to classic Islamic architecture. Nearby is the highly ornate tomb of Mohammed V and a new adjoining mosque. Rabat also has Roman ruins near the Chellah Gate and a Museum of Antiquities on Rue Pierre Parent with many Roman artifacts, including lovely bronzes.

Islamic art can be seen in the Rabat Casbah of the Oudaia, which has a museum, a lovely garden and a pleasant outdoor tea room. Alongside the garden are the shops of master craftsmen—including guitar and violin makers. Above the Oudaia is the walled residential casbah where certain streets are sometimes closed to infidels; boys will escort you to excellent lookout points, the houses of resident European artists and the rug factory that employs young girls under miserable conditions.

On the outskirts of the city is Mohammed V University, with 13,000 students, and a string of resplendent royal palaces stretching for miles to the royal golf course. The summer palace, Dar es Salaam, is open to the public on some Friday and Sunday afternoons. The changing of the royal palace guard can be seen daily from the Mechouar parade ground. When the king is in Rabat on a Friday he often rides his white Arabian charger from the Mechouar to the mosque, accepting homage from the faithful along the way. Across the Bou Regreg River is SALÉ, with fine gates and walls, an interesting Great Mosque and a lively medina. As in Rabat, its bidonvilles are mushrooming.

Night life in Rabat is confined to a few outdoor cafes. The Nomad Club at 16 Zankat Ouarzazate, near the American Embassy, is patronized mostly by embassy staff, other foreigners and businessmen. The US Information Service office in Rabat has a library and an evening jazz club that attracts some young Moroccans. The Peace Corps has its administrative offices in Rabat. Le Bowling Club is for just that.

Accessible by public conveyances from Rabat are the public beaches of Temara and Plage des Nations, five miles north of the city. As in Casablanca, Sunday is devoted to soccer football. The stadium crowds are among the most enthusiastic in Africa. Riding, tennis and golf are available through private clubs and hotels in Rabat, Skhirat and Mohammedia, where there is a casino.

Together with Rabat, Morocco's four "imperial cities" include Meknès, Fez and Marrakesh. MEKNÈS is 100 miles from Rabat along an excellent road which passes through the irrigated agricultural heartland of the country. Its great El Hedim Square, the Mosque of Berrima, the Islamic theological centers of Filali and Bou Inania Medersas, and the Museum of Bab Djamai make this city of 200,000 a stellar attraction. You can stay in the medina or in the new city, but be certain to explore the medina on foot. Take a trip by taxi to the ruins of Dar el Kebra.

A splendid one-day side trip from Meknès is a visit by car or bus to the Roman ruins of *Volubilis* and the adjoining Islamic holy village of Moulay Idriss, burial place of the Sherifian dynasty's 8th century religious leader. The ruins, excellently preserved, recall the time when Morocco was the granary of the Roman Empire and a major frontier post. The mosque of the sacred city of Moulay Idriss may not be entered by non-Moslems, who also must leave the city by nightfall.

Another side trip leads 45 miles eastward from Meknès to the mountain resorts of Ifrane and Azrou, 10 miles apart. Both provide winter skiing, spring and summer hiking in aromatic pine and cedar forests, and traditional Berber settings. From late December to mid-April there is also skiing at Oukaimeden, less than two hours by road from Marrakesh.

FEZ, 40 miles northeast of Meknès, is the oldest traditional city in Morocco and home of the Fassi merchants who dominate the nation's wholesale and retail trade. Fez has fine architecture and exciting markets. Other attractions are the new and old medinas, the Attarine and Bou Inania 14th century Medersas (religious colleges), the Dar Batha Museum of Moroccan Art and Bherratine Medersa dating from the 17th century. The 9th century Karaoyine Mosque is the largest in North Africa—a house of prayer for students from the 1,000-year-old Kairouan Theological University. Moulay Idriss Zaouia is a beautiful tiled sanctuary. Visit the Square of Nejjarine, a festive wonderland of street artists, vendors, musicians and craftsmen. Fez is another city to be explored on foot —search out the potters, weavers, leather workers and other artisans. If you are interested in crafts, be sure to visit the National Institute of Leather and Textiles.

The 290-mile road from Fez to Marrakesh is a pleasant one-day drive by car or bus. Possible stops along the way include the walled town of Demnate with its lively Sunday market, the attractive country town of Beni Mellal with a Friday market, and the dam and lake of Bine el Ouidane for boating.

Of Morocco's four dynastic capitals, MARRAKESH is the crowning jewel. Framed by the Atlas mountains and set in a fairyland oasis of palm and olive groves, Marrakesh is also the gateway to the Sahara and to Black Africa. The Djemaa el Fna, an immense open marketplace, is a daily scene of snake charmers, dancers, acrobats, jugglers and storytellers— enough action here to put any three-ring circus to shame. Side streets off the Djemaa el Fna lead to the covered streets and alleys of the souks, a hundred intriguing caravans of merchandise. The city also has magnificent semi-tropical gardens basking in the rose tints of sun and marble. Here you can see the 12th century Aguedal, the olive gardens of Menara, the 19th century Bahia Palace and its gardens, and the orange groves that surround the walls of the city.

The Islamic architectural splendors of Marrakesh also include the minaret of the casbah mosque, the Koutoubia mosque, the Saadi tombs, the El Badi palace ruins, and the Medersa (Koranic school) Ben Yussef.

The best night life is the free entertainment presented every evening in the Djemaa square. On Thursdays the colorful camel market convenes on the outskirts of town. In mid-May there's a folklore festival.

South and east of Marrakesh are the Atlas and the Anti-Atlas mountains, and beyond them the Sahara. You can drive through mountain passes to the oasis towns of Zagora, Ouarzazate, Tineghir and Erfoud, each of which has a modern government-operated hotel and less expensive facilities. Erfoud in mid-October has a date festival with a colorful display of dancing and pageantry. Don't miss "ahwach," a graceful, undulating Berber women's dance.

Each oasis is inhabited by a Berber tribe or clan with a distinct style of dress, and each has its own casbah, fortress (ksar) with imposing brick towers, and daily market. OUARZAZATE is the most accessible (140 miles of spectacular mountain driving from Marrakesh). It has a youth hostel and a luxury hotel. Nearby is the Berber village of Tifoultout, with its two- and three-story adobe brick houses, casbah and mellah, home of the legendary Black Jews said to have traversed the Sahara nearly 2,500 years ago following their expulsion from Babylon. Beyond this point one road leads north through the Dadès Valley to the oasis towns of Tineghir,

Ksar es Souk and Erfoud at the very edge of the Sahara and then swings west through the spectacular Ziz Valley gorges to Meknès.

Eastern Morocco is at its best from October to April, when the heat is less intense. Each oasis town has its special character. Ksar es Souk is noted for its Foreign Legion frontier drinking atmosphere, Figuig for its Berber crafts, date palms and wild scenery, Tineghir for its olives, fortifications and the nearby gorges of Todgha. Erfoud has a colorful casbah, and there are interesting medieval ruins at Sigilmassa, markets and forts at Rissani. The adventurous may want to push beyond the administrative town of Zagora over rough roads to the beautiful oases of M'Hamid or Foum Zguid.

Another mountain road runs south from Marrakesh 145 miles to TAROUDANT, the walled town at the head of the Valley of the Souss. There you can visit battlements and ramparts, fragrant olive and palm groves, skilled stone carvers, potters and coppersmiths. The farther south you proceed the greater the hospitality you will encounter from a people whose very survival in the desert is a constant struggle.

Out of Taroudant is a road that leads first to the minareted palm grove town of TIZNIT (noted for its Berber inlaid silver jewelry and the nearby beach of Aghlou) and then to the caravan town of GOULIMINE. Here on Saturdays a famous camel market is held and the Tuareg "blue men," so-called for their indigo-dyed cloth headdresses and robes, form their caravans to cross the Sahara. Here also the "guedra" dance is performed by black-veiled women encircled by drummers. TAFRAOUT, a picturesque town, is reached by mountain roads from Goulimine or Tiznit through a valley of rock pinnacles.

The former Spanish port of IFNI, 27 miles by road from Goulimine, was returned to Morocco in 1969 but retains a Spanish flavor. More interesting is the market town of TAN-TAN, 87 miles south of Goulimine by paved road, where at the Governor's Office one can rent bungalows for Tan-Tan beach, 20 miles away. From Tan-Tan to the Spanish Sahara border is 174 miles of desert track; get a camel.

Morocco's Atlantic Ocean resorts and beaches run from Tan-Tan to Tangier, with those north of Casablanca favored during the summer, and those south in the winter. Extending along excellent coastal roads are holiday villages for tourists, luxury hotels, camping sites and good fishing and swimming. AGADIR is the major winter resort. Rebuilt after the 1960 earthquake, it has a fine bay, mimosa-lined beaches and an air of modernity.

Between Agadir and Casablanca lie Essaouira, also known as Mogador, a pretty, whitewashed sardine-fishing port; Safi, a small industrial center and fishing port noted for its excellent potters and good beach; Oualidia, a tiny resort with a lagoon for safe bathing and fascinating underwater goggling, and El Jadida (ex-Mazagan), a place of lovely old Portuguese churches, cisterns, forts and ruins as well as good beaches. Near El Jadida is the fishing village of Moulay Abdullah with the extensive ruins of the medieval Islamic town of Tit, and Azemmour, where there is a fine beach and interesting old ramparts and walls. You can take numerous brief excursions inland from the coastal towns. There's a good road running 103 miles from Essaouira to Marrakesh that passes through Chichaoua, famous for its carpet cooperative and Sunday market.

The most crowded beaches are between Casablanca and Rabat at Mohammedia and Skhirat.

North of Casablanca along the coast road to Tangier, the water is colder, the surf more tempestuous, the beaches less inviting, the tourists fewer and the Moroccans more numerous. Kenitra is a commercial port with a US naval communications station. Nearby a monument commemorates the 1944 Allied landing. Farther up the coast is the pleasant fishing town of Larache, and nearby the ruins of Lixus and the Sunday market town of Ksar el Kebir.

TANGIER, when it flourished as an international city, had many banks, an active casino, and its own jet set and writers' colony. Under Moroccan rule Tangier has become a humdrum commercial city lacking the vitality or traditions of other Moroccan centers. Anyone who has seen Fez or Meknès, Rabat or Marrakesh will be disappointed by Tangier, outraged at its prices and disturbed by the day-trippers who seem satisfied with its shoddy wares. Attractions include strolling along the Boulevard Pasteur, shopping in the Gran Socco and listening to the nightly jazz at the African Rhythm Club.

Tangier also has good beaches at Cape Halabata, Kota and Asilah, a municipal casino with occasional local art exhibits, and a bustling market area. Several tourist nightclubs feature purported Moroccan belly dancing and folklore groups. There is a full range of outdoor sports at several private clubs (Royal Country Club for golf, Yacht Club, Club de l'Etrier for riding), and.an interesting museum at the Sultan's palace in the casbah. Besides an established primary and secondary school, Tangier now has an American-financed technical institute which is to be developed into the University of North Africa. It also has the African Administrative Training Center (CAFRAD), a UN project.

TETOUAN, the former capital of Spanish Morocco, is a more attractive place than Tangier. It has an interesting medina and active markets. The sights include museums of art and archaeology, the palace of the Khalifa and the School of Arts (visitors invited). Nearby, there are fine Mediterranean beach resorts at Martil, M'Diq, Smir and Restingas. Forty miles south of Tetouan is the hospitable mountain town of Chechaouen, home of the proud Rif people. Chechaouen is known for its cafes, tiles, mineral water springs and rug factory. Also in the mountains, 41 miles south of Chechaouen on the road to Fez, is the Rif town of Ouezzane, prominent for its historic mosque, carved balconies and excellent weaving.

The region east of Tangier—the Mediterranean coast and Rif mountains—is the least developed for tourism, but it has a number of interesting hamlets and the attractive Spanish cities of Ceuta and Melilla (described in separate chapter). The coastal road leads to the drab frontier town of Oujda, 15 miles from the Algerian border, which can be crossed by daily train or by road, if you have a visa. If you're heading in this direction you'll come across the cedar and marijuana-growing area near Ketama, the pleasant fishing port of Al-Hoceima and the beach resort of Saidia. Four miles from Oujda are the lovely gardens and spring of Sidi Yahha. The same road takes you to the rugged *Jebel Tazzeka National Park*, the historic town of Taza, and Fez.

Morocco offers many activities for the sports-minded. There are 18-hole golf courses at Marrakesh and Mohammedia and nine-hole courses at Casablanca, Ketama and Tangier. You can climb in the Atlas mountains. There's riding, tennis, yachting, skiing, deep-sea fishing, trout fishing and hunting. For information on hunting (birds, wild boar) write to the Fédération de Chasse, B.P. 374, Rabat. If you want to make arrangements for skiing, write to the Fédération de Ski, Boulevard Mohammed V, Rabat. If you're interested in water sports (there are spear-fishing clubs at Agadir, Casablanca, Kenitra, M'Diq and Tetouan) write to the Fédération d'Etudes et Sports Sous-Marines, B.P. 318, Rabat.

What to Buy

Volumes have been written about Moroccan handicraft. Although the nation's 250,000 artisans face dwindling wages and competition from cheap machine-made products, they continue to turn out magnificent work. Whenever possible visit their workshops and buy directly from the artisans. You can ship goods home safely by surface mail from Casablanca or by air freight from most places in the country. Bargaining is the custom. Take your time, do not show impatience and invite the merchant to share a glass of green mint tea with you (at his expense). Ask to see how the goods are produced (although this may mean visiting sweatshops where adolescent girls toil up to 12 hours a day). Most artisans are organized into guilds, sharing neighborhoods and sometimes schools and religious facilities.

Best known are the rugs and tapestries that come from the High and Middle Atlas mountains and the regions of Marmoucha and Chichaoua. Buy these in Marrakesh or Rabat if you cannot get to the mountains. Woven blankets come from Azemmour. Brocades, silks, jellabas and kaftans are Fez specialties—as are fezzes.

Leatherwork is best in Meknès; it includes handmade shoes and the comfortable, floppy, backless, flat slippers known as babouches. Jewelry comes from Tiznit. Ouarzazate and the south; pottery from Salé, Safi and Fez; muskets, sabers, daggers, copperware, trays and vases from each of the imperial cities.

A quick and easy way to buy is at the government-run Maisons de l'Artisanat in Casablanca and other cities, where there is no bargaining and prices may be 15 to 20 per cent higher than in open markets. Coopartim, a government agency, runs several retail shops including the National Leather and Textile Institute in Fez where you can find excellent buys in wallets, handbags, bookbindings and embossed ottomans (pouffes). The diligent shopper may wish to start his trip by noting prices at Moroccan boutiques in New York, Los Angeles, Paris and elsewhere. Many an "importer" has been born from comparison of these prices with those on the spot.

Moroccan craftsmanship in gold, silver and leather is the finest in Africa. Licensed guides (wearing badges) and free-lancers accost you but their services are not needed unless you are hunting for a particular shop. If a guide helps you find it, the merchant provides a commission and you can throw in a small tip.

Local Attitudes

Morocco is a conservative country dominated by tradition and religion. Get permission before you photograph people, especially veiled women, unless you are at a respectable distance. Miniskirts and similar attire are inappropriate outside cosmopolitan or beach areas. If you receive permission to enter a mosque (most are closed to non-Moslems), remove your shoes. Although hippies are tolerated, complaints are growing about the little money they spend and their effect on local morals.

France and the United States have been the principal sources of public and private economic aid to Morocco. Left-wing Moroccans are critical of US involvement in the economy and its support of King Hassan II, but they are friendly to individual Americans. Peace Corps Volunteers have created considerable goodwill.

Weather, What to Wear, How Long to Stay

Dress to suit yourself but take good walking shoes or desert boots for the mountains and the south. Few hotels require coat and tie for evening meals, but most prosperous Moroccan city men wear jackets (often tweedy) and ties when not in jellaba. Sunglasses, lotions and some sort of hat or sombrero are useful in the south. You'll need a sweater for chilly evenings in Marrakesh and the mountains.

Morocco has four seasons that vary in each part of the country. Winter in Tangier and the north is damp, rainy and chilly. In Agadir it is pleasant with temperatures in the 80's. There is snow and skiing in the High Atlas. Spring, when flowers bloom and fruits begin to ripen, is the best time for Marrakesh, and summer for Rabat and the Atlantic Coast. Summer temperatures soar over 100 degrees in the south. In the fall, particularly September and October, there is temperate weather with light rains in much of the country. Hotel rates rise in the peak tourist seasons (May to September in the north and along the coast down to Casablanca, and December to February at Agadir and Marrakesh).

Some visitors come for a day, others for a week, and a few remain forever. You need a week to see the four imperial cities, highlights of any trip. Although internal flights are cheap and reliable, the country should really be seen by road or rail. Two weeks permit more elaborate exploration of the main cities plus side trips.

Morocco is a great country for lingering, but a month is enough for an extensive and pleasurable visit. Although there are more and more air-conditioned tourist buses, you can still indulge in the leisurely kind of travel that relaxes the body, arouses the senses and stimulates the mind.

Communication

Moroccan postal and telephone services work well by African standards and moderately well by those of Western Europe. International mail takes three or four days to reach North America. Overseas phone service is via Paris. There is direct dialing between the major cities and from Casablanca to Paris.

The national language is Arabic although French has been retained in the secondary schools, universities and administration. French takes you everywhere, Spanish serves in Tangier and much of northern Morocco. English is spoken at most major tourist facilities. Berber in several dialects is also widely spoken.

The press, in both Arabic and French, is strictly government controlled. *Le Petit Marocain* and *La Vigie Marocaine*, both in French, are rather dull. Most educated Moroccans read *Le Monde* and other French papers which arrive on the day of publication. *Newsweek*, *Time* and the Paris *Herald-Tribune* are on city newsstands. The monthly magazine in French, *La Maalif*, provides excellent independent coverage of Moroccan political, social and cultural life. The literary quarterly *Souffles* takes a more radical line. Government radio and TV stations broadcast primarily in Arabic but have regular evening programs in French and Spanish.

There is a nascent Moroccan film industry but so far no noteworthy feature films have been produced. The Ciné Clubs in Casablanca and other cities are good places to meet young Moroccan film enthusiasts. US Peace Corps, Canadian CUSO, British VSO and West German and Scandinavian volunteers, as well as hundreds of French technical assistants, work in Moroccan secondary schools, teacher training and vocational colleges and other educational institutions.

Emergencies

Private physicians and good public hospitals are available in Casablanca. Elsewhere they are fewer and less reliable. The United States has an embassy in Rabat (43 avenue Allal ben Abdellah, tel. 303-61), and consulates in Casablanca (1 place de la Fraternité, tel. 605-21) and in Tangier (Chemin des Amoureux, tel. 159-04).

Spanish Sahara

(Sahara Español)

Profile

STATUS: Overseas Province of Spain. Administered by governor-general responsible to Madrid.

SIZE: 102,700 square miles (about the size of Colorado). Population—between 30,000 and 50,000, mostly nomadic Berbers, plus about 15,000 Spanish (half of them military).

GEOGRAPHY: Vast, flat and monotonous desert on the Atlantic coast. Principal towns—El Aaiún (capital, 9,000), Villa Cisneros (4,000).

CLIMATE: Dry and extremely hot during the day, evenings cool. Sandstorms during March, April and May.

LANGUAGES: Spanish (official), Arabic, some French.

CURRENCY: Spanish peseta (P) divided into 100 centimos. 10 pesetas = about 16 cents; $1.00 = 62.5 pesetas.

VISAS: Required. Available through Spanish embassies and consulates. Fee $5.40. Three passport photos and letter of credit-worthiness from a bank needed. Expect delay while application is sent to Madrid for approval; it is quicker and simpler to apply at the Spanish Government tourist offices in the Canary Islands.

AIRPORT: Villa Bens (EUN), near El Aaiún. Daily flights from Canary Islands, five flights a week from Madrid.

NATIONAL HOLIDAYS: May 1; July 18, Spanish National Day; Catholic and Moslem holidays.

INFORMATION SOURCES: *In US*—Embassy of Spain Information Office,

529 14th Street NW, Washington, D.C. (tel. 202/347-6777); Spanish Consulate General, 964 Third Avenue, New York, N.Y. 10022 (tel. 212/355-4080); Spanish National Tourist Office, 989 Fifth Avenue, New York, N.Y. 10017 (tel. 212/759-3842). *In Madrid*—Ministerio de Informacíon y Turismo, Avenida del Generalisimo 38. *In Canary Islands* —Spanish Tourist Office, Casa del Turismo, Parque Santa Catalina, Las Palmas (tel. 264623).

By *Aaron Segal*

This barren stretch of North African coast and desertland may be the world's most valuable and hotly contested sandbox. It is a place only for those who enjoy the desert, camels, isolation and a dash of intrigue. The Kingdom of Morocco contests Spain's control over these sandy shores where in 1963 one of the largest phosphate deposits in the world was discovered. Oil explorations may yet yield further riches.

Spanish navigators first explored the coast of this territory in the 16th century and the Spanish military have been there since the late 19th century. The country's boundaries were set in a final Franco-Spanish treaty in 1912, but Spain occupied the territory only in 1934, after the Moroccan (Rif) rebellions in the north. Morocco claims the territory on historical and ethnic grounds, and has become more insistent since the phosphate bonanza. Although the Spanish recently ceded to Morocco another stretch of coastal desert to the north, known as Ifni, they are still unwilling to relinquish this richer expanse of Saharan land. Spain has indulged discussion of a possible United Nations-supervised referendum with these options: independence, union with Morocco, or some form of association with Spain. But it is easier to talk about a referendum than to administer it, because Saharans are still mainly a nomadic people who come and go at will across Moroccan and Mauritanian borders.

The country is divided into two regions, Sekia el Hamra, in the north, where the phosphate mines are, and Rio de Oro in the south. The main town in Sekia el Hamra is El Aaiún, the country's capital. The main town in Rio de Oro is Villa Cisneros. But both are little more than administrative and military bases with a combined population of 13,000— principally Spanish civil servants, detachments of the Spanish army and members of the colorful Spanish Foreign Legion.

Elsewhere, except for small fishing communities, the population is on the move in search of pasture and water. The country has a population density of about one person for every two square miles.

Money Matters

The Spanish peseta, valued at 62.5 to $1, is fully convertible. Currency can be exchanged in El Aaiún and Villa Cisneros.

Getting In and Out

Visas or entry permits for one or two days can be obtained from Spanish government tourist offices in the Canary Islands. Applications submitted elsewhere involve paperwork and may be sent to Madrid for approval.

Most visitors take the 45-minute Iberia Airlines daily flight from Las Palmas (Canary Islands) to El Aaiún. The round trip costs less than $22 and permits a peek at the Sahara. There are also five flights a week from Madrid to El Aaiún.

Overland, the only way to come here is across the Sahara. If you don't own a camel, get a four-wheel-drive vehicle. And expeditionary provisions. Even then, you may be turned back by suspicious border guards. There are two routes—from Goulimine in southern Morocco, or from Tindouf in southern Algeria. Both are grueling. Exploratour, located in Summer Place, Westerham, Kent, England, has a London-based tour of Morocco, Spanish Sahara and the Canary Islands that includes a two-day Land Rover trip between El Aaiún and Goulimine.

More comfortable are the twice-a-month cruises from the Canary Islands to El Aaiún. The ships are operated by the Compania Trasmediterranea, whose main office is at Zurbano 73, Apartado de Correos 982, Madrid. Fares from Las Palmas to El Aaiún are $3 to $7.

Getting Around Within Spanish Sahara

The climate is enervating and outside the towns the roads are little better than tracks in the sand, worn by trucks, army vehicles and camels. There are regular flights between El Aaiún and Villa Cisneros and from there to the southern outpost of La Guera, a suburb of Mauritania's booming port of Nouadhibou.

Where to Stay

Near the airport at EL AAIÚN the Spanish Government has constructed the 22-room air-conditioned *Parador*, the first modern hotel in the country. It has a swimming pool. Primarily for overnight visitors from the Canary Islands, it is an attractive but expensive place. Other choices are limited to the very modest *Hotel Ipasa* at Villa Cisneros, or the grubby pensions, or seeking out a sympathetic Spanish family with a spare bed. Exploratour uses its own tents, sometimes Bedouin tents.

Where and What to Eat

Sidewalk restaurants and cafes in the two towns serve Spanish food. Fresh seafood is the best, especially langosta (crayfish), camarones (shrimp) and various kinds of shellfish (mariscos). Try the modern restaurant-bar, *Cabaña de Caballeros*, a favorite of Spanish army officers in EL AAIÚN. In LA GUERA, *Mamacita's La Paella* restaurant also caters primarily to military personnel.

What to See and Do

The two towns of EL AAIÚN and VILLA CISNEROS have little interest beyond their magnificent and virtually empty sand beaches. The sun is intense, so bathing should be confined to early mornings and late afternoons. The headquarters of the Spanish Foreign Legion may be visited.

Those interested in desert technology may want to visit the phosphate deposits at BU CRAA and its new port, the country's most ambitious undertaking. Permission should be obtained from the office of the governor-general in El Aaiún.

Technology contrasts dramatically with the camels, water holes, portable tents (jaimas), traditional crafts and religion of Saharan nomadic life. The lovely Mosque of the Blue Sultan at Semara, a market town 144 miles from El Aaiún, is a fine example of the striking, clean lines of Saharan architecture. Inquire here or in the capital about visiting a nomad encampment, especially for an evening of traditional dancing and perhaps a feast of braised lamb or mutton. Desert hospitality is elaborate.

Fishing is excellent off the empty beaches or in the small boats and trawlers that work the coast. There's some hunting of wild fowl and small game in the dry river beds.

What to Buy

A local specialty is hand-worked copper and silver. It is available in tiny shops in the towns or directly from the craftsmen. Favorite items are intricately worked ankle bracelets, rings and daggers. The weaving of camel hair is another local craft; it's usually a covering material for tents and blankets.

Local Attitudes

Political uncertainty hangs over this military colony and Spanish officials are likely to be curious about visitors who stay more than a day or two.

Ask permission before taking photos or entering mosques.

Weather, What to Wear, How Long to Stay

Along the coast daytime temperatures vary from 80 to 100 degrees, dropping 15 to 20 degrees at night. The interior has the sharp temperature changes characteristic of the Sahara, blazing during the day and at times chillingly cool at night. Except for a rare flash of rain there is no precipitation and humidity is low. Winter months are the most tolerable. Saharan sandstorms are most frequent from March through May.

Casual attire is appropriate but keep miniskirts and bikinis for the empty beaches.

Visitors generally come to the capital on a morning flight from Las Palmas or Tenerife, returning in the afternoon. Two or three days would provide time for trips to Bu Craa and Semara.

Communication

Postal and telephone connections are exclusively between Sahara and the Canary Islands or Madrid; they are reliable but limited. Spanish is the official language, spoken by most townspeople and understood by some nomads. French goes a little way and a Moroccan Arabic dialect (Hassania) furthest.

Emergencies

There is no American or other diplomatic representation. Local medical services are inadequate. Head for Las Palmas or Madrid.

Tunisia

(République de Tunisie)

Profile

STATUS: Independent since March 20, 1956. Former French protectorate.

SIZE: 63,379 square miles (slightly larger than Florida). Population—5,140,000 (mostly Arabs and Berbers).

GEOGRAPHY: 800 miles of Mediterranean coast in north and east, northern half consists of steppes and fertile plateau, southern half Sahara desert. Principal cities—Tunis (capital, 800,000), Sfax (port, 135,000), Kairouan (85,000).

CLIMATE: North is temperate in spring and autumn, hot in summer, cool and damp in winter. Tunis temperatures in the high 80's and 90's in summer with cooler evenings; 50's in winter, dropping into the 40's at night. Saharan heat in south (high 90's to well over 100 degrees).

LANGUAGES: Arabic and French.

CURRENCY: Dinar, divided into 1,000 millimes. 1 dinar = $2.10; $1.00 = 476 millimes.

VISAS: No visa required for Americans visiting four months or less.

AIRPORT: Tunis-Carthage (TUN), six miles from city. Frequent flights to Western Europe and North Africa only. Airport departure taxes—domestic, 200 millimes (42 cents); international, 1 dinar ($2.10). Transport into city—bus, 130 millimes (27 cents); taxi, 1 dinar.

NATIONAL HOLIDAYS: January 18, Revolution Day; March 20, Independence Day; April 9, Martyrs Day; May 1, Labor Day; June 1, National Day; July 25, Anniversary of the Republic; August 3, President Bourguiba's Birthday; August 13, Women's Day; September 3, Commemoration Day; Moslem holidays.

INFORMATION SOURCES: *In US*—Embassy of Tunisia, 2408 Massachusetts Avenue NW, Washington, D.C. 20008 (tel. 202/234-6644); Permanent Mission of Tunisia to the UN, 40 East 71st Street, New York, N.Y. 10021 (tel. 212/988-7200). *In Tunis*—Office National du Tourisme, Avenue Mohamed V (tel. 259217). *In London*—Tunisian Tourist Office, 50-51 Conduit Street, London, W.1; *In Paris*—Maison de la Tunisie, 164 faubourg Saint-Honoré.

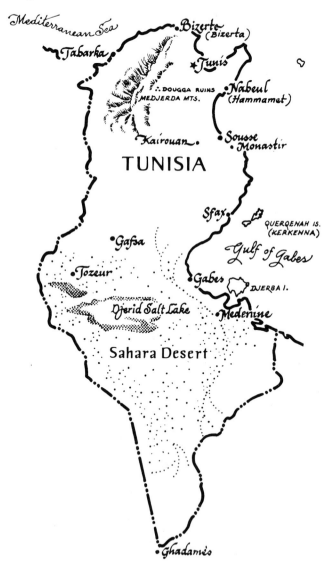

By Aaron Segal

Americans are just beginning to discover what Europeans learned years ago—that this little Mediterranean country wedged between Algeria and Libya is ideal for vacations.

Air fares to Tunisia are relatively low; there's a broad range of hotels and restaurants offering good value; the people are hospitable and cosmopolitan. The country has good beaches, enchanting offshore islands, forests, archaeological sites, water sports, some hunting, a fragment of the Sahara, fine shopping, and enough cultural distinction to make it intriguing but not frightening.

More than 500,000 visitors came in 1972, and the volume is growing by 10 to 15 per cent annually. Mostly the visitors are French, German, Scandinavian and British—with only a sprinkling of Americans thus far. Tunisia has become so popular a holiday resort for Western Europeans that in the high seasons of June to September and December to February some of the major attractions are getting crowded.

Culturally and geographically, Tunisia is isolated from much of the rest of Africa. It is a country to be visited on its own, or perhaps as part of a North African or Mediterranean circuit. It can be included in a broader African itinerary only with difficulty.

Tunisia's population of five million is concentrated along its 800-mile northern and eastern Mediterranean shores, an area of undulating beaches, well-watered fields, seaports and fishing villages. Behind the coast and the central Tell (plateau) is the Tunisian Sahara—lacking the breadth and grandeur of the Sahara of Algeria, Morocco or Libya, but more easily traversed. Beyond the dry highland steppe near Jebel Chambi, the highest peak in the country at 5,066 feet, the topography south and west of Sfax changes into the seemingly endless "chotts"—salt flats at or below sea level with their intricate crystalline textures that often dissolve into mirages. Between the chotts are the exotic oases, islands of life in a stern sand sea, and then a progression of dunes to the southern end of the country.

A strategic mid-Mediterranean location, phosphate resources, and an abundance of olive oil, wheat, wine and cork have attracted invaders as well as visitors throughout Tunisia's history. The Phoenicians came and built Carthage, only to see it crushed by Rome. Rome was in turn followed by Byzantium, Fatimid Egypt, Ottoman Turkey and finally imperial France. As a result of these incursions, Tunisia's architecture, history, culture and genetic make-up are a true Mediterranean mix. Its people are sometimes blue-eyed and blond, sometimes swarthy.

Beginning in 1880, French colonial rule encouraged the development of mining, agriculture and commerce. French settlers promoted French administrative and educational methods, and French values were adopted by the emerging Tunisian elite. But a spirit of nationalism began to take shape early in the 1900's with young leaders urging Tunisians to assert their right to manage their own affairs. Nationalism grew in the 1930's and came to a head during World War II, when Tunisia found itself a battleground for foreign armies. In 1943, after the Allies had taken Bizerta and Tunis, Tunisia's Destour Party, founded by Habib Bourguiba, clamored for basic reform and eventual independence. But when the smoke of battle and nationalist agitation cleared, the French were once more in power. After many ups and downs, including the arrest and exile of Bourguiba, the French at last yielded. In 1957 Bourguiba was elected president of a sovereign independent republic.

Since independence President Bourguiba has followed policies of economic, political and social gradualism intended to advance Tunisian society without violent wrenches. In some areas, such as female emancipation, he has moved fast, abolishing polygamy, increasing educational opportunities for women and promoting birth control as a national policy. His economic policy has concentrated on tourism, light industry and land reform, and he has sought and received extensive American and other Western aid. He re-established cordial relations with France after the Algerian war and the final French evacuation of the Bizerta naval base in 1963. But serious economic problems remain. There is widespread unemployment in a very youthful population. And the nation has yet to find a successor to the elderly Bourguiba and the one-party rule of his somewhat tired Neo-Destour Party.

There is considerable travel literature in French and English on Tunisia. *Tunisia, A Vacation Guide* (Scribner's, 1970), by former British diplomat Michael Tomkinson, is strong on archaeology, sightseeing and history. The *Guide Bleu* in French (Hachette) is a marvel of detail. *Tunisia* by Henri Gault and Christian Milau is a useful little guidebook. More serious works include *Tunisia Since Independence* by Clement Henry Moore (University of California Press) and a series of excellent scholarly volumes on Tunisian history published in French by the two government publishing houses, the Société Nationale des Editions Tunisiennes and the Maison Tunisienne de l'Edition.

Money Matters

The Tunisian dinar can be neither exported nor imported. On arrival travelers are given a currency declaration form to record their foreign currency and their exchange transactions while in the country. Hang on to this form because it must be shown to customs on exit. Service is slow at the airport banks and branches of the Banque Centrale, Crédit Lyonnais, the Société Tunisienne de Banque and others. (Crédit Lyonnais is affiliated with Chase Manhattan and the Société Tunisienne de Banque with the Bank of America.) Banks are open Monday through Friday from 7:30 to 11:30 am in summer, and 8 to 11 am and 2 to 4 pm in winter. It may be easier to exchange at your hotel and accept a slightly less favorable rate. Travelers checks are widely accepted, credit cards less so except at international hotels like the Hilton. It's best to exchange only moderate amounts since you will be stuck with any remaining dinars on departure. Hotel, food and service costs are quite low.

Getting In and Out

Tunisia does not require visas for American, Canadian, British and most Western European travelers holding valid passports and international health certificates. Airport customs inspection is perfunctory and bureaucratic folderol is kept to a minimum.

There are no direct flights from North America but you can make easy connections to Tunis from Casablanca, or Rome, Paris, Madrid, Geneva, Frankfurt, Amsterdam, London, Marseille and other European cities. Air mileage rates permit inclusion of Tunis at no extra expense on tickets from North America to Rome. New York-Rome-Tunis round trips are available for slightly over $300. Alitalia and Tunis Air have daily one-hour flights between Rome and Tunis. Tunis Air, Air Maroc and Air Algérie share a service with several flights a week linking Casablanca and Tunis. These are likely to be heavily booked during summer months, as are the connections with Marseille and Paris. Tunis Air, Libyan Arab Airlines, Lufthansa and United Arab Airlines connect Tunis eastward with Tripoli and Cairo.

Frequent charter flights, especially during winter and summer high seasons, arrive at Tunis and the island of Djerba from London, Frankfurt, Copenhagen, Stockholm and other European points. For example, during the summer of 1972 the Student Travel Association offered charter flights to Tunis at one-way fares of $25 from Rome, $52.10 from London, $45.60 from Paris and $58 from Copenhagen. These flights were open only to students under 30 years of age, but other charter carriers offer comparable rates to travelers of all ages from Western Europe.

However, aside from one weekly British Caledonian flight to and from East Africa, routing to sub-Saharan Africa requires a connection in Rome, Paris, Casablanca or Cairo. At little extra expense one can route an East or Southern Africa ticket from North America to provide for stops across North Africa, including Tunis.

One of the most pleasant ways to arrive or leave is by ship. The Italian Tirennia Line sails weekly from Naples to Tunis. There are connections with ships of the Tirennia Export Line or other lines to the US and Canada. Most Mediterranean cruise ships make at least one overnight stop at a Tunisian port, usually Tunis. The Compagnie Tunisienne de Navigation has some passenger accommodations on freighters to and from Algerian and Moroccan ports and plans to introduce a modern, inexpensive car ferry service between Tunis and Marseille.

At present there are passenger and car ferry services to and from Marseille operated by Navitour (8 rue d'Alger, Tunis); to and from Naples and Palermo by the Tirennia company (Rue de Yougoslavie, Tunis) and to and from Genoa by Anglo-Algerian Coaling Company (5 rue Champlain, Tunis). Prices depend on the size of the car and number of passengers, varying from $50 to $100 a vehicle from Marseille to Tunis, a 48-hour trip. Rates from Genoa and Naples are lower. There are many advantages in driving a car through Europe, shipping it to Tunisia from France or Italy and then using it to see the country. Motorists can drive east from Tunisia to Libya and Egypt or west to Algeria and Morocco and return to Europe via the car ferry from Tangier or Ceuta to Spain.

A good coastal road stretches across North Africa. For entering vehicles Tunisian border officials require only an international insurance card endorsed for Tunisia. They issue their own documents on the spot. Algeria and Libya are tougher on documents. (See Libya chapter for special requirements.) Collective taxis and buses travel between Tunis and the Algerian and Libyan borders, where connections can be made. You can also drive east from the southern Tunisian oases to Ghadamès in Libya, or west to the Algerian Sahara crossing at Nefta on the road to the Algerian oasis of El Oued. Mini-Trek and other overland travel expeditions offer tours that include Saharan travel in Morocco, Algeria, Tunisia and Libya.

Getting Around Within Tunisia

The nation is served by a good and rapidly improving network of paved and all-weather roads and by buses, internal flights and an aging but adequate railway. Internal travel is usually quick and inexpensive.

Two kinds of taxis service the airports and the cities. The tiny metered bébé taxis, usually Renault 4L's or Citroën 2 CV's colored red, blue, orange or green, carry no more than three passengers comfortably. They are handy for scooting around and very cheap, but in great demand and hard to find in rush hours. The larger taxis—Mercedes, Peugeot or other four-door models—are more expensive. Establish the price before you get in. You can also get around in hippomobiles—horse-drawn carriages that operate out of the main squares in Tunis and other cities. Motor scooters and motorcycles are not often seen, although they are cheap and convenient for cities. Ask at the dealers (Vespa or Honda) about rentals.

For getting around within the city of Tunis there are very crowded municipal buses, the ubiquitous—except when you need them—bébé taxis, and trolleys that run along the major avenues. The beach suburbs of Carthage and La Marsa are served by a delightful, creaky wooden trolley-car railway known as the TGM. Its depot is in central Tunis near the Place d'Afrique. The full ride takes 45 minutes, crossing the Lake of Tunis and the port by dike, with stops at each of the major beaches. The TGM costs less than 25 cents one way and is great fun. Mini-taxis charge about $1 to cover the same distance in half the time.

To get you from town to town there are fast collective taxis known as "louages" which operate from the central bus and taxi depots. Regular inter-city buses are slower and crowded but cheaper. (The bus office is at 74 avenue de Carthage in Tunis.) A 300-mile bus trip from Tunis to the border oasis of Nefta via Kairouan and Gafsa costs only $5 but takes 12 hours. The trains are even slower than the buses, but cheap, punctual and usually clean. There is daily train service south from Tunis to Hammamet and north from Tunis to Bizerta. First class has sun blinds and ceiling fans for crowded day-long rides.

Hitchhiking is good in and around Tunis but tiresome and difficult as you go south, where the traffic thins out. It is not advisable for women to hitchhike without male escorts.

You can see Tunisia by using local taxis, louages, buses and trains. But there are obvious advantages in having your own car or renting one, particularly if you want to visit the ruins and other sights of the Sahara. American or international driving licenses are okay. Rentals are available at the airport and in the major cities from Hertz, Avis, Tilden, Carop and a number of other firms. Typical rates are $7 a day and 5 cents a kilometer for a VW 1300, or $45 a week. Driving is on the right, motorists are inclined to be erratic, and the motorcycle police are courteous but quick to fine you on the spot for violating posted speed limits. Drivers also have to keep a sharp eye out for donkeys, camels and other slow-moving beasts of burden.

Tunis Air operates a daily flight between Tunis and Djerba for $14.90 one way. The Société de Transport et des Travaux Aériens (7 rue Charles de Gaulle, Tunis) offers charter air service to other parts of the country.

Small coastal vessels ply slowly and irregularly between Bizerta, Tunis, Sfax, Sousse and other ports.

Many visitors to Tunisia come on all-inclusive package tours that provide full board stays in hotels, some night life and guided bus tours of major sites. This saves wear and tear on inexperienced travelers but it's more fun to make your own arrangements on the spot. You can arrange your own itinerary with the help of these Tunis agencies, among others: Transtours, 14 avenue de Carthage; Tourafric, 52 avenue Habib Bourguiba; Siti Tour, 20 avenue Habib Bourguiba; Stet Voyages, 42 avenue Habib Bourguiba. There are morning and afternoon air-conditioned bus tours of Tunis, Carthage, Sidi Bou Saïd and La Marsa, and longer one- to seven-day tours of the rest of the country. Except in the Sahara, air-conditioning in the buses is unnecessary. The multilingual tours are too often conducted in a rather hasty fashion.

Where to Stay

Tunisia has more than 300 hotels, and scores are being added every year. The range of accommodations assures a choice for nearly every purse and taste. The Embassy of Tunisia in Washington and the Office National du Tourisme can provide a detailed list of hotels classified by category and price. Given the extent of choices and the desire of most Tunisian hotel-keepers to please, it is hard to go wrong. In Tunis, it's best to book only bed and breakfast. Full board or even demi-pension (breakfast and one other meal) at your hotel will deny you the delights of the many good local restaurants.

TUNIS has several luxury hotels charging $20 to $25 a person for demi-pension. The 249-room *Hilton* is on a hill with a commanding view of the city, has transportation to its private beach and local decor. In the center of the city, the 21-story *Hotel Africa* has 162 rooms in the same price range and is a hubbub of activity. The older and comfortable *Claridge* is centrally located on avenue Habib Bourguiba with 110 beds at $15 and $20 and an excellent restaurant, La Pomme d'Api. The highly recommended *Tunisia Palace* and the *Majestic Maison Dorée*, nearby, are slightly less expensive. The 23-room *Hôtel de Suisse* and the 25-room *Hôtel de Bretagne*, both on side streets near the center of the city, charge under $10.

Unless you have business in Tunis you may find it more agreeable to stay at a beach hotel, relying on mini-taxis, guided tours or the TGM trolley to visit the city. My favorite is the little (13-room) *Hôtel Dar Zarrouk* in the beautiful whitewashed village of SIDI BOU SAÏD, 10 miles from the city. It has traditional Tunisian decor, an excellent restaurant with a superb view of the sea, and bed and breakfast prices of $10 to $15, depending on the season. Also in Sidi Bou Saïd is the even smaller and less expensive *Hôtel Boufares*, with the burial site of a local marabout, or holy man, in its courtyard. At the bottom of the hill is the 70-bed *Hôtel Amilcar*, $10 to $15, near a public beach and marina.

The beach suburb of GAMMARTH has three excellent hotels, all in the $15-to-$20 range: the 75-room *About Nawas*, with bungalows and golf course; the somewhat more tasteful and newer 132-room *Baie des Singes*, and the older 50-room *Tour Blanche*.

HAMMAMET is the major beach resort for Tunis, located 36 miles southeast of the city. It has a string of new luxury hotels. The *Tourisme Jeune* has simple facilities that start at $5, but all the others are in the $10-to-$20 range for bed and breakfast. Outstanding across the board is the 206-bed *Orangers* with a full range of facilities. Also attractive and reasonably priced for what they offer are the economy class *Bousten* ($10 to $15 for full board), the luxury *Grand Hôtel* and the gracious *Le Hammamet*. You can rent attractive beach houses, apartments and villas on a weekly or monthly basis. Various real estate agencies in Tunis have listings. (They are known in French as agences immobilières.)

North from Tunis the port city of BIZERTA has an inexpensive *Maison des Jeunes*; the lovely *Corniche Palace*, with its own cypress-lined beach and full board at $12 to $16, and the homey *Petit Mousse* with full board at $10 and a fine restaurant. Heading south from Tunis the first stop is the port and industrial center of SOUSSE where the new luxury skyscraper *El Hana*, with 110 rooms on the esplanade, charges $20 for full board. The 150-room *Jawhara* is in the $10 range and has its own beach. For similar prices the sprawling 458-room *Marhaba* has acres of three-story bungalow blocks and its own pool and beach. The *Maison des Jeunes* and the *Claridge* cater to low-budget travelers here.

Near Sousse is the lovely town of MONASTIR, birthplace of President Bourguiba, and the nearby beach of SKANÈS. The beautiful 148-room *Skanès Palace* charges $20 for full board. The youth hostel (auberge de jeunesse) and *Tourisme Jeune* have inexpensive accommodations. The *Palmiers* and *Ribat* are close to the beach, quiet and comfortable with full board at $10.

Inland from Sousse is the holy city of KAIROUAN. The 62-bed *Hôtel Aghlabites* here has magnificent traditional decor and full board for $15, well worth the price. The *Maison des Jeunes* is in the economy class.

The major road south from Sousse leads to Sfax, Gabès, the island of Djerba and the Tunisian Sahara. In SFAX, the *Hôtel Mabrouk* provides a pleasant $10-to-$15 overnight stop, although lacking beach or pool. There is also the slightly less expensive *Hôtel Oliviers*. The 81-room *Oasis* in GABÈS on the edge of the Sahara is excellent, with cool halls, a fine beach and full board at $15 to $20.

The island of Djerba and the adjacent mainland town of Zarzis are Tunisia's major winter resorts, already beginning to take on a slight Miami Beach flavor with row on row of modern high-rise hotels. On DJERBA the 120-room *Ulysse* charges $18 to $25 for full board in a setting of splendor rivaled by the 120-bed *Sirènes*, with similar prices and a heated mineral-water pool. The *Bousten* and *Sidi Slim* are in the $10-to-$15 range and attract a younger and more modish crowd. The *Sidi Saad* and *Zita* at ZARZIS have comparable prices and provide a little more seclusion.

No one needs to rough it unless he chooses to in the Tunisian Sahara. At NEFTA on the Algerian border the *Sahara Palace* lives up to its name, although expensive at $30 for full board. Local dancing girls perform at night. More modestly priced is the *Mirage*. The *Oasis* in TOZEUR, on the edge of the salt flats, charges $15 for full board and has a pool, interesting architecture and fine service, as does the similarly priced *Jugurtha* at GAFSA, built on the site of an old Roman spa. A special feature of Saharan lodging are the marhals and ksars, traditional brick or dried mud forts that have been converted into hotels. These include the *Relais Mrazig* at DOUZ with 40 beds, the *Relais Nefzaoua* with 50 beds in KEBILI and the *Ghorfa* in TATOUINE, all deep in the Sahara near the Libyan border. Kebili also has the *Hôtel Nefzaoua*, with a real oasis swimming pool.

Perhaps the most remarkable accommodations of all are in the village of MATMATA, 20 miles south of Gabès. Here the Matmata Berbers built underground homes in hollowed-out mountain caves and pits. At $5 to $7 for full board, the *Touring Club* and the more comfortable *Sidi Driss* offer you an underground room, and a cool Saharan one at that.

For the most-limited pocketbooks the Tourisme et Jeunesse Association (1 avenue de Carthage, Tunis; tel. 242693, 248695) provides a list of youth hostels with and without cooking facilities. These charge 25 cents a night and 50 cents a meal. The Maisons des Jeunes (youth centers) are open to older persons at slightly higher cost. During the summer students can also obtain inexpensive lodgings in the residential halls of the University of Tunis as well as the use of inexpensive student cafeterias. Except for organized campsites operated by the hotels, camping is free in Tunis but permission must be obtained from the town council or the local police.

Those primarily interested in sea and sand may wish to consider a vacation village with bungalows, private beaches, water sports and organized excursions, usually catering to young adults of various European nationalities. The village at RAFRAF is admirably simple, convenient by bus to Tunis and well stocked with fresh fish and fruit. Detailed information and prices are available in Tunis from the Touring Club de Tunisie (15 rue d'Allemagne) or the Société Tunisienne des Villages de Vacances (52 avenue Habib Bourguiba).

Hotel and other bills include a 15 per cent service charge and no further tips are expected.

Where and What to Eat

Tunisia has its own rich and varied cuisine based on abundant vegetables, fruit and fish. Although Tunisian dishes are served in most tourist hotels they are spiced down to suit what are considered to be milder palates. Try instead the authentic Tunisian restaurants and make your own decisions about spices. Among the local specialties are brik, a super-light deep fried pastry filled with egg or meat and spinach; chakchouka, a tasty dish of tomato, pimento and onion topped with a fried egg; couscous, semolina grain steamed with a sauce and meat or vegetable; kamounia, cubed liver and stewed meat with gravy; koucha, roast shoulder of lamb; mechoui, roast lamb; mechouia, a diced salad of tomato, egg, olive oil and fish; merguez, a hard and highly spiced sausage; tajine, a heavy square meat, egg and cheese pie; and ojja, an olive oil, scrambled egg, meat and vegetable dish.

Tunisia has abundant fresh shellfish and good tuna, mackerel and perch. Desserts are sweet and sweeter. They include: baklawa, honey pastries; gharaiba, a shortbread; maqrud, a date-filled pastry; bouza and mhalabia, creamy semolina puddings, and many, many others. Desserts are served with demitasse coffee, strong Turkish style, espresso, cappuccino or standard, or with deep-green mint tea with lemon.

Tunisia's strong, inexpensive red wines such as Carthage and Haut Mornag are good buys, as are the medium dry rosés and dry whites. The national drink is boukha, a fiery alcohol distilled from figs and often mixed with a local gaseous lemonade known as boga. Celtic and Stella are cheap local light beers. Ain Garci, a pleasant local mineral water, is preferable to the city drinking water, which is occasionally unsafe. In season, fresh orange, lemon, grapefruit and pomegranate juices are squeezed at sidewalk stands, or electrically mixed with carrots, milk, almonds and other goodies to make orgeat. Another sidewalk treat is lait de poule—electrically mixed raw eggs, ice cream and milk.

The major hotels serve primarily a French cuisine with one or two Tunisian dishes on the menu. For variety, search out the "gargotes"— the small inexpensive Tunisian restaurants.

In TUNIS, good Tunisian food is served at *Le Malouf,* which also features Andalusian music, the *M'Rabet* in the souk (market) of Et Trouk, and the *Palais* on Avenue de Carthage. *Aux Coqs d'Or* on Avenue Habib Bourguiba serves kosher French and Tunisian dishes. The *Strasbourg* next door to Le Malouf has simple Alsatian meals.

Just outside Tunis, try the *Pêcheur* in GAMMARTH for oysters, mussels and clams; the *Lucullus* and the *Vénus* in LA GOULETTE for excellent seafood; the cafe *Saf Saf* in LA MARSA, which has good desserts and a blindfolded camel turning a waterwheel, and the restaurant *Dar Zarrouk* in SIDI BOU SAÏD, with a fine view and good but expensive food. TABARKA, west of Bizerta, has two attractive beach restaurants, *Barberousse* and *Pescadou,* serving king prawns and lobsters. South of Tunis at HAMMAM LIF the *Relais des Coupoles* is a good inexpensive Tunisian restaurant. In HAMMAMET try the modest *Poste* restaurant.

Outside the capital and its neighboring towns, you can search out the gargotes when you tire of the hotel restaurant fare. On the island of DJERBA, the *Hassine Baaziz* in the Place Ferhat Hached is good for grilled fish. Try also *Chez Baccar,* the *Sud* and the *Restaurant de l'Ile* in the Place Hedi Chaker. *Café de la Grotte* in Kahlia Square at MONASTIR is an excellent and charming seafood restaurant.

What to See and Do

TUNIS and its suburbs have a population of over 800,000 and constitute a bustling, attractive metropolitan area. As in most other Tunisian cities and towns the principal street is known as the Avenue Habib Bourguiba. Along it are the leading hotels and restaurants, the tourist agencies and outdoor cafes, the government handicraft shops with their many displays, the 19th century French-style Municipal Theater and the Catholic Cathedral of St. Vincent. Nearby is the Musée de la Monnaie with an interesting display of ancient coins. The Avenue Bourguiba is an easy one-mile stroll from the edge of Lake Tunis to the gate known as Bab El Bahar, marking the entrance to the traditional medina (old walled city), with its winding alleys, busy souks and lovely mosques.

The medina invites leisurely strolling, with or without a guide. You can peek at vaulted and ceramic tiled courtyards, known as zawias, and seek out the streets and souks specializing in various crafts—like the Rue des Teinturiers (wool dyers); the street of the metal workers; the souk Sekajine noted for leather work; the souk of the jewelers; the delightful souk El Kebabjia, where fine silks are found; and the treat of treats, the souk El Attarine, where the perfumers work their wonders with fragrances of rose, jasmin, amber and orange.

Around every other corner in the medina are architectural surprises: former religious schools now converted into apartment houses; the Museum of Islamic Art, open daily except Monday; the 18th century Palace of Dar Hussein, which houses the National Institute of Archaeology and Arts; the Great Mosque of Zitouna opposite the National Library; the Lapidary Museum of Sidi Bou Krissan in the garden of the 11th century El Ksar Mosque, with a collection of Arabic tombstone inscriptions; the Mosque of Sidi Mahrez, near the shops of jewelers and dressmakers; the zawia of Siki Ibrahim, one of the loveliest in Tunis; and for a small tip, access to the roof of the Palais d'Orient, itself a relatively modern bazaar, but with a superb view of the medina skyline. The guidebook by Tomkinson is a useful aid and the National Tourist Office at the medina entrance has guides and maps, but the most fun is getting lost, wandering through the delights of this city within a city.

Above the medina on a hillside is Belvedere Park. It has restful greenery, a small but well-stocked zoo and children's playground, and an attractive pavilion known as the Qubba. On the slopes below the park are the Hilton Hotel and a less-than-chic casino for small-scale gambling. At the opposite end of the medina from the Bab El Bahar, just outside its massive walls, is the casbah with various government ministries, the 13th century mosque and minaret, and the nearby Mosque of Sidi Yusef Sahib and the bustling Bab Souika or "Little Market Gate." Full of cafes and fruit vendors, it is a particularly popular area during Ramadan when Moslems may eat only between sunset and sunrise. The cafes feature special sweet pastries and belly dancing.

A road leads up from the casbah to the hillside site of the National University, agitated in recent years by student-government tensions. From here you can also see Melassine, a slum that has received extensive public housing, and the salt lake of Sejoumi behind the city.

The salt-water Lake of Tunis separates the city from its port and coastal suburbs to the north. A shallow body of water crossed by a four-lane highway and the TGM trolley-railway, it reeks with unpleasant odors. (There are plans for drainage and sanitation.) At one end is the port and industrial town of La Goulette, with its massive medieval casbah and main street full of inexpensive seafood restaurants. The road to Carthage via La Goulette from Tunis is more interesting than the slightly faster highway that goes past the airport.

CARTHAGE is a pleasant suburb with villas, lovely gardens and good beaches. Scattered along its boulevards and streets are Punic and Roman ruins, including the Baths of Antonius, the old Punic ports, and a tophet, or column, marking the site of the temples of Tanit and Baal Hammon.

Summer cultural events take place at the Roman Schola and Theater. On the hill of the domed St. Louis Cathedral are the exuberant gardens of the Carthage Museum (at this writing closed for restoration). A pleasant day can be spent poking about the scattered ruins in Carthage, with time for a visit to the beach and a glance at the secluded but splendid presidential palace.

SIDI BOU SAÏD, next to Carthage, is one of the loveliest villages anywhere on the Mediterranean. Named after a 13th century Moslem leader interred in a small chapel, this dazzling blue-and-white hillside haven has magnificent views of the Gulf of Tunis, an attractive beach near the Hôtel Amilcar at the bottom of the hill, and its own charming Café des Nattes for people-watching and sipping mint tea with pine needles day or night. Gaining prominence as an artists' colony and summer resort, Sidi Bou Saïd has the studio of the talented Tunisian graphic artist and painter Brahim Dahak, whose specialty is camels, depicted in woodcuts.

Air-conditioned sightseeing buses lumber up the steep hills of Sidi Bou Saïd to give tourists a brief look at its splendors. Far better to stay there, renting an apartment or villa, or stopping at one of its two hotels. In any case, take a leisurely day to explore the place. At night during the summer Café des Nattes and the nearby open air nightclub are crowded with Tunisians and tourists, and lively local bands play traditional music. (But the service is abominable; come to sit and look rather than dine.)

LA MARSA and GAMMARTH are attractive beach towns along the coastal road just north of Sidi Bou Saïd. La Marsa has a pier, good outdoor restaurants and the Café Safsaf. Gammarth runs along a cliff road with fine beaches, and has good seafood restaurants at the Sinbad, Tour Blanche and other hotels. Unless you rent a car, you may have to wait a while to find a mini-taxi or crowded public bus to take you back to town.

THE BARDO is a small town three miles from Tunis on the main road to Bizerta. Its 19th century palace houses parliament and the National Museum, which has one of the finest collections of Roman as well as Punic and Islamic art in the whole world. It is open daily except Monday. The Bardo has an exceptional collection of mosaics.

Just off the road between Tunis and Bizerta are the ruins of UTICA, once a Punic port and now six-and-a-half miles inland. Its baths, 6th century BC necropolis and Antiquarian Museum should be seen. Also along the Tunis-to-Bizerta road is the town of Porto Farina with its white sand beach, restaurant and hillside fortress of Sidi Ali El Mekki, and the wine country beach town of Rafraf. BIZERTA, a city of 50,000 and a former French naval base on Lake Bizerta, has a corniche and sand beach, old port area, massive Fort of Spain, modern Congress Hall and 17th century Great Mosque. The Office National de l'Artisanat (ONA) handicraft shop features local carpets, mats and embroidery. It is 40 miles from Tunis, a pleasant day's trip.

West of Bizerta towards the Algerian border are the cork and oak forests of Khroumiria and the mountain village of Ain Draham, noted for pottery, cork products and carved wood. At 2,800 feet, it is cool in the summer and sometimes has winter snow. There's excellent wild boar hunting here. Nearby is the fishing port and newly developing beach resort of Tabarka, with its coral and wood crafts. The road (marked GP 17) from Tabarka to Ain Draham leads beyond to the interesting Roman and early Christian ruins at *Bulla Reggia*.

South of Tunis, after a pleasant one-hour drive, are the beach resorts of Hammamet and Nabeul. Along the road at Hammam Lif there is a mineral water spa. Grombalia is a wine-growing center with its own festival (Fête des Vendanges) in August. Visits to the government co-operative wineries can be arranged from July to October. HAMMAMET is mostly bay, white sand beach and hotel resorts with a small medina and souk for brassware and carpets, Turkish baths and Great Mosque. It is the site of an international cultural festival held each summer in a splendid villa and cultural center that housed General Rommel during World War II. Hammamet hotels offer their own night life.

Just north of Hammamet is the town of NABEUL, best visited on a Friday morning for the market. It has several good hotels, a fine beach and gardens, a youth hostel, and characteristically Tunisian Habib Bourguiba Mosque, renovated by US Peace Corps architects in 1967. The Friday market is a good time to see its earthenware pottery, carpets, chipped stone, haiks (cloaks), sheepskins and other wares.

Several attractive one- and two-day excursions are possible, using either Tunis or Hammamet as a departure point. One leads to Cap Bon, stopping first at Nabeul, then the rug-weaving village of Beni Khiar, the fishing port of Kelibia with its Roman castle, the best-preserved Punic sites in Africa at *Kerkouane*, six miles north of Kelibia, and finally the cape, with its lighthouse and interesting array of birds. The coastal road along the Gulf of Tunis—from the capital to Cap Bon—passes Soliman, a farming town developed by Andalusians expelled from Spain after the 16th century Christian re-conquest; they built here their own Moorish-style minaret, mosque and square. Only 30 miles from Tunis on the same road is the lovely town of Korbous, distinguished for the beach of Sidi Rais and its wines. Nearby is the mineral water spa of Ain Oktor.

Another excursion from Hammamet or Tunis leads inland to the

Roman ruins at *Dougga*, the finest site in Tunisia. You turn off GP 1 at the army town of Bou Ficha, swinging through picturesque Zaghouan, and pausing at the rich Roman ruins of *Thuburbo Maius*, near the town of Pont du Fahs. The MC 28 road leads west from Pont du Fahs to the fertile Mejerda Valley. Here is the market town of Medez El Bab, World War II cemeteries, and the town of Testour, also settled by Andalusians. Testour has an annual June festival of maalouf, classical Andalusian music with a mixture of Arabic and Spanish influences, which takes place in the Café Andalou. The town also has a rug-weaving cooperative, mosque with Moorish minaret, and Spanish tile roofs.

The ruins of Dougga, a fascinating Roman site of the 2nd and 3rd centuries AD, lie south of Testour. Along with an earlier Punic mauso-leum, you will find a temple of Saturn, Roman theater (where the Dougga cultural festival takes place every June), outstanding capitol building, forum, Roman homes, a brothel and baths, including the well-preserved horseshoe of twelve commodes in the communal latrine. Just a few miles south of Dougga off the GP 5 road is the Roman site of Musti, a compact hillside town with a later Byzantine fortress.

While Tunis, Hammamet and the surrounding areas can be seen in short trips, several days are needed to explore the riches of central and southern Tunisia. Road, train and bus lead 87 miles from Tunis to Sousse, with a pleasant stop at Sidi Bou Ali's folklore center (known as Le Bordj), to see local horsemen and jugglers. SOUSSE, population 50,000, has beautiful beaches and people-watching at the Café Olympique. Its ribat (fort) provides a fine view of the medina. There's a good museum, open every day except Monday, with Roman, Byzantine and early Chris-tian mosaics; a Friday afternoon camel market; the July Festival of Aoussou (Neptune) along the esplanade, and just off the Tunis road before entering Sousse, an extensive series of 2nd, 3rd and 4th century Christian catacombs. Hunt for the guide, offer him a small tip, and make sure that he has plenty of candles.

The Islamic holy city of KAIROUAN is 97 miles south of Tunis, 57 miles west of Sousse. Its Great Mosque was begun in the 8th century with the arrival of Islam in North Africa, and next to Mecca itself the city is the holiest place that any North African Moslem may go to on pilgrim-age. Kairouan is also one of the most attractive cities in North Africa, with a population of 85,000 and a renowned industry in rugs, carpets and leather work. Kairouan has interesting souks, a lively medina of cafes and rug-weaving shops, several interesting Islamic shrines, smaller mosques, and minarets. Its architecture is in the classical early Islamic style.

Along the coast just south of Sousse is the small town of MONASTIR, celebrated birthplace of President Bourguiba, whose attractive presidential palace grounds can be visited with a permit from the Tourist Bureau office. The fortress, or ribat, of Harthema is an imposing site with summer evening spectacles of music and lights (son et lumière) to illuminate its walls. A causeway joins Monastir to the island of Oustania, where there are occasional entertainments in the Café de la Grotte. Monastir has a small Islamic museum, a 9th century mosque and the extremely modern Mosque of Habib Bourguiba, an architectural gem. The town has its own beach and esplanade, and enjoys a minor tourist boom. Along the same coastal road farther south is the developing beach resort of MAHDIA.

The excellent GP 1 highway runs 79 miles from Sousse to Sfax. Midway at El Djem, 117 miles south of Tunis, lies the spectacular Roman coliseum, third largest in the world, and better preserved than the one in Rome. The coliseum and amphitheater are magnificent, but the town itself is desolate and some of its inhabitants pester travelers with unnecessary offers to provide guide and other services.

SFAX, Tunisia's second city, has a major port and several industries, and a charming medina featuring metal, woodwork and embroideries. The city is relatively prosperous and rather Westernized. The port handles cereals, olive oil, fruit, fish and phosphate. A 25-cent one-hour ferry ride takes you to the Kerkenna Islands. A budding but still secluded resort, these islands have small fishing villages, good beaches and considerable charm. A few miles west of Sfax is the village of Agareb, which every August stages a fantasia festival of horsemanship, musketry and swordplay, a kind of Arab outdoor Western.

The island of DJERBA, 17 miles long and 14 miles wide, mythical land of the lotus eaters, is 350 miles from Tunis (a 45-minute flight, or a long day's drive via Sousse, Sfax and Gabès). It is reached by a ferry from the mainland at Jorf and a causeway at Zarzis. Djerba owes its international popularity to its superb climate (344 days of sun a year), white sand beaches, and olive and palm groves. The Djerbians are mostly Kharijite Moslems, an egalitarian and austere sect. Aside from its beaches and aquatic sports, Djerba exhibits attractive crafts, including blankets, pottery, jewelry and embroidery. Visit the Monday and Thursday camel market, the 13th century Fortress of Borj El Kebir, the Sheikh's Mosque and a duty-free shop, all in the village of Houmt Souk. Here also, off the Place Mokhtar Ben Attia, is a pleasant nightclub, the Foundouk, and several cafes.

Near Houmt Souk are Hara Khira and Hara Sghira, the Big and Little Ghettos where 2,000 Djerbian Jews live and maintain the famous Ghriba synagogue. Like the other 8,000 Tunisian Jews in Tunis and Sfax, those in Djerba have cordial relations with their Arab neighbors, but lack of economic opportunities prompts many of the young to emigrate to France and Israel. Also on the island of Djerba is the village of El May with its picturesque Mosque of Umm Et Turkia and a Castillian Spanish fort. A four-mile causeway links the island to the rapidly developing mainland beach town of Zarzis.

The oasis town of GABÈS is the gateway to southern Tunisia and the Sahara. The oasis has more than 300,000 palms and several fruit orchards. Local crafts include carpets, wickerwork, wood, amber, leather and silver. But the town itself is rather ordinary. A fine excursion runs south over the 2,000-foot mountains of Matmata to the Berber village in the valley of the same name. In Matmata the local people dig their homes 30 feet deep into the soft soil to escape the Saharan heat. Elsewhere in the region the Berbers built their terraced three- to six-story brick dwellings, known as ghorfas, and their forts.

A longer excursion from Gabès leads west along several chotts to the oasis town of Kebili, which has date palm groves. The Thursday market at the nearby town of Douz attracts Tuareg traders and their camels up from the Saharan interior.

The GP 19 road south from Gabès winds through the town of Medenine to Foum Tataouine, a former convict settlement and still depressing. Tracks take travelers from there into the Ksour mountains to fascinating, rugged Berber villages. South of Foum Tataouine the road becomes a Saharan trail suitable only for four-wheel-drive vehicles. Tunisian military permission is needed to travel beyond the army's Saharan base at Remada. Those who make the trip can travel another 190 miles to the French-built Fort Saint, where the Tunisian, Algerian and Libyan borders join, and if their papers are in order, cross to the Libyan oasis of Ghadamès.

Most travelers who make it to Gabès prefer to continue west to Gafsa, Tozeur and Nefta rather than penetrating farther south into the Sahara. GAFSA, with a population of 50,000, was a Roman site and a Berber stronghold. Its walls are washed a rosy pink, its oasis thrives on date palms and fruits, and its craftsmen specialize in carpets and blankets. Its simple solid brick buildings have striking geometric patterns.

West of Gafsa is the phosphate mining town of Metlaoui, where the Choumovitch Museum houses a 19th century French geologist's collection of fossil specimens. Farther west, towards the Algerian border, travelers can stop at the striking town of TOZEUR, with its brick Sidi Abid Mosque, two minarets, Great Mosque, and lofty orchard garden known as "Paradise." In town near the Sidi Abid Mosque is the "Handicraft

Center of the Jerid and Marvels of the *Sahara*" operated by Amar Ben Taleb Sessi, a shrewd local entrepreneur who offers woven rugs, palm frond furniture and pickled scorpions. His neighbor, Mr. Tijani, operates an interesting snake farm.

NEFTA is an artificial date palm oasis dependent on artesian wells, unlike natural oases that are fed by underground streams or the wadis (dry river beds that catch the run-off of flash floods). Nefta's Sahara Palace Hotel stands on the site of a natural oasis from Roman times, with another garden named "Paradise." The town has a rug-weaving center and several mosques and shrines of the mystical Sufi sect. A hillside road climbs to the Café Corbeille with its panoramic view of the desert and the palm groves.

West of Nefta is the Algerian Sahara, accessible if you have obtained a visa in advance, although there is no place to exchange currency until you get to El Oued. (It's illegal to bring Algerian money into or out of the country.)

A rugged road runs north from Tozeur to the mountain village of Shebika, subject of the fine sociological study by Jean Duvignaud, *Change at Shebika* (Pantheon, 1970), and the Franco-Algerian film, *Ramparts of Clay.*

Much of Tunisia has a climate similar to that of Southern California. Hence, outdoor sports are popular, particularly soccer football, the national passion; every town has its team. There is professional horse racing from October through May at the Kassar Saïd track near Tunis. Several riding stables permit equestrians to try the beautiful Arabian steeds. Camel riding is an acquired skill but at many beach resorts local entrepreneurs offer tourists an inexpensive and safe ride. There is golf at La Soukra, seven miles from Tunis, and sailing from yacht clubs at La Goulette and Sidi Bou Saïd. Deep-sea fishing, water skiing and snorkeling are available at most major beach hotels.

Night life is mostly confined to Tunis and the bars at tourist hotels. Cinemas are popular. Most films are French. There are groups of semi-professional filmmakers and active cinema clubs in Tunis and other major cities. The National Theater in Tunis presents local and visiting (usually French) companies during its November-to-May season. Several touring companies cover the country, often performing at the Maison du Peuple (House of the People) found in most towns. If you speak some French you should be able to find a student to help you understand the Arabic. There are frequent exhibits by local artists at the National Theater and elsewhere in Tunis, including the British Council and United States Information Service libraries, which often have evening cultural presentations. The Palais, Maalouf and M'rabet restaurants in Tunis offer more or less authentic belly dancing, primarily for tourists. Traditional Tunisian dancing is best seen at local festivals.

Interested visitors can see something of Tunisia's many development and social welfare projects. These include the "Enfants de Bourguiba" villages for orphans, the retail and wholesale cooperatives, fisheries projects of the Office National du Poisson, mobile family-planning clinics, and several technical, vocational and teacher training schools. The National Tourist Office in Tunis can help with these visits, while the faculty and students at the university's Institute of Economic and Social Research in Tunis are prepared to assist visiting scholars, discuss their own research and identify projects worth visiting.

What to Buy

Tunisian handicrafts are among the finest in Africa, although perhaps less striking than those of Morocco. The full range at fixed prices can be seen at the department store of the Office National de l'Artisanat on Avenue Habib Bourguiba in Tunis or at ONA branch stores in every major town. Here it is possible to compare prices, pay with credit cards and travelers checks, obtain a 10 per cent discount for purchases made with foreign currency, and have merchandise shipped reliably. However, by bargaining in the smaller shops and great souks, you should be able to obtain prices 10 to 25 per cent below those in the government shops. Bargaining is friendly and opening prices are usually three times or more what the merchant will accept.

Tunisian crafts include handsome carpets, brass, wrought iron, gold and silver, ceramics, wickerwork, embroidery, and traditional and modern textiles. Leather work—including wallets, handbags, book covers, pointed slippers known as babouches, sheepskin and other wares—is less decorative and less expensive than Morocco's. The hand of Fatma and the sacred shape of the fish are emblems of good fortune frequently used in jewelry and embroidery.

Traditional designs have also been adapted into modern textiles including scarves, blouses, flowing robes known as kaftans or jebbas, as well as whole cloth. Attractive rugs and carpets (at attractive prices) come from Kairouan, Gafsa and Gabès. It is advisable to insist on the government handicraft office (ONA) seal, as a guarantee of quality. Another strong medium is pottery, including earthenware pots, ashtrays and pitchers from Nabeul and Djerba. Dainty, wrought-iron bird cages in white and blue are a specialty of Hammamet, Nabeul and Sidi Bou Saïd. The best purchases are made directly from the craftsmen whose workshops are open to visitors. Otherwise scout the government shops and then explore the souks of Tunis and the smaller towns. Beware, however, of purveyors of fake Roman, Byzantine or Islamic "antiques."

Local Attitudes

Tunisia is in the midst of considerable social change, much of it caused by the impact of foreign tourists. Only a few "radicals" question the desirability of tourism itself but there are doubts about what form it should take and concerns over its benefits to Tunisians. While a few crass hustlers do pester travelers, most Tunisians are open, gentle and affable, even when peddling. Some young men wistfully pursue European women whom they believe to be more responsive than the relatively emancipated but still sheltered Tunisian girls. Homosexuality is tolerated among Tunisians and foreigners, a custom going back at least to the days of the Turkish beys. While religion remains an important social bond, there is little fanaticism; virtually all mosques are open to non-believers. Photos can be taken anywhere except inside the mosques. Miniskirts, bikinis and the latest fashions are worn by young urban Tunisians.

American economic aid is appreciated and many of its positive effects are visible. Tunisians display little of the hostility toward American support of Israel that one finds in Algeria and Libya, although everybody sympathizes with the Palestinian Arabs. Discussions can be free and far-ranging, especially with students and intellectuals.

Weather, What to Wear, How Long to Stay

The northern Mediterranean coast where Tunis is located, has a gentle climate with four distinct seasons. Winters can be cold, rainy and damp with temperatures in the 50's and below, although never dipping under 35 degrees. Spring and fall are delightful, with temperatures in the 70's and 80's and cool evening breezes. June through September is cloudless with little or no rain and excellent for the beaches. Temperatures range into the 90's and can go over 100 for several days at a time.

The farther south you go the warmer and drier it gets. Djerba and the Sahara are at their best from November to March; during the summer the heat is intense. May and June are delightful everywhere with blooming flowers and glowing colors. Kairouan, the interior and the south are best explored during the winter, although along the coast one may run into the sirocco wind blowing dust and sand from the Sahara.

Casual attire is the order of the day, especially during the summer and at resorts throughout the year. Dining and entertaining are equally casual but nobody feels out of place in summer lightweight suits or evening dress. During the winter months sweaters and even coats are needed in Tunis. Most homes and offices lack interior heating.

As we've already suggested, Tunisia is best taken on its own rather than as part of a broader tour. One week is enough for a pleasant visit that includes Tunis and its beaches, Kairouan, Djerba and a few coastal towns. Two weeks allows time to look at the Sahara. More and more visitors are renting homes or villas and staying a month or longer.

Communication

The postal service is reliable, although lines are long and service slow. Telegrams, however, often go undelivered. Telephone service has greatly improved in recent years but is still inadequate. Local calls require persistence to make connections, and overseas calls are tedious and expensive, except to Paris.

While Arabic is the official language, French retains semi-official status in government administration, business and education. It is widely spoken throughout the country and will take you anywhere. The tourist boom has prompted a growing interest in English and German but their use is still largely confined to leading hotels. Radio and television broadcasting is mainly in Arabic and French, some in Italian and English.

The media, including the rather dull French-language daily newspapers, La Presse and L'Action, echo the government line. Tunis newsstands also sell Time, Newsweek and the Paris Herald Tribune. The French-language weekly, Jeune Afrique, published by a Tunisian in Paris, has good coverage of North Africa. Worth looking at, especially if you read French, are the delightful and inexpensive children's books of Tunisian tales published by the Société Tunisienne des Editions et Diffusions, as well as the more scholarly titles of the Maison Tunisienne de l'Edition. The Revue Tunisienne des Sciences Sociales is an excellent academic journal published by the Institute of Economic and Social Research at the university.

Emergencies

The American Embassy is at 144 avenue de la Liberté in Tunis (tel. 282566). It maintains lists of competent local doctors and dentists. Hospital facilities in Tunis are adequate but understaffed and overcrowded; the situation is worse elsewhere in the country. Flying to Rome or Paris might be advisable for serious medical problems.

Northeast Africa

Egypt
Ethiopia
Libya
Somalia
Sudan
Territory of the
Afars and Issas

THE REGION AT A GLANCE

From the Mediterranean to the Red Sea, along the Nile basin and against the intrusive Sahara, this is the region of Africa most readily identified with the wellsprings of the Western world. The Egypt of the Pharaohs, Kush of the African iron age and Abyssinian Axum deeded us much of their technology, philosophy, politics and trading patterns. People of the Nile, the Ethiopian highlands and the coasts communicated for thousands of years throughout the entire Middle East and Indian Ocean, across the Mediterranean into Europe, and as far southwest into Africa as Lake Chad. Apostolic Christianity penetrated up the Nile and into the mountains of Ethiopia (Axum), remaining there to this day despite the steady Islamic inundations from Arabia which conquered all North Africa in the 7th and 8th centuries. Today, the cradle of civilization is again a crossroads of conflict.

Perhaps more than any other factor, the River Nile makes this a region. Rising in the Ethiopian mountains and flowing from Lake Victoria, the Blue and White Niles converge near Khartoum, carrying the lifestream of fertility to Egypt, the Sudan and some of Ethiopia. The struggle to master the river's cycles, floods and tides produced some of man's oldest civilizations. It is being reenacted in the hydroelectric and irrigation projects at the Aswan High Dam in Egypt, the Gezira in the Sudan, and Lake Tana in Ethiopia. Along the Nile's shores, lined with

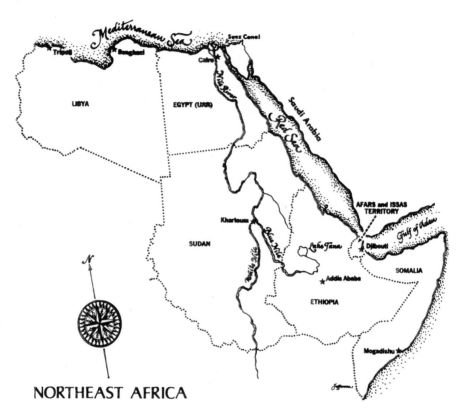

NORTHEAST AFRICA

splendors of the past and diversities of the present, Islam thrives in its most fervent forms, while in the isolation of lofty Ethiopia an ancient Christian society worships according to its own rites and calendar.

To the northwest, Libya surges on the sudden wealth of a petroleum boom. Its uncompromising nationalist regime seeks union with a larger, sobered Egypt, and proclaims Arab and African unity in the current struggle against Israel.

The Red Sea separates the Horn of Africa and the Arabian Peninsula. Somalia, the Republic of the Sudan and the French-held Territory of Afars and Issas (Djibouti) face imposing odds with few and precarious resources in a desert environment. Pride of lineage and an exalted heritage rise above the anachronisms of economics and politics in the Somali nation, still parceled out beyond the odd borders of their republic. The Sudan grapples with the integration of its black minorities and Arab majority after a long, painful civil war. Ethiopia, too, has its minority and secessionist problems, particularly in Eritrea, and its millennia-old

Stained glass window

Abu Simbel Temple, Aswan

Mosque in Tripoli

Africa Hall, Addis Ababa

form of government faces growing challenges from revolutionary young people.

These preoccupations make the Northeast somewhat less comfortable than other regions of Africa. Few foreign travelers have the fortitude or patience to brave the paperwork, political delays and bureaucratic deviousness entailed by a full regional tour. Those who seek exhilaration in historical symbolism, archaeology and modern facilities generally stay in Egypt and Ethiopia. The adventurous, if they prize the romance of the desert and the dignity of its inhabitants, may try Somalia, the Sudan and southern Libya, with Djibouti's French amenities an occasionally welcome break. On the upper Nile, White or Blue, hardy travelers begin a trek northward through a magnificent territory of history and culture so near and yet so far from our own.

PMA

Egypt

(Arab Republic of Egypt)

Profile

STATUS: Republic since June 18, 1953. Loose federation with Libya and Syria formed in September, 1971.

SIZE: 386,661 square miles (slightly larger than Texas and Oklahoma combined). Population—34,500,000.

GEOGRAPHY: The Nile crosses from the Sudan to the Mediterranean and makes cultivation possible on four per cent of Egypt's area, the rest being desert. East of the river is the Arabian Desert; west, the plateau of the Libyan Desert relieved by occasional oases. Principal cities—Cairo (capital, 4,500,000), Alexandria (1,800,000), Aswan, Luxor, Port Said.

CLIMATE: Winter (December to February) temperatures in Cairo in 50's and 60's, Aswan in 70's. Spring (March to May) and autumn (September to November) dry and warm with Cairo temperatures in 80's, Aswan in 90's. Summer (June to August) hot with northerly winds, Cairo temperatures in mid-90's, Aswan well over 100. Little rain.

LANGUAGES: Arabic; English and French widely spoken.

CURRENCY: Egyptian pound (£E), divided into 100 piasters (PT). Piaster divided into 10 millimes. £E 1 = $2.30; $1.00 = 43 PT. There is a special tourist rate of 65 PT for $1.00. £E 1 = $1.54 on tourist rate.

VISAS: Required. Obtainable on arrival in Egypt. Fee $2.30. One photo needed. Two types of visas: one-month visa, subject to renewal, requiring tourist to exchange equivalent of $80; and three-day transit visa.

AIRPORT: Cairo Airport (CAI), 16 miles from city. Frequent flights to and from New York, Europe, the Near, Middle and Far East and many

157

points within Africa. Transportation into city—Egyptair bus, 20 PT (30 cents); taxi, 75 PT ($1.13). Airport departure tax—LE 1 ($1.54).

NATIONAL HOLIDAYS: January 1, New Year's Day; February 22, Union Day; April 30, Sham el-Nesim; June 18, Evacuation Day; July 23, Revolution Day; September 1, Federation Day; December 23, Victory Day; Moslem and Christian holidays.

INFORMATION SOURCES: *In US*—Egyptian Interest Section, Embassy of India, 2310 Decatur Place NW, Washington, D.C. 20008 (tel. 202/232-5400); Egyptian Educational and Cultural Bureau, 2200 Kalorama Road NW, Washington, D.C. 20008 (tel. 202/265-6400); Egyptian Government Tourist Office, 630 Fifth Avenue, New York, N.Y. 10020 (tel. 212/246-6960). *In Cairo*—Government Tourist Information Office, 5 Adly Street (tel. 923000).

By Kristin W. Henry

The lore of ancient Egypt is part of every schoolboy's heritage and the journey to Egypt for many travelers a pilgrimage of sorts to the birthplace of civilization. Yet for modern Egyptians as for the rest of us, the great pharaonic monuments are little more than historical curiosities.

Since the collapse of the last pharaonic dynasty in 525 BC, Egypt has had a fascinating and turbulent history. A succession of foreign invaders left their own landmarks, and these warrant the attention of anyone who wishes to understand the amalgam of influences that make up Egypt. A vassal of the Persian Empire at the time of Alexander's invasion in 332 BC, she was linked thereafter with the Hellenistic civilizations of the Mediterranean for 13 centuries. During this period a majority of Egyptians were converted to Christianity, and the Christian Copts (a corruption of the word "Egypt") remain a vigorous minority to this day. However, the Arab horsemen who invaded the country in the 7th century were destined to leave a greater impact than any of her preceding conquerors. The religion they brought is now embraced by more than 90 per cent of Egyptians, and their language is universally spoken. From 868 Egypt was ruled by locally based Moslem dynasties until 1517, when she was incorporated into the Ottoman Empire.

The modern history of Egypt began, in a sense, with Napoleon's invasion of 1798. His "civilizing" mission was not well received by the Egyptians, and he was forced by the British, then in alliance with the Ottoman Turks, to withdraw his troops after only three years. Nevertheless, his task force of scholars gave Egyptians a glimpse of the science and skill of the outside world, and through their explorations and discoveries helped to spread interest in Egypt abroad.

In the wake of the French departure, Mohammed Ali, an Albanian officer in the Turkish army, emerged as ruler of the country. Relying heavily on foreign advisers, he set about building a national army and developing an agricultural and industrial base, essential prerequisites to his imperial schemes. He got rid of the Mamelukes, the ruling caste under the Turks, by massacring 400 of them at a banquet at the Citadel, and founded his own dynasty in their stead. Despot that he was, Mohammed Ali can nevertheless claim credit for the African continent's first indigenous example of modernization. The trend that he initiated was continued by his successors. However, through their shortsightedness in committing Egypt to projects she could ill afford, such as the Suez Canal, and through profiteering by foreigners, the country was reduced to bankruptcy.

The Arabi Revolt of 1879–1882, sparked by native army officers dissatisfied with foreign privilege in the military, marked in the broader sense the beginnings of the nationalist movement, but in the short run it only precipitated the military occupation of the country by the British in 1882. Initially concerned with salvaging the economy, the British remained the de facto rulers of Egypt for the ensuing 40 years. To their credit, they brought solvency and then prosperity to the country, mainly through fiscal reform, irrigation and other public works, and improving the lot of the peasants. However, they did little to promote industry and education, and by strengthening the foreign superstructure of Egyptian society fed nationalist unrest.

The British fitfully encouraged a measure of self-government in the decade preceding World War I, but shortly after the outbreak of hostilities imposed a protectorate status upon Egypt. After the war, however, nationalist fervor reached such a pitch that the British realized that the protectorate was unenforceable and in 1922 offered "independence by treaty" in its stead. The rights that England reserved for herself, among them the security of the canal and the defense of the country, assured her of a continuing role in Egyptian politics, and for the next 20 years a triangle of forces—the British, the King, and the Wafd (the nationalist party founded by Saad Zaghloul)—jockeyed for power in shifting patterns of alliance and opposition. World War II only aggravated political unrest, and in its aftermath Egypt was left without any effective leadership. While King Farouk wallowed in royal dissipation and the Wafd was rent by internal dissension, Communists and Moslem Brethren (a right-wing extremist group) added fuel to the agitation. Humiliation at Egypt's defeat in 1949 against the newly-established state of Israel as well as aggravation at the continued presence of British troops in the canal zone led to the events of Black Saturday in January, 1952, during which Cairo's Jewish, British, and other foreign establishments were looted and burned. Black Saturday made it apparent to the Free Officers, a clandestine movement within the army, that the moment of revolution was at hand. On July 23 of that year they staged a bloodless coup d'état, and three days later exiled Farouk to Europe.

Gamal Abdul Nasser, the leader of the coup, was proclaimed president of the new republic in 1954 and remained in power until his death of a heart attack in 1970. He remains one of the most controversial statesmen of the 20th century; few leaders have inspired such fervent adulation and such intense dislike within their own countries and abroad.

Internally Nasser continued the struggle against foreign imperialism. He forced the removal of British troops from the canal zone in 1954, nationalized the canal itself in 1956, and in the succeeding years deported thousands of Egypt's foreign residents, confiscating their property and substantial business holdings. In the interest of creating a "democratic, socialist and cooperative society," he initiated a number of sweeping reforms, including land redistribution and the expansion of education. Great efforts were made to develop industry and agriculture. The most impressive technical venture of the Nasser years was the High Dam, which will increase the crop area by about 26 per cent as well as provide abundant electricity for continuing industrialization.

Grave problems remain: unemployment, rural poverty, and a rate of population growth that virtually nullifies advances in agriculture and industry. Nasser must be credited for eliminating to a large extent the class dominance and grossly unequal opportunity that had characterized Egyptian society under all her previous rulers, but at the same time, he must be blamed for failing to develop viable political institutions, for suppressing the right to dissent, and for creating a huge, unwieldy bureaucracy that has become a major impediment to progress.

Nasser's conduct of foreign affairs was influenced by three doctrines: anti-imperialism, Arab nationalism and non-alignment between the two Great Power blocks. His greatest anti-imperialist victory was of course his nationalization of the Suez Canal in the face of the tripartite aggression of Britain, France and Israel. As a result of this, he became a hero not only to the Arab masses but throughout the Third World, and Cairo emerged as the Mecca of revolutionary leaders, particularly from Africa. He then used his new-found popularity to further the cause of Arab nationalism. He was not notably successful. His major experiment in merging with another Arab country, the union with Syria, 1958–1961, was a failure; his attempts to subvert "reactionary" Arab governments usually backfired; and in the name of Revolution he wasted Egyptian troops and resources on a civil war in Yemen that only ended in stalemate. He tried to withstand pressures for a major confrontation with Israel over Palestine but in the end gave in, the prisoner of his own prestige, and led his people to the traumatic defeat of 1967. In his espousal of non-alignment he hoped to accept aid from both power blocs with no strings attached. But as the West grew increasingly disenchanted with his strident anti-imperialism and thwarting of alliances such as the Baghdad Pact, he was forced to rely more and more on Soviet aid. Any pretense of non-alignment was shattered by the Russian military build-up in Egypt after the 1967 defeat by Israeli troops.

After Nasser's death in September, 1970, Anwar Sadat took over the presidency. Under his leadership certain changes in domestic and foreign policy have occurred. Internally, there has been a cautious liberalization.

The activities of the secret police have been curtailed, sequestrations of private property have been lifted, and there is more freedom of the press. The move that has caused the greatest stir was the expulsion in July, 1972 of thousands of Russian advisers.

With the Sinai peninsula occupied by Israel and the Suez Canal completely blocked, Egypt still suffers the consequences of the 1967 war. But the banner of Arab unity, though tattered, still flies. A loose confederation now exists between Egypt, Libya, and Syria (Egypt's new name is the Arab Republic of Egypt), and in July, 1972, plans for a merger were announced between Egypt and Libya.

There is an abundance of books on Egypt covering a wide variety of topics. To cite a few of the best: James Breasted, *A History of Egypt* (Bantam, 1967), the definitive work on ancient Egypt; Pierre Montet, *Eternal Egypt* (Mentor, 1964) and John Wilson, *The Culture of Ancient Egypt* (Phoenix, 1965), less compendious and more readable accounts of the same era; Tom Little, *Modern Egypt* (Benn, 1967), the best general introduction to the modern era with informative chapters on earlier periods, and Anthony Nutting, *Nasser* (Constable, 1972).

The Egyptian Government Tourist Office in New York City has brochures and maps.

Money Matters

There are no limits on importation of foreign currency, but Egyptian money can neither be brought in nor taken out. On arrival you must declare all foreign exchange and jewelry on Form D. Subsequent exchanges through authorized banks and their representatives will be recorded on this form, and you will be asked to present it on departure. Use this form to make all your exchanges at the special tourist rate that gives you 65 piasters for the dollar compared to 43 PT for the dollar at the official rate for other transactions. In order to get a one-month tourist visa, you are required to exchange the equivalent of $80. Although present rules allow you to exchange back into dollars all the unused currency for which you have the original exchange receipts, don't count on it. Instead, plan to spend whatever Egyptian currency you have before you leave.

Banks are open from 8:30 to 12:30 Monday through Thursday and on Saturday, and from 10 to noon on Sunday. Major hotels will accept your credit cards.

The casinos at the Sheraton and Shepheard's also accept foreign exchange, as do the government-run shops specializing in exports.

Getting In and Out

The 1967 war ruptured Egyptian-American diplomatic relations; Egypt is now represented in the US by India. Visas are available on arrival. Unlike Libya and some other Arab states, Egypt does not inquire about religion in its visa application forms, and Jewish tourists are welcome. However, entry is refused to visitors of whatever religion who have Israeli stamps in their passports. (The Israeli immigration officials will, on request, provide travelers with a separate entry form rather than stamp their passports.)

Most travelers arrive by air. There are many flights to Cairo, including several direct flights each week from New York and other major US cities. Cairo can be included on most round-the-world air fares and is an easy stop on tickets from North America to East and Southern Africa. There are frequent flights linking Cairo with Khartoum, Addis Ababa, Entebbe and Nairobi, as well as daily flights to and from a number of cities in the Middle East and North Africa.

If you want to go to Egypt by boat, you can sail from Naples, Athens or Marseille to Alexandria. It is a brief and pleasant trip, accommodations ranging from deck to luxury class. The Egyptian Maritime Company has weekly sailings to and from Alexandria and Piraeus (Athens), Venice and Beirut.

The Italian Line also sails to Alexandria. Details on its schedules are available from the company's offices at 1 Whitehall Street, New York, N.Y. 10004 (tel. 212/797-7000).

For the last few years it has been virtually impossible for foreign travelers to cross the Egyptian-Libyan border by road. However, there is now talk of lifting the restrictions, in which case you will be able to take advantage of the daily bus and taxi service connecting Benghazi with Alexandria.

It is possible to ship a car equipped with the appropriate international documents to Alexandria, but driving for foreigners is limited at present to Cairo, Alexandria, the main highway across the delta connecting the two cities, and the road to Libya up to 60 miles west of Alexandria.

Provided that this route is open to foreigners, you can travel from Egypt to the Sudan by taking a boat from Aswan across the artificial Lake Nasser to the Sudanese border post of Wadi Halfa, where there are connections by train or by Nile River steamer to Khartoum. Boats leave every Monday and Thursday from Aswan. Prices without meals are: first class, £E 8.80 ($13.20); second class, £E 4.60 ($6.90); third class, £E 1.65 ($2.50). Book your ticket through the Sudanese Nile Steamer Company, 8 Kasr el-Nil Street, Cairo.

Getting Around Within Egypt

Egyptair, the government carrier, has daily flights from Cairo to Luxor ($11.25 one way) and Aswan ($15.45 one way). There is service twice a week between Aswan and Abu Simbel ($19.90 round trip). With special permission you can also fly from Cairo to the New Valley ($18.55 round trip) and the Siwa Oasis ($21.90 round trip).

If you have the time, you might prefer to journey by boat or by train. These trips provide a unique opportunity for seeing the Egyptian countryside now that traveling is so restricted outside the main tourist centers. The Cairo-Alexandria train operates 10 or more times daily. It is a two and a half hour ride ranging in price from $1.85 to $3.85 for air-conditioned first class. Five trains a day connect Cairo with Luxor, a 10-hour ride. The same trains take another six to eight hours to reach Aswan. One-way tickets to Luxor run from $4.65 to $10.20, to Aswan from $5.60 to $12.80. If you buy a return ticket, or travel in a group of more than 10, the fares are substantially less. Students can get a 50 per cent reduction on the coaches, but not on the sleepers.

A cruise on the Nile is one of the most delightful river trips in the world. The stretch between Luxor and Aswan is the most popular since it covers the majority of temples. The boats sail only during the winter season (mid-November to early May). For a seven-day trip, including an excursion downstream to the temples of Abydos and Dendara, you have a choice of several boats. The Hilton's two "floating hotels," the *Isis* and the *Osiris*, are luxurious but extravagantly expensive at $300 per person. The *Triton*, operated by the Karnak Travel Agency, 12 Kasr el-Nil Street, is half the price and definitely the best buy. The Eastmar Travel Agency, 13 Kasr el-Nil Street (just around the corner from American Express), runs three less comfortable boats at slightly lower rates.

Trips of 11 to 13 days between Cairo and Aswan are scheduled at the beginning and end of the winter season by the three lines. The rates are only $15 to $30 higher than for the Luxor-Aswan excursion. All rates quoted above include room, board and tours.

Another journey by water can be taken on the hydrofoil from Aswan to Abu Simbel on Lake Nasser. It is a 12-hour round trip starting at 5 am, and not particularly relaxing with the vibrations of the hydrofoil motor drumming in your ears. But most tourists find that the visit to the temple, though it lasts a brief hour, more than compensates for the discomfort. The trip costs $21.40 including a meal and snacks and is scheduled every Tuesday and Thursday. It is advisable to book both the Nile River cruises and the hydrofoil trip well in advance.

Within Cairo and Alexandria taxis are the best means of transportation. They are metered and very cheap, starting at nine cents and charging one and a half cents for every additional sixth of a mile. Most drivers speak a smattering of English, but it is best to make sure the driver understands your destination before you get into the cab. Tipping is not required but you might spare a piaster or two. You can try your luck on the buses, but they are jam-packed and a favorite haunt of pickpockets. The routes, furthermore, are confusing for the non-Arabic speaker. The trolleys are a bit more manageable. At night after the traffic has subsided the horse-drawn carriages (hantours) are a favorite means of transportation in Luxor and Aswan, as well as in Alexandria. Bicycling is also pleasant in Upper Egypt; bikes can be rented very cheaply from a shop on the main square near the temple of Luxor.

The only way to explore certain areas of Cairo, such as the Muski (old bazaar), is on foot. Walking is safe in Egypt during the day; however, in the poorer areas your footsteps may be dogged by urchins shouting for bakshish (honoring the cult of Piast-Ra). At night unaccompanied women should avoid unlit streets outside the center of town.

Where to Stay

The Government Tourist Office classifies hotels ranging from one-star to five-star. These classifications, however, should not be taken too literally; certain one-star hotels are cleaner and more pleasant than the four-star ones. Hotel bills include a 10 per cent service charge.

CAIRO. Cairo offers a wide variety of good hotels. The Sheraton and the Hilton are the most luxurious and expensive, with minimum tariffs of $9 to $15 for a single. The Sheraton is newer than the Hilton and therefore somewhat better kept up (Egyptian labor laws prohibit the firing of employees after six months on the job—which leads naturally to decreased efficiency; furthermore, when imported machinery breaks down, it is difficult to get spare parts). The Hilton is more centrally located and has a wider variety of services for the tourist. The Mena House in the shadow of the pyramids was originally a royal lodge of the khedive Ismail. It was here that Churchill, Roosevelt and Chiang Kai-shek conferred during World War II. The hotel, renovated in 1972, offers singles from $7.50. Two other hotels, the Menial Palace and the Omar Khayyam, were originally royal residences. Prices range from $5.25 a single at the Omar Khayyam and from $6.75 a single at the Menial Palace (there are substantial reductions for members of the Club Méditerranée). The two other good first-class hotels are Shepheard's, not nearly as palatial as the hotel of the same name that was burned down on Black Saturday in 1952, and the Semiramis, with rates starting at $6. When the *Isis* and *Osiris*, the Hilton "floating hotels," are in port you can stay in them for a minimum of $5.25.

Among the less expensive hotels, the following, all of them clean and centrally located, are the best: the *Nile*, $3.75 for a single; the *Golden Hotel*, $1.80; the *Garden City House*, where many visiting academics stay, $3.75 for full board, and the *Windsor*, $2, a charming old hotel where the overflow from the old Shepheard's used to stay.

There are also a couple of attractive houseboats on the Giza side of the Nile with special student rates, $2.25 for half board during the summer season. Check the Eastmar Travel Agency for details.

Youth hostels can be found in Cairo as well as in the other major cities. They charge less than 38 cents per night but are none too clean. The two in Cairo are the Garden City Youth Hostel, Ibrahimi Street, Garden City, and the Koh-I-Noor Youth Hostel, 8 Shukri Street, Pyramids Road, Giza. The offices of the Egyptian Youth Hostel Association are at 7 Dr. Adel Hamid Sayyid Street, Marrouf, Cairo. This organization can give you a list of hostels outside Cairo and help with bookings.

ALEXANDRIA AND WEST. The *Palestine*, situated in the Montaza Palace grounds, and with its own beach, is Alexandria's most luxurious hotel. Singles start at $6. Slightly less expensive are the *Salemlik*, an annex of the Palestine, the *San Stephano* and the *Beau Rivage*, all of which have their own beach facilities.

In the center of town there are three main hotels: the *Metropole*, the *Windsor Palace* and the *Cecil* (readers of Durrell's *Alexandria Quartet* are given a romanticized notion of the latter's hotel lobby; it is, alas, quite ordinary). Rooms at all three hotels are in the $3 to $4 range. Two blocks west of the Cecil and down a side street is the *Crillon*, a comfortable and reasonably-priced pension with rooms overlooking the Mediterranean. Arrangements for other pensions may be made through the Alexandria Tourist Office, Saad Zaghloul Square, Ramleh Station.

Agami and Sidi Abdul Rahman are two resort areas to the west of Alexandria where foreign tourists may go. At Agami you have your choice between *Hannoville* and the *Agami Palace*. Both are reasonably priced but noisy and not particularly clean. You're better off staying in Alexandria and visiting Agami by day. The only accommodations at Sidi Abdul Rahman are at the *Alamein*, an attractive hotel with cabins on the beach (from $5.75).

LUXOR. The best accommodations here are at the *New Winter Palace* and two hotels of colonial vintage, the *Winter Palace* and the *Savoy*. The Savoy is more reasonable than the others, which offer singles in the $5.50 to $7.50 range.

Abdul Rasoul's, on the other side of the river near the Rameseum, offers reasonably clean rooms at very low rates.

Aswan. For turn of the century flavor—wide verandas overlooking the Nile, spacious salons, beds draped with mosquito netting—the old *Cataract Hotel* is unbeatable. One can easily imagine it as a setting for Agatha Christie's *Death on the Nile.* The *New Cataract,* which is slightly more expensive ($7 for a single), pales by comparison.

If these are booked up, you might try the *Calabsha,* the *Amoun,* the *Grand* or the *Abu Simbel,* all in the $3–$4.50 range.

Abu Simbel. There is a small hotel here by the same name, with singles from $5.25.

Tourism is flourishing now in Egypt, after the slump caused by the 1967 war. Alexandria's hotels are crowded in the summer as are the Upper Egyptian hotels in winter. To be safe, book all hotel reservations in advance.

There are a number of good hotels in areas now closed to foreign tourists, i.e. Mersa Matruh, the Faiyum and the Red Sea resorts. Some of these areas are likely to open up soon. Check the travel agencies for hotel accommodations.

All of the above-cited rates may be slightly increased after the 1972–73 season. These are minimum, single-room rates without meals.

Where and What to Eat

Egyptian cuisine includes a number of standard Middle Eastern dishes, among them: kebab, thin slices of charcoal grilled beef or lamb, and kufta, minced meat kebab; homos, tehina and babaganoush, dips made of sesame seed sauce, chick pea sauce and eggplant; dolma, stuffed grape leaves, and honey-almond pastries such as baklava and kunafa.

Egyptians put more heart in the cooking of local specialties. Fool, made of beans and lentils mashed and served with oil and lemon, and koushery, a kind of macaroni pie, are the staple diet of the poor; tamiya, ground bean patties fried in oil, are the poor man's hamburger. Fatta, served with chicken or meat, is a delicious concoction including day-old bread. Pigeon (hammam) is prepared in a variety of interesting ways. Molokheia, a rather gluey soup made of a plant resembling mint, is a favorite among some foreigners; others can't stand it. Do at least try it since it is the national dish par excellence. Um Ali, a pudding with raisins and nuts, is more likely to appeal to most palates.

Imported liquor is expensive in Egypt, roughly $9 for a fifth of whiskey in retail groceries, or 75 cents or more for one shot at the bar. Thus it is a good idea to buy a couple of bottles, preferably quart size, at the tax-free shop on your way through customs entering Egypt. The locally produced rum and zabib, a potent concoction similar to arak, are not bad. Old Egyptian hands have been known, when desperate for a martini, to cut Egypt's own White Cat gin with local vodka and imported vermouth. Stella beer is quite good. There is also a variety of pleasant Egyptian wines; the best are Omar Khayyam and Pharaon (both red), Rubis d'Egypte (rosé) and Cru Ptolème (white). More reasonable and almost as good are Clos Mariut (white) and Clos Matamir (red).

Turkish coffee is much tastier than what goes for "French" or "American" coffee. You can order it "saada" (without sugar), "ziadah" (sweet) or "mazbut" (just right).

A note about health precautions: Egypt is not a clean country. Unless you have a strong stomach, steer clear of the baladi (local) restaurants in the poorer sections of town and little roadside carts selling fool and koushery for a few piasters, picturesque as they are. A glance at the way dishes are washed should deter you from sampling their wares. It is not wise even to buy melons in the street, since they are often injected with water to give them added weight.

Even in the best restaurants, peel all fresh fruit, avoid salads in general, and fish in the summer, unless you know it has been freshly caught. Tap water, surprisingly, is perfectly safe to drink everywhere.

In CAIRO: The restaurants at the major hotels are naturally the most expensive, but at most of them you can dine for under $3.75 per person. The following, which serve both Oriental and Western cuisine, are highly recommended: the two restaurants at the Hilton on the second floor (Rotisserie) and top floor; the second-floor restaurant at the Sheraton; the Semiramis roof and the Mena House terrace (both only open during summer); Shepheard's downstairs club, and the Omar Khayyam.

Outside the hotels, the best restaurants serving European food are Groppi's on Talaat Harb (ex-Suleiman Pasha) Square, the Embassy and the Estoril, next door to each other on the alley linking Talaat Harb Street and Kasr el-Nil Street, and the Rex, on Sarwat Pasha Street just off Talaat Harb. The Fu-Ching, 39 Talaat Harb Street, does its best to produce Chinese food, given the limited ingredients available. There are two mediocre Lebanese restaurants, the Liban, 20 Adly Street, and Sofar, 21 Adly Street, and a Greek restaurant, the Ariston, just off Tewfikiya Square.

All of the above are in the $1.50 to $2.25 range.

Good fish at very reasonable prices can be found at Haj Mahmoud el-Samak, opposite Omar Effendi's on Abd el-Aziz Street. The Sea Horse, halfway to Maadi on the Nile Corniche (three miles south of Cairo center), serves excellent but expensive shrimp and crab. For delicious pigeon at moderate prices, try the *Casino des Pigeons* in Giza just below the New Giza Bridge (southernmost of the four Cairo bridges) overlooking the Nile. Cairo has two pizzerias: one at the *Hilton*, predictably expensive but open most of the night, and a small pizza parlor, *Pizza-Capri*, 31 26th July Street (one block west of the Rivoli Cinema), for the budget-minded traveler.

If you would like to view the pyramids over lunch, and see peasants in the foreground tilling their fields with water buffalo in the age-old way, try *Andreas*, and its excellent grilled chicken, on the extension of the Sakkara road roughly one-quarter of a mile north of the Pyramids Highway. Or, if you are in a more affluent mood, go south several miles along the same road (on your way to Sakkara) to *El-Dar*, for a variety of good Western and Oriental foods. Dinner is also served at both places (El-Dar has a floor show and belly dancer), but the mosquitoes in summer are voracious at night.

For fool and tamiya, the best places are *Domiati*, in Midan Falaki, *Tabi'i*, 35 Arabi Street, and the *Filfila*, just around the corner from the Stella beer depot on Talaat Harb Street. There are kofta and kebab restaurants all over Cairo. To mention just two: *El-Dahaan*, in the Muski, and *Abu Shakra*, about 10 blocks from Tahrir Square.

There are numerous places where you can sit down for a cup of tea and a light snack. The most amusing of them are the two *Groppi's*, at Talaat Harb Square and on Sarwat Pasha Street, favorite watering places of the jet set and retired pashas alike.

In ALEXANDRIA: A few old restaurants preserve something of the cosmopolitan atmosphere the city once had. The most chic is the *Santa Lucia*, on Safeya Zaghlul Street, where you can get fine European cuisine for $2.25 to $3 and dance after dinner to the best combo in town. The ancient woodwork and faded chandeliers of *Pastrudi's*, at 39 El-Horreya Avenue, capture the elegance of pre-war Alexandria at dinnertime; at breakfast (with fresh croissants) the corroded mirrors and vast salons of the cafe on the Corniche just east of Saad Zaghloul Square do the same. The *Union* restaurant, 1 Borsa el-Kadima, has less atmosphere but very good, inexpensive food.

Andreas, on El Geish Avenue just before you reach the Montaza Palace grounds, is noted for its good chicken and fish, for about $2.25 per person.

For seafood, however, the best are the harborside restaurants of Abu Kir 14 miles east of the city center. Here you select your own fish and gigantic prawns caught fresh from the Mediterranean.

What to See and Do

CAIRO. The city of Cairo dates back to 969 AD, when a Fatimid conquering army from North Africa staked out its military capital here. Settlements in the area, however, existed from the time of the pharaohs. Today, with a population of well over four million, Cairo is the largest city in Africa and the Arab world, a huge metropolis of sandstone and concrete relentlessly spreading into the desert and delta. It is an extremely vital city, the cultural and political hub of the Middle East and a major crossroads between East and West. Despite an aura of Westernization, however, it remains Oriental in spirit and proud of its past, clearly evident in its splendid monuments and in the ongoing traditions of its citizens.

To get a proper sense of historical continuity, you might begin with the pharaonic monuments. The sphinx and the Great Pyramids of Giza are about 10 miles to the southwest of the city. Take a taxi or bus from Tahrir Square. Camels are available right at the pyramids for those who want to take a short and bumpy ride. Good horses can be rented for longer rides at two nearby stables, Abdul Aziz (AA) and Mohammed Ghoneim (MG), for about $1.50 per hour. For the adventurous, round trip rides to Sakkara can be arranged either during the day or overnight, camping in the desert. After sunset, there is a son et lumière at the pyramids worth seeing. The narration is corny but the illumination of the pyramids and particularly of the face of the sphinx is fantastic.

Memphis and Sakkara, the name given to the Memphite necropolis, are 10 miles to the south of the Giza pyramids on a good paved road. The sleepy little village of Memphis has little to indicate its former stature as one of ancient Egypt's most important cities. There is, however, a small museum housing one of the two great colossi of Ramses (the other stands in front of the Ramses Railway Station).

The necropolis of Sakkara is the largest and has the longest history of any in Egypt. It also has some of the most beautifully painted tombs. It is best to arrange for a guide beforehand, since you cannot get into many of the tombs without one. Don't waste your time with any of the dragomans (guides) at the site.

The Egyptian Museum in Tahrir Square has many of the treasures of ancient Egypt, including the fabulous Tutenkhamen collection, a number of mummies, some superb statuary and a copy of the Rosetta Stone.

Following historical chronology, your next visit would be to the early Christian quarter in Old Cairo (Masr el-Qadima), across the river from Giza two miles south of the Cairo Hilton. The major sights here are the Coptic Museum, which has a fine collection of early Christian relics, the

4th century Church of Saint Sergius, built on a site where the Holy Family is said to have rested on its flight to Egypt, the Church of El-Moallaqa (The Suspended), built against the old fortifications of Babylon, and the Church of Mari Girgis (Saint George), which has some interesting icons. Also, in the same area, is the Ben Ezra Synagogue, oldest in the Middle East and still serving the remaining Jewish community (of less than a hundred families).

Cairo has some of the most beautiful mosques in the Islamic world. There are over 400 of them, reflecting all the periods of Moslem rule. The following, listed in historical order, should not be missed: the Mosque of Ibn Tulun, El-Azhar Mosque, the Madrasa of Sultan Hassan, the Mausoleum of Kait Bey, the Maristan Qala'un and the Mohammed Ali Mosque.

Dorothea Russell's *Medieval Cairo* and Gaston Wiet's *The Mosques of Cairo*, available at the Hachette and Orientalist bookstores, describe these monuments in detail. The Russell book also provides walking tours for those who want to explore the old sections extensively.

A good, though small, collection of Islamic art can be seen at the Museum of Islamic Art at Ahmed Maher Square on Port Said Street. The Gayer Anderson Museum, right next to the Ibn Tulun Mosque, is also well worth visiting. The home of a wealthy 18th century merchant, built in the traditional Islamic style, it now has a collection of rare Oriental objects and costumes. The Menial Palace and the Gowhara Palace at the Citadel, both belonging to Mohammed Ali, have now been converted into museums as well.

You should pay a visit to the Muski, one of the most famous market areas in the Middle East, if just for its atmosphere. The covered Khan el-Khalili, established in 1292, is the most interesting section, and in its narrow byways you can watch the craftsmen still plying their traditional crafts. If you would like to see a school where these crafts are taught, walk over to the Wikalet el-Ghouri, across from the Muski, just below the El-Ashar Mosque. A medieval inn that once lodged camel caravans, it now contains, in addition to the school, a good collection of Egyptian folk art. Another charming old inn, where a number of modern artists have set up studios, is the Musafra Khan, behind the Hussein Mosque.

Exhibits of modern art can be seen at the Mukhtar Museum in Gezira (just to the right of the Kasr el-Nil Bridge), which displays the work of Egypt's first and best modern sculptor, at the Akhnaton, 6 Kasr el-Nil Street, and at the Beaux Arts Gallery, Midan Falaki. You can check the *Egyptian Gazette* for exhibits at the Goethe Institute and the French Cultural Center.

Superb primitive tapestries are woven at the shop of Ramses Wissa Wassef in Harrania, on the road to Sakkara before the El-Dar Restaurant. Phone 850403 to arrange your visit. Fine, locally woven fabrics can be found in the village of Kirdassa, on the extension of the Sakkara Road a few miles north of the Pyramids Highway.

Other tourist attractions within Cairo itself are the zoo in Giza, and the 200-foot Cairo Tower on the Nile River island of Zamalek. The tower offers a splendid view of the city.

Cairo is one of the great night-time playgrounds of the Middle East. The glittering strip of casinos along Pyramids Highway is the Oriental equivalent of Las Vegas. Two of the most popular spots here are the Tamerina and the Auberge des Pyramides. Gambling, however, is restricted to the clubs at the Sheraton, Hilton and Shepheard's. Cairo's jet set is more apt to frequent the discotheques. The most fashionable at this writing are the After Eight, 6 Kasr el-Nil Street, and the Salt and Pepper, Abou el-Fedda Street, at the northern tip of Zamalek.

The Egyptian film industry, one of the largest in the world, turns out a vast quantity of musical comedies and tear-jerking melodramas. The acting is so heavy that you can understand the plot even without the help of English or French subtitles, which are rarely supplied anyway.

During the winter season, foreign theatrical groups, orchestras, chamber music ensembles, operas, ballets and circuses visit the city. Concerts of classical and popular Arabic music are given regularly, as are performances of the National Folk Dance Troupe.

Sport in Egypt is centered around private clubs. The Gezira Club, once restricted to British members, is still the most fashionable. All the major clubs have tennis, swimming, basketball and horseback riding. (The golfer is advised to use the Mena House links.) The clubs will issue the traveler daily, weekly or monthly memberships at a nominal fee. Soccer matches can be seen at the National Club Stadium in Zamalek and at Nasser Stadium in Nasr City. Horse races are held regularly in the winter at the Gezira Club and the Jhams Club in Heliopolis.

A pleasant few hours can be spent sailing on the Nile, weaving in among the graceful falukkas—pleasure craft of different sizes—and barges from Upper Egypt carrying heaps of clay vessels and other cargoes. Small sailboats are for hire at the Yacht Club on the Giza side of the Nile a few blocks south of the Sheraton; falukkas can be hired in front of Shepheard's. The S.S. *Triton* offers round trip dinner cruises to Helwan, an industrial and resort center 20 miles south of Cairo.

ALEXANDRIA. The city founded by Alexander is now Egypt's second largest metropolis, with a population approaching two million. Once the home of substantial foreign communities, "Alex" in recent years has become fully Egyptian, although its Mediterranean architecture and wide avenues contrast with the character of Cairo. A suggestion of the Alexandria that once was is given in Lawrence Durrell's *Alexandria Quartet*, E.M. Forster's *Guide to Alexandria*, written during the First World War when he was stationed there as a Red Cross volunteer (it is out of print now), and the poems of Constantine Cavafy, a 20th century Alexandrian Greek whose rhymes and subjects thread their way through the city's history in *Passions and Ancient Days* (Dial Press, 1971).

During the summer Cairenes come in hordes to Alexandria to enjoy the 20 miles of white sandy beaches. The most attractive of them are Montaza and Maamura, to the east of the city, and Agami, which lies to the west.

Montaza Palace and its beautiful grounds, a former residence of King Farouk, is well worth a visit. The bottom floor of the palace is now, appropriately, a casino; the top two floors have been converted into a museum containing memorabilia of the royal family, among them the fat king's specially fitted bathroom.

The Graeco-Roman Museum, 5 el-Mathaf el-Romani Street, houses some interesting relics dating back to the 3rd century BC. Unfortunately, the museum is quite run down.

The Graeco-Roman ruins in the city are frankly second-rate. A good deal of historical imagination is needed to reconstruct what was once the greatest cultural and commercial center of the ancient world. Pompey's Pillar, standing among the ruins of the Serapium, is probably the best preserved relic of antiquity. As far as catacombs go, those at Kom el-Sokafa are ordinary. Hardly anything is left of the Roman amphitheater. No traces remain of Pharos, the towering white marble lighthouse that was one of the seven wonders of ancient times. But on its site, at the tip of the peninsula in the eastern harbor, there still stands the 15th century Kait Bey fort. Next to it is the state aquarium, housing exotic species of fish from the Mediterranean, the Red Sea and the Nile. Nearby, there are small boats for hire for a pleasant cruise around the harbor.

Sixty-five miles west of Alexandria lies the World War II battlefield of Alamein, where Montgomery halted Rommel's westward advance. The great desert war is commemorated in a small museum and in the vast cemeteries where 7,500 soldiers rest. The calm of the desert, with the azure Mediterranean stretching into the distance, is in strange contrast to the bloodbath that occurred here. A few miles farther on is the pretty beach of Sidi Abdul Rahman, still relatively unspoiled by tourism. The beach at Mersa Matruh, 200 miles west of Alexandria, is a lagoon shielded from the sea by huge rocks and is reportedly the most beautiful on Egypt's Mediterranean coast. But it is prohibited to foreigners, as are all points west of Sidi Abdul Rahman. Naval bases are nearby.

UPPER EGYPT. Most of the pharaonic monuments are in Upper Egypt, that narrow ribbon of green stretching from the apex of the delta to Aswan. Between Cairo and Luxor there are a number of important sites. Tell El-Amarna, the city chosen by Akhnaton to replace Thebes as capital, the Beni Hassan tombs from the Middle Kingdom (2060–1789 BC), and Ashumein, which contains Ptolemaic, Greek and early Christian ruins, are all interesting. Far more spectacular is the temple of Sethos I at Abydos. Ask to be shown around by the old English lady who calls herself Um Seti (mother of Sethos) in the belief that she is her reincarnation. She has lived in the village since the 1950's and knows the hieroglyphics by heart. Even grander than the temple of Sethos in size if not in decoration is that of Dendera, built in Ptolemaic and Roman times. Bear in mind that all these sites, as well as those between Luxor and Aswan, can only be seen by taking a Nile River cruise.

Even if you are planning to stay just a few days in Egypt, you should include a trip to LUXOR, the ancient Thebes. The monuments here are stupendous, far surpassing those of ancient Greece or Rome. Thebes consisted, in fact, of two cities—that of the living on the east bank of the Nile, and that of the dead on the west bank. All traces of the original mudbrick dwellings on the east bank have long ago disappeared, and all that remain are two grand temples dedicated to the gods, the Temple of Luxor and the Temple of Karnak, where there is an ambulatory sound and light show at night. Perhaps the major attraction on the west bank is the Valley of the Kings, where more than 40 pharaohs were buried in ornate subterranean palaces. Despite the elaborate precautions taken to conceal the burial chambers, the only known tomb to have escaped plundering is that of Tutenkhamen. Since he was only a minor king, his fabulous treasure was probably among the more modest. The other important sites in the City of the Dead are the Valley of the Queens, the Tombs of the Nobles, the Temple of Deir el-Bahri, the Rameseum, Medinet Habu Temple and the Colossi of Memnon.

Three fine Ptolemaic temples, those of Esna, Edfu and Kom Ombo, are situated between Luxor and Aswan.

The present-day fame of ASWAN rests, of course, on the High Dam, but the city is also rich in archaeological treasures. The site was the chief southern outpost of the pharaohs and revered as the place where the advent of the Nile flood was marked. You can take a falukka ride to Elephantine Island, just opposite the center of town, to see the ancient

Nilometer, used to measure the river's depth. There is also a museum here with relics dating back to prehistoric times from the Aswan and Nubian areas. Other short falukka rides can be taken to the mausoleum of the Aga Khan, on the opposite bank, and the Botanical Gardens, on a nearby island. On the west bank overlooking the Nile are the Tombs of the Barons, from the Old Kingdom, and the 8th century monastery of San Simeon. On the east bank is an ancient granite quarry where there lies an unfinished obelisk still attached to the rock bed.

The High Dam, one of the great engineering feats of the 20th century, has been alternately open and closed to foreign tourists. The vast lake behind the dam has submerged many Nubian temples; of those that have been saved, the two at Abu Simbel 170 miles south of Aswan are the most spectacular. These rock-cut temples of Ramses II have now been rebuilt into a new landscaped "false mountain" hundreds of feet above the original site. So precise was the engineering that the first rays of the morning sun still strike the holy of holies in the inner sanctuary. Another lovely temple shortly to be raised is on the submerged island of Philae, a mile south of Aswan between the High Dam and the old Aswan Dam. The waters of the lake lapping against the columns give it a particular charm.

Aswan, with the construction of the High Dam and related industries, has become an important industrial center. Its population has been further increased by the migration of Nubians whose lands were inundated by Lake Nasser. These graceful black-skinned villagers speak distinctive dialects and are noted for their folk art and dance. Examples of their fine-woven basketwork made from dyed date palms can be found in Aswan markets.

The Sinai peninsula remains occupied by Israel five years after a UN resolution urged her withdrawal. The Suez Canal continues to silt, blocked at both ends by sunken ships, with a string of freighters trapped in between. As long as Egyptian and Israeli troops point their guns at each other across the canal, the zone will be closed to tourists. Even the inhabitants of Port Said and Ismailia have gone, leaving their war-blasted cities virtually ghost towns.

The Red Sea resorts of Ein Sukhna and Hurghada, nestled on sandy beaches below the red hills, were famed for their water sports, tropical fish and gorgeous coral; but the entire coast is now prohibited to tourists. Also off limits is the oasis of Faiyum, though there are rumors of its being opened shortly. The oasis is 85 miles southwest of Cairo.

With special permission you may be able to visit the Siwa Oasis and the Kharga and Dakhla oases in the New Valley.

What to Buy

If you are shopping just for souvenirs, there is a wide variety to choose from: camel saddles, miniature leather camels, leather poufs, brass and copper trays, alabaster statuettes and Oriental perfumes. The largest selection of these items is in the Khan el-Khalili bazaar, where long sessions of bargaining over cups of mazbut or chai (tea) is the rule. If you lack time or patience make your purchases at the hotel shops where you pay more but with less discussion.

Gold and precious and semi-precious stones are good buys in Cairo, but to be sure of what you are getting, it is best to visit one of the government-controlled stores, such as Khorasani in Khan el-Khalili. The same goes for antiquities.

The long-flowing gowns known as gallabias, embroidered in silver or gold, can be stunning. If you are planning to stay in Cairo for four or five days, have them made to order. The Atlas Shop in Khan el-Khalili does the best work and has a variety of modified gallabia styles—gallabia dress and coat ensembles, gallabia pants suits, etc. Much of Egypt's famous cotton is now exported, and what remains of good quality on the local market is expensive; however, you can still buy gaily colored pharaonic prints at reasonable prices. If you can get good material, it is well worth having clothes made in Egypt. Ali Yasmine, on Bustan Street near the Goethe Institute, and Adel Luga, opposite Hannaux on Antikhanna Street, rival the best of European dressmakers; and Joe Gaon, 2 Shawarbi Street, turns out first-rate custom-made suits for $33 (it is best to provide him with all materials, including imported linings, thread and buttons).

A number of attractive boutiques are located on Hassan Sabry Street, Zamalek. Among them are Fiametta's, Toi et Moi and Mouche. Leather products in Cairo are inexpensive and of fairly good quality. Kasr el-Nil Street and Talaat Harb Street beyond the Midan are filled with shops selling shoes and handbags.

The old mashrabiya screens, which adorned the traditional Islamic home, are now prized collector's items. With luck, you might find one (for not less than $150) at Hatoun's, in the Muski, or in Khan el-Khalili at the shop of Awad A. M. Hassan, who also has the best old copper and brassware. You should also visit Senouhi, 54 Abdul Khaleq Sarwat Street, fifth floor; its proprietors, Mr. and Mrs. Rashad, have a fine collection of antiques and are thoroughly reliable. They also sell tapestries from Harrania, modern Egyptian paintings and lovely jewelry, much of it designed by them.

Rugs are generally not good buys in Cairo, but if you would like to attend auctions of old rugs, they are held from time to time at the annex of the Russian Cultural Center on Maahid el-Swissry Street, Zamalek.

Before buying any antiquities, check the export regulations with the Egyptian authorities.

Local Attitudes

Whatever the situation along the Suez Canal, most of Egypt does not feel, look or act like a country at war. In Cairo the brick walls in front of doors, occasional sandbags and windows painted blue are reminders that a state of hostility still exists, but its residents go about their daily lives with insouciance. The only formal restrictions apply to travel in closed zones and to photographs of strategic sites: all bridges, airports, harbors, military installations and public utilities. Be careful to heed the photo prohibitions, ludicrous as some of them may seem. When in doubt about a shot, don't take it or you may have your camera confiscated and end up spending a few uncomfortable hours in a police station.

Educated Egyptians generally speak some English and often enjoy the opportunity of speaking to foreigners. Vis-à-vis the United States, the country has a split personality. While the government incessantly condemns US support of Israel and still relies heavily on Soviet military and economic assistance, American oil companies continue to drill, and the American University stands proudly in Tahrir Square. It has often been remarked that Egyptians in their informal friendliness and somewhat broad sense of humor are akin to Americans. Certainly, as individuals, Americans are preferred to Russians, who not only are unsmiling but also are poor customers.

Politics is a favorite topic of conversation, but it is best to let Egyptians take the lead, at least when discussing Arab-Israeli relations. You will find some of the students at the national universities, where anti-government demonstrations erupt sporadically, quite eager to talk.

Visitors are allowed into most mosques except during prayer hours. It is customary to offer 5 or 10 piasters to the custodian (who may or may not issue a ticket) and to leave your shoes outside. You can pad around inside in slippers if the custodian provides them.

Miniskirts invite stares, whistles and the appreciative pinch. Unaccompanied women, even if conservatively dressed, are likely to draw remarks, particularly in the older sections of the city.

Weather, What to Wear, How Long to Stay

December, January and February are the best months for travel. Cairo has warm days and cool nights freshened by breezes off the Nile. Alexandria and the Mediterranean are pleasantly warm from June to August. Temperatures in Cairo at that time are consistently in the 90's, although humidity is low. Luxor and Aswan are hot throughout the year and blaze during the summer with the healthy dry heat of the desert. March through May and September through November correspond roughly to spring and autumn and are generally sunny, pleasant travel months for most of the country. There is very little rain.

Probably the most important item of apparel for Egypt is a pair of comfortable walking shoes. Locally made sandals are inexpensive and of high quality. Summer calls for lightweight wear including a tropical suit if you expect to go to the expensive casinos and restaurants. During the winter there is little or no indoor heating and a coat and sweater are necessary for cool evenings. Pants suits for women are quite acceptable. Pack a bathing suit, whatever time of the year; bikinis are suitable.

Cairo should be seen at leisure in five days or longer. If you have less time you may want to opt for some of the package tours, but keep in mind that you will not be allowed to linger when something strikes your fancy. Using a combination of boat and rail, Luxor and Aswan can be seen in three days, but relaxed traveling demands several more. Alexandria is for spring, summer and autumn lounging on the beaches and a day or more of exploration for its historical sites.

Communication

Al-Ahram, *Al-Akhbar* and *Al-Gumhuriya* are the three Arabic-language dailies, all theoretically under government control. *Al-Ahram* is the largest of them, with a circulation of hundreds of thousands throughout Egypt and the Middle East, and the Friday column of Mohammed Heykal, its prominent editor and a former confidant of Nasser, is an important political weathervane. All the significant stories are translated in the *Cairo Press Review*, available in embassies and at the American University library. The English-language daily, *Egyptian Gazette*, is not very good but does provide schedules of films and local events. *Newsweek*, the Paris *Herald-Tribune* and the London *Times* can be found at the major hotels, but often a week late.

Postal, telephone and telegraph services have not kept pace with the population explosion of Cairo and Egypt in general. Phone service is cheap in Cairo but lines are congested and service shaky; there is a backlog of hundreds of thousands of requests for new phones. Telephone directories are available only in Arabic. Overseas or long-distance calls should be placed from your hotel or the central post office in Ataba Square, open 24 hours a day. Overseas calls require hours of waiting to book a circuit. What's more, they are censored. The postal service is also censored—and inefficient. Avoid requesting money orders by mail, and for the most reliable service, use air letters or airmail postcards posted at the Hilton or Sheraton.

Emergencies

After 1967, when diplomatic relations were broken, the American diplomatic representation in Egypt was reduced to a small Interest Section, officially under the flag of Spain. It is still housed in the old American Embassy building, 5 Latin American Street, Garden City, Cairo (tel. 28219). In case of emergency, the consular office can provide the names of competent physicians and arrange for hospitalization. There are a few good hospitals in Cairo and Alexandria, but most are dirty, overcrowded, and staffed by ill-trained nurses. The Tourist Police are specially trained to help travelers. Their head office in Cairo is at 5 Adly Street (tel. 912644), and in Alexandria at the Montaza Palace Hotel (tel. 6000) and at the harbor. There are also offices at the airport, the pyramids, the main railway station and the Khan el-Khalili bazaar.

Ethiopia

Profile

STATUS: Constitutional monarchy.

SIZE: 457,256 square miles (size of Texas, Oklahoma and New Mexico combined). Population—about 25,000,000.

GEOGRAPHY: Mostly high plateau (8,000 feet); divided by Great Rift Valley; High Semyen Mountains in north. Principal towns—Addis Ababa (capital, 1,000,000), Asmara, Massawa and Assab (main ports).

CLIMATE: Light rains February to April; heavy rains June to September. Temperatures in Addis Ababa range from low 70's to high 80's during the day (March to July warmest months), drop into 50's at night. Somewhat warmer in Asmara. Hot and steamy on the coast, with Massawa often above 100.

LANGUAGES: Amharic (official). English widely spoken, Italian second language in the north.

CURRENCY: Ethiopian dollar, divided into 100 cents. Eth$1.00 = 43 cents. US$1.00 = Eth$2.32.

VISAS: Obtained on arrival in Ethiopia. Fee US$4. Valid for three months. Required—two passport photos, inoculation certificates for smallpox, cholera, yellow fever, and ticket out of Ethiopia. Visas also available from Ethiopian Embassy and Ethiopian Mission to the UN.

AIRPORTS: Haile Selassie Airport (ADD), five miles from Addis Ababa. Frequent flights to and from Europe and East African capitals. Airport departure taxes—domestic, Eth$1.05 (44 cents); international, Eth$3.00 ($1.29). Transport into city—bus, Eth$2.00 (86 cents); taxi, Eth$3.00 ($1.29). Asmara Airport (ASM), six miles from city. Frequent connections with Addis Ababa, Athens, Massawa, Jeddah and Rome.

180

NATIONAL HOLIDAYS: See text (What to See and Do).

INFORMATION SOURCES: *In US*—Ethiopian Embassy, 2134 Kalorama Road NW, Washington, D.C. 20008 (tel. 202/234-2281); Permanent Mission of Ethiopia to the UN, 866 United Nations Plaza, New York, N.Y. 10017 (tel. 212/421-1830); Ethiopian Airlines, 200 East 42nd Street, New York, N.Y. 10017 (tel. 212/867-0095) and 6290 Sunset Boulevard, Los Angeles, Cal. 90028 (tel. 213/466-8830). *In Addis Ababa* —Ethiopian Tourist Organization, P.O. Box 2183 (tel. 47470).

By Morgan Towne

A traveler returning from Ethiopia some years ago described it as "the Tibet of Africa." Ethiopian Airlines has recently taken to calling it "the Hidden Empire." The symbolism is plain—mystery, remoteness, the unusual. These are Ethiopia's chief attractions for the tourist. How long it can retain them in the face of increasing foreign contact and modernization is a question. To anyone who would visit the Ethiopia of legend, the best advice is "Get started today."

Throughout the centuries the vastness and isolation of this rugged, mountainous land have kept it free from colonization and protected its unique culture. Its traditions go back to the Biblical Queen of Sheba, co-founder of the reigning Solomonic Dynasty, and it boasts a 1,500-year-old Christian heritage. Written historical records provide a picture of a Greater Ethiopia at the turn of the 16th century as encompassing five major centers: the Moslem sultanate of Harar, the Ethiopian Christian kingdom of Amhara, the Judaic Falasha kingdom in Semyen, the pagan Galla tribes around Bale, and the southern kingdom of Kaffa.

It was the successful expansion of the Amhara and Galla peoples that laid the basis for the modern Ethiopian nation-state. The Amhara spread their language and Christian beliefs on a north-south axis while the Galla, who were often converts to Islam, spread from east to west. Migration, trade, intermarriage and assimilation brought the diverse groups together. The Amharas emerged in the 17th century as the dominant political leaders, and the Amharic language, with its own distinctive script, became the lingua franca. Closely linked to the religious hierarchy of the church, the Amhara monarchy extended its influence throughout much of the country.

Although subject to periodic warfare with the coastal Somali peoples controlling access to the Red Sea, Ethiopia remained largely aloof from the rest of the world until the latter part of the 19th century. Occasional Portuguese, French and English travelers penetrated the highlands, but it was not until Italy sought a foothold there that the independence of Ethiopia was seriously challenged. In 1896 Emperor Menelik II, rallying the assistance of even his greatest rivals within the country, decisively defeated the invading Italians at Adowa in northern Ethiopia. But he accepted Italy's continued presence in the area now known as Eritrea.

Ethiopia's modern development began with Menelik, who introduced the first roads, schools, electricity, postal service and railways—as well as adding thousands of square miles of new territory in the south and west. He was also the founder of the city of Addis Ababa (New Flower), the modern capital of Ethiopia.

Menelik died in 1913 and was followed by Lij Yasu, who was deposed in 1916, giving place to Empress Zauditu, with Ras Tafari of Harar as regent. With the death of Zauditu in 1930, Ras Tafari became ruler of Ethiopia as Haile Selassie I.

For more than four decades Haile Selassie—King of Kings, Elect of God, Conquering Lion of the Tribe of Judah—has been the dominant force in the country. Under his rule Ethiopia has moved toward effective national unity. He gave the country a constitution, a code of law and a system of justice, and he neutralized the feudal power of the many petty court nobles by nationalizing their private armies. Change and progress, however, have taken a slow and deliberate course in this land so closely geared to traditional values.

Haile Selassie's rule was interrupted in 1935 when Mussolini descended on the country to claim it for Italy. Mussolini's defeat nearly seven years later by a combination of Allied and Ethiopian forces brought the Emperor back to the throne with complete control of his country and an enhanced image in international councils.

Since then he has concentrated his efforts on modernizing his isolated country of 25 million without disrupting the traditional sources of its culture. The economy, based on coffee, hides, tourism, cattle, sugar and light industry, has made gains although hurt since 1967 by the closing of the Suez Canal. The Emperor has introduced many reforms in what remains an absolute monarchy in an aristocratic society, where land is controlled by the nobility and the church. Land reform is a highly controversial subject. Education has been expanded, but much remains to be done before national literacy reaches a satisfactory level.

The Emperor has astutely courted assistance from all corners of the world without compromising Ethiopia's independence. He attracted to Addis Ababa the headquarters of the Organization of African Unity (OAU) and other pan-African organizations, and he himself has been a determined peacemaker in intra-African conflicts. Challenged by a group of dissident university students and young army officers whose coup failed in 1960, the Emperor responded by increasing the prestige and salaries of the 40,000-man army and employing temporizing tactics with the students.

The northern province of Eritrea, an Italian protectorate for many years, which joined Ethiopia in 1952, has been the scene of a secession movement, primarily led by coastal Moslems. Although the Emperor has unified much of the country, Eritrea, with a tradition of education and prosperity, remains an area of discontent.

Born in 1892, His Imperial Majesty is still vigorous, but there is no doubt that the gravest problem facing Ethiopia is this: can any of his possible successors fit the mantle of this remarkable leader? On the answer to this question rests Ethiopia's destiny in the modern world.

Split by the Great Rift Valley, which cuts across Ethiopia and East Africa, the rugged terrain makes communications a constant problem. The central government carefully nurtures its administrative and physical control over the many groups that make up the Ethiopian population. The Galla are the most numerous and the least powerful group politically. The Amhara, light-skinned inhabitants of the central plateau, consider themselves the aristocrats of Ethiopia and occupy the most important posts in government. Their closest competitors for power are the northern Ethiopians called Tigreans. Along the Kenya, Sudan and Somalia borders live various herdsmen and nomads: the tall Borana people of the southern areas and the fierce Danakil of the northeast are probably the best known to tourists.

Three excellent books on Ethiopia (none of which is available inside Ethiopia) are: anthropologist Donald Levine's *Wax and Gold* (University of Chicago Press, 1965), a description of Amhara values and culture; Christopher Clapham's *Haile Selassie's Government* (Praeger, 1969), a candid account of the political scene, including rich detail on who is who; and historian Robert L. Hess's *Ethiopia, the Modernization of Autocracy* (Cornell University Press, paperback, 1970), a good broad introduction to the country.

Ethiopian Airlines and the Ethiopian Tourist Organization have a number of attractive free brochures available describing touristic attractions and cultural traditions, as well as a delightful Amharic-English phrase book. The airline has offices in New York and Los Angeles.

Money Matters

Ethiopia bases its money on the decimal system. The Ethiopian dollar, written Eth$1, is worth 43 US cents. The bills and coins resemble those in the States, with the exception of the rather more exotic 25-cent piece, which is fluted like a pie. Import of currency is unrestricted, but one cannot take more than Eth$100 out of the country. Whatever Ethiopian currency you have left at the end of your stay can either be exchanged, or used (up to Eth$100 worth) at the duty-free shops in the Addis Ababa and Asmara airports.

All foreign exchange transactions are handled by the National Bank of Ethiopia, whose offices are open between 9 and noon on weekdays. Travelers checks from well-known banks will be cashed by many of the leading hotels, restaurants and shops, and major credit cards are also acceptable.

Although imported goods are expensive, Ethiopia in general offers its wares, services and accommodations at very attractive prices.

Getting In and Out

Ethiopian visa and customs formalities are truly simple. A visa will be granted on arrival to any traveler from the US, Canada, the United Kingdom and most Western European countries on presentation of an ongoing ticket and the necessary health certificates (inoculation against yellow fever, cholera and smallpox).

From the US or Europe or the East, of course, one enters Ethiopia by air or boat. Ethiopian Airlines has connections to points that include Beirut, Paris, Rome, Frankfurt and Bombay (the old Karachi and Delhi connections may be reactivated when that part of the world cools down). The closing of the Suez Canal has made sea voyages to Ethiopia lengthy and costly. Passenger service on freighters from Europe to the Red Sea ports of Massawa and Assab is available on the Polish Ocean Lines, Yugoslav Jadranska Slobodna Polovidba Lines out of Rijika and Trieste, the West German Hansa Line, and the Hellenic Line. A quicker and cheaper cruise would be on an Israeli freighter from Eilat across the Red Sea to Massawa.

From African points one flies into Ethiopia by a choice of airlines, connecting three times a week with Accra and Lagos, and more frequently with Cairo, Khartoum and Nairobi. The road trip is the hard way, up through Kenya by four-wheel-drive vehicle. This latter course is recommended only to the hardy, since the "road" is less than that at some points, and various perils await. For details on planning such a trip, write to Ato Lemma Gebregyorgis at the Ethiopian Tourist Organization, P.O. Box 2183, Addis Ababa.

More and more charter flights and tours are becoming available, including some especially attractive package arrangements that include Israel, Ethiopia and East Africa, or Ethiopia, East Africa and India.

The Chemin de Fer Franco-Ethiopien operates passenger and freight service between Addis Ababa and Djibouti (Territory of the Afars and Issas—old French Somaliland) via Dire Dawa, a pleasant 36-hour journey. One can travel up to Djibouti by day-coach for about US$40, with an overnight stop in Dire Dawa. The night trains are fairly comfortable. Fares differ according to the privacy of the sleeping accommodations. Such attractions as colorfully clad tribeswomen selling fruit at the train stops, passing camel caravans, and at least the suspicion that desert shifta (bandits) may pop up at any minute make this an exciting journey. And the lunch at the Awash Station Buffet de la Gare is always a treat.

Getting Around Within Ethiopia

Self-drive car hire is available in all the larger population centers through travel agencies and the Ethiopian Tourist Organization. Both Hertz and Avis serve Addis Ababa. Chauffeur-driven cars are also easy to arrange for, with some notice. Rates vary. Driving is on the right-hand side of the road, and an international license is good to have, though not necessary if your US license is valid.

Ethiopian Airlines offers a bargain US$99 ticket for 21 days of unlimited air travel within the country. You can purchase it through the United Touring Company of Addis Ababa, P.O. Box 3092.

Ethiopian Airlines crews and ground staff have been trained mainly by TWA and are ready to handle anything from 707 jets to the sturdy DC-3's that serve the mountainous interior. In-flight meals and service are good. They also run an inexpensive bus service from airports to downtown hotels.

Elsewhere, buses are also inexpensive—15 Ethiopian cents for a one-way ticket to any spot in downtown Addis Ababa, and only a few dollars for trips into the countryside (one way to Asmara from Addis Ababa, for example, is only about US$10). Though a short trip on a downtown bus can be quite pleasant, a long overland trip may be less so; roads are not always well maintained, particularly during the rugged weather from June to September, and some buses are packed like matchboxes and local music blares non-stop from speakers attached to the bus roof. Word has it, however, that if you must go by bus, the Sati Bus Company, with offices in Addis Ababa's Mercato section, provides the most comfortable and reliable service. For most visitors, travel by car or plane will be the most satisfactory ways to cover long distances.

In Addis Ababa, the popular means of transportation is the little "seicento"—the blue-and-white Fiat that roars up and honks to attract fares. Never get into a "taxi" that does not have the word on its license plate, and never start off without fixing your fare in advance. Most taxi drivers will ask the obvious visitor for anything from 50 Ethiopian cents to a dollar to take him to a city destination, but the going rate is 25 cents—no more, unless the distance is unusually great. The word to use is "Hayámust" (25 cents). "Hámsa" means 50, and "Ant birt" a dollar. Usually a driver who has asked too much will back down with a grin if you stick to "Hayámust." Don't take a taxi after dark, unless you get it through one of the better hotels such as the Hilton. Hotel taxi rates are slightly higher than public rates, but the difference in safety is worth it.

In Asmara "gharries," little one-horse carts with gay paint or tassels, will take you about for a dollar or two. Bicycles (which can be rented) are a favorite means of transport through Asmara's well-paved and graded streets. In Addis Ababa, one occasionally sees a cyclist puffing up a hill or careening down one, but generally speaking the city is not suitable for bikes, both because of the steep hills and because few side roads are smooth enough.

Hitchhiking is up to you and to the risks you are willing to take. In the city few people bother to pick up hitchhikers; in the country there are probably more opportunities.

Walking remains the best way to cover distances by daylight in Ethiopia. Night walking is not recommended, for safety's sake.

Where to Stay

(Prices shown here are in US currency.)

ADDIS ABABA: There are many good places here for the tourist on a restricted budget. To start with the most reasonable, try the YMCA, near Arat Kilo (tel. 13455), where rooms are available from $3.20. The best of the lower-priced hotels are the *Guenet*, *Itegue*, and *Plaza*, where a single room can cost as little as $3.20 to $4. The *Hegue*, which caters mostly to students, has good Ethiopian food and a fine view of the city. The *Ras*, which one might call the Algonquin of Addis for its literary associations (Evelyn Waugh stayed there and described it in his comic novel *Scoop*) and its lively clientele, offers single rooms from $7.60. The Ras has a congenial bar where you can meet a non-jet international set including American and Israeli technical experts and US Peace Corps Volunteers, professional hunters and wandering journalists.

Up the status scale are the *Wabe Shebelle*, *Ethiopia* and *Ghion*, with rooms from $10. At the top, of course, is the *Addis Hilton*, with its tennis courts, boutiques, pool and $13 minimum tariff.

Camping out in public parks or pastoral areas in the city is not recommended, because of the danger of mugging. Reservations should be made in advance at all Addis hotels, if possible, since diplomatic meetings often fill the city's accommodations.

ASMARA: The *Nyala* and *Imperial* hotels are the best in Asmara, and charge just about the same rates as the Wabe Shebelle and Addis Hilton. *Albergo Italia*, close to downtown areas, is much more simpatico and has excellent food. *Albergo Ciaao*, an old hotel that stands near the Provincial Palace, is clean and relatively comfortable, but one cannot get a good night's sleep there when the governor's noisy lions decide to stay up late. Both Ciaao and Italia charge from about $6.40.

Alternatives, if cash is low, are the *White* (single, $4) and the *Hamasien* ($2.40), both quite acceptable. Again, reservations are recommended. There are various pensions available, with rooms as low as $2.

MASSAWA: The *Red Sea Hotel* is beautiful but expensive ($10 for a single). The restaurant here features a superb bouillabaisse. The *Mira Mare* is just about in the same class. Rates at the *Corallo* begin at $5.60. (These hotels have air-conditioning, important because temperatures sometimes hit 120 degrees here.) Many small hotels, the best of which is probably the *Luna*, charge $4 or even less.

ASSAB: The *AGIP* provides excellent service, clean rooms and good meals; singles begin at $6.40. The *Starlite* is also recommended; prices about the same as at the AGIP.

Other Cities: Surprisingly good accommodations are to be found in unlikely rural outposts. The *Abraha Castle* in MEKELLE, Tigre Province, is a case in point—rooms begin at $3.60. The *Ras Hotel* chain runs comfortable hotels (though management varies) in DIRE DAWA, HARAR, BAHAR DAR, AMBO and WOLLISSO. At all the Rift Valley lake resorts cottage complexes offer the visitor comfort and relaxation. The *Grand Hotel* at BISHOFTU and the *Galila Palace* at KOKA DAM, with regular hotel accommodations, are also extremely good.

Students and other budget-conscious travelers will find simple, decent accommodations widespread in Ethiopia at rock-bottom prices. These include the *Touring Hotel* and the *Ras Mengesha* in AXUM, the *Fasil Hotel* in GONDAR and the *Blue Nile Hotel* in BAHAR DAR.

Where and What to Eat

(Prices in US currency.)

As elsewhere in the developing world, fruits and fresh uncooked vegetables present a problem to health unless they have been carefully washed and chlorinated before serving. Peel all fruits anyhow. Raw meat is a no-no, ditto rare and medium-rare. Water is undrinkable all over the Empire unless boiled for 15 minutes; learn to like Ambo, Babile and the other popular mineral waters. Be sure the bottle of mineral water has not been opened before it gets to your table.

The staple dishes of Ethiopia are injerra and wat. Injerra is a pleasant, spongy bread made from teff, a local millet-like grain; wat, a spicy stew of chicken, beef, other meats, or vegetables, is usually seasoned with berberré, a red-hot mixture reminiscent of 100-proof chili powder. If you want a mild dish, ask for alecha wat, which has no berberré, but is moderately spiced with cumin and other herbs. The *Addis Ababa Restaurant*, replete with local color, including the basketware tables called mesobs and folkloric dancers and musicians, is supposed to be the best among the many "national restaurants" in the city. Certainly it is picturesque, for it is quartered in an old thatch-roofed house dating back to the time of Menelik II.

Liquor is expensive in Ethiopia. A good shot of Scotch costs about $1.20 and a bottle $10 or $12. The local wines are excellent and cheap—$1 to $1.20 a bottle for reds like Holletta Rosso and Dukam, slightly less for Guder, Sarris and Makanissa. (Dukam is the best of the lot—a satisfying, full-bodied wine). Tokaj dei Colli, a fruity light wine, is excellent; Claret of Abadir, the only local wine available in a split bottle, is exceptionally fine, but a bit more expensive. Rosatello is a good compromise for the mixed menu. The local sauterne-type wines range from undistinguished to unpalatable. Fenili, an Asmara distillery, makes very acceptable gin and brandy, as well as a wide range of liqueurs and cordials, all reasonably priced. Ethiopia's indigenous beverages—tej, a mead-like distillation of honey, and tella, light beer—are worth trying. Meta and Melotti make the best local commercial beers.

If you are invited to a well-to-do Ethiopian home, you are in for a rare treat. Food is served from the mesob, or basketwork table. Wat is placed on injerra, and eaten with the fingers. Various delicious side dishes, including vegetable and seed mixtures, a soft curd-like cheese resembling ricotta, and of course tej, will accompany the main course. If your host or hostess places bits of food in your mouth by hand, don't refuse—this is a special honor ("gursha"—the same word that is used to mean a gratuity). Eat lightly at first; Ethiopian meals go on and on, and your plate will be filled over and over again—for this too is meant to show honor to the guest. If asked for 8 pm, don't arrive till 8:30. Only the poor, who need a meal, are expected to be on time. For the more fortunate, meals are above all an occasion of politeness and social intercourse.

Restaurants in ADDIS ABABA: Most hotels serve breakfast, lunch, tea and supper. You can eat well in Addis Ababa for less than $4 a day—much less. When hotel food palls, try the following: The Cottage, near the Ethiopia Hotel, lunches and suppers from $1.20, excellent music and food. The Kokeb, next door to Africa Hall, lunches and suppers from $1.60, good food and interesting decor, accent on Ethiopian art. The Villa Verde, off the Bishoftu Road near town, excellent Italian food, and on Tuesdays fresh prawns from the Red Sea, from $1.20. La Taverna at the ReCe Recreation Center off the Bole Airport Road, gourmet Italian food served with style and care, from $2. The China Bar, near the Ghion Hotel and the Hong Kong, off Churchill Road, excellent Northern Chinese lunches and dinners at reasonable prices. The Omar Khayyam, excellent and inexpensive Middle Eastern food in an intimate setting, and, like the equally good Vieux Logis, away from the center of town.

For the slim wallet: *Chez Nourses*, an upstairs spot in the Piazza across from the British Council, for shish kebab and similar delicacies—fill up for under 80 cents. *Oroscopo*, on General Wingate Street off the Piazza, where Signora Emma will feed you from the tavola calda (hot buffet table) for 80 cents or so. *Castelli's* in the Piazza, tavola calda selection for about $1.20, as well as lasagna, veal marsala and local dishes.

Good stops for snacks, cappuccino, pastries: the two *Rendezvous* restaurants—one located in the new post office complex, one in the Finfinné Building at Meskal Square (both central locations). A very passable hamburger or cheeseburger can be bought at either Rendezvous. At this writing the post office Rendezvous is the meeting spot for young international types, travelers off the beaten track, and live wires of every variety—a sort of Ras Hotel Bar for the Coca-Cola set.

ASMARA is heaven for those who like Italian cuisine. Some say that the cuisine at the *Caravel* restaurant is the best in Asmara. *Albergo Italia* is certainly near the top—at $2 or so. *Ristorante da Rino*, downtown, is reasonable—lunch for $1.20, dinner or supper for $2—and absolutely great. The *Imperial* and *Nyala Hotel* dining rooms turn out very fine meals, though the prices are relatively high—$2.40 at least for supper. *Ciaao Hotel* has heavy, dreary dinners, but breakfast is not bad, and they serve prosciutto-like ham that is a delight, as well as delicious omelets.

In MASSAWA, the *Red Sea Hotel* has marvelous, though expensive, meals. The *Luna Hotel*, also Italian cuisine, is more reasonable.

Those who know say that no finer Italian meals can be found than at the *AGIP* in ASSAB, however unlikely that may sound. Prices from $1.20.

In DIRE DAWA, the *Ras Hotel* serves medium-priced, medium-good meals, but "Sabean's" or the *Pensione Omedla* is a great place for family-style Italian cooking—each meal with four or five courses and wine, about $1.60. After dinner, walk to *Courides*, near the railway station, for ice cream, or visit the outdoor *Leuel Ras Makonnen Bar* in the same area.

Tip five per cent in restaurants.

What to See and Do

ADDIS ABABA is a bustling city with a growing population now close to one million. The historic 'seat of the Amhara monarchy, its palaces, churches and cathedrals mingle with striking modern buildings housing international organizations and thousands of the one- and two-room mud and wattle dwellings that shelter its burgeoning population.

Some of the sights: The National Museum, the Ethnological Museum, the new Museum of Natural History, the Institute of Ethiopian Studies, the Haile Selassie I University, the Lion Zoo (where the royal pets can be seen) and Trinity and St. George cathedrals (at Arat Kilo and Meskal Square, respectively). Palace tours can be arranged with the assistance of the Ethiopian Tourist Organization. The Mercato, Ethiopia's largest open-air market, lies in the older part of town, an inexpensive taxi jaunt from most hotels.

The modern face of Addis is reflected in the new government office buildings: the Commercial Bank; the stunning glass skyscraper called Africa Hall, which houses the United Nations Economic Commission for Africa (ECA) and is graced by the stained-glass windows of Afework Tekle and murals by other distinguished artists; and the tall home of the Organization of African Unity. It is good to check the *Ethiopian Herald* each day to see what meetings are being held, what international conference may be on. Often visitors are welcome.

Daily tours of the city are offered by the United Touring Company and other travel agencies.

There are several attractive day or overnight trips from Addis into the surrounding countryside. These can be made inexpensively by local bus or collective taxi or by renting a car or taking an excursion offered by the United Touring Company (UTC), tel. 45609, the Sheba Travel Bureau, tel. 11785, or the Axum Travel Agency, tel. 47907, Addis.

A popular resort is the Koka Dam area, 50 miles southeast of Addis. Here one can picnic under wild fig trees and watch the hippopotamuses in the Awash River below. A 35-mile drive northwest of the capital leads to Mulu Farm, the gift of His Imperial Majesty to Brigadier-General Sanford of Britain, where strawberries are available at Christmas time. Another easy 35-mile drive from Addis leads to Melka Konture, site of a rich prehistoric archaeological dig along the Awash River.

South of Addis is the Lake District, named after a series of lovely mountainous crater lakes in the Rift Valley. A favorite excursion is to the pretty town of Debre Zeit, where there is a hotel overlooking Lake Bishoftu. Farther south for sun and swimming are the mineral baths at Sodere and the Belle Vue du Lac Hotel on Lake Awasa, with a tennis court and inexpensive hut accommodations.

Recreation in Addis is varied. There is a golf club and there are riding facilities (both the Imperial stables behind the Ghion Hotel and a place called Guido's on the Makanissa Road rent horses reasonably). The pool at the Ghion is available free to guests and by ticket to the public, but at the Hilton one must have a year's membership (at US$80) or be a guest or guest of a guest to get in. Tennis courts are open to the public at the Ghion, closed to all but guests at the Hilton.

If nostalgia overcomes you, go out and throw a baseball or football around the American School compound fields off the Jimma Road. You will find other Americans there doing the same. Ask around the Ras Hotel Bar, the China Bar or the small bar in the Ghion—usually someone will be happy to let you be his guest at the recreational facilities there—or will at least tell you how to get in. The Juventus (Italian) and Olympiacos (Greek) Clubs have tennis, squash and other courts and are not too rigid about requirements for entrance.

Soccer football has become a national pastime, and the stadium in Addis is likely to be packed on Sunday for a local or international match. Ethiopians have also developed a passion for long-distance running, especially since their victories at the 1968 Mexico City Olympics. Championship track meets are another local attraction. Polo matches between military teams bring out the elite.

In Addis Ababa everyone entertains, whether at home or at a night spot. Dinner-dancing at the Ras, Hilton, Ghion and Wabe Shebelle is very popular. Ditto the less expensive evening spent at the Sheba, the Zebra, the Disco, the Marathon, the Venus Underground and other low-priced night spots. Discotheques and bars with combos charge a small cover, usually less than US$2. La Mascotte is Addis's sole strip club, with European talent.

Several movie theaters in Addis run almost-new films. The Haile Selassie I Theater gives very interesting folkloric performances, as well as serving as the showplace for traveling artists from all over Europe and the Middle East. Live classical music is rare, and most plays are on an amateur level, with the exception of those given in Amharic by the National Theatre.

The Goethe-Institut, British Council, Alliance Française and USIS will let you know what cultural events they are planning.

Traditional Ethiopian music, which like the language and literature is rich and unique, can be heard daily on both Voice of the Gospel and Radio Ethiopia. Records and cassettes are found at various music shops, the best of which are in the Harambee chain.

For the lone wolf, there are hundreds of little bars where music, liquor and companions are available. Most of the dance halls are out on the Bishoftu (Debre Zeit) Road, close to town. A "tej-bet" is a small bar selling only the local beverages and snacks; a "metat-bet" has music and a larger selection of liquor. In spite of the advice of old Africa hands to find cheap lodgings in the "Desert" or other red light districts of Addis, the budget-watching newcomer will be far better off to drink up his tej and go home, alone or not, to one of the many reasonably-priced hotels in Addis that offer at least a minimum of cleanliness and security.

ASMARA night life is almost non-existent except for the little bars. There are two low-priced nightclubs—the Mocambo and Picadilly. The Caravel restaurant sometimes holds a dinner-dance on Saturday night. Asmara's recreational picture is pretty bleak too. Contact the Chamber of Commerce there and ask advice.

MASSAWA is much livelier. The Trocadero, Marina, Torino, Alhambra and other small bars offer recorded dance music, and the town stays up late. The Red Sea Rest House, a military facility, welcomes the occasional traveler for dinner and drinks; prices are very reasonable, and many English-speaking people go there to meet friends. In Massawa and the nearby Dahlak Islands scuba diving and swimming are the sports. Green Island, an offshore paradise for picnics, can be reached by rowboat. Gurgusum Beach, near Massawa, is planning bigger facilities to accommodate its popularity. Make all arrangements for equipment, accommodation and boats with local firms.

There are several large cinemas in Asmara and two in tiny Massawa. Films have Italian, Hindustani, French, English and other subtitles.

In DIRE DAWA, various small bars feature canned music, and the Ras Hotel holds an occasional dinner-dance.

For the historically and archaeologically inclined, Ethiopia offers several points of interest. Along the so-called Historic Route, which Ethiopian Airlines services at a special tourist round trip rate of $71 for 14 days, lies the heartland of Ethiopian civilization: AXUM, cradle of Ethiopian culture and capital of the legendary Queen of Sheba; GONDAR, fortress city of Fasilidas; LALIBELA, where rockhewn churches built by kings and their angelic helpers form a "New Jerusalem"; BAHAR DAR, site of Lake Tana's island monasteries and Tisisat, the Blue Nile falls. (This trip should be avoided during the "big rains," June to September, as some sites may be inaccessible.)

East of Addis and accessible by air, road and rail, are the cities of DIRE DAWA and HARAR, reached by descending from the steep plateau to the 3,000-foot lowlands near the border with Somalia. Harar is an ancient walled city whose sacred places were entered by Sir Richard Burton, one of the first Westerners to do so, only 80 years ago. It is no longer a "forbidden city," but its charm remains unspoiled and uncommercialized. The site of a government agricultural college (at nearby Lake Alemaya) and a large military training school, it has two colorful markets. A favorite tourist attraction is the Hyena Man, who feeds his nocturnal friends by the light of the moon along the city walls. Dire Dawa, 30 miles north of Harar, is a large, pleasant market town and rail stop. Its wide streets, mosques and shops are best explored by walking.

The trip to Gondar can be combined with an exploratory visit to Lake Tana, source of the Blue Nile. Boat trips by reed boat or "tanqua" can be arranged to many of the island monasteries, and a short jaunt takes one to the Blue Nile Tisisat Falls, which an early explorer called "one of the most stupendous sights in the Creation." A little less than that, they are still memorable and not to be missed. The hotels will book a Land Rover or taxi for $4; the local bus is slow, but only charges 40 cents. (Both fares are round trip.) Near Gondar is AMBOBER, the main center for Ethiopia's Falashas, or "Black Jews," a hospitable people who live a simple rural life attuned to a special form of Judaism based on their own traditions and the Pentateuch. Falasha potters make unique statuettes combining human, angelic and animal characteristics that can be bought cheaply by visitors. These humorous figures are found nowhere else in Ethiopia and collectors prize them. In recent years the dwindling Falasha population has received agricultural and educational assistance from the Israeli Government as part of Israel's extensive economic and technical aid programs in Ethiopia.

The nearly 700-mile drive from Addis Ababa to Asmara traverses the heart of Ethiopia, a grueling but rewarding three-day trip by road or a one-hour flight by Ethiopian Airlines jet. During the dry season side trips are possible along the way to Lalibela and to the ruins of Axum. A city of 250,000 with a large Italian population, Asmara has a distinctly Mediterranean flavor. The city is prosperous, but it is quiet compared to Addis, and the Eritrean secession movement has made it a politically sensitive area with a substantial Ethiopian military presence.

A spectacular 80-mile railway and road descends 6,500 feet from Asmara to the Red Sea port of Massawa. The bus trip costs US$1 each way. As one plunges down the escarpment, military roadblocks are there to remind the traveler of the Eritrean secessionist guerrillas in the area. The air trip is cheap enough, however, and provides a good chance to view the rugged country more safely.

Massawa and its neighboring smaller port of ASSAB are Ethiopia's only outlets to the sea on its own territory. The main Ethiopian naval training base is located here. There are attractive beaches (Gurgusum is the favorite) and good beds of coral with lots of multicolored fish and mollusks for scuba divers off Green Island. Fishing jaunts can be arranged locally.

Ethiopia's natural wonders rival its historic and religious treasures. The High Semyen Mountains in the north beckon the adventurous camper and rock climber. The nation's highest peak, 15,000-foot Mount Ras Dashan (fourth highest in Africa), offers a proper challenge to mountaineers. So does the mountain-top Monastery of Debre Damo, entered only by rope ladder—and then only if you are a man, since not even female animals are allowed within its precincts.

The Omo River Valley of southern Ethiopia, which adjoins the northern Kenya border, is an unspoiled paradise for hunters and photographers as well as the site of exciting new excavations of early man. Free from the commercialism of the typical East African safari spot, the Omo area offers rare species of animals and birds, great herds of kudu, zebra, oryx and the like, and above all, solitude and the sense of adventure. A safari there should probably take a week or two. Write to the Ethiopian Tourist Organization, P.O. 2183, Addis Ababa for information including visits to the prehistoric excavations currently under way.

The *Awash Game Reserve*, a short day's journey from Addis by train or Land Rover, is another exciting place to go with gun or camera. Write the Manager, Wanza Lodge, P.O. Box 3593, Addis Ababa for details on the accommodations there. Ted Shatto, who has been leading safaris in Ethiopia for many years, has a permanent camp with great food at the Awash. His address is P.O. Box 1745, Addis Ababa.

GAMBELA, the jumping-off point for safaris into the game-rich area of Illubabor Province, is the stamping ground of Tom Mattanovich. He can be contacted for reservations or information at P. O. Box 2444, Addis Ababa.

Wildlife and hunting, monasteries and ruins—but there is a changing, modernizing Ethiopia as well. Those interested can explore its new agriculture, growing industry, and export-oriented crafts with the assistance of the Ethiopian Tourist Organization and the relevant government ministries. The College of Agriculture has its experimental field station at beautiful Lake Alemaya near Harar, and the Ministry of Agriculture is pleased to show visitors various model farms and other projects.

Most large factories welcome visitors, as do some traditional art and weaving shops. The Ethiopian Pottery Workshop on the Bole Road in Addis Ababa is a fascinating place for buying and browsing. Ethiopia possesses an impressive hydroelectric potential that is just being tapped at the Tisisat Falls on the Blue Nile and elsewhere. Visits to power stations and project sites can be arranged.

While modernization advances, Ethiopia remains a country influenced to a great extent by its church. Religious festivals are general holidays, with special events, pageantry and celebrations. The official calendar is that of the Ethiopian Church, based on a 13-month lunar year with a plethora of feasts and fasting days. The most important of the feast days is "Timkat," or Epiphany, January 19-20. "Meskal," or the Finding of the True Cross (September 26-27), is a day of giddy rejoicing, on which a huge bonfire festooned with flowers is ignited by the Emperor in Addis Ababa, while the entire army parades and sings, and floats depicting Ethiopia's history roll past. Easter, a week later than the European feast, marks the end of rigorous fasting and is appropriately given over to eating and drinking. Ethiopian Christmas, or "Genna," celebrated on January 7, is really a minor festival, though in Addis Ababa, at least, it bears some of the earmarks of the commercialized Western holiday. Other national and religious festivals are February 19, Martyrs' Day; March 2, commemorating the 1896 Battle of Adowa and Italian defeat; May 5, Liberation Day (Second World War); July 23, Birthday of the Emperor; August 22, Feast of the Assumption; September 11, New Year on the Ethiopian calendar and November 2, Coronation Day.

What to Buy

Ethiopia is a shopper's dream, bursting with fine merchandise at low prices and variety that boggles the mind. Shopping is fun in the giant open-air Mercato in Addis or its smaller counterparts elsewhere. Bargaining is the rule outside the hotels and boutiques, but it is all conducted in good fun and with enjoyment on both sides. Gold and silver work abounds in traditional jewelry, religious crosses, medallions, bracelets, necklaces and countless other forms. Other excellent buys are traditional musical instruments, ikons and other religious relics, and the splendidly detailed frieze panels depicting historical and religious subjects in Ethiopian settings. These paintings as well as Biblical scrolls and other souvenirs can be purchased in the religious centers from the craftsmen themselves or from itinerant merchants. Hides, skins and animal trophies should be bought from licensed taxidermists only, as a cooperative gesture to Ethiopia's conservation efforts. Rugs, baskets and leather work are excellent buys in the outdoor markets.

Start bargaining by remembering that the seller will first ask at least four times what he is willing to take.

Addis Ababa is an increasingly cosmopolitan city with the beginnings of high-fashion shops. Woizero Tsion Andom is Ethiopia's leading dress designer, and her boutique, Tsion Tibeb, located at Meskal Square, is the finest shop offering handwoven Ethiopian materials made into either traditional or high-fashion wear. The lovely Ethiopian fabrics available elsewhere at weavers' shops make striking gifts for use in scarves or light dresses. The jewelry of Teclu Desta in the Piazza is justly famous. Art galleries tend to come and go like shooting stars but the Belvedere Gallery in the Piazza goes on and on, and one can find first-rate arts and crafts there at reasonable fixed prices. Ethiopia's national artist-laureate, Afework

Tekle, has his Studio Alfa in Addis; it can be visited by arrangement. Gebre Kristos Desta, Ethiopia's leading abstractionist, can be contacted through the Addis Ababa Art School. The talented artist Gebros Mehdrin teaches at the Haile Selassie I University, where his work and that of other modern Ethiopian artists can be seen.

The government Craft Centre in Addis is a good place to see a general display of the nation's wares and to arrange, if interested, to visit the workshop of individual craftsmen, including the potters on the Bole Road.

The duty-free shops at the Addis and Asmara airports have an extremely broad range of merchandise, with many imported items, including sound equipment, ready-to-wear suits and jewelry at good prices. For last-minute shopping, one can find traditional Ethiopian crafts too.

Local Attitudes

The political climate of the country is generally comfortable for the visitor provided that he accepts the prevailing order. Radicals will be well advised to keep a low profile, keeping in mind an African proverb that "no flies enter a closed mouth."

The US Army and Air Force Communications Station at Kagnew near Asmara is due to be phased out, but the American presence in Ethiopia is still substantial, and this evokes some resentment among Ethiopian radicals.

The chief characteristics of the Ethiopian temperament are pride and independence. Colonial attitudes will meet here the scorn they deserve— if not some stronger reaction. Remember that most Ethiopians devoutly believe that their Emperor is the scion of Solomon and Sheba. Keep your sense of humor at all times to cope with small frustrations, and keep in mind that Ethiopia is a place where things move slowly, geared to an inner clock at least 3,000 years old. If the traveler realizes this, he will be better able to relax and enjoy his stay.

Religious tolerance is the rule, though Orthodox Christianity is the official state religion. Behavior in Orthodox churches means no slacks or shorts, and women should cover their heads, although this is not absolutely essential. Many churches, especially monasteries, are closed to women, and this rule must be respected. Cameras are tolerated in churches, but some worshippers may be offended. Removing the shoes before entering an Orthodox church, as in a mosque, is a graceful gesture that few visitors seem to know about. It raises murmurs of approval and smiles, and the visitor is much more likely to be ushered up to the front places of vantage.

Weather, What to Wear, How Long to Stay

Take Ethiopia as you find it. Adjust your clothes to the climate, which varies from natural steam heat at Massawa on the Red Sea to almost freezing evenings at times in Addis. If you plan to visit the highlands, sweaters will be needed. Bring light rain gear for the "small" rains from February to April and for the "big" ones from June to September, when it rains for at least a small part of every day, though in between showers it may be sunny and warm.

Light to medium weight suits are appropriate for men and most Western wear is acceptable for women. Miniskirts are worn everywhere, but in rural areas they may evoke catcalls from the young and stern looks from elders. Formal occasions in Addis are very formal: cocktail or evening dresses for ladies, dark suits and even tuxedos for men. Bring an umbrella and good comfortable shoes. Clothing replacements in large sizes are difficult to find, but the Piazza stores in Addis can supply most necessities.

Don't drink the water but do breathe the air—it's absolutely pollution-free, a joy and an elixir.

The many package tours available provide everything from a few days to a month in Ethiopia. Addis alone is worth several days, and the historic circuit of Gondar, Harar, Lalibela and Axum deserves another week at least. Traveling in Ethiopia can be strenuous due to the altitude and it is best to go slowly. Try to avoid the season of big rains, when roads wash out and the going gets gooey. There is enough in Ethiopia to justify making it the focal point of your trip to Africa. It's like no place else—but it's changing fast, so hurry.

Communication

Amharic is the official national language and is spoken throughout the country. English is taught in all the schools and is the second language of instruction in secondary schools and the Haile Selassie I University. It is widely spoken and there is little reason for the casual visitor to learn Amharic phrases, though it is a politeness that will pay off in hospitality and better service. The traditional Amharic greeting is *tenastiling*, which changes to *salaam* in the more Moslem north. *Ishi* means "O.K.," and *yellum* means "no." *Zimma!* will effectively summon a waiter. Italian is a help in the northern provinces of Tigre and Eritrea, though even here English-only speakers can get by.

The government publishes a morning English-language newspaper, the *Ethiopian Herald*, six days a week, as well as the evening *Addis Soir* in French. Both give the official line, as does *Addis Zemen* in Amharic. The Ministry of Information controls communications, cutting some imported films and banning an occasional publication. The Cosmos, Menno and Giannopolous bookshops in Addis have a wide range of imported and local periodicals, including some of the school texts in English issued by the Ethiopian government.

Radio Ethiopia broadcasts in Amharic, several other Ethiopian languages and English, and offers both popular Western and Ethiopian music as well as an occasional program of classics and complete operas. It, too, is controlled by the government. Freer and extremely informative is the daily Radio Voice of the Gospel, a Protestant missionary enterprise that provides its listeners with news, commentary and music, both classical and popular. Television is mostly confined to Addis and its imported features include "Superman" and "The Forsyte Saga." Best local gossip is found in the bars of the Ras Hotel and Cottage Restaurant in Addis and in some of the other popular night spots.

The domestic and international postal service is reasonably good. Allow three to seven days for airmail between Addis Ababa and North America. Send any valuable items air freight via Ethiopian Airlines. Phones are a problem within and between cities but service is improving. In early 1973 a new six-digit dialing system started.

Emergencies

In case of a medical emergency while in Addis Ababa, call the Empress Zauditu Hospital (tel. 48085). It is a Seventh Day Adventist facility staffed by American physicians. There are many other hospitals, but this is by most accounts the best (they use disposable needles), though Princess Tsehaye Hospital's British doctors enjoy a fine reputation too. The United States Embassy at Crown Prince Asfa Wassen Street in Addis Ababa (tel. 10666) has a list of physicians, as does the US Consulate in Asmara at 32 Franklin D. Roosevelt Street (tel. 10855). The Empress Zauditu has a good pharmacy. Also well stocked are the Lion Pharmacy on the Old Churchill Road; the Hilson, next door to the Ethiopian Tourist Organization, and the Central Pharmacy, next door to the Haile Selassie I Theatre entrance, near the Ras Hotel. Most common pharmaceutical products, including birth control pills, are imported and available without prescription though expensive.

Health note: Much of Ethiopia is a high plateau. If your doctor feels that you will encounter physical distress at 8,000 feet or so, stay away from Addis Ababa, Asmara and the High Semyen Mountains, and concentrate on the lowland cities of Dire Dawa, Harar and Massawa.

Libya

(Libyan Arab Republic)

Profile

STATUS: Independent since 1951, first as a federal kingdom; king deposed in September, 1969, and republic established under military rule. Entered loose federation with Egypt and Syria in 1971.

SIZE: 685,000 square miles (a fifth the size of the US). Population—2,000,000 (Arab with small Berber, Tuareg and black minorities).

GEOGRAPHY: Three regions—Tripolitania, Cyrenaica, Fezzan. Varied topography with long stretch of Mediterranean coast, plateaus and extensive lowland which is mainly desert. Principal cities—Tripoli (in Tripolitania, 250,000), Benghazi (in Cyrenaica, 150,000).

CLIMATE: Typically hot and dry year round, with substantial contrasts between day and night temperatures. July to September temperatures in Tripolitania reach over 100 degrees. Winter (November to March) coastal temperatures cooler. Cyrenaica somewhat milder than Tripolitania. Fezzan uniformly hot and dry with cooling evening winds.

LANGUAGES: Arabic (official), some residual Italian and English.

CURRENCY: Libyan dinar divided into 1000 dirhams. 1 dinar = $3.07; $1.00 = 325 dirhams.

VISAS: Required. Available only from Embassy of Libya in Washington. Fee $5.60 (up to 30 days). Two passport photos needed. Two or three days' wait. Extensions available from immigration offices in Tripoli, Benghazi, Sebha.

AIRPORTS: Tripoli (TIP), 21 miles from city, and Benghazi (BEN), 18 miles from city. Frequent connections with Rome, London, Paris, Amsterdam, Athens, Malta, Beirut, Cairo. Airport departure tax—international, 500 dirhams ($1.54). Free bus service from both airports to major hotels.

NATIONAL HOLIDAYS: March 28; May 25; June 11; July 23; September 1, Anniversary of the 1969 coup; September 24, 1971 Federation with Egypt; Moslem holidays.

INFORMATION SOURCES: *In US*—Embassy of the Libyan Arab Republic, 2344 Massachusetts Avenue NW, Washington, D.C. 20008 (tel. 202/232-1315); Permanent Mission of the Libyan Arab Republic to the UN, 866 United Nations Plaza, New York, N.Y. 10017 (tel 212/752-5775). *In Tripoli*—General Board of Tourism and airline offices.

By Aaron Segal

Only the most enterprising traveler will take on Libya. It helps to have a passion for archaeology or power politics and a relative indifference to creature comforts and cold shoulders.

Since its tough young army officers seized power in September, 1969, Libya has become militantly pan-Arabic and pan-Islamic. This means that if you are not one of the faithful, fluent in the language of the Koran, you may be less than welcome. The regime has decreed that all street signs and other public notices must appear only in Arabic, and if that kind of thing drives you to drink you're out of luck because alcohol has also been banned.

Some visitors put up with these and other inconveniences in order to see some of the most interesting Greek, Roman and Byzantine ruins in Africa. Others are curious about the politics of a small oil-rich country determined to exercise its influence in Africa and the Middle East and to change the relations between producer countries and international oil companies.

Libya has three distinct regions: Cyrenaica, Tripolitania and Fezzan. Cyrenaica occupies the eastern half of the coast and shares its inland border with Egypt, with which it has close traditional tries. Tripolitania, separated from Cyrenaica by the Syrtic desert, includes the western part of the coast. It has Libya's largest city, Tripoli, two-thirds of the country's population and most of its new petroleum wealth, and is the more Western in its outlook. Isolated from both these regions is Fezzan in the dry, rugged Sahara interior—all desert with no link to the sea. Its nomadic inhabitants hold fast to Islamic puritanism and ancient customs.

Although the whole country has been predominantly Arab since the 10th century, each region has suffered frequent invasion and conquest over the last 3,000 years. Phoenicians, Romans, Greeks, Byzantines and Vandals all had their turn. In the 16th century, Ottoman Turkey took over and maintained an uneasy hold. At times piracy and smuggling flourished, and in 1807 the United States became involved in its first foreign war, sending its marines ashore at Tripoli to curb the Barbary pirates. Turkey lost Libya to the Italians in 1911, and German and Italian forces under General Rommel ceded this strategic area to the British in 1942. On December 24, 1951, Libya became a united and independent nation under King Idris, hereditary monarch from Cyrenaica. The discovery of oil and natural gas transformed the economy and society and generated a militant nationalism. A cabal of young army officers deposed Idris in 1969 and inaugurated the Libyan Arab Republic.

Led by Colonel Muammar El Qaddafi, the military regime has concentrated on extracting better terms from the Western companies that still control Libya's resources. It has used its more than $2 billion a year in revenue to spur domestic economic development and to make its influence and militancy felt in Middle Eastern politics, especially in the struggle against Israel. Qaddafi has also sought some form of political union with Egypt but progress in achieving this union has been slow.

Wealthy, dynamic and armed to the teeth, Libya nevertheless has an acute shortage of skilled manpower. After the large Italian community was expelled in 1970, Egyptians, Maltese and Tunisians filled some of their posts, thus sustaining Libyan resentment over their dependence on foreigners.

There's a good series of guide books by Philip Ward (e.g., *Tripoli, Portrait of a City*) available from Box 234, Stoughton, Wisconsin 53589, or at the Ferigani bookshop in Tripoli. Those concerned with politics might read John Wright's *Libya* (Praeger, 1969), an unexciting book.

Money Matters

Although the Libyan dinar, officially valued at $3.07, is backed by several billion dollars in foreign exchange reserves, it is illegal for the dinar to be brought in or taken out of the country. Currency can be exchanged at the official rate at the Bank of Libya branches at the Tripoli and Benghazi airports or their city offices. Banks are open daily from 8 am to 1 pm, and also from 3:30 to 6 pm on Wednesday and Saturday. Some travelers may prefer to exchange currency at a slightly less favorable rate at their hotels to avoid the long lines at the banks in the cities. Travelers checks can be exchanged readily but credit cards are not generally honored.

Getting In and Out

Visas are available in North America only from the Libyan Embassy in Washington. It's best to apply in person; even so, expect a three-day delay. Be sure that your passport has a clean, empty page for the Libyan visa; Libya will not share a page. Passports should be in Arabic, or at least have Arabic insertions for your name and address. Libya systematically refuses entry to anyone with an Israeli stamp already in his passport. Visa applications also inquire about religion. Although the government promises to admit Jews who are not Zionists, complications may arise for Jewish applicants who answer the religion question squarely.

Most travelers arrive by air at Tripoli or Benghazi, taking advantage of frequent connections with Western Europe and the Middle East. Onward connections should be reconfirmed. No foreign carriers have airport offices, but in the city the bureaus of Pan American, Alitalia and KLM are recognizable in the welter of Arabic signs.

Although Libya has borders with six countries the only ones easily crossed are the paved coastal roads from Egypt and Tunisia. The other frontiers are in the Sahara, with only occasional camel caravans and supply trucks traveling the sand tracks. If you're coming from Tunisia, there's a daily bus from Tunis to Tripoli. If you're coming from Egypt, you can take a bus (also daily) from Cairo to Benghazi. The buses are cheap and the coastal roads good, but the 24-hour trips can be exhausting. Speedier and more expensive collective taxis from Tunis or Cairo will take you up to the borders where, if your papers are in order, you can enter on foot and get another taxi or bus on the Libyan side. The Egypt-Libya border is often closed to foreigners, however.

Drivers with their own cars, valid visas and international documentation can also enter Libya from either Tunisia or Egypt. But you cannot rent a car in these countries for a trip across the border to Libya. Hitchhiking is difficult because there's not much traffic; besides, you would probably have to pay for a lift.

Saharan crossings are normally made via Niger. The route from Libya into northern Chad crosses terrain contested by the armed guerrillas of the Chadian FROLINAT movement (see chapter on Chad).

Libya is difficult to get to by boat. There are no regular passenger services, although freighters from Malta, Sicily and mainland Italy put in frequently at Libyan ports with a few passengers.

Getting Around Within Libya

There are no street or directional signs in any language except Arabic, no city maps showing changes made since 1969 and not many city buses. Taxis charge a $2 minimum for the shortest ride. Car rentals are ruinously expensive and unreliable.

Fortunately, the cities are not too large to see on foot. If you're lost, you can try buttonholing passersby. You may find someone who speaks a little English (or Italian, if that's any help). If you are looking for a specific address it helps to have someone at the hotel write it out in Arabic.

Travel between cities and towns is less of a problem. Buses leave on all major routes in the early morning hours from central bus depots in Benghazi and Tripoli. Also operating out of these depots are fast collective taxis which zoom away as soon as they have a full load. A one-way trip, 100 miles from Tripoli to the ruins of Leptis Magna, for instance, costs $2 by bus or $2.50 by group taxi.

Libyan Arab Airlines has several flights a day between Benghazi and Tripoli and several flights a week to Tobruk, Sebha, the oasis of Ghadames, the agricultural project at Kufrah, and the natural gas facilities at Marsa El Brega.

The Michelin map of North and West Africa (No. 153) is useful for the countryside. The guide books by Philip Ward have detailed pre-1969 city maps, and the American Embassy has city sketch maps. The Tourist Board is on Haiti Street in Tripoli (tel. 40804).

Where to Stay

Oil prosperity has pushed up prices while accommodations and services are deteriorating in a country rich enough to give low priority to tourism. The expulsion of the Italians lowered both hotel management standards and tourist demand. In TRIPOLI perhaps the best value is to be found at the modest *Hotel Excelsior* with rooms at $5 and up. Around the corner fronting the esplanade and the harbor is the crumbling *Grand Hotel*, a dump at $10 a night. Avoid the *Waddan*, a benighted trap charging $30 per night. The *Libya Palace Hotel* charges upwards of $12 a night for a single room with bath, balcony and breakfast, and has tolerable service.

There is another *Palace* in BENGHAZI. The name is a euphemism. Benghazi also has the *Rex* and *Grand*, also nothing to write home about, but less expensive than the Palace. The government has plans for two large modern hotels for Benghazi but until they are completed clean, comfortable and reasonably priced lodging in that city is indeed hard to find.

Outside the two cities (unless you are a guest of the oil companies) accommodations are simple and rustic, to say the least, except for SEBHA, where the hotel has swimming and tennis facilities.

Where and What to Eat

Libyans seldom eat out and the 1970 expulsion of the Italians put an end to most decent dining. Travelers generally suffer dreary, unpalatable and expensive hotel meals. However, in BENGHAZI there are two reasonable restaurants for Lebanese and Egyptian dishes, the *Shahrazad* and *Omer Al Kayam*. There is a snack bar in the square in TRIPOLI near the erstwhile Catholic cathedral (closed in 1969 and to be converted into a mosque). In Andalus Square, the *Abu Nuaas* serves Libyan food.

Exploring side streets may lead to the discovery of an occasional local restaurant serving the Libyan version of couscous. City water is said to be safe even if it runs brown in hotel taps. Pepsi-Cola with Arabic labels is the leading bottled soft drink. There is no alcohol legally available except in the private homes of diplomats.

What to See and Do

Cities are not Libya's strong points. TRIPOLI is a hodgepodge of Arab, Turkish and Italian architecture. The esplanade and harbor make a pleasant walk. During the evening there are a few coffee houses along the sea front where men sit and sip. (Most Libyan women are veiled when seen at all in the conservative cities and countryside.)

The Castle Museum and old Turkish fort in Tripoli (open from 8 to noon every day except Friday and Sunday) are worth a visit for the Roman mosaics, the Barbary and Ottoman collections, and other holdings. South of the Castle Museum are the bazaar and the old Turkish city with its alleys, courtyards and tiny shops. Shopping or sightseeing is a disappointment here to those familiar with the great markets of Cairo and Tunis.

Tripoli has army and government headquarters. Personal introductions help in meeting the handful of top civil servants, often educated in the US, who run the country together with the young army officers.

Strictly off limits is the Libyan Air Force base near the Tripoli harbor. Here, at what was the American Wheelus Air Base until 1970, Libyan pilots are being trained in Mirage jets purchased from France.

The National University, a cluster of modern buildings, has its campus at the edge of the city. Given a little encouragement its students are willing to try out their English and exchange opinions.

Tripoli is the most convenient point of departure for the magnificent ruins of Sabratha and Leptis Magna. Both sites are open all week—even Friday, the Moslem day of rest. Visitors should take their own food and drink since only snacks are available (and overpriced, at that).

Leptis Magna is an open and well-preserved expanse of Phoenician, Greek, Roman and Byzantine baths, forums, temples, basilicas, churches, palaces and homes. The setting is superb and the splendors of the past easily evoked with the help of an English or Italian guide book sold at the site for 50 cents.

The 9 am bus from the central depot in Tripoli gets to Leptis Magna in two and a half hours. It leaves at 3 pm for the return to the city. The Leptis Magna trip can be a fine picnic outing with time for strolling, sunbathing on the sandy beaches which once served as a Roman port, and even a swim—if you don't mind the sticky petroleum tar everywhere along the shore.

Sabratha, 60 miles west of Tripoli, is also reached by bus or collective taxi from the depot. The distance is shorter than to Leptis Magna but the sights are less impressive. Sabratha has a museum, numerous restored buildings and a fine Roman amphitheater (plus its own guide book). There are picnic tables and a nearby beach.

The government maintains a craft and folk culture center in Tripoli. Dance companies occasionally perform here and in the hotels—all very sedate, no belly dancing. The center can arrange visits to see local dancing in nearby Zawia province. But all nightclubs and similar places of entertainment have been abolished by the regime.

An exception to beaches tarred by petroleum pollution is one belonging to a country club five miles west of Tripoli. It's run by foreign diplomats and Western oil men. There's a similar setup in Benghazi.

BENGHAZI itself is a sprawling, expensive, rebuilt city made rich, although not interesting, by oil and natural gas. From Benghazi you can take a pleasant excursion by bus or collective taxi 140 miles east to the fishing port of Cyrene, with ruins from its period of importance as a Greek and Roman port. The inhabitants of the agreeable nearby village of Susa have retained Greek as their first language.

The coastal road east from Benghazi to the Egyptian border passes through the beach resort of Derna. You may also want to pause at the World War II battlefield of TOBRUK where the German, French and English cemeteries recall the defeat of General Rommel by General Montgomery.

The Islamic heartland of the country and its petroleum wealth can only be seen by journeying to the Sahara. The desert itself is an ever-changing landscape of steppes, dunes, multicolored rocks and dry river beds. The intrepid may take the eight-hour bus ride from Tripoli to the Saharan town of SEBHA, the former winter capital of the monarchy. The colorful oasis of GHADAMES near the Tunisian border can be reached by bus or plane from Tripoli. Here or at Sebha one can see something of the austerity, dignity and hospitality of life in the Sahara.

Another Saharan world is to be found at the desert operations of the major foreign companies or the government-owned Libyan Petroleum Corporation. Inquire at their offices in Benghazi and Tripoli about trips to desert rigs and pipelines.

One of the most interesting desert projects is at the oasis of Kufrah, 500 air miles south of Benghazi, where underground Saharan water irrigates pasture and crop land. The Kufrah Agricultural Development Project, which has its offices in Tripoli next door to the United States Embassy, will arrange visits.

What to Buy

The bazaars in Benghazi and Tripoli are relatively modern and expensive compared to those elsewhere in North Africa. Local crafts have little value but the government has established a crafts center in Tripoli to promote traditional leather work, copper and brass, basketry, ceramics, carpets and tiles. Shops are open every day except Friday, generally closing from noon until 4 pm, and reopening until 7 pm. You can make some good purchases in gold jewelry, brass, rugs, and camelskin and palm fiber products in the Suk al Turk market in Tripoli and the Suk al Zalam in Benghazi.

Local Attitudes

Libya's wealth puts punch behind its Arab nationalist sentiments, but the need for technological help and Western markets for oil and gas means that foreigners must continue to be tolerated. Israel is a particularly sensitive subject. In spite of political strain, Libya and the US maintained diplomatic relations after the 1967 Arab-Israeli War and nearly 200 Libyan students are currently in the US, majoring in business administration and petroleum engineering.

Be sure to obtain permission before photographing anything other than archaeological sites. Mosques are closed to non-Moslem visitors. Islamic holidays, such as Ramadan, are strictly observed.

Weather, What to Wear, How Long to Stay

Most of Libya is hot and dry throughout the year with a rainfall of four inches or less. During autumn and spring, Tripolitania in the west has a hot, dry, dust-laden wind from the Sahara, known as the "ghibli." Winter months are agreeable but from July to September temperatures soar over 100 degrees. Cyrenaica, in the east, has more rain and a somewhat milder, more Mediterranean climate. Casual dress is acceptable throughout the year but miniskirts and pants for women are not tolerated.

The best months for travel are November to March. Tripoli can be seen in one day. Allow another for Leptis Magna and a third for Sabratha.

Communication

A knowledge of Arabic opens many doors, but most top government officials, many of whom were educated in the US, are fluent in English.

The telephone book from the monarchy has been retained and names and numbers are in English in the front of the book. The postal and telegraph services are unreliable in any language and should be avoided. If you need to reach the outside world try phoning.

The local press, radio and TV are in Arabic with the exception of a Benghazi radio station which broadcasts in English, Italian and French daily from 4 pm to 10 pm, and a four-page daily English-language newspaper published in Benghazi which parrots the government's ultra-nationalist line. Foreign-language publications, mostly in English and Italian, arrive with a few days' delay. They can be found at the Ferigani bookshop in Tripoli and the Djerbi bookshop in Benghazi.

Emergencies

Medical facilities and services are inadequate, although the government is trying hard to improve their quality. The American and British embassies in Tripoli have lists of competent doctors and dentists. The US Embassy is near the former king's palace at Garden City, Via Grazioli (tel. 34020).

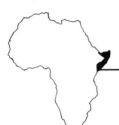

Somalia

(Somali Democratic Republic)

Profile

STATUS: Independent republic since July 1, 1960. Ruled by military and police council. Formerly British and Italian Somalilands.

SIZE: 270,000 square miles (about the size of Texas). Population—2,800,000.

GEOGRAPHY: Rugged and infertile; 1,700 miles of coastline; ranges from mountainous desert in north to flat semi-desert in south. Principal towns —Mogadishu (capital and chief port, 125,000), Hargeisa (80,000), Kismayu (port, 11,000).

CLIMATE: Moderate rainfall from April to August and October to December, dry the rest of the year. Mogadishu temperatures range from 80 to 100 degrees, in the 60's at night. Hargeisa about 10 degrees cooler.

LANGUAGES: Somali, Arabic, some English and Italian.

CURRENCY: Somali shilling, divided into 100 cents. 1 shilling = 15 US cents; US$1.00 = 6 shillings, 65 cents.

VISAS: Required. Application forms available from Somali Embassy or Somali Mission to the UN. Fee $7. Two passport photos needed. Takes several weeks (applications are sent to Somalia for approval).

AIRPORT: Petrella (MCQ), three miles from Mogadishu. Linked with European and East African capitals and Cairo.

NATIONAL HOLIDAYS: July 1, Independence Day, in the north; July 26, Independence Day, in the south; October 21, Anniversary of the 1969 Revolution; Moslem holidays.

INFORMATION SOURCES: *In US*—Embassy of Somalia, 1875 Connecticut Avenue NW, Washington, D.C. 20009 (tel. 202/234-3261); Permanent Mission of Somalia to the UN, 236 East 46th Street, New York, N.Y. 10017 (tel. 212/986-5936).

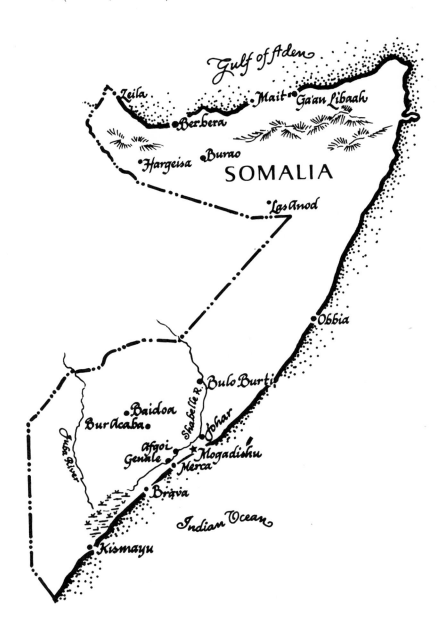

By David Laitin

Somalia attracts few tourists. Its nearly three million people are fiercely nationalistic and have a tradition of independence and defiance. Their country, the easternmost projection of the continent, bordering on the Gulf of Aden and the Indian Ocean, is one of the least fertile and most rugged in all Africa. Those who respond to the desert and to an extraordinary people who have wrested a way of life from the desert may, however, respond to Somalia and the Somalis. Those who are looking for air-conditioned amenities would be well advised to stay away.

The Somali people are tall, range in color from reddish brown to black, have aquiline features and appear to most Westerners quite handsome. Nearly all Somalis are Moslems, and some of their religious leaders claim descent from Aquil Abu Talib, cousin of the prophet Mohammed. The basic and most noble Somali calling is camel herding, and wealth is measured by the number of camels one owns. For the Somali nomad, to drink camel's milk is to be truly happy. Indeed, the word *Somaal* probably comes from *so* (go) and *maal* (to milk). After the revolutionary military coup of 1969, the first song on Radio Mogadishu proclaimed, "Now that there is freedom, we will all be able to drink camel's milk."

Somalia's physical environment probably explains the fatalism and individualism that distinguish the Somali character. From mountainous desert in the north to flat semi-desert in the south, life provides few luxuries. Most of the year the nomad is close to famine and in danger of losing his stock. During the long dry season, the camel herder needs to keep his stock near both grazing land and water holes—usually an arduous trek of 30 miles or more from one to the other. One can be defeated by such a hostile environment—or emerge victorious and proud. The Somalis have done the latter.

Richard Burton's *First Footsteps in Africa*, written in 1856 and available in a 1966 edition published by Praeger, should be read by any prospective visitor. Isak Dinesen immortalized her African friends in *Shadows on the Grass* (Random House, 1961), in which she compared the Somalis to the ancient Icelanders of the Nordic sagas.

The Somalis have a firm belief in their superiority. Going hand in hand with this pride is xenophobia, a characteristic not perfectly suitable for tourism. Europeans will be derisively called "frenji" (Frank) or "galla" (heathen). Arabs, Pakistanis and Kenyans face similar disrespect.

The Somali people have faced expansionist threats from the Portuguese, Ethiopians, Egyptians, French, English and Italians. In 1899 the British became entangled in a guerrilla war with Muhammad Abdullah Hassan, a Somali leader, that continued until 1921 when they bombed his forts from the air. Said a British officer: "It is wonderful how little we have yet managed to impress the Somali with our superior power."

The present northern region (capital at Hargeisa) ultimately became a British protectorate. The southern region, first an Italian colony, then a British colony, was returned to the Italians after World War II as a United Nations trust. The two regions merged in 1960 and became the independent Somali Republic. Neither Britain nor Italy had much effect on the interior of the country.

Modern Somalia is ruled by a military and police council. Its closest foreign ties are with Egypt, Sudan, Libya, the Soviet Union and China. During the Vietnamese war ships flying the Somali flag were spotted trading with North Vietnam, so much of the American aid program was discontinued. The American Peace Corps was asked to leave the country in 1969. Relations with her neighbors—Ethiopia, Kenya and the French Territory of the Afars and Issas (Djibouti)—are at best tenuous, because the Somali Government is committed to reclamation of territory peopled by the Somalis now under her neighbors' jurisdiction. Land travel across these borders can be precarious.

Money Matters

The Somali shilling is not convertible outside Somalia. Exchange currency, therefore, only to meet your daily needs. All the banks were nationalized in 1970 and are operated by the Central Bank of Somalia.

Getting In and Out

Alitalia, East African Airways and United Arab Airlines fly to Mogadishu from Rome, Khartoum, Nairobi and Asmara (Ethiopia). Somali Airlines has flights to Aden.

Entering and leaving Somalia by land can be difficult and sometimes—because of the political situation already mentioned—dangerous. However, there are roads suitable for trucks and four-wheel-drive vehicles connecting Djibouti with Hargeisa in northern Somalia, and Nairobi with the southern Somalia port of Kismayu.

Somali ports receive numerous freighters. Arab dhows travel from Aden up and down the East African coast.

Getting Around Within Somalia

Somali Airlines has a reliable twice-a-week service from Mogadishu to Kismayu, Hargeisa and other towns. From Mogadishu and Hargeisa buses leave regularly to most major towns. Each bus waits at a central spot until it is full before departing, which may mean a five-minute or a five-hour delay. Everyone pays the same price, which is collected midway. Usually the trade truck which also operates from the bus station is a more convenient means of transportation, although you could find yourself sitting on a sorghum bag for 26 hours in order to go 60 miles.

Taxis within Mogadishu are plentiful but not metered—and a price should definitely be established before you enter. They run on regular routes for about 10 cents a trip. This goes up to 40 cents if you want to reach a destination that is off one of the specified routes. There are no reliable auto rental agencies in the country. Hitchhiking is not advisable, but the low-budget traveler will find plenty of inexpensive food, transport and accommodations.

Where to Stay

MOGADISHU has three hotels charging about $8 per couple per night without food. They are the *Croce del Sud*, Italian-run, and the *Juba* and the *Shabelle*, both government-operated. All have clean rooms, good food, bidets and brackish water. The *Hotel Primo Luglio*, relatively clean, has a more Somali flavor and is cheaper. Outside Mogadishu ask at the bus stations about hotels. The *Hargeisa Club* in HARGEISA is adequate and has a distinct British atmosphere. Southern towns such as KISMAYU, BRAVA and BAIDAO have decent government rest-houses for traveling civil servants and other visitors. Rest-houses in smaller towns are ill equipped.

New hotels are planned for the capital.

Where and What to Eat

In MOGADISHU, there are several good restaurants. *Azan's* and *Capeccetto Nero's* are two fairly good Italian restaurants. *Charlie's* and *Abdi's* both serve surprisingly good steaks. *Ming Sing's* serves excellent North Chinese dishes (there is a large staff of Chinese personnel in Mogadishu in connection with a Peking aid program).

But it is the makhaayadda, the Somali tea shop, that gives the visitor the feeling of Somalia. Ali Madowbe, popular restaurateur and amateur politician, owns a makhaayadda, and there Somalis drink tea and talk politics all day. Most Mogadishu makhaayaddas serve "bifstek," "beer," hilib ari, hilib geel and digaag (beefsteak, liver, goat meat, camel meat and chicken). These dishes are usually accompanied by barisse (rice) or basta (spaghetti) and an enormous quantity of subaag (oil).

A Somali treat can be had if you take the Johar bus and disembark six kilometers northwest of Mogadishu—ask for Kilometre Six. There you can enjoy a traditional Somali feast—a large platter filled with goat meat and rice. The moment you dig your right hand into it, you will be "in touch" with Somali food. A Somali student escort to instruct you makes the feast that much more interesting.

A relaxing hour or two can be had at *Mariano's*, where the view from the terrace of the old Arab section of town, Shangaani, is exquisite. Or you can take capuccino and dolce at *Croce del Sud* in true Italian style.

Avoid the tap water and locally produced soda, except for bottled Bravanese or Italian mineral water. Make sure that milk you drink is factory-processed—it will come in a milk bottle and is pasteurized. Tea is safe if the milk and water are boiled. Try to get some fresh camel's milk ('aano geel), which is a taste sensation and need not be pasteurized.

What to See and Do

There are no organized tourist facilities in Somalia. Presumably, the visitor to Somalia wants to see a way of life utterly different from his own. Merely walking through the Somali bush, or through the streets of Mogadishu or Hargeisa, or attempting to communicate with the few English-speaking Somalis can be an experience. Don't expect beautiful sights; there are few. And don't expect hospitality, although if you are taken into a Somali home you are treated with utmost cordiality.

Somalia has 1,700 miles of coastline. Sand dunes line most of the Indian Ocean coast, so access is not always easy, but exploration of the coast south of Mogadishu, at MERCA or at BRAVA, allows you to discover the beautiful fish on the reefs and gigantic turtles on nearby rocks. On most of these beaches you are alone with the world, although various clubs adorn Mogadishu's main beach. (The American Beach Club offers temporary memberships, as do several other clubs). The best skindiving is found 10 miles south of Mogadishu at GESIRA. Snorkel equipment can be purchased near the Croce del Sud Hotel.

The beach at Brava once drew Italian honeymooners. It is quite lovely, and my wife once caught a hammerhead shark there from a 15-foot dhow. The fishermen are more than willing to take you out. Bravanese speak a Swahili dialect, and are more gentle than the Somalis.

GENALE, JOHAR and AFGOI are three Somali towns on the Shabelle River, each a short bus trip from Mogadishu. Genale and Johar have ir-rigation systems and banana plantations—specks of lush green in the desert. Afgoi has an annual stick fight (stunka) which is organized violence involving the whole town. After three days of fighting, everyone is at peace for a year. The dates of these stick fights vary from year to year according to the Islamic calendar. It is a fascinating spectacle and visitors are welcome, although likely to be ignored.

Game hunting is possible in the area of the Juba River and other newly established game reserves, but a license and a rented Land Rover need to be procured in Mogadishu. No tours are available. Don't be surprised, though, if elephants or giraffes cross your road in the Juba Valley. KISMAYU is perhaps Somalia's most beautiful city, and a trip by rented dhow to the off-shore islands to visit the Bajun people is a delightful experience.

If your travels take you to the Red Sea, and you dock at Berbera, leave the burning coast and travel up to GA'AN LIBAAH, a forest knoll, high and cool, just west of Sheikh. Other northern towns, such as AMUD, ZEILA and LAS ANOD possess stone ruins of ancient cities.

MOGADISHU, the capital, is best explored at a leisurely pace on foot. There is no need for a guide; only avoid the midday heat. A walking tour should include the National Museum, the goldsmith shops behind Via Roma, the Dagah Tur market area behind the main bus station, the old Arab section of town known as Shangaani, and the coastal Hammawein section where the weavers of the fine Benadir cloth have their shops. Allow time to stop at the tea shops. Admire but do not enter the mosques, one of which, the Fakhr-Din, is said to be over 700 years old.

The only Western-style night spots in the country are the Bar Lido in Mogadishu and The Club at Gesira. They are the only places where Somalis drink alcohol publicly. Rock music, Somali style, libations and women are all to be found at the Lido.

At the National Theater in Mogadishu, lyric poetry (the classical art form), singing and dancing demonstrate a joie de vivre wholly unexpected in this desert milieu. Most programs are well planned, and even if you don't speak Somali you will catch some of the excitement.

What to Buy

Benadir cloth is woven in a few southern Somali cities. You can watch weavers in the Hammawein section of Mogadishu and to the north of the city. Many speak some English. Their weaving methods, sitting in a pit with the threads stretched out for yards in front of them, are the same as their ancestors'. Four yards of cloth make a ma'awiis, the traditional men's skirt. Bring the cloth to any tailor and for a small charge he will sew it and show you how to put it on. For women, eight yards will make a guntiino. Be sure to get a lesson on how to wear it from a Somali woman.

Just behind Via Roma, where cloth stores abound, you will find a number of gold shops. Here Arab and Indian jewelers work in 22-carat gold and will make things to order. Sidek M. Hagi made a number of things for us, and was quite creative. Small shops in the area sell Somali myrrh and frankincense, which comes from the northern region.

Behind the main bus station (El Gab) is a market area called Dagah Tur, which means "thrown stone." It was from the hill above that Somali nationalists fought the Italians in a bloody uprising in 1948. A monument to that battle stands on the top of the hill, just in front of the new parliament building. At the market, traditional Somali handicraft is available. You can buy a mortar and pestle (moye), a cowhide stool (gumber), a charcoal spoon (dubqad) or a meerschaum stove (bergiiko) —all of which represent Somali functional art. The wooden pillow or head-rest (barshii) used by nomads must be obtained from its carver.

Bargaining is the rule of the market and generally the first price asked by the merchant is twice what he is prepared to accept. Benadir cloth sells for slightly under $1 a yard; a meerschaum clay stove costs about $2. A rug made from the skin of the dik dik, a small member of the deer family, makes a particularly attractive gift. Jewelry carved from the dik dik's horn is also nice. Whatever you buy, try to take it out of the country with you since the postal service is not reliable.

Most businesses are closed between 1 and 4 pm.

Every evening at about five the qat trucks arrive in Mogadishu. Qat is a stimulant and Somali men sit around chewing qat all night long. One chews the leaves of the plant, and keeps some water or tea nearby to counter the bitter taste. You may see a small green leaf in a number of shops in town, a signal to Somalis that the day's qat has arrived. In the north the qat truck rushes through town like the pony express. To be most effective—that is, to have the desired euphoric effect—qat must be fresh. It is legal and costs $1 a bunch. Incidentally, marijuana and other narcotics are not legal and possession probably means jail.

Local Attitudes

While they sometimes marvel at the camera, most Somalis resent being photographed. A photographer can attract a mob in minutes. If your interest is in seeing the Somalis—and not in having Somalis mob you—it would be best to leave your camera at the hotel.

The Arabs have called this country Balad wa Issi, "the land of give me something." You are the personification of wealth in Somalia, and you surely will hear a chorus of "bakshiish issi" (give me something for free). A kumi, 10 Somali cents, is appreciated, but by no means required.

Weather, What to Wear

Men should wear slacks and a short-sleeved shirt. Women should remember that showing the knees in Somalia is not unlike showing the breasts in America. Short skirts are associated with prostitution. No matter what the weather, women should wear below-the-knee skirts and a scarf. April through June is "goo," and the weather is rainy and relatively cool. January to March is "jilaal," the long dry season and extremely hot. July to September is "haggay," a cooler, windier, dry season, while October to December is the shorter rainy season. The weather is hot most of the year, but evenings are quite cool and blankets are needed for sleeping.

Communication

Somali is the national language, spoken by 95 per cent of the population and by nearly another two million persons living in Kenya, Ethiopia and Djibouti. A long-standing controversy between Arabic or Latinate script was resolved in 1972 in favor of the latter. Meanwhile, English and Italian are widely taught in the schools and used in business and government. If you cannot find an English-speaking person in the north or an Italian speaker in the south, here are a few Somali phrases. The language itself is of Cushitic origin and a tough one for most Westerners to learn.

Hello (literally, Is it peace?).	Nabad miyaa?
Answer (literally, It is peace).	Nabad weyee.
Do you speak Somali?	'Af Somaaliga mataqan?
No, I don't.	Maya, ma'aqan.
What do you want?	Mahhaad donaysaa?
I want (camel's milk).	Wahhaan donayya ('aano geel).
Where is the Hotel Juba?	Hotel Juba wa ented?
Where are you going?	Hagad tegaysaa?
I'm going to Genale.	Wahhan tegayyaa Genale.
Who are you?	Ya tahay?
I'm an American.	Maraykin ban ahay.
One, two, three, four, five . . .	Ko, laba, sudehh, afar, shan . . .
Six, seven, eight, nine, ten.	Lihh, todobah, sided, sagal, toban.
One hundred.	Bokol.
How much?	Wa immisaa?
It's 10 shillings.	Wa toban shillin.
Goodbye.	Nabadgelyou.
Yes.	Haa.

There is automatic dialing in the city of Mogadishu, but telephone service elsewhere is poor. Overseas radio-telephone calls can be placed daily between 11 am and 2 pm. The postal service is unreliable and should not be used for important items. The government radio broadcasts in Somali, Arabic, English and Italian. The government publishes newspapers in English, Italian and Arabic.

Emergencies

The general hospital in Mogadishu is understaffed and overworked. The United States Embassy at Corso Primo Luglio, Mogadishu (tel. 216) has a registered nurse and sometimes a physician on duty. In case of serious illness evacuation to Nairobi or elsewhere is advised.

Sudan

Profile

STATUS: Independent since 1956 as the Democratic Republic of the Sudan. Formerly Anglo-Egyptian Sudan.

SIZE: Largest country in Africa, 967,499 square miles (one-third the size of the United States). Population—15,400,000 (more than two-thirds Arab Moslems, remainder Nilotic and Bantu).

GEOGRAPHY: Desert in north, grassland in center, tropical forest in south. Nile River runs length of country from its source in Lake Victoria. Principal towns—Khartoum (capital, 250,000), Khartoum North (135,000), Omdurman (250,000), Port Sudan (79,000), El Obeid, Wad Medani, Kassala, Juba.

CLIMATE: North very hot and dry. Daytime temperatures in Khartoum and Port Sudan range from mid-80's to well over 100 degrees all year, dropping 20 degrees or more at night. South more humid, with moderate rainfall April through September, temperatures somewhat lower (80's and 90's by day, high 60's at night).

LANGUAGES: Arabic (official); English spoken in the cities and south.

CURRENCY: Sudanese pound, divided into 100 piasters (PT). 1 pound = $2.90; PT1 = 3 cents; $1.00 = PT34.

VISAS: Required. Obtainable from Permanent Mission of the Sudan to the UN. Fee $5.80 in person, $6.91 by post. Three passport photos needed; minimum delay of 72 hours; leave passport. Transit visas for 24-hour stay costs $2.95 in person, $4.06 by post. Also available from Sudanese embassies in Cairo and Nairobi.

AIRPORT: Khartoum International (KRT), two miles from city. Frequent connections with London, Egypt, East Africa. Transport into city

—public bus, PT3 (9 cents); taxi, about one pound ($2.90); some airlines have buses. Airport departure tax—one pound ($2.90).

NATIONAL HOLIDAYS: January 1, Independence Day; May 25, 1969 Revolution Day; October 21, 1964 Revolution Day; Moslem holidays.

INFORMATION SOURCES: *In US*—Permanent Mission of the Sudan to the UN, 757 Third Avenue, New York, N.Y. 10017 (tel. 212/421-2680); Embassy of the Sudan, 3421 Massachusetts Avenue NW, Washington, D.C. 20008 (tel. 202/338-8565). *In Khartoum*—Department of Tourism, Ministry of Information (tel. 70932).

By Aaron Segal

Don't go to the Sudan unless you are tough, determined, ruggedly healthy and slightly masochistic. The heat, sand and desolation are not for the faint of heart. But if you are adventurous, if you want to seek out the remnants of lost empires or stand at points of destiny murmuring "Omdurman" or "Khartoum," and scorn the banalities of the beaten path on principle, then give it a try.

In the Sudan near the 9th and 10th cataracts of the Nile the oldest Egyptian civilizations arose more than 4,000 years ago. Great commercial expansion was accompanied by cultural growth, and over the centuries temples, monuments and cities took shape in the punishing heat of the desert winds. The Kushite Kingdom of the Sudan (700 BC to 350 AD) succumbed to Abyssinian invasion, its capital city (Meroë) was torn stone from stone and the land divided into three states called Nubia, Makura and Alwa. Though Christianity entered the Sudan in the 6th century, Coptic influences slowly gave way to those of Islam, and by the end of the 14th century the northern area was almost completely Islamic.

Mohammed Ali Pasha brought Egyptian political control to the Sudan in the second decade of the 19th century. Slaving continued to be the largest source of income and manpower for the Turks, Arabs and Egyptians who were exploiting the land. But in 1870, struggling for dominance, the Egyptian Khedive Ismail Pasha hired the British adventurer Sir Samuel Baker both to subdue rebel leaders and suppress the slave trade, hoping (rightly) to gain the support of Queen Victoria. Later the Bible-toting British General C.G. "Chinese" Gordon was engaged as governor-general of the entire Sudan, with extraordinary powers. From his headquarters at Khartoum Gordon dispensed justice, planned fortifications and attempted to stem the flow of deserters to the ranks of the Mahdi, a Moslem reformer who had attracted thousands to a life of puritanical devotion and self-sacrifice in battle.

In spite of Gordon's own considerable charisma, his starved and depleted forces showed little will to resist when the Mahdi overran Khartoum in 1885 after a 10-month siege. Gordon's head was paraded on a pike, and the Mahdi settled down to enjoy the fruits of his labors in a new capital at Omdurman. Though he died (some say of debauchery) but a few months later, the British did not regain control of the area until 1898, when the steely-eyed Kitchener arrived at Omdurman to avenge Gordon, conquer the tribal dissidents, and set up the Anglo-Egyptian domination that was to last until 1953, when the Sudan was granted powers of self-government. Independence followed in 1956.

Prior to granting the Sudan independence, Britain had assisted the economy of the North by facilitating the export of cotton, hides and gum arabic. The government of the conservative Islamic North was left to its religious leaders. The darker, Nilotic people of the South, who had been introduced to Christianity, were kept apart and were given little economic assistance.

Following independence the Sudan was torn by two power struggles. In the North, civilian politicians, trade unionists, intellectuals and army officers fought for the reins of government, with the army ultimately taking control. Heading the uneasy and divided army regime is President Jaafar el-Nimeiry, who narrowly survived an attempted coup in July, 1971.

Although the Arabs fought among themselves, each of their successive governments sought to impose Khartoum rule and the Islam religion on the southern Sudanese. The result was 15 years of civil war, costing hundreds of thousands of lives and seriously depleting the country's meager resources. The war was ended in March, 1972, with an agreement promising the South extensive autonomy.

With only a trickle of external aid, the government is trying to resettle thousands of war refugees, restore transportation facilities and cope with severe economic problems (including the management of nationalized industries once owned by British, Egyptian and Greek interests).

A history of the country is ably presented in K. D. D. Henderson's *Sudan Republic* (Praeger, 1966) and Alan Moorehead's colorful two-volume account of 19th century explorers, *Blue Nile* and *White Nile* (Harper and Row).

Money Matters

With the exception of British sterling (limited to 50 pounds), foreign currency may be imported and exported at will on declaration; but not a piaster of local currency may go in or out. The Sudanese pound is not convertible outside the country, so exchange money as you need it on a day-to-day basis through the Bank of Sudan. All travelers checks and letters of credit must be declared on arrival.

Banking hours are 8 am to noon.

Getting In and Out

There are frequent flights to and from Cairo and London, and regular connections with Addis Ababa and Asmara in Ethiopia, Entebbe (Uganda) and Nairobi (Kenya). Flying north-south is easy, although planes land in the middle of the night to avoid the stifling Khartoum heat.

The Sudan can be part of a Cape-to-Cairo trip. If you're flying from North America to East or Southern Africa you should be able to include a Sudanese stopover at no additional expense.

Port Sudan, the country's major Red Sea port, is scorchingly hot, swept by sandstorms, and dismal. Since the closing of the Suez Canal few ships touch there. It's more pleasant to take the steamer that plies between Shellal in the northern Sudan and Egypt's Aswan Dam. The steamer, which crosses Lake Nasser, leaves Shellal and Aswan every Monday and Thursday and connects with the trains to Khartoum and Cairo. The cost is $20 first class, $12 second class and $4 third class for a one-day trip on which you provide your own food.

An even more exotic trip out of the country is the twice-monthly steamer from Khartoum up the White Nile to the Southern Sudanese town of Juba—a one- or two-week trip depending on the weather and the thickness of the reeds choking the river. From Juba it is less than 100 miles to the Uganda border by bus. If the cease-fire endures and the border is open, you will be able to enter Uganda (provided that is desirable at the time!) by the same route traversed by Sir Samuel Baker and his intrepid Hungarian wife in 1862. Hitchhikers who are tough and resourceful should be able to make their way as far south as Khartoum; farther south is problematical under present conditions. If you can get to Juba there are trucks as well as local buses to the Uganda border.

It is possible but very difficult to go into or out of the Sudan by road. In addition to the route from Juba to Uganda, there is a route to Ethiopia. This requires putting the car aboard the Nile steamer at Wadi Halfa, navigating from there to Khartoum, following a 250-mile all-weather road from Khartoum to Kassala and the Ethiopian border, and then traversing the highlands to the Ethiopian town of Asmara.

Important: If you intend to stay in the country longer than three days you must report your presence to the police.

Getting Around Within the Sudan

Because of the heat and lack of accommodations, moving overland within the Sudan is a rugged proposition at best. However, one has a choice of rail, motor or inland waterway transport, as well as an inexpensive bus service.

Bus: Service from Khartoum to most major towns is available. For all inquiries on cost ($2 to $10 will cover a one-way ticket to most destinations), call the National Transport Corporation, Khartoum (tel. 71353 and 42078).

Railways: The Sudan Railways run lines from Wadi Halfa on the

Egyptian border to El Obeid, via Khartoum; from Atbara and Sennar to Port Sudan on the Red Sea; and from Sennar to Roseires on the Blue Nile. Whether lines are now open through the southern provinces is a question best answered by the authorities at Sudan Railways in Khartoum. Tickets run about $5 to $15 one way to most destinations for first class accommodations. Second class is crowded and dirty, but costs half the first class tariff.

Inland waterways: It is possible to go by Sudan Railways river steamers to many inland destinations, including Nimule, Kosti and Juba. All reservations must be made in advance. Rates vary and often a trip will include a leg of rail travel.

Motoring: Application to motor through the Sudan must be made to the Undersecretary, Ministry of the Interior, P.O. Box 282, Khartoum, or to your local Sudanese diplomatic representative at least two weeks before setting out. The risks of travel through desolate areas require consultation with the Sudanese Tourist Department in Khartoum. The government strongly advises that travelers should arrange caravans of no less than two four-wheel-drive vehicles, and one of them should be equipped with a winch.

Driving is on the left in the Sudan, and an international driving permit or your US license is sufficient to rent a car. There are more-or-less reliable vehicles for rent in the major towns but quality varies widely, so be careful, especially if you are motoring long distances.

Many otherwise good roads become almost impassable after rains. Make your plans with an eye to the weather. Above all, heed the advice of local authorities. And if you rent a car, hire a driver.

In the towns you can cover short distances by taxi. Yellow with a green stripe, sans meter and usually decrepit, these vehicles can be hired at Khartoum Market Place or hailed on the street. Fares must be decided on in advance: PT25 (75 cents) should cover most local destinations; a full day's hire will cost about five pounds ($14.50). Collective taxis charge PT5 (15 cents) per seat to destinations within Khartoum, Khartoum North and Omdurman.

Where to Stay

Hotels in Sudan leave a great deal to be desired. Air-conditioning is an important consideration.

In KHARTOUM, the *Sudan Hotel* near the zoo has 80 rooms with private baths and air-conditioning and charges $18 for a single bed and breakfast (English style), and $30 for a double. The equally expensive *Grand Hotel* is not as good. A better bet is the less expensive *Hotel*

Khartoum, situated right on the Nile. In the $10-to-$15 price range for bed and breakfast are the *Excelsior*, *Khayam* and *Al Arz*, none of which has air-conditioning. The *St. James Hotel* and the *Royal Hotel* charge $5 or less. Moderately priced and decent lodgings can be found at the *Acropole Hotel* on Quasr Avenue.

Outside Khartoum there is little choice. In the $10-to-$15 price range are the *Juba Hotel* in JUBA, the *Red Sea* and *Olympia Park* in PORT SUDAN and the *Continental* and *El Gezira* in WAD MEDANI. Visitors are better off bringing their own food and using government rest-houses, although traveling civil servants have priority for these accommodations. The Department of Tourism in Khartoum will help you make rest-house reservations. There are youth hostels for students and young travelers from PT25 (75 cents) per day. The Tourism officials will be of help with listings and locations.

Where and What to Eat

There are few restaurants outside the hotels but plenty of coffee-houses. Sudanese specialties include lamb, mutton, partridge and pigeon, and are best sampled, if possible, in a private well-to-do home. If you have no Khartoum acquaintance to offer you a meal, try the cuisine at the *Hotel Acropole*, the *Hotel de Paris* or the *Zola Cafeteria*. Full meals cost about PT150 to 200 ($4.50 to $6). Local beers are not bad, soft drinks are available, and coffee is omnipresent. Imported liquors are expensive: it's $1.50 for a shot of whiskey and a bottle will cost you close to $30.

Don't drink any water that has not been boiled at least 15 minutes; reliable brands of mineral water are your best bet. Avoid fresh vegetables, salads, pastries and buffet dishes that have been cooked and left standing. Hot, well-cooked vegetables and meats served at once are safest; wash and peel all fruits before eating.

What to See and Do

KHARTOUM can be readily explored on foot and by inexpensive local taxis. You do not need a guide although several will try to attach themselves to you. (To avoid bother you may wish to engage one for $1 a day plus tip, depending on his talents.) Walk to the Mogren section where the sinuous White Nile joins the Blue Nile sweeping down from the Ethiopian highlands. There are lovely gardens here and outdoor cafes and a small forest. (Your enjoyment is enhanced if you have read Alan Moorehead's stirring books, *Blue Nile* and *White Nile*, which trace the history of the rivers.) Near the Mogren are the Zoological Gardens with excellent collections of animals, birds and reptiles.

Khartoum, with a population of 250,000, is a modern city with many government offices and commercial buildings. Four museums are worth a visit: the Sudanese History Museum containing remarkable archaeological relics, the Ethnographic Museum, the Natural History Museum and the Graphic Museum. The People's Palace occupies the spot where General Gordon fought and died. Khartoum University, too, should be visited. If you are an "academic" and write for accommodations well in advance, it may be possible to find lodgings on campus.

OMDURMAN lies across the Nile from Khartoum. Here you can visit the house of Khalifa Abdullah, wily successor to the Mahdi, and see the Mahdi's tomb, which Abdullah built to strengthen the Mahdist mystique. The old Dervish fort is nearby, and there is a fine open-air market. War buffs can take a taxi to the battlefield of Karari, some 20 miles away, where in 1898, in the words of the young eyewitness Winston Churchill, Kitchener gave the Mahdist forces "a good dusting."

Soon to be added to the sights of Khartoum and Omdurman are a number of temples salvaged from Abu Simbel on the Sudanese side of the Aswan Dam. They are being transported to the capital and will soon be put on display at the trade-fair grounds.

Students of history should explore the site of Semna, accessible by bus or rail along the river between Wadi Halfa and Khartoum, where two Middle Kingdom Egyptian forts formed the main frontier defense in 1000 BC. The town of Karima, 327 miles north of Khartoum, is the site of several temples and a group of pyramids from the Napatan Period of Egyptian rule; a small museum at neighboring MEROË explains these ruins.

Nine miles east in the village of Ghazzali are the remains of a Coptic Christian monastery and church, Wadi Abu Dom.

Perhaps the most important and interesting ruins of the Sudan are at SHENDI, 112 miles north of Khartoum (a $10 first class round trip train ride). Here flourished the Upper Nile civilization of Kush which had trading routes across Africa, up and down the Nile and across the Indian Ocean from 700 BC to 350 AD. You can visit its capital, now Bagrawiya, as well as several fine temples at Naaga and Musawwarat es Safra. It helps to do a little homework at the Sudan History Museum in Khartoum before your visit. It is a good idea, too, to read a lively book like A Short History of Africa (Penguin, 1966) by R. Oliver and J. Fage, or more specialized works by Peter Shinnie and Basil Davidson.

Hunters and fishermen will find the Sudan well stocked with game and fish. The trick, of course, is to hurdle the formalities and reach the hunting spots unscathed. PORT SUDAN has sailfish, barracuda, greyrock cod, shark, and other formidable adversaries. The Nile can be fished from one end to the other. Look here for the famous Nile perch, notable both for size and delicacy of flavor. Inquire locally at hotels for boats, or at the Game and Fisheries Division, Ministry of Animal Resources, Khartoum.

The Southern Sudan is alive with game animals. Species found here include elephant, buffalo, rhino, giraffe, lion and leopard, as well as many types of antelope. *Dinder National Park*, near the Ethiopian border, features kudu, ostrich and abundant birdlife. In Darfur to the northwest one finds mountain sheep and oryx; in the Red Sea hills ibex abound. Rare species found in the Sudan include white rhino, Nile lechwe, bongo, yellow-backed duiker and giant eland. Hunting season is December to May.

All hunting must be cleared at least three months in advance with the Game and Fisheries Division of the Ministry of Animal Resources. Licenses and permits, game scouts and taxidermy information are all available at Division headquarters in Khartoum and Juba. See local Sudanese diplomatic representatives for permits to bring firearms and ammunition into the country. Nile Safaris, P.O. Box 1802, Khartoum, will be pleased to make advance hunting and fishing arrangements for you. Clear photographic safaris with the Secretary, Cinematographic Board, Ministry of Information, Khartoum.

Sudan Airways can be helpful in advising you on air charter for every kind of safari.

The Sudan's real splendor lies in its cultures and customs. Distinctive regional dress can be seen on the streets of Khartoum and Omdurman. Nilotic people from the South are conspicuous for their blackness, height and slender aquiline features. Many Nubians, traditional cultivators along the banks of the upper Nile, have been moved into and near Khartoum as a result of the Aswan Dam project; their reconstructed villages are worth a visit. The Gezira dam and cotton-irrigation scheme provides a chance to study Nubians and other Sudanese at work.

The peoples of the western Sudan, the area of EL FASHER and Sabanusa, are noted for their camels and horses, swordsmanship, poetry and songs; those of the center, near MALAKAL, have unique marriage, harvest and hunting dances. The Sudanese National Theater and Cultural Center in Khartoum offers displays of arts and crafts and traditional entertainment in the evening. Phone 51549 (Omdurman) for reservations and information. The season runs from October to June.

What to Buy

Sudanese handicrafts are excellent and inexpensive in the bazaars and markets of Omdurman and Khartoum. There is silver and gold work, fine ebony and ivory ware, stuffed animal trophies and leather goods including crocodile shoes and handbags. You'll generally find that hides and skins are well dyed and tanned.

Local Attitudes

Anti-Americanism has been a frequent government theme, especially since the 1967 Arab-Israeli War. American visitors may be troubled by hostile questions. Don't be too upset if Sudanese suspect you of being someone's agent. Since the failure of the 1971 coup, the Soviet Union, which backed the losing side, has become distinctly less popular, although it is still the principal source of arms. Talking politics is the national pastime but visitors should be judicious.

Women are advised not to travel alone. Miniskirts should not be worn. Permission should be asked before photos are taken, except at archaeological sites or in game parks.

Mosques are generally not open to non-Moslem visitors.

Weather, What to Wear, How Long to Stay

The Sudan can be almost unbearably hot. It's incredibly humid in the swampy south, but mercifully dry in the north and center. There are few cooling rains or evening breezes. In Khartoum, January and February are the "coolest" months, with daytime temperatures around 90. From April to October, it's like an oven; daily temperatures are over 100.

The lighter your clothing, of course, the better. Khaki shorts and white shirts are acceptable for men on all but the most formal occasions. Women should dress for the heat (but shorts and miniskirts are out in the Islamic areas of the Sudan).

Travelers willing to take the country on its own terms might spend several days in Khartoum and Omdurman, a week exploring the South, if permission can be obtained, and a week investigating the ruins and archaeological sites. If you're in a hurry, stick to Khartoum. Or skip the Sudan.

Communication

Arabic in a lilting Sudanese dialect is the official language. English is spoken by senior civil servants, army officers and secondary school and university students; it takes you everywhere and is preferred among southern Sudanese who resent the imposition of Arabic and Islam.

Postal, telegraph and telephone services are inadequate and frustrating. Wait until you get to East Africa to mail an important letter or package. The official press and radio are Arabic and militant. British newspapers several days old are available at the airport and leading hotels.

Emergencies

In case of serious medical problems head for Nairobi or Cairo, or try the Medical School of Khartoum University. Diplomatic relations were resumed with the United States in 1972 after a five-year hiatus, and the US Embassy has been reopened at Gamhouria Avenue, P.O. Box 699, Khartoum (tel. 71155-59).

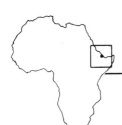

Territory of the Afars and Issas

(Territoire Français des Afars et des Issas —Djibouti)

Profile

STATUS: Overseas Territory of France. Formerly French Somalia.

SIZE: 8,880 square miles (slightly larger than Massachusetts). Population—125,000.

GEOGRAPHY: Harbor on Gulf of Aden; inland, mostly desert with rugged rock formations. Principal town—Djibouti (capital, 60,000).

CLIMATE: Very hot. Temperatures often exceed 100 degrees. From June to September hot, dry hamseen wind blows.

LANGUAGES: French (official), Arabic, Somali.

CURRENCY: Djibouti franc (FD), divided into 100 centimes. 10 FD = 5 cents; $1.00 = 200 FD.

VISAS: Not required for Americans with confirmed reservations and onward tickets staying three days or less. Transit visas (up to 10 days) cost $6. Available from French consulates and embassies.

AIRPORT: Djibouti (JIB), three and a half miles from city. Frequent flights to and from Paris, Tananarive, Reunion, Mauritius, Aden and Addis Ababa. Taxi into city, 330 FD ($1.65). Airport departure tax—400 FD ($2.00).

231

NATIONAL HOLIDAYS: All official French holidays, including May 1, Labor Day, and July 14, Bastille Day; Christian and Moslem holidays.

INFORMATION SOURCES: In US—French Embassy, Press and Information Service, 972 Fifth Avenue, New York, N.Y. 10021 (tel. 212/937-9700). In Djibouti—Office of Tourism, Place Menelik (tel. 2756).

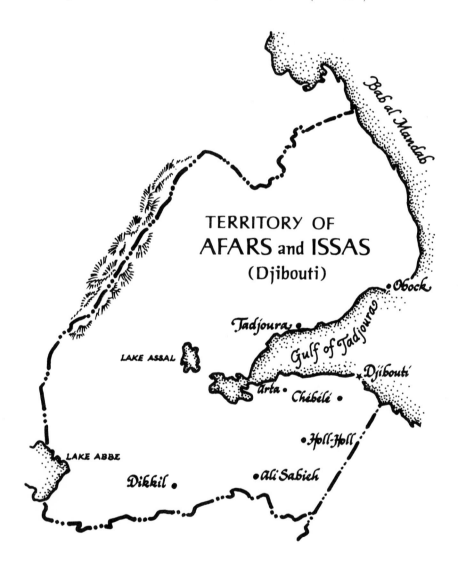

By Aaron Segal

Known officially since 1967 as the Territory of the Afars and Issas, but more commonly referred to by the name of its chief city, Djibouti, this military port enclave on the Red Sea is France's last possession on the continent of Africa. Its remoteness and oppressive heat keep all but the most curious away, but Djibouti is actually a good place to spend a few days relaxing, enjoying water sports, and partaking of French food and drink (not inexpensive). Should its politics come alive, however, as they did on several occasions in the 1960's, this little country could again become a focal point of conflict.

Because it has an excellent natural harbor at the southern end of the Red Sea, Djibouti has been fought over for centuries. Major contestants have been the Christian Amharic peoples of the Ethiopian highlands seeking to secure access to the sea and guarantee the land approaches to their kingdom, and the nomadic Islamic Somali peoples who range up and down the coast and along the interior.

Djibouti didn't become important, however, until the Suez Canal was built in 1875. France, shut out of Egypt, the Sudan and the Arabian Peninsula, settled for this site and proceeded to develop it with port installations and a petroleum refinery. In 1908 the Franco-Ethiopian Railway was completed, winding from the harbor 400 miles to the Ethiopian highlands and Addis Ababa. While Djibouti attracted traders from the four corners of the earth and became a cosmopolitan center, its interior residents, the Afar and Issa peoples, were ignored.

A decade ago the sweep of African nationalism and, particularly, the drive for a united state of Somali-speaking peoples threatened the French hold and caused Ethiopia to fear that the port would fall into the hands of its old enemies. The Somalis, having filtered in over the years, now constituted a near-majority of the port population although they were a distinct minority among the population (125,000) of the entire territory. They supported the Issa, to whom they are related.

France acted quickly to stifle Somali political demands. Thousands of Somali migrants were summarily deported during the 1960's and at the same time the education and social development of the Afar (Danakil) peoples were accelerated. At present Djibouti is an Overseas Territory of France, occupied by a French garrison as part of a strategic communications network from Europe to the Pacific. It enjoys limited internal autonomy and receives aid from France.

Just as the opening of the Suez Canal gave this little country a new future, the closing of the canal has all but sent it back into oblivion. France has tried to counter by pushing tourism, offering generous incentives for foreign private investment and seeking to create an industrial free port. Social unrest could erupt again despite the French troops on hand. Rising Soviet and United States interest in the Indian Ocean and the prospect of a reopening of the Suez Canal mean that France will probably try to hold on to Djibouti for the foreseeable future, especially since its abandonment could prompt a serious conflict between Ethiopia and Somalia. The book *Djibouti and the Horn of Africa* by Thompson and Adloff (Stanford, 1968) discusses these conflicts.

Money Matters

As part of the drive to stimulate trade and tourism the Djibouti franc has been made fully convertible at approximately 200 FD to $1. When you leave it's best to change it back to French francs or US dollars at the Banque de l'Indochine, which has airport and town offices.

Getting In and Out

There are frequent flight connections to and from Paris and the Indian Ocean islands of Madagascar and Reunion via Air France and Air Madagascar. There are also numerous flights to and from Addis Ababa by Ethiopian Airlines and Air Djibouti (one-way fare about $26).

Since the closing of the Suez Canal few passenger ships touch Djibouti but there is irregular service across the Red Sea to Aden by dhow and coastal freighter. Israeli Zim Lines and other freighters that carry passengers to and from the Israeli Red Sea port of Eilat occasionally stop at Djibouti but are more likely to put in at the Ethiopian port of Massawa.

The hitchhiker traveling south from Djibouti can try the irregular local buses and trucks between Djibouti and Hargeisa (a visa for Somalia is necessary), but it's surer to ride the railway west to Addis Ababa and from there to proceed south to Kenya. Single fare including meals for the formidable, lengthy trip is $27 first class (luxurious), $16 second class (comfortable), plus $14.70 for a bed compartment. The train leaves Djibouti at 8:45 pm on Monday, Thursday and Saturday, and arrives in Addis the next day at 6 pm. It is a memorable trip— snaking across the desert, climbing the escarpment walls and passing through the Amharic highlands. There's an excellent dining car.

Getting Around Within Djibouti

Djibouti is divided into four taxi fare zones with the charge of 50 cents for each zone. Automobiles (best are Peugeot) can be rented from

Tavera Auto Ecole Moderne, Avenue Saint-Laurent-du-Var (tel. 3354), or from Bellini, Rue d'Ethiopie (tel. 2869). There are buses within the city and collective taxis to the major inland attractions. Also available for rental are aquatic equipment from Apollo Sports, motorboats from the restaurant Le Relais on the airport road and sailboats through the helpful Office of Tourism, Place Menelik (tel. 2756). It is a good idea to visit that office, pick up their excellent literature (available in French and English) and ask their assistance.

Where to Stay

The town of DjIBOUTI has several good but expensive hotels. Because of the heat, air-conditioning does make a difference. The *Hôtel La Siesta* has 34 air-conditioned rooms, all with private bath (singles at $19 and doubles at $20 to $21), and there's a swimming pool. The *Djibouti Palace*, more centrally located on the Boulevard de Gaulle, has no pool but otherwise offers similar facilities, including television (taped French programs) and a nightclub. Prices including breakfast are $14.75 single and $19 double. Add 15 to 20 per cent for service charges. In the $10 to $15 range with air-conditioning and with or without private bath are the smaller *Continental, Europe, Oasis* and *Mini* hotels. If these are beyond your budget, the tourist office can suggest a family that puts up travelers. Outside Djibouti there's a restaurant and small guest house in the mountain resort of ARTA, 25 miles away, where some city dwellers go to escape the heat.

Where and What to Eat

DjIBOUTI has several good but relatively expensive French restaurants, some of which also offer Middle Eastern fare. These include the *Siesta, Djibouti Palace* and *Oasis* hotel dining rooms, and *Le Relais* on the airport road. Take scrupulous precautions if you eat at any other public place, for the heat and the insects get to most perishable comestibles well before you do.

What to See and Do

The town of DjIBOUTI, with a population of 60,000 (including 10,000 Europeans), can be fun if you take it easy in the 100-degree heat. Stay off the streets, as do most locals, between 11 am and 4 pm. The city has stately Arab houses, an attractive seaside drive (Corniche), inviting sidewalk cafes where you can sip Yemen coffee or mint tea, and narrow streets to explore. Visit the bustling market early in the day, and the port where dhows nudge modern freighters. The French residents are enthusiastic about outdoor sports, and through the Tourist Office you can join their activities, which include riding, pigeon shooting, scuba diving, sailing and parachuting. To avoid the heat head for the white sand beaches, the offshore coral islands of Maskali and Musha, or your air-conditioned room.

Outside Djibouti, there are pleasant excursions by bus or taxi to the palm grove of Ambouli or the summer resort of Arta, with its lovely panoramic view. Lake Assal, 60 miles away, is 500 feet below sea level and is one of the deepest saltwater lakes in the world. This is desolate desert country, pockmarked by deposits of rock salt. Those who enjoy the desert may want to head southwest toward Lake Abbe on the Ethiopian border, where masses of pink flamingos can be seen against a background of strange limestone formations in a sea of yellow sand. Other one-day excursions by bus or rented car can be made to the little coastal towns of the Afar people, including OBOCK and TADJOURA. The towns, built along lagoons and coral reefs, are near the Goda hills and the petrified forest of Day with its remains of giant junipers, wild olives, figs and acacias, the remnants of a glacial age. Outside Djibouti you are likely to see some wildlife—vultures and sea eagles, herons, ibis, pelicans, antelopes and gazelles, but nothing larger.

What to Buy

Djibouti is a free port with good buys in Japanese and European cameras, transistors, binoculars, toys and the like. But be sure that they come with a valid manufacturer's warranty since some firms do not honor claims for goods purchased in free ports. Safer buys are the ornate Afar daggers, Persian carpets, and brass- and bronze-studded chests. Take your time shopping and bargaining, share coffee or tea with the merchant and allow him to arrange the shipping (four to six months to North America by sea). At the Women's Craft Cooperative in town you can purchase inexpensive dolls in local dress, as well as necklaces, basketwork and beads, which you can carry with you.

Local Attitudes

Tourism is important to Djibouti and tourists are welcomed. Many residents will want to talk about politics and discussion is free, but discretion is suggested. American visitors are rare and apt to be objects of curiosity but not hostility.

Weather, What to Wear, How Long to Stay

The climate is one of the hottest in the world. Miniskirts, shorts and anything the French wear are fine, at least in the town.

Djibouti deserves a two- or three-day visit including one day spent visiting the countryside. Be sure to confirm your onward air or train reservations. Overbooking is fairly common.

Communication

French is the official language and the lingua franca, and Arabic is also widely spoken. Somali is the language of the Issa. English is spoken only by a handful of people at the tourist office and in the French government offices.

Mail, telegraph and telephone services are efficient to and from Paris. You can call Paris from 10 am to noon each day. Inter-African communications are poor.

French newspapers arrive daily. The local radio and television stations import most of their programs from Paris.

Emergencies

There are primitive local hospitals and somewhat better French military facilities, but if you have a serious illness head for Paris. The United States has no formal diplomatic representation here.

Mount Kilimanjaro

Olympics poster, Kenya   *Lake Manyara Park, Tanzania*

East Africa

Burundi
Kenya
Rwanda
Tanzania
Uganda
Zanzibar

THE REGION AT A GLANCE

Between the Indian Ocean and the tropical rain forests of Central Africa, nearly 40 million people live in five independent East African states. Part of this region is safariland, where lions doze in trees, elephants have the right of way on highways, and giraffes pose against the snow covered peaks of Mt. Kilimanjaro. Small wonder that over half a million visitors come here every year. Good roads, a broad range of accommodations, experienced tour operators, cooperative governments and magnificent animals all make the region's national parks and game reserves the greatest spectacle of its kind left in this world.

But in East Africa you can also learn something about fast-changing societies and people who are far more than photogenic. Along the coast a rich blend of Africans, Arabs, Asians and Europeans produced over centuries the great Swahili culture of commercial city-states. Pockets of people subsist on agriculture and cattle-raising in the interrupted contours of the interior, collected on temperate highlands and escarpments of the Great Rift Valley, on the slopes of majestic mountains and around the shores of great lakes. A broad, semi-arid tract separates the coast from these valleys and lakes. Where rainfall and soil permit, cultivation of coffee, cotton, tea and other cash crops encroaches upon the domains of the animal herds, domestic and wild.

Although the dream of a united federal East Africa remains unrealized, a common market and several major services (including East African

239

EAST AFRICA

Airways and Railways) are shared by Kenya, Tanzania and Uganda. Of the three, Kenya is the place where Western visitors feel most at home. Its thoroughly modern capital, Nairobi, and its open market economy, excellent communications, sophisticated tourist facilities and achievement-oriented elites make it a congenial place. But wealth in Kenya remains unevenly distributed and the encouragement of foreign investment has yet to enhance prosperity for all. By contrast, neighboring Tanzania has chosen an austere, egalitarian approach to development, with emphasis on national self-reliance and voluntary rural communalism. It is loosely tied to island Zanzibar, where in 1964 African majorities violently wrenched power from their traditional Arab rulers.

Uganda, Burundi and Rwanda, inland republics with compact, spectacular attractions, suffer from social divisions and occasional violence. The recent expulsion of Uganda's middle-class Asian community and the expropriation of foreign property by a capricious military regime have left beautiful Uganda in an atmosphere of insecurity without resolving its fundamental problems. Burundi and Rwanda, neglected wards of Belgium after Germany's loss in World War I, perch on the mountainous western edge of East Africa. The aristocratic Tutsi minority in Rwanda has lost its political supremacy to the Hutu peasant majority, but Burundi's Tutsi military regime clings to power in a turbulent society.

Scene of social ferment, political innovation and natural grandeur, East Africa has so much to see at reasonable costs that only time is a real barrier to a full regional experience. A minimal fortnight permits some game watching, a visit to Nairobi and Dar es Salaam, and a swim in the warm waters of the Indian Ocean. If you have come this far, however, and particularly if Uganda's political tensions subside, a month hardly suffices to cover East Africa.

PMA

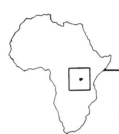

Burundi

(République du Burundi)

Profile

STATUS: Independent since July 1, 1962. Republic since November 28, 1966. Former German colony, administered by Belgium after first World War.

SIZE: 10,747 square miles (about the size of Maryland). Population—4,000,000.

GEOGRAPHY: Landlocked, mountainous. Elevation from 2,500 to 8,000 feet. Fertile plains along the shores of Lake Tanganyika. Principal towns —Bujumbura (capital and port, 100,000), Gitega, Bururi.

CLIMATE: Temperate most of the year. Dry seasons June to August and November to February. Heavy rains in March and April. Evenings in mountains are cool.

LANGUAGES: French and Kirundi (official), Swahili.

CURRENCY: Burundi franc, divided into 100 centimes. 10 francs = 11½ cents; $1.00 = 86.5 francs.

VISAS: Required. Available from Burundi Embassy in Washington and Burundi Mission to the U.N. Fee $7. Three passport photos needed. Delay of several days if applied for in person, several weeks by post. Also available from Burundi embassies in Uganda, Tanzania, Zaïre (two days' wait).

AIRPORT: Bujumbura (BJM), seven miles from city. Regular flights to and from Kampala, Nairobi, Kinshasa and Kigali. Free transport into city by Sabena Airlines microbus. Airport tax, 400 francs ($4.60).

NATIONAL HOLIDAYS: July 1, Independence Day; November 28, Republic Day; Christian holidays.

INFORMATION SOURCES: *In US*—Burundi Embassy, 2712 Connecticut Avenue NW, Washington, D.C. 20009 (tel. 202/387-4477); Permanent Mission of Burundi to the UN, 485 Fifth Avenue, New York, N.Y. 10017 (tel. 212/689-7090).

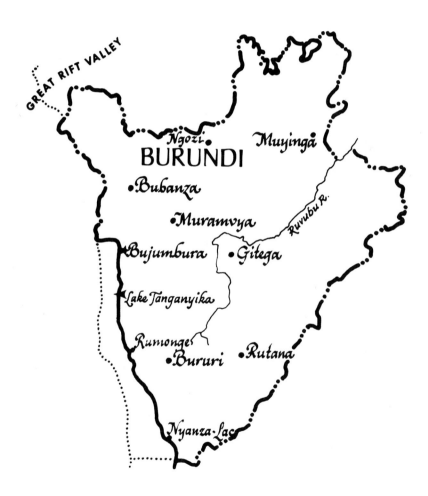

By Aaron Segal

A suspicious government discourages visitors to this beautiful but deeply troubled land, fearing that they might aggravate its already tragic ethnic problems. Tucked into the rugged mountains and craters north and east of Lake Tanganyika are two peoples, the Tutsi and the Hutu, sharing one language and many customs in a tiny, densely populated republic. Yet the Tutsi remain the masters, exploiting the Hutu majority much as they did for centuries under the Tutsi monarchy. Only 14 per cent of the Burundi population, the Tutsi aristocracy now relies on coercion and violence to stay in power. They are all the more apprehensive in view of neighboring Rwanda's 1959 revolution which ended Tutsi mastery in a similar set of circumstances, putting the Hutu into majority control. The stark poverty of an economy based on coffee, cotton and little else feeds the fires of ethnic bitterness.

The Tutsi, nomadic pastoralists and warriors, migrated from the Nile area into the lake region of central Africa between 300 and 400 years ago. In what are now Rwanda and Burundi they found the Hutu, a sedentary, agricultural Bantu people. Not only did the tall and graceful Tutsi look upon all forms of manual labor with contempt, they regarded the stocky and shorter Hutu as natural inferiors on all counts. It's difficult to imagine a situation more favorable to Tutsi economic, social and political suzerainty. The Hutu became vassals in their own land. They cultivated it as serfs, keeping a share of the produce and giving a portion to their Tutsi lords. The Hutu were granted the privilege of caring for the Tutsi's treasured longhorn cattle. Use of land, at least theoretically, belonged to the Tutsi mwami (king) who parceled it out to the ganwa (princes of royal blood), and to his chiefs and subchiefs who in turn subdivided it among their kin.

German colonial rule from 1885 to 1918 strengthened the position of the mwami but achieved little else. The Belgians who administered the territory under a League of Nations mandate and then a United Nations trusteeship (1919–1962) chose, like the Germans, to do so through the mwami and the ganwa, Belgium's main colonial interest being the Congo (Zaïre). It wasn't until 1955 that the feudal land-tenure system was abolished—and then only theoretically, for proposals to implement the change were never written into law. But the traditional social structure, particularly the relationship between Tutsi shebuja (lord) and Hutu mugabire (serf), began to weaken with the conversion to Christianity of large numbers of the population. There were sporadic revolts and in 1959 a serious outbreak of violence.

Burundi and Rwanda shared a common currency and an economic

union under Belgian rule. These arrangements fell apart after independence as a Hutu government came to power in Rwanda and thousands of Tutsi took refuge in Burundi. In Burundi itself Prince Louis Rwagasore tried to bridge ethnic differences with a broad-based anti-Belgian nationalist movement. Elected prime minister in 1961, Rwagasore was assassinated by Tutsi rivals a month after he took office. His successors have been unable to unite Hutu and Tutsi, or to stay in power without recourse to violence. The prestige of Rwagasore's father, the elderly Mwami Mwambutsa IV, proved equally unavailing. The Mwami was deposed in 1966 and a military republic was instituted that year under President Michel Micombero, then a 26-year-old Tutsi army officer.

Tutsi military rule has in turn failed to resolve Burundi's ethnic conflict. Several limited Hutu uprisings were crushed, but in April, 1972, a Hutu-led insurrection caused the death of hundreds of Tutsi and provoked widespread, devastating reprisals. Educated Hutu by the tens of thousands were systematically hunted down and killed. Also slain was the ex-Mwami's son and heir, Ntare V, who had reigned for two months in 1966 and had recently returned to Burundi from exile.

Some observers are convinced that sooner or later, as in Rwanda, the Hutu majority will seize power. The present government seems determined to prevent this from happening. The constant acute tension and the prospects of future violence keep most travelers away. Those who come should first read René Lemarchand's masterful background analysis, *Rwanda and Burundi* (Praeger, 1971).

Money Matters

Theoretically the Burundi franc is tied to that of Belgium and can be converted at the rate of about 86.5 to the US dollar. In practice, since no one wants Burundi francs, they are not convertible outside the country, except at a steep discount. They may be purchased at 10 to 20 per cent below the official rate in neighboring areas of Uganda and Zaïre, but it's illegal to bring them into the country and the penalties are severe. When you get to Burundi change enough currency to meet day-to-day needs. The Banque de la République du Burundi is open weekday mornings, as are the three commercial banks in the capital.

Getting In and Out

You can get to Burundi by plane or by train. Most travelers arrive by air on the thrice-weekly Sabena-Air Zaïre flight that puts down at Bujumbura's airport on its transcontinental journey between Kinshasa-Lubumbashi and Nairobi. There are also regular East African Airway flights from Entebbe and Nairobi to Kigali in Rwanda, where connections can be made to Bujumbura.

You'll probably find customs procedures slow and irksome at Bujumbura's dilapidated airport, but Sabena personnel can help expedite many matters. Call upon them if you need assistance.

If you're coming from Dar es Salaam you can take the three-day train trip across Tanzania to Kigoma on Lake Tanganyika, and a ferry from there to Bujumbura. The train trip is far more exotic than flying, and costs less than $30 for first class accommodations. But the ferry from Kigoma to Bujumbura (a half-day trip) runs only once a week and it's advisable to make reservations before leaving Dar. Belbase, the Belgian firm that handles shipping on Lake Tanganyika, has an office in Dar.

Driving in from East Africa via Uganda and across Rwanda is possible, but not recommended. For one thing you'll need a mass of documents— the East African Automobile Association in Kampala can help you get them, if you insist on coming this way. Driving to Burundi from Bukavu or Goma should definitely be avoided. The lakeside road is impassable in several places, especially during the rainy season, and travelers are subject to harassment and bribe demands from both regular and irregular military forces on the Zaïre side. (Should you find yourself in Bukavu, Air Zaïre can get you to Bujumbura.) A new all-weather road from Burundi to western Tanzania is to be built, but for the time being stick to planes or the train-ferry trip.

Don't, under any circumstances, try to enter Burundi without a visa.

Getting Around Within Burundi

This is not easy. There is only one paved road, leading 30 miles north into the mountains from Bujumbura. The remaining 3,000-odd miles of roadway are not only unpaved, but sometimes impassable. There are probably not more than 5,000 motor vehicles in the whole country. Although a few garages in the capital rent cars, their rates are high and their service is unreliable.

One of the best means of getting to see the country is through the various international organizations that use Bujumbura as a sub-regional center. These include the offices of the United Nations High Commissioner for Refugees, the International Labor Organization, the UN Food and Agricultural Organization, and various foreign missions. These organizations or the Catholic and Protestant missions are often willing to let travelers accompany their officials on trips.

Some areas of the country are open to travelers only by special permit.

Inquire at the Ministry of Interior. However, don't expect to get a permit.

Collective taxis and buses leave for interior towns at frequent—but irregular—intervals from the Place de l'Indépendance in Bujumbura. Much of Bujumbura itself can best be explored on foot. There are inexpensive private taxis to take you to the outskirts and foothills.

Where to Stay

BUJUMBURA has few visitors and accommodations are meager. The *Hôtel Paguidas* in the center of town houses most commercial travelers in an aura of political intrigue; rates here are $10 to $15 a night, and there's a lively bar and a reasonably priced restaurant. The *Burundi Palace* and the *Hôtel Résidence* are cheaper, but they lack the Paguidas's ambiance.

The Baptist Missionary Center has a guest house (primarily for its own guests) and the University of Burundi, five miles out of town, has limited residential facilities. There are also $1-a-night beds of a sort available at bars in the main African section of town (still known, more than 10 years after independence, as la ville indigène—native town).

Outside the capital, accommodations are limited to those that can be provided by Protestant and Catholic missions. These should be arranged in advance whenever possible—and if no fee is charged, by all means leave a small contribution.

Where and What to Eat

BUJUMBURA doesn't have many good places to eat. The restaurant in the *Hôtel Paguidas* is one of the better ones. It specializes in Greek and Belgian dishes. The *Burundi Palace* has an outdoor restaurant that serves Greek food at reasonable prices. *La Crémaillère* is an excellent Belgian restaurant that features fresh Nile perch and other lake fish. There are also inexpensive Indian restaurants.

Try the superb local arabica coffee served at several sidewalk cafes and the local beer (Primus); the soft drinks are not to everyone's taste. Bujumbura's water is said to be potable without filtering or boiling, but you are advised to stick to other beverages.

Night life is limited to a few sleazy bars in la ville indigène.

What to See and Do

You will no doubt spend most of your time in Burundi's capital, BUJUMBURA, and its environs. Situated at the northern end of Lake Tanganyika at an elevation of 2,500 feet, the city is not an unpleasant place, but neither is it one of Africa's most interesting vacation spots. Worth a visit are the African section of town with its daily outdoor market, the port area, the stadium, the Coffee Research Institute and, just outside of town, the university with its spectacular view of the lake. The city is small enough to be seen on foot.

At GITEGA, 45 miles east of the capital, you will find the former royal palace and a small museum of traditional art. You will also have an opportunity on the way to see the intensive pattern of cultivation characteristic of the country and the magnificent-looking but diseased longhorn cattle so highly prized by both Tutsi and Hutu.

Several other interesting excursions are possible from Bujumbura. The road south to RUMONGE and NYANZA-LAC skirts Lake Tanganyika and is an attractive drive. On this road, beyond the Cercle Nautique (yacht club), there's a huge stone commemorating the historic meeting of Henry Morton Stanley and Dr. David Livingstone at Ujiji on Lake Tanganyika in what is now Tanzania. About 70 miles southeast of the capital, just east of BURURI, a lovely little stream flows north into Lake Victoria and the Nile.

The road north of the capital offers spectacular views of the lake and city from the Collège du Saint Esprit (Catholic boys' secondary school) and the Protestant mission at Vugizo. This road leads to the active markets at BUGARAMA and MURAMVYA and beyond to the interesting crafts centers at NGOZI and MUYINGA. The road passes the monument to Prince Louis Rwagasore, the first prime minister, who was assassinated. Colorfully dressed women tend the monument every Monday.

Also worth seeing are the waterfalls of Nyakayi and Rusumu in western Burundi.

There are no game parks in the country—the high population density has eliminated most concentrations of wildlife—but flamingos, pelicans, marabou storks and other birds can be seen on Lake Tanganyika.

The diplomatic community in Bujumbura cultivates a wide variety of sports. There's a local yacht club, swimming in the lake (preferably from a boat away from the shoreline where the risk of bilharzia is greatest), fishing, water-skiing, riding and other outdoor activities. Most of these sports are accessible to visitors who have diplomatic connections.

Cultural life is limited largely to the university. The traditional festivals formerly associated with the monarchy are now staged with the blessing of the republican military regime. There are also festivities on July 1, anniversary of national independence, and on November 28, date of the establishment of the republic. On these and other occasions, Tutsi ("Watusi") dancers perform their majestic leaps in superb costumes. You'll have to inquire on the spot about these celebrations.

What to Buy

Intricately embroidered and beaded baskets of all shapes and sizes, walking sticks and canes, fish nets and traps, and other woven goods are the specialty of Burundi. They can be purchased inexpensively in the open-air market at Bujumbura or at considerably higher prices at the airport gift shop. The Librairie Saint Paul has handicrafts for sale, as well as books and periodicals.

Two exciting markets outside the capital have fine displays of local crafts. The open market at Musinda in the Ruzizi Valley, less than an hour's drive from Bujumbura, features wrought iron and steel ware, including knives, long sabers and spearheads in more than 20 designs. A market at Muramvya in the mountains has excellent buys in drums and cowhide products (and there's a spectacular view from Lookout Point nearby). These markets can be reached by bus, as well as car. Pack a picnic lunch if you go.

Local Attitudes

Burundi is one of the most volatile countries in Africa. Its politics are passionate and bloody, and travelers should exercise extreme discretion in discussing them. Foreigners are mostly diplomats, a few Canadians, Swiss, Belgian and other technical experts and volunteers, and Catholic and Protestant missionaries. Political intrigue is a way of life and visitors are likely to encounter suspicion.

The most important external presence is still that of Belgium, source of external aid, markets and technical assistance. Diplomatic relations with the US have been strained at various times since independence but there is no animosity toward Americans as such.

Weather, What to Wear, How Long to Stay

Its elevation (average altitude for the whole country is 5,300 feet) gives Burundi a most congenial climate. Days are mild and evenings cool. At the capital the average annual temperature is 73 degrees; at higher elevations it goes down to 65 degrees. Precipitation averages 40 to 60 inches a year, with the heaviest rainfall in March and April. June, July and August are the driest months. At least in the mountains, sweaters are needed.

Bujumbura and Gitega can be seen in a stopover of two or three days on your way from East Africa to Kinshasa or vice versa. Exploring the lake country and the Nile sources requires another couple of days.

Communication

French and Kirundi are Burundi's official languages and Swahili is widely used in commerce. It would be unusual to come across anyone who speaks English, but you can manage with some knowledge of French.

Burundi's sole newspaper, *Unité et Révolution*, is published weekly by the government. One of the two radio stations is also government-owned; the other is a Protestant missionary outlet. Some of the missionary organizations publish periodicals of very limited circulation. All media are subject to strict government supervision. The principal source of information, therefore, is "radio trottoir," the gossip of the capital's sidewalk cafes.

Internal and external postal and telephone services leave a great deal to be desired. Some of the most beautiful stamps in the world are issued by Burundi, but don't use them to mail important letters or packages. Overseas radio-telephone connections are through Brussels.

Emergencies

Don't get sick in Burundi. Medical facilities in the capital are poor and elsewhere in the country they are awful or non-existent. Head for Nairobi in case of serious illness.

The American Embassy is on Chaussée Prince Louis Rwagasore in Bujumbura (tel. 34-54).

Kenya

Profile

STATUS: Independent since December 12, 1963. Republic since December 12, 1964. Former British colony.

SIZE: 224,960 square miles (twice the size of New Mexico). Population —10,635,000 (including 150,000 Asians, 50,000 Europeans).

GEOGRAPHY: Indian Ocean coastline; interior rises to 5,500-foot plateau and highlands bordered in east by Aberdare Mountains and west by Great Rift Valley; farther west, low-lying plains along Lake Victoria; north, arid country bordering Ethiopia and Somalia. Principal cities— Nairobi (capital, 500,000), Mombasa (port, 250,000).

CLIMATE: Coast is warm and humid with cool evening breezes; plateau (including Nairobi) and highlands temperate all year with few Nairobi days above 80 degrees or below 60. Long rains March to May, short rains mid-October to mid-December.

LANGUAGES: English and Swahili (both official).

CURRENCY: Kenya shilling, divided into 100 cents. 1 shilling = 14 US cents; $1.00 = 7 shillings.

VISAS: Required. Available from Kenya Tourist Office in New York and Embassy of Kenya in Washington. Fee $3.15. Acquired in 24 hours in person, several weeks by mail. British embassies issue visas where Kenya is not represented.

AIRPORTS: Embakasi Airport (NBO), 11 miles from Nairobi. Frequent direct and transfer flights to and from New York, major European cities, India, Indian Ocean and East and Southern Africa. Transportation into city—East African Airways minibus, 5 shillings (70 cents); taxi, 20 shillings ($2.80—establish fare in advance). Port Reitz Airport (MBA), eight miles from Mombasa. Frequent flights to and from Arusha, Dar es

Salaam, Nairobi, Tanga and Zanzibar. Bus and taxi into city, 8 shillings ($1.14). International airport departure tax—15 shillings ($2.10).

NATIONAL HOLIDAYS: June 1, Madaraka (self-government) Day; 1st Monday in August, bank holiday; October 20, Kenyatta Day; December 12, Independence Day; Christian and Moslem holidays.

INFORMATION SOURCES: *In US*—Kenya Tourist Office, 15 East 51st Street, New York, N.Y. 10017 (tel. 212/486-1300); Permanent Mission of Kenya to the UN, 866 United Nations Plaza, New York, N.Y. 10017 (tel. 212/421-4740); Embassy of Kenya, 2249 R Street, Washington, D.C. 20008 (tel. 202/387-6101). *In Kenya*—Information Bureau, P.O. Box 42278, corner of Queensway and Government Road, Nairobi (tel. 23285); East African Wildlife Society, P.O. Box 20010, Nairobi; Information Bureau, P.O. Box 5072, Mombasa (tel. 5428).

By Aaron Segal

According to a popular song in the Swahili tongue, "God's handiwork is beautiful in Kenya." This description can be endlessly embroidered but hardly improved upon.

A 225,000-square-mile microcosm of the continent, Kenya contains all that is lush, all that is burning and barren; huge lakes, mountains that climb the sky, silver beaches, scorching plains, rain forests, waterfalls, and cool green farmlands, populous animal kingdoms and deserts.

Though Kenya's present popularity with travelers may owe much to tourist promotion, it is just as dependent on the glowing reports of those who have been here. Few return to say that Kenya herself disappointed them—though they may admit that they spent beyond their means or had to take second choice among overcrowded accommodations.

For the traveler with limited time, Kenya remains the best buy on the continent—a lot of enjoyment and a lot of Africa for the price. For the fortunate visitor with leisure to explore on and off the tourist trail, Kenya's variety awaits—all the raw material necessary for an unforgettable adventure in a new culture-time continuum.

The land now called Kenya has been in contact with the rest of the world through commerce since at least the 6th century before Christ, but it was not until about 120 years ago that Westerners began to penetrate its interior. In the interim, slavers and merchants from Arabia, southern Asia and the Persian Gulf mixed with the African populations of the long coast from Mogadishu to Sofala (Mozambique), developing great mercantile city-states with a language and culture called Swahili.

The Western influx began haltingly as missionaries intent on both Christianizing the inhabitants and ridding them of the threat of slavery set up way stations and explored the wilderness that lay between the coast and Lake Victoria. Rebmann and Krapf, two intrepid evangelists, told about Mt. Kilimanjaro and Mt. Kenya—but were laughed at by the Royal Geographic Society; which could hardly have been expected to swallow the story of snow-capped peaks astride the equator.

Competition among the imperial powers in the "scramble for Africa" during the 1880's brought a reluctant Britain gradually into control. Earlier, Joseph Thomson had found a way to Lake Victoria from the coast through Masailand. Thus, Britain could consider building a railway across this hitherto-unknown terrain that would facilitate the transport of men and goods to the territory of Uganda, where Lugard and others of the Imperial British East Africa Company had established what they considered an essential stronghold against the encroaching German and French imperialists.

The successful completion in 1901 of the "lunatic line," as the Uganda Railway's parliamentary foes had dubbed it, opened up Kenya to colonization and economic development. White settlers arrived in force to take advantage of the fertile land and opportunities for investment in a rapidly growing economy. Nairobi, so recently an unsightly railway supply depot, began to take on city airs, and the first tourism was encouraged by Uganda Railway posters advertising "the Highlands of British East Africa as a winter home for aristocrats."

The outbreak of World War I marked the beginning of Britain's troubles in East Africa. A little-known but bloody page in history belongs to the more than 40,000 British and askaris (African troops) who lost their lives there before 1918. For the next three decades, British imperial control seemed secure, despite a steadily gathering African resentment against foreign appropriation of land, jobs and social opportunity, especially the exclusive hold of the settlers over the fertile "White Highlands."

Most troubled by the loss of land and by the racial segregation were the Kikuyu, who make up 20 per cent of Kenya's population. Their grievances erupted in the Mau Mau movement in 1952. After years of bloody struggle, Mau Mau was suppressed militarily, but it brought about major political and social reforms. Not the least of these were an elected African majority in parliament and a government commitment to purchase white settler land for redistribution among the African population.

Imprisoned during Mau Mau, Mzee (Old Man) Jomo Kenyatta, upon release, took the reins of the Kenya African National Union (KANU) and led his party, and his fledgling nation, to independence under his presidency in 1964. With the expansion of tourism, coffee, cotton and tea growing, and light industry, the East African Community, a common market shared with Tanzania and Uganda, has grown rapidly. But this growth has been unevenly distributed, and tensions remain within the Community and among the races and ethnic groups of Kenya itself.

President Kenyatta has managed to balance the loyalties of his own Kikuyu people and those of the Kalenjin, Kamba, Kisii, Abaluhya and others. Most disaffected are the Luo, 15 per cent of the population, who live along the shores of Lake Victoria. Their alienation, and the problem of presidential succession, were worsened by the assassination in 1969 of Tom Mboya, a young Luo cabinet minister and a brilliant trade unionist —and, some thought, Kenyatta's heir-apparent.

The development of government-encouraged African private enterprise is gradually reducing the economic predominance of the resident European and Asian minorities. The latter have been thus far allowed to remain, although they have been denied employment if they failed to acquire Kenyan citizenship. Much depends on the longevity of Kenyatta himself and the handling of his eventual succession. Meanwhile, the economy rises but so does urban unemployment.

Books that will interest the traveler are Kenyatta's own account of his struggles, *Suffering Without Bitterness*, and his anthropological classic, *Facing Mount Kenya*; Rosberg and Nottingham's *The Myth of Mau Mau*; Elspeth Huxley's various accounts of her childhood as a settler and her biography of Lord Delamere, *White Man's Country*; as well as the lyrical works of Ernest Hemingway and Karen Blixen (Isak Dinesen), and fine Kenyan writers like James Ngugi (*Weep Not Child* and other titles). On the practical side, there's *A Guide to Kenya and Northern Tanzania* (Sierra Club/Scribner's, 1971), which covers the obvious tourist attractions. The East African Automobile Association's *Guide* is indispensable to motorists, full of common sense about roads and sights. *Kenya's Coast* by Simon Mollison (East African Publishing House, 1971) is a comprehensive guide to that area, better on beaches and shops than restaurants.

The Shell Oil Company produces the best road maps of East Africa and a series of attractive, inexpensive brochures on East African wildlife, birds, flowering trees, etc., most handy for the parks. Free literature including the official *Hotel Guide* is available from the Kenya Tourist Office in New York or from the Embassy of Kenya in Washington.

Money Matters

Kenya has no limit on the amount of foreign exchange that you bring in, but strictly controls the import and export of Kenya currency. Money can be exchanged at the airport or city offices of Barclays, Standard, Ottoman, Grindlays and other banks, which are open during the week from 9 am to 1 pm and from 9 to 11 am on Saturday. Travelers checks and major credit cards are accepted at large shops and hotels. Tanzania and Uganda currency is available in Kenya from private sources at less than official rates but it is illegal to enter either country with money obtained in this way.

Getting In and Out

Kenya is most easily reached by air, through Nairobi's Embakasi Airport, the busiest in East Africa, or the smaller Port Reitz Airport at Mombasa. The Nairobi airport is served by more than 30 carriers. There are direct flights from New York on Pan American and TWA; from European capitals on most major airlines, and from Zambia, Ethiopia, Egypt, Israel, India, Pakistan and Japan on the national and other carriers. East African Airways flies to both Europe and India and has daily connecting flights from Nairobi to most major cities in Tanzania and Uganda, several flights weekly to Mogadishu (Somalia) and Aden (Yemen), flights south to Malawi connecting to Rhodesia and South Africa, and flights east to the islands of Mauritius, Seychelles and Madagascar in the Indian Ocean. Connections east-west across Africa are less frequent and should be booked well in advance. Sabena and Air Zaïre fly between Nairobi and Kinshasa (Zaïre) via Entebbe (Uganda) and Bujumbura (Burundi), while Pan American and Ethiopian Airlines link Nairobi to Accra (Ghana) and Lagos (Nigeria).

More and more travelers are taking advantage of package tours and charter flights. Some charters offer a New York-Nairobi round trip for $500—less than half the regular fare. Most routes involve an independently booked charter from North America to Europe, then another charter from London (Nilestar, Sea and Sand, etc.) or the Continent (Atlantis). The London-Nairobi charter flights are about $175 each way.

Package tours from North America run from $1,000 to $2,000, depending on length (14–21 days is usual), luxury and scope. Even with the additional cost of a ticket to Europe, package tours from London or the Continent are much cheaper ($400–$800) for similar periods of time, though accommodations are likely to be less posh. The major drawback of package tours is that the tourist usually is hustled from game park to game park, with little chance to see the country and the people.

If you decide to fly on a regular air passage rather than a charter or package tour, your ticket to Nairobi can take you a long way. It should permit at minimum several European and African stops; for a few dollars extra it can also include Dar es Salaam (Tanzania); and for another five to 10 per cent, Johannesburg, Lourenço Marques or an Indian Ocean destination.

Entering Kenya by sea is more difficult. Because of the closing of the Suez Canal, nearly two weeks have been added to ship journeys from North America or Europe to the port of Mombasa. Deutsche Ost-Afrika, Holland Afrika, Scandinavian East African, Lloyd Triestino, and Royal Interocean operate passenger-cargo vessels from various European ports to Mombasa, but it's nearly four weeks around the Cape. Robin Lines and Farrell Lines have limited passenger capacity on their freighter services from the eastern US to Mombasa. There is also a one-week trip between Mombasa and Bombay (India) via British India Lines. Israeli Zim Line freighters and other craft have irregular passenger service connecting Mombasa with Eilat on the Red Sea and other African ports.

East African Railways' overnight train rides between Kampala and Nairobi are comfortable (first class), economical (second class) and unforgettable (third). The dining cars serve adequate meals.

Paved roads connect Nairobi with Kampala and with Arusha in northern Tanzania. East African Road Services runs daily express buses to and from Kampala, Arusha and Dar es Salaam. Hitchhiking is good on the Nairobi-Kampala road, (though travelers should avoid Uganda altogether during the current unrest—see Uganda chapter), but between Nairobi and Arusha there is less traffic. The drive from Mombasa to Tanga in Tanzania is rougher, especially during the rainy season. Hitchhiking on this route is poor.

For road travel between Kenya and Somalia you need special permission from Kenyan authorities to cross the NFD (Northern Frontier District), where a once-active Somali secessionist movement seems to be in quiescence. Two four-wheel-drive vehicles are necessary, and a Somali visa must be obtained in advance. Overland travel between Kenya and Ethiopia is grueling but exciting. It also requires four-wheel drive, or stamina to ride infrequent local buses, as well as careful planning. Roads are passable in the dry season only from January 1 to March 15 and from June 15 to October 15. Request information from the Ethiopian Tourist Association (see Ethiopia chapter) and from the Automobile Association of East Africa, P.O. Box 87, Nairobi.

Getting Around Within Kenya

Nairobi and Mombasa are best seen on foot. If you must ride, however, both cities have municipal bus lines with low fares. Taxi drivers in both cities are aggressive, seldom use their meters and try to charge the limit, especially if their fare is white. If you do use a taxi, settle the price before getting in; 35 cents a mile should cover it.

Nairobi traffic is heavy and since most people with cars go home to lunch, there are four rush hours a day. If you plan to spend much time in the city, consider renting a bicycle or scooter (with a strong lock). Hitchhiking is good both in the city and on the roads leading out. To seek a lift, post a notice at the East African Automobile Association office on Kenyatta Avenue.

You can select a package tour after arriving in Kenya, but this process is cheaper than an all-inclusive package only if you have arrived on a charter flight. In Nairobi the Information Bureau near the Hilton lists many local tour operators, and the choice of tours is enormous—from three-hour jaunts around the city ($3) or through Nairobi Game Park ($6) to rambles over much of East Africa. Some reliable operators include Akamba Tours (Northey Street, P.O. Box 46466, tel. 24674); United Touring Company (Muindi Mbingu Street, P.O. Box 42196, tel. 20911); Archer's Tours (New Stanley House, P.O. Box 40097, tel. 22871); Subzali Tours (Hilton Hotel, P.O. Box 46595, tel. 29573), and— the daddy of them all—Ker, Downey & Selby (New Stanley House, P.O. Box 41822, tel. 20667). East African Airways also offers tours.

Hertz, Avis and most of the tour operators rent both self-driven and chauffeur-driven vehicles. Rentals of self-driven cars start at $5 a day or $30 a week for a VW 1300 or Datsun 1200. Land Rovers cost $11.45 a day or $68.70 a week. Minicabs, on Government Road, has very low rates for small cars.

Driving is on the left in Kenya. Gasoline costs about 70 cents a gallon in Nairobi and twice that in remote areas. Make certain any rented car is equipped with up-to-date maps, a jack and tool kit, a decent spare and an East African Auto Association guide, and that your contract includes towing and repair privileges in case of breakdowns.

If you are going to stay awhile, you might consider buying a car to beat the rental tariffs. Resale is comparatively easy; most franchised dealers for Peugeot, Volkswagen, Toyota and other auto manufacturers will sell you a used car and guarantee eventual repurchase.

Much of Kenya can be seen inexpensively by bus, collective taxi or rail. The Kenya Bus Company has daily express runs between Nairobi and Mombasa, Kisumu, Nakuru and Eldoret. Coast Bus Service on Reata Road runs buses to Mombasa and Malindi.

Collective taxis, usually Peugeot station wagons, will accommodate up to six persons and luggage. The Rift Valley Peugeot Service (RVP) on Latema Road in Nairobi has regular runs from Nairobi to Mombasa, Nakuru, Kisumu and Kericho. RVP taxis leave Nairobi for Mombasa at 7:30 am and 2:30 pm and charge $5 for the 300-mile ride (70 cents extra for the front seat). The route runs through Tsavo National Park, famed for elephants which can sometimes be seen from this road. RVP taxis leave Nairobi at 8 am and 2 pm for the $4 ride to Nakuru and Kisumu. This route passes through the scenic Central Province, the Rift Valley escarpment, the former "White Highlands," Naivasha, and the tea estates of Kericho. You can get off along the way and take a local taxi or hitchhike to the Naivasha Bird Sanctuary or the Lake Nakuru National Park, largely a flamingo sanctuary.

Some of the last steam-powered trains operating anywhere carry freight and passengers on rural runs from Nairobi. East African Railways trips are slow and stately, passing through splendid country between Nairobi and Kisumu, and Nairobi and Kampala. An overnight sleeper trip to Mombasa leaves Nairobi at 6:30 pm and arrives at 8 the next morning. With meals and bedding, the excellent first class accommodations are almost as expensive as an air trip—about $25; second class sleeps six in a fairly comfortable compartment for half the price; third class is cheap but tiring, with wooden benches only.

East African Airways flies daily from Nairobi to Mombasa, Kisumu and Malindi. A bargain for busy travelers is the $140 unlimited-travel ticket allowing you 14 days of flying anywhere within East Africa. Regular round trip fare, Nairobi-Mombasa, is $56.70, but excursion fares are also available at reduced rates. Some of the most interesting spots in Kenya—for example, Lake Rudolf—are best reached by private flights. Charter operators include Air Kenya Ltd, Safari Air Services, and Kenya Air Charters: inquire at the private Wilson Airport, Nairobi; or go to the famous Dambusters Bar at that airport and try to hitch a ride with some departing charter pilot for less than the usual price. Wilson is also headquarters for the Flying Doctor Service. There is an amateur fliers' club there (The Aero Club) that can give you information about renting planes.

The East African Railways & Harbours motorship *Victoria* sails from Kisumu to Port Bell (Uganda) and around Lake Victoria. Make reservations through the railways office in Nairobi. Smaller ships ply the lake between Kisumu and Kavirondo Gulf and also sail to the Rusinga Islands.

If you are a good sailor and want to go to Lamu Island cheaply by sea, take the Kenya Meat Company boat that goes up every 24 hours from Mombasa. At the Old Customs House, Bwana Badi will sell you, for about $6, a one-way ticket that entitles you to deck space. Leaving Mombasa at 4:30 pm, you arrive in the Lamu Straits just as the sun rises and, for another 50 cents, you catch a motor launch or dhow for the ride over to Lamu Town. Be sure to bring your own food and water and a sleeping bag on this exhilarating but sometimes chilly journey.

Where to Stay

Kenya is trying hard to keep up with the swelling tide of visitors. The Ministry of Tourism publishes an annual hotel guide describing accommodations and listing all approved facilities. The best Kenyan hotels meet international standards.

In Mombasa and Nairobi, sign up for bed and breakfast only, so that you will have a chance to try the cities' fine restaurants. Full board is probably best at hotels in outlying areas.

NAIROBI has four luxury hotels—the *Hilton*, the *New Stanley*, the *Panafric* and the *Intercontinental*. All charge between $15 and $25 for single rooms with breakfast. The *Hilton* has overpriced, mediocre food, many boutiques and galleries, a rather attractive decor and a central location. The *New Stanley*, located at the hub of downtown activity, is the home of the bustling Thorn Tree outdoor restaurant. The Long Bar, indoors, is locally famous as the spot where white hunters trap their human prey. The *Panafric*, on a hill outside the city center, is modernistic and slick, with fine cuisine. The *Intercontinental*, also a sophisticated spot, has good food and a pleasant outdoor pool and grill.

If you want to feel that you're in Africa, however, try the colonial-style *Norfolk*, across from the university, within easy walking distance of downtown. Once the focal point of white settler life, the Norfolk retains its charm and freshness. The bar indoors is straight out of Hemingway, and Sunday curry brunch on the terrace is a delightful social occasion. There is a swimming pool and sauna, and both suites and bungalows are set among lovely gardens. Rates begin at a moderate $8 to $13 a day for a single room but climb steeply from there. Nearby is the *College Inn*, where $9 a day will give you bed and breakfast in congenial surroundings frequented by visiting academics. On the other side of the campus on Statehouse Road is the *United Kenya Club*, long a multiracial gathering spot. Fine food, a good bar and tasteful rooms, plus the chance to meet and talk with the Kenyan elite make this an especially appealing spot. Reserve well in advance by writing P.O. Box 2220, Nairobi.

For lower rates, try the *Devon*, on Ainsworth Road near the International Casino, a garden-and-bungalow hotel with a good dining room; $5 to $7 for a single with breakfast. The rustic *Mayfair* on Sclaters Road charges $7 a single for bed and breakfast. These two spots are a bit out of the way; remember to add an extra dollar for taxi fare to and from the downtown area. Nine dollars will buy a comfortably cramped room—and breakfast—for two, with private toilet and shower, at the *Hotel Salama* at the bustling and dirty, but convenient, downtown corner of Tom Mboya Street and Campos Ribeiro Avenue; similar accommodations can be had for a dollar or two less at the *Hotel Gloria*, one block away.

The YMCA near the university, a good place to meet Kenyans, has a swimming pool, game room, dining room, and arrangements for either nightly or long-term rates. Accommodations are for men only.

The YWCA has inexpensive rooms for women and couples. St. Mary's Hostel on Protectorate Road caters especially to women students. Singles with breakfast at the tiny *Hotel Pigalle* on Gulzaar Street cost $7.

Travelers with really tight budgets should try the Nairobi Quaker Center or go to the Sikh Temple off Government Road, where anyone truly in need is welcome to bed and board in return for light household duties. This hospitality, freely given at Sikh temples all over East Africa, should not be abused.

Kenya is also adding to its number of youth hostels, establishments that are often open to older travelers. A new hostel is being completed on Racecourse Road in Nairobi to complement the one at Kabete, seven miles from the city, opposite the Kenya Institute of Administration. The Christian Council of Kenya operates a delightful beach hostel at Kanamai, 15 miles north of Mombasa.

MOMBASA and the Kenya coast offer oceanfront hotels, self-service bungalows, camping grounds and delightful residential clubs. One of the best hotels in all Africa, the 86-room *Oceanic* in Mombasa, begins at $14 for a single bed and breakfast. The *Manor*, reminiscent of the colonial Norfolk in Nairobi, has excellent meals and a pleasant outdoor bar; $8 for a single. The *Hotel Splendid*, with a lively bar and dancing facilities, is $7 for single rooms with bath, breakfast included. The *New Carlton* and *Rex*, though a bit run down, are not bad at the same price. *New Sea Breezes* charges a modest $4.50 per single and the management gives personal attention to its guests' culinary requests. A word about the *New Palm Court*—once a recommended spot for young travelers of modest means, it is now run down and without proper facilities; the *New Carlton*, a sister hotel, is in better shape.

Outside the two main cities Kenyan hotels vary widely in quality, but are numerous. Book in advance if possible.

The coast has become so popular that at times it is unpleasantly overcrowded in the resorts and restaurants. Advance bookings are necessary for the Christmas and Easter holidays and advisable during the peak season of December-March.

Most of the tourist action around Mombasa is not on the island-town of Mombasa itself but on the beaches to the north and south of town, yet within a 20-minute trip by car or hotel-sponsored bus. A favorite among the north coast resorts, across the Nyali Bridge, is the *Nyali Beach Hotel*, with its multi-course meals, graceful verandas and palm-fringed beaches. The atmosphere here, and at most of the beach motels, is largely European, except on Tuesday and Saturday nights when Asian and African locals join hotel residents for semi-weekly poolside dances. Then it's Kenya at its multiracial best. Single rates here begin at around $9, with compulsory full board; doubles begin at $16, run up to around $29.

Other north coast resorts include the pleasant *Mombasa Beach Hotel*, with full-board single occupancy running $20–$30 for two. Farther up the road north to Bamburi (on the way to Malindi) is the cheaper *Whitesands Hotel*, with a variety of accommodations. In the main building, single rooms, full board, run $16; doubles around $12 per person.

Cottages may also be rented for around $20 per day, single; $15 per person per day, double. Rondavels without a sea view go for $12, single; $9 per person double, always full board. At most of the coast hotels there are low-season rate reductions, the off season running from late April through October.

Heading south from Mombasa, across the Likoni Ferry, are two resorts among a burgeoning number being built as the government cuts a road closer to the surf—unfortunately, through the magic of the lush Jadini Forest. The charming *Two Fishes Hotel* at Diani Beach near Ukunda runs about $18 for full-board singles, and there are the usual beach sports facilities. Nearby, the *Jadini* charges $16 for pleasant single rooms with full board. North again, at Turtle Bay, two hotels offer singles with board for $9 to $12—the *Ocean Sports* and the *Seafarers' Club* (where a small membership fee is required). Just outside Mombasa at Bamburi, the *Coraldene Beach* rents self-service cottages with linens at $4 a day per person; the little bar caters to vegetarians and has local dances. In the near-luxury class is the *Dolphin* at Shanzu, charging $16 to $22 for full-board singles. Smaller, prettier and cozier is the nearby *Casuarina*, at $7 to $10, full-board single.

MALINDI, an agreeable little town, is great for swimming, snorkeling and sunning. There are four resort hotels, of which the best is *Lawford's*. While tourists from Western Europe fill most of the hotels, it is possible to find small detached bungalows and campsites near Malindi that are quite secluded. *Kenya's Coast* (East African Publishing House) is invaluable for a visitor to the area.

On LAMU ISLAND, there is an outstandingly good hotel, called *Peponi*. There are also a few acceptable guest houses, the best of which is *Chandara's*. Peponi, which is on Shela Beach, charges $21 a day per person, full board, and will also extend beach privileges to luncheon guests. Chandara's guest house, in Lamu Town facing the seafront, offers clean rooms with the basic amenities for a dollar a night. A boat runs between Shela and Lamu Town; it's a pleasant two-mile walk over the dunes.

Anywhere north or west of Nairobi is called "up-country." Here hotels are the best places to eat and drink, so full board is advisable. In KERICHO, stop at the *Tea Hotel*—one of Africa's finest—for $15 per person with meals. The *Pig and Whistle* in MERU and the *Izaak Walton Inn* at EMBU are less luxurious, but are located in beautiful mountain settings; board and room run from $9 to $13 per person. The *Highlands Hotel* at MOLO, site of polo and fox hunting, is another colonial favorite, with fine old buildings and impressive grounds, golf, tennis and riding. The tariff is a mere $9 per person. Also recommended is the *Naro Moru*

River Lodge on the slopes of Mt. Kenya near a good trout stream; $10 single, full board. Other up-country hotels include the *Outspan* at NYERI, the *Lake Naivasha*, the *New Kisumu*, the *Thomson Falls* and the *Kitale*. NAKURU has the *Midlands* and the *Stag's Head*; the former is cheaper but the latter has better food.

"Safari" is a Swahili word meaning "to travel"—and old-time safaris were rugged affairs conducted close to nature, a far cry from the luxury-lodge tour of today. It is still possible to get the feeling of the real thing in Kenya by staying at the simple yet comfortable campsites accessible through the Ministry of Tourism and Wildlife (P.O. Box 30025, tel. 24221, Nairobi). Usually no special reservations are necessary.

Lodges are listed in the Ministry of Tourism Hotel Guide already mentioned. Two of the best are *Keekorok* in the Masai Mara Reserve on the Tanzania border, and the *Samburu Lodge* in the park of the same name; both charge $16 a day for a single, full board. Slightly less expensive tent accommodations are also available at Keekorok. You can arrange with the Department of Game and Fisheries to camp in a photographic block. A particularly nice one adjoins the Masai Mara Reserve.

In popular Amboseli Park you can see Mt. Kilimanjaro, Masai herdsmen and a wide variety of game. Outside the park entrance at NAMANGA, on the Nairobi-Arusha road, is the gracious and comfortable *Namanga Hotel*, with thatched roof and Masai decorations. Single full board is $14. Inside the park, *Ol Tukai Lodge* offers less-expensive accommodations in small houses with cooking facilities. Two little-known lodges are the *Lake Baringo*, on the edge of the Rift Valley, and the *Maralal*, near the Northern Frontier District. Lake Baringo has fine fishing and swimming and charges $30 a day full board for doubles; the self-service Maralal offers cottages with linens and cooking facilities at $5 per person.

Tsavo Game Park, Kenya's largest, is bisected by the main Mombasa-Nairobi highway. At popular *Kilaguni Lodge* in Tsavo West, single full board is $28 per day. The poor man's equivalent can be found at the *Bushwhackers Safari Camp*; self-service cottages with linens are $5 a person, there is a clear stream and a swimming pool, and you'll see lots of animals.

A camp where you can live royally for $41 a day per couple is *Tsavo Tsafaris East*, known locally as Cottar's Camp, which is located in an isolated spot on the Athi River in the middle of the game park. The camp has excellent food, provides Land Rover safaris, and affords a look at one of the largest concentrations of big game in Africa. You must have a confirmed reservation here to be permitted entry to the park at the Cottar's Camp gate. Book through Silver Spear Tours, Express Transport Ltd, Nairobi.

If money is no object, you might consider staying at the *Mt. Kenya Safari Club* at NANYUKI, near Mt. Kenya. The lodge, built by American oil man Robert Ryan and actor William Holden, has prices that start at $50 a day per suite—but for only $5 you can buy a one-day nonresident's membership that entitles you to enjoy the golf course, tennis courts, pool, bird sanctuary, and other facilities.

Kenya has three lodges where the specialty is midnight game watching by artificial moonlight. The best and most famous is *Treetops*, in Aberdare National Park; package excursions that take you there generally include lunch at the Outspan Hotel in Nyeri. The other two lodges are *Secret Valley* and *The Ark*, pretentious and overpriced at $21 to $33 a night. Treetops charges $26 per person. Reservations should be made well in advance.

Remember, Kenya is not all tourist hotels and game lodges. Especially in the rural areas, there are mission stations, secondary schools, simple hotels and hospitable villagers willing to offer lodging to the traveler. Don't be afraid to ask about modest ad hoc arrangements.

Where and What to Eat

You are not likely to find on the menu of a first-class Kenyan restaurant such African favorites as ugali (maize porridge and spicy stew), banana beer, iroi (a Kikuyu seeds mixture) and goat meat. For these dishes you must generally go to the small cheap cafes of doubtful hygiene in the older quarters of Nairobi and Mombasa. Fortunately, however, more and more Kenyans are dining out these days, and this picture is changing.

In NAIROBI there are several fine restaurants, one of which is the highly praised *Alan Bobbé's Bistro* on Koinange Street, near the New Avenue Hotel, whose own *Topaz Room* has excellent Continental cuisine. The brand-new *Marino Restaurant* on the mezzanine of the International Life House is expensive ($5 and up), but the decor is elegant and the food outstanding. *Lavarini's* on Government Road is an Italian restaurant of the highest quality. *Arturo's*, on the same street, is a congenial and informal spot for family-style Italian meals. The *Steak House*, the *Swiss Grill* and the *Mayfair Hotel Restaurant* all serve excellent meats. The New Stanley's *Thorn Tree Restaurant* has nice hamburgers and salads; the Nairobi *Hilton* serves poor food at rich prices. The international dining room of the *Hotel Ambassadeur* is worth trying —and the *Mandarin* is a good choice if you're in the mood for Chinese cuisine. The most luxurious dining in Nairobi is said to be at the *Kentmere Club*, a converted settler home in the Limuru suburb.

Although the Asian community has decreased, there are still some first-class Indian and Pakistani restaurants in Nairobi. The *Omar Khayyam* on Arwings-Kodhek Road is one of the best. The *Mocha* and the *Curry Pot* are reasonable, as are the *Orientale*, the *Corner Bar & Restaurant* and the *Three Bells*. In a class by itself is Sunday curry brunch at the old-time *Norfolk Hotel* (get there by 12:30 to avoid the mob).

Two small restaurants featuring African food are the *Friends' Corner* on Latema Road and *Iqbal's* nearby. *Tina's* on Government Road and the *Hotel Pigalle* in town serve Kenyan specialties—so does the patio restaurant of the Nairobi City Hall. Cheap snacks are sold in the stalls of the Kariakor Market—try samosas, spicy vegetable-and-meat pies.

Good inexpensive lunches are available at the *Honey Pot* and the *Swiss Cake Shop* on Government Road, the *Café de Paris* on Jevanjee Street, the *Mocha* and the *Pop-in* on Kimathi Street. The adjoining *Sunflower Restaurant* and *Lumu Coffee Shop* near the Catholic cathedral serve health foods. For ice cream and malteds, try the *Sno-Cream* near the university.

MOMBASA has several Indian restaurants that offer good meals from $2 to $4. Among them are the *Curry Bowl* on the Kilindini Road, the *Taj Mahal* on Salim Road, and the nearby *Central Tea Room*. The roof of the *Splendid Hotel* draws raves from connoisseurs of Indian dishes and seafood. For steaks, try the *New Carlton Hotel Grill*. In the center of town, near the *Manor Hotel* (where you can get very good meals in a congenial setting), is the *Fontanella*, an outdoor restaurant with good seafood and passion-fruit juice. Small African restaurants abound on Haile Selassie Avenue near the Peugeot taxi station.

Outside Nairobi and Mombasa, tourist hotels serve standard European fare. The *Outspan* in NYERI, the *Tea Hotel* in KERICHO and the *Mt. Kenya Safari Club* are the best. In MALINDI the small *African Hotel* in the center of town serves good curried fish. At KISUMU, the *Embassy Hotel Restaurant* has excellent curry, and the *Chateau Pereira* has generally good Indian cuisine.

The water is supposedly safe in Nairobi but you might prefer the local beers (such as Tusker's), the wide range of bottled soft drinks or the canned or fresh fruit juices. There's locally manufactured hard liquor, less expensive than the imports.

What to See and Do

NAIROBI is a thoroughly modern, fast-paced city with many attractions. The center of Kenyan government, education and industry, it is also one of the few cities in the world that can boast of animals roaming in a game park five minutes from downtown (*Nairobi National Park*).

Nairobi's population is growing at a rapid rate, as the presence of a sprawling shantytown on the city's outskirts testifies. Happier solutions to the growth problem are seen in the African township public housing projects, such as Jerusalem, Ofafa, Kariakor and Eastleigh, or in the well-to-do suburbs of Karen, Limuru, Westlands and Lower Kabete.

Visitors are welcome on the modern campus of the University of Nairobi near midtown, and at outlying facilities such as the East African Veterinary Research Organization in Kabete and the Agricultural and Forestry Research Center, 15 miles out of town at Kikuyu.

The National Museum off Uhuru Highway in Nairobi has an excellent natural history collection, including displays of the late Dr. Louis Leakey's work on the origins of man. Hours are 9 to 6 daily; admission is 5 shillings (70 cents). The Snake Park on the museum grounds is a fascinating spot; and don't forget to ask at the museum about the activities of local scientific societies, which often sponsor weekend excursions.

The covered Municipal Market near the university is a short walk from the museum. Curios and fresh produce are sold there, and in the bazaar nearby are many small Asian-owned shops where you can buy saris and other souvenir items.

Nairobi is beginning to develop an interesting cultural scene. Donovan Maule Theatre, a semi-professional company, has long been staging versions of London productions in a theater-restaurant setting. Performances in English and Swahili are given by the resident company of the National Theatre and by the university drama group, which tours urban working-class neighborhoods and rural areas. There are several active amateur theater groups, and local schools participate in the annual week-long Kenya Drama Festival. If you can, catch a "Ngomas of Kenya" exhibition of national dance. Classical concerts are given occasionally by the East African Conservatory of Music.

Gallery Watatu on Standard Street displays the works of contemporary East African artists, and wildlife paintings are to be seen at the New Stanley and Hilton Hotels. Studio Arts 68, also on Standard Street, is a fascinating place to browse among artifacts, clothing and art works—all African, all authentic, all for sale at reasonable prices. (Prices here are definitely not the cheapest in town, but you can be sure of authenticity and quality of craftsmanship.)

There are several cinemas in Nairobi, including two drive-ins near the national park, where you can hear lions roar in response to gunshots on the sound track. The Kenya Film Society regularly screens the more serious productions. For listings of these and other current events, check "This Week In Nairobi," a free brochure published by the Nairobi Information Bureau (P.O. Box 42278, tel. 23285), whose offices are near the Hilton Hotel. The bureau will give you free advice, maps and listings of accommodations. It's open during regular business hours.

There is dinner dancing at the major Nairobi hotels, and the International Casino near the National Museum offers good food, gambling and showgirls. There are floor shows as well at the Swiss Grill and Le Chalet. The main attraction at the Equator and Sombrero Clubs is striptease. The Starlite and 1900 Clubs have good combos and a lively clientele. Even livelier are the dives off River Road and in Eastleigh.

Nairobi has a modern Catholic cathedral, an older Anglican cathedral (All Saints), a small Jewish synagogue and a striking Sikh temple. Visitors are welcome inside all mosques except the Ismaili. The Christian Council of Kenya operates an ecumenical conference center in the suburb of Limuru. Its city offices in Church House on Government Road can help arrange visits to interesting projects, including youth and women's clubs in the Nairobi and Mombasa slums, and farm training centers outside the cities. A number of colorful evangelical sects, such as the Dini Ya Israel, worship in the city streets.

If you are interested in Kenyan politics, attend a debate (they are in English) at the National Parliament or visit one of the courthouses. To mingle with Kenyans of every class, sit in the city parks or walk through the 80-acre arboretum on Hospital Hill above the university (but do keep an eye out for pickpockets).

Soccer is a favorite Kenyan sport, played every Sunday at the National Stadium. Track and field competition has gained popularity since the Olympic triumphs of Wilson Kiprogut and Kipchoge Keino; watch for local meets. Auto rallies are enthusiastically supported. The Nairobi office of the East African Automobile Association organizes weekend competitions for local drivers and regular cars. The week-long East African Safari, held every Easter, takes some of the world's best drivers over some of the world's worst roads at the height of the rainy season.

The East African Professional Hunters Association (P.O. Box 528, Nairobi) can provide details on hunting, photographic and fishing safaris, as well as guide you to a qualified hunter with proper safeguards and equipment.

Those who prefer gentler sports can obtain temporary memberships at private clubs offering field hockey (an Asian favorite), golf, polo and tennis. Jamhuri Park is the scene of horse racing and exhibitions, and every September it has a fine agricultural show. There are 18-hole courses at the Sigona and Nairobi Golf Clubs and at Limuru Country Club, where horseback riding is also available. The YMCA will admit nonmembers to its swimming pool for 70 cents (an American dime).

From Nairobi, a major highway runs to Kenya's "second city," MOM-BASA—an ancient island port with a multiracial air, an easygoing pace, and the largest harbor in East Africa (actually, two harbors, on opposite sides of the island). Mombasa can be seen best on foot or by using local buses. City maps, booklets on the history of the area, and other useful information can be obtained at the Information Bureau on Kilindini Road near Elephant Tusk Arch (P.O. Box 5072, tel. 5428).

Stroll through Mombasa Old Town between Makadara Road and the Old Harbour, stopping at craftsmen's shops, mosques and temples, street vendors' stalls and colorful bars and coffee shops. Visit the Jain temple, center of a sect that will eat only food that grows below the ground (sample meals are available on request). At the nearby Ithnasheri temple, a penitential Islamic sect practices flagellation on certain holy occasions. At Mwembe Tayari market, shop for souvenirs or try a game of bao, played with seeds on a wooden board.

South of the Nyali Bridge in the Old Harbour area you will see grace-ful dhows going by, their lateen-rigged sails reminiscent of the Arabian Nights. These vessels regularly make their way up and down the Indian Ocean from the Arabian Peninsula, bringing rugs, chests and metalwork to trade for charcoal and other local products. At Government Square near Fort Jesus, you can find a boatman who will row you out to a dhow for a dollar or two. Dhows at Mombasa (East African Publishing House), or Sons of Sinbad, by Alan Villiers, will give you the background to ap-preciate these lovely but sturdy craft.

Massive, weathered Fort Jesus, built by the Portuguese in 1593, is now open to the public for a few shillings a head. There is a very interesting museum inside, and one can roam the turrets and grounds and look out to sea through slits in the still-formidable walls. Under the seaward side is a small, pleasant public park with benches for sunning or picnicking.

Mombasa is a seaman's town, where most of the after-dark action is in bars and brothels. Along the seafront, stop for a drink at the Star Bar or the Casablanca. The Little Theatre Club, New Florida, and Oceanic Hotel bar attract a more sedate crowd.

Probably the liveliest crowd around that is still within the limits of safety will be found nightly at the Sunshine Day and Night Club, where for a nominal "membership" fee, visitors can mingle unobtrusively, drinking hard or soft beverages or not at all, among the multiracial clien-tele. Female visitors will feel more comfortable if escorted by gentlemen stoic enough not to be lured into back rooms by the pretty young prosti-tutes whose turf this is. In keeping with the warmth of Mombasa, most of the bar girls are friendly—even with women patrons who have come for diversion and the all-night floor show, which ranges from pop singing to limbo dancing to "authentic ethnic" dancing that seems merely an excuse for a state of undress. The mood is relaxed and the atmosphere reportedly becomes mean only very rarely, even though there is drug-dealing and flesh-peddling going on all around the place.

Parks and game reserves:

Kenya's best-known and best-developed parks are the *Masai Mara Reserve*, *Masai Amboseli Game Reserve* and *Tsavo National Park*. All three are located south of Nairobi.

Masai Mara, the newest of the three, is in the southwest corner of Kenya on the Tanzania border. The tourist circuit by road leads from there across the border to Serengeti Park and back to Nairobi by way of Ngorongoro Crater, Lake Manyara and the slopes of Mt. Kilimanjaro. This route affords the most exciting few days of game watching in East Africa. Though the park can be reached by plane, you'll miss half the fun if you don't wind through Masailand by car, close to its people and their animals.

At *Masai Amboseli Game Reserve*, 90 miles from Nairobi on the paved road that leads to Arusha, you can either begin or end the circuit that includes Mt. Kilimanjaro, Mt. Meru Park, Lake Manyara, Ngorongoro Crater, Serengeti Park and Masai Mara. There is a Masai handicrafts center on the road to Amboseli, 10 miles south of the Athi River, turning off the main Nairobi-Arusha highway. Elephant, zebra and rhino are among the animals that throng Amboseli. There are two attractive lodges, and a hotel outside the park at Namanga. Deep in the park is the Masai village of Loitokitok, home of the famous Outward Bound survival training school for young men, and a take-off point for a little-known trail leading up Mt. Kilimanjaro.

Tsavo National Park's 8,034 square miles make it second biggest in the world. Bisected by the Nairobi-Mombasa highway, it is a scrub-and-bush wilderness filled with elephant and other large game. When the Uganda Railway engineers were laying the track to Lake Victoria across these dusty plains in 1898–99, they lost no fewer than 28 men to the rapacious man-eating lions of Tsavo, whose grandchildren seem peaceable enough, though still formidable and numerous. There are hotels at Voi and Mtito Andei on the highway, several campsites, and lodges at Kilaguni, Aruba Dam and Kiboko.

Nairobi National Park is only five miles from the center of the city. You must go there by tour vehicle or car and must stay inside your auto. Late afternoon is the best time to see the lions. There is other wildlife, including warthog and gazelle, and at the main gate a delightful animal orphanage where young strays are cared for.

North of Nairobi near the industrial town of Thika (whose beginnings were portrayed by settler-author Elspeth Huxley in her book *The Flame Trees of Thika*), is *Ol Doinyo Sapuk National Park*, a new reserve with many birds and buffalo.

Aberdare National Park is famous for Treetops Lodge and for its concentration of elephant, buffalo and other big game. There are camping and fishing sites and a scenic mountain road leading from Nyeri to Naivasha that climbs to 10,000 feet through forests, giant vegetation, lakes and waterfalls.

Mt. Kenya National Park can be reached by road from Nairobi via Nyeri and the ranching town of Nanyuki, where you will find the luxurious Mt. Kenya Safari Club and the Silverbeck Hotel. Proceed then by road, foot or pony up the slopes to 17,000-foot Mt. Kenya itself, the Olympus of the Kikuyu deities. Two national park shelters—one at 6,000 and one at 8,000 feet—accommodate campers for $2 a night. Book through the National Parks Department in Nairobi. Only experienced climbers with proper equipment and clothing should attempt Mt. Kenya's toughest peaks, Batian and Nelion, but Point Lenana offers a genuine though less arduous challenge to anyone in good health, warmly dressed. Consult the Mountain Club of Kenya, P.O. Box 45741, Nairobi. Local hotels, like the Naro Moru Lodge, and Snowline Safaris, P.O. Box 82, Nanyuki (tel. 2193), will organize climbing, walking and riding expeditions up the mountain.

On the northwestern border of Mt. Kenya National Park is the town of MERU, and 60 miles northwest of the town itself is *Meru National Park*. Here you can see a good variety of game, including the white rhino. Meru is one of Kenya's least-crowded parks, with good fishing possibilities; and there are both lodge and campsite accommodations available.

Isiolo Buffalo Springs Game Reserve lies just east of Meru and directly north of Mt. Kenya. Reservations at the self-service Buffalo Springs Lodge should be booked in advance through the Kenya National Parks, P.O. 42076, Nairobi.

Samburu Game Reserve, north of Buffalo Springs on the banks of the Uaso Nyiro River, has a luxurious lodge with pool and simpler accommodations as well. Book through Wildlife Lodges Ltd (P.O. Box 47557, Nairobi (tel. 27931).

The *Marsabit National Reserve* is due north of Samburu and Buffalo Springs, and can be reached only by charter flight from Nairobi or by four-wheel-drive vehicle. Set in a rain forest above the desert floor, this reserve is the home of colorful Boran and Somali tribesmen and nomadic herders, many rare species of birdlife, and Ahmed, Kenya's largest and most venerable elephant (protected by a presidential decree). Write to

John Alexander Safaris, P.O. Box 125, Nanyuki (tel. 53), for details on camel treks, safaris and tented camp accommodations in this truly remote and unspoiled area.

If you are willing to undertake the expense of traveling to Marsabit in the first place, a sidetrip that might make it seem all the more worthwhile is a day or two spent at the Lake Rudolf Angling Club on Lake Rudolf, on Kenya's parched Northern Frontier.

Revered by fishermen, who come here to fight for Nile perch and golden perch, Ferguson's Gulf, the site of the Angling Club, is also a bird sanctuary. But even for those whose interest in fishing is nonexistent and whose patience with birdwatching is limited, the resort spot offers a unique glimpse of Kenya's most tradition-bound people, the Turkana.

While it is true that the people who have gathered nearby the Angling Club are among the more outward-looking of their people, having gone so far as to enter the cash economy in a small way, they still evoke the richness of ritual that has given their people such proud bearing even as they slowly starve to death, to be rescued periodically by government food programs. (Rest assured, however, that the Turkana who live and fish near the Angling Club eat as well as the club patrons who daily sample their fresh-caught tilapia, a delicious kind of bream. Turkana staffers also prepare what is probably the only chocolate mousse along Kenya's Northern Frontier.)

A portion of the $20 daily per person fee, full board, goes to the Turkana District Council, as do all fees for dancing and village visits—the only times photographing the people is allowed. Bookings can be made through Bunson's Travel Service Ltd, P.O. Box 5456, Nairobi (tel. 21992). The manager, Mrs. Pat Robertson, is always eager for news from the outside, being limited to communication by radiophone.

To see other peoples of Kenya, ride buses or take a car on excursions outside the major cities. A 20-mile drive west of Nairobi will lead you into the beautiful Ngong Hills, described so movingly by Karen Blixen (Isak Dinesen) in Out of Africa. Here Masai village life goes on in the face of encroaching urbanization.

Driving north from Nairobi on the Kampala road, one encounters a dramatic view of the Rift Valley from the escarpment at Mile 30. On the right side of the road that descends to the valley floor is a tiny Catholic chapel built by Italian prisoners of war captured in Ethiopia. The same road continues to Mt. Longonot, where you can hike to the top of a 9,000-foot crater. For an alternate route, turn right at the town of Naivasha and take the scenic road through the Kinangops Plateau, where African peasant farmers have replaced white settlers. There is good fishing high in the Kinangops at Sasamua Dam, which is the source of Nairobi's water.

At Lake Naivasha, 54 miles from Nairobi, the *Crescent Island Wildlife Sanctuary* staff has recorded 346 species of birdlife. The Marina and Safariland Clubs here will help arrange fishing and boating parties on the lake; or you can camp and hike to nearby Hell's Gate Gorge, with its steam geysers and volcanic rock outcroppings.

A hundred miles north of Nairobi is the soda lake called Nakuru, where thousands of flamingos live under government protection. Above Nakuru there are striking views from the rim of the Menengai Crater, which can be reached by car or foot. Archaeological explorations have been made at Gamble's Cave near Nakuru, Hyrax Hall at Kariandusi, Fort Ternan and the town of Gilgil (which has a Museum of Science). Details and permission to visit digs can be obtained through the National Museum in Nairobi.

From Nairobi it is easy to reach the villages and towns of the Kikuyu. Kiambu is a crowded, semi-urban place. The town of KIKUYU is a cultural center and site of Alliance High School, the prestigious academy where the Kenyan elite have been educated for the last 40 years (nearly half the present cabinet attended this handsome boarding school). The tea projects nearby are worked by peasant cooperatives.

A pleasant road across the hills leads from Kikuyu to President Kenyatta's home and farm in the village of Gatundu and on to the town of THIKA, where you can stop for a drink at the Blue Posts Hotel, swim, and see the Chania Falls and Fourteen Falls on the nearby Athi River.

The road north from Thika to NYERI passes through the heart of Kikuyu country. Stop at the town of Fort Hall to see the church with Elimo Njau's murals of Christ in a rural African setting.

North of Fort Hall at Sagana the road forks: one route continues north to Nyeri and Aberdare National Park; the other leads east to the land of the Embu and Meru peoples and to the important Seven Forks hydroelectric project on the Tana River.

The road to Nyeri is a splendid route for people-watching, and Nyeri itself, at 5,570 feet, is a good place for a rest stop on the way to Treetops.

EMBU and MERU towns are cozy administrative centers, surrounded by coffee and tea farms. At these towns, you can see the Embu dancers, a nationally famous troupe. South of Embu the Kikuyu farmers have prospered from rice-growing on the Mwea Tebere irrigation project.

Fifty miles south of Nairobi is the town of MACHAKOS, the center of the Kamba people, in semi-arid country seldom traversed by tourists. There are farming and ranching projects in the nearby Mboni Hills, and on the road east to Kitui are numerous village self-help projects and harambee secondary schools built by local volunteers. At Wamunyu, Kamba carvers produce and sell their unusual wares.

Another one-day excursion is the 160-mile round trip to Lake Magadi, with its flocks of flamingos and soda deposits. Along the road 40 miles from Nairobi is *Olorgesailie National Park*, where there are well-preserved sites of paleontological excavations by Dr. Leakey and other teams. The park has simple camping facilities. This hot and dusty route is off the tourist beat—but you will be able to see village life without commercial trappings and visit Masai manyattas (mobile encampments).

Longer trips from Nairobi include a jaunt to the ranching town of Nanyuki, off the Nairobi-Nyeri highway. Travel west from here to Nakuru, where the road rejoins the main Nairobi-Kampala highway, through the cattle country around Laikipia, and on to Thomson's Falls, named for the intrepid adventurer who opened up Masailand. Here a four-wheel-drive vehicle can take off over a rough bush road as far as Maralal; regular vehicles can make it to Rumuruti, where a private game farm holds animals for shipment to overseas zoos.

Maralal is located at 7,000 feet in a beautiful setting, traversed by camping and photo safaris; there is also a lodge. From Maralal, four-wheel-drive caravans can set forth for Lake Rudolf. An alternate overland route dips through northwestern Kenya into Uganda and approaches the lake via Lodwar. Most travelers to Rudolf prefer to get there by air charter—ask at Wilson Airport in Nairobi.

East of Lake Rudolf and Marsabit National Reserve in the desolate Northern Frontier District (NFD) are the administrative posts of Wajir and Garissa, where the whitewashed buildings recall Foreign Legion romances. This is camel land, where the nomadic Somalis live.

Many travelers skip northern and western Kenya, which lack major parks or large concentrations of wildlife—yet these areas are beautiful and interesting. Take a car from Nairobi to Eldoret and Kitale in western Kenya, or to Kisumu on Lake Victoria. Collective Peugeot taxis and public buses also make these trips regularly. The roads pass through the old "White Highlands," lush rolling hills, tea estates and the lands of the Kisii people. From Kisumu boating and fishing trips can be made on Lake Victoria. The Luo people, who live in and around Kisumu, have a rich heritage of music and dancing. At Homa Bay there is a model prison where inmates produce excellent handicrafts, and nearby is the small *Olambwe Valley Game Reserve*.

North of Kisumu, scenic mountain roads run through the territory of the Abaluhyas, whose neat villages are clustered in the foothills. Kakamega and Kapsabet are quiet rural centers. European settlers once farmed near Eldoret, Kitale and Broderick Falls; now these towns are the homes of African farmers, many of them Kalenjin-speaking, who have switched from cattle to hybrid wheat and maize. The altitude and open spaces here have helped produce some of Kenya's best track and field stars.

The drive northwest from Kitale to Uganda around Mt. Elgon is one of the loveliest in East Africa. A rougher but equally spectacular mountain road leads north from Kitale to Kapenguria and beyond to Lake Rudolf. You can also turn south at Kapenguria and cross the Cherangani Hills, the Kerio River, and the 8,000-foot escarpment at Tambach, finally descending to the plains at the Perkerra Irrigation Scheme near Lake Baringo. From there a four-wheel-drive vehicle can make it to the isolated lake itself, which has excellent fishing and a comfortable lodge, and to smaller Lake Hannington and a nearby snake farm.

Note: When traveling off the tourist circuit, take time out to visit some of Kenya's rural projects—the resettlement schemes where small farmers have replaced former white settlers; the scenic Egerton Agricultural College near Molo for the training of farm managers; the areas of land consolidation and progressive small-scale farming, especially near Nyeri and Kitale; the self-help harambee schools, and the village polytechnics which provide vocational training in an effort to curb the exodus to the cities.

The Kenya coast is a good place to relax after rushing through the game parks and fast-paced Nairobi. If you travel by road from Nairobi to Mombasa, you can stop in Tsavo Park and make a brief detour at Voi on a good dirt road to see the Taveta Hills people. Near Mackinnon Road 90 miles from Mombasa, there is a simple roadside shrine to the memory of those who built the Uganda Railway.

The beaches south of Mombasa toward the Tanzanian border are less known and less frequented than those north of the city. The Likoni Ferry takes cars and passengers regularly from Mombasa Island to the suburb of Likoni and to Shelly Beach. Along the road to Tanga (Tanzania) is the Shimba Hills National Reserve, a sanctuary for the sable antelope. Just off this route at Tiwi there are self-service beach cottages. At Shimoni, the Pemba Channel Fishing Club will arrange boats for marlin and shark fishing. If you can talk one of the local Shimoni fishermen into it, try to rent a boat to take you across to neighboring Wasini Island, where the mosque reportedly still has its centuries-old porcelain decorations in place and where life goes on in much the same way as when Arab slave traders plied this coast.

North of Mombasa, over the Nyali Bridge, a paved road leads 75 miles to the beach resort of MALINDI. Along the way there are other interesting spots—like Kilifi, where you can fish, sun or swim at the Mnarani Club. Ten miles south of Malindi are the fascinating 15th century ruins of the sultanate of Gedi, an Arab-African town that once rivaled Mombasa. Near Gedi, at Turtle Bay, the *Marine National Park* is a place for snorkeling among the coral reefs. At Malindi itself you will find several resort hotels offering water sports. Professional hunters there will make your arrangements for a Tsavo safari.

Eighty miles north of Malindi is the charming and unspoiled little island and port of LAMU, which can be reached by bus, taxi, air charter and boat (see above). The main feature of Lamu or "Bajun" architecture is the carved door, dating from the city's great mercantile past; many lovely examples are still to be found on the island. Local crafts plying the straits include dhows and mtepes—fishing barks sewn together with coconut coir.

Coast fishing for marlin, shark and sailfish is best in February, when an International Bill-Fishing Competition is held. There's a Malindi Sea Festival in November.

Kenya poses a problem to the person with little time to take in its many wonders. The tourist in a hurry would probably be well advised to stick with an organized package that guarantees a fair share of sights in a limited time. Good bets are the Aberdare Park drive, with or without a stop at Treetops Lodge, and the circuit of Masai Mara, Amboseli and the northern Tanzanian parks. Another circuit might include Tsavo, Mombasa, Malindi and Lamu. You should be able to do a good deal in two weeks for less than $500.

The glory of Kenya is that there is plenty of pampering available for those who need it, and wilderness to spare for those who want to take their Africa straight.

What to Buy

Prices in Nairobi are high. But cameras are a good buy in Kenya, and tourists have duty-free privileges. Try Jon Karmali on Kenyatta Avenue for film processing and photographic equipment; ditto Howse & McGeorge and Elite Studios, both on Government Road.

Clothing shops in Nairobi run the gamut from the bargain-basement prices of the Colpro Store (Kimathi Street) to the chic boutiques in the Hilton and Intercontinental Hotels. The bazaar near Jevanjee Gardens has small shops where you can bargain for saris and other Eastern items. The Central City Market nearby is a good place to shop for souvenirs such as drums, spears and animal skins (skins that must bear the government seal if they are to be exported). In the African markets off the

Pumwani and River Roads you can bargain for better prices, but the stock is limited in variety.

There are art galleries all over Nairobi. Watatu and Studio Arts 68 and the hotel shops are the most reliable. Look for the paintings of Elimo Njau, Robin Anderson's batiks and those of Rebecca Njau, the lino cuts of Hezbon Owiti, Louis Mwaniki's graphics, and the works of Eli Kyeyune and Aspah Ngethe. Check "This Week in Nairobi" to see what exhibits are on.

The colorful kanga and kikoi cloths are cheaper in Malindi and Mombasa than in Nairobi, where they can be seen in profusion at Nation House. There are many Nairobi boutiques where you can have your cloth made up into dresses, robes or skirts—Obeissa's on Muindi Mbingu Street, for example. Abdullah ben Abdullah makes fashionable but expensive safari outfits. (Colpro's safari items are a much better buy for one-time use). Bata Boot stores, with branches all over Kenya, sell good shoes of every description, including safari boots.

Rowland Ward's elegant shop has such exotic items as an elephant's foot stool and goblets engraved with safari scenes. At Zimmerman's equally posh establishment you can buy the finest handbags, shoes and other animal-skin items.

Craftsman's Gallery on Standard Street sells local authentic products such as elephant-hair bracelets and zebra-skin wallets, Masai beadwork and basketry.

Muter & Oswald, near the East African Airways office, holds interesting weekly auctions where you may be able to pick up fine antiques left behind by departing settler families. Beautiful brass items are for sale in the Bazaar Street shops and on the River Road. Camping equipment is best bought from Low and Bonar or Ahmed Brothers. Kenya Bunduki is the leading gunsmith and cutler. Good, cheap, used camping equipment is available at army surplus stores.

Kenya has less to offer in sculpture and other high arts than West and Central Africa or Tanzania. The local crafts can be seen at the Maendeleo ya Wanawake (National Women's Association) on Muindi Mbingu Street. On the Kampala Highway look for inexpensive sheepskin rugs. The Kamba people sell their carvings in an arcade shop at the Hilton Hotel—but you can go to Machakos or to Kilindini Road in Mombasa and get them for much lower prices.

In Mombasa look for souvenirs in the outdoor shops at Mwembe Tayari Market off Kenyatta Avenue. Diguini Road contains many clothing and yardgoods stores full of garments made from local fabrics, kikoi and kanga. Moloo Brothers and the Coast Zanzibar Curio Shop on Kilindini Road are the places to hunt for old books, maps and manuscripts.

Record shops in both Nairobi and Mombasa carry large selections of Kenyan music on 45 and 33 rpm discs, as well as international pop and classical favorites.

Local Attitudes

Kenya swarms with tourists but few venture from the game parks, the coasts and the Nairobi package tours. Kenyans appreciate tourism but want Africans to share more fully in its benefits. Europeans and Asians still dominate the economy, and race relations have been tense in the past. Those who take the initiative to meet Kenyans at the university or elsewhere will be asked many sharp questions, especially about race relations in the United States. There is considerable resentment of America because of Vietnam and the failure of the US Government to take action against the white minority regimes in Southern Africa. Nevertheless, individual Americans are welcomed with warm good-will and interest.

Several thousand Kenyans have returned from university studies in North America. (When he was in the Senate, John F. Kennedy and Tom Mboya, the late Kenyan leader, organized a pre-independence airlift to bring over hundreds of students.) There are still several thousand Kenyan students in the US and Canada, and a small but growing number of American wives of returned Kenyans. At the university, in the senior ranks of the civil service and in business you are likely to meet someone who has been educated in the US.

Britain is still the major external influence. US Peace Corps and British, West German, Scandinavian and other volunteers are active. The Peace Corps offices are on Government Road opposite Malik Street in Nairobi (tel. 27648, 22125). The US Information Service Library in Shankardass House is a good place to meet Kenyans.

Kenyan politics is a sensitive topic, but discussions can be lively. Although they might not want to talk about it in public, Kenyans are concerned about what will happen in the country when President Kenyatta no longer is in power. It may signal the rise of former opposition leader Oginga Odinga, who was released from detention in 1970. His radical views are expressed in his book *Not Yet Uhuru* (Heineman).

Photographing people probably disturbs Kenyans more than talking politics. Many of the Masai expect a small payment for posing—and who can blame them? Ask permission before photographing anyone. Some individuals may not want to be photographed at all.

Nairobi has an increasing crime problem, partly the result of its rapid growth, massive rural influx, and the high rate of unemployment. Pickpockets, car thieves, confidence tricksters and even bank robbers are here, although the streets are generally safe. Still, it's a good idea to lock your car, leave nothing in it, and keep a sharp eye on your wallet and valuables. Leave expensive items in the hotel safe. Women carrying large handbags are a prime target for purse-snatchers. Use one of the colorful local shopping bags made of sisal and known as "kikapus." The police do their best to be helpful to visitors.

Weather, What to Wear, How Long to Stay

Nairobi's temperate climate is considered one of the healthiest in the world. Temperatures seldom rise above 80 degrees or fall below 60; the average range is from 62 to 68 degrees. The warm, sunny, dry season is from mid-December to mid-March, when the long rains begin. The rains continue through May but it's generally clear during the day. June to mid-October is cool, dry and cloudy. Sweaters and jackets are needed in the evening. The short rains fall from mid-October to mid-December; it is a cool and pleasant season.

At the coast the rainy seasons are the same as in Nairobi but temperatures average 10 to 20 degrees higher. It is generally humid. The highlands are pleasant during the day and cool at night, especially above 8,000 feet. Warm clothing is needed at night. Kisumu on Lake Victoria is hot and humid. The Northern Frontier District is dry and warm.

Men wear medium-weight suits in Nairobi and up-country. Lighter and more informal attire can be worn on the coast. Women may have use for cocktail dresses and wraps. Miniskirts are acceptable in cities but impractical in the parks. For safaris jungle green or khaki bush clothing can be made locally or purchased ready-made. Suntan lotions and straw hats are useful and available locally. Most important is a comfortable pair of walking shoes.

Most game lodges have generators and power, so you can take an electric razor.

Two weeks are sufficient to visit the Kenya coast, Nairobi, Tsavo, Amboseli and one other park. The author's choice for a two-week park and wildlife tour of East Africa, rather than Kenya alone, would start in Nairobi, continue through Masai Mara, Serengeti, Ngorongoro, Mt. Kilimanjaro, Amboseli and Mombasa, and then perhaps by air to Kampala for Murchison Falls. If you are interested in the traditions and the evolving society of Kenya, you might spend another two weeks in the Rift Valley, Kikuyuland, lingering in Nairobi and at the coast. A three-week trip more readily combines people, nature and a visit to northern Tanzania. At least a month is needed to see all three East African countries. (See chapters on Tanzania and Uganda.)

Communication

East African Posts and Telecommunications, like the railways and airways, is owned by the three East African governments. The Nairobi post office is the largest in East Africa and service is generally reliable. Allow two to four days for airmail letters to and from North America, and three months for surface mail. Packages can be shipped safely from Nairobi or Mombasa. It's preferable to send packages airmail, or air freight with Pan American or TWA, or with Peck and Barber's moving agency on York Street in Nairobi. You can ask a merchant to ship items you buy from him.

Telephone service is adequate although there is a shortage of pay phones. There is direct distance-dialing between Nairobi and most major East African cities. Overseas calls go through a new telecommunications network that is part of the global Comsat system (Kenya has its own satellite station). Book your overseas calls in advance. Nairobi has 24-hour telex and telecommunications service.

English and Swahili are both official languages in Kenya. English is the language of instruction at the university, in all secondary schools and in some primary schools. It is spoken throughout the country. Kenyans are proud of Swahili, their lingua franca, and use it in trade, local government and mass communications. Grammatical Swahili is heard on the coast, and a rough but easily understandable mixture elsewhere.

A few words of Swahili are understandable even when mispronounced, and your effort to speak it will draw favorable responses. For those willing to try, D. V. Perrot's *Teach Yourself Swahili* (English University Press) and Sharifa Zawawi's *Kiswahili Kwa Kitendo* (Harper and Row) are good introductions. P. M. Wilson's *Simplified Swahili* (East African Literature Bureau) and other brief English-Swahili phrase books are available in Nairobi. Some Swahili words that have crept into standard East African English parlance are: *safari*, trip; *duka*, small general store; *shamba*, small farm; *rafiki*, friend; *bwana*, sir or mister; *asante sana*, thank you; *jambo*, hello; *habari*, how are you; *mzuri*, good or well.

The government-operated Voice of Kenya broadcasts on radio and television in English, Swahili and local tribal languages. TV relies heavily on imported American and British programs but there is an attempt to increase local output.

The daily *East African Standard* is British-owned. The tabloid *Daily Nation* belongs to the Aga Khan. Both newspapers are lively and informative although circumspect in their criticisms of the Kenya government. Each has a Swahili counterpart. The *Sunday Post* and *Nation* appear weekly. Among the scholarly publications are the *East African*

Journal, a monthly, and *Africa,* a quarterly published by the East African Wildlife Society.

Nairobi is becoming a minor publishing center. Local branches of Oxford University Press, Cambridge, Longmans and other overseas firms compete with the East African Publishing House and other indigenous firms to produce books in English and Swahili.

The *International Herald Tribune, Time, Newsweek* and other American publications are easily available at the Standard, Woolworth and other Nairobi bookstores.

Emergencies

Nairobi is a good place to be if anything goes wrong. The US Embassy occupies four floors in Cotts House, an office building opposite City Hall on Wabera Street. The telephone is 27631-9, the address P.O. Box 30137, and there is someone on duty at all times.

There are competent doctors, dentists and optometrists in Nairobi, and the university has a medical school that can recommend specialists. There are excellent facilities at the Kenyatta and Aga Khan hospitals and pediatric services at Gertrude's Garden Children's Hospital. Adequate general hospitals serve Mombasa, Nakuru, Kisumu and other regional centers but if you have medical problems while on safari try to make it to Nairobi.

Pharmacies are well stocked and stay open around the clock on a rotating schedule posted on the front door of every pharmacy in town.

Rwanda

(République du Rwanda)

STATUS: Independent republic since July 1, 1962. Former German colony, administered by Belgium after first World War.

SIZE: 10,186 square miles (about the size of Maryland). Population—3,560,000.

GEOGRAPHY: Landlocked, mountainous (Virunga volcanoes 15,000 feet), with central plateau, swamp and savanna in southeast. Average altitude above 5,000 feet. Principal towns—Kigali (capital, 15,000), Gisenyi, Cyangugu.

CLIMATE: Mild and pleasant in highlands; humid in south. Rainy seasons March to May and October to December (moderate rainfall). Daytime temperatures in the 70's, evenings chilly.

LANGUAGES: French and Kinyarwanda (both official).

CURRENCY: Rwanda franc, divided into 100 centimes. 1 franc = 1 cent; $1.00 = 100 francs. Not convertible outside the country.

VISAS: Required. Available from Rwanda Mission to the UN and Embassy of Rwanda in Washington. Fee $5. Three passport photos needed. Allow two days if applying in person, two weeks by post.

AIRPORT: Kigali (KGL), seven and a half miles from town. Direct flights to and from Athens, Brussels, Bujumbura, Bukavu, Entebbe, Goma, Nairobi and Vienna. Sabena Airlines has free bus into town. Airport departure taxes—domestic, 150 francs ($1.50); international, 250 francs ($2.50).

NATIONAL HOLIDAYS: July 1, Independence Day; Christian holidays.

INFORMATION SOURCES: *In US*—Permanent Mission of Rwanda to the UN, 120 East 56th Street, New York, N.Y. 10022 (tel. 212/753-6010); Embassy of the Republic of Rwanda, 1714 New Hampshire Avenue NW, Washington, D.C. 20009 (tel. 202/232-2882). *In Rwanda*—Ministère de l'Information et du Tourisme, Kigali.

By *Aaron Segal*

This beautiful little country amply rewards travelers who take the trouble to get there. It offers two national parks, a share of sparkling Lake Kivu and an interesting society in which a long-oppressed people have overthrown their former rulers.

Tucked between the mighty Mountains of the Moon and the vast plains west of Lake Victoria, Rwanda is a green land of forests, valleys, steep hillsides and hardy farmers. As in neighboring Burundi, its short, sturdy Hutu people first cleared the forests, tilled the soil and terraced the land. But beginning in the 16th century, the Hutu were gradually conquered by the more militaristic Tutsi, a tall, slender, aristocratic cattle-keeping people who had migrated south along the Nile River.

Although the Hutu peasants far outnumbered the newcomers, they accepted the premise of inequality imposed by the Tutsi. They became serfs in bondage to the Tutsi feudal lords, who in turn were vassals of their king (mwami). This development resembled Burundi's earlier experience, but in Rwanda there was a greater degree of Hutu resistance, especially in the north, less intermarriage between the two peoples, and a more centralized and aggressive monarchy. Europeans came on the scene while the Tutsi were busy consolidating their power.

German colonial rule from 1885 to 1916 did little to change the society. Awarded to Belgium after World War I by the League of Nations, Rwanda and Burundi became administrative and economic appendages of the vastly larger, wealthier Belgian Congo (now Zaïre). Belgium was content to govern through the mwami and the Tutsi lords, curbing only their worst excesses. Under Belgian rule, however, Christian missionaries and schools flourished, planting among young Hutu subversive ideas of equality and justice. These principles were further encouraged by visiting international missions when Rwanda became a UN trusteeship territory after World War II.

Control of land and cattle were the keys to the master-serf contractual relationship between individual Hutu and Tutsi. But in the 1950's, reacting to pressure from the UN, the Belgian administration moved to modify this relationship. By 1958 serfdom, at least theoretically, was abolished. The Tutsi responded by pressing for immediate independence with a monarchical government, on the theory that this would enable them to regain their privileges. They presented themselves as arch antiimperialists, eager to throw off hated colonial rule. Many Hutu, however, preferred continued foreign rule to independence under the Tutsi.

Grégoire Kayibanda, a Catholic-educated Hutu teacher, organized a mass political party (Parmehutu) in the 1950's and directly challenged the power of the mwami. A United Nations mission failed to resolve this conflict, and in late 1959 a series of incidents touched off waves of violence that took the lives of many Tutsi and drove thousands of others into exile in neighboring countries.

The death of the mwami and a dispute over his successor provided the opportunity for Kayibanda, with some help from the Belgian administration, to seize the day. Legislative elections were held and a provisional government was installed under Kayibanda. The newly appointed mwami —from exile—denounced Belgium to the UN.

At independence in 1962 President Kayibanda declared Rwanda a republic, abolishing the monarchy as well as the caste status and other privileges of the Tutsi. Belgian financial and technical aid were critical in keeping the fragile new nation afloat. Rwanda also sought relations with France and her ex-colonies in Africa.

Over the next five years Tutsi groups in exile attempted to overthrow the Hutu republic. One abortive invasion in late 1963 led to another round of massacres of Tutsi and another exodus of refugees. At present about 240,000 Tutsi remain in Rwanda, many still occupying prominent posts, while about 300,000 exiles live in neighboring Burundi, Tanzania, Uganda and Zaïre.

National security remains Rwanda's major concern, but the government has also promoted education and farmers' cooperatives, improved cultivation of arabica coffee (the major export) and introduced tea and pyrethrum as new cash crops. Desperately poor and short of natural resources in this densely populated land, the republic is still dependent on external aid from Belgium and other Western countries. Its plans for tourism and access to the outside world depend in part on close relations with Uganda and Zaïre; Rwanda remains wary of Burundi, where a Tutsi military regime has succeeded the Tutsi monarchy.

Rwanda's social revolution is expertly analyzed in René Lemarchand's *Rwanda and Burundi* (Praeger, 1970).

An excellent French-language tourist guide, particularly useful for visits to the national parks, is available free of charge from the Rwanda Embassy or its Mission to the UN.

Money Matters

The Rwanda franc is supported by Belgium but still unwanted outside the country. Exchange only what you need at your hotel, the government Banque du Rwanda, the private Banque Commerciale du Rwanda or the Banque de Kigali.

Travelers checks are accepted but credit cards are still unknown.

Getting In and Out

Rwanda is reached most easily, albeit expensively, by air. An east-west trip across Africa can sometimes be stretched to include a stop at Kigali, the capital. Kigali can be reached from Kinshasa via connecting flights to Bukavu and Goma (Zaïre) or Bujumbura (Burundi). Most travelers, however, arrive from East Africa and return there. An economy class round trip from Entebbe (Uganda) costs $104; it's $60 more if you fly in from Nairobi (Kenya) and return there.

If you come into Rwanda by road you'll see some spectacular mountain scenery, but the trip is slow and rough whatever route you take. The best route is via the partly paved 300-mile stretch to Kigali from Kampala in Uganda, but Uganda's internal problems have made this road insecure; you must deal with military roadblocks and nasty border officials. Since it is still used by trucks, this route gives hitchhikers a slim chance, but they may be asked to pay for their ride. The longer road from Kampala through western Uganda to the Rwandan border town of Ruhengeri and on to Lake Kivu is beautiful but equally insecure. Incidentally, gasoline is much cheaper in Uganda than Rwanda, so in the unlikely event that you're driving in from Uganda you may want to stock up.

The safest road politically is at present the worst physically. It runs from the Tanzanian railhead and port of Mwanza on Lake Victoria to Kigali. World Bank funds are being used to improve this road and to build a bridge across the Kagera River.

You can drive to Rwanda from Burundi, but dealing with Burundi officialdom can be a nightmare unless you join the weekly automobile convoy operated between Bujumbura and Kigali by the Old East Trading Company. Travelers can either rent a car from Old East or offer to drive a new car being transferred for sale from Burundi to Rwanda.

There are roads leading into Rwanda from Zaïre (skirting Lake Kivu), but on these roads you run the risk of bandits on the Zaïre side, and military and customs officials who behave like bandits.

Once you cross a border into Rwanda, you'll find formalities relatively light. No documents beyond an international carnet (available from the East African Automobile Association) are required. Frequent signs in French remind you that, unlike East Africa, driving in Rwanda is on the right. It used to be possible to rent a car in Kampala for a round trip to Rwanda and back; it may again, if Uganda's security improves.

United Tours in Kampala and Nairobi offers combined air and microbus excursions to Rwanda's national parks and to Albert National Park in Zaïre. This is an expensive but attractive option, especially for those pressed for time.

Getting Around Within Rwanda

Although less than 300 miles separate one end of Rwanda from the other, it's difficult to get around the country. Motorists face rugged mountains, rough roads and a scarcity of facilities. Some prefer to fly, using the services of two private charter firms, Société de Transport Aérien du Rwanda (STAR), P.O. Box 110, Kigali, tel. 5238, and Transafricair (TAA), P.O. Box 352, Kigali, tel. 5318. Rwanda and Burundi are among the few independent African states without their own national airlines.

Local buses and collective taxis are scarce. The government operates a twice-weekly bus service between Kigali and provincial towns (RTP, P.O. Box 619, Kigali, tel. 5294). Hitchhikers sometimes can get rides with European technicians, teachers and volunteers, who also may offer overnight accommodations.

The major hotels have excursion tours to the two national parks. They also arrange car rentals, as do Transintra travel agents (P.O. Box 383, tel. 5287), Rwandamotor (P.O. Box 448, tel. 5294), Solliard (P.O. Box 335, tel. 5660) and the Peugeot, Citroën, Renault, Opel and Volkswagen dealers, all in Kigali. The additional expense of a driver is often justified on longer trips.

Kigali may be the world's smallest capital, consisting of only a few paved streets, and it's easily managed on foot.

Where to Stay

There are only four hotels in KIGALI, but they offer considerable variety in accommodations, price and atmosphere. The *Hôtel des Mille Collines* (originally named the Impala) is new, Swiss-managed, with 200 rooms in the $20- to $30-price range. It has a swimming pool. The *Wagon Wheel* is old-fashioned, but charges only $10 to $15 a day, including all meals. There are also the first class *Hôtel des Diplomates* (P.O. Box 269) and the third class *Kihovu* (P.O. Box 98).

The beach resort town of GISENYI on Lake Kivu has the delightful *Hôtel Edelweiss*, where prices are modest and the cuisine excellent. The *Palm Beach Hôtel*, facing the lake, and the *Beau Séjour* are also reasonable.

Kagera National Park has a lodge with full catering facilities ($15 per person per night) near the entrance at Garibo. The park also has camping accommodations.

In addition to these commercial facilities, travelers can sometimes be put up at the guest house in Kigali operated by the Baptist Mission Center. Similar accommodations are provided by the University of Rwanda, located 84 miles south of the capital at BUTARE. Elsewhere in the country, Catholic and Protestant missions can often provide overnight shelter. By all means leave a contribution if no fee is charged.

Where and What to Eat

There are few restaurants outside the hotels. It might be a good idea to bring along some canned goods if your plans include travel outside the capital. You'll have no trouble, however, finding fresh vegetables. Just head for the nearest outdoor market. The local diet, by the way, features yams, milk dishes, and millet and sorghum. Try the excellent national bottled beer, brewed with water from Lake Kivu. The local tap water should be either boiled, filtered or avoided.

A word should perhaps be added about the importance of beer in the culture of Rwanda. It is drunk on all important occasions—marriages, funerals, contract negotiations and divination rites. It is sometimes a medium of exchange and frequently offered as a gift. To refuse beer is a serious insult. Reed straws are usually provided for drinking the home-made brew from a communal pot.

What to See and Do

Rwanda has one excellent national park and another that's quite good. It also has a fine shoreline along deep-blue Lake Kivu, much striking mountain scenery and an interesting rural life. If it were easier and cheaper to get in and out, the country's travel value would jump. As it is, the government is trying hard with Swiss capital and technical assistance to put its attractive little country on the international tourist map.

KIGALI is a tiny and improbable capital, surrounded on all sides by the terraced hillsides and fragrant eucalyptus and pine forests that grace the entire country. It has a small but lively outdoor market, several embassies and government office buildings, and little else. Night life is confined to the hotels and a few small bars.

A lovely but treacherous mountain road runs 120 miles from Kigali to GISENYI on the shores of Lake Kivu. Along the way one can visit hillside coffee farms, self-help schools and other community development projects. The Kigali offices of Socori, the National Cooperative Society of Rwanda, can help arrange visits to the new tea estates near this road. The densely populated countryside is dotted with missions, chapels and red-brick schools among its green hills.

Gisenyi is a charming resort town magnificently situated at the northern end of Lake Kivu and almost surrounded by lofty mountains. It has an interesting local market, good hotels and several boutiques selling handicrafts. There are water sports, including swimming at a bilharzia-free beach, water skiing, boating, scuba diving and some fishing. When enough tourists are present and willing to pay, the hotels will arrange for a performance of traditional Tutsi ("Watusi") dancing.

Two miles from Gisenyi along a lakeshore road is the larger resort town of Goma in Zaïre. Its hotels and bars have a livelier and more African night life than those of Gisenyi. It is wise to use local taxis rather than to risk problems with Zaïre border officials over a rented car—unless you plan to go through Goma on a four-hour drive north to Zaïre's outstanding Virunga National Park (see chapter on Zaïre).

Rwanda's own excellent *Parc National des Volcans* (Volcano National Park), two hours east of Gisenyi by road, contains the massive non-active volcanic peaks of Karisimbi, Bisoke, Sabyinyo, Gahinga and Muhabura which poke their crests 8,000 to 10,000 feet above the crater lakes and lush valleys. It's a strange sensation to enjoy springlike mountain freshness a few miles south of the equator. The park has extraordinary tropical and temperate vegetation and exotic insect life. The views, the air and the forests are all meant for relaxed hiking and climbing, activities arranged through the Gisenyi hotels, with or without porters and guides. Guides are useful for one- or two-day climbs, particularly if you want to seek out some of Africa's last remaining gorillas, shy creatures who cling to the mountaintops. It was in this area that the American zoologist George Schaller worked on his exciting book, *The Year of the Gorilla*.

Kagera National Park in northeast Rwanda can be reached by road or air from either Kigali or Gisenyi. The park entrance at Gabiro is 60 miles from Kigali just off the main road to Uganda. While lacking the wildlife concentrations of East Africa's major parks, Kagera has the advantage of fewer visitors and a better chance to see its buffalo, zebra, eland, lion, antelope, hippo, crocodile and abundant bird life. On the western border of the park is the *Mutara Big Game Hunting Reserve* (Zone de Chasse du Mutara) where licensed hunting is permitted.

South of Kigali the main road to Burundi is a scenic drive that permits stops at GITARAMA, 30 miles away, former home of the mwami and the royal family, and at BUTARE, 84 miles south. Here is the modest national university with its museum of Rwandan history and culture, a social science research center, and medical school (administered with the help of French-Canadians). There's a guest house there.

CYANGUGU (pronounced Shan-goo-goo), another attractive beach resort, is on the southern shores of Lake Kivu. It can be reached by road from Gisenyi on a scenic but rough drive following the lake, or from Kigali via Butare on a road passing through a beautiful tropical rain forest. Smaller and less developed than Gisenyi, Cyangugu has its own beach, water sports and market.

Five miles away, in Zaïre, is the major resort of Bukavu. Once a week a steamer leaves Bukavu for the two-day trip on Lake Kivu to Goma with a brief stop midway at the Rwanda lake town of Kibuye. The cruise on Lake Kivu provides a refreshing day or two of leisure along one of the most beautiful and pure bodies of water in the world, deep and clear blue, rimmed by thick forests and towering volcanic peaks.

Those who have time should go on beyond the parks to visit the smaller towns and villages, sample traditional rural hospitality, and examine the changes and continuities since independence.

What to Buy

Rwanda, like Burundi, specializes in embroidered, woven and beaded work. Best are the baskets, which come in all sizes and designs, beaded walking sticks and canes, beaded agricultural implements such as scythes, even beaded spears and lances, and traditional pipes. All these items can be purchased at the outdoor markets (with a minimum of bargaining) at prices well below those prevalent in East Africa. Also available are one- and two-kilo bags of the fine local arabica coffee which OCIR (Office des Cultures Industrielles du Rwanda), the national coffee marketing agency, will ship home for you (via Belgium, where it is roasted).

Local Attitudes

Rwanda is a land of hardworking peasants who cling to their steeply terraced hillsides and longhorn cattle. Courtesy, respect and hospitality are important elements of their culture and should be reciprocated.

Educated Rwandans are sensitive about the ethnic violence that has marred their country's recent past. If, however, you tread lightly on that topic and show interest in the positive social and economic changes since independence, Rwandans—secondary school and university students in particular—will be eager to talk.

Rwanda has aligned itself with other moderate pro-Western independent African states. Americans, who are little known, evoke curiosity and interest, and little or no hostility.

Weather, What to Wear, How Long to Stay

The March-to-May and November-to-December rainy seasons are mild and not uncomfortably wet. Evening temperatures can drop below freezing in high altitudes and a sweater or coat is needed there all year round.

Casual clothes are fine. Miniskirts and other modern Western attire are more likely to cause bewilderment than offense.

Despite Rwanda's small size, there is plenty to see. Allow a week to explore the country.

Communication

Kinyarwanda, a Bantu language, shares official status with French, while Swahili serves as a lingua franca (but not nearly as extensively as in East Africa proper). Many Rwandans have worked as migrant laborers in Uganda and a few have picked up a little English. To get around on your own, however, you'll need at least a rudimentary knowledge of French.

Postal service is not good. It's best to mail anything of importance or value from Kenya. The telephone service, too, leaves much to be desired. Overseas connections, via radio hookup, are through Brussels.

There are no regular local newspapers and the government radio is not informative.

Emergencies

Medical and dental facilities are grossly inadequate. If you need medical help, get on the first plane to Nairobi.

The United States has an embassy on Boulevard Central in Kigali (tel. 5601).

Tanzania

Profile

STATUS: Tanganyika became independent on December 9, 1961. Joined with Zanzibar on April 26, 1964 to form the United Republic of Tanzania. (Zanzibar is treated in a separate chapter.)

SIZE: 362,688 square miles (slightly smaller than Texas and New Mexico combined). Population—13,000,000.

GEOGRAPHY: Stretches from thin coastal strip of sand and mangrove swamp across plateau and highlands nearly 1,000 miles inland to Lake Victoria and Lake Tanganyika. Mt. Kilimanjaro (19,340 feet), highest in Africa, and Mt. Meru (15,000 feet) in the north. Principal towns—Dar es Salaam (capital and port, 300,000), Tanga (60,000), Moshi (40,000), Arusha, Mwanza.

CLIMATE: Coastal area has high humidity, temperatures from 80 to 95 degrees, ocean breezes. Central plateau hot and dry. Highlands cool. Long rains March through May, short rains November and December.

LANGUAGES: Swahili and English (both official).

CURRENCY: Tanzanian shilling, divided into 100 cents. 1 shilling = 14 US cents; $1.00 = 7.1 shillings.

VISAS: Available from Embassy of Tanzania and Mission of Tanzania to UN. Fee $3.15. Valid for 30 days. Two passport photos needed. Acquired in 24 hours in person, four weeks by mail. Visa also obtainable from Tanzanian Tourist Office, IPS Building, Kimathi Street, P.O. Box 8610, Nairobi, Kenya (tel. 26888).

AIRPORTS: Dar es Salaam Airport (DAR), eight miles from city. Frequent flights to and from Addis Ababa, London, Lusaka, Nairobi, Rome and Zanzibar. Transportation into city—bus, 5 shillings (70 cents); taxi,

291

15 shillings ($2.10). Kilimanjaro Airport (JAR), 31 miles from Arusha. Connections with Dar es Salaam, Tanga, Nairobi and Mombasa only. Bus fare to Arusha or Moshi, 15 shillings. Airport departure tax—15 shillings ($2.10).

NATIONAL HOLIDAYS: January 12, Zanzibar Revolution Day; April 26, Union Day; May 1, International Workers Day; June 21, Maulid Day; July 7, Saba Saba Day; December 9, Independence and Republic Day; Christian and Moslem holidays.

INFORMATION SOURCES: In US—Embassy of Tanzania, 2721 Connecticut Avenue NW, Washington, D.C. 20008 (tel. 202/483-4116); Mission of Tanzania to the UN, 800 Second Avenue, New York, N.Y. 10017 (tel. 212/972-9160). In Dar es Salaam—Tanzanian Tourist Corporation on Azikiwe Street, P.O. Box 2485 (tel. 27671), also in Arusha (tel. 2330); Automobile Association of East Africa, P.O. Box 2004 (tel. 21965).

By *Aaron Segal*

To many East Africa travelers Tanzania is a very special place. The friendliness and zest of her people and the excitement of bold social and humanitarian experiments make the Tanzanian experience memorable.

Though poor in natural resources, Tanzania is second to none scenically. Mt. Kilimanjaro, Mt. Meru, a stunning sweep of coastline, the lush vegetation of the east and lake regions, the arid expanses of the south and varied animal life everywhere put her on a par with highly touted Kenya.

Unfortunately, a lack of publicity and a lag in tourist accommodations have kept Tanzania from attracting the attention she deserves in world tourism. But now strenuous efforts are being made to improve the tourist infrastructure and transport facilities. Best of all, prices are being maintained at a level well below that of more glamorous neighbors. For the safaris, sights, sunning and sea sports that have made Kenya famous—think about Tanzania, too.

Man's earliest home seems to have been in East Africa. The findings of the late Dr. Louis B. Leakey at Olduvai Gorge on Tanzania's Serengeti Plains indicate the existence of human society almost two million years ago. Over the centuries these tribes migrated across Africa's hills and valleys, lingering where water and food were plentiful. Communities of farmers, artisans and fishermen formed in some places, and other tribal groups pursued nomadic existences.

For the past two thousand years, traders and settlers have come from Asia and Arabia across the Indian Ocean to the shores of Tanganyika (mainland Tanzania), developing a series of mercantile city-states and a flourishing coastal culture in the Bantu-Arabic-Hindustani trade tongue known as Swahili. Portuguese warships and slave traders worried the coast from 1499. Two centuries later, Arabs and Persian Shirazi reasserted control and used the offshore islands of Zanzibar and Pemba as headquarters for an accelerating slave and ivory trade that devastated the interior.

By the mid-19th century, European imperialist interests began to crowd out the Sultan of Zanzibar and his traders. In 1890 Germany acquired a protectorate over a vast expanse of the interior. Determined to make colonization pay, she introduced cotton, sisal and other crops, built railways and established a tough military rule. Rebellion came in 1905, when the inland tribes forgot their differences long enough to join in opposing the invaders in the Maji-Maji uprising.

Soon international strife intruded, as the First World War pitted British colonial troops against the Germans in a prolonged guerrilla war (colorfully described in Leonard Mosley's 1964 book, *Duel for Kilimanjaro*). After the Armistice, the League of Nations gave Britain a mandate over the Tanganyika territory, but Britain let the economy drift and continued to concentrate its interest on Kenya, with its white farmer settlers.

At the end of the Second World War, Britain's League of Nations mandate became a United Nations trusteeship, and Tanganyikan political activity took an upswing. Leader of the fight for freedom was Julius K. Nyerere, a Catholic schoolteacher and one of the first Tanganyikans to study abroad. In 1954 Nyerere and his colleagues founded the Tanganyika African National Union (TANU), which soon acquired a million members, swept the Legislative Council elections and began to press hard for independence.

Britain conceded in 1961 and Nyerere was free to begin concretizing his dream of a new society based on egalitarian ideals and genuinely African values. Locally elected officials replaced colonial appointees, private property was restricted, Swahili was made the national language and non-alignment a principle of foreign policy. Opening Dar es Salaam to African nationalist movements, Nyerere has intrepidly opposed minority rule in Southern Africa.

When Zanzibar's revolutionaries overthrew Arab rule in 1964, Nyerere formed a loose union with them, wisely allowing the island maximum autonomy and a full role in national affairs. Thus, Tanganyika and Zanzibar formed the new United Republic of Tanzania.

The nation's 13,000,000 inhabitants include 300,000 Zanzibaris, 60,000 Asians and 20,000 Europeans. The political structure has been based on Swahili culture, a revised legal code and a single-party system. Internally, democratic elections enable voters to choose from among competing TANU candidates—a prerogative they have used to topple cabinet ministers and other prominent leaders.

Nyerere has constantly emphasized the need for self-reliance, agricultural development priorities and profit-sharing among Tanzanians. The Arusha Declaration of 1967 enunciated these principles, placing strict limits on private wealth, imposing austerity on government officials and justifying government majority holdings in most businesses and industries. Since then further restrictions have been placed on private property, and education has been reoriented toward agricultural skills. Ujamaa (cooperative) villages based on communal labor have sprung up all over the country with government assistance.

The boldness, drive and vision of Tanzania's leader is well conveyed in *Freedom and Unity* (Oxford University Press), a collection of Nyerere's essays, and in a sympathetic biographical treatment, *We Must*

Run While They Walk, by William E. Smith (Random House, 1972). Henry Bienen's scholarly study *Tanzania* provides a picture of TANU, while Susan Wenner's *Shambu Letu* is at the other end of the spectrum —a personal account of a year spent in an ujamaa village. *A Guide to Kenya and Northern Tanzania* (Sierra Club/Scribner's, 1971) is a good guide to the major national parks.

Money Matters

Foreign banks were nationalized in 1967 and reorganized under the National Bank of Commerce, with offices throughout the country. Banks are open from 9 to noon on weekdays and 9 to 11 am on Saturday.

Most leading hotels will accept your travelers checks and major credit cards. Retain your receipts for foreign exchange; even some hotels may ask to see proof that you have obtained your Tanzanian currency legally. Since this currency is not convertible outside the country, change only what you need. Should you have a surplus on leaving consider buying Makonde sculpture, a wise aesthetic and financial investment. Beware of persons offering black-market Tanzanian shillings for your foreign exchange; such transactions are illegal and penalties severe, and the effect is detrimental to a struggling economy.

Getting In and Out

Tanzania is accessible by air, boat, road and rail. Pan American operates a weekly service from New York via Nairobi, a wearying 20-hour flight. Several carriers fly to major European cities and to Entebbe-Kampala, Lusaka, Blantyre, Addis Ababa and Cairo from Dar es Salaam (known as Dar). Connections for flights to and from West Africa are made in Nairobi. Although the government has built an airport near Mt. Kilimanjaro to divert some of the traffic, most international flights still land at the capital.

A ticket from North America to East Africa can be stretched at a difference of five per cent or less to include Dar as well as Kampala and Nairobi. Make a point of investigating this, since most airline personnel will not bother to volunteer the information.

Inexpensive charter flights are not yet available with any regularity, but the Denmark-Tanzania Friendship Association runs one from Copenhagen. You can fly charters from New York to Nairobi for $250 one way, then proceed by road or air to Tanzania.

There are daily flights and weekly boat trips between Dar and Zanzibar. Sometimes it is difficult to get on a flight, since tourism to the politically sensitive island is not being encouraged at this time. Persevere, however, and chances are that an hour or two before flight time your reservation will be confirmed. East African Airways runs flights from Tanzania to the major Indian Ocean islands; so do Air Madagascar and Air Comores.

All roads between East and Southern Africa cross Tanzania. The 700-mile road between Nairobi and Dar es Salaam is paved all the way. The trip takes two days, with several chances for pleasant rest stops en route. Daily low-cost bus service via East African Road Services covers this road. Hitchhikers stand a good chance of being picked up here, since private traffic is relatively heavy.

The coastal road from Mombasa to Tanga and Dar is in poor condition during the two rainy seasons (November to May), with little traffic. All-weather roads encircle Lake Victoria and connect to main thoroughfares; but there is little traffic between Dar and the outposts in this corner of the country.

The Great North Road runs nearly 1,000 miles between Dar and Lusaka (Zambia). It is being resurfaced with American and Canadian aid, but takes an extraordinary beating from heavy-duty truck traffic. At Mbeya, near the Zambian border, a rough mountain road plied by local buses leads to the Lake Malawi port of Itungi; but it's safer to cross the border into Zambia at Tunduma and take the road east to Chitipa and the Malawian border.

The border with Mozambique is enclosed by an area used as a sanctuary for FRELIMO guerrillas (see chapter on Mozambique); it can be entered only with permission from the Office of the President in Dar es Salaam.

There are several interesting—but slow—ways into and out of Tanzania. East African Railways runs trains between Dar and Kigoma, on Lake Tanganyika, and between Dar and Mwanza, on Lake Victoria. On Lake Tanganyika, the steamer SS Liemba connects Kigoma with the Zambian port of Mpulungu; another steamer, the Urundi, connects Kigoma with Kalémie in Zaïre. On Lake Victoria, the East African Railways operates boats from Mwanza to Kenyan and Ugandan ports.

Ocean travel to Dar has been hampered by the closing of the Suez Canal. Robin Lines runs a 12-passenger freighter twice monthly from New York; round trip costs $815. Lykes Lines sails from New Orleans and Houston to Dar with passenger freighters; round trip, $705. Lower fares are available on ships from European ports: Eastern Africa National Lines, German African Lines, Polish Ocean Lines and Yugoslav Jadranzka Slobodna Lines. British India sails between Dar and Bombay; Royal Interocean runs from Dar to Singapore, Hong Kong, Japan, Australia and New Zealand.

Getting Around Within Tanzania

In general, travel in Tanzania is best accomplished by air; overland routes can be slow, hazardous and tiring. Unless people-watching and the appreciation of vast landscapes make up for the discomfort (as they do for many who come to East Africa), take a plane.

East African Airways runs regular flights on DC-3's and other craft between Dar and Dodoma, Tabora, Mwanza, Mafia Island, Kilwa, Lindi, Iringa, Mbeya, Njombe, Arusha, Moshi and the new Kilimanjaro airport. A good bargain if you want to see the country by air is the 14-day, $140 ticket for unlimited travel within East Africa. For the most remote spots, try the private flights offered by Tim-Air Charter at Dar and Arusha airports, and by Tanzair out of Dar.

Within the city of Dar es Salaam there's an inexpensive (but inadequate) municipal bus system. The beach hotels outside the city run their own shuttle buses. Taxis are available around the clock at the airport, railway station and the Kilimanjaro Hotel, and with less frequency at major intersections. There are no meters, but prices are fixed at 50 US cents within the city, 15 cents per mile outside, and $2.10 to the airport or university. Drivers usually speak a little English.

If you can rent a bicycle (ask at your hotel), you can get around Dar pretty easily, although the humidity may discourage you from any fast pedaling.

Car rentals start at $6 a day, plus mileage charges, for a VW 1300. Land Rovers cost up to $11.50 a day, with weekly rates from $35 to $70. An international credit card will substitute for a cash deposit at most car rental agencies in Dar. Driving is on the left, and an international license is required. Sometimes a chauffeur, hired at $3 to $4 a day, is a good investment, especially if you intend to travel overland. Main car rental firms in Dar are Hertz on Upanga Road (tel. 20681) and Valji and Alibhai on Bridge Street (tel. 20522). In Arusha, there's a United Touring Company branch on Uhuru Road (tel. 2762). In Moshi, try the Aziz Taxi Service opposite the tourist office (tel. 2336). A large party may find it cheaper to rent a minibus. Be sure the vehicle you rent has a breakdown towing service guarantee and is equipped with a safari kit including jack and spare tires; carry the useful Automobile Association of East Africa Official Touring Guide.

Bus service connects most important towns with Dar es Salaam. Fares are low, but transit is slow and uncomfortable. Also slow but more pleasant are the East African Railways trains from Dar to Kigoma and Mwanza. There are as yet no plans for passenger accommodations on the TanZam Railroad from Dar to Lusaka being built with Chinese aid.

Many visitors like package tours. Unfortunately, most of the East Africa tours leave out the greater part of Tanzania, including the capital, and confine themselves to the northern Tanzanian game parks and a sight of Kilimanjaro. There are tours, however, that concentrate on Tanzania. One is available through the Denmark-Tanzania Friendship Association in Cophenhagen. Another is sponsored by *Ramparts Magazine*.

Once in Tanzania, try the services of the Fourways Travel agency on Independence Avenue in Dar (tel. 21401); mailing address: P.O. Box 2926. Other helpful agencies in the capital city include Kearline Tours (tel. 20607), Subzali Tours (tel. 25907) and the Tanganyika Tourist Service (tel. 23751). In Arusha: United Touring Company (tel. 2587) and Subzali Tours (tel. 2242).

Where to Stay

While new hotels, lodges and rest-houses are going up all over the country, Tanzania still has problems with the quality of service and the coziness of accommodations. In DAR ES SALAAM, the *Kilimanjaro* pretends to be in the luxury class but isn't. It has 200 rooms with bath, air-conditioning, a pool, nightclub, boutiques and restaurant; but the food is bad and the staff surly or inept. Rates begin at $19 for a single and $26 for a double with breakfast. The *New Africa* has air-conditioned rooms with bath, but there is no pool, the restaurant food is high-priced and mediocre, and the rooms start at $14.40 for singles and $26.60 for doubles. A better value is the *AGIP Motel*, centrally located on City Drive, with 57 air-conditioned rooms with showers, and a good restaurant. Rates are $11.20 (single) and $19.60 (double), with breakfast.

If possible, pass up the downtown hotels entirely and stay a few miles out of town along the beach. There is free minibus service at most seaside places, and access to some of the loveliest beaches in Africa. The *Africana Vacation Village and Hotel* is 14 miles out, with 200 attractive bungalows, a beach for swimming and snorkeling and excellent Swiss cuisine. Full board rates are $15 to $18 for singles and $20 to $26 for doubles. The *Kunduchi Beach*, 15 miles from town, is a neo-Arab structure with 100 air-conditioned rooms, all with bath; it has a very attractive bar and restaurant, a pool, beach and a fishing lagoon. Full board begins at $21 (single) and $33.60 (double). The *Bahari Beach*, a strikingly beautiful modern compound whose architect made imaginative use of local materials, is more informal and breezy. Rates begin at $16.80 for singles and $26.60 for doubles. The *Oyster Bay*, four miles from town, is a compromise between beach and city; a modest, friendly atmosphere plus succulent seafood and low rates make it a special bargain. Singles with breakfast start at $7. *Silversands,* 10 miles out, begins at $11 for singles with breakfast. Camping facilities are also available here at low prices.

There are two city hotels that fall outside the usual classifications. The *Skyway,* a stopover hotel for East African Airlines, is located a block from the AGIP, next to the EAA terminal. Rates begin at $10 (single) and $16 (double) including breakfast, but unless getting to the terminal is your main concern, there's no advantage in staying at this drab place. *Luther House,* a church-operated hostel, has cheap rooms, cafeteria meals and a generally young clientele. Here there is a chance for social contacts and hitchhiking tips; posted on the bulletin board are names of people looking for rides or offering them. Prices are $8 for singles with full board. The YMCA has reasonably priced rooms, but even lower tariffs are charged at some of the Asian-owned guest houses west of Independence Avenue and at the African-run hotels near the Kariakoo Market. Sometimes you can get rooms here for less than $2 a night—but remember that your valuables will need watching, the toilet will be "Eastern style," i.e., a hole in the floor, and your door will probably have no latch.

Outside Dar there is a dearth of decent accommodations, except in the Kilimanjaro and Arusha regions. At ARUSHA you'll find several attractive hotels. There's the *New Arusha,* with 72 rooms (bath or shower), a pleasant restaurant, a pool and beautiful gardens; full board rates are $17 for singles and $30 for doubles (the front rooms have a view of Mt. Meru). Somewhat simpler and cheaper is the *Safari,* with 35 rooms, half of which have baths, and a restaurant but no pool. Rates are $9 for singles, $14 for doubles. The *Naaz Hotel* charges $3 for simple accommodations.

On the slopes of Mt. Kilimanjaro, about 25 miles from Moshi, are two gracious hotels set in lovely grounds. The *Marangu* is rambling and comfortable, with full board at $10 (single) and $17 (double), plus camping grounds with the option of hotel meals for campers. The *Kibo,* half-a-mile up the mountain from the Marangu, also has camping grounds, and prices are low here too: $9 to $11 for singles and $17 to $21 for doubles with full board. Both hotels will arrange climbing expeditions for guests.

In MOSHI itself try the excellent *Coffee Tree Hostelry,* which has a restaurant, coffee shop and nightclub. Singles are $4 to $6 and doubles $7 to $20. The *Liberty Hotel* is modest but comfortable; here singles are $3, doubles $6.50. There is also a YMCA hostel at Moshi with daily and monthly rates.

The national parks and reserves offer a variety of accommodations, from simple campsites to luxurious lodges. Four of the most attractive places—the *Lake Manyara Hotel* and the *Ngorongoro, Seronera* and *Lobo* wildlife lodges—have fixed tariffs of $27.50 for singles and $37.15 for doubles with full board. Reservations should be made well in advance, especially for the December-to-May peak season, through Hallmark Hotels (Tanzania) Ltd, P.O. Box 9500, Dar es Salaam (tel. 28181). The Lake Manyara has a pool and a superb view of the plains and park 3,000 feet below. The Ngorongoro stands just on the rim of the crater; the Seronera and Lobo are both on the Serengeti Plains—the Lobo Lodge is tucked into a massive rock formation.

There are also simpler and less expensive lodgings in the major parks. At Ngorongoro Crater Park there is a youth hostel, with bunk beds and kitchen, open to all ages. More comfortable and more expensive (but still cheaper than the two main lodges in the park) is *Ngorongoro Forest Lodge*. Book reservations through Masailand Safaris, P.O. Box 445, Arusha (tel. 2523). There is a campsite about two miles from the Seronera Lodge at Serengeti, and two excellent lodges serve those who can pay the tariff: *Ngorongoro Crater Lodge*, resembling a chalet with beamed ceilings, at $12 to $20 for singles and $22 to $32 for doubles, full board, and *Fort Ikoma Lodge*, a restored pre-World War I German fort perched on a hill. In addition to a pool, the Fort Ikoma offers proximity to archaeological digs. Full board prices are $23 for singles and $35 for doubles.

Arusha National Park, site of the Ngurdoto Crater, has both the *Momella Game Lodge*, with pool, bungalows and full board rates of $11 for singles and $22 for doubles; and the *Ndutu Tented Camp*, where you can rough it in luxury with showers and electricity for about $25 a day. Another comfort-oriented campsite, 80 miles south of Arusha, is the *Tarangire Safari Park*, in the new Tarangire Park on the Masai plains. Full board rates run $18 for singles and $27 for doubles.

Remember that in all parks it is possible to bring your own camping equipment (which can be rented in Arusha); pay the park entrance fee and stay overnight for about $2.

On MAFIA ISLAND (not the Godfather's summer home), a 45-minute flight from Dar, there is excellent deep-sea fishing. Rates at the *Mafia Island Lodge* are high, from $20 for singles to $30-plus for doubles; book through Hallmark Hotels (above); sea sports arranged by Seafaris, P.O. Box 384, Dar es Salaam (tel. 20553). At Mikumi National Park, 200 miles south of the capital, is a new lodge with camping also available in permanent tents, and a bar with thatched roof built around a giant tree. Make reservations through the Oyster Bay Hotel in Dar. Camping can also be arranged through the Chief Park Warden, Mikumi National Park, P.O. Box 642, Morogoro.

The *Railway Motel* in DODOMA has good food and reasonable prices (singles are $11, full board). This makes an agreeable stop on the road to Zambia, as do the *White Horse Inn* at IRINGA ($7 for singles and $13 for doubles with full board), and the *Guest House* at MBEYA (rooms with full board are $6 for singles and $8 for doubles). Government rest-houses are cheap and generally have beds, fireplaces and kitchens, but first choice goes to civil servants. In dire need, ask at secondary schools with boarding facilities and at mission stations—generally they will offer hospitality if they can. As a last resort go to the local police, who will find you a bed somehow.

Friendly East African Airlines drivers will help you find a hotel in the smaller towns, especially if you're arriving at night. They know the small guest houses and they'll run in for you to find out if there's room. A nice tip is in order.

Where and What to Eat

Local specialties are available at most Tanzanian hotels, even when the rest of the menu is European. Dar city water is said to be potable, but if in doubt boil it 15 minutes or drink a bottled brand. In outlying areas no water can be presumed safe. Fortunately, fruit juices are plentiful, cheap and delicious. There is a local wine called Dodoma (not bad) and good commercial beers. Homemade beer (called pombe) can be tasty but a bit risky unless made under hygienic conditions—and its potency varies.

In DAR ES SALAAM the best food for the money, if you like Eastern dishes, is found at the more modest Indian restaurants. For good curries try the *Sheesh Mahal*, in a pleasant setting, and the *Cosy Cafe*, on an outdoor veranda. The *Hindu Lodge* has excellent vegetable curries and the *City Hotel* and *Royal Restaurant* offer good Indian food in plain surroundings. Fine Italian dishes are found at *Bruno's* in the Oyster Bay suburb and at the *AGIP* dining room in town. The *Twiga Room* of the Twiga Hotel, and *Oyster Bay Hotel* restaurant and *Joseph's* have excellent seafood. *Arlecchino's*, near the Avalon Cinema, and the three *Sno-Cream* parlors offer snacks and ice cream.

African food at very low prices will be found in the small restaurants on Jamhuri Street and at the African hotels near the Kariakoo Market. Try ugali na nyama (maize porridge with meat stew), nyama ya mbuzi (goat meat stew with curry) and ndizi na nyama (plantains and meat). Coconuts full of milk with the tops cut off are on sale for a few cents along the streets everywhere in town, as are fried cassava chips spiced with red pepper and fresh fruits of all kinds. Along the coast seafood is plentiful and cheap; the lobsters are especially good. Inland, fresh water fish abound. The Swahili word for all fish is "samaki." If you are camping along the coast, make friends with a local fisherman; a few shillings in the morning will ensure you a fresh fish dinner at the end of the day.

In the outback, eat when you can at restaurants and good hotels. If this isn't possible, be sure that you avoid fresh, uncooked foods and make certain that cooked ones are served at once. Samosas, a delicious meat and vegetable pie, is very tasty if just made, and the shish kebabs sold by local vendors are safe (and delicious) if thoroughly cooked and made of fresh ingredients. Avoid dairy products unless bought through a good hotel or restaurant.

What to See and Do

In terms of physical setting, DAR ES SALAAM is the "haven of peace" its name implies. With a population of over 300,000, however, this government seat, trade center and refuge for rebels is lively enough—a city of vivid colors, multiracial contrast and excitement just below the surface of everyday life. Above all, it is also an ancient port, with that feeling of constant movement and change found only by the sea.

Getting around central Dar is best on foot. (Bus or hired car or taxi can take you short distances to some of the outlying attractions.) Walk along the seafront, enjoying the wild contrasts in architecture (the old German-built post office, the pseudo-Hiltonian Kilimanjaro Hotel, the National Development Building, the City Hall, the Lutheran Church, the old railway station), or watching the dhows unload their cargoes. At the old port, arrange for a fisherman to take you out for the day in an ungalawa (a kind of outrigger canoe) for about $2.

A stroll into town along Independence Avenue will lead past the principal shops. Several blocks to the east is the Kariakoo Market, where local products are bargained for, and TANU party headquarters. The new National Museum near Ocean Road contains excellent displays of contemporary art, Makonde sculpture and musical instruments; also an historical exhibit, and many of Dr. Leakey's finds from Olduvai Gorge. Admission is free and hours are 9 am to 7 pm daily.

On the Bagamoyo Road, 14 miles from the city, is the Village Museum, a collection of traditional homes and architectural styles of all the major ethnic groups in the country. Here craftsmen display their skills, and on Sundays at 3 pm, ngomas (dance exhibitions) are held. Farther along the road you will find Makonde sculptors from the Mozambique border area working away at their strange, dreamlike ebony statues.

The Dar Information Bureau on City Drive downtown, next to St. Joseph's Church, is always ready to help with maps and information.

They may also help arrange visits to ujamaa villages. *Karibu Tanzania*, a monthly publication available there and at most hotels free of charge, is full of current information on sights, events and accommodations.

A good time to be in Dar is around Saba Saba Day (July 7), the commemoration of the 1954 founding of the Tanganyika African National Union (TANU). A week-long festival and trade fair, with singing, drumming and exhibitions—like those of the fantastic Makonde stilt dancers and the snake dancers from Dodoma—make this a memorable experience.

Several public buildings and areas in Dar are noteworthy: the lovely Arab-style State House near the National Museum, which is reserved for honored guests only, since President Nyerere prefers to live in his modest home a few miles away at Msasani Beach; the University of Dar es Salaam's modern campus on Observation Hill, 12 miles from the city, where excellent dance and theater performances are often held; and Mnazi Moja, a large open-air meeting place off Lumumba Street, where public assemblies are common (nearby is Arnatoglu Community Center, a popular gathering spot for young Tanzanians).

For swimming, water sports and picnicking, the beaches in and around Dar are unsurpassed. In town, try the beach along Ocean Road, where dressing rooms are available at the private swimming club. There are good beaches four miles out at Oyster Bay and at Msasani, five miles away near a fishing village; also at Kunduchi (site of a 15th century Arab mosque) and Silversands. The beach hotels offer facilities for day visitors and provide a generous lunch.

At the beautiful harbor entrance near the intersection of Kivukoni Road and Ocean Road, a ferry regularly crosses the port waters; this 10-minute trip is great fun. Across the harbor at Mjimwema Beach are the state-owned petroleum refinery and Kivukoni College, a residential school for TANU activists.

You can sail, swim and fish at the Yacht Club, six miles north of the city. The Gymkhana Club in the city has golf, tennis and cricket facilities. There are also clubs in Dar that offer riding, flying and skeet shooting—ask at the Information Bureau. Soccer matches are held on weekends at the National Stadium in Dar and at many local fields. Bao, a game resembling parcheesi, is played with great concentration along the seafront and in the public parks. Watch the oldsters at it and buy yourself a set with rules at the National Museum.

Night life in the capital is rather sharply divided between Tanzanians and foreigners. Though most hotel entertainment is routine, there are exceptions. On the rooftop of the Splendid Hotel, for example, a Congo jazz band plays nonstop on Friday and Saturday nights. Cover charge is $1, the drinks are cheap, and there are numerous unescorted ladies about. The action gets going around midnight. The Simba Club of the Kilimanjaro, Margot's and the Silversands Hotel have dancing for the tourist trade. Perhaps the most pleasant spot, though, is the recently reopened Forodhani Hotel, with its outdoor veranda overlooking the most picturesque part of Dar harbor. Here, once or twice weekly on the terrace of this former British club, young Tanzanians and foreign visitors mix to dance to excellent live Congo music. In a spurt of puritanical fervor, the Tanzanian Government had stopped Forodhani's musical entertainments for a while but reopened the outdoor facility to the gratification of both Dar residents and interested visitors.

Films in town are generally lightweight Indian and Italian productions, but the Dar Film Society makes an effort to show a better selection (with English subtitles). The Friendship Textile Mill has a drama club, and the Dar es Salaam Players give semi-professional English performances. Try also to see a Swahili-language production at the University's Theater Arts Department, which also has an excellent dance group.

If you want a good look at Tanzania's social and political life, government and university people can help you visit schools, cooperatives, courts or whatever else is of interest to you. Among the social and educational projects in Dar are the evening classes at the Institute of Adult Education, Kivukoni College, the Chinese-built Tanzania Friendship Textile Mill, several self-help public housing projects, and the child care and handicraft centers run by the National Women's Association (Umoja ya Wanawake). The Institute of Education at the university is responsible for bold curriculum reforms under way and can arrange visits to schools. University law-faculty members will be helpful in arranging court visits and describing the new legal code. The offices of the Christian Council at Luther House in Dar will open their various centers of social work.

Along the 126-mile stretch from Dar west to MOROGORO are a number of interesting projects. Eight miles from the city a group of black Americans have founded an African cooperative poultry farm. Thirty or so miles from the city is the National Youth Service training camp, where boys and girls are taught agricultural and crafts skills in a communal setting; and 10 miles farther is the Nordic Centre, comprising an experimental farm, clinic, secondary school and community development program originally funded by Scandinavian governments. The National Agricultural College and experimental station is at Morogoro; get permission to visit from the Tanzanian Tourist Corporation.

A good boat service is operated by East African Railways between Dar and the southern port of MTWARA, once a center for groundnut trade and now a point of export for sisal, coconuts and cattle. There are good beaches here and at Mikindani, seven miles to the south. This is the area where the Makonde sculptors originated. Inland over mountain roads from Mtwara are the rustic towns of Nachingwea, Masasi, Tunduru, Songea and Njombe. Some of the oldest ujamaa villages are in this area.

Easy to reach by road and air is the coastal town of KILWA, 200 miles south of Dar, with ruins of the once mighty Sultanate of Kilwa, destroyed by the Portuguese in 1505.

North from Dar, 45 miles up a partly paved road, is the lovely historic town of BAGAMOYO. Once an Arab slave trading center, this quiet fishing village was the jumping off point for Burton, Speke and Stanley on their way to the interior. Here, too, lay the body of Livingstone, carried a thousand miles by his faithful bearers to be returned by ship to England. The town has splendid carved doors, a fine beach, a private museum of 19th century artifacts (at the Notre Dame mission) and a massive baobab tree where slaves were once shackled. Three miles away is Kaole, with the ruins of a mosque and pillars dating back 800 years.

TANGA, second city of Tanzania, is a port with a population of 60,000, 353 miles from Dar by paved road. Tanga's once-thriving economy has been hurt by the falling price of sisal, and what accommodations and entertainments remain are modest. Thirty-three miles south is PANGANI, an attractive little fishing port with a good beach. Nearby is KIGOMBE, a little village with local scenes painted on the outside of the dwellings. A few miles from Tanga are Persian ruins from the 13th century. Other excursions around Tanga include a trip through the Amboni Sisal Estate and the Mkomazi Game Reserve (really an extension of Tsavo Park in Kenya), or a ride out to the Amboni limestone caves and the Galanos sulphur springs and mineral baths. Consult the Tanga Tourist Association on Independence Avenue, opposite the public library (tel. 2982), for excursion information.

The paved road between Dar, Tanga and Nairobi skirts the Usambara Mountains, site of the picturesque resorts of Soni and Lushoto. These are hill stations 5,000 feet above the sea—good places to cool off and enjoy the forest. At Soni there is a simple hotel near a waterfall; and at Lushoto two hotels (more expensive) with riding, fishing, golf and tennis. Another road through the eucalyptus and cedar leads to AMANI, site of the East African Malaria Research Institute.

The main Dar-to-Nairobi road runs through several dusty crossroads towns such as Korogwe and Same, and along the Nyumba Ya Mungu (House of God) earth dam on the Pangani River, which provides power for the capital. The Pare people who live along this road and in the mountains are sturdy and self-reliant. At SHUME, 21 miles from Lushoto, there is a large stone, Jiwe Ya Mungu (Stone of God), from which one has a panoramic view of the mountains, plains and valleys far below.

Midway between Dar and Nairobi is the Kilimanjaro area, with the two delightful towns of Arusha and Moshi. Roads lead from here west to Ngorongoro Crater, Lake Manyara and Serengeti Park; south to Kondoa, Dodoma and the Zambian border, and east to *Tsavo Park* and Mombasa.

A few miles due north of the road from Moshi to Mombasa is Lake Chala, directly on the Kenya-Tanzania border. It has a little-known and little-used campsite in a small, sturdy, open lodge built on the rim road atop a lake-filled volcano. The setting between Mt. Kilimanjaro and the Tsavo Plains is extraordinary. Every morning local fishermen of the Chagga tribe descend the steep inner walk of the extinct volcano to fish on rafts. This is one of the most interesting, offbeat spots anywhere in East Africa.

MOSHI is a busy commercial town of 40,000 linked by rail and road to Nairobi, Mombasa and Tanga. The Kilimanjaro Native Cooperative Union (KNCU) runs a fine shopping arcade in the city. The Chagga people have profited from their cultivation of quality arabica coffee. Chagga women, often considered the loveliest and most amiable in East Africa, can be admired at the Coffee Tree Hostelry and other Moshi bars and night spots. The town has a cooperative college and training center. You can play golf at the Moshi Club.

Mt. Kilimanjaro dominates the skyline with snow-capped Kibo Peak at 19,340 feet and the lower but more rugged Mawenzi Peak at 16,890 feet. Along its fertile slopes the Chagga cultivate coffee, bananas and other crops and live in neat, well-tended villages. A paved road leads from Moshi 26 miles up the mountain to the Kibo and Marangu Hotels. Behind the Kibo Hotel the Tanzanian artist Elimo Njau has built a studio and cultural center of traditional Chagga materials. The area is superb for mountain trout fishing, hiking and relaxing. The Kilimanjaro Tourist Bureau, P.O. Box 381, Moshi, and the Mt. Kilimanjaro Fishing Club, P.O. Box 10, Moshi, can help with arrangements.

The climb up Kilimanjaro is in reality a long, tough, five-day walk requiring no special equipment or expertise unless you tackle Mawenzi Peak. Hotels provide porters, guides, clothing and meals for the trip, and will reserve shelter in the three huts on the mountain at 9,000, 12,300 and 16,000 feet. You need a good walking stick, walking shoes, sleeping bag, a backpack, warm clothes and provisions for five days. The climb winds through the forest belt, along open grasslands, across a volcanic lava plain and then, for the last 3,000 feet, up a scrabble and rock path. The views are spectacular, the air invigorating and the climb thoroughly enjoyable, demanding only normal stamina and endurance. The hotels charge $70 per person for an expedition with guide and porters. More intrepid climbers can manage on their own. There's no climbing during the long rains in April and May. It's best in January, February, September and October when days tend to be cloudless.

The Sanya Plains and the new Kilimanjaro Airport are along the 67-mile drive from Moshi to Arusha, and on this road, 13 miles from Arusha, is the turn-off for the new *Arusha National Park*. This is one of the loveliest parks in East Africa, consisting of Momella, a former game farm, Ngurdoto Crater and Mt. Meru Game Sanctuary. The films *Hatari* and *The Boy Ten Feet Tall* were shot in a sanctuary at Momella, which has five crater lakes and a fine concentration of bird and wildlife including colobus monkeys, buffalo, rhinos and elephants. The Momella Lodge provides comfortable and friendly accommodations.

Ngurdoto Crater comes close to being the Garden of Eden as Adam and Eve left it. It is an incredibly lush, well-watered, green valley floor teeming with every species of creature except man, who is prohibited from descending the forested road down the steep crater walls. Bring binoculars and a telephoto lens for viewing and photography.

Mt. Meru is barely under 15,000 feet, an easily scaled extinct volcano like Mt. Kilimanjaro, although not snow-capped. The climb takes three days. At its foot, 12 miles from Arusha on the road to Moshi, is the *Mt. Meru Game Sanctuary*, an open-air zoo maintained by the naturalist Dr. von Nagy. Accommodations are available at the Sanctuary Lodge, where Volkswagens can be rented inexpensively for a 30-mile circle tour of the park that includes the Crater, Momella Lakes (six miles north) and the slopes of Mt. Meru. Beware of elephants that come out of the craters and saunter across the road.

ARUSHA is a fast-growing town (30,000) with a delightful climate, set in a fragrant, floral, mountain uplands crossed by swift streams. It is the tourist center of northern Tanzania and the headquarters of the East African Community (EAC), which is responsible for the common market and certain administrative and research services shared by Kenya, Tanzania and Uganda. The Information Office of the EAC at Arusha is pleased to help visitors with literature and appointments. There are also several travel agencies and tour operators.

Arusha has good hotels and shops, a flourishing bazaar, a striking Sikh temple and a meerschaum-pipe factory. Local jewelers sell the semiprecious stone tanzanite, recently discovered near the town. Through the streets wander colorfully attired men who appear to be Masai, but are really members of the Arusha tribe, a rural people who imitate the Masai dress and hair styles.

Lake Manyara National Park is 80 miles from Arusha by paved road—the first stop on the Manyara-Ngorongoro-Serengeti circuit. A soda lake at the foot of the Rift Valley escarpment wall, Manyara attracts more than 300 species of birds. The park itself teems with buffalo, elephants, rhinos and lions. There is camping at the village of Mto wa Mbu at the entrance to the park, or at the luxurious Lake Manyara Hotel on the edge of the escarpment. As in all Tanzanian parks, there is an entrance fee per person and per vehicle, and a park ranger may be engaged to ride along and help find the animals. The park can be explored in normal vehicles except during the rainy season, when four-wheel drive is needed.

The new *Tarangire National Park* is 76 miles south of Arusha, 33 miles below the point at which the road forks westward to Lake Manyara. It has tented camp accommodations. The nearby Masai herdsmen nourish themselves with the milk and blood of their cattle and do not bother the rhinos, oryx, lesser kudu and other game in the park.

Most travelers skip Tarangire to continue 37 miles on a scenic mountain road from Lake Manyara to Ngorongoro Crater. From the 8,000-foot-high rim one can look down into a 100-square-mile grassland roamed by thousands of animals, including the "big five"—elephant, lion, leopard, rhino and buffalo. Here on the floor of the crater a scientific unit studies problems of ecology and conservation. Descending in one of the lodge Land Rovers with driver and guide costs about $10 per person for the day—well worth it unless you want to take your own or rented car down the narrow, tortuous road.

A tough gravel road from Ngorongoro goes 90 miles to Seronera Lodge in the middle of the Serengeti Plains. Descending 36 miles from the crater onto the plains, one reaches the turning for Olduvai Gorge, a multi-tiered layer of exposed shale and stone containing extraordinary fossil beds. Excavations are still underway at this site, where the late Dr. Leakey found the skull of Nutcracker Man (Zinjanthropus boisei), 1,750,000 years old, which can be seen in the National Museum at Dar. There is a small museum at Olduvai.

Serengeti Park has the largest migratory movement of plains animals anywhere in the world. Each year in May or June hundreds of thousands of wildebeest, zebra, gazelle and other animals move from the central plains to the permanent water of the western corridor in mile-long processions, returning in November or December. Described in the book by Dr. Bernhard Grzimek, *Serengeti Shall Not Die*, the migration can best be seen in May. The animals are concentrated on the plains in January or February. At any time of year Serengeti is spectacular. There are comfortable lodges and camping sites and a road north to the Kenyan park of *Masai Mara* across the treeless plains.

The combination of Ngorongoro, Manyara, Serengeti and Mt. Kilimanjaro is unbeatable. But many visitors start from Nairobi, do some or all of this circuit, and unfortunately never make it to Dar or anywhere else in Tanzania. One option is to go on from Serengeti, continuing across the park by a rough but serviceable all-weather road to the shores of Lake Victoria. This rugged trip can also be made inexpensively every other day by bus from the towns of Mwanza and Musoma on the lake to Arusha via Ngorongoro.

Mwanza is a port and railhead on Lake Victoria, center of a cotton-growing region of the Sukuma people. A boat goes out to Saanane Island, a game sanctuary with a charming animal orphanage. Also at Mwanza is the Catholic-operated Institute of Journalism, and the East African Research Institute for Bilharzia. Ten miles south of Mwanza is the village of Kisesa, with a museum containing many historical relics of the 35 different chiefdoms that compose the Sukuma tribe (the largest in Tanzania, numbering over a million). Nearby at Bujora there are festivals on July 7 and November 22 and displays of the iron, wood and basketwork of Sukuma craftsmen. The small port of Musoma, 161 miles north of Mwanza, is near the birthplace of President Nyerere, who is the son of a chief of the small (40,000) Zanaki tribe. Another excursion from Mwanza is by boat to Ukerewe Island in Lake Victoria, where there is a Catholic Institute of Social Research project studying the remarkable irrigation and fishing methods of the islanders.

The road west from Mwanza to Bukoba skirts the shores of Lake Victoria, passing near the *Biharamulo Game Reserve* on the edge of the lake. This is longhorn cattle country, inhabited by once-aristocratic pastoral societies related to the slender, tall Tutsi of Burundi and Rwanda. Bukoba is an attractive port in lovely coffee country on the western shores of Lake Victoria. It is an educational center with a strong local cooperative for ginning cotton and processing coffee.

Mwanza is also connected by road and rail with Dar via the town of Tabora in the dry plateau country of central Tanzania. The Williamson Diamond Mines at Mwadui, 86 miles south of Mwanza on the road to Tabora, are open to visitors by arrangement with the Dar es Salaam offices of the company.

Tabora was a 19th century caravan center for the ivory and slave trade and is now a dusty trading crossroads with a good secondary school. Four miles from the town is the reconstructed home where Livingstone stayed for a year before setting out on his last journey in 1872.

Western Tanzania is best reached by air or train from Dar via Tabora. The end of the line is the town of KIGOMA on Lake Tanganyika. This port town is drowsy and remote, with good lake fishing. There are boat connections here to Burundi and Zambia. The boat from Kigoma across the lake to Kalémie (ex-Albertville) in Zaïre is less regular but interesting (see Zaïre chapter). Five miles south of Kigoma a plaque marks the site of the mango tree at Ujiji where on November 10, 1871, Stanley uttered his famous greeting to Dr. Livingstone. Ten miles north of Kigoma is the new *Gombe National Park*, the lakeshore home of the 200 chimpanzees who were first studied and written about by Jane van Lawick-Goodall. Southeast of Kigoma is the *Katavi Plain Reserve* with a large herd of buffalo, a government rest-house and an airstrip. Katavi can also be reached by road from the lead-mining town of MPANDA, 25 miles away on a branch railway line.

Central and southern Tanzania are most accessible from Dar by road or air. First stop by road from Dar toward Zambia is the town of Morogoro, 126 miles from the capital, site of the National Agricultural College. One can drive into the nearby Uluguru Mountains, where there are trout streams and game birds. The Acropol Hotel is a moderately priced overnight or lunch stop.

Mikumi National Park is 60 miles west of Morogoro, about a five-hour ride from Dar. It has a new lodge and tented camp, and concentrations of wildlife, including hippos. Overnight package tours are available from Dar. Best viewing months are December through March.

Just south of Mikumi is the 19,000-square-mile *Selous Game Reserve*, largest in the world, named after the famous naturalist and hunter, Frederick Selous. The government uses the area as an immense series of hunting blocks for those who would bag large-tusked elephants and large-maned lions. Hunting safaris here are operated by Tanzania Wildlife Safaris, P.O. Box 9270, Dar es Salaam, which also offers hunting, fishing and photographic safaris in other parts of Tanzania.

The Chinese-built TanZam railway runs along the edges of the Selous Reserve on its route through the Kilombero River Valley. Along the railway line at Kilosa, Kidatu and Ifakara there are interesting agricultural projects for sugar cane and other crops.

The hill town of IRINGA is 130 miles west of Mikumi at a major road junction. Here the so-called Great North Road from Zambia and Southern Africa has two branches, one leading east to Dar on the coast, the other north to Arusha and Nairobi. The road north from Iringa is winding and rough. You can make an overnight stop at the railroad town of Dodoma and a brief halt at Kolo, 115 miles north of Dodoma, to see the fascinating Kondoa Irangi Stone Age rock paintings.

Iringa is a pleasant town on the edge of the southern highlands, a cool, rich agricultural zone of tobacco, wheat and other temperate zone crops. The all-weather road that runs 73 miles to *Ruaha National Park* can be rough during its December-May rainy season. The Ruaha River gorges are beautiful, the park full of elephant, impala and antelope. There are campsites and do-it-yourself cottages where travelers bring their own food. Write the Park Warden, P.O. Box 369, Iringa.

The paved road south from Iringa extends 245 miles to the mountain town of MBEYA in one of the loveliest regions of East Africa. Cool and refreshing at 5,500 feet, Mbeya is the center of tobacco, coffee and maize country. Like Iringa, it once had small numbers of white settlers who introduced modern farming and now has many interesting agricultural innovations for Tanzanian farmers. There is trout fishing and hiking in the mountains, limited gold mining in the Lupa River, and interesting trips—northwest to Lake Rukwa and northeast along one edge of the Rift Valley to the truly isolated Rungwa River Reserve. Near Mbeya the "End of the World" view is extraordinary. Another scenic winding mountain road runs 45 miles south to the farming town of Tukuyu and a leprosarium at nearby Makete, a town renowned for its fine handicrafts and lovely waterfalls. Seventy miles east of Mbeya is Tunduma, and the Zambian border, but that is another story.

What to Buy

Tanzania offers many attractive examples of handicrafts at attractive prices. In government shops there is no bargaining, but sometimes a request for a discount proves successful. Private shop owners will bargain, but reductions will be modest. Shop hours are 7:30 am to 12:30 pm and 2 to 6 pm weekdays. On Saturdays shops are open in the morning hours only. Because of the heat, especially along the coast, do your shopping either late or early during the day.

In Dar a good place to begin is at the National Arts Gallery inside the IPS Building on Independence Avenue. A government shop with fixed prices and a wide range of merchandise, it offers traditional paintings, including pictures by the talented Edward S. Tinga-Tinga, clay sculptures, stone carvings and Makonde sculpture—all of the highest quality. Other artifacts include bao sets, children's toys, basketry, models of dhows and reed work. Prices here can be used as a guide in assessing the other shops in town.

The Silver Curio Shop on Azikiwe Street is a good place to find leather goods, animal skins, jewelry, ivory, carved wooden chests and gemstones. Peeras, on Independence Avenue, has an excellent collection of Makonde work at fixed prices and a selection of local gemstones (there is another Peeras branch in Arusha). Moloo Brothers, on Independence Avenue, features curios, as does Lukmanje, where Zanzibari chests are available. Haji Brothers, on Independence Avenue, is a rather expensive jewelry shop.

In most handicraft and curio stores you will find the vibrant, colorful cotton cloth called "kitenge," either as yardage or made up into shirts, blouses and other items. Other good buys include animal-pelt rugs, copperware and handbags made from animal skins. Spears, shields and beadwork said to be made by the Masai are for sale all over town. Many pieces are quite attractive, and if you're not concerned about authenticity buy some—the price will certainly be less than in Nairobi. Kangas (wrap-around cloths good for skirts) and reasonably priced safari outfits are also Dar specialties.

Makonde sculpture—East Africa's most prolific and audacious style, often expressionistic, always imaginative—is for sale at the National Museum, the National Arts Gallery, and from sidewalk vendors, as well as in some of the better shops mentioned here. The work of the contemporary master Pajuba Alale is especially sought after. On the Bagamoyo Road (a $3 round trip taxi ride) you can visit sculptors at work, commission your own pieces or make your selection from among a vast variety. Makonde prices range from $5 to $250, depending on size and quality—a fifth of the New York City cost.

The best gemstones are found in Arusha and Moshi at Peeras and other first-class shops. Meerschaum pipes, made from a claylike mineral found only in Tanzania and Turkey, are manufactured near Arusha; they make rare gifts, and can be bought either in local shops or (at half price for perfectly usable seconds) at the factory.

Arusha has a bustling bazaar with tailors, dressmakers and shoemakers.

Local Attitudes

Tanzanians are proud of their achievements and aims, sensitive about their poverty, and scornful of the capitalist approaches adopted in Kenya and elsewhere, especially with regard to the differences in income that result. They are willing and eager to talk at great length about their country's failings as well as its strong points. Discussion is lively and free, and Americans should expect to hear harsh things said about Vietnam, race relations and the lack of effective American action against white minority regimes in Southern Africa. They may also hear unfavorable comparisons of American and Chinese assistance to Tanzania. Yet anti-Americanism as such is muted, and there is similar criticism of other Western governments, such as Britain and France. While government-to-government relations run in cycles, individual attitudes have been consistently good, especially toward black Americans who demonstrate a genuine interest in what Tanzania is trying to accomplish. Note well: Contacts with the various Southern African nationalist movements based in Dar es Salaam should be made openly to avoid suspicion in a city where rumors circulate freely.

Although socially innovative, Tanzanians are culturally conservative. There is no room for drugs—hard or soft—or other aspects of the counterculture in this hard-working, egalitarian, striving society. Mosques may be entered freely, but shoes should be left outside and attire and behavior must be subdued. Ask permission before taking photos of people, especially of Moslems who may have religious objections, and avoid photos of anything that might be a military installation.

Weather, What to Wear, How Long to Stay

June to September is pleasant, breezy and cool. November to April has high humidity and light winds. Mildew, rust and fungus are problems, especially during the rainy season. The long rains are from March to the end of May with heavy intermittent rains nearly every day, sometimes falling in torrents for hours. The short rains in November and December are usually brief showers.

Dar and other places on the coast are hot and humid. Daytime temperatures averaging 80 to 95 degrees and humidity over 80 per cent are eased by constant ocean breezes. The highlands have milder climates, lower humidity and temperatures, and less rain than the tropical coast. Arusha and Moshi are pleasantly cool and refreshing. Elsewhere on the central plateau the weather is hot, dry and dusty. Lake Victoria and the southern highlands are cool and wet.

A raincoat is useful wherever you are. Tropical clothing is appropriate all year along the coast, with a sweater for evenings. Wash and wear lightweight suits or dresses are all you need for formal occasions. You might require a heavy sweater or coat in highland areas.

Tanzania is a big country and seeing it properly requires lots of time. The parks of northern Tanzania and Mt. Kilimanjaro (even if you don't climb it) are a must, requiring a week or two. Dar is a grand city worth several days, along with Bagamoyo and a flying trip to Zanzibar. Other parts of the country can only be reached by road trips of two or three days or expensive flights. The area around Lake Victoria is anthropologically fascinating, and the southern highlands around Tukuyu and Mbeya are of great scenic interest. The Mikumi, Selous and other game reserves are open and uncrowded but demand several days. To visit social projects requires introductions to government officials and there may be some delay. Altogether it would take at least three weeks to see something of the parks, capital, coast and landscape, and to get an idea of where the country is going socially and politically. The overseas and locally available package tours stick to the parks and mostly northern Tanzania. They give good value. Incidentally, the range of choice is greater when booking out of Nairobi than in Arusha or Dar. Elsewhere travelers are best on their own, using local buses and taxis, taking the train or renting a car.

Communication

Both Swahili and English are official languages, but it is the former to which Tanzanians respond. As literature develops, the gap between written and spoken Swahili is closing. English is used at senior levels in the government, in the university and upper grades of secondary school, and in business and industry. But Swahili is the language of the streets and villages, the radio, parliament, politics and friendly interchange. English will take you everywhere, but the most halting attempts to speak Swahili will make you friends.

D.V. Perrot's *Teach Yourself Swahili* (English Universities Press) is a good introduction to the language. The Foreign Service Institute in Washington has a conversational grammar originally developed for diplomats and Peace Corps Volunteers, and Harper and Row and other publishers have somewhat expensive textbooks and tapes. Simple English-Swahili phrase books can be found all over East Africa.

The government uses Swahili as a key means of spreading political and social consciousness, and "uhuru na kazi" (independence and work), "uhuru na umoja" (independence and unity), "ujamaa" (a national sense of family), "maendeleo" (development) and "mwananchi" (fellow citizen or comrade) are common terms.

Government radio has programs in English and Swahili with local news, plays, farm hints and music; but BBC short wave is better for overseas news.

The government-owned newspapers are in English with Swahili counterparts. The old *Tanzanian Standard* and *The Nationalist* have been combined into one paper, *The Daily News*, giving the government line. There is also a weekly, the *Sunday News*. If you prefer, the two Nairobi daily papers, *Nation* and *East African Standard*, are available.

The university has several noted academic journals, and the Tanzania Publishing House on Independence Avenue publishes attractive books in English and Swahili in association with Macmillan's. Several book-stores carry *Time*, *Newsweek* and many British periodicals. Television is considered an undesirable luxury that socialist Tanzania has decided to forgo.

The posts and telecommunications are operated in cooperation with the East African Community. Local mail service is reasonably reliable. Airmail letters take five days to reach North America, surface mail six to eight weeks or longer. Telephone service is tolerable within Dar, Arusha and Moshi but poor between cities except where there is direct distance-dialing, as to Nairobi. Overseas cable and radio telephone service is erratic. It's usually booked through Nairobi and should be reserved well in advance. The major communications problems occur on calls to re-mote areas of Tanzania, especially during the rainy season when tele-phone, telegraph and mail service may falter.

Emergencies

The US Embassy is in the National Bank of Commerce Building on City Drive, P.O. Box 9123 (tel. 22775). The Agency for International Development offices are nearby in Luther House on City Drive (tel. 22531) and the US Information Agency offices and library are in the Abdulla Building on Independence Avenue (tel. 24104). The embassy has lists of competent physicians and dentists in private practice. The government-operated Aga Khan and Muhimbili hospitals are under-staffed and overcrowded, although they offer most services and facilities.

Outside Dar, medical facilities are inadequate. If an emergency arises that can't be taken care of by anything in your first-aid kit, enlist the help of local police or missionaries in getting back to Dar as soon as possible, or, if closer, Nairobi.

Uganda

STATUS: Independent since October 9, 1962. Republic since October 9, 1963. Former British protectorate.

SIZE: 93,981 square miles (about the size of Oregon). Population—about 10,000,000.

GEOGRAPHY: Landlocked. Mainly plateau with lush green landscape around northern shores of Lake Victoria, drier plains near Sudan border. Snow-covered Ruwenzori range in west rises to 16,000 feet. Nile River originates in Lake Victoria, fed also by Lakes Albert, Edward and George. Principal towns—Kampala (capital, 250,000), Entebbe (administrative capital), Jinja, Mbale, Mbarara, Tororo.

CLIMATE: Pleasantly temperate in areas adjacent to Lake Victoria. Kampala and Entebbe temperatures average 85 during the day, 60 at night. Rainy seasons are March to May and August to September, with intense rain a few hours a day. Northern Uganda is hotter and drier with a shorter rainy season.

LANGUAGES: English (official), Luganda, Swahili.

CURRENCY: Uganda shilling, divided into 100 cents. 1 shilling = 14 US cents; $1.00 = 7 shillings.

VISAS: Required. Available from Embassy of Uganda and Permanent Mission of Uganda to the UN. Fee $3.15. One passport photo needed. Allow 24 hours if applying in person, several weeks by mail. Visa valid for 12 months.

AIRPORT: Entebbe (EBB), 22 miles from Kampala. Frequent direct flights to and from Athens, Brussels, Bujumbura, Cairo, Dar es Salaam, Kinshasa, London, Nairobi and Rome. International airport departure tax—15 shillings ($2.10). East African Airways has microbus service from airport to leading hotels in Entebbe and Kampala and Kampala airlines terminus; free for arrivals from outside Africa, $2.80 for all others.

NATIONAL HOLIDAYS: January 25, Second Republic Day (anniversary of 1971 coup); October 9, Independence Day; Christian and Moslem holidays.

INFORMATION SOURCES: In US—Embassy of the Republic of Uganda, 5909 16th Street NW, Washington, D.C. 20011 (tel. 202/726-7100); Permanent Mission of Uganda to the UN, 801 Second Avenue, New York, N.Y. 10017 (tel. 212/689-3780). In Kampala—Uganda Tourist Board, P.O. Box 4241 (tel. 41288); Uganda Wildlife Development Ltd, P.O. Box 1764.

By Aaron Segal

There are two reasons for not visiting Uganda for a while. The first is that the military government of President Idi Amin is incapable of effectively disciplining its own troops, who are notorious for their menacing and abusive treatment of travelers and Ugandans. The second is that the economy is in the grip of a severe depression, aggravated by the expulsion in late 1972 of most of the country's Asians who dominated commerce and industry.

Tourism here, to say the least, is not what it used to be.

When and if these conditions change Uganda may return to its position as one of Africa's most attractive countries for visitors. It is a beautiful land, with a pleasant climate, good hotel facilities and convenient internal transportation. The three national game parks are among the best in Africa. The population includes some of the most interesting and talented peoples in Africa.

Landlocked Uganda sits on a high plateau astride the equator on the northern and eastern shores of Lake Victoria, the world's second largest inland sea. It is a land of fertile valleys, towering snow-capped mountains, magnificent lakes and waterfalls, dense forests and vast plains teeming with wildlife. It's in Uganda that the Nile River begins its journey to the ocean, wending its way from Lake Victoria through the lowlands of northern Uganda to the dense swamps of southern Sudan.

The early populations of Uganda had developed agricultural societies with extensive earthwork construction during the last millennium. As waves of settlers descended the Nile to these fertile grasslands, five related, highly centralized and prosperous kingdoms took form over a period of several centuries. They were the Buganda, Bunyoro, Busoga, Toro and Ankole. The Buganda kingdom (Buganda is the kingdom, Baganda the people, Luganda their language) rose by the mid-19th century to dominate the others. Its king (kabaka) greeted Arab traders and European explorers who brought guns and their religions.

A fierce struggle developed among the Baganda, however, with Christian converts fighting Moslem converts. The conflict gave British colonizers a pretext for intervention and, subsequently, an opportunity to expand their influence. In 1894 Uganda became a British protectorate. Six years later a railway to the ocean through Kenya was completed, facilitating coffee and cotton exports.

Throughout British rule the Baganda, although only 20 per cent of the population, enjoyed a privileged position. Colonialism served to enhance the importance of the kabaka, his court and chiefs. The other Bantu kingdoms near Lake Victoria sought the same treatment from the British but failed to get it. In the north the Nilotic Acholi and Lango cattle-keeping peoples, who had more egalitarian societies, were neglected.

Unlike the political situation in Kenya and Tanzania, no united nationalist movement developed. Indeed, the Baganda considered secession —or some form of federalism—which would assure their dominance.

As independence grew closer in the 1950's, complex constitutional negotiations and electoral politics produced a startling outcome. Milton Apolo Obote, a Lango teacher from the north, put together a loose national political party that won the last pre-independence elections in 1962. An independent federal state was formed—but only after Buganda was assured of its autonomy. The kabaka was designated president of the country with Obote as prime minister.

As Obote strove to extend his fragile political base a showdown occurred with the kabaka. In 1966, Obote called in the army, headed by the rough and ready Idi Amin, a World War II veteran up from the ranks. The army won and the last kabaka, "King Freddy," fled to England, where he died several years later.

Having crushed Buganda, Obote moved swiftly to institute a unitary state by arresting his political opponents and eliminating the other minor kingdoms. He later made a bid for popularity by nationalizing foreign-owned businesses and expelling thousands of Kenya Africans employed in Uganda. These, along with some other measures, however, failed to reconcile the Baganda to the loss of their kingdom and political instability continued.

While abroad in January, 1971 Obote was deposed by Amin. Amin's military government at first pleased Britain and other Western powers, which had been unhappy with Obote's policy of nationalization and his militancy over Southern African questions. The Baganda were encouraged to believe that the monarchy might be restored when Amin allowed the late kabaka to be re-buried in Uganda.

Yet Amin, like Obote before him, could neither concede to Uganda's many ethnic demands nor build a strong national political party. Instead he expanded the army and packed the officer corps with men from his own home area near the Sudan border. This favoritism led to violent clashes between pro-Amin and pro-Obote troops and further deterioration of a staggering economy dependent on tourism, light industry and the export of coffee, cotton, copper, sugar and tea.

Unable to build a political base or to halt the economic decline, Amin has lashed out at scapegoats at home and abroad. Border clashes occurred with Tanzania, where Obote took refuge, in the summer of 1971. In November, 1972, an invasion attempt by Ugandan exiles based in Tanzania was repelled. The Israelis, prime suppliers of military aid and major creditors, were ousted in 1972. The British also took their lumps.

Internally the prime targets were the 60,000 Asians, most of whom had rejected Ugandan citizenship after independence in favor of remaining British subjects. Politically inactive, generally aloof and conspicuously well-to-do, the Asians had long been a source of irritation, Amin ordered their expulsion by November 8, 1972, and a reluctant and racially tense Britain dropped its own strict immigration quotas to absorb many of them. Their removal has done little to reduce Uganda's basic ethnic rivalries or to tame the unruly army.

Uganda faces the future with its economy battered, its people still deeply divided, and power in the hands of an erratic army leader unable to control his own troops. But other African states have rebounded from situations that were worse. It would be premature to suggest that travelers should write this country off.

Uganda's colorful past is depicted in Alan Moorehead's immensely readable *White Nile* and the scholarly *Buganda in Modern History* by D. A. Low (University of California Press, 1971). Some background to recent events is provided by *Portrait of a Minority: Asians in East Africa,* edited by Dharam and Yash Ghai (Oxford University Press).

Money Matters

The Uganda currency is virtually worthless outside the country. Tight foreign exchange controls prohibit its being brought in or taken out. This is no country for risking the black market or trying to smuggle in Ugandan currency available at sharp discounts in neighboring countries. Instead exchange what you need legally on a day-to-day basis. Service at Standard, Barclays, National and Grindlays and Bank of India offices can be painfully slow, as it is at the airport bank office at Entebbe. Changing at hotels is faster, but be sure to retain your receipts and exchange control forms in order to leave the country without incident. Credit cards are accepted at major hotels. If you are stuck at the end of your visit with inconvertible Ugandan currency, the airport bar and curio shop can lessen the damage.

Getting In and Out

There are more than 30 flights a week to Entebbe airport on the shores of Lake Victoria. While there are direct flights from Athens, Brussels, London and Rome, many travelers prefer to make Nairobi their initial arrival point and then connect with East African Airways' several daily flights to Entebbe. Most air tickets from North America or Western Europe to East or Southern Africa can be stretched at little or no extra expense to include Entebbe.

If you can, arrange to be met at Entebbe airport by a hotel or travel agent representative to help steer you through customs. Otherwise be patient, declare your foreign exchange, and stick to the East African Airways microbus as your best way of clearing the military roadblocks between the airport and Kampala. The bus costs $2.80 unless you are arriving directly from outside Africa, in which case it is free. It stops at leading hotels and the airlines terminus in Kampala.

Entebbe is not a good airport at which to make connections. Especially unreliable are the east-west flights to Kigali (Rwanda), Bujumbura (Burundi) and Kinshasa (Zaïre). Even for north-south flights try to make your connection in Nairobi, where there is less risk of delay.

One of the most pleasant ways to arrive (or to leave) is by rail. East African Railways has daily service linking Kampala with both Nairobi and Mombasa in Kenya. The three-class train with dining car takes 15 hours to go from Mombasa to Nairobi. The Nairobi-to-Kampala train trip is 24 hours. The first-class fare (with a sleeper) is $15, second class is $8, and third class on a crowded bench, roughly $5. The train winds through the scenic Kenya highlands and the lush grasslands of southern Uganda. Winston Churchill rode it in 1908 as a young journalist and wrote: "Uganda is a fairy tale. You climb up a railway instead of a beanstalk, and at the top there is a wonderful new world. The scenery is different, the vegetation is different, the climate is different, and most of all the people are different from anywhere else in Africa."

Road travel between Nairobi and Kampala is faster but less scenic than the train. The entirely paved 407-mile highway is a drive of about 10 hours with numerous agreeable places to stop along the way. Unfortunately, it is still too expensive and bureaucratically complicated to rent a car in Nairobi and drive it to Kampala, or vice versa. However, if you're coming from Nairobi and you're planning an East African stay of one month or more it might prove economical to purchase a used car from a reliable dealer in that city, where prices are considerably lower and the choice greater than in Uganda, and then re-sell it privately or by pre-arrangement to the dealer in Nairobi. Driving into Uganda requires a certificate of insurance, vehicle registration and Kenya re-entry permit. The Automobile Association of East Africa publishes an excellent road guide and can help with documentation.

For hitchhikers, posting a notice or checking the bulletin board at the offices of the Automobile Association in Nairobi or Kampala is a good way to get a lift.

East African Road Services runs a daily bus between Nairobi and Kampala for about $10. It's a 12-hour ride with few stops. Hitchhikers have good prospects on this well-traveled route.

If you're driving, there's a scenically spectacular route that branches north off the Nairobi-to-Kampala highway at Eldoret in Kenya to make a 150-mile loop around 14,000-foot Mt. Elgon. This road descends a stretch of the Rift Valley escarpment and winds around the forests and waterfalls on the slopes of the mountain. It's a drive you won't forget.

While arriving or leaving by road from Kenya is a relatively easy and agreeable journey, it becomes an adventure when you try it from neighboring Rwanda, Zaïre or the Sudan. The all-weather roads between Kampala and Kigali and Ruhengeri in Rwanda pass through lovely green hills with some truck and private car traffic. Uganda army roadblocks and harassment of travelers make these roads risky. Several all-weather roads connect Virunga National Park and the towns of northeastern Zaïre with Uganda's Queen Elizabeth Park. Here travelers need to obtain visas and other documents well in advance since they are not available at border posts on either side, where military and customs officials are prone to ask for bribes and otherwise bother visitors.

The most exciting entry route is from the Sudan—involving road, rail and Nile River steamer. This route was reopened in 1972 after the end of hostilities in the southern Sudan but it is subject to periodic closings; visas and travel permits should be obtained well in advance. After ascending the Nile by steamer from Khartoum to Juba, travelers can proceed by bus to the Ugandan border town of Nimule, connecting there with another steamer south, or with local buses.

The hazards of road travel between Uganda and its western and northern neighbors can be reduced by group arrangements. The United Touring Company, with offices in Nairobi and Kampala, offers microbus package tours of three to seven days that include western Uganda and game parks in either Rwanda or Zaïre.

A less strenuous mode of travel is provided by East African Railways and Harbours steamers on Lake Victoria which connect Port Bell near Kampala to the Kenya port of Kisumu and the Tanzanian ports of Mwanza, Musoma and Bukoba. It's a relaxing but not very interesting one-week trip costing $60 first class, including meals and cabins, and considerably less for second or deck class where you provide your own food. The boat connects at Mwanza with the 48-hour train ride to the port of Dar es Salaam in Tanzania, and at Bukoba or Musoma with bus service leading toward the Tanzanian coast. While Tanzanian-Ugandan relations remain tense it is advisable to rely on the lake steamer to travel between the two countries rather than drive on the Kampala to Bukoba road, where the Ugandan army is particularly nervous.

Many overseas travelers purchase an East African "safari," a package tour that usually starts and finishes in Nairobi, involving a Nairobi-Entebbe flight and a visit to one of Uganda's game parks. Uganda travel agents are eager to promote competitively priced package tours that make Entebbe the first point of entry in East Africa, with at least a week in Uganda and two Ugandan game parks included in the two- to three-week safari. The advantage of focusing an East African trip on Uganda, rather than Kenya, is that, when domestic conditions are stable, its attractions are less crowded and its hotels less expensive. The Uganda Tourist Board (P.O. Box 4241, Kampala) has attractive free literature on Uganda-based tours. You can also get tour information from Uganda Wildlife (Kampala Road, P.O. Box 1764).

Getting Around Within Uganda

Uganda has an extensive internal transportation network with the choice of air, rail, road and boat travel. There are more than 1,000 miles of paved roads, but road travel suffers from a shortage of qualified mechanics and spare parts. The most serious problem, however, is the lack of discipline in the army. Freewheeling soldiers are a menace to travelers.

City taxis scamper over Kampala's green hills, but their meters seldom function; hence, bargaining is customary, and prices should be agreed upon before entering. The standard daytime fare to go anywhere within the city is 5 shillings (70 cents), doubling or tripling at night. Public buses are crowded but cheap. Other towns can be easily managed on foot or by renting a bicycle through the hotels.

As long as the army remains rambunctious, air travel is the safest way to reach the national parks. Travelers can arrange to be met at the airports. Four-wheel-drive vehicles can be rented inside the parks. East African Airways flies to Murchison Falls. It also flies to Kasese, where travelers are met for the 40-mile drive to Mweya Lodge in Queen Elizabeth Park. It also has a charter service, as does Caspair, to reach Kidepo Park and other points.

Between cities and towns the Uganda Transport Company and other carriers operate fast, cheap, regular bus services. For instance, the 50-mile trip from Kampala to Jinja takes less than two hours and costs less than $1 one way. Faster but slightly more expensive than the buses are the collective taxis, usually Peugeot or Mercedes station wagons carrying four to eight passengers. The buses and taxis travel to every part of the country. If you're on the highway you can simply wave down a large white Peugeot station wagon on the road. The Kampala bus and taxi park, like smaller parks in the other cities, is a lively center.

Renting a car in Kampala is not cheap, but—in ordinary times—it is an excellent way to see the country. An international or national driving license is required and a small refundable deposit must be made. In Kampala, the United Touring Company (tel. 3079), Hunts Travel Services Ltd (tel. 3616), Impala Tours (tel. 56931), and other travel agencies are in the car rental business. For about $4 a day extra you can get a chauffeur, not really needed unless you plan to drive at night outside Kampala, an unsafe proposition, or are uncomfortable about driving on the left. Use your own auto club membership to obtain the map and other services available from the East African Automobile Association office in Kampala. Should you have a minor accident involving a pedestrian, the police advise that you go directly to the nearest police station. Motorists who stop risk being beaten by enraged bystanders.

An alternative to auto rental is to book one or more of the domestic tours operating out of Kampala. These are available through most of the travel agencies including the government-owned Uganda Safaris Ltd, P.O. Box 2844, Kampala (tel. 41571). A three-hour tour of Kampala covers the major sights and costs $4; a one-day tour from Kampala to Jinja and back, including lunch, costs $16, and there are tours ranging from two to five days ($65 to $250) covering one or more of Uganda's national parks. Most hurried travelers take the two-day, one-night, $65 tour of Murchison Falls Park.

For travel by rail there's East African Railways' main line, which runs from Nairobi and Mombasa to Kampala, and from there extends 250 miles westward to the town of Kasese near the Kilembe copper mines. From Kampala to Kasese is an overnight trip. The train leaves Kampala on Sunday, Tuesday and Thursday at 6 pm and arrives as Kasese at 9 the next morning. It's luxurious in first class, but the train is less interesting than the same trip by road. There are second and third class trains that leave Tororo, near the Kenya border, for the 24-hour journey to Soroti and Pakwach East on the banks of the Nile in northern Uganda on Monday, Wednesday and Friday.

While not the quickest way to get around the country, there are several relaxing boat trips. The Lake Victoria steamer takes a week for its circle trip, stopping at several ports. A smaller vessel, the African Queen, makes two trips a day from Gomba Marina near Kampala to the Makusu Islands in Lake Victoria, a pleasant picnic outing. Local inquiries can also help to locate small steamers and motor launches that carry passengers and freight on Lakes Albert and Kyoga and up the Nile above Pakwach as far as the Ugandan border town of Nimule.

Where to Stay

The country has an excellent chain of comfortable, reasonably priced government-owned hotels operated by Uganda Hotels Ltd. There's one in nearly every major city or town. Uganda Hotels also runs the attractive lodges in the national parks, but you can choose less expensive camping and hostel facilities there as well. Budget-wise travelers can also find government rest-houses and camping sites. Brochures and reservations for hotels and lodges in the Uganda Hotels chain are available through P.O. Box 7173, Kampala (tel. 43863).

KAMPALA has two luxury hotels that are pretentious and overpriced. The *Nile Hotel*, also known as the *Uganda International Conference Centre*, doubles as a luxury hotel and a government meeting place. It charges $14 to $20 for single rooms with bed and breakfast and $23 to $29 for doubles. It is near the equally expensive 14-story, 300-room *Kampala International Hotel* on Nakasero Hill. This hotel was formerly known as the Apolo, Obote's middle name. The nearby *Grand Hotel Arcade* is older and friendlier. It has a good restaurant, 102 spacious rooms with baths, and bed and breakfast rates of $11 for singles, $20 for doubles. (Its service may have deteriorated after the expulsion of its Asian management.) Down the street is the smaller *Speke Hotel*, 41 rooms with bath, and bed and breakfast prices of $10 for singles, $20 for doubles. It features an attractive outdoor garden and restaurant, the Hacienda Grill, a popular evening drinking spot. The *Silver Springs Hotel* has 55 double rooms with baths, a pool, and "Jambo" outdoor garden for drinks and Sunday night dances.

Kampala has never had many inexpensive hotels or boarding houses and the loss of the Asians has reduced their number. Low-budget travelers can check the *Lodge Paradise* on Salisbury Road just around the corner from the railroad station. They can also try for a room in one of the dormitories at Makerere University, especially during vacations.

Visitors with academic connections should try to stay at the university guest house, which has attractive bungalows and bargain prices. It is often full, so write well in advance to: Manager, University Guest House, Makerere University, P.O. Box 7062, Kampala. Academics on short research visits can sometimes find a place in the apartments of the Makerere Institute of Social Research, P.O. Box 16022, Kampala.

Outside Kampala the chain operated by Uganda Hotels provides the most attractive accommodations. Prices are uniform at $14 for a single room, full board, and $9 for bed and breakfast, $24 for a full board double room, and $17 for a double room and breakfast. The *White*

Horse Inn at KABALE in the mountains 50 miles from the Zaïre border is an outstanding hotel in a gorgeous setting. The *Crested Crane* at JINJA, the *Hotel Margherita* at KASESE (near the copper mines) and the *Acholi Inn* at GULU are all excellent. The *Rock Hotel* at TORORO makes a convenient overnight or rest stop on the Nairobi to Kampala drive. The *Mt. Elgon Hotel* with a view of the Sipi Falls at MBALE and the spacious *Lake Victoria Hotel* at ENTEBBE near the lake are both delightful, restful spots. Other hotels in this chain are at LIRA, SOROTI, KITGUM, MASINDI and MASAKA.

There are only a few privately owned hotels outside Kampala and their future is uncertain given the economic decline and current government policies. The two best are at FORT PORTAL, a picturesque town situated at the foot of the Ruwenzori range in an area of rich tea estates. The *Mountains of the Moon Hotel*, five miles east of the town in a splendid floral setting, is very good with full board single rooms for $10 and doubles for $19. The *Ruwenzori Tea Hotel*, in town, has a lively bar and full board single rates of $11. The *Parkway Hotel* in MBARARA is a comfortable rest stop with bed and breakfast singles from $6 to $8 and doubles from $11 to $14.

Two tiny remote private hotels rate special mention. The *Travellers' Rest* at KISORO near the Zaïre border has seven double rooms (four with bath), a superb view, an eccentric German proprietor who is a world authority on gorillas, and guides to help seek out the homes of the shy chimpanzees and gorillas that live in the nearby mountains. However, the food here leaves something to be desired.

A veritable Shangri-la is the *Islands Guesthouse*, 210 miles southwest of Kampala near the town of KIKAGATI. This is an exquisitely designed hideaway on an island in the fast-moving Kagera River. Cars are parked on the mainland and access is by a suspension pulley with a bucket seat. The fishing is superb, the hippo and bird watching extraordinary, and the sense of seclusion and comfort unmatched. Full board rates are $17 for singles, $28 for doubles. There are only four double bedrooms. Ask at the Uganda Tourist Board in Kampala about reservations and the security of road travel in what has been a troubled area.

Uganda's three national parks can be enjoyed in expensive comfort or at bargain rates for simple facilities. Entrance to the parks costs $3 per adult except on the first weekend of each month when the fee is 70 cents per person. At Murchison Falls Park, *Paraa Lodge* charges $18 a day for a single with full board, $30 for a double. It is in the center of the park on the banks of the Nile. Farther north the newer and more modern *Chobe Lodge* has the same rates for its 35 double rooms, each of which has a view of the river, hippos and the Goragung rapids. The fishing is excellent at Chobe (a 145-pound Nile perch was landed here). Near Paraa Lodge is a 30-bed dormitory for students and others at $1.40 per person and a tented campsite that charges $6.50 per day single, bed and breakfast. (Campers bringing their own tents and equipment pay only 70 cents per person). There is also a campsite near the Chobe Lodge. There are plans for a third lodge at Pakuba.

The *Mweya Safari Lodge*, with 60 beds and a panoramic view, serves Queen Elizabeth Park. The costs are $18 for full board single rooms and $30 for doubles. Also in the park is *The Country Inn* on Lake Edward, with single bed and breakfast rates of $6. Near the Mweya Lodge there's a dormitory that charges $1.40 per person, and, like its Murchison Park counterpart, has cooking and toilet facilities, as does the tented campsite. Scheduled for completion in 1973 is a new lodge at ISASHA near the southern entrance to the park, where at present five bungalows can be rented for $2 per person with no extra charge for an out-of-this-world view of the river and mountains.

Kidepo Valley National Park in northeast Uganda is the newest and least known—a wonderful wilderness. It is scheduled to have a modern lodge in addition to the present *Apoka Rest Camp*, which has 46 double-bedded bandas (bungalows) with bath or shower and flush toilets. The charge is $6 per night per bed. No food is provided, but victuals can be purchased at the park store, and local cooks can be hired for $1 a day. Those who want to rough it will also find three campsites in this park.

The Toro Game Reserve is at the southern end of Lake Albert, near Queen Elizabeth Park and the town of Fort Portal. Ideal for fishing, its *Semliki Lodge* on the Wassa River offers bungalows and tents and charges $6.50 a person for bed and breakfast.

The Uganda Government operates a number of catering and non-catering rest-houses, primarily for civil servants traveling on official business but also open to the public. Rest-houses come with beds, hot and cold running water, and usually electricity. Non-catering rest-houses have kitchens and utensils and travelers provide their own food. The catering rest-houses charge $4 a person full board. The best are at ARUA, LIRA, MOROTO and SOROTI.

Local governments also run rest-camps and campsites. The former usually consist of a hut or bungalow with or without beds. Visitors furnish their own bedding, mosquito nets, oil lamps, kerosene and insect spray, and usually a camp bed. The Uganda Tourist Board has a list of rest-camps and campsites and information on bookings. It is also often possible to find a bed or cot at a boarding secondary school.

Hotel bills include a service charge and 10 per cent government tax, but small tips of two or three shillings are appreciated by the domestic staff. Most hotels will serve early morning (6 am) tea in your room unless you request not to be disturbed. Shoes left outside your door at night will be shined.

Where and What to Eat

The expulsion of the Asians was a blow to good dining, since it was they who ran most of the better restaurants outside the hotels. Such favorites as the *Hindu Lodge, Bat Valley* and *Shazhan* in Kampala have closed. Or, if they've been reopened, we can't vouch for their quality.

In KAMPALA there are still some attractive restaurants, though at this writing their future is precarious. *Chez Joseph* is a good French restaurant with a varied menu and meals for $3 to $5 without wine. The *Phoenix* and *Canton* are good, moderately priced Cantonese restaurants. There is a smorgasbord lunch on Sundays at the *Silver Springs Hotel* (with public access to its swimming pool for a small fee). The owners of the *Three Stars* bar and restaurant will prepare Greek food ordered in advance. Good spots for morning coffee, a quick lunch or afternoon tea include the second floor coffee shop of the *Kampala International Hotel, Christos'* bakery on Kampala Road, the coffee shops in the SCM and Uganda bookstores in the center of the city, and the *City Bar.*

Take note that restaurants in the leading Kampala hotels, as well as the national park lodges, sometimes require coat and tie at the evening meal. Also there is a tendency for meal hours to be rigid in the hotels. Lunch is served from 12:30 to 2 pm and dinner from 7 to 9 pm. Travelers have been known to go unserved or to be restricted to cold plates if they arrive late.

Few restaurants serve Ugandan food. The staple of the Baganda and their neighbors is matoke—fried or steamed mashed plantains served with greens, peanut sauces, vegetables or meat. It can best be sampled at private homes. Invitations come relatively easily from the elite of the capital. When invited it is customary to bring a bottle of liquor or some other token. If you can't wangle an invitation and you'd like to sample Ugandan food, try the roadside bars and cafes near the bus and taxi depots. They serve matoke, peanut, banana and maize soups and porridges, as well as chicken, goat, lamb and rice dishes. Most of these places also offer curries, prepared in a mixture of Indian and African styles. One of the better roadside cafes is on the traffic circle near Makerere University.

The city water is drinkable and the light Nile and Bell beers are good.

The Ugandan Government has sought to curb the illegal manufacture of semi-lethal alcohol by issuing its own bottled concoction known as "waragi," which comes in rum and gin flavors at less than $2 a bottle. Waragi goes well with tonic or bitter lemon.

Homemade beer ("pombe" in Swahili), usually brewed from bananas, is a favorite rural drink.

What to See and Do

Most visitors shunt in and out of the airport at ENTEBBE, seldom pausing in this very attractive former capital town, which still houses many government ministries. Entebbe has a superb botanical garden, a pleasant outdoor zoo, a fine panoramic view of Lake Victoria, a first-rate golf course and good fishing and boating. (Swimming is confined to pools because of the risk of bilharzia in Lake Victoria). You might also want to see the city's East African Virus Research Institute.

The road from Entebbe to Kampala winds 22 miles through a pretty countryside with coffee and cotton farms (known in Swahili as "shambas"), roadside shops ("dukas"), modest brick and wood homes and several churches and schools. Just off this road 10 miles before Kampala is the Catholic church at Namugongo, consecrated by Pope Paul on his visit to Africa in 1969. It's a quiet and restful spot dedicated to 22 Baganda martyrs executed between 1885 and 1887 for their new Christian beliefs, and recently canonized.

KAMPALA, the capital and principal city, is built on a cluster of seven hills. Kololo Hill is a lookout point with a fine view; Nakasero Hill has the modern parliament building and the new Nile Hotel and Conference Center; Makerere University, one of the oldest universities in Africa (offering degrees since 1938) is on Makerere Hill; Mulago Hill is the site of the hospital and medical school of the same name; Bugalobi and Mbuya Hills are the province of the Uganda army. On the edge of the city, the Namirembe Anglican Cathedral and Rubaga Catholic Cathedral are on facing hills, not far from the Bahai temple, the palace and tombs of the former kings of Buganda, and the Kibuli mosque. There's a daily guided tour of the city. Below the hills lie the bazaar, major shopping streets, post office and banks. The Bombo Road to Makerere passes an open area with a fascinating colony of fruit bats whirring in the trees.

The Uganda National Museum in Kampala has a fine display of traditional art and crafts, excellent historical exhibits and occasional performances of traditional music and dance. The National Theater has frequent performances by the excellent national choral and dance groups and amateur and semi-professional presentations of plays, including those of Ugandan novelist and playwright Robert Serumaga. The Uganda Arts Club has a permanent display of the work of its members in the foyer of the National Theater. The Nommo Art Gallery in Kampala, open daily including Sundays, features exhibits of the work of contemporary East African artists. It is a good place to meet students and intellectuals, as are the Uganda and SCM bookshops in the center of the city. Other examples of the work of Ugandan artists are the carvings in the parliament building, the stained glass at St. Paul's Cathedral and the Bank of India's wall mosaic depicting all the major currencies of the world.

Makerere University has beautiful grounds, a good library, a School of Fine Arts that can be visited by phoning in advance (tel. Kampala 2471), and attractive mosaics in the campus Chapel of St. Francis.

The university is also a lively center for lectures and debates. It also has weekend dances.

Kampala has some of the most enjoyable and informal night life in Africa. The nightclubs feature dance bands, lots of attractive girls, inexpensive beer and low cover charges (70 cents). Dress is casual and anyone from an office clerk to a cabinet minister may turn up. The merriment really begins about 11 pm and continues most of the night. Depending on the band that is playing and the mood of the customers, the Susana Club at Nakulabye, three miles from the center of Kampala, the White Nile in the suburb known as Kibuye, the New Life in Mengo or any of several other clubs may be the fashionable spot. Ask cab drivers for suggestions, and don't hesitate to invite them in for a drink. Feel free to ask anyone to dance (and don't be startled if your companion is similarly invited or if males dance together during a temporary shortage of partners). The Kampala, Grand and other hotels also have dance bands and bars, but these tend to be sedate, catering mainly to non-Africans. There are several cinemas and one drive-in movie. Popular types of private entertaining are "sundowners" (outdoor cocktail parties usually lasting from 6 to 9 pm) and dinner parties.

Soccer football is played on Sunday at Kampala's National Stadium and on innumerable open fields in the city. Omweso, a board game somewhat similar to parcheesi, is a Baganda favorite played outdoors by young and old. Players generally are pleased to teach visitors the rules. Boxing in Lugogo Stadium in Kampala is another crowd favorite.

The outskirts of Kampala are ideal for short excursions. Don't miss the tombs of the kabakas at Kasubi Hill, tended by women who expect a small tip for showing you the interesting thatched buildings. Your shoes must be left outside and no photography is allowed.

Visiting the countryside around Kampala, with its small Baganda towns, can be a very pleasant drive or bus trip. You can visit schools and health centers, local courts, and (if arranged through the Uganda Coffee Marketing Board in Kampala) coffee farms and processing plants. Nearly 50 per cent of Uganda's crop is sold to the US, where it is used in instant and freeze-dried coffees. The stately Baganda women dress traditionally in flowing "busuti," ankle-length dresses with raised shoulders and bustle dating back to 19th century missionary styles. For relaxation the men favor long white gowns known as "kanzu."

A pleasant day or weekend destination is Lake Nabugabo off the Kampala-to-Masaka road, the only fresh-water lake in Uganda sufficiently safe from bilharzia to be swimmable. It is possible to rent bungalows there from the CMS Mission on Namirembe Hill in Kampala. You might also visit the exclusive Budo secondary school, in a lovely setting 10 miles west of Kampala, or take a weekend cruise on the *African Queen* to Makusu Island in Lake Victoria. The island is known for its brilliant array of wild orchids.

Kampala is also a convenient starting point for trips to Uganda's three famous parks. The most spectacular is the 1,594-square-mile *Murchison Falls Park*, reached by scheduled flights from Entebbe or a pleasant 150-mile drive from Kampala via the town of MASINDI. (Near Masindi at Butiaba on Lake Albert there is good fishing.) Road travelers to Murchison should keep in mind that the river ferry to Paraa Lodge stops at 6 pm.

The park is open plains country with abundant wildlife. At the lodge you can take a motor launch up the Nile to the foot of the falls. Here the waters of the Nile cascade 140 feet down into a river pool through a gap 20 feet wide. A footpath leads to the head of the falls. The combination of the falls, the elephants, crocodiles, hippos and other beasts browsing on the shores, and the boat trip, especially at sunset, is truly magnificent.

The Chobe Lodge in the eastern part of the park has fishing, river rapids, salt licks and plenty of big game.

Queen Elizabeth Park, in the southwestern part of the country, is smaller than Murchison but has larger concentrations of hippo, elephant and buffalo, magnificent waterbirds and, in the Ishasha area, lions that take their siestas in trees. Its volcanic terrain and open lakes, against a backdrop of the Mountains of the Moon, are physically more impressive than the plains of Murchison. The park is accessible by good roads—it is 272 miles from Kampala—and by scheduled rail and air service to the town of Kasese. It is easy to drive through the park in ordinary cars with no need for four-wheel-drive vehicles that consume excessive amounts of gasoline. You can take a pleasant trip on a launch on the Kazinga Channel, booked through the lodge. In each of the parks rangers are available at $1 a day to help spot game.

Uganda's third and newest park is *Kidepo Valley* in the rugged northeast, near the Sudanese border. It is a two-hour flight by chartered plane from Entebbe or 490 miles by road from Kampala via Tororo and Moroto. The latter town is the market center for the Karamajong, a striking pastoral people who wear long black cloaks and little else while herding their cattle.

Kidepo Valley Park is for those who want wildlife, scenery and reasonable comfort in a true wilderness setting. It features all the standard big game plus rare species such as greater kudu, reedbuck, eland and cheetah. The dry season is from April to October; at other times of the year four-wheel-drive vehicles are needed. As in the other parks these can be rented on the spot. Economy-minded travelers can try hitchhiking or taking local buses to the park entrances and from there seeking out other travelers willing to take you aboard their vehicles. (You might offer to share their rental costs.)

Uganda has much more to offer in addition to its three parks, including many interesting sights en route to the parks. The most spectacular scenery in Uganda is along the roads leading west from Kampala to Queen Elizabeth Park and the fabled Mountains of the Moon.

The main road southwest from Kampala leads 80 miles to MASAKA, a pleasant coffee town. A side road runs from Masaka to the Lake Victoria port of Bukakata and a boat connection to the Sese Islands, center of traditional Baganda craftsmen, and Nkosi Island, site of the Sitatunga Swamp antelope sanctuary.

The paved major road at Masaka goes 85 miles to the hillside town of MBARARA, center of the Ankole people. Like the neighboring Tutsi and Hutu of Rwanda and Burundi, the Ankole are divided into tall, slender cattle-keepers known as Bahima, and short, sturdy farmers known as Bairu. Unlike the Hutu and Tutsi, however, the Ankole have avoided internecine conflict. The palace of their traditional ruler is at Mbarara. A side road south from Mbarara runs 45 miles to the town of Kikagati, where there's fine fishing on the Kagera River, and the delightful Islands Guesthouse, mentioned earlier.

There's a 90-mile all-weather road west from Mbarara to KABALE that offers an extraordinary panorama of deep blue crater lakes and steeply terraced green hillsides. The town of Kabale, at 6,000 feet, has cool nights warmed by the fires in the excellent White Horse Inn. At lovely Lake

Bunyoni nearby there is a renowned island leper colony and an ecumenical church conference center. This is a resort area, too, and there are facilities for boating, tennis, golf, and horseback riding.

Another spectacular 50-mile drive runs from Kabale to KISORO, near the Zaïre and Rwanda borders. The road climbs to the Kanaba Gap, at 8,000 feet, where the view is breathtaking. To the south are the Bufimbiro volcanic mountains, known as the "cooking pots" and still smoking. The tiny hotel at Kisoro can arrange for you to make the easy half-day climb up the slopes of Mt. Muhavura or Mt. Mgahinga to see the fantastic lichen, ferns and butterflies and perhaps catch a glimpse of the shy chimps and rare gorillas whose ways are brilliantly described in the paperback by George Schaller, *The Year of the Gorilla*.

To get to Lake Edward, Lake George and Queen Elizabeth Park you can leave from either Kabale or Kisoro. It's an all-day drive either way. The drive from Kabale is easier but the route from Kisoro traverses the dense Impenetrable Forest. It also crosses the heavily populated Kigezi District with its hard-working Bakiga farmers and steep terracing. By this route you enter Queen Elizabeth Park at the secluded Ishasha rest-camp.

A paved road winds north from Queen Elizabeth Park to the copper-mining town of Kilembe (the mines can be visited), the tea estates around FORT PORTAL, and the Ruwenzori Mountains. Fort Portal is a lively town with two good hotels. The hotels can help arrange visits to the nearby tea estates and factories or to the palace of the former omukama (king) of the Batoro people. The Batoro share this district with their enemies, the tough mountain Bakonjo and Bwamba peoples.

There are several one- or two-day trips you might make from Fort Portal, including a rugged 55-mile mountain drive to Bundigbuyo to see the hot springs and the Ntandi Pygmies in the Ituri Forest. (A word of caution about the Pygmies: Unless visitors are quick to offer cash or cigarettes they've been known to slash tires, pick pockets and throw stones.) Other excursions include the southern end of Lake Albert for fishing, the Semliki Safari Lodge on the Wassa River and the *Toro Game Reserve* for fishing and hunting.

Fort Portal is also a good base for climbing or walking trips in the *Ruwenzori Mountains of the Moon*. Unlike Uganda's other mountains, these are strictly for experienced, well-equipped climbers. The seasons are limited to June through August and December through March, when the rains and snows subside. The Uganda Mountain Club, P.O. Box 2927, Kampala, will help arrange for guides, porters, maps and huts. (Make sure the club verifies the reliability of the porters; we hear some climbers have been robbed.) Two weeks are needed to climb the glaciers and the twin 16,700-foot perpetual snow summits of Margherita and Alexandra Points. There's a less demanding six-day walking trip that includes a stop at the hut at Lake Kitanda, a beautiful spot.

Fort Portal is connected to Kampala by a 200-mile paved road passing through the market town of Mubende. A more interesting all-weather 230-mile drive runs between Fort Portal and Masindi and from there to Murchison Park.

The circuit by road from Kampala to western Uganda, Queen Elizabeth Park, Fort Portal and back via Murchison Park can be managed in five to seven days. A similar length of time is needed for a road trip through eastern and northern Uganda, including Kidepo and Murchison parks.

The trip east starts out on the main Kampala-to-Nairobi highway and passes through sugar and tea estates, tropical forests, and the farms of the Baganda and Basoga peoples. The industrial town of JINJA is 50 miles from Kampala. There is sailing here on Lake Victoria and golf on the lakeshore (if your ball lands in a hippo footprint you can pick it up without penalty). Visits are possible to the Owen Falls hydroelectric project, which dams the Nile as it exits from the Lake. You can also visit a strip steel mill, textile plant and other industries. Outside the town a plaque commemorates the site where John Hannington Speke first found the source of the Nile in 1862.

The border town of TORORO is 131 miles from Jinja on the main road to Nairobi. It is dominated by an easily climbed 500-foot rock that provides a view of the countryside. The town is an educational center and includes several modern secondary schools built with US aid.

MBALE is 28 miles north of Tororo in the foothills of Mt. Elgon. It is the home of the prosperous Bugishu Coffee Cooperative Marketing Society. The 14,178-foot mountain is an easy three-day climb with hut and other facilities available from the Uganda Mountain Club in Kampala. A spectacular road winds 120 miles around the mountain from Mbale to Kitale in Kenya, taking in Sipi Falls and other sights.

From Mbale it is due north to the Kidepo Valley Park. The route passes through the cattle market town of MOROTO (200 miles from Mbale) where Karamajong, Turkana and other perpetual cattle rustlers turn out excellent crafts in the local hoosegow. The atmosphere is Wild West, African style. Kidepo Park is 160 miles north of Moroto by all-weather dirt road.

At Mbale, too, you can take the railway or road 91 miles northwest to SOROTI, center of Teso District. There's a major agricultural research station here, and the new East African Flight Training Center for African pilots. Interesting late Stone Age paintings are nearby at Nyiro. The Teso people are formerly pastoral Nilo-Hamites who have taken to cultivating cotton and other crops.

Continuing on a northwesterly route, you will come to LIRA, capital of Lango District, 79 miles from Soroti. It is an undistinguished little town except for the Tea Room restaurant, which at last report had excellent African food.

More interesting is the cotton-ginning town of GULU, 65 miles northwest of Lira. It is the major seat of the Acholi people who, like the Lango, are tall slender Nilotics. Their open, relatively democratic societies contrast sharply with the highly centralized aristocratic kingdoms of the Baganda and other Bantu peoples of southern Uganda. This is semi-arid cattle and cotton country. Sir Samuel Baker and his wife were the first Europeans to explore this area. At Patiko, 17 miles from Gulu, the remains of their 1864 fort can be seen.

Gulu is a crossroads town with roads leading north to Nimule and the Sudan, west 75 miles to Pakwach and a 1969 bridge over the Nile, and south to Chobe and Paraa lodges in Murchison Park. Gulu is 238 miles by road from Kampala.

The road west takes the traveler into West Nile District, a maze of peoples and landscapes. It is the home of the Azande, Lugbara, Kakwat (President Amin's people) and other groups, each with its own historical and religious traditions. Cotton is cultivated on the plains and tobacco is grown in the rolling hills. There's a small commercial center at Arua near the Zaïre border and white rhino game sanctuaries at Ajai and Mt. Kei in the extreme north.

Whatever your itinerary, you may find it rewarding to stop at schools, district farm institutes for training local farmers, public health centers and local government offices.

On a Saturday night outside Kampala inquire at local rest-houses or hotels about the customary dance, usually featuring a band imported from Zaïre to play Congo music.

When in doubt about a route, a road or a campsite, ask the local or central government police.

Uganda is a sportsman's paradise. You can fish for Nile perch, tiger fish, catfish and rainbow trout in the Mt. Elgon region, and black bass in Lake Mutanda near Kabale. A full range of big game can be hunted, and many species of birds as well. Hunting and fishing safaris are organized by the government-owned Uganda Wildlife Development Ltd, P.O. Box 1764, Kampala, which has access to 14 game reserves. It also offers photographic safaris. Throughout much of the country you can play tennis or golf, go sailing or climb mountains.

What to Buy

Shops are open from 8:30 am to 5:30 pm during the week, with a long lunch hour, and from 8 am to noon on Saturday. Pottery, carved ivory, beadwork, basketry, barkcloth (a Baganda tradition), hides and skins, beaded flywhisks, elephant hair bracelets, necklaces, drums and other musical instruments, wooden carvings and textiles are all strong local wares. They can be bargained for in the Nakivubo Market in Kampala and other outdoor city markets, or purchased at higher but fixed prices at the government's National Handicraft Emporium on Kampala Road or its branch at the Kampala Hotel, at the Uganda Bookshop near the Grand Hotel, and at the Tusitukirewamu Handicraft Shop on Kampala Road which features Baganda items. Occasionally good bargains can be struck with itinerant street peddlers outside the major hotels. It depends on how astute you are.

At the Uganda Museum it is possible to arrange visits to see local craftsmen at work, including weavers of barkcloth. Potters can be visited at the Nakasero Market on the outskirts of Kampala. Uganda's several talented artists sell their paintings and sculptures at the Nommo gallery at 52 Kampala Road in Kampala. The prison in Kampala is also an excellent source for low-priced and well-made drums and other artifacts. Kitenge, a local cloth suitable for dresses and shirts, is available in small shops along Ali Vizram Street in Kampala.

Dressmakers and tailors on Kampala Road can produce a garment made from local cloth in two or three days.

Local Attitudes

In less unsettled times, Uganda has been an open, hospitable country noted for its courtesy and assistance to travelers. However, its recent economic stagnation and political problems have resulted in a charged atmosphere. Kampala, with swelling unemployment, has had a marked increase in armed robberies, particularly house break-ins by gangs known as "kondos." While Kampala streets are generally safe at night, empty homes and unlocked private cars are not.

Politics is the national passion, but foreigners are strongly advised to listen rather than comment. The pros and cons of Obote versus Amin and civilian versus military rule still divide many Ugandans as do other sensitive political issues. The central police force is an efficient and helpful organization, but the army, swollen in numbers since Amin took power, is notoriously ill-disciplined. Outside Kampala, especially in northern Uganda, army roadblocks are frequent and travelers are advised to do what they are told and to ask no questions. Inquire at the Uganda Tourist Board about areas of the country that may be off limits or require special permission to visit, such as camps for refugees from Rwanda, the southern Sudan and Zaïre. Avoid taking photos of military personnel or military installations and don't wear hot pants, miniskirts and maxi-skirts with V slits in front, all of which were banned in 1972.

Government hostility has been concentrated on Asians, Israelis and the British, but individual Americans have been hurt. An American lecturer at the university and a free-lance journalist were killed by army officers in 1971 and a Peace Corps Volunteer was shot at an army road-block in 1972, leading to the withdrawal of all Volunteers. Earlier, the United States had enjoyed a generally favorable reputation.

Weather, What to Wear, How Long to Stay

Uganda is crossed by the equator, but it is set on a gentle, green highland plateau and the climate is moderate. Even during the rainy seasons there is generally only one brief (but intense) cloudburst a day, quickly cleared by the sun. June and July and December through March are the driest months. Much of northern Uganda is dry and hot throughout the year; western Uganda is slightly wetter and cooler than the Lake Victoria area in the south and east.

Lightweight summer clothing is appropriate throughout the year. Most hotels have one-day laundry services, but dry cleaning is expensive and shoddy. Men need at least one lightweight suit for hotel dining. Cool cotton dresses are appropriate for women. Sweaters are useful.

A week is needed just to see Kampala and the Murchison Falls and Queen Elizabeth Parks. A 10- to 14-day stay is enough for all three parks (including Kidepo Valley Park) and a visit to the Ruwenzori Mountains and western Uganda. If you're in a hurry take in Kampala for a day and allow two for Murchison, including the not-to-be-missed sunset boat trip on the Nile, the highlight of many an African safari.

Communication

Generally speaking the postal service is good, the telephone and telegraph service deplorable. Both are provided by East African Posts and Tele-communications, which has its headquarters in Kampala. Air letters require three to seven days to reach North America. Packages can be safely shipped but send them by air unless you are willing to wait four to six months for delivery. There are few public phones, and calls between Kampala and Entebbe are particularly painful. There is direct distance dialing to Nairobi and Dar es Salaam, usually easier to reach than numbers in Uganda itself.

English is the official language, taught in all the primary and secondary schools and widely spoken throughout the country. Swahili is the informal language of the army, the police and many tradesmen, but is frowned upon by the Baganda who still associate its use with the Arab slave trade, and they prefer their own melodic Luganda.

The government's radio and TV stations broadcast in English and more than 10 Ugandan languages.

The daily newspaper, the *Voice of Uganda*, adheres to a pro-government line. More informative is the lively journal *Mawazo*, published at Makerere University, and the news on Uganda found in such Nairobi newspapers as *Daily Nation* and *East African Standard*, both available on the same day in Kampala. *Time, Newsweek* and British publications arrive by airmail at the SCM, Uganda and University bookshops.

Emergencies

The 900-bed Mulago Hospital in Kampala provides training for the medical students at Makerere University and is a well-known center for tropical medicine. As a government facility its services are in constant demand and travelers seeking more attentive private care may wish to try either the Anglican or Catholic hospitals. Outside Kampala medical services are poor except for an occasional Seventh Day Adventist or other mission hospital. The United States Embassy is located in a large building, Embassy House, in the center of Kampala (tel. 54451).

Zanzibar

Profile

STATUS: Became independent December 9, 1963. Joined with Tanganyika on April 26, 1964, to form the United Republic of Tanzania. Remains politically autonomous. Former British protectorate.

SIZE AND GEOGRAPHY: Two Indian Ocean islands, Zanzibar (640 square miles) and Pemba (380 square miles), 20 miles off Tanzanian coast. Both islands are flat, tropical, partly ringed by coral reefs. Population—Zanzibar Island, 200,000; Pemba, 168,000. Principal towns—Zanzibar Town (capital, 68,000); on Pemba—Wete and Chake Chake.

CLIMATE: Tropical. Hot and humid with evening breezes. Wet season November to May. Daytime temperatures over 85 degrees during most of the year, cooling to 70's in the evening.

LANGUAGES: Swahili (official), English.

CURRENCY: Tanzanian shilling, divided into 100 cents. 1 shilling = 14 US cents; $1.00 = 7 shillings.

VISAS: Available from Embassy of Tanzania and Mission of Tanzania to the UN. Fee $3.15. Valid for 30 days. Two passport photos needed. Acquired in 24 hours in person, four weeks by post.

AIRPORT: Kisauni (ZNZ), five miles from Zanzibar Town on Zanzibar Island. Regular East African Airways flights to and from Arusha, Dar es Salaam, Mombasa, Nairobi, Pemba Island and Tanga. Taxi into city, $1.40 one way.

NATIONAL HOLIDAYS: January 12, Zanzibar Revolution Day; May 1, International Workers Day; April 26, Union Day; June 21, Maulid Day; July 7, Saba Saba Day; December 9, Independence Day; Christian and Moslem holidays.

INFORMATION SOURCES: *In US*—Embassy of Tanzania, 2721 Connecticut Avenue NW, Washington, D.C. 20008 (tel. 202/483-4116); Mission of Tanzania to the UN, 800 Second Avenue, New York, N.Y. 10017 (tel. 212/972-9160). *In Kenya*—Tanzania Tourist Centre, I.P.S. Building, Nairobi (tel. 26888). *In Tanzania*—Tanzania Tourist Corporation, Azikiwe Street, P.O. Box 2485, Dar es Salaam (tel. 27671). *In Zanzibar* —Tanzania Friendship Tourist Bureau, P.O. Box 216 (tel. 2344).

By Aaron Segal

Zanzibar is creepy, exotic, mysterious, sweet-smelling and unique. Its super-sensitive government shadows visitors, most of whom merely whisk in and out, taking the authorized guided tour, wistfully pursuing traces of a romantic but evil past that the regime is seeking to eradicate.

The two islands of Zanzibar and Pemba, 25 miles apart, sit in the Indian Ocean about 20 miles off the coast of East Africa. Their contacts with the outside world go back at least 2,000 years; their permanent settlements, mentioned by Greek and Arab historians as the Land of Zinj, were noted for the pungent cloves and other spices that even today give the island a fragrant aroma.

Chinese, Persian, Indian and European traders came regularly to the islands over the centuries, eager for "apes and peacocks," spices, ivory and rare woods. Above all, Zanzibar flourished as a huge slave market for the East, the place where the Arab and Swahili slavers who worked the African interior for the Imam (sultan) of Oman brought their human cargo.

Zanzibar's importance to the East attained its zenith in the 19th century when the islands served as the gateway to East Africa. Such was their wealth and the extent of their commercial and slave trading network that the Omani sultanate transferred its headquarters from the Arabian peninsula to colorful, chaotic Zanzibar in the 1830's. The predatory caravans of Sultan Seyyid Bargash roamed the East and Central African interior to bring slaves and ivory back to Zanzibar. European explorers like Burton, Speke and Livingstone used the islands as their initial base of operations.

As the European scramble for Africa accelerated in the 1880's the sultanate of Zanzibar lost its ephemeral hold over the East African mainland. It turned to Britain for "protection" against French, German and other competitors. Diplomat and scholar John Kirk, British consul to Zanzibar, used all his skills to induce the Sultan to end the "cursed traffic" in slaves in 1876, but domestic slavery on the islands continued until 1897, seven years after Zanzibar had become a British protectorate.

At the turn of the century, its slave trade over and its commerce eclipsed by the development of new ports on the mainland, Zanzibar's fortunes declined. What had been the principal port for all of East Africa was reduced to small-scale trade.

Although the islanders shared Islam, religious bonds were unable to withstand continued animosity in Zanzibari society between the descendants of former slaves and their masters.

Under British rule the former slave-owning Arab families after 1900 turned to copra and cloves and other spices to retain their prosperity. They relied for labor on migrants from the mainland and descendants of former slaves, now tenants on their estates. The British were content to rule through the sultanate. The Arab royal families dominated the civil service while Indian, Pakistani, Goan, Comorean and other merchants controlled trade. Africans provided mostly unskilled labor except on smaller Pemba Island where a group known as Afro-Shirazis (Africans claiming descent from 16th century Persian settlers) had been able to acquire land and to cultivate cloves on their own.

In order to retain power and privilege when stirrings of independence came in the 1950's, the Sultan and his entourage manipulated several elections against the challenge of the largely African mass party led by Abeid Karume, an ex-seaman of limited formal education. Karume and his followers received political and material assistance from the mainland Tanganyika African National Union (TANU), whose leaders were anxious to see the feudal order ended. Although Karume's party won a slim majority of the total vote in the pre-independence elections, the distribution of legislative seats favored the Sultan and his Pemba Island allies.

Thus Zanzibar became formally independent under its Sultan on December 9, 1963. But the real transfer of power took place on January 11, 1964, in a bizarre popular uprising led by an unknown house painter from Uganda named John Okello. The Sultan fled to England, but a reign of terror on the islands claimed hundreds of Arab lives. Self-designated as "field marshal," Okello was quickly shunted aside by Karume, who organized a Revolutionary Command Council and solicited assistance from China and East Germany. Britain and the US shunned the new order.

Partly to alleviate fears of a foreign takeover, Zanzibar and mainland Tanganyika in April, 1964, formed the United Republic of Tanzania. It is an arrangement giving the volatile Zanzibaris control over most of their domestic affairs and an ample share in the political life of the republic.

The new order in Zanzibar has concentrated on reversing the centuries in which Arabs oppressed Africans. The clove industry and the estates have been nationalized, as has most wholesale and retail trade. African children now enjoy preference in the schools. Karume even went so far as to compel prominent Arab and Asian families to marry off their daughters to political leaders (including himself). Such Draconian measures probably account for Karume's assassination in April, 1972, and for reports of persistent resistance to the present regime on the island of Pemba. His successor as president of the Revolutionary Command Council, Aboud Jumbe, a former schoolteacher, seems committed to a less authoritarian political style and to closer relations with mainland Tanzania. Up to now, the favorable world price of cloves (80 per cent of the island's exports) and severe import rationing have helped to offset some of the economic disorganization caused by the massive changes.

The colorful past is magnificently depicted in Sir Reginald Coupland's two-volume *The Exploitation of the East African Empire*, written in 1938 and recently republished by Northwestern University Press. Charles Miller's entertaining account of the building of the Uganda Railway, *The Lunatic Express* (History Book Club, 1971), has a good picture of Zanzibar in reference to East Africa's colonization. Michael Lofchie's authoritative *Revolution in Zanzibar* (Princeton University Press, 1965) is the best account of the new order's birth.

Money Matters

The Tanzanian shilling is the legal currency of Zanzibar. Travelers checks and hard currency are accepted. All exchanges take place through the State Bank, open from 9 to noon. Don't try the black market unless you are willing to risk being locked up for life. Exchange only what you need for your stay, since Tanzanian shillings are not convertible outside the United Republic.

Getting In and Out

Although a Tanzanian visa is generally required in advance, visitors arriving from Kenya who have booked flights through the Friendship Tourist Bureau, the official government agency, should be able to acquire their visas on arrival in Zanzibar. The government prefers visitors to fly in, take the Friendship Bureau guided tour, and leave on the same day. Although it does permit unguided visits and overnight stays, it exerts heavy surveillance in such cases. Special permission is required for a visit to Pemba, but it's rarely granted.

The daily East African Airways flight from Dar es Salaam to Zanzibar takes 20 minutes and costs $14 round trip. There are flights every day except Sunday between Zanzibar and Tanga, Mombasa and Nairobi, and three flights a week between Zanzibar and Pemba. Book early in season.

A more leisurely and most delightful way to arrive is via the five-hour trip on the steamer SS *Jamhuri* which leaves once a week from Dar es Salaam. The round trip costs $10. Passage may be booked through the Friendship Tourist Bureau or travel agencies in Dar es Salaam.

A few luxury cruise ships also put in at Zanzibar (but not Pemba), and an occasional intrepid traveler tries the dhows that still cross from the mainland to the fabled Land of Zinj.

Getting Around Within Zanzibar

The Friendship Tourist Bureau monopolizes all motorized means of transportation allowed to visitors. It uses most of the taxis for its package tours (discussed under *What to See and Do*); all taxis are nationalized. Car rentals, arranged through the Tourist Bureau, invariably include a driver to keep anyone from going astray. Should you manage to obtain permission to visit Pemba Island, be grateful and prudent, and let the Tourist Bureau show you around. On either island, unless you are black and fluent in Swahili, trying to ride the local buses may be asking for trouble.

Fortunately these restrictions do not seriously interfere with getting around or enjoying Zanzibar. The package tour is a good one and the guides and drivers are helpful. Incidentally, much of Zanzibar Town can be best seen on foot.

Where to Stay

The choice and quality of lodgings are limited; you should book well in advance. Once the Sultan's guest house, the *Zanzibar Hotel* is an old Arab mansion with 32 small rooms, some with air-conditioning and private baths. It is near the center of town and charges about $11 per person for full board. The *Africa House* is about $10 per person for full board; it has a terrace overlooking the port and a placid beach. There are several smaller and cheaper guest houses, the best being *Victoria House* with single rooms for about $2.

Where and What to Eat

The revolution has not been good for visitors' stomachs. Most Arab restaurants are gone and dining is confined mainly to the hotels. Take your meals there and stick to the seafood. The fresh Indian Ocean lobsters are excellent. Most meat is imported, inferior and expensive. Hotels and street vendors offer fresh coconuts, pineapples, mangoes, guavas and refreshing fruit juices. Don't drink the water, unless boiled or filtered. Bottled beer and soft drinks are available.

What to See and Do

The Friendship Tourist Bureau offers a three-hour morning excursion for $17 a person and $28 for couples. For groups of three or more the cost is $11 a person. The excursion includes transportation to and from the airport, breakfast and lunch, and a sightseeing tour with an official guide. It stops at the Anglican church built on the site of the former slave market, the fascinating little historical museum in an attractive former mosque, the market, the 19th century Mtoni palace ruins, the Persian bathhouses of Kidichi, and in front of Livingstone's erstwhile dwelling near the fishing harbor (now a youth corps headquarters, entry is prohibited). Usually, if asked, the driver will go on to Mangapwani, site of an historically important "slave hole." Village children will show the way to a cave in a low coral cliff overlooking a small bay where Arab dhows once came by night to carry off their human cargoes.

In the afternoon, you may browse in the few remaining and rather impoverished curio shops of the Old Town. In the small historical museum you'll find some of Livingstone's possessions, superb carved furniture, ceramics, copper and brasswork and pictorial exhibitions dealing with Zanzibar's colorful past.

The winding, narrow, cobbled alleys of the Old Town, a stroller's delight, are full of massive Arab houses with wooden balconies and intricately carved and studded doors. During much of the year the air is filled with the pungent aroma of cloves drying at the harbor. Walking is best in the early morning or the late afternoon, because between 10 am and 3 pm the heat can be oppressive. You might also try to rent a bicycle or motor scooter, both favorite Zanzibari modes of locomotion. They are available at your hotel or from the Tourist Bureau.

Those who stay overnight will want to take advantage of the opportunities for water sports around Zanzibar's many coral reefs and shark-free beaches. There is an attractive beach in town near the Africa House hotel and several beaches that can be reached by taxi (the Friendship Bureau will arrange for cars and drivers and the rental of scuba diving equipment). Browsing among the extraordinary variety of Indian Ocean seashells at low tide on the coral reefs is a favorite afternoon pastime.

The Friendship Bureau operates boat services to nearby Prison Island which once housed troublesome slaves and now has giant tortoises that you can ride. You can also take a boat to Bat Island, where bats sleep after their nightly visits to the Zanzibar fruit trees, and to Grave

Island, where British casualties from the East African campaign against the Germans in World War I were buried.

At times the Friendship Bureau will arrange visits to Pemba Island. Pemba has the ruins of an Arab fort and several medieval mosques and tombs. A reminder of its 16th and 17th century Portuguese occupation are the Pemba bullfights (in which the bull is not killed), held from December to February.

The discreet traveler with a few days to spare can explore, with the aid of the Tourist Bureau, some dimensions of the Zanzibari social revolution. Major development projects, like the low-cost Workers' Housing Estates on the edge of Zanzibar Town, started with East German aid (although built by the Zanzibaris), and several small factories, can be visited only in the company of an official guide. Other points of interest include the Chinese-operated hospitals (ask about acupuncture) and the new secondary and vocational schools.

Night life for the visitor is best confined to drinking in the hotel bars, or taking in films at the inexpensive cinemas. With permission from the Tourist Bureau, you might try the People's Golf Club on the edge of Zanzibar Town, once the haunt of colonial civil servants. The bar here is a favorite of the new elites.

What to Buy

Revolution and nationalization have placed severe restrictions on Zanzibar's imports. Although the price of cloves has boomed, the government has chosen to hoard its foreign exchange and cut foreign trade. Only a few dim and dusty curio shops, not yet nationalized, remain in the Old Town. They carry goods from India, Pakistan and the Far East, as well as local Arab copper trays, coffee pots, basketware, carved ivory and seashells. There is a poorly stocked government crafts shop near the palace of the former Sultan. The now-scarce silver, china, silk and other imported Asian wares are good buys unless you are planning a trip soon to Singapore or Hong Kong.

The best buy on Zanzibar is carving—mainly miniature wooden doors and chests made of teak and studded intricately in brass. A few are made locally, but the best, carried by dhow and steamer from Iran and India, are now more often seen in Dar es Salaam than in Zanzibar. When available, they range in price from $6 to $145. Passengers who come by steamer can easily ship them back via Dar es Salaam or accompany them back; otherwise shipping is expensive and there is a probable four- to six-month transit time between Zanzibar and North America. A more easily portable although less imposing keepsake is a clove pomander—an aromatic orange ball in a gauze bag, with an enchanting fragrance and a deterrent effect on moths and other closet dwellers. It sells for around $1. It can be dusted later with orris root powder to keep the scent fresh.

Local Attitudes

Like most revolutionary governments, Zanzibar's regime is suspicious and puritanical. Miniskirts and similar attire are frowned upon as symbols of decadent Western culture. Drugs are taboo. Take these strictures seriously: Zanzibar is the last place in the world where you'd want to get arrested. The remaining Arab and Asian minority communities are fearful of close contact with foreigners; it is best to ask few questions about the regime. Do not take pictures unless an official Friendship guide advises that you may do so. Zanzibar's revolution is basically African rather than communist, but Americans are still officially considered hostile.

Weather, What to Wear, How Long to Stay

Zanzibar is hot and humid, with the saving grace of evening breezes. Light tropical attire, with shorts for men and slacks for women, is appropriate.

Most visitors take the one-day package tour, hitting the principal sights and allowing their imaginations to reconstruct the rest. The prevailing air of secrecy, governmental control and isolation doesn't encourage a much longer stay.

Communication

Swahili (at its purest here, linguists say) is the official and living language. English is taught as a second language in the schools and is familiar to most children and merchants.

Postal and telephone services are poor. Calls off the island are placed through Dar es Salaam, and, like the mail, are censored—albeit inefficiently. The local press and radio use Swahili, but Tanzania's English-language paper is available.

Emergencies

Try not to have any on Zanzibar, but if you do become ill or find yourself in difficulty, go to the US Consulate on Tuzumgumzeni Square, five minutes' walk from the Zanzibar Hotel (P.O. Box 4, tel. 2118).

Central Africa

Cameroon
Central African Republic
Chad
Congo (Brazzaville)
Equatorial Guinea
Gabon
São Tomé and Principe
Zaïre

THE REGION AT A GLANCE

An immense Congo-Zaïre river basin embraces the fertile heart of Africa, bounded on the north by increasingly dry terrain through the Lake Chad area to the Sahara and on the south and east by grassland savanna and a richly endowed hill country. Gabon to the west is thick forest up to its deserted coast, and Cameroon to the northwest straddles several productive zones of geography and society.

Large-scale Bantu migrations southward from the Cameroon-Lake Chad region centuries ago pushed remaining groups of Pygmies into the dense equatorial forests, while great Bantu kingdoms formed on the southern savannas. Today, Zaïre (the former Belgian Congo), Cameroon and Gabon are among Africa's wealthiest nations, luckier in resources and technology than their neighbors. The Central African Republic (CAR), Chad, the People's Republic of the Congo (Congo-Brazzaville), Equatorial Guinea, and Portugal's Atlantic islands São Tomé and Principe all depend on modest monocrop exports and/or foreign assistance to sustain low living standards.

Everywhere in Central Africa, the tenacity of European interests, the rudimentary state of communications and the needs of an underprivileged population have complicated government policy. Powerful Zaïre

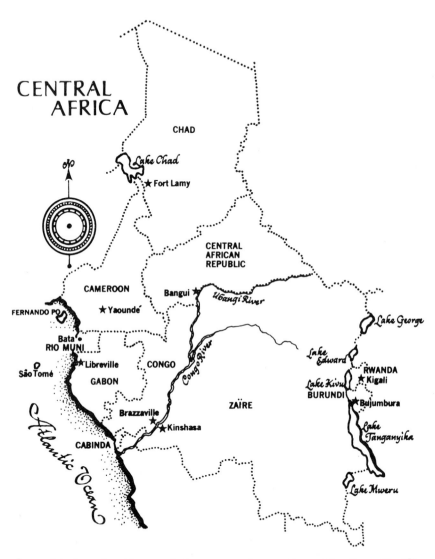

CENTRAL
AFRICA

CHAD

Lake Chad

★ Fort Lamy

CENTRAL
AFRICAN
REPUBLIC

CAMEROON   Bangui ★   *Ubangi River*

FERNANDO PO   *Lake George*

★ Yaoundé

Bata   *Lake Edward*
RIO MUNI

Lake Kivu   RWANDA
São Tomé   ★ Libreville   CONGO   ★ Kigali
                                                               BURUNDI
GABON   ★ Bujumbura

ZAÏRE
Brazzaville
CABINDA   ★ Kinshasa   *Lake Tanganyika*

Atlantic Ocean   *Lake Mweru*

Congo River

has yet to breach wide gaps between people over its vast territory. It still
suffers the effects of disastrous civil wars that plagued its birth for seven
years from 1960. A new reign of "African authenticity" aims at enhanc-
ing national control over Zaïre's mineral wealth, hydroelectric potential
and volatile population, aided but not dictated by foreign investors.
Cameroon continues the slow merger of former French and former British trust territories joined constitutionally in 1961. Chad remains agitated
by rebellion among Moslem northern peoples, a particular example of the

Wedding party, Cameroon

Zaïre River fisherman

Congo drummer

Gabonese policewoman

hostility that has raged throughout the Sudanic latitudes between Moslem North and animist-Christian South. Gabon lived through early challenges to its civilian regime and now relies on foreign entrepreneurs to exploit its rich natural resources. The CAR and Congo-Brazzaville have military regimes seeking to cope with fundamental poverty. Social unrest prevails in Equatorial Guinea, an island-mainland former colony of Spain. Remote São Tomé remains the property of absentee Portuguese landowners.

Traveling Central Africa is perhaps as toilsome and time-consuming as in any inhabited region of the world. It's a long voyage by air or sea from anywhere. A few fine places of accommodation and service, some good game watching, hunting and fishing, pockets of high cultural achievement and of distinct economic interest stand separated by unbroken expanses of forest. Prices are abnormally high for lodgings, meals and anything imported (except in São Tomé). Roads, railways, river transport and air links are largely inadequate (except in parts of Cameroon). Driving is arduous and a knowledge of French a virtual necessity. Even dedicated visitors usually confine their sojourn to a country or two—Zaïre for business or for its splendid lake-mountain country bordering on East Africa; Cameroon, CAR or Chad for animals; Gabon or São Tomé for fishing.

Even if you don't undertake the entire difficult region, you will find natural sublimity, vigorous traditional life, social strength and economic aspirations throughout Central Africa—enough, indeed, to challenge any traveler's imagination.

PMA

Cameroon

(République Unie du Cameroun)

Profile

STATUS: Independent since 1960. Federal Republic established in 1961 uniting former French Cameroun and UN Trust Territory of Southern Cameroon. Became United Cameroon Republic in 1972.

SIZE: 183,581 square miles (slightly larger than California). Population—6,180,000.

GEOGRAPHY: Low coastal plain and equatorial forest in southwest, plateau in center, savanna in north, rain forest in east. Principal cities—Yaoundé (capital, 110,000), Douala (port and industrial center, 320,000), Nkong-samba, Victoria (port), Garoua, Buea (capital of West Cameroon).

CLIMATE: Coastal area hot and humid throughout the year; Douala temperatures in 80's and 90's, 70's at night; heavy rains May through October. Yaoundé, on central plateau, cooler and drier with average temperature in 70's. Northern savanna hot and dry.

LANGUAGES: French and English (both official but French predominates), pidgin English, numerous African languages.

CURRENCY: CFA franc. CFA 100 = 40 cents; $1.00 = CFA 245.

VISAS: Required. Available from Embassy of Cameroon and Mission of Cameroon to the UN. Fee $5. Two passport photos needed. French embassies and consulates issue visas wherever Cameroon not represented. Visitors can acquire visa on arrival but must show ticket out of country.

AIRPORTS: Douala Airport (DLA), three miles from city. Flights to and from West African capitals and Marseille, Paris and Rome. One flight a week from New York. Free buses to leading hotels. Taxi into city, $2.00. Yaoundé Airport (YAO), two miles from city. Frequent flights to and from Douala and Fort Lamy (Chad). Taxi, $2.40. Airport departure taxes—domestic, $1.20; within Africa, $2.40; outside Africa, $6.00.

351

NATIONAL HOLIDAYS: January 1, Independence Day; Christian and Moslem holidays.

INFORMATION SOURCES: *In US*—Permanent Mission of the United Republic of Cameroon to the UN, 866 United Nations Plaza, New York, N.Y. 10017 (tel. 212/355-1838); Embassy of the United Republic of Cameroon, 1705-07 New Hampshire Avenue NW, Washington, D.C. 20009 (tel. 202/265-8790). *In Cameroon*—National Tourist Office, P.O. Box 266, Yaoundé (tel. 41-06).

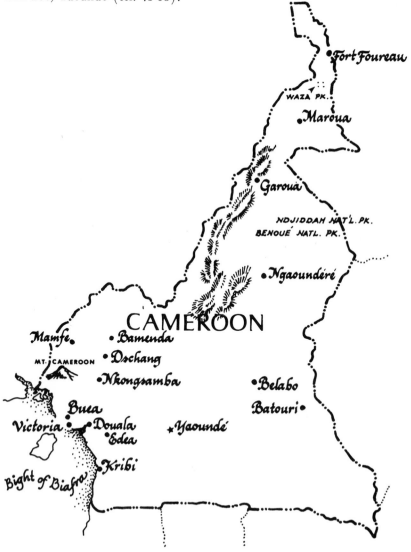

By Aaron Segal

Cameroon is a land of great diversity in both people and geography. Its many attractions include beaches, tropical forests, broad savannas full of wildlife, temperate mountain zones and a variety of cultures. Yet Cameroon is not for everyone. If you're an experienced traveler—with a working knowledge of French—you can do well. Others will find that the tourist organization is embryonic, first class hotels are few (and expensive), and some places of interest are accessible only by bouncing over rough roads or taking small planes.

The resourceful traveler, however, will be rewarded by a view of Africa in microcosm—for this is a land of distinctly different peoples, with their own cultures, architectural styles, crafts and languages. Along the steamy tropical coast are the Douala, mainly fishermen and traders, while in the densely populated west are the Bamiléké, enterprising farmers and merchants. Their neighbors include the Bamoun, a partly Islamicized group of fine craftsmen, living along the plateau. In the savanna country of the north are numerous animist groups called the Kirdi, and various Moslem peoples, including the once all-conquering Fulani (Peuhl), who have matched their building skills and pastoral economy against a harsh environment. And tucked away here and there in the rain forests are various Pygmy groups.

Cameroon acquired its name after 1472 when the Portuguese navigator Fernando Po found shrimps in the estuary of the Wouri River and dubbed it "Rio dos Camarões," after the Portuguese word for shrimp. The word subsequently was applied to the whole territory.

Colonial rule began in 1884 following a treaty of protection between King Akwa of the Douala and a German trading firm. German title over the coast and much of the interior was confirmed by European powers at the Berlin Conference of 1885. The Germans built railways, started plantations and encouraged missionaries.

But German rule ended after World War I when the League of Nations carved up the colony and mandated sections to the French and British. The French got most of the coast, the fertile plateau and the entire north, and the British took what was left, an isolated and mountainous western strip, which it administered as an adjunct of Nigeria.

The French built a railway from Douala to Yaoundé (completed in 1927), and developed the cultivation of coffee, cotton, palm oil, pineapple and cocoa. The British section slumbered economically except for the development of the port of Victoria and some banana plantations. After World War II British and French rule was extended under UN trusteeships.

The UN presence contributed to the emergence of nationalist movements seeking independence and reunification of the two trust territories. The French were the first to be directly challenged. The insurgents were the militant, pro-independence UPC political party, which drew its primary support from the crowded, land-hungry Bamiléké. But the UPC was forced underground, its guerrilla activities were crushed, and most of its leaders were killed or forced into exile, including Félix Moumié, who was mysteriously poisoned in Geneva.

While mopping up the guerrillas the French conceded political reforms. In 1958 they permitted a national election, won by Ahmadou Ahidjo, a Moslem school teacher from the north. Ahidjo, a moderate, favored gradual independence while retaining close economic, political and cultural ties with France. He became the pre-independence prime minister and in May, 1960, when the country became an independent republic, he took office as its president.

In the British-administered section discontent grew at the prospect of remaining a neglected and remote part of Nigeria. In 1961 a plebiscite was held under UN auspices and a majority in the more populous southern area voted in favor of federation with the Cameroun Republic. The northern part of the British trust territory, however, chose to remain part of Nigeria.

The bilingual Federal Republic of Cameroon (spelled Cameroun in French) was born on October 1, 1961, the only example of post-independence unification of former British and French colonies in Africa. The English-speaking west, with a population of 800,000, had limited autonomy until June, 1972, when it was incorporated into a united republic as one of six regions of a highly centralized state.

President Ahidjo, who was re-elected in 1965 and 1970, has assiduously cultivated the political support of major ethnic groups and geographic regions but he has not hesitated to suppress his critics and opponents. Ties to France remain close. A rapidly growing economy is based on agricultural and forest exports, light industry for the local market, and the giant aluminum and hydroelectric project at Edea.

An interesting group of Cameroonian writers, several of whom live and write in France, emerged in the 1950's and 1960's. They include the comic novelist Mongo Beti (*Mission Accomplished*, *King Lazarus*), the musician, composer and short-story writer Francis Bebey (*African Music*), and the satirical novelist Ferdinand Oyono (*The Old Man and The Medal*, *Boy*).

The politics of Cameroon and its recent history are analyzed in two scholarly works: *Cameroun, An African Federation* by Neville Rubin

(Praeger, 1971), and *Cameroon Federation* by Willard Johnson (Princeton, 1970).

Money Matters

Cameroon belongs to the Equatorial African monetary zone along with Gabon, Chad, the People's Republic of the Congo (Brazzaville) and the Central African Republic. These countries share a CFA franc backed by the Bank of France and convertible into French francs and other hard currencies. Currency can be exchanged at the Douala and Yaoundé airport banks, or their city offices, and at leading hotels at a slightly less favorable rate. Banks are open during the week from 8 am to 12:30 pm.

Getting In and Out

The most practical way to reach Cameroon is by air. Douala is a major West African airport with several flights a week from Paris and Rome and once-a-week service jointly operated by Air Afrique and Pan American from New York. There are frequent flights on Air Afrique, UTA, Alitalia and other carriers to West African cities but only one east-west transcontinental flight a week, on Ethiopian Airlines to Addis Ababa.

Yaoundé has a much smaller airport and the only international flights here are from Fort Lamy in Chad and Bangui in the Central African Republic. Travelers concentrating on northern Cameroon sometimes fly in via Fort Lamy, which has good connections with Paris. Air Afrique and UTA offer excursion and package tour fares for visits to Cameroon with either Douala or Fort Lamy as the point of arrival.

A word of caution: Both the Douala and Yaoundé airports are notorious for overbooking flights and stranding passengers. If possible, double and triple confirm reservations.

Although there are no passenger-cargo or cruise ships that stop regularly at Douala, there is frequent traffic out of this busy port to Marseille and to other West African ports. Inquiries at Lagos (Nigeria), Takoradi (Ghana), Dakar (Senegal) or Abidjan (Ivory Coast) are likely to turn up a passenger-carrying freighter.

Entering the country by road from any neighboring country other than Chad requires time, patience and stamina. Fort Lamy is across the river by ferry from Fort Foureau, Cameroon, and local buses, rental cars and package tours are available between Fort Lamy and the towns of north Cameroon. Hitchhikers can try the traffic from Fort Lamy or Bangui, or on the all-weather route from Maiduguri and major northern Nigerian cities. It has some bus and frequent truck traffic. Coastal roads between Nigeria and western Cameroon and from Cameroon south to Gabon and

Equatorial Guinea are in very bad shape, often washed out completely during the rainy season.

Getting Around Within Cameroon

Internal air travel is excellent and relatively inexpensive. Cameroon Airlines has three or four flights a day on the one-hour service between Douala and Yaoundé ($40 round trip). There are also regular flights to Garoua, Maroua and Ngaoundéré in the north, and non-scheduled flights via Cameroon Air Transport from Douala and Yaoundé to Tiko, Buea and Bamenda in the west. Air charter service is also available at both Douala and Yaoundé.

Cameroon passenger trains are first rate. A luxurious night train with sleeping cars runs from Douala to Yaoundé; there is also a slower train in the morning. The railroad is being extended north toward the Central African Republic border, and when this section is completed the trip from Yaoundé to Ngaoundéré, across the plateau into savanna country, should be a traveler's delight.

Major cities are linked by speedy and generally reliable collective taxis, usually Peugeot station wagons. They leave from car parks (known as taxi-gares) whenever they have a full load. Rates are slightly higher than those charged by the riskier microbuses that follow the same routes. Caution: Both these modes of transportation should be avoided at night.

You may prefer to rent a car. Prices range from $5 to $15 a day depending on the make of car and sometimes on the number of passengers it will carry. A driver comes along for another $3 to $4 a day. There's a free mileage allowance of 60 to 100 kilometers (40 to 60 miles) with a 10 to 15 cent per kilometer charge beyond that distance. Gas costs 65 cents a gallon. Rentals can be arranged through major hotels or at the BP station on Avenue Poincaré (tel. 4794) in Douala and the Shell Concorde station (tel. 3309 or 3547) in Yaoundé. Car rentals are also available in Garoua. Driving is on the right.

Hitchhiking is not common in Cameroon, but it's possible along the major roads. If you get stuck, flag down a collective taxi and pay.

Within towns, inexpensive "petits" taxis (tiny Citroën 2CV's or baby Renaults) are available and are recommended over the crowded buses.

Where to Stay

Douala and Yaoundé offer a fairly wide range of accommodations, but outside these two cities travelers find little choice.

Of the dozen hotels in DOUALA, the most expensive is the suburban

Hôtel des Cocotiers with 56 air-conditioned rooms, a restaurant, bar and swimming pool; prices, without meals, are from $14 to $25 per person. The *Akwa Palace* and the *Hôtel de la Résidence Joss*, both in midtown, charge $14.50 for singles and $17 for doubles, but a better buy is offered by the *Hôtel Beauséjour* with singles at $10 and doubles at $12. The other hotels of the city don't compare with these four.

It is essential to reserve your room in advance in Douala, but even with reservations you may be bumped by government priority. One of our contributors found himself, despite confirmed reservations, in the maternity ward of a private clinic—the only empty bed in town. He was awakened at 6 am after four hours of sleep by a thermometer-bearing nurse—quite as surprised as he was. Secondary schools offer inexpensive accommodations during academic holidays and the Catholic and Protestant youth associations (Association des Jeunes Catholiques, Association des Jeunes Chrétiens Protestants) often have a spare cot.

In YAOUNDÉ the Sheraton-operated *Mont Fébé Palace* is a joy. Perched on a hillside two miles from the city, it has 250 air-conditioned rooms with striking views. Free taxi service to town is provided. There's a bar, restaurant, pool, nine-hole golf course and nightclub. Singles begin at $15 a night and go up to $25 for luxury suites; prices include a Continental breakfast served in your room. Less elegant but centrally located are the *Hôtel Central* and the *Indépendance*, both in the $13 to $25 per person range. Rooms can also be had for $3 or even less at the *Flamingo*, *Repos de Mahomet* and *Idéal*. In addition, the university operates a guest house for visiting scholars, and space in the dormitory is available to anyone during school holidays.

At the beach resort of KRIBI there's the oceanfront *Palm Beach Hôtel* with singles at $8 and doubles at $11. Meals here are just $2, without wine. The *Hôtel Kribi-Plage* has cheaper rooms, $4 to $6, but a more expensive restaurant.

BUEA, the capital of West Cameroon, has a very good hotel. It's *The Mountain*, 150 rooms with private bath at $8 single and $12 double, without meals. The port of VICTORIA, also in West Cameroon, has the *Hôtel Miramar*, with air-conditioned rooms at $9 to $12. You can get a good $2 lunch and $3 dinner here (drinks extra). The small *Oceanic* is modest in both price—$6 to $10—and facilities.

Northern Cameroon, with its impressive attractions, is rapidly improving and increasing its lodgings. Still, hotels here tend to be practical and short on elegance. At MAROUA in the far north is the attractive *Relais du Kalao* with 16 air-conditioned rooms at $10 for singles and $11 for doubles. There's no restaurant and it's closed from June 15 to December 1. The more modest 11-room *Hôtel de la Porte-Mayo* has a restaurant and is open throughout the year. At NGAOUNDÉRÉ the 16-room *Hôtel de l'Adamaoua* charges $7 for singles (with bath) and $8 for doubles. It has a restaurant. So does the slightly less expensive *Hôtel des Hauts-Plateaux*. GAROUA offers the new 40-room *Hôtel de la Bénoué*, which outclasses the older *Relais Saint Hubert* with its 15 rooms at $10 single and $14 double, and the cheaper five-room *Hôtel Korman*. The *Hôtel du Flamboyant* at MOKOLO provides a pleasant overnight stop. Elsewhere in the north there are numerous "campements," usually consisting of attractively situated rustic bungalows with refrigerators and cooking facilities used by hunting and photographic parties. Bookings can be made through the Office National du Tourisme, Inspection Nord des Chasses, P.O. Box 50, Garoua.

The plateau towns in the center and west have hotels that cater primarily to weekend visitors from Douala and Yaoundé. The *Ringway* and the *Fort* in BAMENDA are comfortable. A bed also can often be found here at the secondary schools. The *Cheval Blanc* and the *Carrefour de l'Ouest* at BAFOUSSAM are small and friendly. *L'Auberge de Foumban* in the town of FOUMBAN is a small hotel with a nice restaurant. In DSCHANG the emphasis is on outdoor sports at the *Centre Climatique*, which has cabins grouped around a pool. It has tennis courts and an excellent restaurant. Bungalows cost $6 to $10, meals $3.

Where and What to Eat

Good food is likely to be rather expensive throughout the country. In DOUALA, aside from the hotel restaurants, there's Algerian food at the *Méditerranée*, Vietnamese cuisine at the *Lotus* and the *Astor*, Alsatian dishes at the *Relais d'Alsace*, pizza at the *Vesuvio*, and French food at the *Paris*, *Lido* and *Central*. Meals can run from $3 to $10. Cameroonian food can be had at the restaurant in the *Hôtel Beauséjour*.

In YAOUNDÉ the *Mont Fébé*, *Central*, *Indépendance* and *Terminus* hotels all serve excellent but expensive dinners. The *Safari Club* above the Mont Fébé offers equally distinguished food in a delightful location.

Less expensive meals are available at African restaurants in most towns. In these you can sample fresh and dried fish dishes, broiled lamb and mutton, rice and millet and other Cameroonian fare. On the coast fresh shrimp and lobster are specialties; the north is cattle country. Guinness brews a good beer in Douala. City water should be filtered or boiled. Restaurants tend to push expensive French mineral water and wine.

What to See and Do

DOUALA, the country's largest and most important city, is a cosmopolitan industrial center with a busy, modern port on the estuary of the Wouri

River. Its commercial dynamism—sustained at a high level despite tropical weather—is an interesting mix of the energy and enterprise of many ethnic groups. There are six outdoor markets, two of which sell mainly fish. The so-called Lagos Market, in the square of the Grand Mosque, is a thoroughly African place in which everything imaginable is bought and sold. Mostly Nigerian products are sold at the outdoor Grand Marché de Deido (the name comes from pidgin English for "that do," a phrase once used by foreigners to ward off eager salesmen).

Some of the human diversity can be seen by visiting the lively residential sections of Bali and New Bell. One might ask at the hotel about renting a bicycle to join the cycling throngs.

The Douala museum has an excellent ethnographic collection and is well worth a visit. Also of possible interest is the Centre Culturel Africain at the College Libermann, where there is material on the cultural life of the country. The Swiss-sponsored Pan-African Development Institute has an innovative training program, primarily for civil servants. Its French-speaking branch is in Douala with the English-language courses in Buea.

The Douala people are the indigenous inhabitants of the port and the nearby villages. Their fishermen are known for building elaborately sculpted canoes. Ask at the museum and the Syndicat d'Initiative, both in the city hall, near the handsome cathedral, about visits to master craftsmen and dates of festivals, especially those involving canoe races.

Vestiges of Douala's history are scattered about the city, easily seen by a walking, cycling or taxi tour. These include the palace of the pre-World War I king, Manga Bell, built in the style of a Chinese pagoda; the imposing tomb of King Akwa, whose treaty with the Germans in 1884 led to the colonization of the country, and the sacred tree of the Douala people, located near the Rue Bonanjo in the Deido section of town.

Tennis, swimming, fishing, water-skiing and sailing are available through private clubs that offer temporary memberships. The night life is lively with local bands entertaining at the Bodega, Jungle, Castel and Fregate clubs. The private Club Culturel promotes cultural events and contacts between Cameroonians and non-Africans. The six local movies feature French-language versions of "Westerns du Far-West américain."

The road from Douala to the capital city of Yaoundé begins by running south along the coast. Twelve miles from Douala is the lovely beach of Longji, which is safe for swimming but still underdeveloped (there are a few bungalows and campsites). Sixty miles south from Douala is EDEA, site of the vast hydroelectric complex and aluminum smelting plant, the largest industry in the country and one of the most important industrial enterprises in West Africa. Visits to the plant and dam can be arranged through the Alucam offices in Yaoundé or Douala. Visitors planning to stay overnight should ask to stay in Edea's luxurious Alucam guest house, the only decent hotel in this modern company town. Near Edea are a number of lovely lakes and waterfalls and a few Pygmy villages. You can take pleasant canoe trips down the Sanaga River.

At Edea the main road veers east for the 113-mile stretch to Yaoundé. But there's a rougher road that continues along the coast to the beach resort of KRIBI, 55 miles from Edea. From December to May Kribi is sheer pleasure, a leisurely place of palm trees and coconuts, fishing and excellent swimming. At other times of the year Kribi is very wet. Pygmies inhabit the forest behind the town. Several Douala travel agents offer tours that include Kribi.

The capital, YAOUNDÉ, lacks the bustle of Douala but it has its own charm. It is comfortable and scenic. Its 2,000-foot elevation keeps the town green and fresh, and much less humid than the coastal area. The recently built presidential palace is bright and imposing. Nearby, in the Hippodrome section of town, is the headquarters building of the Organization of African and Malagasy States (OCAM), a grouping of French-speaking governments. You can visit the bilingual university; its school of agronomy is innovative, and its medical school has excellent facilities and a dynamic staff. Of interest downtown is the Marché des Artisans near the post office. Take your time here, inspect the masks, carved stools, bronzeware, pots—and enjoy the bargaining.

Take a taxi for $2 up to the Safari Club restaurant, above the Mont Fébé Palace. The restaurant offers a grand panoramic view of the city from its 3,000-foot height. Yaoundé has the night life characteristic of a city of civil servants and diplomats. The nightclubs at the Mont Fébé Palace and Safari Club cater to Frenchmen with money to spend. The more modest bars sometimes have live music. Try Le Chat Noir, especially on weekends.

Yaoundé can be used as a convenient center for brief excursions. A paved road leads 30 miles south to the town of Mbalmayo, which has an active market. You can take a canoe trip here down the Nyong River. Another 80 miles along the same road is Ebolowa, an interesting older town with a German fort, American Presbyterian mission, attractive cocoa estates, and talented ebony and ivory carvers.

Driving east of Yaoundé requires a four-wheel-drive vehicle for the tough one- or two-day trip to the small administrative towns of Batouri and Abong-Mbang. In this vicinity are several Pygmy villages. Visitors should expect to pay a fee for the privilege of taking photographs.

Again, with Douala as a starting point, there are interesting trips to be made west and north of this city.

Fifty miles west along the coast by paved road is the West Cameroon port of VICTORIA. The Cameroon Development Corporation has its headquarters here. Through this agency you can arrange a visit to a banana plantation. Educators may want to visit the Lycée Victoria, one of the country's first bilingual secondary schools. There are swimming, boating and golf facilities at the neighboring beach town of Tiko.

A short distance inland from Victoria, on the slopes of Mt. Cameroon, is the onetime capital city (1901–1909) of BUEA. It has several German colonial buildings of interest and some beautiful flower gardens. With its mild climate, this charming little town of 12,000 offers a welcome relief from the humidity and heat of the coast. From here you can take the two-day walk up 13,353-foot Mt. Cameroon. From Buea, going north, there's a striking mountain road that winds through village after village. High point of this journey is the town of BAMENDA, a crafts center specializing in bronze and brass work and traditional textiles.

The agricultural heartland of Cameroon is the densely populated Bamiléké country, where industrious farmers grow fine arabica coffee. The largest town is NKONGSAMBA with a population of 50,000. It became the terminus of a railroad north from Douala which the Germans began but whose construction was interrupted by the war in 1914 and never resumed. The town is 86 miles by good road from Douala. Nearby are the Ekom waterfalls.

The main Bamiléké town and cultural center of BAFOUSSAM is 161 miles by mostly paved road from Douala. It has several ornamented, sculpted, elaborately constructed meeting halls for Bamiléké clans, some attractive crafts and a flourishing market. Also in Bamiléké country is the mountain resort town of DSCHANG, 40 miles west of Bafoussam by paved road. With its mild climate, sports facilities and magnificent scenery, it is a favorite vacation spot for the affluent.

Neighbors of the individualistic Bamiléké are the highly centralized Islamic Bamoun people. Their traditional capital is at FOUMBAN, 78 miles north of Bafoussam. Here you'll find the palace of the Bamoun sultan, the sultan's museum and another interesting museum of traditional Bamoun art. Craftsmen here specialize in hand-worked aluminum, including statues, table settings, baskets and bas-reliefs in traditional designs. Check with the Ministry of Information in Yaoundé for the dates of Bamoun festivals, when Foumban comes alive with horsemen, musicians and superb dancers.

A highlight of any visit to Cameroon is a trip to the far reaches of the north, the land of stately Islamic societies, exciting crafts and markets, striking architecture, panoramic savanna and wildlife reserves. While the major towns can be reached by air, the most interesting sites require road travel. This entails package tours, expensive car rentals, or reliance on local buses and collective taxis.

NGAOUNDÉRÉ (pronounced En-gwan-dery), with a population of 23,000, is one of the two largest towns in the region. Situated at an elevation of 3,500 feet on the Adamawa Plateau, this interesting market town has a pleasant temperate climate. It is scheduled to be the northern terminus of the Trans-Cameroonian Railway, an extension of the main Douala-to-Yaoundé line currently under construction. The town can be used as a base for excursions to Lake Tison and the Tello waterfalls.

GAROUA (population 25,000), the chief town of the north, lies astride the Bénoué River, 236 miles north of Ngaoundéré. It is an administrative and commercial center with a colorful market featuring goods that come up the river from Nigeria by barge. Hunting parties are organized here. Hunting permits are available through the Inspection Nord des Chasses (Hunting Authority of the North), P.O. Box 50, Garoua.

There are three game reserves for hunting and viewing south of Garoua (but none compares with Waza National Park to the north near the Chad border). The steep upland Bénoué Reserve, 80 miles south of Garoua off the main road to Ngaoundéré, is mostly for buffalo and hippo. The Bouba-Ndjiddah Reserve is 120 miles southeast of Garoua and has rhino, hippo, panther, antelope and crocodile. The Faro Reserve, 140 miles southwest of Garoua on the river of the same name, has hippo, antelope, buffalo and eland.

A serviceable and interesting 200-mile road connects Garoua and Maroua, the chief crafts center of the north. However, there's a longer and rougher road that provides a stunning mountain trip skirting the Nigerian border. This road passes through volcanic hills, through the village of Rhumsiki, which clings to a bare mountainside, and continues to the town of Mokolo, home of the Islamic Mandara people. Other side trips over rough roads from Mokolo or Maroua take you to the mountain villages of Oudjila, Mora, Koza and Tourou, where you will see some of the most striking of the north's architectural wonders. Each village has characteristic conical silos, granaries and chiefs' houses. Out of the bare earth of the mountains the Matakam people who live here devise ingenious terraces for cultivating millet.

MAROUA is a center of the Foulbe (Peuhl) people but is neatly divided into residential quarters, each housing its own ethnic group. The Diamare Museum has a fine ethnographic collection and excellent crafts for sale. Superb tablecloths and embroidered garments are produced and sold at the Coopérative de Tissage. Maroua has a fine market where you can see its jewelers, leatherworkers and other craftsmen at work.

East of Maroua—the road is poor here—is the town of Yagoua, where in May there is a colorful fishing festival on the Logone River. Near Yagoua is the attractive Logone Valley and the town of Pouss, which has the palace of the sultan and some other noteworthy architecture.

Waza National Park, one of the best in West Africa, is 80 miles north of Maroua. It can be reached by direct flight or by road during the dry season. Waza has concentrations of elephant, lion, buffalo, waterbuck, antelope, giraffe and a number of rarer animals. Its 425,000 acres consist of savanna and upland plains that are inundated during the rainy season. This means that you can see thousands of animals migrating during the hot, dusty season. Mid-March to the end of May is the best time to visit. Before and after this period the rains make the plains inaccessible.

The partly paved road north from Waza leads to the Chari River, Fort Lamy (Chad) and Lake Chad. Along the way is the dusty old walled town of Fort Foureau at the Nigerian border, where an all-weather road leads west to Maiduguri (Nigeria), and a ferry crosses the river to Chad.

What to Buy

Bamoun, Bamiléké and Hausa traders carry on their backs and on bicycles the best of Cameroonian and West African crafts. If you miss these traders, don't worry, they'll find you. Gird yourself for zestful bargaining, good fun for all. The northern peoples specialize in leather work and embroidery, crocodile and skin handbags, wallets and briefcases, antelope sandals and pillows. Maroua is noted for its jewelers, weavers and tanners. The Bamoun produce tablecloths, pipes and wooden and bronze sculpture, while the Bamiléké go in for chairs, walking sticks, calabashes adorned with beads, and ceramics. Avoid the curio shops unless you are after genuine antiques—which are expensive but can be exported tax-free.

Local Attitudes

Cameroonians, particularly the elite, can be very French in their attitude toward America and things American—which is to say, politely critical. Western Cameroonians, who have clung to English ways, are eager to meet Americans. But throughout the country you'll find the people friendly and relaxed. In the north, which is predominantly Moslem, miniskirts are likely to offend. And everywhere some discretion should be used in snapping pictures of people. If there's the slightest indication that it's resented, put the camera out of sight. If, on the other hand, there's an indication that you're expected to pay for the privilege of taking a picture, pay up promptly. That's how some people supplement their meager earnings.

Weather, What to Wear, How Long to Stay

Douala is hot, wet and sticky, but Yaoundé, Buea and much of the central plateau have an agreeable temperate climate year-round, with cool evenings, when a sweater may be needed. The rainy season is from April to October. The north is generally hot and dry, with a shorter rainy season. Informal tropical clothing is suitable for the coast and capital.

Cameroon has so much to offer that a minimum of a week is needed to see Douala, Yaoundé, Waza National Park and one or two northern towns (especially on market days). A two-week stay permits a more leisurely tour, including a visit to the beach at Kribi and some time in Bamiléké and Bamoun country. If you speak French and really want to get around a richly diverse country, allow three or even four weeks.

Communication

Under the terms of federation, when British-administered Cameroon joined the Cameroun Republic, the nation became officially bilingual. Senior civil servants are required to know both English and French, but in fact progress in bilingualism is slow. Although the use of French is much more widespread than English, pidgin English goes a long way along the coast and even in the polyglot interior. Secondary school and university students have all studied English and are eager to try it if you encourage them. Nonetheless, a knowledge of French is helpful, especially outside the major cities. In Western Cameroon English prevails.

Telephone service is good within the cities, where there is automatic dialing, and to Paris; otherwise, it's erratic. Packages shipped by surface from Douala should arrive in North America in four to eight weeks.

The daily *Presse du Cameroun* is politically muzzled, as is the government-controlled radio, but there's some excellent Cameroonian pop music on the radio. Outsiders rely for uncensored news on airmail copies of French newspapers and *Time* and *Newsweek*. Another good source of uncensored news (as well as tips on accommodations and local fetes) are the French, US, Canadian, Swiss and West German technical aides.

While in Yaoundé you should drop by the Protestant CLE (Centre de Littérature Evangélique) bookstore. It's the most active publishing house in French-speaking West Africa and carries paperback novels, plays and books of poetry by African writers. You'll also find an excellent tourist guide in French here. Mention should also be made of the well-known bilingual literary quarterly, *Abbia*, which is sponsored by the Ministry of Culture and supported by an active circle of Cameroonian writers in Yaoundé.

Emergencies

The general hospitals in Douala and Yaoundé are fair. In the capital, the privately run Fouda Clinic is very good. Outside the cities, except for an occasional mission hospital, medical facilities are poor.

The United States Embassy is on Rue Nachtigal in Yaoundé (tel. 22-16-33 or 25-05-12). The Peace Corps, with its own staff doctor and nurse, has its offices on the Parc Repiquet (tel. 22-25-34). The US Consulate in Douala is on Avenue Général-Leclerc (tel. 32-31).

Central African Republic

(République Centrafricaine)

Profile

STATUS: Independent since August 13, 1960. Formerly part of French Equatorial Africa. Until 1958 known as Oubangui-Chari.

SIZE: 240,535 square miles (slightly smaller than Texas). Population—2,080,000.

GEOGRAPHY: Landlocked; mostly rolling plateau (averaging 2,000 feet in height); thickly forested Ubangi (Oubangui) River area in south; savanna in east and center. Principal towns—Bangui (capital, 250,000), Bambari (33,000), Bossangoa (38,000).

CLIMATE: Several climatic zones. Rains generally fall from June to October. Hottest months February to April. Temperatures in Bangui range from 85 to 95 degrees, drop to 70 at night.

LANGUAGES: French (official), Sango.

CURRENCY: CFA franc. CFA 100 = 40 cents; $1.00 = CFA 245.

VISAS: Not required.

AIRPORT: Bangui (BGF), three miles from city. Infrequent links with France and with other Central African capitals. Taxi into city, CFA 500 ($2). Airport departure taxes—domestic, CFA 200 (80 cents); within Africa, CFA 600 ($2.40); outside Africa, CFA 1,500 ($6).

NATIONAL HOLIDAYS: August 13, Independence Day; December 1, Republic Day.

INFORMATION SOURCES: *In US*—Permanent Mission of the CAR to the

UN, 386 Park Avenue, New York, N.Y. 10016 (tel. 212/685-2717); Embassy of the CAR, 1618 22nd Street NW, Washington, D.C. 20008 (tel. 202/265-5637). *In Bangui*—Office National Centrafricain du Tourisme, P.O. Box 655; Agence Bangui-Tourisme (Scandinavian SCAC system), P.O. Box 875.

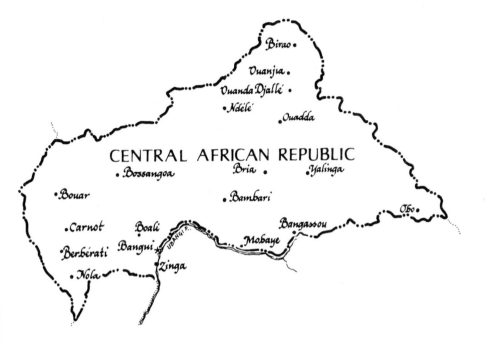

By Philip M. Allen

Traffic to this easily overlooked republic in the middle of the continent is light. The few visitors who do come are mainly businessmen (cotton and mining) and some big game hunters straying from more familiar grounds.

Still, if you are swinging through on a Cameroon-Zaïre or other middle-African itinerary, you might well consider a pause amid the charms of the town of Bangui and its equatorial river environs, a visit to the Boali Falls and a brief exploration of the dense forests with their last remnants of an aboriginal Pygmy population. Without this taste for exotica, however, there is little reason to choose the CAR over more accessible destinations. While the government has begun to consider tourism as a promotable enterprise and has done away with visa requirements for Americans, the inconveniences of travel and paucity of unique attractions will keep foreign traffic at modest limits for some time to come.

About two million people inhabit the CAR's broad plateau, with altitudes averaging 2,000 feet. The territory rests on the thickly forested Ubangi (Oubangui) River area in the south, and separates the Congo-Zaïre-Ubangi basin from the Lake Chad basin in the north. Historically, this terrain represented a crossroads of intra-African migration and conquest, slave trading to the Arab east and a sedentary civilization along the southern riverbeds.

Eventually a common language, Sango, spread over the entire area, notwithstanding the heterogeneity of its inhabitants.

The Banda people of the eastern and central savanna account for about one-third of the CAR population; another third are the Baya farmers of the west and center. Both groups have lived fairly harmoniously with Zande in the east, Sara in the north, the Arabic speaking N'Dele and Bizao in the northeast, smaller Bantu groups (M'Baka, Lissongo, M'Binou), and the river peoples (Sango, Yakomo, Banziri and others). Bangui, the capital and only real city, has a mixed population that includes some French and other Europeans. The Babinga Pygmies, now numbering only a few thousand, keep to their southern forests.

Some 300,000 Central Africans are Christian, most of them Catholic. There is a small minority of Moslems. Virtually all the people observe traditional ancestral religious beliefs and practices, generally classified as animism.

The colonization of this territory began late in the last century, when Germans, Belgians and French began looking into this equatorial heartland from their respective coastal bases in Cameroon and the two Congos. France obtained European endorsement for the boundaries of its

Oubangui-Chari territory by 1911. The landlocked colony was thereupon joined to the more favored coastal territories of Gabon and Moyen Congo (now People's Republic of the Congo), and to the vast expanse of Chad in the north—the whole area forming French Equatorial Africa with its capital at Brazzaville (Congo).

The development of a rudimentary economy based on cotton production and river transport via the Congo's Brazzaville and Pointe Noire represented the essence of French colonial policy in Oubangui-Chari. Forced labor gangs toiled the cotton fields, a thin social surface of French institutions regulated life in this obscure colony and a few privileged Central Africans were trained for civil service jobs, teaching or the clergy. Intermittent nationalist movements harassed French administrators, most notably in the bloody revolt of the Baya people in 1928–31. Political activity became more widespread after World War II under the leadership of Barthélémy Boganda, patriot idealist and subsequently benevolent despot, who founded the Mouvement d'Emancipation Sociale de l'Afrique Noire (MESAN).

Boganda died in a plane crash in 1959 after only a half year as president of the new Central African Republic, "autonomous" within the Gaullist Communauté.

Although real independence didn't come to the CAR until a year and a half after Boganda's death, his reputation as father of CAR nationalism remains unshaken. Two of his nephews succeeded him as president: David Dacko, head of a rather hapless parliamentary regime until December 31, 1965, and Jean-Bedel Bokassa, army chief of staff who overthrew Dacko in order to forestall an alleged Chinese Communist plot. General Bokassa dissolved the parliament in 1966 and now legislates by decree. He has designated himself "President for Life" and behaves with a flamboyance unusual among the generally conservative African chiefs of state.

Bokassa has also taken to twisting the tails of the several foreign powers that take an interest in the CAR. These episodes have been interpreted as resentment (in 1968) against discriminatory privileges for Cameroon and Gabon in the French-inspired Equatorial African Customs Union (UDEAC), a turn to the Left (1969), a reconciliation with the West (1970), new dissatisfaction with France (1971), and a current return to the fold (1972).

Evaluations of Bokassa's statecraft differ widely, except on its unpredictability. His arbitrary acts of cruelty have given him a reputation in Africa and Europe comparable to that of Duvalier in Haiti. But there has been little social turmoil since he assumed power, and his small country has been able to retain French and Western European interest in CAR cotton (one-fourth of national export revenues), coffee and timber. He also has American and Israeli clients for industrial diamonds (now one-half the export total). He receives French aid in exploiting newly discovered uranium deposits at M'Pasou, and from Russia he gets educational and technical assistance.

This is hardly a well-publicized country; even French historical and ethnographical writing is scanty. John A. Ballard devoted a chapter to the CAR in Gwendolen Carter's *National Unity and Regionalism in Eight African States* (Cornell University Press, 1966); Guy de Lusignan has a somewhat more up-to-date treatment in his *French-Speaking Africa Since Independence* (Praeger, 1969). The Hachette *Guide Bleu* for *Afrique Centrale* (Paris, 1962) is authoritative, especially in its essays and capsule descriptions of Central African countrysides, past and present, but it barely notices developments since the end of the colonial period.

Money Matters

Although President Bokassa has talked for some time about printing new, "independent" currency, he seems persuaded for the time being to remain within the Equatorial sub-zone of the CFA system. The CFA franc used here also can be spent in Cameroon, Congo-Brazzaville, Gabon and Chad. The Banque Internationale de l'Afrique Occidentale (BIAO), an affiliate of the First National City Bank of New York, operates here as in all of French-speaking Africa, as does the Banque Nationale de Paris (BNP); the UDEAC complex is served by the Union Bancaire en Afrique Centrale. Banks are open Monday through Saturday, from 7 am to 1 pm. Travelers checks are acceptable everywhere in the CAR, but credit cards are not.

The cost of living is extremely high for Europeans and visitors.

Getting In and Out

Although Bangui Airport receives three flights from Paris each week and one Aeroflot flight out of Moscow, most itineraries include the Central African Republic only as a stopover en route to other points in Africa. However, routing is less easy than it looks. Passengers traveling to or from Zaïre, East Africa, or Nigeria must change planes in Brazzaville (where Americans are not welcome) or Douala (Cameroon), which lies 600 miles to the west as the crow flies and one and a half hours by normal Air Afrique routings. Air access is made all the more uncertain because of General Bokassa's recent withdrawal of CAR participation in the multinational Air Afrique syndicate, without having adequately supplied the country with alternative equipment and organization of its own.

Heavy freight comes into and out of the CAR by the Ubangi and Congo (Zaïre) rivers, for there is no railroad as yet and the roads are either seasonally impassable or difficult. The 1,000-mile trip between Bangui and Brazzaville or Pointe Noire (Congo) is slow and long (five days downstream to Brazzaville in January-June, 10 days upstream; one day less each way during high water season from July to December). The voyage nevertheless evokes echoes from the romances of Congo exploration best exemplified in Joseph Conrad's *Heart of Darkness*, André Gide's *Voyage au Congo*, and the explorer memoirs of Stanley, Savorgnan de Brazza and Heinrich Barth.

Adequate accommodations can be booked on river boats operated by the Compagnie Générale des Transports en Afrique (P.O. Box 125, Bangui). Try to time the trip for the first half of the year (despite the extra day of travel) when countryside and river life are set off best, and don't fail to arrange for a Congo visa in advance. Coming upstream on the Ubangi just below Bangui, everything is off-loaded onto railroad cars to circumvent the rapids between Mongo and Zinga. You can either board a second vessel for Bangui here or take a twice-weekly bus (or hire a taxi) to complete the journey by road.

Hopes for better transportation include (1) a central segment of the UN's projected Trans-African Highway (dubbed by certain wags "Toyota Turnpike" in honor of the Japanese investment in it) that will link Kenya with Nigeria, and (2) a combination rail-river express route through Cameroon to the port of Douala. While both these projects remain for the future, the hardy motorist or hitchhiker can consider one of several inconvenient highway routes across the CAR's borders: an all-weather (and quite beautiful) stretch into the southern Sudan that is in execrable condition; an all-weather road into northern Cameroon at N'Gaoundéré, or a more interesting but frequently washed-out track between Bangui, M'Barki, Berbérati and Yaoundé (Cameroon); a northerly passage to Fort Lamy (Chad) via Bozoum and Bongor that is full of interest for its changing landscape and society but is open on the Chadian side only from January through June; and a direct route to Sarh in southern Chad, also subject to washouts in the second rainy semester but preferred by game watchers and hunters in the dry season.

Getting Around Within the CAR

Air Bangui and Air Centrafrique operate charter flights in and out of Bangui, serving the main centers of hunting and game watching. Scheduled Air Bangui DC-3 service between Bangui and Bakouma (2½ hours) costs about $66 one way, Berbérati (2 hours) $39, Birao in the far north (4 hours) $100, Bouar (2¾ hours) $45. Similar service connects Bangui with Bambari, Bangassou, Bria, Carnot, Ouadda and Ouanda-Djallé.

Almost none of the CAR's 13,000 miles of roads is paved, but their laterite surfaces are fairly hardy. The east-west highways are generally traversable in all seasons, while the north-south routes remain good until the Chad border, except for the northeastern bulge north of Ouanda-Djallé which is accessible only from January through May. The towns are connected by bus routes and collective taxis for hire at negotiated fares. Hitchhikers have little private traffic to count on for free rides. A normal taxi run within town limits should cost about CFA 300 ($1.20). There is no railroad for the time being.

Traffic drives on the right.

Bangui's car rental agencies include Loc'Auto (Renault), Auto Service and the multifarious Agence Bangui-Tourisme. Small vehicles generally rent for about $9 per day with 50 kilometers (30 miles) free and 40 CFA (16 cents) per kilometer thereafter. Large cars hire for about $20 per day, plus 50 CFA (20 cents) per kilometer above the 50 km. allowance. The customer pays for gasoline, which costs from CFA 57 to 61 per liter (89 to 93 cents per gallon). The Auto Brousse Company has Land Rovers and Toyota Land Cruisers to rent for a flat daily fee of $30 to $40. Hire of drivers adds about 1,000 CFA ($4) to the cost, but it is usually worth considering if you can afford the rental in the first place.

Where to Stay

BANGUI has a couple of excellent high-priced hotels, both on the Ubangi River less than a mile from city center. Both are air-conditioned, with swimming pool and night bars. The Rock Hôtel is lower-slung, slightly older and a trifle cheaper (from $16 plus breakfast). The Safari Hôtel has the superior view, especially from its rooftop bar ($18 for singles, $24 for doubles, breakfast included). In the center of town, the Minerva runs from $11 to $13 but has no restaurant. There are no adequate cheap lodgings in Bangui unless you meet someone who will take you home.

Prices outside town are lower, but choices are even more limited. They include inns at BOUAR and BERBÉRATI; guest houses (usually called "hôtels de chasses") with water and electricity at BANGASSOU, BOSSEMBELE, BIRAO, KITESSA, KERRE, the André Felix National Park and administrative centers. There are lodges, primarily for hunters, at OUANDA-DJALLÉ (Hôtel M'Bozolo, used by SAFO Safaris(and at N'DÉLÉ (Hôtel de la Koumbala). There are no Peace Corps or CUSO Volunteers, few missionaries, and few international agencies to call on for private hospitality. Businessmen use the tourist hotels and hunters use lodges or tents.

Where and What to Eat

Both French and African cuisines tend toward the mediocre in most parts of the CAR, and menus are atrociously expensive (averaging around $12 with wine). You have a choice of French, Chinese and African dishes at *La Banquise* in midtown BANGUI, and you can get onion soup on weekends at *Le Pub*, an air-conditioned brasserie. Exotic and plain food is served *Aux Caraïbes*, at *Saraiva* and at *Le Fleuve* on the riverside Boulevard Général de Gaulle. Residents usually do not tip above the service charge on restaurant tabs. And they do not drink the water. Up-country, you may rely on local hospitality, open market produce (mainly cassava or rice), spartan game camp cooking, or whatever you bring along from town.

What to See and Do

Most foreigners visit the CAR for business or hunting. The former spend most of their time in and around BANGUI, a pretty, flower-decked town of a quarter million people on the Ubangi River. Established in 1889 by advance parties of the French administration working out of Brazzaville, this capital of the Oubangui-Chari territory has been neatly laid out on its big rock above the river and around the Place de la République, the European business district. Handsome villas perch on the river palisades, along boulevards lined with bougainvillea, jacaranda, acacias, frangipani and mango trees.

The city has a small museum named after Boganda, a workshop of diamond cutters open to visitors on Mondays and Thursdays, a trade school and artisans' quarters near the colorful Bokassa Market. The Church of the St. Paul Mission, founded in 1894, is now the seat of a bishopric. Dozens of African clans cluster in their own compounds outside the European cité. About 6,000 French, Portuguese, Greeks, Americans, Russians and other foreigners live and work in town. Chadians, Sudanese and Hausa-Foulbe from the northwest control much of the non-European business throughout the CAR. Water-skiing, tennis, golf and horseback riding are available at private clubs, but by invitation only.

Some Central African reality must be sought outside Bangui, at fishing points along the river, or at the tranquil village of BOALI, 60 miles north of town, where you can see the impressive Mbali River Falls, 150 feet in height and 10 times as much in width. Southward, in the Lobaye Forest only two hours by road from the capital, local guides and tour operators from Bangui induce Babinga Pygmies to come forth in dance for paying visitors. To the west, at the edge of the forest, BERBÉRATI (40,000) is one of the CAR's handsomest and most versatile towns, set among coffee plantations and diamond mines, with a mixed population including the Baya (fine carvers), and Moslem Foulbe (Fulani, Peuhl), who celebrate Ramadan month and the Tabaski feast in vigorous style. The landscape north of Berbérati, via CARNOT and BOUAR to the Cameroon frontier, is a composition of forest, grassland, waterfalls, gardens and orchards. Bouar, an old German outpost, has cattle herds of the Bororo Fulani and a prosperous mining economy.

North and east of Bangui is game country—less organized, less regulated and less trodden than in East and Southern Africa, Zaïre, Cameroon or even Chad. The northern savannas include the rare derby eland, as well as buffalo, giraffe, hippo, elephant, lion, panther, leopard, some rhino and many varieties of game birds. Some of the largest elephants in the world herd permanently only 60 miles from Bangui.

Entry permits, licenses and other arrangements may be handled either by the Office du Tourisme or the Agence Bangui-Tourisme, or one of three established safari guide companies (all of which offer package hunting and camera tours). They are Safarafric, which uses the Gounda Domaine (estate) reached via N'Délé (P.O. Box 1078, Bangui); the Société SAFO (Jean Orgeix), which covers the northeast out of Ouandjia (P.O. Box 412, Bangui) and Quintard Cie. (Oubangui Safaris), P.O. Box 22, Bria (in the center-east). River fishing—for Nile perch (capitaine), dogfish, pike, tilapia, and catfish—can be arranged with village fishermen or with boat clubs at Bangui. CAR rivers are fascinating; if you can get near Bocaranga on the Cameroon border, visit the extraordinary waterfalls of Lancrenon on the Ngou River, approachable right to the verge during the dry season (November to May).

Some of the towns in the hunting country have their own points of interest. BOSSANGOA (38,000), 190 miles north of Bangui, is a center of cotton production and diamond mining, with a lively morning market. BAMBARI (33,000) in the center-south, features ivory, copper, ebony and wickerwork sold in the stalls (souks) of Hausa traders from the Niger area. On the Ubangi River at MOBAYE, south of Bambari, you can witness interesting cultural variations and blends, including those of the nomadic Bororo herdsmen, the sedentary Banda with their vigorous cult religions, and other groups that meet on a Sunday in August to celebrate the cotton harvest with dancing and shows of horsemanship.

Except for the game safaris, organized tours are very expensive. A half-day by car with guide around Bangui costs $6; $12 for a boat ride on the Ubangi with stops for swimming; $20 for a forest excursion, including a Babinga Pygmy village and lunch at a coffee plantation; $20 for a day's trip to the Boali Falls, with time for fishing and a picnic lunch. Safarafric operates an overnight tour at its Gounda Domaine for $200, including air travel, local transport and driver.

What to Buy

Except for ivory and some gold jewelry, butterfly specimens and mosaics of butterfly wings, the CAR produces little of value to the collector or souvenir hunter. The Hausa stalls at Bangui's Place de la République have collections of wood, metal, cloth and basketwork from all over Central and West Africa, but these are no bargain and their quality is usually below what you can find in neighboring countries. The work produced at the Centre Artisanal is rather discouraging for those who believe in the future of African creativity. Perroni's shop across from the Bokassa Market in the capital has a good selection of Central African work at fairly high prices. Shops are normally open from 8 am to noon and from 4 to 7 pm, six days a week.

In the north, around N'Délé, you can get fine ironwork, knives, weapons and utensils. At Ippy, 300 miles northeast of Bangui, there are excellent rugs of cotton and wool. Berbérati and Bouar in the west specialize in wood sculpture (especially Banda ancestral statuettes and votive figures) and ivory.

Local Attitudes

Central Africans are by and large charming and tolerant, but little used to foreigners, except for the French. Americans are involved in diamond operations and some small technical assistance projects, but are otherwise inconspicuous. General Bokassa and his eccentricities used to be a subject of mild spoofing, but politics have become sensitive of late, and it's best to play things straight. Do not try to photograph military installations or Bokassa's residence at Bangui; an American with a diplomatic passport was arrested for trying the latter in 1970.

Weather, What to Wear, How Long to Stay

The country covers several different climate zones, equatorial and tropical, forest and savanna. The rains come generally from June to October, with local variations, bringing increasingly cooler temperatures and clear air by day, storms at night. August is the month for despair over the state of the roads, but it also corresponds to good elephant hunting season around N'Délé. The roads are repaired in November and fit for travel early in December, with cool nights and low humidity prevailing through February. March brings increasing heat and good hunting, game watching and fishing into July. The south gets some rain in light showers throughout the November-May dry season.

Prepare for considerable heat during the day most of the year, but with cool winter nights, especially in the north and east. City life is informal in good French overseas style, and bush travel requires standard neutral colors and "roughing it" gear.

Communication

French is the official language, but most people speak only Sango. Few speak English. There's been an improvement in education, but still only one-fourth of school-age children are enrolled in school, and virtually everybody outside Bangui and a couple of other towns is illiterate. Bangui has a relatively efficient post office for mail and telegrams, but all communication passes via Brazzaville or Cameroon, thence via Paris. Messages and packages are best sent from somewhere else.

In the CAR, news is scarce. The national radio and the Catholic weekly La Voix de l'Oubangui carry official announcements of what's going on, to supplement word of mouth at the town bars, markets and shops, where most inquirers repair.

Emergencies

Bangui has a general hospital and a private clinic (Chouaib), but there are few well-equipped health facilities outside the capital—and less than 40 doctors for the entire population. The small American Embassy is located in the center of Bangui on the Place de la République (P.O. Box 302, tel. 20-50). In a medical emergency, fly to Paris.

Chad

(République du Tchad)

Profile

STATUS: Independent since August 11, 1960. Formerly part of French Equatorial Africa.

SIZE: 495,800 square miles (four-fifths the size of Alaska). Population estimates vary between 3,600,000 and 4,500,000.

GEOGRAPHY: Landlocked (1,300 miles from coast). Wooded savanna in south, Sahara desert in north, steppe in interior, Lake Chad (10,000 square miles) in west. Principal towns—Fort Lamy (capital, 160,000), Sarh (ex-Fort Archambault), Moundou, Abéché.

CLIMATE: Hottest months are February to June in Fort Lamy, with daytime temperatures over 100; 65 to 75 at night. Also very hot October to November, only slightly cooler the rest of the year. Rainstorms July to September, dry season December to May.

LANGUAGES: French (official), Sara, Arabic.

CURRENCY: CFA franc. CFA 100 = 40 cents; $1.00 = CFA 245.

VISAS: Required. Available from Embassy of Chad and Permanent Mission of Chad to the UN. Fee $6.25. Three passport photos needed, plus some guarantee of solvency. Also available from French consulates wherever Chad is not represented.

AIRPORT: Fort Lamy (FTL), three miles from city. Frequent links with Cameroon and Paris only. Transportation into city—daytime taxi, CFA 600 ($2.40); night taxis, CFA 1,000 ($4); bus, CFA 500 ($2). Airport departure taxes—domestic, CFA 200; within Africa, CFA 600; outside Africa, CFA 1,500.

NATIONAL HOLIDAYS: August 11, Independence Day; November 28, Republic Day; January 11, National Day; Christian and Moslem holidays.

INFORMATION SOURCES: *In US*—Embassy of Chad, 1132 New Hampshire Avenue NW, Washington, D.C. 20037 (tel. 202/965-1696); Permanent Mission of Chad to the UN, 150 East 52nd Street, New York, N.Y. 10022 (tel. 212/752-0920). *In Fort Lamy*—Office National du Tourisme Tchadien, P.O. Box 763; Tchad Tourisme (agency), P.O. Box 894.

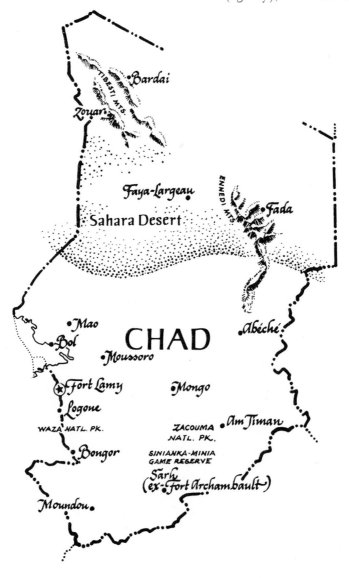

By Philip M. Allen

The fingers of one hand suffice to count the reasons why people might want to visit Chad, a half-million square miles of desert and savanna buried inside the continent 1,300 miles from the nearest seacoast. Three-fourths of the land is unsuitable for farming and much of it can scarcely be used for grazing. In effect, Chad was an interior leftover for France to absorb after the European powers finished scrambling for the more attractive bits of the continent during the final decades of the 19th century. It is still one of the continent's poorest countries.

Africa's fifth largest territory, it has a population variously estimated at between 3.6 and 4.5 million. La République du Tchad, independent since 1960, has had a single party and one president throughout its period of sovereignty. The population consists of Saharan nomadic Toubou and Tuareg, Hausa and Fulani (Foulbe, Peuhl) in the north and west, Bororo herdsmen in the northeast, Wadians and Kanembou farmers and cattle raisers in the east, Kotoko (Boudouma) fishermen around Lake Chad, and, the largest single group, the Sara grain farmers of the relatively well-watered south.

Islam dominates the north and east, with the traditional African religion, animism, prevailing in the south. About one per cent of the population is Christian, most of them Catholic, although the republic's President François Tombalbaye is a mission-educated Protestant.

This broad demographic spectrum corresponds to a range of topography and wildlife that makes Chad an extraordinary experience for explorers of nature and fanciers of game. Chad is in fact the only Central or West African rival to East Africa as a hunter's terrain.

There are other reasons for coming to Chad. A gamut of art and handicraft attracts the collector of good Africana. The bleak northern half of Chad was not always desert: black rock caves of the far northern Tibesti and the sandstone of the northeastern Ennedi Plateau preserve engravings and drawings, and even the oceans of sand have yielded artifacts belonging to a once flourishing green Sahara civilization. At Lake Fitri and along the Chari and Logone Rivers pouring into Lake Chad from the southwest, stone, clay, iron and bronze souvenirs testify to the accomplishments of the Sao kingdom a millennium ago.

Fort Lamy's museum holds evidence of these vanished cultures.

You may also come to see or to fish the remarkable Lake Chad, remnant of a transcontinental sea that once stretched from the Niger to the Nile. Lake Chad is so shallow that three-fourths of its water evaporates in the dry season, shrinking the lake for miles inward.

You don't come to Chad to be comfortable, for it is exceedingly hot, often pestilential, and lonely. And you don't come to admire a national rush of progress, for, unlike Mauritania and other equally obscure territories, Chad has few known resources—physical or human—on which to build, and virtually no institutions or techniques adapted to development. American oil companies have expressed some interest in petroleum deposits in the far north, but exploitability remains uncertain.

This isn't a place to visit in admiration of a harmonious and secure political community either. Stretched 1,100 miles across the Sudanic belt that divides Arab-Berber Islam from Black Africa, Chad suffers from the racial animosities of these latitudes which have plagued Mauritania, Mali and the Sudan Republic as well. In Chad's case, a relatively favored southern majority, supported by the French, controls politics. Some 3,000 French troops have been tied down in fighting alongside Chad's army against a desert enemy in the Tibesti, a grim re-enactment of *Beau Geste* romances and Sigmund Romberg musicals.

The sparse, fiercely independent north has a long heritage of resistance to authority. Toubous (Teda) and Tuaregs, routed by the French after long campaigns lasting through the turn of the century, now compose the core of the rebellion, identified with the North African-based Front for Chadian Liberation (Frolinat). Although the rebellion was allegedly broken with a number of well-publicized defections in 1971, French military authorities admitted that 500 square kilometers of the north remained uncontrolled. In the summer of 1972 there was an epidemic of political arrests and many young intellectuals were exiled, but the rebellion continues. Your hopes of visiting the north for historical research or other purposes depend largely on security conditions and your ability to persuade Chadian or French military personnel to let you through.

In Fort Lamy, Chad's capital, the clamor of rebellion is intermittently echoed in nervous politics. There have been some gestures of liberalization, but President Tombalbaye's control is still severe and uncompromising. The city billets the bored and often racially arrogant French military personnel—an accustomed sight here since World War I, although many now circulate in "civvies." Most of France's annual aid, amounting to some $60 million, must be diverted from economic and social development into military projects. President Tombalbaye's administrative machinery is encumbered by political cronyism, and abuses by the Parti Progressiste Tchadien (PPT) are attributable in part to the regime's obsession with stability. Chad's army is important, busy and loyal.

However undesirable Chad might have been for colonization, France came to value its strategic position both as a land bridge between its Mediterranean and equatorial possessions and as a way station on the air routes between Europe and the West African coast. French dominion in "Le Tchad" supplanted that of Sao, Berber, Hausa, Baguirmi, Wadai, Tuareg and many other masters. Until colonial quiescence settled on its sands, Chad was the scene of constant migration, conquest, invasion and trade. Camel caravans crossed from the Saharan north and Arabic east to the shores of its great lake and back, bearing gold, salt, spices, iron and brass, ostrich feathers, gum arabic and slaves. The seven Hausa states, the empire of Kanem-Bornu and the other powers each were replaced in turn, bequeathing to Chad an Islamic tradition, if little else.

From the advent of World War I—by which time their forces had barely completed the job of "pacification"—the French concentrated on the south, where food and cotton could be cultivated and transported. Germany's loss of Cameroon in that war gave France a keystone to its Equatorial African possessions. Chad (600 miles from the equator at its nearest point) was joined economically to the new Cameroon Trust Territory and administratively to the more manageable colonies of Moyen-Congo (Congo-Brazzaville), Oubangui-Chari (now the Central African Republic) and Gabon.

Just as Chad remains dependent on France for security and for cotton exports, so its impoverished and underprivileged population is dependent on stronger neighbors for access to the coast. President Tombalbaye has protested against perpetuation of Chad's disadvantages, but the country continues to participate in the Central African Customs and Economic Union (UDEAC) and other French-sponsored groupings.

Chad's economy stagnates and its balance of payments deficits grow larger each year. Cotton accounts for 75 per cent of exports, raised with poor productivity and sold in France and Western Europe at declining world prices. Cattle herds find their way only rarely and in half-starved condition over pitiful roads from the thorny Sahel to railheads and markets in Nigeria, Cameroon or the Central African Republic. Some tobacco, rice and peanuts are grown, and the abundant fish resources of Lake Chad are used only for local consumption.

Development of the Lake Chad basin, a long discussed international project, has been stymied by a succession of political distractions in Nigeria, Niger, Cameroon and Chad itself.

Chad is the kind of place that ought to be seriously studied before it is seriously visited. The pertinent bibliography, however, is either romantic (the *Beau Geste* tales, Romain Gary's novel *The Roots of Heaven*, for instance) or recondite (French scholarly articles and monographs on history, ethnography and archaeology). If you read French, you might start with Pierre Hugot's *Le Tchad* (Paris, Nouvelles Editions Latines,

1965) or the excellent essays and vignettes in Hachette's *Guide Bleu* for *Afrique Centrale* (Paris, 1962). You can also write directly for materials and publication lists to the Musée de l'Homme (Palais de Chaillot, Place du Trocadéro, Paris) or the Musée de l'IFAN in Fort Lamy. Some of the early explorers' writings are available in translation—for example, Heinrich Barth's three-volume *Travels and Discoveries in North and Central Africa* (London, F. Cass, 1965) and Gustav Nachtigal's *Sahara and Sudan*, vol. 4, *Wadai and Darfur* (University of California Press, Berkeley, 1972). Contemporary Chad is covered in John Ballard's chapter in *National Unity and Regionalism in Eight African States* (Cornell University Press, 1966).

Money Matters

Chad belongs to the Central African sub-zone of the CFA franc, using the same currency as Cameroon, the Central African Republic, Gabon and the Congo (Brazzaville). You can expect to obtain about 245 CFA francs for your US dollar at the Fort Lamy airport or banks. The Banque Internationale de l'Afrique Occidentale (BIAO), an affiliate of the First National City Bank of New York, is represented at Fort Lamy and Sarh, as it is in most other countries of French-speaking Africa. The same is true of the Banque Nationale de Paris (BNP). Chad's Banque Centrale has offices at Fort Lamy, Sarh and Moundou.

Banks are open only from 7 to 11:30 am, Monday through Friday. You can also exchange dollars or French francs at hotels, restaurants and shops, but at unfavorable discounts. Travelers checks are welcome, but credit cards are not recognized outside of a couple of hotels.

Chad's physical isolation keeps the cost of living exceedingly high for foreigners. Local manufacturing is negligible, and much of what foreigners eat, wear, smoke, read, use in recreation and even for transportation is flown in from France. Beef, fish and millet are usually plentiful, but there are occasional shortages of vegetables and fruits for the entire population. Hence, even the most intrepid backpacker can find himself paying high prices for rare canned goods or skimpy hotel meals.

Getting In and Out

Air Afrique and UTA fly several times each week between Paris and Fort Lamy. You can also take Pan American or other coastal airlines to Douala (Cameroon), and hop to Fort Lamy on Cameroon Airlines. Chad has no railroad or river access, and its road system is strictly for the athletic. Still, if you have the time, equipment and stamina, consider the fascinating 1,150-mile drive across Nigeria and the Cameroon panhandle from Lagos via Ibadan, Kaduna, Kano, Maiduguri (all in Nigeria), and Fort Foureau in Cameroon across the Chari River from Fort Lamy; the road is paved as far as Maiduguri, and "almost all-weather" thereafter (meaning that the rains seldom interrupt traffic for more than 24 hours). The Fort Foureau-Fort Lamy ferry runs all year and takes only a few minutes once you've passed border formalities.

Visas are necessary for Chad; if you are driving in from the west, you need visas from Nigeria and Cameroon as well. They should be obtained before arrival, since security conditions occasionally make Chadian border authorities suspicious of foreigners without appropriate documentation. French consulates issue visas with a minimum of red tape in countries where Chad has no diplomatic representation. Customs controls are normal for the French-speaking world, but firearms should be licensed in advance of arrival, and no ivory can be exported in any form without payment of duties.

Getting Around Within Chad

This vast country has 36 airports for internal travel. Air Tchad flies regularly between Fort Lamy and the main points of economic and tourist interest, charging $65 for a one-way, two and a quarter hour flight to Abéché, $32 for six and a half hour flight to Faya Largeau, $25 to Bongor (1½ hours), $50 to Moundou (1½ hours) and $53 for the three-hour flight to the southern capital and game center, Sarh (ex-Fort Archambault). Air Tchad also provides charter service in aircraft of varying sizes for $120 (in a six-seater Cherokee) to $160 per hour's flight.

If you shun flying, you have few other means for getting around in Chad. There is no railroad and the Chari and Logone Rivers have only freight barge traffic. Private motor boats and wood or papyrus canoes (pirogues) of the Kotoka fishermen can be used for excursions on the Chari or Lake Chad, but the former require "connections" with boat owners and the piroguiers dare to navigate far into Lake Chad only in the dry season (December to May) for fear of sudden storms. During that dry period, however, there is considerable pirogue commerce between the Chadian and Nigerian shores (some of it contraband). It is a hot and uncomfortable excursion.

Motoring around Chad's 20,000 miles of unpaved roads is best done during January and February, the dry period before spring heat builds up and sufficiently late after the floods to allow for repair of the roads in central and southern Chad. The direct route between Fort Lamy and Sarh has the advantage of pavement in spots, but it is dull compared to the rougher tracks via Moundou and Bongor. The east-west route, a link of the Nigerian highway into the Sudan, is open only from November to June. If you have the time and the fortitude, you can improve on the monotony of the Fort Lamy-Abéché stretch by a detour through Bitkine and Mongo in Baguirmi country.

Inexpensive bus service (Unitchadienne and CTT) covers the main routes, usually on a weekly basis when the roads are open—offering a good opportunity to be with Chadians on the move. Hitchhiking doesn't work very well, even during the dry season, for traffic is light and most of it is commercial.

Taxis and unchauffeured vehicles can be rented from Giorgi Didajo (Taxis Texaco), Sympatic Taxis and the Tchad Tourisme travel agency in Fort Lamy. The smallest vehicles (including Volkswagens) hire for $10 to $11.30 per day, with a 50-kilometer free allowance and 12 cents per kilometer above that allowance; larger cars rent for $14 to $16 per day plus 12 cents per kilometer; four-wheel-drive vehicles are $20 to $32 plus kilometrage. Gas costs about 89 cents per gallon (much more in the north). Traffic drives on the right. There is no bus service within the towns. Taxis have no meters and are expensive: in Fort Lamy, a normal errand in town costs about CFA 600 ($2.40), twice that at night.

Travel into the far north is not only rough; it involves the risk of stumbling into zones of rebellion. Check with Fort Lamy military authorities before starting out for the Tibesti or Ennedi regions, and, whether you are aiming at restricted areas or not, follow the Sahara road rules. Travel in a group or convoy with a knowledgeable guide, carrying all your fuel, oil and water needs (supplies are often exhausted once you are there, and an oil change is necessary after every sand storm). Bring equipment for traction over sand and if you are hiring a driver be sure that he has had experience in sand. Beware of the medical problems caused by sand, insects and snakes, extreme dryness and questionable food. (Since the only provisions you can count on purchasing in the Tibesti are dates, you should carry potatoes, onions, fruit, tea and other unspoilable comestibles with you.) It is an obligation in the Sahara to render assistance to any person or vehicle in difficulty. Also, carry extra rations of tea, sugar, cigarettes and other "wampum" to offer guides, caravan leaders and anybody who helps you out.

The government's Office National du Tourisme Tchadien (P.O. Box 763) offers some general assistance to travelers, but it is best to put your question to the commercial agencies (Tchad Tourisme, P.O. Box 894, tel. 34-10; or Socopao, of the international SCAC system, P.O. Box 751, tel. 28-19).

If your main interest is in hunting or watching game, write for information, permits, accommodations, vehicle rentals, guides and safari tours to the government's Direction des Eaux et Forêts et Chasse, P.O. Box 447, Fort Lamy and/or the agency Tourisme et Cynégétique (affiliated with Tchad Tourisme), P.O. Box 88, Sarh. Socopao also has branches in Sarh and Moundou. For special permits or information concerning the Zakouma and Sinianka-Minia reserves, write the government's Direction des Parcs et Réserves, P.O. Box 905, Fort Lamy. The Société Orchape, 6 rue d'Armaillé, Paris 17, operates safaris and rents equipment in Chad. The Chadian Embassy in Washington has lists of guides.

Where to Stay

Accommodations in Chad are designed to suit the businessmen and safarists who compose the bulk of its visitors. FORT LAMY has two good, expensive hotels for foreigners. Both are on the Chari River less than a mile from center city and both were evidently designed somewhere outside of Chad—for their cement walls radiate the 100-degree sunshine throughout the night, air-conditioners notwithstanding. La Tchadienne, the bigger and newer establishment, has 100 rooms, a pool, several bars and a $4 lunch/dinner menu. Its rooms rent for $16 single and $18 double, breakfast included. Le Chari, smaller and slightly older, is a trifle cheaper. The Grand Hôtel in the center of town, occupying what was once an Arab fort, has 11 air-conditioned rooms for $13 single and $16 double as well as 29 non-air-conditioned rooms for half the price. Breakfast costs $1 extra. The veranda bungalows called the Air Hôtel on the Chari River (Diners Club cards welcomed) are barely satisfactory. Noisy and not altogether sanitary lodgings also can be rented around the African market and mosque.

At SARH (ex-Fort Archambault), another good place for foreigners is the all air-conditioned Hôtel Safari, $12 to $14 plus breakfast. The regular hunters' lodge (Hôtel des Chasses) has six non-air-conditioned rooms for $8 to $10 plus breakfast. Lunch and dinner menus, as everywhere in the European circuits, start at about $4. There are Oasis hotels at ABÉCHÉ in the east and BOL on Lake Chad, with rooms for $6.50 single and $10 double plus breakfast. Meals here are slightly less expensive. The Villa de Dougia, a popular luncheon stop on the Chari River near Lake Chad, has adequate accommodations in the $6 to $10 range.

Bush camps, government rest-houses (gîtes) and hunting lodges vary enormously in quality, but all are cheap. The most elaborate are the Campement du Bahr Tinga in the Zakouma Park (four-bed huts at $4 per bed plus breakfast, meals from $3.70 to $4.50) and the Tchad-

Tourisme lodges at BARDAI and ZOUAR. Other places exist at Faya Largeau, Fada, Moundou and Bongor.

Ask the Office du Tourisme for advice on staying at government rest-houses or consult Peace Corps and CUSO headquarters in Fort Lamy on other chances for cheap accommodations. In the Tibesti, unlike other parts of the Sahara, few inhabitants use tents; instead, they construct quick lean-tos against their vehicles, or burrow sleeping trenches into the sand. In any case, use a sheepskin bedroll (faro) or sleeping bag with abundant blankets, as well as protection against insects.

Where and What to Eat

Combinations of French cuisine and local food can be found in the two main towns at $5 and up per meal. Try Chez Cabrini, a pleasant French-Italian-Vietnamese place seven miles outside FORT LAMY, and the Chari Club, where you have to be invited by a member. Le Lotus is probably the best Vietnamese place among several that cater largely to French military personnel. The Air Hôtel, Bar-Restaurant de la Poste, Le Weekend and the major hotels offer a basically French cuisine. The Pizzeria-Baby Scotch discotheque and the Saloon Bar cater to more affluent young clients, while the Lebanese Naufal Sami and the Relais Aériens at the airport serve snacks. The Villa de Dougia is good for meals during an outing along the Chari near the Lake Chad shore. In addition to the hotels, SARH has the Lebanese Sakkal Joseph. Service charges are usually added to the restaurant bill.

Sold at marketplaces are millet and sorghum, couscous, porridge and cakes, rice (in the south) and dates (in the north), along with imported (expensive) juices and soft drinks. The Brasseries du Logone produce a good local beer at high prices to replace the unreliable water of Fort Lamy and countryside.

What to See and Do

Standing strategically at the confluence of the Chari and Logone rivers 80 miles from Lake Chad, FORT LAMY has been a river ford for caravans and Hausa-Fulani pilgrims to Mecca. It was developed by the French into a military post in 1900. The town is very much divided. One section is a sandy, tree-shaded business-residential area of air-conditioned villas constructed in a wagon-wheel arrangement of boulevards extending from the Place de la République. Here are shopping arcades, restaurants and bars for the military, river sports, bowls, horses and tennis for the members of the Chari Club. The other section is a large carré (gridiron) of flat-roofed adobe (poto-poto) houses shielding courtyards where food is cooked, peanuts and seeds are pressed into oil, and families receive traveling relatives from the homelands of Sara, Banda, Bongo, Hausa, Leto, Foung from the Sudan, Toubou from the Tibesti, Boudouma and Bororo.

The African quarter has a splendid morning market, animated by cattle, goats, donkeys, the bright cloth of the market women and the stately procession of shoppers. Nights are usually passed amid the music of flutes and drums. There are soccer football and bicycle races on weekends. The mosque is modest and the cathedral modern. Fort Lamy's museum houses fossils, iron tools and stone objects, bones, pottery and ornamental imagery from the Sao culture and the ancient Tibesti epochs, as well as exhibits of the art and customs of contemporary Chad.

The Sao ruins include the Butte de Sao, an artificial hill of rubble six miles north of Fort Lamy. A $6 riverboat excursion down the Chari to Lake Chad passes curious fishermen's villages, flocks of river birds and an occasional hippo. LOGONE-BIRNI, ruined capital of the Sao Sultanate, lies on the Logone's left bank, 40 miles south of Fort Fouraud in Cameroon (ferry crossing, visa needed), on a path accessible only from January to June. Far from splendid today, it remains a holy place for the Kotoka (Boudouma) descendants of that kingdom, the site of their ancestors' tombs. Twenty miles south of Fort Lamy, the small *Dandelia Reserve* is still a refuge of elephants, with hippos nearby at KOUNDOUL, and a swimming beach on the Chari. (An organized tour costs $18 including picnic lunch).

There's a colorful Sunday market at LINIA, 20 miles east of Fort Lamy.

Lake Chad itself is worth the considerable effort required for exploration. At 800 feet above sea level, the 10,000-square-mile surface makes it the 11th largest inland body of water in the world. At least 150 species of game fish inhabit the lake, and an abundance of wildlife (including ostrich and elegant horned kudus) collects on its banks—especially at the Chari River delta and, farther north, at RIG-RIG. Certain corners of the lake remain virtually unexplored, except by light airplane from above. You can either hire a boat at Fort Lamy and come down the Chari or drive to the tiny port of BOL and charter a boat from there; a government launch is sometimes available. Otherwise the Boudouma (Kotoka) fishermen will rent you a kadaye (canoe) with motor or oarsmen. Carry clothing for full coverage and insect repellent as well. Medical authorities advise against swimming in the lake.

There is also excellent fishing along the lower Logone and Chari, especially in late summer and fall when the waters are flooding over the green banks. Here, you can see a perfection of "hut" architecture in the dwellings of the Mousgoum and the fortified villages of the Mara. The Boudouma and Kanembou of the area are good drummers and dancers.

SARH (ex-Fort Archambault), the Sara capital and the country's second city, is a pleasant but dull agricultural town of broad, shaded avenues. From December through May, this is a departure point for hunting and camera safaris along the rivers and in the savannas of the south. Airlines and travel agencies at Fort Lamy can make arrangements for such a trek, or you can deal directly with Dalat Safaris (P.O. Box 224, Sarh). The south has numbers of the rare derby eland, as well as other antelope, elephants, buffalo, kudu, giraffe, lions, panthers, apes, hyenas, wart-hogs, a few rhinos and innumerable birds. The big game are protected in the Zakouma National Park but hunted at the Sinianka-Minia Estate.

Tours from Fort Lamy provide an overnight stop at ZAKOUMA, with guides and full transportation, for $100 (two and a half days). There is also a three-day tour to Cameroon's Waza National Park, 85 miles from Fort Lamy, costing between $90 and $120 per person, depending on the size of the group (see chapter on Cameroon).

In the area west of the main Fort Lamy-Sarh highway, there are several points of interest: some beautiful houses and granaries of the Kirdi people; dancing and wrestling at the Sunday markets of BANANA and the Monday markets of BONGOR; intricate calabash carving throughout the area; horsemen and their caparisoned steeds at BINDER; the agreeable local capital of MOUNDOU, and the projectile-arched huts of the Mouloui people along the Logone River.

ABÉCHÉ is the busy capital of the Chadian east, frequented by nomads and townsfolk, weavers of camel-hair rugs, musicians and dancers of several ethnic groups. The elaborate ruins of the OUARA, metropolis of the old Waddai (Ouaddai) empire, are 35 miles north of Abéché at the end of an excruciating track. Huge ruined outer walls and inner courts surround impressive remains of the sultans' palace, the great mosque and other proud edifices. The dry, rocky eastern countryside, where there is a variety of social and economic life, has possibilities for hill climbing, crafts shopping and a visit to the great Monday market at OUM HADJER.

When accessible, the north presents an intriguing panorama of town life, oasis, space and wasteland. FAYA LARGEAU, a citadel in the desert of the Borkou, has a colorful·daily market with camel processions and, on festival days, a slow quadrille of Teda (Toubou) women dancers in long silk robes, heavy amber collars and massive silver ornaments. The limestone and sandstone plains of the Ennedi to the east have several bright oases: beautiful BARDAI with its environment of gorges, volcanic craters, sulfur deposits, cliffs and gardens; FADA, close by some of the Sahara's oldest cave paintings; and the Guelia d'Archei near Fada, a narrow canyon with red rock walls and caves inhabited by tribes of dog-faced baboons.

ZOUAR is the green spot of the Tibesti, farthest northern range of Chad, in a silent, tortured, volcanic Sahara of cones and peaks, motley-colored rocks and sand mountains, with cave paintings nearby and a population of proud nomadic Toubous. MOUSSORO at the southern edge of the Sahara is headquarters of the Méharistes, the desert camel patrol that stages camel and horse races at the end of November each year to honor the rains that have come.

The best time to witness Chadian drumming, dancing and musicianship is on Moslem holidays in the north, local fertility and harvest festivals in the south, and Independence Day (August 11) at Fort Lamy.

What to Buy

Central African artistry and craftsmanship can be found at Fort Lamy and in the provincial markets. You can find, for instance, camel-hair rugs (chemle) from the east (Abéché market); decorative cotton cloth (gabak) from the central region (Mongo and Bitkine markets); fine straw and wickerwork throughout the center and east; uniquely decorated calabashes with geometrical patterns, animal figures or initiation symbols along the Logone River (Bongor market); silver bracelets, copper and silver spurs and other jewelry at Abtouyour, Bitkine and Mongo; leather work, wrought iron and wicker at Sarh, as well as ivory (albeit subject to a heavy export tax); well-cast, often amusing brass figures, including anthropomorphic bells (a long-nosed General de Gaulle, arms flung wide above the bell-skirt, and a full-breasted Marianne de France, are especially prized); throwing knives, weapons, bows, lances, swords, flutes, drums and other instruments, as well as amber choker-collars and massive silver jewelry, cotton and wool cloth and copperwork from Morocco in the north (Faya Largeau); fine pottery in the west (Koumra) and central region (Abtouyour, Bitkine, Mongo).

Itinerant traders exhibit many of these articles in their stalls on the edge of Fort Lamy's central Place or in front of the hotels. Bargain for your life. Smaller selections at firm but higher prices are in the shops of the capital, open from 7 am to noon and from 4 to 6 pm, six days a week.

Local Attitudes

In this period of rebellion, Chad has a nervous government and limited tolerance for antics by foreigners. Islamic sensitivities in the north should also be respected. However, if you aren't too interested in the workings of politics and the motives of the distant rebels, you will find Chadians friendly or benignly indifferent to American travelers. Capital city social life divides into (1) informal overseas French style of cocktails and dinner in the big hotels and residential villas, and (2) the tough-talking military ambiance of the downtown bars and Vietnamese bistros.

Weather, What to Wear

Although Chad spreads over several distinct weather zones, you can expect scorching daytime heat everywhere in the country. Rains come in heavy storms at dawn or in the afternoon from July to September (heaviest in August). During the dry season, from December through May, skies are cloudless, night temperatures fall significantly, especially as you go north, and a dry east wind blows steadily. The early part of this period, from late November to February, is the most pleasant season for travel, dry in the daytime, with night temperatures descending to 50 degrees and below, even at Fort Lamy. From March to May, springtime is beastly hot, almost never dropping below 90 degrees anywhere, with blowing dust and irritating dessication in the air. Chad's abundant insect population is renewed with the first rains of June (May at Sarh, July at drier Abéché).

Rain becomes scarce to non-existent by the time you pass the northernmost latitude of Lake Chad; it falls in July and August only. The northern half of Chad displays Saharan extremes of climate: fierce daytime heat with nights in winter that usually go well below freezing. If you are traveling in the Tibesti, carry sweaters, blankets and other wool wrappings, as well as a hat and some sort of face-cloth to protect your skin from the blowing sand. Sweaters are also useful for evenings in Fort Lamy, whether in the cool breezes of garden parties or the brisk air-conditioned indoors. Bush dress can be purchased in Fort Lamy, as can the baggy seroual trousers that are ideal for camel riding.

Communication

French is the official language of Chad, but since the country has one of the lowest literacy and school enrollment rates in the world, the use of even that language is restricted to townspeople and civil servants. Sara has become the basic tongue for the southern regions, and Arabic for the north. A few dozen Peace Corps and CUSO Volunteers are scattered around Chad, and there are quite a few Nigerians (of a community that numbers almost 100,000) who speak some English.

Local and African news is carried daily in the mimeographed *Info-Tchad*, as well as on the national radio. The foreign press is flown in from Paris. For information in English, you can only resort to the US Embassy, USIS library and Peace Corps headquarters next door to the Embassy on Rue Behagle.

Fort Lamy's airport has a reputation for efficiency, and there are 30 post offices in the country, but postal services, freight and other communications reflect Chad's general state of underdevelopment and dependence.

Emergencies

This is not a place to have any. The general hospital at Fort Lamy has French army doctors experienced in tropical medicine, and there are secondary hospitals at Sarh (Fort Archambault), Moundou and Abéché. But even considering the military establishment, the national ratio is only about one doctor to every 75,000 Chadians, and the Centres Médicaux up-country are poorly equipped and understaffed. The US Embassy on Avenue Colonna d'Ornano (tel. 30-91, P.O. Box 413) has a health room open six days a week with a part time nurse. The Peace Corps next door (tel. 34-20, 31-42) has a staff doctor who is available only for genuine emergencies. The Canadian Embassy address is P.O. Box 289.

If in doubt, fly to Paris.

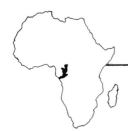

Congo

(République Populaire du Congo)

Profile

STATUS: Independent since August 15, 1960. Declared People's Republic in 1970. Formerly part of French Equatorial Africa.

SIZE: 132,000 square miles (about twice the size of Missouri). Population—915,000 (major groups are Bakongo, Mbochi, Teke, Lari).

GEOGRAPHY: Tropical hardwood forests, Congo River (3,000 miles long). Principal cities—Brazzaville (capital, 200,000), Pointe Noire (100,000).

CLIMATE: Hot and humid most of the year. Brazzaville and Pointe Noire temperatures in the 80's to low 90's all year (60's and 70's at night). Rainy season October to May.

LANGUAGES: French (official), Bantu languages.

CURRENCY: CFA franc. CFA 100 = 40 cents; $1.00 = CFA 245.

VISAS: Virtually impossible for Americans to obtain in the US. Apply in person at the Embassy of the People's Republic of the Congo in Paris.

AIRPORT: Maya Maya (BZV), three miles from Brazzaville. Connected with Paris, Pointe Noire, Bangui, Ft. Lamy, Libreville. Taxi into city—CFA 400 ($1.60) during the day, CFA 800 ($3.20) after 7 pm. Airport departure taxes—domestic, CFA 500 ($2); within Africa, CFA 750 ($3); outside Africa, CFA 2,000 ($8).

NATIONAL HOLIDAYS: May 1, workers holiday; August 15, anniversary of 1964 coup; Christian holidays.

INFORMATION SOURCES: *In US*—Permanent Mission of the People's

Republic of the Congo, 444 Madison Avenue, New York, N.Y. 10017 (tel. 212/889-5060). *In Paris*—Embassy of the People's Republic of the Congo, 57 bis, rue Scheffer (tel. PAS 77-09). *In Congo*—Office National Congolais du Tourisme, Brazzaville (tel. 27-13); Syndicat d'Initiative, Avenue du 28 Août 1940, Brazzaville (tel. 31-78); TCOT Voyages (travel agency), Avenue Patrice Lumumba, Brazzaville (tel. 43-02); Syndicat d'Initiative, facing the Congo-Océan train station, Pointe Noire.

By Lynn K. Mytelka and Aaron Segal

The People's Republic of the Congo is one of Africa's most exotic and, for Americans, least accessible countries. The "little Congo"—not to be confused with its big neighbor, which has changed its name from Congo to Zaïre—broke diplomatic relations with the US in 1965. In 1970 it declared itself Africa's first People's Republic committed to "scientific socialism," and, except for one-day transits, has allowed few Americans in. Curious travelers are required to make a special effort for a chance to glimpse the political and social ferment and the natural wonders of this fascinating country.

Congolese society has not always been this inaccessible. The Congo is the historic homeland of the Lari, an important subdivision of the Bakongo kingdom, whose 16th century emperors eagerly sought alliances and trade with the Portuguese and other European powers. They were rebuffed and the empire later was smashed by slave traders.

During the 19th century European powers squabbled over control of the mouth of the 3,000-mile-long Congo River. The French explorer, Pierre Savorgnan de Brazza, pushed up-river from the Atlantic Ocean and founded in 1879 what became the river port of Brazzaville. Across the river the Belgians built a rival port and city, Léopoldville. Meanwhile, the Berlin Conference of 1885 awarded to Portugal the tiny Cabinda enclave north of the river, thus preventing France or any other nation from controlling the mouth of the river.

Brazzaville (port and city) developed as a trading center for the up-river French colonies. Although more cosmopolitan and liberal than Belgian-run Léopoldville, it was also much smaller and poorer. The first French colony to rally to General de Gaulle in 1940, it was the Free French capital for a short time during World War II.

Independence came on August 15, 1960 under the leadership of the flamboyant defrocked priest, Abbé Fulbert Youlou, who became the first president. The much larger Belgian territory across the river also took the name "Congo" on independence that year, but has since become Zaïre (see chapter on Zaïre). Inclined to high living and conspicuous corruption, President Youlou was overthrown during the "three glorious days" of August 12–14, 1964, when students, teachers and trade unionists took to the streets in protest.

Since then the Congo has had intermittent military rule and constant political instability. The current president, Marien Ngouadi, is a French-trained army officer who heads an uneasy coalition of French-educated Maoist intellectuals, veteran trade unionists and army officers.

Despite substantial exports of tropical hardwoods, bananas, palm oil, cocoa, sugar, potash and petroleum, the Congolese economy needs shoring up with French, Chinese and Soviet aid. Unemployment is widespread in this densely urbanized country. It contributes to continuing ethnic conflict between the minority of Lari and related Bakongo peoples and the majority of Mbochi, Teke and other groups in the less-developed interior.

The government has concentrated on extending education (the Congo has one of the highest literacy rates in Africa) and medical and social services. Both the Chinese and the Russians have built hospitals and provided doctors. French economic interests still predominate, but the government has begun to put pressure on French business and has withdrawn from the French-oriented African and Malagasy Organization (OCAM).

Surprisingly little has been published on this intriguing country. It is covered in a chapter in Guy de Lusignan's *French-Speaking Africa Since Independence* (Praeger, 1969). Hachette's *Guide de l'Afrique Centrale* (Paris, 1962) has background on history and tourist sites, and there are other scholarly studies and memoirs in French.

Money Matters

American travelers checks can be cashed at the Brazzaville and Pointe Noire branches of the two leading French commercial banks in West Africa, BIAO (Banque Internationale pour l'Afrique Occidentale) and BICI (Banque Internationale pour le Commerce et l'Industrie du Congo). Banking hours during the week are from 6:30 to 11:30 am, and 2 to 5 pm. The country uses the CFA franc, as do Cameroon, the Central African Republic, Chad and Gabon.

Getting In and Out

Although few Americans have obtained visas since 1965, it can be done. The best chance for success is a personal application at the Embassy of the People's Republic of the Congo in Paris, located at 75 bis, rue Scheffer, Paris 16 (tel. PAS 77-09). Applicants are required to show a round trip ticket or evidence of sufficient funds to guarantee that they will not be stranded.

It is sometimes possible to spend a few hours in the city of Brazzaville on a transit basis—without a visa—depending on the state of relations between the Congo and Zaïre. Frequent ferry service connects the two capital cities, Brazzaville and Kinshasa, but is often disrupted by political feuds, or limited to nationals of these countries. UTA and KLM have offices in both cities and can arrange for the ferry crossing, with time to roam in Brazzaville before making your flight.

Brazzaville has a major airport served by KLM, UTA, Air Afrique and other carriers. Connections are good to Western Europe and the neighboring former French capitals. The KLM office at Avenue du 28 Août 1940 (tel. 46-46) is particularly helpful.

Pointe Noire is a major port for African coastal and Europe-Africa freighters. There are occasional passenger ships of the Paquet Line out of Marseille. The government-owned Agence Transcongolaise de Communications (ATC) manages the ports of Brazzaville and Pointe Noire. It operates a boat service for passengers and freight going up the Congo River from Brazzaville to the Ubangi River and the landlocked Central African Republic. The same company runs truck transportation from Brazzaville to Dolisie and the Gabon border.

Getting Around Within the Congo

The Congo has a public bus system but the buses are very crowded. City taxis are better. Fares are under $1 for any distance during the day and under $1.50 at night. Automobiles and motorbikes may be rented in Brazzaville from Auto Location, Rue Sergent-Malamine (tel. 31-31), and Auto Service, Avenue du 28 Août 1940 (tel. 32-17); and in Pointe Noire from Taxis Frégate (tel. 21-90). An international driving license and a deposit are required, and a chauffeur is helpful since the paved road stops 45 miles outside the capital.

Lina-Congo provides daily plane service between Brazzaville and Pointe Noire and Dolisie, in the heart of a rich sugar-growing region. There is also a daily 11-hour train connection between Brazzaville and Pointe Noire (one-way fares are $15.60 first class and $12.50 second class, not including meals or drinks in the restaurant car). It's a good way to see the countryside. Collective taxis and passenger-carrying trucks also run up-country and to the coast from Brazzaville. Negotiate prices.

Where to Stay

The cheapest decent hotel in BRAZZAVILLE is the *Petit Logis*, where prices start at $7 a night. The French owners serve fairly good meals. The newest and largest hotel is the air-conditioned, 103-room *Cosmos*, built by the Soviet Union in 1969. It has a nightclub with a live band and the only public swimming pool in town. Single room rates are from $11 to $27 per night. The 52-room *Relais Aériens* caters to airlines personnel and French visitors and has a pool for hotel guests and an attractive river view. Rates are from $15 to $21, including Continental breakfast. The *Hôtel du Beach* is more moderately priced and has a passable French restaurant. There are no readily available inexpensive accommodations.

POINTE NOIRE is a beach city with two oceanfront hotels, the *Atlantic Palace* and the *Victory Palace*. Single room prices range from $11 to $15. The slightly less expensive *Hôtel du Plateau* and the *Hôtel Sole e Mare* are closer to town. Outside these two cities, except for two modest hotels in Dolisie, lodging is uncertain. One must rely on missions, schools, and mining and lumber camps.

Where and What to Eat

The leading hotels in Brazzaville and Pointe Noire have their own restaurants which offer mostly French cuisine. Less expensive in BRAZZAVILLE are *La Pizzeria* for pizza and other Italian dishes, *Pam-Pam*, a snack bar on Avenue Foch where you can get a fairly good steak, and the Vietnamese restaurant, *A. Dong*. POINTE NOIRE has the *Restaurant de l'Aérogare* and *La Rotonde*, a snack bar. African food is served in numerous small bars and roadside restaurants. Local beer and imported (expensive) Evian and Vichy mineral water are available for those who do not have access to boiled or filtered water.

What to See and Do

BRAZZAVILLE stretches for six miles along the broad Congo River (known on the other side as the Zaïre River). It has distinct sections: the administrative center (the Plateau), an essentially commercial area (the Plain), the military quarter (le Tchad), a residential section (l'Aiglon) and an industrial zone of small factories (Mpila). East of the modern city is Poto-Poto, the African residential and trading quarter where scores of ethnic groups mingle in a rich mélange of color, music and conviviality; stretching west along the river is the Bakongo neighborhood.

A visit to Poto-Poto is a must, even for travelers who have only crossed the river to make a plane connection. On the way, stop at the modernistic Catholic Basilica of Sainte Anne of the Congo. In Poto-Poto, stroll in the Moungali and Ouendze markets where such delicacies as caterpillars and boa constrictor meat are on sale. Visitors are welcomed at the Poto-Poto art school (Ecole de l'Art de Poto-Poto) which seeks to combine modern and traditional designs. The Elysée Bar provides a good sample of Congolese dance music and atmosphere, and several small restaurants serve inexpensive meals of saca-saca (cooked cassava leaves) and chicken pili-pili (chicken in chili pepper sauce).

The modest modern sections of the city have broad boulevards but lack the imposing architecture of Abidjan or Dakar. Traders display their wares along the Avenue Foch and in the beach and port area. There is a junior college (Centre d'Enseignement Supérieur) and a teacher training college (Ecole Normale Supérieure). The World Health Organization has its African headquarters here. A huge portrait of Mao hangs over the entrance of the Chinese Embassy.

Night life is sedate and expensive at the major hotels, lively and cheap in Poto-Poto. Numerous outdoor clubs cater to rich and poor alike. Many recover from a swinging Saturday night by attending Sunday services, especially at the new church in the Bakongo neighborhood where Mass is sung in the Lingala language to a drum accompaniment.

Near Brazzaville are several interesting sights. The lighthouse (phare) and Case de Gaulle (built for the General in 1940) offer panoramic views of the river and the city. Organized boat and canoe trips on the river include the fishing village of M'Pila, Congo River rapids, Bouenza and Foulakari falls and the island of N'Damou in mid-river.

POINTE NOIRE is a pleasant port and beach town that has excellent ocean fishing, especially for tarpon. In town is a lively open market and the Cathedral of Notre Dame. There's water-skiing at the Sea Club, on a stretch of beach known as la Côte Sauvage. The road south toward Cabinda leads to Djeno beach and sport fishing. The dense Mayombe forest, one of the world's largest stands of tropical hardwoods, is 140 miles north of Pointe Noire by a road open only in the dry season.

The Congo contains numerous projects built with Chinese, French, Soviet, Cuban and World Bank assistance. These include a textile mill, hospitals, potash mines and technical and agricultural schools. The Office National Congolais du Tourisme in the Plateau section of Brazzaville (tel. 27-13) should be able to arrange visits.

What to Buy

The markets in Poto-Poto and the sidewalk traders in the city display a variety of wares common to this part of Africa. Some of the best sculpture comes from Gabon and the coast. Although the expensive hotels have craft boutiques it is better to shop in the markets, taking your time and bargaining vigorously.

Local Attitudes

Pants for women are fine, but the People's Republic is no place for miniskirts or shorts. It is unlikely that hippie attire will be tolerated.

The official party weekly newspaper, *Etumbi,* carries vituperative articles about United States imperialism; the government paper, *La Voix de la Révolution,* is less militant. Rare American visitors encounter little hostility. The people are curious about world affairs and race relations in other countries. It is probably best not to discuss Congolese politics unless citizens volunteer their opinions. The Chinese, Russians and Cubans in Brazzaville tend to stay in separate groups. The government is not eager to advertise their presence or respond to inquiries about their whereabouts. Resident Frenchmen and officials of the World Health Organization are easier to meet.

Weather, What to Wear, How Long to Stay

The Congo is hot and sticky and light clothes are generally all you need. Probably the best time to visit is from October to February, avoiding both the heavy rains and the long dry seasons.

Unless you are there only to make a flight connection in Brazzaville, a visit to the Congo depends on patient pursuit of a visa and frankness with the embassy personnel about your reasons for visiting the country and your travel plans there. A week should suffice to see Brazzaville and Pointe Noire. If you can, wangle an official invitation, stay longer and try to find out what the People's Republic is all about.

Communication

French is the official language and is spoken in many places. It is almost impossible to find anyone who speaks English. But *Time* and the Paris edition of the *Herald Tribune* are on sale at the Maison de la Presse, a well-stocked bookstore on Avenue Foch in the center of Brazzaville.

Postal services are generally reliable and visitors may receive mail, which should be marked "Poste Restante," at the main post office in Brazzaville, open from 7:30 to noon and 2:30 to 5 pm. Telephones have automatic dialing within Brazzaville and Pointe Noire and good overseas connections to Paris at specified times of day. Packages can be shipped abroad through the main post office.

Emergencies

The United States is officially represented here by West Germany. Americans should check in at the German Embassy in Brazzaville (tel. 27-70) on arrival in the country. Medical services are adequate. There are general hospitals in Brazzaville and Pointe Noire.

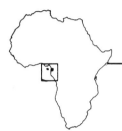

Equatorial Guinea

(República de Guinea Ecuatorial)

Profile

STATUS: Independent republic since October 12, 1968. Former Spanish colony.

GEOGRAPHY: Comprises mainland territory known as Rio Muni (10,140 square miles), the island of Fernando Po (787 square miles) and three small groups of volcanic islands, almost completely barren. Fernando Po (population about 80,000), 20 miles off the coast of Cameroon, is very mountainous. Rio Muni (population about 210,000) is mainly tropical rain forest beyond its coastal fringes. Principal towns—Santa Isabel (capital, on Fernando Po, 30,000), Bata (Rio Muni).

CLIMATE: Hot and humid; equatorial rains.

LANGUAGES: Spanish (official), pidgin English, some French.

CURRENCY: Peseta, divided into 100 centimos. 10 pesetas = about 16 cents; $1.00 = 62.5 pesetas.

VISAS: Required, but difficult to obtain. May be available from Mission of Equatorial Guinea to the UN. Fee $5. Two passport photos needed. Embassies in Madrid, Yaoundé (Cameroon) and Libreville (Gabon) sometimes issue visas.

AIRPORT: Santa Isabel (SSG) on Fernando Po, five miles from city. Frequent flights to and from Bata on the mainland and Douala (Cameroon), weekly to and from Madrid.

NATIONAL HOLIDAYS: October 12, Independence Day; Catholic holidays.

INFORMATION SOURCE: *In US*—Permanent Mission of Equatorial Guinea to UN, 440 East 62nd Street, New York, N.Y. 10022 (tel. 212/759-2193).

400

Santa Isabel

FERNANDO PO I.

Gulf of Guinea

EQUATORIAL GUINEA

Bata

Atlantic Ocean

By Aaron Segal

Once a pleasant pit stop of the Gulf of Guinea, Equatorial Guinea's current political problems and governmental paranoia discourage most visitors to Africa's least-populated independent state.

Although Spain early acquired and still holds the Canary Islands and Spanish Sahara, it had a late start and small success in gaining sub-Saharan colonial territory. The tropical island of Fernando Po and several nearby volcanic specks were acquired as an 18th century afterthought. Named after a 15th century Portuguese explorer, the island was a slave trading station until the abolition of slavery by Spain in 1868. Rio Muni, on the mainland 150 miles to the southeast, was claimed by Spain in the second half of the 19th century but it was fully occupied only after World War I.

by migrant Ibo laborers from Nigeria. The Nigerian immigrants now number almost 50,000—more than half the total population. The remainder includes the indigenous Bubi people and the racially mixed "Fernandinos." The islanders have long been at higher economic and educational levels than the Rio Muni mainland population (mostly Fang and related groups). They even sought to impede independence, preferring Spanish protection to division of the economy with their less privileged continental neighbors.

But the overwhelming numerical superiority of the Fangs (about 200,000 live on the mainland) was the decisive factor in determining political control. With the help of the Spanish Foreign Office, the Rio Muni faction prevailed. Fernando Po was united with Rio Muni as an independent republic in 1968. Federico Macias Nguema, a Fang, became the first president of this shaky new government, surviving a violent clash within the government in 1969. The mood of insecurity was intensified in late 1972 when Gabon occupied Equatorial Guinea's coastal islands, where oil strikes have been anticipated. By the end of the year an Organization of African Unity commission was still studying the dispute.

Since independence the mood of the country has been shaped by isolation, fear and political instability. Although the economy depends on Spanish subsidies for its cocoa and Spanish revenue from the timber industry on the mainland, the government has followed an anti-Spanish and generally anti-Western policy line. It professes to be progressive and socialist, partly to mask its own internal problems, and makes life difficult for unsuspecting visitors in its effort to ferret out alleged conspiracies. Many Spanish residents fled the country after the government began to display its hostility to the former ruling power.

If you're interested in offbeat destinations, Fernando Po may be worth your consideration—provided you can get a visa and don't object to government surveillance during your stay. The island has good beaches, a fairly cosmopolitan mixture of peoples, a 10,000-foot volcanic peak and some handsome Spanish colonial architecture. The capital, Santa Isabel, is served by a new international airport.

Rio Muni has fewer charms, unless you fancy equatorial rain forests. The principal town on the mainland is Bata. It is no wonderland. Ebebiyin and Rio Benito are dull commercial centers.

Money Matters

The local peseta is officially tied to that of Spain. Currency is valued at 62.5 pesetas to $1.00 but is in reality not convertible. Equatorial CFA francs are acceptable; try to use them and avoid exchanging money.

Getting In and Out

Few visitors of any nationality have been able to get visas in recent years. You can try at the Mission to the United Nations of Equatorial Guinea. Your application may have to be approved by President Macias himself. There are embassies at Libreville in Gabon and Yaoundé in Cameroon. Apply in person.

There are no regular cargo or passenger ships to Santa Isabel or Bata. There are three flights a week between Douala and Santa Isabel, and five weekly flights between Santa Isabel and Bata. Irregular flights connect Bata and Libreville, in Gabon. Iberia Airlines operates a once-a-week service between Santa Isabel and Madrid. Small boats go to Nigeria.

Getting Around Within Equatorial Guinea

Santa Isabel can be explored on foot. You may sip coffee in the main plaza in front of the cathedral, walk to the port and beach, and enjoy 12 hours a day of television on free public sets (Spain's last pre-independence gift). Inexpensive local taxis take you to a cocoa estate and to the edge of the rain forest.

Bata can also be covered by walking but it lacks the attractiveness of Santa Isabel. Townspeople use the beach as a garbage dump. There are few passable roads into the interior and no reliable car rental services. A friend of ours managed a trip by public bus and wood-burning riverboat to Acalayoung, the southernmost community. Then for $20 he hired a pirogue that took him a few miles down the Muni River to Cocobeach (named by American missionaries) in Gabon, where he hired a taxi to Libreville. With luck and a knowledge of colloquial French but no Spanish, he was able to travel nearly 150 miles in 12 hours.

Where to Stay

Since independence, the government has made life difficult for the handful of resident Spanish and Portuguese businessmen who run the meager hotels and restaurants. The *Monterrey Hotel* in SANTA ISABEL and the *Gurea* in BATA were once tolerable but there is little current information.

What to See and Do

Strolling, swimming and people-watching in the cafes once made FERNANDO PO a leisurely, stylish experience, but visitors are now closely watched. The few remaining affluent Europeans and Africans live more quietly now. The political crackdown has closed bars and nightclubs. The public television sets are everywhere, broadcasting programs taped in Spain.

BATA was once a jumping-off point for visits to village carvers and sculptors. The masks carved by the Fang are among Africa's finest. At present, permission from the Ministry of the Interior is required for trips out of town.

Local Attitudes

The government is publicly anti-American and anti-Western and suspicious of foreigners. Leave your camera in your suitcase.

Weather, What to Wear, How Long to Stay

The mainland is wet, wet, wet. Rainwear, good walking shoes and light tropical clothes are essential. Fernando Po has cool ocean breezes but is only slightly less humid. March and April are the least wet months for a visit. The length of a stay is determined by government authorities, but two or three days for Fernando Po and one or two for Bata should suffice.

Communication

Spanish is the official language as well as the lingua franca of Fernando Po. Pidgin English is widely spoken. On the mainland the people speak Spanish and, in Bata, some French as well. There are no regular newspapers.

Emergencies

There is a United States Embassy at Santa Isabel at Armengol Coll and Asturias Streets, but it's not likely to be much help. The American Ambassador resides in Yaoundé, Cameroon. In 1970, his chargé d'affaires killed the second-in-command, the only American ever convicted of murder while a diplomat. Since then the post of chargé has been vacant.

Medical services are inadequate.

Gabon

(République du Gabon)

Profile

STATUS: Independent republic since August 17, 1960. Formerly part of French Equatorial Africa.

SIZE: 103,347 square miles (about the size of Colorado). Population— 650,000.

GEOGRAPHY: Equatorial forest rising from Gulf of Guinea to interior plateau. Principal towns—Libreville (capital, 75,000), Port Gentil (40,000), Lambaréné (10,000).

CLIMATE: Equatorial. Heavy rains March to June and October to December. Dry season, June through September; relatively cool with daytime temperatures in low 80's, evening temperatures in the 60's.

LANGUAGES: French (official), Fang and Bantu languages.

CURRENCY: Equatorial CFA franc. CFA 100 = 40 cents; $1.00 = CFA 245.

VISAS: Required. Available from Gabon Embassy in Washington. Fee $10. Three photos and letter of reference needed. Try French consulates wherever Gabon is not represented.

AIRPORT: Libreville (LBV), eight miles from city. Linked daily with Paris and Douala; less frequently with major African capitals. Taxis into city should cost CFA 700 ($2.80) but be sure to fix price before starting. Hotel buses also available.

NATIONAL HOLIDAYS: August 17, Independence Day; November 28, Republic Day; Christian holidays.

405

INFORMATION SOURCES: *In US*—Embassy of Gabon, 4900 16th Street NW, Washington, D.C. 20011 (tel. 202/829-9070); Permanent Mission of Gabon to the UN, 866 United Nations Plaza, New York, N.Y. 10017 (tel. 212/751-2170). *In Libreville*—Office National Gabonais du Tourisme, P.O. Box 403 (tel. 21-82).

By *Philip M. Allen*

This rugged forestland astride the equator lives under a fortunate star. Its mineral and timber resources, protective forest shield, low population density, the unflagging favor of its ex-colonial French patrons, and an open door to Westerners have permitted Gabon to enjoy an economic boom in a smaller, simpler political context than those of Zaïre or the Ivory Coast. Almost all investment and technology come from overseas; if most raw materials and profits pass quickly into foreign hands, enough remains behind to give the Gabonese one of the highest standards of living in Africa. A visit to Gabon has limited but distinct appeal, particularly to hunters and fishermen, surf-riders and skindivers, and to those who admire a neat, successfully exploited primary economy.

Gabon is 100,000 square miles of thickly timbered landscape with lighter savanna and virtual desert on its edges, a mineral-laden plateau in the north and east, a scattering of low-slung mountains, and some splendid beaches on a coastline of river deltas and lagoons. Gorillas, chimpanzees, buffalo, hippos, various antelopes, myriad birds and elephants both large and dwarf (assala) inhabit broad hunting zones, three national parks and four game reserves. The sea and lagoons hold barracuda, sawfish, scad, barfish, cavallys, tarpon and shark. In the rivers and lakes there are Nile perch.

About 180,000 of the 650,000 Gabonese belong to the warrior Fang (Pahouin) people who pushed down from north-central Africa through the Cameroonian savanna into northern Gabon, reaching the Ogooué River a century ago. There are also large groups of Eshira, Mpongwé-Mitsogho in the west and center, Bakota on the edges of Fang territory, Bapounou in the southeast, Adouma and Okandé river peoples, a scattering of smaller Bantu groups and remnants of the aboriginal Babinga Pygmies in the forests where they retreated in front of invading Bantu and Fang. Thousands of imported laborers from neighboring nations work the mines and timberlands, and some 15,000 European residents provide technical know-how and management in exchange for some of the fat of the land.

Almost half the Gabonese are claimed by various Christian churches; Islam has barely penetrated into these forests.

Portuguese, Dutch, French, Belgians and others have splashed about the Gabonese coasts since 1470. France began its explorations of the interior after securing coastal privileges from Mpongwé kings in 1839 and 1842. Libreville, the capital, absorbed a number of slaves freed by the French navy, and France declared the territory as its colony in 1890. Although isolated by its forests from the rest of the continent, Gabon joined Moyen-Congo (Congo-Brazzaville), Oubangui-Chari (now the Central African Republic) and Chad in the French Equatorial African complex (AEF). Educational and missionary activity prospered, and a small Gabonese elite has worked in government and international organizations for several decades.

Gabon participated passively in the post-war evolution of French colonies toward self-determination. It obtained republican status within the shortlived Gaullist Communauté after the referendum of September 1958, and independence on August 17, 1960. Its first president, the autocratic Léon M'Ba, was restored to power by French paratroopers with considerable bloodshed in February 1964 after having been deposed by disgruntled military and civilian elites. M'Ba died in 1967, following a long illness during which he prepared for the succession of youthful Albert-Bernard Bongo. President Bongo has reformed M'Ba's administration and party with a deft, businesslike political touch—but without altering Gabon's policy of cooperation with French and other overseas interests.

There are plans afoot—by French and American interests and Air Afrique's affiliate Hotafric—to develop the new Intercontinental Hotel at Libreville as the cornerstone of an equatorial "Riviera" extending from Cap Estérias to the border of Congo-Brazzaville. To populate the prospective vacation facilities in this remote geographical cranny, Gabon counts on a few very European recreational drawing cards. These include the proximity to one another of good hunting and fishing—along several fine rivers as well as at seacoast sites like Setté Cama and Mayumba. The ambitious 350-mile "Transgabon" railway, still not entirely funded, represents a cardinal point in planning. In addition, Gabon's artistic resources are comparable in quality, if not abundance, to those of most competing tourist citadels (Cameroon, Zaïre, Zambia, Angola) and superior to those of Southern and East Africa. Dr. Albert Schweitzer's famous "bush" hospital at Lambaréné can also be counted on for several hundred visitors each year.

These attractions are limited in scope, however, and the country has some drawbacks as well.

It is hard to get to, with few decent roads and a very expensive internal air travel system. Visa charges for Americans ($10) are far above the going rate. Mediocre French cuisine is offered by overpriced hotels and restaurants, and there are few alternatives for the modest budget. The cost of living for travelers is far above that of East, North and Southern Africa. What's more, the Gabonese bureaucracy can be difficult about visas, hunting-fishing licenses, taxes and the like.

Few Gabonese, unfortunately, have any role in this proposed tourist industry, except as laborers and service personnel. Their villages, economy, religion, dress, cuisine and culture are all viewed either as mere curiosities or as anachronisms irrelevant to the vacation experience.

The ebullient British naturalist Mary Kingsley came to Gabon toward the turn of the century "in search of fish and fetish" and her book, *Travels in West Africa: Congo Français, Cousco and Cameroons* (London, Frank Cass, 3rd ed., 1965), like the writings of Albert Schweitzer (for example, his *African Notebook*, Peter Smith, 1958), provides a sense of how Christian Europeans approached this "primeval" forest country. Brian Weinstein's *Gabon, Nation-Building on the Ogooué* (MIT Press, 1966) is a standard American political science profile of the new state.

Money Matters

The CFA franc used in Gabon can be spent in Cameroon, the Central African Republic, Congo (Brazzaville) and Chad, and can be converted within the franc zone. It exchanges for about CFA 245 to the US dollar. The Union Gabonaise de Banque (UGB) at Libreville, Port Gentil, Oyem and Franceville is associated with Morgan Guaranty as well as the French Crédit Lyonnais and the Deutsche Bank; the Banque Internationale de l'Afrique Occidentale (First National City Bank of New York) and the Banque Nationale de Paris have Libreville and Port Gentil branches, as well as offices throughout French-speaking Africa. Banks are open from 7:30 to 11:30 am and 2:30 to 4:30 pm, Monday through Friday.

Gabon's cost of living for city dwellers and travelers is extremely high, comparable with Abidjan, Dakar and Lagos.

Getting In and Out

To reach Gabon from the United States, you must change planes in France or West Africa. Libreville and Port Gentil have considerable traffic in cargo steamers, including those of the Farrell Lines out of New York, the Compagnie Fabre from Marseille, and the Chargeurs Réunis from Bordeaux. Some cruise ships also call at Libreville, but there is no passenger liner service to Gabon. Parts of Gabon's single international highway—Brazzaville-Dolisie-Lambaréné-Oyem-Yaoundé (Cameroon)—are handsome, but little of the Gabonese section is paved and the rains take a heavy toll in spring and fall. Hitchhiking presents few problems, but traffic is light.

Americans must have visas for Gabon and must show a ticket out. Transit visas are available at the airport and the port of Libreville. If you haven't a tourist visa, come with the intention of leaving forthwith, and extend your transit visa at police headquarters if you like the place enough to pay $10.

Getting Around Within Gabon

Many parts of Gabon are inaccessible by road, or can be reached only during the dry season. The few roads that do exist are served by collective taxis only. Gabon's first railroad is due to begin operations in 1973 between the Belinga iron deposits in the northeast and a new port at Owendo on the estuary just south of Libreville. Gabon's several big rivers have cargo traffic (150 miles up the Ogooué, for example), pleasure boating, canoeing and floating logs, but no passenger boats.

Two internal airlines cover the country's two dozen airfields with scheduled flights, charter arrangements—and rates that suit only international businessmen and government officials traveling on expense accounts. Transgabon flies out of Libreville to Lambaréné (1¼ hours) for $34 one way; to Franceville (2 to 3 hours) for $73; Moanda (1 hour) for $73, and Port Gentil (45 minutes) for $22. Air Gabon shuttles between Port Gentil and eight airfields including Setté Cama (2¼ hours; $41.50). All rates are subject to a 7 per cent tax.

You can rent three-passenger planes for about $80 per hour and 12-seat Dorniers for $225. Round trip safari flights between Port Gentil and Setté Cama cost from $250 to $335 (plus 7 per cent tax), depending on the number of passengers.

Automobiles with or without drivers can be rented at Auto-Service in Libreville and Port Gentil, as well as Garage Bazaille in Libreville; cars without drivers are available at Auto-Gabon in the capital. Small cars rent for $8 a day (60 free kilometers) plus 12 cents per kilometer; larger vehicles cost $14 plus 16 cents per kilometer; Land Rovers cost $20 a day plus 20 cents per kilometer above the first 60 kilometers; Toyota Land Cruisers hire for a flat $40 per day. Gas costs the customer CFA 64.50 per liter for regular, CFA 69 per liter for higher test (1.00 to $1.05 per gallon).

Town taxis are very busy these days; 50 francs takes you anywhere within city limits.

Tours and tourist information are available from the Tourisme et Voyages en Afrique (TVA) agency (international SCAC system, with

Socopao affiliates at Port Gentil and Moanda). The TVA can be reached by writing to Box 161 in Libreville (tel. 21-00).

Where to Stay

The opening of LIBREVILLE's *Gabon Intercontinental* in January 1972 started the country off on the tourist quest. With 154 air-conditioned rooms, a casino, night bar and other amenities the Intercontinental, across the road from the beach, gives businessmen and foreign dignitaries a suitable place to stay, albeit with somewhat less luxury and expense than the Ivoire Intercontinental at Abidjan. The Relais Aériens Français (Air France) mainstay, *Le Roi Denis*, on the beach, is a good second choice in the higher price category at $15.50 to $17.20 for singles, $18 to $20 for doubles. *Le Gamba* at the airport charges about the same for air-conditioned rooms, with a few lower priced non-air-conditioned accommodations; likewise *Le Tropicana*, a thatched-roof beach complex in a palm grove just outside town.

The good *Hôtel Louis*, as well as the *Central*, the *Hôtel Moderne* and the *Glass Hôtel* in town are more modest in accommodations and price, but nothing is really cheap in Gabon.

Le Grand Tarpon is PORT GENTIL's luxury place (a Relais Aériens) on the sea, with rooms from $16.50 to $19. *Le Provençal* and the *Hôtel Hatari* are smaller and better buys ($9 to $12 at the Provençal with air-conditioning). LAMBARÉNÉ has the very comfortable *Hôtel de l'Ogooué* in the center of town with a beautiful view of the river and rooms from $8 to $12. MOANDA's *Hôtel de la Comilog* is an interesting community center for Europeans in an isolated company town. N'DENDE's *Oasis* is small with adequate facilities. Hunting lodges at BOOUÉ and SETTÉ CAMA (Patry Cie., Box 403, Libreville) are satisfactory. There are government rest-houses (gîtes) with minimal facilities at M'BIGOU, FRANCEVILLE, LASTOURSVILLE and MAYUMBA (also a Roman Catholic mission here). The Wonga-Wongué National Park between Libreville and Port Gentil has the Campement du Petit Bam-Bam, with sleeping huts, restaurant and pool.

CUSO Volunteers live in several towns, and a few missionaries will offer beds to wanderers, but inexpensive touring remains a little-known phenomenon in Gabon.

Where and What to Eat

High priced European and international meals can be readily found in LIBREVILLE—the best ones at *Le Surcouf*, *Le Tropicana* and *L'Auberge du Cap* at Cap Estérias. For their ambiance and variety try *Le Shangrila*, *Snack Komo* (bright little night bar next to a cinema), *Le Vietnam*, *L'Oliverade* and *Brasserie de l'Océan*.

Gabonese specialties, based on cassava dough or flour, plantain and fish, can be sampled at *La Case Bantoue* and *Kinguélé*, or in hotels and large restaurants upon 24 hours notice.

Excellent seafood and imported French fare are available in PORT GENTIL at the *Provençal Hôtel*, *Le Café du Wharf* and *L'Esquinade*. LAMBARÉNÉ's *Hôtel de l'Ogooué* has menus starting at $6 with wine.

What to See and Do

For forest fanciers, surf and sea enthusiasts and athletic vacationers, Gabon offers distinguished pleasures, separated by an agreeable town or two. Pressed between estuary and forest, LIBREVILLE is clean, bright, green and modern without being urban, but the economic boom has begun bringing bulldozers to the palm-lined boulevards, and high-rise construction and heavy traffic to what used to be a colonial garden town wreathed in somnolence.

Libreville has a small museum with interesting ivory pieces, the handsome Peyrie Gardens in the center of town, attractive arcades in front of old colonial buildings like the Hôtel du Gouvernement, a harbor with massive okoumé logs afloat, and lively markets (Nombakélé and Mont Boué). In the African residential quarters (Akébé, Glass and Nombakélé) the nights hum with music.

Apart from a number of jumping bars like Le Son des Guitares, La Paillotte (discotheque) and (for scheduled dances) the Cercle des Métis, central Libreville is dead at night. Sports furnish diversions in town as well as outside: the Tropicana Beach (surfing and other pleasures), the Barracuda Boat Club, the pristine beaches across the estuary, horseback riding at the Club Hippique, golf, tennis and pool swimming. The streets are free of beggars.

From Libreville, an attractive road leads 25 miles northward to CAP ESTÉRIAS (Cape Asturias), a rocky, surf-heavy beach with crayfish, oysters and sea urchins to be tasted or caught, a number of fishing villages and (in the morning) up-creek markets to visit. TVA runs a four-hour tour out here for $10. The tour can be increased in time and expense by lunch at the Auberge. Some visitors will be interested in the new port and railway installations at OWENDO, a few miles south of Libreville.

The Mbei River country north of Kango has a cluster of Fang villages, the Kinguélé Falls and a new power dam. Eighty miles in the other direction out of Libreville, the *Wonga-Wongué National Park* can be reached only by air. Here, savanna and forest merge, with a good variety of game (but no hunting allowed), lakes and pools, and a comfortable camp lodge. The cost of Land Rover game runs is about $10 per person.

The hunting season south and east of Libreville extends from December 1 to the end of September; it is driest and coolest between mid-May and mid-September. Several safari packages available at Libreville or Port Gentil include guides, Land Rover and canoe, and gun and equipment rentals as well as room and board. For long hunting expeditions in the *Setté Cama Domaine* (estate) along the coast and in the "desert," savanna and forest south of *Petit Loango National Park*, write Maurice Patry, P.O. Box 403, Libreville. For safaris of less than a fortnight at the *Iguéla Domaine* north of the park, try Jean Chevet, P.O. Box 240, Port Gentil.

Iguéla and Setté Cama also have big game fishing facilities, with a good tarpon season from December to May. The principal hotels can help arrange deep-sea, estuary and river fishing.

PORT GENTIL thrives on its okoumé timber port, its off-shore oil installations, and several lively bars (La Cabane, Safari and L'Esquinade). Otherwise, the town is merely a launching pad for land, sea or river excursions. You can plummet the rapids and prowl the equatorial forests of the Ogooué River accompanied by expert Adouma canoers (piroguiers) from Lastoursville to Lambaréné in three to five days. (Fly from Libreville or Port Gentil to Lastoursville and make your arrangements there.) Or just take an exciting one-day canoe trip with the Okandé people from Booué to Ndjolé (fly or drive in and out, as you please). Ndjolé is the "St. Helena" where the great West African sultan Samory Touré was exiled in 1898 and buried in 1900.

LAMBARÉNÉ is first of all the Schweitzer Hospital, founded in 1913 and established at its present site in 1926. Directed by Dr. Walter Mung since Schweitzer's death in 1965, the hospital retains its "bush" atmosphere on 100 acres of concession land, with places for 600 patients and their families. Both hospital and town reflect their equatorial forest setting—surrounded by the waters of the Ogooué in the rainy seasons (March to June and October to December). It is humid but never excessively hot, and always exploding with flowers. Permits are required to visit the hospital, but you can obtain these through your hotel or tourist office. (No photographs allowed.)

The Hôtel de l'Ogooué in Lambaréné also has a boat for sightseeing on the fascinating river and nearby lakes.

A TVA tour from Libreville takes care of all arrangements, with an overnight stop at the Hôtel de l'Ogooué, for $60 plus air fare (about $56 round trip); groups of 30 can go down and back in one day for $64 per person, including air fare.

When traveling in the Ogooué River area, seek out music and dance at the festivals of the Adouma, Okandé or Mitsogho people—although don't be too confident of witnessing a genuine Bwiti (Mbouiti) cult celebration.

On the north-south highway south of Lambaréné, the town of Mouila is a market center where good masks and other carving of the Bapounou people can be found, as well as abundant big game. The remote village of M'Bigou to the east produces celebrated stone sculptures, small but massive figures reproducing in new craftsmanship the imagery and utensils of ancient wood carving.

Farther south, the Nyanga River waters another handsome valley, especially the area between Tchibanga and the coasts. The spacious lagoon behind Mayumba offers spectacular fishing. The Moanda-Mounana region above the upper Ogooué in the east has enormous deposits of manganese and uranium, in rolling hill country with lakes, waterfalls and antelope-inhabited savanna. Moanda is an artificial mining town of 11,000 with full facilities for African labor and white management, and a cable-car line that carries the manganese from this remote hillside 47 miles to the Congolese railhead of Mbinda.

What to Buy

Gabonese art is of good quality but not abundant. Collectors should look for the subtly carved Fang and Mpongwe masks and statues from the north, "Congolese" Bakota and Bateke wood sculpture from the south, and Bapounou masks in the central west—where ivory, model canoes and ebony are also carved (Mouila market, for example). Koumougari pottery from Tchibanga, stone statuettes from M'Bigou, as well as forest musical instruments, weapons and tools are all worth your consideration.

Gabon, by the way, issues some of the most attractive postage stamps you'll find anywhere.

Some town markets and the itinerant traders' stalls at Libreville have selections of craftwork from all West and Central Africa. Bargain intrepidly for your price. The National Tourist Office has a small gallery and the Masafric store (Avenue du Colonel Parent) features elegant jewelry made in Gabon. Most of Libreville's shops are French or Lebanese-run, featuring chic imports at high prices. They are normally open from 9 am to noon and 4 to 7 pm, six days a week.

Certain antique items, classified as national treasures, must be certified for export by the Libreville Museum.

Local Attitudes

Historically more intimate with Europe than any other part of the world, urban Gabonese live, dress and behave very much like the French. Americans were regarded with suspicion by touchy, pro-French governments in 1964, after the aborted deposition of President M'Ba, and in 1967-68, when the Peace Corps was evicted from the country on still unexplained grounds. Modest American aid commitments and the substantial profits repatriated by mining companies probably don't fully ease the official attitude, but in any case individual Americans have little difficulty enjoying Gabon.

You should get on-the-spot permission to photograph Bwiti cult and other religious rituals.

Weather, What to Wear

The inland forests retain an almost year-round humidity, but Gabon's temperatures are generally quite mild. There are heavy rains from March to June and October to December, and showers throughout the year except for July and August. December to May is a good season for the beach: skies are clear, days are warm, showers come at night. The dry season, from June through September, is relatively cool (evening temperatures frequently in the 60's, daytime heat seldom above the mid-80's), with considerable cloud cover but low humidity. This is the best period for animal watching and town sightseeing. Fishing conditions vary: June to November favors the river fisherman, while October to May is best for sea and lagoon fishing.

Sweaters and heavy garments are necessary in Gabon only for rare nights in the uplands and for Libreville air-conditioning. Raingear is advisable for those who wear such things at home. Loose, comfortable, easily washable clothing is suitable for the entire country, and you never need worry about formality of attire, unless you need a sport shirt or chemise veste for some diplomatic function.

Communication

A small group of privileged and educated Gabonese participate in the Francophone world, although the rate of literacy among the whole population is low. But today an estimated 75 per cent school enrollment guarantees a fairly widespread knowledge of French among young Gabonese. Few people here speak English, however, and in the bush the common languages are Fang in the north and dialects of Bantu elsewhere.

Radio-telephone and telegraph connections function 24 hours a day with Paris, but communications for other destinations are generally inefficient.

Emergencies

Economic prosperity has helped support a relatively good network of health facilities. There are 70 doctors in five main hospitals, including a modern installation at Libreville. The celebrated Lambaréné station is considerably more up-to-date now than it was in the early 1960's when Dr. Schweitzer was criticized for maintaining an anachronism offensive to modernizing Africa. The other three hospitals are at Port Gentil, Oyem and Mouila. The small American Embassy in Libreville stands near the ocean front on Boulevard de la Mer (tel. 20-03).

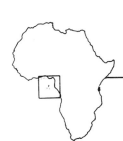

São Tomé and Principe

(Ilhas do São Tomé e Principe)

Profile

STATUS: Overseas Province of Portugal. Administered by governor-general responsible to Lisbon.

SIZE: 372 square miles (combined). Population—70,000 (93 per cent on São Tomé).

GEOGRAPHY: Archipelago in Gulf of Guinea. São Tomé—low, marshy coast rising steeply to mountains (Mt. São Tomé, 6,643 feet). Principal town—São Tomé (capital, 10,000). Principe—mountainous. Principal town—Santo Antonio (port, 1,000).

CLIMATE: Temperatures in the 80's on coast and between 50 and 65 degrees in uplands. Driest season May to September.

LANGUAGES: Portuguese (official), Creole dialect.

CURRENCY: Escudo, divided into 100 centavos (1$00). Not convertible. 10$00 = 37 cents; US$1.00 = 27$00.

VISAS: Required. Available through Portuguese consulates in New York, Boston, Newark, San Francisco. Fee $5.85. Expect delay of three to four weeks while application is sent to Portugal for political clearance.

AIRPORT: São Tomé (TMS), linked twice weekly with Angola only.

NATIONAL HOLIDAYS: June 10, National Day; October 5, Proclamation of Republic; December 1, Independence Day; Catholic holidays.

INFORMATION SOURCES: *In US*—Portuguese Tourist Information Bureau, 570 Fifth Avenue, New York, N.Y. 10036 (tel. 212/581-2450); Portu-

417

guese Consulate General, 630 Fifth Avenue, New York, N.Y. 10020 (tel. 212/246-4580); also 31 Commonwealth Avenue, Boston, Mass. 02116; 10 Commerce Street, Newark, N.J. 17102; 3298 Washington Street, San Francisco, Cal. 94115. *In São Tomé*—Centro de Informação e Turismo, P.O. Box 40, São Tomé (cable TURISMO). *In Portugal*—Palacio Foz, Avenida da Liberdade, Lisbon.

By Philip M. Allen

Equatorial possessions of Portugal since 1470, the tiny, beautiful islands of São Tomé and Principe have been overlooked by tourists and barely touched by the recent winds of political change in Africa. For the traveler, this most obscure of Portugal's "overseas provinces" is an offbeat, inexpensive place of quiet and lovely beaches, great fishing and luxuriantly forested hills.

Portugal counts 83 per cent of the archipelago's 70,000 people as "natives," another 4,500 as "Europeans," and the rest as temporary labor. All came to the originally uninhabited islands in the Gulf of Guinea from other parts of the Portuguese empire—Angola, the Cape Verde Islands, Brazil and Portugal itself. Some of the temporary workers are on four- or five-year contracts; others are prisoners or political detainees from more embattled Portuguese territories. Charges of forced labor in São Tomé were confirmed by a United Nations inquiry in the 1950's and the last of many uprisings by Africans was put down with much bloodshed in 1953.

For centuries, the islands served as a base for the slave trade with Brazil. Sugar cane and other crops were cultivated by Portuguese Jews shipped there from the motherland in the 16th century after refusing to convert to Christianity. The islands now depend heavily on cocoa, but also produce coffee, bananas, coconuts, palm oil, cinnamon and vanilla.

The economy is controlled by several great families in Portugal who seldom visit the islands but do provide certain paternalistic services to their black and mulatto plantation employees. Primary education is nearly universal, although virtually no pupil can afford to attend school past the sixth year. Health care is free, villages and housing compounds are clean and attractive and food appears abundant. However, the population is growing faster than the colonial economy, forcing many young men to emigrate to Angola. Export earnings go to Portugal and imports are at a minimum. Development investment is barely beginning. While racial discrimination is not legally sanctioned, the better jobs are invariably reserved for whites.

Most activity takes place on São Tomé island, three miles north of the equator, containing seven-eighths of the area and 93 per cent of the archipelago's population. Principe is 90 miles to the north, about 155 miles from the Benin coast just east of Lagos (Nigeria).

From 1967 to 1969, São Tomé found itself involved as a supply station for arms, equipment and food destined for the rebel Biafran side in the Nigerian civil war.

The islands' few visitors come either from Portuguese-ruled Angola (which is developing its own tourist industry at a more rapid pace) or from French-speaking Gabon, 175 miles along the equator from São Tomé. They come to a quiet place with lush, dramatically vertical topography rising out of steamy marshes and fine beaches to volcanic heights up to 6,643 feet (Mt. São Tomé).

The capital, also called São Tomé, is a charming and immaculate town with the sultry somnolence of colonial oblivion. Tall green trees burst out of the forest, impinging on coffee and cocoa farms, surrounding the simple tin-roofed cabins of the country people, lining the island's excellent roads, and plunging down steep slopes and ravines. The forest basks in flowers and its steady concourse is with birds. Its streams have trout and crayfish, and at the shores the crescent bays contain an extraordinary variety of game fish and seafood.

Literature on São Tomé in English scarcely exists. There is an informative but strictly official government handbook entitled *S. Tomé e Principe, A Brief Survey* (Lisbon, Agencia-Geral do Ultramar, 1970). It is available from Portuguese Embassy information offices and on São Tomé itself. You'll also find some background information in James Duffy's *Portuguese Africa* (Harvard University Press, 1959); *Portuguese Africa, A Handbook*, edited by David M. Abshire and Michael A. Samuels; and Ronald H. Chilcote's *Portuguese Africa* (Prentice-Hall, 1967).

Money Matters

Portugal has endowed each of its four African "provinces" with a currency, all pegged at identical rates to the metropolitan escudo. São Tomé's money exchanges at about 27 escudos to the US dollar (note the use of the $ symbol as a decimal). These escudos are worthless outside the islands. Dollars and travelers checks are accepted by restaurants and major businesses, but credit cards haven't reached São Tomé yet. The Banco Nacional Ultramarino has offices in the town of São Tomé and in Santo Antonio on Principe island. Bank hours are from 8 to 11:30 am and 2 to 4:30 pm, including Saturdays.

Getting In and Out

Some passenger ships and freighters, mainly Portuguese and Dutch, make occasional calls at São Tomé harbor.

The capital's airfield receives two weekly flights from Angola, connecting with TAP service to Lisbon. Political antipathies make more extensive connections with the African mainland impractical, but there is an occasional Trans-Gabon Airlines charter flight bringing French residents from Gabon.

Immigration and customs are relaxed, but Americans do need visas and the Portuguese are as touchy about clearances here as they are for Angola or Mozambique.

Getting Around Within São Tomé and Principe

Buses and taxis convey traffic over 100 miles of narrow but well-paved mountain roads on São Tomé, radiating from the capital. The great plantations keep their own roads in good condition. The rest of the main island and all of Principe are linked by hard-packed dirt roads and pathways. Santo Antonio, Principe's capital and port, can be reached in a half-day by water or in 35 minutes by air four times weekly from São Tomé (about $17 round trip).

Porto Alegre in the south of São Tomé has a small relief airport with two flights a week from São Tomé.

Just beginning to think about exploiting the islands' tourist potential, the Centro de Informação e Turismo provides information on request. Several shipping agents offer tour facilities, including Cosema (Mr. Carlos Martin de Sousa, P.O. Box 11), or Mr. Eduardo Castela (Box 134), and Casa Inglesa (representing British Hull, Blyth, Box 15).

Cosema rents Mercedes cars for about $5 a day and 6 cents per kilometer, not including gasoline (which costs about 70 cents per gallon). Chauffeur-driven vehicles with free gasoline rent for $23 a day. Stomauto (Germano Castella, P.O. Box 130) also has cars for rent. Boats can be hired from Cosema for island tours.

Where to Stay

Accommodations suffice for current tourist traffic, and they are very reasonably priced. The *Pousada* (government tourist hotel) *São Jerónimo* on the edge of São Tomé town has quite satisfactory full-pension facilities for under $10 per person per day. The *Pensão Henriques* and *Pensão Turismo*, both family guest houses in the town, offer simple meals and lodgings for about $6. *Restaurant Bar Yong* also has simple rooms at very low cost.

The island's principal hotel is the *Pousada Salazar*, perched 2,500 feet above the bay near SITIO DA SAUDADE and the São Nicolau falls. It takes buses 30 minutes to climb the 10 miles from São Tomé town. The *Salazar* has comfortable rooms and bath for $5 single and $6 double; single rooms without private bath rent for less than $4. Good Portuguese food and local specialties cost from $2 to $3 per meal (plus wine).

Downhill from Saudade, the *Presidencial da Trindade* in the mountain village of TRINDADE has rooms without private bath for less than $4 and rooms with bath for $5.50. Like the Salazar, the Presidencial has frequent overnight and weekend guests from the coasts of São Tomé seeking fresher air and recreation in the hills.

In SANTO ANTONIO, Principe, the *Pensão Cabral Sacadura* offers full pension accommodations for about $5 per person.

Where and What to Eat

Menus at the hotels and at the *Restaurant Palmar* near the governor's palace in São Tomé town feature seafood, mountain stream crayfish, pork, chicken or river fish served with beans or rice, pounded cassava or yam and an abundance of fruit. In addition to Portuguese stew (mocótó), local specialties include calúlú, a bean casserole with fish or chicken and spices; jogo, a rice and fish platter with peppers and greens; and fuba, a variation on continental African pounded plantain or cassava, served with palm oil sauce and spices. Sturdy Portuguese "green" table wines are available everywhere in pitchers.

What to See and Do

The old town of SÃo TomÉ arranges its neat, low-slung buildings, plazas, gardens and shops behind a rather sultry bayside esplanade. An hour's walk, with pauses at a couple of cafes, acquaints the visitor with the capital and its few places of note (Esplanade Gardens, Republic Square, the governor's residence, the Catholic church, a couple of explorers' statues). Fishing villages and suburbs of tin-roofed palmwood cabins on stilts, garden patches and chickens line the roads from São Tomé, which lead out to the great plantations.

The center and most of the humid southwest consist of virtually untouched timber. The ocean winds have borne the seeds of coconut palms and baobabs from drier Africa, along with breadfruit, mangoes, bananas, guavas, malagueta, ocas, mangrove, ironwood, rubber trees, cinchona, kola nut trees and trumpetwood from the humid climes. Glorious ferns, bougainvillea, extraordinary cannas, crotons and coleae—all in constant bloom—carpet the ground.

The roça (plantation) Rio do Ouro near GUADELOUPE village in the north welcomes visitors to its impressive fields, handsome experimental gardens and small zoo. You can obtain permission to visit from the resident manager. On the road south from São Tomé town, pretty square-sailed fishing boats line the beach at PRAIA MELÃO, and by turning inland from there, you pass a little "fetish temple" at CRUZEIRO on the right-hand side of the road just before turning off for Trindade.

Principe island is less rugged in topography but more primitive than São Tomé, with few roads and little electricity. Its port capital, SANTO ANTONIO, is a neat, sleepy town. Three miles south of São Tomé island, the geodesic equator passes through the tiny island of ROJAS (Gago Coutinho) where a coconut plantation provides a living for about 100 people. The path of the equator through Rojas is marked by two monuments.

The islands have few animals of interest, but their bird life and ocean fishing are among the richest in the eastern Atlantic. Local fishermen will take visitors out for a modest fee for a try at barracuda, sailfish, marlin, tarpon, Alison shark, giant mackerel, bonito, sawfish, sea perch, sea bream, snapper, kingfish, herring, sardine, sole, tuna, and even whales, grampus, manta ray, dolphin and sea turtles.

A courtly, archaic Portugal blends with attenuated African rhythms and dance to produce a countryside Creole culture of carnival, mime and pageantry on one hand, and a calypso-like insular high-life in the towns. The Congo dance and "tchólóli" use traditional mime, allegorical or mythical characters, fanciful wired headdresses of crepe paper, flowers, birds and bells, and the resources of drum, gourd rattle, bamboo scraper and flute to arrive at a stately, yet vivacious and brisk, dance theater. Many local groups also perform the "socopé" and "tuna" dances in colorful costumes and with ceremonial patterns like the minuet, alternating with abandoned, driving movement. These performances can be seen on some Sundays in the countryside and during pre-Lenten carnival time (or some other special occasion) in the town square.

What to Buy

São Tomé and Principe produce little of special interest—except for the fascinating wicker construction (bird cages in the form of cathedrals, for instance) and votive carvings that African families seldom consent to put on the market. There is a standard supply of beads, shells, tortoise-shell fans and mother-of-pearl jewelry, both in the shops and at the Maritime Station where boys hawking cheap necklaces descend on all strangers.

Local Attitudes

The islanders lead quiet, conservative lives, decorous in their habits, fervent in their religion, whether Catholic or animist. They are hospitable, tolerant people, and are not offended by reasonable foreign ways or curiosity. Portuguese political and military sensitivities exist, but political tempers are low—at least for the moment.

Weather, What to Wear, How Long to Stay

Visitors to the shores and hills of São Tomé must be prepared for a 20-degree variation in temperature between the two locations. The driest and most auspicious season for visiting is from mid-May to mid-September. However, the temperatures average 80 degrees on the coast (with high humidity) year-round, and between 50 and 65 degrees in the uplands. The "winter" rains usually come in sudden showers, but occasionally last for several days. Unless you are traveling independently, you haven't much choice of itinerary. Three days between flights suffice for the shores, hills and fishing expeditions, and another three for a sail to Principe (flying back to São Tomé in time to connect with the return flight to Luanda). Two weeks here requires unusual dedication to deep-sea fishing or diving, or a strong interest in plantation agriculture and bird life.

Communication

While Portuguese is the islands' language, the non-European majority speaks a Creole dialect that many Portuguese cannot understand. Some English is taught in the schools, but few pupils are exposed to it long enough to master it. Some businessmen and civil servants speak enough English or French to be helpful, but life is seldom so complicated that visitors require more than that.

Emergencies

São Tomé has good medical facilities, some of them established by plantation proprietors or missions. A good road and telephone system—and even the presence of a rather bored military contingent—might come in handy for crises. Complicated problems are treated in Luanda or in Lisbon. There is no American representation in the islands.

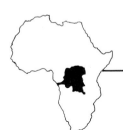

Zaïre

(République du Zaïre)

Profile

STATUS: Independent republic since June 30, 1960. Formerly Belgian Congo, later Democratic Republic of the Congo (Congo-Kinshasa).

SIZE: 905,567 square miles (equivalent of US east of Mississippi). Population—about 20,000,000 (about 65,000 Europeans).

GEOGRAPHY: Zaïre (Congo) River equatorial basin with low-lying forest, higher grassland plateau in south, mountains in east and west. Principal cities—Kinshasa (capital, 1,400,000), Lubumbashi (300,000), Luluabourg (400,000), Kisangani (180,000), Matadi (seaport, 80,000).

CLIMATE: Equatorial zones, mostly hot and humid with considerable rainfall. Substantial higher, cooler and drier areas, especially in east and south.

LANGUAGES: French (official), Lingala, Kizaïre (Kikongo), Tshiluba, Kingwana (Kiswahili).

CURRENCY: Zaïre (Z), divided into 100 makutas (k). Z1 = $2.00; $1.00 = 50k.

VISAS: Required. Available from Embassy of Zaïre and Zaïre Mission to UN. Fee $4.00 to $8.00 for tourist visa (fee depending on length of stay); transit visa $2.00 (up to eight days' stay). One passport photo and letter of responsibility needed. Takes two days; apply in person if possible.

AIRPORTS: N'Djili Airport (FIH), 14 miles from Kinshasa. Frequent connections with Western Europe, New York and South Africa, fewer within Africa. Taxi into city, Z2.50 ($5). Lubumbashi Airport (FBM), four miles from city; infrequent connections with Europe and Zambia.

NATIONAL HOLIDAYS: May 20, National Party Day; June 30, Independence Day; November 17, Army Day; Christian holidays.

INFORMATION SOURCES: *In US*—Embassy of the Republic of Zaïre, 1800 New Hampshire Avenue NW, Washington, D.C. 20009 (tel. 202/234-7690); Permanent Mission of the Republic of Zaïre to the UN, 400 East 51st Street, New York, N.Y. 10022 (tel. 212/758-8060). *In Kinshasa*—Office National du Tourisme, Hôtel Memling, P.O. Box 1399 (tel. 224-17).

By Philip M. Allen

Under its former name—the Congo—the country stood for much that was rough and untamed in the center of Africa. Now the former Belgian and Kinshasa Congo epitomizes vitality under growing discipline and a vision of general prosperity for 20 million people. Its great river coils and surges through a coalescence of powerful diversities that compose one of Africa's most surely developing nations. Also one of the most expensive and frustrating for visitors.

From 1482, when Portuguese Diego Cão found a highly organized and advanced Kongo kingdom commanding the river estuary, until after Henry Morton Stanley publicized his trek from East Africa to the Congo's mouth in 1877, Zaïre was a little-known territory interesting to Europe only as a source of slaves, suspected raw materials and challenging natural grandeur.

The past century gave free rein to the ambitions of foreigners like Leopold II, King of the Belgians, who owned this enormous territory personally from 1885 to 1907 (when he deeded it to the Belgian nation); Stanley, who represented Leopold and acted for himself; the compassionate imperialist David Livingstone; Conrad's fictional Kurtz; European industrialists, would-be Tarzans and white mercenary gunmen. Now, finally, Zaïre's enviable resources are becoming the fruitful property of Zaïrois (also sometimes known as Zaïreans).

This political-economic renaissance is reason enough for a visit (and indeed increasing numbers of American, European and Japanese businessmen are crowding government offices and the new Intercontinental Kinshasa). But there is more to Zaïre than development statistics. There is also strong artistry and music-making in town and countryside, one of Africa's finest national parks, and a variety of impressive landscape from the magnificent Mountains of the Moon to the great equatorial forests along the river.

Zaïre has disadvantages as well. You are not always treated politely and you won't always be comfortable. Hands are extended for bribes (matabish) everywhere you go. Hotels, trade and government agencies are disorganized. Transportation and communications are a mess. The country is expensive and its capital, Kinshasa, is provincial, pretentious, unsympathetic in the center—albeit animated enough on the outskirts where Zaïrois live.

At present, a compulsory "cultural revolution," baptized "Recours à l'Authenticité" (return to authenticity), has caused confusion over the names of people and places, aroused antagonisms at home and abroad (particularly with some of the powerful Catholic clergy of the country), and provoked skeptics to warn of atavism and mystification in a state destined for modernity.

Visitors must beware of a Z20 ($40) daily exchange rule: on leaving the country, you must show exchange receipts amounting to this sum multiplied by the number of calendar days (or fraction thereof) spent in the country. If your certificates fall short of the total, you are obliged to make up the difference on the spot, or you may be refused permission to leave.

Although bribery and fast-talking have been known to help get around the rule, some people prefer to skip Zaïre.

Self-government came in 1960 to the old Belgian Congo, big as all of Western Europe, but real independence was achieved only a decade later under fire and brimstone. For that vast, lugubrious "heart of darkness" derided by Joseph Conrad, Vachel Lindsay and the dying Dr. Livingstone, the butt of our cannibal jokes and Tarzan myths, modern life began with a mock republic tortured by secession in the south, rebellion in the east, foreign intrigue everywhere, and corrupt politics at the roots.

Its tragic nationalist Prime Minister Patrice Lumumba died under mysterious circumstances in 1961, while UN troops, Belgian colons and dissident tribalists kept the new nation at bay. Erstwhile Katangan secessionist leader Moïse Tshombé, Lumumba's opposite in everything, died in 1969, after four years of exile. Durable President Joseph Kasavubu died in retirement, a symbol of immobility and inefficacy under pressure. In all, a half-million Zaïrois went to less-publicized deaths between 1960 and 1968.

But in November, 1965, a new military dictatorship under General Mobutu Sese Seko (then Colonel Joseph-Désiré Mobutu) began to end the ordeal. By mid-1967 Mobutu's regime had inaugurated a period of stability, internal cohesion and social change, converting its own status into that of an elected government of the single-party Mouvement Populaire de la Révolution (MPR). In October, 1971, the wealthy, hapless Congo became independent Zaïre, named for its great river in the old language of the coastal peoples.

All ethnic communities of middle Africa inhabit this continental heartland, and indeed nobody knows for sure whether 18 million or 22 million people live there. The Zaïrois speak over 200 languages, ranging from Swahili in the east to a panoply of Bantu tongues (more than half the total) spread throughout the land. There are something less than 100,000 Pygmies in the Ituri and Kivu forests.

Christianity claims at least one-third of the Zaïrois, most of them Roman Catholic, although at least two million belong to indigenous, syncretic churches like the Kimbanguists (followers of the latter-day Prophet Simon Kimbangu) which blend Christian doctrine with traditional African (animist) principles and rituals.

An industrial proletariat, schooled to the sixth year in mission institutions, was fostered by the Belgians for service in mines, plantations and factories. After the ravages of rebellion and economic chaos, there has been a quick, new, very impressive growth of younger, technocratic elites to man the higher posts that "Congolese" had never hoped to occupy.

Apart from the important human dynamics, Zaïre's strength derives from copper in Shaba (ex-Katanga) Province, produced at a rate of nearly 500,000 tons a year (fifth ranking in the world), as well as cobalt and industrial diamonds (world leader in both), zinc, tin, manganese, bauxite, timber (mahogany, teak, ebony), ivory, small amounts of gold and other precious metals, and, lately, oil.

Hydroelectric power from the Zaïre River is potentially the greatest in the world (one-sixth the total world potential). Zaïre's immense basin of forestland, plateau savanna and mountain fringes permit a wealth of food and export crops (palm oil, cotton, rubber, coffee, cocoa, tea, tobacco, sugar cane, fruits), with beef cattle in the east, south and western panhandle.

With a colonial heritage of industry and plantation agriculture and since 1967 a stable national currency, Zaïre struggles with transportation, communication and bureaucratic inefficiencies throughout the enormities and diversities of the new economy. Mobutu's regime seeks remedies through combinations of self-reliance (nationalization of major industries, state participation in other enterprises, rapid advancement of nationals— frequently at the cost of considerable initial disorder), foreign initiative and international aid. American commitments from 1960 to date approximate one-half billion dollars, and private American interests have invested in mining and metallurgy, chemicals, diamonds, automotive assembly, grains, rubber, electronics, equipment manufacturing, oil drilling and hotels. The US is also Zaïre's leading supplier and second customer (after Belgium). The French, Italians, Japanese, West Germans, British and others are also participating in the Zaïrois "miracle."

Once a closed colonial preserve, subsequently tormented by corruption and fratricide, Zaïre is still a nation in flux, where all is energetic, nothing permanent, complete or perfect. It's a marvelous, but not an easy, place to visit. And that $40 rule is meant to keep out the bargain trade.

To start coming to terms with this immense republic, you might follow the scrupulously historical approach of Jan Vansina in *Kingdoms of the Savanna* (University of Wisconsin Press, 1968) or the contemporary political science approach of Crawford Young in *Politics in the Congo, Decolonization and Independence* (Princeton University Press, 1965). "The old horror" is best witnessed by Europeans in Henry Morton Stanley's *Journals*, Joseph Conrad's novel *Heart of Darkness* and André Gide's *Voyage au Congo*; the new in Conor Cruise O'Brien's *To Katanga and Back* (Simon and Schuster, 1962) and Catherine Hoskyns's *The Congo Since Independence* (Oxford, 1965).

Money Matters

The term "Zaïre" now stands for the republic, for the river and, since 1967, for an internationally traded currency, pride of the nation. One Zaïre, divided into 100 makutas, equals two American dollars. Each likuta (the singular form of makuta) is further subdivided into 10 sengi, which have little practical value for foreigners, prices being what they are. Zaïres can be exported only in limited quantities (Z200 unless otherwise authorized).

International airports at Kinshasa and Lubumbashi have exchange facilities. The official Office des Changes (Boulevard Lumumba in Kalina-Kinshasa) is open from 8 to 11:30 am, Monday through Saturday, while the Banque du Zaïre (affiliated with Morgan Guaranty), the new locally owned Banque de Kinshasa and the Société Zaïroise de Banque (affiliated with the Bank of America) are open from 8 to 11:30 am, five days a week. Travelers checks are universal coin and the recognizable credit cards will be honored in major hotels and shops.

Getting In and Out

A place of many portals, Zaïre provides several options for travelers, although nothing is simple. Big jets of Sabena, Air Zaïre, UTA and other lines come into Kinshasa regularly from Brussels, Paris and cities in Africa—although connections within the continent remain imperfect, thanks to differing French, British and Belgian transportation legacies. There are two weekly Pan American connections directly with New York, West Africa and Johannesburg. Lubumbashi in the south and Bukavu in the east also receive a small number of regionally oriented flights.

The border with Portuguese Angola is closed to passengers, precluding the cozy Old World Benguela Railway from Lobito on the coast to the Shaba copper country. However, combinations of road, rail and boat penetrate arduously through the Great Rift Valley and the mountainous lake country on Zaïre's eastern frontier to Kalémie (ex-Albertville) and other border stations. An overnight Lake Tanganyika cruise on the CFL company's 1926 steamer *Urundi* between Kalémie and Kigoma (Tanzania) is a rare experience of colonial *dolce far niente* for approximately $10.

The Zambia-Rhodesia Railway enters Zaïre at Mufulira between the Zambian and Zaïrois copperbelts. Zaïre's own Voie Nationale combines road, waterway and track to buckle the southeastern mining districts to the country's only seaport at Matadi, on a narrow panhandle at the foot of the immense western escarpment.

Matadi lies 100 miles up the Zaïre estuary, which separates Angola from Zaïre for a while, then narrows into perilous spirals and rapids after Boma, a timber port and former capital. The estuary passage is sailed by numerous international cargo ships, including Farrell Lines from New York (18 days to Matadi) and from Great Lakes ports in spring, summer and autumn (Farrell Lines Kinshasa office, P.O. Box 8753). The only all-passenger service to penetrate the continent through this artery thus far is Raymond and Whitcomb's African Quest winter cruises.

In 1975 a new rail segment of the Voie Nationale will permit embarkation or disembarkation at Banana on the Atlantic coast, with a new railroad bridge across the river at Matadi, on the way to the capital. The river is traversable between Kinshasa and Brazzaville (Republic of the Congo), just downstream from the lakelike bulge once known as Stanley Pool, now redesignated Malebo Pool. However, current political animosity between Brazzaville and Washington makes this portal either closed or perilous to Americans and the confusion in Brazzaville-Kinshasa relations has kept the ferry inactive for about half the past five years.

If you are hitchhiking, the only likely routes for free rides are in the south (with Zambia) and the east via Bukavu (with Uganda, Rwanda and Burundi). All overland border crossings require visas for each country touched.

Never arrive at Kinshasa by air on a Sunday unless you happen to be flying with the chief of state. Everything in town is dead, except that the airport (at N'Djili, 14 miles from town) remains its swarming, terrifying, venal, confusing self. If you have the time, confirm and reconfirm all reservations, hotel, transport, flights, and on departure get to the dreary airport very early before check-in time.

Once processed through what can only euphemistically be called "formalities," the visitor faces a storm of putative taximen demanding his patronage to town and beyond. Your only safe recourse is to choose an unoccupied vehicle, preferably an STK Mercedes taxi in apparent good condition with a meter that seems functional, and head steadfastly for it, baggage in hand. It's far better to have somebody meet you at the airport.

Although travel brochures refer to "complimentary airport transportation," few travelers have enjoyed such service. If you see the Air Zaïre microbus parked outside the air terminal, you can try to take it, but it's often reserved.

These lapses, among many others, indicate the distance Zaïre must still cover before it is ready to render satisfaction to the fastidious tourist traffic that it deserves. There are other things to watch out for: visa applications still ask for documentation of respectability (any letter of sponsorship will do). Visas cannot be obtained at airports without encountering appeals for bribes (don't comply). Customs, immigration, health controls and baggage handling at N'Djili continue to betray a penchant for disorder, venality and indignity that discredits the nation.

Getting Around Within Zaïre

Mileage figures for Zaïre's roads, rails and waterways run impressively into the tens of thousands, but the experience of getting around on them is something else again. A national development priority calls for major improvement in transportation, for even the precious minerals must emerge from the interior over a variety of fragmented, inefficient and inadequate systems. To travel over this giant land requires time and patience, as well as some tolerance: roads are seldom paved and usually in deplorable condition; trains and buses, operated by young public monopolies, don't run on time; Air Zaïre, now a ward of Pan American, remains staffed and managed below the level of its expensive equipment and priced far above the level of anybody's business.

One-way plane fare between Kinshasa and Bukavu (6:40 hours) is $356, Kisangani (4:20 hours) $116, Luluabourg (4 hours) $77, Lubumbashi (3:15 hours) $148.60, Moanda on the beach (2:20 hours) $38, and Mbuji-Mayi (4 hours) $82.20. A one-hour flight to Matadi Airport costs $23.40, but that's only the beginning of the journey, since the Matadi field stands one hour by truck over a rutted-laterite hairpin road to the ferry slip and an indefinite period of time from truck to rickety launch to a bus into town. Moreover, Air Zaïre food and service are wretched and schedules largely fictitious. Hence, Zaïre's 175 airports are often better served by a half-dozen assiduous private charter services and aero-clubs, but none of these is any bargain either.

However you travel, petty officialdom does its best to complicate things for you—with troubles in ticketing, reservations, permits, passes, taxes, office hours and the like. Yet it's impossible to stay in one place if Zaïre is going to be visited at all; you must simply get used to expecting annoyances, and rejoice when they don't turn into disasters.

The River Zaïre, Africa's third longest, grapples this land, courses over its soils, plunges into titanic electrical power reserves, and irrigates a gigantic basin. The river determines access in the north and west, just as the lake and mountain system opens and closes the east. Once at Matadi, the port, you are confronted upstream by 200 miles of falls, rapids and gorges, forcing everybody and everything to move overland up to Kinshasa. You can cover this ground either expensively by car (hitchhiking is possible, especially if you ask at the Hôtel Métropole and at the freight forwarders who send new cars and truck cargoes up to the capital by road), or more cheaply with the Zaïrois by bus. You can also take the curious, folksy, swaying rail trolley car called La Micheline, which leaves Matadi after lunch on Thursday and starts out in beautiful river landscape, becoming duller as it climbs in six hours or more to Kinshasa.

From Kinshasa, the public OTRAZA line operates river boats along the 1,100-mile trek via Mbandaka to Kisangani (ex-Stanleyville), capital of the northeast (Haut-Zaïre Province). This was Conrad's boatway into the "Heart of Darkness," through forests, waterscapes and canoe-commerce that remain as interesting as they were then. The stern-wheelers leave Kinshasa weekly, take seven or eight days to reach Kisangani, at a cabin fare of about $60 first class (other classes ride on deck or in towed barges). Food is good—much of it caught out of the river or purchased from canoes alongside—and accommodations adequate.

Make your bookings two or three weeks in advance if you can at the OTRAZA offices, Boulevard du 30 Juin, P.O. Box 98, Kinshasa (tel. 247-61). It's a trip you'll remember.

The seven cataracts of ex-Stanley Falls stop navigation 25 miles southeast (upstream) from Kisangani, and the circuit must proceed overland through the northeastern forests. The railroad or road from Kisangani to Ponthierville allows you to resume river travel, or you can continue eastward to the superb lake and mountain country on East Africa's frontiers, and subsequently into the drier, mineral-rich savannas of eastern Kasai and Shaba (ex-Katanga). A shorter way from Kinshasa into the south starts with smooth river or rough road passage to Ilebo (ex-Port Francqui) followed by a 750-mile southeasterly rail journey to Lubumbashi in Shaba, only parts of which are worth the trial.

Lubumbashi is linked by paved road south to Zambia, southwest to the mining town of Kolwezi (ex-Jadotville) and the Angolan border, and by all-weather roads north to the Lofoi Falls and the largely undeveloped Upemba National Park. Much of Shaba's mineral wealth passes out directly by rail through Angola to the port of Lobito. But while Portugal maintains sovereignty over Angola, Zaïre has political reasons to improve her Voie Nationale between Lubumbashi and Matadi or Banana, as well as the roads and bridges between Lubumbashi, Luluabourg and Kinshasa. Until these plans are realized, however, air travel remains the only rapid way of traversing Zaïre.

For the road, STK (Société des Transports Kinois) rents air-conditioned Mercedes taxis with chauffeur for upwards of $20 a day plus 20 cents per kilometer, plus gas, which costs about 45 cents a gallon. Autoloc in Kinshasa and agencies at the Okapi and Intercontinental hotels also rent vehicles; Autoloc's Volkswagens and other cars without chauffeur cost $12 to $16 a day plus 12 cents per kilometer and gas. Traffic drives on the right in Zaïre, at least most of the time. Once you've seen some of the roads and the traffic around Kinshasa, Matadi and Kisangani, you'll understand why Zaïrois drivers are uniformly skillful—all the poor and mediocre ones are dead.

Trucks and bush taxis, as well as more comfortable public buses (on approximate schedules) push into most places, even during the heavy rains. Hence hitchhiking and inexpensive public transit are feasible, if wearying and uncertain, alternatives. If you want to read or work on the bus, taxi or Micheline, take earplugs for defense against the constant blare of the radio (not all the music is good Congo jazz). Otherwise, getting around spacious Kinshasa involves very crowded public buses or hiring a car or taxi (expensive).

STK meter taxis in town cost 10 makutas (20 cents) per trip plus 8k (16 cents) per kilometer. Short hops in taxis without meters should cost 50k ($1), but if there isn't a meter, bargain the fare in advance, as taxi drivers have a merited reputation for rapacity, both in their driving and their salesmanship. Official American employees run their own inexpensive private VW-bus taxi service dispatched from the US Embassy.

Travel information in Kinshasa and other main cities is geared to air safaris, big towns and businessmen's hotels; there's little for the offbeat request. The Office National du Tourisme maintains a stock of literature at its Memling Hotel office and at headquarters on the Boulevard du 30 Juin just beyond the main post office. A number of travel agencies issue bulletins on what to do in the country and how to do it through them. The most capable of these include Agetraf, AMI and Menno (a subsidiary of the Menno Agency in Ephrata, Pennsylvania).

Where to Stay

At KINSHASA, where in 1970 the best a tourist could get was a shabby and unreliable old colonial detention house known as the Memling, there are now two solid hotels of international caliber and a number of smaller hostelries. Prices in the list that follows are unusually susceptible to change (upwards) and, unless otherwise noted, do not include breakfast, service charges (usually 10 per cent), taxes (another 10 per cent) or supplements for using the air-conditioners.

In Kinshasa-Kalina, 10 minutes from midtown, a new *Intercontinental* exemplifies that chain's plush, standardized accommodations and services aimed at American businessmen ($16 to $22). A bit farther out, on a lofty terrace in the chic Binza residential suburb, the UTH *Okapi Hôtel* ($14 to $18) offers some luxury, a swimming pool, terrace and other bars, and withdrawal from the bustle of Kinshasa.

In the center of the city, the old four-square *Regina* surrounds its aged courtyard like a Belgian school building, with equally outmoded utilities ($12 to $14). For the undemanding, there are also the superannuated *Memling* ($10 to $14; no credit cards), the cheaper *Bonanza* and the *Terminus*. Rather than patronize a dump, try the modest, clean, restaurantless *Excelsior* on Avenue du Port next door to Air Zaïre headquarters (where many travelers must willy-nilly pass much of their time seeking to straighten out "connections") for $13 including service, tax and breakfast.

For cheap lodgings, ask the Tourist Office for a list of pensions and guest houses in town or try the inexpensive, orderly compound of the Union Mission House on Avenue Banning (often filled by missionary families on their way to or from their posts). The National University (ex-Lovanium) has guest and dormitory accommodations, but it's awfully far out of town if you don't have ready transportation.

A network of resort hotels, businesslike pensions, safari camps and cheap digs has barely begun to develop in the provinces, not quite keeping step with the Zaïre boom. There are some 700 Christian missions scattered throughout the country as well. Most regular hotels out of town are less expensive than the Kinshasa establishments—for instance the *Mangwé Beach* at MOANDA on the Atlantic, the *Excelsior* at BOMA two hours downstream from Matadi ($4 to $5) and even the bleak Iberian monastery style *Métropole* at MATADI where five flights of crudely air-conditioned rooms with rudimentary conveniences surround a spacious, echoing courtyard ($7). KISANGANI has an air-conditioned government guest house that charges $6 to $9. LULUABOURG's *Hôtel Atlanta* costs about the same. There is a rest-house at the Yangambi Agricultural Station on the river downstream from Kisangani.

In the south, LUBUMBASHI has several expensive hotels that have seen better days. They include the *Sabena Guest House*, the *Hôtel Lubum-*

bashi and the once illustrious *Hôtel Léopold II* (cheaper at $4.50 to $6); the *Hôtel du Katanga* is a good buy. If you are a student, the university on the edge of town may be able to put you up.

The tourist grounds of the east are better off. Offering vacation comfort at fairly reasonable prices are the *Hôtel du Lac* at KALÉMIE (ex-Albertville) on Lake Tanganyika ($6 to $9), the government-operated, recently renovated *Royal Residence* at BUKAVU ($7.50 to $9), the *Mutwanga* in the like-named valley below the Ruwenzori Mountains, northern lakes, the thatched bungalows of the *Hôtel de la Rwindi* in the Virunga National Park, and the rebuilt *Relais* at BUTEMBO. The *Hôtel des Grands Lacs* at GOMA beween Lake Kivu and Virunga Park ($4 to $6) and the *Hôtel Riviera* at BUKAVU ($4.50 to $6) are both almost a bargain.

Where and What to Eat

Dining in European style generally proves a minor disappointment in Zaïre, but several rather expensive Kinshasa restaurants are comparable to the French kitchens of Abidjan, Douala and Dakar—and they are certainly a cut above the "European cuisine" of English-speaking Africa. Menus and prices are seldom posted outside restaurants, so be prepared to spend upwards of $5 for any main platter and even more for a bottle of wine. Tips are usually 10 per cent when not added to the bill.

Among the best in KINSHASA is the *Brussels*, next to the Regina Hôtel complex, an elegant, dignified, expansive place with the atmosphere of a gentlemen's club. The *Pergola* not far away offers excellent specialties including game, tournedos béarnaise, Congolese meals, and Indonesian nasi goreng, served in and around a handsome garden. The OAU restaurant on Mt. Ngaliema is handsome and expensive. *La Devinière* up in the Binza district is particularly attractive at night, with excellent service, superb imported food and high prices ($20 with wine). The *Okapi Hôtel* restaurant is distinguished and equally expensive.

There's respectable food at *Le Grill* (moderate-priced lunch), the Zoo *Restaurant* (lunch specialties in garden setting), the *Memling's* big dining room (beef fondue), and the forest-lake tavern at Ma Vallée, 10 miles outside town. *En Plein Air* serves good fondue high above the river. *Chez Nicola* offers sumptuous pizzas for $5, good shish kebab and Italian meals in its own pleasant garden. There is an inexpensive pizzeria on the Boulevard du 30 Juin with sidewalk tables.

Visitors should try the excellent traditional dish called moambe, consisting of chicken cooked in palm oil sauce, with rice, cassava greens and peppers (pili-pili sauce for those with sturdy digestions). It's available in the courtyard of the *Taverne Grecque*, a decent, less expensive midtown

place, at the Pergola and the restaurants of the African residential quarter
(La Cité). Crayfish (cossa-cossa) is a delectable specialty at Matadi, and
palm wine is called sambwa. Walkers and budget travelers can buy fish
in a banana-leaf platter, coconuts, peanuts or fruit of all sorts on the
squares, market places and beaches of the capital. The Boulevard du 30
Juin has the Brauhaus-like *Café de la Paix* for good food and drink and
several sidewalk cafes that serve soft drinks and beer, beer, beer. Most
habitués prefer local Skal or Simba beer above the weaker Primus or the
expensive imports. Water is fairly safe in hotels, but you're better off
using it only to wash with.

What to See and Do

From the vitality of Kinshasa's jazz bars to the quiet rustling of the
Virunga Park and the Ituri, from the surge of industrial power at Inga
across from Matadi to the gardens and domestic privacy of Lubumbashi,
a traveler in Zaïre crosses frontiers of life in a country bigger than life.
People here have long been masters of the plastic arts, music, costume
and body decoration, but they pursue very different ways in different
settings across the country.

KINSHASA is big, with well over a million people, and rivals Lagos as
sub-Saharan Africa's largest metropolis. It joins several old villages and
green patches in a riverside landscape surrounded by an eroded, ugly
plain, but it hasn't yet jelled into a city, as Lagos has, or Dakar or Dar es
Salaam. It has the muscle of heavy and light industry, administration and
commerce, but remains dusty, rambling and unconvincing as a metropolitan capital, perhaps because so few Zaïrois live inside it. The laboring
population resides under a sea of tin-roofed shanties in La Cité, crowding
rapidly and suffering from unemployment even while the nation booms.

The government quarter is monumental and ugly, the commercial
center alternately decaying and slick. Undistinguished, antiseptic contemporary buildings are beginning to cover the rubble of the 1960's and
to overshadow the bleak cement of the colonial town, but the improvement is in neatness and glitter, not in style. And the electricity fails nearly
every day, with or without rainstorms.

The zoo is ordinary and the Parc de la Révolution mediocre, but one
is very glad to have them in downtown Kinshasa, which dies every evening and all day on Sunday. The authenticity campaign has resulted
in the removal of all statues of non-Zaïrois (Belgian notables, explorers,
etc.); they are to be housed in a new museum being built for the purpose.

Here and there in Kinshasa, an institution or district strikes its special note: the river port installations where all imaginable products are off-loaded on their way between Matadi and the interior; several important churches of the Kimbanguists and other African Christian sects; the huge Grand Market (best on Sunday) and the morning market on the Avenue du Plateau; the first locomotive to complete the arduous trip from Matadi in 1896, now on display at the railroad station; the Binza quarter with a Beverly Hills sense of domestic well-being; the luxurious OAU cluster of handsomely decorated villas, gardens, restaurant and sports facilities on a wooded hill once named after Stanley (now Mt. Ngaliema).

Come in early July to catch the great annual Fikin Fair, with its panoply of nature, technology and craft, domestic and international, and its crowds of well-dressed, supremely alive Zaïrois. If you do come then, check and double-check your hotel reservation.

Kinshasa produces a smooth, cosmopolitan, yet traditionally anchored jazz enthusiastically heard and danced to in the multitudinous bars of the Cité (where you had best be escorted by Zaïrois) and a few places in the city center like the Ouififi, A Côté and the posh Vatican. Less idiomatic music can be heard at the tourist favorite Showboat (with a floor show), and at La Cave (discotheque with swinging atmosphere), Suzanella and La Perruche Bleue. Don't bother going to any of these clubs before 10 pm, but if you enjoy bar hopping, this is the best place in Africa for it. In the Cité, start at Vis à Vis or Le Petit Bois and go on wherever your escort takes you.

Kinshasa is also an excellent town for athletics, with swimming and boating on the river, swimming in the OAU pool ($1 admission), tennis at public courts (Funa sports complex, $1.40 entrance fee), golf, riding, sport flying and fishing (especially upstream at Kinkolé). There are spectator sports like soccer football, cycling and karting. All are readily accessible through a hotel concierge or enterprising travel agent.

If you have an hour, take the river ferry to Brazzaville (round trip $4) across the Malebo Pool with its water hyacinths; don't try to enter Brazzaville without a visa, however. Ramshackle public boats also cover the pool on full-day excursions with swimming, fishing and catered lunch. In dry seasons, there is a stirring day's Land-Rovering and rugged hiking to the 250-foot-high Inkisi Falls at Zongo, 60 miles downstream from Kinshasa.

Kinshasa National University (once Lovanium), on its suburban hill-top, sends its graduates down into the civil service matrix, and its students down to lose bloody battles with Mobutu's security forces. The university has a Museum of African Culture, a geological museum and a marvelous collection of crucifixes. Nearby is the sportful artificial forest lake Ma Vallée (no swimming, but good boating and picnicking in thatched pavilions), patronized mostly by Europeans. A 40-minute drive (or a longer but prettier boat ride) brings you to the President's showpiece experimental farm, NSELE, with spectacular rows and squares of growing things, an authentic Chinese pagoda, swimming pool and dock, and MPR party headquarters. The fishing town of Kinkolé, halfway between Kinshasa and Nsele, is being modernized into another kind of showpiece by the government.

There are extraordinary butterflies at the popular picnic place called Black River 50 miles northeast of the city.

Westward from Kinshasa, road and rail pass through flower-spangled MBANZA-NGUNEU (ex-Thysville) where a grotto contains the rare, pink and white "blind fish." A unique flower plantation and an impressive Catholic cathedral can be visited 10 miles away at Kisantu. The dense Mayombe Forest and the sculptured tombs at Tshela and around Boma, capital of Leopold's Congo, as well as the gigantic dam site at Inga on the plateau across from Matadi port, adorn the Zaïre's right bank between the final falls and the Atlantic beaches at Banana and Moanda.

MATADI, sole deep-sea port imbedded in the river, seems small for its job. The town comes crumbling down to the grey, disturbed river, steep and rocky, lucid but hot before and after the rains, with a light little gem of a central Place, a concentrated essence of open market at the town's summit, rather photogenic withal. At the bottom on the muddy bank called "Venice," small river ferries just nibble at crowds of trucks and people waiting (on both sides) to cross; don't be hurried, for here the surge of projects and passions of people on the move justifies some delay.

Above the town, the river drops toward its ocean level, racing past Stanley's old house (now reachable only after a stiff climb from a bold boat) and the rock that marked Diego Cão's 1482 penetration in Portugal's name. On one of many scenic ridges above the river outside Matadi, the isolated village of PALA-BALA has an unusual cemetery of ceramic grave markers and a cottage industry of blackware pottery.

The human reality of Matadi is loud, tough, physical, conforming poorly to the quaint and delicate flavor of its buildings. At night the seaport folk rock to versatile bands at Jacqui's Bar or Mickey's, or drink beer at the Guest House outdoor café or upstairs at the Métropole. Whores roam in T-shirts and seamen talk tough over Ping-Pong and beer. Two obscure communes on Matadi's hilly flanks shelter Angolan refugees displaced by the guerrilla rebellion against Portugal just a couple of miles away across the border from town. These are grim, rather hostile settlements, without the signs of hope that pervade Zaïre's own towns.

Western Kasai country to the southeast of Kinshasa ranges over a number of lost valleys, like the Kwango with a sparse beauty of flowers, waterfalls and lakes, rarely seen by tourists. You can take the OTRAZA steamer to KIKWIT (four days, $44 with full pension in a double cabin), drive or hike through the gorgeous countryside of the Bambala people from there. North of Ilebo (ex-Port Francqui), the Kasai is still dense, undeveloped forest. And to the east, above big LULUABOURG (400,000), is the country of the Bakuba people, makers of handsome dwellings, fine carvings and woven cloth. Farther east, MBUJI-MAYI (275,000) dominates a nest of attractive towns at the edge of an easier Kasai countryside, pretty, populated, opened by rail and road, with lake oases and gaily decorated houses of raffia. The land rises into a drier plateau here, studded with diamonds and other minerals, free of equatorial humidity.

Handsome and comfortable cities of Shaba like Lubumbashi and Kolwezi, or Mweka with its fine museum of Kuba art, have grown rich on copper and show it in flowers, trees and a superb (if seasonally arid) plateau landscape. When it was called Katanga, Shaba Province was the scene of the immediate post-independence secession movement and of United Nations armed intervention. Its copper mines continue to provide nearly 70 per cent of the nation's foreign exchange earnings and most of the wealth of the province. The new name of the province literally means, "copper." LUBUMBASHI, the provincial capital (formerly Elisabethville), has the country's second university campus, as well as broad, tree-lined boulevards, elegant residential quarters and modern office buildings, all reflecting copper revenues. Entertainment is concentrated on weekend nights when the hit Zaïrois band of the week performs at one of the outdoor clubs. Ask at your hotel, at the USIS or among students to learn of the latest favorites.

The northeasterly route from Kinshasa, dominated for more than a thousand miles by the river and its special forest life, passes great experimental gardens at Eala near Mbandaka, an agricultural research station at Yangambi, the low-lying country of primeval Lakes Leopold II and Tumba, and by Kisangani, the heart of the rapids where Wagenia fishermen cast and draw from rolling canoes.

KISANGANI itself (180,000) still struggles with the economic aftermath of war that all but destroyed its breadbasket and plantation agriculture of palms, cotton, coffee, rice and timber carried by river ships to Kinshasa. Its skilled and white-collar classes were massacred by the rebels, but a young university, begun by Protestant churches but now one of three national campuses, plays a central role in the revival of town and province.

Zaïre has little organized hunting or sport fishing. You can travel with a guide from Kisangani through the thick Ituri Forest where Pygmies dwell among trees 150 feet in height. Zaïre's unique okapi antelope is studied at Epulu station just west of the Mambasa crossroads. From here you can proceed eastward to the Kilo gold mines near Bunia off Lake Albert, or northward to the *Garamba National Park* with a fine stock of okapi, white rhino and giraffe. Lake Albert in the Ubangi corner of the country is one of the world's great Valhallas of lake fishermen. The 28 caverns and Venus Ladder of Mount Hoyo are also worth your visit.

Coming southward, you enter more classic tourist country, nonetheless beautiful for all that. BUKAVU stands poised on five fingers of land pointing into luxurious bays. Pretty GOMA is the point of departure for safaris into the delightful ambiance of the Kivu. This is marvelously situated lake country spectacular for scenery, fertile for plantation agriculture. It has a string of attractive towns, an excellent temperate climate, good accommodations for visitors, water sports on and in the lakes, a treasury of water fowl, with gorillas, okapi, white rhinos and less rare beasts in the high Kahuzi bamboo forest and the savanna plains around three fine lakes (Albert, Edward and Kivu).

About 20 miles north of Bukavu off the road to Goma is a scientific research station doing interesting work in seismology, agriculture and zoology in a lovely setting overlooking Lake Kivu. The Intore warriors perform their rituals at the request of touring visitors, and the small people who dance for organized tours near Beni are all recently out of the Ituri. Snow-capped Peak Marguerite, third largest summit in Africa (16,800 feet), in the Ruwenzori range (Ptolemy's Mountains of the Moons), can be climbed in five days, through a shifting welter of plant life (non-volcanic, hence quite rare) and wildfowl. The Virunga range to the south divides the Nile Basin from the Zaïre-Congo and offers two climable volcanoes, Nyragongo and Nyamulagira, most recently in eruption during 1967, and source of the black earth of Goma's lush plain.

In the *Virunga* (ex-Albert) *National Park*, mountains seal off the reserves of lions, elephants, buffalo, hippos, antelopes, hyenas, apes, boar and other game, making this 200-mile-long reserve one of the most diverse and nearly perfect nature agglomerations in the world. It is best visited in July and August. Lake Edward on the park's eastern border, has extraordinary coveys of birds. There are thermal springs (Mayi Moto) throughout the park, especially between Rutshuru and Rwindi.

Roads don't serve much in this region, unless you have four-wheel drive, but air hops are available to Goma or Bukavu from most big towns. For backpackers, the up-river boat trip to Kisangani puts you where you can hitchhike or ride cheaply to Bukavu.

Visitors baffled by the variety and complexities of Zaïre travel can choose among some good, if expensive, organized tours to be booked as an alternative to feeling one's way around. From Goma, several different tour packages cover the Kivu-Virunga Park area in one to seven days at prices from $35 to $350 per person. Agencies and airlines can book customers on these tours. Kinshasa can also be circumnavigated by a half-day guided taxi tour costing $10; it's not worth the price unless you are at a loss for a framework in which to locate the emergent attractions of an otherwise difficult city. There are also tours out of Kinshasa to the university, Nsele and Ma Vallée, and to the Zongo Falls (all day, with picnic and Land Rover transport for $22, which isn't bad).

What to Buy

Shops are well stocked in Kinshasa and Lubumbashi, less well so in Kisangani, Bukavu and other towns hit hard by the war. These disparities tend to increase despite equalization efforts by the government, as trade follows established patterns of investment and affluence. Workshops have sprung up in the suburbs of prosperous cities. Craft centers encourage reproduction of traditional arts, not always with fortunate results. Kinshasa shops are usually open from 8 am to noon and from 3 to 6 pm (not Saturday afternoon). The Ecole des Beaux Arts in the Commune de St. Jean has a Sunday morning sale of student work, both African and Western in style, some of it of respectable quality.

The greatness of Congolese carving continues in villages and on the edge of forests in Bas-Zaïre country, among the Bakuba of the Kasai, the Baluba of the south, and the northeastern people. Middlemen usually buy the local work for resale at higher prices in the Kinshasa markets, but you can find or commission fine pieces if you look hard. In browsing about the country, keep your eyes open for gorgeous green malachite stones in the south and east; forged metalwork, wicker, pottery, woven cloth, Christian imagery in stone carvings among the Bas-Zaïre of the west; carved utensils of the Jaga (Yaka) and the masks and musical instruments of the Pende in the southwest; bronzes and jewelry of Shaba in the south; carved vases in the Kivu; the popular "Kasai velvet" cloth around Luluabourg and the iron and horn figures of the Bakuba.

Tie-dyes and block prints are imaginatively done at Kinshasa, although you usually have to comb through piles of shoddy imports to find an authentic bolt in the open markets. Ivory is available in most towns, but export is taxed—and customs officials do inquire about ivory as you are leaving the country. You can also stuff your sacks with the usual African souvenirs in wood, metal, skin, leather or straw, assembled by traders here from all of Central Africa.

A reliable shop for Zaïrois art at fixed prices is run by Catholic nuns on Avenue Fuchs around the corner from the American Embassy. Kinshasa's Ivory (Souvenir) Market, spread along the sidewalks of Place Braconnier in midtown, requires strong consumer resistance and a stomach for ruthless bargaining (aim at paying about one-third the asking price). Here you can come out with some decent ivory, wood and metal pieces if you look past the slicked, botched and uglified junk that most foreigners are presumed to admire. Around the Boulevard du 30 Juin, the Maison du Fétiche and Imp Kiloba sell similar merchandise at fixed, high prices. In any case, you will have to accept a less imaginative way with ivory than in countries farther east and an inferior bronze-casting style than in the metalwork of West Africans along the Gulf of Guinea.

Kinshasa is the center of a new wave of Congo jazz, sophisticated meshes of traditional African music with a strong, drumming, danceable beat, topical lyrics and Afro-American-Caribbean influences. If you dig this sound, or if you seek stimulating gifts for the hip at home, get a couple of 45 rpm disks by continentally popular stars like Seigneur Rochereau, Dr. Nico or Maître Franco and his O.K. Jazz combo.

Local Attitudes

It's impossible to generalize for the immense panorama of Zaïre. But the regime still emits atavistic or puritanical bursts against resident foreigners, removing monuments to Europeans, erasing by fiat all trace of the suddenly humiliating name "Congo," enforcing Draconian morality for the sake of modernity, justice or self-determination. Yet Zaïre encourages foreigners to come, and is sensitive to their influence on its evolving finances and world reputation.

In many places Americans are treated with special cordiality for what is regarded as their nation's constructive role in Zaïre's stability and prosperity. About 2,000 Americans live in various parts of the country. Still, visitors should avoid brazen pronouncements on the nation's recent civil strife, its historic exhibitions of brutality, its experience with white mercenaries, the imposition of one-man military dictatorship and one-party rule, and the compulsory reversion to African nomenclature under the current authenticity campaign. These issues are far more complicated than many writers and commentators have portrayed them.

Weather, What to Wear, How Long to Stay

Low altitudes of the Zaïre basin on both sides of the equator ensure regularly hot, humid weather with considerable rainfall. North and south have almost contrary seasons, however. From June to September, Kinshasa, Lubumbashi and most of southern Zaïre are relatively cool and dry in the evenings, although near the river (as at Kinshasa), the days are sticky, hazy and glaring under perpetually overcast skies. At this time, northern Zaïre is having its rainy season, with brilliant air and blue skies between downpours. Rain falls hardest in the central basin and in the south during February-April and October-November, but here too skies are clear between storms. The Bukavu-Goma Kivu area enjoys an ideal climate, with moderate rainfall and temperatures that favor wine grapes and other temperate zone fruits.

Your wardrobe should obviously defend you against both humid and dry heat, but you should also anticipate evening chill in the eastern hills and even at Kinshasa in July and August (and in the air-conditioned offices and salons of the affluent). If you are dealing with government, university or big business officials, some Western formality prevails. Suits and ties are worn to offices whatever the weather; luncheons, cocktail parties and dinners require an effort to "dress." If you are traveling outside those circles, however, relax with the Zaïrois.

A fortnight suffices for any three Zaïre regions, provided you travel by air. If you want to know the river, the terrain, or the rarities of this enormous country, you must add at least another week for transportation alone.

Communication

Telephone, cable and postal services are expensive but improving as a new American communications system becomes operative. Domestic service remains dreadful, even within towns, and Kinshasa's electric power fails constantly. If you must send vital messages or money in or out, the best way is through an international bank.

With four regional languages (Lingala, a quasi-official lingua franca for Kinshasa and the north; Kingwana, a form of Kiswahili, in the east and south; Ki-Zaïre or Kikongo in the western panhandle; Tshiluba in the Kasai and southeast), as well as a school tradition of French, Zaïre is nonetheless taking remarkably to the lures of English, the language of "international success." You will find some English-speakers in the eastern regions bordering on Uganda, Tanzania and Zambia, around American mission stations, Peace Corps installations and especially among the cosmopolitan young technocrats who represent burgeoning government agencies in their dealing with the world of trade, industry and development finance. Outside the game parks, in fact, the most frequent visitors to Zaïre are representatives of American firms or agencies interested in the boom. French is still the way to get around Zaïre, but lack of it should not deter you.

There are nine lively daily newspapers in French, at least 40 other periodicals in a variety of languages, a national press agency, fervent national radio, and a flood of promotional literature gushing from the presses of Kinshasa.

Emergencies

Although services lag behind needs, the major centers have adequate government and mission hospitals, military rescue squads and other resources for crises. The American Embassy is located on Avenue des Aviateurs in Kinshasa (tel. 258-81/86). There are consulates in Lubumbashi (Boulevard Elisabeth, tel. 23-24), Kisangani (Avenue Eisenhower, tel. 29-57) and Bukavu (Avenue Mobutu, tel. 25-94).

West Africa

Cape Verde Islands
Dahomey
The Gambia
Ghana
Guinea
Ivory Coast
Liberia
Mali
Mauritania
Niger
Nigeria
Portuguese Guinea
Senegal
Sierra Leone
Togo
Upper Volta

THE REGION AT A GLANCE

A golden chronicle of great indigenous kingdoms and untrammeled culture unfolds in West Africa, between the vast Sahara and the Gulf of Guinea. In the Sudanic interior, the Moslem patricians of the medieval western Sudan exerted their peace and their wealth over enormous empires known successively as Ghana, Mali and Songhai. On their borders were Kanem, Bornu and the Hausa-Fulani emirates in the east, vigorous forest kingdoms and democracies to the south (Cayor, Ashanti, Dahomey,

445

WEST AFRICA

Benin, the Yoruba city-states and the Ibo communities, for example),
and the inveterately unvanquished Saharan Berbers (Tuaregs and others)
in the Saharan north.

When Europeans came to the Guinea coast in the late 15th century,
they found Africans ready to do business in gold, grain, pepper, ivory,
palm oil, timber and slaves—but without ceding control over their territories to the strange newcomers. West Africa's center of gravity began
nonetheless to move southward from the interior plateau savannas in the
16th century down the great rivers toward the maritime coasts. It has
remained there ever since. Imperial Europe occupied the region in the
late 19th century, working by preference the agricultural and mineral resources closest to the coast. The interior Sudanic belt became poor, des-
siccated, thinly populated, out of touch with modernity. But from
Mauritania to Lake Chad, down the curving River Niger from Guinea's
Fouta Djallon hills to the oil palm deltas of Nigeria, this is the terrain
where religion, sculpture, music, dance, poetry and community are different articulations of the same vivid high culture.

Southward in the forests, the old commercial powers regrouped under
colonialism to combine great artistic energy with a rush of urbanization,

Lagos harbor

Weaver, Mali

University of Ghana

Young vendor, Nigeria

technology and trenchant Western influence. New leaders emerged for the new nations as colonial control receded after World War II.

Isolated in the coastal center, Liberia was settled a century and a half ago by black people freed from American slavery; their Afro-American republic dates from 1847. A new Ghana emerged in 1957 in the British Gold Coast colony, once the dominion of the proud Ashanti nation and still imbued with the grace and pageantry of old. Africa's most populous territory, Nigeria, had to win its unity in the tragic 1967-70 "Biafran" civil war but has emerged with prospects of enormous power and general prosperity.

Guinea first broke from the 1958 Gallic vision of a French-speaking Commonwealth. Things have gone hard for Guineans since then, but two years later, Senegal, Mauritania, Mali, Upper Volta, Niger, the Ivory Coast, Togo and Dahomey had all negotiated their "transfers of power" from General de Gaulle's government. French influence remains alive in most of their economies and cultural institutions.

Smaller British holdings in Sierra Leone and the Gambia brought the number of independent West African states to 14 by 1965. Only Portugal retains its possessions here—the coastal part of war-torn Guinea-Bissau and the impoverished Cape Verde Islands.

Despite its diversities, the West African region represents Africa's historical, economic and cultural epitome. The vitality of its coasts, the effervescence of its cities, the traditional ebullience of its rural regions and markets, and the brooding souvenirs of the interior Sudan—these are in the authentic greatness of an Africa that is both new and old.

The traveler's experience here is uneven: accommodations, food and services are sometimes superb, sometimes deplorable; communications remain oriented toward London or Paris, functioning less well among African countries; former British and French territories have yet to develop habits of cooperation that would encourage trade and travel; visas are still required for most visitors and the climate is usually better somewhere else.

You will encounter a complex polyrhythm of daytime warmth, refreshing rain and night brightness. The same powerful music beats through the lives of 100 million West Africans in the worldly, ebullient high-life jazz of their cities and the fervent communal spirit of the land.

PMA

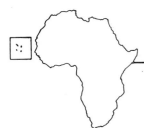

Cape Verde Islands

(Ilhas do Cabo Verde)

Profile

STATUS: Overseas Province of Portugal with governor-general responsible to Lisbon.

SIZE: Archipelago made up of 10 islands and five islets with a total land area of 1,557 square miles. Most important islands: Santo Antão (301 square miles), São Vicente (88 square miles), Santiago (383 square miles), São Nicolau (132 square miles), Sal (83 square miles) and Fogo (184 square miles). Population—260,000.

GEOGRAPHY: The islands are the highest visible points of a vast volcanic chain 283 miles from the West African coast. Arid, rocky, mountainous. Principal towns—Praia on Santiago Island (capital, 17,000), Mindelo on São Vicente (25,000).

CLIMATE: Temperate. Average temperatures range from 65 to 80 degrees.

LANGUAGES: Portuguese (official), Lingua Creola (widely spoken local dialect derived from Portuguese), some English.

CURRENCY: Escudo (1$00), divided into centavos. 10$00 = 37 cents; US$1.00 = 27$00.

VISAS: Required. Application forms available from Portuguese consulates in New York, Boston, Newark and San Francisco, also from Portuguese Embassy in Washington. Fee $5.85. Expect delay of three to four weeks while application is sent to Portugal for approval. Less delay obtaining transit visa (valid for stay of up to eight days).

AIRPORT: The airport on Sal Island (SID) receives regular flights from Lisbon and three flights a week from Portuguese Guinea (Bissau).

NATIONAL HOLIDAYS: June 10, National Day; October 5, Proclamation of the Republic; December 1, Independence Day; Catholic holidays.

INFORMATION SOURCES: *In US*—Portuguese Consulate General, 630 Fifth Avenue, New York, N.Y. 10020 (tel. 212/246-4580), also 31 Commonwealth Avenue, Boston, Mass. 02116, 10 Commerce Street, Newark, N.J. 07102 and 3298 Washington Street, San Francisco, Cal. 94115; Embassy of Portugal, 2125 Kalorama Road NW, Washington, D.C. (tel. 202/265-1643).

By Aaron Segal

Those who have a taste for quiet seclusion in a rugged, remote and somewhat forlorn setting will enjoy these isolated islands. Lying nearly 300 miles off the West African coast west of Dakar, this chain of 10 volcanic islands and five uninhabited islets has watched the world pass it by.

The 260,000 islanders are the racially mixed offspring of laborers from Angola and elsewhere in West Africa, Portuguese traders and administrators, and seamen from around the world. Resourceful and vibrant, the Verdeans have evolved a distinctive Creole dialect and a rich tradition of dance, music and poetry.

These islands, tragically, have no regular and reliable natural sources of water. Droughts are frequent, arable land scarce and jobs desperately short. Thousands of islanders are forced to emigrate in search of employment, education and other opportunities. Money sent home by emigrants is the principal source of income for many families. Wherever they are—whether in Angola, Mozambique or Portuguese Guinea as minor civil servants, or as merchant seamen at the four corners of the earth, or in the mill towns of Massachusetts as factory workers, Cape Verdeans gather together and recall with nostalgia the bittersweet quality of life in their lovely but stricken islands.

Uninhabited prior to their discovery in 1460, these islands are considered by Portugal to be the most assimilated of its several "overseas provinces." Verdeans have been favored over other Africans by the Portuguese in employment as civil servants in Angola, Mozambique and Portuguese Guinea. Their posts, to be sure, are minor ones.

Fishing, agriculture, exploitation of salt deposits and tourism have all lagged in development while emigration continues. Located near major shipping routes between West Africa and North America, and Europe and South America, the islands have done a little business providing ships' supplies. Recently there has been talk of constructing facilities to service the petroleum vessels that take the longer route around the Cape of Good Hope since the closing of the Suez Canal.

Many Verdeans are bitter at what they consider to be Portuguese neglect in developing the islands. At least some have joined or are sympathetic to the African Independence Party of Guinea and Cape Verde (PAIGC) whose aim is to unite the West African mainland territory and the islands into a single independent state. While war rages on the mainland, strict military and police controls have kept the islands relatively quiet. Portugal allows no public discussion of independence and indeed uses the islands to confine political prisoners from its other African possessions—and from Portugal as well.

Money Matters

The escudo is the currency of the islands, and theoretically it is equal in value to the Portuguese escudo. However, the Cape Verde escudo is not accepted outside the islands and it is better to meet your expenses with Portuguese escudos. Foreign currencies and travelers checks can be exchanged at the Banco Nacional Ultramarino (National Overseas Bank), with offices at Praia and São Vicente.

Getting In and Out

Visa applications must be approved in Lisbon. This can cause considerable delay. The quickest and simplest procedure is to request a transit visa valid for a stay of up to eight days. The most serious travel problem is the scarcity of ongoing connections. TAP flies three times a week to Portuguese Guinea and daily except Sunday to Lisbon, but there are no flights to anywhere else in West Africa.

Access by sea is not much better, except for freighters. The Sociedade Geral de Trasportes operates a passenger and cargo service between Lisbon and the island ports of Praia and São Vicente. Portuguese freighters to Angola sometimes call.

Getting Around Within Cape Verde

The tiny islands are mountainous, but each is easily negotiated by a combination of walking, cheap taxis and public buses. English-speaking taxi drivers can be hired by the day for informal tours.

Cape Verde Air Transports (TACV) runs local flights in small planes between Praia, Sal and São Vicente airports, and to the airstrips on the smaller islands. São Vicente is the center of a regular inter-island passenger boat and mail service. Cheaper sail and motor boats also operate around the islands, but without fixed schedules.

Where to Stay

While plans for tourist expansion have been talked about, present facilities are few and modest. They're all inexpensive. There is a transient hotel for passengers at Espargos Airport on SAL ISLAND, but much nicer is the *Estalagem Morabeza* guest house in the town of Santa Maria. The *Porto Grande* is a businessmen's hotel in the town of Mindelo on São VICENTE ISLAND. Also on this island is a simple boarding house in Baía das Gatas. The *Praia Mar Inn* is a plain commercial hotel in the town of Praia on SANTIAGO ISLAND. Also in Praia is the friendly pension, *Sol Atlantico*. Low-budget travelers will almost certainly find a family to put them up by inquiring at the neighborhood bar or the Tourist Office in Praia (Centro de Informação e Turismo). Since the hotels and pensions are small, advance reservations are a good idea.

Where and What to Eat

Food has been the happiest expression of the encounter between African and Portuguese cultures. Hotel and pension restaurants are adequate, but the best meals are to be found in Verdean homes. Creole dishes feature fresh seafood, especially lobster and other crustaceans, served with generous portions of rice, beans and sweet potatoes, and complemented with fresh bananas, pineapples and other fruits, and the excellent locally grown coffee. The water is safe (some of it has been converted from sea water), but imported Portuguese wines and beers are cheap.

What to See and Do

These islands are for relaxing. They offer quiet pleasures—sipping coffee and wine in port cafes, admiring the grace and poise of the Verdeans passing by, and exchanging stories with island locals whose worldwide travels and experiences are likely to put yours to shame.

SANTIAGO is the most populated island. It has the provincial capital, Praia, a town of 17,000. The island has two good beaches for swimming and underwater fishing (São Francisco and Tarrafal), a lively market and an agricultural research station at the town of Orgãos. You can take a beautiful mountain drive to Trindade, which has fine views.

SAL ISLAND is the arrival point for international air travelers. Santa Maria beach is 11 miles from the airport. The town has a lobster fishing fleet. Also on Sal are the Pedra Lume salt-pans, set in the crater of an extinct volcano.

São Vicente is where the big ships arrive, taking advantage of the fine natural harbor at Porto Grande. The main town of Mindelo has a population of 25,000. There is a good beach at Baía das Gatas. The island offers agreeable town strolls and mountain drives.

Each of the lesser islands has its attractions, but all still lack overnight accommodations, unless one stays with local families. Fogo Island has a half-moon shaped 9,279-foot volcano that last erupted in 1951. Brava Island is greener and cooler than the others, and it has medicinal springs. Santo Antão has fertile valleys and panoramic mountain views, while São Nicolau has the colorful village of Ribeira Brava. Its whitewashed tile-roofed architecture is characteristically Portuguese.

Night life revolves around friendly neighborhood bars. There are cinemas in Praia, Mindelo and Espargos. Each of the islands has its special saints' days and local festivals. These and other occasions feature the performance of distinctive Verdean songs and dances which effectively blend African and Portuguese influences. Best known are the moving, nostalgic "morna" and "coladeira," both expressions of regret at the need to migrate. Cape Verdean folk music can be heard in small bars and clubs.

What to Buy

Imported goods are expensive and local crafts limited. There is some weaving, embroidery and lacework, as well as locally manufactured shoes, cigarettes and pipe tobacco.

Local Attitudes

Travelers, except for seamen, are still rare, and Verdeans—because of their own extensive emigration—are likely to ask if you know an uncle, cousin or brother in New York, Boston, Lisbon, Paris or Montreal. The islanders are ready to be photographed and to welcome you into their homes. If you must discuss politics, be discreet. Political police and informers may be listening.

Weather, What to Wear, How Long to Stay

The islands are tropical, but ocean breezes keep temperatures in the 70's most of the year. September can be hot and February cool, but more annoying are the harsh northeast winds that blow throughout the year.

Except on Santo Antão, which is green, the landscapes are rugged and arid, and the light rains that should fall from August to October often fail.

Casual attire is normal, but the islanders are not ready for miniskirts or hot pants. However, shorts for men and slacks for women are acceptable. Unless you are on a ship passing through, you may want to slow down and relax for several days, taking in some of the islands and absorbing the atmosphere.

Communication

A soft, lyrical, Creole-Portuguese dialect serves as the working language. It is less guttural than the Portuguese spoken in Portugal, and the islanders are proud of their several distinguished novelists and poets who have captured on paper their distinctive speech. Many men speak some English as a result of having traveled as seamen or migrant workers. You are likely to find an occasional Verdean who has retired to his island home after years of work in a Massachusetts factory.

Postal and telephone services to the outside world are slow and must go through Lisbon. Inter-island communications are carried mostly by small boats rather than electronic devices. Three private radio stations provide music. There are two official weekly papers in Portuguese.

Emergencies

The two small hospitals at Mindelo and Praia are grossly inadequate. Serious illness would necessitate hopping a TAP plane to Lisbon. There is no American diplomatic representation on the islands.

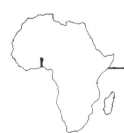

Dahomey

(République du Dahomey)

Profile

STATUS: Independent since August 1, 1960. Former French colony.

SIZE: 44,696 square miles (slightly larger than Tennessee). Population— 2,685,000 (Yoruba, Fon and Adja in south, Fulani, Somba, Bariba and Denda in north).

GEOGRAPHY: Coastal zone—low, sandy, with lagoons, thinned forest, savanna. Rugged escarpments and Atakora mountain range in far north. Principal towns—Porto Novo (capital, 85,000), Cotonou (economic capital and port, 130,000), Abomey (42,000).

CLIMATE: Two zones. South humid with steady temperatures in the 80's; two rainy seasons, March to July (heaviest in June) and September to November; dry seasons July to September and November to March. North is drier, with day-night temperature contrasts.

LANGUAGES: French, Fon, Yoruba and other African languages.

CURRENCY: CFA franc. CFA 100 = 40 cents; $1.00 = CFA 245.

VISAS: Americans require visas. Available from Embassy of Dahomey and Mission of Dahomey to UN. Fee $1.30 (up to 15-day stay), $2.60 (up to three-month stay). Two passport photos needed. Available from French consulates where Dahomey is not represented.

AIRPORT: Cotonou (COO), four miles from city. Airport departure taxes —domestic, CFA 100 (40 cents); within Africa, CFA 500 ($2); outside Africa, CFA 1,500 ($6). Linked by frequent flights with major West African neighbors and directly with Paris and New York.

NATIONAL HOLIDAY: August 1, Independence Day; Christian holidays.

INFORMATION SOURCES: *In US*—Embassy of the Republic of Dahomey, 2737 Cathedral Avenue NW, Washington, D.C. 20008 (tel. 202/232-6656); Permanent Mission of the Republic of Dahomey to the UN, 4 East 73rd Street, New York, N.Y. 10021 (tel. 212/861-3700). *In Cotonou*—Office du Tourisme, Avenue Général LeClerc, P.O. Box 89.

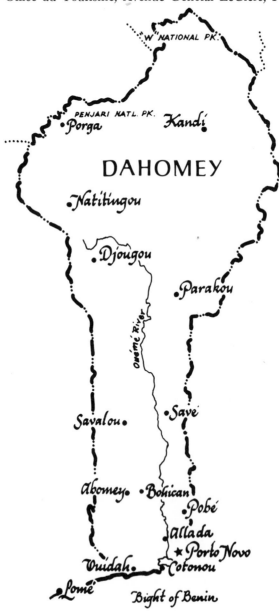

By Philip M. Allen

On a small wedge of poor land, drumstick-shaped with its narrow part toward the south, the Dahomean world contains dramatic concentrations of two cultures: the wellsprings of vital West African tradition and the bright, cosmopolitan ethos of France. Administrative institutions, military place-names and overseas commerce epitomize Dahomey's French pole, as do the elegant cuisine, well-groomed women, sun-bleached Riviera architecture of Cotonou, and the schooling of generations of Dahomeans. At the other pole, ancestral tradition lives in family compounds among elaborate pantheons and religious cosmologies, at convents of fetish priests and priestesses, in decaying palaces of the old city-states, and in the conserved royal arts and village crafts that make the region of Abomey a treasury of West African civilization.

Dahomey's history typifies the struggles of West African kingdoms among themselves and against European powers. At 18th century trading posts like Ouidah and Porto Novo on the Bight of Benin, Portugal and France dealt in slaves with the rulers of Dahomey, the royal Fon (Adja) of Abomey. In 1894 the 250-year-old kingdom of the Fon succumbed to superior French technology and proud Dahomey became a colony.

France, during her rule, educated many Dahomeans to become the intellectuals and skilled professionals of West Africa. Thousands left their country, where suitable jobs were unavailable, for clerical and professional work throughout the French empire. Many of them were later evicted from their privileged positions during waves of nationalistic fervor and the Dahomeans were obliged to return to a land of marginal fertility and irregular rainfall.

The coasts are sandy and the central forests are gone except for patches around Savalou, Zagnando and Allada. Vast palm groves annually yield decreasing amounts of oils for export, and crops of peanuts, coconuts, fish, timber and crafts barely support the 2.7 million Dahomeans propped against the powerful mass of western Nigeria. The nation's subsistence is mortgaged to France.

Politically independent of France since 1960, Dahomey has barely survived 12 years of governmental chaos and bankruptcy. During the first decade of independence, national governments succeeded one another every year through force. Dahomey's procession of regimes has been preoccupied with survival and has yet to gear up for tourists, join the larger cooperative circuits for trade and travel, or master a soaring cost of living.

The traveler finds himself in Dahomey often as an afterthought to Nigeria, Ghana or the Ivory Coast. Those who come may discover not only the waving palms and white beaches of the coast but also the bit of France that prevails at Cotonou (Dahomey's capital in all but title), or the deep reserves of animist spirit dwelling in village circles and family compounds at the roots of West Africa.

Dahomey has been extensively studied by French scholars, but little has been written about the nation in English. There is Melville J. and Frances Herskovits's *Dahomean Narrative, A Cross-Cultural Analysis* (Northwestern University Press, 1958) as well as a few specialized historical and political studies.

Money Matters

A charter member of the West African CFA system, Dahomey's currency converts at about CFA 245 to the US dollar. Travelers checks are welcome in hotels, restaurants and a few Cotonou shops. Banks offer better exchange rates than the commercial emporia. In Cotonou you have the choice of the Banque Nationale de Paris (BNP) and the Banque Internationale de l'Afrique de l'Ouest (BIAO, partly owned by the First National City Bank of New York), both of which cover most other French-speaking West African countries, and the Société Dahoméenne de Banque which is also represented in Porto Novo.

Banks are open between 7:30 am and noon and between 2:30 and 5 pm, Monday through Friday.

Inflation rages along the entire West African coast, as seriously in Dahomey as anywhere else. Particularly for people who depend on imports and expect European standards in goods and services, costs can be high. Even basic food prices (corn, cassava, yam, sorghum, sugar, etc.) have been rising of late. The careful and thrifty visitor can avoid expensive hotel shops, however, and instead patronize artisan workshops, barrestaurants, tailors, laundries, barbers and other moderately priced places in Dahomean quarters. He can also bring his imported goods with him from neighboring Togo, which is cheaper.

Getting In and Out

Porto Novo, Cotonou, Ouidah, and Grand Popo are situated along the paved coastal highway between Togo and western Nigeria, an attractive road for entering and leaving Dahomey. Delays at the Nigerian frontier can extend travel time between Cotonou and Lagos to over three hours. On the western side, Dahomey and Togo have recently eased controls to permit Cotonou-Lomé traffic to make the trip in less than two and a half hours. (Travelers should note the time change on this border: Dahomey is an hour ahead of Togo.)

Dahomey is also bisected by a north-south road, tarred and maintained in random segments along its route from Cotonou to the Niger border. Official buses run twice weekly from Cotonou's motor terminal to Niamey, capital of Niger. In the north, an alternate but occasionally flooded route leads through fascinating hill country from Natitingou to Porga on the edge of the Pendjari game reserve and into Upper Volta. Taxis licensed to cross national borders can be engaged quite cheaply: $2 suffices for a Cotonou-Lomé trip.

Travelers who wish to economize—but without undergoing the risk and discomfort of the lopsided old Renault mammy-wagons—can join the rapid, hardy Peugeot 404 collective taxis that regularly convey nine passengers and baggage on long-distance treks. Other vehicles are available for hire in the capitals, but they are considerably more expensive than taxis and charter only on a round trip basis.

Cotonou receives a Pan American jet from New York, as well as regular Air Afrique and UTA flights connecting major European and African centers. The quiet little airport, four miles outside town, is served by assiduous taxi drivers and courteous immigration/customs authorities, but can become pandemonium when large groups arrive or leave.

Two rarely exploited avenues should appeal to travelers with time, initiative and a liking for waterways. (1) Shipping at Cotonou's deep-water port includes Farrell Lines freighters out of New York and cargo vessels of all nationalities, in addition to Paquet passenger ships from Marseille. Travelers may book passage to or from Cotonou through a vessel's local agent or directly with the ship's captain. (2) The large Nokoué Lake behind Cotonou and Porto Novo forms part of an extensive West African lagoon system navigable by sailboats, canoes and shallow-draft motorboats from Cotonou to a point 100 miles east of Lagos (Nigeria). While no commercial lagoon transit lines traverse the Dahomey-Nigeria border, enterprising travelers can arrange delightful inland waterway passage (three hours by motorboat between Lagos and Cotonou via Porto Novo and Badagry) by inquiring at the residential boat club in Cotonou, the Motorboat Club or Yacht Club at Lagos, or at any of the major fishing ports on the lagoon.

Used as a crossroads between the larger coastal nations, Dahomey has become rather particular about its visa and customs prerogatives. Americans seeking to enter without a visa—even in direct transit—have been subjected to delays and occasionally rejected at frontiers. It is wise to get your visa in advance at Dahomean embassies, or through French consulates in cities where Dahomey has no representation. While visas are required for the lagoon passage to Nigeria, formalities tend to be superficial at these water border posts.

Getting Around Within Dahomey

Without benefit of asphalt (aside from the two trunk roads), Dahomey nonetheless seems a nation easily and entirely on the move: in official buses on the north-south highway and coaches hired from the government's Office du Tourisme; in fast, collective bush taxis, rickety mammy-trucks, regular mini-taxis or hired cars from Locauto or Locar Benin companies at Cotonou; or by bicycle, hitchhiking, and on foot. Some northern roads are awash in the rainy season, but the international borders, parks and places of interest usually remain accessible. Hitchhikers can find drivers easily on the busy east-west coastal road but usually must wait at hotels or filling stations along the north-south route where most of the traffic is commercial. The hotel at Pendjari National Park rents Land Rovers for game runs.

Taxi rides within Cotonou and Porto Novo cost CFA 50 (about 20 cents), although some of the Citroen 2CV's will settle for half that fee if the trip is brief. Fares for passing beyond the bridge in east Cotonou, or penetrating the outskirts of town, should be negotiated with the driver in advance.

Cotonou and Porto Novo lend themselves to bicycling. Ask at your hotel about department stores or garages willing to rent a wheel. Canoes take on passengers at lagoon ports such as Abomey-Calavi; bargain over the fare and be sure that the canoe pilot has agreed to a round-trip price.

Dahomey also has a national railway network. Trains originating at Cotonou make the 275-mile, eight-hour run to Parakou three times a week, with several attractive possibilities for stops along the way (most notably in Bohicon-Abomey). Another line runs daily over the coastal sand spit to Porto Novo (20 miles), then north to Pobé (67 miles). A third train proceeds every day westward to Ouidah (25 miles) and ends at Segbohoué (36 miles). Particularly if combined with more flexible one-way trips by rented car or taxi, these train facilities permit an aesthetically agreeable "feel" for the southern Dahomean countryside. The rolling stock is aged but adequate, and the passage is cheap: first-class accommodations to Parakou cost about $8; the crowded second class costs $5.

Few airfields in Dahomey get regular service. Air Cotonou flies a DC-3 twice weekly between Cotonou, Parakou, Kandi and Natitingou, and in the dry season has a flight between Cotonou and Porga near the Pendjari park. The Aero Club of Cotonou has small Piper aircraft for rent.

To discover what's going on, visitors may consult the daily *Daho-Express* or inquire at the Office du Tourisme (Avenue Général LeClerc, P. O. Box 89) or at the Syndicat d'Initiative in Cotonou. Personnel at the American Cultural Centers in Cotonou and Porto Novo and at Peace Corps headquarters are well informed, as are the leisurely habitués of the Hôtel du Port swimming pool, the more swinging bars and the Mawule snackbar in the center of Cotonou.

Where to Stay

COTONOU provides a surprisingly wide range of accommodations considering its size and traffic; moreover, most of the up-country centers have at least a shelter of sorts for travelers. Until the new, luxurious *Hôtel de la Concorde* opens, it is the *Croix du Sud*, tucked in a palm grove near the beach halfway between the airport and town, that remains the favorite of visitors for comfort and serenity. Clean but less than elegant single rooms rent for $12 to $14 per night.

For swimming and night life, the younger clientele favors the small, modern *Hôtel du Port* on the beach, with a few double rooms at $13 and air-conditioned bungalows at $16 per night. Gourmets and aficionados of Cotonou-town prefer the older *Hôtel de la Plage* on the central fishing beach. It features excellent food in its garden restaurant, a new swimming pool, and rooms renting for $11 single and $18 double. (Suites run considerably higher.) All three hotels are air-conditioned.

For tighter budgets, rooms can be rented at the *Pam-Pam Restaurant* in the center of town between the business district and the Dahomean quarter, as well as at *La Florida* with a Swiss kitchen, *L'Asie* with Vietnamese food, *Le Provence*, a small colonial-period hostelry in the oldest part of town—all with or without air-conditioning at the client's option. Campers park in palm groves on the beach and Peace Corps Volunteers sometimes rough it for about $3.50 per night at the *Hôtel Babo* or the Nokoué in the Dahomean quarters.

PORTO NOVO is so close to Cotonou and so overshadowed by it that it has but one rudimentary hotel—*Les Députés*, run by the government and not always open to transients. The *Motel* at ABOMEY has adequate accommodations at $5 per room, but the nearby rail junction of BOHICON boasts three establishments: the *Hôtel Bohicon*, the *Hôtel des Députés* and a motel. PARAKOU offers a choice between the *Hôtel des Routiers* at $4 to $6 per person and the *Buffet-Hôtel de la Gare* with somewhat more impressive conveniences at $6 to $8 per person. DJOUGOU in the northwest near the Togo border has a motel with rooms at $3 per night. Most of these places lack hot water, and electricity is rationed.

There are government rest-houses (gîtes) with minimum facilities at SAVÉ, BEMBÉRÉKÉ, KOUANDÉ, NATITINGOU, ALLADA, NIKKI, SAVALLOU and KANDI. Some serve meals, but it is always advisable to inquire at the government tourist office in Cotonou before starting off for any of these shelters.

The *Hôtel Tourisme et Safari de la Pendjari*, in the national park on the Upper Volta border, has 28 comfortable double rooms with air-conditioning for $6 per person. It has a swimming pool and offers a full pension arrangement for about $15. The simpler Porga Camp near the Pendjari, open from mid-December to the end of May, has 100 beds at $3 each, as well as private double rooms for about $5. There are as yet no accommodations on the Dahomean side of the tri-national "W" park.

Backpackers are advised that schools normally do not permit visitors to occupy their dormitories, but hospitable Dahomean families, Catholic missions and Peace Corps Volunteers can be found in or near most towns.

Where and What to Eat

Good French and African meals appear on a variety of menus through-out Dahomey. In COTONOU, the *Hôtel de la Plage* offers the widest range of French food, complemented on Tuesdays by an Oriental menu. The other major hotels do well for a price. (Be prepared to spend upwards of $4 for a set menu at lunch or dinner, excluding wine.) Le *Provence* offers simpler French fare at lower rates, and the *Pam-Pam* has an open brasserie atmosphere with authentic French food. *Paris-Snack*, for those who can ignore the name, proves to be intimate and rather chic with most of its food flown in from France. *Chez Pepita* serves delicious paella, fish soup, lobster and other seafood on a pleasant garden patio. Le *Capri* (Chez Maria) prepares pizzas and fish. La *Florida* makes good meat and cheese fondues.

At the airport, C. O.'s (Charley Oscar's) appeals to the affluent European discotheque crowd. Banquets can be staged at the attractive Chaumière on the airport road outside town.

To the east of Cotonou, in a charming outdoor setting on the Porto Novo road, Les *Trois Paillottes* manages to combine a standard bourgeois French menu with good Dahomean food; e.g., pounded cassava and yam (foufou), roasted plantain, fried corncakes (akassa) in fiercely spicy sauces, fish, chicken and meat stews, fruit fritters, and on Sundays a couscous.

More urban combinations of Dahomean fare with "biftek et frites" can be found at *L'Intimité* and *Le Tontin*, both popular with students and Peace Corps Volunteers. *Mawule*, opposite the Monoprix store in central Cotonou, serves inexpensive French sandwiches with draught beer. *La Gerbe d'Or* pastry shop serves ice cream and other sweets that almost justify their astronomical prices.

PORTO NOVO denizens dine privately or "go out" to Cotonou; meals can be ordered in advance at the *Hôtel des Députés*. For an offbeat experience, there is a perfectly acceptable, inexpensive African menu (which includes chicken and beef) scrawled on a blackboard in the busy courtyard of *Le Bon Souvenir* cafe on the road to Porto Novo's suburban Lycée Béhanzin. Good meals can be enjoyed at the *Abomey Motel*, the *Hôtel de France* in Bohicon and Parakou's two small hotels.

The water is doubtful in Dahomey, but French and Maghreb wines and bottled mineral water can always be found. The local beer (paradoxically called Sobrado) is of a good Alsatian strain. Palm wine and a slightly fermented corn beer are sold in the markets.

Dahomey's waiters expect little more than a nominal tip, and most restaurants add a service charge to the bill. Any gratuity beyond that is a grace note.

What to See and Do

Dahomey's landscape is hardly what attracts visitors, although the scenery does change from palmy beaches and lagoons into thinned forest and savanna, ending with the rugged escarpments and the exciting Atakora mountain range in the far north.

COTONOU has been a fortified French commercial town since 1863, but it remains quieter and less well knit than most overseas French capitals. The enthusiastic walker will pass through congested urban quarters, between compounds and beachfront villas, modern business places and proletarian suburbs.

The most ambitious structures—the 21st century office building attached to a flying saucer conference hall built for the defunct multinational Union Africaine et Malgache, a couple of neo-Babylonian parliament and presidential palaces, a deserted four-lane boulevard and four luxurious villas near the Croix du Sud hotel—were all built about independence time to anticipate a sovereign patronage that comes here but rarely.

Between the egregious Grande Place, designed to beat the Place de la Concorde in Paris, and the exciting lagoon market, which operates every fourth morning at Abodki-Condji on the outskirts, stands an incipient city, a lagoon bridge, and an epoch of history. Here people meet to drink and dance at the Canne à Sucre, the Calebasse, the Lido and the Excelsior; Europeans go to the Poster Club at the Hôtel du Port and to C. O.'s at the airport. Quieter Dahomeans patronize their own bars in the carrés where beer and palm wine course the night through. There's soccer on Sundays in Akpakpa, boxing in town, tennis for the elegant, swimming for the paying guest, and the infinite pounding ocean for everybody (although swimming in the heavy surf is risky).

West of Cotonou, a 15-minute drive to ABOMEY-CALAVI (not to be confused with the larger and more important Abomey to the north) takes you to the new National University, supported by France. From here, a short motor launch or canoe trip brings you to GANVIE, on Lac Nokoué, largest and best articulated of West Africa's lagoon villages. The palmwood houses of 10,000 inhabitants cluster on stilts among the shallow waters of the lagoon, with a marketplace, a temple, huts for smoking akadja fish, a souvenir shop and bar where an elder welcomes visitors. If you are being paddled around, it is prudent to invite the oarsmen in for a beer before the return trip. Another stilt village, AGUÉGUÉ, flooded only during the rainy season, is reached by canoe from Porto Novo in two hours of paddling.

Farther west, the road links Cotonou with OUIDAH, vegetating port for the French and Portuguese slave trade to Cuba, Bahía and the Antilles. The São Jão fortress here was a Portuguese enclave tolerated by the French until Dahomean independence, when it was expropriated by heirs of Portugal's former slaves. Ouidah's museum has an interesting pictorial account of slaving on these coasts and in Brazil. Fort William was occupied by the English during their season here. These monuments to an epoch of inhuman commerce fit as easily into ordinary Ouidah as the Temple of Pythons, a dilapidated but active shrine of an ancient cult.

ATHIÉMÉ, two hours by road from Ouidah, produces crayfish and crabs, fruits and flowers, and a wealth of roadside clay effigies. These so-called "mud" sculptures are images of village pride, adorned monuments to the powerful and the beautiful, or they are dramatizations of Legba, eccentric protector of communities, placed by villagers to advertise civic virtues or to ward off incivility. They abound along the pathways and even the highway between Cotonou and ALLADA, center of medical and religious training for what Westerners call fetishism.

To the north of Allada, at ABOMEY (80 miles from Cotonou), the partially restored 100-acre palace of the Fon dynasty serves as a museum to the glories of embattled kings, the strength of their political symbolism, and the royal domination of bronze casters and coppersmiths, weavers and carvers. Historical bas-reliefs on the palace metopes depict the dynasty's course through thick and thin. Their imagery is repeated in primary colors on the delightful appliqué tapestries sewn for tourists at Abomey today. Artisan quarters in the museum's courtyard, the royal burial chambers and the weapons and protective armor of King Guezo's royal Amazons may be seen in the company of knowledgeable French-speaking guides supplied by the museum.

The town of 30,000 inhabitants lives in the presence of its powerless monarch, heir of Ali-Agbo, who succeeded the tragic King Gbehanzin after the battles of the 1890's had been lost to the French. With luck, visitors may see the King and his court at festivals and celebrations; even without luck, the indigenous spirit of Dahomey emerges in its miniature bronzes, tapestries, museum activity and the clay statues of the roadsides.

PORTO NOVO, technically the nation's capital, but honored only by a few ministries and schools, represents an old West Africa of city-states. Here the Yoruba Toffa dynasty resisted British, French and Dahomean Fon, and here, in the eastern quarter of town, sculptors fashion masks for the secret Gueledé society, statues of ancestral energy, and myriad carvings, many of them imitative and worthless, some of them exemplary of the great fecundity of the Yorubas. There are also potters, dyers, tanners and smiths in these guild districts of Porto Novo, a fine collection of Yoruba art in the crowded IRAD Museum (sister of the Fon institution at Abomey), a fading shell of the Toffa palace by the lagoon, and a perpetual market more vast and busy than the invisible economy of Porto Novo would seem to warrant.

Shabby, two-story balcony houses testify to a former prosperity, and great families live in compounds separated from the world by high walls. The narrow lanes of a dozen communes around Porto Novo resound at night to drumbeats and the cries of societies of guardians—inexplicable to the stranger, menacing to the intruder.

Porto Novo is no place for casual tourists, except those who linger momentarily by day at the museum or the lagoon, or who relax by the Bar du Soleil on the fine beach outside town. Otherwise someone who knows the place must unfold it to you, for its slumbering, guarded privacy can be penetrated these days only by a combination of prosperity and love—and Porto Novo has little left of either.

In the midland of Dahomey, between withered forest and foothills, stands the dusty railhead PARAKOU. Then, to the northeast, are BEM-BÉRÉKÉ and KANDI, capitals of the Bariba people, whose rites of passage, seasonal festivals and fantasias performed by horsemen are kept remarkably alive. Similarly, in the far northwest, a picturesque hill country between Natitingou and Fada N'Gourma in Upper Volta, cut by gorges and cascades, mountains and rivers, the magnificent Somba people inhabit their traditional turreted fortress houses, and celebrate the perfection of body and soul in an environment that, for all its beauty, brings them mainly deprivation and struggle.

Within this landscape lies the relatively rich game reserve of the Pendjari, a photographer's pleasure camp from Christmas to the rains of mid-June. Eastward, the "W" National Park, on a frontier corner occupied by Niger and Upper Volta, has an increasing but still disappointing stock of game compared to the reserves of Southern and East Africa.

What to Buy

Much Yoruba carving comes into and out of Porto Novo. Fon bronze casting usually follows worn patterns of the old royal art, producing animals, dancers, and balancing acrobats in series, but a coppersmith at Abomey, if offered a good price, can cast a unique piece of fantasy by the "lost wax" technique, either for his own pleasure or the customer's.

Gay, simple appliqué tapestries also come out of Abomey bearing standardized portrayals, in primary colors, of Fon dynasty history. In dealing with a tapestry artist, however, you might induce him to improvise an original cloth. Jewelry, musical instruments, wood engravings and inlaid furniture continue to be made in Abomey's workshops.

Dyed cloth and ceramics, basketwork, beaded charms and the traditional African "chess" game (here called hagi) are available for pittances in the Dan Tokpa market on Cotonou's lagoon. Decorated pirogue paddles can be found in Ganvié's souvenir shop on stilts. Woven blankets, skins and leather, lead figures and small animals in bone come down from the north to be sold, their prices increasing as they approach Cotonou. Kiosks of itinerant traders near the central market and the port entertain the serious bargainer. There are souvenir stalls in the Maison du Tourisme (Avenue Général LeClerc) and at the hotels.

Jewelers in Dahomean carrés fashion attractive rings and bracelets. A tour through the craftsmen's quarters in Porto Novo produces excellent opportunities to buy masks, statues, jewelry, embroidery, tinware, brass, pots, leather, dyed cloth, wickerwork and the like. Inexpensive tailoring and embroidering for booboos, dashikis, or sarongs (pagnes) can be readily arranged in Cotonou or Porto Novo.

Local Attitudes

Dahomeans are tolerant. Their code of hospitality and courtesy renders an invitation to dine, or to enter a home, almost compulsory. Traditional religious buildings and personnel, however, should not be photographed without consent. In driving, avoid killing stray animals and snakes: one never knows whose cult will be offended. If you do transgress, offer a sum of money in compensation.

Weather, What to Wear, How Long to Stay

The best time for visiting the coast is in July and August, after the rains and before the intense heat. Early winter (November to January) is fairly dry and cool (70 to 85 degrees), especially in the north, but is subject to the dusty harmattan wind. Heat mounts until the spring rains (April on the coast, June in the interior). Temperatures vary little in the south. Evenings in the north turn considerably cooler (50 degrees) than the daytime heat suggests. In towns where the French have left their mark, men are likely to think first and foremost of comfort, while women seem inclined to take pains with dress.

A relaxed visitor on a short leash won't be at all distressed simply to enjoy three days of food and drink around Cotonou, including a paddle out to Ganvié and an overnight run to Abomey via Allada and Ouidah. The dedicated student of West Africa, however, should visit the museums in Porto Novo and Abomey, call at the university to find congenial guides for explorations around Porto Novo, Allada, Ouidah and Abomey, and go into the little-known northland of the Bariba and Somba peoples. He couldn't possibly terminate his stay in less than a fortnight.

Most people fit neither of these extremes and should probably devote a week to Dahomey. Traveling east-to-west by road or lagoon adds a day in transit, and to leave the country by the northern route requires two more days. For game fanciers, the Pendjari merits two days, but in the "W" National Park you must either live in tents or cross over for accommodations on the Upper Volta or Niger side.

Communication

French is indispensable in towns where the numerous educated Dahomeans live. Visitors to villages, however, often encounter no European language whatever. Peace Corps and Canadian CUSO Volunteers are dispersed throughout the country, and there are a few US AID employees in the south. A bit of French and an interpreter for Fon should suffice for the serious traveler.

Dahomey's communications belong to the overseas French system, which provides barely adequate radio, telephone and telegraph service to Paris, Abidjan and Francophone Africa. There's intermittent service to

Nigeria and virtually nothing to Ghana or to Europe outside Paris. Public telephones function from post offices, hotels and administrative buildings.

Emergencies

Southern Dahomey is well equipped for medical and other emergencies; larger hospitals in the main towns have capable Dahomean and French doctors, but medical supplies and diagnostic resources are scarce. In the north there are virtually no adequate facilities. One can almost always call from a post office to a medical facility or to American officials in times of necessity. The American Embassy (tel. 26-93), the USIS cultural center and Peace Corps headquarters are in the residential section of Cotonou.

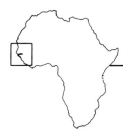

The Gambia

Profile

STATUS: Independent since February 18, 1965. Republic since April, 1970. Former British colony and protectorate.

SIZE: 4,361 square miles (twice the size of Delaware). Population— 360,000 (half Wolof).

GEOGRAPHY: Flat country along Gambia River banks. Principal towns— Bathurst (recently renamed Banjul, but still generally known by former name; capital, 33,000), Georgetown.

CLIMATE: Tropical. Bathurst temperatures range from mid 60's to high 80's; hotter up-river. Dry, cool season from November through March. Heavy rainfall in summer.

LANGUAGES: English (official), several African languages.

CURRENCY: Dalasi, divided into 100 bututs. D1.00 = 52 cents; $1.00 = D1.92.

VISAS: Required. Available from British Consulate General in New York. Also issued by Senegalese offices in New York and Washington, Gambian diplomatic offices in London and Dakar, British consulates wherever the Gambia is not represented. Fee $5.60.

AIRPORT: Yundum (BTH), 16 miles from Bathurst. Linked with West African neighbors and once weekly with London. Also, numerous charters from northern Europe. Taxis into city, D7.00 ($3.64); no buses except for organized tour groups. Domestic and international airport departure taxes, D2.50 ($1.30).

NATIONAL HOLIDAYS: February 18, National Day; Christian holidays.

INFORMATION SOURCES: *In US*—British Consulate General, 845 Third

Avenue, New York, N.Y. 10022 (tel. 212/752-8400). *In Bathurst—* Chief Tourist Officer, Office of the President, The Quadrangle (tel. 2891, ext. 25); Information Kiosk, opposite MacCarthy Square; WingAfric Ltd, 1 Independence Drive, P.O. Box 101 (tel. 8371).

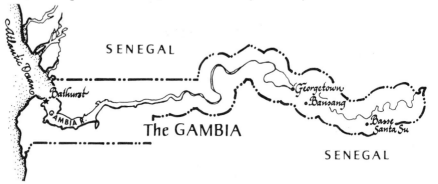

By Philip M. Allen

Whether seen through history or on holiday, Africa's smallest nation represents many things to many men. For the British it was an admirably strategic appendage colonized at the mouth of an accessible river and "protected" along 300 serpentine miles inland. For the French it is still an Anglo-Saxon bore, and for the Senegalese it's a 4,000-square-mile enclave in their patrimony, inhabited by the same Mandingo, Wolof, Dioula, Serer and Fulani people, but governed by foreigners. The Gambian enclave stands in the way of Senegalese communications and behaves disrespectfully toward Senegalese market controls, customs ordinances and import quotas. To other Africans, a Senegambian tongue in cheek, this diminutive beachhead also represents for some 5,000 sun-loving Scandinavians every balmy winter virtually all there is to Africa.

European powers first fought over the broad estuary at Bathurst and its hinterland 400 years ago to obtain slaves. Britain won and remains the independent Gambia's mainstay in trade, finance and technical assistance. But its victory engendered another in the series of artificial West African frontiers running arbitrarily inland from a coastal trade "factory."

Peanut-sized and peanut-shaped, the Gambia depends on peanuts (groundnuts) for nine-tenths of its export revenues. It even manages to sell back to Senegal at high prices the produce that Senegalese peanut growers have illicitly traded in Bathurst. In return, Gambian shopkeepers (Lebanese mostly) offer imports of cloth, electrical appliances, vehicles, hardware, whiskey and cigarettes at relatively low prices to consumers with ready cash from Senegal's inflated and rigged economy.

This sunny, breezy and practical little republic lives on its good climate and its wits, attracting tourists at a rate far beyond the normal West African standard and seeking good relations with everyone. The Gambia maintains only a tiny army (despite occasional growls from the Senegalese bear), an amorphous diplomatic service, and no university or other extravagant national institution. Its "airlines" waste no resources on planes or schedules; they merely sell tickets and charge for services to other people's operations.

Sir Dawda Jawara became prime minister on independence in February, 1965, acceding to the presidency in 1970 when the Gambia became a republic by referendum. A Moslem of the Mandingo people who once ruled great medieval empires inland, Jawara manages to sustain national identity on the Gambian territorial sliver despite a startling diversity of population. His majority includes the Moslem Wolof, Moorish, Lebanese and Dioula traders; his opposition relies on Bathurst's Christian Creole class (Aku), who descend from freed American slaves originally settled in Sierra Leone.

These 360,000 Gambians compose a hospitable and liberal nation, bright, gentle and tolerant. Its assets rival those of the most stable and sun-drenched Caribbean paradise, and that has influenced the Gambia's current ambition to promote tourism. Despite some prudish tongue-clucking from Aku and British residents and from French-speaking neighbors, the Gambians have evidently failed to become corrupted by the flocks of sun-hungry Scandinavians who migrate to this seaside oasis on cheap vacation charter deals. In fact these physical pilgrimages out of northern Europe—marshaled by Stockholm's Vingresor Club—cause most Gambians to rejoice in visions of neo-Caribbean, post-Rivieran and super-Canarian prosperity. Vingresor and its Gambian partners are also encouraging visitors from outside Scandinavia, and are building hotels to absorb them.

Foreign criticism has nevertheless provoked some reflection within the Gambia. Nobody can prove the existence of a single nudist or confirm suspicions of sexual and narcotic promiscuity, but some Gambians worry over moral deterioration, lagging initiative and excessive dependence on tourism.

Visitors will readily note the expansion of rather over-priced accommodations in the Gambia, the improving appearance of Bathurst, rapidly rising imports offset by foreign exchange from visitors, and new employment in building and service trades. Craftsmen, jewelers, tailors, taxi drivers, hairdressers, guides and hotel employees are all doing well, although the quality of service remains as depressing as elsewhere in insufficiently trained West Africa.

Not much general information has yet appeared on the Gambia. J.M. Gray's A History of The Gambia (Cambridge University Press, 1966) is the best book on the subject up to independence. An informative but poorly edited official Gambia Year Book can be obtained through government channels. A Tourist and Trade Guide is available from the African Advertising Agency, P.O. 574, Bathurst (D2.00, $1.04).

Money Matters

The Gambia departed from imperial British tradition by adopting right-hand drive just after independence and by converting to the decimal system in 1971. This conversion turned the old Gambian pound into dalasi (a convenient corruption of "dollars," if you will), divided into bututs. D1.00, or 100 bututs, equals about 52 cents. Bank rates, however, are around 55 cents for one dalasi and D1.86 for the dollar. For quick calculation, two dalasi or 200 bututs should be worth a little more than your dollar. Gambian currency cannot be imported or exported.

The Standard Bank of West Africa (an affiliate of Chase Manhattan) is the oldest in the Gambia, with branches up-country as well in Bathurst. Hours are 8 am to 1 pm Monday through Friday, 8 am to 11 am on Saturday. Standard and the recently opened French Banque Internationale du Commerce et de l'Industrie (BICI), which also has afternoon hours from 2 to 4 Monday through Thursday, accept travelers checks and hard currency.

Hotels and shops offer less favorable rates for your dollars or travelers checks; a few now recognize the major credit cards.

Getting In and Out

During the superb winter vacation season, from January through April, companies like Vingresor in Stockholm, Spies in Copenhagen and the British Far Horizons organize heavily booked Boeing 727 charter flights to Bathurst on a membership basis. A fortnight, all-inclusive round trip out of Stockholm costs about $400. Some people are predicting a comparable London package for around $280. Regular flights from London by British Caledonia, Ghana and Nigeria Airways, as well as Air Senegal, cover the West African coast from Lagos (Nigeria) to Freetown (Sierra Leone) or Dakar (Senegal), calling at Yundum Airfield, 16 miles from Bathurst. This World War II bunkering strip is currently being enlarged and modernized to handle large jets.

Customs and immigration services are push-pull, click-click for the charter customers, but officials turn a bit sluggish (although not at all unfriendly) for the individual visitor unless an influential friend tugs at their sleeve.

Bathurst's 12-mile-wide estuary invites travelers in from the sea. The cruise ships *Regina Maris*, *Irpinia* and *Fiorita* (Chandris Lines) bring in 2,000 British and Scandinavian passengers from Dakar and the Canary Islands each month during tourist season. Raymond and Whitcomb's African Quest tour calls six times each winter with American passengers aboard the Greek *MTS Apollo*, sailing between Dakar and Matadi (Zaïre). Passenger liners of the British Elder Dempster Line (Unilever) out of Liverpool come once every six weeks. During peanut export time, which coincides with the winter tourist season, passage can be arranged on Unilever, Norwegian and other flag freighters through local agents or ships' captains.

Until the advent of Scandinavian heliotropism, travelers usually saw the Gambia fleetingly while driving through the area between northern Senegal and southern Senegal (called the Casamance). Some doubtless fell victim to the charm of the country or got bogged down in the swampy countryside during the rainy summer. But most motorists merely made a pleasant 100-mile detour through Bathurst, often emerging with quantities of luxury imports to filter through the porous customs frontier to Senegal.

With the completion of a paved northern approach to the Barra-Bathurst ferry, traffic can now cross the Gambia at two different places: via the improved Transgambian Highway 115 miles east of Bathurst (300 miles to Bathurst from Dakar) and by way of the coastal road which is about 100 miles shorter between the two capitals. The Barra ferry takes 20 minutes to cover the three-mile neck of the Gambia River estuary, leaving from Barra at 9:30 am, 12:30, 3:30 and 6 pm, and returning from Bathurst at 8:30 and 11 am and 2:30 and 5 pm (Sunday afternoons at 4 only).

Hitchhiking is fairly good on both routes, especially over weekends.

Senegal-Gambian pledges of cooperation in tourist promotion and border control may ultimately make the trajectory more convenient for travelers. For the time being, however, you need a new (or multiple-entry) visa every time you cross a line.

Getting Around Within the Gambia

The country has only about 150 miles of paved road, including its brief segment of the Transgambian Highway from Senegal to Senegal, and the 115-mile link between Bathurst and that highway. Half the unpaved roads are strictly seasonal, hence only for four-wheel-drive vehicles from mid-July to early November. There are no regular passenger bus lines. All available buses are used for tours. Generally, wherever a vehicle can penetrate, you will find a "place (collective) taxi" or mammy-wagon. Once filled for the run, a one-way jaunt by place taxi from Bathurst to suburban Serekunda, Bakau and other nearby places costs about 14 cents per seat. It's 35 cents to Yundum Airport and $1 to Brikama (22 miles). Negotiate fares for anything longer than that.

Bathurst swarms with taxis, all licensed and fairly reliable but without meters. Prices for standard taxi runs are posted in all hotels: about 35 cents for a short run in the city (50 cents if you've called the taxi by phone), $1.35 for an hour's hire within town. You can also join excursion taxi parties that leave from hotels for the beaches and other attractions. Almost all traffic on local roads is commercial; the hitchhiker must usually pay for his ride. Considering the thoroughly flat character of the Gambian landscape, you can do very well by renting a bicycle from Vingresor.

A 484-mile cruise on the Gambia River aboard the creaking 500-ton steamer *Lady Wright*, together with chickens, goats, peanuts and sacking, vegetables, salt blocks, bicycles, machinery and people, is worth the four and a half day round trip between Bathurst and Basse Santa Su. "The Lady" leaves Bathurst on Saturday evening, arrives Tuesday morning and returns to Bathurst by Thursday afternoon, making two dozen hooting, people-thronged stops each way. Most travelers are satisfied with a one-way passage (cost: from $13.50 to $18.50 depending on privacy of bedrooms and plumbing facilities, plus about $2 per day for tasty, rather sloppy, food; bring your own whiskey or wine).

In the dry semester you can make one 250-mile trip by road to or from Basse, either non-stop in a place taxi at about $4 per seat or by renting your own taxi for about $50 (sharing the expense with traveling companions and stopping along the road wherever you please). Vingresor's Bathurst agency, WingAfric, offers the whole package, with return by bus and an overnight stop at Jappeni, for about $48. Avoid going up the steamy river in the summer rains, when human activity diminishes and insect life increases. However, hurry if you still want to do the cruise on the *Lady Wright*, which seems much older than her 22 years. She is due to be replaced in late 1973 by two new tourist boats. Book your passage with the Director of Marine, Wellington Street, in Bathurst.

There's another way of "doing" the river in wintertime: take a taxi from Bathurst four miles out to Denton Bridge, where the decorated "groundnut cutters" unload their peanut sacks, returning empty up the river. Sail with them as far as you like and take either the *Lady Wright* or a taxi back.

Where to Stay

The rush of low-budget, highly organized northern European tourism has crammed all hotels to capacity during the November-to-March season, encouraged the construction of three new hotels in the last two years, and transformed the Gambia's style of accommodation—no more colonial "grace," no real luxury, less attention to cuisine, high rates for shabby rooms, everything oriented to the beach. Do not come during the season without a confirmed reservation. If you have trouble, throw yourself on the mercy of the official tourist office first and Vingresor (on Leman Street) next.

The hotels in BATHURST and vicinity:

Sunwing, Cape St. Mary, the newest Vingresor-Gambian-British collaboration, 160 rooms occupying a fine beach peninsula beyond the suburb of Bakau; simple public rooms and with the Gambia's very first swimming pool. Rooms cost about $13.50 for singles, $20 for doubles, with breakfast; a $2.75 supplement for air-conditioning (seldom needed).

Fajara, built in 1971 on its own beach by Vingresor and the Gambian Government; plenty of room here, no air-conditioning, prices slightly less than at the Cape St. Mary Sunwing.

Palm Grove, on the Cape Road two miles out of town, small and simple but with sitting rooms as well as bedrooms and its own beach. Singles are $12, doubles $18, with a surcharge for air-conditioning.

Wadner Beach, a large, handsome new beach hotel two miles out on the Cape Road; owned by the Swedish proprietress of Radio SYD. Has a more heterogeneous clientele than the Vingresor establishments, good food, no air-conditioning. Singles cost $8 ($11.50 for half pension), doubles $13.

Atlantic, on the marina within walking distance of town, Bathurst's oldest hotel (1954) with several buildings and chalets, an open palm court in front (floodlit at night), two lively bars and a terrace in the rear, poor plumbing and sanitation, and for no fathomable reason walled off from the ocean. Avoid the Grill Room, a suburban luncheonette at steak house prices with fussy British service. Singles rent for $11, doubles for $19 (a reduction of about $2.80 is in effect off-season).

Hotel de la Paix, Atlantic Cape, a small Lebanese place without air-conditioning; double rooms for $15.

Uncle Joe's (Joe Cates), on Cameron Street in the center of town, with six non-air-conditioned rooms, minimal in comfort, but inexpensive and with congenial table d'hôte. Singles rent for $5 to $8, doubles for $9 to $14.

Three other humble hotels, which belong to the Adonis Group, set high rates by virtue of the heavy tourist demand. They are *The Adonis* on Wellington Street at the edge of town, a good place to eat, drink and meet friends (it charges $10 to $15 for singles, $14 to $18 for doubles, and boasts 24-hour service); the *Banjul,* relatively new, in center city; and the medium-sized *Carlton* on Independence Drive.

The *Chief's Rest House* on Leman Street in Bathurst is usually reserved for political personages and civil servants.

Traveling up-country in the Gambia puts you at the mercy of government accommodations or private arrangements. There are few schools in the hinterland to offer lodging and only a few Anglican and Methodist missions. (The missions have headquarters in Bathurst; inquire there for latest information on possible accommodations.) Government resthouses, charging about 30 cents per night for beds and wash basins, are found in the following towns: JAPPENI, BRIKAMA, KEREWAN, BWIAM, GEORGETOWN, FARAFINI, MANSA KONKO (slightly better than the others), BASSE and BARRA. You must bring your own bedding, food and utensils. Check with the Ministry of Local Government at the Quadrangle in Bathurst or with the office of the district commissioner in these provincial capitals.

Where and What to Eat

Although the Scandinavians have tried to relax the boiling and parching of "European" cuisine in this part of ex-British Africa, hotels in the BATHURST area are still motivated by a fierce desire to avoid offending non-African clients. The result is a compromise between Lebanese shashlik and smorgasbord. Of the European places, *Wadner Hotel, Adonis, Uncle Joe's* and *Club 98* try hardest.

Yet Gambian cuisine is itself so varied and exquisite that no discriminating traveler should agree to more than bed-and-breakfast accommodations at Bathurst. At simple places like the Lebanese-owned *Gambia Restaurant* on Wellington Street, the *Super Bird* just outside town, another *Gambia Restaurant* at Bakau eight miles from Bathurst, and some rough-and-ready urban dumps like *Nioukabouka* on Peel Street, *Saravah* behind the Adonis Hotel, Malick Secka's *Lion's Head* on Hagan Street, and (weekends only) *The Caribbean* on Primet Street, you can have inexpensive chicken and jollof rice stewed in tomatoes and vegetables (bena chin); chicken or beef and rice in groundnut stew with green beans (domodah) usually served with millet dumplings (chere); meat or smoked fish cooked in palm oil with vegetables (plasa); Lebanese meat pies; millet with meat and beans (bassi nyebe); pounded cassava (fufu) in a variety of sauces, and so forth. There is palm wine, beer or water.

Wherever you are dining look for fresh lobster, crab, mullet and other seafood from the area. Don't pay more than $3 for a steak—filet costs about 35 cents per pound in the market.

What to See and Do

Whether you observe from the decks of the *Lady Wright*, from a groundnut cutter boarded at Denton Bridge, or from a motor canoe rented in shore villages such as Bintang or Kaur, there is a world of pageantry to be seen along the Gambia River and its creeks. The Mandingo people of these villages move with the shifting fishing, cattle and peanut seasons; flocks of European birds join the Gambia's feathered wealth during winter; the farther upstream you go the better the chances for seeing hippos and crocodiles.

At Barra village near the ruins of Fort Bullen across from Bathurst, washerwomen work among tame "sacred" crocodiles, like those at Kartong Pool at Bakau. Along the north bank, around Kaur, Georgetown and beyond, the Senegambian circles of stones still cause head-scratching on the part of historians too sober to suppose that Anglo-Druids of two millennia ago took winter vacations. Twenty miles up-river from the capital, the baobab-bedecked ruins of James Island's old slave fort (1651) speak in muffled tones of battles and explosions, cruelty and piracy. If you hire a motor canoe, don't pay more than $3 per hour and be sure you know how many freeloaders your boat is carrying, for they affect its speed and range.

Winter visitors regard the Gambia as a crystallization of balmy beach, constant sun and repose. You have your choice of beach situations— calm warm surf in the estuary east of Cape St. Mary, or a cooler, rougher Atlantic to the west; perfect privacy on untouched sands 16 or 17 miles outside town at Tanji or Brufut, versus the dressing huts, refreshment stands and passing parade on the beaches within two and three miles of Bathurst.

Great sport fishing awaits off the estuary (barracuda and tigerfish as well as turbot and herring) and there is some bird-watching or bird shooting among the savannas and mangrove banks of the river—egrets, herons, flamingos, rollers, parakeets, hoopoes, jacanas, bee-eaters, sunbirds, pelicans, sand grouse, rock pigeon, green pigeon, guinea fowl, teal, duck, spurwing goose, snipe and many more. The meager forests and inland marshes contain their modest quantity of panthers, monkeys, baboons, hyenas, boar and snakes. You can come upon some of these in a quiet ramble by taxi to *Aluko Park*, 12 miles from Bathurst. It's open from 8 am to sundown every day, admission D2.00.

The best game park in the vicinity, however, is Senegal's *Niokolo-Koba Reserve*, due east of the Gambia. Air Senegal flies from Bathurst with 12-seat charters, but it is cheaper and more fun to drive in from Bathurst through the Casamance, coming back via Tambacounda and eastern Senegal.

For the student of development, the government will gladly display its cattle raising projects operated out of GEORGETOWN, 195 miles from Bathurst, or the intensive rice cultivation projects.

BATHURST itself, with 33,000 people, occupies a sandy peninsula curling back into the Gambia River estuary like the toe of a jester's slipper. The town lies between its beaches. Its activities center around MacCarthy Square, an old parade grounds and stadium next to government headquarters in the impressive Quadrangle. Colonial quaintness persists at State House, with its bougainvillea and hibiscus, and in the peeling balconied town houses along Wellington Street by the port, some dating from the years of Portuguese trading. There is little glass and aluminum modernity.

Everything is found close together in this town. Birds and fishing boats still frequent the south shore of the peninsula, along Bond Street. Albert Market, on Wellington Street, has abundant stocks of food (mainly fish and various flour heaps and herbs), but it is even more remarkable for the superb appearance of its Wolof and Mandingo clientele. Artisans ply a dozen trades in the side streets and at the admirable crafts market near the Quadrangle. But the developing world's willy-nilly urbanization has brought this calm, open, four-square town its share of whitewashed, rusty tin-roofed shanties, open sewers and muddy lanes.

Cricket remains Bathurst's sport of passion and soccer football is also taken seriously here, as everywhere in West Africa. The tourist office of WingAfric can help you get a temporary golf club membership. Bakau and Serekunda have wrestling tournaments on weekends (watch for announcements in the newspapers and on Radio SYD). Festive political rallies with dancing and singing take place at Brikama, President Jawara's handsome village 22 miles from Bathurst, and there are experimental gardens to visit on the nearby estate of the chief of Kambatai. One of the safest, most beautiful and lonely beaches, at Gunjar, 40 miles south of Bathurst, spreads next to a village where fishermen return in the afternoons with their catch and where Moslem devout come for pilgrimages at local shrines.

The Gambia celebrates Christian and Islamic holidays impartially. On

Christmas Eve, young men and boys dressed in fanciful navy costumes parade through Bathurst's streets carrying elaborate lanterns and home-made ship models, some of them 20 feet in length and festooned with colorful streamers and glowing with candles and torches. They sing, dance and drum until the early hours of Christmas morning.

Night life tends to be surprisingly tame in Bathurst, considering the influx of Europeans on holiday. Scandinavians and Englishmen content themselves with a beer and a stroll after dinner in the deliciously cool evenings—unless called to some organized merriment. The best shows are staged by the Super Ballets Africains, who present an ebullient pastiche of West African stage dancing, acrobatics, drumming and song—usually at Club 98, a well-appointed European restaurant-discotheque in Bakau by the sea. Young Gambians are more frequently found drinking beer or dancing to the Rover Band at the Bambooland Club in Serekunda, at the Omar Khayam or the Casuarina Club in Fajara—all suburban places —or in town on weekends at the rougher Caribbean and Africano bars.

As you might expect, Vingresor's WingAfric offers a gamut of orga-nized tours, at considerable saving for parties of 20 persons or more. They include: Bathurst city with visits to craftsmen's workshops and schools ($4.50); "festivals" of song and dance, sport and hospitality staged at one of several recruited Mandingo villages near Bathurst ($6 including re-freshments); taxi to *Aluko Nature Reserve* ($5); beach party at Gunjur ($6 including picnic); Club 98 evening barbecue with performance by Super Ballets Africains, followed by dancing ($7 all inclusive); deep-sea fishing tours ($9 for half day, $13 for full day); overnight bus tour of the Casamance to Ziguinchor ($41, plus visa fees); three-day river cruise on the *Lady Wright* to Basse, return by taxi ($48, everything included); a shorter river trip to and from Jappeni ($40); excursion by air charter to Senegal's *Niokolo-Koba Game Park* and return, with two game runs, overnight, and full pension at Simenti camp ($100).

What to Buy

Mandingo weavers carry on a tradition dating back to medieval Ghana. Their unique broadloom cloth, called "thub," comes in fast-dyed 12" by 84" strips ready for tailoring. Tie-dyes and batiks (which cost about $1.40 per yard) can be found at tailors' shops, or on the backs of itinerant Dioula traders, or at the government crafts center (where print-making is demonstrated to visitors). The center also offers good silver, snakeskin articles and musical instruments. A ready-made, handsomely embroidered African style shirt can be bought outside the Albert Market for $4.

Gambian filigree jewelry in gold and silver is justly prized; most of it is made in shops on Lancaster Street, Bathurst, although some comes in clandestinely from Senegal. Albert Market stalls offer pretty painted chests and decorated picture frames, glass bird cages, leather goods and straw. The leather workers can be visited in their shops on Allen Street. Few tourists fail to pick up a wicker basket or straw sun hat. And few fail to acquire something of the country's wood carving—although its inspiration falls far short of the strong original carving of Mali and the easterly forests. A couple of Gambian artists paint picturesque African scenes for visitors. Their works are shown at Gallery 5 in town.

The Lebanese shops in Bathurst display their merchandise in the dim recesses of decaying old balcony houses along Wellington Street and inside town. Bookshops are ill stocked; the Methodist and New England shops have the best selection of Africana, but most of their trade is in stationery and picture postcards. Business hours are normally from 8 am to noon six days a week, and from 2 to 5 pm except Saturday.

Local Attitudes

Contrary to rumor, Gambians permit no more audacious behavior by foreigners than any other Islamic African country. Bathurst has hordes of tame tourists, few hippies, no conspicuous nudists and only an occasional "swinger." Bikinis, miniskirts and bar-hopping have had little effect on the sedate tone of Bathurst. Some Gambian children pester tourists for coins and call "Toubab" (meaning "White Man" although guides tell you it means "Hello, friend") at any foreigner who walks their ghetto streets. A sincere display of interest in how Gambians live will bring out genuine, if surprised, pleasure on the part of your hosts.

Smuggling and bribery survive as private rituals here, like sex, pursued without bursting into scandal. But it is foolish for non-residents to engage in such enterprises without knowing how to manage the business, and in any case the prices for things they want are attractive in the Gambia only when contrasted with prices in Dakar or Conakry, not Las Palmas, Lomé or even Europe.

Another word of caution: Dolphins belong in the sea. Gambian fishermen resent any harm that comes to dolphins from anybody, burnoosed or bikinied.

Weather, What to Wear, How Long to Stay

The Gambia is a warm country by day. Shorts, slacks, short-sleeved shirts and sandals are standard tourist attire, with a sun hat for noontime and a sweater, jacket or full-length dress for winter nights when temperatures may drop to the 60's. While government and upper-bourgeois dignitaries cleave on occasion to the formality of shirt and tie (without jacket), most Gambians dress either in European cottons or in their national booboos, kaftans and lappas. Tourists may envy their elegance but usually settle for a dashiki shirt. Suit yourself.

If you don't mind plenty of company, come in the November-through-March tourist season. Skies are blue all day, only midday is hot, and Vingresor has yet to pay off on its guarantee to refund the fare of any client who can measure rainfall at Bathurst during that season. The Gambia would like to expand its tourist business into a year-round trade, but summer is humid, even though Bathurst temperatures seldom go above 90 degrees. Up-river things begin to get very steamy in March, June rains help only somewhat, and temperatures run 20 to 25 degrees higher than on the coast.

The European travel organizations emphasize the moderate-priced attractions of a fortnight on the Gambia beach, with exposure to village and river life and a chance to tour the interior, the Casamance, or the Niokolo-Koba Park in Senegal. With two weeks or more to spend, assuming you are not beach-bound, you might consider driving in from Dakar, taking the Gambia River cruise one way after visiting Bathurst, touring the Casamance (see chapter on Senegal), and going out by road to the Senegalese railroad at Kaolack—with Bamako, Timbuktu and the River Niger waiting in Mali at the end of the fortnight. Admittedly, chances of accurately coordinating schedules between the Gambia and her French-speaking neighbors are not encouraging. You can plan the trip in Dakar, verifying through WingAfric in Bathurst, and use Gambian taxi or place taxi rentals for most of your road travel.

Communication

English is official in the Gambia, but most of the population, especially up-river, speaks very little of it. Even Vingresor's locally hired guides are only a cut above "pidgin" levels in Swedish or English. Educated Gambians are suave and communicative, but education lags behind West African standards generally.

Although practically every sociable visitor who strays from his herd has made friends in this country, there are other ways to know what's going on. Radio Gambia is perhaps the weakest of them, remaining dependent on canned BBC programming and government "enlightenment." Probably the most popular radio station in all West Africa calls itself Radio SYD (formerly Radio Caroline when it broadcast from sea on the ship *Cheeta II*). A licensed commercial station, SYD pries listeners away from official programs in the Gambia and Senegal by broadcasting nothing but rock, soul and jazz, with a smattering of non-political news and advertising in English, French and Swedish (the language of its owners).

The government's Information Office publishes an informative *Gambia News Bulletin* three times weekly. In addition to several mimeographed periodicals, *The Gambia Echo*, a four-page weekly aligned with the Bathurst political opposition, prints international as well as local news and comment.

A satisfactory postal and telephone service functions within the country, with connections to London and Dakar, but communication from Bathurst with any other place in the world may be difficult. It's best to send your packages from somewhere else.

Emergencies

Full-scale hospitals exist only in Bathurst and Bansang, but the government maintains a network of health centers that dispense pills and first aid. Vingresor provides medical services to its clients, but if you encounter serious problems go to Dakar or London. The American Embassy is a one-man show on Cameron Street, open from 9 am to 1 pm six days a week (tel. 526). The emergency police telephone number is 222.

As noted in the profile, the name of the Gambia's capital has been changed officially from Bathurst to Banjul, but the new name has not yet gained currency internationally. In making travel arrangements it would be less confusing if you continue—for the present—to refer to the city by its former name.

Ghana

Profile

STATUS: Independent since March 6, 1957. Republic since July 1, 1960.

SIZE: 92,100 square miles (slightly smaller than Oregon). Population—8,725,000.

GEOGRAPHY: A coastline of 350 miles, thick forest, cocoa plantations, rolling hills and savanna plateau. Volta River merging into man-made Volta Lake in east. Principal towns—Accra (capital, 750,000), Kumasi, Tamale.

CLIMATE: Warm, high humidity. Accra temperatures range from 80 to 90 degrees (January to May hottest months). Northern temperatures range from 85 to 100 degrees (January to May hottest months). Evenings are cool.

LANGUAGES: English (official); Twi, Ewe, Akan languages (Fanti, Ashanti).

CURRENCY: New cedi, divided into 100 pesewas. NC1.00 = 81 cents; $1.00 = NC1.23.

VISAS: Required (even for direct transit through country); 14-day visitors' visas available from Ghana Embassy in Washington and Ghana Consulate General in New York. Fee $2.25. Three passport photos needed. Three days for processing. Longer stays require clearance from Accra. Visas available from British consulates where Ghana is not represented.

AIRPORT: Kotoka (ACC), five miles from Accra. Frequently linked with Western Europe (especially London) and West Africa. Airport departure taxes—domestic, NC0.50 (40 cents); international, NC1.00 (81 cents). Taxi into city, NC1.00.

NATIONAL HOLIDAY: March 6, Independence Day; Christian holidays.

INFORMATION SOURCES: In US—Embassy of Ghana, 2460 16th Street NW, Washington, D.C. 20009 (tel. 202/462-0761); Embassy of Ghana, 565 Fifth Avenue, New York, N.Y. 10017 (tel. 212/986-0500). In Accra— National Tourist Corporation, P.O. Box 3106 (tel. 28933 or 27114, cable TOURISM GHANA); Principal Secretary, Ministry of Information (P.O. Box M-41).

By Philip M. Allen

Keystone of the nations grouped around the Gulf of Guinea, this is West Africa's most attractive destination for English-speaking travelers. In increasing numbers American, Canadian, European and African visitors are discovering the beauty of Ghana's coast, forest regions and hill country, the color and romance of its festivals, the appeal of Gold Coast and Ashanti traditions, the quality of African cooking, and the charm of its eloquent and amiable people.

The first European territory in Black Africa to achieve independence, Ghana rode the postwar winds of change under its spellbinding leader, the late Kwame Nkrumah, galvanizing the entire continent. Nkrumah envisioned a union of free African territories confronting the world powers. The former British Gold Coast adopted the name "Ghana" at independence in 1957 to recall the great Sudanic empire of a thousand years ago.

But Nkrumah's Ghana, only eight million strong, spent its leadership resources prematurely and disastrously. The president's militant anti-colonialism, his neutralist foreign policy and pan-African ideology seemed radically quixotic and even pro-Communist to many Western observers. His chosen appellation, Osagyefo (the Victorious), appeared megalomaniacal and discredited his policies. By the mid-1960's, Ghanaian militancy threatened stability in neighboring countries—French-speaking Ivory Coast, Upper Volta, Niger and Togo—where conservative regimes depend on continuing exchanges of privileges with France. As Ghana sought to force the pace of pan-Africanism, it alienated two dozen new governments preoccupied with consolidating their respective holds on freshly minted national territories and institutions.

Inside the country, grand projects and grandiose monuments were financed on overly optimistic predictions of world prices for Ghana's cocoa crop, which accounts for one-third of world production. Nkrumah's cronies salted away the proceeds. The country amassed a foreign debt of three-quarter billion dollars, equal to three years of export revenues. In February, 1966, while Nkrumah was out of the country, Ghana's British-trained military leaders deposed him and turned the nation to more modest destinies. Nkrumah died in April, 1972, after six years of exile in Guinea.

In October, 1969, the generals returned Ghana to a freely elected civilian government headed by the sociologist Kofi Busia, long an opponent of Nkrumah, as prime minister. Because of international debts, however, even the development of hydroelectric energy on the Volta River, the expansion of cocoa production and the increased exploitation of bauxite, manganese and timber resources failed to resolve the deep financial crisis. In January, 1972, the two-year experiment in civilian rule was terminated when the army again took control. Politics have been suspended and the military caretakers, led by 40-year-old Col. Ignatius K. Acheampong, grasp for new solutions.

But for serious travelers, Ghana offers remarkable riches. It has the cultural concentration of Dahomey and the contrasting landscape and natural wealth of Nigeria and the Ivory Coast, with a population better adapted than any for showing these advantages to visitors. The climate is as temperate as any in West Africa. Its people have a greater spirit of enterprise and greater pride in their culture than one sees in their French-speaking neighbors. Ghana's 350 miles of coastline are liberally sprinkled with cliffs, beaches, palm trees and castles (European fortresses dating back to the days of slave trading and competitive scrambling). The interior of thick forest, cocoa farms and rolling hills leads up to the Sudanic plateau. In the center live the heirs of the Ashanti nation, masters of the land and mines behind the Gold Coast until conquered by the British in the late 19th century.

The Ashanti, with their Fanti, Ga and Twi neighbors to the south, the Ewe to the east and the Gonja, Dagomba and Hausa people in the north, compose a spirited, elegant and productive nation. Ghana spends nearly 25 per cent of its budget on education. It has remained a member of the British Commonwealth and opened its doors to foreign industry and investment. Its tourist facilities are multiplying. But the millennium anticipated by successive regimes has been deferred by harsh financial realities, the futile rivalry of powers and factions, and the excessive ambition of past leaders.

Ghana's grandeur and tragedy have been described by many writers and political figures. Ayi Kwei Armah's surrealistic novel *The Beautyful Ones Are Not Yet Born* (Heinemann, 1968) has won wide acclaim. Nkrumah wrote a half-dozen works, including his fascinating *Autobiography* (Nelson, 1957). The books of Kofi Busia, W. E. Abraham, Kofi Awoonor and the dramatist Efua Sutherland rank with the best of West Africa. Scholarly works include David Apter's *Ghana in Transition* (Atheneum, 1964) and a comparison edited by Philip Foster and A. R. Zolberg entitled *Ghana and The Ivory Coast, Perspectives on Modernization* (University of Chicago Press, 1971). The Anglo-Ashanti wars are recounted by Alan Lloyd in *The Drums of Kumasi* (Longmans, 1964). W. E. F. Ward's *A History of Ghana* (Allen and Unwin, 1966) is a useful introduction. The Ministry of Information in Accra has a comprehensive collection of official papers and reports.

Money Matters

Ghana's currency reflects its strained economy and has fluctuated widely in value. The non-convertible new cedi, divided into 100 pesewas, equals 81 cents. Banks and hotels sometimes give more for hard currency but often decline to exchange leftover cedis. Change only what you need as you go along. A 10 pesewa piece (worth 8 cents) is often called a shilling. Three international banks have headquarters on High Street in Accra and branches in most major Ghanaian towns. They are the Ghana Commercial Bank (also offices in London and Lomé, Togo), Barclays Bank DCO, with its world network, and the Standard Bank of West Africa, affiliated with Chase Manhattan. Travelers checks are honored. Merchants are reluctant to accept credit cards, partly out of apprehension over future variations in the exchange rate.

Currency controls at frontiers are directed against the black market and contraband traffic in goods and money between Ghana and its CFA franc neighbors. Cedis are not permitted into or out of Ghana. You must declare foreign currency on arrival and departure, although unlimited quantities can be carried in either direction. Keep your exchange receipts in case of examination on leaving the country. Airline offices and the duty-free shops at Kotoka Airport accept only foreign currency.

Between 1963 and 1971, as Ghana struggled to refinance her international debt, to adjust to the decline of world cocoa prices and to accumulate resources for lagging investment, the cost of living doubled for city dwellers and others in the "modern" economic sector. Prices in hotels, shops, travel agencies, "European" restaurants and other tourist facilities now approximate the inflated prices of Abidjan, Dakar and Lagos. You can economize somewhat by trying to book lodgings in government rest-houses, eating good Ghanaian food, using public conveyances and buying everything possible (after prolonged bargaining) in the open markets. Some things may be in short supply. Essential imports (rice, soap, etc.) have become increasingly scarce since the government's repudiation of its $600 million private debt; exporters have been unable to obtain guarantees and importers are now being investigated to detect alleged habitual fraud.

Getting In and Out

There is constant land, sea and air traffic in and out of Ghana. Kotoka International Airport, five miles northeast of Accra, is a West African pivot point for a dozen airlines. It is one of Africa's most luxurious and comfortable terminals, with a full array of shops, bars, travel agencies, airline offices and a newly renovated hotel. Charter flights between London or New York and Accra are numerous and convenient, especially for educational travel groups during the summer.

Takoradi, the cocoa port in the west, and Tema, the industrial harbor 17 miles east of Accra, receive ships of many flags carrying passengers. They include Farrell Lines out of New York, Ghana's Black Star Lines from Canadian East Coast and Gulf ports, and Elder Dempster vessels from Liverpool, all on frequent schedules. The few passenger vessels between Ghana and Europe are usually booked solid from June to September. However, a talk with a ship's captain or shore agent may turn up possibilities.

You can also enter and leave by road. Taxis, collective taxis, mammy-wagons and rented cars travel West Africa's most important paved highway along the coast from Lagos (Nigeria) through Dahomey and Togo into western Ghana beyond Takoradi. There the highway ends, at least for the foreseeable future. Backpackers can cross the border into the Ivory Coast at Half Assini if the private ferry is operating and the border posts are open (inquire about this at Accra or Abidjan before starting out). Motorists must take a semi-circular detour requiring about 14 hours between Accra and Abidjan via Kumasi, the Dormaa-Ahenkro border crossing and Abengouro (Ivory Coast). There is an enjoyable but rough interior road crossing on Ghana's eastern border at Dafo and Klouto (Togo) just east of the great Volta Lake.

Land and air connections are poor between Ghana and its northern neighbor, Upper Volta. Ghana's 525-mile north-south axis, paved between Accra and the border, is traveled by state buses as far as Bawku or Navrongo; trucks and collective taxis continue into Upper Volta. Traffic drives on the right in all neighboring countries, but changes to the left for Ghana.

Documentation requirements for visitors are strict. Americans need visas even for direct transit through the country. Since Ghanaian consulates insist on a two-to-three day processing period even for short-term visitors' visas, it's quicker to apply at British consulates in non-Commonwealth countries where Ghana is not represented.

Getting Around Within Ghana

The country has 14,000 miles of road, less than half of them paved. There are also some 6,000 miles of dry-season tracks, mostly in the underdeveloped north. The coastal highway between the Togolese border and Takoradi has considerable commercial and pleasure traffic, as do the north-south arteries from Accra-Tema through Kumasi in the Ashanti center, and from Accra to Akosombo and the eastern shore of the Volta Lake. The State Transport Corporation (STC) sends sturdy Mercedes buses and tourist coaches into most parts of the interior on fairly firm schedules. Seats are reserved. Taxis and perilously loaded Morris lorries—made over into mammy-trucks ("tro-tros"), and painted with proverbs and admonitions from Ghanaian and Biblical folklore—also ply these roads, but on flexible schedules.

Hitchhiking is fairly easy on the main arteries but elsewhere suffers from the paucity of non-commercial traffic.

Chevrolets and Peugeot 404's (the latter excellent for rough roads) are available for hire with drivers at the State Transport Corporation in Accra (P. O. Box 384) at NC12.50 ($10) for the first 50 miles and 25 pesawas (20 cents) for each additional mile. The United Trading Company (UTC Motors) in Accra and Kumasi charges similar rates for large vehicles but less for smaller General Motors Opels. Tarzan International Services also rents Opels, Datsuns and Vauxhalls at lower rates. Speedway Travel and Tours rent Opel Kadetts for about $6 a day and 15 cents a mile after the first 40 miles; larger Opel and Peugeot 404's rent for $7.30 plus 19 cents a mile; Chevrolet and Mercedes cars rent for $9 and $10, plus 20 cents a mile. The UAC Car Hire Service in Accra and Kumasi has comparable arrangements. In all cases the customer pays for gasoline. Overtime allowances for drivers are charged by all companies. None has a one-way rental plan.

In towns, taxis with yellow fenders are owned by the State Transport Corporation. Taxis are unmetered. They are authorized to charge up to 20 pesewas a mile or fraction thereof, but passengers should fix the price of any trip with the driver before starting. Taxis sometimes pick up additional passengers, dropping each off in turn. In Kumasi taxis are both cheap and plentiful.

Railway and internal air routes follow the road system over the densely populated forest triangle between Accra, Kumasi and Sekondi-Takoradi. Ghana Airways, with rates that compare favorably with most internal African airlines, flies Fairchild F-27's several times daily to Kumasi (one way costs $14), and Fairchild and Hawker-Siddeley planes four times weekly to Takoradi in the west ($14) and Tamale in the north ($32). The national railroad covers much of the area inside the Accra-Takoradi-Kumasi triangle. Most trains have first class accommodations as well as cheaper facilities. Ghana Airways has DC-3 charter service to more remote places and to destinations outside Ghana.

The new man-made Volta Lake system above Akosombo can be crossed at a dozen points between Yeji and Ada on car ferries or launches. For pleasure boating make your own arrangements in the lake ports.

The National Tourist Corporation publishes a small *Official Guide* as well as brochures and maps. An unofficial and somewhat amateurish *Ghana Tourist Guide* can be obtained by writing to P. O. Box 7774, Accra. The Tourist Corporation and Ghana Airways publish national and city maps. Moxon Paperbacks (P. O. Box M-160) and Moxon's Atlas Bookshop in Accra have several helpful publications including *Your Guide in Ghana*. The Ghana Publishing Corporation (Accra, Tema) also has a number of booklets including *Ghana's Main Towns and Cities* and A. A. Opoku's *Festivals of Ghana*. The Ministry of Information and Tourism issues a variety of handbooks and periodicals on the country. But official tourist policy seems obsessed with sterilizing, cellophaning and air-conditioning Ghana rather than making its unique qualities accessible.

The Ghana Hotels and Tourist Corporation (Indusco House, Barnes Road, Accra) owns most of the hotels and provides advice on accommodations. The Chief Game Warden of Mole Game Reserve (P. O. Box 8, Damongo) furnishes details on his bailiwick. The Chief Transport Officer (Ring Road, Accra) advises on official bus service and government rest-house accommodations up-country. The Automobile Travel Association of Ghana (Fanum Palace off Kojo Thompson Road, P. O. Box 7047, Accra, tel. 239-53) helps members of international automobile clubs with travel arrangements. On arrival, pick up a copy of each Accra newspaper available. They are entertaining, helpful in setting the stage, cost virtually nothing and take very little time to peruse. USIS's library is uptown at the corner of Tudu and Kojo Thompson Roads. To locate a festival, ceremony or art exhibition in time to attend you sometimes have to consult all these sources.

Several travel agencies compete for tourist patronage in Accra. Scan-travel, which also has a branch in Takoradi, represents American Express (CFAO Building, High Street, P. O. Box 1705). Other agencies include: Intertours and Cargo Services, at Mona House, Liberty Avenue (P. O. Box 6704); Express Travel Agency, at Casanova Building, Tudu Road (P. O. Box 2625) also in Kumasi; and Universal Travel and Tourist Services at Republic House (P. O. Box M-99).

Where to Stay

Lodgings are no bargain in Ghana. Anything of quality is high priced; almost anything low priced is shabby and unsanitary. The State Hotels Corporation manages comfortable but generally expensive hotels in Accra, Tema, Kumasi, Takoradi and at the Volta Lake. Each State hotel either provides sports facilities or can make arrangements for you. Accommodations are especially scarce during school vacations and the European holiday season, so it's best to reserve well in advance.

In Accra, the *Ambassador* represents standard large-hotel convenience in a tranquil garden 15 minutes' walk from the center of town. It has a pleasant open air restaurant, several high-spirited bars (good places to get to know the Ghanaian city elite), a rooftop casino, beach club, spacious public rooms and leisurely copious British breakfasts. But food and service are mediocre and rooms overpriced at $14 for singles and $20 for doubles (including breakfast).

The State Corporation's *Hotel Continental*, along the road to Kotoka Airport, is a former Intercontinental. It has comfortable rooms and its own casino, terrace bar, gardens and fountains and a cabaret nightclub. Prices, food and service are similar to the Ambassador's. The *Star Hotel*, on the 4th Circle Road, is an old favorite among Accra's sophisticates. This is the State Corporation's medium-priced hostelry ($6.50 singles, $10.50 doubles). The brand new *Hotel President*, privately owned, is also in this range.

Moderately priced accommodations in Accra are shabby, but try the *Avenida Hotel* on Kojo Thompson Road or the *Washington* downtown, both with rates comparable to the Star but in a more central location; *Kob Lodge* on Ring Road Central; the *Bosumtwi Hotel* where double rooms can be had for $5.50 (singles at $4), and the *Victoria*. For truly low budgets, shop along Airport Road at places like the *Nkwadum Bar and Rest House*, the *Date* (a dance bar with rooms), and the modern YMCA or YWCA on High Street between midtown and the ocean. There is a clean, cheap youth hostel in the Tesano section north of town.

On a hilltop at Greenwich longitude above the industrial port of Tema, 19 miles from Accra, the State Corporation runs the *Meridian Hotel*, Ghana's only nearly luxury establishment. Its rates are slightly lower than those of the Ambassador and Continental, but it has an empty feeling that reflects Tema's still unfulfilled destiny. The Meridian's Zero Room is well appointed for small-scale performances of superb Ghanaian drumming and dancing, and the Skyview Bar looks down over the harbor.

At Legon, north of Accra, academic folk may find lodgings at the University of Ghana Guest House or the *Ford Foundation Flats*. Student residences at all three Ghanaian universities are usually occupied during summer vacations by overseas educational groups, including many Americans. Many US students spend a year here.

In Kumasi, the State Hotel Corporation runs the large reasonably priced but inconveniently located *City Hotel* ($6.50 singles, $10 doubles), with a casino and shopping gallery. The *Hotel de Kingsway* is in about the same price range and better located. The *Tourist Cottage Club* charges $3.50 to $5 per room. There is also a University Guest House.

The State Corporation's handsome and well-managed *Atlantic Hotel* ($6.50 singles, $10 doubles) overlooks the harbor at TAKORADI and has a casino and golf course. The charming little *Volta Hotel* at AKOSOMBO near the great dam has air-conditioned rooms with fine views of the Volta Lake for about the same price.

The *UST Motel* on the beach at ELMINA is a popular resort where the $4 to $6.50 prices go up another cedi on weekends. Academic people may be housed at Cape Coast University near Elmina. BOLGATANGA in the north has the old *Hotel de Bull* ($3 a person). TAMALE has the *Tufou* and the *Chandiba*, NKAWKAW the *Hotel Nkawkaw*, KOFORIDUA an inexpensive YMCA Motel. At DAMANGO, the *Mole Game Reserve Motel* charges from $4 a single with minimum facilities to $7.50 for greater privacy. It has a swimming pool and an inexpensive menu.

The Ghana Government operates motel-like catering rest-houses (usually $5 to $6.50) at Cape Coast, Tamale, Sunyani, Kumasi and Kpandu. Service is good and the bars are filled with local beer drinkers. Most of these houses are tucked into the outskirts of towns and are difficult to find or to book, since they are intended for traveling civil servants. It's often worth the effort to stop by or ring them up before settling for less comfortable or more expensive accommodations. Rest-houses in smaller towns may also accommodate visitors (usually 50 cents a bed), but don't serve food. Requests for these accommodations must be addressed to the appropriate Regional Administrator. Some of the nicest non-catering rest-houses are located at AMEDZOFE overlooking the Volta Lake 30 miles north of Ho; VANE, on the side of the same hill; MPRAESO, six miles above Nkawkaw on the Kwahu escarpment, with a pretty view, and Fort Metal Cross in DIXCOVE, where the old cannons and parapets still loom over the fishing cove and village.

For accommodations at religious missions, inquire at the Catholic Youth Organization (P. O. Box 76), the Presbyterian Young People's Guild (P. O. Box 777), the Methodist Youth Fellowship (P. O. Box 403) or at YMCA or YWCA offices, all in Accra. Other cheap beds at secondary schools, bar-restaurants and private residences (including Peace Corps and Canadian CUSO Volunteers) require on-the-spot requests.

Where and What to Eat

Good news for the discriminating diner in Ghana: the overboiled, overpriced European menus can be avoided here. Even the hotels, which assume that all foreigners want soggy vegetables, sad meat and pallid custards, now provide one or more Ghanaian dishes (sample them at the *Palm Inn* of the Ambassador, for instance). Try groundnut (peanut) stew or palm stew with rice, pounded yam (fufu) or fried spiced plantain (kelewele), jollof rice, agushi "soup" (a melon seed sauce), or one of the many leaf stews with or without hot sauce, and palm wine. Some are acquired tastes but can become habit quickly.

In ACCRA, the *Black Pot Restaurant* on Ring Road East has an enormous multinational menu and reasonable prices. It is situated in an old Accra house with fine Adinkra tapestries and beautiful Bolgatanga crockery. Run by Anglo-Ghanaian publisher-businessman and long-time aficionado of Ghana James Moxon, it is quite probably the best African restaurant. Try any chicken or Guinea fowl dish, baked cassava fish, palmnut soup, turtle au gratin, Shama pigeon, venison, chichinga (shish kebab) or any of the standard West African platters. The rum punch is elegant, the palm wine pure and the fruit desserts magnificent.

Simpler meals are available at very modest prices at the *Date Hotel*, *Club 10 Bar*, *The Eagle*, the YMCA and YWCA, or at cheap but hygienically risky "chop bars" on all major roads just out of center city Accra. Other possibilities are *The Point* on Tema Road (with tangy roast chicken and salads, and a fine view), Lebanese food at the *Diplomat* (a particularly good buy at lunch) or *Le Rêve* on Liberation Circle, *George's Chicken Bar* in Tudu, *Edwards* and *Uncle Sam's* on Kojo Thompson Road, *Talal's* off Liberty Road and *Fawzi's Snack Bar*. For good African and Chinese fare try the *Mandarin* across from the Black Pot on Ring Road East, and the *Biscay*. Inexpensive Indian curries are served with music at the *Maharaja* on Pagan Road above the Glamour Department Store, and (more expensive) at Saturday lunch time in the Swiss *Le Chevalier*. There are Italian platters at *Piccolo Mondo* (with discotheque) in Republic House; French food at *Le Baron* on the Trade Fair site, and Swiss-Viennese meals at *Maxim's* on Achimota Road. Excellent spit-roasted chicken is served on a high pavilion at *Restaurant May* near the Botanical Garden at Aburi.

KUMASI has *The Cabin* on the Accra Road, a delightful, inexpensive place run by three women—one Ghanaian, one Chinese and one Filipino. There are also the *Top High*, the inexpensive Lebanese *Chicken Bar* near Hotel de Kingsway, and the *Friday Club* at Abrepo Junction.

On the coastal highway at the turn-off to WINNEBA is the *Blue Star* roadhouse for Ghanaian "chop" and beer. At CAPE COAST try the locally popular *Green Hill Restaurant*. At NKAWKAW the *Hotel Nkawkaw* has good roast chicken.

Low-budget travelers can get by on locally grown fruits, some vegetables (wash them carefully), excellent roasted plantain bananas at roadsides, and abundant fish.

If you must eat in hotel dining rooms stuff yourself on an English breakfast and settle for fish and chips at other times.

What to See and Do

Ghana's attractions include a bustling, shabby capital with splendid night life; two dozen castles studding a 350-mile Gold Coast; fairs and festivals occurring almost weekly during much of the year; color in local markets; jeremiads painted on the lintels of mammy-trucks; the Volta Dam and its huge man-made lake; country-wide facility in English and a radiant heritage of sculpture and metal casting, music and dance.

Greater ACCRA (with Tema) claims 750,000 inhabitants with standards of living ranging from shanty poverty and khaki rags to big bougainvillea bungalows and stunning high fashion. The Ussher Town and Victoriaborg sections have some admirable new buildings like the public library and the Ghana Commercial Bank. Fort James and Fort Ussher, both dating back to the 17th century, now serve as prisons. The white monolith of Christiansborg Castle, taken by the Danes from Portugal and refashioned by a parade of successors, houses major government offices and can be visited on certain days with permission from the National Tourist Corporation. Its sea wall shades the grave of American-born W. E. B. DuBois, distinguished black American scholar and NAACP director and editor. The Trinidadian George Padmore, another eminent pan-Africanist, is buried inside the castle grounds.

Accra's National Museum, north of the Ambassador Hotel, has one of Africa's richest collections of sculpture, historical regalia and golden Kente cloth from Ashanti. The National Science Museum also merits a visit. Nkrumah's titanic but empty Black Star Square is used on ceremonial occasions. His luxurious state house (called "Job 600") was occupied only once, briefly, by the African statesmen for whom it was built. Now his Flagstaff House residence is again army headquarters. The zoo nearby is open to the public.

The Arts Center on 28th February Road has crafts workshops, a sales shop, an active theater, orchestra and choir, and occasional exhibitions of paintings. Here and at theaters in town or at the university, you may see performances of Ghanaian folk operas composed and directed by Sacque Acquaye, or Experimental Theater Workshop productions led by the poetess Efua Sutherland. Theatrical performances are given at secondary schools and local cultural associations outside Accra.

Everybody in Accra goes to the central Makola Market where genial, proverbially wealthy "market mammies" control trade and hold court in genuinely matriarchal style. The Christmas rush here is a marvel of ringing bells and joviality.

Musical bars like Club 10, the Lido, Tip-Toe, the Metropole, La Ronde and the Star Hotel jump until dawn with rock, soul and (alas, less and less) Ghanaian high-life, an urban improvisation of African and Western music. The Bokum Hotel occasionally has good floor shows. There is "international" entertainment from time to time at the Continental and the Ambassador. The latter's outdoor dance floor attracts a glittering clientele.

The capital is flanked by its own beaches and has hot springs near Fort Ussher. Soccer football, Africa's passion, is played on Sunday afternoons at the stadium near Black Star Square. There's horse-racing at the race course nearby, and polo. Try the Ambassador Hotel's Beach Club, just off Black Star Square, whether you are staying at the hotel or not. Its water is relatively unpolluted and the company attractive.

The 600-square-mile metropolitan area of Accra includes Legon, nine miles to the north where the University of Ghana—oldest and most classically European of three national universities—rises handsomely over lofty hills. The Ghana Dance Ensemble is housed there and under the guidance of the Ghanaian musicologist J. H. K. Nketia some fascinating experimental music is emerging from the blend of rural tradition and urban idioms. Browse in the university's gardens and bookstore.

Fifteen miles north of Legon, on the plateau at Akwapim Ridge, are the lovely botanical gardens of Aburi, with the Peduasi Lodge, residence of former Ghanaian presidents Nkrumah and Akufu-Addo, and a landscape of waterfalls and tropical forest. Restaurant May near the gardens has a fine view and on weekends attracts gorgeously gowned patrons.

TEMA also lies in the metropolitan area. Its spankingly modern port opened in 1962, and there is a Kaiser-Reynolds aluminum smelter plant, but the communities planned around it are unfinished and its industrial potential is not yet fulfilled. The terrace bars and casino of the Meridian Hotel and the El Passo and Talk of the Town bars are friendly.

Visitors to the castles of the Gold Coast might write for information to the Inspector of Monuments, P. O. Box 41, Elmina (tel. 12). More casual tourists can visit the most prominent castles in a day's 150-mile drive between Accra and Takoradi. These include the Portuguese-built Elmina, named in 1482 after the gold mines that first lured Europeans here. It is now occupied by the Ghana Mobile Police who conduct regimented tours. Elmina stands above a lively fishermen's beach and has some of the finest ocean swimming in Ghana. Christopher Columbus visited Elmina in 1482. Near Elmina, at Cape Coast, is the 1662 Carolusburg, Britain's colonial headquarters for much of the 19th century. Fort Amsterdam, 70 miles from Accra, built in 1630, is undergoing restoration as a slave trade monument by a group of black American residents. Other popular castles on the route are at Shama, Komenda, Anomabo, Apam and Saltpond.

The Gold Coast motorist can pause at beaches, fishing villages, schools and towns like Winneba, an educational center near a forest of deer, with a restaurant and facilities for bathers. The town of CAPE COAST (44,000) is an animated city of fishermen, once a slaving capital and now the home of one of Ghana's three universities. The international cocoa port, TAKORADI, with its residential adjunct SEKONDI, has a population of 80,000, a beach club, several dance bars and the sporting and social facilities of the Hotel Atlantic. At fishing villages along the way you can arrange to be rowed out over the surf, watch net casting or the return of the fishermen, and do some diving or fishing on your own.

East of Accra the highway runs across the Volta River delta, past mangrove lagoons and marshy areas, to Lomé, capital of Togo. Fifty miles upstream at AKOSOMBO, the Volta Dam closes 3,300 square miles of a man-made lake that extends 250 miles northward to the confluence of the White and Black Volta streams. Travelers can cover the lake in rented boats, cross by ferry between Kpandai and Dumbai or eastward from Yeji, drive around the handsome hilly region off the eastern shore, and visit the huge but underdeveloped *Kujani Game Reserve* on the west bank. South of the lake near KOFORIDUA, Tafo has a well-known Cocoa Research Institute. KPANDU on the eastern shore is a center of pottery, ivory and wood carving. North from Yeji, there are remains of an old slave market at SALAGA and rice growing projects at the garden-filled town of TAMALE in the Moslem north.

KUMASI, capital of Ashanti, 162 miles northwest of Accra, was rebuilt after the British destroyed it in 1874 during their half-century of warfare against the 200-year-old empire. It is still a major inland trade and educational center, and a living textbook on Ghanaian history and culture. Kumasi has the inextricably earth-bound sword of Okomfo Anokye, founder of the realm, and an old Ashanti fort now used as a military museum. You may be able to call on the Asantehene (emperor) in the highly traditional Manhyia Palace. The zoo and the Asafo market warrant lengthy visits. The University of Science and Technology here is more specialized than the two coastal universities. Wood carvers and brass casters work in the National Cultural Center, surrounded by gardens and an open air museum. Night spots include the As Usual, Jamboree, Star-nite and Atomic Paradise clubs.

Twenty miles south of Kumasi, the sacred Lake Bosumtwi (pronounced "Bosomchwi") is encircled by beautiful hills, cocoa plantations and close-knit villages. Bonwire village is the home of Kente cloth, a resplendent fabric of bold primary colors interwoven with golden thread, seen widely throughout Ghana despite its ostensibly prohibitive cost. Weavers work on complicated looms behind their homes, fashioning four-inch-wide strips in a variety of traditional patterns that are sewn together to make gowns, togas, flags, ceremonial canopies and wall hangings.

At OBUASI, 40 miles south of Kumasi on the road to Takoradi, visitors may inspect a working gold mine (the product more frequently ends up in the weaves of Kente than in the national treasury). There are smaller gold operations at Tarkwa, an hour's drive from Takoradi.

Ghana's northern and upper regions are predominantly Moslem, relatively underdeveloped and underpopulated. They include centers of high pageantry like Tamale, Gambasa, Navrongo, Bawku with its Togolese market, and Yendi. BOLGATANGA has a large crafts market, and eastward toward the GAMBAGA Scarp the Tongzuzu rock formations create a dramatic landscape. There is a pond of sacred tame crocodiles at Paga, 22 miles away.

The *Mole Game Reserve* north of Damango, 420 miles inland from Accra, is best visited in the dry winter and early spring. Fly to Tamale and drive the last 92 miles by taxi or pre-arranged rented car. The motel at Mole makes guides available. Game, while plentiful, includes few large cats or elephants.

West African drumming, instrumental music and dancing reach their zeniths among the Ashanti, Fanti, Ewe, Twi, Ga and northern peoples of Ghana. The universities and national cultural centers (especially those at Tamale, Ho, Tema, Bolgatanga, Sekondi and Kumasi) are seeking to sustain these traditions among young Ghanaians. With government encouragement local festivals have remained frequent and popular, many of them featuring religious pageantry, horsemanship, musketry, dancing and durbars (assemblies of chiefs and their people). Most festivals celebrate historic victories, vital initiations, or moments of communion with the living dead (in secular terms, commemoration of ancestral tradition). Harvest festivals occur in August and September, but there are many ritual occasions throughout the year. Calendars maintained by the National Tourist Corporation can be consulted.

Ghana is the easiest country in West Africa for good casual conversations, getting invited to homes, meeting kings and courtiers, observing how people work and live, tend their cocoa trees, resolve conflicts in communal style, and study at the many schools throughout the country.

Government agencies and international organizations are glad to conduct visits to their development projects. Scantravel and other agencies operate a bus tour of the capital and Legon for $3; a nine-hour excursion to Aburi and Akosombo via Tema, with a visit to a cocoa farm and lunch, for $15; an eight-hour tour of the Gold Coast as far as Elmina with lunch, for $10; and a two-day visit to Kumasi and Ashanti country by air, including accommodations at the City Hotel, guides and transportation, for $55.

What to Buy

Ghanaian markets exhibit some of West Africa's finest carvings, brass casting, weaving, textile printing, dyeing and batiks, pottery and musical instruments. You can also find metalwork, leather and wood from Upper Volta, and brasses and textiles from Dahomey. Modern Ashanti miniature goldweights cast in brass, Kente, Adinkra and other fine cloths, handsome carved stools and canes, and reproductions of Akwa-Ba fertility dolls carried in the gowns of young Ashanti women all follow important Ghanaian traditions.

Examples of these wares are available in Accra at the Arts Center at Victoriaborg, the Africa House on Castle Road, the open Makola Market, Shop One on Liberation Circle, the Gloy Art Gallery, La Boutique Africaine, The Loom, and (for foreign currency at high prices) the airport shops.

Fine filigree jewelry, some of it imported from interior countries, also appears at these places and at shops in the major hotels. La Boutique Africaine (Casanova Building in Tudu Road, Accra) will pack and ship. The best places to buy Kente cloth and to see it made are Bonwire village and Kumasi. Or try the Opoku Kente Weaving Centre in midtown Accra. The cheapest complete robe or toga of Kente cloth with gold thread costs about $150, although you can buy short strips for sashes, ties or decoration—an excellent and easily transportable gift for friends and relatives at home. Kente robes without gold thread are considerably cheaper.

Records of Ghanaian experimental music are found at university bookshops, and high-life selections in department stores like Kingsway, UTC, Glamour, Leventis and CFAO. West African literature is stocked at Simpson's and the Atlas Book Shop (Moxon's) near the Ambassador Hotel. Ghana's growing publishing industry produces lovely children's literature in English, recipe books, folk tales, detective stories and scholarly titles. Accra shops are generally open from 8 am to noon and from 2 to 5:30 or 6 pm; some close on Wednesday and Saturday afternoons. The general department stores are fun to browse in, but prices are high and one misses the joy of bargaining.

In Kumasi, market women and tradesmen offer some of the best artifacts. Many good items can also be found at moderate prices in the Crafts Shop of the National Cultural Center (proceeds go to the museum), the City Hotel shop and at places around the Hotel de Kingsway and the post office. The Bolgatanga market in the Upper Region displays fine pottery, raffia basketry, woodwork, canes and leather goods at reasonable prices. Tailoring is expert; if you have time, buy your shirt or dress materials by the yard in the open markets, and have the dashiki, booboo or kaftan made in Ghana.

Local Attitudes

Ghanaians are amiable, dignified, open and helpful people, with little reticence toward foreigners. Accra alone has some 7,000 non-African residents, white and black, some of them expatriates devoted to Ghana. The country is visited by thousands of Americans each year. Hundreds of Ghanaians have attended American colleges. Many Ghanaian women wear miniskirts in town and bikinis on the beach, although in the Moslem north clothing styles are more conservative.

Weather, What to Wear, How Long to Stay

Ghana is a warm country (except for winter evenings in the north) with fairly constant sun and wide rainfall variation between regions. March is the hottest month. The spring rains bring waves of insects. Only December and January are truly dry at Kumasi under the dusty harmattan winds. The coast suffers constant humidity. Still, Accra's climate is tolerable—more comfortable than Abidjan or Lagos, less so than Lomé or Dakar. If there's a best season for visiting Ghana it is doubtless August to September, when harvest festivals are abundant and temperatures low, thanks to the rains, which end in July (though they begin again in late September for a few weeks). The upland game areas have low humidity and low grasses in January and February.

The major tourist circuit, although by no means the only one, starts and ends in Accra, covering the Gold Coast westward to Takoradi, the Obuasi gold fields north to Kumasi and Ashanti; depending on time available, either (a) farther northward into Volta River country and the Mole Reserve to Tamale and beyond, before turning south to the Volta Lake, Kpandu, Akosombo, and Accra via Aburi, or (b) a more abbreviated return southeastward from Kumasi to the southern portion of the lake at Akosombo, and back to Accra via Aburi. The shorter tour requires at least one night in Takoradi, two nights in Kumasi and a fourth night in Akosombo; Accra and vicinity easily round out a full week of southern Ghana. The longer routes depend largely on taste, finances, the scheduling of local festivals, and pluck. Travelers arriving by ship at Takoradi or Tema have little difficulty arranging similar circuits by taxi, rented car, hitchhiking, or a combination of rail, air and road.

The quickest and most expensive sojourn devotes one full day to the road from Accra via Akosombo to Kumasi, flying back to Accra for the second day, with a third day spent on the Gold Coast castle route, flying back to Accra on the 6 pm flight from Takoradi.

Communication

Almost all Ghanaians have been to school. Most people under 30 speak some English, which is the official language and principal language of the press, radio and TV.

The country has a fairly good internal telephone and telegraph system, and is linked by radio with 40 countries, generally through London. Communications with French-speaking neighbors are deplorable. There are Telex connections with 53 countries. Unless a dealer will ship purchases for you, do not mail your packages from Ghana.

American and Canadian technicians, businessmen and volunteers are sprinkled throughout Ghana, and many North American teachers and students come to the country's universities for a year of study or on summer programs. The national press is lively and informative although obsessed with parochial issues. Foreign periodicals come in regularly and radio reception is good in Accra. The bimonthly *Legon Observer* provides serious commentary on national affairs. *Transition*, Africa's liveliest intellectual magazine, once published in Uganda, now comes out six times a year from Accra.

Emergencies

Ghana's National Police can be helpful in difficulties. Health services and hospitals are adequate, particularly around Accra, Kumasi, Akosombo and Legon (the University Medical School). There are emergency telephone numbers in each locality (999 in Accra). The United States Embassy is located at Rowe and Liberia Roads, on the edge of downtown Accra (P.O. Box 194; tel. 6681-5). It has a health unit staffed by a registered nurse.

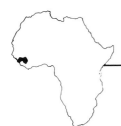

Guinea

(République de Guinée)

Profile

STATUS: Independent republic since October 2, 1958. Former French colony.

SIZE: 94,925 square miles (about the size of Oregon). Population—about 4,000,000.

GEOGRAPHY: Flat coastal tropics in west, high plateau (uplands) and Fouta Djallon mountains in north, eroded Sudanic zone with several green valleys in east, fertile forests and Nimba Mountains in southeast (Mt. Nimba 5,675 feet). Principal towns—Conakry (capital, 250,000), Labé (30,000), Kankan (35,000), Kindia (45,000).

CLIMATE: In Conakry, low 90's most of the year, low 70's at night. Heavy rains June to October, with cooler daytime temperatures (low to mid 80's). Temperatures in Labé about 10 degrees lower, with moderate rainfall May to October.

LANGUAGES: French (official), Peuhl (Fula), Mendé and other African languages.

CURRENCY: Syli. 10 sylis = 44 cents; $1.00 = 22.7 sylis.

VISAS: Required. Available from Guinean Embassy in Washington. Fee $5. Three passport photos needed. Allow two weeks for processing.

AIRPORT: N'Bessia (CKY), eight miles from Conakry. Taxi into city, $8. Airport departure taxes—domestic, $2.40; within Africa, $4; outside Africa, $6. Links with Algeria, France, Soviet Union and West African capitals only, but flights are irregular.

NATIONAL HOLIDAYS: May 1, Labor Day; September 28, date of 1958 referendum against French Communauté; October 2, Independence Day; major Moslem festivals.

INFORMATION SOURCES: In US—Embassy of Guinea, 2112 Le Roy Place NW, Washington, D.C. 20008 (tel. 202/483-9420); Guinea Mission to the UN, 295 Madison Avenue, New York, N.Y. 10017 (tel. 212/532-5513). In Conakry—Ministère de l'Information et du Tourisme (tel. 21.25); Syndicat d'Initiative et du Tourisme, P.O. Box 609.

By Philip M. Allen

Suspicious of neighbors, strangers and many of its own people as well, Guinea is usually given a wide berth by most travelers in Africa. For the time being at least, the Guinean government formally discourages tourism and does not welcome journalists or other explorers of the political and economic landscape. Visitors are usually restricted to Conakry.

Yet, excluding Guinea from your itinerary means missing one of the most interesting and dedicated experiments in African independence. Guinea is a beautiful nation of energetic and colorful people. It took its birthright to self-determination literally and uncompromisingly in 1958 but has been obliged to be rhetorical and compromising ever since. It is in fact West Africa's only rival to Tanzania in the search for original and indigenous avenues to national development. Its failures have been tragic but its effort honorable. Nevertheless, policy and public paranoia are too intimate for comfort—a condition that can scarcely be appreciated firsthand by foreigners without aggravating fears of subversion.

Historically part of the vassal territory of the great medieval empire of Ghana, northern and eastern Guinea provided a power base for Ghana's successor, the dynasty of Mali's 13th century Emperor Sundiata Keita. Subsequently, the Mandingo and Malinké people who had ruled all of Mali remained in control of what we now call Guinea, south and west of the Songhai empire. Their forest and hills also kept them relatively secure from the invasions of Berbers, Tuaregs, Toucouleur, Mossi and other outsiders.

A confederation of Moslem Peuhl (Fulani) emirates developed in the Fouta Djallon uplands of the northern interior after the shrinking of Malian power in the mid-17th century. This brotherhood held firm against Saharans, Europeans and forest Africans. Like the Hausa patrimony on the eastern Niger, it provided a cradle for vast campaigns of Islamic militancy, much of it conducted by fire and sword. Ousman Dan Fodio from Sokoto, El Hadj Omar the Toucouleur, and the Malinké Moslem Samory Touré led different waves of the jihad (crusade for Islam) throughout the Sudanic savannas behind the Gulf of Guinea.

It was at Bissandougou in eastern Guinea that Samory the Almamy (sultan) established his bastion against French expeditions in 1870, carrying his Napoleonic campaigns into what is now Mali, Senegal, Upper Volta and the Ivory Coast until his capture and exile in 1898. In Guinea itself, Samory had followers who kept the French from totally "pacifying" la Guinée Française (so declared in 1891) until 1911–1912.

His modern descendant, President Ahmed Sekou Touré, has personified Guinean nationalism since the mid-1950's in defiance of France.

The French came to the Guinea coast two centuries after the pathfinding Portuguese—who were known in the Conakry-Boké area since the 1450's. By assiduous cultivation of coastal rulers and forceful expeditions into the interior, France built its Conakry foothold into an attractive port for Peuhl caravans and other commerce. Conakry, now the nation's capital, rose in successful rivalry with the British and Creole base at Freetown (Sierra Leone).

On criteria of education and health services, economic development and political participation, France's colonial record in Guinea was undistinguished. Guinea's resistance to empire, the absence of an indigenous middle class, and the post-World War II development of vigorous labor unions around an incipient mining industry all led in 1958 to the act that Gaullist France regarded as treason: alone of all French territories on three continents and three oceans, the Guineans voted (by 97 per cent) against joining the dependent Communauté proposed in the French referendum of September 28, 1958. Only four days later, as a consequence of its repudiation of metropolitan ties, Guinea became formally independent, the second republic (after Ghana) in sub-Saharan Africa to obtain its sovereignty since World War II.

Within a few weeks, the real French response was felt, a reaction so vindictive that for all her self-reliant nationalism and her considerable natural resources, Guinea still has not overcome the initial damage: Frenchmen left Guinea by the thousands—businessmen, technicians, civil servants, teachers—taking their property, equipment, record books and finances with them. Even telephones were uprooted and shipped back to France. Paris has since come to a cool, fragile modus vivendi with Sekou Touré's regime.

Immense bauxite reserves have been mined for several years. In 1971 more than one million tons were mined, and this is expected to quintuple. Private American investment in bauxite comes to nearly $200 million. The USSR is responsible for Conakry's Polytechnic Institute, the closest institution to a university in Guinea. Production of iron ore, diamonds, timber, beef, rice, bananas and tropical fruit is growing, but prosperity has not come. Food supplies fall short of demand, mining activity has not induced industrialization in other sectors, the state is seriously in debt, black marketing and smuggling have aggravated the country's economic misfortunes. Almost 500,000 Guinean refugees now live in Senegal, Liberia, the Ivory Coast and France.

Much of the trouble is "political." Although pursuing an aggressive revolutionary vision of modern Africa and a militant socialist, neutralist ideology, Guinea's one-party regime (Parti Démocratique de Guinée, PDG) has been plagued by troubles at home and by diminishing Guinean influence in African and international forums. Governing with enormous personal vitality, President Touré has made enemies everywhere by his criticisms of more conservative African nations, his often magnified disputes with Europe, Russia and the United States, and his effusive welcome of the late Kwame Nkrumah after the latter's deposition as Ghana's president in 1966. Nor did the breakdown of legal due process in 1971 and 1972 win him any new friends.

Conakry has for years been the principal extra-territorial base of the anti-Portuguese African Party for the Independence of Guinea-Bissau and the Cape Verde Islands (PAIGC). As this rebellion increased in success (see Guinea-Bissau chapter), relations between Sekou Touré's Guinea and the Portuguese authorities to the northwest deteriorated into violence. A crude and outrageous "Bay of Pigs" attempt to storm Conakry in November, 1970, by Portuguese-supported guerrillas (many of them exiles from Guinea) evoked widespread sympathy for Sekou Touré. The regime, however, dissipated this support by indiscriminate domestic purges, executions, expulsions of foreign residents (especially West Germans) and publicized bloodbaths, all committed under the authority of kangaroo "peoples' tribunals." The International Commission of Jurists condemned Guinea in January, 1972, for permitting this collapse of legality. The institutions of state, built so laboriously after the abandonment of Guinea by France in 1958, have been crippled by the elimination of the new Guinean managerial elite.

This constant bleeding of resources, the refusal of agriculture to respond to development schemes, ill-conceived measures to bolster the economy by foreign "donors" as well as Guineans, the lagging payoff from bauxite and other mining enterprises, and capricious political policing by a nervous regime have all rendered today's Guinea an uncomfortable place to be in.

The republic's population includes a sample of every group represented on the Gulf of Guinea and in the Sudanic interior, as well as some 4,000 foreigners (half of the 1958 French colony alone). About one-fourth of the four million Guineans belong to the Islamic cattle-herding Peuhl of the Fouta Djallon range and the northeast. Another million are identified with the agricultural Mendé-speaking people of the forests and wooded savannas of the south (including Malinké and Mandingo communities). Many of these southerners are Moslem (like Sekou Touré, and Samory before him) but retain a strongly ancestral animist culture. The coastal

Soussou (Susu) are another quarter-million. The foreign community is composed of those French and Lebanese traders who remained in their "ruined paradise" after the great exodus of 1958–1959, in addition to expatriate teachers and technicians from many countries of East and West Europe, China and the United States.

Guinea's complicated story has yet to be fully—and objectively—told. Essential contemporary sources include Sekou Touré's own writings; see his *L'Afrique et la Révolution* (Paris, Présence Africaine, 1966). Ruth Schachter Morgenthau's *Political Parties in French-Speaking Africa* (Oxford, 1964) and Guy de Lusignan's *French-Speaking Africa Since Independence* (Praeger, 1969) put the politics into broader perspectives. For deeper appreciations of the Guinean experience, the works of novelists and poets Camara Laye and Fodeba Keita can be strongly recommended; there are translations of Laye's two best books *The African Child* (L'Enfant Noir) and *Radiance of the King* (Le Regard du Roi), published by Collins (London, 1965) and Macmillan (New York, 1970), respectively.

Money Matters

On leaving the Franc Zone in 1960, Guinea kept its own franc until 1972, then created the syli, not convertible outside Guinea, not for export or import. Change your money only at accredited stations (Conakry airport and other customs offices, the banks and major hotels), and keep all receipts. All banking facilities are national: the Crédit National pour le Commerce, l'Industrie et l'Habitat, with 28 branches throughout the country, provides the best services for travelers. It is open from 8 am to 1 pm, six days a week.

Guinea suffers from a chronic shortage of foreign exchange; hence, all imports and services required by travelers are in short supply and expensive. Shortages and rationing have led to a serious black market in currency as well as imported commodities and to the smuggling of some Guinean products like beef and diamonds across frontiers into zones of convertible currency. You can spend dollars and other foreign currency at a new cooperative exchange in Conakry, operated with Yugoslav assistance. It has a wide range of merchandise at reasonable prices.

Getting In and Out

Guinea is connected with East and West Europe and other African countries by French UTA, Air Afrique, Sabena, Air Mali, Aeroflot, Czech

CSA and East German Interflug, but flights are infrequent. Conakry is a busy port, however. Farrell Lines freighters come here from New York. There are no international railroad or river connections with Guinea, although barges and other shallow-draft vessels can navigate the Niger River between Siguiri and Bamako (Mali) in the May-to-January high water season.

All overland routes are rough, and all borders strictly policed by Guineans anxious to keep out "fifth columnists." However, with sturdy vehicles, you can drive to or from Freetown (Sierra Leone); Dakar, Kaolack and Tambacounda (Senegal) across the Gambia River and by the western edge of Senegal's Niokolo-Koba National Park; and Monrovia (Liberia) via Nzérékoré in the beautiful Nimba Mountain region. If you are driving, be sure that your visa is in order and that your vehicle's documentation is impeccable. Also, be sure that all traveling companions are "harmless" looking to this nervous regime, that you are carrying no firearms, and that you can communicate with border guards in French. Hitchhikers and backpackers often wind up in jail, no questions asked. The experience can be extremely unpleasant.

Do not try to enter Guinea without a visa. Journalists and other prospective visitors likely to aggravate Guinea's image abroad will be systematically refused entry, and there are times when no foreigner can get a visa unless he is especially *persona grata* with Conakry authorities. Guinean embassies in Washington and other capitals usually have to consult with the foreign ministry in Conakry before issuing visas: hence, be prepared to pay for a cable and to wait two weeks for a reply. In France, the Mali embassy represents Guinea.

Getting Around Within Guinea

The 400-mile National Railroad between Conakry and Kankan in the east provides an extraordinarily varied and colorful experience for passengers who can put up with the ancient, ill-kempt, obsolete equipment. The route passes through the southern foothills of the Fouta Djallon, with superb changes of scenery, crossing the Niger River near Kouroussa. A handsome but only partially smooth highway runs parallel to the line of rail. Two newer railroads, both privately operated for the benefit of the bauxite mines, connect Fria with Conakry (95 miles) and the Boké mines at Sangaredi with the new port at Kamsar. But neither railroad carries passengers as yet.

Eight airfields in the country are connected on regular flights by Air Guinée, using a hodgepodge of Czech, Russian and American equipment. One-way passage from Conakry to Boké (35 minutes) costs about $18; Conakry to Kankan (1 hour, 40 minutes), $38.50; Conakry to Nzérékoré (2 hours), $56.50. The other airfields are at Labé, Kissidougou, Macenta and Siguiri. Only Conakry's N'Bessia airfield takes the larger jet planes.

Less than 300 miles of Guinea's 8,000 miles of road are paved, mainly on the east-west axis out of Conakry. Many of the roads into areas of interest to travelers (Labé and everything beyond in the Fouta Djallon, Siguiri in the northeast, Macenta and Guéckédou in the south near the Liberian border) are poorly maintained in the dry season, slippery or flooded in the July-to-October rains. Inexpensive government buses run between towns and in Conakry, using poorly maintained equipment (spare parts being agonizingly scarce for all imported machinery). There are a few taxis in the towns. If you can find one, the fare is about 50 cents per trip within city limits; trips outside must be negotiated. Peugeot sedans can be rented from the Agence Charbonneaux in Conakry for about $30 per day plus gasoline, which costs about $1.25 per gallon. Backpacking is a rugged delight in this beautiful country, but there are so few private vehicles, and so many suspicious authorities, that hitch-hiking cannot be recommended.

There are no travel agencies, but the Ministry of Information and Tourism and the UTA and Air Guinée agencies in Conakry can be helpful in planning a visit.

Where to Stay

You haven't much choice. In CONAKRY, the Hôtel de France and the Russian-built Hôtel Camayenne are both situated handsomely on the sea, but are deteriorating and expensive. Single rooms without air-conditioning or private bath rent for $11, with air-conditioning $15; doubles are $15 and $22. These rates do not include breakfast. The Camayenne has suites and rooms with sitting rooms for slight additional cost. The Hôtel N'Bessia, near Conakry's airport (eight miles from town), is all air-conditioned and offers bed and breakfast for about $13 single and $21.50 double.

There are virtually no commercial hotels up-country. The government operates a network of rest-houses (gîtes); however, you will need authorization from local party or administrative officials to stay in one. These include a tourist camp in the Kakoulima Range about 40 miles east of Conakry, and rest-houses in the mountain spa of DALABA, the central junction town of DABOLA, PITA in the Fouta Djallon, DINGUIRAYE and KÉROUANE in Malinké country, and KISSIDOUGOU and GUÉCKÉDOU in the south. Ask at the Ministry of Information for exact locations of accessible gîtes and how to obtain authorization to use them.

Where and What to Eat

Imported food and drink are very expensive, and there is a chronic shortage of meat despite the herds of cattle, sheep and goats that roam the interior. Water can be drunk in Conakry, but it's safer to take locally produced fruit juices, mineral water or Sobragui beer. Guinean staple foods, varying with the landscape and ethnic composition of the countryside, are cassava (foufou), millet and rice. Chicken is served with delicious peanut sauce and spices, and the spiced fish is also excellent. These local dishes are available at Guinean restaurants near major marketplaces in towns, as well as *Petits Bateaux* in Conakry. The hotels and the restaurants—*Royal St.-Germain, Paradis, Le Grillon* and *L'Oasis*—struggle valiantly to produce French and Oriental menus.

What to See and Do

Like many capitals, Conakry reflects the mood of the nation. It is a very pretty town perched on Tumbo Island off Kaloum Peninsula, surrounded by blue ocean, with green spaces, flowering trees, broad avenues and palm lined beaches. But this tropical paradise of a closed colonial society has gone to pot since 1958, and nobody denies it. Independent Guinea has been occupied with things other than the beautification, or even proper maintenance, of its capital. There has been little major construction—only the Chinese-built People's Palace and the cinema on the neck between Tumbo Island and mainland Conakry, the vast Polytechnique ("University") built by the Russians, the two new hotels and one office building. The president's palace and other major government edifices are holdovers from the colonial administration; they are suitably modest.

What little traffic there is on the streets is as shabby as the roads and buildings. Comfortable villas on the sea road (Corniche) and in the suburbs compare strikingly with the disorder of teeming Boulbinet, where most of the population lives in heaps. But the handsome Conakrians in their bright booboos, head-ties and gandouras provide an even sharper contrast with these drab surroundings, and there are no beggars on the streets, unlike the capitals of richer African nations. Outdoor dance-halls like the Paillotte and Jardin de Guinée are full of life.

There is plenty to keep a roving sightseer busy. Come during the Quinzaine Artistique—the annual cultural fortnight usually staged by the PDG at the end of the rainy season in October. Or if you're lucky at some other moment, you can see Fodeba Keita's justly renowned "Ballets Africains," as well as theater, dance and music from all parts of the country. Meander along the beautiful coasts in either direction from town and listen to the singing of the Susu fishermen. Dig the jazz and rock music at the Eldorado or the Hotel N'Bessia. The great Miriam Makeba (Mrs. Stokely Carmichael) lives in Conakry and occasionally sings at important festivities. Explore the handsome landscape behind Conakry, including the 3,000-foot, forested Mt. Kakoulima, the waterfalls and caves of Kakimbon and the Taban Valley. You can visit banana plantations at Coyah, 30 miles from the capital, a textile mill at Kilometer 28, a Yugoslav-built furniture factory in Sinfonia, trade schools, training projects and other installations that can be identified for you by the Information Ministry. If you have a genuine interest in the revolution being conducted in neighboring Guinea-Bissau, you might write for an appointment to the PAIGC office (P. O. Box 98) in Conakry.

Conakry's indispensable excursion is a boat trip to the ILES DE LOS ranging from three to six miles off Tumbo Island. You can take a public launch at the port, or you can hire canoes at fishing beaches. The islands include the elongated Kassa, which is nearest the town (bauxite mines here have been producing ore for Canada since 1952), and Tamara (excellent beaches, rocky shores, steep hills and magnificent ferns and woods with monkey colonies, an idyllic place for hiking and picnicking). Between these two islands is luxuriant, gorgeous little Roume, once a slave trade and smuggling depot and later British headquarters for anti-slaving activities. Roume is thought by some to have inspired Stevenson's description of "Treasure Island."

Superb but difficult roads lead north from Conakry into the hill country of the Fouta Djallon, enhanced by a bracing climate, waterfalls, and cliffs to climb. LABÉ, 3,000 feet in elevation, a center of Fula (Peuhl) resistance to French occupation from 1892 to 1905, is now a government conference center and potential tourist resort. DALABA, south of Labé, and MALI to the north, are also pleasant hill towns. In the far north, the Coniagui and Bassari people farm, fish, hunt and conduct their sacred initiation rites in the tradition of their ancestors. Festival time around YOUKOUNKOUN comes in February to March and August to September. This is also good hunting country, if you can get permits from a gun-shy government. Chances are better across the border in Senegal.

Guinea's southeast has its own kind of fascination. There are beautiful forests in the Kissidougou-Guéckédou-Macenta triangle; excellent orchestral music and dancing by the "bird-men," stilt-walkers and masked spirits of numerous Malinké and Tomo villages by their sacred forests in the dark of night; fervent dance ceremonies of the Guerzé (Kpelle) people of the forests and Nimba Mountains around NZÉRÉKORÉ. BEYLA, sitting high in the hills north of Nzérékoré, east of Macenta, where Samory held out after retreating from the Soudan (Mali) before the French, is another good place for hunting, mountain climbing, hiking and cool relief.

The central Guinean axis between Conakry and the Mali Republic traverses hill country and archaeological diggings around KINDIA, a former vacation spa for the French and now Guinea's second city. Kindia has several specialized schools, a fruit research institute at nearby Foulaya and a new Russian bauxite mining concession scheduled to begin operating in 1974. The road continues through the exciting mountain landscape of the Peuhl people to DABOLA, where the songs of Moslem troubadors recall the crusades of El Hadj Omar Tall and his Tidjani Moslem Brotherhood. In 1850, Omar founded the town of DINGUIRAYE, 65 miles north of Dabola, and his mosque there is a point of pilgrimage for the Tidjani faithful.

KANKAN is Guinea's interior railhead with a beach on the Milo River, a trades school and the national Teacher Training College (Ecole Normale Supérieure). Between Kankan and Beyla to the south is Malinké holyland, blending ancestral religion with Islam. Here was the spiritual source of Samory's militancy and his last refuge from 1889 to 1893.

SIGUIRI, in the Sudanic northeast, stands near the site of Niani, capital of the Empire of Mali under its dynastic founder Sundiata Keita (1230–55); before that it had been for centuries Malinké metropolis of the southern region of the ancient empire of Ghana. Here mines of gold that shored Ghana's and Mali's power are still worked, and Malinké troubadors (griots) still sing the old chronicles of their nation's greatness.

Theater, poetry and music have become partially politicized for new national ends under the PDG as the Guinean revolution struggles against its polar enemies of indigenous superstition and mindless imitation of Europe. But the traditional function of the griot has had a revival. After consulting with the PDG Section Culturelle at Conakry, or with local party officers, you can visit griot villages like FADAMA, DJÉLIBAKORO and KEYLA in Malinké savanna country, and attend festivals or tournaments of traditional song, legend and dance.

North of Conakry is the modern and industrial town of FRIA, with the great aluminum plant owned by Olin Mathieson with French, British and West German partners. Farther up the coast, the new aluminum complex at SANGAREDI near Boké follows a somewhat different organizational pattern, with the Guinean government holding 49 per cent, Harvey Aluminum 26 per cent and smaller participation by ALCOA, Canadian and European interests. Boké also represents an interesting experiment in harnessing foreign investment for general development purposes: the consortium is responsible for physical and social infrastructure in the entire Boké-Kamsar port area. This activity is worth a visit by anybody concerned with development; consult the Office de Boké (OFAB) headquarters in Conakry.

At Boffa, halfway along the coast between Boké and the capital, family names like Lightburn, Curtiss, Faber and Wilkinson recall the years when this village was a port for American slavers.

Women play important roles in modern Guinean public life. Much production, buying and selling is organized in cooperatives. These and other vital features of the Guinean revolution may be studied by calling on responsible officials at PDG headquarters at the People's Palace; write or phone the administrative secretary of the party for authorization to enter the Palace.

What to Buy

Guineans are creative in traditional carving, especially the Guéré and Baga people who work in wood, and the Kissi, in stone. They also produce embroidery from the Fouta Djallon (marketed in Dabola), Fula jewelry and raffia weaving. Malinké musical instruments, prized by collectors, include calabash rattles (gboroi), drums and tambourines, ivory or horn trumpets (pouvogui), lyre mandolins (konigui), as well as more universally West African griot instruments like the calabash harp (kora) and calabash resonated xylophone (balafon).

State bookstores carry approved revolutionary literature, including Sekou Touré's writings and the works of many other "progressive" African authors. You can also obtain excellent recordings of Guinean music there. In general, however, valuable commodities are scarce, many craftsmen and merchants preferring to sell (legally or otherwise) in neighboring CFA franc or Liberian dollar zones, or outside Africa entirely. Conakry shops are open from 8 to noon, 3 to 6:30 pm; department stores are open continuously from 7:30 am to 3 pm. The airport has a duty-free shop.

Local Attitudes

For the time being at least, revolutionary Guinea is a very sensitive state. Party agents are everywhere and strangers are suspect, citizens of "capital-

ist" countries particularly so. An honest interest in Guinea and its problems will often, but not always, be appreciated, and political opinions are
more likely to be resented than rebutted. Guineans get little news of the
outside world, except through propaganda organs like the newspaper
Horoya and the national radio (Voix de la Révolution). Do not take
photographs of any subject that may be even remotely official without
permission from local police or army personnel.

Americans enjoy on-again off-again relations with Guinean authorities;
we are sometimes regarded as "better" than the French or the Russians,
willing to help Guinea if only to make money out of bauxite, and so on,
but at other times even individual Americans may become the target for
the regime's nervous outbursts. Half of Guinea is Moslem, and miniskirts, like political opinions, are taboo.

Weather, What to Wear, How Long to Stay

Guinea's general rainy season lasts from June or July through October
(May to November in the forest). Rain comes in great bursts between
periods of sunlight in the forests and on the coasts, diminishing in the
Fouta Djallon range. The coasts have constant humid sea breezes except
for winter (December to February). Dry, cool evenings prevail in the
uplands from October to April. The dry harmattan wind blows on northeastern Guinea during January. Hence, you should be prepared for heat
during most of the year, heavy rain for the summer semester in the lowlands and relatively cool evenings for the winter months up-country.
Both the French colonial heritage and the PDG revolutionary ideology
discourage formality in attire.

Winter is the best time to visit Guinea, but if you can make it earlier,
inquire at Guinean embassies concerning the dates of the Quinzaine
Artistique in Conakry and the season for festival music in the north
and the south. Unless you have professional reasons for staying longer,
10 days is probably maximum time for Conakry and up-country Guinea.

Communication

Left almost without contacts in 1958, Guinea has slowly evolved plans
for improving its radio, telephone and telegraph links, both domestic
and international. But shortage of foreign exchange and disagreements
with technical assistance agencies have hampered progress. Don't depend
on any kind of communication with the outside world from here.

Getting around linguistically is no easy job in today's Guinea. There
are no Peace Corps (since 1967) or CUSO volunteer programs and few

English-speaking technicians outside the Boké and Fria industrial complexes, where American, Canadian and British companies have representatives. It is PDG policy to downgrade French as a vehicle of communication; hence it is taught less thoroughly in Guinean schools than in more Francophile countries like Senegal and the Ivory Coast. Literacy and literature are being promoted in several vernacular languages, but schooling is by no means universal as yet. Many of the French-speaking elites have been purged or driven into exile.

Press, film and radio are monopolies of the PDG state. Recent purges of key personnel have weakened their quality, even as organs of propaganda, but the visitor can learn more or less what is worth knowing of current events through the radio and the daily *Horoya*, in French. No foreign newspapers are available in Guinea, except those that come on postal subscriptions.

Emergencies

Only Conakry is equipped for medical care. All such services are state-owned and operated. There are about 100 physicians in the entire country. Villages have at best a brigade sanitaire operated through the PDG. The state pharmacies carry few brands recognizable by Americans. The US Embassy in Conakry (2nd Boulevard and 9th Avenue, P.O. Box 603, Conakry; tel. 415-20/24) keeps a low profile, but can be helpful with advice.

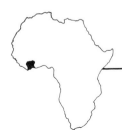

Ivory Coast

(République de Côte d'Ivoire)

Profile

STATUS: Independent republic since August 7, 1960. Formerly part of French West Africa.

SIZE: 127,520 square miles (slightly larger than New Mexico). Population—4,500,000 plus about 1,000,000 migrant African workers and 50,000 Europeans.

GEOGRAPHY: Southern half is coastal rain forest thinning out and rising to low savanna plateau in northern half. Mountains in west. Principal towns—Abidjan (capital, 450,000), Bouaké (105,000), Daloa (65,000), Man (52,000), Korhogo (25,000).

CLIMATE: Hot and humid on southern coast, with variations in temperature and lower humidity as you go north. Dry season December through March. Abidjan temperatures in the 80's year round, 70's at night.

LANGUAGES: French (official), several major African languages.

CURRENCY: CFA franc. CFA 100 = 40 cents; $1.00 = CFA 245.

VISAS: Required. Available from Ivory Coast Embassy in Washington; Development Office in New York; Honorary Consulate, Los Angeles. No fee. Four photos needed. Round trip ticket, other proof of solvency, 48-hour wait. Transit visas obtained on arrival at airport, valid for 24 hours. Visas available from French consulates where not represented.

AIRPORT: Port Bouet (ABJ), 10 miles from Abidjan. Frequent connections with Western Europe and West African capitals; two flights per week with New York. Airport departure taxes—within Africa, $2.40; outside Africa, $6. Transportation into city—taxi, about $5.60; hotel buses (Hôtel Ivoire bus, $1.40).

515

NATIONAL HOLIDAYS: May 1, Labor Day; August 7, Independence Day; Christian and major Moslem festivals.

INFORMATION SOURCES: In US—Ivory Coast Embassy, 2424 Massachusetts Avenue NW, Washington, D.C. 20008 (tel. 202/483-2400); Ivory Coast Development Office, 521 Fifth Avenue, Suite 1604, New York, N.Y. 10017 (tel. 212/869-1700); Permanent Mission of Ivory Coast to the UN, 46 East 74th Street, New York, N.Y. 10021 (tel. 212/988-3930); Honorary Consulate, 9000 Sunset Boulevard, Suite 1402, Los Angeles, Cal. 90069. In Abidjan—Ministère d'Etat chargé du Tourisme, P.O. Box 20.949; Office du Tourisme (c/o Ivory Coast Travel Agency, ICTA), 9 avenue Barthe, P.O. Box 1173 (tel. 22-26-75); Syndicat d'Initiative, P.O. Box 1173.

By Philip M. Allen

Solid though it may seem, the Ivory Coast is a fragile composition of unequal societies held together by a national prosperity and single-party politics. For the visitor, it blends natural beauty and flourishing economic activity, sustained ancestral tradition and modern urban luxury, communities of people caught at widely varying points in an uneven process of social change.

The indigenous population comprises some four and a half million Ivoirians, mainly from these ethnic groups: the Agni and Baoulé in the east and center; Malinké, Dioula, Dan, Guéré and Gouro in the west, and Lobi, Senoufo, Bobo and Koulango in the north. In addition, there are almost a million migrant workers from Upper Volta, Niger, Mali, Guinea, Dahomey, Togo, Nigeria and Liberia, and 50,000 Europeans (mostly French). The immigrant groups provide professional, technical or muscular skills in a booming economy that has insufficient manpower of its own.

The republic is governed by a strong Parti Démocratique de Côte d'Ivoire (PDCI) regime with a genius for settling disputes by palaver (dialogue). Successful production and marketing of coffee, cocoa, timber and tropical fruits have for years attracted international capital.

Indeed, foreign investment is evident in every aspect of the economy, helping exploit modest manganese, diamond and newly discovered iron resources, financing large-scale hydroelectric and other major installations, and developing rubber, cotton, peanuts, tobacco, oil palms and fisheries as well as a relatively broad base of consumer industries.

Visitors may be fascinated by Ivoirian modernity or repelled by its materialism. They may be enthusiastic about its moderate pro-Western pragmatism or exasperated by ideological compromising. Otherwise, the Ivory Coast from the tourist viewpoint is first and foremost a glittering capital city Eldorado called Abidjan, and secondly, if at all, a typically paradoxical parcel of contemporary West Africa.

Visitors who come for wildlife are usually disappointed and the Ivoirians you encounter may strike you as "cold" compared to other West Africans. But for vacation pleasure and shopping, mixed with the excitement of a booming economy and a rich cultural heritage, this place rates high. (And so, incidentally, do the prices.)

Historically, the southern, forested half of the Ivory Coast remained immune to conquest by great neighboring West African empires like the Ashanti to the east, the Mossi in the northeast and the several Moslem realms to the north and west. But the northern half was decimated by slave trading and warfare. Immigrants settled the forests in small, heterogeneous groups and are today a patchwork of communities and clans. Among the most important of these groups are the Baoulé people, brought by Queen Alba Pokou to the forest center around Bouaké in the mid-18th century.

Until late into the 19th century, the European powers were content with control over ivory, timber and slaving on the coasts. By 1898, when French expeditions penetrated the interior of what France had already claimed as a colony, they encountered the remnant forces of the Malinké Sultan Samory Touré, who had opposed their "pacification" campaigns for almost 30 years, and captured him near the present town of Man.

After a half century of out-and-out economic exploitation, French policy changed favorably in the post-World War II period. From the mid-50's, Paris tacitly permitted the Ivory Coast to achieve gradual economic pre-eminence among the territories of former French West Africa. Abidjan's star rose in the firmament of what was once a West African federation dominated by Senegal's capital, Dakar.

The business-like and highly influential Ivoirian President Félix Houphouet-Boigny, a physician and Baoulé noble, began his political career as spokesman for syndicates of Ivoirian coffee and cocoa growers. His name received the suffix Boigny in testimony to the hammer-like force of his politics, but since 1944 Houphouet has helped harmonize French policies with moderate political evolution in West Africa.

When independence came to the Ivory Coast in August, 1960, it brought additional compensation for loyal alignment with France. French educational institutions multiplied in what had been an essentially undisturbed African culture. France has bought Ivoirian coffee and cocoa at pegged prices and has defended these products in the European Common Market and other world markets. Frenchmen have come to Abidjan to trade, teach and settle, especially after their political "disappointments" in more militantly nationalist societies like Algeria and Guinea. France stations troops at Abidjan to help Houphouet's security forces keep the peace, and has looked the other way on several occasions when the regime found pretexts to expel large numbers of non-Ivoirians.

In 1950 French engineers cut a permanent canal from the sea across the tricky sand bar at Vridi into Abidjan's lagoons, thus opening the capital to ocean-going vessels and putting it on a par with its principal West African competitor ports, Dakar and Lagos. Investment and aid followed, still largely, but not exclusively, from France.

Production has soared each year since independence. The balance of payments runs a surplus of $80 million per year. Food processing and chemical and textile industries now contemplate broader markets in

Abidjan's hinterlands. The United States ranks second as a trade and aid partner; Japan, Canada, West Germany, Italy and other Western European countries are increasing their activity annually. With his eye on further capital and commercial participation, Houphouet has launched a controversial movement in conservative Africa for a political dialogue with South Africa. The present five-year plan nevertheless calls for domestic public investment, not foreign capital, to assume the major burden of development financing, and it anticipates a greater Ivoirian share in economic management than has been the case thus far. These policy reversals are cited by Abidjan's friends as a form of successful "self-reliance."

An affluent first-generation Ivoirian elite has grown up on this expansion of industry, education and trade. It swells an overgrown civil service and tends to pattern its leisure on French styles of consumer living. But the schools that turn out increasing numbers of white collar youth remain poor imitations of French models, failing to satisfy the labor demands of an expanding economy and aggravating a serious problem of unemployment. Moreover, falling international prices for some Ivoirian exports, substantial repatriation of earnings by foreign businesses and personnel, and a growing international debt that is just beginning to come due have begun to jeopardize a still fragile and essentially agricultural economy.

The hinterland behind Abidjan is checkered with prospering plantations and stagnating peasant holdings. Thousands of semi-educated youths flock to cities where there are no jobs for them. The Agni people in the east have been stirred by secessionist impulses for a decade, precipitating a number of bloody conflicts with police and army. Confrontations have also occurred with students and other organized groups in sporadic demonstrations. The inflationary economy has boosted the Ivoirian cost of living to one of the world's highest. Houphouet's regime recognizes these potential threats to security. The program of dialogue with discontented groups continues, and a new austerity campaign seeks to curb excessive government spending and extravagance by civil servants.

To most visitors Abidjan, the capital, reflects the happy results of a comfortable and productive relationship with the West. Its shining new structures and brilliant waterscapes, its yellow beaches and domesticated rain forest, its hillsides covered with European villas and its flanks of bustling, colorful African suburbs are delightful to anybody who can take the sultry climate and the high prices. Anticipating an annual flow of tourists expected to reach 120,000 by 1980 and 500,000 soon thereafter, Ivoirian, European, Israeli and American partners are developing just east of Abidjan a lagoon pleasure paradise of luxury hotels, beach clubs and sporting facilities in a section already called the "Riviera."

For the more discerning traveler, however, Abidjan often appears to be a brilliant billboard screening the powerful but neglected reality of Africa. Behind the Riviera a rich natural and cultural patrimony remains accessible, at least for the time being. Ivoirian Africa has been summoned to serve the future and supply the mass of capital, but it is not yet overwhelmed. Within the thick forests and plantations of the country's center, the savannas of the north and the mountain country of the west, Ivoirians can still be identified by what they do, what they make and how they live as people of the African present.

Most of the literature on the Ivory Coast is in French, including the works of Bernard Dadié and other Ivoirian authors. A good introduction to the political scene appears in Aristide R. Zolberg's *One-Party Government in the Ivory Coast* (Princeton University Press, 1964, 1969), and in *Ghana and the Ivory Coast*, edited by Zolberg and Philip Foster (University of Chicago Press, 1971).

Money Matters

The Ivory Coast is a bellwether of the West African CFA zone, dependent on Paris but nonetheless leading the economies of its French-speaking neighbors. The dollar fluctuates here between 240 and 250 CFA francs. Hotels, shops and restaurants will exchange currency, but they take a healthy discount. You're better off at banks and at the Port Bouet Airport. Travelers checks are common currency and credit cards are recognized at many hotels, restaurants, shops and car rental agencies.

Represented throughout French-speaking Africa, the Banque Internationale de l'Afrique Occidentale (BIAO), part owned by the First National City Bank of New York, has offices in Bouaké and Daloa, as well as Abidjan. The Banque Internationale du Commerce et de l'Industrie (BICI), affiliated with the Bank of America and the Banque Nationale de Paris, is another major Abidjan institution. American Express is located on the Boulevard de la République. Banks are open from 8 to 11:30 am and from 2:30 to 4 pm five days a week, and 8 to 11 am on Saturday. Foreign currencies are welcome in any quantity, but may have to be declared on arrival. Leftover West African CFA francs can be spent in Senegal, Mauritania, Upper Volta, Niger, Togo and Dahomey.

Prices in Abidjan are astronomical (about double those in France) for such things as transportation, imported canned goods, vegetables and meats, film, phonograph records and tapes, clothing and sportswear, manufactured equipment and accessories, medicines, cosmetics, paper items of any type, and skilled services (still often performed by Europeans). You can't avoid these high prices by simply skipping Abidjan, although basic living costs are considerably lower in the provinces. If your budget is limited, better avoid the country or plan to pass through quickly.

Getting In and Out

All West African airlanes lead to Abidjan. Air Afrique and UTA operate two flights a day to and from Paris. Pan American and Air Afrique fly twice a week to and from New York. Abidjan is linked with major European capitals twice or three times weekly (UTA, KLM, Sabena, SAS, Swissair, Alitalia), and with African capitals by regular flights of a dozen airlines.

Two other methods of access ought to be considered if you have the time: (1) by ocean steamer through the Vridi Canal into the lagoon and the inner precincts of the capital, or (2) by railroad down from the grasslands of Upper Volta to the forests and the coast.

Shipping agents in the United States, Europe or West Africa can help travelers book passage on the occasional packet boat of the Nouvelle Compagnie Française de Paquebots (11 days from Marseille or Bordeaux), or on freighters to and from Abidjan. The Farrell Lines (represented in Abidjan by UMARCO, P.O. Box 1559) takes about 18 days from New York, somewhat longer from the Great Lakes, for about $400; Delta Lines also sails here from the Gulf Coast, and Paquet Lines connects Abidjan with Marseille.

The Abidjan-Niger Railway (which never reaches the Niger) runs four times weekly between the Ivoirian capital and Ouagadougou (Upper Volta) on a scheduled 27-hour, 700-mile trip through the forest to Bouaké, the savanna to Katiola and Ferkessedougou, up the escarpment into the low-lying plateaus of the three Volta rivers to Bobo-Dioulasso (Upper Volta) and Ouagadougou. It has a good catering service and the fares are reasonable: $27 for one-way first-class accommodations; meals are extra and a sleeper (couchette) costs $11. If you do the trip in Spartan style, second-class without sleeper, you pay about $10.

Abidjan is a treat to approach by air. The vista is a mosaic of water and woven palmtree tops and the city bursts excitingly out of this lagoon tapestry. Spacious, modern Port Bouet Airport is 10 miles southeast of Abidjan center. It has a striking Lattier sculpture suspended from the lobby ceiling. Customs and immigration are normal but you encounter a mob scene of taxi drivers and minibuses. It's best to be met, rent a car at the airport or take a hotel bus. When driving in you pass the original port settlement of Treichville and cross one of two fine bridges into the Plateau peninsula, Abidjan's business and administrative heartland. Air Afrique's multinational headquarters is here.

About the roads: Highways cover interesting but difficult terrain between the Ivory Coast and the Niger River at Bamako (Mali). There is a partially paved road paralleling the railway into Upper Volta. The border road to Guinea-Conakry is beautiful but rough, and the border itself is rigorously policed by the Guineans. Compagnie Transafricaine buses travel the roads to Upper Volta and Mali twice weekly, and you can hitchhike if you have great patience. There is a paved roundabout circuit to Ghana through beautiful Agni and Ashanti country around Abengourou, but there is no coastal highway between these two important neighbors and no regular bus or collective taxi service across the border. A privately operated passenger ferry between Half Assini in Ghana and Adiaké below Aboisso in the Ivory Coast, once a favorite crossing point for backpackers, suspended operations in 1971; canoes may be available.

Visas are required for Americans and Canadians. Ivoirian forms are a complicated nuisance (bring along three sheets of carbon paper if you're going to fill them out at a consular office) and for some reason four photographs are needed. You may also have to show a fully paid round trip ticket and/or letter of sponsorship or financial solvency, and the whole process takes at least 48 hours. You can trust the consulate with your passport, but if applying by mail, allow plenty of time (a week minimum) for the process. Only 24-hour transit visas are issued on arrival at the airport. In countries where the Ivory Coast does not have diplomatic representation, visas can be obtained from French consulates —with fewer formalities. The trouble is that with its economic boom, the Ivory Coast is represented in most places you're likely to go to.

Getting Around Within the Ivory Coast

Air Ivoire, affiliated with France's UTA Airlines, operates expensive regular DC-3 service between Abidjan and Bouaké (190 miles in one hour and 20 minutes for $32 one way), Korhogo (2½ hours, $40), Man (3½ hours, $38), Sassandra (one hour, $29), as well as San Pedro, Bereby, Daloa and Tabou. It will also charter DC-3 and smaller aircraft to those towns and to a number of airfields like Ouango-Fitini in the Bouna Game Reserve, Yamoussoukro (President Houphouet's home town and plantation residence), Bondoukou on the Ghana border south of the Bouna Park, and Gagnoa in the forest-plantation-hunting territory.

The railroad link with Upper Volta creates a north-south axis through almost 400 miles of the Ivory Coast, with local service to Agboville (two hours) and Bouaké (7¼ hours, $6.70 one way first class, $2.40 second class). There are also sleeper accommodations. This is a good choice for quick one-way runs in and out of Abidjan if you decide to drive, hitchhike or go by bus, plane or taxi the other way. Navigation on the country's four rivers is restricted to canoes and motorboats.

Hertz, AutoLoc, Air Service (Europcars) and Transcoop offer car rental facilities at the airport and in town. There are agencies also in Bouaké, Daloa, Gagnoa, Man and Sassandra, but no one-way rental deals. Rates are high: $9.50 per day plus 6 cents per kilometer for the smallest, self-driven vehicle, usually a Fiat 600 (the first 60 kilometers are free), up to $21 per day and 10 cents per kilometer for an American car or Fiat 2300. Air-conditioned cars are available. These rates do not include gasoline which costs 80 cents per gallon (88 cents for high test). Chauffeur service adds an additional $4 per day, and is usually worth it, for town traffic is heavy, bush roads are tough, and your driver is often a help in negotiations en route. The companies require credit card guarantees or a refundable deposit of about $160. There is a Michelin "red" map for the Ivory Coast (No. 175).

Hardy, low-budget travelers may prefer the rude but convenient 15-seat Renault buses or the eight-seat collective taxis. Or you can bargain with taxi drivers in town. Trunk roads are in fairly good shape, with over 1,200 miles of hard surface from Abidjan to Bouaké, Bouaflé and Abengourou on the main routes fanning out from the capital. Travel on other roads is dusty in the dry seasons, muddy and occasionally interrupted by washouts during the rains.

Taxis in Abidjan are painted bright orange. They charge an initial 40 CFA (16 cents) plus 20 CFA (8 cents) per kilometer. Town buses are usually jam-packed, but charge only 20 CFA (8 cents) per ride. Hitchhiking is easy along the paved coastal road to Grand Bassam and the north-south axis as far as Bouaké, as well as on the Abidjan-Abengourou highway toward Ghana. Middle-class Ivoirians and many foreign vacationers, businessmen and technicians pass along these routes. Beyond these roads you must scramble a bit for a free ride by asking at garages, hotels and town halls, but most of the traffic is commercial, and Ivoirians themselves either pay or walk. Vehicles drive on the right.

The Ministry of Information and Tourism, usually working through the nationally owned Ivory Coast Tourist Agency (ICTA), publishes quantities of promotional literature for investors and visitors. Their tourist documentation heavily emphasizes the appeal of Abidjan and the *dolce far niente* of mass vacationing. They adopt the patronizing French term "folklore" to refer to African music and theater, and their English translations are embarrassing to say the least. If you read French, order your materials in the original.

For bookings and transportation, the government gives free rein to the commercial agencies, including its own ICTA, 9 avenue Barthe; Delmas-Vieljeux on Avenue Barthe; Transcap on Avenue Houdaille; American Express on Boulevard de la République, and Socopao of the international Scandinavian (SCAC) system on Boulevard de la République.

If you plan to drive a car, the Automobile Club de la Côte d'Ivoire (P.O. Box 394, tel. 22.73.60) offers useful advice.

Where to Stay

A spurt of post-independence building has resulted in a scattering of clean, efficient, rather sterile hotels in town and in the provincial capitals.

ABIDJAN's pride and joy is the Intercontinental's *Hôtel Ivoire*, a veritable citadel of luxury on the Bay of Cocody, 15 minutes by car from center city. Situated on a promontory topping town and lagoon, the Ivoire has a huge pool, boat landing, paddle-boat pool, gymnasium, sauna bath, theaters, tennis courts, bowling alleys, ice skating rink, casino, seven restaurants, a supermarket, travel agencies, nightclub, a glassy, cavernous lobby, the continent's largest and most reliable outlet for West African arts and crafts, enormous corridors and elegant rooms in both the main building and the 33-story "Ivory Tower" annex from whose summit on a clear day guests can actually see Africa.

The hotel provides many services, including a free minibus shuttle to and from the center of town. Single rooms rent for $17 to $22 per night, doubles from $24 to $34, and suites from $26 to $80—plus taxes. All meals are extra. Here is the archetype and anchor of the Riviera tourist scheme which promises to line the Ebrié Lagoon with more establishments for vacationers eastward from the Ivoire.

Abidjan also accommodates less glamorous tastes. Virtually next door to the Ivoire the discreet Air France *Relais de Cocody* has its own discotheque, swimming pool and good restaurants (including a thatched chalet at water's edge) overlooking the lagoon and the impressive Abidjan Plateau. Single rooms rent from $13 to $16, doubles from $13.50 to $25, cabanas from $16, suites from $21 (all meals, service and taxes extra).

In town, the *Hôtel du Parc* occupies a convenient location close to business and government offices, with a popular sidewalk cafe, one of

Abidjan's best French restaurants, shops and airline agencies. Rooms are simple and businesslike, renting from $9 to $15.50.

The quieter but shabbier *Grand Hôtel* on the bay at the edge of the city center across from Treichville has a good restaurant, a rooftop bar and simple rooms with air-conditioning and bath for $7.50 to $10 singles and $8.80 to $15 doubles.

The most comfortable of several good hotels in the environs of Abidjan is the *Palm Beach* at Vridi, two and a half miles from the airport, with rooms and bungalows from $12 to $18. It has good seafood, a large swimming pool and tennis courts on the beach. Less expensive competitors include *Les Tourelles*, with swimming pool, and the *Hôtel de la Pergola* on the Boulevard Marseille ($8 per room). The *Hôtel de France* near the main railroad station in Treichville has 50 air-conditioned rooms without private bath for $10 to $14. For stricter budgets, you must settle for outside midtown, with resultant transportation costs. Try the *Hôtel International* on the Airport boulevard ($6 to $10), the *Hôtel Atlanta*, 15th Avenue in Treichville ($6 to $8), the *Hôtel Haddad* in Treichville ($5 to $6), the *Bon Séjour* in Marcory ($3 to $5) and *L'Humanité* in Adjamé ($3.50).

Beyond the vicinity of Abidjan, hotels become simpler and relatively cheaper, but there are few chances to save money on accommodations except for government campements administratifs under the authority of local sous-préfets in all principal towns. In YAMOUSSOUKRO, the *Relais Shell*, *AGIP Motel*, and the *Hôtel Relais* all have decent lodgings and good food for $7.50 to $12.

At BOUAKÉ, the old *Provençal* has 32 air-conditioned rooms for $10, with good food and a sidewalk cafe. The smaller but more modern *Motel du Lac* rents for $8.80 per room. The *Buffet-Hôtel de la Gare* (operated by the railroad) has non-air-conditioned rooms for $3.50 to $5, air-conditioned rooms for $8.50.

To the east, ABENGOUROU boasts a pretty, brand new *Hôtel Indénié* with full air-conditioning and swimming pool ($10 to $15). Abengourou's campement administratif is adequate and cheaper.

There is a campement at AGNIBILEKROU just off the border northwest of Abengourou. BONDOUKOU farther north has the reasonable *Hôtel Mon Zanzan*.

West of Bouaké, DIMBOKRO, TOUMODI and BOUAFLÉ have rest-houses near game areas. DALOA has the small *Oasis* ($4 for non-air-conditioned rooms, $8 for air-conditioned) and the *Hôtel des Ambassadeurs* (44 air-conditioned rooms for $10 to $12).

GAGNOA, crossroads of coffee caravans, has the *Hôtel Fromager* (fully air-conditioned, $8 to $10), as well as the simpler *Hôtel-Bar Caluas* and

Le Cottage (with air-conditioning at $10 and without air-conditioning at $3.50).

A fine new *Hôtel Les Cascades* at MAN with full air-conditioning, swimming pool, terrace bar and pretty waterfall, costs from $10 to $15.

In GOUESSESSO, the *Hôtel des Lianes* is a tourist village built in proximity to a community of Yacouba people, usually taking group parties at negotiated rates.

At SAN PEDRO, the *Hôtel l'Horizon* is expanding from 10 to 40 rooms and is likely to be in the $10 to $15 category for single rooms, as is the *Motel ARSO*. The *Club Avicam* on GRAND LAHOU beach is attractive.

In the north, the rustic old *Relais Senoufo* at FERKESSÉDOUGOU has air-conditioners in its bungalows for $7.50. KORHOGO, capital of Senoufo country, offers the excellent new *Hôtel du Mont Korhogo* and the *Motel AGIP*, both fully air-conditioned, starting at $6 per night; *L'Escale* is cheaper. Hunting lodges at OUANGO-FITINI on the northern edge of the Bouna Game Reserve are fully equipped and comfortable.

Finding a cheap private bed depends on the luck of your contacts— with Peace Corps or CUSO Volunteers, mission personnel, or some hospitable Ivoirian family.

Where and What to Eat

Ivoirian affluence, a burgeoning French population and tourist interest have sustained a high level of cuisine in Abidjan and at other centers of the Ivory Coast, although all but the simpler African restaurants import many of their foodstuffs and charge accordingly. Even the nastiest flea-bag hotel in a trucking crossroads town will have a most palatable, full-course French menu, often with an African dish or two.

Close to the port and beaches of ABIDJAN, there are several fine seafood restaurants including the rustic and unpretentious *Bar des Pêcheurs* by the fishing port, the *Palm Beach Hotel* and *Le Lido* at Vridi, the *Taverne Bassamoise* at Grand Bassam, *La Vigie* on the road to Bassam, and *Le Lagon* on Ile Boulay in the lagoon west of town. Elaborate French tables are set at *La Petite Auberge* (extremely expensive but good) off the airport road, the "climatisé" (air-conditioned) restaurant of the *Hôtel du Parc* and *La Chaumière du Banco* in the Banco rain forest (an excellent place at dinner when the rather eccentric "patron" is in a cordial mood). The *Relais de Cocody* has a good pair of restaurants, and the *Hôtel Ivoire* gives you seven to choose from.

More bourgeois French food can be obtained at the *Brasserie Abidjanaise* close by the Plateau park, the *Grand Hôtel*, *L'Aquarium* by the swimming pool on Cocody Bay across from the Relais and the Ivoire,

Le Vieux Strasbourg, Le Coq Hardi on the Route de Marseille, Le Cabanon and Chez Francis, both on the way to the airport. For tighter budgets, try the Hôtel des Anciens Combattants on the Plateau above the stadium, Valentin on Avenue 16 in Treichville, the Restaurant de la Bourse in Treichville (bouillabaisse on Fridays), Chez Pépé near the main railroad station which offers provincial French menus from $2.50.

La Pizza de Soriente on the Boulevard de Marseille outside Treichville charges haute cuisine prices for simple Italian dishes but also has a moderate menu served in a delightful garden of thatched cabanas. The rather expensive midtown Kentucky Bar has copious French provincial specialties in a city bistro atmosphere (late evening is best). Slightly cheaper snacks are obtainable at the Ivoire bowling alley, the Café Calao at the Parc Hotel, the Ascot Bar on the Plateau and several brasserie-cafes along the main avenues.

More exotic fare is offered at Le Baobab, a good Senegalese restaurant in Marcory east of Treichville; La Babouya, a superb Mauritanian salon on Rue No. 7 in Treichville; Le Baalbeck, a Lebanese emporium with nightclub above the Plateau stadium; Le Dragon, a good Chinese restaurant on the Plateau; La Baie d'Along, an attractive Vietnamese place in Marcory on the lagoon; Madinina, in Treichville, for Martiniquais food; Le Calalou 421, a Togolese restaurant in Cocody not far from the Ivoire, which caters carefully to European visitors, and the Zoo Restaurant, which also prepares African specialties.

At a host of places in African suburbs like Adjamé, Treichville and Attiecoubé, you can eat simple Vietnamese food, or range over a choice of African dishes like foutou (plantain or yam with palm oil or peanut oil sauce), Senoufo chicken, jollof rice, atieké (pancakes or porridge made with cassava flour) and drinks like bandji (or Bangui) palm wine, lemouroudki (lemon juice with ginger) or tchapalo (millet beer).

Good French wines are sold at major restaurants and supermarkets for stiff prices (comparable to prices in the US). Heat spoilage in transit reduces the number of drinkable good white wines to a rarity, whereas table wines and tougher North African vintages stay "cool" and within budgetary reach. City water is dreadful, although restaurants and hotels usually serve it safely filtered. Since you can never be sure, however, try locally reconstituted milk, Ivoirian pineapple juice, locally bottled soft drinks, imported mineral water (expensive) or the quite drinkable local beers (Bracodi or Solibra).

The hotel network up-country provides simple food, mixing European and an occasionally piquant African menu. Restaurants like Le Dauphin at DABOU, L'Auberge du Bongo at N'DOUCI, the Relais Routier Shell at

YAMOUSSOUKRO, Le Refuge at BONDOUKOU, the Relais Senoufo at FER-KESSÉDOUGOU, the inexpensive Comoé Bar at ABENGOUROU, BOUAKÉ'S Hôtel Provençal and MAN's Fraternité Matin and ONU merit their good reputations.

Most places add a service charge of between 10 and 15 per cent to your bill but, as some waiters insist, this surcharge goes to "le patron" or "le chef." If this seems to be the case, good service might well deserve to be rewarded directly by an extra five per cent.

What to See and Do

Visits to the Ivory Coast invariably start at ABIDJAN. The capital keeps nearly a half million people rocking on the waves of its prosperity. It covers the shores and peninsulas of several undulating lagoon bays, connected by the Vridi Canal with the Gulf of Guinea three miles from the city's central Plateau. While numbers of resolutely urban Europeans still live in midtown apartments, the Plateau loses the entirety of its African working population every day at nightfall.

Abidjan has also already lost most of its magnificent old forest, but a few trees rise to 100 feet above three generations of building characterized by: (1) low, open colonial terrace structures now nearly extinct, followed by (2) flat, rectangular, air-conditioned offices and villas of the independence period, now becoming dwarfed by (3) leaping high-rises competing for sky like an African Manhattan. But it is a colorful Manhattan, with its own small "Central Park," its intimacy with water, the flash of Africans and the flair of the French. Even police cars are painted reddish-orange with green and white striped roofs.

Across the bay, reached by a semi-circle of boulevard, the Hôtel Ivoire complex resembles a glassed-in Rockefeller Center, self-contained and scintillating. Around the Ivoire, the gentle hills of Cocody are planted with decorative villas of the affluent and the fortunate, Africans and foreigners, businessmen, diplomats and government dignitaries.

Treichville and Adjamé on the southern and northern projections of the city, respectively, house most of the African working people. Each section is sub-divided into quarter after quarter of Baoulé, Agni, Senoufo, Malinké, Mossi, Dioula, Hausa, Bambara, Yoruba and virtually all the other West African ethnic groups. Here, and in smaller suburbs like Attiecoubé and Koumassi, they live within their various transitional urban cultures, harboring young unemployed immigrants of their own clans, sharing great outdoor markets, mosques and teeming city buses. At night this circumference of ethnic suburbs glows with the vitality of family suppers, cult music and the leisures of city men.

Between the central Plateau and Adjamé, is the old French IFAN Museum (now the National Museum). It is small in size, enormous in its collection and qualitatively notable for locally carved loom bobbins, musical instruments and sculptured plaques. The museum is open daily except Tuesday from 9 am to sundown (closed from noon to 2). West of the Plateau on Banco Bay is the impressive wood port, its magnificent logs floating at the flanks of ships just below the contemporary Babylonian architecture of President Houphouet's palace. Both Adjamé and Treichville have enormous, colorful and well-structured open markets, best visited in the fresh of the morning. They are not to be missed.

The university has a drama group that performs African as well as French plays, and experiments a bit in traditional and modern theatrical adaptations (although not to the extent that the Nigerians and Ghanaians have gone in developing new forms). There is a collection of traditional musical instruments and an occasional performance at the Ecole des Beaux Arts, a cinema club that sometimes shows the films of young Ivoirian directors, and a number of art galleries, including the sculptor Lattier's studio. The Cultural Center at Treichville also has evenings of Ivoirian theater.

Traveling players and headline cabaret entertainers come to the Ivoire from France (admission is high). Dance troupes come into town at government bidding for major holidays and VIP visits. Night life swings along Boulevard Delafosse in Treichville and at a sprinkling of discotheques in Cocody, the Plateau and Adjamé. But be careful—drinks, including local beer, cost a minimum of $3. The half-dozen cinemas on the Plateau are carpeted, the Hôtel Ivoire has a casino, the cafes are open in the evening (sit at rear tables if you wish to escape some of the hawkers, hustlers and shoe-shiners who swarm around tourists). With its comfortable facilities, its opportunities for sport and the proximity of water and forest, Abidjan is immensely attractive for drinker, dancer, gamesman and city stroller.

For beaches, fishing and water sports, you can start off from the Hôtel Ivoire's own dock, or drive out through Treichville to nearby old fishing towns like Port Bouet and Grand Bassam, or to the Palm Beach Hotel, for snorkling or water-skiing. You can hire a boat and go fishing for sailfish (the world record catch was set here in 1961), swordfish, marlin, barracuda, scad (merou), bonito, cavallys (carangue), shark, dorado, mullet, tuna, carp and pike. In creeks off the lagoon are crocodiles. October to May is the best season for all types of fishing.

GRAND BASSAM itself, 25 miles along the sand spit to the east of Abidjan, has an air of charming decay, with large old counting houses and verandaed administrative buildings, and sculptured tombs dating back to well before the turn of the century when this was the capital of the unexplored territory. A few ivory carvers and busy fishermen in the Azuretti quarter help the weekending beach crowds keep Bassam animated. The pre-Lenten carnival is particularly interesting for its synthesis of African-Christian traditions.

Here, as on most ocean beaches of this coast, heavy surf and tricky undertow make bathing a bit risky; and the lagoons close to Abidjan are badly polluted. For safer water fun visitors go farther out—in speedboats and cars—to Assinie, for example, a row of fishing villages close to the Ghana border, with both lagoon and ocean beaches (here the Club Méditerranée has opened a new vacation village for 450 people); or to Ile Boulay in Banco Bay to the west of town; or farther west to Dabou, Tiemba near the curious Tiakba stilt village and Jacqueville, all palm-lined old slaving towns with a prosperous plantation hinterland and an air of old world innocence.

Beyond the western lagoons, beaches become more nearly private, but there are good accommodations, attractive old traders' buildings and sporting facilities at GRAND LAHOU, 100 miles from Abidjan, where you can also go inland to see elephants, or fish with falcons from canoes on the Bandama River. Some of the best lagoon fishing (red carp, barracuda, whitefish) takes place in the lovely region of FRESCO, 125 miles west of the capital. Knowledgeable sportsmen also like the charming town and region of SASSANDRA, an hour's flight or a six-hour drive away, in an area of small game and big surf. SAN PEDRO farther west is a newly planned booming port for timber and iron ore; it already has beach, fishing and hunting facilities.

On the north shore of the Ebrié Lagoon 10 miles to Abidjan's east, stands quiet and quaint BINGERVILLE, Grand Bassam's successor from 1900 to 1933 as territorial capital. The forest road from Abidjan passes coffee, cocoa and banana plantations, the Dahlia Fleur Company's impressive gardens of orchids and other flora, and the graceful buildings of Abidjan's university. The university, established in 1964 after seven years as a French junior university, is still very French in its approach to Africa's education and technology, and a source of youthful dissent. Dissenters are treated severely at times by state authorities. Somnolent Bingerville has a school and gallery for young sculptors in the heavy, monumental tradition of the school's late founder, Professor B. Combes, and an orphanage that welcomes visits to its workshops. A tiny automobile ferry links Bingerville and Grand Bassam, permitting an excellent full day's excursion into lagoon, forest, city and ocean.

Only a few minutes beyond Adjamé in the north of Abidjan the *Banco National Forest* represents what the Ivory Coast was before the emergence of plantations, roads and cities. This is a well-preserved zone of 10,000 acres for hikers, picnickers and meandering vehicles. It has a fine arboretum, a little zoo, fishing pools and about 40 miles of difficult dirt road. Warriors and women of Banco villages like Yassap and Anyama have become used to putting their best feet forward in dance for the benefit of bus tours.

A solitary visitor can sometimes share the Banco morning with small antelopes and monkeys, but the foliage here is generally too dense for game watching. This is better done—although by no means with the same frequency of success as in East and Southern Africa—in the marshlands around Dabou (45 miles from Abidjan) or Gagnoa (180 miles), and particularly in the northeastern savannas at the *Bouna Game Reserve*, a growing haven for antelopes, small-tusked elephants, buffalo, hippos, monkeys, crocodiles and occasional big cats. Bouna is visitable between mid-December and mid-July, although rains begin to interrupt the pleasure in May. In the dry season, any sturdy car can cross the reserve without difficulty on north-south and east-west axes, but the park's animals are widely dispersed and several different excursions may be necessary to make the visit worthwhile. The excellent Ouango-Fitini Lodge and other small camps make this feasible. Hunting season (not in Bouna) is open from November to June; gun permits are issued by the Ministry of the Interior and hunting permits by the Service des Eaux et Forêts (apply through an Ivoirian consulate or travel agency).

Proceeding by road, rail or air northward from Abidjan, you pass Sikensi near the village of Gomon where a marvelous satirical-religious festival takes place in April. You then pass through plantation country to YAMOUSSOUKRO (four hours from Abidjan by road), an elaborately planned town thriving in the luster of President Houphouet, its native son. Every Wednesday an exuberant market fair brings forest and savanna dwellers together in Yamoussoukro. You can also visit the president's experimental plantations, as well as mosques, jewelry workshops and a nearby lake of crocodiles. There are elephants and other game to the south of Yamoussoukro.

If you continue northward for two more hours from Yamoussoukro, you reach BOUAKÉ (105,000), economic center of Baoulé country. It has the Gonfreville textile plant, silversmiths and tailors, tobacco and transport sheds, busy marketplaces, an occasional horse race, and an interesting Benedictine monastery outside town.

The savanna opens up north of Bouaké, with fields of grain, circular thatched houses, Mangoro pottery at KATIOLA, a handsome mosque surrounded by rice fields at FERKESSÉDOUGOU, weavers, carvers, musicians, an artisans quarter and a big open market at the ancient Senoufo capital of KORHOGO (25,000). This is a place for music, with Senoufo orchestras and balladeers who rank among the most creative in Africa. Normally, however, you must pay to have a performance staged for you. Near Korhogo are clusters of productive villages like Koni with ironsmiths who make elegant human statuettes, Kassoumbarga with ironsmiths and a 17th century mosque, and Waranié-Né, a town of weavers of rough-textured, figuratively etched Korhogo cloth, highly prized by collectors of West African crafts. The Senoufo people are also among the most prolific carvers of the continent. Great spirit masks adorn their festivals of fertility, initiation and burial during the dry season (October through March).

In the east, between Abidjan and the Bouna Reserve, live the Agni (or Ndénié) people, close cousins of the Ashanti across the border in Ghana. This is also a country of coffee plantations and a culture of panoply and ceremony, feasts and harvests. There is an especially beautiful yam festival at BONDOUKOU and other Agni and Koulango centers in November and December. You can rent canoes for an exhilarating run on the Comoé River west of ABENGOUROU, the Agni capital. The village of Zaranou, 30 miles from Abengourou, has creative carvers (especially of stools), tapestry makers, dancers and musicians, as well as an historical museum dedicated to Captain Binger, one of France's first explorers in the interior. In the northeastern corner of the country, the Lobi people live in conical-roofed fortified huts often decorated with geometrical designs or folk figures.

Traveling into the northwest from Abidjan, on a long but pleasant detour around Yamoussoukro, GAGNOA, BOUAFLÉ and DALOA stand at crossroads of the Guéré, Gouro, Bété, Baoulé and other peoples. Each follows its traditional style of building, of cultivating the sacred earth and of creating objects of religious fertility. Daloa (65,000) is especially good as a market for sculpture, ivory and ironwork, and for the dancing of the Bété people. There is a charming little Don Bosco Museum with an art shop at DUÉKOUÉ, halfway between Daloa and Man.

At the end of this road, before it trickles dustily into Guinea, the strong but very different artistic styles of the Dan (Yacouba), Guéré and Malinké people animate the Ivory Coast's most varied landscape near the pleasant city of MAN (52,000), a nine-hour drive from Abidjan. Here the hills rise as high as 4,000 feet, above waterfalls and rocky gorges. There is an interesting but breathtaking sinuous 12-mile track to the top of Mont Ton Koui (3,924 feet), passing a quick-changing procession of flora and rapidly flowing water to a radio tower (265 feet high) which can also be climbed with permission from the local government radio manager. Another three-mile road out of Man leads to the stony base of La Dent (the Tooth) de Man, which can be scaled only with full alpine equipment.

The wealth of this northwest area is in its ebullient cultural variety—stilt dancing in Man and its nearby villages; Goua initiation dances and acrobatics at Biankouma; minstrel storytellers, education-initiation ceremonies, and warrior processions of the Gouro in Dianflé near Bouaflé; masked theater of fire and brimstone, amusement and fertility, and the manipulation of snakes at DANANÉ. You deal with troupe leaders or village elders to arrange for a performance unless you come upon one during a festival, fair or national holiday.

Man's night bars, La Paillotte and La Calebasse, bring echoes from cosmopolitan West Africa and Afro-America into this rich, remote cultural pocket. The tourist village established by the government at GOUESSESSO, 30 miles north of Man via the important market town of BIANKOUMA, provides attractive accommodations, sporting facilities and good food 1,900 feet in altitude, where air-conditioning is unnecessary. Gouessesso is a point of departure for explorations of this fertile countryside, particularly during the festive post-coffee harvest season in March, April and May.

The partnership of government and overseas agencies has packaged a number of rather expensive tours, excursions and circuits, the best of which include (1) a five-day outing from Abidjan to Yamoussoukro, Dabou, Man and Gouessesso, going up by road and flying back from Man ($235); (2) a well-planned overnight trip by road into Agni country to Abengourou and Zaranou, where Agni royalty takes part in ceremonies of welcome ($78); (3) several different day-long excursions by a combination of road and speedboat to the Assinie beaches, or to Dabou and Jacqueville, etc. ($28 to $39); (4) a four-day Senoufo country journey by air from Abidjan to Korhogo and its circumference of villages, returning by rail from Ferkessédougou ($12). During the January-April dry season, the Senoufo excursion can be lengthened by three days in the Bouna Game Reserve for an additional $78.

In addition there are several tours of Abidjan, Banco Forest and environs by minibus, private car or motorboat, costing from $7.50 to $30 per day. If you like tours, ask for further details and bookings through ICTA or other Abidjan travel agency, or airline. In most instances, you can get guides who speak at least some English.

All but the most hurried traveler should consider the Ivory Coast in terms of a circuit including Upper Volta and Ghana, two closely related yet contrasting neighbor states. The Ouagadougou-Abidjan train provides one pleasant overland link, and the road via Abengourou and Kumasi (in Ghana) offers another for those who prefer to avoid flying when they have the chance.

Breaking up the train ride for a couple of days around Korhogo can be managed easily, provided transportation is available in Korhogo. (Tell an Abidjan travel agent or the Syndicat d'Initiative in Korhogo of your interest in renting a vehicle, or else wait until you're there and dicker with a taxi driver for a daily rate). Once in Abidjan, the northwest route can be accomplished in three days minimum, driving one way, flying the other, with at least two full days for the area around Man, Danané, Biankouma and Gouessesso.

Doing the beaches and/or the game parks depends entirely on your enthusiasm for what they offer. If you are seeking wildlife and landscape, you're best advised to fly to Bouna Game Reserve, Bouaflé for hunting, Sassandra for fishing and game, or Man for a combination. If you want to visit a succession of African communities, then drive, take buses or hitchhike in leisure northward or westward from Abidjan, remembering that the capital itself merits a solid, although expensive, week of time. If you are interested in social and economic development, call at the UN and UNICEF agencies in Abidjan, as well as specialized government services and the African Development Bank headquarters; consider trips to San Pedro to visit the new port project, the Bandama Dam at Kossou and the related resettlement programs, the rice-growing activity around Ferkessédougou, and the educational television studios at Bouaké.

What to Buy

Because many Ivoirians continue diligently in their artistry—and because artifacts from neighboring countries tend to fetch higher prices in Abidjan than at home—this is indeed a good place for the collector and curio hunter. Some of the best West African carving, new and occasionally old, can be acquired here. Major shopping centers give you choices in masks, ancestor statues, loom bobbins, utensils, stools and musical instruments. They are products of the Dan, Guéré, Gouro, Senoufo, Baoulé, Malinké, Bété, Bobo and Agni. Some are imported from the Bambara, Dogon, Yoruba and Fon. Mask styles vary enormously, even among contiguous Ivoirian groups like the Dan, Guéré and Gouro. If you chance upon a valuable old piece, you must get export clearance from the National Museum (P.O. Box 1650).

Some original ivory carving—combs, bracelets, animal figures and bas-relief tusks—is still done by the Gouro and Kaya in the region of Zouénoula and Vavoua between Man and Bouaké, as well as at Grand Bassam, east of Abidjan. The brass-bronze casting of Dahomey, Upper Volta and Ghana is well represented in Abidjan's shops. Gold jewelry comes from the lagoon area, Touba in the west, and from Niger, Mali and Senegal. Excellent printed cloth, handsome tapestries and weaves from the entire West African coast, particularly Fon (Dahomey) and Agni appliqués, Senoufo dyed weaves from Waranié-Né, blankets from Upper Volta, colorful Baoulé cloth from Tiébissou, N'Douci and Dimbokro, as well as manufactured linens and blankets from the Gonfreville mills in Bouaké suit both aesthetic and utilitarian tastes.

There are also leather-work items and skins from the north, basketry and wickerwork from the entire territory, balafons (gourd-resonating vibraphones), horn trumpets, drums and stringed instruments from north and west, the Hagi (Bao or Wari) African parcheesi game (often with elaborately carved and expensive boards), feathers, beads and raffia costume adornment, pottery from Katiola, Dimbokro, Touba and Séguéla, and much more for your collection.

In town and village markets you have a chance to deal close to the source of production, at prices that are generally lower than Abidjan's (although not too much lower, since the sophisticated craftsmen know what their work can sell for in town). The emporia of Abidjan include kiosks of the itinerant Dioula merchants in front of the Hôtel du Parc, where any tourist is regarded as fair game. Stick to your guns in haggling, retreat one day to live and fight another day, and pay what you must for what you really like.

Selections and price tags are safer in the vast, reliable gallery of La Rose d'Ivoire, a concession on the lobby floor and basement of the Hôtel Ivoire, where trinkets and curios are modestly labeled, and worthy objects go for worthy prices. (Many of the latter are locked in a corner "cabinet" which you should ask to have opened for you.) You cannot use credit cards here, however. Rose d'Ivoire has a branch shop at the Nour al Hayat shopping complex on the Plateau behind the Hôtel du Parc. La Gallerie Tai in the same complex also has a collection of genuine African art for prices that are fair, although higher than those reached at the end of a weary bargaining session under the trees.

Chic shops for clothing, sportswear and leisure needs are located at the Ivoire and on the Plateau between the Parc, the Nour al Hayat center and the Avenue Barthe (banker's row). Excellent African materials are displayed in the main town markets. In Abidjan, try the wholesale arcade behind the Air Afrique main agency on Avenue Général de Gaulle, or the markets of Treichville and Adjamé. There's excellent tailoring (especially in Treichville) for kaftans, booboos, dashikis and other interesting items of apparel.

A few good bookstores around the Parc offer recent periodicals from France and the United States, as well as a variety of French and African literature, history and scholarly research, all at high prices. Abidjan shopping hours are usually from 8 to noon and 3 to 7 pm, six days a week.

Local Attitudes

Years of association with Frenchmen have made many Ivoirians accustomed to European manners. They are hardly to be shocked by what American visitors might do, think or wear. The more chic the fashion, male or female, the more admired—on city streets, at least. The Baoulé and Ivoirians in general have a reputation for dourness among other Africans and visitors; their officials seem unusually pompous as well, but many individual Ivoirians are warm and spontaneous.

About one-fifth of the population is Moslem, with sensitivity to décolletage and to over-exuberant behavior around mosques. Among rural Ivoirians it's best to ask consent before photographing people and ceremonies, or before entering a private or religious building. Politics are openly discussed, but the government is conservative, controlling dissent without entirely suppressing criticism.

Weather, What to Wear

No amount of luxury or sophistication can disguise the climate of the Ivory Coast: it is hot and humid, with wider variations in temperatures and lower humidity as you proceed north and northwest out of the coastal forests. The dry season runs from December through March (a little longer in the north). Bouna Reserve is best in February and March, when heat begins to build up in anticipation of rain. March and April are also festive post-harvest seasons around Man and Korhogo. August and September, while damp, are cooler on the coast, and the rains diminish somewhat at this time, returning with full force in October and November.

Generally speaking, the rainy season has its advantages, for daily average humidity on the coasts remains about the same, temperatures are lowered by precipitation, and the rain usually falls in heavy showers separated by bright periods of fresh sunshine. Many of the up-country roads are mucky, however, so that the summers are less convenient for getting around. Also, half the French residents are away on European vacations at that time and many of their restaurants and shops are closed. October to May is the best season for sport fishing. The north has one rainy season, from May to September, with temperatures rising steeply by day and falling sharply by night. The northwest mountain region around Man has more even temperatures and gets rain fairly evenly for most of the year. Rain stops only in December and January.

Sweaters are essential not so much for the cool nights (except on the savannas and in the western hills) as for the intense air-conditioning of government offices, shops and restaurants in the capital. The Ivoirian elite tend to dress extremely well, in both European and African styles, wearing dark, relatively formal clothes for office, dining and circulating around town. Ministers and high officials expect their callers to stick to protocol in Abidjan, so if you are there on business, carry a quickly foldable jacket and pocketable tie to slip on and off as you shuttle from chilled office to sticky outdoors and back. For women, French modes prevail among those who can afford Parisian prices, but a well-tailored and well-carried booboo or kaftan always passes. Outside of Abidjan's formal circles, if you are not dining with a local big shot, feel free to dress comfortably in restaurants, bars and theater.

Communication

French is the language of government and commerce, and tends to unify the diverse Ivoirian people. English ranks as a second language, taught without really being spoken in most schools. It can be used in major hotels, some government offices, among Peace Corps and CUSO Volunteers and international technicians.

A 24-hour radio-telephone and Telex service connects Abidjan with most major Western countries, some of them via Paris. A new satellite link has improved the old colonial radio network. Abidjan's telephone system has been strengthened and enlarged, but service remains behind demand in this fast-moving place. Inter-city links are very poor. With patience for elaborate postal and customs procedures, you can mail packages safely from Abidjan. Try to time your mail drops to the US for the Wednesday evening Pan American direct flight. The major shops (e.g., La Rose d'Ivoire) will mail purchases for you.

Ivoirian newspapers and periodicals, all of them in French, rank among the worst in Africa for chauvinism and sycophancy. The national radio and television, using packaged French entertainment, and the government party's daily newspaper Fraternité Matin nevertheless wedge some information between adulation of government ministers and soccer stars.

Emergencies

Some social services have begun to catch up with the growth of population and activity, but even in Abidjan, medical and hospital facilities are inadequate. The Plateau's general hospital is a mess; if you need help, try the University Hospital Center, the private Clinique du Plateau or the Treichville Hospital. There are few Ivoirian but plenty of French doctors in town (dentists also), and everything about medical care is expensive; hence, it's best to carry insurance. Precautions are especially important outside Abidjan, where the only fully equipped hospitals are at Bouaké, Daloa and Korhogo.

The American Embassy in Rue Jesse Owens on the Plateau has a part-time American nurse, as well as off-hours duty personnel; they can call on a Peace Corps doctor in case of emergency (tel. 32.25.81).

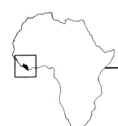

Liberia

Profile

STATUS: Independent republic since July 27, 1847.

SIZE: 43,000 square miles (slightly larger than Tennessee). Population—1,400,000, including 45,000 "Americo-Liberians."

GEOGRAPHY: 350-mile coastal area with lagoons and tidal creeks; plateau grassland rising to 3,000 feet; low mountain ranges in north. Principal towns—Monrovia (capital, 120,000), Harper (15,000), Buchanan (iron ore port).

CLIMATE: Hot and humid; daytime temperature 90 degrees, dropping 20 degrees at night. Rainy season from May to November, heaviest rainfall along the coast.

LANGUAGES: English (official).

CURRENCY: US dollar.

VISAS: Required. Available from Liberian Consulate in New York and Embassy of Liberia in Washington. Fee $2. Two passport photos needed. Takes 48 hours.

AIRPORT: Robertsfield (ROB), 38 miles from Monrovia. Frequent connections with West African capitals, four times weekly with New York, infrequent links with Western Europe. All airport departure taxes $3.00. Bus ($5) or taxi ($10) into Monrovia takes one hour.

NATIONAL HOLIDAYS: January 7, Pioneers' Day; May 14, National Unification Day; July 26, Independence Day; Christian holidays.

INFORMATION SOURCES: *In US*— Liberian Consulate General, 53 West 43rd Street, New York, N.Y. 10036 (tel. 212/687-1025); Embassy of

Liberia, 5201 16th Street NW, Washington, D.C. 20011 (tel. 202/723-0437). In Monrovia—Department of Information and Cultural Affairs, Camp Johnson Road (tel. 22011).

By *Philip M. Allen*

Africa's oldest republic is also the only nation on the continent founded by Americans.

In 1816 the American Colonization Society, a philanthropic group chartered by the US Congress, began organizing ocean caravans of free blacks who wished to return to the West Africa of their forefathers. In 1822, after being refused admission to Britain's Sierra Leone colony, the first shipload arrived at Providence Island at the mouth of the Mesurado River. They settled on land deeded by local kings on the Grain and Pepper Coasts. Despite the hostility of nature and the truculence of European powers, the colony outgrew its island and spread to the banks of the Mesurado and Saint Paul rivers. The capital was named Monrovia after the fifth president of the United States, and the republic (proclaimed on July 27, 1847) was modeled on the principles and institutions of James Monroe's America.

Later arrivals founded plantations and towns among the mangrove deltas and rain forests on the coast. While England, France, Portugal, Belgium and Germany carved up the remainder of West Africa into colonial territories, the American immigrants survived in obscurity. Their descendents, called "Americo-Liberians," became the nation's aristocracy and, in the frontier tradition of white America, adopted paternalistic attitudes toward the Vai, Kru, Gola, Kpelle and Mandingo people living in the interior, who remain Liberia's underprivileged majority.

The national economy developed slowly. Lebanese merchants took over the retail trade and small manufacturing. Half a century ago large-scale rubber production was developed for export to the United States. But Liberia received little to compare with the investment that Europe, in its own interest, was committing to neighboring Ivory Coast, Sierra Leone and Guinea. The country remained deeply in debt through the 1960's. Except for rubber export, its ties with the United States were essentially symbolic—in government structure and titles, the dollar currency, a preference for bourbon whiskey and the national flag (a one-starred Old Glory). The republic took a generally conservative approach to African and international affairs, particularly under the late William V. S. Tubman, Liberia's president from 1944 until his death in 1971.

Liberia is now entering a new, less provincial phase, with prospects of general prosperity and the hope of finally integrating its interior "tribal" majority into a modern economy. The country's gross national product and trade equilibrium have improved dramatically, thanks largely to production from Africa's largest iron mines (70 per cent of Liberia's exports), registration of the world's largest merchant fleet (much of which never calls at Liberian ports), discovery of oil, establishment of an industrial and warehousing free port at Monrovia, and an open door financial policy favorable to American and West European investors. The United States now takes about one–fourth of Liberia's exports (but is also involved in mining operations for European markets) and supplies one–third of its purchases. International debts are being repaid. Liberians have revealed gifts for management, organization and enterprise, as well as an underlying cultural vitality, that belie the old images of stagnation, hopeless corruption and elite extravagance.

Under a strongly centralized government, political and economic participation has spread to Africans of the interior, whose relations with the "Americos" have always been complicated. Liberia's Bible–quoting Establishment is splintered through a dozen sects of American Protestantism and Freemasonry; President William Tolbert is himself a practicing pastor. But the sons of the colonists also have been profoundly influenced by West African animist tradition, including powerful "secret" societies like Poro, a fellowship that acknowledges no non-African heritage.

For some time to come, Americans will go to Liberia for personal or family reasons, on official, industrial or scholarly business, but not for conventional tourist motives. Despite the great charm and hospitality of Liberians and the recent surge of their economy, the country remains physically difficult to penetrate and hard to enjoy without using special "handles" of some sort; Liberia is best visited if you "know somebody" there.

For background reading, try Charles Morrow Wilson's *Liberia, Black Africa in Microcosm* (Harper, 1971) or the more critical J. Gus Liebenow's *Liberia, the Evolution of Privilege* (Cornell, 1969), and for a sense of its republican past, Hollis R. Lynch's biography of West Africa's eminent pioneer statesman, *Edward Wilmot Blyden, Pan-Negro Patriot, 1832–1912* (Oxford, 1967).

Money Matters

This is dollar country (Liberia has its own coins, however). Travelers checks and major credit cards are welcomed. Commercial banks include the Bank of Monrovia (affiliated with the First National City Bank of New York), which has five rural branches for up-country business; Chase Manhattan, which has offices at Monrovia and Harbel (headquarters of the mammoth Firestone rubber industry); the Bank of Liberia (associated with the Chemical Bank of New York), with offices in Monrovia, Buchanan and Ganta, and the Commercial Bank of Liberia (correspondent of Barclays, Manufacturers Hanover Trust and Bank of America).

Hours are from 8 to noon, except on Friday when banks remain open until 2 o'clock.

Despite free port trading and open door financing, Liberia is an expensive country. Prices compare with New York for canned goods, meat, cosmetics, medicines, clothing, accommodations, jewelry, foreign newspapers, dairy products and other items of interest to travelers. Fish, fruit and some vegetables provide a partial relief for the low-budget visitor. In the interior prices are lower but goods are scarce.

Getting In and Out

Isolated from the road links which France built among its former West African colonies, Liberia can be entered over rough forest tracks in the northwest corner from Sierra Leone, or in the north at Ganta from beautiful but desolate southern Guinea, and in the northeast Guéré country from the Ivory Coast.

American Farrell Lines freighters carry passengers on 14-day runs between New York and Monrovia with good accommodations and food for about $500 one way. Ghana's Black Star Lines, somewhat cheaper, connects with Canadian and Gulf Coast ports. Several lines, including British Elder Dempster, sail along the coast to and from Liverpool.

Pan American flies four times weekly into Robertsfield Airport, 38 miles from Monrovia, on its long circuits between New York and African points south and east; Air Afrique makes a similar round trip once a week. Swissair comes in twice weekly and Ghana Airways links Robertsfield and Monrovia's Spriggs-Payne Field almost daily with other coastal capitals between Lagos and Dakar. Bus service over the hour-long stretch between Robertsfield and the capital is irregular, and costs $5. Taxis cover the route for double that price but will settle for $6 or $7 when traffic is sparse (particularly if the taxi man hopes that he can become your private driver in Monrovia).

Customs regulations at border stations and at Robertsfield are standard. If you are crossing by road to or from Guinea, however, your documentation, baggage, currency and vehicle papers must be impeccable for the strict Guinean controls (see chapter on Guinea).

Getting Around Within Liberia

Even the exploitation of iron ore and rubber resources has not transformed Liberia's internal transportation systems. Only about 200 miles of roadway are paved; laterite secondary roads frequently wash out in rainstorms and raise heavy dust clouds when dry. Most roads connect the ports of Monrovia and Buchanan with the north central region, but traffic is either commercial or nonexistent. The hitchhiker should wait for the weekend and try to find a Monrovian driving to or from his country place.

Mammy-wagons and bush taxis (here called "money buses") make these runs frequently and cheaply, but without fixed routes or schedules. They are usually crowded with people and freight. A four-hour trip (Monrovia to Gbarnga, for instance) costs $3.50 to $4. Of the three private railroads covering some of the same terrain, passengers are accommodated—but only by invitation of the Liberian-American-Swedish Minerals Company (LAMCO)—over the 200-mile line from the northeast tip of the country above Sanniquellie to the ore port of Buchanan. This is about the most interesting route scenically in a country that changes little in landscape or climate across the interior. Liberian National Airlines operates scheduled flights to the principal interior towns and three other companies provide non-scheduled or charter services.

Monrovia's taxis are numerous and enterprising, incessantly honking and sneaking in close; but their drivers exhibit skill, patience and courtesy unusual in hackmen. They accept 25 cents for short in-city hops and 50 cents for runs into close suburbs or the port-industrial zones. Drivers do not expect tips, but they enjoy showing visitors around (frequently with their own companion in the front seat) and you might reward them for tourist services not strictly in the line of driving. The Mensah Company at the Ducor Intercontinental Hotel rents vehicles with or without driver. The Yes Transport Service rents from midtown headquarters and some of their Mercedes vehicles are air-conditioned. Driving is on the right. Gasoline costs 45 to 50 cents per gallon and can be bought only in towns or occasionally, in bottles, at roadside stands.

Where to Stay

Accommodations are in short supply, even in MONROVIA. For years the *Ducor Intercontinental Hotel* has had things its own flamboyant but musty, flaking, fading and mildewed way. The Ducor's high balconies and terrace bar offer a splendid view from Mamba Point (one of several hills that burst out of the Liberian coastal plains). The hotel has central air-conditioning, a popular swimming pool and a nightclub, but a new, less cavernous interior and a bit of competition would improve its looks and service. The Ducor's prices reflect its international pretensions ($18.50 for a single room, $22.50 for a double, $25 and up for suites; plus a 10 per cent service charge).

The alternatives are few. *The Travellers Roost* recently opened in the arcade on Broad Street, Monrovia's principal artery, with simple, clean, attractive, air-conditioned rooms for $12 (single) and $18 (double), plus 10 per cent service charge. The less stylish *Carlton Hotel*, also on Broad Street, charges $10 (single) and $16 (double) with air-conditioning, plus 10 per cent. The YMCA on Broad Street and YWCA in suburban Sinkor have limited accommodations, usually occupied by students. Simple, clean rooms are available above the *California Bar and Restaurant* on Gurley Street off Broad Street ($7 for a double, non-air-conditioned but with comfortable facilities) and above *Julia's Restaurant* ($8, double).

In addition to government rest-houses at ZORZOR, SALALA, KAKATA, HARPER, TCHIEN, GANTA and SUAKOKO, there is a hotel at GBARNGA near Cuttington College; an *Airport Hotel* at ROBERTSFIELD convenient to the Firestone complex at Harbel; the *Lofa Motel* at ZORZOR; the *Louisa* in BUCHANAN. On occasion, Cuttington College's guest facilities at Suakoko can be used. Otherwise, traveling in the interior requires either invitations from local hosts or full sleeping pack and food rations.

Where and What to Eat

Domestic hospitality among Liberians sets a brisk pace for dining, with honorable traditions of generosity and good American cooking, soul as well as white. In MONROVIA, *Salvatore's Italian Restaurant* on Broad Street at the foot of Mamba Point below the Ducor has the best European meals. *Lords Restaurant* a few blocks farther down Broad Street toward midtown offers a cosmopolitan menu in exemplary West African-Lebanese style, with typical dining-out prices. Limited wine selections run at about New York levels in a country that drinks mostly beer, palm wine and softer beverages. Liberia's Club Beer is good. Monrovia's water, although filtered, often becomes contaminated and is considered unsafe to drink.

The *Ducor Hotel* offers daily African specialties that are worth sampling if you are staying there: jollof rice, palm cabbage, cassava and plantain with good peppery sauces. *Chopsticks Restaurant* on Gurley Street just off Broad Street has a varied oriental menu for $2.50 to $3. The *Gondole* and the *Diana*, both in the business center, and the *Johnny Walker* on Gurley Street vary the experience of dining out in Monrovia. *Julia's* is a small, pleasant place for pizza and wine on Gurley Street. Cheaper places with simple menus occupy "Sing-Sing Road" (Carey Street). These include the *Atlantic Rasputin*, *Oscar's*, the *A. M. Restaurant* and the pleasant, air-conditioned *Senegalese Restaurant* where jollof rice, pepper soup, fufu or steaks can be ordered for 50 cents to $1 per platter. There is also couscous at the Morocco. The US Embassy Recreation Center operates an American snack bar on UN Drive.

Restaurants are scarce outside Monrovia, but there are "cook shops" in towns. Rice, fruit, boiled eggs, roasted corn and plantain bananas can often be found at bus stations, rural markets and Lebanese stores along the road. The *Coo-Coo Nest* serves simple meals at TOTOTA near the president's farm. The *Tamba Bar* serves meals in BUCHANAN. The mining and rubber concessions have dining rooms for staff and guests.

What to See and Do

Liberia should be visited in the company of Liberians with time and attention to spend on their guests. The capital, MONROVIA, sprawls from its republican palaces (Presidential, Parliamentary and the Ducor Intercontinental) out into seas of rusted tin roofs, cadavers of old buildings and aborted new ones. Even Broad Street is gap-toothed and rubbled. Monrovia hasn't yet absorbed enough capital to permit it to rise up or fill out its shell after the fashion of Abidjan or even Accra. Businessmen and civil servants occupy a ring of suburbs, in houses that transcend the condition of streets, landscaping or city services.

On Providence Island, the original Americo-Liberian settlement, a small museum has been installed in a house between town and port. The island is scheduled for development as a tourist complex with new accommodations, shops and amusements. Across the river from town, past a crowded and interesting shantytown, is the free port, a bustling spot without much fascination. A visit to the municipal courts, located near the president's palace and the university, provides vivid insight into Liberia's informal, highly personal style of justice.

Walking in the early morning and at market closing time brings you into contact with workaday Monrovians. In the side streets, shanty shops, barbers and tailors attend their clientele under exuberant "pop art" signboards. The Lebanese textile quarter on the edge of town is also busy. A few discreet beggars and hustlers patrol the street, but they are nothing in comparison with other West African capitals.

The beaches around Kenema outside Monrovia are pleasant refuges, although the Atlantic surf makes bathing dangerous most of the year. There is little skindiving or deep-sea fishing off the Liberian coast. At Scheffelin, 16 miles from Monrovia just inside the beaches, the government has established a cultural center with a dozen buildings in traditional style. There's usually some good sculpture and cloth for sale here, and an outdoor stage where visitors may see the Liberian National Ballet, a fresh young troupe featuring superb drumming and vigorous dancing.

The official Department of Information and Tourism schedules ballet performances for groups of 50 or more. Inquire there or at a tourist agency about joining such a party, and about any events being held at the Executive Pavilion in downtown Monrovia.

Fifty miles from Monrovia at Harbel, the 90,000-acre Firestone rubber plantation, largest of its kind in the world, welcomes visits scheduled in advance (tel. 216-74). Firestone's public relations personnel conduct informative tours of two to three hours. Liberian employees of Firestone will freely discuss the company's personnel policies, long criticized for alleged tardiness in advancing Africans.

Iron-mining companies have constructed communities for employees and families at Bong, 100 miles north of Monrovia, and at Yekepa in the far northeast. A company invitation is needed for a visit to LAMCO operations at Nimba near Yekepa, but it's worth the effort for the view of three countries on the drive up the Nimba Mountains.

Cuttington College, a private church-sponsored institution at Suakoko in central Liberia, and the University of Liberia in Monrovia both stage theatrical and choral evenings. Cuttington has a collection of African art and history on exhibition.

Research facilities for students of West African and black culture can be found at the Booker T. Washington Institute at Kakata (in rubber-growing country north of Harbel), and at the Tubman Center for African Cultural Research at Robertsport on the coast 75 miles northwest of Monrovia. (Robertsport is not to be confused with Robertsfield, both named for Liberia's first president.) Lake Piso near Robertsport is a favorite spot for weekend outings. The president's farm at Totota, 73 miles northeast of Monrovia, has a small zoo where weekend motorists frequently repair for picnics. Harper, a lost plantation and port on the Ivory Coast frontier, has a small museum and library, Our Lady of Fatima College and a new stadium.

To visit the industrial axis northeastward (by taxi or rented car), plan on a four- or five-day circuit from Monrovia to the Firestone plantation at Harbel (overnight at Robertsfield or at Gbarnga, 140 miles from Monrovia); then north to Totota for the president's experimental farm and zoo, Suakoko where Cuttington College is located, Ganta and Sanniquellie (rest-house, 88 miles from Gbarnga); then, if invited, to the new LAMCO company town of Yekepa on the slopes of the Nimba Mountains. Return via the 180-mile iron-ore road along the St. John River to the port of Buchanan; and from Buchanan back to Monrovia via Robertsfield (another 100 miles).

The lush but monotonous forest landscape is interrupted by a variety

of plantation and mining enterprises, and by villages with different decoration, crafts, clothing and body adornment. This is by no means an
ideal scenic promenade, but Liberia isn't ready for the casual tourist.

For another four-day route, drive from Gbarnga (three and a half
hours out of Monrovia) to Zorzor on the Guinean border (another four
hours), then to Voinjama and finally to Koindu (Quendu) across the
Sierra Leone border, where the Sunday market features fine tie-dye cloth.

Monrovia swings at night, particularly in the jazz citadels of Sing Sing
Road. Look in at The Wave and the Groovin' Workshop any night after
11 for rock, jazz and high-life music. The bars, dives and cheap restaurants of this fascinating quarter include such places as the Jolly Love
Bar, the Mermaid, the Can Can, the Safari, the Black Rock and the
Flaminco (sic). Most of them have music and a young, multiracial
clientele (including Peace Corps Volunteers). There is also a nightly
show of African dance at the Liberian Jungle on Bushrod Island.

Scantravel operates half-day guided tours of Monrovia as well as longer
excursions to Totota, Bomi Hills, the Bong mining range and Buchanan
by bus, private car or air charter. Meager tourist traffic has kept the rates
high for these tours, but they are good ways to see the country if you do
not have a personal host.

What to Buy

Liberia exhibits and still produces a rich selection of traditional West
African art—sculpture, musical instruments, Dan metalwork, jewelry,
pottery of the Krahn and Grebo people, soapstone carvings of the
Mende, dolls, utensils and cloth. Sale of these items is haphazard. Many
good products slip away to bigger markets in the Ivory Coast or abroad.
Expeditions into the hinterlands produce authentic work at the lowest
prices for knowledgeable buyers; for information ask at the Tubman or
Booker T. Washington institutes at Robertsport and Kakata. Dealers
roam Monrovia looking for customers, and will find you if you advertise
your interest with hotel personnel or at the cultural center in Scheffelin.
If you bargain well, prices for excellent Bambara and Dogon carvings
from Mali, as well as Guéré, Mende, Bassa, Kru, Dan and other Liberian
forest sculpture run considerably lower than in Abidjan or Dakar. Contemporary urban artists are turning out interesting paintings and abstract
sculpture. The Department of Information has studio addresses.

The shops of Monrovia, most of them in central Broad Street, have
little to offer but the convenience of fixed prices. Safari International
Crafts and Designs in the shopping arcade at Broad and Gurley Streets
offer handsome tie-dyes from Liberia, Guinea and Sierra Leone at stan-

dard prices (about $2 per yard and up). Afri-Craft in the same arcade has similar cloth and tailored dresses. Lebanese textile shops on Waterside carry a wide variety of tie-dye cloth and prints at good prices: $1 to $2.25 per "loppa" (2 meters by one meter) for prints, $4.50 to $6 for tie-dye. Local tailoring is inexpensive and good; this is the place to have your booboo or dashiki made.

Wadih Captan and other bookstores carry West African literature as well as records from Nigeria and Ghana. The Liberian government has issued a 12-inch LP collection of traditional Liberian music; it's one of the best introductions to West Africa's great musical heritage. Shopping hours are from 8 am to noon and 2 to 6 pm Monday through Friday, and to noon on Saturday.

Local Attitudes

There is nothing especially touchy about Liberians. The "Americos" are fond of American customs of speech, dress and thought. Up-country people display West African ease, hospitality and tolerance. There are about 4,500 American businessmen, missionaries, Peace Corps Volunteers and technicians in Liberia.

Weather, What to Wear, How Long to Stay

Entertainment is usually informal but the Monrovian bourgeoisie dresses with chic taste, and if you are a guest of the government you are likely to be invited to black-tie parties. Women may have use for long gowns and are advised to buy them (African style) in Monrovia or have them made from Liberian cloth. Sweaters come in handy on the up-country plateaus and in Monrovian air-conditioning. Otherwise, prepare for heat and humidity.

A visit to Liberia usually starts and ends at Robertsfield Airport. Two days and three nights in Monrovia and four days to a week by road in the neglected interior are usually sufficient.

Communication

English is Liberia's language and it is spoken more extensively than any of the country's several vernaculars. But accents and pidgin constructions often pose problems for the uninitiated visitor. Literacy is low in West African terms, but school attendance has been increasing in recent years. Peace Corps Volunteers are found in the hinterland and at the bars and terraces of Sing Sing Road. Most other visitors here are Americans, English-speaking businessmen, government officials and mariners.

International telephone links reach the United States, Britain, Nigeria and France, but all service, including domestic, involves delay, line breaks and poor fidelity. Telex and cable are more efficient.

The *Liberian Star* and *Listener's Daily* keep up with local activities. Local radio and television are amateurish. The Voice of America broadcasts to West Africa from here.

The USIS cultural center is on Broad Street.

Emergencies

Liberia has 32 hospitals, at least one in every province. In addition there are 160 clinics operated by religious missions, business-industrial concessions and the government. The John F. Kennedy Medical Center outside Monrovia is a modern, fully-equipped hospital associated with the University of Liberia's Medical School. The American Embassy at Mamba Point has duty personnel for off-business hours and a health unit with an American doctor in residence (tel. 229-91).

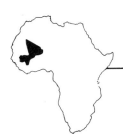

Mali

(République du Mali)

Profile

STATUS: Independent republic since September 22, 1960. Federation with Senegal 1959-60. Former French Sudan.

SIZE: 464,000 square miles (the size of Texas, Oklahoma and New Mexico combined). Population—about 5,000,000.

GEOGRAPHY: Landlocked and butterfly-shaped. Large parts desert and semi-desert. Well-timbered savanna in south. Principal towns—Bamako (capital, more than 200,000), Mopti (15,000), Ségou (35,000), Kayes (35,000), Timbuktu (14,000).

CLIMATE: Rainy season from June to September. Fresh and dry season from November to February (average temperature in Bamako 77 degrees, freezing nights in Sahara). Hottest season from March to June (afternoon temperatures reach 120 degrees).

LANGUAGES: French (official), Bambara and other African languages.

CURRENCY: Malian franc (FM). FM100 = 19 cents; $1.00 = FM520.

VISAS: Required. Available from Embassy of Mali and Malian Mission to the UN. Fee $8. Two passport photos needed. Takes 24 hours. Visas valid for single entry and eight-day visit (extension obtainable in Mali at the Office Malien du Tourisme).

AIRPORT: Bamako Airport (BKO), two miles from city. Three flights weekly to Abidjan, Dakar, Paris; less frequent within rest of West Africa. Taxi into city, FM200 (38 cents). Airport departure taxes—domestic, FM200; within Africa, FM1,000 ($1.90); outside Africa, FM3,000 ($5.70).

NATIONAL HOLIDAYS: January 20, Army Day; May 1, Labor Day; September 22, National Day; Moslem holidays.

INFORMATION SOURCES: In US—Embassy of the Republic of Mali, 2130 R Street NW, Washington, D.C. 20008 (tel. 202/332-2249); Permanent Mission of the Republic of Mali to the UN, 111 East 69th Street, New York, N.Y. 10021 (tel. 212/737-4150); African Explorers, Route 9, Parlin, N.J. 08859 (tel. 212/356-3434 or 201/721-2929). In Bamako—Office Malien du Tourisme, P.O. Box 222.

By Philip M. Allen

Of all the places off the West African travel beat, Mali is probably the richest in spirit, but it is hot, remote, uncomfortable, not especially cordial to tourists, and no bargain. You can come here seeking resurrection—of civilizations in ruins, of religions in legend and myth, of art in dancing and sculpture—but not for a resurrection of the body. For the scholar-traveler, Mali recalls everything that West Africa was before the center of trade and power gravitated southward to the coasts; in this sense, it is attractive enough to spend weeks in, discomforts notwithstanding. For more casual visitors, it is at best good for a few hot days in wintertime.

This enormous landlocked Sudanic nation has over five million people (nobody is quite sure of the exact total). They include Bambara and Malinké in the west, cliff-dwelling Dogon and Mossi in the south, pastoral Peuhl (Fulani) and Bozo fishermen in the center, Songhai farmers and Bella herdsmen in the east and nomadic Berber Tuaregs roaming the Saharan north. Their nation struggles with mortgages of dependence, disunity and poverty. Yet at times Mali rises above its burdens to creativity and to recollections of a proud history.

Mali was central to the centuries of trade around the great northern curve of the Niger River and through the surrounding Sahara. By the time Europeans arrived in force, 90 years ago, it had already known a millennium of great empires ranging from Lake Chad to the Atlantic, from forest to the Saharan mountains beyond the Niger. It saw Moslem holy wars and foreign explorations, and became a courtesan of gold and firearms, a source of slaves and a cradle of resistance to domination. Kingdoms ebbed and flooded along the Niger's banks from Ségou to Gao and invaders stormed the Senegal from St. Louis to Kayes. The great Arab traveler Ibn Batuta wrote admiringly of the place in 1352. Trade moved in and out of Timbuktu and Mopti, Tessalit and Sikasso. Toucouleur cavaliers under El Hadj Omar brandished the swords of Islam and the Almamy Samory Touré, great warrior sultan of the entire Upper Niger, defied the French invaders until 1897.

Mali has always been a homeland of idiomatic cultures—Black Islam, Bambara and Dogon animism, Tuareg mysticism—even while evolving politically from a rough French frontier to a neglected interior sibling of Senegal to an independent republic in September, 1960. A party-dominated socialist workshop for eight years under its first president, Modibo Keita, Mali experienced a military takeover in November, 1968. Led by Colonel Moussa Traoré, the present regime in Bamako seeks unity, embracing no ideology, denying no connection.

Mali still depends on Senegal to ship its goods through the port of Dakar, on France to support its franc, and on Algeria, Mauritania, Guinea, Ivory Coast, Upper Volta, Niger and Senegal to keep its seven borders quiet. Virtually self-sufficient in food, it cannot finance development needs by its modest exports of peanuts, cotton, cattle and fish. It thus accepts assistance from France, Russia, China, Israel and West Germany—from any source, in short, that can help organize a modern economy. Disgruntled wage earners, the unemployed, and restless civil servants have made increasing difficulties for the regime.

The literature of Mali's medieval Sudanic kingdoms is growing. For a start, try Basil Davidson's *The African Past* (Grosset and Dunlap, 1967) and E. W. Bovill's *The Golden Trade of the Moors* (Oxford, 1968), as well as the more recent West African histories (Davidson, Fage, and French texts like those of Cornevin, Boubou Hama, Jean Rouch). The new sense of historical glory has been debunked in Yambo Ouologuem's baroque novel *Bound to Violence* (translation of *Le Devoir de Violence*, Harcourt, 1971). For more recent Mali, there is Webster and Boahen's *West Africa Since 1800* (Longmans, 1967), William J. Foltz's *From French West Africa to the Mali Federation* (Yale, 1965) and Guy De Lusignan's *French-Speaking Africa Since Independence* (Praeger, 1969).

Money Matters

Mali applied for Franc Zone orthodoxy in 1968 after a period of financial autonomy, but France demands an arduous retraction of virtually all socialist measures taken in 1960-68 before it will grant full convertibility to the Malian franc (FM). Approximately 520 Malian francs are equivalent to the US dollar. The Bamako Airport makes exchanges, as do hotels and banks, the latter open only from 8 to noon. Malian francs are worthless outside the country, and you can bring unlimited amounts of foreign currency in and out: hence, convert only what you need. Credit cards are accepted by major hotels. Anything imported into Mali is expensive—including packaged food, beverages, clothing, cosmetics, medicines, photographic supplies, manufactured equipment and spare parts-- but economies are possible for the subsistence-oriented backpacker.

Getting In and Out

The seven borders of Mali are penetrable by several means. Most choices trade convenience against charm. Few are the "desert ships" that make their way in caravans these days to Timbuktu. Sahara tracks follow middle longitudes from Oran and Adrar to Gao, crossing the Mali-Algeria border above Tessalit (see chapter on Algeria). Elaborate Sahara travel precautions, including contact with police authorities, are necessary. You can come down in convoys of Jeeps or Land Rovers, or on trucks carrying dates, sheep, salt and other commodities from the Sahara to Niger River ports. Avoid driving in the Malian north between June and mid-October because of washouts.

Roads entering from east (Upper Volta) and west (Senegal) cross an alternation of attractive and monotonous country, and at considerable cost in comfort. The Kita-Kayes stretch of the western road is traversable only between December and May. The road up from Abidjan, while rugged, is the most interesting of all. If you are driving into Guinea, be sure that every piece of documentation and all baggage are above suspicion.

Twice weekly, the Dakar-Niger Railway carries passengers along the Senegal and Baoulé Rivers to Kayes, Bafoulabe, Kita and the Badinn-Ko Forest to Bamako (764 miles in 26 hours). Train accommodations are shabby but adequate and cheap ($30 one way with sleeping accommodations in first class, $17 in second) and the food is good.

Navigable from St. Louis (Senegal) to Matam and beyond during the summer-autumn flood season, the Senegal River is a slow and rarely utilized means of access for visitors. The Niger River has no border-crossing passenger craft.

Jet aircraft come to Bamako from Paris (10 hours), Dakar (3 hours), Abidjan (3 hours), Upper Volta, Niger and Eastern Europe. Propeller craft hop from airport to airport over the picturesque intra-African routes from Bobo-Dioulasso (Upper Volta), Conakry (Guinea) and Monrovia (Liberia). Visas and evidence of return or onward passage are required on arrival at Bamako's cavernous airport. It's best to apply in person at Malian consulates or French embassies where Mali is not represented.

Getting Around Within Mali

Some Malian features are accessible only by road and some Malian roads exist only in the dry semester (January through June). Paved roads are rare outside the cities, but in the broad zone between the flooding rivers and the sweeping Sahara, dirt roads are passable most of the year.

Buses and "cars rapides" (collective taxis) cover many of the routes between towns, but from Mopti to the doorsills of the Bozo fishermen around Djenné, for example, you need a pirogue (canoe) in the December-January Bani River flood season. To visit the Dogon people in their amazing cliff habitats beyond Bandiagara, you can hire four-wheel-drive vehicles at Mopti to go as far as Sangha. The rest of the way is on foot.

Bamako's taxis are few but enterprising. They accept FM100 (20 cents) for hops within town and go most places for a bargained price. Town buses cost a nickel. Cars can be rented with or without driver as reasonably here as anywhere in West Africa, particularly if you are content with a Citroën 2CV ($5 per day, with 60 free kilometers, 8 cents per kilometer beyond that). The cars are available at Jacquard et Cie., or at Bamby-Auto in Bamako. You pay for gasoline at FM100 per liter or about 72 cents per gallon. The government Tourist Office rents Land Rovers by the day in Mopti, Gao and Timbuktu; about $20 plus hire of driver.

To hitch rides in any town, ask at police prefectures or at local garages. Unless you come upon the rare international technician or missionary driving your route, you settle for a truck. This involves a nominal payment and lending a hand with the work. Traffic drives on the right.

Air Mali shuttles in old but scrupulously maintained aircraft between Bamako and Gao (5 hours, $72 one way), Mopti (2 hours, $34.40), Timbuktu (3 to 3½ hours, $48.50) as well as Kayes, Goundam, Nara, Kanieba, Niori and Ségou. Private companies rent small aircraft.

The Dakar-Niger Railroad goes westward from Bamako through beautiful Malinké country (twice-weekly express to Kayes, 310 miles, costs $8 in first class), and also eastward from Bamako to the Niger River port of Koulikoro, 36 miles downstream. On Tuesday nights from early July until February or March, while the river is high, one of three steamers sets out at Koulikoro for Mopti. Beginning in late August or September it pushes as far as Gao, 786 miles downstream, stopping at Kabara, the port of Timbuktu. Try to travel on the newest of the boats, the *General Soumaré*, but on any of the three, first or second class accommodations are relatively comfortable and meals are adequate. You will meet many more Malians in second class. Fares for the full five-day trip (six for the upstream return) are about $76 for air-conditioned first class, $52 for second class (four to a cabin, not air-conditioned, ordinary food). Third and fourth class accommodations are on deck and in steerage; you provide your own food ($6 for the full trip in fourth class). You can go on a segment of the journey for proportionately reduced fares. Buy your tickets at the Cie. Malienne de Navigation offices (P.O. Box 150) in Bamako, and check schedules carefully. If the boat-train connection looks tight, don't depend on it; take a taxi out to Koulikoro early in the day and stroll around the park.

Principal source for travel information is the government's Office du Tourisme, P. O. Box 222, in Bamako. UTA and Air Mali provide travel services, as does the Régie du Chemin de Fer (P. O. Box 260), but the best travel agency is Socopao (SCAC Scandinavian travel system), Rue Baba-Diara, P. O. Box 176, Bamako.

Where to Stay

Mali is an underdeveloped but ripening tourist terrain. At BAMAKO, there was once only the *Grand Hôtel*, pride of overseas France. It was for a time a run-down setting for ghost dramas, but it has been renovated. And it has some competition. Air-conditioned rooms at the Grand cost from $9 to $11.50 (single), non-air-conditioned from $5. Breakfast and service (15 per cent) are added to the bill. Food is fairly good, with menus starting from about $2.50 (plus wine). There is a sizable air-conditioned *Motel de Bamako* two kilometers outside town, with a dance bar and the Grand's rates, but breakfast and service are included. The small *Hôtel Majestic* in the center of town adheres to these rate levels, and also has non-air-conditioned rooms for about $5.30 (breakfast not included). All three accept major credit cards.

Accommodations in the exotic provinces are rudimentary and comparatively cheap. GAO in the east has the *Hôtel Atlantide*, with single air-conditioned rooms at $5.30, doubles at $6.75, and non-air-conditioned rooms at half those rates (service included). A full pension for town-touring visitors costs only $7.50 per person (air-conditioning is extra). The *Hôtel Vignat et Garcia* is even more modest.

TIMBUKTU's air-conditioned (it often breaks down) 18-room *Hôtel de Tombouctou* and the *Motel de Sévaré*, several miles east of MOPTI, offer moderate comfort at prices comparable to those of Gao's Atlantide. At KAYES, there is the *Hôtel-Restaurant du Commerce* and at SIKASSO the *Hôtel-Restaurant de Sikasso*; both places are better for food than for lodgings.

A system of government rest-camps is evolving. The Dogon cliffs are reached from a small camp at SANGHA which has room and board for $6 per day. MOPTI's own camp is cheap, although not much more so than the Motel de Sévaré.

For the game reserves, rude but adequate camps run by the government's Direction des Eaux et Forêts have kitchens, refrigerators and dormitories. These include the *Baoulé* at the edge of Boucle de Baoulé Park northwest of Bamako, the *Madina* inside the same park 30 miles from BAOULÉ (100 miles from Bamako), and *Missira* serving the Fina reserve between Baoulé and the capital. There is an attractive government rest-house at SAN on the Niger River between Ségou and Djenné, and less desirable places at SÉGOU, SIKASSO and BOUGOUNI.

American missionaries scattered around Mali occasionally offer hospitality and there are Canadian teachers here with CUSO. See the USIS officers at the US Embassy in Bamako for advice on such non-commercial lodging possibilities. Backpackers can camp at various sites for $1 to $2, or obtain other cheap possibilities through the Office du Tourisme or local authorities.

Where and What to Eat

Many reasonable restaurants prepare simple French menus with locally produced ingredients, including good beef, mutton or chicken, varied with rice, fish, couscous, sauces and fruits. Simple hotels, airport restaurants and camps serve this basic diet. Frogs legs are a Bamako specialty. Remoter areas in the north may test the traveler's capacity for dates, millet porridge and curdled milk. (The less tolerant traveler brings his own provisions.) Fermented grains, fruits and palm wine provide strong beverage alternatives to beer and vin ordinaire, both expensive imports. Water requires filtering, at least, so avoid it to be safe. Locally canned tamarind and guava juices are excellent.

In BAMAKO, L'Aquarium prepares scrupulously French menus with provisions largely imported by air (hence expensive). Majestic and Grand Hôtel food is good. There is French provincial cooking at Le Berry and good meals in a riverside setting at Les Trois Caimans. Le Lido, four miles outside town, is a weekend and evening favorite with Europeans and affluent Malians. Malian staples like millet dumplings and rice, spice and fruit dishes with meat or fish, can be found near town markets, sometimes for as little as FM100 (20 cents).

What to See and Do

Two special experiences should be considered by any traveler with sufficient spirit and time. The first is the nearly 800-mile Niger River trip between Koulikoro (near Bamako) and Gao, cruised by passenger boats from September through February (shorter stretches open from July through February). The second is the Bandiagara cliff world of the Dogon people. Both trips go to MOPTI, 335 miles downstream from Bamako, a bustling port for fish and salt at the confluence of the Niger and the Bani rivers. Flood waters cut the town into three islands connected by dikes. This is Peuhl country, with tall men and elegant women. It has intricate streets inhabited by cattle, donkeys and goats, a market for good jewelry and West Africa's finest blankets and a mosque patterned after the 13th century prototype at the holy city of DJENNÉ, upstream on the Bani. (The river steamers don't go to Djenné, but piroguiers and Bozo fishermen can row you into this most attractive town.)

The Niger steamers stop at Ségou, capital of the Bambara people. They are grain farmers, musicians and poets—and perhaps Africa's most brilliant carvers of masks and statuettes. If you have time at Ségou, the Chinese-built textile complex, Comatex, is interesting to visit.

After three days and 576 miles, the boat stops at Kabara, port of TIM-BUKTU (Tombouctou in French), walled metropolitan wonder of the 16th century Islamic world. Forbidden for centuries to infidels until French René Caillé found it during its senescence in 1828, Timbuktu has come to symbolize the "nowhere" of romanticism. The historical reality, described in Brian Gardner's The Quest for Timbuctoo (Harcourt Brace, 1968) and Horace Miner's The Primitive City of Timbuctoo (Doubleday, 1965), was a commercial metropolis where intellectuals from all parts of the Arab and Berber worlds came to study, where black Songhai, Mandingo, Toucouleur, Malinké and Mossi lived, worked and fought with Tuareg, Almoravid and Arab, where books were published and markets dealt in gold, spices and ivory.

Still a place of mood and trade, Timbuktu has a mixed population, several public buildings and many private mansions of the glorious epoch a half-millennium ago.

The moods of Timbuktu emerge during a prosaic stroll in the warm, silent sands of night to the Sankoré University mosque, the Sidi Yahia and 1325 AD Dyinguere-Ber mosques, the tombs of Malian kings and the houses where African merchants and European "discoverers" lived side by side. From December to May hundreds of camels stream into the city bearing huge salt bars from government mines at Taodenni in the Sahara to be loaded onto river craft bound for southern Mali. The chants, flute melodies and drumming of the camel drivers hover over their camps outside town.

The visitor has only a few daylight hours to see Timbuktu while the boat is moored at Kabara. Eight-passenger Land Rovers are available for this period for about $30. The glimpse satisfies most tourists. If one lacks historical imagination, the place can be merely dirty, dry and disappointing, a sandy rubble of heat and insects. In fact, the river journey is itself a bore for many, an experience to be endured for the later telling. Frankly, there aren't five days of intrinsic beauty in the landscape, which changes from thorn-bush savanna to baobab Sahel to sheer desert, or in the activities of boatmen and the frantic haranguing of the market ports. Impatient travelers should make the downstream run from Mopti to Timbuktu, fly back to Bamako or hop eastward by DC-3 to Gao.

GAO is a kaleidoscopic, polyethnic marketplace on the Sahara's edge where camel caravans and trucks meet the river traffic with cargoes of salt, meat, dates, wool and cotton. Capital of the Songhai empire, which flourished on gold and the slave trade from the 14th to the end of the 16th centuries, Gao has a ruined mosque, tombs of its Askia dynasty and marble grave markers of 12th century Moslem inhabitants. The Songhai still produce men of magic and healing who are employed throughout West Africa.

Downstream from Gao in an area of poor roads leading into the Niger Republic is the charming and little-known game park of *Ansongo*.

Communities of the Dogon nest in the Bandiagara cliffs and caves around Sangha, south of Mopti, among narrow ledges, plains of baobab trees and gigantic rock formations. The regular three-day tours from Bamako guarantee some dancing at Sangha, but only with much perseverance do you get a chance to see into the extraordinary life of the Dogon. There is sublime verticality here of cliff, crop and choreography, a Manicheistic dualism of good and evil, light and dark, male and female, and a fervent faith in ancestral survival technology.

In the far north, a few miles over the Mauritanian border in fact, the millennium-old capital of Ghana at Kumbi-Saleh lies in ruins. Seventy-five miles by exceedingly rough road from the Nara airfield, Kumbi-Saleh can be visited only after elaborate preparation. You'll need a knowledgeable guide. Here and in the Djouf region to the northeast, archaeology is restoring the physical context of medieval West African civilization.

BAMAKO, with almost a quarter-million inhabitants, is set in the broad, hilly Niger valley with tree-lined avenues, parks, bright colors and vivid odors. New compared with other Sudanic capitals, it is not yet a metropolis to rival coastal centers like Abidjan or Dakar. Bamako can be only shabby, stuffy, dirty and irritating to visitors immune to the quiet vigor of its handsome people, the modest virtues of its Ethnological Museum and zoo, its burgeoning market and riverbank bustle and the colonial feeling of its terraced hillsides. Near the Great Mosque is a Centre Artisanal where craftsmen work in gold and silver, ebony and ivory, leather and snakeskin. Veranda-fringed government buildings tower over the town on the Koulouba fortress hill, and new districts have sprung up across the long Niger River Bridge.

City people drink beer and dance at *Trois Caimans* and *Le Village*, take to the hills, lakes, and the *Lido Restaurant*'s swimming pool outside town on weekends (*Les Daltons* at the Lido has dancing and occasional entertainment), or they simply sit outdoors at night around brazier cookers, talking, smoking, chewing. Saturday nights pulsate here and in most towns with drumming, flute-playing and singing. If you are lucky, you may catch the fine Malian National Dance Troupe at home between its international tours.

Westward from Bamako, the eroded Mandingues Hills and the National Park at the Baoulé River are inhabited by giraffe, buffalo, antelope, gazelle, derby eland and leopard. The park is especially good from December to March, but Mali is not auspicious territory for hunting (which requires licenses) or animal photography. Fishing is especially good during the winter, when big Nile perch (capitaine), catfish and dog-fish flash in the rivers. The stretch between Bamako and Koulikoro is one of the best for fish. For river fanciers, a cruise up from or down to Senegalese and Mauritanian ports offers a more tropical set of notes than those of the Niger passage. You can explore the Senegal River terrain by road, passing into colorful Kayes, former capital of the French Sudan, entrepot for gum arabic and peanuts, and one of the hottest river ports in creation.

Between Bamako and Kayes, the road and railway proceed through a lovely countryside of waterfalls, lakes and forests; it is the home of the Malinké and Peuhl people, of animal and river spirits. At Bougouni south of Bamako, where the savanna almost thickens into forest, there is great Bambara music and dance—on schedules found only on the spot.

Soccer football is important to inhabitants of most major towns. Local Europeans use the rivers for sail-boating, fishing, canoeing and water skiing. Swimmers risk encountering the bilharzia liver fluke. Club members at Bamako can invite you to tennis or horseback riding. Movies provide the conventional distractions.

There are several patterns of sojourning in Mali. The busy, demanding traveler, if he comes here at all, flies into Bamako and samples the river cruising, landscape viewing and heritage hunting from a base in the capital. These purposes are respectably served by small-group tours run by the Office Malien du Tourisme, Socopao and the various airlines. The tours take groups of four to Dogon country for five days, for about $85 per person. They combine Dogon cliffs and the Niger River to Timbuktu for one week at about $80 per person (in groups of four), not counting one-way air travel between Bamako and Timbuktu (about $48.50). Traveling under these auspices insures seeing dancers, village life and nomadic tent hospitality, not always available without such sponsorship.

Using air links when necessary you can "do Mali" on your own in upwards of a week, with much to show for it. Enter the country by the Senegal River at Kayes, coming to Bamako by rail. Proceed to Mopti and Ségou by bus or car. Drive or paddle, depending on the season, to Djenné, and penetrate the Bandiagara in a durable vehicle. Take the Niger River boat up or downstream between Koulikoro, Ségou, Mopti, Timbuktu and Gao. To linger a night inside one of these historic sanctums usually involves making up the rest of the river route by air. Once in Gao, fly out to the Niger Republic and points south, or move intrepidly toward the Sahara.

What to Buy

Bambara, Dogon and Malinké wood carvers have created some of the greatest sculpture in Africa. Their traditions have slackened somewhat, but not expired. Almost no legitimately old sculpture remains, but excellent new masks, tchi-wara (antelope) head pieces and statuettes come from the villages where such items have long been carved. Authentic masks require approval for export, but carved granary doors (Dogon and others) are still available.

Tuareg leather work and weapons are found in Timbuktu and Gao; copper and steel utensils and wax statuettes in Timbuktu; embroidery, pottery and bookbinding in Djenné; splendid blankets, rugs, jewelry and pottery in Mopti; curiously symbolic basketry, shawls in black, indigo or red, metalwork, and the occasional good carving in Ségou, Bougouni, and Bamako.

At the capital's Centre Artisanal, Bambara carvers are busy imitating Bambara carvers, sometimes with subtle and expressive results. Here too you can find good gold and silver jewelry, tapestries, leather and skins. Before buying gold jewelry, be sure that the piece is stamped with the official imprimatur of the Service des Mines. The National Tourist Office in Bamako exhibits samples of what the enterprising shopper can procure.

Freelance traders accost all obvious visitors and you can occasionally find a rare work of art through these channels, but Mali's poverty and obscurity have discouraged artists and middlemen from retailing here; instead, they often repair to the more affluent emporia of Abidjan, Dakar and abroad.

City shops close for three or four hours at midday.

Local Attitudes

Malians take no special pains to attract tourists, but their traditions are dignified and hospitable. French overseas informality has not yet rubbed off on this independent, austere, Islamic nation. But there is little sensitivity to the behavior or dress of foreigners. Nevertheless, use of a camera requires a special permit, obtainable from the police at Bamako. Inquire about this at the consulate that issues your visa; it's an old requirement, but sometimes harshly enforced. Even with a permit, ask permission before taking pictures of people or ceremonies and avoid anything conceivably of "military interest." Ask consent before entering mosques in remote localities. Americans are not well known around Mali and many students and city people resent what they understand to be the United States position in the world, but these generalities seldom inhibit a traveler's experience.

Weather, What to Wear

Whether riding the flood tides or flying into the dry Sahelian spring, you will encounter heat, dust and insects. In the summer around the rivers, there is rain. Bamako is fiercely hot, day and night, from March to June; it is cooler, especially at night, from December to February. The sandy harmattan blows off the desert in late winter. Harvest festivals occur in October.

Although you can't do everything in a single season, the best time to take on Mali's roads, rivers, game parks, fishing beds and heat is the winter. You need sandals for the sand and sturdy shoes for hiking the Bandiagara or the waterfall country west of Bamako. Exploring the parks, camps and archaeological digs requires you to carry your own bedding, mosquito netting, water and food. Carry cigarettes, sugar, tea and other luxuries to exchange for desert hospitality. Westerners, in their khaki shorts and light shirts, frequently admire the richly embroidered, flowing booboos of Malian women and the gandouras of the men, but seldom feel at home in the raiment of so distinctive a culture.

Communication

Mali is plagued by poor communications, domestically and externally. International messages pass through Paris, indeed seeming at times to have trouble finding their way even there. Telegrams from the Bamako Post Office seem to reach their destinations more surely than radio-telephone calls, even to France, Cairo or French-speaking Africa.

A few schooled city folk understand a little English and an occasional amateur guide has been to the United States or Nigeria. But without French the traveler is fairly reduced to reticence, and even with French he often lacks conversational partners outside the major towns. The few English speakers in Mali live at embassies, the technical assistance missions, the schools with Canadian CUSO teachers and at rare up-country mission stations.

Emergencies

Mali is not a place to court problems. Arduous communications, extremely poor sanitation and cumbersome services impose caution on a visitor. All localities have hospitals or dispensaries, and there are a few French or French-trained doctors around Bamako, but chances for adequate treatment diminish the farther you get from the capital. The American Embassy (corner of Rue Testard and Mohammed V, tel. 46-63, 48-34) has a health unit with a nurse. If complications develop, fly to Dakar or Abidjan.

Mauritania

(République Islamique de Mauritanie)

Profile

STATUS: Independent since November 28, 1960. Former French colony.

SIZE: 419,231 square miles (slightly smaller than Alaska). Population— 1,170,000; majority are Moors (Arab-Berber).

GEOGRAPHY: Mostly desert; Atlantic coastline in west, Senegal River valley in south. Principal towns—Nouakchott (capital, 45,000), Nouadhibou (port, 20,000).

CLIMATE: Saharan. Slight rainfall from July to October in Nouakchott. May to November hottest months (high 90's), December and January "coolest" months, with Nouakchott temperatures in 80's dropping into 60's at night. Nouadhibou generally 10 degrees cooler.

LANGUAGES: Arabic, French.

CURRENCY: CFA franc. CFA 100 = 40 cents; $1.00 = CFA 245.
(Important—Mauritania adopted a new currency as this book went to press. See note at end of the chapter.)

VISAS: Required. Available from Embassy of Mauritania and Permanent Mission of Mauritania to the UN. Fee $7.20 for up to three-month stay; transit visa $2.00 for less than three-day stay. Two passport photos needed. Visas also available from French consulates where Mauritania not represented.

AIRPORTS: Nouadhibou Airport (PTE), two and a half miles from city. Linked with France, Dakar, Conakry, Casablanca and Canary Islands. Taxi into city, CFA 150 to CFA 200 (60 to 80 cents). Nouakchott Airport (NKC), two and a half miles from city. Linked with Dakar and

Algiers. Airport departure taxes—domestic, CFA 200 (80 cents); within Africa, CFA 600 ($2.40); outside Africa, CFA 1,500 ($6.00).

NATIONAL HOLIDAYS: November 28, Independence Day; Moslem holidays.

INFORMATION SOURCES: In US—Embassy of Mauritania, 2129 Leroy Place NW, Washington, D.C. 20008 (tel. 202/232-5700); Permanent Mission of Mauritania to the UN, 8 West 40th Street, New York, N.Y. 10018 (tel. 212/947-8655). In Nouakchott—Office du Tourisme, Secrétariat-Général à l'Artisanat et au Tourisme, P.O. Box 246; Socopao, P.O. Box 361.

By Philip M. Allen

The visitors Mauritania tends to attract are only the most sober business-men and the most romantic addicts of space, sand and stars. For this is a lonely, wasted land, a continental shoulder where Saharan sands blow westward to the Atlantic and southward to the green tropics of Black Africa. Put it on a West or North African itinerary only if you enjoy poking into inhospitable dunes or want to know an austere Islamic desert people for whom hospitality has evolved into an art of survival.

Several thousand visitors witnessed the 1973 solar eclipse here.

Berber Sanhadja tribes planted Islam here in the 8th century. In the 11th century came the Almoravid crusaders and two centuries later Arab invaders, pressing against the marches of the great Sudanic African kingdoms, turning them south and converting many to Islam.

The Moors, descendants of these Arab and Berber settlers, yielded their territory to France at the turn of the last century but reinherited control of today's Islamic Republic, independent since 1960. The Moors today occupy the upper stratum of a caste and vassalage system in this western part of the transcontinental Sudanic belt that divides northern "white" and southern "black" latitudes from the Atlantic to the Red Sea. The largely nomadic, totally Moslem population of over one million Mauritanians includes, besides this aristocratic Moorish majority, the related "blue" Tuaregs of the deserts (so called because the indigo dyes used on their turbans often discolor their skin) and some 300,000 black farmers of the Senegal River area on the southern border. Their president since before independence has been Mokhtar Ould Daddah, a sedate, sagacious, Paris-trained lawyer who has recently begun to challenge French domination over Mauritania's economy.

This is sublime country, cruel to the unwary, a broad terrain of over 400,000 square miles, regarded by the noble, nomadic Moor as a birthright. It is a land of golden dunes and luminous seacoasts, busy fringes and an empty desiccated center where civilizations prospered in a once greener Sahara. Its features include copper and iron ore, eroded mountain ranges roamed by cattle, sheep and goats, and farmland along the Senegal River peopled by the Toucouleur, Peuhl, Wolof and Sarakollé, many of them just out of bondage to the Moors. Mauritania has a touch of Gallic culture in its towns, Arab Islam in its soul, and a blend of conflict and creativity in its past.

An economy once based on palm dates, milk, meat, fish, wool and camel's hair, with salt and the coveted gum arabic of the acacia tree for export, now looks forward to modern prosperity from the iron resources around F'Derik and Zouerate and the copper of the Akjoujt hills. A syndicate of French, British, German and Italian partners (MIFERMA) mines the iron at a rate due to reach 12 million tons of ore annually. MIFERMA also operates the country's only railway and mans the modern port installations at Nouadhibou (ex-Port Etienne). Another consortium (SOMIMA) works the copper of the accessible interior northeast of Nouakchott, the capital city. There is also a search underway for offshore oil deposits.

Mauritania takes less than 10 per cent of the 300,000 tons of tuna, mullet, herring, bonito, ray, whale, crayfish, gurnard and other fish caught annually by Europeans, Japanese and North Africans in the waters off her coasts.

Aristocratic Saharans send their sons to schools and jobs in Dakar (Senegal) or France. But eventually they expect their French partners to convert foreign enterprise to Moorish benefit.

To help shore its political future, the Islamic Republic assiduously maintains its foothold in the Arab fraternity. For a decade, President Ould Daddah has had to fight opposition to Mauritania's very existence from a Moroccan monarchy yearning for imperial re-integration, but this battle now seems won by the Mauritanians.

Little has been written about this country in English. Try Alfred G. Gerteiny's *Mauritania, Survey of a New Nation* (Pall Mall, London, 1967) and the standard histories of the medieval Sudan and French West Africa. Literature in French, however, is abundant, particularly from archaeologists, explorers and soldiers of the late 19th and early 20th centuries. Some of the romance of Mauritania of a few decades ago emerges in Antoine de Saint-Exupéry's *Terre des Hommes* and *Courrier Sud* (These works are translated, respectively, as *Wind, Sand, and Stars* and *Southern Mail*.)

Money Matters

Until the completion of financial negotiations begun with the French in 1973, Mauritania remains in the CFA franc's western sub-zone. The Banque Internationale d'Afrique Occidentale (BIAO), an affiliate of First National City Bank of New York, has branches in five Mauritanian cities and throughout West Africa. Airports do not have exchange facilities, and the banks observe customary Mauritanian leisure by staying closed every afternoon and all day Saturday. Hotels and restaurants can convert dollars, although at less favorable rates than banks. Unlimited quantities of CFA francs can be brought in or taken out of Mauritania, making it convenient to visit the country either before or after stops in Senegal or other CFA areas. Mauritania's very limited economy and the absence of traversable roads from the port of Nouadhibou to the interior require that the bulk of the country's equipment and consumer goods be trucked or flown in from Dakar; hence, prices are astronomical for much of what Europeans and travelers consume.

Getting In and Out

Mauritania's three geographical facets—Sahara, Atlantic coast and Senegal River—present as many portals for the enterprising few who come here. Foreigners bent on business seldom stir beyond the modest conveniences of Nouadhibou, the iron ore port, or Nouakchott, the capital, and their respective airfields. UTA Airlines and Air Afrique fly twice weekly between Nouadhibou and Paris, and there is a flight each week to and from Casablanca (Morocco) and Las Palmas (Canary Islands). Air Mauritanie and Air Afrique connect Nouakchott and Nouadhibou with Dakar, which has daily connections with Paris and three weekly round trips to and from New York.

Instead of "dropping in" on Mauritania, however, you can drive up from Senegal covering the 190 miles from St. Louis to Nouakchott in less than five hours over paved roads and via the ferry at Rosso (which operates from 7 am to 12:30 and from 3 to 6 pm). Or you can plod more heroically by four-wheel-drive vehicle (preferably in a convoy) down through the Sahara from Tindouf (Algeria), east of the Atlas mountains. The Senegal River steamer *Bou El Mogdad* brings a few visitors upstream from St. Louis or downstream from Mali to Mauritanian river ports Kaedi or Rosso; if you enter this way, you should arrange ground transportation in advance to get anywhere else in Mauritania.

Ore carriers and tankers deposit a maritime tourist or two at Nouadhibou, and soon there will be a deep-water port at Nouakchott. But tourism remains primarily an airborne trickle.

Visas cannot be obtained at airports unless you have arranged for such delivery in advance. You should have a ticket for return or onward travel upon entering Mauritania but otherwise there are no special problems at immigration, customs or airports.

Getting Around Within Mauritania

Travel among these shifting sands can be a challenge. There are no buses, camel trains are slow and sporadic these days, and anything else requires time, fortitude and funds. Some town taxis (but not all) have meters;

in any case, short runs within Nouakchott cost from 50 to 150 CFA francs (75 to 200 CFA in Nouadhibou), and you can bargain for reasonable rates on longer trips. The amazingly sturdy Citroën 2CV can be rented at Etablissements Lacombe in Nouakchott (agencies in Nouadhibou, Rosso and Kaedi) for $14 per day; larger cars cost from $16 to $20, Land Rovers about $40 per day.

You also pay for gasoline, which costs CFA 44 per liter (about 63 cents per gallon).

Only 300 miles of road is paved in all Mauritania (the Rosso-Nouakchott-Akjoujt artery). Other roads, like the Akjoujt-Atar-Chum track, can be managed with discomfort but no great peril in normally sturdy pleasure cars. Most of the remaining roadways, particularly in the north and east, consist of ephemeral tracks easily effaced by the wind. Here, you need four-wheel drive, spare parts, repair kits, extra fuel and oil, water and other provisions, as well as sand tracks and a guide. The somewhat firmer roads in the more populated south are often flooded in the July-to-October rains. Service stations, food and water can be found only in towns or villages.

France and the EEC are beginning work on a road between central and eastern Mauritania, but completion is years away.

Camel caravans willingly take passengers from oasis to oasis at modest cost, but you must be willing to share a stern, hard life, live on dates and milk, and dispense with all Western notions of time.

The 420-mile railway from Nouadhibou to F'Derik and Zouerate primarily serves the iron mines. Trains occasionally carry passengers, but you should inquire about the availability of such accommodations well in advance. MIFERMA company permission is needed to use the road from F'Derik to the Zouerate mining center.

Given the distances that separate Mauritania's pockets of activity, air travel has become virtually indispensable to the young nation. Air Mauritanie covers much of the immensity by DC-3 and Ilyushin-18. A one-way flight between Nouadhibou and Nouakchott (210 miles) costs CFA 7,050 or about $28.20; Nouakchott to F'Derik (413 miles) costs CFA 13,200; Nouakchott to Aïoun El Atrouss in the fascinating southeast (430 miles) costs CFA 13,750.

The Nouakchott Aero-Club has small craft for charter at hourly rates ranging from CFA 8,000 ($32).

The best source of travel information is the National Tourist Office in Nouakchott which has mimeographed English translations of some basic French materials. The Socopao travel agency in Nouakchott (P.O. Box 361) is linked with Socopao Dakar and the international SCAC-Scan-travel network.

Where to Stay

In Nouadhibou, the *Clupea*, a social center as well as lodging, is close to town and beach. It's a comfortable, up-to-date place renting from $13 to $16 per room, with good food (but expensive at $8 minimum), and a night music bar. Be certain to make reservations, for that's all there is in Nouadhibou and the place is frequently booked up.

In Nouakchott, the *Marahaba*, once a covey of caverns around a courtyard, has been expanding the number of its rooms to 65, putting in a swimming pool, new bars and a tent for traditional Mauritanian tea taking. Air-conditioned rooms rent from $10 to $15; meals cost from $4 to $6. The smaller *Hôtel El Amanne* in central Nouakchott charges about the same rates as the Marahaba, but its meals are slightly cheaper. Likewise for *L'Oasis*, which has superior food. The *Hôtel Gomez* has a few non-air-conditioned rooms at less than $10, plus standard $10-to-$16 accommodations.

There are few choices outside the two main towns. Atar has the renovated and inexpensive *Hôtel du Tourisme*. There are government rest-houses (gîtes d'étape) at Rosso (rather expensive), Chinguetti (primitive) and Kaedi. Air Afrique manages a camp for hunters and game watchers at Keur-Massene on the Senegal River estuary ($24 for full board). There are no youth hostels or mission rest-houses—or other decent cheap accommodations, for that matter—until the government puts its other broken-down gîtes into shape. Unless you are somebody's guest or are prepared to camp out, there is no way to avoid spending money for lodgings.

All hotels add 15 per cent to your bill for service. If you are staying in a nomadic camp, bring sugar cones, cigarettes and tea to exchange for hospitality.

Where and What to Eat

Mauritanian hospitality is dignified, fraternal and unselfish. It tends to emphasize the privacy of villa, camp or tent, and the intimacy of tea time, leaving the preparation of public fare to the French. Couscous, pigeon pie, mutton and chevon (goat meat), dates, spiced fish and other seafood all come tastefully, if expensively, out of hotel kitchens. The most frequented of these are the grill room of the *Clupea* in Nouadhibou and the *Oasis* in Nouakchott. Millet is a staple in couscous or porridge.

Water is scarce and rather hazardous throughout Mauritania. Visitors are well advised to stick to a favored brand of imported mineral water or beer instead.

What to See and Do

Mauritania's interior appeals primarily to the romantic and historical imagination, whereas the coastal and river towns offer some of the more ordinary pleasures of beach, fishing and tempered sun. An agreeable tranquillity and a fair dry climate recommend NOUADHIBOU (ex-Port Etienne) to the beachcomber and fisherman, but the town itself is rudimentary and artificial. Mulatto (Imraguen) fishermen and enterprising Canary Islanders ply these waters from September through March, and the ordinary angler can virtually dip a pail full of fish from Nouadhibou's wharf or a small sailboat on Lévrier Bay (available at $6 to $8 per day). Around ILE D'ARGUIN, where the celebrated *Medusa* shipwreck occurred in 1816, are perhaps the world's richest fisheries.

The marine oriented visitor can also repair by boat to caves of the huge, rare angel seal at Cap Blanc, or watch the drying and smoking of fish in town.

Hotter and less breezy, NOUAKCHOTT, the capital, was literally planted on the sands of an old ksar (fortified village) in 1958 and is still growing to its full height (up to that year, the Mauritanian colony was administered from St. Louis in Senegal). The town is white, four-square, clean and dull. China is financing a new deep-water port here, as well as irrigation and rice projects. The camel market and rug-weaving center are worth a visit. The coasts north and south of Nouakchott consist of fine but treeless beach with good surf fishing and bathing. Five miles from town, at Tarfayat El Mansour, a complex of bungalows and water sport facilities is soon to be built. A half-hour north of Nouakchott stands a baobab tree associated with Saint-Exupéry's *Little Prince*. Another sports center is planned for the CAPE TAMIRIS area, halfway between Nouakchott and Nouadhibou. From the cape, you can boat out to the pretty Ile des Oiseaux (Isle of Birds).

For the time being, the most credible reason for coming to Mauritania lies along age-old tracks swallowed by the sands behind these coasts. Reminiscences of Moorish glory and Saharan prehistory are emerging from the desert, prodded by archaeologists and aerial photographers. They include rock paintings in the Adrar range and the ancient copper mines of AKJOUJT, center of renewed mining activity around a completely new town; the ruins of AZOUGUI and its Almoravid tombs; the tools, jewelry and buildings of long-buried civilizations in the north and east.

Salt caravans still come in and out of ATAR, prosperous, walled, rosy-tinted oasis, traditional staging area for southbound invasions, now only five hours from Nouakchott by all-weather road. The caravans of this region cross sensational landscapes changing in form and color as the sun burns its way across the sky between tent encampments and isolated ksars.

The ksar of CHINGUETTI, half-ruined holy city of Islam three hours east of Atar, is a point of pilgrimage and meditation. Its rugged 13th century Moorish mosque has a minaret reminiscent of the Koutoubia at Marrakesh. Its decorated stone buildings line narrow alleyways in a setting of fragrant palm groves and a brilliantly colored emptiness beyond.

Amid its ruined gardens, the ancient university capital of OUADANE, another 60 miles by track eastward from Chinguetti, still has its mosque, some handsome houses, and a rare manuscript collection of the epoch of trans-Saharan trade. Near Ouadane, at Richat, are large concentric craters of unknown origin.

The sparse, mountainous middle country of Mauritania eastward and southward from Ouadane is rewarding to admirers of sheer space, a topography sculpted by wind, sand and time. Back in the Nouakchott latitudes, tracks lead from Atar into the aristocratic hill country of the TAGANT, with green valleys (wadis), fine oases, little emerald-hued lakes, palm groves and date trees, domestic flocks, camels, tiny gazelles and fennecs (desert foxes), breathtaking mountain passes at Moudjaria and Batha, vegetable gardens and a fine tradition of poetry and art in the villages. TICHITT, ancient center of salt production, stands 125 miles east of Tagant's capital of TIDJIKDA, a six-day trek by camel. Tichitt retains some of its towers, arches, subtly hued stone and chalk walls. The lost, surviving town and its eloquent ruins testify to a Saharan style of building that is Islamic in its geometric imagery but untrammeled by the Arabic or Hispanic influences of Moslem architecture nearer to the Mediterranean and Red seas. The minaret of Tichitt's mosque affords a broad view of town, cliffs and oasis.

Other sites of historical interest lie farther to the south: at KUMBI-SALEH, capital of the great medieval empire of the Soninkés called Ghana, more easily reached from Mali than from Mauritanian towns; in the difficult mountain terrain at TAMCHAKETT near ruins of the flourishing 16th century cities Togba and Aoudagost, their populations composed by centuries of interzonal and interracial trade, warfare, enslavement and industry. Far to the east, on the latitude of Tamchakett and of Timbuktu, OUALATA (Walata), perched on a peak, commands another desert valley. Its narrow alleys separate houses of a unique decorative style, with arabesques and expressive lines set by finger reliefs in wet colored clay on reddish stone walls. If lucky, you can hear the night singing of Sarakollé hunters in the camps around Oualata.

The southern salt trails from Nouakchott to Rosso lead into Senegal past pastures, villages of carpet weavers, wood carvers and chest makers, acacia savannas with gazelle and waterfowl, the camps of nomadic lords who still claim their feudal dues from dark-skinned subordinates. It is a short airplane hop or long sand trek from Rosso, river port and ferry crossing for salt, gum arabic and tea, to BOUTILIMIT, with its Institute of Islamic Studies. The river basin is Mauritania's granary for rice and millet, as well as its green forest and lake country, where cattle and sheep thrive, in addition to the camels, goats and donkeys of the north. From July to December, the river is navigable from St. Louis (Senegal) into Mali, with a variety of village life and vegetation that make the steamer journey worth considering (see Senegal chapter).

What to Buy

Without displaying great abundance, Mauritanians take pride in fine workmanship—in patterned rugs and blankets stoutly woven from wool and camel's hair at Miderda, Boutilimit and the north; in metal inlays and carvings on panels and chests, intricate silver bracelets and necklaces, copper and brass pieces, elegant "Moroccan" dyed leather, stringed instruments of the griot troubadours, drums and tambourines, daggers, swords and pistols from the north, and shells on the coast. A solid silver tea service is a good investment for those who can use it or store it. Tooled leather saddles are also a good buy.

Each town has workshops where local products can be found or commissioned. There is a government-sponsored Centre Artisanal at Nouakchott and the souks of the Forjno jewelers at Nouadhibou. The Office Mauritanien du Tapis can advise on rug purchases or arrange visits to weaving centers. Shops are normally open in towns from 9 am to noon and from 3 to 7 pm, six days a week.

Local Attitudes

This is a fervently Moslem country. Islam is the state religion, and much of its practice is said to be "pure." Women are expected to be modestly clothed, and those mosques that are open to "infidels" must be visited unshod. Yet where the French have made their impression, informality and Western amenities are tolerated. Visitors can bring in a bottle of spirits and hotels stock beer and vin ordinaire. Americans are rare in Mauritania, particularly since the departure of embassy and Peace Corps personnel in 1967, but private Americans are accorded the same kind of courtesy Mauritanians extend to anyone else.

Weather, What to Wear, How Long to Stay

A complete visit to Mauritania involves as much desert slogging as the traveler can bear, with patience and stamina required for rough, hot, often empty spaces of time and place. The best season to come is the dry winter time (November through March), after which the desert winds bring new sand into the coast. Nouadhibou stands in the way of strong trade winds from February through July. The sun turns blistering everywhere from May through October, except on the humid Senegal River, but nights are always cooler. The hunting season is from November to June.

A varied wardrobe, for changes between daytime heat and brisk night, obviously makes the most sense. You'll need sturdy shoes and sandals for walking. Rain gear is useful only in the southern river basin during the steamy summer. Europeans and Americans sometimes try the loose trousers (seroual), veil-tunics (derrah), turbans (aouli) and leather sandals of the Moors, very practical garments for the temperature contrasts of the Sahara, the oven heat of the interior, and the sandy and salt breezes of the coast. Mauritanian women wear an ample one-piece cotton booboo called the "mefala," frequently dyed indigo like the masculine seroual and derrah.

Given 10 days or a fortnight, with Land Rover and/or dune-jumping aircraft, the more contemplative or romantic traveler probably will pause a few days at Nouadhibou and Nouakchott, if only to cool off after the mammoth interior circuit from south to north (Akjoujt, Chinguetti, Ouadane) and north to south (Tagant, Tichitt, Tamchakett, Oualata). For the normal traveler coming or going, the land route to St. Louis and at least a few miles of the fascinating river can be covered in a couple of days, leaving time for the seemlier delights of Dakar and the adventures of Mali and the River Niger.

One week is an honest minimum for Mauritania. If you don't have time or temperament for some of the arduous interior, you probably shouldn't be going at all.

Communication

A knowledge of French or Arabic, the national language, is needed for traveling in Mauritania. A bit of pidgin English can be heard on the docks of Nouadhibou and some school English emerges from younger Moorish patricians. Telephone and radio links are with Paris, Dakar and the Mediterranean, but all communications are rudimentary. Mail your packages from somewhere else.

Emergencies

Nouakchott, Atar and Aïoun El Atrouss have hospitals, and Nouadhibou has a good Polyclinic for MIFERMA personnel but available to others in emergencies. There are smaller medical centers in 15 other towns as well as dispensaries and bush medical stations, but the whole country has only 35 doctors and all its facilities are overtaxed. There has been no official American representation here since 1967. Hence, a visit demands scrupulous observance of precautions. If you need consular assistance, go to the French or West German embassy at Nouakchott.

Currency change: On June 1, 1973, Mauritania left the CFA franc zone and adopted a new currency called the Ugiya. The Ugiya is pegged to 5 CFA francs (about 2.5 US cents at this writing).

Niger

(République du Niger)

Profile

STATUS: Independent republic since August 3, 1960. Formerly part of French West Africa.

SIZE: 489,200 square miles. Population—4,016,000. Main groups are Hausas, Djermas, nomadic Tuaregs and Fulani (Peuhl).

GEOGRAPHY: Landlocked and mainly desert. Semi-desert savanna belt along southern border. River Niger flows through western corner. Principal towns—Niamey (capital, 90,000), Zinder (30,000), Maradi (22,000), Agadès.

CLIMATE: Hot and dry. Rain in south from June to September (cooler temperatures). Also cooler from December to January. Cooler at night (especially in northern desert). Day temperatures in Niamey range from the 90's to over 100 degrees.

LANGUAGES: French (official), Hausa and other African languages.

CURRENCY: CFA franc. CFA 100 = 40 cents; $1.00 = CFA 245.

VISAS: Required. Available from Embassy of Niger and Mission of Niger to the UN. Fee $6.25 (one week to three month stay). Transit visa free (up to one week stay). Two passport photos needed.

AIRPORT: Niamey (NIM), seven and a half miles from city. Linked infrequently with France and West African capitals (primarily Abidjan). Transport into city—free hotel transport, few taxis, private car for two, CFA 2,000 ($8). Airport departure taxes—domestic, CFA 200 (80 cents); within Africa, CFA 600 ($2.40); outside Africa, CFA 1,500 ($6).

NATIONAL HOLIDAYS: May 12, Political Party Day; August 3, Independence Day; December 18, Republic Day; Moslem and Christian holidays.

INFORMATION SOURCES: *In US*—Embassy of the Republic of Niger, 2204 R Street NW, Washington, D.C. 20008 (tel. 202/483-4224); Permanent Mission of Niger to the UN, 866 United Nations Plaza, Suite 570, New York, N.Y. 10017 (tel. 212/421-3260). *In Niamey*—Office du Tourisme, P. O. Box 612; Syndicat d'Initiative, Chamber of Commerce building on Government Square.

By Philip M. Allen

A republic of loose-jointed parts, bigger than Texas and California combined, Niger sprawls half over the Sahara, half onto Sahelian grassland, suffering from thirst, lacking a true center of gravity. Uranium and iron ore deposits (and a possibility of oil and copper) give signs of change, but today's Niger territory remains inchoate and unperturbed much as it was 600 years ago when great kingdoms flourished to the east and the west. It was taken but not entirely subdued in France's campaign to join her western and central African interior territories at the end of the last century.

Formally created a colony of France in 1922 Niger became independent in 1960.

It attracts few visitors and no crowds, but has an authenticity that transcends usual tourist delights. The rich diversity of its Sudanic cultures remains intact for travelers who can put up with heat and discomfort in order to approach what almost seems a leftover from pre-colonial West Africa.

The republic is named for the world's twelfth largest river, which flows through 300 miles of flatlands on its western edge, from the curious "W" bend near the Upper Volta frontier into a potent and burgeoning Nigeria. To avoid confusion with the more numerous Nigerians of the formerly British neighbor, most writers refer to Niger's four million people by the French designation, Nigériens. Half of them are Hausa-speaking farmers and traders of the Sahel; the rest include sedentary Djerma-Songhai, Peuhl (Fulani) herdsmen, and the nomadic desert people, Tuareg and Toubou, of the immense north. United by politics and by Islam, they inhabit an open country easy to penetrate, difficult to know, and impossible to cover.

The land runs from exhausted level plains into the uranium-rich Aïr mountains of the Sahara. It has an economy based on peanuts and beef cattle, Maradi red goats, dates, and ragtag fishing in Lake Chad and the Niger River. There are horses in the south, donkeys in the east, camels in the north, and a heritage of trade over the entire terrain. Three-fourths of the population clings to the semi-fertile savanna along the southern border.

Sickness and drought attack constantly; no forests remain; little industry has moved in, for the country lies 600 miles from the sea; education and training are hard to get, and students show constant signs of restlessness over their bleak future.

For better or worse, the Niger Republic, unproductive, landlocked, and hemmed in by seven neighbors, depends on France for viability and modernization. The French mine Niger's uranium, tin and gypsum, furnish most of its investment capital and technical aid, manage its institutions, govern its currency, buy its cotton and peanuts at pegged prices, and sell most of what Niger imports. In mid-1972, however, Niger began pressing France for a more favorable share of mining proceeds and greater participation by Nigérien labor; many French technicians and a French ambassador were sent home.

In 1925 France chose to establish the territorial capital at Niamey, a fishing village on the Niger fortified against the Mossi of Ouagadougou, the Hausa of Zinder and Nigeria, the Songhai of Mali, the ubiquitous Fulani cavaliers, and all other African threats to European control. Still the capital, Niamey has grown a bit in its time. It houses 90,000 people in a variety of domiciles from thatch and adobe to garden villa. It boasts a fine star-shaped cluster of administrative buildings, a few hotels, some green places, and Africa's greatest open-air museum.

The lovely palace of the former colonial governors is occupied now by President Hamani Diori, one of a half-dozen remaining presidential comrades of the original Gaullist fraternity that brought independence to 14 former French colonies in 1960. Currently serving his third five-year term, President Diori governs a civilian, single-party state where very little has happened to change the old Niger territory. He has dealt skillfully with traditional rivalries—between north and south, Djerma and Hausa, Saharan white and Sudanese black, desert Tuareg and the rest of the world—and has steered a conservative course with French indulgence. West Germany, Canada and Italy also participate in the mining and transportation development projects on which Niger depends for its economic future.

Niamey's new bridge over the River Niger was built with US aid.

Little has appeared on Niger in English. You can best begin with the standard histories of West Africa (Oliver and Fage, Basil Davidson, Webster and Boahen), supplemented by chapters in collections like Michael Crowder's *West Africa Under Colonial Rule* (Northwestern University Press, 1968), Virginia Thompson's essay in G. M. Carter's *Nationalism and Regionalism in Eight African States* (Cornell University Press, 1966), Richard Adloff's *The French-Speaking Nations* (Holt, Rinehart and Winston, 1969) or Guy de Lusignan's *French-Speaking Africa Since Independence* (Praeger, 1969). If you read French, you can find considerable historical and ethnographical material; seek out the excellent and abundant works of Boubou Hama, an historian who is also president of Niger's National Assembly.

Money Matters

The CFA franc circulates in Niger, is convertible and moves freely from one part of the Franc Zone to another. Travelers checks are accepted readily enough in the towns, but credit cards usually evoke only shrugs, except in car rental agencies and other sophisticated business places. Banks belong to the usual overseas French networks. They are open from 8 am to noon and 4 to 6 pm. The cost of living for people who depend on imports and European-style services is outrageously high—a consequence of landlocked isolation, inadequate communications, market stagnation, bureaucratic inefficiency and monopolistic wholesale-retail merchandising supported by high tariffs.

Getting In and Out

For the time being, only two kinds of visitors come to Niger: official or private businessmen dealing with Diori's government and the rare desert trekker following the longest, most desolate pathways in Africa. The first category enters by big jet from Paris or Abidjan (Ivory Coast), the second by Land Rover, Jeep or Toyota over the sands of the western Sahara, the ancient Hoggar Track from Algeria (see chapter on Algeria for a discussion of trans-Saharan roads).

Niamey's new airport receives four round-trip flights each week between Europe and Abidjan or Cotonou and one round trip between Madrid and Lagos.

You can hitchhike or ride a sequence of unscheduled buses between Niamey and western Nigeria, or through Hausa country between Zinder and Kano (Nigeria). The Nigerian roads and railways carry quantities of Niger's cattle and peanuts through Kano to the port of Lagos. Remember to get your Niger visa and some CFA francs ahead of time if you are crossing this way into Niger. Without a visa, you risk rejection at the frontier, and no other currency is recognized by Niger's antediluvian border bureaucracies. At this writing, the first trans-Niger river boat was soon to begin a run between Niamey and Port Harcourt (eastern Nigeria)—a potentially significant development that should open the lower river to increased interior trade, lowering Niger's currently astronomical transportation costs, and eventually providing access and egress for passenger traffic as well.

The western road artery from Ouagadougou (Upper Volta) is both rugged and monotonous, but it permits interesting detours into the national game parks of Dahomey, Upper Volta and Niger. Canada, which will supply the river boats for the new Niger-Nigeria links, is also constructing a 290-mile paved east-west highway from Zinder to Gouré and ultimately to Nguigmi on Lake Chad; this route will improve communications between Niger and neighboring Chad. Chad-Niger communications are currently dependent on the Nigerian roads and infrequent, circuitous air connections through coastal capitals. From Niamey to Dahomey, a sadly deteriorated international road carries a sizable amount of Niger's imports and exports by truck. Niger's new mining industry may warrant an improvement of that highway.

Visas are not available on arrival; even at the airport you may be forced to leave within 24 hours if you arrive without one.

Getting Around Within Niger

Most roads within Niger are perpetually rough, dusty and humdrum most of the year, and rained out along the waterbeds in the summer. As with the Sahara crossing, pluck and precaution are necessary. Even the Niamey-Zinder national highway remains unpaved in spots, although this deficiency is to be corrected soon. Take extra gasoline on any long trip since filling stations are more than 100 miles apart in some regions. Bring water for yourself and your vehicle, a good tool kit, spare tires, and plenty to read in case you must wait for help.

Public SNTN buses (so-called "Transniger") plunge daily along the 600-mile stretch of national highway between Niamey and Zinder. They regularly go to Ouagadougou and Parakou outside Niger as well. The bus rides are slow, crowded and wearying, but full of life. Bring something to drink with you and stock up on fruit, peanuts and crackers at intermediary bus stops. Market trucks (called "mille kilos"), found near all town markets, sell rides over the same terrain. Find out first what the bus fare is, then haggle with the truck driver for less—especially if he makes you ride in back with the freight.

The Nigercar Company (Route de Gamkalley, P. O. Box 715, Niamey) has the largest selection of rental vehicles, with or without driver. Rates are high: about $12.80 per day for a Volkswagen beetle, plus 8 cents per kilometer (12.8 cents per mile) each day after the first 60 kilometers, and you pay for the gasoline (about 22 cents per liter, or almost 80 cents a gallon). Larger cars cost proportionately more; weekly rental rates and package itinerary deals offer very little saving. All rates rise for trips outside Niamey. You might find more merciful prices at R. Jillade (Place du Grand Marché, Niamey) or at the Navalon Garage at the Hôtel Terminus.

In any case it's wise to hire a driver who knows the territory and speaks the languages (at least Hausa). It adds very little to the bill (about $2 per day in town, less than $5 for overnight jaunts), and he could become a friend. Also bring an internationally recognized credit card or other guarantee of solvency in order to avoid Nigercar's $120-to-$200 refundable deposit.

Taxi fares are about 100 francs (40 cents) for normal runs inside Niamey, where most streets are unnamed; you must use major buildings and landmarks for orientation. The tri-national (Niger, Upper Volta, Dahomey) "W" game park can be reached by Land Rover or Peugeot 404 (don't try a low-slung American car) via Diapaga in Dahomey (visa necessary), or by government-owned Air Niger DC-3 (about $18 for a one-way flight from Niamey to the airfield 33 miles from Tapoa camp), or by a five-seat air charter of the Transniger Company (about $30 per passenger if the plane is full).

Boat passage to the park and accommodations at the camps should be arranged through the Direction des Eaux et Forêts (P. O. Box 246, Niamey), or through a Niamey travel agency like Transcap (P. O. Box 522), Socopao (Box 560), or Société de Voyages et Tourisme (Box 481).

Air Niger's DC-4 and DC-3 also fly three times each week between Niamey, Zinder, Tahoua, Agadès and Maradi, as well as to a number of hinterland airstrips. A Niamey-Agadès one-way ticket costs over $100; Niamey-Zinder, about the same distance by air (460 miles), costs $66. These planes can be chartered for about $120 and $140 per hour, respectively.

The Office du Tourisme du Niger (P. O. Box 612, Niamey) represents the nation officially to visitors but isn't 'terribly efficient or well equipped. Whenever in a large town, travelers may seek out the Syndicat d'Initiative for advice on what's going on, how to get to places, make purchases, and the like.

American Peace Corps headquarters are in Niamey on Avenue Salaman; the USIS is opposite the Grand Marché.

Where to Stay

NIAMEY offers a fair choice of accommodations; outside the capital, you are roughing it. For aesthetic reasons, many travelers prefer Air France's shabby, medium-sized Grand Hôtel standing high on a bluff overlooking the river and only a short walk from most of the sprawling town. Its third- and fourth-floor balconies are admirably placed for sunset viewing over the Niger. Evenings turn pleasant in the hotel's terrace gardens. A double room with bath here costs about $18.50, breakfast and service charges included.

For greater modernity and comfort, many Americans prefer the Hôtel

Le Sahel, a bit farther away from things but also close to the river, next to an Olympic-size swimming pool and with somewhat more tempting cuisine. Here a double room costs about $15, all charges included. (Single occupancy runs only about $2 cheaper per night at both Le Sahel and the Grand, thus compensating travelers with companions or singles willing to double up.)

Between Le Sahel and the Grand, the *Terminus* has a new swimming pool to go with its old rooms. There's a nice garden for open-air dining. Here you have a choice of non-air-conditioned rooms at $5.20 single and $7.50 double, with air-conditioning tripling the price. In midtown, the *Rivoli* offers air-conditioned single rooms from $11 and a sidewalk cafe. Three miles outside Niamey, *Les Roniers*, a favorite with motorized and/or athletic visitors, has 10 rooms and several bungalows, all air-conditioned, starting at about $15 per double, breakfast and service included. The guest is surrounded by tennis, swimming, riding, volley-ball and gymnasium facilities. Small, cheap Nigérien hostels come and go in Niamey; check with Peace Corps headquarters to find the latest avatar.

At ZINDER, the venerable *Hôtel Navalon* accommodates transients around its attractive courtyard, with shower bath and optional air-conditioning in its clean rooms for $10 per room. MARADI's *Hôtel Niger* (formerly Chaureau) has a comparable tariff for similarly modest offerings. At Dosso, the *Hôtel Djerma*, a French establishment previously known as Les Routiers, has a couple of clean rooms with air-conditioning for $8 and four without air-conditioning at half the price. The hotel also has a swimming pool and a French menu. In AGADÈS, the visitor can choose between the air-conditioning and auspicious location (opposite the mosque) of the *Hôtel de l'Aïr* at $12 per room ($9 without air-conditioning) or the rougher accommodations of the *Boudon* at $4. As elsewhere in Niger, the tariff includes breakfast, taxes and service. The *Auberge des Hirondelles* at DOGONDOUTCHI and the government campement in BIRNI-NKONNI, east of Niamey along the Nigeria border, have respectable and cheap accommodations.

Tapoa Camp stands just inside Niger's "W" Park on a cliff overlooking the Tapoa River about 100 miles south of Niamey. Attractive thatch-roofed bungalows with electricity and water rent for about $3.50 per night. Upper Volta also has a camp on its portion of the "W."

Only 30 miles downstream from Niamey, the picturesque village of SAY can be reached by road or canoe through a landscape devoid of everything but grass and animals. Accommodations at the Say Camp cost about $2.50 per night. In Tuareg and Songhai country upstream on the Niger, the Ayorou Camp has rooms and bungalows with a modicum of sanitary facilities for $3.50, and a restaurant on a terrace over the river.

Throughout southern Niger, one can find hospitable local families, Peace Corps and other technical personnel, school authorities, and (in 15 places) American Baptist missionaries who may furnish lodgings if asked on the spot. Better yet, consult the Tourist Office, Peace Corps headquarters, Baptist Mission and other central sources in Niamey before starting out; you can thus confirm locations and willingness to accommodate, and bring messages or other useful items to your hosts. The National Tourist Office can provide a list of government rest-houses (campements) in most towns along the national east-west road; some of them are findable and acceptable, others not. Always wire ahead to be sure of accommodations in Niger's hinterland.

Where and What to Eat

Meals are always expensive, not always copious, but frequently excellent. There are seasonal shortages of vegetables, fruits and other staples, but beef is plentiful, rice is often in surplus, and river fish (perch, carp, catfish and others) are served in a variety of ways. National dishes usually involve a base of millet or sorghum, cooked in porridge or cakes, or diced into couscous with spicy sauces. Few restaurants or canteens offer Nigérien meals, however, partly because the French prefer their own cuisine, partly because Islamic tradition stresses domestic rather than public dining. Stalls in all town markets offer rice and sauce very cheaply, although the hygiene is questionable.

Markets and bus stops invariably feature crackers, sometimes even bread and roast chicken, fruit and peanuts.

In NIAMEY, several good Vietnamese restaurants are fairly reasonable ($2.50 and up, not including wine). Try the *Miam Miam Bono*, the *Saïgon* and *La Baie d'Along*, as well as *Le Kasbah* for Algerian couscous. *La Flotille* has a Russian menu. The better French places include *Les Roniers* outside town (expensive), the gardens of the *Terminus* and, during luncheon, the *Rivoli*. The *Sahel Hôtel* has a good restaurant with a pizza menu and a lovely view of the Niger River. *Le Pigalle* is less expensive.

Out of town, the standard Nigérien-French menu consists of beef or roast chicken, fried potatoes, sometimes canned beans or tomatoes. For variety when in BIRNI-NKONNI, try the honest improvisations and Vietnamese platters at *Madame Wright's*. At MARADI, the Lebanese *Maradaoua* offers the standard menu for 100 francs (40 cents). In ZINDER, *L'Oiseau Bleu* serves meals and has music for dancing on Saturday night. *Boudon's* meals at AGADÈS are moderately priced for a hotel; the emphasis is on mutton. Menus at the game park camps are fixed and dreary; they equal the rooms in cost.

Water in Niger is unsafe to drink. All restaurants, local bars and some bus stops sell beer and soft drinks, sometimes cold if the electricity is on, but for a minimum of 100 francs (40 cents) because of the weight of the imported bottle. Salads and fresh vegetables may be contaminated, although they are hard to avoid in the otherwise ill-provisioned interior; some people who eat such things with insouciance elsewhere in Africa tend to avoid them in Niger.

What to See and Do

Many visitors to Niger, realizing the ardors of logistics, settle for Niamey and its environs, but it's a pity to penetrate no farther.

NIAMEY presents itself as a disorganized, rather green but often smelly place, set against the slow life of the Niger. The market is extensive and colorful, the mosque mediocre and the white Sudanese buildings of state admirably harmonious with Sahelian sand. The middle class consists of top civil servants and about 2,000 foreigners (French and Lebanese businessmen plus the usual capital city expatriates); most Nigériens are poor. Niamey's original fishing village still leans against the river banks, its flat-roofed banco (adobe) houses pressed into the dry clay for refuge from the sun.

The city's people are tall, dignified, fully robed, often devoutly Moslem. Its women are not yet admitted to the roles that they might play in a new nation. A two-year College of Science was recently opened, strictly coordinated with other French-oriented universities in Africa. Night life is scanty, expensive and dull, but the HiFi and the Fofo discotheques (the latter in the Sahel Hotel) are diverting. There are some sporting events, including horse-racing and camel-racing, soccer football, and boxing. The US Embassy Recreation Association has a swimming pool and other sports facilities, a snack bar and twice-weekly exhibitions of American films, open to US government employees and their guests.

The best reason for coming to Niamey is the 60-acre open-air National Museum, a jewel of a place between river and town. Here, under the inspired direction of Pablo Toucet, each major ethnic group of the republic has its own quintessential village compound; the animals of the country occupy their ground in an open zoo; Niger's art and music are well represented; the botanical exhibitions include a 30-foot fossil tree. Everything in the museum is alive: craftsmen work and sell there, French-speaking guardians inhabit the model villages constructed by their kinsmen, costumes revolve on mannequins in well-lighted show-cases, Nigérien music sounds through the park, lights play on the delightful buildings at night, school children are introduced to an admirable condensation of their cultural heritage, and the people of Niger circulate at a rate of 150,000 annually through their greatest national institution. The museum is open until sunset, with special openings on specified evenings. Admission is free.

Consult the Tourist Office, or Mr. Toucet himself, if you wish special tours, explanations or privileges.

If you're interested in innovative educational schemes, consider asking the Ministry of Education (preferably through the USIS Cultural Officer) to arrange a visit to Niger's pioneering but highly controversial Educational Television Project (still, after seven years, in the experimental stage), or to the somewhat unorthodox, but still French, National Administration School, and, if you are up to the trip, to one of the itinerant schools installed among nomadic groups up-country.

From Niamey, the river runs through grasslands and gorges to the 4,000-square-mile "W" National Park. Game is increasing here; sailing, canoeing and fishing have become popular. Hunting is prohibited throughout the republic, however, until the herds build up, and swimming or water skiing involves risks of an encounter with the deadly bilharzia liver fluke. If you hire a boat at Niamey and motor upstream toward the Malian border, you will come upon shoals of fish, herds of hippos, ostriches, giraffes and antelopes descending to drink from the river at sunrise and sunset. The shores around TILLABÉRY are good farm land, and have interesting cliff formations. You can stop at villages perched atop river islands.

If you go far enough upstream, or drive 150 miles north from Niamey, you can visit a splendid Sunday market at AYOROU, which brings in the Berber-Tuareg "blue" camel drivers and cavalry celebrated in much Western pulp fiction and operetta. Ayorou also attracts traders in canoes from far upstream in Mali, and whatever tourists the capital happens to have on weekends. If you prefer to avoid other travelers, try the less well known market at FILINGUÉ in an equally interesting area 115 miles northeast of Niamey.

The Tuaregs conquered most of this territory once. They resisted French colonization into the 1920's, and they still avoid paying livestock taxes to the several independent African states over which they drive their herds. Their life is a tough, incessant march across the boundless desert in search of pasture and water. Many Tuaregs in western Niger have recently become sedentary, tempted out of the tent by prospects of steady income from cash crops, of education, and supplies accessible through government cooperatives. Nevertheless, their villages exude an inexorable sense of movement—of women at work, of blue-veiled men strolling between hut and "palaver shelter" (their new communal judicial-legislative "tent"), of tired donkeys and camels, goats and guinea fowl. On Independence Day (August 3), at the end of Ramadan month, and at other festive times in the main towns, fantasias of horsemen (Songhai, Dosso and Fulani, as well as Tuareg) and camel races revive the pageantry of Sudanic empires and Moslem holy wars before the "pacification" campaigns of the Europeans.

Fully 650 miles by road from Niamey, little AGADÈS opens a northern world of Sahara mountain and desolate, beautiful, arid plains. On the wild high plateaus of the Aïr, sand-eroded peaks gesture grotesquely at the sky, which never sheds a tear. You can climb the Taruadji, Bagzan, Agalek and Tamgak Mountains, going up as high as 6,000 feet to preside over a landscape of silence. In the important uranium area north of Agadès, you can also visit a new town at ARLIT, with 6,000 mining industry people and a full range of civic facilities where five years ago there was hardly a footstep.

At IFEROUANE in the far north, reachable by air or camel-back, ancient portraits in the stone of the Tamgak mountains commemorate the animal life of a once greener, perhaps gayer, Sahara.

An ancient power on the great central trade route of medieval Africa, Agadès still lives as a market town for salt, a bit of tin mining and craftsmanship. From here the archetypal Cross of Agadès, reproduced a thousand times in filigree gold or silver, circulates throughout West Africa. Here the motley ensembles of the living southern Sahara converge to trade, to take water, occasionally to sell a gaunt animal from their precious herd, or to congregate at the superb 16th century mosque. Land Rovers can be rented at Agadès for about $30 a day for overnight camping trips to Iferouane, Igouloulof, Timia, and the Aïr plateau. Try to find a guide who can double as driver. Three or four passengers can share the costs.

Southward in the Sahel, rain falls for a few weeks in the summer; in that season, herdsmen drive their cattle from east to west, and from west to east in the winter. MARADI, flourishing on the crossroad between Niamey, Zinder, and Nigeria's Katsina and Kano, has a technical high school and a training center for leather workers and tanners. The United States buys little from Niger but imports the skins of Maradi's red goats.

A very old Hausa citadel, ZINDER is Niger's second city, still a place of trades and crafts, but once the commercial capital of a million square miles of Sudan. The work of artisans, the marvelous Thursday market and the constant confluence of nomads and townspeople stir Zinder in spite of decades of isolation—caused when the colonial barrier to British Nigeria went up, the Sahara caravan trade virtually disappeared, and Niamey received the nod from France's territorial administrators. You can visit the old sultan's palace, the erstwhile Foreign Legion fort portrayed in *Beau Geste* and the potters and leather workers at their trades. On Sundays, see the bustling market and gardens of MIRRIAH, a few miles east of Zinder.

Farther east, Lake Chad washes the stilts of fishing villages. Here you can accompany fishermen in their papyrus canoes and try your hand at lake angling.

Songhai minstrelsy, Djerma and Tuareg dancing and other justly celebrated expressions of Nigérien artistry are rarely seen by tourists; the country isn't organized yet for public displays. There are Moslem festivals, private celebrations and government command performances, however, that you may search out—watch carefully for them and inquire repeatedly.

Your best chances are the shows staged irregularly at the Niamey National Museum.

The travel companies operate a few simple, relatively inexpensive tours around Niamey and into the river country and (by air) to the Aïr mountains. These serve at least to familiarize travelers with the town and its environment. The agencies and National Tourist Office can advise about the availability of package transportation to the game areas.

What to Buy

The filigree Agadès cross in gold or silver, as well as Tuareg rings and ear pendants, can be obtained in northern Niger where they originate, but they are also available in many other parts of French-speaking West Africa. Government regulations fix gold and silver prices by weight, so that you can seldom be tricked if you know the official rates and the weight of the piece that interests you. Some traders and artisans allow discounts if you bargain seriously, but usually the piece is worth the going price.

Nigériens also make excellent dyed leather goods from a wide variety of skins; Tuareg saddles and goatskin articles from Maradi are much prized. You can find good pottery, especially at Zinder, lovely stringed instruments (look for a Songhai inzad harp), carved calabashes, multicolored wool blankets from Dori, Macina and Tillabéry, colorfully embroidered skullcaps, iron weapons and tools, and miniature animals in terracotta or bone covered with skin. (Caution: Importation of such objects into the United States may be prohibited.) Songhai-Djerma weaving is elegant, expensive and worth it, especially if you bargain diligently in the markets after studying the fixed prices and controlled quality of comparable cloth at the National Museum. Some local printed cloth is available, but most prints are imported and expensive; wait for Nigeria and the coast (although a piece of cotton, crudely indigoed with the dye that turns Tuareg faces "blue" and thus gives them their nickname, would be something of a trophy).

Geometric decorations on doors, panels and wooden chests testify to Koranic influence in Nigérien design. Wood carving is generally scarce and mediocre.

Niamey's museum crafts center is the best starting point for shoppers, but don't miss the Grand Marché or the smaller crafts market in town. Other shops are usually open between 8 am and noon, six days each week, and from 4 to 7 pm on Monday through Friday. Zinder's shops feature leather work, pottery, decorated knives, jewelry, basketry and ornate chests. Bargain with perambulating traders or deal with the artisan in his workshop—including El Hadji Garba for leather.

Local Attitudes

A predominantly Islamic country without large numbers of foreigners, Niger is not unfriendly to visitors. Women should avoid displays of flesh, and photographers should ask permission before snapping people or rituals anywhere in the country. Travelers on government business keep Niamey's hotels busy, but other visitors are scarce. You have the place to yourself—which is one of its delights. Americans, when they are identified at all, enjoy a good reputation in Niger.

Weather, What to Wear, How Long to Stay

Niger is always hot in the daytime, but often cool at night—especially in the chill of the northern desert. The middle months of the dry season, from November through February, are the coolest and hence most agreeable for a visit, although the harmattan brings sand from the Sahara. This is also the post-harvest period when marketing and town life are at their most animated, and the season when the animals gather at water holes. Between March and the June rains, Niger's landscape becomes fiercely hot and dusty, but marriage ceremonies and street dances in May herald the rains and are worth watching if you don't mind the heat. The summer rains cool things a little and wake the river out of the slow pools into which it settles during the winter.

Only in November can you get both low grass for game watching and high water for river boating.

Radical changes in temperature between midday and evening, especially during December and January, call for sweaters or light jackets in your otherwise tropical wardrobe. Some young foreigners have taken to the traditional flowing booboos of the Nigériens with happy effect in the heat. Local tailors can make these expertly for you, and local people should instruct you how not to look silly in them. Generally, however, the custom for visiting men follows the French example of bared leg and short sleeve (long-sleeved shirt or "chemise veste" for evening formality), and for women light dresses and slacks. Sandals and sun hat suit the needs of one's extremities.

Neckties and stockings have virtually disappeared from Niger, except in cool season diplomatic circles.

With a week or more of time, if you are reconciled to flying expensively over long areas of unremarkable landscape, or to using four-wheel drive, you can devote three days to Agadès and some of the north country, two days to Zinder and Hausaland, and the remainder to Niamey. The Niger banks to Tillabéry and Ayorou upstream, or to Say and the "W" downstream, require a longer sojourn.

Communication

French and Hausa are the languages of passage here. Arabic has traditional and religious importance, but is seldom spoken. The Tuaregs have an ancient language of their own, with a considerable literature of erotic poetry. In any case, English does little good, except among some 60 Peace Corps Volunteers and a number of Canadians working in several major aid projects, all primarily in the south. Less than 10 per cent of Nigérien children attend school regularly; hence, even French is limited to a tiny fraction of the population. A few phrases in Hausa are very useful, particularly if you are traveling for any length of time in the West African interior.

Mail and messages proceed slowly. It's unwise to send valuable packages out of the country from here.

The only press in Niger is government-dominated and not very informative; nor is the radio.

Emergencies

A land as broad, sparse and poor as Niger, with its withering climate, is inevitably handicapped in dealing with foreigners' personal or medical problems. Niamey and Zinder hospitals have fairly well equipped operating facilities, but are plagued by hygienic vicissitudes and personnel shortages. Medical stations are separated by great distances, and the small American Embassy in Yantala on the outskirts of Niamey (P.O. Box 201, tel. 26-64, -70) has neither doctor nor nurse. Army and police forces are small and under-equipped. Travelers should take care about immunizations, hygiene and diet, and should not expect much from any facility. When in doubt, fly to Abidjan or Paris.

Nigeria

Profile

STATUS: Independent since 1960. Federal republic within the British Commonwealth since October 1, 1963.

SIZE: 356,669 square miles (slightly larger than Texas and Oklahoma combined). Population—more than 60,000,000 (major groups are Ibo in east, Hausa-Fulani and Tiv in north, Yoruba in west).

GEOGRAPHY: Long forested coastline on Gulf of Guinea. Savanna and desert scrub in central plateau and north. Crossed by Niger and Benue river system, with broad delta in east. Principal cities—Lagos (capital and port, 1,000,000), Ibadan (650,000), Kano, Zaria, Enugu.

CLIMATE: Hot in all regions, but humidity varies. In Lagos (on coast), day temperatures are in low 90's; high humidity even at night. In Kano (inland), middle 90's to over 100 degrees during the day, cool at night. Rainfall from March to October—extremely heavy in summer—with little rain the rest of the year in the north.

LANGUAGES: English; major regional languages are Hausa, Yoruba and Ibo, among many African languages.

CURRENCY: Naira, divided into 100 kobos (pronounced "korbors"). 1 naira = $1.53; $1.00 = 65 kobos.

VISAS: Required. Available from Embassy of Nigeria in Washington and Nigerian Consulate General in New York. Fee $2.18. Apply well in advance, delays up to six weeks are common.

AIRPORTS: Ikeja Airport (LOS), 15 miles from Lagos. Regular flights to and from West Africa, London, Rome and New York. Kano Airport (KAN), linked regularly with London. Airport departure taxes—domestic and international, $1.28.

NATIONAL HOLIDAYS: October 1, Independence Day; Christian and Moslem holidays.

INFORMATION SOURCES: *In US*—Consulate General of Nigeria, 575 Lexington Avenue, New York, N.Y. 10022 (tel. 212/752-1670); Embassy of Nigeria, 1333 16th Street NW, Washington, D.C. 20036 (tel. 202/234-4800). *In Lagos*—Nigerian Tourist Association, 47 Marina, P.O. Box 2944 (tel. 20-335).

By Philip M. Allen

Sheer size, economic power, immense creativity and destructiveness inevitably attract attention to Africa's big republic. Travel to Nigeria is increasing and will reach a climax in January, 1975, when Lagos plays host to an anticipated 100,000 visitors at the four-week Festival of Black Arts and Culture.

But the rewards of a visit to Nigeria come only with effort and tolerance on the part of the visitor. Nigerians are their own masters, even more so since winning their 1967–70 war of secession and realizing a postwar oil boom. Hospitable and affable as individuals, collectively enterprising and ambitious, they speak of a "renaissance of tourism" without as yet setting up the appropriate machinery or having the temperament for it.

Possessing one of the most venal petty bureaucracies in Africa, the least satisfactory network of hotels, the most crowded cities, perilous traffic, grasping tradesmen and rapacious street hustlers, Nigeria has yet to develop the accommodating mood that a tourist industry requires. So much the better then for tough, individualistic travelers who insist on confronting a nation's true visage without compromise.

For the holiday vacationer accustomed to comfort and amenity, almost anywhere else will do better.

Three centuries ago Nigeria exemplified African civilization: the northern territory contained migrating fragments of Sudanic empires, the Yoruba and Benin south had a cluster of city-states ruled by divine kings, and the east included the agrarian democracies of the Ibo people. This complexity of character survived a century of shadowy British colonialism and it remains intact now after 12 turbulent years of independence as a federation.

Despite a federal constitution constructed to respect the political, religious and cultural disparities among almost 300 ethnic-linguistic groups, Nigeria was to endure the holocaust of civil war less than a decade after independence. Six years of wasteful and corrupt post-independence politics had failed to satisfy conflicting regional demands; two bloody military coups d'état in 1966 inflamed rivalries among East, West and North. Eastern Nigeria, dominated by the Ibos, declared itself to be the Republic of Biafra in May, 1967, and defended its claim to independence for two and a half agonizing years before capitulating to federal forces in January, 1970.

Although assisted materially by Britain and Russia, and supported politically by most African and other British Commonwealth nations, Nigeria won through its own military efforts. Now, facing new vicissitudes, Africa's biggest nation displays a rare self-confidence born (like that of Algeria and Zaïre) out of an ordeal by fire.

Prior to 1966, each of Nigeria's three major ethnic groups had its own geo-political region—the 14 million Hausa-Fulani dominating the enormous Northern Region, the eight million Ibo in the East, and the 10 million Yoruba in the West (which includes the capital city of Lagos). Following the second 1966 coup, the military government headed by Major General (then Colonel) Yakubu Gowon divided the republic into 12 states in order to weaken the three monoliths and enhance federal control. While this arrangement has succeeded, many Nigerians still refer to the North, East and West when talking about their country. Gowon's military regime is a benign one, but refuses to permit a resumption of civilian politics before 1976.

The postwar recovery program has developed a great deal of economic activity, particularly in the densely populated coastal areas. The more sparsely settled North, Islamic since the 14th century, retains its traditional structure, although subject to important changes.

Blessed with a multiplicity of agricultural and climatic zones and a variety of marketing advantages among its large, concentrated population, Nigeria looks forward to prosperity. It is able to produce sufficient food and raw materials for subsistence, to support Africa's largest base of indigenous industry, and to export crops and minerals in proportion to its imports of equipment, technology and consumer goods. Since well before the Biafran secession, however, the country's economic hopes have been fixed on reserves of petroleum that are now earning over a billion dollars annually. Nigeria has become the world's sixth largest exporter of oil.

This federation of northern Hausa, Fulani and Tiv, western Yoruba, eastern Ibo and Rivers people, and several dozen smaller ethnic factions, has tested its strength in more than political and economic terms. Nigeria is Africa's leader in literature, theater, painting and sculpture, music (both traditional and urban), pageantry and craftsmanship. These achievements and the vitality they express make Nigeria a stimulating place to be in at any time. There is excitement in the West's ebullient cities and traditional market towns, and in an ancestral culture compromised, but never converted, by European Christianity; in the dense and oil-rich East, pulling itself together after the humiliation of war, and in the Islamic North, now carved into six states without diminishing its wealth of art and ceremony.

For further insight into Nigeria's complexities there is an abundance of literature, notably the novels of Chinua Achebe, the plays and poetry of Wole Soyinka, John Pepper Clark and other Nigerian writers, as well as the memoirs of important political figures like Nnamdi Azikiwe and Obafemi Awolowo, and many studies by foreign scholars—including Michael Crowder, Thomas Hodgkin, Ulli Beier, William Fagg, Paul Bohannan, Robin Horton, E. W. Bovill, Gerald Moore and others.

Money Matters

Breaking with the Sterling zone in January, 1973, Nigeria replaced its pound with the naira (worth half the old pound or about $1.53). Import or export of Nigerian currency is strictly prohibited and severely punished. Dollars are not accepted except at banks and exchange offices at airports, hotels and the like; a merchant who takes your dollars probably has illegal intentions about converting them. Banks remain open from 8 am to 1 pm weekdays and close on Saturday at 11 am. The Bank of America, the Standard Bank of West Africa (Chase Manhattan affiliate), Barclays Bank DCO, the International Bank of West Africa (affiliated with the French BIAO and First National City Bank of New York) all have offices in major towns.

High import duties, taxes and inefficiency combine to exert strong upward pressure on the cost of living in the so-called "modern sector." Be prepared to pay premium prices for tourist items, including, of course, hotel accommodations.

You can economize by spending a good deal of your visit outside Lagos and living simply, taking your cue from Nigerians.

Getting In and Out

Situated in Benin's crook, at the heart of western and central Africa, Nigeria can be reached in a dozen ways. (1) By road: easily from the west across the charming coasts and dense forests of Yorubaland; adventurously across the Saharan and Sahelian wastes through Tamanrasset (Algeria), Agadès and Zinder (Niger) to Kano; laboriously in the east from western Cameroon to Enugu in Iboland; even more laboriously from Fort Lamy (Chad) through Maiduguri and Nigeria's most nearly deserted regions. (2) By sea to Lagos and Port Harcourt, both crowded with tankers and freight commerce, but little used for passenger traffic. (3) By inland lagoons from Cotonou and Porto Novo (Dahomey) to the old slave port of Badagry; in late 1973, the Niger River should be open for passenger travel between Port Harcourt on its delta estuary and Niamey (Niger). (4) By air into Lagos, or Kano in northern Nigeria.

Flight connections to and from Lagos are tolerably good along the West African coast (especially for Cotonou, Accra, Douala and Monrovia) and with London, Rome and New York. Crossing Africa is time-consuming and expensive, but there are four flights a week between Lagos and Addis Ababa (Ethiopia) and five to Nairobi (Kenya).

No regular road or rail service connects Nigeria externally, but you can rent cars or taxis to cross borders, and ride local buses to the frontiers. Farrell Lines freighters sail to Lagos out of New York, Ghanaian Black Star Lines from Canadian or Gulf of Mexico ports, and Elder Dempster or Nigerian Lines out of Liverpool. Passenger vessels charge $130 in second class, $353 in first class for the round trip between British ports and Lagos, somewhat more to Port Harcourt.

Kano is the commercial center of the central Sudan, the largely Islamic belt that runs between Sahara and forest from Senegal in the west to the Republic of the Sudan in the east. This area contains more than 30 million Hausa-speaking people within Nigeria and neighboring Niger, Dahomey and Chad. Irregular buses and trucks ply north from Kano to the Niger border and its trading center of Zinder. If you are taking this route out of Nigeria, arrange your Niger visa beforehand in Lagos and obtain some of Niger's CFA francs in the market or banks of Kano. Over the border neither travelers checks nor foreign currencies are accepted.

A rough road leads eastward from Kano to Maiduguri, capital of the Northeastern State and railhead for a packet train to southern Nigerian ports. Buses, bush taxis or trucks will get you—with patience and some luck—from Kano to Maiduguri and from there to Fort Lamy (Chad) on a 154-mile road that may be washed out in the rainy season. It's a trip you are bound to remember.

Clearance procedures at Nigeria's airports, road frontiers and port facilities can be among the most dilatory and aggravating in Africa. Much depends on the mood of customs and immigration officials who, while quite intelligent, are apt to be arbitrary, irresponsible, arrogant and venal. They will insist on proper documentation and appropriate respect from you, but would often prefer to harass you for a small bribe (called "dash") than apply the book strictly. Many practiced travelers simply offer the dash and get on with their business, but the more enlightened practice is to refuse—loudly and indignantly if necessary, appealing to superior officers or just playing dumb as the circumstances warrant. Dashing is illegal and the government is trying to wipe out the practice. Whatever their particular needs, the officials with their hands out are earning salaries far above the average Nigerian's income. If you have something to hide, the rules are off, but if you are "in order," you can resist corruption.

An American should never arrive without a visa and an exit ticket.

Apply in person for the visa, avoid sending your passport in by mail, and be prepared for long delays. If you can't have the visa stamped in your passport, have a Nigerian travel agency or sponsor arrange for entry and get cable confirmation. Never tell an immigration officer that you may not have a hotel reservation: you might find yourself confined to the airport grounds.

Getting Around Within Nigeria

Traveling about the country has all the uncertainty and adventure of getting in and out. Nigeria Airways connects all major towns by Friendship F-27 or comparable planes on schedules more honored in the breach than the observance. Several private companies and aero clubs, in addition to Nigeria Airways, provide non-scheduled and charter service over a wide network of airfields.

Traffic conditions are monstrously hazardous in cities and on most highways. Narrow and ill-kept roads, with excessive traffic, hordes of pedestrians without adequate walkways, defective vehicles in all sizes and shapes, audacious motorists—all give your adrenal glands a workout.

Gray-uniformed drivers pilot reconditioned (but relatively safe) Greyhound and newer Mercedes buses of the government-owned Midwest Lines over the roads between Lagos, Ibadan and Kano, and between Lagos and the east as far as Warri. Their fares run higher than those of the jammed inter-city taxis and mammy-buses (flat-bed covered lorries with a life expectancy of about two years; remnants line the sides of every highway). The latter are cheaper, provided that you bargain your way on, because the long-distance starting fares quoted to foreigners by taxi and private bus drivers start at about double what Nigerians expect to pay. One-way trips in the big buses cost about $3 between Lagos and Ibadan; private vehicles charge about $2.35. Lagos to Benin City should be bargained to about $6, to Enugu about $8.50 and to Port Harcourt about $7.65.

There are car rental facilities at Lagos, Ibadan, Kaduna, Kano, Jos, Enugu, Aba and Port Harcourt. Rates are high—insurance premiums alone justify that—and vehicles are often in poor condition. Driving a rented car yourself can involve complications if the vehicle breaks down or suffers an accident. Hence, the best way to rent is through a major travel agency on a written contract and include a good Nigerian driver. Otherwise, take public transportation.

Travel agencies in Lagos include Scantravel, John Holt and Umarco, all on Yakubu Gowon (ex-Broad) Street, and Transcap on the Marina.

Nigeria recently switched to rightside driving with an attendant increase in confusion and accidents.

Town taxis abound; unless there is a meter, don't close the taxi door before having agreed on the fare. Usually taxi drivers and their inevitable front-seat companions (friends, apprentice drivers and others) make good informal guides, although their recitals tend toward the melodramatic.

Hitchhiking is uncommon but not unknown. The availability of rides suffers from publicity given to highway crime and fatalities. Also, many drivers insist on charging a fee equivalent to mammy-bus fares.

The vast area still known as "The North" can be reached from Lagos by train six times a week. The slow but steady 28-hour journey to Kano—whether by first class sleeping compartment ($44.50 one way) or in inexpensive second ($22.20) or third class ($11.20)—can open your eyes to Nigeria and the Nigerians. The trip can be broken with stops at Ibadan or Oshogbo, centers of Yoruba culture, at the administrative city of Kaduna, capital of the North-Central State, and at the university town of Zaria in the once powerful Zazzau Emirate. Visitors with time and the interest take the train one way and either fly or drive back.

A more varied itinerary involves a second, long, but fascinating train ride between Kano and Enugu (almost 20 hours) and on to Port Harcourt (33½ hours) over the steep escarpment south of Jos, at fares slightly higher than the Kano-Lagos trip. Good Nigerian meals cost from 85 cents to $1.25 in the restaurant cars, slightly more if served in one's compartment. European food is more expensive and not worth it.

Waterways add considerable allure to traveling in Nigeria, but you must make your own arrangements. To explore the lagoon system, including Badagry Creek behind Lagos, for example, inquire at the capital's several boat clubs, at the Federal Palace Hotel, or at larger creekside villages. More than 700 miles of the Niger and Benue rivers, including the large man-made lake behind Kainji Dam, are scheduled to have regular passenger boat traffic by 1974. In Lagos, there is a ferry service between the midtown marina and the port area of Apapa, as well as launches to Tarkwa Beach from the Marina and the Federal Palace Hotel on Victoria Island.

The Nigerian Tourist Association, a trade syndicate at 47 Marina in Lagos, provides information on travel, festival schedules and accommodations, but with a heavy promotional touch. Nigerian consulates and Nigeria Airways offices outside the country distribute some of the association's materials. The Federal Ministry of Culture and Information on Yakubu Gowon Street in Lagos has policy responsibility for tourism, but does little for visitors. The larger travel agencies are competent and knowledgeable, although their foreign managers may wax cynical about the country's defects.

Universities at Ibadan, Zaria, Ife, Nsukka and Enugu, as well as at Akoka on the mainland outside Lagos, act as cultural centers and clearinghouses for the kinds of information serious travelers wish to have. Their bookstores have maps, local information and good collections of Africana. Other cultural institutions exist, but the pre-civil war association of artists, musicians, writers and theater people in the Mbari Clubs has disintegrated into essentially local phenomena.

Travel in the North is more difficult than elsewhere in the country. Few tours include even Kano as a stop, although its airport has direct flights to London, Rome and across Africa to Khartoum and Cairo. You are therefore probably on your own; so much the better. Use local transportation, preferably bus, air and rail, and avoid driving yourself unless you are with someone familiar with road conditions. Familiar figures in these parts include UN, British, Canadian, Italian, American and Scandinavian experts of one kind or another (in livestock and construction programs, especially). Chances are good that by frequenting the government rest-houses you will find a traveler with a car and space for an extra passenger.

A few words of Hausa help along the way in the North, even if they are only simple greetings. There is a *Teach Yourself Hausa* text published in London, but casual travelers will be well served with an inexpensive English-Hausa phrase book sold at bookshops throughout Nigeria.

Where to Stay

Nobody who knows Nigeria ever plans a visit there to enjoy its hotels or restaurants. The former are almost without exception overpriced, overcrowded and poorly managed, while good food is restricted to spicy, idiomatic Nigerian dishes. In Lagos and other big towns, hotel structures and service continue to deteriorate as their prices rise and electricity and water breakdowns increase. Yet Lagos suffers from a desperate scarcity of accommodations. You must book early if you expect to stay at lodgings of your choice in the capital. Although the government intends to expand capacity for the 1975 Black Culture Festival, you should reserve accommodations months ahead of time for that event.

One formula for saving money as well as gastronomic integrity in a hotel involves (a) taking early morning tea with biscuits, (b) eating everything on the (British) breakfast menu, (c) lunching on fruit and peanuts from the market and (d) dining in a Nigerian restaurant.

There are two additional sources of housing you might look into. The first is the network of government rest-houses maintained in almost every major town for the benefit of touring civil servants. The second is the possible availability of university and teacher college guest houses at Ibadan, Ife, Zaria and Nsukka, normally reserved for academic personnel. The official rest-houses, booked through the appropriate state government, usually provide a decent minimum of comfort (overhead fans and mosquito nets, for example, but no air-conditioning). They have only mediocre plumbing and sometimes (in Bida, for instance) lack electricity. They serve honest Nigerian food together with the usual parody of European cooking, and permit casual acquaintance with a variety of local and traveling Nigerians. We recommend the rest-houses (sometimes simply for lack of alternatives) in Ibadan, Oshogbo, Kano, Kaduna, Bauchi, Jos, Minna, Maiduguri, Obudu, Okitipupa, Onitsha and Nsukka. They charge between $2 and $10 per night.

All rest-houses, guest houses and certain religious missions (which often charge for room and board) are heavily booked during festival seasons, school vacation periods and official congresses. Tourists with reservations can be bumped at any time if a senior dignitary of the sponsoring institution shows up. During summer holidays, you may find university dormitories booked by visiting educational travel groups.

So, back to the hotels! Collective experience suggests the following tentative array of accommodations and rates for room and breakfast, with a sincere caveat about prices which often prove ephemeral (or, rather, perpetually susceptible to upward revision).

In LAGOS:

Federal Palace Hotel, on Victoria Island, Nigeria's only genuine luxury establishment, astronomically expensive, with an atmosphere of politicking and wheeling-and-dealing reminiscent of pre-1966 Lagos; a good swimming pool, boat service to Tarkwa beach, a casino, night entertainment, handsome gardens and shops, a Chinese restaurant, good service and a comfortable terrace for munching pizza or sandwiches while watching the ships sail by.

The *Bristol*, on Martins Street in downtown Lagos, very much a businessman's place (no children allowed), with a brusque British manner and rates that rise before your very eyes. At last look, single rooms cost about $17 and doubles $29. The lunch menu includes Nigerian food.

The *Ikoyi Hotel*, a friendly but down-at-the-heels haven for families and expatriates in Lagos's principal upper-class island suburb. It has a pleasant terrace bar, a cool inside bar and swimming pool (lots of children). Somewhat more reasonable tariffs prevail than at the Bristol or Federal Palace ($14 to $16 for singles, $23 to $26 for doubles).

The *Mainland Hotel*, deteriorating in condition and service from the day it opened (1966), on the wrong side of Carter Bridge for people with center-city business and an allergy to traffic jams, but rather nicely located for contemplation of lagoon traffic and neighborhood life. Rates approximate those of the Ikoyi Hotel.

The *Excelsior*, in Apapa, about the same price category as the Mainland and Ikoyi, offers a pool, shops, a casino and nightclub. For those who prefer to reside in the port area, since Apapa is connected with Lagos by tortuous roads and crowded but interesting ferry launches.

Cheaper accommodations in Lagos can be had at the *Wayfarer Hotel* on Campbell Street and the *Niger Palace* in the popular suburban Yaba district. There is also the *Lagos Airport Hotel* in Ikoyi, with air-conditioning, tennis courts, swimming pool and casino, but 40 minutes at the least from center-city. The airport complex also has the less expensive *Binitie Guest House and Cafe*. For pot luck on minimum budgets, inquire at Anglican, Baptist or Methodist mission headquarters in Lagos, or at Lagos University and the secondary schools on the mainland.

In IBADAN:
The *Premier*, Ibadan's one international hotel, nicely perched on a hilltop between the city center and the university, with a pool, casino, banking and car-hire facilities, a mediocre overpriced restaurant that tries to be all things to all guests, and prices from $10 to $15 for singles, $17 to $25 for doubles.

The *Green Springs Hotel*, a modest motel-like place with swimming pool on the Ife Road; a favorite for middle-range accommodations but inconveniently located.

Senior Staff Guest House at Ibadan University, mainly for academic personnel and university guests; heavily booked, charges $12 per day for bed and breakfast and provides shuttle service to town.

Otherwise, the government catering rest-house or the *Lafia Hotel* on the Abeokuta Road.

In IFE: University guest houses, which charge approximately $9 for bed and breakfast. *Mayfair Hotel*, a good African place.

In OSHOGBO: The *Ebenezer*, in the middle of things, with a bustling bar-lounge, but shabbier and less comfortable than the government rest-house just outside town.

In KANO: The *Central Hotel*, recently expanded; poor food, inadequate service and high rates (about $15 for singles, $20 for doubles). Same management as the Lagos Bristol and Ikoyi. *Hotel de France*, less expensive, caters to Nigerian businessmen. *Usman's Memorial Hotel*, just inside the gates of the Old City (Sabuwar Kofar); inexpensive, with a predominantly Nigerian clientele. The Kano state government runs the new luxury *Bagauda Hotel* at Lake Bagauda, 30 miles from the city.

In KADUNA: *Hotel Hamdala*, air-conditioned and lively, with a pool, a zoo, a jumping night-bar, but shabby accommodations. Overpriced at $17 for singles, $30 and up for doubles. Cabins annexed to the hotel can be rented for upwards of $11 per person.

In BAUCHI: *Wikki Warm Springs Hotel* (Yankari Game Reserve).

In Jos: *Hill Station Hotel*, quiet and neat, but more expensive than the heavily booked Vom government catering rest-house.

In MAIDUGURI: The *Yerwa Hotel* and the *Race Course Hotel*, both clean and simple places.

In NEW BUSSA: *Kainji Motel*, reasonably priced in a splendid location by the Kainji Dam.

In OBUDU (near the Cameroonian border): The *Ranch Hotel*, a holiday place, with full pension for $16. There is also a government rest-house.

In ILORIN: *Unity Hotel*, a solid place.

In OWERRI: *Phoenix Hotel*, comfortable. Small new hotels are now sprinkled around the East-Central Region (ex-rebel Biafra).

In ENUGU: *Hotel Presidential*, formerly the place to stay, but a war casualty; was to be reopened some time in 1973. The government rest-house is always crowded. Private arrangements are advisable if you are spending the night here.

In PORT HARCOURT: *Presidential Hotel*, packed by oil-company employees; boom-town prices.

Each of the northern cities has a "sabon gari," or neighborhood of strangers, usually inhabited by non-Moslem merchants and workers from southern Nigeria. These districts contain inexpensive combination bar-nightclub-restaurants offering a quick meal and a cheap but not necessarily clean or quiet bed. During school holidays, chances for a bed are good at the schools or colleges and the residential halls of Ahmadu Bello University in Zaria. At other times travelers in the North take pot luck.

London's respect for northern Islam kept the number of Christian missions to a minimum here, but the Sudan Interior Mission, an evangelical group that provides valuable medical assistance, particularly in the treatment of eye diseases endemic in this region, has decent and inexpensive lodgings at its hospital in Kano and sometimes at outlying mission stations in Jos and elsewhere. No smoking or drinking in the mission facilities. American Peace Corps, Canadian CUSO, British VSO and other volunteer or technical aid personnel may also come through with a night's lodging.

Where and What to Eat

The best that can be said of the food at European and tourist hostelries is that it's wholesome, for it's hard to get poisoned with over-boiled meals tasting everywhere of brussels sprouts and cabbage. Since town water should almost always be boiled, many travelers use up their calorie allowance on good local beers (Star, Top, Golden Guinea), mixing them with Guinness stout for a square but liquid meal. Nigerians drink palm wine and use kola nuts for hospitality and stimulation; both are pleasant acquired tastes for foreigners.

Nigerian cuisine requires metabolic adjustments for many Americans, but with a proper frame of mind and control over the chili-pepper seasoning, you may enjoy fufu (yam or cassava dough prepared with sauces), garri (cassava porridge), palm oil chop (chicken or beef in red palm oil served with rice or fufu and fruit), groundnut stew, moin-moin (stews with white beans), egusi soup (melon seed sauce), jollof rice (chicken, vegetables and sauce with rice), and in the north a variety of mutton dishes. If you don't wish to lose face by asking to "go mild," just request your pepper on the side. "Chop" is a generic pidgin word for food.

Hotels and catering rest-houses serve these interesting dishes, but at some spots you must be rather insistent to get them. In the North, street vendors offer chicken cooked on skewers and rubbed with red pepper and delicious (if eaten fresh) fried bean cakes (akara). Other Northern specialties include Nile perch (giwan ruwa) and makwa ruwa, a species of partridge usually roasted. Superb roast ram is prepared during the Feast of Idd al Fitr at the close of Ramadan. Try the splendid goat's meat dishes, including gigot (leg) of goat and goat's liver, the pepper "soups" (sauces) with rice, yam or millet, and the curries and groundnut (peanut) stews featured throughout West Africa. Goat's milk is a delectable recourse if you are in a non-alcoholic Moslem situation and have reason to distrust the water.

In LAGOS, the *Koriko Bar* in the Martins Street sidewalk complex at the Bristol Hotel serves curry puffs, sausage rolls, moin-moin, Congo meat (snails) and sandwiches at prices from 25 cents to a dollar, while a whole pepper chicken costs about $2 and hamburgers about 85 cents. The Koriko is frequented by city Nigerians with a little money to spend and time only for quick lunches or long beers. The *Cathay Restaurant* on Yakubu Gowon Street near Tinubu Square has one of the fullest and best Chinese menus in the non-Asian world, but at New York prices. Curry at the *Domo Hotel* on Saturdays and the *Ikoyi Hotel* on Sundays can become a ritual for aficionados. The *Maharani* on Martins Street serves Indian and Middle Eastern dishes. A few restaurants prepare good Western cuisine ("European" almost always means "bad British"); they include *Antoine's* off Yakubu Gowon Street, *Quo Vadis* at the top of Western House with its superb view, and the *Federal Palace Hotel*. All are expensive. Tarkwa Bay has a simple Nigerian restaurant that serves chicken and fish and chips. The *Bagatelle* is interesting at night and the *Airport Hotel Restaurant* is open 24 hours a day.

IBADAN offers Lebanese style international menus at the *Yesmina* and Lebanese table d'hôte at the *West End Club* (bring your own wine or beer), where the roof garden affords a good view of Ibadan at night. The *Cocodome* at Cocoa House, Dugbe, is an overpriced Lebanese place with a swimming pool and bar that are popular with Europeans. The University of Ibadan Guest House has a lively Staff Club for members or resident guests, and a public restaurant upstairs that serves fair meals at reasonable prices (about $1.65). The *Premier Hotel* charges too much for poor food and far too much for wine. If you are looking for Nigerian "chop," ask local friends for advice or, failing a friend, try the *Osamare-Na*. Otherwise, you might as well save your money: eat lots of fruit and nuts and drink beer until you are somewhere else.

In KANO, the *Pink Peacock Night Club* has good but expensive Pekingese food ($6 per person plus service for dinner), while the *Albarmaki* on Club Road prepares decent Lebanese dishes at moderate prices. Europeans dine out at the private *Kano Club* and the *Airport Restaurant*, both so-so. The *Dambalta* on Galadima Road has good African chop for less than $1.

Elsewhere, rest-houses and roadside bars have Nigerian food.

What to See and Do

Nigeria's ubiquitous and overwhelming attraction is people—great quantities of them in perpetual animation. The best way to watch people is of course to walk, especially in the smaller towns, or to hire a bicycle in the cities. Visit the daily markets, the stalls and shops of craftsmen, and try to be as unselfconscious as you can about the fact that Nigerians will be looking at you with reciprocal curiosity and, frequently, with hopes of acquiring some of your money.

Education is a national passion in Nigeria. Total strangers will ask you to help arrange scholarships for young Nigerians (some of them qualified) who cannot otherwise continue in school. Already several thousand Nigerians are alumni of American colleges and universities. If you visit a secondary school, teacher training college or other institution you will encounter people eager to display what is going on. Set up such a visit a day or two in advance with the headmaster or headmistress of the school.

Despite increasing industrialization, a majority of Nigerians still live in villages, albeit with high degrees of organization and cultural sophistication. English-speaking school children usually flock to your side, offering to show you around, and elders may extend a traditional welcome of kola nut and palm wine. It's well to be carrying something for reciprocation.

Nigeria's intellectual life revolves around its universities and local cultural centers. Generally speaking Nigerian artists and writers welcome overseas visitors, for their works often receive more attention abroad than at home. The Institutes of African Studies at the Universities of Ife and Nsukka and the Ori Olokun Cultural Center at Ife have frequent lectures, discussions and theatrical presentations. Ibadan is a cultural center with Yoruba and English-language theater, opera and dance. The Nigerian Institute of International Affairs in Lagos also stages art exhibits and cultural presentations.

Nigerian night life centers around informal bars, usually with live music. Dress is casual, beer the standard drink and conversation lively. Young women, whether accompanied or not, may be asked to dance by anyone, and where there is a shortage of women, men may dance together or solo. Let your inhibitions go and relax with cold beer, loud and lively music, and plenty of animated talk. The person with whom you strike up a casual conversation may be a school teacher, army officer, civil servant, businessman or office clerk.

Small Nigerian-owned factories in the towns, hospitals and some technical assistance projects in the countryside may prove interesting to visit, depending on your tastes and time. Make arrangements through federal or city authorities or local businessmen's associations, and if accompanied by an interpreter to translate in the vernacular, consider taking in a local law court.

LAGOS, with 700,000 inhabitants officially, but certainly more than a million at any given time, presides over the federation and the West without dominating either. This elongated island a few hundred feet across Carter Bridge from mainland Yaba and Apapa is an accumulation of urban excitement and urban blight, charged with constant energy yet contaminated by poverty and filth; it is purposeful in action, theatrical in art and artistic in theater, but also a scene of paralyzed traffic, intimidating con-men, persistent beggars and pimps. The beautiful harbor front (Marina Drive) is congested and dirty, the main shopping streets cluttered, torn up, unsanitary and crowded. An African city much like some in America, from which the affluent retreat out of air-conditioned offices to cool quiet suburbs on other islands (Ikoyi and Victoria), leaving the shell of a modern business sector to slumber in the night and a ring of colorful ghettos to seethe and swelter. But even then no part of Lagos is deserted: night people are everywhere—the homeless and the restless, celebrants and sinisters inhabit the streets from dusk to dawn.

Surrounded by slums on Lagos Island are a number of flamboyant, exuberantly decorated town houses of the so-called "Brazilians"—descendants of freed slaves who returned to West Africa from Brazil in the late 19th century and subsequently prospered in trade. The blend of African and Latin American styles of this "old nouveau riche" class is depicted in Antonio Olinto's novel, *The Water House* (London, Rex Collings, 1970). The Benin-style palace of the Oba (king) of Lagos can be visited nearby, flanked by waterside markets. The Lagos National Hall has an interestingly carved historical frieze on its iroko wood doors. Near the race course, administrative and sports center of Lagos Island, is the Nigeria Museum (open from 9 am to dusk every day). This is one of Africa's greatest museums, with admirably displayed, unmatched collections of bronzes, wood and stone sculpture, ivory, ancient terracotta and recent pottery. Behind Martins Street near the Bristol Hotel, a huge cloth market sprawls among shanty residences and stalls of utilitarian bric-a-brac.

Visitors circulate with difficulty in the rubbled, muddy suburbs of the Lagos laboring majority (Yaba, Apapa, Surelere, Abute-Metta and others), but these are the neighborhoods made by the Lagotians for themselves, and here they are seen as they really are. The suburbs also display extraordinary night energy in beer bars with high-life bands, cinemas, Yoruba-language theater, casinos for the wealthy or the ambitious, and sidewalk gatherings under lanterns for talk or checker games. For fun and music, try the Caban Banboo, Afrispot, the Gondola, Sure-Lere Nightclub, the Blue Note and the Cool Cats Inn, or the more expensive tourist favorite El Morocco in the Excelsior Hotel, all on the mainland.

In midtown Lagos are the Palace Landen, the Maharani and a current sensation, the New Can Can Club, down a sinister alleyway from Customs Street across from Glover Hall Theater near the Marina; the New Can Can features Godwin Omabua's idolized music, the suggestiveness of high-life matching the club's smoky and rather innocent "vice." It offers fair food, ample drinks, mediocre entertainment and a bevy of friendly, unaffected, graceful hostesses—a formula that led one of our dignified American correspondents to urge that the New Can Can be "franchised right across the United States." As in all the popular high-life bars, come no earlier than 10:30 to catch the action, but not much later than that if you want a table at a reasonable distance from the band.

There is considerable sport in Lagos. There are clubs for tennis, polo, soccer football and water sports, and you can take a ferry launch from the Marina or the Federal Palace Hotel to the calm beach of Tarkwa. Other beaches like Lighthouse and Bar Beach are fascinating for people-watching but the heavy surf makes swimming dangerous.

Yoruba villages on the outskirts of the capital bustle with a very different kind of life from that of Lagos; yet it is the same set of village sons who divide their weeks between the two worlds. Here, art and religion are identified with activity: a mask is to be danced, a drum to be played, and a shrine to be built. You can sense a bit of this "animism" in the villages along Badagry Creek, part of the Benin fresh-water lagoon system, and in BADAGRY itself, 42 miles toward the Dahomean border from Lagos, with its old market, its former slave quarters and a cemetery for early Christian missionaries. Across the lagoon from this inland port is a spit of coconut palms and lovely terraced ocean beach.

Traditional "country" standards animate Yorubaland's larger city-states like Ibadan, Ile-Ife, Abeokuta, Oyo, Ede and Oshogbo. IBADAN is a hilly fortress built during the Yoruba wars with Dahomey in the 18th and 19th centuries. Uninteresting then to Europeans, it grew spontaneously into a great rail hub and swollen market town of 650,000 people (or perhaps double that number, nobody really knows). Ibadan's beautiful university was the first in Nigeria and is among the most respected classical European academies in English-speaking Africa. Its Institute of African Studies frequently has excellent exhibitions. Ibadan has developed a buoyant dramatic and literary tradition, with Africa's most celebrated playwright Wole Soyinka (formerly a pillar of the original Mbari Club and now on the university faculty) and lively troupes like Duro Ladipo's and Herbert Ogunde's which blend rich Yoruba legend, mime, dance and music with Western proscenium-theater format. There is a mammoth cloth market every 16 days at Ibadan, a great daily market that transforms itself into a fascinating new bazaar at night, the Oba's palace, several bustling nightclubs (especially the National Club for good dance music), large family compounds of the urban Yoruba, a whirl of masks and drumming at the Egungun festivals held periodically between January and June, and lake upon lake of tin-roofed houses to be gazed on from the hills. The International Institute of Tropical Agriculture at Moor Plantations is an all-Africa research center assisted by American foundations.

Yorubaland stands even more clearly defined in the smaller cities of the southwest:

ABEOKUTA, under the sacred Olumo rock, has the Alaka palace, cloth market, great July festival of the drums in honor of Ogun the warrior-hunter and the pioneering Aro Psychiatric Hospital and the self-help Mayflower Secondary School; both institutions welcome visitors.

ILE-IFE is the holy city where the Yoruba nation was born. Some of the great kingdom's marvelously expressive bronze royal portraits are held in the tiny museum by the palace of the Oni (king). Ife has a young university with a musical theater tradition of its own (inspired by the playwright-composer-actor Ola Rotimi), a fine Institute of African Studies that hosts a theater-music-art festival in December and January, and a cluster of shrines including the tall leaning stone phallus, called the Oranyan Staff, near the middle of town.

OYO is a place of weavers, leather workers and calabash carvers, historically an aggressive citadel against the Dahomeans and now a thriving market town. Visitors should browse in the workshops (although, to be sure, families of the Oyo craftsmen give prospective customers little peace) and see the Alafin throne in the Oba's palace. The town of ISEYIN has guilds of cloth makers and an experimental cattle ranch. EDE houses a permanent exhibition of talking drums and other traditional instruments of the Yoruba.

A confluence of local genius and resident European patrons has made the market town of OSHOGBO (130,000), lying 160 miles northeast of Lagos and 30 miles north of Ife, into one of West Africa's most exciting living theaters. Sculptors, masons and metal forgers are constantly at work on the several forest shrines to the protecting Oshun River spirit, shrines that theoretically lose value once the creative work has stopped. The Mbari-Mbayo artists' movement continues here in a rather run-down gallery and theater where two generations of Nigerian painters and sculptors, poets, playwrights, designers and performers helped spark Nigeria's cultural renaissance. A small museum donated by Ulli Beier, one of several European men of art who lived and worked in Oshogbo, is crammed into a charming house on the outskirts of the town. Several chapters in Beier's prize-winning book *Contemporary Art in Africa* (Praeger, 1968) are dedicated to the Oshogbo movement. Another important European artist, Suzanne Wenger, now a priestess of Oshun, lives in a beautiful forest-like house in midtown; her expressionist wood and stone sculptures, like those of Twins Seven Seven, Adebisi, Buraimoh, Afolabi, Olatunde and other Oshogbo artists, adorn many places of the city. Dance and music reach an apotheosis during the magnificent Egungun festival at Oshogbo in August, when it is very difficult to get even standing room, much less a place to sleep in town. A "pop" art collection, housed in a small gallery near the Ataoja's (king's) palace, emphasizes the continuity in West African aesthetics between the religious masterpiece and the honest functional imagery of urban society.

ILORIN, Yoruba gateway to the Islamic North, has a great market which, like few others, becomes particularly animated at night. Eastward from Ilorin, near the village of Esie, another museum houses some of the thousand extraordinary stone sculptures of still undetermined origin found in the region.

Focus of any visit to the Nigerian North should be the city of Kano, as close to Old Testament Jerusalem in flavor and smell as can be found, yet with its distinctly African character. The smaller commercial and religious cities of Sokoto, Katsina, Bida, Zaria and Maiduguri each sustains an ancient emirate in a land that has been Islamic for centuries.

KANO is not to be missed. Its walled Old City, at the end of ancient Saharan camel routes to the Maghreb, Arabia and Turkey, exudes a thousand years of Sudanic life. On foot, you can explore the artisans' quarters, watch the intricate dyeing and weaving of the famous Kano cloth, the working of leather and forging of metals; you can pass through narrow streets with thick-walled Sudanic houses, and wend your way among the intricacies of markets, with camels, goats, sheep, Tuareg tribesmen from the Sahara in indigo capes and cloaks, and bejeweled little Hausa girls majestically bearing ceramic wares on their heads. You can climb the tower of the Central Mosque for a panoramic view of the old and new cities, including during harvest season four-story pyramids of peanuts heaped in the sun awaiting shipment southward.

Kano is really three cities. The old walled town dominates, flanked by the white mosque and anchored by the 800-year-old Emir's palace (not open to the public, but appointments can be made to call on the Emir). Friday is a day of great color and ceremony around the mosque, which can be visited. At the corner of Emir Square stands the fine old Makama Madawaki town house, now a museum of Hausa and Fulani art. Official permission is needed for non-Moslems to lodge within the walls of the Old City, but all are free to explore during the day. A favorite time is March and April when the end of Ramadan is celebrated with processions of horsemen, acrobats, jugglers, snake dancers and the roasting of lambs and goats. There's a special children's day when tiny Hausa tots decked out in their finery are hauled about in carts pulled by adults.

Near the Old City, reached on foot or by rented bicycle or taxi (bargained price between $1 and $2, depending on the extent of your trip), is the Township. Here are the government buildings, large department stores (Kingsway and Leventis), Younis's Lebanese ice cream parlor, British Council and US Information Service libraries and overpriced restaurants. Less planned and more vibrant is the sabon gari (strangers' town) of small shops, cheap bars and crowded housing for the non-Hausa laborers and traders of the area. The new Kano University campus is just outside the city.

Extending from Kano like the spokes of a wheel are roads leading to other traditional centers of the North. The most accessible is ZARIA, 111 miles to the south, a walled and turreted city (170,000) with its own Emir's palace, fine crafts, spectacular Moslem religious festivals, and on the outskirts the modern campus of Ahmadu Bello University.

The spiritual heartland of the Hausa-Fulani peoples is SOKOTO whose Emir (the Sardauna) is religious head of this huge province of Islam. Reached by an adequate 300-mile road from Kano or by regular flights of Nigeria Airways, Sokoto is the most traditional city of all. It has two mosques, the Sardauna's palace, magnificent leather work and the tomb of the crusading 19th century Fulani Emir Usman Dan Fodio.

The city of KATSINA is 193 miles north of Kano, with its 14th century walls encircling scenes of great variety. A recent book by Gretchen Dihoff, entitled *Katsina, Profile of a Nigerian City* (Praeger, 1970), provides excellent background for the trip.

History fanciers will want to visit the grave mound of the first kings of Katsina, on the road to Daura, 50 miles east. At Daura itself is the lovely well where the hero Bayajidda killed the snake that terrorized the town, receiving its queen in marriage as his reward and beginning a dynasty that founded the seven original Hausa states. Thirty miles northwest of Katsina near the border with Niger is the Jibiya market, one of the liveliest in Africa. It attracts Fulani and Tuareg traders on horses and camels, traveling medicine shows purveying herbs and amulets, and fine displays of old coins used as jewelry, as well as local and imported cloth.

A more adventurous trip covers 370 miles by bus, car or air from Kano to MAIDUGURI, seat of the Kanuri peoples whose empire and rulers—the Shehu of Bornu—preceded and rivaled those of the Hausa. The Shehu's palace, a fine market, mosque and craftsmen's quarters make this city of 90,000 on the road to Chad an interesting place to visit.

Much of the North is Islam in Africa—traditional, stately, proud, hierarchical, representing a millennium of common civilization and language. Yet there are things about the North that are new, like the $300 million hydroelectric dam on the Niger River at Kainji, site of a planned iron and steel complex. The 500-square-mile Kainji Lake is a scenic delight, situated near the small *Borgu Game Reserve*.

Another facet of modern Nigeria can be glimpsed at KADUNA, 164 miles south of Kano on the salubrious Bauchi Plateau, capital of the

North Central State and administrative, industrial, communications and educational center for the North. Modernity and tradition meet on the polo fields and handball courts of Kaduna, frequented by civil servants and army officers. Top Nigerian bands play at the Hamdala Hotel.

Two smaller resort towns, Bida and Jos, supplement the attractions of the North. BIDA lies on the borders of Hausaland, slightly north of the Niger River. Many of its 20,000 inhabitants are Christian. Its craftsmen specialize in Nupe glassware—including bangles made from beer bottles—as well as cloth, silver and basketry.

Jos stands 4,000 feet high, 173 miles west of Kaduna on a winding road climbing from one plateau to the other. A tin-mining center, Jos is capital of Benue Plateau State and treasure ground of the hill-dwelling "old people" whose settlements pre-date the coming of the Hausa and perhaps even the Yoruba. The Jos Museum has a small but outstanding collection of regional art, displays of Nok terracotta heads from a tradition of trans-Sudanic cultural contact that dates back more than 3,000 years, a zoo, and examples of crafts from the Tiv and other peoples of the plateau. The cultural diversity and subtlety of these animist societies have made the area a happy hunting ground for anthropologists and serious travelers.

Off the Maiduguri road 100 miles east of Jos is the *Yankari Game Reserve*, open from November through June, with a good lodge, a few hippos, but otherwise a paucity of animals compared with the great parks of East Africa and even nearby Cameroon.

Northern night life revolves around combination bars and small hotels that offer live music or records. In Kano, Kaduna and Jos, watch for a performance by Mamman Shata, the recording star of Hausaland. Hausa students, civil servants and school teachers, most of them fluent in English, are often delighted to guide you through a memorable cabaret evening, sharing their culture with you. A lively group of intellectuals frequents the Kaduna Writers Club, which publishes an English-Hausa literary magazine, *Images*, and is hospitable to visitors. Bars in smaller towns often feature gogge music (calabash-resonated violin and drums) accompanying itinerant professional dancers.

Nigerians from all parts of the country attend the annual fishing festival held in mid-February at Argungu, southwest of Sokoto. Only on this day is fishing permitted in the Argungu River, which is specially dammed for the event. You can bring a car from Lagos to Gusau by rail, drive 115 miles to Sokoto and then another 64 to Argungu.

During the rainy late summer the proud, tall, handsome Fulani herdsmen celebrate the ceremony of "Sharo" in their villages. Young men evince their manhood to prospective brides by smilingly accepting blows of the cattle-herding staffs that Fulani men carry.

While all of Nigeria exults in soccer football, polo is a popular sport in the North with traditional and colonial roots. A Saturday or Sunday afternoon game, usually between military contestants in Kano, Katsina, Kaduna and other northern towns (also in Lagos) is an exercise in pageantry.

Movie going is about the same anywhere, but in Nigeria it provides enjoyment more because of the audiences than the films. Most cinemas are open-air, with the cheapest and best seats on benches below, and a balcony at twice the price for local elites. Selections include musical comedies from India as well as ancient Italian and Hollywood shoot 'em ups, although the Nigerian Calpenny Productions Company has begun to produce full-length features based on national themes. The audiences are uninhibited and take an active part in the drama, cheering underdogs and booing the Tarzans, the police and other symbols of intimidation.

Eastern Nigeria, still restructuring itself from the ruins of war, can indulge less in the luxury of tourist entertainment. The region remains a cauldron of Ibos, Kalabari, Ibibio, Efik, Ejaw and other vigorous people beginning to prosper on oil wealth and reconstruction investment. A visit to schools reveals the astuteness of the Ibo people.

The coal-mining hill town of ENUGU, capital of the pre-war Eastern Region, then of rebel Biafra, and now of the East Central State, has once again become the center of an area producing food, timber, minerals and art. It has a campus of the University of Nigeria. Thirty miles to the north, NSUKKA has the main university campus, with a new Institute of African Studies headed by the novelist Chinua Achebe. The dry season festival at Afikpo, southeast of Enugu, features dancing and wrestling. Farther south, at Arochukwu, the Ikeji festival in September recalls ceremonial episodes in Achebe's novels. Ikot Ekpene, east of the industrial town of Aba, continues a heritage of fine Ibo sculpture, including enormous slit drums of iroko wood. Umuahia, 37 miles north of Aba, has the fine Queen Elizabeth Hospital, a government college (secondary school) and other facilities restored since the war.

At the steamy, crowded delta town of PORT HARCOURT, the petroleum and tanker business preoccupies almost everybody, but there is escape in the rain forest, and by canoe among the mangrove lagoons of the Niger. The town of Calabar, east of the delta, is pleasant and attractive, an old seaport with a rich mercantile past, several fine old houses and an interesting market.

West of Enugu, the inland river port of Onitsha, after an eclipse during the civil war, will soon reopen West Africa's greatest daily market. Onitsha's festival takes place in December, when the king traditionally "shows himself" to his subjects. The Enugu-Onitsha road passes through Awka, home of the skillful carvers of stools, chests, canes and other artifacts. Fine pottery comes from Okigwi, 60 miles south of Enugu on a detour route to Awka and Onitsha.

On the forest road between Lagos and Enugu lies BENIN CITY, circled by its dry moat, clinging to a royal tradition that was suppressed by Britain 80 years ago as punishment for recalcitrant slave trading by the Bini aristocracy. The capital of legendary Atlantis according to some, citadel of Edo-Yoruba power that once extended from Lake Chad to Dahomey, holding a worthy reputation in the reports of seafarers from Renaissance Europe, Benin's royal traditions survive in shards. Some of the celebrated bronzes, cast to honor divine kings, are still in the museum (many are in Lagos, or England and elsewhere); part of the Oba's palace stands with heroic sculptures in clay on its walls; some of the houses of the mercantile and military aristocracy are there. Metal workers and other artists still inhabit their quarters. The Oba (king) shows himself at the Igwe festival in mid-December, still a time of impressive festivity. The Olokum Theater performs modern adaptations of tradition—a theatrical style characteristic of southern Nigeria's creative momentum.

Eighty miles to the north of Benin is a fine crafts museum at Owo, another center of carving, weaving, metalwork and calabash decoration. On and off these roads of the Nigerian midwest, guides can show you handsome, elegant, decorative shrines and powerful images sculpted in clay. A good preparation for this experience is offered by Ulli Beier's book *Nigerian Mud Sculpture* (Cambridge, 1963). The delta ports of Sapele and Warri are interesting centers of wood carving south of Benin.

The foregoing paragraphs represent a bare catalogue of what Nigeria has to show the traveler. You may inquire at universities and the museums in Lagos and Jos about other museums and collections, the promotion of crafts, the activity of Mbari and other creative groups, the mosques, shrines and temples in existence and underway, diggings at Jos, Esie and Meghane, rock paintings of Birnin Kudu and Gaji, the varied music and dance of this very culturally-rich nation.

What to Buy

Practically everything that Africa produces can be found here and there in Nigeria, with its varied cultures and tradition of making, buying and selling. Ebony and ivory are scarce, however, and old pieces of sculpture cannot be exported from the country without a waiver by the Antiquities

Department of the Nigerian Museum at Lagos. Most contemporary woodwork is trash, but interesting new sculpture can be acquired at its sources—the Igun and Isbesanma Street workshops at Benin, for example, the Guelede Society mask makers in Yoruba towns, Kalabari and Ibo villages, and in Oshogbo and Ikot Ekpene. Mixed in a mass of imitative Western daubing and cheap exotica are some magnificent paintings of the Oshogbo school and by other Nigerian artists; Mbari houses in Benin and Oshogbo, and several galleries in Lagos and Ibadan, show good canvases in traditional, expressionist and surrealist styles.

Bronzes are still being fashioned, sometimes with originality, by the immensely fecund Yoruba and Benin people. Terracotta and pottery work goes on in Aba, Enugu, Sokoto, Jos, Benin City and other centers. Bida craftsmen produce delightful Nupe cloth, glass and cast metal. Fine gold, silver and tin alloy jewelry and beadwork (including the highly valued "coral" necklaces) come from the North, as well as from Lagos, Bida and Benin (silver teaspoons are a specialty, for example). Kano, Sokoto, Jos and Oyo are centers of leather work (bags, wallets, "pouf" cushions, slippers, belts and the like), while carved and decorated calabashes from Oyo are prized by those who can carry or ship these bulky but weightless gourds. Delicate, lightweight miniatures of village scenes, boating parties and chessmen are carved from thornwood at Shagamu on the Lagos-Ibadan road; they are available at their place of origin or in Lagos.

Practically every important town has its traditional style of cloth and its cloth market, with Ibadan setting the pace for Yoruba prints and dyes, and Kano exhibiting some of the richest textured work in the North. There are capable tailors everywhere, as well as utilitarian furniture makers, carpenters and metal workers.

Nigeria's publishing industry is booming. Attractive books on African history and culture are available from the presses of the University of Ibadan and University of Ife. Ibadan's University Bookstore is admirably stocked with these as well as more popular works from local branches of overseas publishers.

The Church Missionary Society (CMS) and the Kingsway Department Store bookstores are about the best in Lagos.

Urban Nigeria has its share of high-priced shops (around hotels and at Kano Airport, for instance), department stores and trader kiosks—all of which display local arts, crafts and manufactures. Lagos shops are normally open from 8:30 am to noon and from 2:30 to 6 pm, although many stay open through lunch hour, closing about 4:30; all close on Saturday by one o'clock.

The Hausa trader circle in front of Lagos's Ikoyi and Federal Palace

Hotels and the Midwest Crafts Shop at Benin are among the more convenient places to look for authentic Nigerian products. There is a Bronze Gallery at 39 Campbell Street in Lagos, a Nigerian Women's Craft Council on Tafawa Balewa Square and an Exhibition Centre on the Marina. Itinerant backpacking hawkers will seek out all foreigners in the smaller towns (and sometimes the bigger ones as well), offering a little wheat with their sacks of chaff.

You must patiently insist on quality merchandise (frequently something that is brought to you only on a second visit), and haggle over price.

Local markets and artisan workshops are ideal sites for selecting and bargaining—a leisurely ritual of exploration, examination, praise for the craftsman's work, protestations of one's own poverty, and patient negotiations. Whatever your pride of purse or shopping technique, remember that if the starting price is always hiked higher for foreigners than for Nigerians, so too is the anticipated final price: we're all supposed to be both wealthier and more eagerly acquisitive than anyone else.

Local Attitudes

In spite of its military government, its recent civil war and the conservative inclinations of its Moslem communities, Nigeria remains a wide-open, liberal society, tolerating a freedom of manner and speech that more austere African nations rigorously suppress. Nigerians are riding on a wave of pride these days, however, and they exhibit a decreasing tolerance for foreigners who tell them what to do and how to do it. Discretion is important, therefore, when doing business with Nigerians and their official agencies, even those that are sloppy and mismanaged. Photographers are officially enjoined against taking pictures of subjects that "put Nigeria in a prejudicial light," on the grounds that the country suffered enough bad publicity during and just after the civil war. Photographing military installations and personnel without express authorization is taboo.

Sidewalk smugglers, deformed beggars and dash-takers hound a foreigner's footsteps in many Nigerian towns, and crowds are said to be full of pickpockets, purse-snatchers and other thieves. Extra caution may be wise, especially in the bustling, fast-moving towns of the southern part of the country.

Americans occasionally encounter Nigerians in the West and the North (some of them civil servants) who still resent the support many United States newspapers, religious organizations and philanthropic groups gave rebel Biafra during the civil war, although the American government assisted the Nigerian government non-militarily. Bitterness has been expressed in visa delays and other harassment of American travelers, but these incidents seem to have declined.

Weather, What to Wear, How Long to Stay

All Nigeria's climatic zones are likely to be hot during the day in the dry winter (November through March), but there are great variations in humidity and in night temperatures. The North is generally dusty during this period, as the harmattan desert wind fills the air with sand and, in the plateau areas, lowers night temperatures into the 40's. The southeastern area gets the steadiest and heaviest rainfall, but the coast around Lagos remains humid most of the year, with storms from April through July and during September and October. There is a cloudy period on the coasts without much precipitation in August and early September.

The best time to travel the entire country, therefore, is in November and early December. Avoid traveling during school vacations if you depend on hotel or government rest-house accommodations; at the same time, those vacations permit low-budget voyagers to find cheap lodgings in the vacated school dormitories. April to June are the worst months for travel. The mid-summer and autumn showers have a relatively cooling effect if you can time your sorties to take advantage of them.

All wardrobes should include the coolest cottons plus a sweater and some rain gear. Men have the privilege of dressing to their comfort, except in certain pretentious European hotels that demand a coat and tie (or alternatively, Nigerian national dress) at dinner. Women dress as they please in the south, but should stick to dresses and slacks among conservative Moslems of the North. Long flowing robes, often embroidered (agbadas in Yoruba country, full rigas or tunic-like yarsharas among the Hausa, booboos or bubas elsewhere) can be purchased ready-made or be tailor-made. They are useful against the heat, although Westerners tend to get laughed at if they carry Nigerian garments poorly, having failed to learn the correct drape of national dress.

A minimum stay in Nigeria is over a week for anybody interested in the depth and variety of the country. You will have to select your spots carefully and cover some of them by air. Official delays and schedule lapses are almost inevitable even for the most careful planner. A half dozen sites in Yorubaland can be covered only by road in an intensive four-day tour. Lagos repels many visitors after two or three days, but deserves that much time at least. There are some who don't want to leave.

Benin and the East are distant, difficult to cover and usually omitted by travelers pressed for time. You can make Lagos-Benin City and return in two days by road, but it's a pity to pass up the midwest and some of Iboland if you have more time than that. Whatever you do in West Africa, consider reserving some time for Kano, the favorite city of many an Africa traveler. Its palaces, markets and mosques warrant a leisurely day, or better, two or three. A week permits visits to Jos and plateau country, with a stop at Zaria and the university. At least two weeks are needed to take in Sokoto, Jos, Kaduna and Katsina in addition to Kano— a fortnight that conveys the variety and coherence of the Nigerian North.

Communication

English provides the cultural cement for the Nigerian federation, although primary schools and oral traditions keep Hausa, Yoruba, Ibo and other vernaculars very much alive. Pick up a phrase book for the major vernacular when you go. Pidgin English is lingua franca along the whole Benin Coast, and is used in the works of Wole Soyinka and other authors. University and secondary school students, and unemployed semi-educated Nigerian youths on almost all streets of all towns enjoy speaking with visitors, and if encouraged, will show them around or invite them to an evening's diversion. These services are not always performed without a motive. Nigerian youths are extraordinarily enterprising and ambitious and you must always be prepared to encounter a young Nigerian's fervent hopes for help in advancing his education and/or traveling to America.

Literary output is part of the great vigor of this nation. It ranges from elegant lyrical poetry, drama and fiction, to the inexpensive, crudely written moral-adventure fiction exemplified in the penny novelettes found at Onitsha and other markets. A fairly vigorous English-language press helps keep readers informed about the passing show, particularly if it is scandalous. The most readable of the newspapers are the *Daily Express* and *Daily Sketch* of Ibadan, Lagos's *Daily Times*, and especially the *New Nigerian* of Kaduna. Periodicals from the US and England arrive with reasonable promptness in Lagos and Kano. Several excellent social science journals and the intellectual quarterly *Observer* are published in Ibadan.

Nigerian television carries an unusual variety of programs compared with most African networks, including an occasional original work of theater. The Nigerian Broadcasting Corporation (NBC) is a popular medium for local information and the latest tunes.

Telephone, postal and telegraphic communications have been overloaded and sadly inefficient for years. Telex connections are probably most effective for getting messages out of the country and telegrams are best from city to city. The Pan American central city office in the Standard Bank building has become a Saturday morning mail drop for correspondents eager to see their letters safely through the postal machinery and onto the direct Saturday evening flight to New York. It's wisest not to ship packages or other valuable items from here. A new satellite system will soon link Lagos better to the outside world than it is to the rest of Nigeria.

Emergencies

All Nigerian towns have hospitals but most are too crowded and overworked to perform complicated services for foreigners. The medical colleges of Lagos and Ibadan universities, the Ahmadu Bello University Medical Clinic at Zaria, mission hospitals at Kaduna, Jos and Kano, the American Baptist Mission at Ogbomosho in the West, and the Queen Elizabeth Hospital at Umuahia in the East offer somewhat more sophisticated treatment than the general hospitals. Services in Eastern Nigeria are still not back to normal following the civil war. The American Embassy, located at No. 1 King's College Road near the race course in Lagos (tel. 573-2018), has Marine guards and embassy staff on duty through weekends and holidays. It also maintains a medical unit for official personnel and dependents (headquarters of a regional State Department doctor) at Western House not far from the embassy. American consulates are maintained at Ibadan (Barclays Bank Building, tel. 24101) and Kaduna (5 Ahmadu Bello Way, tel. 3373-6).

Portuguese Guinea

(Guiné)

Profile

STATUS: Overseas Province of Portugal with governor-general responsible to Lisbon. Part of country controlled by African nationalists.

SIZE: 13,948 square miles (slightly larger than Maryland). Population—800,000 (98 per cent Africans, remainder Mestizos and Portuguese).

GEOGRAPHY: Mostly mangrove swamps and tropical rain forests. Principal towns—Bissau (capital, 50,000), Bolama, Cacheu.

CLIMATE: High temperatures all year (80's and 90's, dropping to low 70's at night). Dry season December to May. High humidity May to November, heaviest rainfall in June and July.

LANGUAGES: Portuguese and Creole based on Portuguese.

CURRENCY: Escudo (1$00), divided into 100 centavos. 10$00 = 37 cents; US $1.00 = 27$00.

VISAS: Required. Available through Portuguese consulates in New York, Boston, Newark and San Francisco, also Portuguese Embassy in Washington. Fee $5.85. Expect delay of three to four weeks while application is sent to Portugal for approval. (See text for entry via PAIGC-held zones.)

AIRPORT: Craveiro Lopes (BXO), seven miles from Bissau. Regular flights from Lisbon and Cape Verde Islands. Expensive taxi service only.

NATIONAL HOLIDAYS: June 10, National Day; October 5, Proclamation of the Republic; December 1, Independence Day; Catholic holidays.

INFORMATION SOURCES: *In US*—Portuguese Consulate General, 630

Fifth Avenue, New York, N.Y. 10020 (tel. 212/246-4580), also 31 Commonwealth Avenue, Boston, Mass. 02116, 10 Commerce Street, Newark, N.J. 07102 and 3298 Washington Street, San Francisco, Cal. 94115; Embassy of Portugal, 2125 Kalorama Road NW, Washington, D.C. (tel. 202/265-1643). *In Guinea*—Secretary-General, PAIGC, B.P. 98, Conakry, Republic of Guinea. *In Bissau*—Centro de Informacão e Turismo, P.O. Box 294.

By Aaron Segal

At present the only visitors to this small, swampy country on the West African coast—an "overseas province" of Portugal—are likely to be war correspondents. This is because Guinea-Bissau, or Portuguese Guinea, is the site of a protracted war between Portugal and the African Independence Party of Guinea and Cape Verde (PAIGC). (Don't confuse this country with its independent southern neighbor, the Republic of Guinea, or with independent Equatorial Guinea.)

As a result of the war there are two ways to visit this country. One is as a guest of the Portuguese government, taking the war correspondent's tour of the combat zones. The second is as a guest of the PAIGC, entering the country from one of its sanctuaries in neighboring Senegal or the Republic of Guinea and going on a walking tour with the African guerrilla warriors.

The nationalist side of the war, including a detailed account of daily life in the liberated areas (as much as half the countryside), has been sympathetically depicted in two books: *Liberation in Guiné* (Penguin, 1970) by the British historian and journalist Basil Davidson, and *Armed Struggle in Africa* (Monthly Review Press, 1970) by the French journalist Gérard Chaliand. The writings of the late PAIGC leader Amilcar Cabral, considered by some observers one of the outstanding leaders in Africa, have been published in English under the title *Revolutionary Struggle in Africa* (Monthly Review Press, 1970). Available by writing to the American Committee on Africa, 164 Madison Avenue, New York, N.Y., 10016 are prints of some of the numerous documentary films made with the cooperation of the PAIGC.

The Portuguese side of the war and defense of their record can be found in a book by their former foreign minister and ambassador to the United Nations, Franco Noguiera, *The UN and Africa* (Praeger, 1968). Jim Hoagland, foreign correspondent of the *Washington Post*, wrote an excellent and balanced series of articles which appeared in his paper in February, March and April, 1971.

Portuguese Guinea is a territory the size of Maryland, consisting largely of mangrove swamps, tortuous estuaries, tropical rain forest and a handful of offshore islets. What is the war all about? The Portuguese claim that their continued presence here is justified by rights going back to the 15th century. They argue that the mainland and the Cape Verde Islands are overseas provinces of metropolitan Portugal whose inhabitants exercise the full rights, privileges and responsibilities of Portuguese citizens. They point to Eastern European aid for the PAIGC as proof that the rebellion is Communist-dominated.

The mainland population is overwhelmingly African, but also includes racially mixed persons (mestizos) from the Cape Verde Islands and Portuguese civil servants and troops. The PAIGC, fighting for a united independent state of Portuguese Guinea and the Cape Verde Islands, contends that Portuguese rule exploited rather than developed the country, which indeed is largely poverty-stricken and illiterate.

The fighting has been going on since 1962 when an anti-colonial war of liberation was launched. Portugal responded with a commitment of 30,000 troops, but each year the insurgents, led by the PAIGC, have gained control over an increasing area. Of all the anti-colonial movements in Portuguese territories, the one in Portuguese Guinea appears to be the most effective. Portugal seems to be fighting to protect its historic hold in West Africa and to avoid the domino effect which a defeat here might have on its much more valuable possessions in Angola and Mozambique. Despite Cabral's murder in 1973, the war goes on.

Economically the country has few resources—unless oil is discovered offshore. The war has sharply reduced the limited production of peanuts, palm kernels and palm oil, rice and tropical hardwoods.

Money Matters

The currency consists of Portuguese metropolitan escudos as well as local escudos (27 to the US dollar), confusing because a "dollar sign" is used as a decimal point (e.g., 27$00 equals US$1.00). Stick to Portuguese escudos since the local escudos are not convertible. All foreign exchange transactions are made through the offices of the Banco Nacional Ultramarino (National Overseas Bank). The PAIGC relies on barter in the liberated areas and if you are their guest you have no need to spend money.

Getting In and Out

There are regular flights via TAP from Lisbon and the Cape Verde Islands to Bissau, Portuguese Guinea's capital. There are no air or road connections between the Portuguese-occupied territory and independent African states; the only way out of Bissau is by air or ship back to Lisbon or to the Cape Verde Islands 300 miles offshore. Journalists and other official visitors will be met on arrival.

Going in with the guerrillas requires writing to the Secretary-General, PAIGC, P.O. Box 98, Conakry, Republic of Guinea, explaining your motive for visiting and giving credentials if you are a journalist, filmmaker or otherwise professionally interested in the revolution. The PAIGC will try to obtain a visa from the supersensitive government in Conakry. A simpler but probably less usual route is to seek out the PAIGC office in Dakar, after obtaining a Senegalese tourist visa.

Getting Around Within Portuguese Guinea

Although the Portuguese have paved a number of interior roads and there is regular bus service from Bissau to some towns, your best bet is to rely on the air force or local subsidiary of TAP to fly you around. Most official tours include military bases and one or two fortified villages where peasants have been re-grouped to limit their contacts with the PAIGC. The PAIGC, on the other hand, walks its visitors. Some have gone in for several days or weeks, camping out with soldiers and villagers in the liberated area. The PAIGC is interested in having its story told abroad and encourages film coverage.

The Portuguese, incidentally, also permit their visitors to photograph extensively.

Where to Stay

As an official government guest you might be put up in the residence or guest house of the governor-general. Commercial hotels in the capital, BISSAU, include the Grande, International and Miramar, all modest and not particularly recommended. Cheaper are the pensions, including the Caldense and Central. There is a small inn on the island of BUBAQUE and several pensions in the town of BAFATA.

The Catholic diocese in Bissau and up-country mission stations sometimes can provide rough, inexpensive accommodations.

Where and What to Eat

BISSAU is a commercial port with a population of roughly 50,000, including Portuguese officials and small businessmen. Most restaurants double as bars. These include the Ajuda Esplanada, the Riviera, Solar do 10 and the Pelicano. Don't expect anything fancy but do ask for the local dishes. Local favorites include roast duck (bringe), peanut soup served with chicken or fish (caldo de mancarra), shellfish stew (conforbate), peanut soup (chabeu), a rice, tomato and onion concoction (mafefede), and oysters served with rice and various sauces (pitche-patche de ostras). These dishes come with lively red peppers (piri-piri).

Desserts feature heavily sugared candies and puddings made from peanuts, cashew nuts and coconuts, as well as local fruits. Imported Portuguese wines and beers are also available.

The PAIGC looks after the culinary needs of its visitors, providing some interesting local dishes with rice, peanut, millet and yam bases.

What to See and Do

BISSAU itself is a sleepy port and military base with a massive stone and coral fortress, and an interesting ethnographic and historical museum. The Information and Tourist Center (Centro de Informacão e Tourismo) on Rua Dr. Vieira Machado (tel. 3282) can help arrange appointments with government officials and visits to the local dockyard and small factories. Aside from the Gato-Nègro snack bar and several cinemas there is little night life in Bissau or anywhere else in the country.

There are several beaches near Bissau including Prainha, Tor and Suru. Much of the coast consists of creeks, swamps, estuaries and offshore islands. Launches from the port of Bissau visit the islands of the Bissago archipelago, including the beaches on the island of Bubaque. Other recreational facilities, including a swimming pool, are accessible at the Portuguese Officers Club (Club Militar) in Bissau.

Local Attitudes

No visitor is regarded as detached or impartial. Either side will want to know where you stand and what you think. The Portuguese are likely to emphasize the differences among Portuguese Guinea's peoples—the island-dwelling animistic Bissagoes, the pastoral Fula, the agricultural Mandingo and Balanta—while the PAIGC underlines the common desire of these people to be rid of Portuguese rule. The PAIGC takes pride in the schools, dispensaries and other activities it has established in the rural areas under its control.

Each side has a grudge against the United States, although not against individual Americans. The PAIGC insists that US arms sold to Portugal—for European use only, according to NATO arrangements—are turning up in Africa, and that US loans support the Portuguese war economy. The Portuguese are bitter that the US has not formally endorsed their "anti-Communist struggle" and has supported UN resolutions urging independence. An American visitor to either side will be subject to much hard questioning.

Communication

The lingua franca of Portuguese Guinea is a delightful, lyrical Portuguese-derived Creole language. It is the working language of the PAIGC, used in their spirited songs and poems. Portuguese officials and many Africans are likely to know some French. Knowledge of English is limited to a handful of Portuguese army officers trained in the US. Postal, telephone and telegraphic services to neighboring countries are nonexistent. To the outside world they go through Lisbon, and are almost certainly monitored by Portuguese authorities.

Emergencies

Only France, Belgium and Lebanon have formal representation here and no one represents the US. The city of Bissau has both a civilian and military hospital but they are likely to be busy. If you get in trouble or are taken ill, the best bet is to head for Lisbon on the first plane out. The PAIGC has medical assistants and simple dispensaries in the liberated area, and rural hospitals with physicians in the refugee zones of the Republic of Guinea and Senegal.

Mouride mosque, Touba, Senegal

Senegal

(République du Sénégal)

Profile

STATUS: Independent republic since April 4, 1960. Former French colony, part of French West Africa.

SIZE: 75,955 square miles (slightly smaller than South Dakota). Population—3,780,000 (80 per cent Moslem).

GEOGRAPHY: Mainly savanna with tropical river forest country in north and south, virtual desert in eastern center. Principal towns—Dakar (capital, 600,000), Thiès (90,000), Rufisque (65,000), St. Louis (50,000).

CLIMATE: Driest and coolest period from January to April with temperatures in upper 60's. Hot from May to December (temperatures in upper 80's). Rainy season from mid-June to mid-October.

LANGUAGES: French (official), Wolof, Peuhl (Fula), Mandé and other African languages.

CURRENCY: CFA franc. CFA 100 = 40 cents; $1.00 = CFA 245.

VISAS: Required. Obtained from Senegalese Embassy and Senegalese Mission to the UN. Also available from French consulates wherever Senegal is not represented. Fee $3.60 (for up to three-month stay). Two passport photos needed. Transit visas (72-hour stay) available gratis at airport on presentation of departure ticket.

AIRPORT: Yoff (DKR), nine miles from Dakar. Regular and frequent links with New York, France, Western Europe, Brazil, Argentina and West Africa. Airport departure taxes—domestic, CFA 600 ($2.40); outside Africa CFA 1,500 ($6). Transport into city—bus, CFA 50 (20

629

cents); taxi, CFA 1,000 ($4); limousine for eight, CFA 250 each ($1). Beware of rapacious taxi drivers at airport.

NATIONAL HOLIDAYS: April 4, Independence day; Christian and Moslem holidays.

INFORMATION SOURCES: *In US*—Embassy of Senegal, 2112 Wyoming Avenue NW, Washington, D.C. 20008 (tel. 202/234-0540); Permanent Mission of Senegal to the UN, 51 East 42nd Street, New York, N.Y. 10017 (tel. 212/661-8866). *In Dakar*—Bureau d'Accueil, Délégation Générale au Tourisme, 28 Avenue Roume (Place de l'Indépendance), P.O. Box 1412 (tel. 239-50).

By Philip M. Allen

Dakar, the capital of capitals, comes first along the airways and shipping lanes from Western Europe and North America to Black Africa. Senegal has priority also for those interested in the heritage of France in Africa, the accomplishments of Africans in a French cultural universe, and for some of Africa's own spirit after generations of European presence. Here is a mixed African patrimony of theater and music, science and proverbial wisdom, the excitement of cities, the curiosities of countryside, and the profundities of Islam.

The Senegalese are a varied population of Wolof (more than a third of the total), Peuhl (Fulani), Serer, Mandingo, Dioula and Toucouleur (Tukulur), with smaller communities of Lebou, Sarakollé, Bambara, Bassari and Moors from Mauritania. They inhabit a country relatively at ease with strangers and accommodating to the far-ranging tastes of travelers.

Until it gained independence in 1960, Senegal was the oldest French colony in Black Africa. Moslem for nine centuries, unified 500 years ago by the Djolof kings of sandy Cayor, Senegal survived intact in the western lee of the great Sudanic African empires of Ghana, Mali and Songhai Gao. It has witnessed the gold trade of the medieval Sudan, the invasions of Moors and Berbers, the slaving of Portuguese and their African collaborators from the mid-15th century, and the military incursions of a half dozen rival European powers that ended by 1814 with France on top.

From the outset, France's colonial policy of "assimilation" flourished in the atmosphere of Senegal's four favored coastal communes: St. Louis, Rufisque, Gorée Island and Dakar. While the Sudanic interior required campaigns of "pacification," these towns received dowries of French political institutions, sizable communities of French settlers, and French systems of trade, finance and education. Considerable industry came to the colony and French citizenship was eventually accorded black Africans and racially mixed persons (métis).

In order to centralize administration, colonial headquarters were transferred in 1902 from St. Louis to Dakar, a railhead and the westernmost point on the continent. From 1909 until 1958, Dakar stood with Paris and Algiers as a capital of empire, presiding over a Federation of West African colonies.

Dakar's strategic port and airfield were used by Free French and Allied forces in World War II.

Participation in Europe's conflicts hastened the growth of nationalism in Senegal as elsewhere. The Federation began to break up in the 1950's as each territory agitated for autonomy. Guinea-Conakry went its way in 1958, seven others a year later, and the former Soudan broke with Senegal in September, 1960, becoming the Republic of Mali. When Senegal gained its own sovereignty on April 4 of that year, it was at the cost of her privilege as a regional seat of power in Overseas France.

With the breakup of the West African Federation, Dakar also lost her economic hinterland. Abidjan, capital of the wealthy Ivory Coast, has competed successfully for investment, international trade and political influence. Senegal has sought to form new combinations among its independent neighbors and is now counting on the benefits of a recent series of agreements with the Ivory Coast. But thus far these associations have failed to pay dividends.

Dakar, on its superb peninsula, now presides only over a single nation of less than four million. It has a great port, a huge civil service and impressive French institutions, as well as considerable industry. But it is handicapped by a shortage of natural resources, dependence on a fickle peanut crop, rampant inflation and unemployment. Living standards for Senegal's peasantry and urban poor are actually declining.

The roots of France hold fast in the economy and urban culture of Senegal. France remains the principal point of reference for the port, banks and trading companies of an overseas-oriented economic system, and for Dakar's proud, French-subsidized university, the law courts, the army and all communication networks. Now a privileged partner and source of substantial economic aid, France dominates the processing and exportation of Senegal's phosphates and peanut oils, and the importation of consumer goods and equipment. Continued poverty and dependence on France have caused unrest among students and wage earners, as well as among the less articulate peasantry.

Attacked by critics as the incarnation of French colonial assimilationism, Senegal's poet-philosopher-president, Léopold Sédar Senghor, exemplifies his own theories of cultural cross-breeding (métissage). Senghor has been for 40 years a leading advocate of black civilization (Négritude) and a patron of its poetry and music. He is also one of 20th century France's most important intellectuals and a Roman Catholic. Senghor has sought to inter-breed several traditions: Islamic, traditional African and French. To these he has added elements of advanced technology (which he often identifies as American) and a strictly controlled economy of private and state enterprises (which he styles African socialism).

Even while awaiting the fruition of Senghor's statecraft, Senegal is a fascinating land to visit and to know. Some 50,000 non-African residents, many of them third-generation Frenchmen and Lebanese-Syrian traders, plus another 50,000 foreign visitors, students and laborers, give to this small nation a cosmopolitan style and geniality that cannot be quenched in economic doldrums.

Full-length treatment of Senegal in English is scanty, but there are many specialized articles and essays on the country's history and politics, as well as recent studies of Islam in Senegal (by Lucy Behrman and by Donal Cruise O'Brien) and an excellent assessment of the French impact in Michael Crowder's Senegal, a Study of French Assimilation Policy (Methuen, 1967). The copious French literature on Senegal includes a 1972 Hachette Guide Bleu, treating the country thoroughly.

Senegalese writers and filmmakers have eloquently documented the beauty and perplexity of their country. Some of Senghor's poems and essays have been translated (for instance, in A Book of African Verse, edited by John Reed and Clive Wake, a Heinemann African Writers Series paperback, which also includes selections from the fine Senegalese poets David Diop and Birago Diop). Cheikh Hamidou Kane's beautiful novel Aventure Ambiguë has been translated (Ambiguous Adventure, Walker, 1969), as has at least one of Ousmane Sembène's strong political novels (Les Bouts de Bois de Dieu, translated as God's Bits of Wood, Doubleday Anchor Books). Sembène's films are the best known of a new crop of moviemakers. His work is well worth seeing by anybody planning a visit.

Money Matters

A capital of CFA franc country, Dakar has several French banks with international affiliations. These include the Banque Internationale de l'Afrique Occidentale (BIAO), partly owned by the First National City Bank of New York, with branches in St. Louis, Ziguinchor, Kaolack and Tambacounda. There is also a wide network of West and Central African counterparts.

Banking hours in Dakar are from 8 to 11 am and 2 to 4 pm, Monday through Friday, plus Saturday mornings. The airport, hotels, shops and Chamber of Commerce also offer exchange facilities. While hotel keepers, merchants and taxi drivers welcome hard currencies, they tend to quote highly imaginative rates of exchange—always in their own favor. So it's best to use banks. CFA francs bought in Senegal can also be spent in Mauritania, Ivory Coast, Upper Volta, Niger, Togo and Dahomey.

As a result of heavy taxation and tariffs, as well as governmental and private price fixing, Senegal's cities are extraordinarily expensive. Any imported commodity gets sold at bounty prices and even local products—food, services, textiles, crafts, theater tickets and the like—cost more than comparable items in, say, the Gambia, Mali, Liberia or Upper Volta.

Getting In and Out

Dakar's seaport and airport (at Yoff) are among the busiest gateways of Africa. Aircraft and ships from France, Latin America and New York, as well as the rest of Africa and Europe, land here. There are three direct Dakar-New York round trip flights each week, and daily air connections with Paris. Pan American offers excursion rates for 10- to 14-day round trip visits from New York.

American Farrell Lines and Delta Lines are among the companies calling with cargo and occasional passengers at Dakar. Fortnightly Farrell freighters cost about $355 for excellent accommodations on round trips between New York and Dakar. The French Paquet Lines operates three-class passenger ships from Marseille twice monthly ($110 to $330).

Parallel to a very rugged east-west highway, the old colonial railroad links Dakar with Bamako, capital of landlocked Mali, but the 24-hour train ride (arriving at Dakar Monday and Friday mornings) can be tedious for impatient travelers. The ancient pathways of conquest lead down from the western Mediterranean through Morocco and Mauritania, crossing the Senegal River by ferries at Rosso, with Dakar a modern oasis at their terminus.

Getting Around Within Senegal

Outside the concentrated Dakar-Cape Verde neighborhood, Senegal's points of interest are well spread out. Forested river country, hills and game savannas lie up and down the coast and beyond the broad central desert, which can be crossed or circumvented as you wish. Only one fourth of the country's 5,500 miles of road is paved, mainly in the west.

Car rental agencies (Hertz, EuropCar, Avis-Senegal Tourisme, Sintra, LocAuto, Sama) are available to fill your needs, but at stiff rates: $10 per day for 70 free kilometers, plus 6 cents per kilometer for mini-cars, double that rate for large vehicles ($5 surcharge for air-conditioning). You buy gasoline at 50 CFA francs per liter (72 cents per gallon). Drivers can be hired for $6 extra per day.

Taxis, buses and bush taxis (usually the sturdy six- to eight-passenger Peugeot 404 station wagon) cover the highway spokes emanating from Dakar's railway station on Avenue Malick Sy near the medina. When full, bush taxis charge CFA 750 ($3) between Dakar and St. Louis, 60 cents between Dakar and Thiès, $1 to M'Bour, $2 to Kaolack, $4 to Bathurst (The Gambia) or to Ziguinchor in the southern Casamance. Dakar's taxis have meters: CFA 40 (16 cents) is the basic charge, plus CFA 20 (8 cents) per kilometer; double rates at night. Bargain a price for longer hauls. Traffic drives on the right.

The railroad serves Thiès, Kaolack and Touba from Dakar daily, St. Louis also daily, Tambacounda and Kidira twice weekly on the run to Mali (with sleepers and air-conditioned coaches). The Dakar-Thiès run (45 miles) costs about $1.45 in first class, 55 cents in second; Kaolack (120 miles) is $4.54 in first class, $1.84 in second; St. Louis (165 miles) is $7.80 in first, $2.14 in second. The 24-hour run to Bamako (770 miles) costs about $32 in first class.

Senegal River boats of the French Messageries Maritimes run twice monthly between St. Louis and Podor; they proceed as far as Matam during the high-water summer season when some river basin roads are awash. The Cosena Company's ship *Cap Skirring* carries passengers between Dakar and Ziguinchor at the head of the Casamance River estuary; the trip takes less than 24 hours, and costs about $26 (one way), good meals included. The ports of Dakar and Gorée Island are linked by an hourly ferry that costs CFA 150 (60 cents) for round trips. The Gambia Republic is crossed by road in two places between northern Senegal and the Casamance, using ferries that operate only in daylight hours.

There are regularly scheduled one-hour Air Senegal flights from Dakar to Bathurst, the Gambian capital, for about $22 one way, to Ziguinchor for $25, St. Louis for $15, Kédougou for $51, Matam for $37, Podor for $31, Tambacounda for $34 and the Simenti game camp for $41. Air Senegal also provides charter service to the Simenti Hotel airfield at the Niokola-Koba National Park, which can be reached as well by rented vehicle from rail junctions at Kaolack or Tambacounda. Air Senegal charters five-passenger Pipers for $108 per hour and Cherokees for $81.60.

The official Délégation Générale au Tourisme maintains a tourist reception office on Dakar's Place de l'Indépendance. The Chamber of Commerce stands across the square. The Touring-Club du Sénégal assists members of international automobile clubs. Fifteen airlines and as many shipping lines and travel agencies have offices in Dakar. Socopao Voyages (also in Kaolack), Usima-Voyages and Transcap, all French-owned, offer the most complete services.

For information about national parks, write Le Conservateur des Parcs Nationaux, P.O. Box 37, Tambacounda; for hunting information, La Direction des Eaux et Forêts, Parc Forestier et Zoologique de Hann, P.O. Box 1831; concerning arts and artisan crafts, L'Office Sénégalais de l'Artisanat, Village Artisanal de Soumbedioune, P.O. Box 3162; on deep-sea fishing, Le Centre de Pêche Sportive de Dakar, P.O. Box 3132— all in Dakar.

Where to Stay

Dakar's official list of hotels includes 25 establishments with a total of 900 rooms. There are at least another 30 outside the capital, not counting camps or rest-houses. The costs that follow, converted into dollars for convenience, include a 10 to 15 per cent service surcharge, but not breakfast (which costs from $1 up) unless so specified.

DAKAR's luxury trade is served for the time being by only two establishments, both aging. La Croix du Sud, a businessmen's hotel in the center of the city, has one of West Africa's best-known restaurants. Air France's beachfront Hôtel N'Gor, near the airport at Yoff, 20 minutes from midtown, has intriguing split-level apartments, terraces and all manner of sporting facilities. Both charge a minimum of $14.50 for air-conditioned single rooms with private bath. Double rooms range upwards from $19 and suites from $23. Croix du Sud prices do include Continental breakfast.

Lunch and dinner prices begin at about $4 (less wine) at both hotels. The Croix du Sud also offers an interesting American plan from $21.50 per day for singles and $36 for couples (full pension), or $17 for singles and $27 for doubles (half-pension). But Dakar has so many good places to eat that only the half-pension really makes sense.

The Place de l'Indépendance is to have a 264-room luxury palace— UTH's Hôtel Teranga. There will also eventually be an Intercontinental Hotel on Cap Manuel, five minutes from the center of the city, and a Sheraton in the Fann suburban residential district.

Less luxurious but pleasant accommodations are available in central Dakar at the Touring Hôtel and the Hôtel Clarice (with English management and a nice snack-bar) and at the Village N'Gor on the beach. All charge about $8 minimum for single rooms.

Cheaper and rather shabby alternatives are the Vichy, once a midtown favorite of cognoscenti, but now rather run down and over-priced, the Majestic on Independence Square and the more moderately priced Plateau and Central in midtown, the Métropole overlooking the port, and Relais de l'Espadon on Gorée (all from $6 for singles). Air-conditioning usually involves a surcharge at most of these places. If you don't want to be charged during Dakar's many cool nights, have the desk clerk note your wishes on the registration form.

Hostels, inexpensive furnished rooms, family pensions and flop-houses are scattered around Dakar, particularly in the palisades area above the port, behind neighborhood restaurants in the older parts of midtown, and in the medina (African quarter) on the edge of the city. Before making compromises with sanitation, try *Mon Logis*, a French family pension with excellent food at 57 Rue Blanchot (third to fifth floors) for $3.50 to $5 a night, or the *Atlantic*, 52 Rue du Dr. Thèze, for $5 upwards.

East and south of Dakar, THIÈS has the small *Hôtel du Rail* (from $6), the very modest *Etoile du Sud* and the *Rex*. Down the southern coast, bungalows stand on a pretty site at the *Hôtel-Restaurant de l'Hippo-campe* at LA SOMONE ($2 per bed, $8 for full pension); M'BOUR offers the *Relais 82* and the *Hôtel-Restaurant de la Petite Côte* (both from $4).

East of Thiès, DJOURBEL has the *Hôtel du Baobab* for $5 upwards, as well as camps at DIOKOUL, LINGUÈRE and TOUBA (available by authoriza-tion of the district prefect).

At KAOLACK to the south, there is the *Paris* ($5 up), the *Hôtel-Restau-rant du Tourisme* at nearby KAHONE, and government rest-camps in the Sine-Saloum delta.

On the northern coast, by the road to St. Louis, a new tourist beach center has opened at M'BORO. The *Hôtel du Lac* there offers rooms from $6 up.

ST. LOUIS's major hotel is the seaside *Résidence*, with good rooms renting upwards from $6 per single ($4 supplement for air-conditioning) and a menu from $3.50. There is also the *Hôtel de la Poste* in the center of St. Louis with an animated sidewalk cafe for $4 upwards, and the smaller *Hôtel de Paris*. Along the river, RICHARD TOLL and PODOR have only government rest-houses, but there are Air Afrique hunting camps in the delta at MAKA-DIAMA and KEUR MASSENA (across the Mauritanian border) and the small *Hôtel du Fleuve* (Chez Fadel) at MATAM ($5 up).

ZIGUINCHOR, capital of the Casamance, has the small *Hôtel-Restau-rant Aubert* ($6 up, with air-conditioning), the still smaller *Provence* ($8) and the cheaper *Said Doumith* and *Escale*. There are Casamance vacation cabins at the *Centre de Nema* ($2 up), the hotels *Relais Fleuri* and *Bérenguier* at BIGNONA, and two camps at CAPE SKIRRING. The *Grand Hôtel Skirring* is under construction at the Cape.

In eastern Senegal, TAMBACOUNDA offers the *Hôtel de la Gare* ($4). NIOKOLA-KOBA PARK visitors stay at the good *Hôtel de Simenti* with air-conditioned rooms for $6 up and bungalows for $3.50 and $4 per person. The park also has the somewhat cheaper *Hôtel de Niokolo-Koba* without air-conditioning, and a government camp at Badi near the park entrance. Backpackers out of town may find lodgings at secondary schools, reli-gious missions and international volunteer residences.

Where and What to Eat

Most of the hotels listed in the preceding section serve standard French meals. In DAKAR, good Continental restaurants include the *Croix du Sud*, *Mon Logis* (a pension), the *Relais de l'Espadon* on Gorée and, for less elaborate cuisine, the *Métropole* and the *Majestic*. Other good places include the *Lido* (with its swimming pool), the *Vesuvio* (Italian), *Le Lagon* (seafood on a pier over the Bernard Inlet on the edge of town), *Le Folklore* below the Vichy Hotel, *Le Ramatou* near the airport, the chic Lebanese *Cellier Ali Baba* down the street from the Croix du Sud, the excellent but expensive *Chevalier de Boufflers* on Gorée Island, the *Brasserie Colisée* on Avenue Lamine Guèye for a wide variety of menus and *Café Protet* on the Place de l'Indépendance.

A number of small neighborhood bistros in the port area, the charming Creole courtyard restaurant of the *Hôtel St. Louis* and the modest *Taverne des Boucaniers* on Gorée serve decent meals at lower prices (about $2.50 and up for five-course menus, excluding wine).

Outside the capital, the better European kitchens will be found at *La Petite Côte* at M'BOUR, the *Auberge des Cocotiers* in CAYAR, the *Poussin Bleu* in THIÈS, the *Aubert* in ZIGUINCHOR, the *Hôtel de Paris in* KAOLACK and *La Résidence* in ST. LOUIS. Meals at these provincial places seldom cost less than $5.

Beyond this array of French cuisine, Senegal has good Lebanese and Vietnamese restaurants (*Kim Son Marcel, Eurasie* and *Le Farid* in Dakar, for example) and offers a brilliant spectrum of dishes from the Wolof, Serer, Peuhl, Mandingo and other African people of the country.

The national platter, usually encountered at lunch, is thiébou diène (pronounced "cheeboodjin")—a bouillabaisse combining fresh and dried fish, rice and oil, vegetables and hot pepper, sometimes with snails. You can also taste rice prepared in various sauces (nététou, niébé), chicken yassa (lemon, onion and pepper sauce), or chicken mafé in peanut oil stew, foufou (fish or meat with cassava or plantain dough and okra), stuffed mullet and couscous variously garnished. Fish is abundant, as are tropical fruits and fresh drinks like palm wine, ginger beer blended with mint, sugar and spices, or kinkiliba leaf tea, as well as alcoholic treats for non-Moslems.

An invitation to a méchoui—a barbecue of sheep or goat, often celebrated with music—is to be cherished. If you lack such invitations from the hospitable Senegalese, try these dishes at restaurants like the *Baobab*, the *Hôtel St. Louis*, the *Niani* and the *Ramatou* in "European" Dakar and at a hundred places of pot-luck and work-a-day dining wherever Senegalese congregate.

Dakar's water is filtered but considered unsafe by American standards. Up-country try another kind of beverage, even if only the over-priced bottle of French mineral water. French bakeries, by the way, are part of urban Senegal's pride.

Restaurant checks usually carry a 10 per cent service charge, but if you want to reward the waiter for superior service, add a few coins.

What to See and Do

Senegal divides into three sections: (1) river forest country in the north and the south, (2) eastern grasslands with the Niokolo-Koba Park and the Sahara-like Ferlo, (3) the Cape Verde peninsula and coastal areas around the capital city.

DAKAR is a place of administration and commerce, expensive in its European style, poverty-stricken but lively in its African character. The city's restaurants, shops, galleries, tall bleached office and apartment buildings, the graceful presidential palace and elegant new parliament building, the handsome university, mosques, lovely marine drive (Corniche), handsome middle-class residential sectors and low-cost suburban housing developments all satisfy a sightseer's interest in properly arranged, moderately exotic and suitably modern urban Africa. The government has declared war on the squadrons of beggars, lepers and contraband hustlers (bana-bana) who have heretofore dogged tourists' steps throughout the city.

There are safe beaches at N'Gor and Bernard Inlet (Anse Bernard) and water sport facilities at N'Gor, the Lagon Restaurant pier, and Air Afrique's Centre de Pêche Sportive at the Espadon Hotel on Gorée, as well as splendid skindiving off Gorée, the Almadies Point, and the shore islands and inlet called Les Madeleines.

Inside the city, behind the port, is the old Mediterranean district of petits blancs (lower middle-class whites). Also located in this area are garages and small restaurants, wholesalers and appliance shops, and the intensely alive Kermel Market for food, flowers and cloth. This leads into the fashionable area and business center of the Place de l'Indépendance.

Beyond the Place runs the animated commercial Avenue William Ponty, crossed by Avenue Lamine Guèye (ex-Avenue Maginot) with legions of Lebanese textile dealers, and at the intersection, the lordly but teeming Sandaga Market.

Following Rues Thiers, Carnot or Félix Faure off the Place, you can wander through the old quarters of Africans, Creoles and "Portugalese" from the Cape Verde Islands and Guinea-Bissau. Their gridironed streets run into Avenue Lamine Guèye and then Place Tascher, with the National Assembly and the IFAN Museum's magnificent collection of carvings, architectural treasures, pottery, cloth and musical instruments from all of West Africa.

Past a quiet residential section, you come (by taxi, bus or bicycle) upon ruined fortifications at the coast, followed by the government's big, commercial but diverting Artisan Village at Soumbedioune and the neo-Grecian Musée Dynamique on the Corniche (special exhibitions on irregular schedules). From here you have a view of rugged off-shore islands in a superb blue sea, and an alternation of rich and poor quarters from Soumbedioune through Fann (site of the university), Ouakam, the Yoff Airport and the resorts of N'Gor, off the wild Pointe des Almadies.

The University of Dakar is a vintage French institution, now operating under nominal Senegalese authority. It welcomes American students seeking a year of study abroad, even if only to polish their French.

Most intriguing of these sections is the low-lying, virtually treeless, sandy, gridironed medina, designed for Africans by colonial authority, thus enabling Europeans to have the rest of Dakar to themselves. With its colorful and cluttered market, its occasional villa, a heavy traffic of the occupied and the idle, the boggy ruts of the rains and the choking sands of the rainless periods, this slum surges, splutters and resounds with the polyrhythms of Africa in a setting no African would have built. In their poor, single-story family dwellings, colonies of Wolof, Dioula, Toucouleur, Peuhl, Moor and Hausa create their own moods of daytime despair and nighttime revival.

This alternating black and white checkerboard of Dakar ceases by the time you enter the island atmosphere of GORÉE, 20 minutes by launch from the port (Pier No. 1). Less than a thousand islanders of both colors and cultures inhabit this old settlement, a melting pot of trading and slaving. They dwell within solid, harmonious, pastel- or white-walled compounds under orange tile roofs, without motor cars or industry. Gorée displays a dignity of survival through five centuries of slaving, piracy, bombardments and successive occupations by British, Dutch, Portuguese and French.

Last of the island's mangled forts, the 19th century Castel of Nassau and St. Michel was put out of action by British warships in 1940. Perched on an exhilarating cliff at the southern tip of the island, it has subterranean corridors and ruined World War I batteries. Climb to the Castel for a view over its battlements, or down the muzzle of a cannon, out to sea, bay and the shore of Senegal. An alley of baobabs leads back down from the fort to Gorée village, with its quiet, sandy lanes, its beach, deep-sea fishing center and restaurants, its pretty mosque and St. Charles

Borromée Church, and its police prefecture built as a Portuguese church in 1482. There is a small marine museum and a historical museum presenting an orderly educational display of West African chronology.

The House of Slaves, where hundreds of thousands of captives awaited transportation over the Atlantic, is a monument to 300 years of ignominy. Its grim dungeons lie directly under what were the graceful living quarters of the European commandants, surely within earshot. Near the Slave House is the studio of a talented young Senegalese artist, Souleymane Keita. Gorée can be thoroughly covered on foot in less than an hour but deserves a full day of meandering, cafe sitting and reading, and bathing in the calm cove. Avoid weekends and Thursdays, when everybody else is here and when swarms of self-appointed child guides harry you at every corner. Come soon, for the government has reportedly adopted plans for new tourist constructions to dramatize Gorée as an historical and cultural pilgrimage point.

Dakar is also a place of excellent, albeit expensive, theater. The glamorous Daniel Sorano Theatre has resident drama and ballet troupes. The Senegalese National Dance Company, one of Africa's most polished troupes, performs here, and entertainment by internationally known foreign artists is also offered. Movies in Dakar tend toward run-of-the-mill Western, detective and cowboy stuff, but the Cinema Club and government, university or embassy showings occasionally feature a film of Sembène, Johnson Traoré, Momar Thiam or other African directors. In the commercial cinemas, owned by international syndicates, these indigenous artists seldom get a viewing.

There are also a couple of struggling cabaret-theaters (e.g., Le Café-Théâtre on the Rue Diouf), discotheques of the affluent young (La Case at Soumbedioune, Ferlo, 732), dancing at the big hotels and at the rough dance bars of the big port town. Late evening medina activity centers around beer and rock music at the Moulin Rouge, Le Mali, Cannibale 2 and the Miami. There is a casino on the N'Gor road. Soccer football and a slow, ceremonious style of wrestling draw Sunday afternoon crowds to the stadiums.

The travel agencies operate numerous tours of Dakar and environs, as well as longer excursions to beaches, game parks, rivers and forests. A half-day organized survey of the city can be useful for the newcomer. The ocean drives, beaches, lighthouse, university area, crafts market at Soumbedioune and Musée Dynamique are all beyond easy walking distance and rather expensive to reach by taxi. Town buses are clean but crowded and bicycling is only for pedalers who don't mind heavy traffic.

The major agencies like Socopao and Usima guarantee a glimpse of music and dancing on their weekend village tours out of Dakar. Guides are improving both in their command of English and in their awareness of the country, but they still have far to go professionally. Tours tend to dwell excessively on the undazzling modernity of Dakar—the National Assembly, the hulk of a cathedral, the hideous, huge Administration Building, and the plastic superficiality of the modern Moroccan mosque.

Within a two-hour driving radius of Dakar, along the coasts of Cape Verde and into the peanut-growing interior, are to be found towns, beaches (with dangerously heavy surf, unfortunately) and countryside in striking variety. N'GOR VILLAGE with a pretty central square and mosque; N'GOR ISLAND, a surfing and skindiving resort; basalt rocks, deep-lying fish sources and oyster beds at LES ALMADIES, westernmost point of the peninsula; the powerful lighthouse of LES MAMELLES (The Mammaries), 350 feet above the tiny village of Ouakam (visitable in the afternoon); the zoo at HANN—all lie within a brief range of the city.

Thirty-five miles out along the northern coast, the return of fishermen to the beach of CAYAR in their boats with triangular sails creates a splendid scene of trading in cargoes of tuna, sole, mackerel, shrimp, bonito, ray and other merchandise. Closer to town, the beach at SOUMBEDIOUNE, between the Crafts Village and the Musée Dynamique, has a similar if less orchestrated fishermen's return. You can join an Air Afrique fishing boat from Gorée (reservations at Air Afrique's Place de l'Indépendance office) for a quest of barracuda, sailfish, tuna, bass, red mullet, marlin and bluefish.

The CAPE VERDE circuit encompasses the old mill and port town of RUFISQUE; SANGALKAM, with a botanical garden; THIÈS, an industrial town where textile design and printing have been stimulated by Senegal's best-known painter, Papa Ibra Tall; the Catholic museum at N'GUEKOKO at the mouth of the Somone River; the monasteries of KEUR MOUSSA and KEUR GUILAYE, with their exuberant African-Christian frescoes and Senegalese music accompanying holy offices; the experimental ranch at BAMBYLOR; the fishermen's town M'BOUR; and JOAL, birthplace of President Senghor, an old Portuguese mission town between fisheries and oyster beds with long flat patches of earth (tanns), celebrated in Senghor's poetry. The pretty lake island of FADIOUTH, with its Catholic cemetery of shells and its shellwork artisanry, can be reached by a causeway or by canoe from Joal.

Proceeding south by track, the Sine-Saloum river marshes contain islands, beaches, megalithic monuments of unidentified origin, and hospitable villages like N'DANGANE (rest-camp), FOUNDIOUGNE, TOUBACOUTA and MESSIRAH. You can hire canoes at these places.

Once over the ferry and past the river enclave of the Gambia (see separate chapter), the motorist or bus rider enters a more dense, humid, greener domain: the isolated CASAMANCE of the Malinké (Mandingo) people and the immigrant Dioula. There is superb dancing at OUSSOYE village and at AYOUNE where the genial Queen Sybeth welcomes visitors by her sacred grove.

A two-hour cruise on the *Cap Skirring* or another boat on the splendid estuary of the Casamance River to ZIGUINCHOR quietly penetrates the peace of mangrove swamp, river foliage and wildlife.

Ziguinchor, a former Portuguese slave port, nests inside palm groves, fruit orchards, gardens and peanut plantations. The little regional capital is especially lively during the winter peanut marketing season. Its circumference of villages is well worth exploring for their traditional housing, farming methods and pure cultural styles.

At the sea end of the road, after the tropical *National Park of the Lower Casamance*, CAPE SKIRRING boasts a warm sea striking upon a fine wild site, fine sand and fresh sea breezes. These qualities are soon to be marketed as a new tourist center.

If you are invited by the African Party for the Independence of Guinea and Cape Verde (PAIGC), the nationalist movement that occupies about two-thirds of Portuguese Guinea-Bissau (see that chapter), you may visit PAIGC schools, a medical center and housing settlements for 60,000 Guinean refugees. Some bold foreigners are escorted at night by PAIGC members across the border southeast of Ziguinchor, through sections patrolled and occasionally raided by Portuguese troops, to a PAIGC-adminstered area bordering on the independent Republic of Guinea.

Back in Senegal, a flat peanut-growing area of baobab trees and cactus east of Thiès includes the holy Moslem city of TIVOUANE, residence of the Tidjane Brotherhood's caliph; the artisan center of DJOURBEL, with a handsome mosque and flowering gardens in the midst of dry brush savanna; TOUBA, with its spacious and sublime mosque, capital of the Mouride sect whose chief marabout (caliph) remains influential in Senegalese economic and social life, and the commercial center of TAMBACOUNDA on the edge of the Ferlo Desert, where only the herds of the Peuhl can survive.

Tambacounda, 293 miles from Dakar, opens the road southward through dry savanna to the edge of the Fouta Djallon mountains and into poor, scantily populated country that includes one of West Africa's best game reserves, the *Niokolo-Koba National Park*. Antelopes (including the gigantic derby eland), buffalo, monkeys, birds, lions, hippos and crocodiles are best seen along the park's western waterholes as the terrain dries out in late winter and spring. The hunting season runs from late December to May. South of the park, at the eastern sources of the Casamance River, live the Bassari and Coniagui, an untamed, isolated, intensely active hill people.

Senegal's northern reaches, from St. Louis around the great curve of the Senegal River, speak in a different mood than Cape Verde, Casamance or the Islamic east. At the former colonial capital (1814 to 1902) of St. Louis are to be found balconied homes and once prosperous business houses, which were erected as early as 1638 on the trade in gold, ivory, gum arabic, leather, wax, slaves and firearms. St. Louis retains its gridiron form, its important fishing industry and a mixed population. The town and its spit of protecting land, called La Langue de Barbarie, still exude an atmosphere that inspired much French romantic literature.

The river-island setting is laced by bridges. Worth a visit are the fishermen's quarters at Guet N'Dar on the southern end of the Langue de Barbarie, the jewelry, cloth and spice stores, a Moslem fishermen's cemetery with net-draped tombs, a great 19th century mosque and churches of a readily converted Creole bourgeoisie. There is a natural history museum in the Senegal Research and Documentation Center.

From St. Louis, the roads go into Mauritania or follow the river upstream along the northeastern then southeastern curve into Mali. In the river delta at MAKA DIAMA, 20 miles from St. Louis, is an Air Afrique hunting reserve with birds, crocodiles, hippos and wart hogs. The reserve is open from mid-November to the end of May. Twice monthly, a Senegal River steamer leaves St. Louis for the old trading port of PODOR, reached in six days, and in high water (August through October) it travels as far as MATAM, 10 days upstream, the old fort of BAKEL, and KAYES in Mali.

The boat cruises through the dense bird sanctuary of DJOUDJ northeast of St. Louis, past the national rice basket and lake area at RICHARD TOLL, by DAGANA with its old French fort and steamy ROSSO over the ferry crossing in Mauritania.

The riverscape contains squadrons of fishing craft, crocodiles and water birds, hippopotamus herds in the north and east, and a string of Senegalese and Mauritanian ports with their own hold on river commerce. One-way travelers can go on into Mauritania and Mali, or fly back to Dakar from Matam (460 miles), the millet grain capital of the east, or from Bakel (438 miles).

Fortunate travelers may be able to adjust their itineraries to coincide with a local festival. Occasions of traditional music and pageantry are less easily discovered in Senegal than in, say, Ghana, except for Christian and Moslem feast days. Despite President Senghor's celebration of Négritude and Negro arts, assimilated Senegalese are not inclined to display their "pagan" heritage to foreigners with pride. Catholics have a Whitmonday pilgrimage to Popenguine on the coast south of Dakar and hold a festival for St. Francis Xavier at Fadiouth on the first Sunday in December. Moslem Senegal observes the Islamic calendar, including Ramadan and the Tabaski feast, as well as the Mouloud pilgrimages of the Tidjane sect to Tivouane on the Prophet's birthday and the assemblage of the Khadria sect at N'Diassane one week later. Touba's great Mouride festival is the Magel. Senegal's Islamic leaders (marabouts) have enormous political and economic importance. Having a conversation with one, or with an articulate follower, can be a most enlightening experience for a visitor.

Ancestral African festivals take place according to the natural cycles of planting and harvest, maturity and death. Certain styles of dance and spirit invocation belong to different settlements or regions, with New Year carnivals ("Fanal") at St. Louis and Ziguinchor, the "Fil" festival preceding the rainy season at Touba-Toul near Thiès, the "Houmabeul" at Oussoye (Casamance) in September, harvest festivals in the Casamance and the Mandingo areas of the Niokolo in March, Mandingo initiation ceremonies in February, Bassari initiations in April and May, the Merediyo animal festivals of the Torodé Peuhl around Toumbacounda in June and July, and Mandingo fish festivals at Ghanikoye (20 miles from Tambacounda) in May. The Tourist Bureau in Dakar may be able to advise more specifically on the year's festivals.

For those with a more pragmatic curiosity, Senegal has several interesting rural development projects which can be visited after contact with program headquarters in Dakar—in most cases, the Animation Rurale section of the Prime Minister's Office, whose controversial and embattled program to mobilize agricultural communities for development is often sabotaged. American AID and Peace Corps offices, Canadian CUSO personnel, the French SATEC (technical assistance contractor) and the International Labor Organization (ILO) in Dakar can also lead you to several interesting field projects.

What to Buy

Senegalese creativity, especially a marvelous sense of decoration, is represented in abundance in Dakar. Various shops and traders' stalls along the Avenue William Ponty (where you must bargain for your life) and the Craftsman's Village at Soumbedioune (bargain here, too) have filigree jewelry (including reproductions of the Agadès cross), leatherwork, pottery, weaving, musical instruments and other commodities. Don't be put off by Soumbedioune's plentiful but hideous wood carvings. Mauritanian silver jewelry and stones, tea services and carved chests are available at La Cour des Maures, 69 Avenue Blaise Diagne in Dakar. Prices for massive and filigree jewelry weighing over five grams are held within bounds by government rules based on weight; the crafts office at Soumbedioune can give advice on price ranges within these norms. The Dakar Kermel Market also has gold and copper jewelry, stones, shells and amulets up for bargaining. You may occasionally come upon very old jewelry at the medina market.

Every town's marketplace has its supply of wicker baskets and straw figures, as well as textiles, shells (near the coast), horn objects and leather (in the interior). Papa Ibra Tall, artistic patron of Thiès cloth, Souleymane Keita of Gorée, Younousse Seye and other painters exhibit occasionally at Dakar. An excellent bronze caster, Cheikh Diop Mahone, produces statuary in the tradition of the old Djolof kingdoms by the lost-wax method at his personal gallery in Djourbel.

All Senegal sustains a rich heritage of minstrelsy (griots), festival dance (especially in the south), and drumming. With perseverance and luck you may find a good example of the region's unique stringed instruments (kora or khalam), a forest drum or a gourd-resonating xylophone (balafon) of the Wolof, Mandingo or Serer people. On Gorée and at Soumbedioune, small dolls in plastic (or better ones in felt) depict the gorgeous dress of Senegalese women. Original tapestries are found at Thiès.

The works of Senegal's writers, a good selection of Africana, and French literature, are available in a half dozen bookstores off the Place de l'Indépendance and Avenue William Ponty. There is no domestic publishing industry, so book prices, like those of all other imports, run well above metropolitan or North African prices.

Dakar offers excellent barbering and hairdressing, tailoring and French fashions—all at prices that presuppose a genuine, nay desperate, need for such things.

Local Attitudes

Although 80 per cent Moslem, Senegal is accustomed to dealing with Europeans, and the very gentle Senegalese show little offense at the customary liberties of strangers. Young French men and women long ago accustomed residents to miniskirts, bikinis and other abbreviated costumes. The country's women, in their attractive gowns and head-ties (mounsor), are virtual works of art. They can be photographed and indeed should be, assuming they consent to hold still for the camera.

Politics are earnestly discussed wherever educated Senegalese get together, and although the government has discouraged an organized opposition and independent press, private speech remains remarkably free.

American policies in Vietnam and toward Africa have given the United States an unenviable reputation among many educated Senegalese and French students at Dakar, but official policy is amicable and individual Americans are seldom embarrassed under non-political circumstances.

Weather, What to Wear, How Long to Stay

Tolerable weather and auspicious geography conspire to put the Cape Verde area on virtually any West African itinerary. The driest and coolest period for Senegal comes between January and April. Dakar is usually brisk then, the ocean waters clear, the game reserves open. Even the Casamance is relatively dry in winter. While this is not the best time for an ambitious Senegal River steamer trip, it is good for a trek around the river's accompaniment of roads and tracks. Rains come in the misnamed "hivernage" from mid-June to mid-October, alleviating some heavy, mid-day heat, even at Dakar with its fairly constant trade winds. Ocean fishing is good from July through October.

Despite steamy summer days along the rivers and dry heat elsewhere, visitors to almost any corner of Senegal will encounter cool evenings in winter. Rains normally come and go in vigorous thunder showers, except in the Casamance, which gets steady summer precipitation. A varied wardrobe is thus necessary. Most things can be bought in Dakar—expensively for imports, economically for attractive Senegalese garments. Informality serves travelers well in most parts of the country. Even in the dressy restaurants at the N'Gor or Croix du Sud, for example, men appear in open-necked shirts and shorts, women dine in slacks. French women dress their best on weekend evenings at clubs, restaurants and parties, and the Senegalese city elite look good practically anywhere.

Dakar is the starting place for a Senegal sojourn of any length or form. Here, your feet are on Senegalese ground, information and communications are available. The capital and its environs are easily worth a week, but if you don't care for cities you should still consider a full day for the immediate suburbs, plus a day for Gorée and the rest of Cape Verde.

Excursions by road out of Dakar add one day at least for Rufisque-Thiès-Joal-Fadiouth and return, another (by road or rail) to Touba and back, one more for Cayar and the northern coasts. Continuing from Cayar to St. Louis entails one or more days in the old town, and then the Senegal River which could take anywhere from a full day (Richard Toll, Dagana, the game areas and back) to a fortnight along the northern and eastern borders. The quickest way to Niokolo-Koba Park is by air (regular flight or charter) from Dakar to Simenti, but you can also have a car conveyed by rail from Dakar to Tambacounda and drive it from there.

Going southward in greatest haste, you must allow one day to Joal and Kaolack, another for the detour to the Sine-Saloum river country, a third for the Gambia (crossing the river at Bathurst), two days for the Casamance, returning to Dakar in two days via the Transgambian Highway at Mansa-Konko, Nioro-du-Rip (which has curious royal tombs) and Kaolack. This would consume about half of a fully rounded fortnight tour of Senegal, about the least you can do if you want balanced benefits out of the experience.

Communication

French is the language of national Senegalese and European affairs, but even in this veteran terrain of Francophonia, with its impressive literary tradition and educated elites, only one-tenth of the population can answer a traveler's more complicated questions in French. City schools are turning out large numbers of readers of English these days, and there are Peace Corps and CUSO Volunteers as well as English-speaking Gambians along the coast and in the south. Nevertheless, travelers outside Dakar cannot expect to get along very well without French.

Senegal's radio-telephone communications are satisfactory with Paris, French-speaking West Africa, Bathurst (the Gambia) and New York; they weaken deplorably beyond that network. Post offices handle telegrams, telephone and correspondence efficiently. You can mail packages with relative confidence from the main post office.

Dakar's daily newspaper, Le Soleil, although uncritical of authority, is a well-edited source of information. There are also specialized weekly periodicals and the foreign press.

Emergencies

Dakar has two relatively modern hospitals (Hôpital Principal and Hôpital Dantec), a few private clinics and the pioneering Institut Pasteur for rare problems. St. Louis and Djourbel have major hospitals. Elsewhere hospitals and dispensaries are frequently unsanitary and crowded and doctors are scarce. The American Embassy, AID regional headquarters and USIS are all located in the BIAO Building on the Place de l'Indépendance in the center of town, but will be moving to a new site. The Embassy maintains a health unit with a full-time nurse. There are Marine guards at the Embassy on 24-hour duty (tel. 263-44).

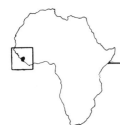

Sierra Leone

Profile

STATUS: Independent since April 27, 1961. Republic since April 19, 1971. Former British colony and up-country protectorate.

SIZE: 27,699 square miles (slightly smaller than South Carolina). Population—3,100,000 (Temnes, Korankos and Limbas in the north and center and Mendes in the south account for two-thirds of the population).

GEOGRAPHY: Atlantic coastal plain in west and south rising to high rocky plateau. Southern half of country heavily forested. Principal towns —Freetown (capital, 150,000), Bo (30,000), Kenema (10,000), Makeni (8,000).

CLIMATE: Tropical, with temperatures averaging over 80 degrees and high coastal humidity. Rainy season from May to October with heaviest storms from July to September.

LANGUAGES: English (official), Krio (Creole), African languages.

CURRENCY: Leone (Le) divided into 100 cents. Le 1.00 = $1.30; $1.00 = Le .77.

VISAS: Required. Available from Embassy of Sierra Leone in Washington and Consulate General of Sierra Leone in New York. Fee $1.74. Transit visa fee 21 US cents. Three passport photos needed; also, assurance of return ticket and proof of financial support while in Sierra Leone.

AIRPORT: Lungi (FNA), 18 miles across Sierra Leone River to Freetown. Well connected with West African capitals, less frequently with Western and Eastern Europe and North Africa.

NATIONAL HOLIDAYS: April 27, Independence Day; Christian and Moslem holidays.

INFORMATION SOURCES: *In US*—Embassy of Sierra Leone, 1701 19th Street NW, Washington, D.C. 20009 (tel. 202/265-7700); Consulate General of Sierra Leone, 919 Third Avenue, 22nd Floor, New York, N.Y. 10022 (tel. 212/935-1701). *In Freetown*—National Tourist and Hotel Board, 28 Siaka Stevens Street; Scantravel (Scanship Ltd), Cline Town; Aureole Travel Agencies, Rawdon Street.

By *Philip M. Allen*

Sierra Leone's government and the international tourist industries are only beginning to consider the country's potential for tourism and they tend to concentrate almost exclusively on the mass appeal of its superb beaches. Until planning matures, Sierra Leone's facilities for travel will remain inferior to those of better-organized neighbors like Ghana, the Ivory Coast and the Gambia.

Today Sierra Leone can be recommended mainly to those individual travelers interested in the decadent elite Creole towns of the peninsula, the neglected urban communes of Freetown's slopes and the unexploited savanna of the interior.

The Creole communities of Freetown and neighboring villages on the peninsula of Sierra Leone were formed by thousands of former New World slaves and Africans freed from slave ships, all transported to West Africa by Britain. The country's name descends from a 16th century Portuguese description of the "wild hills" behind Freetown, on one of the largest natural harbors in the world. The Creole immigrants and a handful of European merchant settlers on the peninsula became middle-class subjects of the British Crown in 1808, and the trading territory behind the coasts was linked to the peninsula as a protectorate at the end of the century.

The entire country became independent on April 27, 1961. Ten years later, after a national referendum and several military changes of government, the civilian regime of Siaka Stevens declared Sierra Leone a republic within the Commonwealth. Stevens is the first and current president. He governs in an unsteady political atmosphere, under a state of emergency prolonged by decree through 1972 and with elections postponed from 1972 to 1973.

A national commission may recommend a change of name to Songhay or another patriotic African designation.

Sierra Leone's population includes about 100,000 Christian descendants of Freetown's Creole immigrants and some 650,000 Moslems; the majority are essentially animist—Mende-speaking people in the south, and Temne, Koranko, Susu, Limba and other smaller groups in the north and center. There are small communities of Europeans (mostly British) and mercantile Lebanese.

The colony-protectorate distinction survives, by the way, in a customary reference to Freetown and the peninsula as the "western area" and the interior territory as the "provinces."

National mines in the eastern interior yield about one-fourth the world's production of diamonds (gems and industrial stones). The smuggling of diamonds into Liberia and Guinea has been keeping Sierra Leone's earnings lower than they should be.

Iron ore from the Marampa area, bauxite, rutile and a variety of agricultural products from the well-watered interior constitute the remainder of the republic's economic wealth.

You can prepare for a visit to Sierra Leone by reading Christopher Fyfe's A History of Sierra Leone (Oxford University Press, 1962) and Martin Kilson's Political Change in a West African State (Harvard University Press, 1966). Freetown atmosphere emerges admirably but anonymously in Graham Greene's wartime novel The Heart of the Matter (Penguin) and his older Journey Without Maps (Heinemann, 1936, reprinted in 1961 by Viking Press). A.P. Kup's The Story of Sierra Leone (Cambridge University Press, 1964) is a charming book for Sierra Leonean schools.

Money Matters

The leone is technically worth one-half the pound sterling, but you invariably get less than full rates for your dollars. Banks are only slightly more generous in exchange than the hotels and restaurants. Barclays Bank of Sierra Leone maintains four offices in Freetown and eight more in the provinces. The State Bank of Sierra Leone is near the Post Office in an extremely handsome building. The Standard Bank of West Africa, affiliated with Chase Manhattan and the international Standard system, has offices in Freetown and at Fourah Bay College. Banks open at 8 am and close at 12:30 for the day (11 am on Saturday). Currency in your possession must be declared on arrival and departure and the equivalent of only Le 50 (about $65) can be taken out in bank notes of any nationality. So you should confine your wealth to travelers checks or bank drafts.

Freetown's cost of living is rising at about five per cent each year. Everything touched by tourists—accommodations, food and drink, transportation, medicines and cosmetics, film, even postcards—runs as high in price here as in the other inflation-ridden economies of West Africa.

Getting In and Out

Almost everybody enters Sierra Leone by the beautiful harbor of Freetown—even airborne travelers, since the international airport at Lungi is separated from the capital by a nice, hour-long ferry ride across the estuary. Sierra Leone Airways buses shuttle between the Paramount Hotel and

Lungi Airport to meet all incoming and departing flights. Travelers should ride the bus for it has priority on the ferries.

The port of Freetown receives passenger ships and freighters, which travelers may consider using for access and egress. Farrell Lines freighters arrive every two weeks with passengers from New York ($950 round trip). The Ghanaian Black Star Line sails more cheaply between Freetown and Canadian or Gulf ports. Elder Dempster Lines also carries passengers to and from Liverpool (two classes).

Travel by road from neighboring Guinea and Liberia proves wearying to all but the most robust motorists, and visas and customs formalities on the Guinea side of the border are particularly complicated (see chapter on Guinea).

Americans require visas for Sierra Leone and should not expect to get them at the airport.

Getting Around Within Sierra Leone

The government's Road Transport Corporation (RTC) acquired new equipment in 1971 when Sierra Leone changed to right-hand drive. Hence, despite a paucity of paved roads up-country and a constant traffic snarl in town, the daily bus service out of Freetown to Bo, Kono, Mattru, Segbwema, Makeni or Kenema is comfortable and safe. Avoid the perilous mammy-wagons unless your motive for travel is to enjoy prolonged, inexpensive human contact. The railroad system, which primarily served the mining industry, is now being scrapped in favor of anticipated improvements in the roads; its passenger service had already been allowed to deteriorate.

Taxis swarm over hilly Freetown. Their drivers take you anywhere for a price—which should definitely be agreed upon before starting out. A brief trip in town costs 40 Leonean cents (about 56 US cents), a one-way visit to the outskirts runs twice that much, and a 10-mile jaunt from midtown to Lumley Beach or Cape Sierra costs Le 2 (about $2.60). Drivers of the larger, newer taxis have been known to obtain as much as $40 for a full day's rental, but the visitor ought to bargain for about half that price. Hitchhiking is difficult amid the largely commercial traffic of Sierra Leone. Sierra Tours Company has cars for hire.

In addition to the ferries, there are small, decorated launches serving for transport on the estuary and up the few navigable miles of river behind Freetown.

Sierra Leone Airways operates regular round trip flights between Hastings Field, 14 miles from Freetown, and the provincial capitals. The company also charters 17-passenger Heron aircraft at high rates. Its offices at Delco House in Freetown act as agent for most other airlines serving West Africa. There is a branch office at the Paramount Hotel.

Little travel literature is yet available. Hans M. Zell's delightful *Freetown Vademecum* (published by the Fourah Bay College bookshop as a handbook for new faculty) has become a local collector's item. The Ministry of Information issues a useful promotional brochure titled *Sierra Leone in a Nutshell* (available through Sierra Leone embassies and consulates). A crudely edited *Sierra Leone Yearbook* produced annually by the Freetown *Daily Mail* is obtainable in Freetown. The rather under-equipped National Tourist and Hotel Board (28 Siaka Stevens Street, Freetown; tel. 67-25) plans to issue new folders. Travel agencies specialize in getting visitors in and out of the country, and in occasional one-day excursions for cruise ship passengers.

Where to Stay

Sierra Leone has a few hotels of modest international class, but their rates are high and food mainly deplorable. All are in the FREETOWN area. The newest and best place is the *Cape Sierra Hotel*, on a lovely beach 10 miles outside Freetown, waiting for a European tourist invasion. The attractive central building is flanked by three commodious boxes containing 75 rooms, all air-conditioned and with private baths. Rates are about $16.50 for single rooms and $28 for doubles, including breakfast, with a 10 per cent service charge. It offers a beach, swimming pool, casino and nightclub, crafts shop and nearby golf course. There's minibus service to town and a fishing boat for guests.

The kitchen is governed by an Austrian chef whose cuisine is superior to most in English-speaking West Africa, but service crawls. Lunch menus start at $3.50, dinners at $4.20.

The *Paramount Hotel* has dominated expatriate social life in Freetown for years. It perches on a ridge above the historic Cottonwood Tree, and has a good cloth shop, travel services, a quiet lounge and terrace bar, but the rooms are shabby and management is uninspired. Lifeless formality and the fussy clatter of "British" service pervade the dining room, where heavy "European" dishes cost about $3.50 and far superior African dishes are almost as dear. Air-conditioned rooms rent for about $20 (single) and $35 (double), suites from $46, including early morning tea and breakfast.

Service adds an automatic 10 per cent. Although registration forms admonish you not to tip, try to get a waiter or porter out of your room without his coin.

More modest hotels serving the Freetown area include *Brookfields*, with 44 rooms and eight chalets (some with private bath) renting from $10.80 (single) and $16.80 (double), including breakfast. Lunch menus start from $2.10, dinner from $2.80. Full pension is available from about $16 per day. Across the estuary, the *Lungi Airport Hotel* is a newly renovated establishment with 40 air-conditioned rooms, all with private bath, renting at $11.20 (single) and $16.80 (double), breakfast not included; meals are inexpensive (good African dishes can be ordered for about 70 US cents).

For even less expensive lodgings, try the *City Hotel*, a meeting place from Graham Greene's time when it had no competitors, or the *Lido*, the *Ratcliffe*, or the *Lamar* (which has the benefits of air-conditioning and good Lebanese food).

The only hotels in Sierra Leone's provinces are *Denby's* in the town of Bo and *Adam's* in MAGBURAKA, both rather primitive. You may try to find private lodgings with local residents, missionaries, secondary schools during vacations, or Peace Corps and Canadian CUSO personnel. Or obtain permission from district officers to use government rest-houses. These vary considerably in facilities and condition. Avoid the dilapidated rest-house at Shenge, but don't hesitate over the enormous, rather spooky barn with its splendid view at the Musaia Agricultural Research Station, or the charming rest-house at the Kasewe Forest Reserve. Freetown's Hotel and Tourist Board can identify rest-houses and the authorities to be addressed in seeking permission to use them.

Where and What to Eat

To escape from the monolithic weight of overseas British cooking, try the jollof rice, fufu, shrimps Freetown and other delicious African dishes at the *Paramount Hotel* (expensive), the *Lungi Airport Hotel*, the *Cline Town Club*, and *Queen's Restaurant* in FREETOWN. The more acceptable "European" restaurants include the *Cape Sierra Hotel*, the *Cape Club*, eight miles out of town on Whiteman's Bay, where you can get chicken, fish and chips and sandwiches served under palm trees—and dance in the evening; the *Atlantic Club*, on the beach one mile short of Cape Sierra, and *La Tropicana*, in the Roxy Theater building (center Freetown), which serves steaks and pepper chicken. Chinese food is available at *The Casino*, where the bar comes alive at night, and the *Cathay*, in Trelawney, which has an inexpensive lunch menu. The *Kit Kat Bar and Nightclub* opposite the Odeon Theater provides auspicious ambiance for meeting friends and getting to know Freetowners.

Freetown water tastes quite good, but so do the local beers, especially when mixed "half and half" with Guinness stout. Wines are overpriced.

Tipping depends on the quality of service and, since most waiters in Sierra Leone try hard, we usually offer about 10 per cent.

What to See and Do

Founded in 1792, FREETOWN now shows its age, its conglomerate population and its poverty. Few new buildings adorn the capital. The State Bank, the Post Office, and the Parliament Building are handsome hillside exceptions. Despite abundant running water along its slopes, Freetown possesses only rudimentary sanitation systems. Europeans reside in hilltop or beach refuges outside the tumbling town. Most of Freetown's colorful, balconied, West Indian style houses stand in a siege of shanties and sheds. They are worth looking at, as are a few old forts, churches, mosques, Lebanese shops and other modest features of an old city where several cultures met and settled down together.

The stalls, bars and markets of Freetown's several communes pulse with the errands and recreation of urban dwellers—especially in the early morning and evening when the center city shrivels up. Four-towered mosques are animated by the faithful at prayer and fretful young scholars. Handsome women stroll in lappas or miniskirts. Stalls are stocked with bright, cheap utilitariana, heaps of fish, cassava flour and spices. Exuberant urban folk art enlivens the signposts and advertisements for master barbers, "governing" tailors and "sympathetic" funeral homes. A blare of soul and high-life music accompanies the walker's steps through the Krootown, Kissy Road, Cline Town, Tower Hill and, farther out, Congo Town districts.

Near the huge and ancient Cottonwood Tree where emancipated exslaves received their new deeds of freedom is a tiny gem of a museum with a nice selection of soapstone images (nomoli), dyed and woven cloth, masks of the Bundu secret society, musical instruments, currencies, charms, canes and historical mementos.

Fourah Bay College, founded in 1827 by the British Church Missionary Society, nests high on the "wild mountain" overlooking town and bay. Now the main campus of the University of Sierra Leone, Fourah Bay has long been a training ground for clergy, teachers and other professionals from all of English-speaking West Africa.

Njala College, 100 miles east of Freetown, is the other, primarily agricultural, campus.

The national dance troupe, one of Africa's best, has had extensive international experience in its several years of existence, but manages nonetheless to remain close to its sources. The troupe dances for major tour groups and official occasions. The individual visitor has to be alert and lucky to attend a performance; ask about it when you get to town.

Freetown celebrates Moslem as well as Christian and national historical anniversaries. On the night of Idd al Fitr at the end of Ramadan, there is a parade of lanterns and illuminated kites through the city, with singing, dancing and conviviality throughout the night.

Out along the hilly and forested peninsula behind Freetown, quiet villages sporting noble names like Regent, Gloucester, Hastings, Waterloo and Wellington testify through broad streets and solid old houses to a prosperous time of colonial and Creole trade. The erstwhile slaving "factory" at Bunce Island in the river across from Freetown dates from 1670, although its present ruins are more recent. To reach the island, launches must pick their way with great care past submerged wrecks and rubble.

The slender peninsula has hills rising almost to 3,000 feet, and 30 miles of unpopulated beaches, most of them safe from sharks. Lumley Beach, one of the most idyllic in West Africa, will eventually be developed for tourists; for the time being its sands have few occupants. Across the estuary from Freetown, the villages around Lungi Airport contain handsomely decorated, square cement houses. Some of them— temples and mosques—bear pagoda-like upper stories with splashes of color on their walls.

There is some game on the up-country savanna, an alternation of hill country and grassland rising to rich forested plateaus at over 4,000 feet. Two game reserves are planned for the Koinadugu district in the far northeast.

Fine dancing and drumming can be observed at Rotifunk and Moyamba, southeast of Freetown, if district authorities are notified in advance of your interest in attending performances. Ramadan celebration in Moslem areas and the Sunday market at Koindu on the Liberian border (gorgeous tie-dye cloth) are especially interesting. But Mende and Susu initiation ceremonies can seldom be witnessed by outsiders (unless you have friends who invite you discreetly).

By applying for permission at the National Diamond Mining Company headquarters in Freetown you may be able to visit mining operations in the Sefadu-Yengema area 180 miles east of Freetown. Along the railroad line, 153 miles southeast of Freetown, the provincial capital and diamond buying center of Bo has little to offer travelers, but the Bo School has been an educational center for sons of the provincial elite since 1906. Farther on, 40 miles from the Liberian border, the boom village of Kenema, which mushroomed to a population of 10,000 during the diamond rush of the mid-50's, attracts a spirited variety of labor and market people. Kenema is also the site of the Forest Industries Corporation's furniture factory.

What to Buy

Mende and Temne masks are among the most sought-after styles of African sculpture, but good pieces long ago became hard to obtain. Unfortunately, their place has been assumed by cynical grotesques manufactured for tourists, rather than by honest modern work or decent reproductions of authentic styles. Thus there is little good carving on display in the stalls by the hotels and main post office of Freetown. Small steatite (soapstone) nomoli figures can still be found in Freetown, and occasionally in Mende country where they originate, but there are government restrictions on the export of nomoli or other carvings dating from earlier than 1939.

Sierra Leone cloth, however, is abundant. It is of excellent quality and design, and inexpensive (much of it selling for $2 per yard and less). There are elegant prints and batiks, subtle weaves with geometric motifs, and satin tie-dyes, often sold in two-yard by one-yard bolts called "lappas" (sarongs). Raffia is used for making hammocks. The Small Industries Centre on Tower Hill invites inspection of the manufacture of some of these fabrics and has a sales room.

Among valuable rarities offered in Freetown are hand-stitched Creole carpet slippers, colorful cloth kites, and handsome fruit baskets with geometric decoration.

The Arts and Crafts Centre on Water Street in Kissy dockyard has a fair selection. The tiny (and dingy) shop of the Musa Saccoh Brothers on Walpole Street contains a few first-rate items for low prices if you bargain vigorously. Reliable selections of Sierra Leone cloth can be found at higher prices in shops in the Paramount and Cape Sierra Hotels. Browse in the colorful Morgan Pharmacies, especially in the original store at Westmoreland and Upper Brook Streets. The best of several bookstores in Freetown is run by Fourah Bay College. Imported consumer goods are handled largely by the Lebanese entrepreneurs.

Local Attitudes

Political instability has given Sierra Leone an undeservedly negative reputation among foreigners. The government remains authoritarian and touchy, and Americans have been treated with unnecessary suspicion from time to time. These difficulties, however, do not seriously hamper relations between travelers and an essentially hospitable, friendly and tolerant population.

Weather, What to Wear, How Long to Stay

Sea breezes and the harmattan desert wind make January and February best for a Freetown visit. Shorts, slacks and cotton shirts or light dresses are all in order. Freetown businessmen and civil servants usually go without jackets but wear ties during the day. The Paramount Hotel and some of the clubs require a tie (but not a jacket) at dinner. Otherwise, sheer practicality should govern wardrobe decisions on this hot, humid coast and in the dry but warm interior.

Two or three days suffice for a conventional visit to Freetown and environs. By renting a taxi, or combining bus travel with hitchhiking, you can spend an interesting week exploring the peninsula, the beaches and neighboring creek country, and have time enough for Freetown, Lungi, Port Loko, Moyamba and other towns in the western area. Bus or air penetration into the provinces requires another four or five days to be worthwhile.

Communication

Among educated Sierra Leoneans, English is the customary language. Most coastal people use a pidgin dialect called Krio (Creole) and the majority of the interior's inhabitants speak no English at all. The Peace Corps maintains one of its larger programs here, with volunteers throughout the country. Domestic and international communications are heavily overworked but the telephone system is being improved. Freetown's press is in a most ragged state, specializing in sycophantic reporting of what the government wants the public to know, as well as opinion-mongering. *The Nation* is the liveliest of the bunch. A good radio network and a television service (confined to Freetown) broadcast standard information without much originality. You'll find friendly exchanges of information at these gathering places: Fourah Bay College, the British Council and USIS libraries, and the bars at the Paramount, City Hotel and Kit Kat Club.

Emergencies

Sierra Leone is no place for crises. Medical facilities here are below the standard of others in Africa. Freetown and Bo have the only specialized hospitals but missions and mining companies operate medical units in the provinces. There is a hospital for paying patients at Hill Station above Freetown and a large Protestant mission hospital at Segbwema. The Government Hospital at Kenema is ill-equipped. If your problem is urgent, better fly out to London or Dakar (Senegal).

The American Embassy and USIS offices are conveniently located just below the Cottonwood Tree in the center of Freetown on Walpole Street (tel. 6481).

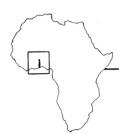

Togo

(République du Togo)

Profile

STATUS: Independent republic since April 27, 1960. Former German colony, later French trust territory.

SIZE: 21,850 square miles (about twice the size of Vermont). Population —2,000,000 (principal groups the Ewe-Mina and the Kabré).

GEOGRAPHY: 30 miles of coastline on Bight of Benin, Gulf of Guinea, extending northward to lagoons, mountains and wooded savanna. Principal towns—Lomé (capital, 120,000), Anecho (13,000), Palimé (18,000), Atakpamé (13,000), Sokodé (18,000).

CLIMATE: Two rainy seasons, April to July and late September to November. Temperatures in 70's and 80's all year, humidity high on coast.

LANGUAGES: French (official), some English in west, African languages.

CURRENCY: CFA franc. CFA 100 = 40 cents; $1.00 = CFA 245.

VISAS: Required. Available from Embassy of Togo and Permanent Mission of Togo to the UN. Fees—for visit of one to 14 days, $1.80; 15 to 30 days, $2.70; one to three months, $5.40; three to six months, $10.80; 50 per cent charge for multiple entries. Three passport photos needed.

AIRPORT: Lomé Airport (LFW), three miles from city. Linked by regular shuttle with Cotonou (Dahomey), less frequently with other West African capitals and Paris. Airport departure taxes—domestic, CFA 100 (40 cents); within Africa, CFA 500 ($2); outside Africa, CFA 1,500 ($6). Taxi into city, CFA 300 ($1.20).

NATIONAL HOLIDAYS: January 13, National Day; April 27, Independence Day.

INFORMATION SOURCES: *In US*—Embassy of Togo, 2208 Massachusetts Avenue NW, Washington, D.C. 20008 (tel. 202/234-4212); Permanent Mission of Togo to the UN, 800 Second Avenue, New York, N.Y. 10017 (tel. 212/490-3455). *In Lomé*—Office National du Tourisme, Rue d'Anecho, P.O. Box 1177 (tel 40-26); Touring Club, Rue de la Mission, P.O. Box 61 (tel. 2647).

By Philip M. Allen

This slender chip off the old imperial block is a favorite of connoisseurs. Pressed between larger occupants on the Bight of Benin, Togo seems sunnier and milder than most of its neighbors and less expensive for visitors. It has an exuberant, articulate population, decent accommodations and sufficient distractions to charm many an unsuspecting transient into prolonging his stay.

German Togoland emerged out of Europe's scramble for territory a century ago. Even then it was little more than a corridor projecting 370 miles northward from trading beachheads at Anecho and Togoville. But the World War I peace settlements divided that sliver into western British and eastern French mandates under the League of Nations. Britain's jurisdiction ended in 1956 with the controversial incorporation of British Togoland into what became Ghana. The eastern trust territory, after a period of association with French West Africa, attained independence in 1960.

Togo's narrow stretch of beachfront, lagoon, mountain and wooded savanna is populated by two million people from some two dozen ethnic groups. Fishing villages occupy 30 miles of palm-lined beach. Verdant riverbeds are crossed up-country by the Fazao and Togo mountain ranges. In pockets of this topography are the Ewe, Mina and Adja-Quatchi people of the south, the Akposso, Bédéré and Adele in the center, the Kabré, Cotokoli, Bassari and Hausa of the north. Impressive regal pageantry and occasional outbursts of animosity affirm the identity of each.

Their land is blessed by a pleasant summery climate and deposits of exceedingly pure phosphate behind the coastal lagoon at Anecho. A deep-water free port was opened in 1968 to handle phosphate and eventually iron ore shipments—under protest from neighboring Dahomey, which had hoped to see Togo's economy joined to her own less-endowed system. The few social and economic advantages that might have brought these two Benin mini-states into union have virtually vanished: each now has its own embryonic university, its national airline, its own foreign trade and diplomatic service. They have, however, agreed to co-operate on border policing and customs control. With its free port, its non-discriminatory trade policy and low import duties, Togo enjoys a cost of living considerably below those of high-tariff Dahomey and Ghana. As a result, their common borders are repeatedly penetrated by contraband, to the benefit of the Togolese balance of "trade" and the irritation of her struggling protectionist neighbors.

Nevertheless, prosperity approaches the Togolese with wary steps. Their nation is too small to support an industrial market, too diverse to be easily united. It is still susceptible to the tugs of Ghana on their common Ewe populations and to the blandishments of the French on behalf of Dahomey. Wages are improving, but salaried labor makes up barely five per cent of the work force. Small cash crop farmers are gaining from expanded production of cocoa, coffee and palm products, but these exports remain vulnerable to international market fluctuations, and most agriculture in Togo still amounts to subsistence planting and nomadic herding. Both Germany and France are providing substantial economic assistance but the phosphate industry, the port and other objects of Western aid have yet to prove their value to the average Togolese.

Progress has been costly in political terms and beset with uncertainties. Togo's only democratic regime collapsed in January, 1963, with the assassination of the strongly nationalist Ewe President Sylvanus Olympio, first victim of what was to become an epidemic of African coups d'état. Following a period of civilian government propped up by the military, Togo's army reasserted its will in January, 1967. Gen. Etienne Eyadema, a 26-year-old corporal when he led the coup against Olympio, governs as president of a single-party state friendly to France, in alliance with a new non-political, technocratic generation of civilians and military elite. A northern Moslem, Eyadema has a tight hold on Togolese politics and has stilled chronic antagonisms between the southern Ewe-Mina people, part-Christian, largely animist, and accustomed to dominating, and the Kabré-Losso of the underprivileged north.

German and French visitors are increasing in the little country that manages, despite its fragility, to exhibit a smiling and sturdy personality. As much as any country in West Africa, except perhaps Liberia, Togo is open to the initiative of both young people and strong women—in the marketplace, in education and in government.

There's little literature on the country in English. You might have a look at the Togo chapter in Guy de Lusignan's *French-Speaking Africa Since Independence* (Praeger, 1969).

Money Matters

Togo participates in the West African CFA system without special quirks. Travelers checks pass smoothly and dollars are accepted gladly in many places, but credit cards are virtually useless. There is no bank at the airport, but the Union Togolaise de Banques, the Crédit Lyonnais, the Banque Nationale de Paris, the Deutsche Bank and the Banque Internationale d'Afrique Occidentale (BIAO, partly owned by First National City of New York) are open from 7:30 to noon and from 2:30 to 5 pm, Monday through Friday. Comparatively low prices prevail.

Getting In and Out

Lomé, the capital, and Anecho are both on the handsome highway that follows the coast from Ghana through Dahomey to western Nigeria. Americans require visas even to cross Togo in direct transit, so you might as well stay awhile, if only to amortize the nuisance of visa procurement. Most surface traffic enters and leaves the little country by this road, although devotees of landscape, camping and smuggling often find alternatives. There's the dusty north-south axis between Lomé and Upper Volta, as well as the former British Togoland road which crosses the Ghana border near Palimé, heads northwest toward Kpandu on the great Volta River in Ghana, and connects with Accra and Kumasi.

The new free port receives only a trickle of passengers on ore-carriers and other cargo vessels. Your chances are better if you go to Tema (Ghana), Lagos (Nigeria) or Cotonou (Dahomey), which get more frequent passenger and passenger-cargo ships. Taxis and rented cars are readily available between these ports and Togo.

Likewise with air travel: instead of wrenching itineraries to accommodate the rare flights in and out of Lomé, it's far more agreeable to use the airports in Accra or Cotonou and drive to Lomé in a couple of hours. Be sure you have visas for all countries touched en route and that the car or taxi engaged at the airport is documented for border crossing.

Getting Around Within Togo

Few roads are paved other than the east-west coastal highway, and only a few miles of the road between Lomé and the north. Teletaxi (Boulevard Circulaire, P.O. Box 1542, Lomé) rents cars with or without driver at reasonable rates. You can also rent vehicles in Lomé at the Garage du Centre (tel. 30-10) and the Syndicat National des Transporteurs Routiers (Rue Champ de Courses). Hitchhiking is practical along the coast and around the capital, less so in the sparsely traveled interior. Mammy-trucks and collective taxis crisscross the entire territory at low fares and with minimal comforts.

The national railway between Lomé and Blitta in the center traverses a pretty countryside for 170 miles. These trains often carry private automobiles over the rugged stretches of hill country around Atakpamé, where the roads north become better. Buses and bush taxis also shuttle between Blitta and Sokodé. A rail spur connects Lomé with Anecho (27 miles) and the phosphate installations. A third track runs northwest from the capital toward the Ghana border as far as Palimé (73 miles), crossing the rich farmlands of the Ewe people.

Air Togo flies to Sokodé and to Sansanné-Mango between the central mountains and the picturesque northern plains. It charters flights as well, but ground transportation predominates in Togo.

The Office National du Tourisme, the Touring Club, Suvuto Travel Agency (16 rue d'Alsace-Lorraine) and Chargeurs Réunis (Rue Maréchal-Gallieni, P. O. Box 34, tel. 26-11) can help arrange travel from Lomé. Togo does very little publicizing of itself; a few modest brochures are available through its embassies and in the literature of the Conseil de l'Entente, the Abidjan-based association of Upper Volta, Niger, Dahomey, Togo and the Ivory Coast.

Where to Stay

Without a vast gamut of styles to choose from, Togo manages to be accommodating and hospitable. LOMÉ's major hotel is Le Bénin, a big, rambling place one mile outside the city center in a setting of palms and white sand, with a swimming pool, full air-conditioning, sports facilities and a terrace bar which looks out to the sea. Le Bénin's rooms, which should be more comfortable than they are, rent from $8 for singles through $26 for suites. In the center of town there's the older and less sporty Hôtel du Golfe with its delightful courtyard restaurant and scent of Lomé's constant humidity in the rooms; a double room with air-conditioning and a sitting room rents for about $12 (half price without air-conditioning). The Hôtel de la Plage, on the beach not far from Le Bénin, offers rooms without air-conditioning for $4 to $6. L'Auberge Provençale, on the west side of town virtually at the Ghanaian border, has five rooms at reasonable rates.

Twenty miles outside Lomé, the Hôtel-Restaurant du Lac has three chalets in a garden, with lake sporting facilities, for $6 per person. On the coast road by the new port, the Foyer des Marins (seamen's club) offers clean, comfortable, basic facilities for about $2.50 per person. In a similarly moderate category are the spartan accommodations for $2 at Edith's Inn, a former Peace Corps hostel run by former PCV's Edith and Charlie Simpson. It's a favorite with young Americans. The government constructed 14 handsome villas with gardens on the beach east of Lomé to house chiefs of state at the 1972 African-Malagasy Common Organization (OCAM) meeting; these are to be the nucleus of a 250-room tourist complex, but are reserved now for "important" guests.

Hotels are rare in the provinces. They include very small establishments at ATAKPAMÉ, PALIMÉ and SOKODÉ. With official permission, you may bring bedding with you to government rest-houses at TSÉVIÉ, MISSAHOË, SOKODÉ, and BASSARI in the hilly hunting country, and at

LAMA-KARA, KANDÉ and DAPANGO in the northlands. A few church missions and volunteer groups (American, French and German) take in travelers if requested. If you're backpacking, stop at Peace Corps headquarters in Lomé or at Edith's Inn for advice.

Where and What to Eat

Food is good in both the African and French hostelries of LOMÉ—especially at Le Lac, 18 miles east of the city. Good meals can be obtained for upwards of $3 in the patio of the Golfe in midtown, at L'Auberge Provençale on the sea, Las Vegas, the Alsatian Mini-Brasserie, and the 421, which features high-life music and dancing. The 4e Zone has Chinese food, Le Ramatou has African dishes and the Paris-Snack a French menu with music. The Foyer des Marins serves German meals—sausage, sauerkraut, German beer—for about $1.50. Edith's Inn, filled with young people, has inexpensive menus with beer on tap, and they can also dish up a hamburger, pizza, pork with fried rice and banana splits for nostalgic Americans.

Water in Lomé is relatively safe, but mineral water and the excellent Germanic Benin beer (on tap at several places in town) are preferable. Tipping beyond the usual established service charge is unusual in Togo, but a few extra francs should be given whenever service has been particularly good.

Outside Lomé restaurants are rare, but all provincial hotels cook and think French, and all towns have their canteens or cook shops. Many travelers pack provisions, including bottled water, to supplement the fruit, eggs, peanuts and cereals usually found along the road.

What to See and Do

A good deal of travel pleasure is concentrated into Togo's slender frame particularly during festive seasons (July in the north, elsewhere at various times). All paths ultimately lead to the sands of LOMÉ, the modest capital, a relatively new town at the border of former British Togoland (now Ghana). Created a capital city in 1920 by the French, Lomé took precedence over the old slave port of Anecho which had been used by the German administration. It is simple, genial, intimate with both sea and lagoon, hardly a metropolis in any sense, but one of West Africa's most pleasant capitals.

Although the town was spruced up for the OCAM meeting in 1972, some of its streets are still sand and rut. A railroad bisects Lomé into business areas with family compounds, and an administrative middle-class residential district to the west. The monuments of national administration stand along the Route Circulaire. An impressive Independence Monument raises its arms in lyrical solemnity—the dance of Africa hovering above the new juridical state. Flowering trees and gardens enliven the middle-class quarters on the west, and the fenced compounds of Togolese family life sparkle with sounds and odors in the center of town. Morning market is especially lively on Wednesdays and Saturdays. There is an incipient national university modeled on French traditions in the capital. Lomé night life pulsates without pretense, absorbing Western modes into the beat of urban African high-life music. A variety of bars includes Le Rêve, Watusi, Maquina-Loca and 421, Edelweiss, Edith's Inn, Mini-Brasserie, 4ᵉ Zone and the Benin Hotel's Seventh Heaven.

There are no guided tours in Togo. A half-day's taxi ride around Lomé with stops should cost about $10 after some bargaining.

Along the coast road, the chain of palm groves and thatched fishing villages leads past the ancient Portuguese and French slave center at Porto Seguro to ANECHO, an inland port at the edge of a productive agricultural and mineral region. Behind the coast, Lake Togo is part of the extended lagoon system that parallels the Benin coast from Nigeria to Ghana. It is well stocked with fish, has a good bathing beach and facilities for boating. Nearby is a ritual-rich sacred forest by the historic village of Togoville.

Togo's landscape opens out to the northwest in the direction of PALIMÉ, surrounded by hill country producing coffee, cocoa and fruit. There is an interesting Tuesday and Saturday market here. The 300-foot cascades of Kpémé seven miles north of Palimé, the forest around Missahoë and Chateau Viale, and a two-hour climb up 3,500-foot Mount Agou all recommend this western stretch of Togo to weekenders, explorers or leisurely motorists.

The straighter northern route leads from Lomé through TsÉVIÉ, where a brief detour brings you to the colorful fishermen's village of Abobo, with animist priest monasteries and a lively tradition of dance and drum. The road climbs from Tsévié through a mountainous world of coffee and cocoa plantations and tea groves around ATAKPAMÉ; the Teacher Training College (Ecole Normale) here operates interesting experimental programs in languages and mathematics.

This fertile rolling land becomes semi-desert northward around SOKODÉ in the cattle country of the Cotocoli people. At Bafilo the road passes the great Aledjo Fault, a deep gash in the granite, and then enters little LAMA-KARA, industrious granary of northern Togo. Here, in a bracing climate, volcanic hills rise above curiously pockmarked river and lake palisades. They hold the villages of the Kabré, who celebrate the cycles of nature and of youth and age with dance, drum and sport. Their most exciting festivals and wrestling tournaments occur in July and August.

A difficult track leads to NIAMTOUGOU, which has a massive market every six days, then passes the Keran gorges between the Fazao cliffs of Togo and the Atakora range in Dahomey. The landscape around KANDÉ is a kaleidoscope of rock, grass and baobab, with an intriguing variety of people and fortified villages on the rim of Togolese savanna.

What to Buy

If Togo is disappointing at all, it is in the quality of indigenous goods for sale. The markets at Niamtougou, Atakpamé, Lama-Kara and Sokodé exhibit worthy items of local artisanry, but most good work is minor in key—finely carved stools, tables and boxes, as well as some clay modeling and basketry. Openwork silver jewelry is elegant, and you may be attracted by certain idiomatic novelties of local craftsmanship—including comic masks cut from coconut shells, intricately linked wooden "marriage chains," anthropomorphic dish lids, the graceful aklama statuettes of the Ewe people, and Siamese-twinned figures in vase or ashtray form.

The brass and bronze, religious carving, ivory, bone figures, and much of the jewelry and printed cloth sold near the hotels usually originate in Dahomey, Upper Volta or some other West African cultural fountainhead. Still their prices in Lomé may well be most reasonable after earnest bargaining. Start your search at the Mamas Galerie de l'Art Nègre. For textiles, try the Lomé market and, if in search of Kente cloth from Ghana and other chic, seek out a charitable women's shop called (ugh!) Togo-à-Gogo. Imported beverages (including whiskey), clothing and electrical appliances are cheaper here than in other parts of West Africa. Shops are open from 8 to noon and 3 to 6 pm, except Saturday afternoon.

Local Attitudes

An easygoing people accustomed to foreigners, the Togolese impose few taboos on the traveler. Religious ceremonies and people at their tasks can be photographed, but a request for permission is always appropriate. Americans enjoy a favorable reputation among Togolese who know us mainly through an effective Peace Corps program.

Weather, What to Wear, How Long to Stay

Visits to Togo are usually part of larger itineraries encompassing Nigeria, Ghana, Ivory Coast and possibly other countries. Once West African nations develop cooperative one-way car rental facilities with border-crossing conveniences to match, Togo might well become a kind of Switzerland or Luxembourg for continental travelers. For now, the options are untidy or expensive, involving round trip car renting, one-way taxi or rail passage.

Count on at least three days around the coast, two days on a circuit to Palimé, and two more for the road-rail exit into the north, ending either in Upper Volta or at the Pendjari Park. In any case, don't merely scoot by air over the country, even if you must travel in the rough rains and relative heat of the spring (August and September are the best months).

The humid warmth of the coast presents no special challenge in selecting a wardrobe. You can choose freely between comfort and style, and probably will want a little of both. Like Ghanaians, town Togolese dress smartly in their traditional styles, and many young Westerners affect these handsome prints, weaves and brocades without inhibition. On the hills and in the northern plains, sweaters are necessary for evenings, especially when the winter harmattan is blowing.

Communication

Togo had its brief German period and then 40 years under France. It calls itself polylingual, but only with the educated can one communicate easily in a European language. Some Togolese, especially the Ewe in the Lomé-Palimé area, understand a little English, thanks to Ghana's proximity and to scattered Peace Corps personnel. (The Ewe have their own highly developed literary culture, interesting in itself.) Educated Togolese, of course, speak French, and can be both helpful and entertaining. Thus, with modest facility in French or the help of a guide, Americans should have no problem getting around in Togo.

Information about what's going on is provided by the *Togo Presse*, a conscientious, informative newspaper edited by Polycarpe Johnson.

Telephone and telegraph connections are sometimes satisfactory, sometimes not.

Emergencies

Hospitals and medical posts on the coasts and around the major towns are adequate for small problems. There is telephone service from post offices for emergencies. The American Embassy and Peace Corps headquarters are located behind the business area of Lomé, Rue Vauban, (tel. 29-91).

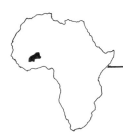

Upper Volta

(République de Haute-Volta)

STATUS: Independent republic since August 5, 1960. Formerly part of French West Africa.

SIZE: 105,900 square miles (about the size of Colorado). Population— 5,500,000. More than half are Mossi or related; 17 per cent are Moslem, 10 per cent Christian.

GEOGRAPHY: Plateau savanna, landlocked, 500 miles from Gulf of Guinea coast. Principal towns—Ouagadougou (capital, 150,000), Bobo-Dioulasso (80,000), Koudougou (35,000).

CLIMATE: Uniformly hot and dry, minor variations between river valleys in south and virtual Sahara in north. For most of the year the temperature range is from 90 to over 100 degrees, dropping 20 degrees at night. Rainy season May to October (especially heavy in August).

LANGUAGES: French (official), Moré (Mossi), other African languages.

CURRENCY: West African CFA franc. CFA 100 = 40 cents; $1.00 = CFA 245.

VISAS: Required. Available from Voltan Embassy in Washington and Permanent Mission of Upper Volta to the UN. Fee $2. Two passport photos needed. Allow 48 hours. Available from French consulates wherever Upper Volta is not represented.

AIRPORT: Borgo Airport (OUA), five miles from Ouagadougou. Infrequently linked with Paris, Abidjan, Dakar and Niamey. There are taxis and Indépendance, Buffet and Ricardo hotel buses into city.

671

NATIONAL HOLIDAYS: August 5, Independence Day; December 11, Republic Day; Christian and Moslem holidays.

INFORMATION SOURCES: *In US*—Embassy of Upper Volta, 5500 16th Street NW, Washington, D.C. 20011 (tel. 202/726-0992); Permanent Mission of Upper Volta to the UN, 866 Second Avenue, 6th floor, New York, N.Y. 10017 (tel. 212/758-1595). *In Ouagadougou*—Office du Tourisme, Hôtel de l'Indépendance, P.O. Box 624 (tel. 28-01); Socopao, P.O. Box 379 (tel. 26-25).

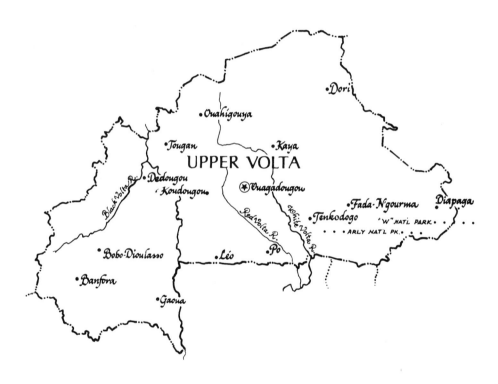

By Philip M. Allen

For a country relatively unconcerned about travel and tourism, Upper Volta has quite a bit to say for itself.

Arid, landlocked, overpopulated, pre-industrial and poor, plagued from independence (1960) through 1965 by a prodigal political regime, this Sudanic republic of five and a half million Voltans (Voltaïcs) owes most of its livelihood to luckier coastal territories. Upper Volta is used to seeing its best manhood migrate for jobs to the Ivory Coast and Ghana. Droves of Voltan cattle take to the southerly roads every week, to be re-fattened and then slaughtered in the stockyards of Abidjan and Accra. Manganese, copper, iron and bauxite are eventually to be mined, but France calls this tune, and Ivory Coast has the seaport. Precious water filters through eroding grasslands to the great Volta Dam in Ghana. Upper Volta itself earns only the remittances received from its stronger partners for these vital but unimposing exports.

But with knowledge, luck and some courage, the traveler can penetrate beyond these discouraging realities into a proud past, a vital culture and a pleasant country of savanna and open forest populated by dignified, gifted and energetic people. In Ouagadougou, the capital's Mossi people still celebrate their centuries of imperial influence over these savannas; their emperor, the Moro Naba, remains a socio-political factor in the young republic. Other kingdoms rose and fell in the territory, but half the Voltan nation is Mossi or closely related. The remainder include Bobo, Lobi and Mendé-speaking people, the Dioula in the south and west, the Gurmanché grain farmers in the east, and the Moslem Fulani, Tuareg (Berbers) and Bella in the north.

Politically and culturally, the Mossi held firm against Moslem invasions, but one-sixth of the Voltan population became Moslem during the epoch when the three Volta Rivers were crossed and re-crossed by traders, slavers and marauders. Less than 10 per cent are Christian.

Following its conquest of the western Sudan, France "pacified" the Upper Voltan regions over a 15-year period, ultimately incorporating them into the Senegal-Niger colony in 1904. In 1919 France conferred on Upper Volta the status of an overseas territory, but in 1932 the country was dismembered and parceled out to wealthier neighbors. It was put back together again in 1947.

The highly respected Ouezzin Coulibaly led Upper Volta's political revival, as part of the moderately nationalist Rassemblement Démocratique Africain (RDA) movement. But Coulibaly died before the new republic obtained its independence in 1960 together with the majority of France's African possessions. He was succeeded by flamboyant President

Maurice Yameogo, whose self-indulgence and inefficacy brought labor unions and other demonstrators into the streets in 1966. The result was a nationalistic military regime of implacable austerity under Colonel (now General) Sangoulé Lamizana. In late 1970 the military regime re-opened the avenues of parliamentary politics, permitting multiparty elections and the establishment of a civilian administration headed by Prime Minister Gérard Kango Ouedraogo (a hallowed family name among the Mossi). Lamizana remains chief of state.

The three Volta rivers—White, Black and Red—flow through a predominantly flat plain that is green with foliage in the southern valleys, brown with rushing torrents during the summer rains, beige with millet and sorghum at harvest time, and gray with livestock along the sloping hills. Pockets of the southeast and southwest have quantities of game, although the safari conditions cannot compare with those of East Africa or even those of nearby Chad and Cameroon. Towns like Bobo-Dioulasso (familiarly known as Bobo), Kaya and Ouagadougou (Ouaga) flower in season, but their heat is almost always unseasonable.

The best reasons for visiting Upper Volta come from interest in the preservation of an historical and cultural dignity that is rare in the former colonies of the French. The classic text through which to approach this kind of travel experience is Elliott P. Skinner's *The Mossi of Upper Volta, the Political Development of a Sudanese People* (Stanford University Press, 1964).

Money Matters

There are no special problems in Upper Volta's currency regulations, but no special conveniences either. The CFA franc, shared with the Ivory Coast, Senegal and other ex-French territories, floats here with French support at around CFA 245 to the dollar. Ouagadougou has branches of the overseas French banks—Banque Internationale d'Afrique Occidentale (BIAO), partly owned by the First National City Bank of New York and the Banque Nationale de Paris (BNP). They're open five mornings a week. Hotels have exchange facilities; airports do not.

Geographical isolation, low consumer demand, and monopoly commerce help keep the cost of living high in this impoverished, import-dependent economy.

Getting In and Out

Upper Volta is a traditional but neglected crossroads for interior Africa. Ouagadougou is joined three times a week by jet flights from Paris,

Abidjan (Ivory Coast) and Niamey (Niger). Twice-a-week flights cross the western Sudan from Dakar (Senegal) and Bamako (Mali). The latter also stop at Bobo-Dioulasso, the western commercial center of Upper Volta. Travelers cannot fly into or out of Upper Volta without passing through one of these capitals of the French-speaking world.

A rough road crosses Upper Volta from Mali in the west to Niger in the east, branching off for Abidjan in the Ivory Coast. There are northern dirt roads linking Upper Volta with the trans-Saharan routes via Gao (Mali) and Niamey, as well as a good paved road from Ouagadougou to Ghana's main north-south axis. Compagnie Transafricaine buses run twice weekly between Upper Voltan cities and Abidjan, Bamako, and Niamey, providing rugged, lengthy but exhilarating contact with the West African interior. There is no border-crossing bus service into Ghana (not part of the French-speaking world), but you can take collective taxis across the frontier at Po, as thousands of Voltan laborers do, or pay for a ride in a truck.

Or else rent a car in Ghana and drive to Ouaga and back.

A slow, exotic train (the Abidjan-Niger) travels 700 miles in 27 hours every other day across the kaleidoscopic West African landscape between Abidjan and Ouagadougou. It climbs from the forests of the Ivory Coast through the plateau escarpment and dry savanna of the Senoufo people to Bobo-Dioulasso and Ouagadougou. First-class accommodations in a sleeper-car (couchette) cost about $38 one way. Few travelers have time or the inclination for a round trip. Even strict budgeters with gregarious motives tend to choose the couchette, which is $11 more than the basic coach fare ($27 first class, about $10 in second). Meals cost extra but the food is quite good.

Small charter aircraft bring passengers over the borders into and out of the Arly Game Reserve, as well as the Dahomean Pendjari Park at Porga and the Niger River "W" National Parks. However you travel, you will need visas for all countries touched.

Getting Around Within Upper Volta

Road travel around Upper Volta is for the hardy voyager with a sturdy vehicle, and even then only in the dry season from September to June. Transafricaine buses cover the rural network between towns, as do Renault mammy-trucks and collective bush taxis with heavy loads of passengers and merchandise. The Desplats Company in Ouagadougou rents Renaults and Peugeots at rates from $10.80 to $12.40 a day (50 free kilometers) plus 8 cents a kilometer and 15 per cent tax. Air-conditioned Peugeots hire for $14 to $16 in town, $18 to $20 (including an obligatory chauffeur) in the bush. Customers pay for gas at about 80 cents a gallon. Land Rovers at Arly Park rent for $48 a day. These rates reflect the rigors of Upper Volta's roads, the scarcity of spare parts and good maintenance, and the high price of fuel.

Taxis are unmetered. A normal run within city limits costs 50 CFA (about 20 cents). For anywhere farther you must bargain before the cab starts off. Hitchhikers sometimes starve before a ride comes along; better pay for the Transafricaine.

The railway to the coast also runs shuttles between Ouagadougou and Bobo-Dioulasso on a daily schedule ($8 first class one way). Air Afrique and Air Volta offer regular flights between the two towns (one hour, $43.20 one way). Air Volta and the Aero-Club of Ouagadougou charter flights to the country's 30 smaller airfields ($115 an hour for five- or six-seat Cherokees).

Official information helps only slightly in Upper Volta. The government Office du Tourisme, based at Ouagadougou's Hôtel de l'Indépendance, sponsors tours and has a modicum of travel literature in French. The Syndicat d'Initiative at Bobo (Box 166) can be helpful in the west. The Socopao Agency, affiliated with the SCAC system, arranges travel in Ouaga (P.O. Box 379; tel. 26-25), Bobo (Box 319) and Koudougou (Box 86). Socopao also operates the hunting lodge at Arly.

Hotel bars and swimming pools, stocked with affable if somewhat cynical expatriates and Voltan elites, can be veritable fountains of information and cautionary advice if you have a gift for mingling—but keep a grain of salt on hand.

Where to Stay

Public lodgings are limited for the most part to Ouagadougou, Bobo-Dioulasso and the game parks, except for rudimentary rest-houses in a dozen smaller towns. The landscape ranger should bring tenting and bedding gear with him when he penetrates the northlands and the east.

In OUAGADOUGOU the *Hôtel de l'Indépendance*, large, air-conditioned, jerry-built, is virtually monopolized by the coming and going of Europeans and affluent Africans. Single rooms rent from $10 to $14, double rooms from $14 to $18 in the main building and almost twice that much in the private, comfortable bungalows across the swimming pool. These prices include service and taxes, but not breakfast. The hotel does not accept credit cards.

Less expensive, less conspicuous, but clean and quiet lodgings are available at the *Buffet-Hôtel de la Gare* (run by the railways) in the center of Ouagadougou. It has bungalows and a swimming pool, as well as superior food. Price is $11 a room, single or double, not including breakfast; 10 per cent service or taxes; no credit cards. The *Hôtel Central*, a small establishment on the marketplace, charges $7.50 to $8 plus breakfast, 10 per cent service and taxes. Diners Club cards are accepted.

Outside Ouagadougou near a water reservoir, the pleasant *Ricardo Restaurant*, a sporty nightspot, has six air-conditioned rooms for $8 to $10, and a swimming pool. Ricardo offers transportation to airport and town whenever possible, but you'll feel marooned there without your own vehicle.

In Bobo-Dioulasso, the centrally located *Royan* has a dozen adequate, air-conditioned rooms for upwards of $10, plus service and taxes. It has a swimming pool and snack bar but no restaurant. The *Hôtel Provençal* is cheaper. Socopao's *Hôtel d'Arly* in the National Park has air-conditioned bungalows for $6 (plus breakfast, 10 per cent service and taxes). Meals cost from $4, full daily pension is $7.50 a person (you pay a $4 supplement if occupying a bungalow alone). There is a swimming pool.

Outside of an occasional spare bed at a government lycée or training school in a major town, there are few cheap lodgings in Upper Volta unless you are invited to stay with a Voltan family, or Peace Corps or Canadian CUSO Volunteer. Government bungalows and dormitories at Diapaga (on the tri-national Niger "W" Park) and in the Arly Reserve, 45 miles from Diapaga, are open from early December to the end of April. They offer a minimum of comfort for approximately $2 a night, with simple menus at moderate prices. The camps are often heavily booked in advance of the season. For reservations write directly to the Direction des Eaux et Forêts, Ministère de l'Economie Nationale, Ouagadougou. Except for the campement at Fada N'Gourma, the government's other rest-houses (gîtes) are shabby.

Where and What to Eat

Good Voltan beef or chicken, some river fish and vegetables, rice and local fruits are expensive in European restaurants, less so elsewhere. Anything in a bottle, from North African and French wines to soft drinks, mineral water and imported beer, runs up the tab. Unfiltered water should always be shunned, but local beer (Bravolta) is reasonable.

In Ouagadougou, meals at the *Central* and *Buffet* hotels are slightly cheaper than those at the *Indépendance* (about $4 to $6 as opposed to $6 or $8 for à la carte service, excluding beverage). Fixed menus run about $3.50 everywhere. *Ricardo's* Spanish specialties (order in advance) and the French food at the *Eau Vive* are about the best in and around the capital. Good, cheaper meals are available at the *Croix du Sud* on the road to Po and the *Don Camillo* in town.

At Bobo, the *Eau Vive, Auberge* and the *Normandie* are good. When at home, Voltans cook tempting combinations of millet or cassava, fish and meat, peppers and other spices. Restaurants seldom feature such dishes, but some will gladly oblige if you request an "African dish" in advance. There are also the usual cheap West African canteens around marketplaces throughout the country, especially those with Transafricaine bus stops.

What to See and Do

The vast majority of Upper Volta's visitors come to transact business in the two main towns. You should reserve time for a bit of cross-country travel and/or hunting, however—particularly from January through April when the tall grasses have dried sufficiently in the eastern parks, the southwest and the Black Volta basin.

Once in town, inquire about the traditional festivals with music, dance and horsemen. They may occur in November for harvest celebrations, around February in Islamic areas celebrating the end of Ramadan, in April for the Moslem tabaski (sheep) feast, or at various times on a shifting calendar for initiation and fertility ceremonies.

OUAGADOUGOU rambles uncertainly around its administrative axis (wistfully called the Champs Elysées). Elite life is centered at the Indépendance, but the focus of capital tradition is the palace of the Mossi king, the Moro Naba. The building itself has little beauty but visitors can obtain permission there (at the Secrétariat) to attend a weekly re-enactment of the outdoor "Naba goes to war" ceremony every Friday morning at seven. Accompanied by royal musicians, courtly pomp and venerable regalia, the Moro Naba ("Sun on Earth") and most of the Mossi aristocracy of the capital play their hereditary roles in homage to an unforgotten past.

French-speaking guides are sometimes available for visitors.

Ouagadougou's National Museum, although neglected, has a good sample of the rich artistic production of these savannas. A large neo-Romanesque Catholic cathedral stands near the palace. Modern European offices and residences co-exist with the flat-roofed banco (adobe) dwellings of the Mossi. The vast, elegant covered city market will thrill all six senses.

Although Upper Volta has no full-scale university yet, the government has tired of seeing Voltan students expelled (usually on political grounds) from universities in places like Abidjan and Dakar. With massive French assistance, the capital's Centre d'Etudes Supérieures (Lettres) is to evolve into a national university.

A few miles outside Ouagadougou, city dwellers stroll or picnic in the so-called Bois de Boulogne, another bit of nostalgic nomenclature. Farther out to the north and west, the grasslands are interrupted by lakes, streams, cascades and marshes, populated by small game animals and birds. There are elephants and baboons south of the capital on the road to Ghana. At SABOU, 50 miles down the road toward Bobo-Dioulasso, semi-tame crocodiles bathe in the pools and snap at chickens tugged on fishing lines by wading children.

BOBO itself gives the visitor a concentrated view of Sudanic urban life and custom in action. It is an old trading center for slaves, spices, kola nuts and gold. Now brisk commerce is conducted by a variety of people in colorful dress at animated markets, amid a solid architecture that includes a delightful porcupine-towered mosque. The strong religious tradition of the Bobo is expressed in lofty masks with stunning circular faces, and by rich heritages of legend and music.

Nearby villages like KOUMI and KOULIMA house important guilds of carvers and dancers in a countryside of green river valleys. In the Borodougou Cliffs only nine miles from town are the caves of a troglodyte people. There is a reservoir of hippos 50 miles to the north. The 220-foot high Farfiguela Falls are found 70 miles to the southwest near BANFORA, a national bread-basket and center of excellent village dancing and drumming (at TENGRELA and MANGADARA, for example). There are curious lace-like rock formations at SINDOU, 30 miles west of Banfora. City dwellers come to swim in the cool forest springs outside KOU, near Dinderesso, 10 miles from Bobo. An experimental Taiwanese rice project operates at Kou.

Arly National Park (season ticket $4), a northern extension of Dahomey's Pendjari Reserve, can be reached by air or over a rough but beautiful road out of FADA N'GOURMA (140 miles east of Ouagadougou). It is only 30 miles from the tri-national *Niger River "W" Park* (named for the double bend of the Niger River at the park's northeastern corner). All three parks suffer from neglect and poaching, but Upper Volta, Dahomey and the Niger Republic are making efforts toward conservation. Big game includes some elephant, buffalo, lion, cheetah, leopard and hippo. Antelopes, monkeys, warthogs, birds and smaller animals are abundant.

Official tours leave Ouagadougou for the nearby Mossi village country. Rarely patronized by the stray tourist in town, these excursions are rather expensive. The one-day Ouaga-Sabou-Koudougou-Ouaga circuit costs $40 a person, not including meals. A one-day animal run in the little *Po Reserve* near Ouagadougou costs $60 plus meals. There is also a two-day air tour into the Arly (December through April) for about $90, including accommodations and meals. Airlines and travel agencies in Ouaga or Bobo can book these tours for you—or you can go directly to the Office du Tourisme. For hunting in the Bobo area (December through June), write to Monsieur Charlot, P. O. Box 190, or the Syndicat d'Initiative in Bobo-Dioulasso.

What to Buy

The creative and industrious population produces an alluring variety of sculpture and artifacts. The best are often found in the villages where they are made to be used. They include the glamorous polychrome masks of the protecting spirit (Do) of the Bobo people, handsome stools and ancestral statuettes of the Lobi, stylized antelope masks of the Kouroumba, woven blankets and rugs (look for them at the Catholic mission on the Bobo road in Ouaga), exuberantly brocaded skullcaps, tooled leather, beadwork, pottery, wickerwork and fine gold jewelry.

Practically every visitor to Ouagadougou takes back a few miniature warriors and dancers cast in lead or bronze—occasionally an entire chess set of them ($25 and up). Drums, balafons (calabash resonating vibra-phones), and stringed instruments of the Mossi, Senoufo and other musical peoples can also be found. Seek out the musician or craftsman himself, rather than relying on the markets, for when he decides to dispose of his best work, he usually sells to itinerant middlemen who carry it toward the readier cash markets of Abidjan, Dakar or Accra. Most such purchases require stern bargaining.

Shops like those in the Hôtel de l'Indépendance complex (where the Office du Tourisme maintains a semi-official outlet) are usually open from 8 am to noon and from 4 to 7 pm. The crafts market near the Hôtel Central stays open from dawn to sunset.

You can also make purchases during visits to the Centre Voltaïc des Arts near the main post office and at the Centre de Tannage (leather work) on the Niamey road.

Cloth is a good buy in Ouaga and tailoring a bargain.

Local Attitudes

Voltans are outgoing and cordial, both in towns and countryside, although Mossi royal traditions emphasize hierarchy, protocol, privacy and ceremony. American visitors are welcome. Moslem areas of the west and north impose the usual constraints on diet, behavior in holy places, and inhibitions for women. Miniskirts are forbidden by law.

Weather, What to Wear, How Long to Stay

With Sahara-edge landscape in the north and green valleys along the southern rivers, Upper Volta possesses a fair range of climates, but nowhere is the country genuinely cool in daytime. The most nearly comfortable visiting period extends from December to February when the harmattan winds blow dryly (but with dust) and evenings are cool. Game viewing is good from mid-January.

The heat begins to return in March, becoming fierce by June, when rains fall intensively on the savannas. The rains persist through October, with the heaviest storms in August.

Normal hot weather garments are needed in almost all of Upper Volta almost all of the time. Cool evenings occur in December and January to the north of Ouagadougou. Otherwise, sweaters and jackets are useful primarily for air-conditioned offices and salons. Rain gear is desirable during the summer.

Both Ouagadougou and Bobo-Dioulasso are easily encompassed in a single itinerary, whether by air, rail or road. Hiring a car in each town allows the visitor to spend a full week roaming up-country, either returning to bed and board each night or camping out. A two-day visit to Arly and its Dahomean neighbor Pendjari is usually sufficient for game watching. A fair itinerary would thus involve entering via the railway from Abidjan as far as Bobo-Dioulasso, then road or rail to Ouagadougou, and leaving the country after 10 days over the parklands of the Pendjari to Dahomey, or alternatively through the "W" to Niger.

Communication

A small expatriate community and a growing number of educated young Voltans speak French. Most of the English speakers are Peace Corps and CUSO Volunteers and their pupils scattered around the country. Some Voltan laborers have returned from Ghana with a few words of English.

The single weekly newspaper, *Carrefour Africain*, is well edited and informative, especially compared to the dreary quasi-official press in most former French colonies. The official mimeographed *Bulletin Quotidien* appears daily, with useful information on what's going on.

Postal and telephone services are improving, but are still generally inefficient. To get your valuable packages home, it's safer to take them with you when you leave.

Emergencies

As in other countries of the interior, special services depend on luck. Ouagadougou's Yalgado Ouedraogo Hospital is partly modern, but most towns have scarcely adequate medical facilities for their own populations. Petty officials manage to be as exasperating as anywhere else, but the "man in the street" can be helpful. The army may be available for assistance outside the capital.

The small American Embassy (P.O. 35, tel. 21-91, 23-73) is in the residential section of Ouagadougou. An American nurse who has duties in several countries is stationed there.

Southern Africa

Angola
Botswana
Lesotho
Malawi
Mozambique
Namibia (South West Africa)
Rhodesia
South Africa
Swaziland
Zambia

THE REGION AT A GLANCE

In a geographic area two-thirds the size of the United States, Southern Africa combines some of the most magnificent natural endowments with the most convoluted social relations on earth. The industrial wealth and communications networks commanded by the white minorities that rule here are the furthest Africa has gone in economic development. But the clash between those minorities and the disenfranchised African majorities involves vast issues of social justice, dramatizing the economic and political weakness of Africans and aggravating their multiple frustrations in a white-dominated world.

Europeans began occupying Africa in this far southland during the mid-17th century. The original Cape Town Dutch, who have evolved into the ruling Afrikaners of South Africa, were followed by British and other Europeans. Together or separately, they conquered Hottentot, Xhosa, Zulu, Matabele, Shona, Swazi, Tswana and Sotho—Africans with claims to the rugged land of the dry coasts and the agreeably temperate

SOUTHERN AFRICA

high central plateaus. When other Europeans were scrambling for the rest of Africa, Afrikaners, British, Germans and Portuguese were already ensconced in South Africa, the Rhodesias, South West Africa (Namibia), Angola and Mozambique.

After World War II, the south remained under minority rule as far as the southern Congo (Zaïre). But as three dozen new countries attained independence through the late 1960's, Northern Rhodesia became sovereign Zambia, British Nyasaland became Malawi, and the three obscure British High Commission protectorates emerged as Botswana,

Gorongosa Park, Mozambique

Women work crew, Lesotho

Ruins of Zimbabwe

Lesotho and Swaziland—all under majority rule in a still strong sea of white power.

The Republic of South Africa holds hegemony in the south. It is the wealthiest and most powerful country on the continent, its ruling minority of whites benefitting from industry, mining, efficient agriculture, world trade and cheap labor, and its regime committed to an impassioned doctrine of strict racial segregation. Botswana, Lesotho and Swaziland, reluctant economic satellites of South Africa, seek to minimize the penetration of their neighbor's apartheid ideology. Namibia (South West Africa), formally a United Nations trust territory, has been virtually incorporated into South Africa.

Portugal clings to Angola and Mozambique, becoming increasingly dependent on South African assistance as it grapples with African guerrillas and its own poverty. A white minority regime, outnumbered 20 to one by Africans, dominates (Southern) Rhodesia in defiance of Britain and the United Nations, but with South African and Portuguese support. As in South Africa, African nationalism remains fragmented in Rhodesia, denied legal channels for grievances and yet unable to use violence successfully in the overthrow of established government.

On the edges of these conflicts, independent Malawi and Zambia scramble for whatever leverage geography and their own resources permit. Refusing to continue its traditional dependence on communications with the white-ruled south, Zambia relies on abundant copper exports to help finance new links to East Africa. Less endowed economically, Malawi has become reconciled to the superior power of her neighbors.

You cannot travel this region without some exposure to social conflict. For all foreigners, the terms of politics, rebellion, economic divisions and racial ideology influence the experience of an exceedingly varied subcontinent where visitors are courted, facilities good, societies productive and the elements of nature often bountiful. The rewards of this kind of trip are great, but so are the strains—for in many ways the conscience. of mankind is at stake in the outcome of the Southern African drama.

PMA

Angola

(Província de Angola)

Profile

STATUS: Overseas Province of Portugal.

SIZE: 481,353 square miles (almost twice the size of Texas). Population—6,000,000 including about 500,000 Europeans.

GEOGRAPHY: 1,300 miles of coastline in South Atlantic, rising into several plateau zones. Desert area in south. Exclave of Cabinda across Zaïre River to the north. Principal towns—Luanda (capital and port, over 500,000), Lobito (second port, 100,000), Nova Lisboa (80,000), Benguela (60,000).

CLIMATE: Varies from humid, tropical climate in north to dry and temperate in central plateau zone and desert climate in southern strip. Generally dry and cool from June to September (high 60's on coast). Warmer, rainy season from October to May (85 degrees maximum). Rainfall light on coast, up to 55 inches in the interior.

LANGUAGES: Portuguese and various Bantu languages.

CURRENCY: Angolan escudo (1$00), divided into 100 centavos. 10$00 = 37 cents; US $1.00 = 27$00.

VISAS: Required. Available through Portuguese consulates including Portuguese Consulates General in New York, Boston, Newark and San Francisco. Fee $5.85. Expect delay of three to four weeks while application is sent to Portugal for clearance.

AIRPORT: President Craveiro Lopes (LAD), two and one half miles from Luanda. Hotel buses into city are free, taxis cost 25$00 (93 cents). Airport departure taxes—domestic, 10$00 (37 cents); international, 30$00 ($1.11). Frequent flights to Cape Town, Durban, Johannesburg, Lisbon, Lourenço Marques and Salisbury.

NATIONAL HOLIDAYS: June 10, National Day; August 15, Luanda Day; October 5, Proclamation of the Republic; December 1, Restoration of Independence Day; Catholic holidays.

INFORMATION SOURCES: *In US*—Portuguese Consulate General, 630 Fifth Avenue, New York, N.Y. 10020 (tel. 212/246-4580), also 31 Commonwealth Avenue, Boston, Mass. 02116, 10 Commerce Street, Newark, N.J. 17102, 3298 Washington Street, San Francisco, Cal. 94115; Embassy of Portugal, 2125 Kalorama Road NW, Washington, D.C. 20008 (tel. 202/265-1643). *In Luanda*—Centro de Informação e Turismo de Angola (CITA), Largo Diogo Cão 7, P.O. Box 1240 (tel. 72021-2).

By Philip M. Allen

A promised land for European settlers, Portugal's Angola is making impressive efforts to attract tourists as well. The country is large and beautiful, but at present it appeals primarily to white vacationers without strong political sensitivity. Angola's multiracial policy combines paternalism and "assimilation" in a way that has proven costly to Portugal, unreal to most resident Europeans and intolerable to African nationalists.

The huge territory of over six million people, governed by Portugal as an overseas province, is managed by its minority of 500,000 whites, installed in plantations and mining concessions and in the pleasant ports of Luanda (the capital) and Lobito. Portugal's control is seriously challenged by Africans well inside Angola's borders with Zaïre and Zambia. Guerrilla forces of the People's Liberation Movement (MPLA) claim substantial territory in the east, where few Europeans live. The MPLA and two other nationalist movements also campaign outside Angola for self-determination. They are especially concerned about indirect Western support for Portugal's continued sovereignty over African territory.

Much has changed in the relationship between Portugal and Africa since the first caravels from Lisbon called in 1484 at the court of the Manicongo near present-day São Salvador and the Portuguese visitors carried news of Congo-Angola back to Europe. A century of mutual respect gave way to a long season of slaving for Brazil, and subsequently to dogged colonization. Now Lisbon supports a large army to cordon off the nationalist-occupied zone, maintain security in the towns and protect homesteaders along the irrigated and mineral-rich central plateaus.

Industrial diamonds in the northeast, iron ore from Cassinga in the south, oil from the northern coasts and the exclave of Cabinda (north of the Zaïre River estuary) and coffee concessions on the highlands all attract white immigrants.

Unlike the older generation of landowners and professional city people, the new immigrants from Portugal often occupy the lower echelons in Angola's economy, where they come into competition with the black majority. This source of conflict has aroused racial antipathies that contradict the official policy of assimilation. Today only a handful of privileged Africans and mestizos (persons of mixed racial descent) have achieved the status of "assimilated person," with rights and responsibilities equal to those of the white Portuguese.

As part of an ambitious development program, the government woos tourists with new facilities, lavish traveler services (among the best in Africa) and extensive advertising of Angola's shores and countryside, which indeed are lovely. More agreeable and flexible than South Africa's officialdom, better organized for travel than Zaïre or other nearby Black African countries, the Portuguese have lightened controls, increased information services, facilitated currency exchange, provided competent guides and transportation to places of interest, and in general behaved as if their African "province" were here to stay.

An examination of Angolan history and its current condition appears in a book by Douglas L. Wheeler and René Pelissier, *Angola* (Praeger, 1971). Readers may wish to pursue the African nationalist case further in *The Angolan Revolution*, Vol. I, edited by John A. Marcum (MIT Press, 1969) or Ronald Chilcote's *Portuguese Africa* (Prentice-Hall, 1967). The conservative viewpoint is represented in *Portuguese Africa, A Handbook*, edited by David M. Abshire and Michael A. Samuels. The Portuguese Government argument emerges clearly in Michael Chapman's *Angola on the Road to Progress* (Luanda, Angola Consultantes Lda., 1971), which is distributed by Portuguese agencies abroad.

Money Matters

Angola has its own currency, not valid outside the country, but of equal exchange value with the Portuguese escudo. Important towns have branches of the Banco Comercial de Angola (a Barclays Bank affiliate) and the Banco de Credito Comercial e Industrial. The Banco Totta-Standard de Angola is associated with the Standard Bank system and Chase Manhattan. All banks close for the day at 11 am (10 am on Wednesday and Saturday).

Dollars and travelers checks are accepted by hotels, restaurants and major shops so the visitor ordinarily needs only a small quantity of escudos at a time.

The cost of lodgings, food, transportation and services is relatively low in Angola—at a par with costs in South Africa and Rhodesia, but far lower than in Zaïre or Zambia. Imports from outside Portuguese Africa, however, are expensive. As increasing numbers of white settlers take jobs at higher wages than those paid to African labor, the cost of services and other prices are starting to rise.

Getting In and Out

Regular jet flights link Luanda's President Craveiro Lopes Airport with Lisbon, Johannesburg, Salisbury, Windhoek and Mozambique. Road access is unreliable. The borders with Zaïre and Zambia are usually closed and the main road up from South Africa through South West Africa

(Namibia) traverses the "homeland" of the Ovambos (see Namibia chapter). Authorization to travel across such areas is rarely given. Cruise ships, Union Castle and Belgian Line passenger vessels and passenger-cargo vessels call frequently along Angola's 1,300-mile coastline. The Portuguese merchant marine carries passengers between Lisbon and Luanda or Lobito on the comfortable vessels *Principe Perfeito* and the *Infante D. Henrique*.

Portuguese consular agents issue visas for visits of three days or more. Allow three weeks at least for a visa or have your ticket show less than three days' transit, arranging to extend your stay once you're in. Avoid indicating on your visa application anything that might suggest that you could be "trouble"—that is, a journalist, for example, interested in political or racial conditions.

Certain areas of Angola remain out of bounds unless you are explicitly authorized to enter them. Of the several game reserves, for instance, only Quiçama near Luanda is generally open.

Getting Around Within Angola

Air taxis and the government's Divisão dos Transportes Aéreos (DTA Angolan Airlines) cover most of the routes between Luanda and the main cities, as well as the resort areas of the south. One-way fares from Luanda to Lobito cost about US$29, to Cabinda $28 and to Nova Lisboa $36. Narrow-gauge tracks push into the central highlands from Luanda, Lobito and Moçamedes. The 80-mile Amboim Railway is privately owned, as is the venerable Benguela Railway from Lobito to the Zaïre border. Angola has been paving its roads—especially where they facilitate military movements—but there still are enormous stretches of virtually trackless country.

Buses cover the long distances, but the railroads are more fun. Large and small cars can be rented in Luanda from Auto Touring, Jante 13 and Automoveis de Alaguer de Alameda for upwards of US$10 per day and 5 cents per kilometer (8 cents per mile), not including gasoline (about 72 cents per gallon). Travel agents or TAP Airlines can arrange car delivery at the airport or hotel. Drive on the right in Angola. Metered taxis in the towns charge 4$00 (15 cents) for the first kilometer plus one escudo (4 cents) for each additional one-sixth kilometer. They can be hired for about US$5 per hour.

Information on Angola is disseminated abroad through Portuguese consulates and TAP Airlines offices. You may also write or visit the Centro de Informação e Turismo de Angola (CITA) at Largo Diogo Cão, P. O. Box 1240, Luanda; if a member of an automobile club, consult the

Automovel e Touring Clube de Angola (ACTA), P. O. Box 5466, Luanda. If you can read a little Portuguese, let these sources know, for the materials in that language are far superior to the English versions; they include an excellent cultural and travel quarterly entitled *O Turismo*.

Where to Stay

Hotel construction booms in Angola. A government classification system keeps price reins tight, so that accommodations are still reasonable. However, hotel price quotations ordinarily do not include breakfast or the automatic 10 per cent service charge, the 3 per cent tourist tax or the optional 50 escudo ($2) nightly charge for air-conditioning. Tourists will do well to reserve on half-pension outside Luanda, allowing some flexibility but still saving a little on hotel costs.

At LUANDA: *Hotel Tropico*, Luanda's best, a luxury establishment that opened in February, 1973, in the center of the city; 200 rooms with bath; singles from $17, doubles from $25. *Grande Hotel Universo*, first class; singles from $6, doubles from $8; full pension $5 above room rent. *Hotel Turismo*, first class, preferred by businessmen; singles from $8.50 to $15; doubles from $14 to $21; half-pension for $3 additional per day. *Hotel Presidente*, just opened on Bay next to harbor entrance, first class. *Dom João II*, residential hotel; singles from $5.50 to $17; doubles from $18 to $23; full pension supplement $6; menus start at $3. *Hotel Globo*, second class, center of Luanda; rooms $7 to $16; full pension at $4 supplement; avoid the bug-ridden Annex. Third class hotels scattered throughout Luanda charge between $3 and $9 per night: try first at the *Pensão Sirius*, a clean, very Portuguese place not far from downtown, where a full pension costs $3.50 to $5 per day. *Luso, Paris* and *Grand Hotel de Luanda* are also worth looking at. Early in 1973, the luxury *Panoramico* opened on Luanda Island. For campers: Municipal camp ground in pine grove on Luanda Island near cafes and beach.

At LOBITO: *Infante de Sangres*, first class; singles from $7, doubles from $12. *Terminus*, second class, between residential and business districts; rooms from $5.50 up. *Belo Horizonte* and *Turismo*, both second class.

At BENGUELA: *Hotel M'Ombraka*, second class, handsome; rooms from $6.50. *Luso* (residential), *Continental* and *Tamariz*, all third class.

At MALANGE, inland from Luanda: *Turismo* and government *Pousada Victoria*, both second class; singles from $4. *Hotel Angola*, third class, cheaper. *Pousada Duque de Bragança*, pleasant, small inn overlooking waterfalls at Duque de Bragança north of Malange; singles from $7, doubles from $12, including breakfast.

At Sá da Bandeira: *Grand Hotel da Huila*, first class resort establishment; singles from $3. *Pousada de Turismo da Huila*, first class; singles from $2.50. *Hotel Metropole*, second class. *Hotel Turismo*, third class.

At Nova Lisboa: *Residencial Hotel*, singles from $6, doubles from $10. *Hotel do Planalto* (airport hotel) and *Ruacana Hotel*, both second class; singles from $4, doubles from $11. *Esplanade*, third class.

At Moçamedes: *Hotel Turismo*, second class; singles from $5, doubles from $7.50. *Hotel Moçamedes*, second class; singles $5.50 to $8, doubles $10 to $14.

At Luso: *Luso Hotel*, second class; *Hotel Continental*, third class.

At Villa Robert Williams: *Hotel Comercial*, third class.

At Silva Porto: *Hotel Girão*, second class.

At Novo Redondo: *Hotel Praia*, second class.

At Cabinda (north of Zaïre River): *SICAL Company Guest House*, second class. *Grand Hotel de Cabinda*, third class; singles from $7, doubles from $10.

At Quiçama and Cameia Game Reserve: Camps; adequate but no meals available.

Where and What to Eat

Seafood is superlative here, particularly the large and slender prawns (gambes) and the squid. Angola has a range of fruits, vegetables, grains and meats from the interior to augment basic Portuguese cooking. It is hard to find Mediterranean-style neighborhood bistros or fishermen's bars in Luanda, where most working people return home for the long tropical lunch hour.

Hotel and restaurant food is reasonable in price, however, and the sidewalk cafes also serve meals.

You can get excellent seafood at the *Tamariz*, *Mar e Sol* and *Barracuda* on Luanda Island. Portuguese meals can be ordered at *Vilela*, the *Caverna* and the *Restinga* on the island. Angolan platters (Portuguese with African influence) are found at *Mãe Preta* and *Veleiro* on the island and several small places on the Estrada da Conduta. The *Club Naval* on the island offers fashionable dining and entertainment for gentlemen in coats and ties, and their ladies.

Among the hotels in Luanda, the *Universo* has a reputation for good food. There are rustic restaurants on Mussolo Island and at the Cuanza River estuary.

In the towns, water is safe to drink. Bills include a 10 per cent service charge; residents seldom tip beyond that, but another 5 per cent is warranted for superior service.

What to See and Do

With a population already over the half-million mark, LUANDA exudes Mediterranean urbanity much like the former Algiers of the French. Sloping up from a curving bay, with an arcaded business marina, a sprinkling of pastel-colored buildings and an occasional wrought iron veranda, the capital is pleasant and busy—and a bit sterile.

It was a slave port for 300 of its 400 years. Few Africans live or work in the city's heart now, for European immigrants have the jobs in markets and restaurants, at the wheels of trucks and taxis, and behind counters. Most of Luanda's school children are either white or of mixed blood; a rare black person leaps the hurdle of "culture." The stevedores and porters are African, Africans build houses and repair streets, but in Luanda multiracialism seems to consist primarily of the occasional mixed marriage and the ubiquitous government posters. Yet Luanda's plazas and avenues, its splendid, clean, multi-tiered market, and flower-festooned town houses are decidedly attractive.

The Angola Museum stages temporary exhibitions of paintings and sculpture to augment its standing collection of animal dioramas, historical and religious curiosities, and rather mediocre African art. There is a mineralogical museum and a zoo; the 17th century Fort São Miguel, now an army barracks, with a fine view from its high esplanade; a 17th century cathedral and several other admirable old churches, and a bull ring.

Luanda Island (Ilha de Luanda), connected with the city by a short causeway, contains a growing luxury of beach villas, cafes, smart hotels and visitable artisan workshops. The closer beaches are becoming crowded as the growing population seeks its pleasure, for the water is warm (80 degrees in February and March) and the cafes are open to sea breezes. In November Luanda hosts the Grand Prix d'Angola automobile races.

Lusitanos and the Star Travel Service offer a variety of tours. The railway out of Luanda opens the region to hunting and game watching; these savannas are the last remaining haunts of the giant royal sable, a monumental black antelope. Quiçama National Park, 45 miles south of the capital, is Angola's only accessible game reserve as of 1973. Hunting season opens August 1 and runs through the end of December. For permits and information write the Direcção Provincial dos Serviços de Veterinaria de Angola (Largo Diogo Cão, P. O. Box 527, Luanda) or the Clube dos Caçadores de Angola (P.O. Box 5145, Luanda).

Color and pageantry, missing in the antiseptic sunlight of the capital, appear in some of its night spots. Here, the city borrows from the older towns and villages where aesthetic "assimilation" has produced interesting mixtures of courtly Portugal, carnival exuberance, sad fado singing, street accordion sounds, and Africa's musical verve. Creole dance styles—merengue, rebita and others—are seen nightly in Luanda at the Muxima, the Adego do Aires and Pes Molhades da Corimba clubs, and on Sundays, festival days or during Carnival season. Inquire about schedules at the CITA office. Luanda night life is otherwise undistinguished—although there is expert fado singing at the Belo Horizonte.

A fine harbor in a curiously shaped bay, LOBITO is 600 miles south of Luanda. Washed by Antarctic currents, it has less ocean swimming, diving and fishing than the capital. The town has few points of focus for the visitor, but it serves as a launching pad for hunting and game watching, and for the 838-mile adventure of the Benguela Railway. This elegant Old World conveyance ploughs twice weekly with pampered passengers through Angola's rich plantation and mining regions, stopping at BENGUELA, founded in 1617 and now stagnating in Lobito's shadow. The town has an old fortress, a handsome palace, the Church of Notre Dame do Populo, and a standing exhibition of local agriculture, ocean life and artisanry at the Chamber of Commerce.

A hurried traveler may ride this far (34 miles), spend a day at Benguela, and return by local train or car to Lobito. The interested voyager can push on 350 miles to NOVA LISBOA, the capital of the interior, elevated and prosperous, with its new jet airport, museums of ethnology and art, the Quissala Fort and a zoo. You can go on to SILVA PORTO, cattle center on the Bié plateau, past the Cuemba River falls and the *Cameia National Park* (open by special permit only) right up to the Zaïre border (which cannot be crossed).

Down the coast 475 miles from Lobito, the iron ore port of MOÇAMEDES (12,000) enjoys a Mediterranean climate and has good fishing. The fine Church of Santo Adrião and a fisheries museum are here, and you can also see the *Weltwitschia mirabilis*, a rare stemless plant. From Moçamedes you can ride into the Namib Desert and you have another opportunity for railroading up the escarpment into the iron mining plateau. The Moçamedes track twists up 6,000 feet in 227 miles through the Tundavala to SÁ DA BANDEIRA (20,000), a popular mountain vacation spot on the Huila plateau. The museum here contains agricultural, historical, and scientific displays. The bracing air of the highlands, with waterfalls, green valleys and town gardens, entices sportsmen and health-seekers alike.

In the historically and culturally rich savannas of the Lunda people, 1,000 miles east of Luanda, the town of DUNDO has a most extraordinary museum, known to aficionados of African art. Its great collections of sculpture, artifacts and recorded music belong to Diamang, the world's second largest diamond company, which works the area primarily for industrial gems. Even when this region is open for travel (which is not always the case), the only convenient means of access is by air. Requests to visit the Dundo collection should be addressed to the headquarters of the Companhia dos Diamentes de Angola (Diamang, Rua dos Franqueiros 12, Lisbon 2, Portugal). The company maintains an excellent guest house for visitors.

CABINDA, the Zaïre River estuary exclave, is enjoying an oil boom (Gulf Oil is involved). Timber and tropical fruits are also exploited here. It is a fine place for ocean fishing and one of the few remaining natural habitats of gorillas.

Ocean sports are especially rewarding at Benguela and Moçamedes, in the Cuvo estuary at Novo Redondo (where the interior ravines and forests are also attractions), and in the Cuanza estuary on the edge of the Quiçama Park. Catches include tarpon (sometimes exceeding 200 pounds), marlin, tuna, swordfish, barracuda, sailfish, bonito and kingfish. Tiger fish and leopard fish provide sport in the fresh water streams. Fishing craft and tackle can be hired in the ports.

What to Buy

Good Kongo or Lunda sculpture, heir to great artistic traditions, is hard to obtain in Angola. Knowledgeable acquaintances or professionals from the Labor Institute in Luanda can direct collectors to the rare sites of continuing traditional production, located particularly in the north. The statuettes, masks and other carvings usually offered for sale are the uninspired glazed grotesqueries that are sadly becoming the hallmark of "modern African art." The official Artesano installation at Luanda and the crafts workshops on Luanda Island show an occasional piece of good workmanship, particularly among less expressive or minor media, such as casket inlay work, leather and raffia, masks, musical instruments (especially thumb pianos), walking sticks, basketry, and horn decoration. Prices for such items are lower than in West Africa or Zaïre, and the classifications are accurate. A commissioned piece from an artist on the island, and particularly from a Lunda or Tchokwe village of the north, can turn out extremely well.

Ivory and semi-precious gems are available in the cities as are animal hides (at the Artesano and the Casa dos Peles). Shops are open from 8 am to noon and from 3 to 7 pm, except Saturdays. Local painters are shown at the museum, but they are less exciting than the artists of Nigeria or Mozambique.

Local Attitudes

Angola is filled with security zones and military restrictions, but little of the guerrilla warfare is noticeable in the coastal towns. Excursions and photography outside the customary tourist routes should be cleared in advance with CITA, the Automobile Club or local authorities. European Portuguese persistently call attention to what they are doing for the "natives," whereas Africans generally maintain silence concerning their welfare and attitudes toward the nationalist cause. It is very difficult to obtain a genuine conception of what is going on in the far reaches of the country, and any sign of interest beyond ordinary tourist curiosity may rebound against you. Inside Angola, you hear very little praise or criticism of American policies toward Portugal.

Weather, What to Wear, How Long to Stay

Angola's climate varies from region to region. You encounter sultry tropical weather in the northern lowlands; temperate weather at the inland stations, with higher temperatures from October through April. Luanda is cool (mid 70's) from June to September and really wet only in March and April. Summers (our winter) at the southern coasts (Lobito and Moçamedes) are bathed in mist from the clash between warm air and the cold Benguela current atmosphere.

Tourists generally come between May and September (the Cacimbo season), and most of them are introduced to Angola's sun and seafood during a ship's one-day stop in Luanda or Lobito. Given more time, even en route between West and Southern Africa, you can extend your experience profitably by a week's excursion on the coast and by rail into the interior, flying or driving back.

If you go to the Dundo Museum or to Sá da Bandeira, you must add at least two extra days to the trip.

As in Portugal, women don't wear miniskirts, bikinis or hot pants to church; otherwise, Mediterranean informality prevails.

Communication

The existence of much tourist literature in English should not encourage an exaggerated impression of the country's linguistic versatility. In fact, Spanish and French are rarely heard around Luanda, much less English. However, at the main hotels and big businesses you will find people who can communicate well enough in English, and elsewhere a combination of basic "Romance" vocabulary and ordinary tourist hand signals will see you through. You will enjoy the interior better with a bilingual escort and/or a Portuguese-English phrase book.

There are four daily newspapers plus several dozen other periodicals, all in Portuguese. The foreign press is scanty. Telephone and radio-telegraph are unsatisfactory, even to reach Lisbon and Johannesburg, and there are no links with independent Black Africa.

Emergencies

Medical services are adequate through most of the territory, especially where European city folk or settlers have staked their claims. Luanda has two general hospitals. The diamond and plantation concessions maintain medical stations up-country. The American Consulate General is at Avenida Paulo Dias de Novais 42, Luanda (tel. 72494, 73155).

Botswana

Profile

STATUS: Independent republic since September 30, 1966. Former British protectorate.

SIZE: 220,000 square miles (slightly smaller than Texas). Population—648,000.

GEOGRAPHY: Mostly undulating sandhills of Kalahari desert and stretches of grass and woodland; swamplands in north, rolling plains in east. Principal towns—Gaberone (capital, 14,000), Serowe, Francistown.

CLIMATE: Generally sub-tropical. Dry winter season from May to September, warm days, cool or cold evenings. Summer is hot but tempered by prevailing northeasterly breezes. Rainy season from October to April.

LANGUAGES: Setswana and English (both official).

CURRENCY: South African rand, divided into 100 cents. R1.00 = $1.33; $1.00 = R0.75.

VISAS: Not required, but transit visas needed for entry and exit through South Africa, Rhodesia or Zambia.

AIRPORTS: Gaberone (GBE) and Francistown (FRW), both linked only to Johannesburg and Lusaka.

NATIONAL HOLIDAYS: September 30, Independence Day; Christian holidays.

INFORMATION SOURCES: In US—Permanent Mission of Botswana to the UN, 866 United Nations Plaza, New York, N.Y. 10017 (tel. 212/759-6587); Embassy of the Republic of Botswana, 1825 Connecticut Avenue

NW, Washington, D.C. 20009 (tel. 202/332-4994). *In Botswana*—Government Information Services, P.O. Box 51, Gaberone.

By Ivar Nelson

In the early 19th century, the central highlands of Southern Africa were a swirling chaos of inter-tribal war and migration. Spun out of the vortex were eight groups whose movement west ultimately was blocked by the inhospitable Kalahari desert. They settled along the tributaries of the Limpopo River, built villages and grazed their herds of cattle. But their future was uncertain. On the one side was the danger of destruction by stronger Africans; on the other, absorption by the rapidly growing Boer (Afrikaner) state in the Transvaal.

The century-long struggle that followed was led by three generations of the Khama family, hereditary chiefs of the Bamangwato, largest of the eight groups. Also playing major roles were David Livingstone, a zealous Scottish missionary, and Cecil Rhodes, an archetypal English imperialist.

Livingstone, famous for naming the great Zambezi falls after Queen Victoria, for his exploration treks and his meeting with Stanley in the Congolese forests, was important long before that for using the gun and the Bible, two great tools of British imperialism, to gain breathing space for what is now independent Botswana. With his father-in-law, Robert Moffat, he helped drive off bands of Sotho raiders and converted the powerful Mzilikazi, who later founded the Matabele nation farther north.

Yet the real danger to the growing Botswana state and to British hegemony in Southern Africa was to come not from native Africans but from the Boers, European invaders who had made their famous trek inland from South Africa's Cape Province. Their vision of an expanding Afrikaner Republic conflicted directly with Cecil Rhodes's dream of a Capetown-to-Cairo railroad connecting the links of British empire. With the Germans in South West Africa (now Namibia), the Boers in the Transvaal and the Portuguese in Mozambique, there was only one route north for the British: through Livingstone's mission station and the Limpopo territory of the eight tribes known together as the Batswana.

In 1885, the area became the Bechuanaland Protectorate. Rhodes got the railroad through to his future namesake, Rhodesia, but lost control of Bechuanaland to the Crown. The Bamangwato king, Khama the Great, a Christian convert, remained on the throne.

Reluctantly protected and benignly neglected, Bechuanaland continued under English control for more than 80 years. In the 1960's, with new nations emerging throughout Africa, Seretse Khama, grandson of Khama the Great, pressured the British for release of the protectorate. Independence was granted on September 30, 1966.

Botswana has a booming frontier atmosphere. Trucks cut across the plains to newly discovered diamond mines. Settlements spring up over-night. Urbane Batswana officials, bush families and white hunters min-gle on gravel streets of small desert towns that could be used as sets for Hollywood westerns.

Botswana's prospects are promising, both because of its mineral wealth and the adroit leadership of President Sir Seretse Khama, once exiled by the British (after marrying an Englishwoman) and later knighted by them. Once an impoverished people dependent primarily on cattle rais-ing, the Batswana are now mining diamonds, copper, nickel, salt, potash and soda. What's more. they are improving agriculture by extensive irri-gation, developing several light industries and encouraging tourism.

A geographical quirk gives Botswana more room for political and economic independence than either Swaziland or Lesotho. Surrounded, like Swaziland and Lesotho, by white-dominated states, Botswana does have physical contact with Black Africa at a single point—at Kazungula in the northeast corner of the country, where the ferry crosses the Zambezi River into Zambia. The US Government approved a $12 mil-lion loan in 1972 to build an all-weather road from the capital of Gabe-rone to the ferry crossing, defying the claims of Rhodesia and South Africa over this potentially strategic border point, and making it easier for people and goods to enter Botswana without South African or Rho-desian scrutiny.

Botswana politics and society are discussed in Richard Stevens's *Lesotho, Botswana and Swaziland* (Pall Mall, 1967). The romance, mar-riage and ensuing cause célèbre of the president and his English wife are related in John Redfern's *Ruth and Seretse* (1955). Two books by Laurens van der Post, *The Heart of the Hunter* (Morrow, 1961) and *The Lost World of the Kalahari* (Penguin), offer sympathetic accounts of the life of the Bushmen of Botswana.

Money Matters

The financial ties with South Africa are many. Central to them all is the use of the South African rand ($1.33 to R1) in both countries. US cur-rency and travelers checks can be exchanged at the four branches of Barclays Bank and Standard Bank in Gaberone (the capital), Francis-town, Lobatse and Mahalapye, and at the President Hotel and Holiday Inn in Gaberone. Make sure you are carrying rands if you leave any of these areas because the dollar doesn't necessarily talk in isolated petrol depots. Don't depend on your credit card to pull you out; it will be accepted only at safari and tour services, and not always there.

Getting In and Out

Getting to Botswana is easy, getting around the country somewhat more difficult. South African and Botswana Airways fly from Johannesburg to Gaberone and Francistown several times a week. Botswana Airways and Air Zambia also serve these two towns from Lusaka in Zambia, but schedules vary and should be checked on the spot. The Brazilian airline, Varig, recently initiated a Botswana safari tour from New York via Rio de Janeiro, and the country is featured in other African educational, hunting and game-viewing tours.

A slower but more exotic entrance into Botswana is the Rhodesia Railways train from either Cape Town, South Africa or Bulawayo, Rhodesia. The passenger train is racially segregated in Rhodesia and South Africa, but not in Botswana.

Entering Botswana from Zambia is uncomplicated. (Entering through Rhodesia or South Africa, where the police are ultra-sensitive to "suspicious" travelers, may involve a thorough inspection of your baggage.) Livingstone (Zambia) and Kasane in northern Botswana are connected by a short flight; charter flights may be available if the scheduled service is not operating. The more traditional and picturesque method is to take the gravel road along the Zambian side of the Zambezi River from Livingstone, then the ferry to Botswana at Kazungula. Hitchhikers can check at gas stations in Livingstone about trucks making this run.

Driving from either Rhodesia or South Africa to Botswana has the benefit of well-traveled, tarred roads. Bulawayo, in Rhodesia, is about two hours from Francistown and Johannesburg/Pretoria about four and a half hours from Gaberone. There are dirt tracks that connect Botswana to both Angola and Namibia (South West Africa), but only pack animals are known to make the Angola connections. Lorries do drive from Ghanzi to Windhoek in Namibia.

The Botswana police maintain border posts at most entry points including those with South Africa, where the South African police are also in evidence. In both cases, make sure you check the hours when the border is open (usually from 8 am to 6 pm).

If you are coming through Rhodesia, South Africa or Zambia, you will need a visa for whichever country you cross through and another to get out again. You can't get them in Botswana, so plan ahead.

Getting Around Within Botswana

Botswana is an enormous, generally empty land where transportation is easy only in the well-populated eastern edge. There, both a good gravel road and the railroad connect Lobatse and Gaberone in the south with Serowe and Francistown in the north. You can travel cheaply on the railroad twice a week or on buses over the parallel road.

Striking out into the hinterlands of Botswana is for those durable of body and strong of mind. A regular sedan can make the gravel road from Gaberone via Francistown to Maun, but you'll need four-wheel drive to reach Ghanzi or Kasane. The deep ruts often make steering both impossible and unnecessary. Joubert Transport in Francistown runs a twice-weekly road service to Maun. Kennemayer's Garage in Gaberone rents Jeeps and Land Rovers. Your American driver's license is good for six months. Driving is on the left.

For the adventurous with a high comfort index, Botswana Airways flies several times a week to Kasane, Maun and Ghanzi. You can also rent small planes at either Lobatse or Francistown for trips within Botswana. A five-seater rents for 35 cents a mile per person.

Hitchhiking through the desert lands of Botswana is possible but must be well planned. Check in with the central gas station in each town to find out when the next trucks are heading in your direction. The farther you get into the bush, the longer is the wait for a truck.

Where to Stay

The most unusual of Botswana's many attractive hostelries is the *Crocodile Camp*, five miles north of MAUN. Perched on the edge of the immense Okavango Swamp, its cool reed huts and exotic foods (would you believe truffles?) are the kickoff for hunting and other safaris in dugout canoes along the Okavango waterways. Full board is $6.65. Within the Okavango, the *Kwai River Lodge* provides more luxurious lodgings at higher prices. It can be reached only by plane or boat from Gaberone or Maun.

In Maun itself, there is and always has been *Riley's Hotel*, a living relic of colonial days when the sun never set on the British Empire. Chances are your companions in the trophy-strewn bar will be hunters or anthropologists. Full board is $8. Riley's also rents vehicles.

For the true Frank Buck experience, however, you'll have to go to GHANZI and the *Kalahari Arms Hotel*, as isolated a place as any in the Sahara. The hotel is actually a guest house, with eight rooms and no electricity, but not as uncomfortable as it sounds. Full board is $6.65.

Still exotic but more accessible and more comfortable is the *Chobe Safari Lodge* at KASANE in the Chobe National Park, one of the world's few remaining untrammeled game parks. Located one mile from Kazungula, the uneasy meeting point of two white-ruled and two Black African countries, the lodge charges $8 for full board and requires reservations in advance (P.O. Kasane). Kasane also has a campground with water and a store.

The hotels in the major towns of Botswana are comfortable but un-inspiring. In GABERONE there's a new *Holiday Inn*, with its familiar sign and food, monotonous design and a casino. The *President Hotel* (about $14.60 single, full board) has a good bar, an à la carte restaurant and a reputation for being pro-apartheid. The other hotel in town, the *Gaberone*, is cheaper ($6.65 bed and breakfast), slightly run down and more relaxed.

Farther south in LOBATSE, the *Lobatse Hotel* is cheaper (full board $8.30) than the colonial *Cumberland* ($10.65 bed and breakfast). The latter has a good restaurant and is a favorite among Europeans.

FRANCISTOWN's two hotels are unexciting, The *Tati Hotel* is $6.65 with full board and the *Grand Hotel* is slightly more expensive. MAHAL-APYE, PALAPYE and SEROWE have one hotel each. The only one worth noting has the name of *Chase-Me Inn* (in Mahalapye).

Where and What to Eat

Eating out in Botswana is strictly functional. There are few restaurants as such, although several of the hotel dining rooms have à la carte meals. Gaberone has a mediocre Chinese restaurant. The hotels usually serve British colonial-style menus with five stodgy courses. In the game lodges and safari camps you might be able to get zebra or antelope steak. The Batswana eat maize meal and grilled beef. They drink a maize brew, "twala." Try to find the real stuff because the commercial twala, called Heinrich's Chibuku, pales in comparison.

The farther you get from the bigger towns, the more likely it is that the people you meet will invite you into their homes. If you go to a Batswana village, slow your pace and, if you find someone who can speak English, linger awhile to talk with the people. Someone may invite you in for some twala or tea.

The water in all the main towns is good. Imported liquor is expen-sive. Be careful of the pork. At the hotels, lunch is often the heaviest meal of the day.

What to See and Do

The Batswana are undergoing rapid change, as Western styles and technology come into contact with traditional culture and family rela-tionships. Their autonomy is complicated further by proximity to and dependence on white-supremacist South Africa. These transformations and dilemmas influence the experience of any visitor to this wonderful country.

GABERONE itself is symbolic of these changes. As you walk its paved streets and pass the pleasant, multi-arched parliament, remember that nothing, not even a hut, existed here 10 years ago. It is the place to check on transportation, get maps, licenses and permits (if necessary), change money and get oriented.

The new and unpretentious National Museum provides an introduction to traditional Batswana culture and the natural resources of the country. Its exhibits of art and sculpture from all around Africa are well worth seeing. The Gaberone campus of the University of Lesotho, Botswana and Swaziland is also of interest.

Beyond mushrooming Gaberone is the frontier. Hundreds of miles of track lead to exotic places of the Kalahari, still visited only by the truly adventurous. You can now fly to some of them.

Evocative of what Humphrey Bogart had to deal with in "The African Queen," the Okavango Swamp lies remote and forbidding in the northwest section of the country. In a strange reversal of the usual order of things, the Okavango River, seventh largest in Africa, comes out of Angola and disappears by spreading out into the Kalahari desert. The result is 6,000 square miles of small waterways with hippos, crocodiles, pythons, thousands of strange birds, rare species of game, and people totally out of touch with the rest of the world.

And you can visit it. From MAUN, you can hire a dugout canoe and paddler for $1.30 a day, but you need your own equipment. Unless you know what you are doing, it is easier to have the safari arranged by Ted Wilmot at his Crocodile Camp, near Maun (P.O. Box 46, Maun). Safari South (P.O. Box 40, Maun) also organizes trips into the Okavango with equipment, canoes and paddler/guides.

Another way into the swamp is from the *Moremi Wildlife Reserve*, three hours by road north of Maun. You can base your forays into the reserve at the Kwai River Lodge there. The lodge also provides equipment and canoes.

The best time for the Okavango is June to September. The tsetse flies and mosquitoes will have you for dinner the rest of the year. The Ngamiland Trading Company at Maun provides food and other provisions.

Two hours south of Maun is Lake Ngami, a bird reserve turned pink by thousands of flamingos.

All of western Botswana, from the Okavango south through Ghanzi to the South African border, is the home of the Bushmen, one of the few remaining peoples in the world relatively unmarked by modern ways of living. Light grass covers the undulating sand of the Kalahari, which, while not a true desert, would seem totally uninhabitable. Yet more than 6,000 Bushmen make it their home.

If you can endure 30 hours in a Land Rover over rough trails, go northwest of Maun, around the swamp to the Tsodilo Hills. Here, 30 or so miles from the Angola border, are more than 2,000 Bushman rock paintings, probably the largest collection in the world and the least known. Their colorful stick-like animals and leaping hunters cover the undersides of huge granite boulders. *National Geographic* has magnificent photos of them in its June, 1963, article on the Bushmen. The Tsodilo Hills paintings are also eloquently described in Laurens van der Post's moving book, *Lost World of the Kalahari*.

GHANZI, in the middle of the Kalahari, is the point of most modern contact with the Bushmen, and the home of their more urbanized members. East and south of Ghanzi are the *Kalahari* and *Central Kalahari Game Reserves*, two huge, undeveloped tracts that together cover one-eighth of the country. They are evidence of the government's effort to protect Botswana's vast herds of wild game. From Ghanzi a sand rut road reaches Kanye near Gaberone after 400 miles. Along the way are the exotic towns of Tsabong and Tshane, homes of the Botswana police camel patrol. Yes—camel patrol.

The easier run between Maun and Francistown on the gravel road passes two other rougher game reserves, both in large salt pans, or depressions, in the plains. The larger, the *Makgadikgadi Pan Game Reserve*, has huge flocks of flamingos and other birds and large herds of antelope, zebra and other game, all of which exist on a smaller scale at the *Nxai Pan Park*. Both have the advantage of being neglected by tourists.

In the north of Botswana is the *Chobe National Park*, the most accessible of the game reserves and one of the most modern. Yet, compared with the heavily traveled reserves of East Africa, it is largely unspoiled. Elephants abound, strange birds flock along the banks of the Chobe (later the Zambezi) River where tiger fishing is excellent. The retired white hunter who manages the lodge there takes people for a three-hour boat ride up the river every morning. The puku antelope and the red lechwe are found in the Chobe Park.

For the adventurous there are campsites at Serondelas, 11 miles upstream from Kasane, and game blinds on the Ngwezumba River in the center of the park. The Muzungula Tree, under which Livingstone preached when he was at Chobe River, is still standing near the ferry.

The eastern strip of Botswana, along the railway, is the center of its national culture. SEROWE is the traditional capital of the Bamangwato people and site of the Bamangwato royal burial grounds. KANYE to the south is another traditional town, rich in art and architecture. A visit to either Kanye or Serowe, not on the usual tourist itineraries, helps to convey some of the history of this proud nation. Both are communities of about 40,000.

LOBATSE in the south is much smaller and of interest as the site of the large slaughter house of the Botswana Meat Commission. Every year, nearly 200,000 head of cattle are processed through Lobatse. This accounted for 85 per cent of the country's total exports before the mining industry began.

South of Gaberone and 30 miles west of Ramotswa Station, is the site of Livingstone's home on the Kolobeng River. Near it stands the Mothalsa Tree, another of the great fig trees used as meeting places by Livingstone.

One of the most fascinating educational experiments in Southern Africa is the Swaneng Hill School near Serowe. Started in the mid-sixties by Patrick van Rensburg, a political refugee from South Africa, it has used a highly successful work/study program to help Batswana students support themselves while learning. Now a government school, its staff is composed of people from all over the world. They welcome visitors who can give labor and support to the school in return for a bed or a meal. A similar school has now been started by the government in Shashi, south of Francistown.

Botswana's encouraging economic future rests directly on two new mines, each of which may merit a visit from those interested in mining, town planning and multiracial living experiments. One is the $30-million diamond mine at Orapa that South African De Beers began working in 1971. The other is at the Selebi-Pikwe complex southeast of Francistown, where British and American financial interests will be extracting copper and nickel.

FRANCISTOWN is the jumping-off place for the mining area and for most of the game reserves to the west. It's one of the fastest growing towns in Botswana and a little chaotic.

If you want to go hunting, Botswana is one of the few places left where you can do it relatively cheaply. The season runs from April 1 to October 31, and a day on a hunting safari will cost about $100, including the various permits. You will need a permit from the Botswana Embassy to import guns into the country and a license for the hunt. The Chief Game Warden, P.O. Box 131, Gaberone, will provide any information you might need.

Some hunting agents, in addition to those near Maun mentioned earlier, are: Botswana Hunters, P.O. 68, Francistown; Bamangwato Safaris, P.O. 60, Serowe, and Kalahari Tours, P.O. 197, Lobatse.

What to Buy

Botswana is one of the best places on the continent to buy animal skins. They are usually in good condition and quite cheap. A full-size zebra skin goes for about R100 ($133). Fortunately, the controls on killing game and exporting skins are fairly strict. The skins are available through the government-run Botswana Game Industries, P.O. Box 118, Francistown, or one of its outlets in Maun and Gaberone.

Out in the Kalahari you can get such oddities as ostrich egg water containers and fringed majumboro shirts from Bushmen and other traders. There is a thriving curio industry throughout Botswana that makes excellent Batswana utensils, baskets, carvings, rugs and fabrics for the tourist.

Local Attitudes

The Batswana are a warm and courteous people. If you are interested in their culture and their development, you'll find them eager and open hosts. Americans are usually well received, partly because of the favorable impression of Peace Corps Volunteers and partly because there are fewer of them than British or South Africans. The Batswana are conservative in the best sense of the term. Freakish behavior or dress will put them off until they get to know you.

Weather, What to Wear, How Long to Stay

Northern Botswana tends to be hot and humid, the south and west pleasantly warm and dry. The best times for a visit are between April and October, after the rainy season.

A singular contribution made by South African whites is the safari suit. Originally khaki but now any color, worn with either long trousers or shorts, this two-piece all-purpose outfit for men and women is acceptable for informal wear in most of Africa, and has become standard traveler's garb in Botswana. You can buy safari suits in Francistown or Gaberone. Otherwise, make sure you have light, loose clothing for the desert and sweaters for the cool nights.

If you have only a few days, spend one in the Serowe area getting to know the Batswana and the others at Chobe National Park on the way through to Zambia. A flying trip to Maun requires three days if you want to get into the Okavango. You will need 10 days to two weeks for a road safari through the Kalahari to Maun, Ghanzi and back to Kanye. Any good hunting trip would take at least a week, preferably two.

Communication

All Batswana who have been to school, and some with little formal education, speak and understand English as a second language to their own Setswana. Learn the Setswana greetings; it will help to break down the cultural barrier.

You can get in touch with the outside world fairly easily from Gaberone or Francistown, which have telephone, telegraph and mail services through Johannesburg. If you are going to send or receive anything that might upset the South Africans, make the package look as innocent as possible. The South African police watch communications and can open envelopes if they wish. Telephone hook-ups overseas can be made with only a small delay.

Airmail from Gaberone to the United States will take between five and seven days; allow much more time from anywhere in the interior.

Emergencies

The American Ambassador to Botswana, also accredited to Lesotho and Swaziland, resides in Gaberone. The US Embassy is located in the Barclays Bank Building in Gaberone, P.O. Box 90 (tel. 318). Other diplomatic missions include the British, Nigerian, Zambian and Chinese (Taiwan), and United Nations Development Programme representatives. The 1,300 police in Botswana are well trained, polite and efficient.

There are good government hospitals at Gaberone and Ramotswa and a Seventh Day Adventist Hospital at Kanye, which operates a flying doctor service throughout the country. There are dentists in Gaberone and Francistown.

Visitors to tsetse fly areas should have a blood test before leaving the country. Malaria is also a problem during the October-to-May rainy season, especially near the Okavango Swamp. If you plan to be there during those months, start taking a suppressant several weeks earlier.

Lesotho

STATUS: Independent since October 4, 1966 as a constitutional monarchy. Former British High Commission territory.

SIZE: 11,720 square miles (slightly larger than Maryland). Population—1,040,000.

GEOGRAPHY: Landlocked (surrounded by Republic of South Africa). Barren and mountainous, elevation from 5,000 to 11,000 feet. Principal town—Maseru (capital, 15,000).

CLIMATE: Temperate. Days warm, nights cool. Mountains cold to freezing all year.

LANGUAGES: English and Sesotho (official).

CURRENCY: South African rand, divided into 100 cents. R1.00 = $1.33; $1.00 = R0.75.

VISAS: Americans do not need visas to enter Lesotho, but do need South African transit or entry visas to reach it. No fee or passport photos required. Expect at least four weeks' delay. Available from South African consulates in New York, Washington, New Orleans and San Francisco (see South Africa chapter for addresses).

AIRPORT: Maseru (MSU). Three flights a week from Johannesburg. Many international airlines operate to and from Johannesburg.

NATIONAL HOLIDAYS: March 12, Moshoeshoe's Day; May 2, Birthday of the King; 1st Monday in July, Family Day; 1st Monday in August, National Tree Planting Day; October 4, Independence Day; 1st Monday in October, National Sports Day; Christian holidays.

INFORMATION SOURCES: In US—Embassy of Lesotho, Caravel Building, 1601 Connecticut Avenue NW, Washington, D.C. 20009 (tel. 202/ 462-4190); Permanent Mission of Lesotho to the UN, 866 United Nations Plaza, Suite 580, New York, N.Y. 10017 (tel. 212/421-7543). In Maseru—Department of Information, P.O. Box 353; Maluti Treks & Travel, P.O. Box 294.

By Ivar Nelson

In 1823, a young Sotho leader named Moshoeshoe retreated with his followers, depleted and exhausted from fighting with the Matabele, to a small, naturally fortified mesa in the mountains. From his safe haven on this mesa, called Thaba Bosiu, or "Mountain of the Night," Moshoeshoe created a united Basuto nation from a scattering of small villages and wandering bands. Adopting European military tactics, including firearms, he developed such strength that he first stopped the advance of the Afrikaner trekkers, and then convinced the British Crown to protect his people from being absorbed into the new Boer republics.

Out of Moshoeshoe's dream has come Lesotho—independent since 1966 and a member state of the United Nations with a population of one million. But the gap between appearance and reality makes a tragedy out of the struggle of the proud and tough Basuto to be free.

For this barren and mountainous country is an African land-island completely surrounded on all sides by white supremacist South Africa. This, in turn, imposes on Lesotho a reality of economic and political dependence on its all-powerful neighbor.

Unable to earn a living from the eroded and infertile mountain slopes, which were left to them after the white settlers took the productive plains in what is now the Orange Free State in South Africa, over one-half of Lesotho's men must migrate to South Africa to work as seasonal labor for white-owned mines and farms. The government is trying to change this and a fertilizer plant and light industry manufacturing tires, candles and carpets have been built in the last few years.

Moshoeshoe's land is for the adventuresome in search of unusual scenery, mountain climbing and trout fishing—who don't mind rough living and who will respond to the happiness and determination that mark these rugged people. Few books on Lesotho are available. Its position in Southern Africa is discussed by Jack Halpern in *South Africa's Hostages* (Penguin) and by Richard Stevens in *Lesotho, Botswana and Swaziland* (Pall Mall), both somewhat out of date. The government is eager to have people visit and has attractive travel literature available.

Money Matters

The South African rand (fully convertible at $1.33 for 1 rand) is also the money of Lesotho. There are no exchange controls between Lesotho and South Africa, and no black market. American dollars and travelers checks can be cashed easily at the Standard or Barclays banks in Maseru, Mohales Hoek or Leribe, or at the Holiday Inn at the edge of Maseru.

Otherwise, carry sufficient cash with you, because there are few other places in the country where you can change money easily.

Getting In and Out

In spite of international law, you cannot get into or out of Lesotho without passing muster for the thorough and slightly paranoiac South African police. This will take place both when you apply for your South African visa, which you need to get to Lesotho, and also again when you land on South African soil.

Even if you get only a transit visa and stay inside Jan Smuts International Airport and fly on directly to Maseru, the South African police can search you. Note: Before going into Lesotho, make certain that your South African visa is good for one more entry into South Africa. Otherwise you will find yourself in Lesotho with no way of getting out.

Don't plan on going to Lesotho if you have ever publicly expressed your feelings about South Africa's racism or if you look like a freak. South Africa won't let you through. On the other hand regular American tourists will not be hassled. Americans do not need an entrance visa to enter Lesotho itself.

Any blacks experiencing difficulties should contact the Lesotho Ambassador at the Lesotho Embassy in Washington. He is committed to having black Americans visit Lesotho.

You can now fly three times a week (Monday, Wednesday, Friday) on a $26 round trip from Johannesburg to Maseru (94 miles on South African Airways), or take a train/bus combination that goes through Bloemfontein to Maseru. The latter is slow going.

You can also drive on paved roads through the pleasant geography of the Orange Free State.

Caution: If you are driving, make sure that the road you are planning to take has a border post that is open when you want to go through. The usual hours are 9 am to 6 pm. There are no separate Lesotho customs; South Africa has already taken care to see that you don't bring in any Beatles records, TV sets or copies of *Playboy*.

Getting Around Within Lesotho

It is not easy to move around in Lesotho. If you have the money, and it's really not that expensive, the best idea is to hire a small plane from Basuto Air. In the far reaches of the mountains that is often the only way to get somewhere other than by walking or by horseback.

Lesotho is a country of many mountains and few roads. If you intend to go off the few main roads around Maseru, drive a Land Rover or a VW. Cars and Land Rovers can be rented in Maseru from Maluti Travel Agency (tel. Maseru 2554). Buses go on daily, but irregular, schedules from Maseru to the larger villages. Hitchhiking often means the back of a truck, but if you can take it it's still the best way to get to know the country and the people.

Where to Stay

The *Holiday Inn* stands on the outskirts of MASERU in all its antiseptic glory. Prices are high for Africa ($15 for a single) and its 220 rooms are usually full of white South African tourists. Reservations are needed for all weekends and holidays, and months in advance for Easter and Christmas.

The rambling *Lancer's Hotel* in the center of Maseru has the slower pace of its British colonial heritage. Its more reasonable rates ($10 a night for bed and breakfast) attract businessmen, officials and volunteer types. If you need comfort, and Holiday Inn and Lancer's are full, drive 19 miles north to the *Blue Mountain Inn* at TEYATEYANENG, a most enjoyable place, or cross the South African border on the outskirts of Maseru and stay at the *Riverside Hotel* (whites only).

Mission stations, the university at Roma, and local bars can provide less expensive, simple lodging.

There are also hotels of varying quality at LERIBE (*Mountain View*), BUTHA BUTHE (*Crocodile Inn*—very good), MOHALES HOEK (*Mount Maloti*), QUTHING (*Orange River*), MAFETENG (*Bataung*) and QOCHA's NEK (*Maluti*).

Where and What to Eat

The only restaurants in MASERU are the two hotel dining rooms. You can eat American and à la carte (the same menus as in Memphis, Tennessee) at the Holiday Inn or plod through seven-course British meals at Lancer's. You get cheaper meals throughout the day at the *Maseru Cafe*. Tip high (10 to 15 per cent)—they need it.

The average Basuto farmer can only afford to eat a hominy-like mush. It is not recommended for a steady diet, but try it once, especially with the variety of greens they add on top. To wash it down, get either "joala," a mead made from maize, or "marahrah," a wine (made from grapes).

If you make friends with any of the students at the university at Roma, you may be able to join them in their dining hall or even find a bed for the night.

What to See and Do

Lesotho is mountains. If you get vertigo—don't go. The mountains, although defrosted, offer spectacular scenery. Go east out of Maseru on the Mountain Road.

The first fork to the left will take you up to Thaba Bosiu, where Lesotho history began. There is often an old man there who will guide you over the paths that Moshoeshoe blocked to turn back the Afrikaner settlers. Give him a small tip afterwards (25 cents).

The second fork to the right will take you up to the University of Botswana, Lesotho and Swaziland at Roma. Although the students don't really raise much of a fuss, the government used to consider it a hotbed of dangerous political activity. Immediately across from its entrance is the Observatory, run by a fascinating priest who plays the zither. Stop in, he'll show you around.

On up the Mountain Road for another hour you come upon one of the oldest evidences of the early African people—the Bushman paintings. Men throw spears, cattle are herded and wild game cavort in color on the underside of huge boulders. Don't let your guide throw water on the paintings to bring out the colors because this may cause erosion; use a flashlight.

Maluti Treks, the tour operators in Maseru, can arrange a number of unusual trips into the mountains. An overnight trip will take you by small plane to a grass landing strip in the center of the mountains. From there you continue by pack horse to Semonkong Falls, or on other pony treks.

The same outfit will also take you trout fishing near the Oxbow project in northern Lesotho, involving travel by both Land Rover and Basuto pony. You'll get good fishing in clear, icy waters.

The latest kick for Southern African sports enthusiasts is skiing at Sani Pass in the winter (July). Tows and ski equipment rentals should be available. Not exactly Chamonix, but fun.

While moving around Maseru, go past the prime minister's official residence. It's a much enlarged version of a rondavel—the round, thatched hut that the Basuto all live in. If you are in Maseru for the Sabbath and are up early enough, the service at the Catholic cathedral has surprisingly good music and singing.

Night life in Maseru means eating, drinking and then visiting the casino at the Holiday Inn around 10 o'clock to play roulette (the European board with one zero) or blackjack. Coat and tie are required. Minimum bet: 75 cents. If you are in Maseru on Sunday, go to the soccer football matches in the national stadium.

What to Buy

The Basuto herd Angora goats, and the rugs and blankets that they weave with the mohair are durable and attractive (they were trained by Swedes). Most are woven at Kopano outside Maseru and at the Royal Lesotho Weavers in the industrial area of Maseru.

Also in the industrial area is Basuto Sheepskin, which makes rugs, slippers and coats, and the Kolonyama Pottery, a firm making bowls, vases and pitchers.

All of these things can be bought at the Basuto Hat in Maseru, which is the marketing agent for crafts from all over Lesotho. Prices are cheaper at the place where the things are made and where you can bargain.

There is a local outdoor market near the stadium where people sell pottery and tin crafts as well as vegetables and fruits.

While the world's sixth largest diamond (601 carats) was found in Lesotho at Lets'eng-la-Draai on the road from Butha Buthe to Sani Pass, and diamond mining is a growing activity, you can't buy them there.

At Teyateyaneng, north of Maseru, Tully's Trading Center weaves tufted mohair rugs with intricate and colorful designs. Tully's is right across the road from the Blue Mountain Inn.

Local Attitudes

Peace Corps Volunteers have swarmed all over Lesotho for the last five years, so Americans are no curiosity, even in the back valleys. The political climate is still sharply divided between those who support Leabua Jonathan's government, which nullified the last election, and those who won that election—the Basuto Congress Party. Members of the Basuto Congress Party don't love the United States because we continue to support Jonathan. Be respectful and friendly, act with good sense and remember that the people of Lesotho are more conservative in dress than most young Americans.

Weather, What to Wear, How Long to Stay

Maseru is at 5,000 feet and has a temperate climate, but the seasonal reverse of ours in the States. The days can be very warm but the nights cool. The mountains of Lesotho rise to 11,000 feet and are cold to freezing throughout the year. Sweaters and woolens are useful whatever the season.

If you want to go fishing, plan on staying a week. You'll need several days for any of the trips into the mountains. The same holds true for things to do around Maseru itself (Bushman paintings, Thaba Bosiu, weaving). If you have a Land Rover or an expendable VW, it's a hair-raising trip to follow the route of the annual auto safari over the mountains (by way of Butha Buthe) to Natal in South Africa.

Communication

English and Sesotho are the official languages of the country, and many people speak both. Telephone, telegraph and postal services from Maseru to South Africa or the rest of the world are reliable although not always speedy. Most of the tourists you will run into will be South Africans, often Afrikaners from the Orange Free State.

Emergencies

There's an American embassy in Maseru (Kingsway, P. O. 333, tel. 266) headed by a chargé d'affaires (the Ambassador resides in Botswana), a USIS library and a British high commission. For medical care, ask the desk clerks at the Holiday Inn or Lancer's Hotel to recommend physicians. Serious medical problems are probably better handled in Johannesburg.

For non-political problems, the Lesotho Mounted Police are prompt and efficient. They receive training and technical assistance from the South African Police, with whom they exchange information.

Malawi

Profile

STATUS: Independent since July 6, 1964. Republic since July 6, 1965. Former British Protectorate of Nyasaland.

SIZE: 45,483 square miles (about the size of Pennsylvania); one fifth consisting of Lake Malawi. Population—4,500,000.

GEOGRAPHY: Plateau, mountains and the beautiful Lake Malawi. Principal towns—Zomba (capital, 20,000), Blantyre and twin city of Limbe (combined population of 125,000), Lilongwe (future capital, 20,000).

CLIMATE: Moderate temperatures throughout the year, ranging from 65 to 85 degrees (though hot and humid in southern lowlands). Rainy season from November to March.

LANGUAGES: English and several Chichewa-related languages.

CURRENCY: Malawian kwacha, divided into 100 tambalas. 1 kwacha = $1.30; $1.00 = 77 tambalas.

VISAS: Not required. 90-day visitors permits issued on arrival and presentation of passport, health certificate, onward ticket and proof of solvency.

AIRPORT: Chileka (BLZ), 11 miles from Blantyre. Frequent flights to and from Johannesburg, Salisbury, Nairobi and Lusaka. Transport into city—Air Malawi microbus, 1 kwacha ($1.30); coach, 60 tambalas (78 cents); taxi, 4 kwachas ($5.20).

NATIONAL HOLIDAYS: March 3, Martyrs' Day; May 14, Kamuzu Day—President's Birthday; July 6, Republic Day; Christian holidays.

INFORMATION SOURCES: In US—Permanent Mission of Malawi to the UN, 777 Third Avenue, New York, N.Y. 10017 (tel. 212/755-8470);

Malawi Embassy, 2362 Massachusetts Avenue NW, Washington, D.C. 20008 (tel. 202/234-9313). *In Malawi*—Department of Tourism, Delamere House, P.O. Box 402, Blantyre (tel. 2811).

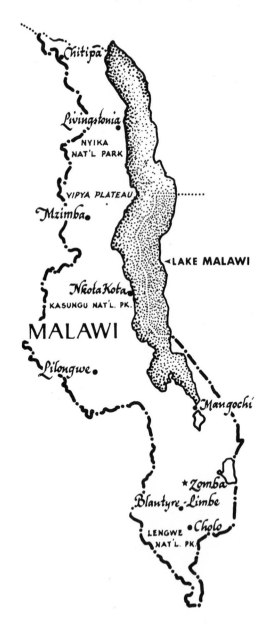

By Aaron Segal

This handsome little country on the western shore of Lake Malawi provides an excellent opportunity to get acquainted with a developing African nation in a minimum of time and with a minimum of difficulty. Independent only since 1964, the former Nyasaland Protectorate is busy modernizing its economy, constructing a new capital and overcoming a scarcity of natural resources with agricultural and community development projects. If you tire of watching nation-building, you can sightsee, meet friendly Malawians, relax with water sports, and enjoy the temperate climate and breathtaking views from the mountains and plateaus.

Although a convenient stop on trips between Eastern and Southern Africa, Malawi has not yet drawn swarms of visitors and is still relatively inexpensive.

Malawi's modern history began in the 14th century, when the shores of Lake Malawi became alive with trading activity. But when David Livingstone got there in the 1850's he found a stricken land, preyed upon by Arab slavers. The slave traders and European missionaries clashed and in 1891 Britain established a protectorate over the territory. Christianity and missionary education took an early and deep hold, but colonial rule failed to develop the economy. Thousands of mission-educated Africans, unable to find jobs in the country, left to work in the mines of South Africa and on the farms of Southern Rhodesia.

In 1953 the British compelled the country to join the Central African Federation, dominated by white-ruled Southern Rhodesia. The embryonic nationalist movement formed the Malawi Congress Party to protest membership in the federation. Composed primarily of young men, the party recognized the need for an older, nationally respected figure to unite the country, take it out of the hated federation and lead it to independence. The party's choice was Dr. Hastings Kamuzu Banda, who had left the country 40 years earlier as a boy. He had received a medical degree from Meharry College in the US and practiced medicine in England and Ghana.

Dr. Banda's return in 1958 electrified the country. Britain, after initial resistance, agreed to dissolve the federation and granted independence in July, 1964. The new nation was called Malawi, the name of a 16th century trading people who lived along the lake. Dr. Banda moved swiftly to build a broad political base and to crush some of his colleagues who were soon chafing under his authoritarian rule. He became president "for life" and established close and cordial relations with South Africa and Portugal.

President Banda argues that landlocked, densely populated Malawi must cooperate with its stronger and richer neighbors for access to the sea, export markets and jobs for its migrant workers. This policy is offensive to many African nationalists, but it has brought economic aid and technical assistance from South Africa, which in turn has helped consolidate the aging Dr. Banda's power.

A good historical account of the country is provided by Robert Rotberg in *The Rise of Nationalism in Central Africa: The Making of Malawi and Zambia* (Harvard University Press, 1966). A broad survey of the country can be found in *Malawi* by John Pike (Praeger, 1968). The Department of Tourism's free annual *Malawi Holiday Guide* is useful.

Money Matters

Malawian currency is not convertible, so travelers should acquire only enough to cover their expenses. In February, 1971, the new "kwacha" currency was introduced. Kwacha means "it is dawn" in the Chichewa language. One kwacha, consisting of 100 tambalas, equals approximately $1.30. Kwachas come in red 1K, green 2K and blue 10K notes. Some of the old Malawian non-decimal pounds, shillings and pence are still in circulation, making things a bit complicated. The new kwacha equals 10 shillings of the old currency.

Travelers may neither import nor export more than 20K. Currency can be exchanged at major hotels, the airport bank, the National Bank of Malawi and the Commercial Bank of Malawi. Bank hours in Blantyre-Limbe are 8 am to 12:30 pm weekdays except Wednesday (8 to 11:30 am), and 8 to 10:30 am on Saturday. In smaller towns without banks travelers checks can be cashed at the offices of district commissioners. Major credit cards are honored at the leading hotels.

Getting In and Out

US and Canadian citizens visiting Malawi for no longer than 12 months do not need a visa. Customs inspection is perfunctory and pleasant.

BOAC, Air Malawi, South African Airways and TAP operate regular flights between Blantyre and Salisbury (Rhodesia), Johannesburg (South Africa) and Beira (Mozambique). There are flights from London both direct and via Nairobi and additional service between Zambia and Malawi from Salima to Lusaka and Ndola. Zambia Airways flies once a week between Blantyre and Mauritius.

You can drive to Malawi along mostly paved roads from Salisbury and Lusaka and all-weather roads from Beira. Hitchhikers will find substantial truck traffic on these routes but may be asked to pay. Those seeking rides should check bulletin boards at the Automobile Association offices in Blantyre, Salisbury, Lusaka and Beira. Drivers with space often list a "lift." You can post your own notice of a desired ride at no cost.

United Transport Company operates an inexpensive daily bus service between Blantyre and Salisbury. But it runs along a stretch of road across Mozambique which has been the scene of fighting between Portuguese troops and African nationalists and there's the possibility that the road may be mined.

Malawi Railways runs a regular passenger and freight train between Beira and Blantyre, a slow but interesting journey. Check with the Malawi Railways office in Blantyre (tel. 50011) about the new but still irregular passenger service to the port of Nacala in northern Mozambique, a very scenic trip (see chapter on Mozambique).

Getting Around Within Malawi

The country is small and internal transport steadily improving. Most Malawians rely on buses and so will economy-minded travelers. In the twin cities of Blantyre-Limbe the municipal buses run frequently and charge 14 cents.

Six bus companies service most of the country. Check at the Blantyre bus depot for routes and schedules. The intercity buses are slow, usually crowded and uncomfortable, but the passengers are friendly and the fares are cheap ($1 to $5 one way depending on distance).

Near the frequent bus stops, there are added attractions for travelers. Conveniently located bars sell chibuku, a local beer made from maize. While disembarking passengers argue about ownership of the chickens and goats on the roof rack and boarding passengers struggle to load their luggage, there is usually time for a few beers in a bar. Singing on the bus is another popular way of passing the time, together with exhorting the driver to go faster. Keep an eye on your baggage to make sure it's not unloaded along the way.

Taxis are more expensive and, of course, quicker. They are metered in Blantyre-Limbe and charge 40 tambalas (52 cents) for the first mile and 24 tambalas (31 cents) for each additional mile. Taxis are stationed at major Blantyre hotels or can be summoned by phone (tel. 2604). Elsewhere collective taxis operate from the bus stations between cities and towns, departing whenever they fill up with passengers.

Automobile rentals are available in Blantyre from the United Touring Company, Hall's Garage and other firms. Driving is on the left. Drivers must be at least 18 years old and have an international license. Small cars can be rented for 5K a day ($6.50) and 10 tambalas (13 cents) a mile after the first 25 miles. Weekly rates start at 30K ($39) and 10 tambalas per mile (13 cents) after the first 175 miles.

Hitchhiking is good throughout the country except in the northern region where traffic is sparse. Malawian drivers may expect to be paid the equivalent of bus fare but rarely ask outright for money.

Malawi Railways has a pleasant and inexpensive daily train from Blantyre to Salima near Lake Malawi. This train connects with the new diesel service to Nacala, in Mozambique.

A most delightful journey is Malawi Railways' seven-day, 654-mile round trip boat ride on Lake Malawi. The 620-ton *MS Ilala II* takes nine cabin class passengers, and also has second and deck classes. It leaves from Monkey Bay in the south (which you can reach by road, rail or air). The boat goes up the Malawian side of the lake, stopping at small towns and mission stations. At Karonga, near the Tanzanian border, it turns around. Round trip cabin class passage costs 41K ($53.30) plus about $5 a day for meals. Second class and deck accommodations are much cheaper. Passengers can get off along the way.

Air Malawi schedules frequent and inexpensive internal flights from Blantyre to Lilongwe, Salima and Monkey Bay. Air Malawi, Capital Air Service and Leopard Air run charter flights to more remote areas.

Where to Stay

Malawi offers accommodations in a broad range of prices. In BLANTYRE, the 193-bed government-owned *Mount Soche Hotel* is air-conditioned and elegant. Single rooms, with breakfast, begin at $14. Down the street is the sprawling but comfortable 95-bed *Ryall's Hotel*, with single rooms including breakfast at $11. Here, as in many former British colonies, early morning tea is brought to your room unless you specify otherwise. In nearby LIMBE, a good compromise between European and African style hotels is the *Continental* (sometimes still known by its old name, the *International*). It charges $5 to $7 for bed and breakfast, and has excellent food and a pleasant bar patronized by Malawians. The old and stately 65-bed *Shire Highlands Hotel* charges $10 for a single, including breakfast.

The 24-bed *Nash Hotel*, just behind Ryall's, has an attractive Indian and Malawian atmosphere and single rooms for under $5. The YMCA and YWCA provide simple hostel accommodations. Cheap beds can also be found during school holidays at Soche Hill Teacher Training College or Churchill College of the University of Malawi. The government rest-house in Blantyre is a bargain, but as at rest-houses elsewhere, traveling civil servants have priority and it is best to book in advance through the Department of Tourism.

The future capital of Lilongwe and the present capital of Zomba each have limited but attractive accommodations. In LILONGWE, the 83-bed *Lilongwe Hotel* caters mainly to businessmen and charges $5 to $13 for singles including breakfast. The *Fourways* is much cheaper and has a friendly bar. Six miles from ZOMBA on the edge of a lush plateau, the 36-bed *Ku Chawe Inn* has spectacular views across the plains of Mt. Mulanje and Lake Chilwa. Single rooms with breakfast here cost $8 to $13. Trout fishing and bird watching are nearby. The *Welcome Hotel* in town is cheaper.

Lake Malawi is the country's star attraction. Along its shores are several hotels which cater primarily to white Rhodesian and South African tourists. Each hotel offers swimming, boating, snorkeling, water skiing, fishing and other outdoor sports. At MANGOCHI near the southern end of the lake, the 50-bed *Club Makokola* has air-conditioned cottages from $10 a person, with breakfast. Nearby the new government-operated *Nkopola Lodge* has 52 beds in a hotel and family chalets. Rates are similar to the Makokola. North of Mangochi near SALIMA, the 60-bed *Fish Eagle Inn* charges $5 to $8 a person for bed and breakfast. Prices are similar at the 113-bed *Grand Beach Hotel*. The *Monkey Beach Hotel*, on the cove of that name, has 32 beds in the hotel and chalets at $5 to $6 a day including breakfast. It features a guardian hippo which plays in the lake, keeps the crocodiles away from the beach and makes a unique companion for swimmers. Like the Grand Beach Hotel, the Monkey Beach has camping facilities.

At CAPE MACLEAR, the *Golden Sands Holiday Camp* has both camping facilities and simple rooms.

The major hotels generally add a five per cent service charge on bills but additional small tips to staff for personal services are customary.

All district centers have cheap and moderately clean government resthouses which are under the auspices of the Ministry of Trade, Industry and Tourism. Payment for lodging is in cash only. Each rest-house provides bed and service at $2.50 a night for adults and $1.25 for children under 12 years of age. Visitors purchase their own provisions which are cooked by the rest-house staff at no extra charge. All the rest-houses have kitchens, refrigerators, cooking utensils, crockery and cutlery, bathrooms, hot and cold running water, firewood when needed (at no extra charge) and nearby gasoline pumps. Campers using rest-house facilities pay about 60 cents a night each. They may also use the facilities of most religious missions at no cost.

Where and What to Eat

The major hotels serve the best meals, which cost from $3 to $8 a person without wine. In BLANTYRE the *Ndirande Restaurant* in the Mount Soche Hotel and in LIMBE the *Balmoral* in the Shire Highlands Hotel are both good. Less expensive food can be found in Indian and African cafes and restaurants in most towns.

Fresh fish from Lake Malawi is delicious. Try chambo (similar to perch), rainbow trout and catfish. Fish and chicken are often served "piri-piri" with pepper and sauces in Mozambican style. Fresh fruits such as pawpaws, mangoes, oranges, pineapples, bananas and avocados are delectable. Home-grown Malawian coffee and tea are excellent. The city drinking water is safe. The Danish Carlsberg Company has a brewery in Malawi.

What to See and Do

Malawi's charm lies in its countryside, its lake and its people. Administration and commerce are centered in BLANTYRE and the twin town of Limbe (since 1966 administratively part of Blantyre). A brief stroll on Victoria Avenue near the Blantyre post office will convey some of the flavor of this relaxed and attractive place. Limbe is more businesslike. The tobacco auctions held there between April and October are fascinating to watch.

For a pleasant half-day outing, take a bus, rented car or taxi to Chichiri, located nearly midway on the five-mile stretch of the Kamazu Highway connecting Blantyre and Limbe, and also administratively part of Blantyre. Chichiri has a complex of government offices. The Malawi Museum, with displays of local crafts and natural and historical material, is well worth a visit. Soapstone sculptors work on the lawn and their products can be purchased on the spot. The museum is next to the headquarters of the Malawi Congress Party and across the street from the current main campus of Churchill College of the University of Malawi. Nearby are the 50,000-seat Kamuzu Stadium, the Kwacha National Cultural Centre and Independence Arch.

Christianity plays an important role in Malawian life. Sunday services in both the cities and countryside are major events. President Banda, an elder of the Scottish Presbyterian Church, may turn up at a Blantyre service. The imposing St. Michael's Church, constructed by self-taught builders and workmen between 1888 and 1891, should be seen.

On Saturday nights, dances are often held at Soche Hill Teacher Training College or Chancellor College of the University of Malawi. They are fun and less expensive than the European-style night life at the Flamenco Club near Chileka Airport and the Mount Soche Hotel. You can drink, dance and meet educated Malawians at the Central, Continental and Chigamula bars. Salaries are paid at the end of the month and bars swing for the next week. Outside Blantyre night life is mostly confined to bars, hotels and local dances. There are cinemas in Blantyre-Limbe.

Several brief pleasant excursions can be made from Blantyre. The Shire River cataracts, sulphur baths and Kapachira Falls are 32 miles away on a good road. There are tea estates at Thyolo, the Mpatamanga Gorge off the main road to Salisbury, and the Mfunda Falls near Matope.

Forty-six miles southwest of Blantyre is the *Lengwe National Park*, open from May 1 to December 31. These 50 square miles of flat, open country are home to the rare nyala antelope, kudu, buffalo, impala and elephant. If you want to stay overnight, book accommodations for the Lengwe Game Camp through the United Touring Company in Blantyre (tel. 30122). Bring your own food.

ZOMBA is a lovely little town 43 miles by paved road from Blantyre. Its state house, parliament building, market and botanical gardens are worth a visit. Zomba has scenic views from the lush 7,000-foot Zomba Plateau, and spectacular butterflies, birds and flowers, as well as excellent trout fishing. Currently the seat of government, Zomba will house the national university when the capital moves to more centrally located Lilongwe.

The scenic mountain road leading south of Zomba to the Mozambique border is a convenient starting place for hikes around and up 10,000-foot Mt. Mulanje. This cedar and pine forest country was beautifully described by South African writer Laurens Van der Post in his book, *Venture Into the Interior*. Prospective climbers should get in touch with the Mulanje Mountain Club (P.O. Box 240, Blantyre) and ask the Department of Tourism for its leaflet on the mountain. Fishing licenses are required only for trout. Fishermen should consult the Angling Society of Malawi (P.O. Box 744, Blantyre).

The newly-designated national capital of LILONGWE is nearly 200 miles from Blantyre by a mostly paved road. You can make the trip overnight by bus, or take your time and detour from the route near the pleasant mountain town of Dedza to see the Chencherere Stone Age rock paintings. Lilongwe is becoming a well-planned modern town of government offices built around the existing trading center. Those interested in town planning might want to contact the Capital City Liaison Officer's headquarters on Chilambala Road (tel. 2350) to see plans and building sites.

Good roads lead west from Lilongwe to Zambia, east to Salima and Lake Malawi, and north to Kasungu and the Vipya and Nyika plateaus. The *Kasungu National Park*, 116 miles by an all-weather road from Lilongwe, is accessible from May 1 to December 31. On its 800 square miles of gentle plains you can see elephant, antelope, buffalo and zebra. There is a camp for day visitors. The new Lifupa Game Camp has a swimming pool and nine rondavels (thatched-roof bungalows) with electricity for overnight guests. Book through International Travel and Tour Co., P.O. Box 247, Lilongwe (tel. 2278).

Few travelers go beyond Kasungu to the northern region, scenically the most striking part of the country. There are no hotels but most towns have comfortable government rest-houses. The 67-mile drive between Mzimba and Mzuzu across the 7,000-foot Vipya Plateau is a visual feast of landscapes, birds, wildlife and colors, especially between August and November when wildflowers bloom.

The farther north one goes the more spectacular the scenery becomes, with mountain views across Lake Malawi to the Mozambique plains. The 360-square-mile *Nyika National Park*, open all year, offers bird watching, and has eland, zebras, roan antelope and occasional lions and leopards. Lodging is available in the park at the Chelinda Game Camp's four chalets and six double bedrooms. Book through the Director of Forestry and Game, P.O. Box 182, Zomba (tel. 797). The park is located at an altitude of 7,000 feet; evenings are frosty in June and July.

Near the Nyika Park along a spectacular escarpment road is LIVING-STONIA, mission center of the Free Church of Scotland. The center is situated on the Khondowe Plateau, 2,500 feet above Lake Malawi. All the original buildings, dating back as far as 1894, are intact. Nearby are Manchewe Falls and a series of caves where archaeological excavation has begun.

Lake Malawi is a deep blue gem, 355 miles long and 10 to 50 miles wide. It is Africa's third largest lake, after Victoria and Chad, and the tenth largest in the world. Accessible by car, bus, rail and plane from Blantyre, the lake is delightful for water sports.

Along its shore travelers can relax or explore Malawian history and rural life. One place to start is MANGOCHI (formerly Fort Johnston) at its southern end, 133 miles from Blantyre. The town has several historic buildings and a new Lake Malawi Museum with exhibits of traditional canoes and other lake craft. From Mangochi an all-weather road runs 42 miles north along the lake to Monkey Bay, departure point of the *MS Ilala II* for lake cruises. Just beyond is Cape MacLear, site of the original Church of Scotland mission station in 1875. There are interesting ruins here and water sports are good.

Although new lakeshore roads are planned and existing routes are being improved, the boat trip on the *MS Ilala II* is the most enjoyable way to see the lake. It includes stops at NKOTA KOTA, a large traditional village noted for its fishermen, crafts and dances; the historic cathedral on Likoma Island; the port and beach of Nkhata Bay, and the charming, quiet town of Karonga. If you wish to stop overnight, there are rest-houses and mission stations along the way.

Lake Malawi is lined with interesting villages. You can see village women perform graceful traditional dances such as the "Chiwoda," which has social and political implications. Young men and women volunteers operate several rural training centers and agricultural settlements through the Israeli-assisted Malawi Young Pioneers youth corps. Promising cotton and rice irrigation schemes for small farmers function near Salima. The Department of Tourism can help arrange visits to the schools and numerous agricultural and community development projects.

Sportsmen can obtain temporary memberships for private clubs in Blantyre-Limbe, Zomba and Lilongwe which offer golf, tennis, field hockey and other recreation. Sailing and fishing are splendid on Lake Malawi, at Mudi Dam near Limbe, Kamuzu Dam near Lilongwe, and elsewhere. Hunting is for small game only. Duck shooting is excellent on Lakes Chiuta and Chilwa, south of Lake Malawi.

What to Buy

Malawi produces a broad range of traditional crafts, including wood and soapstone carvings, woven and embroidered baskets, fish nets and traps, beadwork, pottery and musical instruments. These can be seen on display at the Curio and Handicraft Centre and the Arts and Crafts Centre in Blantyre, where prices are fixed. Better buys are available from the craftsmen themselves, or in the town markets, or from itinerant vendors. Locally grown and manufactured tea, coffee, cigarettes and peanut-based candies also make attractive gifts.

Shops are open during the week from 8 am to noon and 1 to 4 pm, and on Saturdays from 8 am to 12:30 pm. Bars and restaurants are open weekdays from 4 to 10 pm, and on weekends until midnight.

Local Attitudes

Malawi has always been a conservative country and President Banda has made it more so. Signs in the airport and elsewhere remind visitors that "according to Malawi custom, it is not regarded as proper for a woman to publicly expose any part of her leg above the knee, except when the wearer is engaged in a form of sport for which such clothing is customary." Miniskirts and shorts are therefore out. Even long pants for women are frowned on. If you look like a hippie or possess marijuana or other drugs, you can expect trouble and may not be allowed into the country. If you are driving and the president's car approaches, pull to the side of the road, whatever your direction, or his.

But it's easy to meet people and make friends in Malawi. The Blantyre Youth Centre, Kwacha National Cultural Centre and the Kamuzu Stadium—where soccer is played on Saturday—are good places to meet young people. So are the secondary schools, teacher training colleges and the university. Feel free to discuss almost all subjects but hold criticism of Dr. Banda and his policies for private occasions. Gossiping about the colorful president and his Amazonian female companions is a favorite but discreet national pastime.

Malawians are used to foreigners. The country teems with non-African advisors and experts of one kind or another. There are British, French Canadian, West German, Dutch, Scandinavian and a few US volunteers; Chinese from Taiwan are teaching rice growing, and white South Africans are helping to plan the new capital. Britain remains the principal influence and educated Malawians are most familiar with British ways and institutions, although they are interested in America and Americans. There is no hostility here and if you have a technical skill or are a qualified teacher you might even find a job. However, long hair and sloppy dress will not help job-hunters. These characteristics were cited by President Banda as reasons for sharply reducing the number of Peace Corps Volunteers after 1970.

Weather, What to Wear, How Long to Stay

The climate is moderate throughout the year, and there are few sunless days. Visitors to the Zomba plateau and the northern mountain areas will need sweaters for cool evenings. Casual attire is fine except for the few Blantyre hotels that may insist on coat and tie for dinner. Women often try the colorfully printed "chirundu," a long, flowing wrap-around traditionally used by Malawian women and suitable for dresses or skirts. The chirundu, also known as the "chijaga," is worn with colorful bandana head scarves called "duku," and blouses with national symbols and designs called "malaya." Traditional dress for Malawian men is called "chikwemba," a wrap-around cape or cloak resembling a Roman toga. It is worn at home or in rural areas. Western attire is favored for offices.

You will need a week to visit Blantyre, Zomba and the plateau, and Lake Malawi. Allow at least another week for the lake cruise. South

African Airways offers 10- to 14-day package tours from Johannesburg; Air Malawi has "Skylake" holidays from Lusaka and Ndola, in Zambia. United Touring and other agents offer domestic tours. But Malawi and Malawians are best discovered on your own.

Communication

English, Chichewa and the related dialects of Citumbuka and Chinyanja all have official standing. The government hopes that English and these national languages will serve as unifying forces among the linguistically different but culturally related Malawians. English is taught throughout the school system and widely spoken everywhere.

There is no television yet but the Malawi Broadcasting Corporation has radio programs in English and the national languages. The two semi-weekly newspapers, the *Times of Malawi* and the Congress Party's *Malawi News*, adhere to the government line. The Times bookshop in Blantyre carries airmail editions of British and South African papers, as well as *Newsweek* and *Time*, and an excellent collection of books about Malawi. There are smaller bookstores in the other towns.

Postal service is reliable but slow. Packages shipped from landlocked Malawi will take four to six months to get to North America unless they go by air. Telephone service works within Blantyre but calls to other parts of the country or abroad are difficult.

Emergencies

Queen Elizabeth Hospital in Blantyre has adequate staff and facilities for any but the most complicated illnesses. There is a small United States Embassy at Nyrho House on Victoria Avenue in Blantyre (tel. 438).

Mozambique

(Província de Moçambique)

Profile

STATUS: Overseas Province of Portugal.

SIZE: 303,771 square miles (similar in shape to California but almost twice as large). Population—7,500,000.

GEOGRAPHY: 1,500 miles of Indian Ocean coast; grasslands, tropical forest, savanna and plateaus in the interior, Mulanje mountains in the northwest. Principal cities—Lourenço Marques (capital, 500,000), Beira (port, 80,000), Quelimane.

CLIMATE: Southern half is pleasant and dry from May to September (daytime temperatures in 70's, 50's at night), about 10 degrees warmer the rest of the year, with moderate rainfall. North generally hotter and drier.

LANGUAGES: Portuguese (official), some English in southern half, Bantu languages.

CURRENCY: Escudo (1$00), divided into 100 centavos. 10$00 = 37 cents; US$1.00 = 27$00.

VISAS: Required. Application forms can be acquired from Portuguese Embassy in Washington or consulates in New York, Boston, Newark and San Francisco. Fee $5.85. Expect delay of three or four weeks while application is sent to Portugal for approval.

AIRPORTS: Gago Coutinho Airport (LUM), five miles from Lourenço Marques. Frequent direct flights to Lisbon, Salisbury, Johannesburg, Beira and Nampula. Sacadura Cabral Airport (BEW), eight miles from Beira. Frequent direct flights to Lisbon, Salisbury, Luanda (Angola), Blantyre (Malawi), Lourenço Marques, Quelimane, Nampula. Depar-

ture taxes both airports—domestic, 10$00 (37 cents); international, 50$00 ($1.85). Both airports have free buses to leading hotels, as well as public buses and taxis.

NATIONAL HOLIDAYS: June 10, National Day; October 5, Proclamation of the Republic; December 1, Independence Day; Catholic holidays.

INFORMATION SOURCES: *In US*—Tourist Information Bureau, 570 Fifth Avenue, New York, N.Y. 10036 (tel. 212/581-2450); Portuguese Consulate General, 630 Fifth Avenue, New York, N.Y. 10020 (tel. 212/246-4580), also, 31 Commonwealth Avenue, Boston, Mass. 02116, 10 Commerce Street, Newark, N.J. 07102, 3298 Washington Street, San Francisco, Cal. 94115; Embassy of Portugal, 2125 Kalorama Road NW, Washington, D.C. 20008 (tel. 202/265-1643). *In Lourenço Marques*—Centro de Informação e Turismo, 1179 Avenida da República, P.O. Box 614 (tel. 5011).

By Aaron Segal

White-controlled Mozambique is a popular vacation retreat for white Rhodesians and South Africans, and for good reasons: it offers good beaches, hotels, restaurants, game parks, reasonable costs, and a comfortable compatibility with the Portuguese who run the country. But vacationing and tourism are confined largely to the southern half of Mozambique, which also contains the majority of the population. North of the Zambezi River, which bisects the country, a guerrilla war of liberation is being fought. The pro-independence forces turned to violence after Portugal repressed all political activity.

Ninety-five per cent of the seven and a half million Mozambicans are blacks and mulattoes, most of whom live in a condition of poverty and illiteracy. There are about 150,000 European settlers and some 50,000 people whose origins are in India, Pakistan, Goa and Macao. And 50,000 Portuguese soldiers.

The history of Mozambique, first visited by Vasco da Gama in 1498, has been cruel and violent. Portuguese plunderers and slavers destroyed what had been a well-developed coastal society of Afro-Arab communities prospering on trade with Asian and Arab countries; later, Portuguese business interests came along to expropriate much of the land in the interior.

Until recently, Portugal did little to develop the economy, relying instead on Rhodesian and South African interests to build roads and rail and port facilities, while collecting taxes from Mozambican laborers recruited for work on farms and mines in Rhodesia and South Africa. Education and social services for Africans were almost totally neglected.

Faced with a nationalist challenge, Portugal is finally making an effort to develop Mozambican resources. Industry and tourism are being promoted and a program of road-building is under way, including an all-weather route between the two principal cities, Lourenço Marques and Beira. Dwarfing all the other enterprises is the giant $400-million Cabora Bassa hydroelectric project tapping the Zambezi River at Tete (near the Rhodesian border). Since its main purpose is the transmission of power 900 miles to South Africa, which has helped finance its construction, the dam has become a hated symbol of racial exploitation for Mozambique's liberation movement and its sympathizers.

The anti-colonial movement is spearheaded by the Liberation Front of Mozambique (FRELIMO), organized in 1962 by the late American-educated Eduardo Mondlane as a clandestine political, educational and military force. Guerrilla activity began in 1964 and has had increasing success, although Dr. Mondlane was assassinated at Dar es Salaam in 1969. Rebel activity is concentrated in the thinly populated northern districts of Cape Delgado and Nyasa, near the Rovuma River border with Tanzania (which provides sanctuary for the guerrillas). Fighting has also broken out in the Tete district, near the Cabora Bassa project.

However, visitors to Mozambique, who generally confine themselves to Lourenço Marques and Beira, both south of the combat zones, see little evidence of challenge to Portuguese supremacy, nor any sign of the war, for that matter, except for the ubiquitous Portuguese soldiers. The government-controlled press reports nothing but glowing accounts of Portuguese victories.

Background on the struggle between the nationalists and the Portuguese can best be found in two opposing accounts, Mondlane's *The Struggle for Mozambique* (Penguin paperback) and *Portuguese Africa: A Handbook*, edited by D.M. Abshire and M.A. Samuels (Praeger, 1969). Luis Bernardo Honwana, a young Mozambican writer, has written an interesting book of short stories, *Who Killed Mangy-Dog?* (Heinemann, 1969).

Money Matters

Mozambique has its own escudo. The exchange rate is about 27 to the US dollar. One thousand escudos is equal to one conto, worth about US$37. This currency is not convertible, even to metropolitan Portuguese escudos. Note that the escudo is written with a "dollar sign" following the denomination so that 27$00 equals US$1.

Hotels in the cities will accept dollars, South African rands, most Western European currencies, travelers checks and major credit cards. Pay with these or change only what you need for your stay. The leading banks are Barclays, Standard and the Banco Nacional Ultramarino. They are open from 8 to 11 am, except on Wednesdays and Saturdays when they close an hour earlier.

Getting In and Out

Visas for a stay of 90 days can be obtained from Portuguese consulates in the US, but the process is quicker at Portuguese offices in Malawi, Rhodesia or South Africa, where there's only a two- or three-day wait. Transit visas allow a stay of three days to make flight connections. Officially the government makes no racial distinctions on visa applications but in practice it is likely to be more wary and slower about visas for black Americans.

Airport customs inspection is usually cursory.

Air Travel: If you're coming from Europe, there are direct flights to Beira and Lourenço Marques from Lisbon. You can make good connections to Mozambique from other parts of Southern Africa that receive international flights. There are several departures daily from Johannesburg to Lourenço Marques, including various lower-fare excursions. TAP operates a regular service from Luanda (Angola) to Lourenço Marques via Salisbury (Rhodesia).

Mozambique is a desirable maximum-mileage destination point on a North America-to-Africa air ticket. You can stop in Europe, fly down the West African coast making several stops, visit South Africa, use Lourenço Marques as the high point of your ticket for computation purposes, then return via East Africa and Europe. For $819 you can purchase a 17- to 45-day round trip TAP excursion ticket from New York to Lourenço Marques permitting stopovers in Beira and four other cities. Round up any 15 friends or strangers for a group and this fare becomes $689.

For surface travel there is an excellent paved highway from Johannesburg to Lourenço Marques (slightly over 400 miles) and daily express bus service as well as rail connections with South Africa, Swaziland and Rhodesia. Union Castle Line passenger ships out of Southampton often stop at Lourenço Marques and two Portuguese lines, Companhía Nacional de Navegação and Companhía Colonial de Navegação, have a regular passenger service between Lisbon and Lourenço Marques, which is also a port of call for many cruise ships.

Getting from Mozambique into independent Black Africa involves complications. A Portuguese visa in your passport may provoke strict questioning about the purpose of your trip, especially in Zambia and Tanzania, and particularly if you exit from Mozambique through Rhodesia, the easiest way out. An alternative is the weekly flight from Beira to Blantyre, capital of independent Malawi, which has a working relationship with Portugal and does not care where you are coming from. You can also take the 20-hour train ride from Beira to Blantyre (relaxing and scenic but too long), or the new train from the northern Mozambican port of Nacala to the junction with Malawian Railways at Liwonde.

One interesting but risky exit route is the road that crosses central Mozambique and extends to the new bridge crossing the Zambezi River at Tete near the Rhodesian border. There is bus service to Salisbury on this route, and enough truck and passenger traffic to give hitchhikers a fighting chance. It permits a stop in Tete and a visit to the nearby Cabora Bassa project, as well as a chance to see something of Mozambican village life. However, this is a zone of increasing FRELIMO guerrilla activity. Roads are sometimes mined and ambushes do occur. Vehicles travel in armed convoys.

FRELIMO has taken some journalists and sympathetic visitors to the areas it holds near the Tanzanian border. FRELIMO headquarters are in Dar es Salaam, Tanzania.

Getting Around Within Mozambique

To get from place to place in Mozambique, most travelers use the excellent and inexpensive facilities of DETA, known also as Air Mozambique. There are several daily flights between Lourenço Marques and Beira at $57.50 one way, and regular service to smaller towns. Most major hotels offer free transportation to and from airports; DETA has airport bus service (about 55 cents), and airport taxis charge about $1.50 to $3 depending on whether it is day or night.

Within the cities there are metered taxis, operated mainly by white Portuguese settlers. Rates are low.

Car rentals are available at both airports. Albatroz Motors, which has offices at Gago Coutinho Airport and also at 267 Avenida Fernão Magalhães in Lourenço Marques, has Valiant sedans for $4 a day, 6 cents a kilometer, and VW minibuses for $7 a day and 14 cents a kilometer. At Sacaduro Cabral Airport, Auto Flecha rents VW-1300's for $4.10 a day, 6 cents a kilometer. International driving licenses are needed, auto renters must be 21 years old or over, and a $35 deposit is required. The Auto Clube de Moçambique, which has offices in Beira and Lourenço Marques, can help motorists affiliated with international auto clubs. Driving is on the left.

Guided sightseeing tours of Lourenço Marques and environs are available through major hotels, and the Albatroz, Wagons-Lits/Cook and Turismo travel agencies. A three-hour tour of the city costing $2.70 includes museums, churches, botanical gardens, the town hall and beach areas. A five-hour evening tour runs $20 to $25 and includes dinner and drinks at a leading restaurant plus nightclub visits. A four-hour daylight excursion to the village of Vila Luisa, costing $4.40, includes a glimpse at wildlife. There's also a full-day trip to nearby Inhaca Island for swimming, fishing and skindiving at a cost of $20 per person for parties of five or more.

Hitchhiking prospects are poor except on the exit roads to South Africa, Rhodesia and Malawi. Local buses and trucks carrying passengers run along the coast. Except for the paved highways leading to neighboring countries, roads are rough and driving is difficult.

Where to Stay

Lourenço Marques and Beira have a fair range of accommodations, open to all visitors but influenced by white Rhodesian and South African tastes. Hotel breakfasts are English style and substantial. Hotels offer full-board rates, but you are better off with bed and breakfast or bed and one meal, which will permit you to sample the local fare.

Hotel bills usually include a 15 per cent service charge but an extra 10 to 15 escudos directly to porters and servants will get you better attention.

Reservations are advisable at leading hotels during the crowded July-to-September winter high season. Rates shown here are likely to be raised in the high season. All hotels are multiracial but there are few black guests.

In LOURENÇO MARQUES, there are three luxury hotels located in the hillside residential area adjacent to the beaches and yacht club. Each has its own swimming pool, preferable to the shark-infested surf. The best is the Polana (165 air-conditioned rooms) with its active night life; rates are $9 to $11 for a single, $14 to $30 for a double. The Hotel Cardoso is in the same price range but less luxurious. The Girassol is still luxury class but a notch cheaper.

Downtown, near the harbor, shops and markets, are the new and excellent Turismo and Tivoli hotels, both with good restaurants; rates are $8 to $9 for a single and $13 to $15 for a double. Less expensive is the nearby Hotel Tamariz with $6-to-$8 prices for a single including breakfast. There are several seamen's hotels near the docks that are combinations of brothel and bar—cheap, but watch your wallet.

BEIRA's hotels are also grouped according to their central or beach locations. Downtown is the *Hotel Embaixador*, 108 rooms with private baths and air-conditioning; bed-and-breakfast singles at $5 and doubles at $9. Other good downtown hotels are the *Miramar, Savoy* and *Beira*. The excellent new hotel, the *Mozambique*, in the center of town, has 200 rooms; singles from $8, doubles from $15.

The Beira beach area, between the airport and the city, is known as the Estoril. Hotels here include the lovely *Dom Carlos*, which has its own beach and a fine restaurant. Singles begin at $13 (add $7 per person for full board). Less expensive is the nearby *Estoril Motel* which has rooms with cooking facilities for those who prefer to do it themselves. Similar arrangements can be found at the *Motel Santa Luiza* and at the Estoril camp grounds.

Outside Beira and Lourenço Marques there are simple and cheap pensions, guest houses, bungalows and commercial hotels ranging in price from $5 to $10 per person per night. There are no youth hostels, but travelers can try Catholic and Protestant mission stations. Between Lourenço Marques and Beira, there are campsites and pensions at the beach towns of JOÃO BELO, SAN MARTINHO DO BILENE and CHANGUENE. There are commercial hotels in INHAMBANE and VILANCULOS and pensions and bungalows on the offshore fishing island of SANTA CAROLINA. Farther north look for the pleasant *Vera Cruz Hotel* at QUELIMANE, the attractive *Pousada de Moçambique* on MOÇAMBIQUE ISLAND, the modest but decent *Hotel Tete* in TETE, and the *Lys Residencial* and the *Pousada Baía* in PÔRTO AMÉLIA.

Where and What to Eat

Mozambique cuisine blends African and Portuguese recipes to produce delectable seafood and chicken dishes, generally known as "piri-piri" for their sharp hot sauce. This can be accompanied by inexpensive Portuguese wine or good local beer such as Impala, a light lager, or the sharper La Laurentina and 2M.

In LOURENÇO MARQUES the *Sheik* restaurant in the Polana district is excellent, and the *Zambi* along the beachfront has fine seafood. Also recommended are the *Khalifa, Costa do Sol* and *Piri-Piri*. The snack bar of the *Cervejaria Nacional* (National Brewery) has excellent beer and shrimp.

Good sidewalk cafes and restaurants abound in both Lourenço Marques and Beira, where meals cost as little as $2.

In BEIRA, one of the best places is *Johnny's*, near the docks, run by Johnny the Greek, whose specialty is jumbo prawns, great with cold local beer or Portuguese wine. Other good restaurants in Beira are the *Arcadia*, *Pic-nic*, *Emporium* and *Oceania* and the *Dom João Hotel Restaurant*.

City water is safe to drink.

What to See and Do

LOURENÇO MARQUES is a bustling, sprawling capital, full of interesting tropical architecture. The best buildings are those of Pancho Guedes, the distinguished Mozambican architect and wood sculptor. The affluent decorate the exteriors of their residences with verve and color. In contrast, there are fetid ghettos that house the poverty-ridden mulatto and black population. Many of their shanties are exuberantly painted, too, but tourist guides rarely consent to take you there.

The downtown area has a lively covered market that sells fresh fruits and vegetables, tasty local almonds and cashew nuts, carvings, bread jewelry and animal skins. The Xipamine (pronounced Shi-pa-mina) market on the outskirts along the Rua dos Irmãos Roby has a more African ambiance. Most of the city's department stores feature South African goods. You can find bargains in the back street Chinese and Pakistani shops carrying Oriental wares.

A stroll can also include the strikingly anachronistic railway station and World War I victory monument. With special permission you can visit the big modern port, where 50 per cent of the traffic is with South Africa. The town hall and historical museum feature splendid antique European furnishings and relics of Portuguese colonial conquests. You can see fascinating mosaics, sculpture and painting by Mozambican artists—including the ebullient genius Malangatana—in the attractive Banco Nacional Ultramarino building. Stuffed animals in extremely life-like settings and a special exhibit on the gestation of the elephant from foetus to birth are among the excellent attractions of the Alvaro Castro Museum of Natural History.

The university, limited to technical education, is along the seafront. Lining the beach in the Polana residential section are splendid private homes and an exuberant modern church, São Antonio da Polana. The yachting, swimming and tennis clubs along the marina make their facilities available to temporary visitors.

There is formal, all-white and expensive night life at the beach hotels, which feature dance bands and occasional nightclub acts. Livelier (and multiracial) are the Beira Club, Moulin Rouge, Media-Luz and other clubs near the port on the Rua Araujo (pronounced Ar-ow-joe) which give it a "sin street" reputation.

Art enthusiasts may visit the Lourenço Marques studio of Valentine Malangatana, a prodigious painter of dreams, legends and myth in a wild expressionist palette that brought him to the attention of the great architect Pancho Guedes when Malangatana was only a golf caddy.

The Portuguese are proud of their record in penal reform. A persistent visitor, perhaps with the assistance of the US consulate, may be able to obtain permission to visit Machava Prison, a few miles from Lourenço Marques, which houses many captured nationalist guerrilla fighters. The work of artist-prisoners is offered for sale at Machava. Especially interesting are the wood sculptures of the prolific and imaginative Makonde people of northern Mozambique, prominent among the FRELIMO partisans.

Among Mozambique's main attractions are hunting, fishing and game viewing. Big-game and fishing safaris in Mozambique are probably easier to arrange and less expensive than anywhere else in Africa, although prices are still steep if you are determined to kill an elephant, lion or other big beast. A one-week hunting safari costs $2,000 and up per person, not including air fares. This price includes guaranteed kills of several major species, mounting of trophies, services of a professional hunter and entourage, and some impressive living comforts in the wilderness. Fishing, photo and hunting trips can be arranged by airlines (TAP) and car rental agencies (Albatroz Motors). There are travel bureaus in Lourenço Marques specializing in safaris, including Mozambique Safari-land, P.O. Box 1378 (tel. 2172) and Nyasaland Safaris, P.O. Box 2255 (tel. 6526). However, most hunters start from Beira, which is closer to the game parks. There you can book with Safrique, P.O. Box 216 (tel. 3734); United Safaris, P.O. Box 270 (tel. 2091); Cotur, P.O. Box 329 (tel. 2519); Safaris Outfitters of Mozambique, P.O. Box 75 (tel. 2459), or Agencia de Viagens e Turismo, P.O. Box 1343 (tel. 3152).

Safari operators will take care of licenses, itineraries, guides and all other details. The hunting season in most areas is from April through November.

The *Maputo Game Sanctuary* is only two hours from Lourenço Marques by car (you'll need a four-wheel-drive vehicle). There's an overnight rest camp in Maputo charging $5 per person. Visitors bring their own food. If you prefer, you can book a tour at your hotel for six persons at $20 each. You'll be picked up at 6 am and returned in time for dinner, having crossed the Catembe River by ferry and looked at elephant, hippo, rhino, buffalo and other animals.

Other road trips from Lourenço Marques go to the Kruger National

Park and Mala Mala Game Reserve in South Africa, the Swaziland game sanctuary of Miliwane, and the tourist spa and gambling casino at Mbabane (see chapter on Swaziland).

Coastal fishing in Mozambique is superb. The fishing camp at Punta da Ouro south of Lourenço Marques specializes in barracuda. The Paradise Islands offer the best opportunities in the world for black marlin.

BEIRA is a sleepy coastal town. UN trade sanctions against neighboring Rhodesia have reduced its activity as a port. It is now principally an air and rail terminus, a beach resort for Rhodesians, and a departure point for hunting, fishing and game viewing safaris.

If you're in Beira, you should visit *Gorongosa National Park*, one of the largest (5,000 square miles) and finest of the African animal parks. While the game areas in East Africa are often dry, bare and brown, Gorongosa charms visitors with its rivers, creeks and green rolling hills. Its combination of marsh and savanna sustains a variety of animal life— zebra, wildebeest, lion, kudu, elephant, hippo, buffalo and many of the other most popular species—in larger numbers than in many East African parks. Since Gorongosa receives relatively few tourists and is not yet threatened by agricultural encroachment, the atmosphere is quiet and undisturbed.

There are daily tours at $27 per person that leave for the park from Beira at 5 am; you can devote a full day to game viewing and return at 5 pm. These tours can be booked at Beira hotels or through the Safrique travel agency in downtown Beira. A more interesting 27-hour trip costs $36 per person, and like the one-day tour puts four to eight persons in a microbus. It leaves Beira at 2 pm and returns the next day at 5 pm after a night at the Gorongosa rest camp in a comfortable thatched-roof hut (rondavel) with porch and shower.

Gorongosa can also be reached by renting a car in Beira and driving 87 miles (about two hours) on a paved road to the camp. Keep in mind that you must arrive before 5 pm when the park gates close. There's an entry fee of $1.40 per person and $2.80 per car. The rest camp rates are $7 to $11 per person with all meals, and the camp includes a swimming pool, restaurant, bar and gift shop. Once in the park you are free to travel on but not off the dirt roads. For a small fee, a local guide will help you spot game. The park is a photographer's dream. A visit should include the Hippo Bar, where from a platform built on stilts you can watch the hippos doing their thing in nature's own bathtub.

Few travelers get beyond Lourenço Marques, Beira and Gorongosa. Yet along the coast there are scores of quiet, secluded beaches with good swimming and fishing and interesting adjacent attractions. However, buses and inter-city taxis are few, and hitchhiking is very difficult due to the lack of traffic. The alternatives are to rent a car or to fly.

The road north along the coast from Lourenço Marques takes you to the town of João BELO, near the Indian Ocean mouth of the Limpopo River. Along the nearby river is the Limpopo settlement for irrigation farming, a rather unsuccessful attempt to settle Portuguese and African farmers close together. A lovely salt water lagoon marks the beach of San Martinho do Bilene, 116 miles north of Lourenço Marques on the coast road. Another 35 miles north are the sparkling beach resorts of Xai-Xai (pronounced shy-shy) and Changuene, each with campsites and simple, inexpensive hotels. In the town of Zavala, a three-hour drive from Xai-Xai, the Chope dancers and musicians perform their world-renowned polyrhythmic xylophone timbila music on Sundays.

Between the commercial town of INHAMBANE and the port of Beira lie the offshore Paradise Islands of SANTA CAROLINA, SANTA ISABELLA and BAZARUTO. You can drive to the mainland fishing port and beach town of VILANCULOS and take the launch, or fly from Inhambane or Beira. Santa Carolina is particularly well known for its fishing.

Some of northern Mozambique above Beira is a war zone where travel is restricted, although visitors have been flown in to visit Portuguese military bases. However, the coastal and inland towns and nearby plantations, estates and game reserves are accessible and, so far, free from strife. The *Marromeu Buffalo Reserve* near the Zambezi River is nearly 300 miles north of Beira along rough but serviceable roads. Farther up the river are the Sena Sugar Estates and it is possible to go by river paddle-boat from there downstream to Luabo and the tiny port of Chinde. North of the Zambezi lies the coastal port of QUELIMANE, center of a vast coconut and copra plantation area, with its own palm-tree-lined beach and the pleasant Vera Cruz hotel. (An all-weather road leads from Quelimane to neighboring Malawi through the border town of MILANGE and the adjacent lush highland tea estates.)

North of Quelimane travelers are rare and Portuguese settlement sparse. This is an area where Arab trade and Moslem presence have had considerable influence until recent times. Unlike southern Mozambique, where white Rhodesian and South African tourists have brought the English language with them, a Portuguese-English phrase book is useful north of the Zambezi, especially for dealing with the Goan merchants who may speak a little English.

Along the coast north of Quelimane is the pleasant fishing port and beach of Pebane. However, the stellar attraction is the picturesque island of Moçambique just across from the coastal village of Lumbo. It's a 16th century major Arab and Portuguese port and trading station, an anachronism whose forts, ruins and narrow streets and alleys speak of other civilizations. Rickshas carry visitors to the 17th century São Sebastião fort, Misericordia church and chapel of São Francisco Xavier. Across the harbor is the village of Mossuril, where the inhabitants have preserved many ancient Islamic customs. Travelers find attractive accommodations at the Pousada de Moçambique, and the nearby beach is a fine spot for seashell collecting.

Tete, far inland on the upper reaches of the Zambezi, a 17th century trading outpost, had some of the same charming lost-in-time quality as Moçambique Island until it was selected as the site for the Cabora Bassa project. This $400-million enterprise involves damming the 1,700-mile Zambezi River at one of its narrowest points, rendering the river partly navigable downstream and providing some prospects for local irrigation and mining. Its main purpose, though, is to provide power for South Africa.

All this construction activity has created a boom in Tete travel. There are now all-weather roads from Beira, Salisbury and Blantyre, and regular flights by DETA. This is now a war zone, however.

The northern port of Nacala, one of the finest natural harbors in the world, is the starting point of a nearly completed railroad to the tea estates of the Mulanje mountains and a link with the Malawi railways. A passenger service between Malawi and Nacala was initiated in 1971 on an irregular basis. The train, when it runs, passes through fantastic mountain scenery around Entre-Rios (also called Malema), Ribáuè and the principal mountain highland town and military base of Nampula. Each of these towns has inexpensive guest houses (pousadas).

The last large beach in the north is Pôrto Amélia, with fine fishing and seashells. It has two reasonably priced places to stay in—the Lys Residencial and the Pousada Baía.

What to Buy

The Portuguese have done little until recently to encourage African handicraft. The African art boutiques feature local wood and ivory sculpture and many items from South Africa and Swaziland. The Afrikan Souvenirs shop in Beira has mounted animal skins and such hunting trophies (not to everyone's taste) as elephant foot ash trays. Wider choices at lower prices can be found at the Paraiso Africano in downtown Lourenço Marques. Shops are open daily from 8 am to noon and 2 to 6 pm, and on Saturdays from 8 to noon. Itinerant African vendors sell carvings, masks, flywhisks, beaded work and other items on the down-town streets at virtually all hours. Most of these items are commercial kitsch for the white Southern African tourist trade.

Local Attitudes

Language and social barriers make contact with Mozambican Africans difficult. It's just as well, because many of them fear the wrath of the secret police if seen talking to foreigners. About the only opportunities for social encounters with Mozambicans occur in the bars in the African sections of the two main cities, or in the "African" bar found in most interior towns (where another bar usually caters to local whites).

The Portuguese are generally wary of Americans, whom they regard as favoring Mozambican independence, partly because the late FRE-LIMO leader, Dr. Mondlane, was educated in the United States, taught school in America, and had an American wife. Officials parrot the government line. Few white people are willing to express personal opinions about local conditions. You may be able to talk to non-Portuguese missionaries who are active in the interior.

Weather, What to Wear, How Long to Stay

From May to September the weather in southern Mozambique is balmy and dry and there's ocean bathing in both Beira and Lourenço Marques. Casual and lightweight dress is appropriate with a light sweater or jacket for evenings. Clothes should be a bit more formal if you stay at a resort hotel and wish to dine there (men are often required to wear coats and ties). From October to April the weather is rainy and warmer. The interior is several degrees hotter but less humid than the coast and the north is dry and quite warm.

A week will suffice for Lourenço Marques, Beira and Gorongosa. A traveler who really wants to investigate Mozambican life and society will need two or three weeks more for visits to the north, Tete and some of the interior settlements. And a smattering of Portuguese would help.

Communication

Portuguese is the official language but English is widely spoken in the two major cities, especially at hotels and restaurants. Hundreds of thousands of Mozambican Africans have worked in Rhodesia or South Africa and consequently have learned some English. Postal and telephone services are slow and sometimes censored. Communication with South

Africa and Rhodesia is better than it is within Mozambique. There are pro-government Portuguese-language newspapers in Beira and Lourenço Marques, where the English-language South African papers are on sale. Private Radio Lourenço Marques (Radio LM) is the best jazz and rock music station in Southern Africa; it broadcasts in English.

Emergencies

The US Consulate General in Lourenço Marques is at 3 Rua Salazar (tel. 6051/3). There are decent medical facilities at the Miguel Bombarda Hospital in Lourenço Marques and at the Rainha Amélia Hospital in Beira, but head for Johannesburg in case of anything serious.

Namibia

(South West Africa)

Profile

STATUS: Administered by Republic of South Africa under League of Nations mandate, since withdrawn by United Nations.

SIZE: 318,099 square miles (twice the size of California). Population—650,000.

GEOGRAPHY: 1,500 miles of barren coast (Namib Desert). Plateau (3,600 feet) 60 to 100 miles from coast; fertile grassland, mountains between Namib and Kalahari deserts. Principal towns—Windhoek (capital, 70,-000), Keetmanshoop (17,000), Lüderitz (8,000), Walvis Bay (port, 25,000).

CLIMATE: In Windhoek, temperatures (October to February) 75 to 85 degrees. Moderate rainfall in January, February and March. Winter (May to September) temperatures about 10 degrees lower, frequently in the 40's. Walvis Bay slightly cooler, virtually dry all year.

LANGUAGES: German, English, Afrikaans.

CURRENCY: South African rand, divided into 100 cents. R1 = $1.33; $1.00 = R0.75.

VISAS: Required. Available from South African consulates in New York, New Orleans, San Francisco, Washington (for addresses see South Africa chapter). No fee. No passport photos. Allow four weeks.

AIRPORT: Windhoek (WDH). Frequent connections with Johannesburg and Cape Town, less frequent with Angola, Frankfurt, Madrid, Paris and Canary Islands. No airport departure taxes.

747

NATIONAL HOLIDAYS: April 6, Van Riebeeck Day; May 31, Republic Day; October 10, Kruger Day; Christian holidays.

INFORMATION SOURCES: *In US and South Africa*—(see South Africa chapter). *In Namibia*—South West Africa Publicity and Tourist Association, P.O. Box 1868, Windhoek, South West Africa.

By *Philip M. Allen*

To visit or not to visit Namibia poses issues of political taste. So, for that matter, does the very name of the place. The United Nations calls it Namibia, in deference to African wishes. The Republic of South Africa, which refuses to yield control over the territory, calls it South West Africa.

British and German trading agents vied for footholds along this lengthy, desolate coast during the latter half of the 19th century. In the 1885 European agreements partitioning Africa, England settled for a 474-square-mile enclave at Walvis Bay halfway along the coast, while Germany took the mass of surrounding territory, adding a strategic panhandle in the northeast, called the Caprivi Strip. In 1909, following the Boer War, the Union of South Africa inherited Britain's title to Walvis Bay (see South Africa chapter), and after Germany's World War I defeat, South Africa obtained a League of Nations mandate for the South West Africa colony.

Foreign travelers usually come here, if at all, between visits to Angola and South Africa on some large Southern Africa circuit. Cruise ships and other vessels put in for water at Walvis Bay and sail off after permitting a few hours on shore.

But white South Africans regard the big territory as an attractive offbeat vacation spot, and they are the masters in the land.

Pretoria now administers the huge, sparsely settled but mineral-rich territory, in defiance of the United Nations General Assembly, as a virtual extension of the Republic of South Africa. The UN has renamed the territory after its coastal Namib Desert, the world's most nearly absolute wasteland, and has sought in vain since 1966 to reassert international authority over the trusteeship. Its juridical "sovereignty"—as successor to the League of Nations—has been upheld by the International Court of Justice, and General Assembly majorities annually vote solemn but unenforceable condemnations of South Africa's refusal to honor UN supervision of its trust. In July, 1972, however, South Africa agreed to cooperate with a special New York-based representative of the UN responsible for reporting to the Secretary General on Namibia's political progress.

South Africa holds de facto control over the territory, investing heavily in mining and transportation, and gradually extending domestic apartheid legislation into the disputed territory. An undercurrent of Namibian nationalism, much of it affiliated with the South West African Peoples Organization (SWAPO), resists South African policy in the northern zones, largely reserved by Pretoria for eight of the 11 Bantustan "homelands" that are eventually to receive non-white people from half of the territory's habitable area.

Visitors with white skins and unobjectionable politics are welcome in Namibia. Those who come find it hospitable, although 500 years of mariners have called this 1,500 miles of desert shore the "Skeleton Coast."

A relatively fertile, grassy interior, dramatic mountain formations, and a fairly temperate climate help support Namibia's 650,000 inhabitants (less than one-sixth of them white) between the Namib and Kalahari deserts. Most Ovambos theoretically occupy their own semi-autonomous northern "homeland," but white-owned industry has been obliged to contract for increasing numbers of them to work outside the reserve. Ovambo protests against forced settlement, indirect rule and migrant labor conditions have increased dramatically and have taken the form of strikes and occasionally of violent guerrilla tactics.

Beside the 200,000 Ovambos, Namibia's interior is inhabited by Berg-damaras and their former masters, the Hereros, now tragically depleted in numbers and status, along with a few Bushmen and their more numerous relatives, the Nama. Traditional animosity between these groups has helped the government in pursuing its separate ethnic homeland program.

Windhoek and other towns contain about 100,000 Germans, Afrikaners and English-speaking South African whites. There are large colonies of "Coloured" (anybody of mixed blood, according to South Africa's litmus), including about 10,000 proud, pious and self-reliant Basters of Rehoboth, a settler group of cattle ranchers who bought their own "homeland" south of Windhoek in 1870.

The economy is based on copper, lead and zinc mining, fishing and fish processing, relatively uncomplicated diamond extracting, farming, and herding of cattle, goats and sheep. Agriculture confronts obstacles: the north receives as much as 22 inches of rain per year, while the central interior gets half that much, and the coast less than an inch. Succulent crayfish, labeled for American consumers "rock lobster tails," come from here. So do quantities of pilchards, tuna, snoek and game fish, taken by Russians and Spaniards among others. Some are brought for salting to Walvis Bay and then shipped abroad, often through an intermediary country to overcome boycotts of South African products. Namibia also produces karakul skins for "Persian lamb" coats, beef and mutton, salt for treatment of fish and millet for local tables.

United Nations, World Court (ICJ) and South African Government archives contain oceans of literature on the intricacies of the territory's status, history and socio-economic circumstances. If you're interested in the fundamental issues, read Muriel Horrell's balanced report for the South African Institute of Race Relations, *South West Africa* (Johannesburg, 1967) and John H. Wellington's *South West Africa and Its Human Issues* (Oxford, 1967).

Money Matters

Financial conditions in Namibia are patterned after those of the Republic, with the identical rand (R1 = $1.33) and branches of the same major banks (Barclays, Standard of South Africa). The cost of living, although rising as South Africa suffers inflation, nonetheless remains quite reasonable for so remote a territory. Windhoek prices are usually higher than those of the coast or countryside.

Getting In and Out

Namibia is certainly not inaccessible. South African Airways and other airlines have regular service between Windhoek and major cities of the Republic, as well as a weekly flight to Luanda (Angola) and weekly connections to Paris and Madrid. Flights cover the 1,000-mile distance between Johannesburg and Windhoek in 2 hours 45 minutes at a cost of about $50 one way.

Separated from the Walvis Bay enclave only in international law, the territory uses that port for all shipping. Swakopmund's old, unreliable harbor has been closed. You can pass by road or rail between South West Africa proper and Walvis Bay without formality. The port receives its share of bunkering and watering traffic, fish-oil tankers and freighters. Union Castle's coastal liners call here regularly, and there is a growing number of cruise visits to Walvis Bay on South Atlantic and Indian Ocean itineraries.

Overland travelers enjoy weekly railway coach service to or from Cape Town or Johannesburg through DeAar Junction to Karasburg and Seeheim in Namibia, branching off there for Lüderitz on the southern coast, or continuing to Windhoek, Walvis Bay or Tsumeb in the north. A one-way passage between Cape Town and Windhoek costs about $47 first class and $31 second class; Windhoek-Johannesburg fares run about one dollar less.

Road access from the Republic is equally feasible. Most main routes are fully paved, but the distances can prove wearying. If you are a respectable-looking white male with the patience of Job, you may hitch-hike these routes.

Visa regulations and other requirements follow those of the Republic of South Africa. They are inflexible and indeed prohibitive for non-white travelers or known critics of their system. The Ovambo homeland, the diamond fields and certain other sites can be visited only with express authorization from the Ministry of the Interior in Windhoek.

Getting Around Within Namibia

Despite the heat and great distances, travel through most of inhabited Namibia is quite convenient. The north-south road between Tsumeb, Walvis Bay and Karasburg is entirely tarred, and the Etosha Game Park tracks are passable. Railway travel—segregated as in South Africa—costs little for standard comfort: Windhoek to Swakopmund one way (265 miles) costs a little over $10 for first class, under $7 for second class; Windhoek-Tsumeb is under $16 for first class, about $11 for second class.

Air routes link the capital with a half dozen domestic airports. Transportation from Windhoek over the 350 miles to Etosha Park is available by bus, rented automobile or rail. Also you can travel by air to Tsumeb (280 miles; trains can carry your car to that point), and by bus or pre-reserved car from there. South African Railways, the motor clubs, travel agents, or the official tourist office at Windhoek can assist with travel arrangements and accommodations, including government permits for Etosha. You can obtain your own permit from the Director, Nature Conservation and Tourism, Private Bag 13186, Windhoek.

Taxis are readily available in the towns. You can rent cars at rates comparable to those in South Africa from Avis or United Car (Hertz) in Windhoek, or from Troost Taxis in Swakopmund and Walvis Bay. Tour facilities are offered by Basie Maartens Safaris, Oryx Safaris and South West Africa (SWA) Safaris in Windhoek, by Holiday Farm at Etemba, Botswangola Safaris in Omaruru and Windhoek, and Freddie Troost in Walvis Bay.

Published information for travelers is scarce. South African tourist literature includes South West Africa only as an afterthought.

Where to Stay

German, British and Afrikaner hospitality combines felicitously in the good—but racially segregated—hostelries of Namibia. Advance booking should be observed at Swakopmund during the March-to-August beach season and at Windhoek year-round. Modern facilities, air-conditioning and private baths are scarce, but hotel rates are reasonable and sanitation irreproachable.

The following tariffs are for single rooms, breakfast included, converted to approximate dollar equivalents (add 10 per cent service charge); the more expensive rooms usually have private bath.

At WINDHOEK: *Hotel Continental*, large, international quality; $6.50 to $10.50. *Thuringer Hof*, German establishment; $5, private bath from $7.50 to $12. *Berg Hotel*, 10 rooms; $4 and $5. *Grand Hotel*, $6 to $11, air-conditioning. *Safari Motel*, new and rather chic; $8 to $12, air-conditioning. *Grossherzog*, venerable, Teutonic, the cheapest; $7 for full pension.

At SWAKOPMUND: *Hansa Hotel*, in the center of town, completely German and gemütlich; $6.50 to $11; copious German table ($2 lunch menu, $3.25 dinner) with good selection of South African, German and French table wines. *Fürst Bismarck*, ramshackle German provincial near the beach; $6 and $7; inexpensive German food with German beer on tap. *Atalanta*, small, across the street from the Hansa; $7.15. *Schuetze*, old, modest; $4.50 to $7. Numerous pensions and boarding houses, as well as semi-furnished municipal bungalows for families, rent for $6 per day (usually fully booked well in advance); for all listings write Town Clerk, Swakopmund.

At WALVIS BAY: *Mermaid*, the best buy; $5 to $10; restaurant. *Flamingo*, the largest, good for clean, simple accommodations; $4.30 to $10.50. *Atlantic*, $4 to $6.50. *Desert Inn*, Narraville, outside town; cheap at $2.50 and up.

At KEETMANSHOOP: *Union Hotel*, $4 to $8.

At LÜDERITZ: *Kapp's*, $4.50 to $7; *Rummler's*, $4.50 (no private baths or restaurant).

Holiday bungalows at AI-AIS and OSTEND BEACH.

ETOSHA PARK: Four rest-camps including an old German fort at Namutoni; water, bedding and provisions available, but the guest should bring his own kitchen utensils, blankets, flashlights; book accommodations through Senior Tourist Officer, Private Bag 12175, Windhoek.

ETEMBA: *Holiday Farm*, attractive bungalows in Herero country 25 miles from Omaruru; $6.50 for full pension (plus surcharge if you stay less than four days).

Where and What to Eat

While not especially imaginative, food at hotels is generally pleasant and plentiful, with South African or German emphasis on seafood, beef, potatoes, wine and beer. Try the excellent German pastry in bake shops and at tea rooms like the *Schweizerhaus* above the beach in SWAKOPMUND. The *Airport* and *Daan Viljoen Park* restaurants are on Windhoek's outskirts. The general dining pattern, however, is in homes or at hotels and boarding houses. Such elaborately titled places at the *Steakhaus zum Seeteufel* in Swakopmund turn out to be tea rooms that prepare take-out bags of frankfurters, hamburgers and curried chicken for the bungalow crowd. Water is safe to drink. A 10 per cent tip is standard.

What to See and Do

Cool ocean breezes, perfect sand in impressively lofty dunes, good fishing and skindiving, flocks of sea birds, and a somewhat diluted Bavarian resort atmosphere make little SWAKOPMUND (7,000 permanent residents) so idyllic that the whole territorial administration moves there from Windhoek for January and February. The town is built on smooth yellow sand, with broad avenues, and its baroque towers and tiled roofs make a pretty sight when approached over the 20-mile dune road from Walvis Bay. Pristine pastel houses and a profusion of bakers, beer signs and hairdressers all bespeak a rustic Germany before wars, before colonialism, perhaps even before races and their conflicts.

Swakopmund has a fascinating little museum of Namibian sea and desert items (open daily, including Sunday, from 10:30 to 1:30 and 4 to 6, plus Saturday evenings), a sheltered beach and a large municipal swimming pool, sports facilities, some well-known boarding schools, a lighthouse on the dunes, several monuments of wartime pride and sorrow, German bookshops and an occasional chamber music concert.

WALVIS BAY burrows three feet below sea level behind a rampart of dunes, a creation of merchant man, with trees and shrubs imported as at Swakopmund into the Namib's oblivion. Its population is one-third "European," to crowd the sandy 18-hole golf course on the dunes. A desert harbor until World War II, "Whale-Fish Bay" has grown prosperous on fishing and trade, but the town remains unremarkable for all that. Visit the village of "Coloured" fishermen, landowners and permanent residents of Walvis Bay—distinguished from "Africans" who are permitted here only as temporary labor under apartheid's rules. Pink flamingos inhabit the salty marshes behind the dunes.

CAPE CROSS stands 80 miles to the north, across empty sands and salt deposits near a gathering place for seals and a flourishing sealskin industry. This is where the first European, the Portuguese Diogo Cão, planted his southernmost staff in 1484. Cape Cross is accessible by permit only—and only during periods of the year not devoted to slaughtering and skinning. In the interior, lofty Brandberg rises to 8,500 feet in a bed of rock carvings, cave paintings and the petrified forest of Aurus. These sites in a transitional veld between desert and savanna can be reached out of the "garden town" of OMARURU (pop. 3,000) which has rock paintings at Paula's Cave (seven miles from town).

WINDHOEK perches high and a bit heavily on an altitude of 5,400 feet. The capital's 70,000 people are about half white, half non-white. The latter include many of the remaining Herero people—tall, high-caste patricians of Namibia who were disinherited early this century in the name of *Kultur*. Subsequently, Herero women adopted their mistresses' Teutonic fashions; they still walk with great dignity along Windhoek's streets in long skirted gowns and turbans. The Hereros, the trees and flowers of overseas Germany, the handsome parks and monuments and the Maytime music of Carnival, all enliven Windhoek.

Safaris leave from Windhoek between April and November for the *Etosha* and the *Kalahari-Gemsbok* parks. The small *Daan Viljoen Game Park* is 12 miles west of town, and there is an interesting transit game camp with zoo at OKAHANDJE, 43 miles north of Windhoek.

Among several castles on the Windhoek's hilly circumference is the Alte Feste (1890), which now houses an historical museum. The State Museum nearby contains some important items of natural history, ethnology and geology. Both museums are open from 8 to 12:45 and 2 to 5, Monday through Friday, and on weekend and holiday afternoons. Windhoek's public gardens have a rockery of meteorites collected throughout the territory, which seems to attract an extraordinary number of such objects. Visitors interested in advanced techniques of recycling may pay a visit to Windhoek's water and sewage plant.

To the south, KEETMANSHOOP commands the karakul sheep district. Its experimental farm and several pretty churches deserve a visit. Three hours to the southwest is the impressive Fish River Canyon, 15 miles long and a half-mile deep, one of the few streams in Namibia that flood. In June and July campers come to AI-AIS, 30 miles south of the canyon, for the hot waters and solitary sojourns of the place.

LÜDERITZ, along the southern coast on the rim of the forbidden diamond reserve, is cool, dry as dust, but pretty, with a small port for fishing and lobstering, and a good beach at Ostend.

The far northland is tribal homeland, including OVAMBOLAND, favored by nature and South African investment, but deeply troubled politically and socially. Grain waves in the fields and cattle roam among baobab trees. Few tourists are authorized to enter the homeland, but you stand a slim chance of a permit to go through by road in transit to Angola (with appropriate Portuguese visa and all the other trappings). If allowed in, visit Ovamboland schools, and the "black capitalism" project started by the South African Government at OSHAKATI to absorb excess labor and set the homeland on its feet economically. TSUMEB is the transportation hub of the north, a center for copper, lead and zinc mining. Sixty miles beyond Tsumeb begins the 15,000-square-mile *Etosha Game Park*, with a major stock of elephant, lion, giraffe, rhinoceros, cheetah, antelope and bird life. The park is open from March through October. The best time to visit is after July.

What to Buy

Aside from diamonds, which are no more accessible here than anywhere else, Namibia produces a vast array of semi-precious gems—beryls, tourmalines, tiger's eye, aquamarines, rose quartz, chalcedony and topaz, for example. Trustworthy gem shops are located in Swakopmund and Windhoek. Karakul lamb and seal skins from Cape Cross are sent to Europe for processing, but good inexpensive coats can be found at Keetmanshoop and Windhoek. Available art work is negligible, although some German dealers in the towns turn up valuable carvings from West Africa from time to time. There is the usual supply of beads, canes, inlaid plaques and other African handcrafts, called "curios" in this part of the world. Big game skins, including zebra, are abundant here and probably at lower prices than anywhere else in Africa.

Local Attitudes

While political and racial discussion touches tender nerves everywhere within South Africa's dominion, the Germans and expatriate Afrikaners of Namibia seem on the whole less defensive than some of their more embattled counterparts in the Republic. Moreover, Afrikaners tend to display less resentment toward English speakers here than in Johannesburg and the Transvaal countryside. Still, any vocal denunciation or conspicuous violation of policy is likely to result in detention for the resident and expulsion for the visitor. Perhaps the worst offense is trespassing on restricted diamond fields or the Ovambo reserve. For physical safety, abstain from treading on the Namib's coastal dunes: the sand crusts are brittle and the chances of struggling out from beneath them are unpromising.

Weather, What to Wear

While most of Namibia spreads out under a scorching sun, temperatures on the plateaus and coasts frequently require sweaters. Walvis Bay's temperatures seldom top the mid-80's and Windhoek occasionally gets to 90 degrees or so in the October-to-February austral summer, but their lows, in May through August, frequently reach down into the 40's. Rain gear is worth bringing only to Windhoek and the north in January, February and March. Otherwise, normal dry temperate and tropical clothing is appropriate for the entire territory.

Different seasons are most appropriate for touring in different parts of the territory: April to June for Windhoek and environs; August to October for Etosha Park. Cool currents along the Atlantic coast keep Walvis Bay, Swakopmund and Lüderitz pleasant (although susceptible to fog) for most of the year, particularly in the summer season from November to March. This is the period when rain (what there is of it) falls on the warmer interior. Light sandy winds blow on the coasts in June and July.

Communication

Windhoek and Swakopmund are good places to practice your German, but English is an official language, too, recognized throughout the territory. Windhoek newspapers come in English, German and Afrikaans. The Cape Town press is flown to Windhoek and Walvis Bay daily. Main telephone and telegraph networks link with trunk lines in South Africa.

Emergencies

True to both German and South African custom, Namibia has excellent medical and other emergency facilities. "European" hospitals exist in over a dozen centers and there is an average of one doctor for every 5,000 inhabitants. "Non-whites are also taken care of," the guides declare. The nearest US consulate is at Cape Town.

Victoria Falls

Rhodesia

Profile

STATUS: By virtue of a unilateral declaration of independence (UDI) in 1965, Rhodesia asserted its independence of Great Britain—a status not recognized by Britain or any other state. In 1970 the regime declared the country a "republic."

SIZE: 150,820 square miles (slightly smaller than Montana). Population—5,400,000, including 250,000 whites, 24,000 Asians and Coloureds.

GEOGRAPHY: Landlocked; central spine of highveld (4,000 feet) sloping to Zambezi River and lowveld plains in the north, Victoria Falls in the northwest, Limpopo River and plains in the south, and Inyanga Mountains in the east. Principal cities—Salisbury (capital, 400,000), Bulawayo (250,000), Umtali.

CLIMATE: Hot in October, slightly less so November to March, the rainy season. Sunny and temperate rest of the year.

LANGUAGES: English (official), Shona, Ndebele.

CURRENCY: Rhodesian dollar, divided into 100 cents. R$1.00 = US$1.52; US$1.00 = 66 Rhodesian cents.

VISAS: Not required.

AIRPORT: Salisbury (SAY), nine miles from city. Frequent flights to Beira, Blantyre, Johannesburg, Lisbon and London. Transportation into city—bus, 25 cents (38 US cents); taxi, R$1.45 (US$2.20).

NATIONAL HOLIDAYS: July 10, Rhodes's Day; July 11, Founders Day; September 12, Pioneers Day; October 23, Republic Day; November 11, Independence Day; Christian holidays.

INFORMATION SOURCES: *In US*—Rhodesia National Tourist Board, 535 Fifth Avenue, New York, N.Y. 10017 (tel. 212/986-6838); Rhodesia Information Office, 2852 McGill Terrace NW, Washington, D.C. 20008 (tel. 202/483-4468). *In Salisbury*—Rhodesia National Tourist Board, Cecil House, 95 Stanley Avenue (tel. 29051).

By Aaron Segal

Travelers to Rhodesia will find well-organized tourist facilities, excellent roads and internal communications, plenty of outdoor sports in a temperate and equable climate, plus two truly outstanding attractions: the great stone ruins of Zimbabwe and Victoria Falls.

Having said that, it must be pointed out that Rhodesia is a sorely troubled (and troublesome) country. Since 1965, when it unilaterally declared its independence from Great Britain, it has been an international "outlaw." Political and economic sanctions voted in the United Nations have been supported, in principle at least, by all UN members except (not surprisingly) South Africa and Portugal.

The issue is minority rule. A quarter of a million white Rhodesians, more than half of whom were born elsewhere, exercise repressive political and economic domination over nearly five million black Rhodesians, 15,000 persons of racially mixed descent ("Coloureds" in local parlance) and 9,000 Asians.

Also involved from the mother country's point of view is Britain's leadership of a largely non-white Commonwealth and, far from a trivial consideration, British "face." The mother country is therefore a strong supporter of UN sanctions, which theoretically are intended to break the rebellion. Britain declines to use military force.

Actually, Rhodesia has been an unruly colony for a long while. Between 1890 and 1918 it was the de facto property of Cecil Rhodes's British South Africa Company. Called Southern Rhodesia to distinguish it from the northern territory named for Rhodes (now the independent Republic of Zambia), it continued to be administered by the company until 1923, when it became a self-governing colony. From that day to this, it has been less than subservient to the wishes of Whitehall.

White explorers reached what is now Rhodesia early in the 19th century, but impressive African civilizations occupied the territory since at least the 8th century, the period of the earliest stone buildings at Zimbabwe. During the 16th century a new kingdom, known as Rozwi, defeated and partly assimilated that of Zimbabwe. It was defeated in the early 19th century by roving Ngoni-speaking groups. One of those groups, the Ndebele (also known as the Matabele), settled near the present city of Bulawayo, dominating the earlier Shona residents.

Cecil Rhodes had already made a fortune in South African gold and diamonds when in the 1880's he became interested in the great African heartland lying beyond the Limpopo River. His motives were partly mercenary, partly patriotic. He hoped to find gold and minerals here to rival the wealth of Kimberley and the Rand, and to add to his vast fortune through land sales to settlers. He was also motivated to preempt Portuguese, German and Boer designs upon the area.

Rhodes promoted settlement of the new territory and on September 12, 1890, (a date still celebrated by white Rhodesians as Pioneers Day) a camp was established at Salisbury. When the Ndebele realized that the settlers had come to stay, rather than just mine the soil, they fiercely resisted. Nor were they at all happy with Rhodes's clever tactic of employing Shona, whom the Ndebele regarded as their natural subordinates, as policemen. "To whom," asked an emissary of Lobengula, the Ndebele king, "do the Shona belong?"

The Ndebele directed their frustration first against the Shona, whom they accused of "disrespect." When the settlers came to the support of the Shona, armed conflict with the Ndebele became inevitable. The war was fought by the British South Africa Company without British support, and many Africans (as well as a few whites) lost their lives before the Ndebele were subjugated. That was in 1893–94. In 1896–97 the settlers had another war on their hands, this time with their former allies, the Shona, as well as the Ndebele. And again the whites demonstrated the superiority of firearms. Atrocities on both sides marked these conflicts and long-lasting mutual distrust resulted.

Although the settlers were disappointed in the mineral wealth of the territory, they prospered through commercial agriculture (tobacco originally) and stock farming, and eventually mining and light industry. They were aided immensely by cheap African labor and a series of laws and tax measures, such as the one that reserved for whites 50 per cent of the land (including, of course, the most fertile areas and the cities) and the tax laws that imposed on Africans the steepest burdens, forcing many to leave their small farms to work for pittance wages.

Generous land grants spurred the rate of white settlement. In 1922 the settlers rejected union with South Africa. Railway lines to Mozambique and South African ports helped the landlocked colony to survive.

The British Government in 1953 encouraged the formation of the Central African Federation, composed of Southern and Northern Rhodesia and Nyasaland, at least partly to temper the settler influence through association with two territories ruled by British colonial officials. As Africans acquired majority rule and demanded independence in Northern Rhodesia (now Zambia) and Nyasaland (Malawi), the federation foundered. It was dissolved in 1963, leaving the white settlers of Southern Rhodesia still in complete control, thanks to a restricted franchise that gives whites 50 times the voting strength of blacks.

As Britain fretted and African nationalists sought to organize against severe police repression, a majority of white settlers led by Prime Minister

Ian Smith moved inexorably toward UDI (unilateral declaration of independence). The step was taken on November 11, 1965.

The two major African nationalist parties—the Zimbabwe African National Union (ZANU) and the Zimbabwe African Peoples Union (ZAPU)—have been bitterly divided and thus far ineffective. Both parties are illegal and their leaders are in jail or in exile. However, mounting incidents of sabotage caused Rhodesia to close its 400-mile Zambezi River border with Zambia in January, 1973 (even tourists are not permitted to cross).

UN economic sanctions have hurt tobacco and other exports, but the economy is growing with back-door help from Portugal and South Africa. The US Senate's decisions in 1971 and 1972 to allow the import of Rhodesian chrome were a major blow to the sanctions policy.

Intermittent negotiations between the British and Rhodesian governments have been unsuccessful. In 1971–72 they broke down after a British investigating team, the Pearce Commission, reported that Africans were overwhelmingly opposed to any deal that would perpetuate white settler rule. The commission's mere presence sparked widespread anti-government rioting.

Although Rhodesia lacks the rigid ideological outlook of South Africa on racial matters, it is moving in the direction of apartheid. Non-white visitors are not barred, but neither are they welcome.

Most literature on the country is highly partisan. Lewis Gann provides a pro-settler *History of Southern Rhodesia*, in contrast to the pro-African versions offered by Nathan Shamuyarira in *Crisis in Rhodesia* and Stanlake Samkange in *Origins of Rhodesia*. Doris Lessing's *Martha Quest* is a vivid fictional account of her own childhood in colonial Rhodesia. Critical pro-African accounts of contemporary Rhodesia can be found in the pages of *Africa Today*, a quarterly published by the Center on International Race Relations at the University of Denver.

Although not recognized diplomatically by the US, the Rhodesian government maintains an information office in Washington and a tourist office in New York, both of which have copious travel and other government literature (see *Profile* for addresses).

Money Matters

The Rhodesian dollar is exchangeable only in South Africa, Botswana, Angola, Malawi and Mozambique. In spite of economic sanctions and the shortage of foreign exchange there is little or no black market within the country and only a slight discount available in South Africa. The official rate of exchange is one Rhodesian dollar to US$1.52, making the US dollar worth about 66 Rhodesian cents. Banks are open from 8 am to 2 pm, except on Wednesday and Saturday when they close at 11 am. Barclays, National and Grindlays, the Standard Bank, and the Netherlands Bank of Rhodesia all have branches around the country and extensive overseas affiliations. Major credit cards and travelers checks are accepted. While residents of Rhodesia are subject to strict controls on export and import of currency, travelers are free from restrictions.

Getting In and Out

Rhodesia does not require visas from holders of United States, Canadian, British and various other Western European passports. However, writers, journalists, photographers and recognizable opponents of racism may be refused entry at airports and immigration stations; it's best to list your profession as "businessman," "housewife" or "mathematics teacher."

Rhodesia is most easily reached by air. The South African Airways' flight from London to Johannesburg stops at Salisbury. Air Rhodesia and South African Airways operate several flights a day between Salisbury and Johannesburg, some with special excursion fares. Air Rhodesia and TAP Portuguese Airways fly between Salisbury and Bulawayo, Rhodesia's main cities, and Beira, Lourenço Marques and Vilanculos (Mozambique). TAP also flies three times a week between Salisbury and Lisbon via Luanda (Angola). Rhodesia can be included at no extra expense on tickets between North America or Europe and South Africa.

Union Castle, P.O. Lines and other passenger cruise ships operate between Southampton and South Africa, and these sea vacations can be combined with flights to Rhodesia. Normally these arrangements involve a package tour that includes Salisbury, Victoria Falls, and if desired, other Rhodesian national parks.

Rhodesia is also accessible by road and rail. There are comfortable first and second class passenger facilities on Rhodesia Railways to the Mozambique ports of Beira and Lourenço Marques, a pleasant but much slower trip than by car. Although primarily for freight, there is also a long rail run across Botswana from South Africa. Excellent paved roads connect Beira with Bulawayo and Salisbury. Another first-class road links Salisbury to the South African heartland including Pretoria and Johannesburg, crossing the border at Beit Bridge, where the customs and immigration post is open from 6 am to 8 pm. Express Motorways Company, P.O. Box 3298, Salisbury, offers comfortable bus service between Salisbury and Johannesburg twice a week. Hitchhiking for well-groomed white males is also good on roads to Beira and Johannesburg.

Traveling north to independent Black Africa benefits from daily flights on Air Malawi and Air Rhodesia between Salisbury and Blantyre (Malawi). At Blantyre you can connect to flights to Zambia, East Africa, and the Indian Ocean island of Mauritius. Pedestrians used to cross the Victoria Falls bridge from Rhodesia to Livingstone (Zambia) and connect there with flights, buses or trains to Lusaka. Travelers wishing to visit neighboring Botswana may do so by a rough but all-weather road from Bulawayo to Francistown and Gaberones (both in Botswana) or by an exciting 50-mile drive from Victoria Falls to the lodge in Botswana's Chobe National Park (see chapter on Botswana).

Getting in and out becomes politically complicated only for visitors who plan to go north from Rhodesia to independent Africa. Rhodesia has cordial relations only with neighboring Malawi. There is constant tension with Zambia, whose government is determined to reduce its economic dependence on Rhodesia. Travelers with Rhodesian entry permits or stamps in their passports may encounter hostility or even refusals of entry in some African countries, although much depends on the mood of the individual immigration officer. It is prudent either to save Rhodesia for the end of your trip or to ask the Rhodesian immigration officials not to stamp your passport. There are no document problems entering Malawi from Rhodesia, but the Zambians and others may want to know what you were doing there.

Getting Around Within Rhodesia

The best way to see the country, unless you're with a tour group, is by car. Many white Rhodesians own two cars and trailers (known as caravans). There are more than 2,000 miles of two-lane paved roads linking the major cities and towns and another 1,000 miles of roads paved with a single-lane tar strip. The latter can be treacherous, since someone must get off the paved strip when two cars meet.

Although imported gasoline from South Africa is expensive, auto rental rates are still reasonable. Avis (10 Sinoia Street in Salisbury and at the airport), for example, charges US$4.20 a day for a Toyota Corolla or $25 plus 8 cents a mile by the week. Hertz, York Car Hire and Southern Cross Safaris also operate auto rental agencies in Rhodesia. If you have one of their credit cards or a card accepted by them, no deposit is required. Minimum age for auto rental drivers is 16 provided that the contract is endorsed by someone over 21 and that the driver has an international license. Driving is on the left.

Inter-city bus service is infrequent and uncomfortable except between Salisbury and Bulawayo. Rhodesia Railways, however, offers good and reliable passenger service and Air Rhodesia has many domestic flights. Rhodesia United Air Carriers operates a charter service out of Salisbury and has spectacular flights from Victoria Falls over the falls and river.

In Salisbury and Bulawayo taxis operate from stands at or near the major hotels and office buildings. They can also be summoned by phone. Taxis are metered; the rate ranges from 14 to 35 US cents for the first mile, plus 35 cents for each one-seventh of a mile thereafter. City buses are crowded and inconvenient, operating mainly between African areas and industrial zones. Heavy traffic makes bicycle-riding dangerous.

Much of Rhodesian tourism is based on organized package tours. Prices, accommodations and efficiency compare favorably with package tours available elsewhere in Africa. Some of the most interesting and most reasonably priced tours are operated by Rhodesia Railways and by Air Rhodesia (its "Flame Lily" holidays, for example).

Tours range from a three-hour sightseeing bus trip around Salisbury to a six-day visit to Kariba Dam, Wankie National Park and Victoria Falls. A one-day coach trip from Salisbury to the ruins of Zimbabwe costs $30; a five-day tour runs about $175. These typical prices can be beaten if you can find several persons to share the costs of a rented car, but not otherwise. Unless you want to book a package from South Africa or Mozambique that includes transportation in or out of the country, it's best to make tour arrangements after you arrive in Rhodesia. Besides Air Rhodesia and Rhodesia Railways, attractive tours are offered by United Touring Company (also agents for Hertz) and Southern Cross Safaris.

Where to Stay

Rhodesia has a number of good, moderately priced hotels. There's an official guide to hotels, national park rest-camps, caravan and camping sites available without cost from the Rhodesian tourist office in New York and from the Registrar of Hotels, Department of Tourism, Cecil House, 95 Stanley Avenue, Salisbury. Although complete hotel segregation is not yet the law of the land, most hotels are racially exclusive. The guide does not indicate which of the quality hotels will accept non-white guests; it only lists several hotels that "cater especially for African visitors" which are generally located in African townships. The only way to avoid embarrassment is to inquire in advance. Outside the capital multiracial hotels are particularly hard to find.

SALISBURY has three distinguished hotels that are (at least at this time) multiracial. The centrally located Jameson (130 rooms) charges from US$10 to $15, breakfast included; it offers radio and TV in each room, a very good outdoor buffet luncheon and a reasonable restaurant.

The *Ambassador* (89 rooms) on Union Avenue charges $8 to $12 for rooms with private bath and TV; it caters especially to businessmen. *Meikles Hotel* (213 rooms), an important political and business hub overlooking Cecil Square in the center of the city, is the largest and best hotel in the country; rates are $14 to $16 in the east wing and $8 to $12 in the modest west wing with its inferior view, both including breakfast.

Salisbury has several inexpensive downtown hotels in the $8-to-$10 range (breakfast included) like the *Queens* and the *Norfolk*, plus numerous hotels and boarding houses with weekly and monthly rates. And there's the simple and clean YMCA hotel with bed and breakfast at $2.50 and the YWCA residential club at $3.

The *Federal Hotel* (Kudzanayi) on Salisbury Street, several blocks from the city center, has only seven rooms but advertises itself as "completely international and multiracial." Its bed-and-breakfast rate is only $4 and it is a good place to meet Africans, but it is really more a bar than a hotel. The University of Rhodesia guest house and student residences, although far from the center of town, are multiracial and inexpensive.

The second city of BULAWAYO has the comfortable and modern *Southern Sun* with 190 air-conditioned rooms at rates from $9 to $25, breakfast included. *Grey's Inn*, a family hotel, is more modest with 22 double and eight single rooms at rates of $7 to $10 with breakfast. The *Carlton* is equally central and slightly cheaper.

VICTORIA FALLS has the luxurious *Casino Hotel* with 107 air-conditioned rooms at $14 for bed and breakfast. The 152-bed air-conditioned *Victoria Falls Hotel*, a delightful restored 1905 building, offers excellent accommodations; its rate for bed and breakfast is $12. *Peter's Holiday Motel* with 45 double air-conditioned rooms at $8.50 is a little farther from the falls.

If you're driving between Salisbury or Bulawayo and Victoria Falls, the *Gwaai River Hotel* in WANKIE DISTRICT is a welcome stop for good food and rooms. It charges $4 to $6 for bed and breakfast and boasts a bar with a sign declaring that "all the water served on these premises has been personally passed by the Manager."

Two hotels serve visitors to ZIMBABWE. The *Zimbabwe Ruins*, within walking distance of the ruins, has 41 rooms and charges about $9 for room and full board. *Sheppards Hotel*, a short drive from the ruins but closer to water sports at Kyle Dam, has 26 double rooms with bath at $7, breakfast included. Both hotels have swimming pools, a welcome feature after a day spent tramping around the ruins.

Some of the most attractive accommodations in the country are to be found at the 250 chalets, cottages, lodges and tents in the national parks. Such facilities are to be found at Victoria Falls, Wankie, Kariba, Matopos and other parks. They are in principle open to visitors of all races and can be booked through the National Parks Central Booking Office, P.O. Box 8151, Causeway, Salisbury (tel. 26087), or at the parks. Chalets come with one or two bedrooms and communal showers, toilets and kitchens. The rate is $2 a night per person and includes use of cooking utensils. Cottages have their own kitchens, baths and toilets, and the rate for them is $2.40 a night. Tents, available only at Falls Camp at Victoria Falls, cost $1.40 a night, including use of communal kitchens, toilets and showers. Bring your own cutlery and crockery to these accommodations, but for $3.50 per person you can get a two-room lodge with kitchen, stove, bath, toilet, utensils and crockery.

At most population centers elsewhere in Rhodesia you can find comfortable and inexpensive hotels. For instance, at UMTALI the *Cecil* and the *Wise Owl* are both pleasant, with the latter more of a motel. Nearby in the Inyanga Mountains the *Montclair* and the *Troutbeck Inn* come close to the luxury class in facilities with reasonable prices. At the eastern end of Lake Kariba the *Cutty Sark* and *Kariba Heights* are air-conditioned hostelries with swimming pools and equipment for other sports, including a chip and putt golf course at the Cutty Sark. Accommodations in the game parks are discussed in greater detail in the section *What to See and Do*.

This is one of the few places in Africa, it might be noted, where good dry cleaning is available. Beauty parlors also are good. The customary tip is five to 10 per cent, the same as for hotel and restaurant service.

Where and What to Eat

Unfortunately, food in Rhodesia does not come up to the standards of its hotels. At best it can only offer reasonable facsimiles of French, Italian and Chinese cooking. Unless you stop at an African hotel, you won't have an opportunity to sample African dishes. A few Asian- and Coloured-owned combination bar-cafes that serve curries and stews are to be found on the edges of the downtown districts of both principal cities.

Rhodesian breakfasts are English-style, which is to say substantial. Lunches are often a buffet and evening meals are heavy, often preceded by an extended cocktail hour (called a "sundowner"). Afternoon tea, with sandwiches and pastries and tea with milk in the English manner, is a widespread custom. Even more so is drinking, usually in hotel public bars and cocktail lounges. (Ladies welcome, but generally not non-whites.) Local beers are good, but the preference is for Scotch—one way of demonstrating that UN economic sanctions have not worked. Public bars close at 9:30 pm Sundays, 10:30 pm other days.

The best dishes are likely to be fresh rainbow trout from the Inyanga Mountains, shrimps and prawns flown in from the Indian Ocean and served "piri piri" in the Mozambican style with succulent sauces, and good, solid Rhodesian beef and steaks.

The best restaurants in SALISBURY charge $5 to $6 per person, wine (usually South African) included. The *Bamboo Inn* on Manica Road has good Chinese food; *La Fontaine* in Meikles Hotel specializes in Continental cuisine; the *Colony* in the Windsor Hotel is known for its beef and steaks. Outside Salisbury there isn't much to whet the appetite, although there are numerous coffee shops and snack-bars serving inexpensive meals. Hotel meals, like those at the huge *Victoria Falls* dining room, are often accompanied by dance music (often loud and only faintly "Africanized" for local color) and slow archaic British service. Major hotel restaurants in BULAWAYO are as strong on roast beef as those in the *Cecil* and *Selborne* hotels. UMTALI is the place for fresh mountain trout, specialties of the outlying *Montclair Hotel* and the *Troutbeck Inn*, where you can do your own fishing, and of the *Hotel Cecil* in town.

What to See and Do

"This was the most wonderful sight I had witnessed in Africa," wrote David Livingstone of the falls that he first saw in 1855 and named for Queen Victoria. Called Musi-o-tunya ("smoke that thunders") by the Africans, *Victoria Falls* is indeed spectacular.

"We came in sight," Livingstone recounted, "of the columns of vapour, appropriately called 'smoke,' rising at a distance of five or six miles, exactly as when large tracts of grass are burned in Africa. Five columns now arose, and bending in the direction of the wind, they seemed placed against a low ridge covered with trees; the tops of the columns at this distance appeared to mingle with the clouds. . . . The whole scene was extremely beautiful. But though we were within a few yards of the falls, I believe that no one could perceive where the vast body of water went; it seemed to lose itself in the earth. At least I did not comprehend it until, creeping with awe to the verge, I peered down into a large rent which had been made from bank to bank of the broad Zambesi, and saw that a stream of a thousand yards broad, leaped down a hundred feet, and then became suddenly compressed into a space of fifteen or twenty yards. . . ."

The falls are best viewed from the Zambian side of the bridge across the Zambezi. Before 1973 you could have crossed the bridge by car or bus or on foot. It's still best to see the falls on foot, exploring on the Rhodesian side the eight downstream gorges, the footpath through the rain forest, the Chain Walk path and other trails. You will need a rain-coat or bathing suit, a cover to keep camera and film dry, and a flashlight if you want to approach the falls at night. The best time, however, is in the afternoon, when the sun is behind the Rhodesian side. The view from the air and a river cruise will help put it all in perspective.

Rhodesian United Air Carriers has a 15-minute flight over the falls in a small plane for $8 that's especially appealing to photo fans. The same firm also offers a $25 one-hour flight that includes some great views of wildlife on the Wankie game reserve. The two-hour sunset cruise on the Zambezi leaves at 5 pm. The teetotalers' cruise costs $2, while the "sun-downer" cruise costs $4.50, drinks included. In the dry season, hippos and other game are abundantly visible.

There are other tours from Victoria Falls—to a crocodile farm, to a private game reserve, to the village of Shangaan Mushu. The latter, of-fered by United Touring Company, includes a good barbecue and dancing by the Ndawa and Makishi people. The dancing is much less phony than most "tribal dancing" for tourists in Africa.

Driving to the falls permits game watching in the *Wankie* and *Victoria Falls National Parks*, if that interests you. Otherwise, you can take Air Rhodesia's one-day weekend tour ($45 from Salisbury). Air Rhodesia also has more expensive two- and three-day tours with overnights spent at the Victoria Falls Casino, the only place in Rhodesia where gambling is legal (roulette, chemin de fer and baccarat are offered).

The other great attraction is Zimbabwe, a source of pride to Africans. The ruins are located 18 miles south of Fort Victoria, which in turn is 274 miles south of Salisbury and 179 miles east of Bulawayo. Tours leave from all three towns, but it is probably more interesting (and cheaper) to go by rail, air or bus to Fort Victoria, rent a car there from United Touring or Southern Cross Safaris, and take in the ruins on your own.

These ruins were stumbled upon in 1868 by an American big game hunter, subsequently pillaged for treasure, partly explored in the 1920's, and today stand in brooding solitude. Some of them dating back more than a thousand years in all probability, the impressive ruins comprise an "acropolis"—a massive fortification with intricate passageways, nu-merous rooms, and evidence of gold smelting—an elliptical "temple" or great enclosure and the footings of many stone houses. Walls reach 32 feet in height and 16 feet in width. The stonework was fitted without mortar—stone or wooden lintels were used—and there appears to have been an extensive drainage system. Zimbabwe is one of the world's major archaeological treasures. The book *Zimbabwe* by Roger Summers (Thomas Nelson, 1963) will be of interest to visitors.

Near the ruins, incidentally, is an aloe garden that flowers in July and August. At nearby man-made Lake Kyle there's fishing, water skiing and game watching, and at *Musahandike National Park*, 24 miles west of Fort Victoria, you can enjoy fishing and boating.

For the rest of Rhodesia, starting with the capital city:

SALISBURY is a modern commercial center with broad avenues, rows of skyscrapers and an agreeable climate. The flowering jacaranda trees, scarlet flame trees and flamboyants add to the enjoyment of strollers.

Cecil Square is the site of the first settler encampment in 1890. The city contains several interesting museums including the Queen Victoria Museum, which has a fine natural history collection, the Rhodes National Gallery, where African artists and craftsmen work and exhibit, and the National Archives Building with its exhibits of Rhodesian history. The botanical gardens are also worth a visit. If Parliament is in session, you can sit in the public gallery.

Another view of Rhodesian life may be gained by a visit to the African townships. It is instructive to visit and compare white and African urban schools and medical facilities. African students at the University of Rhodesia, one of the few multiracial institutions left, can also provide a glimpse of what it's like to be black in Rhodesia. If you are white, you can get an invitation to a white Rhodesian home through the Salisbury and District Publicity Association's "Meet the Rhodesians" scheme. The association is located at 84b Rezende Street (tel. 21315). Sightseeing bus tours of the city and the townships are available at $4 per person for three hours.

Night life in Salisbury is sedate and largely confined to hotel bars and nightclubs. There are occasional amateur classical music concerts at the National Theatre, as well as visiting and local semi-professional theatrical groups. Le Coq d'Or on Baker Avenue offers a floor show, usually with talent imported from Europe, as do the hotels.

Pleasant nearby excursions include the *Ewanrigg National Park*, 25 miles north of Salisbury, with its 60-acre garden of aloes and cacti, best seen in June-August when they are flowering. Lake McIlwaine, 20 miles southwest on the Bulawayo Road, has yachting, water skiing, fishing, and bird and small game watching. Swimming is advisable only where posted notices indicate that the water is free of bilharzia. You may also enjoy the Borrowdale race track. Tembo Village, the replica of a 19th century African village, has tribal dancing put on strictly for the tourists. Mermaid's Pool, a resort on a river 25 miles from Salisbury, also has staged tribal dancing. Seven miles from the city on the Widdicombe Road are the giant balancing rocks, precariously perched boulders clinging to one another. A more interesting trip is 80 miles north to the Sinoia Caves and the deep-blue underground pool. Visits can also be arranged to tobacco farms, cattle ranches, citrus groves and agricultural stations.

BULAWAYO, Rhodesia's second city, is a primarily industrial community. The National Museum here has interesting wildlife and geological exhibits, as well as Rhodes memorabilia. The city is host to an annual trade fair, usually in late April. There are dreary African townships here, worth a visit by the sociologically inclined. The city, it might be pointed out, has an excellent municipally operated camping and trailer (caravan) site.

Excursions in the area include Maleme Dam for fishing and picnicking, and at Khani, 14 miles west of Bulawayo, the ruins of a large settlement with stone steps and paths leading to the remains of a fantastic hilltop palace. You may also want to visit the Jesuit Cyrene Mission and the Anglican Hope Fountain Mission for a look at rural African education, and some interesting student art.

South of Bulawayo is *Rhodes Matopos National Park* with its magnificent granite hills and weird rock outcroppings. Stone Age Bushmen left their delicate rock paintings in caves here (at Pomongwe, Bambata and Nswatugi); here the Ndebele made their last stand against the settlers in 1896, and here Cecil Rhodes chose to be buried. Today herds of wildebeest, zebra, warthog, ostrich and rhino roam the plains.

FORT VICTORIA is the first town settled by the Pioneer Column in 1890. Having stopped to rest here on their long trek to Salisbury, the pioneers left behind a contingent of British South Africa Police to erect an earthen fort. Today the town has a population of 13,000 (2,600 Europeans) and is the center of the region's mining and ranching industry. It has little of note for tourists except that it is near the Zimbabwe Ruins, which must be seen, and the *Kyle National Park*, which has a game reserve well stocked with buffalo, giraffe, sable, water buck, impala, wildebeest, kudu, reedbuck and hippo and some rare species like the nyala, oribi, blesbok, hartebeest and the square-lipped white rhino. The game reserve is on the shore of Lake Kyle, behind the dam constructed in 1961. The area has since been developed into a recreation spot for boating, water skiing and fishing. There are comfortable thatched stone lodges (equipped with servants and electric lighting) and on a hilltop overlooking the lake there are camping and caravan sites.

From Fort Victoria there is a 192-mile road that runs east and north to Umtali, near the Mozambique border. Along the route, at Chipinga, a branch road leads 18 miles to the Mt. Silinda forest and the United Church of Christ Mission, an educational complex in a lovely rural setting near the Zona Tea Estate. It is open to visitors.

UMTALI is a pleasant town with two good hotels—the Cecil and the Wise Owl—a regional museum and a modern little theater. Just south of Umtali is the *Vumba National Park*, set in the beautiful Vumba Mountains. More rugged and spectacular, however, are the Inyanga Mountains north of Umtali. Amid these mountains are the *Rhodes Inyanga* and *Mtarazi Falls National Parks*, which can be reached via a 75-mile road skirting the Mozambique border. There are mountain streams full of rainbow trout, the park campsites are excellent, and for the luxury-minded the area has two fine hotels, the Montclair and the Troutbeck Inn. In the mountain village of Vukutu there is a workshop of talented soapstone sculptors.

Just across the northern border of the Rhodes Inyanga National Park is Inyanga Village, where you can get permission from the District Commissioner to visit the African Weaving Centre at Rugare Mission. There are attractive natural wool rugs for sale here. Accessible from Inyanga Village are the Nyahokwe Ruins and the Van Niekerk Ruins, miles of only partly explored walls and terracing in a splendid setting.

The Zambezi Valley in the northwest is noted for its Kariba Dam, a 420-foot high structure opened in 1961. The damming of the Zambezi River provides power for the Zambian Copperbelt, as well as Rhodesia, and it has created the 2,000-square-mile Lake Kariba, largest man-made lake in the world. The lake, excellent for fishing and boating, is becoming a major tourist attraction. Of special interest to anglers is the tiger fish, unique to Rhodesia. Roaming on the shores are elephants and other game. On the eastern end are accommodations for every taste, including two air-conditioned hotels, the Cutty Sark and Kariba Heights. Air Rhodesia has six flights a week to the town of Kariba from Salisbury, with onward connections to the Wankie National Park and Victoria Falls. You can also drive to Kariba from Salisbury (five hours on a tarred road).

Wankie National Park, as big as the state of Connecticut, is below Victoria Falls in the western part of the country and is on the itinerary of tours to the falls. The park has a large number of elephants, specimens of 50 other types of game and a wide range of birdlife. Within the park guides are available for game viewing drives. Observation platforms near waterholes provide up-close viewing. On the edge of the park is the new Southern Sun Safari Lodge, a luxury establishment where you can see big game from your bedroom balcony or the glass-fronted dining room. Less elaborate but comfortable accommodations are available in the Main Camp and Sinamatella Camp, open all year, and Robins Camp, closed during the main rains, November through May.

Hunting in Rhodesia is tightly controlled and not nearly as good as in neighboring Botswana or Mozambique. The best opportunities are in private game areas owned by the following companies: Matabeleland Game Safaris, P.O. Box 2217, Bulawayo; Nampini Safaris, P.O. Box 95, Victoria Falls; Rhodesian Safaris Ltd, P.O. Box 191, Salisbury; Rosslyn Farms Ltd, Private Bag 5, Wankie, and Zambezi Hunters Ltd, P.O. Box 1938, Salisbury. These agencies will provide all equipment. But reservations should be made well in advance.

If you're interested in a game viewing or photographic safari get in touch with one of these agencies: Kazungula Safaris, P.O. Box 3938, Salisbury; Camera Africa Safaris, P.O. Box 3676, Salisbury, or Abercrombie South Safaris Ltd, P.O. Box 2997, Salisbury.

Fishing is excellent throughout the country. There are 56 angling clubs belonging to the Rhodesia National Anglers' Union. You can get full information by writing to the Union at 42 Baines Avenue, Salisbury.

Information about other sports activities—and there are many, including golf, tennis, rugby, cricket, polo, riding and soccer football—can be obtained from the National Tourist Board or from the local publicity office in each town.

What to Buy

It is technically illegal to import into the US anything from Rhodesia except chrome. Since Rhodesia has no bargains, either in crafts or manufactured goods, this is not likely to cause the traveler a crisis of conscience. Neighboring countries offer better prices for carvings, animal skins and other African artifacts, as well as wider selections.

There are, however, three exceptions: copperware, jewelry made from semi-precious gemstones (also sold uncut), and the ingenious soapstone and granite carvings by young African artists working at the Rhodes National Gallery in Salisbury, at Victoria Falls and in the countryside.

There are also attractive picture postcards and color slides—gifts which you can safely purchase without concern over sanctions.

Business hours are from 8 am to 5 pm, 8 to 11 am Saturdays.

Local Attitudes

Most white Rhodesians support UDI and are convinced that the rest of the world misunderstands and misjudges them. They feel that by their own hard work and talents they have built a fine country that would be destroyed under African majority rule. At the same time, they often express the view that they are doing their best for the Africans and their advancement. They will go out of their way to argue these points, often stressing their commitment to Christianity and Western values as blocks to the spread of Communism in Africa. A handful of white liberals and some businessmen concerned about the effects of economic sanctions don't share these views, but even they are convinced that a quick transfer of political and economic power to Africans would spell disaster for Rhodesia as they know it.

Africans have few chances to speak for themselves. The chiefs are appointed and paid by the government, the militant nationalist leaders are either under detention or in exile, and other people are wary of the consequences of speaking freely to strangers. The American-educated Methodist Bishop Abel Muzorewa, of the African National Council, has emerged as the most effective public spokesman for the under-represented majority, humiliated by contemptuous racial policies.

The government prefers visitors who stick to the game parks, opt for packaged tours, and leave impressed with the efficiency of the country and the low prices of their holiday in the sun. Like some independent black African states, Rhodesia has a reputation for expelling journalists and others who ask sensitive questions or seek out critical points of view. It's best, therefore, to listen and not argue.

White Rhodesians are conservative socially as well as politically. Their dress is drab, their cities dull and their conversation provincial. (The more lively whites take their own holidays at the more swinging, less inhibited beach resorts of Mozambique.) Hotels and restaurants are likely to insist on coat and tie for both lunch and dinner. Miniskirts are acceptable, but any behavior that smacks of "hippieness" (including, of course, smoking grass) is out. And remember that there's no American representation in the country.

Weather, What to Wear, How Long to Stay

A gentle temperate climate is one of Rhodesia's main selling points. The sun shines four to 10 hours a day throughout the year, the humidity is low on the plateau, and the rainy seasons short with annual rainfall 20 to 40 inches in many parts of the country. The coolest months are June and July when sweaters are welcome during Salisbury evenings. October is the hottest month but on the plateau the temperature rarely exceeds 90 degrees; the lowveld is generally hotter and more humid. The rainy season begins at the end of October and lasts until late April. Rarely does it rain more than a few hours a day but raincoats or umbrellas are useful. Winter is technically from May to August but a coat or sweater is needed only at night and early morning. Coat and tie are customary in the cities. At the game parks and in the rural areas dress is much more casual, although hotels still may stick to the coat and tie rule.

Especially if you use the guided tours, a week is sufficient to see Victoria Falls, Zimbabwe, Kariba and something of Salisbury. Victoria Falls and Zimbabwe can even be crowded into three days if you fly. You may want to stay longer to visit other ruins, the Inyanga Mountains, Wankie and Matopos, unless you prefer to see more of Africa that is African. In which case, push on.

Communication

Postal service to South Africa, Europe and North America is good, to the rest of Africa virtually non-existent due to sanctions. Air letters take a week to reach North America. Telephone service is good too, with direct distance dialing to many parts of the country and to Zambia. Radio-telephone links to London are fast and generally reliable; overseas calls also may be placed through South Africa. Telex service is direct to South Africa and Zambia and through the Telex exchange in Salisbury for overseas connections.

English is the official language, spoken throughout the country by all races, a majority of Africans having had at least some exposure to it in school or at work. The government-operated radio and television programs are in English, Shona and Ndebele. TV operates from 5 to 10:30 pm and carries a mixture of local variety shows and imported programs.

The privately owned *Rhodesian Herald* is the leading newspaper, mildly critical at times of the government but carefully censored, as are all publications, local and imported. The various chambers of commerce publish a number of trade journals, and the government printing office and the Department of Statistics release what the government wants known about the economy and such sensitive subjects as imports-exports and the balance of trade. The Rhodesia Science Society puts out an informative journal on natural history and geography.

Emergencies

Rhodesia has competent doctors and dentists, concentrated mostly in Salisbury and Bulawayo, and the Salisbury General Hospital has excellent facilities. There is no US diplomatic or consular representation. The American Embassy in Pretoria and the US consulate in Johannesburg look after national interests and the nearly 1,000 Americans in Rhodesia (mainly missionaries and businessmen) from a distance.

Republic of South Africa

Profile

STATUS: Union created in 1910, granted sovereignty by Britain in 1934. Republic since May 31, 1961.

SIZE: 472,359 square miles (the size of Texas, Oklahoma and New Mexico combined). Population—21,314,000 (includes 14,000,000 Africans, 4,000,000 Europeans, 2,000,000 Coloureds and 500,000 Indians).

GEOGRAPHY: Bordered on west, south and east by Atlantic and Indian Oceans, on north by Namibia, Botswana, Rhodesia and Mozambique. Four provinces: Cape of Good Hope in west and south, Natal in east, Orange Free State in center, Transvaal in north. High inland plateau, hill country of Natal falling sharply to the coasts. Lowveld in eastern Transvaal. Drakensberg mountains (11,000 feet) in Natal. Principal cities—Pretoria (capital, 500,000), Cape Town (1,000,000), Johannesburg (2,000,000), Durban (750,000).

CLIMATE: Temperate. Seasons reverse of US.

LANGUAGES: Afrikaans and English (both official); African languages.

CURRENCY: South African rand (R), divided into 100 cents. R1.00 = $1.33; $1.00 = R 0.75.

VISAS: Required. Available from South African consulates in New York, New Orleans and San Francisco. No fee. No photos needed. Takes four weeks for whites, longer for blacks, if issued at all.

AIRPORTS: Jan Smuts Airport (JBN), 17 miles from Johannesburg. Well connected with East, Central and West Africa, Western Europe, North and South America, Indian Ocean and Australia. Transportation into city—bus, 55 cents (73 US cents); taxi R5.00 ($6.65). D. F. Malan Airport (CPT), nine miles from Cape Town, and Louis Botha Airport (DUR), 12 miles from Durban, both well connected by direct and transfer flights (via Johannesburg) with most major cities.

NATIONAL HOLIDAYS: April 6, Van Riebeeck Day; May 31, Republic Day; 2nd Monday in July, Family Day; 1st Monday in September, Settlers' Day; October 10, Kruger Day; December 16, Day of the Covenant; Christian holidays.

INFORMATION SOURCES: *In US*—South African Consulate, 655 Madison Avenue, New York, N.Y. 10021 (tel. 212/838-1700), also 225 Baronne Street, New Orleans, La. 70112 and 120 Montgomery Street, San Francisco, Cal. 94104; South African Tourist Corporation, Rockefeller Center, 610 Fifth Avenue, New York, N.Y. 10020 (tel. 212/245-3720); South African Airways, 605 Fifth Avenue, New York, N.Y. 10017 (tel. 212/421-6477), also branches in Chicago, Houston, Los Angeles, San Francisco and Toronto. *In Pretoria*—South African Tourist Corporation (Satour), President Centre, 265/9 Pretorius Street, Private Bag 164; National Parks Board, P.O. Box 787 (game park information).

By Philip M. Allen

An intense social drama dominates and may even obliterate the attractions of South Africa for serious visitors. Here is a varied beauty of towns and landscape, with lofty mountains, golden beaches, a prairie wilderness in the interior Karroos, and a generally temperate climate. South Africa has some wildlife, although not so much as East Africa, and bountiful waters for ocean sport. It is well organized, comfortable and cheap for white visitors, with cultural and athletic events in Western traditions. More than 20,000 Americans take advantage of these assets annually in what has become a major world tourist industry. For the conscientious traveler, however, they must be weighed against the rigid enforcement of a repugnant racial doctrine (apartheid), a denial of opportunity and even citizenship to the majority, official blindness to the realities of interdependence among communities and a continuing erosion of civil liberties.

South Africa is a large and complicated country. No visitor can see enough of it with sufficient concentration to arrive at a fully balanced verdict. Yet even for Americans reluctant to judge another society (perhaps until our own is in order), some reaction is almost inevitable. Here, black visitors are unwelcome unless officially invited.

Some historical background is crucial to an understanding of South Africa's world.

On April 6, 1652, Jan van Riebeeck and a handful of fellow Dutchmen established a refueling and victualing station for the Dutch East India Company at Cape Town on the maritime pivot between the Atlantic Ocean and the Indies. A monument to van Riebeeck in Cape Town's Heerengracht credits him with bringing "civilization to Southern Africa."

Nobody claims seriously any longer that the Cape was devoid of human inhabitants when the Dutch first settled there. The indigenous Bushmen and Hottentots were characterized, however, as pacific and complaisant, ready to intermarry with Europeans and often to cede land when requested, but less than willing to work on the Dutch farms. Malays and Malagasy were soon brought in as labor, most of them in bondage. Interbreeding took place with local Europeans and Africans. Although interracial sex has been a punishable crime for the last century, whites and non-whites had by then produced a "Coloured" or mulatto population that today amounts to almost two million people.

In addition to the two million Coloureds, most of whom live in Cape Province, contemporary South Africa has a half-million Indian residents whose forebears had been brought to Natal on the east coast to labor on the sugar plantations. The African population (called "Bantu" in

South African legal parlance, although it is applied to a variety of ethnic and linguistic groups) amounts to a majority of almost 70 per cent (14 million). The not quite four million "Europeans" or whites total slightly less than 20 per cent. To make its racial policies work, the government encourages white immigration, but the black population continues to grow at almost twice the rate of the white.

Holland was not the only European interest at the Cape in the 17th century. Portuguese had been there as early as 1486 but had not stayed. French, Spanish and British were on the way, however. The Dutch outpost needed security in addition to food productivity for the Company's ships. The refreshment station grew into a garrison and a colony as more Dutch arrived and as Huguenots joined the Calvinist-Protestant settlement in refuge from Catholic France. Although that group has by now largely abandoned the Cape, it was the foundation of the Afrikaans-speaking community of white South Africa today.

As Afrikaner literature declares, the English have pursued Dutchmen in South Africa for the last three centuries. Britain occupied the highly strategic Cape several times during the Napoleonic wars, annexing it outright in 1814. British soldiers, tradesmen, administrators and missionaries so antagonized the sensibilities of the settled Dutch that by the late 1830's hundreds of families undertook a Great Trek into the interior, seeking farmland and pasture, a sanctuary for their stern religion and "puritan" way of life. This movement brought the "Voortrekkers" or "Trekboers" (pioneer farmers) into conflict with Xhosa, Tswana, Zulu and other African occupants of the land that ultimately became the northeastern part of Cape Province, Natal, Orange Free State and the Transvaal.

The treaty rituals and warfare that ensued for decades closely resemble our own mid-19th century pioneer history—a likeness that inspires some South African apologists to identify their current situation (and solutions) fallaciously with those of the United States.

Although the decisive battles were won by the Boers, South Africa was not entirely safe for Afrikaner civilization. British force of arms and settlers crowded them out of the Natal coast and pushed them farther north from the Cape. When diamonds were found at Kimberley (Orange Free State) in 1866, and two decades later when enormous gold deposits were discovered on the Witwatersrand around Johannesburg (Transvaal), their republics were literally invaded by British and other European fortune hunters, financiers and tradesmen—people whose motives and morality were anathema to the Afrikaners. The inevitable rivalries led in 1895 to the Jameson Raid, a quixotic attempt by

Cape Colony Governor Cecil Rhodes to overthrow Boer rule on the Witwatersrand, and shortly thereafter to the agonizing Anglo-Boer War of 1899-1902. In 1910, to crown the postwar settlement, the Transvaal and Orange Free State were joined with British Natal and Cape Province into the autonomous Union of South Africa, within the British Commonwealth. In 1961, once the Commonwealth's consensus had swung against South Africa's white-monopolized racial policies, an act of the Union Parliament declared South Africa a republic outside the Commonwealth.

For Africans living in the territory, the hostilities between Europeans meant only further expropriation and subjugation—except for the three enclaves of Basuto, Swazi and Batswana that came under British protection until acceding to independence in the 1960's as Lesotho, Swaziland and Botswana (see separate chapters). The ensuing prosperity of South Africa had very different implications for its own African population. Rather than being confined to tribal reserves, which has always been the destiny reserved for Africans by the Afrikaner leadership, one-third of the "Bantu" population has been employed on the white-owned farms and ranches of the interior (producing beef, mutton, leather, grains, wool, sugar, wine and tropical as well as temperate zone fruit); another third is employed in the mining and industrial complexes on the Witwatersrand and beyond.

Industrialization has been based not only on diamonds and gold (in both of which South Africa remains the world's leading producer) but on substantial deposits of iron, coal, copper, manganese and other minerals; on almost $3-billion in investments from Britain (plus nearly another billion from the United States and sizable infusions by other Western investors); on the initiative and technology of South African and foreign entrepreneurs, and on the cheap labor of Africans, Coloureds and Indians. South Africa is the most intensively industrialized nation on the African continent. It has attracted new white immigrants as well as temporary (non-immigrant) African laborers, thus strengthening the hold of "Europeans" and allowing "non-whites" to be assimilated only on the lowest rungs of the economy.

At present, while English-speaking whites control most of the industry, the Afrikaners (53 per cent of the white population) dominate national politics, the civil service, agriculture and the large state industries like iron and steel, armaments and coal. Their principal goal since the end of World War II has been the development of South Africa along lines of multinationalism, not to be confused with its opposite, multiracialism. The system called apartheid (separateness) depends on Afrikaner solidarity and the complicity, tacit or otherwise, of portions of the English-speaking white community, the 130,000 Jews and the Italian, Portuguese and other European immigrants. Blacks have no effective voice.

At the root of the apartheid theory is the proposition that distinct racial groups have distinct personalities and thus constitute distinct "nations." Cohabitation among such nations results, so the government believes, in inevitable weakening of the respective national cultures and/or in a subjugation of one race by another. The theory was put in sharp terms by the Minister of Bantu Administration speaking in Parliament at Cape Town on February 3, 1972:

"Every Bantu in South Africa, wherever he finds himself, is a member of his specific nation and not a member of the nation of which I am a member. The Bantu in the White areas—whether born there or allowed to come there—are there for the labour they are allowed to perform. Basic civil rights are enjoyed by each Bantu person only in his own national bond and linked to his homeland and not to mine. Those Bantu who are in White South Africa are treated here as cohesive communities. While he is there, secondarily, we ensure his liaison with his homeland in every way possible." (*The Daily News*, Durban, February 4, 1972.)

The South African Government seeks to avoid the dangers of "national" cohabitation by overt physical separation of white, black ("Bantu"), Coloured and Asian in their respective territories ("homelands"). However, the homelands reserved for the 70 per cent of the population that is black amount to only 13 per cent of the territory, including none of the urban, mineral or agricultural wealth of developed South Africa. Moreover, the authorities have not yet announced how or where they propose to resettle the two million Coloured or the half-million Asians who have no semblance of an "original" African homeland outside the cities of South Africa, which are reserved exclusively for whites.

"Petty apartheid" affects virtually everybody's daily life—in signs on the doors of all kinds of public facilities designating which race may use them, in the crowded upper sections of double-decker buses whose lower areas are reserved for the few whites traveling those lines, and so on. However "cool" the holiday brochures may sound, petty apartheid is the manifestation of a deep and systematic humiliation of the majority by a racist minority. Some of the brutal aspects of enforcing apartheid have been more widely felt of late. Student protests in 1972 against educational apartheid were repressed with harsh police action. Suddenly, the massive South African military and security machine, used for so long to crush dissent among blacks, was felt by whites.

Critics of apartheid insist that physical separation of the races can never work in South Africa so long as the Republic requires cheap black labor and that the real issues involve the control of South Africa's wealth by a racial minority at the expense of the majority.

If you can speak frankly with black South Africans—difficult because most of their leaders are either in exile, in prison or in fear of police informers—you will learn of apartheid's realities: of urban Africans forced to leave their residences for rural backwaters that they often have never seen but which are identified as their homelands; of a "pass" system that punishes their unauthorized presence in the towns and industrial complexes reserved for whites; of the hardships worked on African laborers, who are prohibited from residing close to their work, who earn only a fraction of white salaries in comparable jobs, and who are excluded from middle-level positions reserved for whites.

South Africa's bibliography is legion, but the country's own writers provide the best beginning. Leo Marquard's *The Peoples and Policies of South Africa* (Oxford, 4th ed., 1969) represents the most serious, exhaustive, critical and patriotic introduction. See also Pierre van den Berghe's *South Africa, A Study in Conflict* (Berkeley, University of California Press, 1967). Alan Paton's several impassioned books include political writings in favor of multiracialism and a charming presentation of South Africa for young students, yet readable at any age, titled *South Africa and Her People* (London, Lutterworth Press, revised 1970). Ernest Cole's *House of Bondage* (Random House, 1967) is an eloquent indictment of the system, magnificently illustrated by Cole's own photographs, from the viewpoint of a self-exiled black South African. The official view of South Africa's accomplishments is provided in the attractive literature available through South African tourist and diplomatic missions abroad. The independent South African Institute of Race Relations, now being investigated by the South African Government for possibly having aided black groups, produces the *Annual Survey of Race Relations in South Africa*, which furnishes documentation on the country's problems. A recent American book is Jim Hoagland's *South Africa: Civilizations in Conflict* (Houghton Mifflin, 1972). Another important new book is *No Neutral Ground* (Thomas Y. Crowell, 1973), a bitter account by Joel Carlson of his years as defense attorney for black South Africans. Most of these are banned in South Africa.

Excellent novelists and poets, black and white, have studied their country with intense imagination. Some of the best examples are found in the works of Ezekiel Mphahlele, Alan Paton, Peter Abrahams, Laurens van der Post, Nadine Gordimer, Alex LaGuma, Lewis Nkosi, Dennis Brutus and playwrights Athol Fugard and Cosmo Pieterse.

Money Matters

South Africa's rand, supported by gold holdings and occasional gold market sales, was devalued with the dollar in 1971. Currency controls restrict the amount of rands brought in and out of South Africa in bank notes (R50 if traveling by air, R100 if by road or rail), but you may carry unlimited quantities of travelers checks or foreign bank notes.

Barclays Bank DCO, the Netherlands Bank of South Africa, American Express, the Standard Bank of South Africa, First National City and the Volkskas all have branches in major towns. Bank are open between 9 am and 3:30 pm except for Wednesdays and Saturdays, when they close at 1 pm and 11 am respectively. In the interior provinces, banks may close for lunch between 12:45 and 2 pm. You can cash foreign currency at airports, hotels and major shops as well. The Diners Club is popular and its cards will be honored in more than 1,000 places in 140 towns.

Getting In and Out

Johannesburg-Pretoria, Cape Town and Durban, South Africa's biggest cities, stand at the points of a long triangle in the eastern half of the country, with several major urban mining and agricultural centers spaced among them. The transportation network is the best on the African continent. Jan Smuts Airport, 17 miles from Johannesburg, as well as other international airports at Cape Town, Durban, Port Elizabeth and East London, receive dozens of flights each day from London, Paris, Frankfurt and Lisbon. There are also flights from New York via West African capitals or Rio de Janeiro, from Australia via Mauritius, and from a broad Southern African circumference as well. The ports of Durban, Cape Town, Port Elizabeth and East London are busy with passenger traffic, much of it from the United States, South America and Great Britain (New York-Cape Town freighter passage can cost as little as $250 one way by Hellenic Lines, somewhat more by Robin or Farrell Lines, or the South African Marine Corporation).

Roads leading from Mozambique, Swaziland, Rhodesia, Botswana, Lesotho and Namibia (South West Africa) also carry a large volume of visitors.

South African Airways is not permitted to overfly most independent Black African states; hence, its direct flights to and from London and other parts of West Europe take longer than comparable flights by European airlines. BOAC offers a New York-Johannesburg air/drive holiday that includes 500 miles in a rented car.

Strict enforcement of exclusion regulations against persons of undesirable race, politics or profession complicate South Africa's visa and immigration processes. Visas for Americans are issued free of charge after satisfactory establishment of eligibility, proof of adequate funds and of return or ongoing transportation afterwards. Multiple-entry visas should be obtained by visitors intending to travel into and back from Swaziland, Lesotho, Mozambique and other neighbors. No visas are issued at borders or airports except for direct transit to contiguous countries. Canadians and some other Commonwealth citizens can enter South Africa without visas, if they are white. Visa applicants might wish to conceal such occupations as writer, journalist, photographer and film or television executive—unless they are sure of a welcome from authorities in advance. The safest occupations for Americans to list are investor, financier, industrialist, corporation lawyer and housewife. If you are a Japanese businessman, South African law declares you an honorary white person.

Getting Around Within South Africa

South African Airways and a number of other carriers conduct extensive jet and Viscount flights between all major towns; a Johannesburg-Cape Town one-way flight takes two hours and costs R47 (about $62.50); Durban-Johannesburg takes 50 minutes and costs $56.

Travel by rail can be a treat, however, with new equipment, good catering and good service on long tracks over a changing countryside. The most illustrious of the special South African Railways journeys proceeds by luxurious, all-first-class "Blue Trains" between Cape Town and Johannesburg (1,000 miles in 24 hours). The fare ranges from $70 to $120 one way, double for round trip. You must reserve weeks in advance. The Trans-Karroo Express follows the same route at $58 one way and $96 round trip. The Orange Express travels between Cape Town and Durban for $70 one way and $117 round trip (first class). The Trans-Natal night train connects Durban and Johannesburg for $32 one way, $60 round trip (first class). All other rates, based strictly on mileage, are markedly cheaper than these special trains. If you can adjust your schedule, try to leave and arrive at coastal centers during the day, for the landscape is best around the escarpments behind the coast. Further information and reservations are available at the South African Railways office in New York. National headquarters are on Wolmarans Street, P.O. Box 1111, Johannesburg; in town, call 22-1359/1368.

Coaches, buses, taxis and rented vehicles set out from every major town in South Africa over 15,000 miles of paved roads and twice that number of unpaved miles. Traffic drives on the left in South Africa. Tourist routes and commuter arteries can be extremely crowded and are also subject to one of the world's highest rates of traffic fatalities and drunken driving. Avis, United Car Hire (Hertz) and Hunks Car Hire are the major auto rental agencies in the Republic. They offer a number of convenient one-way packages at rates comparable to American tariffs; rental ranges from $4 to $12 per day, depending on the size of the vehicle, plus five to 26 cents per mile, plus gasoline (about 55 cents in the cities for regular, 10 cents additional for premium and 10 cents above that in the interior). Petrol stations become rare on the longer routes between cities; fill up frequently and/or carry an extra supply. You can rent small cars at lower tariffs from the Mini-Car Hire and Budget Car Hire companies (the latter has offices in Cape Town, Johannesburg, Durban, Port Elizabeth and Pretoria).

Any valid US state driver's license can be used if it carries the photograph and signature of the bearer and if the bearer is over 23 years old. Otherwise, international driver's permits are necessary. Credit cards may be used for the otherwise stiff deposit for automobile security and insurance (around $65). Camping is facilitated by convenient campsite locations, liberal regulations and special government brochures.

Hitchhiking is easy—if the thumber is white, neatly dressed and clean-shaven.

Taxis in South African towns are supposed to ignore hailers, departing only on assignment from stations and telephone dispatchers. Most are designated for whites only, others for "non-whites." All usually charge about 52 cents for the first mile and six cents for every quarter-mile thereafter. Town buses are also segregated; in fact, many innocent white visitors learn by insult that they can't take that merry jaunt around Cape Town on the top deck of a double-decker bus; tops are "beneath" them.

Much useful information on travel in South Africa can be obtained from a variety of sources, particularly from the state-controlled South African Tourist Corporation (Satour) in New York, Beverly Hills and South African cities. Maps and other road materials are provided to automobile club members by the Automobile Association of South Africa, P.O. Box 596, Johannesburg. Hunting licenses and other official services may be requested from the Department of Tourism, Private Bag 262, Pretoria. Game park information and reservations are obtainable from the National Parks Board's Pretoria office.

Fifteen daily newspapers in English offer considerable enlightenment on what's going on in South Africa. All towns have either a Visitors Bureau or a service in the Town Clerk's office to assist in necessary local arrangements. You can acquire non-official information about travel conditions from students or from missionaries in the Anglican, Lutheran, Methodist and Catholic stations around the country.

In addition to the official brochures, the Union Castle Company has a dry but thorough *Guide to Southern Africa*, edited by John Norton (London, Robert Hale, 1972). There is also a Shell *Tourist Guide to Southern Africa, 1971-72*, available at bookstores, or through the Shell travel club, or from the publisher, Chris van Rensburg, P.O. Box 25277, Marshalltown, Transvaal, South Africa.

Where to Stay

The Government Hotel Board has virtually completed its task of grading over 2,000 hotels, motels, botels (sic) or boatels, pensions and inns in the Republic. Its ratings use a range of one to five stars, signifying satisfaction of minimal criteria to impeccable luxury. The rating book is available from all tourist offices. Be careful, however, to gauge both prices and specific features before automatically choosing a multi-starred establishment over a lesser-graded one, or a mini-starred place as inevitably less costly than a more bespangled house. Many otherwise highly rated hotels are "private," hence not licensed for alcoholic beverages; others are licensed only for beer and wine, or for bar service to diners only. These places ordinarily accept few or no short-term clients. Some dumps are so rated but charge high prices nonetheless.

Although government ratings note segregation only by omission, you may assume that graded hotels accept only white clients, except for official black visitors. Even in the so-called African homelands, some places offer little more than back-door service to Africans, for fear of offending white clients. For "acceptable" visitors the number, range and quality of accommodations and service are among the best and most economical in Africa. A "luxury" lodging can be regarded as anything costing above R8 ($10.65) per night.

A few customs you'll have to get used to: early morning tea or coffee automatically replaces Continental breakfast unless you notify the management of your wish to remain undisturbed until breakfast time. Some hotels will not quote rates for bed and breakfast, while others quote nothing else. Women may not be seen at cocktails except for those sedate places designated as "Ladies' Bars," where stiffness and formality are often excruciating, and where the bottles behind the counter are empty, since a Lady is not permitted to witness drinks being poured in public. Bar service closes at 11:30 pm. Full pension rates and other American Plan arrangements can be highly advantageous financially for those who don't much care to explore dining facilities outside the hotel. In some cases the meal supplement (less wine) comes to about $1.50 per day.

The following selection only skims the surface. Rates are quoted per person per night, minimum to maximum range during peak season, bed and breakfast included (unless otherwise noted); a service charge is added only where noted. At some but not all places, per capita rates are reduced for double-occupancy rooms. Low-budget white travelers will find good accommodations at YMCA, YWCA and youth and student hostels in most towns.

In CAPE TOWN:

Heerengracht, the newest big luxury palace just off the port; $17.30 and up without breakfast. *Mount Nelson*, Orange Street near the museums and botanical gardens; with tennis courts and pool, a jewel of a place for Old World accommodations and dining; $14.65 to $18.65 (doubles from $21.30) plus 10 per cent service. *Arthur's Seat Hotel*, at Sea Point suburb; near shops, golf course and bowling green; $11.30 to $13.30; full pension $17.55 to $19.55. *Metropole*, Long and Castle Streets in town; $8 plus 10 per cent service. *Tudor Hotel*, just off Greenmarket Square in city center (not licensed); $5 (without private bath) to $6.30 (with). *Settlers Club*, Victoria Street; for members only; very reasonable rates; apply for membership a few days before intending to move in.

Outside Cape Town, among a covey of inns; *Lanzerac*, in an idyllic setting at Stellenbosch; $8, full pension $14.65 plus 10 per cent service.

At BLOEMFONTEIN:

Bloemfontein Hotel, $12 plus 10 per cent service. *President Transito*, $6 (without private bath), $10 to $13.30 with.

At ORANGEKRAG near Orange River Hydroelectric Project:

Hendrik Verwoerd Dam Motel, $7.65; full pension $9.

At KIMBERLEY:

Savoy, $8 to $26.60; full pension $12.65 to $31.25. *Horseshoe*, smaller; $4.65 to $7.65; full pension $7.65 to $11. *Grand Hotel*, $4.65 to $6.65; full pension to $8.65.

In JOHANNESBURG:

Carleton and *President*, both big, new, with all imaginable facilities; $14.65 to $18.65 without breakfast, plus 10 per cent service. *Quirinal*, in Hillbrow; $11.30 to $16. *Rand International*, $14.40 without breakfast. *Dawson's*, small and central; $12.65. *Langham*, large and traditional; $10.65. *New Library Hotel*, $8.65. *Cranbrooke*, $6 to $7.40.

Outside Johannesburg: *Balalaika*, in Sandown; cottages in a garden setting with pool; $10.65 to $21.30. *Holiday Inn*, Jan Smuts Airport; $10 to $19.95. *Casa Maria*, at Berea; gardens, pool; $11.65 to $16. *Kyalami Ranch Hotel*, in Bergvlei; with horseback riding, garden restaurant, pool, tennis; $10 to $14.

In PRETORIA:

Assembly, near shopping area and Bingers Park, with pool and bowling green; $6 to $10. *Residensie,* smaller; $7 to $8; pension $8 to $9.

In EASTERN TRANSVAAL:

Kowyn, at Graskop; $6.65; pension $8. *Floreat Motel,* at Sabie; $5.35 without breakfast.

In DURBAN:

Edward, most elegant of many luxury places on the "golden mile" beachfront; $16.55 to $18.15; pension from $22.95 to $24.30. *Edenroc,* well situated; $10 to $13.30; full pension $13.30 to $26.60; 10 per cent service. *Claridge's,* large establishment; $8 to $8.65; pension $9.65 to $13. *Empress,* conveniently located near shops and beach; $6.65 to $10.65. *Killarney,* huge place with pension plan only; $5.65 to $6.35. *Alexandria,* on Point Road; among the better buys; $3.35 to $4; full pension $4.65 to $5.35.

At HLUHLUWE GAME RESERVE:

Zululand Safari Lodge, $10.65 to $14.65; full pension $17.30 to $21.30. *Holiday Inn,* $6 to $9.30, without breakfast. Rest-camp, ample for families, in the midst of fine parkland; everything provided but food.

At EAST LONDON:

Deal's Hotel, $10.65 to $12; full pension $13.30 to $16.*Weaver's Hotel,* on seafront near Orient Beach with fine view; $6.25 to $8.40; full pension $7.85 to $10.

At UMTATA, Transkei:

Savoy, a somewhat better buy than other accommodations available; $5 to $5.35; full pension $7.30 to $8.65. *Grosvenor,* $5.50 to $6.65.

At PORT ELIZABETH:

Elizabeth, new establishment on Beach Road; $13.60 to $14.90; 10 per cent service. *King Edward,* old former luxury place on Green in upper town; $6 to $10.65; full pension $7.30 to $12. *Markham,* in center city; $6.65 to $8.65.

At KNYSNA and PLETTENBERG BAY resorts:

Formosa Inn, in garden setting at Plettenberg Bay; $8; pension $11.30. *Henties Botel,* Knysna; $5.35 to $6.65. *Beacon Island Hotel* (ne plus ultra); recently opened.

At OUDTSHOORN, Garden Route:

Holiday Inn, pool; $6.65 to $10. *Riempie Motel,* full facilities and good service in a bare kraal-like setting; $6 to $7.30.

Where and What to Eat

Food is generally well prepared at South Africa's hotels and restaurants. The British tradition has tended toward elegant dining, but with malicious influence on the taste of beef dishes. Dutch, Afrikaner, Asian and

African chefs vary the menus at lower prices. Try some Afrikaner specialties—for instance boernors sausage, bobotie (spiced meat casserole),
sosatie (spiced meat on skewers), sout ribbetjie (salted mutton chops),
biltong (dried meat), braavleis (barbecue), tomato bredie stew, konfyt
(stewed fruit in brandy), and koeksusters (glazed doughnuts), as well as
elegantly spiced Cape Malay dishes, curries, kebabs and chutneys, hot
pepper sauces, mealies (African corn), abundant fruit in all seasons
(mangoes, papayas, avocados, granadilla or passion fruit, as well as citrus
fruits and apples). South African white wines outrank their Mediterranean competitors and are moderate in price—as are good domestic
sherries and brandies—although chauvinistically overrated in comparison
with white Burgundies or Rhine/Mosel wines. Most South African reds
are only drinkable and the rum is poor.

The cities have a variety of good restaurants and "cafes" (which sometimes refers to take-out food delicatessens). There is little in quantity or
quality along the stretches of road between towns and resorts. Genuinely
exciting meals are usually found at the formal and fashionable hotels
like the Edward in DURBAN and the Mount Nelson in CAPE TOWN. In
addition, Cape Town has the Florentine Grille in the Grand Hotel,
Hildebrand's, Rossi's, the Cafe Royal, a string of Greek restaurants,
Chinese food at the Nanking and Dragon Inn, the Harbor Safe Inn for
seafood with hot peri-peri sauce, the Constantia Nek and several other
excellent old Cape Dutch inns in the wine-growing environs of the city.
Plaza España in the hilly fishing village of HOUT BAY serves good paella
and seafood.

The Janina is one of PRETORIA's best restaurants. In DURBAN, in addition to several posh hotels, there are the Caprice, Napoleon, Beach Blue
Waters, the Playhouse Tudor Room, "67" and Oyster Box Grill. PORT
ELIZABETH offers simple rough food at the Fingerlik and Chinese meals
at the Hong Kong.

JOHANNESBURG's wonderful Indian restaurants are off limits to "Euro-
peans" now, but you can dine well at Dawson's Hotel, the Prospect, the
Palazzo (Tollman Towers Hotel), the Colony (Hyde Park Hotel), the
Mirabelle (Casa Mia Hotel), Spaghi's, the Three Vikings, the Kyalami
Ranch on Pretoria Road out of town. There is good French food at
André's, Italian at Franco's and the Pizzeria Bella Napoli and Arrivederci,
both in Hillbrow, Spanish at España Cani.

Most department stores have lunch bars of sorts, but no alcohol. Before sitting down in an unknown place, verify the license; you can often
bring your own wine into unlicensed restaurants. Bars stop serving at
11:30 pm and remain closed on Sunday except in licensed hotels. Where
service charges are not added to the bill, tipping is about 10 per cent.

Tipping is regularly practiced for taxi drivers, porters, room servants, doormen, filling station attendants and hairdressers (but not theater ushers). The usual rate is 10 per cent of the basic charge, or a casual gratuity of 10 to 15 South African cents when there is no base.

What to See and Do

A full South African travel experience includes considerable time in Cape Town, Johannesburg, Durban and some smaller places, using the cities as points of departure for broader excursions, covering some of the exciting eastern landscape, a game park or two, a bit of beach and/or other sports for which the country is well suited. Opera and symphonic music are mediocre by international standards. Putting together the museum collections of Cape Town, Johannesburg and Durban would produce a rich holding of European painting and sculpture and painting by Westernized African artists. There are some creditable white South African versions of prevailing Euro-American styles. In certain rare pieces of sculpture, the presence of potent, symbolic abstraction testifies to African influence.

Night life sparkles here and there, mostly in musical comedies, and occasionally in little-theater groups like that of Athol Fugard in Cape Town. Audiences are strictly segregated, but whites can attend performances of black theater, or hear the lilting urban music of South Africa made famous by such performers as Miriam Makeba, Dollar Brand, Hugh Masekela and King Kong. A fascinating style of protest "ragtime" and the poignant pennywhistle blues of the African beer gardens (shebeens) may remind the visitor of jazz created by black musicians for black audiences elsewhere in the world. Otherwise, South Africans are little inclined to public gaiety. Their bars close early and a serious urban crime rate keeps many people off the streets at night. Theater and film are mercilessly censored against any semblance of infectious political, racial or sexual liberalism. The results are often incoherent and not worth attending. For related reasons, South Africa still has no television, but the government promises to begin TV service in 1976.

CAPE TOWN, one of the world's most beautiful cities, is South Africa's oldest and most cosmopolitan settlement. A third of its nearly one million people are white (mainly English-speaking) with a relatively liberal constitutional heritage. Fifty per cent belong to the ebullient urban communities of Cape Coloured, many of whom are being forcibly moved out of their city and are encountering new color bars as Cape Town succumbs to the general pattern of apartheid. The remainder is composed of smaller clusters of Moslem Malays and Africans ("Bantu"). Cape Town's famous old "District Six," the Coloureds' multifaceted, respectable and riotous, solemn and sinful town within town, has been declared a white suburb and has lost virtually all its original inhabitants and charm. The government is systematically reducing opportunities for contact between the increasingly isolated races. All but a handful of Coloured students are being forced to leave the University of Cape Town to attend the segregated University College of the Western Cape.

The Cape Town that Coloureds must leave sits comfortably in its marvelous mountain-peninsular setting, with lovely botanical gardens and a cluster of museums and old public buildings in the center of town. The flat midtown zone between Table Bay and the slopes of Table Mountain is fairly easy to cover on foot for the heavy skirt of suburbs contains the bulk of the population, all races included. The city center has a number of splendid examples of 17th and 18th century domestic architecture, notably the Koopmans-de Wet House (a museum of antique furnishings and historical pieces from old Cape Town); the Old Town House, containing a collection of Flemish and Dutch painting; the Martin Melck House, once the Lutheran Church vicarage, now the property of an antique dealer; and the old slave hostel cum Supreme Court building which now houses the fascinating Cultural History Museum. Superb lifecasts of Bushmen and their society, a kind of Kalahari Madame Tussaud's, head the list of extraordinarily fine exhibitions of African civilization as well as natural history in Cape Town's South African Museum, the Republic's finest. Most museums and galleries charge a small admission fee and are open from about 10 am to about 5 pm.

Table Mountain's 3,500 feet can be climbed, but only with great caution and in the company of a veteran mountaineer, for many an alpine tourist has been lost in sudden dense cloud formations which Vasco da Gama dubbed "the tablecloth." Cable cars climb from the foot of Kloof Nek when wind velocity permits, to give visitors a chance at one of the world's most exhilarating views over two oceans of different hue, two bays and a fine city. It's a half-hour by cable from midtown to the top; the admission fee is R1.

The air of this handsome city is being invaded by serious industrial pollution, sometimes spoiling what has always been a thrilling approach into Table Bay from the sea. Waterfront commercial real estate has been expanded and a screen of smog-enveloped, plastic and sexless medium-high-rise edifices is fast emerging from erstwhile bayshore and pierside, surrounded by parking lots and cement walks. Thus Table Bay and Table Mountain are also becoming "separated." The intensity of suburbanization has caused increasing traffic problems as well.

Starting from Cape Town, you may set aside at least two days for explorations along the lovely Cape Peninsula and to the wine-growing area inland. A rapid drive down to False Bay, past beaches, exurban villa districts and the Anglo-South African naval station at Simonstown, passes fascinating formations of cliffs and peaks always in proximity to the sea. The route can include the beautiful Cape Dutch colonial farmhouse Groot Constantia, now a museum of antiques; continuing to the *Good Hope Nature Reserve* at the tip of the Peninsula and returning to Cape Town takes a full day in all. At Rondebosch on the slopes of Devil's Peak, flanking Table Mountain, is the University of Cape Town, where the student population of 5,000 is made up mainly of English-speaking South Africans, with a sizable foreign contingent. At Groote Schuur Hospital near the campus on what was once Cecil Rhodes's estate, Dr. Christiaan Barnard performed his first heart transplant operations.

In old Cape Dutch country north of Cape Town, you can taste wines (free samples if you appear serious) at the KWV Farmers' Winery near STELLENBOSCH; the town, founded in 1679, has a large Afrikaans university, more classical in academic tradition and conservative in politics than Cape Town University. Franshoek, Saldanha Bay, Paarl and Hermanus are among the interesting towns in the fishing grounds, vineyards and beach areas of the inland Cape. You can swim in cool Atlantic Ocean water at Clifton Beach—popular with bikinied sun worshippers—or in warm Indian Ocean surf at Muizenberg. Cape flora are justly renowned, thanks to the area's escape from Ice Age depredations. An extraordinary range of flowers and blossoming trees comes alive in late August for six to eight weeks, drawing thousands of visitors.

A similar grandeur, although less flowery, adorns the famous (but rather ill-titled) "Garden Route," traversing sensational mountain and beach landscapes east of Cape Town almost as far as Port Elizabeth (500 miles). In the Little Karroo (prairie), OUDTSHOORN represents a good overnight stopping place near the Cango dolomite caves and several diverting ostrich farms. Southward stand the agreeable Indian Ocean havens of Knysna, Wilderness and Plettenberg Bay, and the handsome old spa of George.

The manganese and iron ore entrepot PORT ELIZABETH (400,000) is hilly and quietly commercial, with good beaches and hotels at Humewood two miles south. Port Elizabeth offers a pair of entertaining dolphins in the aquarium, a snake park and a rare breed of small fierce elephants at *Addo Park*, 45 miles to the east.

The port of EAST LONDON (125,000) is a highly conservative, sports-minded town with an enormous new township for African laborers miles distant from the city and four racially delimited beach zones (white, "Bantu," Coloured and Asian). There would be little cause for visiting East London were it not for its aquarium and little gem of a museum, with a splendid presentation of African bead-weaving, and the distinction of having the original four-legged coelacanth fish in captivity; this example of a 300-million-year-old "missing link" species, presumed extinct for the last 60 million years, was caught offshore in 1938.

At 4,400 feet, in the center of South Africa's plateau, BLOEMFONTEIN (200,000), capital of the Orange Free State, is Afrikaner to the core. Destined to become rich on a new gold bonanza, the town has an interesting fort and a museum with extraordinarily complete dinosaur bones.

KIMBERLEY (100,000), 100 miles to the northwest, is the town where Cecil Rhodes began amassing his unprecedented fortune during the diamond rush of the 1860's. You can stroll from the center of town to the "Big Hole," nearly a mile in circumference and over 3,000 feet deep, from which some 14.5 million carats of diamonds have been extracted. The currently active De Beers mine can also be visited on weekdays by applying to the company or to the town publicity manager at City Hall. Among Kimberley's several small museums, the most remarkable contains the Duggan-Cronin collection of photographs of "Bantu" people.

DURBAN is always another story. Its three-quarters of a million population is composed one-third of Indians now doomed to ostracism from the town they once almost owned, one-third of Zulu and other African peoples, and the rest of mainly English-speaking whites. This is South Africa's greatest port, center of vacation beach life and most pronounced combination of exotic and materialistic cultures.

The town of flowering trees and handsome hillside suburbs lives off a huge harbor with its protecting bluff and howling humid winds. The Indian market and temples stand near the center of town where Indians cannot now own property, and their segregated university on the hillside —all but empty—awaits 2,000 Indian students.

Durban's downtown includes the excellent Local History and City Museums and the Municipal Art Gallery, all in the City Hall complex. Nearby, there is a crowded Old House wedged in between modern apartments, and crammed to its verandas with antiques. To get to the spice-permeated Indian Market, you walk under arcades past automobile dealers and shoe stores. It is a busy, careless city whose old Oriental flavor is fast disappearing as the exotic buildings come down and the long shoppers' avenues fragment into sterile splinters of storefronts and display windows. The abbreviated side streets by the shore have a windblown character, and the golden beachfronts are fringed by surfboard riders who seem to glide right into the city's heart on the waves of the Indian Ocean. On the beach is an impressive snake farm and one of the world's finest aquariums, with three levels of viewing, an exciting 11 am feeding operation by divers, and a "separate homeland" tank for sharks; the aquarium is open until 9:30 pm and charges 50 South African cents admission.

On some Sunday afternoons, there is Ngoma dancing at Durban. Zulu rickshaw men in fantastically improvised costumes vie with one another to wheel bwanas from the steps of the luxury beach hotels. The Shembe Zulu festival at Indana, 20 miles inland, occurs on the weekend nearest July 25, with a remarkable interpenetration of African and Christian ritual that itself refutes the tenets of cultural apartheid. You can attend the festival either as part of a tour group marshaled by the Durban Visitor's Bureau (Church House, Church Street), or alone after securing a permit from the Chief Bantu Affairs Commissioner at Durban or the Department of Bantu Administration and Development in Pretoria. There is a smaller Shembe Zulu festival toward the end of January. Zulus also celebrate their Festival of First Fruit toward the end of March at Mafunza, 28 miles from pretty PIETERMARITZBURG, capital of Natal Province. For more mundane pleasures, there is horse racing in Durban every Saturday and, in July, on Wednesdays too.

Behind Durban the Natal farming land became white property. An hour's ride into that hinterland, however, opens up the lovely Valley of the Thousand Hills where Zulus live amid beauty and poverty, too close to the urban surge ever to be reconciled to the government's program of bucolic tribalism. Zulu women string their beads and carve their canes for tourists, send their sons to Durban for work in spite of official discouragement, and send their daughters to dance (barebreasted, of course) for busloads of tourists. Avoid the vulgar "Valley of the Thousand Hills" guided excursion to fake kraal-land and trashy "curio" shops, but do take a bus or drive into the Valley and beyond into Zululand itself, the designated tribal homeland 75 miles north of Durban.

The coasts of Natal, with their fine beaches, the sugar estates behind them and excellent Zululand game reserves, border on sensational mountain country—the Drakensberg. Here are rugged peaks up to 11,000 feet, bursting across the frontier into Lesotho. There's snow for good skiing at Sani Pass, which is accessible from the resort towns of Himeville, Underberg or Bulwer; there is a ski lift and a chalet at the top of the pass.

The lovely eastern Transvaal, with its sharp slopes, waterfalls and canyons, neighbors *Kruger National Park*. While not quite the equal of some East African parks, Kruger is big, well stocked and meticulously administered, with a visitor flow reaching 150,000 per year. All but the southern part of the park (Gates Numbi, Crocodile Bridge and Phalaborwa) closes from mid-October through April. There is an admission charge to Kruger. Write early to the Director, National Parks Board, P.O. Box 787 (cable: NATPARK), Pretoria, for reservations, giving exact dates as well as numbers of adults and children.

South Africa now has several other parks, including the *Kalahari-Gemsbok* in Bushman country on the Namibia (South West Africa) border, the *Royal Natal Park*, the new *Golden Gate Highlands Park*, and several private reserves. The *Hluhluwe* (pronounced shloo-shloo) *Reserve*, 180 miles from Durban, has carefully built a fine game herd including the once nearly extinct white rhino. A favorite with visitors, Hluhluwe is big (57,000 acres), set in fine scenery with kudu, buffalo, wildebeest, zebra, abundant birdlife, giraffe, antelope and warthog, in addition to black and white rhino; there are no lions. Accommodations are attractive and guides helpful. You can hunt by permit from April to October; write Zululand Safaris, P.O. Box 79, Hluhluwe.

People in South Africa adore sports, from cricket and bowls (on greens) to golf, tennis, soccer and rugby. Every town has a stadium and every weekend is dedicated to one form of competition or another. Scottburgh and Umkomaas golf courses are among the world's best links.

Racial segregation in sports, the law of the land, cost South Africa its participation in the Olympic Games, Davis Cup tennis, Commonwealth field competition and other international events. Seeking to rejoin world competition, the government has opened a few events and teams to invited "non-whites," but for most purposes, permanent or temporary membership in an all-white club is needed to take part in organized sports.

A fast-growing, dull city that turns beautiful in October when 60,000 jacaranda trees bloom, PRETORIA has passed the half-million mark. It is the Republic's capital. South Africa's best zoo is in Pretoria, also an outdoor cultural history museum. The tours take you to a pretty Ndebele village (permit obtainable Monday through Friday mornings from the Bantu Commissioner, Room 6, corner of Von Wielligh and Struben Streets, Pretoria) and to the Cullinan or Premier diamond mines, where visitors are welcome.

On certain Sundays, tourists may attend "Bantu" mine workers' dances in a designated mine laborers' compound. African workers recruited without their families on 12- to 18-month contracts from neighboring countries perform staged "tribal" dances in highly artificial style before all-white audiences. Tickets and information are available through travel agencies, city publicity offices and the Chamber of Mines in Pretoria and Johannesburg.

On a hill four miles south of Pretoria stands the most significant and revered shrine to that state of mind known here as the Voortrekker—the Afrikaner pioneer who fought his way up from the Cape into the Transvaal and Orange Free State to pursue his livelihood, his Old Testament religion and his xenophobic ethics in solitude. The huge monument has a marble frieze of pioneerdom, a hero's hall, altar and eternal crypt, an Anton van Wouw statue of an Afrikaner mother shielding her child from "African barbarism," all encircled by the laager of wagons and thorn trees that still symbolically defends the race. It can be visited from 9 am to 5 pm except on Sunday morning when it would not dare compete with another (related) religion, and Tuesday morning, the only time when "non-whites" are allowed to come to see it.

JOHANNESBURG, with almost two million people, stands for bigness and material progress in South African society. Its population is a mixture of Afrikaner and English-speaking whites, black Africans from all the southern continent's ethnic groups, and a sprinkling of Asians and Mediterranean immigrants. The skyline seems to have shot up overnight but it began growing with the discovery of gold on the Witwatersrand in the 1880's. As the buildings rise, the margins of town are increasingly defined by smokestacks and slag piles.

This is the corporate home of the mining, industrial and commercial syndicates that own white South Africa. It is a place of money, of power, of expensive living and strict segregation, of an uneasy, suspicious modus vivendi between social groups and political factions, native Afrikaner and "foreigner." The Africana Museum, Geology Museum, Railway Museum, War Museum, Art Gallery and zoo (all of them mediocre), the English-speaking Witwatersrand University with its excellent planetarium, the Snake Park and Lion Park, the nearby sanctuary and botanical garden, the wealthy residential Hillbrow section with its discotheques, several fine hotels—all enliven European life in an industrial city whose spirit cannot rival Cape Town or Durban, a city that waits for its elements to jell and its blood to warm. In short, a "second city."

The Anglo-American Corporation has a permanent mining exhibition in its headquarters at Johannesburg to help tell the success story of South Africa. South Western African Township (SOWETO) as well as other "Bantu" suburbs that the authorities will let you visit, the "locations" of migrant workers and distant "homelands" of banished Africans tell of its tragedy.

Literally hundreds of packaged tours beckon to travelers interested in avoiding the burdens of planning and operating their own circuits. All these can be bought at reasonable rates compared to the cost of car hire or taxi rental. A dozen major firms organize these packages in addition to those of the public South African Railways and South African Airways. The biggest include United Touring Company in Johannesburg, Cape Town, Durban, Port Elizabeth, East London, Kimberley and Windhoek (Namibia, or South West Africa); Southern Cross Safaris in Durban and Johannesburg; Springbok Safaris in Johannesburg, Cape Town and Durban; Grosvenor Tours Ltd in Johannesburg, Cape Town, Port Elizabeth and Durban, and numerous specialized operators of hunting safaris, photographic tours, ornithological expeditions, city sightseeing and the like. Satour can provide lists and details.

South Africa: The Silenced Majority

Finding pleasant things to see and do in South Africa is easiest for affluent white visitors uninterested in politics. What about seeing something of the life of more than 80 per cent of the population? It can and should be done but involves taking some risks in a racist police state.

First, there are some things that will not get you into trouble. A dramatic glimpse of working conditions can be obtained by visiting the "non-white" concourse of major commuter railway or bus stations in cities like Johannesburg at morning or evening rush hours (6 to 8 am, 5 to 7 pm). Compelled by law to reside in African townships miles from all-white cities and to observe rigid curfews in the cities, hundreds of thousands of African workers pack into incredibly crowded, dangerous commuter buses and trains for this daily journey. Under these conditions, it's easy to understand why South Africa has one of the world's highest rates of fatal train accidents.

For blacks who fall afoul of the law, the most common offense is an irregular pass book—an identity card and residence and travel permit requiring regular endorsement by employers and Bantu administrators. These offenses are tried in "pass courts" that deport 500,000 Africans each year to their tribal "homelands," where jobs and land are scarce. The courts in Johannesburg, Pretoria and other cities can be visited during any weekday from 9 to 5 without prior permission. Even though most proceedings are conducted in Afrikaans, you can still obtain unequaled insight into the workings of the South African judicial system and the living conditions of urban Africans.

Some municipalities operate guided tours of urban black residential areas—including a popular Johannesburg tour of the beer halls, shops, schools and showplace private homes in SOWETO where 200,000 Africans live in an immense sprawl of identical houses that they are not permitted to own. Since townships are fenced off and guarded—and they are frequently separated from the white cities by open spaces—it is difficult to make illegal private visits unless you are black. Visitors can obtain permits from city offices of the Bantu Administration to join an escorted visit to schools or hospitals or, if their reasons are plausible, to attend meetings of black professionals (lawyers, doctors, nurses, teachers) in the townships.

Government officials and employers encourage visitors to admire the efforts made in sanitation, health, education and recreation for the benefit of African laborers, many of whom are attracted here by the availability of jobs or better pay than in their own neighboring black- or Portuguese-governed territories. A full-day free visit to a gold mine can be arranged by applying (at least 14 days if not several months in advance) to the Public Relations Officer, Transvaal and Orange Free State Chamber of Mines, P.O. Box 890, Hollard Street, Johannesburg.

The working conditions of black employees and the labor relations practices of American-owned firms in South Africa have received considerable attention in the United States. These employees are denied by law the right to bargain collectively or strike. They nevertheless experience very different treatment from firm to firm in regard to wages, pensions, medical care, promotions, job training and related matters. Frank and Hirsch Company of Johannesburg, distributor of Polaroid products, and the Gillette Razor Company are among the more progressive enterprises that will discuss their programs of equal pay for equal work, job training and employee welfare. The American-South African Chamber of Commerce in Johannesburg can provide information and facilitate visits to other plants, including those of Ford, Chrysler and General Motors.

The official side of issues can best be clarified through calls at Department of Bantu Affairs offices, in discussions with bilingual journalists of the pro-government Afrikaans-language press (*Die Burger* or *Der Transvaaler*, for example), in visits to businessmen arranged through Chamber of Commerce or municipal Publicity Officers, in talks with clergy of the Dutch Reformed Church, or with leaders of conservative student groups at Stellenbosch and other universities.

In addition to the safe and officially encouraged experiences, several small, courageous liberal organizations can help visitors see and do some things that are legally permitted but considered by the government to be suspect. The National Union of South African Students (NUSAS) has branches at each of the English-speaking universities and headquarters at the University of Cape Town. It does what it can for interracial contact among young people, operates December-to-February vacation construction projects in some of the homelands, and participates in a few "inner city" social welfare projects in the "outer cities" of the black proletariat. It can also put visitors in touch with the (black) South African Students' Organization (SASO) and other black student leaders.

The Progressive Party, a Cape Town-based opposition, uses its single parliamentary seat to attack government policy from a multiracial standpoint.

The Christian Institute of South Africa, 35 Jorissen Street, Braamfontein, Johannesburg, with branches in other cities, is an ecumenical organization dedicated to building contacts along non-racial lines between South African Christians and their respective churches. The Institute's community centers and welfare projects are among the country's few genuinely multiracial activities. For a visitor the Institute can facilitate contacts with black churchmen, including those in some of South Africa's many dynamic independent churches. The Catholic and Anglican churches also operate schools and social welfare projects of interest.

The South African Institute of Race Relations (Auden House, 68 de Korte Street, P.O. Box 97, Johannesburg) has an outstanding research staff that publishes the *Annual Survey of Race Relations in South Africa*, the finest document of its kind. It holds interracial conferences, discussions and workshops and is in touch with black professionals and academics. The Institute of African Studies at the University of Cape Town is another well-equipped research center.

The Black Sash Organization (37 Harvard Building, Johannesburg) is a civil liberties and humanitarian group of white women. A visit to a Black Sash social welfare or legal advice office in any major city provides unsurpassed insight into the plight of South Africa's silenced majority.

In Cape Town, Durban and other coastal cities, professional and social organizations serve the Asian and Coloured communities who are, like Africans, denied the right to vote. Among these organizations are the government-appointed Coloured Persons' Representative Council, the South African Indian Council, the (Coloured) Labour Party and several professional groups.

It is possible but difficult and often time-consuming to obtain permission to visit the homelands or to see something of African rural life. In some cases the political officer at the US Embassy or consulate can assist with the authorities. Apartheid legislation makes it illegal for whites to visit African residential areas, urban or rural, without express permission for each visit from the Department of Bantu Affairs in Pretoria (P.O. Box 384) or its local offices. This authorization also applies in the case of Coloured or Asian residential areas, except for those that are still left within town limits. Permission is rarely given for unescorted visits to the distant rural homelands.

If you can get a permit to visit a rural homeland, you may be interested in the "tribal colleges"—which include Fort Hare University, one of the oldest and most distinguished schools in the country. You will no doubt be escorted, but you can ask questions. You might include in your visit crowded lower schools, where teaching is in the "tribal" vernacular (with increasing instruction fees as pupils advance in grade), the "border industries" which allow African labor to work just outside the homeland (but in white-owned enterprises, at lower wages than whites receive, with long hours and few fringe benefits, and with every inducement to spend their pay in white border areas) and the hospitals, which remain inadequate to cope with high malnutrition, infant mortality and other miseries in these already overpopulated and under-productive subsistence areas.

The main Durban-to-Cape Town highway passes through a section of the TRANSKEI "homeland" of the Xhosa people, but you need a permit from the Bantu Administration to leave the public road. On Mondays and Fridays you can join a tour of a Xhosa village and kraal near UMTATA, capital of the Transkei, with dancing staged for your benefit; these are arranged by Mr. Lester Hunter, Umtata Agencies and Tourists' Paradise (P.O. Box 232, Umtata). If you are driving a rented car and mistakenly take a wrong turn or two, you may see a good deal more of "homeland" conditions. Umtata's Bunga (parliament) is worth a visit.

Perhaps the most interesting "homeland" is Zululand where Chief Gatsha Buthelezi, one of South Africa's most articulate black leaders, challenges the government to implement its protestations of sympathy for African people. The poverty, overcrowding, soil exhaustion and depression of these areas are described in a recent book by Father Cosmas Desmond called *The Discarded People* (Penguin, 1971). A Catholic priest who traveled extensively in the reserves, Father Desmond has been placed under house arrest indefinitely and denied the right to receive visitors or to write for publication because of this book (which is, of course, banned in the Republic).

Seeing and doing some things in South Africa is illegal, entailing the real risk of arrest or deportation. The rural areas where convict labor is widely employed, as well as many mines, are strictly off limits. Interracial sex is an offense by law, although punishment is usually reserved for blacks. Violations of petty apartheid incur severe reprimands and fines. Integrated private parties are rare—less so perhaps in the intellectually dynamic atmosphere of Cape Town—and risky, except when the government wishes to entertain visiting African or Asian VIP's. There are no hotels, restaurants or bars where whites and blacks may legally meet except the Holiday Inn at Johannesburg's airport.

There is no African press except for some white-owned tabloids that dramatize sex and violence.

What to Buy

Under official encouragement to return to "tribal ways," Africans in South Africa continue to produce vast quantities of elaborate and attractive patterned beadwork, carved canes, ivory and soapstone carvings, woven blankets and pottery. These and other artifacts (salad servers, poor quality masks and drums, spears, etc.) are sold in markets, in the reserves (the best places to buy them) and at city shops specializing in what Southern African whites insist on calling "curios." The most reliable of these emporia include J.R. Ivy in Johannesburg, Cape Town and Durban, as well as Gainsborough Galleries and Sieradaki's in Johannesburg, but there are dozens of others. Most stores are open from 8:30 to 5 pm Monday through Friday, and on Saturday mornings. Prices are fixed in shops and markets, but bargaining is the rule with individual traders. Handicrafts centers have been opened on some of the main tourist routes as well.

Uncut diamonds can be purchased only from licensed dealers. Semiprecious stones—especially rare ones like the so-called tiger's-eye (silicified asbestos) and Transvaal jade—are also excellent buys in South African jewelry and curio shops. Most of Africa's available animal skins appear at good prices, either in cured or ornamental condition. South African wines are inexpensive and the industry is exceedingly export-minded at the moment. Safari clothing and other gear for the vacationer come well made and moderately priced in the major department stores. Malay tailors in Cape Town can cut you a fine suit out of yard goods. Spices of India and Malaysia perfume the markets of the coasts.

One of the finest bookstores in the world for Africana—including reprints of 19th century travel memoirs and even some controversial literature about South Africa itself—is Struik's at Wale and Loop Streets, Cape Town.

Local Attitudes

South Africa's many taboos are inherent in the racial-sexual dogmas of apartheid. Racially mixed society can be tolerated legally only under rare circumstances in certain places (diplomatic soirees, the Cape Town establishment, authorized meetings, etc.). This is not habeus corpus country; residents are frequently "detained" for months and longer without trial. Irritating foreigners are thrown out of the Republic with regularity. The informer system is effective in circles regarded as seditious.

Petty officials here, as everywhere, lack a sense of humor—only here they seem to have more to be humorless about. Better not provoke police, immigration officers, customs officials, guards or transport agents even in jest or by negligence. If you can't put up with petty apartheid, don't go. The burden is on visitors to adapt to separate buses, doorways, post office windows, elevators, beaches and toilets for people of separate skin color. Flamboyance about sex or feminine freedom also gets on some South African nerves, although the big cities have now seen their mini-quantum of miniskirts, the discotheques their array of dashing decolletage, and the beaches their bikinis. Away from Cape Town and Durban, tolerances prove much lower, and the informal, inquisitive, English-speaking foreigner is sometimes regarded instinctively as a potential subversive.

Weather, What to Wear, How Long to Stay

The best seasons to come are spring and fall (fall and spring to us). The summer climate (December to March) is seldom unbearable anywhere in the country. Cape Town winters turn cool and wet, but the best time for up-country game parks is from July to mid-October, and you can ski on the Drakensberg in June, July and August. The Natal and Cape beach seasons reach their peak in December and January, but the winter months also bring them a brisk trade out of the cold, damp interior.

Transportation lying well to hand, travelers may improvise their own itineraries. The standard package tours take between three and four weeks to cover the essential terrain between Cape Town, Johannesburg and Kruger Park, plus the eastern angle to Durban, Swaziland and the Garden Route. Few such tours include the enormous distances of the western Cape or South West Africa (see Namibia chapter).

In any case, a 10-day minimum should be planned for any thorough experience of the beautiful and painful world between Cape Town and Johannesburg. Remember that between these two are 1,000 miles and a difference of 6,000 feet in altitude.

Given the formality of many South Africans, the varieties of sport, and the variations in temperature, humidity and altitude, the visitor's wardrobe must include a wider range of costume here than in other African destinations. Jacket and tie are essential for men in many hotels and city restaurants— even for lunch and cocktails in some places. Women tourists find themselves immersed willy-nilly in a relatively "dressy" milieu. Contrasts of temperature between day and night on the Karroo, in high Johannesburg or Oudtshoorn and at the sea-level resorts warrant a greater variety in the suitcase or backpack.

Communication

English and Afrikaans are the official languages of a largely bilingual white population. Afrikaners fought for generations to obtain parity for their language, a derivative of Dutch, and they resent remarks about its provinciality. Africans usually prefer English (Cape Coloureds speak Afrikaans), and the government promotes the use of "tribal" vernaculars in the homelands.

Cities are linked by direct dialing telephones. International mail moves quite rapidly in and out of Cape Town and Johannesburg. Postal services are reliable, except that letters from or to "certain" persons may be opened and read by other persons. Telegraph lines and radio connect the parts of the sprawling Republic and link them with much of the circumference of African, Rhodesian and Portuguese-ruled territory. Communications with London are excellent.

Emergencies

Doctors in South Africa are listed in the yellow pages of telephone books under "Medical Practitioners." The state of their science is quite advanced and there are relatively plenty of them to go around. Ambulances can be summoned by calling fire stations. Medical care and hospitalization are not free services in South Africa; you should therefore have international health insurance coverage.

The United States has an embassy in Pretoria (Thibault House, tel. 3-3031), and consular offices in Johannesburg (Shakespeare House, tel. 834-1181), Cape Town (Broadway Industries Centre, Heerengracht, tel. 3-7061) and Durban (Norwich Union House, tel. 2-8388). Duty stations are manned during off-hours; USIS cultural centers accompany the diplomatic missions. The embassy moves to Cape Town during the January-May parliamentary season.

Swaziland

Profile

STATUS: Independent since September 6, 1968, as a constitutional monarchy. Former British protectorate.

SIZE: 6,705 square miles (slightly larger than Connecticut). Population—410,000.

GEOGRAPHY: Landlocked; bounded on north, west and south by South Africa, on east by Mozambique. Rugged hills and pine forests in western uplands; lowlands (scrub plains) in center. Coastal escarpment in east. Principal towns—Mbabane (capital, 15,000), Manzini (commercial center).

CLIMATE: Uplands are temperate, 50 to 75 degrees with cooler nights. Lowveld (lowland) is hot and dry.

LANGUAGES: English and Siswati (official).

CURRENCY: South African rand, divided into 100 cents. R1 = US$1.33; US$1.00 = 75 cents.

VISAS: Although Americans do not need visas to enter Swaziland, they need South African or Portuguese (Mozambique) transit or entry visas to get to Swaziland. No fee or passport photos required. Expect at least four weeks' delay. Available from South African or Portuguese embassies or consulates (see chapters on South Africa and Mozambique).

AIRPORT: Matsapha (MTS), near Manzini. Frequent flights to and from Johannesburg, Durban and Lourenço Marques.

NATIONAL HOLIDAYS: September 6, Independence Day; Ncwala (harvest festival) in December or January; Christian holidays.

INFORMATION SOURCES: *In US*—Permanent Mission of Swaziland to the UN, 866 United Nations Plaza, Suite 420, New York, N.Y. 10017 (tel. 212/371-8910); Embassy of the Kingdom of Swaziland, 4301 Connecticut Avenue NW, Washington, D.C. 20008 (tel. 202/362-6683). *In Swaziland*—Swaziland Government Information Services, P. O. Box 464, Mbabane. *In Johannesburg*—Swaziland Publicity Office, Winchester House, Loveday Street.

By Ivar Nelson

The Swazis are experts in the art of political survival. Beset by the Zulus in the early 19th century, they married their princesses to Zulu chieftains to end the harassment. Threatened by Afrikaner expansionism later on, they warded off a complete takeover by bringing in the British to balance the power. Caught in the middle of the Boer War, they kept alive by remaining neutral and afterwards convinced the British to protect them permanently from South African encroachment.

A land island between Portuguese-ruled Mozambique and white supremacist South Africa, Swaziland is now a politically independent country and member state of the United Nations. The Swazis have maintained their ethnic and cultural identity, but they still pay a high price in economic dependence on British and South African business. The asbestos, iron and coal mines, the pine forests and pulp mills, the sugar and citrus plantations, and the growing tourist industry have brought wealth to Swaziland. The story of Swaziland since independence is, and will be, how well the Swazis manage to acquire for themselves the full economic benefits of their rich country. At the moment, half of the land and all of the mines, industries and businesses are controlled by non-Swazis. With the exception of 10,000 whites and a few thousand Coloureds, all the 410,000 people in Swaziland are Swazis. A unique British colonial law of the 1930's restricted residence in Swaziland to Swazis and whites, thereby barring Asians and other Africans.

Until quite recently, the Swazis were relatively untouched by European influence, and have retained their own culture, ways of life and political structures. Their traditional ruler, the Ngwenyama, Sobhuza II, is also King of Swaziland under the new constitutional monarchy established when the country became independent in 1968. Now more than 70 years old, Sobhuza II is still the alert and active leader of the country, the fountainhead of all power.

Two good books which deal in depth with Swaziland's history and political situation are Jack Halpern's *South African Hostages* (Penguin, African Library, 1965) and Richard Stevens's *Lesotho, Botswana and Swaziland* (Pall Mall, 1967). Both are rapidly losing their timeliness, however. A marvelous ethnography is Hilda Kuper's *The Swazi, A South African Kingdom* (London, International African Institute, 1952), which affectionately describes the Swazis' traditional customs. *Swaziland* by Chris Potholm (University of California Press, 1972) is also recommended. Although oriented to the interests of the South African tourist, *The Guide to Swaziland* by Bruce Andrews has useful travel information.

Money Matters

Swaziland is part of South Africa's currency area and there are no currency restrictions between them. The South African rand ($1.33 to 1R) is the currency of both countries and easily exchanged for dollars. There are Standard and/or Barclays banks at Mbabane, Manzini, Havelock, Nhlangano, Big Bend and Tshaneni. The banks are open all weekdays and Saturday mornings. In addition, the Royal Swazi Hotel and the Holiday Inn will exchange currency. They also accept credit cards.

Getting In and Out

Physical access to Swaziland is relatively easy. Being allowed to go there is something else. While Pan Am and South African Airways fly directly from New York to Johannesburg (22 hours), it is more comfortable to fly to London, change planes and then fly to Johannesburg. You can also fly to Lisbon, and then on to Lourenço Marques in Mozambique.

Whether you come into Swaziland through South Africa or through Mozambique might depend on whether you are more acceptable to the Portuguese or the South Africans. You must pass inspection by one or the other to get to Swaziland. Be sure that you apply for an exit transit visa together with your entry transit visa.

If you are "non-white" or a former Peace Corps Volunteer or look like a hippie freak or have ever publicly criticized apartheid, the South Africans will be suspicious and probably turn down your visa request. In this case you can try the Portuguese, who are more lenient and have fewer files, or cut your hair and try to sneak in the back door by asking for your visa at the South African consulate in Rio de Janeiro or Salisbury. The average white tourist will be handled courteously and efficiently.

There is always a chance that the South Africans will not let you into their country but will give you a transit visa to Swaziland. This permits you to join a select fraternity of travelers who are restricted to Jan Smuts International Airport while waiting to catch a flight on to another destination. The fact that you are technically not in South Africa, but in an international airport, does not protect you from the scrutiny of the South African police. If you are anyone other than the average tourist (e.g., black or young and bearded) expect them to search your luggage thoroughly before you continue to Swaziland.

Once in Joburg (Johannesburg) or LM (Lourenço Marques) you can fly, drive, take the bus or hitchhike to Swaziland. There are flights from both places to Matsapha Airport in Swaziland several times a week. The flights take about 45 minutes. You can also fly up from Durban every other day. A VW bus will be at the airport to take you to your hotel.

There are occasional charter flights from Luxembourg or Switzerland to Johannesburg or Lourenço Marques for much less than the commercial fares. Information is available from Luxavia (formerly Trek Airways), Grand Building, Trafalgar Square, London.

You can rent cars in Joburg and LM and drive to Swaziland. Mbabane, the administrative capital, is about four hours on paved roads from Joburg and three hours (partially paved) from LM. Express buses from LM make the same trip daily. Hitchhikers will find sufficient traffic. Both drives display vividly the contrasts between the different countries. From Joburg, you come through the heart of the Afrikaner veld. At the Swaziland border the terrain becomes rugged, green, hill country. Coming up from the Mediterranean laziness of Lourenço Marques, you don't leave the red tile warmth of Portuguese architecture until, at the Lomahasha border post, you jump abruptly to the dualistic mixture of British and Swazi culture. Suddenly you see efficient police posts and orderly service stations, now run by purposeful Swazis.

The South African border post at Oshoek on the Joburg road is open from 7 am to 10 pm. The Swazis don't have a post there, only a big welcome sign. The closing time of the Oshoek post was changed from 6 to 10 pm at the request of South Africans who wanted to leave Joburg after business hours and still be able to gamble at the casino in Swaziland that night. The Swazis and the Portuguese both have border posts at Lomahasha that are open from 7 am to 8 pm. In relaxed Portuguese fashion, they close for breakfast and lunch.

Getting Around Within Swaziland

Swaziland is small—a good hop-skip-and-jump will get you almost anywhere in the country. The roads (some tarred but mostly gravel) can be negotiated by all vehicles, even American cars. However, a VW or Land Rover can take you off the roads and onto cattle tracks which wind back into the bush.

It's best to have a car while in Swaziland. If you cannot bring one with you, rentals are available from Hertz at the Royal Swazi or from Swazi-Safaris Ltd in Manzini. The car papers, insurance and licenses that allow you to drive in either South Africa or Mozambique are also valid in Swaziland. Your American driving license is good for six months. Driving is on the left.

If you want to meet Swazis, ride the buses that go irregularly between the larger towns. Hitchhiking is easy.

Distances in Swaziland are too short for using charter planes for internal travel, but the wealthier traveler might want to use one for connections with South Africa or Mozambique. If you want a charter in Swaziland, call Swaziland Air Services in Mbabane (tel. 6302 or 2576).

Where to Stay

The hotel business in Swaziland is booming. Since the discovery that Calvinistic Afrikaners will pay for a little more sin than is permitted in their own country, South African tourism in Swaziland has been expanding. Swaziland's main attraction for its neighbors is legalized gambling at the Casino.

The hotel connected to the Casino is the largest and most expensive in the country. Owned and managed by South Africans, the *Royal Swazi Hotel and Spa* in MBABANE contains the Casino and is surrounded by a very good 18-hole golf course. It fronts on one of the most magnificent views in Swaziland, and is rapidly becoming one of the most luxurious hotels in Southern Africa. You pay for it. Single rooms, midweek, are $11, and $18 on weekends and holidays. Doubles, midweek, are $18 and $28 on weekends. Meals are not included.

Americans won't have to look far for familiar sights. In fact, they can see the familiar *Holiday Inn* sign blinking in the night. The Holiday Inn is next to the Royal Swazi golf course. It is exactly like the one out on the highway in your home town. Rooms are cheaper than at the Royal Swazi. Singles are $8 during the week and $11 on weekends; doubles are $12 and $17.

The dozen other hotels in the country are of older vintage and have a much warmer and more personal feeling. Originally built for colonial administrators and occasional traveling businessmen, they have depended until recently on their possession of the liquor monopoly in their town. Most still have two bars, which legally separated black from white drinkers until the early 1960's. With tourism picking up, most are expanding and becoming more active.

At the *Highland's Inn* in PIGGS PEAK, you are in the midst of the second largest man-planted forest in the world and right up the road from a crazy jerry-built sawmill. Single rates start at $6.30, with dinner and breakfast. The *Assegai Inn* in the mists of HLATIKULU reeks of pith helmets and mementos of King George VI, who once visited there. You can usually get a good story from the American ex-merchant ship captain who operates the *Robin Inn* in NHLANGANO, but the accommodations are not the best.

The commercial center of MANZINI has several hotels, some—like the *Paramount*—for playing and some—like the *George*—for sleeping. Rates at the George are $6 (single) and $8 (double), including breakfast. There's an annex with rooms for $4 a day.

The hotels with real character, however, are in MBABANE, still the center of government administration.

With dart board, horseshoe bar, fireplace and dark wood paneling, the *Tavern Hotel* is a little bit of old England. The hotel has bathrooms and separate residential huts in the garden near the swimming pool. Prices are $7.45 for singles and $9.45 for doubles, without food.

The most pleasant hotel in Swaziland is just on the outskirts of Mbabane on the winding road down toward Manzini. This is the *Swazi Inn*, where comfortable rooms and an open dining room overlook the whole length of Ezulwini Valley, including the twin peaks known as Sheba's Breasts at the far end. It's very popular and reservations are necessary for weekends and holidays. Rates are reasonable at $6.65 (single) and $9.30 (double) with dinner and breakfast.

The nearby *Highlands View Hotel*, which has been improved recently, offers moderately-priced lodgings.

The *Bend Inn* in BIG BEND ($6) and the *Impala Arms* in TSHANENI ($6.65) are good businessmen's overnight stops in those sugar-producing areas. Prices include breakfast and dinner. The *Forester's Arms* in the forests of MHLAMBANYATI is more of a short vacation spot for families. Doubles with two meals start at $7.30.

Camping is easy in Swaziland. In addition to the open country, most of which is unfenced, there are facilities at the Mlilwane Game Sanctuary and at the Timbali Caravan Park (run by Forsyth Thompson, one of the few Europeans who truly know the Swazis). Simple and clean, the Mlilwane camp has huts and camping sites at $2.70 a night ($2 under age 16). They should be reserved in advance. Write or call Terence Reilly, Mlilwane Game Sanctuary, P.O. Box 33, Mbabane (tel. 6211).

Where and What to Eat

No one comes to Swaziland because of its food. Most of the hotels serve a combination of British and South African cooking that has about as much character as a franchised hamburger. The Portuguese, who are slowly moving into Swaziland from Mozambique, may help to improve the fare. The Portuguese-owned *Moçambique* is the best restaurant in Swaziland. It's one block off the main road in MANZINI. Try its grilled shrimp and green wine (vinho verde). Across the road from the casino in EZULWINI is the *Chinese Garden Restaurant*.

The Swazi farmers eat cornmeal mush as a regular diet and drink "twala," a maize beer. The commercial twala is pretty poor, but the home brew has a kick, and is quite good once you are used to it.

There are small delicatessen/cafes in both Mbabane and Manzini where you can get sandwiches and coffee. Usually, you will have to eat in a hotel for lack of an alternative.

The more friendly Europeans might invite you home for dinner, or more likely lunch, which is the big meal of the day. Visiting friends and relatives is common among Swazis, but spontaneous and informal. Out on the Swazi farms, however, you may be invited for tea, twala or food if you spend some time there.

What to See and Do

Knowing the Swazis and knowing Swaziland can be two different things, as much of the country's tourist industry is run for and by white South Africans. This is certainly true of the entertainment complex at the Royal Swazi Hotel in MBABANE. Government officials, who are the only Swazis with cash wealth, are prohibited from gambling, leaving only a few Portuguese to challenge the South African monopoly at the roulette and blackjack tables. The casino doesn't get moving until after midnight, so allow for a late night.

A long-standing way of ending a night's gambling is to make your way to the mineral springs at the edge of the golf course, strip down and wade into the warm, magnesium waters. Not surprisingly, the springs are called "cuddlepuddle" in the local jargon. During the day they are the basis for a thriving health spa run by a vivacious Dane, Jenny Thur.

Believe it or not, there will be a second casino in southern Swaziland in the near future. Night life in Mbabane has had a major breakthrough; there are now two nightclubs. The Penguin is the older and is open every night after 9.

If you're a sports enthusiast, you'll find many opportunities to expend your daytime energies. The Royal Swazi's 18 holes are the best of a half-dozen golf courses in the country. All the leading hotels have tennis courts. There are squash courts in Mbabane and Manzini. There's polo on Sundays, soccer football in the national stadium and swimming at most of the hotels and in the town pool in Mbabane.

The real excitement, however, is getting a horse and riding in the hills. The feeling of silent peace in the forests and the exhilaration of freedom in the open grasslands are incomparable. Horses can be obtained through the Royal Swazi, the Tavern or the Forester's Arms. Don't fish or swim in any of the rivers without making absolutely sure they are free of bilharzia. The fast-moving water in the gorges is usually safe.

The African heritage in Swaziland is fascinating and unique. The Stone Age sites near the Komati River, the traces of early haematite (iron ore) workings at Bomvu Ridge near Oshoek, and especially the Bushman paintings testify to the achievements of this black man's country long before the whites ventured around the Cape of Good Hope.

Visit the Queen Mother's compound at LOBAMBA, talk to Swazis about the comradeship of contemporaries (age sets) and their family relationships and you will learn of a vibrant society only very recently affected by the intrusion of European customs. If you can, arrange your trip to permit attendance at a Swazi ceremony. The sacred "Ncwala" marks the harvest in December or January and celebrates unity and kingship (date set every year). The "Umhlanga," or reed dance, on the second Monday in July is a paean by Swazi girls to the Queen Mother, who is known as the Ndlovukazi (she-elephant). Both rituals are striking displays of communal spirit partially open to the public; no movie cameras.

The Swazis live in a narrow landscape with tremendous variation. The rugged hills, winding roads and pine forests of the uplands are fun to wander in. Go northwest from Mbabane towards Oshoek, then turn right on the road to PIGGS PEAK through open sheep country as far as Forbes Reef, an old abandoned gold town. You can see the remains of the mines if you turn off the main road to the left.

At the District Officer's headquarters in Piggs Peak, ask for directions to the Komati Gorge off the road to Balegane. You'll have to walk several miles, but the great channels carved out of the granite by the river are well worth it. Another day's trip for hikers is a visit to the Ndlozane Gorge near Grand Valley in the south. Unfortunately the Bushman paintings near Piggs Peak have been defaced, but there are many others throughout Swaziland (such as those near Sandlane). Inquire at the Swaziland Tourist Office, P.O. Box 451, Mbabane.

Authorities have made a major effort to bring back to Swaziland the many types of game which used to be plentiful. The *Mlilwane Game Sanctuary* is like a large, open zoo. Most of the animals are relatively tame and wander freely through the 10,000 acres. You can even approach the eight white rhinos (actually dark gray in color) and shake their horns in friendship. Terence Reilly, the originator and game warden of Mlilwane, is also developing another sanctuary set aside by Sobhuza II at Ehlane on the road to Lomahasha.

Those visitors interested in the social and economic factors that are suddenly changing Swaziland from a traditional, slow-moving, agricultural society to a booming, hectic modern country can see the transformation themselves. Visit Anglo-American's big open-pit iron mine at Ngwenya and see Swazis operating digging machines the size of houses. The Commonwealth Development Corporation's pulp mill at Usutu and sugar mill at Tshaneni reflect the diversity of the country's agricultural potential.

Education in Swaziland culminates at the local campus of the University of Botswana, Lesotho and Swaziland at Luyengo, which focuses on agricultural training.

Demonstrating the viability of multiracial education to the white supremacists across the border is the Waterford/Kamhlaba School near Mbabane, whose students come from all over Southern Africa.

What to Buy

Good functional handicrafts are traditionally Swazi. The woven mats are well made and almost indestructible. The wooden salad bowls, however, are easier to ship. Swazis still dress primarily in traditional cloth garments. These "mahias" are available in the larger stores everywhere. The King often wears one in a bright red-orange.

The burgeoning tourist markets carry endless numbers of spears, Swazi battle axes, shields and staffs. The largest market is in Mbabane, but you will see them also at Oshoek, Manzini and Lobabba.

While not originally Swazi, the tie-and-dye center in the SEDCO Estate in Mbabane does beautiful work in shirts, dresses and cloth. If you have the money, you can get soft, exquisitely woven mohair blankets and draperies in brilliant colors at Coral Stephen's in Piggs Peak.

You can bargain (in fact, you are expected to) in the market, but not usually in the shops.

Local Attitudes

The Swazi police are beautiful—clearly there to help you and not to oppress you. Competent and courteous, they have their hands full dealing with the influx of South African tourists who see Swazi roads as their private race course. Unfortunately, the road down Malagwane Hill outside Mbabane provides a fatal lesson for too many. Repress your urges and take it slowly, especially in the evening mists.

Both the Swazis and the whites in Swaziland are quite conservative. Going braless or getting stoned at the Ndlovukazi's royal enclosure (kraal) or the Mbabane Club is not the way to ingratiate yourself with the citizens. Although the American Peace Corps has broken the ice and people are not as shocked by odd deportment as they used to be, remember that Swaziland is more like Levittown than Greenwich Village.

The Swazis are a dignified people and do not lend themselves to "staged" photographs of anthropological exotica. If you want to begin to know these wonderful people, go far from the Royal Swazi Hotel to any small kraal. Find somebody who can speak English and sit down for a long time and talk.

Weather, What to Wear, How Long to Stay

The climate of upland Swaziland (like its people) is moderate with rare bursts of temperament. Usually the temperature is between 50 and 75 degrees, with the cooler nights requiring sweaters or light coats. Fires are often used to dry things out in Mbabane, chosen by the British as their administrative center for its climatic resemblance to the misty, damp English countryside.

The lowveld is hot, dry and generally unpleasant for everything but sugar cane, humped cattle and cotton. For visiting Manzini, the game parks or other lowland areas, bring your lightest and coolest wardrobe.

If you want to escape from the world and relax, stay in Swaziland for a month and let your metabolism slow down while you play tennis, swim, ride horses or stroll around. For the fast-moving tourist, however, three or four days will suffice for a good view of the tiny country. One day could be spent visiting a Swazi village and examining its handicrafts, one hiking into the Komati Gorge, looking at the Bushman paintings or riding out on the veld, another touring the Mlilwane Game Sanctuary or Ndumu Game Reserve and another sporting and gambling at the Spa.

Take-A-Tour of Swaziland, P.O. Box 485, Mbabane, has minibus trips around the country.

If possible, leave Swaziland through the back door at the Goba Border Post and drop down to Oro Point on the Mozambique coast. The reefs and white sand beaches are unforgettable.

Communication

Siswati and English are the two official languages of Swaziland and many Swazis speak both. All phones, telegrams and mail go out to the world through South Africa. On one hand, this means that communication is relatively swift. On the other, it means that everything can be perused by the South African authorities if they wish. And they often do wish.

Telegrams are sent at the post office, which is open from 9 am to 4:20 pm. Mail to the United States takes from five to seven days. Phone calls to the outside have to be booked in advance, usually only an hour's wait except on holidays.

American Peace Corps Volunteers are everywhere. You'll find them in almost every school and community development project in the country. They and the British volunteers usually welcome guests, but cannot be used as though they were an extension of the US Travel Service.

Emergencies

There are only three diplomatic missions in Mbabane, with the American, Portuguese and the United Nations Development Program all in Embassy House near the broadcasting station. The British High Commission is 100 yards up Allister Miller Street in a modern version of a Norman castle. The US Embassy address is P.O. Box 199, Mbabane (tel. 2272).

The South Africans don't have diplomatic representation in Swaziland. They don't need it, since they exert their influence in almost every other way. If you are in trouble with your South African visa, ask help from the American vice consul.

Medical care in Swaziland is very good and getting better. In Mbabane, there are a government hospital, a private clinic, at least a dozen doctors and three dentists. Treatment is free at the hospital if you cannot pay.

Zambia

Profile

STATUS: Independent republic since October 24, 1964. Formerly known as the British Protectorate of Northern Rhodesia.

SIZE: 290,586 square miles (slightly larger than Texas). Population—3,900,000, plus 50,000 whites, 12,000 Asians.

GEOGRAPHY: Half the country covered by forests. Elevation from 3,500 to 7,000 feet. Victoria Falls in south on border with Rhodesia. Principal cities—Lusaka (capital, 250,000), Ndola (150,000), Kitwe, Livingstone.

CLIMATE: Daytime temperatures moderate all year, rarely exceeding 90 degrees. Winter nights (May through August) quite cool, often dropping into 30's; otherwise evening temperatures in 60's. Moderate rainfall November through March.

LANGUAGES: English (official), six major Bantu languages.

CURRENCY: Kwacha (K) divided into 100 ngwee (n). K1 = $1.40; $1.00 = 71.5 ngwee.

VISAS: Required. Available from Zambian Mission to UN and Zambian Embassy in Washington. Fee $3.15. Also obtainable from Zambian embassies or high commissions in Nairobi, Addis Ababa, Kinshasa and Dar es Salaam.

AIRPORT: Lusaka (LUN), 15 miles from city. Frequent flights to and from Rome, London, Blantyre, Dar es Salaam, Nairobi and Ndola. Transport into city—coach, K.75 ($1.05); taxi, K6.00 ($8.40); car (two or three people), K3.00 ($4.20).

NATIONAL HOLIDAYS: May 1, Labor Day; May 25, Africa Freedom Day;

817

1st Monday and Tuesday in July, Unity Days; August 9, Youth Day; October 24, Independence Day; Christian holidays.

INFORMATION SOURCES: *In US*—Embassy of the Republic of Zambia, 2419 Massachusetts Avenue NW, Washington, D.C. 20008 (tel. 202/265-9717); Permanent Mission of the Republic of Zambia to the UN, 150 East 58th Street, New York, N.Y. 10022 (tel. 212/421-7820); Zambia National Tourist Bureau, 150 East 58th Street, New York, N.Y. 10022 (tel. 212/758-9450). *In Lusaka*—Zambia National Tourist Bureau, Century House, Edinburgh Square, P.O. Box 17 (tel. 73667).

By Aaron Segal

Zambia is worth your attention because of its economic and political vitality and the interesting mixture of peoples sharing in the trials of this emerging nation. And if you want more, there's Victoria Falls, one of the most extraordinary sights on the face of the earth. There are many other natural attractions too—including Luangwa National Park, Kafue National Park, Kalambo Falls and Lake Tanganyika.

Zambia is one of the most urbanized countries in Black Africa, with 40 per cent of its people clustered in the capital of Lusaka and the towns along the Copperbelt, the source of its major industry. It is the third largest producer of copper in the world.

But it is a landlocked country, dependent for transportation on hostile neighbors. The prosperous economy is narrowly based and fragile with high costs everywhere, making it considerably more expensive for travelers and residents than East Africa.

Known as Northern Rhodesia until it gained independence in 1964, the country had been colonized in the late 19th century by the British South Africa Company of Cecil Rhodes. Rhodes saw Northern Rhodesia as a link in his vision of a Cape-to-Cairo railway whose trains would whistle "God Save the Queen." The territory was twice as large as Southern Rhodesia, but there was far less white settlement, even after the discovery in 1920 of the enormous riches of the Copperbelt.

For years, however, it was dominated by white-controlled Southern Rhodesia, and in 1953 it was forced into an amalgam called the Central African Federation, a contrivance by Europeans intended to defend their influence against the threat of rising nationalism in this part of the continent. Eleven years later, under the leadership of Kenneth Kaunda and his United National Independence Party, the country was finally able to break loose from the federation—and from its status as a British protectorate. On independence it repudiated the association with the name of Cecil Rhodes and took the name Zambia (from the Zambezi River).

In 1969 the Zambian government acquired a majority ownership in the copper mines and other industries. Copper has remained a mixed blessing. It provides 95 per cent of export revenues but it has drawn many young people from rural areas, with a consequent decline in agriculture. High wages for a few, including the remaining non-Africans, have caused envy and unrest. Worst of all, the export of copper depends on rail lines and ports controlled by the Portuguese regimes of Angola and Mozambique and white Rhodesia.

To work its way out of this dependence, Zambia has joined with

Tanzania in arranging a $400-million interest-free loan from China to build a 1,200-mile railroad from the Copperbelt to the Tanzanian port of Dar es Salaam (a project rejected by the US, Britain and the World Bank). Zambians look forward to the completion of the TanZam Railway in 1974. Until then, the white rebel regime of Rhodesia has closed the Zanbezi border, allegedly in retaliation for Zambia's willingness to let African nationalist guerrillas use bases within Zambia. There's no knowing how long the border will be closed.

At the same time the government seeks industrial diversification and the expansion of education. Secondary school enrollment is growing, and the University of Zambia, established in 1965, is rapidly making up for the pre-independence shortage of university-trained Africans.

Hostility among Zambia's many ethnic groups remains always close to the surface. The predominant tribes are the Lozi of Barotseland, many of whom were trained as clerks by early European missionaries and administrators, and the Bemba of the Northern Province, who provide much of the labor for the Copperbelt. The Lozi and the Bemba have become influential in the political affairs of the country. But conflicts persist and President Kaunda's hopes for a real sense of national unity have not yet been realized.

Zambia's political and economic problems are analyzed in a fine book by Richard Hall, *High Price of Principles* (Praeger, 1969). Brian Fagan discusses the archaeology and history of the country in *A Short History of Zambia* (Oxford University Press). The Zambia National Tourist Bureau office in New York has attractive brochures and an excellent *Zambia Travel Guide*.

Money Matters

Like its little neighbor Malawi, Zambia calls its currency the kwacha, meaning "dawn" in the Cinyanja language. It is converted at one kwacha (K) to $1.40, with each kwacha divided into 100 ngwee (pronounced en-gway), each worth 1.4 US cents. The kwacha is generally unwanted outside Zambia and while there is no black market within the country travelers may be offered kwachas at a discount in neighboring countries. But it is illegal to enter (or leave) the country with more than 10 kwachas.

You can exchange currency at the airport banks, hotels or the offices of Standard and Barclays banks in town. The banks are open from 8:15 am to 12:45 pm, except on Wednesday when they close at noon and on Saturday when they close at 11 am. Credit cards and travelers checks are accepted at major hotels.

Getting In and Out

The new airport at Lusaka receives several flights a week from London via BOAC, Caledonian and Zambian Airways; there are two flights from Rome, where Zambian Airways and Alitalia operate a combined service, and one on UTA from Paris.

Zambia is a good stopping point on trips between East and Southern Africa. There are regular flights from Nairobi (Kenya), Dar es Salaam (Tanzania) and Blantyre (Malawi). To go west across Africa you can fly from Lusaka to Nairobi or from Ndola to Lubumbashi in Zaïre and from there by Air Zaïre to Kinshasa, thence to various points in West Africa. However, the Ndola-to-Lubumbashi service is often interrupted.

Heading south requires a little maneuvering as long as the Rhodesian border remains closed to tourists. It was possible to fly to Livingstone on the Rhodesian border and cross the international bridge to the town of Victoria Falls on the Rhodesian side, connecting there with flights, trains or buses to Salisbury, Bulawayo and Johannesburg. However, most travelers heading south from Zambia make air connections in Blantyre (Malawi) where there are regular flights to Salisbury and Johannesburg and once-a-week service to Beira in Mozambique. There is one weekly flight between Lusaka and Gaberone in Botswana; private planes can also be chartered for this run.

To enter by boat, you can travel East African Railways from Dar es Salaam to Kigoma on Lake Tanganyika and from there take the Liemba steamer to Mpulungu in Zambia, a journey that Livingstone himself might have envied. More luxurious and faster is the combined air-sea safari offered by Union Castle Line on its England-to-South Africa passenger cruise which, for an extra $1,000, provides a five-day round trip from Cape Town to the Luangwa Valley Game Reserve in Zambia or to Victoria Falls and Lusaka.

The most interesting routes in and out are by road. Coming from or going to East Africa along the Great Northern Road, there is asphalt from Lusaka to the Tanzanian border town of Tunduma and an interesting drive across the flat, dry country of northeastern Zambia. The road on the Tanzanian side is rougher and chewed up by heavy petrol tankers and trucks hauling railroad construction equipment.

Two all-weather roads connect with northern and central Malawi. There's a paved road running 80 miles from Lubumbashi in Zaïre to Ndola. A good highway links Lusaka and Salisbury, Rhodesia (a six- to eight-hour drive), crossing the Zambezi River near the Kariba Dam. There are regular bus services on all these routes, except the suspended 80-hour Express Motorways special from Johannesburg to Lusaka.

Hitchhiking was easier coming in from Rhodesia, where traffic was heavy, than from Tanzania. To get a ride from Rhodesia, one used to post a notice or check the bulletin board at the offices of the Automobile Association in Salisbury or Bulawayo.

If you want to hitchhike out of Zambia, drop in at the Automobile Association office in Lusaka or Ndola.

Getting Around Within Zambia

Zambia Airways offers good internal flights to Livingstone, Ndola, Mpulungu and Lake Tanganyika in the north, the Luangwa Valley and elsewhere.

The national railway, coming up from Mozambique and Rhodesia, operates daily trains with sleeping accommodations on the 500-mile run from Livingstone via Lusaka to the Copperbelt and then beyond to Zaïre and Angola. Unfortunately, the railroad has a poor safety record.

The cheapest way to get around within Zambia is by bus (Central African Road Transport is the main bus-line operator). The buses fan out from Lusaka to all parts of the country. The National Tourist Bureau operates an excursion bus tour from Lusaka to Livingstone and Victoria Falls, a 280-mile trip that is a good bet for the hurrying traveler. It also offers bus tours of the Kafue River area, Kariba Dam on the Zambian side, and the Luangwa Valley Reserve. The Lusaka-to-Victoria Falls tour is particularly recommended—it's well planned, comfortable and interesting.

Zambia has good north-south roads (mostly paved). Driving licenses are issued to visitors for 90 days. Car rentals are available from leading hotels and agencies in the main cities. In Lusaka, there's Ridgeway Car Hire Service, P.O. Box 929 (tel. 73968), and Central African Motors, P.O. Box 672 (tel. 73181). You'll find branches of the Central African Motors agency in Kitwe, P.O. Box 2795 (tel. 2390), and in Ndola, P.O. Box 105 (tel. 3621). Also in Ndola is Rent-a-Car, P.O. Box 2123 (tel. 2865). Rates are high, international borders cannot be crossed, and gasoline costs nearly $1 a gallon, reflecting the cost of trucking or piping it 1,200 miles from Tanzania.

Driving is on the left-hand side of the road, traffic is heavy, vehicles are often improperly maintained, drivers are frequently reckless, and extreme caution is needed at all times. Night driving is particularly hazardous. The rate of automobile accidents in Zambia is among the highest in the world, especially along the Copperbelt.

Hitchhikers once got to Victoria Falls if they could get a ride to Livingstone. But Luangwa Valley, Kafue and Kariba are still hitchhikable.

Where to Stay

Zambia has concentrated on luxury hotels, which tend to be overpriced and inefficiently serviced. In Lusaka they are sometimes overbooked. Personal services such as hairdressing are also expensive and inexpertly administered. The *Intercontinental* in LUSAKA has air-conditioned rooms with TV and also features a pool, bar and restaurant. Prices begin at $20 (single with breakfast). The *Ridgeway* has comparable facilities and rates, albeit slightly less "class" with a friendlier and less commercial atmosphere. A better buy, but still overpriced, is the centrally located *Lusaka Hotel* at $15 a night (single bed and breakfast). The University of Zambia has a guest house and dormitories but is inconveniently located seven miles south of Lusaka. Modest accommodations in town can be found at the YMCA-YWCA and sometimes at the Evelyn Hone College of Further Education.

In LIVINGSTONE, the gateway to Victoria Falls, is the *Musi-o-Tunya Intercontinental Hotel*, which takes its name from the Tonga words for the falls, "smoke that thunders." Magnificently situated facing the falls, it has lavish facilities and prices that match ($30 a day single and $40 double, with breakfast). You don't have to pay those rates, though. There are nearby camp grounds, a cheap, clean and comfortable government rest-house and delightful cottages with showers, running water and cooking facilities. Other hotels in the town are the *North Western, New Fairmount* and the *Chalets*, with prices in the $10 to $15-a-day range for a single, including breakfast.

Prices at Copperbelt hotels are also high, although facilities and service are somewhat better than in Lusaka. The *Hotel Edinburgh* in KITWE is a businessman's treat at $20 a night, as is its counterpart, *The Savoy*, in NDOLA. More moderately priced accommodations in Ndola ($4 to $10) are available at the *Elephant and Castle* and the *Rutland*.

Much better value can be found off the commercial circuits. South of Lusaka on the road to Kafue National Park are the pleasant weekend retreats of *La Hacienda Hotel* and the *Leisure Bay Motel* (both at $10 per single room) on the shores of Lake Kariba. In the far northern town of MBALA (26 miles from Lake Tanganyika) one finds the quaint *Grasshopper Inn* on the road to Kasaba Bay. The game parks have their own lodges and camping facilities, which we discuss later. On the road to Luangwa Valley, 200 miles from Lusaka, is the government hotel at KACHALOLA, good only for a drink and a meal. Farther east on the main road to northern Malawi and its lake resorts is the *Lundazi Castle*, surely one of the strangest hotels anywhere in Africa. Now government-run, it was built by an eccentric Englishman as a replica of a medieval castle.

Another exotic hotel is the new *Lyambai* with 22 rooms with private baths, 400 miles west of Lusaka at MONGU, capital of the Lozi Paramount Chief. Elsewhere, in nearly every minor town or trading center, there are government rest-houses with modest accommodations. Mission stations and secondary schools are also often available for housing.

Where and What to Eat

Good restaurants are mostly confined to the hotels and are expensive. The *Intercontinental* hotels in LUSAKA and LIVINGSTONE serve Continental cuisine at $6 to $10 without drinks. The *Copper Chalice* is a supper club outside Lusaka with moderately good but expensive meals and a lively Congolese dance band providing African, Latin and Caribbean rhythms. Also in Lusaka are *La Gondola*, with a nightclub, the *Woodpecker Inn* and the *Lotus Inn* (Chinese).

Copperbelt hotels tend toward bland English meals. Ask for fresh fish, especially tilapia, bream, karpenta or catfish, from Lake Tanganyika. In the cities are Indian restaurants and near the bus depots are African bars and restaurants with maize beer, nshima (a cornmeal and beef stew) and mealie-mealie (a mushy meat or fish and corn flour dish). The water is drinkable in the cities and the bottled beer is excellent.

What to See and Do

LUSAKA, once a sleepy administrative center, has become a cosmopolitan city of 250,000. Short on municipal planning, it is unattractive and sprawling. There are no public buses and you may have to take taxis to see some of the sights. (Hitchhiking is easy, particularly for well-groomed males with short hair.)

The broad thoroughfare of Cairo Road, with its modern office buildings, however, is a pleasant walk, and a short stroll across a bridge over the railway tracks leads to the open-air market, with interesting shops selling traditional medicines (herbs, roots and charms). Freedom House, which houses the representatives of some Angolan, South African and Rhodesian nationalist movements in Zambia, is also nearby.

Lusaka is dotted with new government buildings. Worth a visit are the copper-domed Mulungushi Conference Center, completed in 1970, the National Assembly buildings, and the university, all south of the city. Excellent copper industry exhibits can be seen at the Geological Survey Museum.

The National Tourist Bureau runs daily city bus tours from its attractive office at Century House on Edinburgh Square off Cairo Road (tel.

73667). The tours include the Anglican Cathedral; the Zambia Gemstones Polishing Works, where precious and semi-precious stones are displayed for sale; the 30-acre Munda Wanga gardens, with a fine aviary and 300 varieties of exotic plants; and the Chilanga research station of the Game and Fisheries Department, where baby elephants, domesticated elands and rare red lechwe antelopes can be seen.

Lusaka is a dull town, with little night life. What there is of it is found at the hotel bars, one or two supper clubs catering mostly to non-Africans, a private (non-African) amateur theater group and a few cinemas. However, at the university a dynamic student group runs the open-air Chikwakwa theater, an effort to take culture to the masses. The performances are quite exciting. Zambia has excellent dancing and a fine national dance company. There are occasional performances in Lusaka and regular shows in Livingstone that are first rate. Check with the National Tourist Bureau for time and place.

Thirty-five miles south of Lusaka is the modern town of KAFUE, designed by the famous Greek architect, K. Doxiadis. Kafue is to become a major industrial center and several factories are already in operation. Of particular interest are the new Kafue dam and hydroelectric project.

A leisurely drive 84 miles south of Lusaka by paved road takes you to Lake Kariba, the largest man-made lake in the world. Crossing its 420-foot-high dam takes you into Rhodesia (but this route was closed in 1973). Along the lake are resort camps and a motel at Siavonga, and campsites at Sinazongwe and Chipepo. The attractions here are fishing and bird watching. Boating facilities are also available, but be careful not to drift over toward the Rhodesian bank lest you be grabbed for espionage.

Five hours by road and 45 minutes by air from Lusaka is the town of LIVINGSTONE near Victoria Falls. The town has the Livingstone Museum with its superb archaeological, art and historical collections, and the Maramba Cultural Center, where traditional craftsmen ply their trades in ersatz village huts (if you arrive at the right time you can see them changing from Western clothes to traditional dress). There is a daily display of dancing. Near the Cultural Center is Livingstone Game Park, with about 400 easily viewed animals. Although the park is small, it offers, in addition to the usual varieties of wildlife, aviaries for indigenous birds and enclosures for small mammals not normally seen in the larger parks.

Victoria Falls is seven miles west of Livingstone. The falls, twice the size of Niagara's, are 350 feet high and 5,700 feet wide. This extraordinary formation is part of the mighty Zambezi River crashing through on its

1,700-mile trip to the Indian Ocean. During the rainy season (March to May), mist off the falls impairs viewing. At any time of the year you need a raincoat and sandals, or if so inclined, a bathing suit.

The falls are one of the most stunning natural attractions on the face of the earth, and are best viewed from the Zambian side of the river (although there is a broader and less expensive range of hotels on the Rhodesian side). The sight is absolutely unworldly when there is a full moon, but on moonless nights the falls are floodlit. The best view is from the Eastern Cataract between 10 and 10:30 pm. Down-river is an ancient baobab called the Lookout Tree, where the falls can be seen from a platform.

An added attraction of a trip to the falls is the daily "sundowner" or cocktail cruise, an hour and a half trip up the river on the SS Makumbi, a luxury launch operated by the National Tourist Bureau that takes you past hippos, elephants and crocodiles browsing on the river banks. There are also Saturday and Sunday luncheon cruises.

On the other side of the river, 50 miles west of Livingstone by all-weather road, is the hotly contested Caprivi Strip where the Botswana, Namibia, Rhodesia and Zambia borders join at one-car ferry crossing. The Chobe National Park lies on the Botswana side of the river (see chapter on Botswana) but is most easily reached from Livingstone.

Zambia's major parks:

The Luangwa Valley Game Park, after Victoria Falls, is Zambia's best attraction and one of the finest game parks in Africa. Extending over 6,000 square miles, it teems with wildlife during the May-to-November dry season. It is one of the few parks where you can leave your car and, accompanied by an armed guard, approach the game on foot (children under 12, however, are not permitted to do this). Reached directly by air or a 340-mile drive from Lusaka, Luangwa Valley has two fully catered lodges, Mfuwe and Luamfwa, and four smaller camps where you supply your own food. The National Tourist Bureau has tours to Mfuwe Lodge by air from Lusaka at $30 a day plus round trip air fare ($45). Norman Carr, hunter turned conservationist, offers a one-week Wilderness Trail tour for groups of six at $150 per person.

Kafue National Park, 200 miles southwest of Lusaka, is one of Africa's largest. The Kafue River winds through the park and offers fine fishing. Visitors can see great herds of antelope, buffalo, elephant and other game grazing on its banks. Ngoma Lodge, which has 10 chalets, costs $25 a day for full board, but there are also facilities for camping. You may wish to stay overnight in Safari Village in the bush, and spend an evening game viewing from a Land Rover the nocturnal predators such as the leopard, cheetah and hyena. A group of American conservationists is developing a new 2,400-square-mile wildlife refuge near Kafue for the red lechwe antelope and other swamp creatures.

Hunting and fishing are important tourist attractions in Zambia. Hunters must obtain a Tourist's Import Permit for firearms and ammunition at point of entry. It is valid for six months, and must be returned to the customs officer on departure. Shooting expeditions can be arranged in the Kafue and Luangwa game parks.

Game fishing is good along the Zambezi, especially near Mambova, at the junction with the Maramba River. Lake fishing is also excellent. At Lake Tanganyika, particularly from December to March, you can try for Nile perch, tiger fish, vundu (giant catfish), goliath tiger, lake salmon and kupi.

North of Lusaka is the 70-mile-long and 20-mile-wide Copperbelt, containing the richest source of copper ore on the continent. You can explore this area by rail or road. You might want to stop first at the army garrison town of KABWE (ex-Broken Hill), where there are interesting archaeological excavations. Next comes NDOLA, site of the giant Bwana Mkubwa mine and, with a population of 150,000, the third largest city in Zambia. The National Tourist Bureau in Lusaka can arrange visits to the mines and also to the Northern Technical College and other vocational training institutes that have helped make Zambian miners among the most skilled and highly paid workers on the continent.

KITWE, 50 miles farther north, is the commercial and industrial center on the Copperbelt. It is an attractive city, noted for the Nkana copper mine and excellent sports facilities (Kitwe is Zambia's major center for horse-racing). The Christian Council of Zambia operates the Mindolo Ecumenical Center for interracial gatherings and adult education here.

The Copperbelt is of keen sociological interest. Its white mine executives and technicians enjoy high wages and amenities, and organize their lives around such outdoor sports as auto- and horse-racing, golf, fishing, hunting, tennis and water skiing at Mindolo Dam near Kitwe. The Copperbelt's nearly 600,000 Zambians include many who left far-off villages for the bright lights and better wages of this area. The trade union halls, UNIP (United National Independence Party) youth centers, company sports grounds and numerous bars are their meeting places.

A change from the pressures and industry of the Copperbelt is provided by the calm seclusion of Lake Tanganyika, 650 miles north of Lusaka. It is accessible by twice-a-week flights from Ndola or Lusaka and by road. Situated on this immense inland sea are two charming lodges, Kasaba Bay and Nkamba Bay, each charging $18 a day per person, full board. There are also camping facilities nearby. At Kasaba Bay there is lake fishing, sunbathing, cruising on the lake (if you wish to swim, avoid the bilharzia-contaminated shore), and fine game watching as elephants, hippos and lesser fry wander past the lodges for an evening drink and stroll. The best season here is from December to March.

Twenty-six miles south of Kasaba Bay is the small resort town of Mbala. Kalambo Falls, a sheer 726-foot drop, is nearby. It is a nesting place of the rare and singularly ugly marabou stork.

Most visitors concentrate on Zambia's physical attributes and neglect its peoples. Its 73 ethnic groups speak six major languages and offer an extraordinary diversity of cultures. The Bemba in the northeast are noted for their industry and political skills, the Lunda and Luba for their carvings and crafts, the southern Tonga are fishing folk, and the Lozi specialize in architecture, boats and baskets. These and other Zambian peoples have their festivals and ceremonial occasions. The Tourist Bureau can assist with information.

The most spectacular ritual takes place each year in February or March when the Litunga, or Paramount Chief of the Lozi, moves his court and capital from the Zambezi River flood plains to high ground at Mongu. The accompanying Ku-omboka pageant of canoeing, dancing and festivities is great fun. The move back takes place in July and is interesting but less impressive.

What to Buy

Zambia's finest crafts, including bowls, cups and jewelry, are made of copper. There is much wood carving, although of varying quality, including drums, bowls, masks and animals. Finer items are malachite eggs, uncut and semi-precious stones and fine Barotse reed baskets. Shops are open from 8 am to 5 pm during the week and 8 am to 1 pm on Saturdays. Original jewelry is on show at the Copper Boutique of the Intercontinental Hotel in Lusaka.

Most handicrafts are dying out in the villages, but professional artisans still work in the Maramba Cultural Center in Livingstone. If you're looking for genuine Zambian items, you're better off buying here than from street vendors, whose wares may come from East Africa or Zaïre.

Local Attitudes

Urban Zambia has ethnic differences, intense party politics and a concern over the country's dependence on white-ruled Southern Africa. However, most of the time conversations are free and relationships easy. The most sensitive subject is Rhodesia, whose white settlers defied Britain and the UN in 1965 by declaring the country independent. There is bitterness in many quarters that Britain and the United States have not been sufficiently severe toward the Rhodesian government. Americans may run into some harsh questions about their government's policies toward Southern Africa, especially from university staff and students.

Weather, What to Wear, How Long to Stay

Zambia is elevated plateau country at 3,500 to 7,000 feet. May to August is the cool, dry season when temperatures range from 30 degrees in the evening to 80 degrees during the day. September to November are the hottest months, with daytime temperatures in the 80's and 90's. The rainy season, March to November, means a few hours of rain each day.

Attire is casual. Many Zambian men follow the style of President Kaunda in wearing a khaki bush jacket and matching trousers. Evenings can be chilly, especially in the game parks, and a jersey or jacket is advisable. For women, light summer dresses, miniskirts and slacks are fine in town or country. The most important traveling item is a pair of comfortable walking shoes.

At least a week is needed to see Victoria Falls, Luangwa Park and something of Lusaka. Two weeks permit visits to the Copperbelt and Kariba Dam. Package tours offered by the Zambian National Tourist Bureau and several private tour operators in Lusaka may be attractive if you are in a hurry.

Communication

English is the official language and is used throughout the country. Postal services are good and generally reliable but ship packages air freight to make certain of their arrival. Direct dialing within and between major cities generally works. Most overseas calls go via Nairobi.

Zambian Broadcasting Corporation has limited local television programming, mostly imported. Zambian Radio broadcasts several hours a day in English and the six major African languages. There are two lively daily newspapers, the semi-official *Times of Zambia* and the tabloid *Zambia News*. Kingsway department stores in Lusaka, Ndola and Kitwe have bookstores with collections of current British, American and South African periodicals.

The bookshop at the University of Zambia in Lusaka has a good collection of local scholarly publications.

Emergencies

Medical services are adequate but facilities overcrowded at Lusaka Central Hospital. The US Embassy (tel. 50222), Independence Avenue and Livingstone Road in Lusaka, can help with the names of competent medical personnel. Serious illness may require treatment in Nairobi or Johannesburg.

Health tips: You aren't likely to get sick if you take reasonable precautions. Lusaka and the Copperbelt are virtually malaria-free, but the disease is widespread elsewhere. Pools are the only really safe places for swimming—natural water courses and dams are infected with bilharzia.

Indian Ocean

Comoro Islands
Madagascar
Mauritius
Reunion
Seychelles

THE REGION AT A GLANCE

Five island groups flung over a tropical sea have played their historical roles as outposts of empire for Portugal, Holland, Britain and France and are now warming under more modern suns. Maritime and strategic priorities long ago ceased to dramatize this zone under its periodic monsoon and typhoon influences. Some of them uninhabited before Europeans came to settle—as well as to raid enemy shipping and to trade along the great eastern sea routes—the islands remain dependent on British or French patronage for their budgets, their educational and social institutions and their monocrop economies.

Only Madagascar, the world's fourth largest island, and tiny Mauritius, the world's most acutely overpopulated, have attained sovereignty thus far. But everywhere indigenous nationalism has begun to make itself felt. Madagascar's seven million people have a new government seeking for the first time in their 13 years of nominal independence from France to chart new directions for national politics, economics and cultural transformation. Mauritius, the only Commonwealth member to have joined the French-oriented sphere of African states, balances these European allegiances against strong claims of its Indian, Pakistani and African communities. Reunion, an Overseas Department of France, keeps reform pressures suppressed while seeking prosperity within the metropolitan French system. The Comoro Islands recently stunned the

831

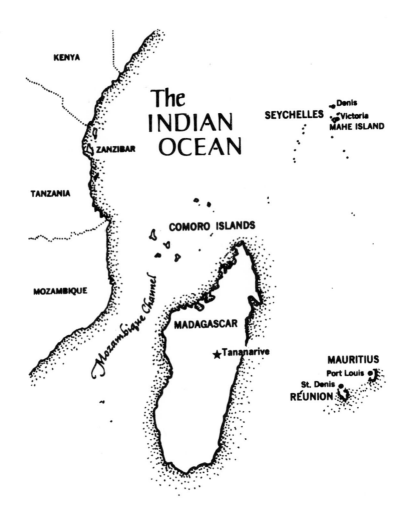

micropolitical world by petitioning France for independence. To the distant northeast, the Seychelles electorate is split between a majority in favor of continued colonial subordination to Britain and a sizable nationalist minority.

In 1965, Britain detached certain obscure atolls from Mauritius and Seychelles to form a virtually unpopulated strategic possession, the British Indian Ocean Territory. The territory includes Aldabra Island, a prized destination for fanciers of exotic wildlife and elaborate coral formations.

Mauritius bay

Comoro Island dhow

Merina woman

Tanararive street

Notwithstanding their new political self-consciousness, all the island groups receive increasing numbers of visitors with rare warmth, charm and solicitude. Composed of successive arrivals of African, Asian and European people, their societies grew in the tropical sun and the ocean breezes, forming special ways of life. Roman Catholicism and African animism combine in the Creole melting-pots of Reunion and Seychelles, and in the large "colored" minority of Mauritius. Hindu and Moslem Indians retain their fundamental cultural identities on Mauritius, and Chinese trader communities flourish throughout the region. The four Comoros reflect four differing modes of insularity, cemented by Islam, the Swahili language and French colonial power. Madagascar is an entire world to itself—beautiful, creative, hospitable, musical.

This is the dead-end refuge of the lemur and the tenrec, the giant land tortoise, rare butterflies and a multitude of unique natural creations. Its landscape contains forests of orchids, acres of ylang ylang and other perfumed flowers that spice the air, golden beaches, lava fields and coral rock, granite hills and extraordinary formations made by volcano and sea. It is the region of quiet, merry people with inward grace and inate toughness, a pious sense of hope and an elegant, eloquent literature.

Its distance from American points of origin excludes the Indian Ocean from standard travel itineraries. However, a growing number of British and South African "packages" bring tourists to Seychelles and Mauritius; French groups are also increasing their traffic to the area. Americans with sufficient reach can buy a round-trip (or round the world) air ticket with Mauritius as high point, allowing coverage of most of Africa in the coming and going. Or ship on a freighter or cruise vessel (preferably outside the January-March typhoon time), but don't settle for single days in port. These islands are rare inside and outside. Once you're in the mood, they might claim you for keeps.

PMA

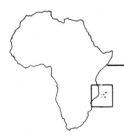

Comoro Islands

(Iles Comores)

Profile

STATUS: Overseas Territory of France. Administered by elected Government Council under resident French High Commissioner.

SIZE: Archipelago totaling 838 square miles. Population—275,000 (1972 estimate). Half living on Grande Comore, about 90,000 on Anjouan, 25,000 on Mayotte, 10,000 on Moheli.

GEOGRAPHY: Four major islands of volcanic origin midway between East Africa and Madagascar. Wide variety of topography, coastline, soils and climates. Principal towns—Moroni on Grande Comore (capital, 18,000), Mutsamudu on Anjouan (9,000), Dzaoudzi on Mayotte (4,000).

CLIMATE: Tropical maritime, varying according to altitude and among islands. Sunny most of year. Rainy season from October to April (cyclones and intense heat in February and March).

LANGUAGES: Swahili, French (official), Arabic (religious).

CURRENCY: Comorean CFA franc. CFA 100 = 40 cents; $1.00 = CFA 245.

VISAS: Required. Available from French Consulate General in New York. Fee $3.92. Two passport photos, onward ticket necessary. Takes 24 hours.

AIRPORT: Moroni (YVA), on edge of town. Taxis into city. Linked with Madagascar, Tanzania, Djibouti and Paris.

NATIONAL HOLIDAYS: July 14, French National Day; November 11,

835

Armistice Day; May 1, Labor Day; May 8, end of World War II; Moslem and Christian festivals.

INFORMATION SOURCES: *In US*—French Embassy, Press and Information Service, 972 Fifth Avenue, New York, N.Y. 10021 (tel. 212/737-9700); French Consulate General, 934 Fifth Avenue, New York, N.Y. 10028 (tel. 212/535-0100); French Government Tourist Office, 610 Fifth Avenue, New York, N.Y. 10020 (tel. 212/757-1125), also Chicago, Los Angeles, San Francisco. *In Moroni*—Office du Tourisme, P.O. Box 71.

By Philip M. Allen

A southern outpost of Islam, eastern flank of Swahili, the four Comoro Islands stand between northern Mozambique and northern Madagascar, and belong to France. This archipelago of uncommon beauty is only just beginning to attract the attention of others besides the few sportsmen who have been diving and fishing in these waters for decades.

The causes of this obscurity are historical. As the 19th century Great Powers ate away the Sultan of Zanzibar's dominions, the tiny Arab-Shirazi emirates on the islands of Grande Comore, Moheli, Mayotte and Anjouan withdrew successively from the "protection" of Zanzibar to that of France. They have remained French by flag and by trade ever since. The old Arab oligarchs now share power with French businessmen and together they have held these enchanted isles as their private preserve. And it is an enchanting preserve indeed—a quartet of scented lands, with boutres, dhows and goélettes crisscrossing a clear green sea, and legends of freebooters and shipwrecked *misérables*. Comorean mythology crosses Arabian motifs with Malagasy and East African.

Although totally Moslem, the Comoreans are descended from a mixture of peoples who show combinations of East African, Malagasy, Arabic and Persian influences in both their bloodstream and culture.

Each of the four islands was formed at different times by underwater eruptions. Each has a distinctive topography, climate and economy. But as neither variety nor beauty is sufficient to feed a rapidly multiplying population, a diaspora of over 100,000 enterprising Comoreans has collected in Madagascar, Zanzibar and Tanzania, where job opportunities are more plentiful than at home.

The Comorean colony was declared an Overseas Territory of France in 1947, and it has anxiously clung to this status, fearful of the consequences of a possible French withdrawal. Constitutional changes of 1961 and 1968 allowed some internal autonomy, but the archipelago's governance still rests with a high commissioner from Paris and its livelihood depends on 500 French residents, small French subsidies and even smaller tastes for exotic products like copra, spices, perfume oils, sisal and vanilla.

Most opposition to French and feudal privilege has come from students and overseas residents. A Comorean Liberation Movement (Molinaco) is based at Dar es Salaam. But economic stagnation, unemployment, French indifference and an elitist educational system have turned domestic politics around. Elections in December, 1972, gave a strong majority to pro-independence forces behind Premier Said Mohamed Djaffar. France continues to divide and rule the islands, however, and still keeps a couple of Foreign Legion companies stationed there as guarantors of "stability."

Largest of the islands is Grande Comore, which contains the territorial capital of Moroni and a great active volcano, the Khartala. This is a strange island of black lava, ringed by white coral beaches and cut into several "climates" by a pair of mountain crests. Here, no rivers run, no wells surge, and the soil, though fertile, cannot hold water. Cisterns must catch the water that Grande Comore drinks, yet on the windward north there is a tropical forest of mahogany, ebony, palisander and takamaka, and the south is rich in coffee, cocoa, copra and cloves. Along the upper slopes of the 10,000-foot Khartala (whose last eruption occurred in 1965, for the eleventh time in a century), rain falls in virtually constant sheets.

Anjouan, second largest and most densely populated of the islands, holds water admirably and produces remarkable perfume plants—patchouli, jasmine, lemon grass, basilic violet, palma rosa and ylang-ylang. Their olfactory perfections adorn an island already likened to a pearl. Yet, while high green basins (cirques) flank M'tingui mountain (6,300 feet) the three corners of this triangular island remain dry and bare as a desert atoll.

Tiny Moheli with 10,000 people, fine forests and pastures, represents a potential breadbasket for the territory. But, with the demands of world trade the determining factor, the island primarily produces copra.

Mayotte (once called Mahore) in the south of the archipelago is only 150 miles from Diego Suarez. It lies low-slung and fertile inside a superb lagoon entirely surrounded by thick coral reefs. Pamanzi Island, across a strait from Mayotte proper, presents a vista of magic peace and undisturbed flora, while Dzaoudzi on its narrow rock, once capital of the Comoros, has their only secure all-year, deep-water port facilities.

There is literally nothing written in English on the Comoros except passing references in histories and memoirs of the Indian Ocean, Zanzibar and Madagascar. Air Comores puts out a flossy promotional book entitled *Isle of Perfume*, with an execrable translation of the original French text, but even this is hard to find outside the archipelago. French writing on the Comoros tends to be highly specialized, governmental, obsolete, or all three.

Money Matters

Administered until 1947 as part of France's Madagascar colony, the Comoros still maintain banking and other important ties with their larger neighbor. The Comorean CFA franc is pegged at 50 CFA to one French franc; hence, about 240-245 francs to the dollar. The Banque de Madagascar et des Comores, based in Tananarive, handles most of the banking in Moroni, Mutsamudu and Dzaoudzi. The cost of living for foreigners is somewhat lower than in Madagascar, but there is less to buy and life is generally simpler.

Hotels accept travelers checks.

Getting In and Out

Each island has a small airfield linked with Moroni, on Grande Comore, which in turn is connected to the outside world. One-way passage between Moroni and Tananarive costs $80; Dar es Salaam is $85. If you are in Kenya and wish to go to the Comoros via the Seychelles, you can make arrangements in Nairobi or Mombasa for Air Kenya's non-scheduled Navaho flight to carry you from Mahé (Seychelles) after taking BOAC there; then in due course fly out with Air Madagascar or Air France to Tananarive.

Messageries Maritimes passenger liners out of Marseille call several times each year at Moroni and Mutsamudu, as do freighters of the French, Scandinavian and other lines in the Indian Ocean Shipping Conference. Unless you are lucky, however, you'll probably have to change ships at an East African or Malagasy port. Arab sailing vessels (generically called dhows), once thick athwart the monsoons from here northward as far as Oman, still travel between the Comoros, the East African coast and Madagascar. Their masters (nakhodas) will gladly take on passengers, but be prepared for a rather rough voyage.

Getting Around Within the Comoros

Air Comoros hops regularly from island to island and has four-seater sport planes for charter. Outriggers and dhows ply constantly between and around the islands, taking paying guests wherever they wish to go, even into some rather risky moorings. Passage can be arranged at any sizable port or in fishing villages. The price is determined by bargaining with the boat's master.

Each island has some all-weather road, but only Grande Comore is extensively paved. Here, buses shuttle between Moroni and the beach town of Itsandra. The hardy taxi-brousse (bush taxi) does the rest of the conveying. The foreign trading companies on each island will sometimes furnish trucks or cars, and in any case can advise visitors on finding appropriate vehicles, including a four-wheel drive, which is necessary for interior probing.

Mayotte's three-island complex is linked by ferry service in early morning, at noon and at 5 pm. The French companies also usually have, or can help locate, French-speaking guides.

Where to Stay

There is little tourist traffic and the business community ordinarily cares for its own guests, so Comorean hotels are few. Grande Comore offers a choice: the graceful, white *Hôtel Itsandra*, a few miles outside MORONI on a brilliant green cove, with canoes, bathing and a full array of recreational facilities (13 of the 24 rooms are air-conditioned, renting for about $12); or the older, rougher *Hôtel du Khartala* across from Moroni's airport (singles $4.50, doubles $5.50).

A new *International Nautical Center* has bungalows at MALOUDJA BEACH near Mitsamiouli, 25 miles north of Moroni (singles $10, doubles $16; full pension $17 and up).

A similar choice exists at MUTSAMUDU, capital of Anjouan. The new *Al Amal* is the elegant, air-conditioned counterpart of the Itsandra, on a cliff overlooking the sea ($12 per room). Decent food and accessibility, but far more simple accommodations, are offered by the older *Hôtel-Restaurant de l'Escale*.

Three choices at Mayotte include the new, sporty, rather expensive *Hôtel de la Marine*, with bungalows, at DZAOUDZI. The *Hôtel du Rocher*, also at Dzaoudzi, an older place, charges $3.50 per person, and offers a prospect of the sea. There are cheap accommodations at the *Hôtel Saadani* in MAMUTSU on the principal island. For the hiker or motorist, Mayotte offers a couple of empty shelters (gîtes) at CHICONI and SADA that require full camping paraphernalia.

Little Moheli has no hotels, but private rooms and apartments can be rented by writing M. Dominique Lauret at Fomboni, or by asking around after one gets there.

Where and What to Eat

The traveler dines without ceremony but well at the hotels, particularly at *L'Escale* in Mutsamudu, the *Itsandra* and the *Maloudja Center* on Grande Comore, as well as at the cafe-restaurant *Foucault* in Mamutsu on Mayotte.

Crayfish (langoustes) abound in season, and there are more ways to enjoy goat's meat than most Americans think. Fish, cassava, rice, corn, sweet potatoes, plantain bananas, peanuts, cape peas and breadfruit, along with pineapples, mangos, papayas, avocados and cane sugar, go into the diet of those who eat what the Comoros produce. A tradition of professional cooks enables Comoreans to satisfy the demands of fussy Europeans as well as appetites for couscous, barbecue, spiced and peppered sauces and rice.

What to See and Do

At Moroni, on Grande Comore, where practically every trip starts, there is whitewashed Islamic solemnity, enlivened by the intrigue of narrow alleys, the green and orange gowns of the women, market stalls of fruit and vegetables in all colors of the rainbow, and the drums of the Comorean night. The minaret of the Vendredi Mosque offers a splendid view of the town's unhurried arabesques, its port of pirogues and boutres, the grand green sea, and the hulking Khartala in the hinterground. Quick ears catch sounds of music from the tom-toms of a nocturnal neighborhood festival (particularly the stately chorus lines of the northern Irougoudjani quarter), or from an itinerant professional troupe celebrating some event of yesterday or today, or from the launching of a new boutre to the encouragement of drumming and song. Light-skinned Comorean nobles in their foyers perform and patronize classical Arabic music like patricians of old Persia or salon aristocrats of Europe. For the visitor with a sophisticated musical ear, an invitation is very much worth accepting.

At Mitsamiouli, colorful ancient emirate on the northern cape, the slowest of saber dances (with palm fronds for swords) and a dance of welcome for foreigners are performed, but must usually be "commissioned." Nearby, the Trou au Prophète cave at Maloudja holds tales of pirate machinations and miraculous landings. The tombs and mosques of Tsoueni and the Miracle Mosque at Bangoi Kouni attract the faithful on pilgrimage. Sterile women allegedly can be cured at the Bangoi Kouni mosque, said to have been built without human hands (thanks to the materials of a wrecked ship supplied by Allah).

South from Moroni, a fertile coastline again breaks into white coral beach at CHINDINI and around FOUMBOUNI, capital of a vigorous emirate. A mill of the Société Coloniale de Bambao at SALIMANI processes vanilla, copra, ylang-ylang, perfume blossoms and cocoa. The fishermen of ICONI build fine outrigger canoes for the high seas. Women of the fishing families of M'BACHILE prepare coconut fibers for strong nautical rope.

The great clouded dome of the Khartala can be climbed in two days. A guide and porters (if desired) at $2 per day plus rice will be furnished by the Société Anonyme de la Grande Comore at Moroni. The SAGC also helps in outfitting the excursion and conveys the climber by a steep road to its estate at Boboni, where you meet your guides and take to the trail early. Before nightfall the path crosses a soggy, spongy tropical belt and you will undoubtedly be happy to see the SAGC's chalet, La Convalescence.

Once at the top, the climax of the trip is a fascinating descent into the fuming crater.

After Grande Comore, Mayotte Island is the place to dwell, with its reef-guarded villages and beaches, rushing rivers, perfumed botanical paradise at tiny Pamanzi Island and the old French fortifications around the interesting ex-capital DZAOUDZI. All the Comoros offer excellent possibilities for skindiving and spear fishing, but the colorful, limpid coral lagoon of Mayotte beats everything, especially during the high tides of August and September. Boutre races and skillfully burlesqued "steer fights" add dimensions of entertainment at Dzaoudzi and MAMUTSU, but you must be alert to learn of their occurrence. Residents circulate in boats or squeeze past one another on the "Boulevard des Crabes," a narrow mile-long dike between Pamanzi and Dzaoudzi. Charter flights are beginning to arrive on Mayotte with vacationers of the Club Méditerranée, as well as Italians and South Africans.

Moheli Island today slumbers after turbulent 19th century court intrigues and Great Power gamesmanship. It has only six miles of coastal road, but its beaches can be reached by four-wheel-drive vehicle or on foot from Fomboni. The pretty fishing village and copra center of NIOUMACHOI is accessible by boat in a lagoon filled with fish and a beach abounding in shells. Shirazi tombs at FOMBONI mark the presence of Persians here a half millennium ago. The town's main street is lined with kapok trees.

In the attractive islets to the south, facing Nioumachoi, dwell mainly wild goats and the ambitions of tourist developers.

The lovely landscape of Anjouan Island rises in a matter of minutes between Mutsamudu, Bambao and Domoni, from scented, luxurious vegetation into the temperate climate of a jagged center. The Arabic village of DOMONI has narrow cobblestone alleys winding past medieval mosques and intricately carved doorways. Nearby, in fishing grounds of barracuda, grouper (mérou), cabot, cavallys (carangue), perch (capitaine) and shark, the second known coelacanth was caught in 1952 and several more since then. An ungainly, 300 million-year-old link in evolution's chain, the coelacanth had been thought extinct for the past 70 million years.

MUTSAMUDU, Anjouan's capital of 8,000 people, is probably the archipelago's most impressive town, with its serpentine alleys, 17th century terraced houses, trellised windows and carved, studded doors. A citadel growls over the truculent sea, the ancient tombs are conical in shape, and the town's mosques have odd cylindrical minarets. As on Grande Comore, the frequent tom-tom parties sometimes include saber dances and slow, sinuous lines of traditional choreography. Anjouan's women appear in brightly colored full-length chiromani, which serve as gown, blouse and veil.

You can visit the perfume plant of Al Amal at Mutsamudu.

What to Buy

Products of fine handicraft are obtainable only in small quantities, for some of the traditional skills are dying out in the islands. A few ornately carved chests, doors, panels, tabletops and bookstands (porte-coran), as well as copies of the beautiful studded doors of southern Islam, can be found in the government crafts center at Moroni or at the artisans' workshops on Anjouan. Handsome leather slippers, finely embroidered skullcaps (coffias), prayer rugs, pearl and gold necklaces, filigree bracelets and pendant earrings also are available. Multicolored inexpensive basketwork with abstract design abounds on all islands. But the delicately decorated ceramic incense burners from Foumbouni have become rare, and the printed cloth is imported.

The Sakalava fishermen at Chiconi (Mayotte) and their Arab counterparts at Iconi (Grande Comore) carve intricate models of boutres and pirogues in sizes to fit the tourist suitcase and beyond. Shells and conches adorn some beaches, including valuable mother-of-pearl burgon shells at Moheli. Sada on Mayotte is a center of jewelers. Craftsmen on Anjouan make unique, stylized dolls in local dress, as well as delicate jewelry, and at Sima, on the western tip of Anjouan, the Société MacLukie fashions a unique and interesting style of furniture out of "porcupine wood" (coconut palm trunks).

Local Attitudes

Affluence tends to have its way in poor territories like the Comoros where devout Moslem servants cook the despised meat of the pig and care for the reviled pet dogs of Europeans. Hence, restrictions on behavior for visitors are relatively light. Photographing the brilliantly garbed but veiled Comorean women sometimes poses problems, but they will usually not take great offense if the subject is approached with discretion. Mosques can be visited.

Americans have no particular reputation, good or bad, except among some of the local French.

Weather, What to Wear, How Long to Stay

The Comorean winter (May to October) blows relatively cool and dry. It's the best time for a visit here—and in Madagascar, Seychelles and the Mascareignes as well. Some of the finest deep-sea fishing in the world can be undertaken from October to December, however, and there is sunshine all year around, even during the bitter-hot typhoon season of February and March.

Comorean dress glitters either with color (chiromani sarongs) or with subtle embroidery on white (kandjon gowns). Foreigners don't usually imitate these styles, for French overseas custom calls for brevity and comfort. Going up the Khartala on Grande Comore and Mt. M'tingui on Anjouan requires blankets, sweaters, heavy socks and durable trousers to protect against severe cold, dampness and thorns.

Few travelers make the Comoro detour for less than a week, and all but single-minded fishermen include it in a swing through East Africa, the Seychelles and Madagascar. One week is a good, realistic sojourn for the archipelago.

Communication

English comes in a poor fifth or sixth among the languages used on the Comoros. Swahili is the language of trade, administration and sociability; most Comoreans can get along in Malagasy as well. Arabic is the scholar's tongue, and French the avenue of communication with the political metropole.

Some fragile radio links exist with France and Madagascar, but to other parts of the world even postage runs dear. There are telephones on Grande Comore and Anjouan, but most people simply carry their messages in person.

Emergencies

Facilities and services are very limited, even at the medical centers in Moroni and Mutsamudu. Four smaller hospitals and several rural stations are not equipped for much beyond first aid. Fly to Tananarive or Paris if you have serious problems.

There is no American representation in the archipelago.

Madagascar

(République Malagasy)

Profile

STATUS: Independent republic since June 26, 1960. Former monarchy, conquered by French in 1896.

SIZE: World's fourth largest island, 230,500 square miles (one and a half times the size of California). Population—about 7,000,000.

GEOGRAPHY: High central plateau area, tapering to coasts in west, falling off abruptly to coasts in east. Forests in east, heavily eroded (lateritic) moors in south, west and center. Principal towns—Tananarive (capital, 350,000), Tamatave (principal port, 62,500), Majunga (70,000), Diego Suarez (naval base, 44,000).

CLIMATE: Summer rainy season from November to May, cooler dry season from June through September. Constant rainfall on east coast (hurricanes from January to March), drier in west and central plateau. Tananarive daytime temperatures are in the 70's and 80's year round; evenings are cool, often dropping into the 30's in winter. Tamatave is about 10 degrees warmer.

LANGUAGES: Malagasy; French in the cities.

CURRENCY: Malagasy franc (FMG), supported by French franc. FMG 100 = 40 cents; $1.00 = FMG 245.

VISAS: Required (not available on arrival). Fee $2.00 (for up to three months' stay). Three passport photos needed. Available from Malagasy Embassy in Washington, UN Mission in New York and Honorary Consuls of Madagascar in Chicago and San Francisco. Issued by French consulates wherever Madagascar is not represented.

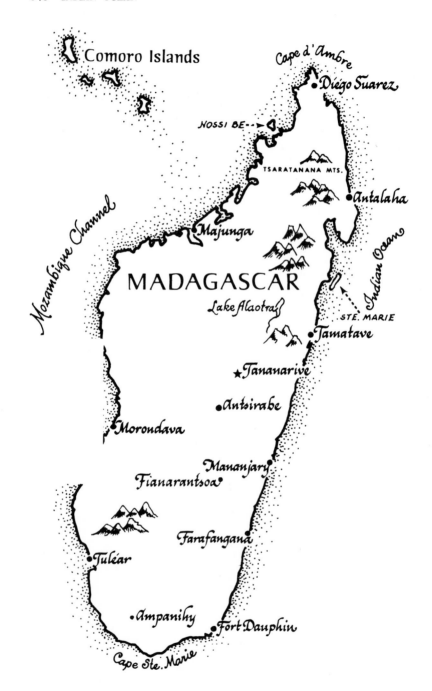

Comoro Islands

Cape d'Ambre

Diégo Suarez

NOSSI BE

TSARATANANA MTS.

Antalaha

Majunga

Mozambique Channel

MADAGASCAR

Lake Alaotra

Indian Ocean

STE. MARIE

Tamatave

★Tananarive

Antsirabe

Moroudava

Mananjary

Fianarantsoa

Farafangana

Tuléar

Ampanihy

Fort Dauphin

Cape Ste. Marie

AIRPORTS: Ivato Airport (TNR), 11 miles from Tananarive. Frequent connections with France and French-speaking Indian Ocean airfields, fewer with East Africa, eastern and southern Europe. International airport departure tax—FGM 1,500 ($6). Transport into city—taxi, $4 to $8, depending on size of vehicle; airport bus, $1.40.

NATIONAL HOLIDAYS: June 26, Independence Day; October 14, Republic Day; May 1, Labor Day; Christian holidays.

INFORMATION SOURCES: In US—Embassy of Madagascar, 2374 Massachusetts Avenue NW, Washington, D.C. 20008 (tel. 202/265-5525); Permanent Mission of Malagasy Republic to the UN, 301 East 47th Street, New York, N.Y. 10017 (tel. 212/752-1076). In Tananarive—Commissariat National au Tourisme et aux Arts Traditionnels, Place de l'Indépendance, P.O. Box 610 (tel. 228-85, 262-98, 257-34); Madagascar Air Tours (subsidiary of Air Madagascar), Hilton Hotel, P.O. Box 3874 (tel. 241-92, 265-15).

By Philip M. Allen

Tourist tracks to this veritable continent, where the traveler's palm (ravinala) is the national symbol, are unfortunately limited. Doubtless, however, travel will begin in earnest once intercontinental air connections and air tariffs improve. Madagascar is already a three-star destination, worthy of a journey in itself, but ships take a month to get there from Europe so long as Suez remains closed, and airline programming is still a virtual monopoly of Air France and its affiliate Air Madagascar. As a result, travelers find difficulty lingering here en route to any place but another Indian Ocean island.

Madagascar covers over a quarter-million square miles, sometimes rich and populated, mostly desolate, infertile, tortured by erosion. This is a special civilization of quasi-autonomous settlements and isolated economic activity strewn like pellets of an archipelago over a red-rock sea. The Great Island's seven million people are correctly called Malagasy (singular and plural), and so is their language, but the place itself is Madagascar or the Malagasy Republic, never "Malagasy" alone. The population is hospitable and handsome, the capital city, Tananarive, perched on the high central plateau, is a beautiful jumble of exotic worlds, and the island itself is a dreamland for artists, photographers and wanderers.

A single language, subject to some local variation, binds 18 ethnic groups into the Malagasy nation, unified for almost 200 years. The solidifying force was supplied in the late 18th century by the Asian (Malayo-Polynesian) Merina monarchy of the High Plateau around Tananarive. The proud, mostly Protestant Merina fought the invading French in 1895-96 and led sporadic movements of resistance against French colonial administrations, climaxed in the still mysterious island-wide revolt and massacre of 1947-48. Normally hospitable and pacific, acquiescent to a fate laden with taboos that seldom play fair with them, the Malagasy share one essential culture and honor one world—the world of the happily living dead.

French style is imperfectly assimilated in Madagascar, and delicately fused with Asian introspection and grace, as well as the politics and poverty of Africa. Educated Malagasy admire France's egalitarian mythology and cultural mystique however sullied by monopolistic tradesmen and supercilious bureaucrats. Politically and economically, the ex-metropole continues to pay many pipers and call many tunes. Frenchmen are at home here, as they used to be in Algiers and still are in Dakar and Abidjan. From 1960 until 1972, the Malagasy repeatedly elected a pro-French, conservative government espousing a benign brand of social welfare, bound hand and foot to overseas commerce and finance, unable to conquer under-development.

These policies were seriously challenged for the first time on the island in 1971 and 1972; the nation witnessed a bloody uprising in the impoverished southwest, followed by violent riots of students and labor unions at Tananarive, and scapegoat purges of politicians and foreign diplomats. In May, 1972, President Philibert Tsiranana, whose longevity and equanimity had seemed eternal, finally ceded his executive powers to a new government dominated by senior military officers under veteran Merina General Gabriel Ramanantsoa.

The regime has pledged austerity and a kind of New Deal, opened Madagascar's doors to East and West, and begun to renegotiate France's multifarious "privileged relations" in Malagasy economics, education and security.

The Great Island raises multitudes of cattle and quantities of rice and coffee; it produces more vanilla than any other place in the world and more cloves than any except Zanzibar; it mines graphite, chromite, mica, nickel, fissionable metals and bauxite, as well as large numbers of semi-precious stones—but none of these things is done efficiently enough, or with adequate returns for Malagasy, to overcome the mass poverty that prevails.

Chinese and Indian communities (of 10,000 and 15,000 respectively) ply their businesses quietly throughout the country. Americans employed at the nearby NASA tracking station frequent the capital city of Tananarive. Europeans and American missionaries run hospitals, schools and churches in most corners of a half-Christianized country. Europeans come in increasing numbers on holiday or business. All these vazaha (foreigners) are conspicuous as only the affluent can be in a pool of poverty.

But the tolerant, poetic, musical Malagasy set the pulse and character of this bewitching land—in the pyramidal thatched rooflets and umbrellas that shelter one of the world's mightiest markets, the Zoma (Friday) of Tananarive; in the sweep of a lamba (shawl, for men and women) over thin-boned, graceful shoulders; in a special appreciation for the ubiquitous horned and humped zebu cattle; in a complicated cuisine based on rice, and in the wisdom and ritual of a culture affirming ancestral precedent, family solidarity, love of rhetoric, power of taboo, and reverence for the intricate order of the created universe.

Travelers rarely come to Madagascar for a single, definite tourist purpose; it's too far away and too expensive for that. The beaches and water sports hardly surpass Caribbean, Mediterranean or other Indian Ocean facilities. Urban and economic centers are widely separated and their accommodations uneven in quality. Craftsmanship is better in West and Central Africa, where the music is also more exhilarating. The finest literature, theater and religious ceremony depend on the lovely but difficult Malayo-Polynesian tongue of the Malagasy. There is some hunting and good fishing, but not enough to draw the sportsman interested in nothing else. That exotic evolutionary abortion, the Malagasy lemur, is rigorously protected, as well it deserves to be. Millennia of geographical isolation have deposited an unduplicated stock of animals, butterflies and plants here, but few safaris are organized to explore this extraordinary natural endowment.

Madagascar's romantic history of seaborne migrations, warfare, piracy, internal empire and foreign colonialism has been well documented in French. In English the standard place to start is Nigel Heseltine's *Madagascar* (Praeger, 1971), a respectable introduction to the island's physical and social background, weakest in its treatment of contemporary politics and economics. O. Mannoni's much-discussed *Psychologie de la Colonisation* has been translated as *Prospero and Caliban* (Praeger paperbacks, 1964).

A few poems by the great Jean-Joseph Rabearivelo, Flavien Ranaivo and Jacques Rabemananjara have been translated in various anthologies of African verse.

Money Matters

Malagasy francs are no longer convertible outside the island. French francs and US dollars will be accepted or exchanged at the airport, hotels and main shops, but not in the markets. Among the several banks, all of them French, the Banque Nationale pour le Commerce et l'Industrie (BNCI), owned by the Banque Nationale de Paris, has agencies in various parts of Tananarive (including the Hilton Hotel) and 14 other places on the island.

The Banque de Madagascar et des Comores (BMC), owned by Crédit Lyonnais, is also conveniently located.

General Ramanantsoa's new government has imposed some price ceilings on what has been a dramatically inflationary economy. Tananarive prices for accommodations, food (especially imports), liquor, medicines and cosmetics, film, all paper items and some services are almost equal to those of French-speaking West Africa and well above the levels prevailing in Paris or American cities. Living costs outside the capital are substantially lower, however, and the budget-conscious traveler can manage fairly well on rice, beef, chicken, vegetables and fruits, locally bottled beverages and inexpensive accommodations.

Getting In and Out

Madagascar lies 260 miles off the coast of Mozambique. Access is primarily by air. Travelers also arrive via Messageries Maritimes passenger liner from Marseille, and sometimes on freighters of the Robin Lines from Baltimore, the Scandinavian Lines and the Compagnie Havraise rounding the Cape of Good Hope. Tamatave, the island's principal port, as well as half a dozen other ports around Madagascar's circumference, link it with Europe, the coasts of Africa and the other Western Indian Ocean islands.

Air France and Air Madagascar operate five round trip flights each week between Paris and Tananarive (increasing frequency in the June-to-August French vacation period), taking about 11 hours with stops variously at Majunga in Madagascar's northwest, Nairobi (Kenya), Dar es Salaam (Tanzania), or Djibouti (Territory of the Afars and Issas) and Athens. These flights continue or connect to Mauritius, Reunion and the Comoro Islands. Air Madagascar flies once each week to and from Lourenço Marques (Mozambique) and Johannesburg (South Africa), while South African Airways has a weekly Johannesburg-Durban-Tananarive round trip. Unless you can join a Club Méditerranée or other rare charter, you must pay a minimum of $133.80 one way between Tananarive and Nairobi, $103.50 from Dar es Salaam, $514.30 from Paris and $145.30 from Johannesburg.

American and Canadian visitors must arrive with a valid Malagasy visa. Customs and immigration controls follow normal overseas French patterns.

Getting Around Within Madagascar

To cover the island's widely separated pockets of activity, you must either have time and stamina for spartan overland travel or funds for an expensive air network. No quantum of weeks will let you see all of Madagascar and no lifetime suffices to "know" the place. You can bounce among 68 airports on scheduled or chartered Air Madagascar flights (DC-4, DC-3 and smaller craft), and usually find surface transportation and accommodations at the other end. Since most air circuits begin and end in one day at Tananarive, many flights leave the capital at ungodly hours. Nine weekly flights between Tananarive and Majunga cost $32 (one way), Tamatave (twice daily) $20; Nossi Be (daily), Fort Dauphin (three times weekly), and Tulear (five times per week)—all $52. Air Madagascar offers some seasonal excursion rates between Tananarive and resort areas like Nossi Be and Sainte Marie Island.

The national railway runs on beautiful itineraries daily between Tananarive and Tamatave, Tananarive and Lake Alaotra, Fianarantsoa and Manakara (the splendid coffee railway) and four times daily between Tananarive and the resort capital of Antsirabe to the south.

The Great Island's knobby, lateritic contours, its expanses of emptiness and rudimentary roadways prove forbidding to fastidious travelers, and challenging even to the rough rider. Many roads in the east and the northwest are washed out by rain between November and April; others are temporarily cut. Road excursions are thus normally restricted to the paved areas around Tananarive, the 260-mile highway along the plateau vertebrae south to Fianarantsoa, and the rather monotonous newly paved limb from Tananarive to Majunga in the far northwest.

Adequate European vehicles can be hired with or without driver from a number of firms, including Hertz, on Tananarive's Avenue de l'Indépendance; Avis, represented by Madagascar Air Tours agencies at the Tananarive Hilton, Nossi Be and Majunga, and some modest local garages. Standard rentals cost from $10 to $12 per day plus about eight cents per kilometer. Drivers are available for $4 additional per day (occasionally an additional two cents per kilometer) and are often worth their weight in gold. In addition to these fees, you also pay for taxes (about six per cent) and gasoline, which is about twice the American price. Most agencies offer some reductions for long-term rentals and you can get a car for a half-day at Nossi Be for $10, all included. But no firm rents for one-way trips. Few Tananarive taxis are equipped for an extended journey outside town.

There are buses, however, along the infinitude of routes from Tananarive to the southern coasts. Hitchhiking almost always costs some fee or share of expenses. For circulation within Tananarive, small taxis (2CV, Renault 4L, et al.) charge 50 francs (20 cents) per short trip, 100 francs for anything involving the Hilton Hotel or a suburban destination, and double the regular fare after 8 pm. Larger taxis start at 100 francs. It is always advisable to carry a decent map of Tananarive (available at bookstores, the Hilton Hotel and the BNCI Bank) for the streets interlace like a plate of spaghetti, and the taxi drivers frequently know addresses only by the quartier (district), not the street number.

The National Tourist Service (Commissariat National au Tourisme) is understaffed, unsophisticated and less helpful than it should be in so lovely yet complicated a country. The government relies on French-managed travel agencies whose expertise is largely restricted to the capital city. Madagascar Air Tours (Hilton Hotel) and Transcontinents (Avenue de l'Indépendance) are the most experienced.

The Chamber of Commerce on Rue Colbert and the Syndicat d'Initiative just above it on the Place de l'Indépendance (never to be confused with the Avenue de l'Indépendance, site of the great Zoma market several hundred feet below the Place) can be helpful in contacts with tradesmen and artisans throughout the island. For road travel the Automobile Club de Madagascar at Tananarive (P.O. Box 571), with chapters in all provincial capitals, can also be useful, if you are a member of an automobile club at home. A certificate from the Tananarive club permits out-of-town hotel and restaurant discounts. Its annual *Guide Routier et Touristique* contains current information for travelers on most itineraries in Madagascar and neighboring islands. The Secretariat of the Indian Ocean Tourist Alliance (ATOI) is on Rue Amiral Pierre (tel. 262-62) near the Place de l'Indépendance; the ATOI may be of help in organizing visits including Mauritius, Reunion and the Comoros.

Where to Stay

In TANANARIVE: Accommodations and meals cost more than in East Africa, although somewhat less than in Abidjan, Dakar and other West African cities. (Costs outside the capital are substantially lower, but rooms and facilities tend to be simpler and older.) Unless otherwise noted, rates do not include breakfast, taxes or service charges.

A new *Hilton Hotel* nests near jacaranda-fringed Lake Anosy at the lower rim of town. Ask for a room with view uphill to the Rova (Queen's Palace), although the rear rooms look over interesting new government buildings, housing developments and rice fields. The Hilton has several restaurants and bars including a pleasant "Bistrot," a pool, spacious lobby lounges and smiling personnel. Rooms cost $20 to $23 per night and are inhabited by American, South African and business-tourist clients other than Malagasy or French. The latter tend to prefer older, mustier accommodations at the *Colbert, Sélect* or *Hôtel de France* (all $8 to $20), located closer to the city's center, or the *Lido* ($5.50 to $8), which sits right on top of the great Friday market. A new luxury *Hôtel Panorama* is scheduled to open in 1973 on the suburban hills east of downtown Tananarive.

Cheaper, rougher accommodations are available in the center of town at the *Hôtel Glacier* ($3 to $5); the *Mellis*, a renovated Greek business-man's place ($4 to $8, all charges included); the *Terminus* at the foot of the Avenue de l'Indépendance across from the railroad station ($3.50 to $5), and quite a few other modest establishments, often situated above restaurants.

The island is a hive of hotels, rooming houses and restaurants, most of them catering to Europeans or traveling Asians, since Malagasy almost invariably lodge among family. If a town has no regular hotel, its officials or church representatives can usually find you a place to stay. There are impromptu camping grounds everywhere. Provincial hotels often date from well before independence (1960) and many have not been "modernized" or, in some cases, even cleaned since then.

Unless otherwise identified, the establishments listed below are rugged and satisfactory for health and comfort without luxury or impeccable hygiene. Upper prices usually indicate a surcharge for air-conditioning, which isn't always needed. Prices are given for room only; hence they will be supplemented by taxes, service charges and breakfast tariffs. If you are staying longer than three or four days, try to "bargain" a discount from *le patron*, and always look for reductions offered to Automobile Club members. Also, anticipate an inflationary rise in price.

North of Tananarive:

Nossi Be—*Les Cocotiers* (formerly Bellevue) on a fine beach, with good food, facilities for fishing, skindiving, boating, etc., $7.50 to $10 per bungalow. *Palm Beach Hotel*, with 58 bungalows, terrace dining area, a salt-water pool and full range of water sports facing, alas, the least of the island's beaches ($16 for singles, $20 up for doubles). A dozen bungalows on a nice beach at the Village d'Ambatoloaka rent for upwards of $6 per person.

DIEGO SUAREZ—Fairly rough going at the *Hôtel de la Poste* and the *Tropical* (same management) for $6 to $8. The *Nouvel Hôtel* isn't that new, but has good food and a garden for about the same rates.

MAJUNGA—Your choice is between flaking old-town hotels with "atmosphere" like the *Hôtel de France* ($3.50 to $10), the *Hôtel Fitarikandro* ($3 with inexpensive meals and dancing) or the newer bungalow arrangements like the *Village Touristique* jutting into the sea at the aborted Port Schneider ($3.50 up); or the *Guimbretière* beach bungalows at AMBOROVY (five miles out of town) for $10 per cabin.

Smaller-town accommodations include AMBALABONGO's popular (with duck hunters and fishermen) *Hôtel Carlton* ($3, but be sure to confirm your reservation) and the good Greek *Hôtel Glacier* in the town of AMBATO-BOENI ($3 up).

East of Tananarive:

TAMATAVE—*Les Flamboyants* for luxury accommodations; *Hôtel Joffre* for the old-fashioned; an ocean view and good food at *Casa Maria* ($8). AMBILA-LEMAITSO—*Relais d'Ambila*, a good beach resort place ($4 to $5, with bungalows for $6 to $7). FOULPOINTE—*Hôtel-Motel de Foulpointe*, $5 to $6. SAINTE MARIE ISLAND—Bungalows on Bety-Plage, villas and rooms in private homes available through the Syndicat d'Initiative. AMBATONDRAZAKA—*Hôtel Alaotra*, recently renovated (from $5 per room).

South of Tananarive:

ANTSIRABE—The gigantic renovated *Hôtel des Thermes* (where Mohammed V, Sultan of Morocco, was exiled in the 1950's) has reopened under government management. *Hôtel Truchet*, with good food and rooms at a variety of prices from $3 to $12; the *Trianon* and *Veromanitra*, simpler, with Malagasy food ($2.50 to $4).

FIANARANTSOA—*Hôtel Moderne du Betsileo* (Chez Papillon, one of the best on the island), $6 to $9; *Hôtel des Voyageurs*, small with boules (pétanque) court and library, $3.50; *Sud-Hôtel* (interesting bar, good food), $3 to $8. AMBALAVAO—*Hôtel Verger* (rustic, old French provincial place with fine food), $4, cheaper in the Annex. IHOSY—*Hôtel Verger* (not as distinguished as its sister establishment in Ambalavao), $4 to $5. BERAKETA—*Le Relais* (good food), $5; Annex from $1.50. FORT DAUPHIN —*Hôtel de France* (large, renovated), $3 to $5; *Dauphin* (smaller, good food), $5 to $12; cottages at Libanona Beach, $10; other cottages available through American Lutheran Mission in Fort Dauphin.

TULEAR—*Motel Capricorne* (in agreeable suburban gardens), $6 to
$10; *Tropical* (in town), $3 to $7. MORONDAVA—*Grand Hôtel*, $3 to $9;
Village Touristique, $5.50.

A note for backpackers: Ask about government gîtes (shelters) at town
halls and sous-préfets' offices, or seek out local missionaries, school directors, syndicats d'initiative, or general store operators (French, Malagasy, Chinese, Indian or Greek merchants who constitute the backbone
of local initiative). You might arrange such board in advance at Tananarive through the American Lutheran missionaries (at the Imprimerie
Luthérienne, P.O. Box 538), the Ligue Laïque d'Enseignement (for
school facilities), the Ministry of the Interior for gîtes or the Chamber
of Commerce. Canadian CUSO Volunteers teach at Malagasy schools,
but there is no Peace Corps on the island. Camping makes good sense
throughout the island whenever the rains don't threaten to spoil cool,
starry nights. June to October is especially good. Local markets provide
adequate cheap rice (or cassava or corn, in parts of the west and south),
beef, fish, fruit, occasional vegetables (which had better be carefully
washed) and peanuts.

Local stores carry bottled water and beer, and canned goods like sardines
and liver pâté, which are expensive.

Where and What to Eat

TANANARIVE excels all of Eastern and Southern Africa for French cuisine,
local and Creole dishes, as well as Chinese and Vietnamese meals. Until
you get to Abidjan or Dakar, you will find no better French restaurant
for food, service and ambiance than *La Taverne* at the Hôtel Colbert
($4-to-$6 menus, plus superb hors d'oeuvre, à la carte specialties, and a
good choice of wines including the Taverne's own Malagasy vintages).
The *Café de Paris* on the arcaded Avenue de l'Indépendance is swathed
each Friday by Tananarive's great Zoma market—a good place to lunch
on that day and to survey an excellent wine list at any time. Other
worthy French restaurants include *Chez Audier* on Rue Colbert uphill
from the south end of the Zoma, the *Relais Normand*, the *Select Hôtel*
overlooking the Zoma, *Chez Grégoire* to the east of center-city, the
Relais Aériens at the lake of Ambohibao near the Ivato Airport, with a
bikini-adorned swimming pool, and quite a few more.

The *Agip Motel* and *The Pizzeria* at the midtown Hôtel de France
serve Italian food.

European palates are intrigued by the occasional zebu filet, spiced
Malagasy or Creole sauce, or Indian Ocean specialty, to prove how far
France can come from Europe and yet stay French. The *Terminus* and

Acropole hotels and *La Cabane* are among a number of less expensive French places. A host of Vietnamese restaurants include *Le Pavillon de Jade, Le Grand Orient, Kim Son* and two called *Doan Van Bien.*

Tananarive has a few authentically Malagasy restaurants, including the *Buffet de la Gare* at the railway station, *La Rotonde* (an annex of Chez Grégoire), *Restogasy* on route No. 7, and the *Tantely* nightclub on the Route Circulaire just below the center of town. Your best bet is a home invitation, but these and a number of other restaurants (especially outside Tananarive) offer good examples of an authentic cuisine of rice, fish, pepper-onion-tomato sauces (rougaille), smoked pork (kitoza), cassava leaves, delicate bouillon with stew (romazava), fruits and rice cider (ranovola).

Tap water is safer here than in most of Africa, but still may be questionable. Local bottled water, soft drinks and wines are inexpensive, and local beer (Three Horses or Amstel) is excellent.

Many good provincial restaurants, most of them with mixed culinary styles and with rooms for rent as well, adorn the Great Island landscape. The following are among the best.

Near Tananarive:

Le Marseillais at AMBALAVAO (halfway down to Antsirabe, crayfish and Mediterranean specialties; reserve tables if you're going on a Sunday or holiday); *Au Rendezvous des Pêcheurs,* also at Ambalavao ("Chez le Grec," preferred by some habitués over Le Marseillais; reserve here for Sundays and holidays, too). *Bar-Restaurant du Syndicat d'Initiative* at AMBOHIMANGA (by the old citadel of the Merina dynasty; open weekends and holidays only, with a Malagasy dance troupe). *Le Relais du Lac* at MANJAKANDRIANA (French cuisine, inexpensive). *Motel Walter* at ANJIRO (near Manjakandriana, on the road east to Tamatave). *Bel Air Hôtel* near the IVATO AIRPORT and *La Riviera* at AMBOHIDRATRIMO (another sacred hill, eight miles out of town, with weekend dancing). Both Bel Air and Riviera have good Malagasy as well as French food. *Chez Madame Bouissou* at FARATSIHO (between Antsirabe and Lake Itasy). *Au Rendezvous des Chasseurs* at ANDOHORANOFOTSY (excellent garden ambiance and specialties, six miles south of town).

ANTSIRABE and southward:

Hôtel Truchet (French), *Veromanitra* (Malagasy), *Buffet de la Gare* (Malagasy, for as little as 60 cents), *Hôtel Diamant* and *Leung Hine* (both Chinese) and *Le Fleuve Parfum* (Vietnamese) in Antsirabe. *Hôtel Naturel* in BETAFO; *Grand Hôtel Chez Théo* at AMBOSITRA (Greek and rustic French specialties). *Hôtel Moderne du Betsileo* and *Sud Hôtel* at

FIANARANTSOA (both expert in several styles, moderate prices). *Hôtel Verger* at AMBALAVAO. *Le Relais* at BERAKETA (Malagasy dishes from 40 cents up). *Le Dauphin* in FORT DAUPHIN (seafood specialties). *Hôtel des Bougainvillées* at MANANJARY (Asian, Malagasy, Creole dishes).

East of Tananarive:
Grand Hôtel at MORAMANGA (game, fish and Malagasy specialties). *Hôtel Alaotra* at AMBATONDRAZAKA (French and Creole styles). *Casa Maria* (seafood) and *Hôtel Joffre* at TAMATAVE.

In the north:
Hôtel Maeva at MAEVATANANA (Malagasy); *Hôtel Carlton* at AMBALA-BONGO (32 miles north of Maevatanana, in hunting zone, with game, Creole and Chinese specialties). *Hôtel Glacier* at AMBATO-BOENI. *Hôtel de France* and *Nouvel Hôtel* (curry), *Kohinoor* (excellent Indian-Pakistani food from 40 cents per platter) at MAJUNGA; *La Soucoupe Volante* at AMBOROVY (beach resort five miles from Majunga). *Hotel Palm Beach* at NOSSI BE. *Nouvel Hôtel* and *Le Saïgonnais* at DIEGO SUAREZ; *Escale du Nord*, 20 miles north of Diego (Malagasy).

What to See and Do

Time and purse alone dictate the traveler's options. So diverse and so rare is Madagascar that experience will often create its own tastes. Only the ancestors have the time and resources to know this whole land, with its dreamlike desolation, its urban jumbles, its fastidious blend of spirituality and traditional technology, the sobriety of its social life and the hilarity of its festivals. Yet the traveler can sample these delicacies in their world unto itself and, as the proverb warns, once sipped, the waters of Madagascar will draw him ineluctably back.

The capital and environs:
For all but the few who come by sea, TANANARIVE is Madagascar's point of arrival and departure, the hub of transport, matrix of institutions, minotaur of finances. The hilltop capital spills over slopes 4,000 to 5,000 feet high surmounting a landscape of green rice fields and pounded red promontories that is Imerina (land of the Merina people). On Fridays, when it swells to 10 times its daily size, Tananarive's Zoma market monopolizes the center of town, engulfing the modern city's Parisian perfumeries, Madras modes, shaded cafes and arcaded chic shoppes.

Tananarive is made of yellow stone and red earth, laced with stone staircases, planted with pastel-green, yellow and pink houses one on top of the other. Durable walkers can clamber most of the capital on foot, although inexpensive taxis provide welcome relief from the sheer uphill climbs and the long beautiful ridge circuits. Drive up to the calm, period-piece summit palaces of the old kings and queens (the Rova, or citadel), now a most expressive, if thinly stocked, historical museum (open Tuesday, Thursday and Saturday from 2 to 5 pm, Sundays and holidays from 9 to 11 am and 2 to 5 pm). And then stroll back down via old lanes and twisting steps, virtually through the gardens and henneries of the city people (who enjoy having passersby), past lovely round-faced children and fragments of musical language coming out of doors and gateways.

You'll find a nice little zoo and fine botanical garden at Tsimbazaza on the southern flank of the city, spread around the Franco-Malagasy Orstom Ethnographic Research Center (open Tuesday, Thursday and Sunday from 2 to 5 pm); ask at the Orstom building to see a most extraordinary collection of butterflies.

The suburban university affords a sensational view of undulating Imerina on one side and the city on the other. From here, after decades of subservience to an imposed French ideal of higher education, young Malagasy faculty members and students boiled over into the streets of Tananarive in May, 1972, demanding a new government that would permit greater self-determination for their national institution, and were shot down by the troops.

There are art shows at three or four galleries in Tananarive, horse racing on Sunday and several specialized libraries for the scholar. During slack work periods, the Bendix Company technicians based at the American Embassy are glad to show people around their NASA tracking station at Imerintsiatosika, 30 minutes west of the capital. Local friends or hotel people may be able to get you guest privileges for tennis or golf at one of the European clubs, or for riding at the Etrier stables in Mahamasina near the central stadium. Cock-fights are staged surreptitiously on Sundays in certain suburbs; a Malagasy friend might be willing to take you.

Night life in Tananarive is largely imported. Unless it's a family affair or a theater performance in their own language at the huge Tranom' pokonolona (House of the People) in the slum market district of Isotry, the up-to-date Malagasy drink and dance with the Europeans at the latter's places sprinkled throughout town and suburb. Le Baladin is a current favorite for good food and swinging music. There are pianists (like the superb Malagasy stylist Jeannot Rabeson) at the Hilton's Papillon Bar (first drink costs $1.60, whatever it is). Le Caveau is the oldest and most genial of the clubs. Le Cellier Chez Jean Louis serves good food, fine wines and piano music. The Casino on Avenue Foumbey-rolles has the standard games, as well as food. La Rotonde (Chez

Grégoire) stages Malagasy dances on Friday nights (book at Madagascar Air Tours). Les Relais Aériens discotheque is at Ambohibao. And the taxi girls wait at Tantely (Malagasy restaurant) and Le Cannibale.

A 15-mile drive through inundated rice fields and red clay villages brings the traveler to the sacred hill of AMBOHIMANGA, a well-preserved palace enclave of good King Andrianampoinimerina, founder of the so-called Hova (Merina) imperial dynasty. At AMBOHIDRATRIMO, eight miles northwest of Tananarive, another sacred hill has interesting clusters of royal tombs on an exalted promontory.

The southern plateau:

By far the most popular of several overnight road trips out of Tananarive leads to cool, collected ANTSIRABE (56,000), a handsome plateau spa with light industry set in a fertile rolling landscape of lakes and pine forest. Water skis furrow over legendary Lake Andraikiba and nearby picturesque Betafo. Star-crossed lovers are still leaping into the black lethe of the Tritriva crater. The renovated Victorian Hôtel des Thermes —Marienbad out of Charles Addams—is the center of recreation for visitors. There are several good bars and a casino in Antsirabe, but camping around these hills and lakes is a delight, and you can rent bicycles for a romp in town.

Knowledgeable motorists usually break the Tananarive-Antsirabe journey at AMBATOLAMPY, for a stroll over tree-shaded lanes, for brook fish, duck, frogs legs or crayfish at one of the restaurants. A bit farther off the road, picnickers stop at pretty ANDRAMASINA, in a town park by mountain rapids. Fishing is excellent all around these hills.

A somewhat rougher return from Antsirabe carries travelers west of Tananarive into the lovely volcanic lake country of ITASY, site of experimental livestock operations and of carefree weekend explorations around Soavinandriana, Faratsiho and Ampefy. For those who prefer to have their insouciance without discomfort, the Itasy excursion can be made from Tananarive and back over better roads.

Too many of the curious simply double back after a couple of days at Antsirabe, never learning the merry pleasures of Monsieur DuBois's Auberge de la Forêt, his fruit orchards and winery at Ambalamanakana, near the woodcraft and straw-weaving center of AMBOSITRA, 60 miles south of Antsirabe. At Ambositra, in four or five major ateliers, the glistening inlay woodwork, carvings and utensils of an old guild craft are worth visiting, however slick and middlebrow the styles. You can camp on the Père DuBois grounds at Ambalamanakana. Side trips out of Ambositra by four-wheel-drive vehicle take you into splendid mountain terrain.

The road continues good past FIANARANTSOA and AMBALAVAO, 260 and 290 miles south of Tananarive, centers of the astute, musical Betsileo people, who tend cattle, grow rice on ingenious terraces and even produce wines. Atop Fianarantsoa, a loosely built, hillside provincial capital of 50,000, dominating a spectacular topography, is the ruined Rova established in 1830 by the Merina imperial armies as a fortress against Betsileo revolts.

On the outskirts of Fianarantsoa, affluent residents (some of them Malagasy) have landscaped their own lakeside plots at Sahambavy for watery weekend fun. Forty miles to the northeast, RANOMAFANA (the name means "warm water") offers salubrity and beauty in a tropical forest, with waterfalls, the excitement of an occasional boar hunt, trout fishing and more sedate lawn sports, butterfly collecting and orchid-watching. The small Hôtel Thermal de Ranomafana was seriously damaged by a hurricane in 1972 and is at least temporarily closed.

In the red and white brick town of AMBALAVAO (12,500), 30 miles south of Fianarantsoa, craftsmen bring their wrought iron, silk cloth, cottons, zebu cattle and carvings to market, where there is usually good music as well. In a workshop near the Catholic Church, a dozen skilled women press dried leaves and petals into thick rice fibers to make the decorative sheets, stationery, fragile purses, place mats and book jackets of rare Antaimoro paper. Only hardy and well-equipped travelers push much farther than Ambalavao, along a dwindling road into the decimated masses of the south.

The south:

The pavement stops at ANKARAMENA, 35 miles south of Ambalavao and the road narrows to an often single, corrugated track for most of the great triangle extending from there to Fort Dauphin and Tulear. At places outside those cities, the asphalt returns again, but not for long— except for a 90-mile strip between Tulear and Sakaraha. Landscapes change from the fuzzy, gouged lateritic moors of the central plateau into dustbound ridge and plains where even laterite has worn away, leaving bald stone groveling in dead sand, or heaving gigantic knuckle bones at the sky. Rivers bear the sole conceivable stuffs of life, and when water runs near the roadside, the traveler peers through luxuriant green foliage back into nature's own graveyard.

The first call after Ambalavao is the flowering crossroads town of IHOSY (6,500), ringed with cotton and peanut farms, cactus, coconut groves and innumerable cattle herds of the athletic and fun-loving Bara people. The customary "grand tour" plunges south from Ihosy over the purple, windswept Horombe Plateau, into desert, cactus forest and dry savanna, fringed by files of spectral, lymphoid baobabs, occasional dec-orated stone tombs merging Christian piety with ancestral pageantry, and mountainous termite hills like some Pythagorean tumulus. Walkers trudge the road from nowhere to nowhere, and goats gradually replace cattle on the rubbled pastures of Capricorn. Settlements become more sparse, monocultural and poverty-stricken as you pass through the Tropic.

Local festivals, usually in May and June, bring out the best of these places. Their local notables can help arrange visits to markets, festivals or funerals, farms and cooperatives, schools and churches, local artisans and small industries.

The provincial ports of FORT DAUPHIN and TULEAR, each 450 miles from Tananarive as the crow flies, dwell in a calm, slow charm. Their dark-skinned populations of Antandroy, Tanosy, Mahafaly and Vezo-Sakalava, their staple diets of corn and cassava, create a relatively "African" atmosphere.

Tulear (40,000) is more spacious, greener, poorer, gayer and warmer than Fort Dauphin. It sits lower and more brightly on its palm-lined beach, safer from the typhoon blasts of January and February. Some plucky skindivers plumb the pink and white coral reefs off Tulear, accompanied by vast varieties of fish and only a few sharks (so they say).

Fort Dauphin (13,000), site of the first ill-fated attempt by Europeans to colonize Madagascar in 1642, rises dramatically on peaks, cliffs and escarpments. The ruined 17th century fort of the massacred French settlers under Etienne de Flacourt is still there. The port does a brisk trade in meat (on and off the hoof) with France's Reunion Island, and in sisal, mica and eventually bauxite with Europe.

Between the two southern capitals stands some rugged but relatively populous country, with a few interesting towns like AMBOASARY (sisal plantations and a private woods with lemurs and bats), AMPANIHY (mo-hair rug mill and garnet mines), EJEDA (large American Lutheran hos-pital), and BETIOKY (syndicated Mahafaly wood carvers), as well as spectacular windblown Cape Ste. Marie and Faux Cap (False Cape).

The west:
Air Madagascar is about the only way to get in and out of major west coast towns like MOROMBE, BELO-TSIRIBIHINA, MAINTIRANO and even MORONDAVA, center of Madagascar's most audacious efforts at organizing communities for agricultural production and exportation. While the vast region around Morondava is less interesting to tourists than other parts of the Malagasy countryside, it contains some of the rarest of the island's cultural treasures—namely, several royal "Vezo" tombs tucked in forest glades, their stone bulwarks surmounted by jubilant, brazen wood sculp-

tures portraying the perfect (admittedly "pagan") union of erotic love and immortality.

The north:

A classic week's tour package treats vacationers to the exotic delights of French-speaking, oriental Tananarive and a Polynesian beach nirvana at NOSSI BE off the far northern coast. That island will eventually have a jet airstrip, well-paved roads, modern hotels, new beach bungalows and a casino. If you can't wait for these boons of modern tourism you can still bask or dive in the limpid, placid, reef-protected surf, wander in motorboats from island to island, climb old craters, collect shells and coral along several beaches, paddle in outrigger canoes (pirogues à balancier), motor through sugar cane, coffee and pepper plantations, see lemurs at the Ampasindava Reserve, imbibe the fragrance of ylang-ylang and other perfume scents at sunrise, visit the rum distillery at Dzamandzar (free samples), the perfume plant at Ampasimenabe, or the government oceanographic station, promenade the neat little port town of Hellville, and feast on steak, fish, chicken, French wines and cheeses at the Palm Beach Hotel or Les Cocotiers.

For boats, snorkeling equipment, water skis, tennis facilities and other sports see the Marine Service at the Palm Beach or the Syndicat d'Initiative in Hellville. For a pirogue ride over the surf, take a taxi to Ambatoloaka village and talk things over with an elder on the beach.

DIEGO SUAREZ (44,000), still a French naval base (shared, to be sure, with Madagascar's rudimentary navy), springs out from its immense bay, site of a pre-emptive British occupation in 1942 that is still deplored by some (Vichy) French. Diego's steamy climate is relieved by ocean breezes.

A serpentine 45-mile drive from Diego brings visitors to the sacred lake at Anivorano-Nord inhabited by "tame" crocodiles who are reincarnations of inhospitable townsfolk of an ancient Indian Ocean Gomorrah. As drums beat the invitationals, the beasts emerge from their dark depths to collect chunks of meat posted on the shore for them. The ceremony is good, but costs as much as $68 for each "production"—hence the experience is best approached in numerous or affluent company. Tuesdays, Thursdays and Sundays are the crocodiles' days off.

MAJUNGA (70,000), the northwestern capital, can be reached by air on the Nossi Be route, or by twice-weekly jet landings from East Africa. The seedy, four-square colonial port sleeps in the economic shadow of Tananarive and Tamatave, but Indian merchants retain a lucrative foothold, Arabs and Swahilis draw their picturesque boutres and dhows into the little sailing harbor, and 20,000 Comorean immigrants from the enchanted but poverty-stricken islands to the north decorate Majunga's Mahabibo district with their flowery robes, white fezzes (coffias), golden earrings and whitewashed mosques. Legions of pousse-pousse (ricksha) drivers ask only 50 cents to cart a visitor at leisure's own pace all day over the handsome shore drives and boulevards; do plot the route and establish the fares in advance, however, and add a tip if the driver has "poussed" hard.

Majunga has always been a place of relaxation and sport for well-off Europeans and Indian commerical families. You can frolic in the surf at Amborovy Beach five miles north of town near the airport, or play tennis free of charge at the Tennis Club on Avenue Mahabibo.

The east:

Madagascar's east coast, from Diego Suarez to Fort Dauphin, is fertile, voluptuous and wet, exposed to pounding typhoons during January, February and March, and to showers much of the remaining time. It is also a long swath of disconnected activities, difficult to cover in one course without doubling back several times to Tananarive and Fianarantsoa. You can fly to Diego Suarez, to the isolated vanilla country around Antalaha, Sambava and Andapa, to the coffee region east of Fianarantsoa, to Fort Dauphin and of course to Tamatave itself, all with considerable back-tracking to the capital.

The island's main port, TAMATAVE (62,500), spreads pristine and prosperous on its lush coast, a town of sport and society, full of lively, historical reminiscences of warfare on land and sea, pirates and corsairs, diplomacy and intrigue. The immediate coastal area and hinterlands are extravagantly tropical, with palm-fringed beaches giving way to mangrove and, farther inland, to thick, almost anthropomorphic, vegetation, abundant food crops, banana trees, the ravinala (traveler's palm), raffia, coffee, cloves, pepper, sugar cane and vanilla orchids.

Vacationers from Tananarive sometimes tempt the pounding, shark-filled surf, but they more frequently settle for sand and safety in the calmer waters of the Pangalanes canal. AMBILA LEMAITSO is one of the island's most popular beaches, reachable by rail and sport plane as well as by the rough trunk road (less than half paved) that rudely connects Tananarive and Tamatave. The pretty village of FOULPOINTE, 35 miles north of Tamatave, has not only a safe and salubrious beach, but also the interesting ruins of old fortifications from the days of Indian Ocean maritime warfare.

Seeking offbeat privacy for fishing and soul-searching, the traveler coud hardly find a better spot than ILE SAINTE MARIE, an unspoiled French-Malagasy preserve with a colorful history of torrid loves and piracy. This little-known island has idyllic beaches behind coral reefs. Attainable by air from Tananarive and Tamatave, Sainte Marie can also be reached by driving 140 miles up the handsome coast on a road that's paved as far as Fenerive, and continuing by auto-ferryboat from Manompana.

There are a few reasons for preferring the 200-mile, 12-hour road trip between Tananarive and Tamatave, notwithstanding the hairpin curves and wickedly rutted road surfaces. Not only is the coast lovely and the intervening forest glorious, but you also have a variety of pleasant stops along the upper (interior) part of the way. These include LAKE MANTASOA, 40 miles from Tananarive, where over a century ago a shipwrecked French genius named Jean Laborde created for the Merina queens a Jules Verne-like industrial park, zoo and pleasure garden; PERINET and ANJIRO, departure points for a day's meander among the lemurs, butterflies and orchids of the forest escarpment.

The expensive Tananarive-Tamatave railway is the government's reason for keeping the highway in discouraging condition. Passenger trains pass daily in each direction and on special dates a comfortable "Micheline" coach gets added to the usual rolling stock. At Moramanga, another track goes to the agricultural district of Lake Alaotra and AMBATONDRAZAKA, center of major international projects in rice, cassava, tobacco and peanuts.

To the south, a parallel railway cuts down from Fianarantsoa to the small coffee port of MANAKARA, with round trips daily over one of the most laboriously constructed tracks in history. The line (not duplicated by roads) traverses a primeval rain forest, especially interesting around Beromazava station, with its own stock of lemurs, butterflies, waterfalls, orchids and vines, bananas and gigantic foliage.

In autumn (April to June), Malagasy life abounds with harvest celebrations, family reunions, sacrifices and initiation ceremonies—occasions for renewal of faith in a personal and intimate, yet sacred, universe. Oratory is the bread of these festivals, and music the wine. In the succeeding months, the island becomes dry and cool enough for many families to conduct their famadiana, in which selected honorable ancestors receive handsome new garments (lambamena) and literally participate in a festival of kinship.

Government agencies and travel offices can sometimes alert travelers to country fairs, but the famadiana is a family matter. Air Tours and other travel agencies are short on improvisation, but they offer a number of package tours that serve to acquaint the visitor with the Great Island—provided you want to pay a premium for such guidance. Among the better excursions (with approximate prices) are a two and a half hour Tananarive circuit for $3, a Malagasy dinner with dance performances for $10, a three-hour guided trip to Ambohimanga for $15, a day at Lake Mantasoa for $35 (plus lunch), a day at Lake Itasy for $40 (plus lunch), a day at Antsirabe for $42 (plus lunch). There is a four-day plan for Nossi Be costing $105 plus air fare (another $105 round trip); a three-day tour to Antsirabe and Fianarantsoa by road, then to Manakara by train and return to Tananarive by air ($90 plus transportation); and a four-day air excursion to Fort Dauphin and Berenty (Amboasary) with a visit to the private sisal plantation and lemur forest for $177 (including air fare—reductions in off seasons and special rates for couples).

What to Buy

With luck and attention to what local informants say, you might discover in your travels an especially interesting drum, gourd-resonated guitar or violin, a brilliant wood composition from inaccessible Iakora in the south, a miraculous pair of votary statuettes from Maintirano in the west, a massive silver necklace hammered out of antique doubloons in the southeast (these appear occasionally in Tananarive shops), a selection of butterflies at Anjiro or Perinet in the east, or a densely woven well-patterned mohair rug from Ampanihy. Straw work, bamboo, embroidery and cloth are among the island's most common virtues. Lambas (shawls) for men or women range from elegant cotton-silk weaves (arindrano) of the Betsileo, which can cost as much as $80 in the markets of Ambalavao and Fianarantsoa, to delicate white silks of the Merina and gayly striped cotton weaves (lambamena, literally "red lambas") meant primarily for re-shrouding ancestral remains, but worn by the well-draped quick as well.

The Malagasy have yet to acquire the knack of "packaging" their culture for tourists. Their profound philosophical reserve prevents them from boasting about their prowess. But without ever leaving Tananarive you can find many things. Ceremonious haggling in the Zoma (where bargaining is virtually obligatory) easily produces a gay, practical straw hat or basket (soubique), embroidered blouse or place setting, a set of miniatures of costumed hira gasy (strolling players and musicians), a twisted cane of polished "sacred" banyan wood from Vezo country in the south, a wood-inlay panel from Ambositra, or even a stuffed baby crocodile or blowfish. You can listen to an expert streetcorner concert on the valiha (bamboo zither, the national instrument) before clinching the purchase.

Decorated valihas with 16 double-stopped strings cost only a couple of dollars. For garnets, beryls, amethysts, onyx, quartz crystals and a multitude of other semi-precious stones, you can bargain in the stalls of the Zoma, or, to be certain of quality at somewhat higher prices, patronize the Taillerie de la Grande Ile shops in the Hilton Hotel and on Rue Auguste Ranarivelo in the Ankadifotsy suburb. Another good place for gems is Antsirabe's Hôtel Trianon. The Hilton's bookstore is one of the few outlets on the island for the unique pressed rice paper designs (papier d'Antaimoro). The bookshop also has a selection of valiha zithers. The Motel Walter at Anjiro east of Tananarive is owned by a butterfly expert who sells good selections.

You may also pick up Ampanihy mohair rugs, silver necklaces, Comorean filigree jewelry, and other rare acquisitions at the small shops along the Rue Amiral Pierre beginning at the Place de l'Indépendance in the upper city. Most of the wood carving on sale is imitative junk, but occasionally you can spot a handsome piece from Betioky or Ampanihy in the south, Ambositra on the plateau, or the coasts. Shops always close at noon for lunch and siesta.

Local Attitudes

The uprisings of 1971 and 1972 notwithstanding, Madagascar's population deserves its reputation for amiability and hospitality. An erratically puritan government banned miniskirts in 1967, and women are seldom seen wearing shorts in public, but aside from these restrictions French casualness and Malagasy tolerance combine to encourage comfort and informality.

It is a privilege for a vazaha (foreigner) to be invited to a family religious ceremony; ask consent before taking pictures.

Weather, What to Wear

Madagascar is an all-weather place, brilliantly cool and dry on the High Plateau from June through September, sultry and humid on the rainy east coast, drier and tropical in the west. Tananarive in summer (November through April) is a burst of bougainvillea, mimosa, flamboyants, jacaranda, frangipani and poinsettia. Unless under the influences of a coastal hurricane (cyclone) coming out of the southeast, each summer day's rain is usually well timed, and the sunlight between showers is a blessing to outdoorsmen and photographers.

The rains are less benign on the east coast, especially during the January-to-March hurricane season. All beaches are best during the cool season between June and October, when a sweater is advisable and, in Tananarive and other high altitude places, even a topcoat can come in handy. This is also a period for dressing up at parties among the Malagasy elite, the Europeans and other privileged persons of the capital. Civil servants and teachers wear jackets and ties in their offices most of the year, and French women return from European vacations in September with the latest in fashion. If you are circulating below these levels or remaining outside the capital, you will find sport shirts, light dresses and slacks very much in style.

Communication

There isn't much English spoken around Madagascar, except in the major facilities of the capital, where the essential delights are rather for the eye, palate and nostrils than the ear. This is technically "French-speaking Africa," and bookstores bulge with volumes from Paris and Malagasy literature in French, but even French doesn't always work in the remoter countryside of this eminently cultivated civilization. While thoroughly accustomed to being told that the French language has been given to them for the expression of their noblest thoughts, the Malagasy are proud of their own language and will beam joyfully at the vazaha who uses a few strategic words correctly. A Malagasy-English dictionary is available in bookstores.

Canadian CUSO Volunteers, Bendix-NASA personnel in Tananarive, a few dozen American missionary families scattered around the south and on the plateau, and a rising number of South African and European tourists complete the roster of English-speakers in the country.

Communications are archaic (radio-telephone around the island and abroad), although Telex and postal services are reliable. Count on three months for packages mailed to the United States by sea.

Most of the island's lively press is published in Malagasy, but the radio has full-time programs in French. Two quite professional French-language papers, the daily *Courrier de Madagascar* and the Catholic Church weekly *Lumière*, furnish considerable information—but little advance notice of festivals and other events around the island.

Emergencies

The breadth and diffusion of the Great Island make crises difficult to treat if they occur outside major population centers. Each provincial capital has a general hospital and there are small medical stations spread around the island as well, but these are usually rather archaic pre-independence establishments with few facilities for sophisticated diagnosis or treatment. In addition to the ancient General Hospital where conditions of sanitation and service are deplorable, the capital has a French military hospital (Girard et Robic), a small Catholic Clinique des Soeurs and a University Medical Center. There is also a part-time American nurse on duty at the United States Embassy (Rue Rainitovo, Antsahavola district, tel. 212-57). Outside Tananarive, several important mission hospitals serve needs over wide territories. They include excellent American Lutheran institutions at Ejeda and Manambaro (near Fort Dauphin), both in the south.

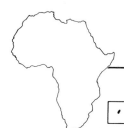

Mauritius

(*Ile Maurice*)

Profile

STATUS: Independent member of the British Commonwealth since March 12, 1968. Former British colony.

SIZE: 720 square miles (smaller than Rhode Island). Population—approximately 850,000.

GEOGRAPHY: Part of Mascareigne Archipelago, with scattered island dependencies. Approximately 1,250 miles from East Africa, 500 miles east of Madagascar. Central plateau rising to 1,900 feet with peaks up to 2,700 feet. Steeply descending rivers. Principal towns—Port Louis (capital, 150,000), Curepipe (55,000), Beau Bassin-Rose Hill (75,000).

CLIMATE: Maritime tropical, with high humidity and heavy rainfall on plateau, especially January to May; fierce cyclones January to March. Coasts are drier and 10 degrees warmer than plateau. Highest coastal temperatures, January to March, are in the upper 80's.

LANGUAGES: English and French (official); Creole (French patois mixed with African and Asian languages) is lingua franca.

CURRENCY: Rupee, divided into 100 cents. 1 rupee = about 20 US cents; $1.00 = about 5 rupees.

VISAS: Required. No fee. Available from Embassy of Mauritius and Mauritian Mission to UN, also consulates in London, Paris and New Delhi, and British consulates wherever Mauritius not represented.

AIRPORT: Plaisance (MRU), 18 miles from Curepipe, 27 miles from Port Louis. Extensive links with South and East Africa, Paris, London, Madagascar, Egypt, India, Australia and Reunion Island. Hotel buses and taxis to the cities. Airport departure taxes—domestic and international, 12 rupees ($2.40).

NATIONAL HOLIDAYS: March 12, Independence Day; June 2, Queen's birthday; Hindu, Moslem and Christian holidays.

INFORMATION SOURCES: *In US*—Embassy of Mauritius, 2308 Wyoming Avenue NW, Washington, D.C. 20008 (tel. 202/234-5436); Permanent Mission of Mauritius to the UN, 301 East 47th Street, Suite 3-C, New York, N.Y. 10017 (tel. 212/754-1288). *In Mauritius*—Mauritius Government Tourist Office, Cerné House, La Chaussée, Port Louis (tel. 2-1846/7).

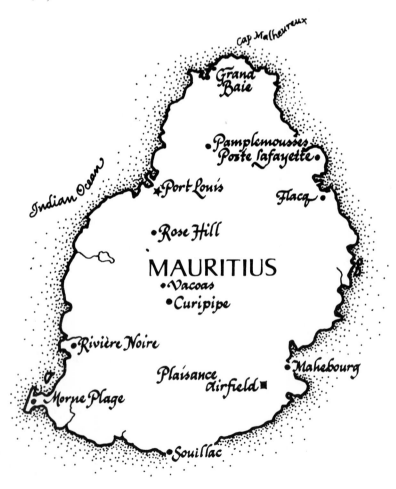

By Philip M. Allen

One of the world's most hospitable islands now looks to visitors to help save its 850,000 people from Malthusian catastrophe. Mauritius is overcrowded, socially agitated and devoid of resources save for its one main crop, sugar.

Despite these problems and the island's remoteness—in the middle of the Indian Ocean, about 1,250 miles from the African mainland—travelers in increasing numbers are coming from South Africa and via East Africa from Europe. They come for tropical warmth and splendid coral-protected beaches, to climb curious volcanic peaks, to poke into Indian Ocean history and to observe the ethnically divided population of Asians, Europeans and Creoles who fill this small green island to its brim.

Until the early 17th century Mauritius was occupied only by tropical timber and strange insular fauna like that amiable swanling, the dodo bird. Then came Dutchmen seeking a way station between the Cape of Good Hope and Malaysia. They named the place after their sovereign, Prince Maurice of Nassau. In 1721 the French changed the Dutch name to Ile de France and began to settle it with planters, retired sea captains and African and Malagasy slaves. It soon evolved into a French powdered wig society prospering on spices, sugar cane, slavery and east-west sea traffic. Here Paul met Virginia, Virginia left Paul, returning tragically and too late to his Creole arms in the pages of Bernardin de Saint-Pierre's idyll *Paul et Virginie*.

During the Napoleonic period, the island harbored nests of buccaneers and noble corsairs (Baron Surcouf, for example) whose patriotic function was to prey on British shipping. The island in 1810 yielded to an invasion by superior British forces, leading to 158 years of Pax Britannica.

British rule changed the nationality of Mauritians, converted their island's name back to the original Dutch, endowed it with a massive sugar cane industry and left the religion, privacy, decadence and economic privileges of its French-speaking citizens untouched. Independence was won after a long, vigorously contested process in March, 1968. But to this day one per cent of the population (the white families and their corporations) owns 70 per cent of the land.

A sugar monocrop of over 600,000 milled tons annually (barring cyclone devastation) keeps the island solvent but dependent on the vicissitudes of the international market. Mauritius still relies on the good will of Britain, principal customer for sugar at pegged prices and major source of aid.

Freed in 1835, the African, Malagasy and by then numerous mulatto ex-slaves took to the hills and coastal villages, causing the British administration to import thousands of Hindu canefield laborers from India. Hindus now form the majority of the island's population. Mass immigration and colonial economics turned Mauritian life into a human drama that impresses even the most casual visitor. The master-slave relationship has left as a legacy a strict color bar between two exceedingly French (and Roman Catholic) "communities": one white, elegant, patrician, snobbish; the other ranging over all shades of non-white, exuberant and poor. They live apart from the rural Hindu mass on an island surface already the most densely populated agricultural landscape on earth. Moreover, 130,000 Moslems from India, most of them urban workers and traders, and 25,000 reclusive Chinese shopkeepers, keep their respective distance from the Hindu and colored Creole.

This cramming of ethnocentric and often hostile communities into an ever-tightening space has produced declining living standards, aggravated unemployment, frustrated school leavers, increasing dependence on imported food and domestic unrest. Street riots have been common, strikes even more frequent, and opposition leaders have been jailed under the state of emergency declared in December, 1971.

To meet these nightmares, the coalition government headed by Prime Minister Sir Seewoosagur Ramgoolam, a Hindu physician, seeks crop diversification, employment expansion, family planning and promotion of foreign investment. It welcomes anybody who promises to spend money, buy sugar, pay for schools and social services, accept emigrants, or offer any other relief for the island's problems. A welcome economic upturn occurred in 1972.

Tourism may help. The French-sponsored Indian Ocean Tourist Alliance and German, South African and American vacation projects are expected to create 18,000 new jobs out of the 130,000 needed by 1980. Here, where sugar cane covers 45 per cent of the land surface and where people already seem to inhabit all the remainder, visitors still find some of the world's loveliest landscapes. Mauritius offers coral reefs and lagoons, casuarina-fringed beaches, broad level plains under curious sharp mountain peaks, green forests stocked with deer, plummeting rivers, rushing waterfalls, defunct volcanic craters, shooting stars, ubiquitous rainbows, a chronicle of buccaneers and shipwrecks, a culture of poets, and a deft, French-speaking people in their bittersweet, delightful, partly English-speaking country.

Besides *Paul and Virginia*, Mauritius has inspired much romantic prose, including Joseph Conrad's "A Smile of Fortune" (in '*Twixt Land*

and Sea) and parts of his *Personal Record*. More scholarly approaches have been made by Burton Benedict in *Mauritius: Problems of a Plural Society* (Praeger, 1965) and in a classic government report by Richard M. Tutmuss and B. Abel-Smith, *Social Policies and Population Growth in Mauritius* (Methuen, 1961, reprinted 1968).

Money Matters

The Mauritius rupee, worth about 20 US cents, is importable in quantities up to Rs 700 ($140) and exportable up to half that amount. Internationally oriented businesses (most of them are) recognize both travelers checks and the credit card. Sir William Newton Street in Port Louis, the island's capital, contains the major banks, including the venerable Mauritius Commercial Bank Ltd (10 offices throughout the island) at P.O. Box 25 and the (rather confessional?) cable address: EGO. Barclays Bank DCO also has 10 Mauritian offices.

Despite heavy reliance on imported food, consumer items and equipment, trade is balanced and prices have remained relatively moderate in Mauritius for the past decade. Part of this stability has depended on artificially high sugar prices, which could drop, and on low wages, which are under fairly consistent attack by well-organized and increasingly militant trade unions.

Getting In and Out

Flung afar though it is, Mauritius can be reached fairly easily. Some European and American tourists make it the tail-end of an East African holiday. Or it can be the high-mileage point on a round trip air ticket, offering considerable flexibility in itinerary for about $1,000 to and from London or Paris. Charter arrangements are available from England, France and Germany. Air Mauritius serves primarily the Mascareigne Archipelago (Mauritius, Reunion and Rodriguez islands).

Plaisance Airport lies off Blue Bay in the lovely southeast corner of Mauritius. Diametrically across the island is Port Louis, the capital and sole port of a nation that survives on foreign trade. Port Louis is reached by Messageries Maritimes passenger ships coming monthly from Marseille via Cape Town, Madagascar, Reunion and occasionally the Comoros. Robin Lines freighters (with deluxe passenger facilities) sail fortnightly from New York, taking about 25 days to reach Port Louis. Cost is approximately $915 round trip.

British, French and ships of other flags connect Mauritius with Africa, Asia, Australia and Europe.

Getting Around Within Mauritius

All nine towns on the island are linked by a network of paved roads. The flowered transversal boulevards are heavily traveled, especially as the Port Louis middle class circulates among offices, shops or counting houses and the cooler residential plateaus. Buses cover every traversable stitch of the island, as do wild, flapping taxis propelled by skillful Creoles (7 US cents per mile, more at night). The Mauritius Touring Company rents appropriate, left-hand-drive vehicles at Port Louis and Curepipe. Small Morris cars cost about $3 a day plus 6 cents per mile; chauffeurs cost an additional $2 a day. International licenses are acceptable. Hitch-hiking is good. Mauritius has no railroad and no navigable rivers.

Mauritius' main island dependency, Rodriguez, has a thrice-weekly small-plane link with Plaisance Airport and a fortnightly passenger boat (350 miles, 36 hours); this is a sleepy, hot, humid place of coral-reef beaches, hills and small farms in the direct path of every hurricane. The rest of Mauritius' oceanic diaspora is hard to reach from the main island unless you rent a fishing yacht or clamber aboard one of the boats owned by a fishing, copra or guano company.

Only the most avid fisherman or curious island-hopper goes to the Cargados Carajos shoals (Saint Brandon), a place of sea birds, turtles, green lagoons and coral reefs. Agalega and the distant atolls of the Chagos archipelago (including Diego Garcia) no longer belong to Mauritius, having been preempted in 1965 by the British for strategic purposes.

The government's Tourist Office (MGTO) issues several informative brochures in English, available abroad from Mauritian embassies. A monthly "Coming Events" bulletin published by the MGTO can be helpful once you are on the island. For travel services there is the Mauritius Travel and Tourist Bureau in Port Louis and Curepipe, as well as several private agencies, including Rogers and Co. Ltd, P.O. Box 60, Port Louis. The Automobile Association of Mauritius, 2 Queen Street, Port Louis, can be helpful to motorists.

Where to Stay

New tourist establishments are burgeoning on the beaches and in the heartland. Most of the bigger spots are operated by a part-Mauritian international syndicate called New Mauritius Hotels Ltd. More modest places usually reflect investment by local tradesmen, Chinese especially, but there are a few French provincial inns too. Because of heavy jet traffic and considerable charter business during the June-September vacation season, it is wise to get advance reservations through the Mauritius Travel and Tourist Bureau (Sir William Newton Street, Port Louis; cable: TRAVEL), a quasi-official coordinating agency. However, arrival during the eminently agreeable May-June or October-December seasons permits a choice of lodgings at reduced prices, and, frankly, the hit-and-run tourist will always find a place to sleep on this hospitable island. Children cost less to lodge than adults; beach bungalows entail good savings for families and large groups; room prices usually include a sturdy British breakfast.

PORT LOUIS, typical of a bustling Oriental seaport abandoned by its affluent denizens after business hours, has a raft of seedy hotels and a few more respectable places. Take a look at the old *Hotel National*, a meeting place for the Mauritian intelligentsia with single rooms renting for $3 without private bath and $7 with bath. The *Ambassador Hotel* is larger, newer and more expensive at $8 for singles and $10 for doubles (air-conditioning costs a dollar more). The Chinese-run *Golden Tourist* charges $2.50 for a single room without bath, $4 with (doubles are about $2 more). For air-conditioned comfort, the *Hôtel des Touristes* is the best buy at $5.75 for singles and $6.25 for doubles (cheaper accommodations available for $3 and $4.50, respectively).

There is a somewhat more elegant choice in the plateau residential capital of CUREPIPE, starting with the handsome *Park Hotel*, an old French colonial mansion with annexes, sitting in its own cool, quiet garden, which has singles from $7 to $11 and doubles from $10 to $13 (food is mediocre). The *Vatel*, a modernized favorite in center Curepipe with French cuisine and night life, charges upwards of $8 for singles, $11 for doubles. *L'Auberge du Petit Cerf* offers moderate pension lodgings and good cooking at $3 per person ($5 for full board). The *Hong Kong Hotel* pleasantly represents what its name suggests ($3 up). The modern, quiet *Hôtel des Mascareignes* specializes in larger groups at negotiated rates.

The *International Hotel* at ROSE HILL, halfway between Port Louis and Curepipe, is convenient to the nearby Plaza Theater, where Mauritius' most important shows take place. Rates are $4 without private bath, $6 with, $7 for doubles.

Most tourists usually stay on one beach or another. Proceeding clockwise from Plaisance Airport by Mahébourg in the southeast, the sandy and coral circumference of the island includes the following hotels:

Le Chaland on an idyllic beach at BLUE BAY, four miles from the airport, with air-conditioned rooms and bungalows for upwards of $11 single and $14 double, as well as water sports, horseback riding and night life.

Tourist Rendezvous, an inexpensive motel at PLAINE MAGNIEN near the airport, with rooms at $3 single and $5 double and Chinese menu. *Le Morne Brabant Hotel* at MORNE PLAGE, on two miles of golden beach beneath 1800-foot cliffs, a fully equipped pleasure dome of well-appointed bungalows and rooms, offering demi-pension at $14 for non-air-conditioned singles ($18 with air-conditioning) and air-conditioned doubles at $26, with a casino and facilities for deep-sea fishing, horseback riding, golf, tennis, water skiing, scuba diving in the lagoon or ocean. The *Dinarobin Pierre Desmarais Hotel* is not far off, with a pool, a shopping arcade and other facilities. *Motel Relais de Lamivoie* at RIVIÈRE NOIRE, with a pool and weekend dancing in the region of Creole fishermen, has rooms with bath and air-conditioning for $13. *Sea Blue Tourist Hotel,* close to Port Louis at POINTE AUX SABLES, has singles for $4 and doubles for $6.

The *Trou aux Biches Village Hotel* on a quiet lagoon in the northwest recently played host to French-speaking African chiefs of state (OCAM). A new Club Méditerranée 250-bed tourist village stands nearby at POINTE AUX CANONNIERS.

Isle de France at GRAND'BAIE in the extreme north, with another lovely beach on the edge of an exciting hinterland, has rooms at $7 single and $10 double without air-conditioning ($9 and $12 with). Here you can bathe either in the lagoon, hotel pool or the deep little cove of Peyrebeyre, a favorite of avid swimmers. Nearby Pointe aux Piments is a popular embarkation site for fishing and skindiving. *Merville* has bungalows with kitchen for $8 to $12 per day (two persons).

Kuxville, near the historic northern CAP MALHEUREUX, has family bungalows with kitchen, laundry and other facilities at $9 to $12 for doubles (small extra charge for additional persons); boats and canoes are for hire. A nearby Chinese grocery helps keep the kitchens stocked.

Touessrock, on Lièvre Islet at TROU D'EAU DOUCE south of Flacq, has better food (especially seafood) than most of the competition, but less remarkable rooms with full pension rates from $10 to $12 for singles, $18 to $22 for doubles.

If you belong to an international youth organization, you may obtain inexpensive lodgings through the Mauritius Youth House in Port Louis. Roman Catholic students can be housed through the Port Louis diocese. Other backpackers may try school dormitories in the central towns during vacation season.

Boarding houses are the next cheapest bet ($3 up), but it's well to get a recommendation from either the Tourist Office or Chamber of Commerce, for many of them are fleabags.

Where and What to Eat

Good Chinese and Indian fare, fresh seafood, and Creole rice and sauces compensate for the mediocrity of most Mauritian hotel cuisine. Venison in season and camarons (fresh water crayfish, usually sautéed in hot sauce) are rare treats. Creole specialties include baked fish with hot sauces like sacré chien (damned dog), or simply rice and curry.

Moderately good exceptions to dyspeptic European fare are served at Vatel and Le Petit Cerf in CUREPIPE (reserve in advance at both places); Flore Mauricienne, a modern complex of eating places, bars and a gift shop in PORT LOUIS, where you will also find the Café de la Cité, an old town house serving Creole food, and the National Hotel with its Creole specialties; the Isle de France at GRAND'BAIE for seafood and Creole stews; Touessrock at TROU D'EAU DOUCE for seafood; the International Hotel at ROSE HILL for Indian dishes.

Curepipe and especially Port Louis have an array of hot, grimy, dimly lit, tough-talking bars and Oriental food houses. These include the relatively tame Tropicana, Rio and Hong Kong at Curepipe; Soopee (Pakistani), Lai Min (Cantonese) and Porte Bonheur in Port Louis, as well as a Chinese businessman's meeting place (also popular with Englishmen) called Soleil Levant. The Magic Lantern in Rose Hill has decent food and dancing to a good band. The Beach Hotel at Pointe aux Sables also has dancing and serves home grown Chamarel coffee.

What to See and Do

Mauritius' landscape lacks the savagery found on Reunion; its rural habitations are slatternly, rusty tin-roofed shanty towns frequented by pariah dogs. But its coasts vary between canefields and coconut or banana palms, with bamboo thickets and coral sands; its interior is cut by rivers, ravines, regions of aloes, acacias and tamarind. Mountain deer are hunted from June through August around the waterfalls and pools near Moka on the plateau; at Souillac, where Rochester Falls carves grotesque shapes in the soft lava stone; at the Cascade de la Vierge in the east, and at the private Yemen Reserve on the Black River (Rivière Noire) in the southwest.

At CAP MALHEUREUX and other coastal points, you may await the noontime return of fishing boats with their often embarrassingly small catches from the depleted lagoons. Or watch the building and repair of boats at GRAND GAUBE. Fishermen here will take guests out for about $1 per half day (double or more in a motor canoe) as they pursue their tough, discouraging quest for capitaine, leaping mullet and colorful coral-hugging fish.

At MORNE, across the island, sportsmen seek blue marlin (a record 1100-pounder was caught here in 1966), becuna, barracuda, cavallys, red snapper, sole, yellow and black tuna, kingfish and manta ray. The best fishing season is from October to March.

Some of the world's most exciting scuba diving and spear fishing take place along these reef-protected coasts and open bays. The Mauritius Underwater Group, headquartered in Port Louis, explores these sea beds and the submerged wrecks of numerous ships. It also publishes a special guide, available from the Tourist Office. Boats and gear can be hired at Bigafi Ltd in Port Louis or at the Chaland, Morne Brabant and other beach hotels. Among many excellent swimming beaches, Poste Lafayette in the northeast is probably the most beautiful and the western Tamarin is best for surfing. The Grand'Baie Yacht Club stages sailing regattas July through October. Several beach hotels have horseback riding, and there are golf courses at Vacoas on the plateau and Morne Beach.

You can also hike and climb over Mauritius' contorted lava hills, poking up out of flat green plains. Experiences range from fairly simple alpinism at Le Pouce and Lion Mountain to the difficult ascent of the Pieter Both (2,700 feet) behind Port Louis. Colonel Alexander Ward, a resident enthusiast, has published a helpful 28-page guide to a dozen cliffs and ridges called *Climbing and Mountain Walking in Mauritius*, available from the Tourist Office.

Creole fishermen around FLACQ in the east make music to an African beat as they work. On weekends across the island, around Grande Rivière Noire, they dance the sega, a Mascareigne calypso with both courtly and "apache" ingredients, accelerating from sedate shuffling to wild, pelvic undulations while the ravane drums pulsate and the rum flows.

The island is liberally sprinkled with mosques, pagodas, blue-and-gold Hindu temples and mighty Catholic churches and shrines. Hindu communities undertake pilgrimages for holy water to the Grand Bassin Crater lake during the festive nights of Maha Shivaratree in February; they celebrate the Divali festival of lights in October-November. Tamil-speaking Hindus stage fire-walking and sword-walking rituals at their Cavadee festivals in spring and fall. The Chinese wolf dance occurs periodically at Port Louis, and the Moslem New Year is celebrated in a procession of wood and bamboo towers called ghoons.

PORT LOUIS provides a four-square setting for an organic jumble of life. Laid out in the classic French gridiron pattern, the seaport has never been either monumentally impressive or mysteriously "Oriental." Today it is a crowded, smelly, busy and yet attractive place where no Englishman would ever think of living and which prosperous Frenchmen regard as a necessary business evil. French governors lived at Pamplemousses and later at Réduit, the current governor-general's residence, uphill in a park near Moka, with beautiful lawns between cliffs and sea (visitable on an irregular schedule).

In town, a few pretty Creole houses are tucked behind bamboo shelters or flowering trees, distinguished for their wrought-iron balustrades and verandas. The port quarter spreads from Chinese store to Chinese store, redolent of spices and deals. There are statues and souks, a Catholic and an Anglican cathedral, a bustling market and docks that caught Joseph Conrad's attention, shabby Fort Adelaide on a great mound close to town, a dignified Town Hall, an old theater, and the immense, colorfully decorated Jummah Mosque. The Hippodrome on the Champs de Mars is one of the first race courses in Britain's colonial world (1812); from May to October it is a Saturday afternoon magnet for the robed, the ragged and the bowler-hatted. Government House is in part authentically 18th century colonial; its esplanade, the Place d'Armes, opens gracefully onto the harbor. But the best building in town is the Mauritius Institute, with a library, a small art gallery and a fascinating natural history museum that emphasizes marine biology.

CUREPIPE, with its entourage of dormitory suburbs, is damp, prosperous, ringed by small, white, ornately decorated cottages behind bamboo palisades, green with lawns and envy. Shops, banks, restaurants, Indian and Chinese jewelers and clothiers are here, as well as hospitals and other big dull buildings in colonial and contemporary style. There is a nice botanical garden at Curepipe, and a copy of Prosper d'Epinay's passionate statue of Paul and Virginia in front of the Town Hall. The Trou aux Cerfs crater dominates the town, with its own view of sea and canefields, blue hills and lakes. You can drive along the crater's rim.

A sugar mill is interesting to visit, especially at night during milling season (October-November). Private companies are glad to show guests around. Try the Flacq United Estates factory in the east or the Saint Pierre mills closer to the towns. Nearby is a highly reputed Sugar Research Institute. The University of Mauritius, still in its infancy, started as an agricultural college and retains a mission for technical studies.

A fine historical museum and scattered monuments around MAHÉBOURG recall the days of Franco-British sea rivalry, as well as the first settlements of the Dutch and French, before Port Louis came into its own. Mahébourg, with its splendid bay setting, was never completed despite intentions to build it into a capital; it decays languidly amid its broad avenues and memories.

Northeast of Port Louis, PAMPLEMOUSSES ("grapefruits") has garden treasures from everywhere, including cinnamon, clove and nutmeg trees, palms of every variety, and the enormous Victoria Regia lily which can indeed hold a newborn babe in its tray. Domesticated deer, statues, a replica of a 19th century sugar mill, and the chateau of Mon Plaisir also inhabit these indescribably lovely gardens. The decaying village is haunted by 18th century souvenirs and has the Church of Saint Francis (1756), the island's oldest.

The interior is best probed by road from Vacoas near Curepipe, starting in crisp, silvery morning light, before clouds begin to build up on the hills. You drive past Mare Longue reservoir into the Massif de la Rivière Noire, with wild dense forestland, exciting views from cliff lookouts, and bizarre geological figures at Le Chamarel near Grande Case in the southwest. The north-central country boasts luxurious open forest, lakes and sea panoramas around La Nicolière, and, farther north, the spice trees and flowering royal guavas on the road between Grand'Baie and Pamplemousses. There is a little cliff museum of coral that used to be the home of poet Robert Edward Hart (died 1954) near Souillac in the south.

What to Buy

Mauritians have a proud artisan tradition, but handicrafts tend toward industrial and utilitarian objects such as baskets, tortoise-shell implements, pottery and Indian jewelry, as well as some carved wood and abundant seashells. There are Chinese imports in great number, particularly around the port and, for higher prices, in the shops of Curepipe; these are good places for jade, ivory, carved teak and embroidered textiles, assuming you are going no farther east than Mauritius. The sega drum (ravane) is more a style of playing than of carving, but sega recordings complement any collection of Caribbean calypso, West African high-life or Congo jazz. Aside from Paris, there is no better place to acquire the works of Mauritius' proud poets, Malcolm de Chazal, Edouard Maunick and Robert Edward Hart.

The Export Processing Zones recently established at Port Louis by the government produce exportable toys, electrical appliances, furniture, jewelry and clothing, manufactured by foreign enterprises with an eye on African and Asian markets. Some of these items should be available at duty-free rates to travelers on the island.

The best shops for souvenirs include the Mauritius Boutique and the Cottage Industries showroom in Port Louis, the Commercial Centre in Rose Hill, Handicrafts Ltd in Curepipe's business arcade and Corinne on Royal Road in Curepipe. Export permits are required for precious stones and metals and for works of art, as well as for any accumulation of goods exceeding 1,000 rupees (about $200), excluding personal effects and clothing.

Local Attitudes

Mauritius is crowded, true, but not fussy. It doesn't stand in the way of people who seek buried pirate's treasure or who explore the hulks of wrecked ships off the northeast coast—although the odds of discovering anything by now are slight. Catholic, Hindu and Moslem religions are practiced with great seriousness on Mauritius, with important political implications as well. Respect for religious beliefs and taboos is essential when you are in villages and countryside. Americans are not well known.

Private property is hallowed here. You can fish, hunt, swim and hike on private domains with the permission of owners—a necessity, for example, for a walk or ride through the lovely forest area from Magenta at the foot of the Trois Mamelles (prudently translated by an American writer as "Three Udders") to Tamarin off the west coast, past deer, monkeys, water cascades and luxuriant vegetation. It's the property of the Reunion Sugar Estate near Vacoas.

Weather, What to Wear, How Long to Stay

A tropical climate in microcosm, Mauritius is agreeably warm on the coasts but hot in the north and windy in the south, and always damp in the afternoons on the central plateau. The entire island turns cool and relatively dry in our summer months (June to October). Trade winds refresh the beaches, stage cloudy theatricals over the heights, and bring heavy rain from January to May with occasional hurricanes (called cyclones) in January-February-March.

Variations in temperature and humidity are striking between Curepipe on the plateau and Port Louis or the beaches. Sweaters, raincoats and hats will do, in addition to summer clothing. The more dignified hotels of British tradition, like the Park, request gentlemen to don jacket and tie for dinner, but the beach resorts have done away with such ceremony. Women are free to dress pretty much as they please. European and Creole residents are never seen in saris, kimonos, dashikis or booboos, but that doesn't prevent visitors from wearing what they choose.

Except for travelers who are passing through briefly—in the course of an East Africa, Southern Asia or world tour—the average stay is a week to 10 days. If you've got anything else to do in life or anywhere else to go, that's probably long enough. If not, you're bound to stay longer.

Communication

English is an official language rarely heard in this ex-British colony, except among civil servants, but it will get you around the island fairly well. The lingua franca is a Franco-Malagasy-Bantu patois called Creole. The cosmopolitan whites and Creoles speak, think and wear nothing but the best Parisian.

Post offices and telephones are located around all the towns, sometimes in police stations, Chinese shops or restaurants. Cable, radio and telex communications function adequately, considering the distances between Mauritius and any other place. English measures are still used in confusion with old French counterparts and decimalia.

Newspapers include *The Mauritius Times* for the English-reading population and *Le Mauricien* and *Le Cernéen* (both over a century old) for the cultivated Francophone. *Le Militant* expresses the viewpoint of the radical opposition. The Mauritius Broadcasting Service carries news and transmits BBC and RTF productions on wireless and screen—when it isn't striving to provide equal time to all the island's linguistic groups. The Mauritius Central Information Office issues a weekly *Bulletin* in English and French.

Emergencies

This is a rather healthy place for visitors, free from malaria and other diseases endemic to Africa and South Asia. Hospitals on the central plateau suffice for most problems; there is an impressive medical center at Quatre Bornes. A small American Embassy is maintained in Port Louis, Anglo-Mauritius House, 6th floor, Intendance Street (tel. 2-3218).

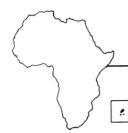

Reunion

(La Réunion)

Profile

STATUS: Overseas Department of France.

SIZE: 969 square miles (slightly smaller than Rhode Island). Population—450,000, mostly Creole.

GEOGRAPHY: Mountainous, oval-shaped island of volcanic origin; part of Indian Ocean Mascareigne Archipelago, 440 miles east of Madagascar, 170 miles west of Mauritius. Principal towns—Saint Denis (capital 100,-000); Saint Paul.

CLIMATE: Tropical maritime, with contrasts in temperature and humidity between coasts and hills. Warm with rains from December to mid-April, occasional cyclones in January and February.

LANGUAGES: French and Creole patois.

CURRENCY: CFA franc (Reunion). CFA 100 = 40 cents; $1.00 = CFA 245.

VISAS: Not required.

AIRPORT: Gillot (RUN), three miles from Saint Denis. Regular flights to and from Paris, Madagascar and Mauritius. Taxi service into city.

NATIONAL HOLIDAYS: July 14, French National Day; May 1, Labor Day; May 8, end of WW II; November 11, Armistice Day; Catholic holidays.

INFORMATION SOURCES: *In US*—French Embassy, Press and Information Office, 972 Fifth Avenue, New York, N.Y. 10021 (tel. 212/737-9700); French Government Tourist Office, 610 Fifth Avenue, New York, N.Y. 10020 (tel. 212/757-1125), also in Chicago, Los Angeles, San Francisco. *In Saint Denis*—Office de Tourisme, Rue Sainte-Marie (tel. 21-14-66); Syndicat d'Initiative, Rues Amiral-Lacaze et Bontaunay (tel. 21-24-53).

By Philip M. Allen

The first requirement for visiting Reunion is to have heard of it; the second is to find it (just inside the Tropic of Capricorn, 400 miles east of Madagascar); the third is to arrive solvent after paying Air France's monopolistic tariffs. Once here you will find Reunion a multicolored, sensationally beautiful island with an obscure but rich history. For the visitor, it combines provincial French creature comforts, Creole exoticism and varieties of outdoor sport.

Uninhabited while Arabs, Portuguese and Dutch mariners moved about the Mascareigne Archipelago, Reunion acquired its first settlers from the beleaguered French colony of Fort Dauphin on Madagascar in the mid-17th century. They patriotically called the island Bourbon, but the French Revolution changed the name and the Second Republic liberated its Malagasy and African slaves (1848)—although not before white masters had begun converting most of the island's population into mulatto Creoles. Indentured field hands from India, Chinese traders and Moslem-Indian artisans—even British naval occupiers (1810–15)—came here, but the growing population, now nearing a half-million, remains furled in the Tricolor.

This is an Overseas Department of France, 7,000 miles from Paris, with representation in the French parliament and a vital place in the French budget. Reunion is administered at Saint Denis, the capital, by a prefect who is responsible to the French Ministry of the Interior. French Frenchmen, French Creoles and French Asians are packed into 23 communes and workers' suburbs along the coasts of Reunion, and in chains of family domiciles and small farms strung out along the tree-lined roads that traverse the island's great inhospitable central rock.

If some early masters of Reunion were people of questionable virtue—freebooters, political exiles, convicts and exportable ladies—they surely redeemed their reputations by naming most of their towns after Catholic saints. The church is powerful and pervasive here, and people are more sober than the usual Creole image suggests. Christian festivals vie with "Malabar" dancing and fire-walking, and even with the all-popular sega dance, as cultural phenomena. Reunionnais family life dominates, and the island's abundant and handsome children are all dutifully sent to school.

Reunion lacks the land and the jobs needed for its burgeoning population. For years politics have been bitter, elections farcical, the winners conservative, the leftist oppositions harassed. The income gap between a small oligarchy of sugar magnates and a huge sub-proletariat of poor whites and Creoles is spreading. Most Reunionnais seem to agree that this overcrowded and resourceless little place, with a relatively high but declining living standard, can avoid revolution or chaos only by remaining constitutionally and economically tied to France. Thus, Paris continues to foot Reunion's bills, paying four times the world's going price for its sugar and monopolizing its imports. France also provides development subsidies, most of which must go into housing, education and social services for a population growing at a rate of 3.8 per cent a year, virtually the fastest in the world.

Reunionnais grow most of what they eat, and, in addition to sugar, they sell some geranium essence, vanilla, and perfume extracts like ylang-ylang and vetyver to French purchasers of such exotica. Everything but food comes in by plane or ship from Madagascar and France.

Unlike Mauritius, the island has little organized tourism. Most visitors are French people coming from central Madagascar, seeking good beaches and a strong, congenial dose of provincial France far from home.

Nothing of consequence has been written about Reunion in English. But it is treated in Auguste Toussaint's *History of the Indian Ocean* (1961; English translation published by Routledge and Kegan Paul, London, 1966) and in Alan Villiers's stirring Indian Ocean chronicle *Monsoon Seas* (McGraw-Hill, 1952). The island has influenced its share of French literature (Mahé de la Bourdonnais's *Mémoires* from the mid-18th century are fascinating, as are George Sand's *Indiana* and poetry by Baudelaire and the island's famous literary son, Leconte de Lisle). The standard French profile, aging fast, is J. Defos du Rau's *L'Ile de la Réunion, Etude de géographie humaine* (Bordeaux, 1960).

Money Matters

Paris keeps this overseas department at a financial distance through a special CFA franc convertible at 50 CFA to the French franc. You will get between 240 and 245 CFA francs for your dollar (less in restaurants, hotels and shops), but if you have any CFA left over at the end of your visit, change them into French francs or other Franc Zone currency instead of paying the stiff discount for buying dollars.

The two main banks are the Banque de la Réunion (Rue Jean-Chatel, Saint Denis) and the Banque Nationale pour le Commerce et l'Industrie (Rue Juliette-Dodu, Saint Denis, and several other towns). The latter is owned by the Banque Nationale de Paris and affiliated with the Bank of America.

Travelers checks are accepted readily here, but credit cards are regarded as an American device to take over the world.

Getting In and Out

Air France and its affiliate Air Madagascar fly regularly into Gillot Airport near Saint Denis for a Paris-Reunion round-trip price (lowest fare) of $1,044. A wider choice of routes and carriers is available via Mauritius (see that chapter), a good choice for high mileage point on your round-trip air ticket (without that, you pay $33 for the 150-mile flight from Reunion to Mauritius, one way, tourist class.)

The sole seaport is at Pointe des Galets, 12 miles from Saint Denis. It is visited regularly by Indian Ocean "Conference" vessels belonging to the Nouvelle Compagnie Havraise Péninsulaire (NCHP), the Compagnie Messageries Maritimes (passenger liners and freighters), the Scandinavian East Africa Line, the Clan Line and the Robin Line (US). A New York to Reunion round trip by deluxe Robin Line freighter costs about $900. Freighter passage can be arranged in the European, Malagasy or African ports touched by these partners, particularly during sugar export season. But what used to be a pleasant 24-day passage from Marseille through the Suez Canal now takes twice as long around the Cape.

As in France itself, no visas are necessary for a visit of less than three months.

Other entry formalities are minimal unless you are importing live plants or other potential menaces to the touchy sugar cane group.

Getting Around Within Reunion

Mobility within the island poses few problems. There are no trains or navigable rivers, but official buses, taxis operating out of each town, French-manufactured automobiles (renting at $10 to $12 per day plus 4 cents per kilometer; $4 for chauffeurs) and obliging truckers carry passengers over the nearly 1,000 miles of good road. The few routes into the formidable crests and cirques (high volcanic basins) of the interior are paved and graded. The coastal roads, crossing a succession of palm-lined beaches, black lava cliffs and forest, attract most voyagers. Quick detours can be made from these roads into plantations and genuine wilderness. Backpackers can combine travel by bus, hitchhiking, footpath and mountainous track almost at will.

Two aero clubs based at Gillot rent their planes for lofty surveys of this extraordinary landscape.

At the Syndicat d'Initiative in Saint Denis, travelers can obtain information and advice on seeing the island. The Automobile Club is also helpful in this regard. The Service des Eaux et Forêts arranges for guides and shelters. The capital's main travel agency, Transcontinents (Rue

Mât de Pavillon), can make reservations and furnish vehicles with or without drivers. A section of the Madagascar Automobile Club's *Guide Routier et Touristique* is devoted to Reunion.

Where to Stay

True to its French culture, Reunion leaves nothing to be desired in hospitality. Each town usually has at least a country inn, as well as Chinese or Creole restaurants with rooms for the less fastidious. All hotels are small and most have only a few rooms with private bath and other luxuries. All serve decent food, and all prices include breakfast, service charges and taxes.

Saint Denis has the biggest and most stylish hotel, the 40-room *La Bourdonnais*, named after the great 18th century French governor. Singles are $11.50 (non-air-conditioned) and $14 to $18 (air-conditioned); doubles, $13.50 and $15 to $20, respectively. The cheaper *Hôtel Bourbon* has a highly regarded kitchen and the new *Touring Hotel* is well equipped. Rooms above bars and restaurants provide the cheapest lodgings in town, and there are also many boarding houses with rooms from $2.50 up. Just outside Saint Denis, on the slopes of La Montagne, Air France has built another of its modern *Relais Aériens Français*, with a chic bar, swimming pool, car rental facilities and the like (singles $13 to $16, doubles $15 to $20).

At Cilaos, the island's major mountain resort, the impeccable *Grand Hôtel* presides over a group of lesser hotels in a breathtaking setting. Grand Hôtel prices are $10 to $14, with good food. The others include the *Hôtel des Abeilles*, *Auberge du Hameau* and *Hôtel du Cirque*. On the Plaine des Cafres, along the mountain route toward active volcanos and sounding seas, *Lallemand* offers moderate accommodations ($5 to $6) and a good kitchen. On the northeast coast, at Sainte Suzanne, the *Hôtel le Bocage* nests near a setting of waterfalls.

At the island's principal sport beach, Saint Gilles les Bains, together with several more modest hostelries, the *Boucan Canot* provides complete resort facilities, with sailing and skindiving, good food and reasonable prices. *La Souris Chaude* is a new bungalow hotel at Saint Gilles ($12 for two persons) with a swinging clientele and a swimming pool. At Saint Philippe on the southeast coast *Le Baril* has bungalows for $6, plus water sports, horseback riding, hiking in an extraordinary forest, and good food.

For the pack-carrying climber, Reunion has scattered several adequate hill shelters (gîtes) at La Roche Ecrite, the most beautiful of many beautiful lookout peaks; near Cilaos at the foot of the Piton des Neiges, and on the way to the great volcano, at the Pas de Bellecombe, 7,500 feet up.

Catholic youth may find hospitality through the Saint Denis diocese.

Where and What to Eat

With public dining a revered custom in French Reunion, the choice ranges from perfectly authentic metropolitan cuisine in the top spots to checkered-cloth satisfaction in the more modest bistros and auberges, plus a gamut of Chinese, Vietnamese, Malagasy and Indian fare. Reunion offers interesting seafood dishes, great peppery condiments like rougail, curry and "cari" (curry *sans* curry), a special way with lentils, dried fish as a flavorer for rice and cornmeal, succulent palmiste (palmetto) and a strong local rum. Also, you must try café bourbon, an arabica legacy of colonial days that some coffee drinkers regard as the best in the world.

Although bars and snack shacks are rare on Reunion, a traveler's sudden hunger and thirst can be satisfied at any Chinese grocery.

Among the more notable of Reunion's restaurants, with menus around $2.50 to $4, SAINT DENIS offers (in addition to the inexpensive Oriental places): *Le Rallye*, a popular meeting place serving Malagasy and Creole dishes and Moroccan couscous at reasonable prices; *La Ferme*, a typically Continental country place with a good wine list; the *Café de Paris* for outdoor dining; *Le Safari* for late supper; *P'tit Paul* for Creole fish at cheap prices; the *Bar de la Piscine* (at the city's salt-water swimming pool, a favorite watering hole for bikini-clad youth), where a Saturday couscous is served. *Le Bosquet*, new place outside town, serves good Creole, French and Malagasy food on a terrace for $3.50 per person.

The port town of POINTE DES GALETS has several Chinese, Vietnamese and Creole restaurants with menus from $2 up. SAINT ANDRÉ, 20 miles east of the capital, also has a number of small places.

HELL-BOURG, the quiet, flowering hilltop spa, has the *Salazes*, which offers a fairly expensive but scrupulous cuisine featuring palmistes and suckling pig. Near PLAINE DES CAFRES, at kilometer marker 27, the *Auberge du Volcan* offers excellent food and wine in a rustic setting. SAINT PIERRE includes *La Taverne* and *Le Fin Gourmet*, as well as numerous Chinese, Indian and Creole places and several fishermen's bars.

At MANAPANY LES BAINS, *Le Manapany* has fine seafood. Northward on the sea, by SAINT GILLES LES BAINS, the *Cabane Bambou* serves seafood specialties under a cool, thatched roof; *La Souris Chaude* and *Lallemand* are excellent, while the *Chic Escale* and *Les Cocotiers* betray their French names with authentic Chinese food, and the *Loulou Fils* plies a less spendthrift crowd with lodgings and audacious "Oriental" food. Among many good places at LE TAMPON, on the way up or down from the plateaus, *La Paille en Queue* serves paella, duckling and curry worthy of southern France, and *Chez Claude* has a fair table d'hôte.

In this family-oriented provincial society, where the affluent "go out" only to dinner parties and private clubs, public night life tends to cluster around the larger hotels. Dining is sometimes combined with such collateral diversions as bowling, discotheques, charity benefits or entertainment by itinerant performers. For evening drink and song there are the *Arc-en-Ciel*, *Scotch Club* and *La Cave du Mandarin* at SAINT DENIS, the *Relais Aériens* at LAMONTAGNE, *Moulin Rouge* at SAINT JOSEPH, the *Grand Hôtel* at CILAOS and *Boucan Canot* at SAINT GILLES LES BAINS.

What to See and Do

SAINT DENIS is a bright, orderly municipality between sea and cliff. But the town is changing. White veranda-decked Creole houses are giving way to clean mass housing projects (cités) and public buildings very unlike the domestic rural citadels from which the new immigrants come. Two-thirds of the town's population is under 25.

A walk along the sea promenade (Barachois) and a climb on the cliff, especially at sunrise or sunset, help you appreciate the town's good figure. Its Hôtel de Ville and Préfecture are admirable; statues and churches point up Reunion's pious insularity; the hippodrome helps accelerate the pace of life.

The Dierx Museum in the erstwhile episcopal residence has elegant collections of historical pieces and impressionist paintings. The animated shopping alleys are particularly interesting just after dawn when families go to market. The handsome Museum of Natural History (open on Thursday and Sunday only) stands in the former royal botanical garden with its spicy recollections of the 18th century experiments of Pierre Poivre. For the rainy day, there is a fascinating and accessible collection at the Departmental Archives (Rue Roland-Garros) of mementos of the East India Company, buccaneers and corsairs, the inspired administration of La Bourdonnais and Napoleonic War sea battles.

Uphill from the capital, the residential suburbs of LA MONTAGNE and azalea-bathed LE BRÛLÉ lure city employees home to the foot of the Roche Ecrite (7,500 feet). The rock is climbable after a five-mile hike from the end of the road.

A bit farther along the road to the port, past Possession, site of France's first flag-planting in 1645, travelers pay their respects at SAINT PAUL, first capital of the East India Company colony and birthplace of the Parnassian poet Leconte de Lisle. The town is full of historical and literary reminiscences, has a pretty lake and an impressive hinterland of ponds and bush, celebrated by Leconte de Lisle, George Sand and Baudelaire.

SAINT GILLES LES BAINS, on a peninsula southwest of Saint Paul, is Reunion's favorite seaside resort. It has coral sand, hotels, restaurants and water sport. The Saint Gilles Club Nautique offers sailing and bathing opportunities at its beach.

Deep-sea fishing expeditions start from SAINT PHILIPPE in the southeast corner of the island. There is good trout fishing at TAKAMAKA near Saint Benoît, and excellent eel fishing in the Poules d'Eau pond near HELL-BOURG in the center.

Seething craters, jagged peaks, gorges, waterfalls, lava piles, caverns, inaccessible cirques and eroded hills—alternating with orchid forests, cane fields, farms and pastures—draw tourists out into Reunion's superb, if economically depressed, countryside. Interior points of pilgrimage include Hell-Bourg and the Piton des Neiges (10,000 feet, but snowless).

CILAOS is a major spa at the end of a stunning 25-mile spiral road that passes dahlia beds, cane fields and tobacco plantations, then traverses pretty hamlets to the southern foot of the Piton des Neiges. The Plaines (plateaus) des Cafres and des Palmistes spread above a good roadway between southwest and northeast coasts where all climates, all vegetation and almost all Reunion can be sampled in one drive.

The most obscure crannies of these lacerated hills harbor the descendants of former African and Malagasy slaves (maroons), as well as a curious blue-eyed, blond-haired, barefoot race of "petits blancs" living out their own scenario of Tobacco Road in the almost impenetrable refuges chosen by their impoverished ancestors.

The most exhilarating trek leads to a funereal and silent landscape east of the Plaine des Cafres where the Piton de la Fournaise, five miles of smoking crater 8,600 feet high, occasionally pours out its molten innards toward (fortunately) the sea. A road is being built to the top. Grand Brûlé's smoking crests are reachable from the road out of the Plaine des Cafres after a strenuous hike along astonishing varied rock configurations, with staggering glimpses of sea and luxuriant growth, rushing streams and canyons.

Other points of interest include SAINT PIERRE, exuberant, polyglot, colonial backwater, patronized as the "capital" of the south, with a fishing port, sugar mills, colorful markets and an ancient quay for Arab dhows; SAINT BENOÎT in the northeast, a staging place for the rough foot passage into the trout-laden ravines of the Rivière des Marsouins and the Takamaka falls; SAINT LOUIS, hot but fertile sugar-bowl, and the less known, wildly varied southern coasts between SAINT BENOÎT, SAINTE ANNE (a bizarre concrete church), SAINTE ROSE by the tropical forest,

Bois Blanc, and the lost village of Saint Philippe on the edge of a weird, spongy soil wood, with lovely blue sea and cane fields on its outer edges.

Those who seek quieter beaches than the Saint Gilles complex can relax on black sands and coral at Etang Salés-les-Bains or on red rocks at Manapany farther down the west coast. Visiting one of the island's 13 sugar mills and rum distilleries is a particularly impressive experience at night during milling season between August and November. Any of the companies based at Saint Denis can set up a tour. The biggest installation is at Saint Louis, but the Sucrerie de Bourbon has several mills closer to Saint Denis. There is an interesting sugar research experimental station near La Bretagne east of Saint Denis.

What to Buy

Sturdy, practical and pious, the Reunionnais scarcely compete with their Malagasy and African neighbors in the arts. Their island produces little for tourist souvenirs. Lovely shells and conches populate the beaches; "fanjan" flowerpots are carved out of heavy roots in the highlands; mountaineer women around Cilaos produce elegant lace and embroidery, best purchased on the spot. For Indian jewelry, semi-precious stones and African and Malagasy products try Au Zoma in Saint Denis.

Local Attitudes

Although clerical and provincial compared to other French-speaking societies, the Reunionnais decline, like all good Frenchmen, to impose unreasonable constraints on other people's behavior. Americans are not particularly well known on the island.

Weather, What to Wear, How Long to Stay

Reunion's rugged topography pushes to lofty but climbable central peaks that divide the island into two climatic zones: a green, humid northern/eastern hemisphere relieved by the alizé tradewinds (hence called "Vent"), and a drier, occasionally burnt volcanic landscape fringed by tropical beaches and bush ("Sous le Vent"). From mid-April through November in this part of the Indian Ocean, the air is relatively dry and fresh at the coasts, with a genuine chill on the temperate slopes and an almost Alpine feeling at the top. In hotter, humid austral summer, January-February especially, Reunion attracts a couple of heavy cyclones (typhoons) each year.

Garments are chosen largely in view of (a) the informality of French tropical life and (b) radical variations between warm humid coasts and chilly peaks. Men tend to wear the briefest and most comfortable combinations day and night (shorts, sandals, open-necked shirts, slack suits), while women are more inclined to dress for evening presentability. A day on the east coast almost always involves rain, and even the most comfortable drive over the Plaines, or to Hell-Bourg or Cilaos, calls for sweaters, hats and sturdy shoes. Mountain-climbers must double their coverage in this respect, and should carry bedding.

Rather common here is the two- to three-day stop between planes connecting Madagascar, Mauritius or Paris with East Africa, Australia and/or South Asia beyond. The island's dimensions serve this kind of sojourn well, but at the expense of visiting mountain peaks, volcanos and remote hamlets.

For the energetic and dedicated vacationer, Reunion is worth a fortnight or more; and the price, international air travel aside, can be moderate. Food isn't expensive, accommodations are adequate and a combination of travel by rented car, bus, hiking, hitchhiking and cable car provides an exhilarating passage from summit to shore and peak to peak.

Communication

Postal and telecommunications are reasonably efficient and inexpensive around Reunion, or between the island and most parts of the Franc Zone community. They are rare and dear to other parts of the world, however, and telephone service with Madagascar is restricted to only one and a half hours on weekdays. Public telephone booths are open from 8 to 11 am and 2:30 to 5:30 in the afternoon, until 4 pm on Saturday, and never on Sundays or holidays.

In provincial and Creole France, English is rudimentary wherever it exists. Yet a few words of French go exceedingly far in this unsnobbish society.

News circulates readily over Reunion's extensions of French radio-television. Among an array of politically oriented publications is the daily *Journal de l'Ile de la Réunion*, which carries the most general kind of information and lists physicians and pharmacies on duty. The weekly *Voix des Mascareignes* has useful social and economic material.

Emergencies

Saint Denis has a large medical center. Saint André, Saint Joseph, Saint Paul and Saint Pierre have local hospitals. If problems become serious, fly to Paris (a 12- or 13-hour flight). There is no American representation on the island, but the British have a consulate on Rue Jean-Chatel.

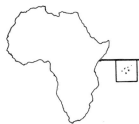

Seychelles

Profile

STATUS: British colony since 1810. Limited self-government since 1970.

SIZE: Archipelago of 85 islands totaling about 180 square miles in an oceanic area of 150,000 square miles. Population—56,000, three-fourths on Mahé. Majority of population is Creole (mixed African, European and Asian), with small European, Indian and Chinese minorities.

GEOGRAPHY: 30 granite islands, 55 coral atolls in western Indian Ocean north of cyclone belt, just south of equator and 1,000 miles east of Kenya coast. Principal town—Victoria (capital, on Mahé Island, 15,000).

CLIMATE: Warm and sunny. Temperatures on Mahé between 75 and 85 degrees; coolest from June through September, warmest in March and April. Rainfall moderate on granite islands (rainy months December and January), light on coral islands.

LANGUAGES: English (official), French widespread, Creole universal.

CURRENCY: Rupee (Seychelles), divided into 100 cents. Rs 1.00 = 19 US cents; $1.00 = Rs 5.40.

VISAS: Not required.

AIRPORT: Mahé (SEZ), seven miles from Victoria. Regular flights to and from London, Nairobi, and Asian capitals. Taxis into city.

NATIONAL HOLIDAYS: June 2, Queen's Birthday; Christian holidays; Bastille Day (July 14) celebrated by French community.

INFORMATION SOURCES: *In US*—British Information Service, 845 Third Avenue, New York, N.Y. 10022 (tel. 212/752-8400); Lindblad Travel, 133 East 55th Street, New York, N.Y. 10022 (tel. 212/751-2300). *In Seychelles*—Department of Tourism, P.O. Box 56, Victoria, Mahé.

By Philip M. Allen

Minor cults of foreigners have fallen in love with these sun-drenched islands and decided never to leave. They include retired Englishmen seeking clubby comradeship and ease of life; Old World *grandes familles* who prospered here on slavery until 1835 and now endure the coming of the English, the tourists and democracy with languorous disdain; and some erstwhile oceanic adventurers who settled down close to the monsoons. The majority population consists of 50,000 handsome, gregarious, fervently Catholic Creoles. They descend from former slaves and masters of the old French Seychelles colony, from Africans and Malagasy freed on the islands by 19th century British slave-chasing frigates, and from mariners who found respite in the warm little haven of Victoria and the arms of its local women.

Things have changed in the Seychelles (pronounced say-shells), for there's a new jet airport, a steeply rising rate of tourism, and some sensitivity to the political realities of underdevelopment. Despite these impulses the islands are still a place of good fellowship where there's almost enough food on the trees and in the sea, and where if there's little work, it's too ill paid to be regretted. Although skillful as fishermen and sailors, the enterprising sons of Seychellois go elsewhere to find jobs, leaving their lovely homeland to the elderly, the lotus eaters and the vacationers (20,000 of whom are expected in 1973, 150,000 annually by 1978.)

Some 85 islands—two-thirds of them coral atolls with scant population, the rest forming a unique cluster of granite isles—poke out of pleasant waters from a long submerged continental shelf a thousand miles east of Mombasa. A gentle tropical climate gives the archipelago its "Garden of Eden" reputation—an image perpetuated by visitors like General "Chinese" Gordon in 1881, King Prempeh of Ashanti, exiled here from 1900 to 1924, Archbishop Makarios, in exile during the mid-1950's, Noel Coward, Alec Waugh and Ian Fleming. The main inhabited islands (Mahé, Praslin, La Digue, Silhouette, Curieuse, Félicité and Marianne) romp with one another in sea, cloud and spray like "seven sisters," as the first Portuguese called them. The French later named them Seychelles after a Paris political figure of the time.

The Seychelles waited centuries to receive their first settlers, for the archipelago was off the beaten tracks of coast-hugging Arab dhows and Europe's east-west passages between the Indies and Cape. Beginning in 1768 French soldiers, farmers, foresters, tortoise hunters and their slaves came from the populated Mascareigne islands of Ile de France (Mauritius) and Bourbon (Reunion). Later arrivals included deported terrorists and exiles from the French Revolution. American whalers knew the Seychelles, as did pirates and official French corsairs who preyed on merchant ships (mainly British). After several changes of hands during the Napoleonic Wars, Britain seized the archipelago in 1810 along with its mother colony Mauritius, and has governed unobtrusively ever since, doing little to "de-Frenchify" the place.

Britain's governor in Victoria, the capital, acts through an elected parliament. The incumbent Chief Minister, James R. Mancham, and his majority Seychelles Democratic Party (SDP) demand more economic aid from London without agitating for what they regard as perilous political independence. The opposition People's United Party seeks independence and closer affiliations with East Africa.

Seychelles's influence once extended to a number of coral reefs and atolls that are now part of the strategic British Indian Ocean Territory. These include Aldabra, famed home of giant tortoises and green sea turtles, Farquhar Island and Desroches of the Amirantes group. There are British fishing and ecological research stations on beautiful Aldabra, accessible only by sea.

Books on the Seychelles offer more pleasure than depth. Start with Guy Lionnet's *The Seychelles* (Stackpole Books, 1972) and Australian Athol Thomas's *Forgotten Eden* (Longmans, 1968). Burton Benedict has published a scholarly *People of the Seychelles* (HMSO, 1968).

Money Matters

The Seychelles rupee is supported by sterling. Barclays and the Standard Bank operate at Victoria. Prices for services and imported goods have risen remarkably over the past few years; freight costs add about 50 per cent to the basic price of canned goods, for instance. Currency imports are unrestricted, but Seychelles currency can be exported only in small amounts (about $20) and other currency is limited to $650. Carry travelers checks or bank drafts.

Getting In and Out

Mahé Airport, completed in 1971 on a bed of dredged sea and coral, receives five weekly VC-10 flights from London via Cyprus, Entebbe-Kampala and Nairobi. The 6,000-mile trip costs $475 one way (tourist class). Mahé is also a stop on a BOAC circuit to Colombo, Hong Kong and Tokyo. Non-scheduled Wilkenair service by eight-seat Navaho aircraft connects Mahé with Mombasa, the Comoros and Madagascar.

The Seychelles are a pleasant interruption on long sea runs from continent to continent. Silhouette Island surges beautifully out of the sea when approached from Mombasa on the way to Port Victoria. There is regular traffic with the Durban and Mombasa-to-India freighters of the Royal Interocean Lines, the British India Line and the Shipping Corporation of India.

The Lindblad Travel Company offers an 18-day tour to the Seychelles from New York via London and Nairobi, with a week's cruise of the islands aboard a sailing schooner, or alternatively a week's cruise of the outlying Amirantes group by small motor vessel. The $1,350 price includes economy air fare New York-to-New York in the winter slack season. Prices are higher in the summer. You can also extend your stay in the Seychelles or East Africa within the terms of your 45-day excursion flight ticket.

Getting Around Within the Seychelles

New roads are being built to augment the few miles of paved surface and passable dirt thoroughfares on Mahé. Praslin has a new tarred transversal road, but La Digue still uses oxcarts. Taxis wait under shade trees in Mahé's Victoria town and diesel mammy-wagons (camions) cover the Mahé roads regularly with a diverse burden of people, wares and animals.

Government launches and private schooners, or pirogues, with or without motors, are indispensable for island-hopping. There is a thrice-weekly ferry service linking Mahé, Praslin and La Digue (round trip costs about $2 and takes three hours) with less frequent runs to less-populated places. Victoria's port area is ticket office, travel agency and vehicle rental office. The Seychelles Travel Services Company is Victoria's most professional agency. You can rent serviceable Japanese cars there when taxis are scarce.

Where to Stay

Seychelles's hotel situation is changing rapidly as the islands gear up with British and South African capital for the coming tourist boom. At Beau Vallon above VICTORIA, the new *Coral Strand Hotel* is well set on the beach, charging about $25 per day, full pension. The *Reef Hotel* charges a little less and offers modern conveniences and access to sport (there's a swimming pool). It is situated on the water seven miles from Victoria, near the airport. Similar rates prevail ($20 and above for full pension) at the handsome new *Vista do Mar* at GLACIS, 15 minutes from Victoria, and the resurrected *Pirates Arms Hotel* in town. There are also the tiny but scrupulous *Northolme* rooming house (with its own beach) and the *Fisherman's Cove*, a well-managed cottage complex with excellent service, both charging about $5 per room, $10 for full pension.

Praslin Island's *Côte d'Or* costs about the same. La Digue Island has only rooming houses and a steadily booked ($2) government rest-house.

Backpackers can camp anywhere under palm trees, or ask around for inexpensive rooms to let. The Teachers Training College near Victoria sometimes has a bed to spare, and Catholic students may be lodged with help from the Diocese of Victoria.

Where and What to Eat

Shanty cook-shops in Victoria's side streets prepare standard Creole fare —curried rice with fish, lentils, dumplings, hot sauces and fruit, often cooked in slightly rancid local coconut oil (copra), anathema to gastronomes. Fish is abundant, and for those who acquire the taste, salted shark meat substitutes well for scarce beef. Delectable turtle meat, crayfish and soups come to the tables of the affluent. Coconuts, breadfruit, bananas and mangos fall in one's lap. *The Black Parrot* is a good Chinese restaurant on Praslin Island. Demand Creole food at your hotel.

In addition to British gins and whiskeys there is a variety of local liquors: calao (palm wine), bacca (sugar cane spirits) and toddy or calou (femented coconut juice).

What to See and Do

Until the tourist boom catches on, most travelers come to the Seychelles to enjoy what one of its leaders has termed "primitive peace and primitive comfort." Visitors include sea sportsmen, bird watchers, shell collectors and island fanciers in general. There is little hunting but more than 800 species of fish swarm over the shallow ocean bottoms (rarely deeper than 40 fathoms) between islands. Spear fishing is prohibited.

Three-fourths of the people live on Mahé, 17 miles long and five wide. The rolling countryside is dotted with tin-roofed villages, occasional villas and coco palms, and dominated by the green, 3,000-foot-high Morne (bluff) Seychellois. The island was named for the great French Governor Mahé de la Bourdonnais, who sent the first boats here from Mauritius.

The only town is Victoria. Despite a shanty-town appearance it is clean and cheerful, adorned with birds and flowers. The huge Cathedral of the Immaculate Conception lords it over the town. Roman Catholicism operates here in warm, emotional forms, an imported religion that has assimilated the African intuition of the nearness of heaven.

Westerners are intrigued by Seychellois beliefs in gri-gris (amulets) and les bonhommes du bois (healers and soothsayers) despite their ra-tional education and Christian piety. The energetic visitor may prowl through island nights on the trail of the isolated bonfire where the forbidden "moutia" is danced to the accompaniment of drumming and singing. This ceremony has much the same cathartic value for Seychellois as the real calypso of the Caribbean, the sega dance of the Mascareignes and the ritual jazz and voodoo of other African societies seldom witnessed in their true form by outsiders.

However, more common diversions on Saturday nights and Christian festivals include dancing and drinking at Creole toddy clubs, where the atmosphere is easygoing but dignified. Sedate Europeans sip highballs at their own places. There are no regular theaters or concerts. Some intrepid foreigners dig for buried treasure at shores and coves once frequented by buccaneers. Those who fancy more traditional sports watch soccer football or play golf, tennis and squash.

A US Air Force satellite tracking station has been a major employer and object of occasional political agitation on Mahé since 1963. There is also an agricultural research station across the island from the airport. A few settlements are strung along Mahé's thin beaches, their fishing boats housed under thatched shelters, their lives dominated by church, school, the dukas (shops) of the Indians or Chinese, and the bacca or toddy clubs.

Creole life in Victoria is characterized by evening strolls, dignified Sunday promenades, incessant conversation and gracious manners. It is more rustic on the outlying islands, but no less sociable. Praslin, La Digue and Silhouette, facing Mahé across the channel, are populated mainly by the families of fishermen and absent emigré workers. PRASLIN's Vallée de Mai has a rare black parrot and unique palm trees which grow canopy-wide leaves as well as the bizarre coco de mer nut; brought by tides to all shores from Mombasa to Bombay, the huge coco de mer's voluptuous "pelvic" shape has been imagined an archetype of sex from out of the oceanic depths, and its meat is of course prized as an aphrodisiac. Not irrelevantly, General Gordon published proof that the original Biblical Garden of Eden was situated in this Vallée de Mai.

LA DIGUE is a charming island of boat builders. COUSIN ISLAND is a reserve for rare birds and tortoises, and COUSINE, nearby, is a snorkeler's paradise. These are among the granite outcroppings of the archipelago, more luxuriant and varied in vegetation than the coral atolls. But the atolls too have their attractions. They are places of extraordinary shells and birdlife, good fishing, snorkeling and peace.

Boats are available at almost every settlement. Proprietors of coconut groves, copra mills, guano pits and fisheries are hospitable to visitors.

Conveyances range from simple pirogues paddled by Creole gondoliers for a couple of dollars a day to motor launches and schooners hired in the larger ports or at the Victoria Yacht Club. Fishing launches are scarce during the high season (November to April) and should be booked well in advance through your hotel.

What to Buy

Seychellois are excellent craftsmen, good with tropical woods, basketry, tortoise shell, palm wood and other local materials. But the islands produce neither the art of their European masters nor that of Africa, Madagascar and other points of Creole origin. Artisan shops in Victoria are beginning to accumulate a stock of souvenirs.

Local Attitudes

The reputation here for easy virtue is accurate but rather misleading. There is a piety about the Seychellois that is merry but far from promiscuous, and a decorous insularity that sometimes baffles outsiders. Until you get used to the place, you can only be cautioned against losing your patience or your head.

Weather, What to Wear, How Long to Stay

Almost unchanging warm weather makes the Seychelles an ideal year-round retreat for the sun seeker. Located north of the great cyclone paths, Mahé and her sisters sit in frequent doldrums, but eastern monsoons blow refreshingly between July and October. Hotter northwestern monsoons come from November through April.

Tourists should dress lightly for the tropical climate, but sweaters are needed occasionally in the hills. Reef walking requires strong shoes. Unless you are entertained by His Excellency the Governor or fall into the white man's club set, casual clothing is adequate. The Seychellois dress in scrupulously neat European style, but most visitors come here precisely to avoid formality.

A Seychelles tour can be planned in advance but the sportsman, beachcomber or health-seeker usually improvises his itinerary on arrival. Many people simply wish to be able to say they've been to the Seychelles, although the islands' growing tourist prospects are bound to weaken the rarity of that boast.

An inquisitive, patient traveler should seize any chance for a week or two on these balmy berths, and the sooner the better.

Communication

With three-quarters of Mahé's children registered in schools, English is the first international language. Most islanders understand French as a distantly related dialect of their own Creole—a patois similar to that of Mauritius, Reunion and Haiti, but more strongly influenced by Swahili and Bantu languages.

Communication with the outside passes through the Cable and Wireless Ltd, a complex of Telex, radio-telephone and telegraphic circuits which functions bravely between major islands and with Nairobi (if often at a sacrifice of clarity) whatever the language used.

The government radio depends on BBC for international news, but the islands produce several periodicals: the official *Seychelles Bulletin* (daily), *Le Seychellois*, a bilingual thrice-weekly put out by the farmers' association, weekly journals of the political parties, and an illustrated fortnightly issued by the Catholic Diocese of Victoria. For Europeans, the clubs, the hotels, the port and the exceedingly general "general" stores (dukas) in Victoria's center are valuable information exchanges. Until the airfield opened, news used to arrive from Europe weeks late, and most Seychellois preferred it that way. Now London papers come in regularly.

Emergencies

This is quite a healthy place with few of the tropical diseases known on the African continent. There is a major hospital in Victoria. Residents are most helpful to anybody in difficulty, but precautions are advisable since you will be far from any metropolitan facility. Most of the outlying atolls are not linked with Victoria, even by radio. There is no American representation in the archipelago aside from the tracking station on Mahé.

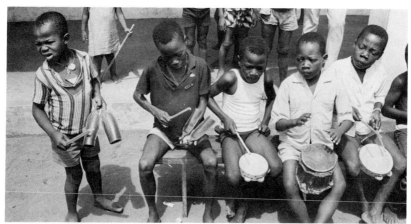

Dun-dun jam session, Nigeria

Moor of Mauritania

Nigerian masks

Tunisian woman

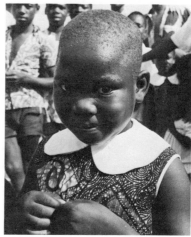

South African girl

Dahomean village girl

Young Masai cattle-keeper, Tanzania

Guinean boy with Koran tablet

Classroom in Mauritania

Glossary

This list includes major ethnic groups and languages of Africa, unfamiliar names for clothing, food, animals, plants, art works, musical instruments, and other special terms found in this book or generally encountered in Africa travel.

ACHOLI (a-*cho*-lee)—Nilotic cattle-keeping and cotton-growing people of northern Uganda.

ADINKRA (*ah*-din-kra)—A fine cloth woven in Ghana.

AFARS—See Danakil.

AFRIKAANS (ah-free-*kahns*)—Language developed from 17th century Dutch; one of the official languages of the Republic of South Africa.

AFRIKANER (ah-free-*kah*-nur)—In the Republic of South Africa, an Afrikaans-speaking descendant of Dutch settlers. Afrikaners are also known as Boers (farmers) and as Voortrekkers (referring to early 19th century migrations from Cape Province into the South African interior).

AGBADA (ag-*bah*-da)—Yoruba name for the full-length, two-piece patterned robe worn by men, primarily in western Nigeria.

AGUSHI (a-*goo*-shee)—West African melon-seed sauce accompanying cassava, yam and other main dishes. Spelled "egusi" in Nigeria.

AGNI (*ahn*-yee)—A people of the eastern Ivory Coast (also called Ndénié) noted for brilliant pageantry and festivals.

AID (Agency for International Development)—US government agency responsible for the foreign economic aid program.

AKASSA—Boiled flour served with various sauces in Dahomey and Togo.

AKU—Christian Creole people in Sierra Leone and the Gambia who are descendants of 19th century freed slaves.

ALIZÉ (ah-lee-zay)—French term for trade winds, used particularly in the Indian Ocean.

AMERICO-LIBERIANS—Descendants of 19th century settlers from the US (many of them emancipated slaves) who compose the social and political elite of Liberia. Their culture retains many links with its American origins.

AMHARA—The dominant people of Ethiopia, approximately 30 per cent of the total population; mostly Coptic Christians.

ANIMISM—Traditional African philosophy and religion based on the belief that all objects in the natural world are infused with the energy of creation, that energy and matter are essentially the same. Divinity, ancestors and other spirits have physical manifestations (often in mask dancing and other ceremonies as well as natural phenomena) just as human beings and all other created objects have spiritual energy, or "soul." These realms interpenetrate, intercede and interfere with one another in human life.

ANKOLE (an-koh-lay)—Cattle-keeping people of western Uganda composed of tall Bahimas and short Bairu who share a common language (Runyankore) and culture.

APARTHEID (a-pahr-tayt)—In Afrikaans, "separateness"; official policy of racial segregation and separate racial development in the Republic of South Africa.

ARTISANAT (ahr-tee-zah-nah)—French term for any of a variety of handicrafts or the workshops of artisans.

ASHANTI—A major people of central Ghana who enjoyed hegemony over other Akan-speaking peoples until the British conquest of the Gold Coast. A culture of distinctive style in music, art, textile design (including Kente cloth), and festivals.

ASIAN—This term has much narrower reference in Africa than is usual. It identifies persons of Indian or Pakistani origin residing in East and Southern Africa and Indian Ocean.

ASKARI—Swahili term for soldier or night-watchman.

ASSIMILATION—The policy, especially in French and Portuguese overseas possessions, of granting social status to indigenous individuals or groups that have become Europeanized or otherwise "qualified."

AUBERGE (oh-behrjh)—An inn, usually offering meals as well as lodging. Youth hostels are known as "auberges de jeunesse."

BA—Prefix in many Bantu languages meaning people. For instance, Ba-shiru means people of the Shiru tribe. The singular prefix is "m"; Mshiru, therefore, means a person of the Shiru tribe.

BAB (bahb)—Gate in Arabic; often used to refer to the principal entrances to the older, walled parts of cities.

BABAGANOUSH (ba-ba-ga-noosh)—Sauce made from chickpeas and eggplant often eaten with the flat, fresh Arabic bread known as pita; served as an appetizer in North African restaurants and in Lebanese restaurants in sub-Saharan Africa.

BABOUCHE (ba-boosh)—Backless and heel-less leather slipper, often brightly colored and decorated, worn in North Africa.

BAGANDA—A people two million strong who live in southern Uganda around Kampala. Their language is called Luganda.

BAKLAWA (bah-klah-vah)—A very sweet pastry made from honey and almonds. A favorite in North Africa and the Middle East. (Also spelled "baklava.")

BAKONGO—A people numbering several million living in northern Angola, Congo-Brazzaville and Zaïre (where they are called Bazaïre). Their language is Kikongo.

BAKSHISH (bok-sheesh)—Arabic for charity or alms; the cry commonly uttered by street urchins and other beggars in Egypt, Morocco and Somalia.

BALADI (bah-lah-dee)—Egyptian Arabic for cheap restaurants where hygienic standards often leave a great deal to be desired.

BALAFON (bah-la-fohn)—West African xylophone with gourd resonators; used in orchestras and to accompany story-tellers.

BAMBARA (bahm-bah-rah)—An industrious and creative agricultural people of western Mali; producers of some of the most highly-prized wood sculpture in Africa.

BAMILEKE (bah-mee-lay-key)—A people of the highlands of central Cameroon. They are noted for their imaginative architecture and masks.

BAMOUN (bah-moon)—A partly-Islamic people of central Cameroon known for their furniture-making, carving and trading skills.

BANA-BANA—Street hustlers in West African cities, especially visible in Dakar.

BANCO—Adobe or stucco used in construction throughout Africa.

BANDA—Swahili for thatched-roof cottage, often found in national parks in East and Southern Africa.

BANTU (*ban*-too)—A group of African languages widely spoken south of the line from Cameroon to Kenya. Also the people of this linguistic family.

BAO (baow)—Swahili for wood; refers to a game similar to Parcheesi played in East Africa with seeds and a carved wooden board. Different versions of this game are found throughout Africa under other names (e.g., Wari, Hagi).

BAOBAB (bay-oh-bab)—A large, stubby-branched, thick-trunked tree bearing a gourd-like fruit; native to Africa.

BAOULE (*baow*-lay)—A major agricultural people of southern and central Ivory Coast; related to other Akan-speaking people like Agni, Ashanti and Fanti. Excellent carvers.

BARKCLOTH—Woven cloth made from the bark of certain trees. Sold at gift shops in Uganda and elsewhere.

BEMBA—A major people in northern Zambia. Many work in the Copperbelt.

BERBER (*berr*-burr)—Nomadic or semi-nomadic mountain people who have lived in North Africa and Sudanic West Africa since prehistoric times. Their language is also known as Berber.

BHANJI (*bahn*-jee)—A term used frequently in East Africa for local varieties of marijuana. Also known as "gangi."

BICHE (beesh)—French slang for a bribe, frequently used in Zaïre and West Africa. Also French for female deer. "Tête de biche" often refers to carved antelope head-dress for masks in Bambara initiation ceremonies (chi-wara), reproduced for sale throughout West Africa.

BIDONVILLE (bee-doh-*veel*)—French for urban shantytowns found throughout Africa.

BILHARZIA—Disease (schistosomiasis) caused by blood flukes which burrow into the skin of people who enter water infected by human and animal waste.

BINI (bee-nee)—The predominant people in the Midwest State of Nigeria and formerly of the historic kindom of Benin. They are still "ruled" by their traditional Oba (king).

BLESBOK—Large antelope having a blaze on its face; found in South Africa.

BOBO—Highly artistic farming people inhabiting the forest and savanna areas of western Upper Volta.

BOMA—Swahili word for government office building.

Fish traps; in background, Lagos

Traffic in the Sahara Desert

Baby-carrying, Ivory Coast

West African village

Equatorial forest track

BOOBOO—Full-length robe of various materials worn throughout tropical Africa. Also spelled "buba," "boubou" and "bubu."

BOULE (bool)—French lawn bowling game (also known as "pétanque"), played wherever the French presence has been felt in Africa.

BOUTRE (boo-tr)—See dhow.

B.P. (or Boîte Postale)—French for post office box.

BRAZILIANS—Descendants of freed slaves who returned to West Africa in the late 19th century from Brazil. They have retained some Brazilian customs and are known as skilled craftsmen and merchants.

BREADFRUIT—Large tropical fruit that can be baked and eaten like bread.

BRIDE-PRICE—Traditional payment of goods or money by bridegroom or his family to consummate a marriage. If the marriage is dissolved the bride-price is customarily returned. (Known as "dot" in French and by a variety of other terms, such as "lobola" in South Africa.)

BRIK—Hot meat and vegetable pastry, usually served as an appetizer in North Africa, especially Tunisia.

BUI-BUI (bwee-bwee)—Black full-length cloak and veil worn by Moslem women along the East African coast and in Zanzibar.

BUNDU (boon-doo)—A secret society among the Mende of Sierra Leone and other West Africans, known for their voluminous helmet masks. Also a Swahili word used in East Africa to refer to remote rural areas.

BUSH BABIES—Small mammals related to the lemur, often domesticated as house pets.

BUSHMEN—One of the earliest peoples of Africa, dwindling in number since Bantu migrations forced them out of forests and savanna country into the Kalahari desert of Botswana, Namibia and South Africa.

BUSH TAXI—See collective taxi.

BUSUTI—Full-length gown with ruffled sleeves and a bustle worn by Baganda women in Uganda.

BWANA—Swahili for mister or sir. The formal term of address for adult strangers. Less formal is "rafiki" for friend or, in Tanzania, "mwananchi" (mwa-na-in-chey) for comrade.

BWITI—A syncretistic cult in Gabon, using strong animist symbolism, music and dance in an otherwise Christian liturgy. Also spelled "Bouiti."

CALABASH—A dried gourd, often elaborately carved and decorated. Used for bottles and bowls in West Africa and elsewhere.

CALIPH—Islamic title taken after the death of Prophet Mohammed by reigning descendants.

CAMPEMENT (kamp-mah, French)—Camping ground often found in national parks, usually has bungalows with running water and sometimes refrigerators and cooking facilities.

CARNET DE PASSAGE (kar-nay duh pas-sahj)—French term used internationally for the customs document permitting automobiles to cross national borders.

CASBAH—Literally, "citadel" in Arabic; now usually the walled residential area of Arab cities.

CASSAVA—Tuberous starchy plant used as a food staple in West, Central and Southern African forest areas; eaten in cereals and dough with a variety of sauces, as in gari and foofoo.

CASSE-CROUTE(kass-kroot)—French for snack (literally "crust-breaking") often served at small restaurants, sidewalk cafes and rural grocery stores in French-speaking countries.

CFA (Communauté Financière Africaine) Franc—Currency based on the French franc, used in Senegal, Dahomey, Niger, Ivory Coast, Upper Volta, Togo, Cameroon, Gabon, Chad, Central African Republic, Congo-Brazzaville, Reunion and Comoro Islands.

CHAGGA—A people living on the slopes of Mt. Kilimanjaro in Tanzania; noted for their fine coffee and beautiful women.

CHEMISE VESTE (shuh-meez vehst)—French for a man's white shirt tailored to be worn tails out; acceptable for many cocktail parties and restaurants in tropical areas.

CHIBUKU—A beer made from maize; popular in Malawi, Rhodesia and South Africa.

CHOP—West African pidgin for a meal or food generally. Also used as a verb: "go chop," to eat.

CHOPE (tcho-pee)—A people of southern Mozambique known for their dancing and orchestral music featuring xylophones.

CHOTT (shott)—Dried salt lakes on the North African plateaus.

CITÉ (see-tay)—French term for specific sections of cities—as "la cité indigène," or African quarter; "la cité universitaire," student residential district.

COCO DE MER (koko-d'mair)—Enormous nut of coconut palms in

Seychelles. Occasionally washes up on South Asian shores where its fruit is regarded as an aphrodysiac.

COELECANTH (see-luh-kanth)—Indian Ocean fish weighing up to 130 pounds, thought at one time to have become extinct 300 million years ago. First identified in 1938. Still occasionally found, it brings a tidy sum from museum collections.

COFFIA—Arabic term for the skullcap worn by Moslems. Often finely woven and embroidered.

COLLECTIVE TAXI—Passenger vehicle (often a Peugeot station wagon seating eight) widely used between cities and villages. Called "car rapide" in French-speaking countries.

COLOURED—Official South African designation for a person of racially mixed ancestry. (More than two million persons in the Republic of South Africa are so classified.) The term is used informally throughout Southern and East Africa to refer to persons of mixed African and white origin. (Elsewhere designated as Creoles, mulattos, métis, or mestizos.)

CONGO JAZZ—Popular urban music style which originated in Kinshasa (Zaïre) in the 1960's.

COPTS—A Christian sect, nearly 10 per cent of the population of Egypt, whose origins go back to a 4th century theological schism. Copts are related to the Orthodox Church of Ethiopia.

CORNICHE (kawr-neesh)—Road following the line of high bluffs overlooking the sea or ocean.

COUSCOUS (koos-koos)—Steamed semolina served with a sauce, meat and vegetables in North and West Africa.

CREOLE—People of mixed European and African background, also their culture, language and cuisine. Also used to refer to communities of descendants of 19th century freed slaves in the Gambia and Sierra Leone.

CUSO (Canadian University Service Overseas)—Volunteer technical assistance program similar to United States Peace Corps.

DAN—Accomplished musicians, dancers and sculptors of the coffee-growing forest area in western Ivory Coast and Liberia.

DANAKIL (dan-a-keel)—A proud and rugged nomadic people of northeast Ethiopia who survive in one of the world's least hospitable desert environments. Also known as Afars.

DASH—Slang term in West Africa for a bribe, often demanded by petty officials for performance of services.

DASHIKI—Open-neck shirt with short sleeves, usually brightly patterned and often with embroidered borders.

DEMI-PENSION—Hotel and boarding house arrangement entailing a flat rate for room, breakfast and one other meal.

DHOW—Arab sailing vessel used off the east coast of Africa and the Indian Ocean in the trade with the Persian Gulf and Arabian peninsula. "Boutres," "goelettes" and "baggalas" are types of dhows.

DIK-DIK—A diminutive antelope, native to eastern and southern Africa. Also known as "duiker."

DINKA—Cattle-keeping herders of the southern Sudan.

DIOULA (djoo-la)—A dynamic people of Upper Volta who have set up trade routes and settlements from Senegal to the Ivory Coast. Also spelled "Jula."

DJERBIANS (d'jer-bee-ans)—An austere, egalitarian sect of Moslems whose center is the Tunisian island of Djerba. Djerbians are prominent in business in North Africa and France.

DJERMA—A major group of middle Niger people, living around and upstream from Niamey, capital of the Niger Republic. Part of the Songhai empire which dominated the western Sudan in the 15th and 16th centuries.

DODO—Large, flightless, defenseless, now extinct bird identified with the history of Mauritius, where it used to dwell.

DOGON (do-gahn)—Cliff-dwelling people of southern Mali, known for their elaborate cosmologies, grain-growing technology, initiation and festival dancing, and superb sculpture.

DOMODAH (do-mo-dah)—Groundnut stew with chicken or beef and rice eaten in the Gambia and Senegal.

DOUALA (dwa-lah)—Fishing people and town dwellers of the Cameroon coast.

DRAGOMAN (drah-go-man)—Egyptian guide, sometimes licensed, often not.

DUKA (doo-ka)—In Swahili, a small general store; in East Africa and Indian Ocean often owned by Asians (persons of Indian or Pakistani origin) or Chinese.

DUN DUN (duhn-duhn)—Matched set of drums, including talking drum, used at courts of Yoruba kings.

DURBAR—Grand social, legislative and judicial assembly of chiefs and

Rural railway station, Ivory Coast

Ferry, Sierra Leone

Camel freight, Ethiopia

Cargo boats on Niger

Walking along Rift Valley in Kenya

people in North and West Africa. Formal occasion often involving pageantry and horsemanship.

EAC—East African Community. Common market of Kenya, Tanzania and Uganda.

EBONY—Hard, heavy tropical wood, black with white skin. Sculptors generally retain small patches of the skin to show that the wood is genuine ebony.

ECA—United Nations Economic Commission for Africa, headquartered in Addis Ababa.

EGUSI—See agushi.

ELAND—A large antelope with long spiralled horns and a dewlap at the neck.

EMIR—Hausa-Fulani sultan in northern Nigeria. Sometimes used as a title of honor for descendants of the Prophet Mohammed.

ERITREANS—Christian and Moslem peoples of northern Ethiopia; major centers, Asmara and Massawa. Resistant to central rule from Addis Ababa.

ESSENCE (ess-sahs)—French for gasoline.

EWE (ay-way)—A people in coastal area of Ghana and Togo; prominent in Ghana army and police.

FADO—Portuguese song style, often sentimental.

FALASHA—Jews of western Ethiopia, descended from 16th century Judaic kingdom. Now numbering about 25,000, they cling to Old Testament rituals and elaborate traditions. They receive assistance from the government of Israel.

FALUKKA (fah-loo-kah)—Graceful, traditional sailing vessel on the Nile.

FAMADIANA (fah-mah-dee-ah-nah)—Malagasy religious ceremony involving disinterment of selected ancestors and their return to the tomb. Associated with intense festivity, music and dance. Known in French as "retournement des morts."

FANG—A major people of Gabon and southern Cameroon noted for the incisive lines of their wood carvings. Also known as Pahouin.

FANTASIA—French term for North African festivals that feature displays of horsemanship, often accompanied by sharpshooting and swordsmanship.

FANTI—Inhabitants of southwestern Ghana, allies of Britain in· 19th century wars against Ashanti (to whom they are closely related culturally).

FATMA—The five-fingered hand of fate, of pre-Islamic Berber origin. A favorite motif in Islamic jewelry, architecture, amulets and other art forms in North, Northeast and West Africa.

FERNANDINO—Inhabitant of the island of Fernando Po (Equatorial Guinea); of mixed European and African origin.

FETISH—A great variety of objects which contain and transmit the magical properties of a cult.

FEZ—Brimless, flat-crowned felt hat, usually red and ornamented with a black tassel.

FLAMBOYANT—Large poinciana tree with scarlet or orange flowers seen mainly in West and Central Africa and the Indian Ocean.

FON—Forest people of central Dahomey noted for imaginative metal sculpture and tapestries. Former rulers of the Dahomean kingdom, they maintain elaborate royal traditions.

FOOL—Staple food of Egyptian working class; made of mashed beans and lentils and served with oil and lemon.

FOULBE—See Fulani.

FRELIMO—Mozambique Liberation Front, a nationalist movement fighting the Portuguese. Headquarters in Dar es Salaam, Tanzania.

FUFU—West African dish composed of pounded steamed yam or cassava, usually served with a sauce containing fish, chicken or meat. Also spelled "foufou" or "foofoo."

FULANI—Cattle-herders and town-dwellers of West African Sudan, particularly concentrated in northern Nigeria, Niger and Cameroon (where some are called Bororo and others Foulbe), Senegal and Guinea (where they are known as Peuhl). Also known as Fula. Their early 19th century crusade for Moslem reform resulted in conquests from the Senegal River to Lake Chad.

FUNDI—Swahili for any kind of skilled craftsman. For instance, an auto mechanic is called a "fundi wa motokaa."

GALLA—A major people of Ethiopia, mostly living south and east of Addis Ababa. Partly Islamicized. They are herdsmen, farmers and soldiers.

GAMBES (gahm-bez)—Portuguese for shrimp.

GANDOURA—A flowing, usually embroidered, full-length gown worn by men in Mali, Guinea and other West African countries.

GARGOTE (gar-gut)—Popular French term for inexpensive restaurants in North Africa.

GARI—Cassava or yam porridge served with a variety of sauces in West Africa, especially Nigeria. Also spelled "garri."

GCE—General Certificate of Education. A secondary school completion diploma awarded in many former British colonies, often based on Cambridge or West African exams.

GÎTE (jheet)—A shelter; often a rest-house reserved for official guests, but also frequently available to travelers at modest cost.

GNU (nyoo)—Large antelope with big head, long tail and horns that curve down and out.

GOANS—People originating from former Portuguese colony of Goa, now part of India. Usually Roman Catholic. Many are in business in Mozambique and East Africa.

GOFIO (gawf-yo)—Staple flour used in Canary Island cooking.

GOLD COAST—Colonial name for contemporary Ghana. Several dozen castles and forts remain on the coast from its slave trade era.

GOUDRON (goo-droh, French)—Tar or pitch, as on a surfaced road.

GRAFFITO—Ancient inscription on rocks or cave walls, found in dry and desert areas of North, East and Southern Africa.

GRIOT (gree-oh)—In French-speaking West Africa a composer and singer of historical sagas and songs of praise; a troubador.

GRIS-GRIS (gree-gree)—Protective amulet worn in West Africa. In English-speaking countries known as "juju."

GROUNDNUT—Peanut-like root, a major West African export. An essential ingredient and source of protein in many favorite African foods.

GUANCHE (gwan-chay)—Indigenous Berber inhabitants of the Canary Islands, now almost entirely absorbed by the Spanish population.

GUAVA (gwa-va)—Tropical fruit from which a delectable juice can be made.

GUM ARABIC—Sap of the acacia tree growing in arid parts of North and Sudanic Africa. Used in adhesives and pharmaceutical products.

HABARI—Swahili greeting: How are you? The customary response, "mzuri" (em-zoo-ree), means good or well.

HAMMAM—Egyptian Arabic term for pigeon, often served as a delicacy, skewered or baked into a flaky meat pie with sweet sauces.

HAMSEEN—Swahili for wind.

HARAMBEE—Literally, in Swahili, "to pull together"; self-help project or institution. National motto of Kenya.

Nigerian shanty-town

Street in Lome, Togo

Desert track, Mozambique

Downtown Accra

HARMATTAN (*har*-mah-tahn)—Dry winter wind that blows from the Sahara Desert over West Africa.

HAUSA—Major cattle-keeping people of northern Nigeria, eastern Niger and, in smaller merchant communities, most other West and Central African nations. Almost entirely Moslem, particularly since early 19th century when their emirates were conquered by the militantly Islamic Fulani. Also, primary or secondary language of nearly 50 million people in West Africa, with a literature going back to the 10th century.

HAYA—A people known in Swahili as the Wahaya, who live in western Tanzania. They are coffee farmers and fishermen.

HEREROS—A major people of Namibia who resisted German colonial rule, suffered enormous losses, yet continue to resist white South African domination. Herero women are noted for their dignified bearing and unique long-skirted gowns.

HIGH-LIFE—Popular dance and music style in urban West Africa, especially Ghana and Nigeria.

HOTTENTOT—Inhabitants of Southern Africa, almost completely absorbed during European settlement. Many of South Africa's Coloured are part Hottentot. Also known as Khoi-Khoin.

HUTU (*hoo*-too)—The majority people of Burundi and Rwanda who historically were dominated by the cattle-owning Tutsi. The Hutu now control the Rwanda government but remain subordinate in Burundi.

IBIBIO (i-*bee*-bee-oh)—Agricultural people of southeast Nigeria closely related to the Ibos. Known for their subtle sculpture, strict social organization and commercial skills.

IDD AL FITR—Celebration of the end of Ramadan, the holy month.

IDD AL IDHA—See Tabaski.

IDD AL KEBIR—Feast and pilgrimage preceding Ramadan.

IFAN—Institut Fondamentale d'Afrique Noire. Includes cultural and scientific research centers and museums established under French colonial rule and now operated by African governments with French support. Known as "IRAD" in Dahomey.

INDIGÈNE—French for "native," but used slightly less pejoratively than the English; as in "quartier indigène" (African district of a town).

IROI (ir-*oh*-ee)—A Kikuyu dish in Kenya with ground maize as main ingredient; served as a porridge.

IROKO—Sacred mahogany-like tree of the Yoruba and other prolific sculptors of West Africa.

ISMAILI—Follower of the Moslem sect headed by the Aga Khan; mainly in Kenya, Tanzania and Madagascar, usually of Indian or Pakistani origin.

ISSA—An Islamic people, closely related to the Somali, who live in the French-ruled city of Djibouti.

ITHNASHERI (ith-na-shair-y)—A puritanical Moslem sect of Indian origin that practices self-flagellation. Its mosques are in East Africa.

JACARANDA—A tropical tree with bright blue flowers. Found in most parts of Africa.

JAIMAS (ha-ee-mas)—Berber and Arabic word for spacious tents made of animal skins used by nomads of Morocco and Spanish Sahara.

JAMBO—Swahili greeting equivalent to hello.

JELLABA (djeh-lah-bah)—Long gown worn by men in North Africa. Also written "gallabia," "jebba," and "djellaba."

JIHAD (djee-had)—A crusade or holy war for Islam.

JOLLOF RICE—West African dish of rice cooked in a rich tomato sauce; served with green peas, pepper sauce, beef and fried plantains.

JUJU—Term used widely in English-speaking West Africa to refer to a fetish object or charm. Known as "gris-gris" in French.

KABYL (kah-beel)—Berber people of the mountains of Algeria centered around Tizi-Ouzou and the Kabylie region. They played a leading role in the Algerian revolution.

KAFTAN—North African woman's garment with long sleeves, sometimes ties in at the waist and often has dolman sleeves.

KALENJIN (ka-lenn-djin)—A linguistic group in western Kenya and Uganda consisting of different peoples including the Kipsigi, Kara-majong, Pokot and Suk.

KAMBA—More than a million in number, these sturdy cultivators, carvers and soldiers live northeast of Nairobi in Kenya. They speak a language closely related to that of the Kikuyu, the predominant people of Kenya.

KANGA—A colorful textile of East Africa.

KANURI—Pastoral inhabitants of northeastern Nigeria and other territories around southern Lake Chad. Their empire of Bornu ruled throughout the region from the 10th to 19th centuries.

KANZU—Full-length white robes favored for relaxation by the Baganda men of Uganda.

KAPOK (ka-pak)—Tree fibers of silken texture, used as stuffing and ornamentation.

KARROO—Vast, arid tablelands of red clay soil in South Africa.

KENTE CLOTH—Elaborately patterned hand-woven cloth made mainly by the Ashanti in Ghana. Often has strands of gold thread.

KI—Swahili and Bantu prefix meaning "language of." The Swahili language is correctly known as "Kiswahili." "Kiingereza" is the Swahili term for English, literally "the language of the English people."

KIKAPU (ki-kah-poo)—Swahili and Kikuyu term for decorated and woven purses, shopping bags and baskets, often made from sisal.

KIKUYU—Largest single group in Kenya (about two million). These people live in and around Nairobi and the nearby highlands. President Kenyatta and many other leading Kenyan figures are Kikuyu. Also spelled "Gikuyu."

KIMBANGUISTS (kim-bang-ists)—Members of an important syncretistic church based in Zaïre; doctrine and liturgy blend Protestant Christian elements into an animistic African structure.

KIPSIGI (kip-see-ghee)—People of the highlands of northeast Kenya. Tall and athletic, the Kipsigi have produced several Olympic champions, including Kipchoge Keino.

KISSI (kee-see)—A people of Liberia and Sierra Leone. Also refers to thin wrought-iron bars used as currency in parts of West African interior. Also spelled "Kisi."

KOLA NUT—Seed about the size of a chestnut; contains caffein and is used for hospitality in West Africa.

KORA—West African harp with calabash resonator.

KORAN—The holy book of all Moslems, believed to have been dictated by God (Allah) to his prophet (Mohammed) in the 7th century.

KOUBBA (koo-bah)—Arabic for mausoleum, usually of a saint or holy man.

KPELLE (k'pell-lay)—Agricultural forest people of Guinea and Liberia. Called Guerze in French.

KRAAL (crawl)—Village in Southern Africa, usually surrounded by a stockade for cattle; or simply a cattle enclosure.

KSAR—Fortified site in North Africa and Mauritania, sometimes still inhabited and used for defense.

Kuba—A highly hierarchic Bantu group of the Zaïre savanna whose magnificent sculpture and other art reflect the importance of kingship and lineage.

kudu—A large antelope. The males have long, corkscrew-shaped horns sometimes used as trumpets by musicians in East, West and Southern Africa.

kufta (koof-tah)—A favorite Middle Eastern and North African dish of minced meat, often lamb, served in a stew. Available at Lebanese restaurants through much of Africa.

laager (lah-gher)—Afrikaans words meaning "camp." Refers historically to the grouping of ox-wagons in an enclosure for defensive purposes during 19th century Boer (Voortrekker) migrations. Now connotes a conservative, stockade-like attitude or mentality.

lamba—Traditional shawl, often full-length, embroidered or elaborately woven, worn by almost all Malagasy. The "lambamena" (literally, red lamba) refers to luxurious burial shrouds that drape a family's ancestors in the world of the dead.

Lango—Nilotic cattle-keeping and cotton-growing people of northern Uganda, closely related to their Acholi neighbors.

lappa—Any cloth of various patterns used as a skirt or sarong in West African forest regions. Also, a cloth measure (one meter by two meters). Also spelled "loppa."

laterite—Sterile reddish soil formed in tropical regions by the decomposition of underlying rock. Often refers to road surfaces.

lemur—Nocturnal mammal existing almost exclusively in Madagascar. Often mistaken for monkey.

lost wax—Traditional West African method of casting metal sculpture. In French, "cire-perdue."

Lozi (loh-zee)—Hierachically-structured society of western Zambia. The former Lozi kingdom was known as Barotseland.

Luhya (loo-yah)—A farming people, also known as the Abaluhya, who live on the Kenyan slopes of Mt. Elgon.

Lunda—A Bantu-speaking people of Zaïre, Zambia and Angola. Separated from the Luba realm in the 16th century, they founded a monarchical empire—glorified in strong, royal wood sculpture—that dominated the southern savannas into the 19th century.

Lou—A tall, Nilotic people, also known as "Jaluo," who live along the Kenyan shores of Lake Victoria and rank next to the Kikuyu as the most numerous in Kenya.

Rural bus stop, Ethiopia

Chopi dancers

Tent of nomadic Mauritania family

Makonde sculpture   Merowe pyramids, Sudan

MAGHREB (mah-*greb*, Arabic)—Literally, "setting sun"; a name for the western countries of North Africa (Morocco, Algeria, Tunisia).

MBARI (um-*bah*-ree, Ibo)—Creativity; applied to network of artists' and writers' clubs in Nigeria.

MAISON DES JEUNES (may-*zohn* day *zhun*, French)—Cultural and social association of young people.

MAJUMBORO (ma-*joom*-boh-roh)—Colorful fringed shirt worn by the Bushmen and other peoples of Botswana.

MAKONDE (ma-*kahn*-day)—A people of northern Mozambique and southern Tanzania noted as carvers of expressionist sculpture and masks, and as vigorous dancers.

MALACHITE—A green copper stone used in jewelry and ornamental architecture. Found in Central and East Africa.

MALAGASY (mah-lah-*gah*-see)—The people of Madagascar and their language. Their country is correctly known as the Malagasy Republic, never as "Malagasy" alone.

MALAY—People of Malaysian origin, of whom about 50,000, mostly Moslems, live in and around Cape Town, where they migrated in the 19th century.

MALINKÉ (ma-*link*-ay)—See Mandingo.

MALLAM (ma-*lahm*)—Arabic title for a Moslem scholar or religious dignitary, usually an older person. "Ulema" also used in North Africa. "Mwalimu" (mwah-*lee*-moo) is a Swahili word meaning a learned person, often a teacher, not necessarily a Moslem. For instance, President Nyerere of Tanzania, a Catholic ex-schoolteacher, is often referred to as Mwalimu Nyerere.

MAMMY-WAGON—Small bus, inexpensive, usually unscheduled and often crowded, used for urban-rural transportation in West Africa. Known also as "tro-tro" in Ghana, "money-bus" in Liberia, "taxi-brousse" in French-speaking countries.

MANDINGO—A creative people of the forests and savannas of West Africa, ranging from Senegal to Guinea. Descendants of the great medieval Sudanic empire of Mali and 19th century alliance ruled by Sultan Samory Touré, their musical and poetic traditions remain strong today. Also known as Malinké and Mandé.

MANGO—Tropical fruit, sometimes as large as a grapefruit, with hard nut and juicy pulp.

MANIOC (ma-*nyok*)—French for cassava.

MANYATTA—Masai word for the mobile encampments sheltering their families and livestock.

MASAI—A proud, physically impressive people of the grasslands of Kenya and Tanzania whose diet includes the blood and milk of their cherished cattle.

MASCAREIGNES (mas-kah-*rains*)—Indian Ocean archipelago including Reunion, Mauritius and Rodriguez islands.

MASHRABIYA SCREEN—A classic traditionally carved screen found especially in Egypt; now valuable collector's item.

MATOKE (ma-*toh*-kay)—See plantain.

MAZBUT (*maz*-buht)—Egyptian Arabic for strong Turkish coffee, often served in demi-tasse cups. Order it "saada," without sugar, or "siadah," sweet. "Mazbut" also means just right.

MBIRA (em-bee-rah)—See thumb piano.

MEALIE-MEALIE—Southern African term for corn-based rations often fed to migrant farm and mine workers.

MECHOUI (*mesh*-wee, Arabic)—North and West African festive meal of lamb or kid, often roasted whole.

MEDERSA—Arabic for a religious college or seminary for advanced theological studies. Known as "madrasa" in Egypt and Libya, "medersa" in North and West Africa.

MEDINA—The older, walled sections of North African cities.

MEERSCHAUM—A special clay, found mainly in Tanzania and Turkey, used for the manufacture of pipes, stoves and other products.

MENDE (*men*-day)—One of the principal peoples of Sierra Leone and Liberia, known for their powerful sculpture in wood and stone.

MERINA (*mair*-neh, Malagasy)—The largest and once dominant people of Madagascar, descended from sea-borne immigrants from Malayo-Polynesia over a milennium ago. Astute, disciplined, with vivid culture, they speak Malagasy, the lingua franca for the island.

MÉTIS (may-*tee* or may-*tees*, French)—Persons of mixed African and European ancestry. "Mestizo" in Portuguese, "mestro" in Spanish.

MOAMBE (moo-*ahmb*)—National dish of lower Zaïre-Congo River area; usually prepared with chicken, groundnut sauce, vegetables and spices.

MOAZABITE (mo-az-a-*beet*)—A puritanical Islamic sect whose center is in Ghardaia in the Algerian Sahara and whose followers are noted for their business acumen.

MOIN-MOIN—White bean purée, steamed, served with garri, rice or other West African staple.

MONSOON—Indian Ocean winds that blow steadily from northeast to southwest from October to March and in the opposite direction from April to September. Arab, East African and South Asian sea trade has been organized on the strength and regularity of these winds for over 2,000 years.

MOORS—People of mixed Arab and Berber ancestry whose forefathers (Almoravids) ruled Spain from the 8th through the 15th centuries, and also conquered much of the western Sahara and Sudan. Applied to dominant population of Mauritania today.

MORAN—A Masai young man, usually between the age of 18 and 35, who belongs to the warrior-herdsman group.

MOSSI (mah-see)—A major people of Upper Volta with strong traditions of court pageantry. Their kings (naba) render traditional homage to the Moro Naba of Ouagadougou who retains social influence even in the contemporary republic.

MOULOUD (moo-load)—Anniversary of the birth of the Prophet Mohammed. A major holiday in Islamic countries.

MOURIDE (moo-reed)—Member of Islamic sect of Senegal led by Marabout of Touba, whose mosque is among the most beautiful buildings in Africa. His economic and political influence remains strong.

MOUSSEM (moo-sem)—Festival or holiday honoring a local Moslem saint.

MPLA—Popular Movement for the Liberation of Angola, the most important of the three Angolan nationalist movements fighting the Portuguese. Headquarters are in Lusaka, Zambia.

MURRAM (moor-um)—Black clay surface of unpaved roads in East and Southern Africa. Treacherous when wet.

MZEE (em-zay)—Swahili term of respect and endearment for older people, usually reserved for men. For instance, President Kenyatta of Kenya is affectionately known as Mzee Kenyatta.

NDEBELE (en-da-bay-lee)—Also known as Matabele, these people migrated to Rhodesia in the 19th century from South Africa, conquered the local Shona, and then fought and lost to the British settlers whose rule they continue to resist.

NÉGRITUDE—The cultural, political and economic values characterizing black civilizations; French-language literature and philosophy celebrating these values. Expounded in writings of President Leopold Senghor of Senegal.

NGOMA (en-go-ma)—A Swahili word meaning to drum or dance. May mean a dance performance.

NILOTIC—Persons living along the Nile River Basin. The Luo, Acholi and Lango of East Africa, who speak related languages, were once part of a broad migration south from the upper Nile.

NOMOLI—Small soapstone (steatite) figures of ancient origin placed as protective charms in farmed plots of the Mende and Kissi people in Sierra Leone, Guinea and Liberia. Also called "pomdo."

NSHIMA (en-shee-ma)—Rhodesian maize mush or porridge, sometimes served as a stew with meat and vegetables.

NUBIANS—Dark-skinned Egyptians and Sudanese of the Nile region. Many villages were inundated by the construction of the Aswan dam and villagers resettled. They are noted for their craft, fishing skills, distinctive dialect and customs, possibly traceable to the ancient Nubian dynasties.

NUTCRACKER MAN—Oldest African yet known. The skull, dating back almost two million years, was found by the late Dr. Louis S. B. Leakey in Olduvai Gorge and is now on display at the National Museum in Dar es Salaam, Tanzania. Less familiarly known as Zinjanthropus Bosei.

NYAMA—Swahili for meat or animal. "Nyama wa mbuzi" means goat meat, "nyama wa kuku" means chicken meat.

NYANJA (nee-ahn-dja)—People of central Mozambique and Malawi whose language, Cinyanja (pronounced chin-yan-ja), is widespread throughout Southern Africa.

OAU—Organization of African Unity, the association of all independent black African states. Organized in 1963. Headquarters are in Addis Ababa.

OKAPI—Short-necked relative of the giraffe with zebra-like stripes on its legs. Now lives only in northeastern Zaïre.

OKOUME (oh-koo-may)—An important tree of Central Africa, also called "gaboonwood," used in sculpture and exported (especially from Gabon) for plywood.

OVAMBO—People of northern Namibia and southern Angola. Recruited as mine laborers and herdsmen for European-owned enterprises.

PAGNE (pah-nye, French)—Toga-like garment in a wide variety of colors, materials and designs.

PAIGC—African Independence Party of Guinea (Bissau) and Cape Verde, nationalist movement fighting the Portuguese.

Loading steamer on Lake Tanganyika

Dahomean craftsman

Pygmy family, Burundi

Village meeting, Botswana

South African workers

PAILLOTTE (pie-yote, French)—Thatched-roof cottage, often referring to rustic restaurants or guest houses.

PALAVER (Portuguese origin)—A meeting for the discussion of problems. Used in West Africa, often to describe village councils.

PALISANDER—A hardwood resembling rosewood; grown in tropical African forests and used in sculpture as well as fine carpentry.

PALM WINE—Strong, yellowish syrup of palm trees. A popular beverage in West and Central Africa. Also called "bangui," "bandji," "sambwa," "calao," and other names.

PAPAYA—Large, melon-like, yellow-skinned fruit; a breakfast delight often served at hotels in East Africa. "Papaw" or "pawpaw" is the smaller fruit of a similar tree grown in temperate zones.

PARADOR—Spanish for government-operated hotels, often historic buildings converted for tourist needs. Found in Spanish Sahara and the Canary Islands.

PASTILLA—Also known as "b'stila." Pigeon pie. See hammam.

PATCHOULI—Patch-leaf, an aromatic plant used for moth protection and (in extract form) as a perfume base. Grown in the Comoros and Reunion.

PCV—United States Peace Corps Volunteer.

PENNYWHISTLE—Blues-influenced city music of South Africa. The name comes from the cheap mouth organ or flute which is its melodic instrument.

PEUHL—French for Fulani.

PIDGIN—A simplified speech, based on English, used for communication among millions of people of different languages in Cameroon, Ghana, Nigeria, Liberia and other West African countries.

PIED NOIR (pyay-nwarh, French)—European settler in Algeria. Numbering one million at the end of the Algerian war of independence (1962), the majority emigrated to France and other countries.

PIRI PIRI (peery-peery)—From the Swahili word for pepper, used in Southern Africa to designate hot and pungent sauces, often of red pepper, chopped tomatoes and onions, served with chicken, fish, rice, curries and many other dishes. Called "pili-pili" in Central Africa, "rougail" in the Indian Ocean and "piment" in French.

PISTE (peest, French)—Track or trail. When the reference is to a road, it means one that is unsurfaced, narrow and little traveled.

PLANTAIN—Tropical fruit similar to the banana, but requiring cooking.

Consumed in various ways: as toasted chips, in a stew with meat and vegetables ("matoke" in Uganda), as dough with sauce ("killewelle" in Ghana), and in other forms throughout tropical Africa.

POMBE (pom-bay)—Swahili for beer, either homemade from bananas, corn or other ingredients, or commercially brewed.

PORO—Secret society of men with educational responsibilities and strong social and political influence in many West African countries.

POTO-POTO—A style of art blending Western forms with traditional African subjects and vitality. It takes its name from the Poto-Poto neighborhood in Brazzaville. Also a term for the adobe clay used in much construction throughout West and Central Africa.

POUF (poof, French)—An ottoman of dyed, embossed leather in North and West Africa.

POUSADA (poo-sah-da)—Portuguese for a small, usually family-operated hotel or inn. "Posada" in Spanish.

POUSSE-POUSSE (poos-poos)—French for ricksha, a conveyance still used in the Indian Ocean islands and South Africa.

QAT—A mildly stimulating leaf legally chewed by Somalis.

RAFFIA—A low-growing palm indigenous to Madagascar, now found throughout tropical Africa. The leaf stalks yield a fiber used to weave articles such as baskets, mats, hats and nets.

RAIN FOREST—Forest of rapid tropical growth, dense vegetation and normally 70 or more inches of rain annually. Central and West African rain forests near the coast and the forests of the Congo-Zaïre interior have giant hardwood trees. Other rain forests are found on São Tomé, the east coast of Madagascar and the coastal strip of Tanzania and Kenya.

RAMADAN—Moslem holy month of prayer and fasting (during daylight hours).

REEDBUCK—Yellowish antelope about the size of a small deer. Males have short, forward-curving horns.

RIBAT—Arabic for a castle or fortress.

RIFFIANS—Mountain people of northern Morocco who speak a Berber dialect. Known for their resistance to Spanish colonialism and their independent spirit.

RIFT VALLEY—A 6,000-mile-long canyon descending from the Arabian Peninsula and cutting across Ethiopia and East Africa, 50 to 100 miles wide at many points. The valley is dotted with crater lakes, its walls marked by steep escarpments.

ROMAZAVA (roo-mah-*zah*-veh)—National dish of Madagascar, literally meaning clear broth, served with rice, meat, green herbs and spices.

RONDAVEL—Thatched-roof bungalow housing visitors to South African national parks.

SACRED CROCODILE—Usually identifies those aquatic reptiles believed to embody spirits of ancestors, as in Dahomey and Madagascar.

SAFARI—Although any trip is a safari in Swahili, the term usually refers to a hunting or photography tour of East African game parks.

SAHEL (*sah*-el, Arabic)—Literally, "street" or "corridor"; applied to the very dry strip of West African savanna south of the Sahara, and inland from the humid coast.

SALAAM (sa-*lahm*, Arabic)—Salutation, meaning "peace," used in North and East Africa, northern Ethiopia and Madagascar. Also Swahili.

SAMOSA (Swahili)—Meat and vegetable pie served in East and Southern Africa and Lebanese restaurants elsewhere.

SANSA—See thumb piano.

SARA—A major people of southern Chad. Noted for elaborate facial scarification and other body decoration.

SAVANNA—Grassland region with scattered tree growth grading into either open plain or woodland; found especially at the edges of the tropics where rainfall is seasonal. Most large game herds and domesticated animals graze in savanna country.

SCAC—Scandanavian Travel Services Consortium. Operates a network of travel services, primarily in West Africa.

SCHISTOSOMIASIS (skis-toe-so-*my*-a-sis)—See bilharzia.

SEGA—Calypso-like dance music popular among Creoles of Mauritius and Reunion.

SENOUFO (sen-oo-foo)—Agricultural people of West African savanna (especially Ivory Coast), known for powerful religious sculpture and music.

SEROUAL (seh-roo-*ahl*)—Voluminous trousers worn by men in North Africa and western Sudan, often handsomely striped or embroidered.

SHAMBA (Swahili)—In East Africa, a small farm.

SHEBEEN—Illegal bars in segregated areas of South Africa. Often run by women.

SHEIK—Arabic term for chief or local ruler.

SHIFTA (Somali)—Guerilla fighters; in particular, those supporting Somali nationalism.

SHIRAZI—Persons living in Zanzibar claiming descent from Persian settlers and retaining certain of their customs.

SHONA—Also known as Mashona, the majority people in Rhodesia. They are farmers and industrial workers.

SIMBA—Swahili for lion. Sometimes used to refer to rebel or guerrilla movements.

SIROCCO—Hot, dry, dust-laden wind blowing across North Africa.

SISAL—Tough, cactus-like plant used for the manufacture of rope and twine; important exports from Kenya, Tanzania, Madagascar and Mozambique.

SOMALI—The Somali-speaking people, numbering over three million in Somalia and in the neighboring areas of Ethiopia, Kenya and the Territory of the Afars and Issas.

SORGHUM—Tall, corn-like grass bearing edible grains, prepared in porridge, cakes and dumplings; a staple food in West Africa savanna territory.

SOTHO (soo-too)—The people of Lesotho, sometimes identified as Basuto, many of whom work as migrant laborers in South Africa. Their king is known as Moshoshoe. Their language is Siswati.

SOUK (sook, Arabic)—Open or partly covered market with many stalls and vendors. "Soko" in Swahili.

SUDAN—The vast arid region south of the Sahara and Libyan deserts and extending from the Atlantic to the Red Sea. As a geographic term, it covers an area much larger than the country known as the Sudan. The western Sudan was the region of such powerful medieval empires as Ghana, Mali, Songhai and Kanem-Bornu.

SUKUMA—The largest population group in Tanzania, numbering about a million cattle-keepers and cotton-growers in the western part of the country.

SUNDOWNER—Late afternoon drink. In East and Southern Africa a cocktail party, often outdoors.

SWAHILI—A widely spoken and written language in East Africa, northern Mozambique, eastern Zaïre (there called Kingwana), the Comoros and other territories. Basically a Bantu tongue with additions from Arabic, English, Hindustani and other languages. The first language of several million persons in Zanzibar and along the Kenyan and Tanzanian coasts, and a lingua franca for perhaps 70 million persons. Written in Latin script, with a literature going back several hundred years.

SWAZI—The people of Swaziland, whose king is known as Sobhuza.

TABASKI—Moslem festival commemorating the consent of Abraham to sacrifice his son Isaac. The miracle which spared Isaac is symbolized by a feast of lamb or kid meat. Also known as Idd al Idha.

TAJINE (tah-djeen)—A fried meat, cheese and egg pie eaten throughout North Africa.

TALKING DRUMS—Drums that reproduce the words and cadences of tonal languages such as Yoruba, the Akan languages of Ghana, and many Central African tongues. Besides the precise simulation of speech, talking drums are used to transmit code messages and to lead masks, dancers and other performers in traditional ceremonies.

TAMIYA—A popular Egyptian dish of ground bean patties fried in oil.

TANZANITE—Semi-precious stone recently discovered and now commercially mined in Tanzania.

TARMAC—A bituminous binder for roads; used as a generic term in English-speaking countries for paved road surfaces.

TAXI-BROUSSE (taxi brooce, French)—Literally, bush taxi. See collective taxi and mammy-wagon.

TAXI-GARE (taxi garrh)—French for taxi station or rank, used in Africa to indicate depots for city taxis and taxi-buses (taxi-brousse) traveling between towns.

TEJ (tehdj)—Ethiopian national drink made from distilled honey. Tastes somewhat like mead.

TEJ-BETS—Popular, cheap bars that sometimes double as inns or brothels. The latter are especially prevalent in the red-light district of Addis Ababa.

THIÉBOU DIÈNE (chee-boo djin)—A fish soup with rice and peanut oil, vegetables and spices; Senegalese national dish.

THUMB PIANO—Small wooden box, often decoratively carved, one edge of which has flexible metal strips plucked by the thumbs. Known by many names throughout Africa (especially "sansa" in West Africa, "mbira" in East Africa and "chisanzhi" in Angola).

TIDJANI—Followers of a North and West African Islamic religious sect whose leader lives in Senegal. Collectively these people, who number in the hundreds of thousands, are known as Tijanniya.

TILAPIA—Delicious freshwater fish of the bream family. Often stocked in inundated rice fields for insect control.

TIV—Inhabitants of the savanna area around the Jos plateau in central

Nile Hilton, Cairo

Hotel Ivoire, Abidjan

Inter-Continental, Lusaka

Hippo Bar, Gorongosa Park

Ambassador, Accra

Nigeria. They are an industrious people who work the tin mines, take pride in military accomplishments and produce imaginative artifacts.

TOUBAB—Common West African term for "white man."

TRIPTYQUE (trip-teek, French)—More commonly known now as a "carnet de passage en douane." A passport for an automobile enabling the owner to pass through customs without having to post a bond or pay duty when temporarily importing it into a foreign country.

TSCHOKWE (choke-way)—Also known as Chokwe, these people live in Eastern Angola, Zaïre and Zambia. They are among the finest carvers and dancers in Africa.

TSETSE—A fly whose bite causes tripanosomiasis (sleeping sickness). Although there is not yet an effective cure, control measures have restricted the range of the insect to less densely populated bush country in tropical West, Central and East Africa.

TSWANA (t'ss-wah-nah)—The predominant people of Botswana, themselves a merger of eight 19th century chiefdoms. Many work as migrant laborers in South Africa.

TUAREG (twah-regg)—The famous "Blue Men" of the Sahara whose distinctive desert cloaks are dyed with indigo. Nomadic Berber cattle-herders, merchants and warriors, the Tuareg and their caravans cover thousands of miles linking the markets of North and West Africa. They have a long history of resistance to authority, defiance of political boundaries and preference for their own unique way of life. Their written language has a considerable body of traditional poetry.

TUTSI (toot-see)—The aristocratic minority in Burundi and Rwanda who for centuries dominated the majority Hutu and still do in Burundi. Also known as Watutsi (Watusi) in relation to their ceremonial dances. The Tutsi average more than six feet in height. They revere their long-horned cattle, subject of much lyric poetry.

TWA (t'wah)—Dwarf-like Pygmies of Zaïre, Burundi and Rwanda who have interbred with other groups and turned to farming. They are servants and court jesters to the Tutsi royalty of Burundi and Rwanda.

TWALA—In Botswana and Rhodesia, a local beer, usually homemade from maize.

UDEAC—Economic and Customs Union of Central Africa, comprising Cameroon, the Central African Republic, Chad, Gabon and Congo-Brazzaville.

UDI—Unilateral Declaration of Independence. An act by which the white minority regime of Southern Rhodesia in 1965 declared its independence from Great Britain.

UGALI—Swahili and Kikuyu term for a stew made from maize, meat and vegetables. "Ugali na nyama" means maize stew with meat (usually beef).

UHURU (oo-hoo-roo, Swahili)—Freedom or independence. "Uhuru na Ujamaa" (freedom and unity) is the national motto of Tanzania. "Uhuru na Kuzi" (freedom and work) is a popular post-independence slogan in East Africa.

UJAMAA (oo-dja-mah, Swahili)—Unity. In Tanzania it characterizes government policies, especially with regard to communally owned and operated agricultural settlements, known as ujamaa villages.

UNGALAWA—Swahili for outrigger canoe fitted with sails. Used along the East African coast for fishing.

VALIHA (vah-lee-eh)—Cylindrical zither, usually made of bamboo sections strung with wire or cord; a major solo instrument in Madagascar.

VELD (velt, Afrikaans)—Open grasslands in Southern Africa. Lowveld refers to hot, humid plains country, highveld to the drier and more elevated plateau.

VETYVER—An East Indian grass grown in the Indian Ocean. Its long, aromatic roots have value as a perfume base, insect repellant and weavable fiber. Also spelled "vetiver."

VIETNAMESE—During colonial times many Africans served in the French army in Indo-China. Some returned with Vietnamese wives, and other Vietnamese, as French citizens, emigrated to Africa. Vietnamese restaurants are found in many cities in nearly every former French colony.

VOUDOUN (probably Ewe origin)—Sometimes applied to a whole system of magical practices having roots in Africa. In West Africa, and especially Dahomey, refers to spirits intermediary between humans and the higher deities.

VSO—Voluntary Services Organization, an international agency that provides volunteers to assist developing countries.

WANAWAKE (wah-nah-wah-kay)—Swahili for woman. Some of the best handicraft shops are operated in Kenya by the Maendeleo wa Wanawake (National Women's Development Association) and in Tanzania by the Umoja wa Wanawake (National Women's Unity Movement).

WAT—Ethiopian national dish made of chicken, beef and/or vegetable stew served with red-hot berberre, a pepper-based powder.

WATERBUCK—A large species of antelope living in marshes and reedy places in Central and Southern Africa; the males have long, ringed, forward-curving horns.

WHITE RHINO—Rare, two-horned, square-lipped species now limited to parts of Central and Southeast Africa. Tallest of the rhinos (sometimes six feet high at the shoulder). Its color is actually gray.

WILDEBEESTE—See gnu.

WOLOF (woh-loff)—Also spelled "Ouolof" in French. An important kingdom, ranging along the coast of Senegal and the Gambia. Its language has become a lingua franca for both countries.

XHOSA (kh-oh-sah, first syllable a plosive click)—Southern Bantu people of the Transkei and other parts of South Africa. Their songs have been recorded by Miriam Makeba.

YLANG-YLANG (ee-lahng ee-lahng)—An aromatic tree, found in the Comoro Islands and Madagascar, among other places. Its blossoms yield oil used to make perfume.

YORUBA (yaw-roo-bah)—Predominant people of western Nigeria and eastern Dahomey, numbering about 10 million. Noted for their theatre, art and fashions, for city-state organization and forest agriculture.

ZULU—A very numerous cattle-raising, Bantu-speaking South African people in the Natal area around Durban. Under their great King Shaka, early in the 19th century, the Zulu began to acquire their formidable reputation as warriors.

Appendix

I

AGENCIES SPECIALIZING IN AFRICAN TRAVEL

Adventureland Safaris, 735 North La Brea Boulevard, Hollywood, Cal. 90828 (tel. 213/933-9579). Associated with SAS. East and Southern Africa; safaris in Zaïre led by naturalist Jean-Pierre Hallet.

Adventures Unlimited, 19 East 45th Street, New York, N.Y. 10017 (212/986-6686). East and Southern Africa.

African Explorers, Professional Building, Route 9, Parlin, N.J. 08859 (201/721-2929). West Africa.

African Safari Holidays, 2949 Bathurst Street, Toronto 399, Canada (416/781-8215). East Africa.

African Tenting Safaris, P.O. 582, Lynbrook, N.Y. 11563. East and Southern Africa, primarily for young persons.

African Tourist and Travel Association, 114 East 32nd Street, New York, N.Y. 10016 (212/725-5726). Sponsored by group of African governments. All regions.

American Express, Tour Department, 770 Broadway, New York, N.Y. 10003 (212/677-1111). All regions.

American Travel Abroad, 250 West 57th Street, New York, N.Y. 10019 (212/586-5230). Associated with Air Afrique. North and West African tours.

Brien Merriman's Africa, 136 East 57th Street, New York, N.Y. 10022 (212/752-0730). East and Southern Africa, including camping and hiking.

Club Méditerranée, P.O. 402, Farmingdale, N.Y. 11735. Operates resorts in Algeria, Egypt, Ivory Coast, Mauritius, Morocco, Tunisia.

Club Tours (National Parks and Conservation Association, Travel Department), 18 East 41st Street, New York, N.Y. 10017 (212/532-7075). Associated with Sabena Airlines. East African tours.

Thomas Cook and Son, 587 Fifth Avenue, New York, N.Y. 10017 (212/688-4000). Offices throughout US and Canada. Tours of West and East Africa; Cape Town to Cairo tour.

Di Carlo Travel Bureau, 151 West 40th Street, New York, N.Y. 10018 (212/695-7570). Associated with Iberia Airlines. Canary Islands, Swaziland, South Africa and Namibia.

Eastours, NY, 1140 Avenue of the Americas, New York, N.Y. 10036 (212/490-2040). Student tours to East Africa, and Indian Ocean via Israel.

Embassy Tours, 505 Fifth Avenue, New York, N.Y. 10017 (212/661-6100). East African tours.

Europacar Tours, 136 East 57th Street, New York, N.Y. 10022 (212/751-3250). Associated with Swissair and Avis. East and Southern Africa.

Donald L. Ferguson Travel, 219 Palermo Avenue, Coral Gables, Fla. 33134 (305/446-3525). All regions.

Four Winds Travel, 175 Fifth Avenue, New York, N.Y. 10010 (212/777-0260). All regions.

G.T. Travel, 104 East 40th Street, New York, N.Y. 10016 (212/867 4044). Tours and charter flights to East and Southern Africa.

Hemphill Travel, 1201 West 4th Street, Los Angeles, Cal. 90017 (213/482-8420). East and Southern Africa; Cape Town to Cairo tour.

Henderson Travel Service, 931 Hunter Street NW, Atlanta, Ga. 30314 (404/522-6886). East and West Africa.

Kuoni Escorted Tours, 11 East 44th Street, New York, N.Y. 10017 (212/687-7197); other offices in Chicago, Los Angeles, Toronto, Associated with TWA. East and Southern Africa.

Lindblad Travel, 133 East 55th Street, New York, N.Y. 10022 (212/751-2300). Extensive luxury safaris and tours.

Linden Travel Bureau, 136 East 57th Street, New York, N.Y. 10022 (212/421-3320). Photographic tours of East Africa.

Lion Country Safari African Tours, 8800 Moulton Parkway, Laguna Hills, Cal. 92653 (714/837-1200). Tours of game parks in Southern Africa.

Lissone-Lindeman, 500 Fifth Avenue, New York, N.Y. 10036 (212/279-7100). All regions.

Maupintour, 270 Park Avenue, New York, N.Y. 10017 (212/687-7773). Morocco and Canary Islands.

Merriman and Finnerty, 15 East 48th Street, New York, N.Y. 10017 (212/752-0730). Ethiopia, East and Southern Africa.

Nilestar Tours Africa, 200 Park Avenue, New York, N.Y. 10017 (212/986-2666); other offices in Chicago, Los Angeles, London, Nairobi. Tours and charter flights to East Africa.

F. Oliviera Travel Agency, 265 Rivet Street, New Bedford, Mass. 02744 (617/997-9361). Associated with TAP. Angola, Mozambique, South Africa.

Orbitair International, 20 East 46th Street, New York, N. Y. 10017 (212/986-1500). East and Southern Africa.

Percival Tours, 5820 Wilshire Boulevard, Los Angeles, Cal. 90036 (213/936-2171) and 48 East 43rd Street, New York, N.Y. 10017 (212/867-6900). Photographic safaris and tours of all regions.

Raymond and Whitcomb, 400 Madison Avenue, New York, N.Y. 10017 (212/759-3960). Tours featuring cruises circling Africa.

Safari Outfitters, 8 South Michigan Avenue, Chicago, Ill. 60603 (312/346-9631). Hunting and photographic safaris of East, Central and Southern Africa.

Scantravel West Africa, c/o WDI, Mundy, 350 Fifth Avenue, New York, N.Y. 10001 (212/868-0420). West Africa.

Simba Safaris, 400 Madison Avenue, New York, N.Y. 10017 (212/371-1164). East Africa.

Sunny Land Tours, 166 Main Street, Hackensack, N.J. 07601 (201/487-2150). Egypt, Kenya and Morocco.

Travcoa Africa, 111 North Wabash Avenue, Chicago, Ill. 60602 (312/332-0950). All regions.

Travel Go Round, 516 Fifth Avenue, New York, N.Y. 10036 (212/867-3835). North and West Africa.

Travelworld, 515 Madison Avenue, New York, N.Y. 10022 (212/759-3720). Associated with Air France for tours of East Africa.

United Touring Company, c/o WDI, Mundy, 350 Fifth Avenue, New York, N.Y. 10001 (212/868-0420). East and Southern Africa.

Uniworld Travel, 62 West 45th Street, New York, N.Y. 10036 (212/697-1133). East and West Africa.

U.S. Student Travel Service, 866 Second Avenue, New York. N.Y. 10017 (212/421-6680). Student flights and camping tours of East Africa.

AIRLINE TOURS

Most airlines serving Africa have package tours with lodgings and ground travel arrangements. Their New York City offices are given here.

Air Afrique, 683 Fifth Avenue, New York 10022 (tel. 212/758-6300). French-speaking West Africa and Ghana, Liberia, Nigeria. Also, with Ethiopian Airlines, 28-day tour of East and West Africa.

Air India, 345 Park Avenue, 10022 (935-5090). East Africa and India (22 days) via New York and London.

Alitalia, 666 Fifth Avenue, 10019 (262-4422). East, Central and Southern Africa; tours originate in Rome or elsewhere in Europe.

BOAC (British Overseas Airways Corp.), 245 Park Avenue, 10017 (983-3113). East Africa, Southern Africa and Indian Ocean islands of Mauritius and Seychelles; tours originate in New York and London.

East African Airways, 576 Fifth Avenue, 10036 (757-2327). Owned jointly by Kenya, Tanzania and Uganda. East African tours, originating in London, other European cities or within East Africa.

El Al Israel Airlines, 850 Third Avenue, 10020 (751-7500). Combined tour of Israel and East Africa offered jointly with Ethiopian Airlines.

Ethiopian Airlines, 200 East 42nd Street, 10017 (867-0095). Represented elsewhere in US and Canada by TWA. Tours of East Africa; combined tours of Israel and Ethiopia (with El Al), of India and East Africa (with Air India), of Europe and East Africa (with Alitalia) and of East and West Africa (with Air Afrique).

Japan Air Lines, 655 Fifth Avenue, 10022 (758-8850). East Africa via London and Frankfurt.

KLM Royal Dutch Airlines, 609 Fifth Avenue, 10017 (759-2400). Tours of all regions.

Lufthansa German Airlines, 680 Fifth Avenue, 10022 (357-3910). East and Southern Africa.

Pan American World Airways, Pan Am Building, 10017 (973-7700). East and West Africa. Combined tour (with South African Airways) of Rio de Janeiro, South Africa and Amsterdam.

Sabena Belgian World Airlines, 720 Fifth Avenue, 10019 (957-2800). Tours of all regions.

South African Airways, 605 Fifth Avenue, 10017 (421-5952). South Africa and Rhodesia. Combined tour (with Pan Am) of Rio de Janeiro, South Africa and Amsterdam.

Swissair, 608 Fifth Avenue, 10020 (995-3800). Morocco, East, West, Southern Africa.

TAP Portuguese Airways, 601 Fifth Avenue, 10017 (421-9229). Angola, Mozambique, South Africa and Rhodesia via Portugal.

TWA (Trans World Airlines), Tour Department, 605 Third Avenue, 10016 (557-3000). East and Southern Africa.

UTA French Airlines, 509 Madison Avenue, 10022 (421-7250). East, West, Southern Africa.

Varig Brazilian Airlines, 485 Lexington Avenue, 10017 (883-6161). Tour of Botswana via Rio de Janeiro and Johannesburg.

OVERLAND TOURS

Several London-based firms offer organized tours with four-wheel-drive vehicles from the Mediterranean Coast to East Africa, or the other way around. These tours take from seven to 12 weeks to cross the Sahara and Central Africa, camping out part of the way. They're conducted on regular schedules between November and May. Tour members consist of 10 to 15 men and women, usually of several nationalities, and a tour guide and mechanic. Members are expected to be healthy in body and spirit and to assist with cooking and other chores. One-way prices, including food, vary from $600 to $1,000, with extra charges sometimes tossed in for extending the tour to South Africa or to major East African game parks. You can sign up for tours going in either direction (or on a round trip) through agents in New York, Nairobi, Johannesburg, London and other European capitals.

Across Africa Safaris Ltd, P.O. Box 49420, Nairobi, Kenya (21593). Booking agents for several overland tours from East Africa to Europe.

Encounter Overland, 12 Egerton Gardens, Knightsbridge, London, S.W.3. 12-week overland trips between London and Johannesburg.

Minitrek Travels, 5/7 Kingston Hill, Kingston-upon-Thames, Surrey, England. Overland from Marrakesh to Nairobi, 57 days. Two, three and four week overland trips to Ethiopia, Morocco, North Africa.

Overland Trip, 39 Lansdowne Gardens, London, S.W.8. 47-day trips between London and Nairobi.

Penn Overland Tours, 330 Sutter Street, San Francisco, Cal. 94108 (415/391-5728); and c/o University Travel, 44 Brattle Street, Cambridge, Mass. 02138 (617/864-7810). London based firm with two-month overland tour from Marrakesh to Nairobi, and four-week Algiers to Timbuktu and Nairobi to Johannesburg tours.

Safaris, NY 7, Southside, London, W.S.4. London to East Africa tours.

Siafu Expeditions, 60/61 Abbey House, 2/8 Victoria Street, London. 12 weeks overland from Tunis to Nairobi with a firm whose name is the Swahili word for driver ants.

Tourist Centre, 64 Joubert Street, Johannesburg (23-4701). Books overland tours from South Africa to Europe.

Cesia Travel Service, Room 520, 415 Lexington Avenue, New York, N.Y. 10017 (212/697-5771). Booking agent in the US for Encounter, Minitrek, Overland Trip and Siafu tours.

II

CRUISES, PASSENGER SHIPS, FREIGHTERS AND FERRIES

(You can often combine passenger ship and passenger-carrying freighter travel with air trips at discount prices: for instance, with a sea and air ticket from Europe to Africa and/or from Africa to Australia. The leading shipping companies also belong to Inter-change Lines, a syndicate that sells interchangeable tickets at discounts—10 per cent on round trips—to promote connections between ships and airlines.)

Cruises

French Line, 555 Fifth Avenue, New York, N.Y. 10017. Around-the-world cruise with stops in Africa.

Italian Line, 1 Whitehall Street, New York, N. Y. 10004. Cruises from Florida to Caribbean, African and South American ports.

Lindblad Travel, 133 East 55th Street, New York, N.Y. 10022. Indian Ocean cruises.

Norwegian-American Line, 29 Broadway, New York, N.Y. 10006. Cruises from Florida to South American and African ports.

Paquet Lines, 119 West 57th Street, New York, N.Y. 10019. Two- and three-week cruises between Marseille and Dakar.

Raymond and Whitcomb, 400 Madison Avenue, New York, N.Y. 10017. Cruises circling Africa and Mediterranean cruises.

Siosa Line, 450 Seventh Avenue, New York, N.Y. 10001. West African cruises.

Freighters to North and Northeast Africa
(from North America)

American Export Isbrandtsen Lines, 26 Broadway, New York, N.Y. 10004. New York to Casablanca, Tunis and Tripoli.

Concordia Line, c/o Boise-Griffin Steamship Co., 90 Broad Street, New York, N.Y. 10004. New York to the Canary Islands and Alexandria.

Hellenic Lines, 39 Broadway, New York, N.Y. 10006. New York, New Orleans and Houston to Tripoli.

United Arab Maritime Line, 2 rue de l'Ancienne Bourse, Alexandria, Egypt. Toronto, Hamilton, Montreal and Quebec to Alexandria.

Yugoslav Line, c/o N.E.W.S. Shipping Co., 17 Battery Place, New York, N.Y. 10004. New York and Norfolk to Casablanca and Tangier.

Freighters to West and Central Africa
(from North America)

Black Star Line, c/o F. W. Hartmann & Co., 21 West Street, New York, N.Y. 10006. Ghana line. Houston, New Orleans, Montreal and Halifax to Dakar, Freetown, Monrovia, Takoradi, Lagos and Douala.

Farrell Lines, 1 Whitehall Street, New York, N.Y. 10004. New York to Dakar, Conakry, Freetown and Monrovia.

Freighters to East and Southern Africa
and the Indian Ocean (from North America)

Christensen Canadian African Line, c/o Kerr Ltd, 468 St. Johns Street, Montreal. Montreal or Halifax to South Africa, Mozambique and Kenya.

Farrell Lines. New York to South Africa, Mozambique and Kenya.

Hellenic Lines. New York, New Orleans and Houston to South Africa, Mozambique, Kenya, Djibouti and Sudan.

Lykes Lines, 1300 Commerce Building, 821 Gravier Street, New Orleans, La. 70012. (In New York, Lykes Brothers Steamship Co., 17 Battery Place.) Gulf of Mexico ports to South Africa, Mozambique, Kenya and Tanzania.

Nedlloyd Pacific Africa Service, c/o Transpacific Transportation Co., 650 California Street, San Francisco, Cal. 94108. (In New York, 5 World Trade Center.) Los Angeles to South Africa, Mozambique, Kenya, Tanzania and Djibouti.

Orient Overseas Line, 311 California Street, San Francisco, Cal. 94104. (In New York, c/o WDI, Mundy, 350 Fifth Avenue.) Los Angeles or Florida to South America and South Africa.

Robin Line, c/o Moore-McCormack Lines, 2 Broadway, New York, N.Y. 10004. New York to Namibia, South Africa, Mozambique, Tanzania, Kenya and sometimes Madagascar and Mauritius.

South African Marine Corp., 17 Battery Place, New York, N.Y. 10004. New York, Boston, Mobile and Houston to South Africa.

Passenger Ships and Freighters to West and Central Africa (from Europe)

Compagnie Maritime Belge, Agence Maritime Internationale, 1 Meir, Antwerp, Belgium. (In New York, c/o Belgian Line, 5 World Trade Center.) Passenger ships from Antwerp to Tenerife, Matadi and Lobito.

Dafra Line, c/o Agence Maritime Wall, 18 Falconplein, Antwerp. Freighters from Antwerp to Las Palmas, Tenerife, Pointe Noire, Matadi and Boma.

Elder Dempster Lines, c/o Killick Martin, 20 Mark Lane, London. Passenger ships and freighters from Liverpool to Las Palmas, Freetown, Monrovia and Lagos.

Nautilus Line, c/o Keller Shipping, Holbeinstrasse 68, Basel, Switzerland. Freighters from Genoa, Marseille and Naples to West African ports.

Nigerian National Shipping Lines, c/o Killick Martin, London. Freighters from London or Liverpool to Nigeria, Ghana, Sierra Leone and Senegal.

State Shipping Corp. (Black Star Line), 32-38 Dukes Place, London. Freighters from London or Liverpool to Ghana, Nigeria, Sierra Leone.

United Yugoslav Lines, Zupanciceva 24, Piran, Yugoslavia. Freighters from Venice, Trieste and Rijeka to Dakar, Abidjan, Conakry and Tema.

Passenger Ships and Freighters to Southern Africa (from Europe)

Companhía Colonial de Navegação, 63 Rua São Juliao, Lisbon. Passenger ships and freighters from Lisbon to São Tomé, Angola, South Africa and Mozambique.

Holland-Africa Line, c/o Nedlloyd, 5 World Trade Center, New York, N.Y. 10007. Passenger ships from Rotterdam and Southampton to South Africa and Mozambique.

Lauro Lines, c/o E. H. Mundy and Co., 87 Jermyn Street, London; or c/o Armatore, Via Cristoforo Colombo 45, Naples. Passenger ships from Southampton via Genoa and Naples to South Africa, Australia and New Zealand.

Lloyd Triestino, Piazza dell'Unita d'Italia, Trieste, Italy; or c/o Italian Line, New York. Passenger ships from Trieste, Venice and Brindisi to Walvis Bay, Cape Town, Durban and Beira.

Messageries Maritimes, 3 place Sadi-Carnot, Marseille. Passenger ships and freighters from Genoa, Marseille and Naples to South Africa, Indian Ocean ports and Australia.

P & O Line, Gravel Lane, London. Passenger ships from Southampton to Lisbon, South Africa and Australia.

Port Line, c/o Blue Star Line, 3 Lower Regent Street, London; or c/o Norton Lilly and Co., 90 West Street, New York, N.Y. 10006. Freighters from England to South Africa, Mozambique, Australia and New Zealand.

Union Castle Lines, 19-21 Old Bond Street, London; or c/o WDI, Mundy, New York. Passenger liners from Southampton to South Africa.

Passenger Ships and Freighters to East and Northeast Africa (from Europe)

Compagnie Maritime Belge, Antwerp. (In New York, c/o Belgian Line.) Freighters from Antwerp to Mombasa and Dar es Salaam.

Deutsche Afrika Linien (German African Lines), 2 Hamburg 50, West Germany. Freighters from Hamburg, Bremen, Rotterdam and Antwerp to Nacala, Mombasa, Dar es Salaam, Tanga and Mtwara.

Eastern African National Shipping Line, c/o Cayzer, Irving and Co., 2-4 St. Mary Axe, London. Freighters from England to Mombasa, Dar es Salaam, Tanga and Zanzibar.

Hansa Linien, Schlachte 6, Bremen, West Germany. Freighters from Rotterdam or Antwerp to Djibouti, Massawa, Assab and Port Sudan.

Hellenic Mediterranean Lines, Piraeus, Greece. Steamers from Marseille to Alexandria.

Turkish Maritime Lines, Denizyollari Isletmesi, Yolcu Salonu, Sirketci, Istanbul, Turkey. Passenger steamers from Barcelona to Alexandria.

United Arab Maritime Line, Alexandria. Passenger ships from Piraeus and Venice to Alexandria.

Ferries to Morocco

Gibraltar to Tangier; trips once or twice daily.

Algeciras (Spain) to Tangier; one or two trips a day. Málaga to Tangier; five trips a week (daily July 15-October 9). Reservations: Limadet Lines, 3 rue Henri Regnault, Tangier.

Lisbon to Tangier; biweekly. Southern Ferries, Portland Terrace, Southampton, England.

Marseille to Tangier, continuing to Casablanca. Paquet Lines, New York.

Ferry to Algeria

Marseille to Algiers, Oran, Skikda; once or twice a week. C.G.T.M. Line (Compagnie Générale Trans-Mediterranée), 61 boulevard des Dames, Marseille.

Ferries to Tunisia

Marseille to Tunis; two or three times a week. C.G.T.M. Line.
Genoa to Tunis; weekly. D.F.D.S., 8 Berkeley Square, London.
Naples to Tunis via Palermo; weekly. Tirrenia Line, c/o Italian Lines, New York.

Ferries to Ceuta and Melilla

Algeciras to Ceuta; once or twice a day. Almeria to Melilla; three times a week. Málaga to Melilla; six times a week. Companía Transmediterranea, Zurbano 73, Apartado de Correos 982, Madrid.

Passenger Ships and Freighters
(from Asia to Africa)

British India Navigation, c/o Smith Mackenzie, Kilindini Road, Mombasa, Kenya; also P & O Building, Leadenhall Street, London, E.C.3. Passenger ships from Bombay to Seychelles, Mombasa and Dar es Salaam.

Shipping Corporation of India, Steelcrete House, Dinshaw Wacha Road, Bombay, India. Freighters from Bombay to Mombasa.

Royal Interocean Lines, Prins Hendrikkade 108-114, Amsterdam, Holland. Freighters from Japan, Hong Kong and Singapore to East, Southern and West Africa.

III

EDUCATIONAL TOURS

These come in a variety of forms, some emphasizing formal education (usually with lectures and seminars directed by African faculty members) and offering academic credit. The following organizations have experience in the African educational tour business.

American Forum for International Study, 15 Columbus Circle, New York, N.Y. 10023 (tel. 212/581-7888). Three-week summer study tours of East and West Africa, co-sponsored by University of Massachusetts. Two-week trips to Ghana during December and January.

American Youth Hostels, 535 West End Avenue, New York, N.Y. 10024 (212/799-8510). Summer camping and minibus tours primarily for high school students. East Africa, Morocco and Western Europe.

Association for Academic Travel Abroad, 280 Madison Avenue, New York, N.Y. 10016 (212/679-5280). Summer study tours of West and North Africa, co-sponsored by American University and other universities.

Audubon Society African Workship, Cahill-Laughlin Tours, 20 East 46th

Street, New York, N.Y. 10017 (212/986-1500), or local Audubon Society chapters. Three-week summer tours of East African bird and wildlife sanctuaries.

Educational Expeditions International, 68 Leonard Street, Belmont, Mass. 02178 (617/489-3030). Three-week trips throughout the year led by anthropologist, archaeologist or natural scientist.

Educators to Africa Association, African-American Institute, 866 United Nations Plaza, New York, N.Y. 10017 (212/421-2500). Summer seminars for teachers.

Experiment in International Living, Putney, Vt. 05346 (802/257-7751). Summer programs in Liberia, Ghana and Sierra Leone.

Explorers Club, 46 East 70th Street, New York, N.Y. 10021 (212/628-8383). Three-week summer scientific expeditions in East Africa. Scholarships for high school and college students, especially those from minority groups.

Foreign Study League, Box 1920, Salt Lake City, Utah 84110 (801/487-1761). Four-week summer study tour of East Africa and Europe for high school students. Study tours also organized for adult organizations.

Friends World College, Study Travel Department, Lloyd Harbor, Huntington, N.Y. 11743 (516/549-5000). Six-week summer tours for small groups to Southern and East Africa and Israel. Emphasis on meeting people, visiting rural areas, studying race relations. Also, visits to wildlife areas.

Institute of International Education, Division of Study Abroad Programs, 809 United Nations Plaza, New York, N.Y. 10017 (212/867-0400, ext. 471). Summer seminars, primarily for teachers, at University of Ghana.

National Parks and Conservation Association, 1701 18th Street NW, Washington, D.C. (202/667-3352). Three-week tours of East African national parks and ecology projects throughout the year for groups of 10-15.

Ramparts magazine, 2054 University Avenue, Berkeley, Cal. 94704 (415/845-8807). Three-week summer tour of East Africa focusing on Tanzania.

Scholastic International, 50 West 44th Street, New York, N.Y. 10036 (212/867-7700). Summer tour (42 days) for high school students; four weeks of study in Nairobi plus stopovers in Europe.

Students Abroad, 771 West End Avenue, New York, N.Y. 10025 (212/928-7878). One-month nature tour of East Africa for high school and college students; camping, hiking, climbing Mt. Kilimanjaro.

Syracuse University, Program of East African Studies, Division of International Programs Abroad, 335 Comstock Avenue, Syracuse, N.Y. 13210 (315/476-5541). Summer seminars for teachers and others in East Africa. Includes four weeks at University of Nairobi and two weeks in the field.

Teen-Age Safaris, P.O. Box 14662, Nairobi, Kenya. Summer camping and climbing trip led by American teachers living in East Africa.

University Experiments in Foreign Exploration, P.O. Box 898, Chapel Hill, N.C. 27514. Seven-week summer camping trips to remote areas of Morocco, Algeria and Tunisia. Primarily for undergraduates.

STUDY PROGRAMS AT AFRICAN UNIVERSITIES

Several African universities have initiated programs specifically for American students. Information about these programs can be obtained from the African-American Institute, 866 United Nations Plaza, New York, N.Y. 10017 (tel. 212/421-2500). This agency also provides information on scholarship assistance and sells (for $3.75) a directory of African colleges and universities.

American sponsors of study programs:

American Institute for Foreign Study, Dept. T-AYE, Greenwich, Conn. 06830 (203/869-9090). Administers a one-year program at University of Nairobi (Kenya).

California State Colleges (International Programs), 5670 Wilshire Boulevard, Los Angeles, Cal. 90036 (213/938-2981). One and two semester programs in Ghana.

University of California at Santa Barbara (Education Abroad), Santa Barbara, Cal. 93106 (805/961-2311). Coordinates programs at Universities of Ghana and Nairobi for students at University of California campuses.

DePauw University (African Studies Center), Greencastle, Ind. 46135 (317/653-9721). Coordinates for group of midwestern colleges a one-year program at University of Dakar (Senegal). Proficiency in French required.

Kalamazoo College (Africa Program), Kalamazoo, Mich. 49001 (616/343-1551). Undergraduate programs in Liberia, Kenya, Nigeria, Ghana and Sierra Leone.

Kenyon College (Middle East Program), Gambier, Ohio 43022 (614/427-2244). Program at American University in Cairo.

Macalester College (International Programs), St. Paul, Minn. 55101. (612/647-6221). Programs in East Africa.

Note: Individual arrangements often can be made with African educational institutions. Extensive programs in African studies on undergraduate and graduate levels are offered by the University of Ghana, Fourah Bay University College (Sierra Leone), the University of Nairobi (Kenya) and Makerere University (Uganda).

WORK AND SERVICE OPPORTUNITIES

Many African states invite the services of skilled persons, especially those willing to work themselves out of a job by training their African replacements. However, with unemployment widespread and work permits hard to obtain, there are few opportunities for foreigners without specific and needed skills. Don't go to Africa expecting to find a job after you get there.

Information is available from these organizations:

•American Council of Voluntary Agencies for Foreign Service, 200 Park Avenue South, New York, N.Y. 10003 (tel. 212/777-8210). Has a Directory

of African Technical Assistance Programs of Non-Profit Organizations ($3).
´ Association of American Medical Colleges (Division of International Medical Education), 1346 Connecticut Avenue NW, Washington, D.C. 20036 (202/466-5100). Lists organizations utilizing American physicians.

Canadian University Service Overseas (CUSO), Ottawa, Ontario, Canada (613/237-0390). Recruits Canadian university graduates to teach for two years in African secondary schools or to perform other jobs.

Catholic Relief Services, 350 Fifth Avenue, New York, N.Y. 10016 (212/594-9300). Administers American Catholic programs overseas.

Commission on Voluntary Service in Action (Youth Service Projects), 475 Riverside Drive, Room 832, New York, N.Y. 10027 (212/870-2707). Provides information on work camps, community service, study seminars and individual service in ecumenical church projects around the world.

● Crossroads Africa, 150 Fifth Avenue, New York, N.Y. 10011 (212/675-4080). Launched in 1958 by the late Dr. James Robinson, Crossroads Africa has sent hundreds of young Americans to African countries each year to work on such projects as the construction of village schools or clinics. Participants are expected to pay a substantial portion of their costs, but scholarships are available.

● Institute of International Education (Teaching Abroad), 809 United Nations Plaza, New York, N.Y. 10017 (212/867-0400). Provides information on teacher exchanges and other opportunities for teaching jobs.

International Executive Service Corps, 545 Madison Avenue, New York, N.Y. 10022 (212/688-6400). Advises retired businessmen on opportunities for short-term consulting and other assignments.

● International Voluntary Service Organization, 1555 Connecticut Avenue NW, Washington, D.C. 20036 (202/387-5533). Progenitor of the US Peace Corps, this multi-national organization recruits skilled persons for assignments in Africa and elsewhere, usually for one or two years.

● Mennonite Central Committee (Personnel Services), 2 South 12th Street, Akron, Pa. 17501 (717/859-1151). Recruits teachers, agriculturalists, mechanics and others.

National Council of Churches (Board of Foreign Missions), 475 Riverside Drive, New York, N.Y. 10027 (212/870-2200). Clearinghouse for overseas programs of several Protestant denominations. Emphasis on laymen with technical skills and religious commitment. Several churches, including Adventist and Methodist, also have denominational service programs.

Peace Corps, 806 Connecticut Avenue NW, Washington, D.C. 20006 (202/382-2841). Increasing emphasis is being placed on older and more experienced volunteers with technical skills, although more than half the volunteers currently serving in Africa are liberal arts graduates teaching in secondary schools.

Trans-Century, 1789 Columbia Road NW, Washington, D.C. 20009 (202/462-6661). Recruits teachers for African colleges (two-year contracts).

United Church of Christ (Specialized Ministries), RD 2, Pottstown, Pa.

19464 (215/326-4975). Arranges placement in summer work camps.
● United Nations (Division of Personnel), New York, N.Y. 10017
(212/754-1234). The United Nations Development Program and specialized UN agencies (like UNESCO and the World Health Organization)
have openings in Africa for qualified personnel on two-year assignments.
The UN also has initiated its own multi-national program for volunteers.

IV

SUGGESTED READING

The reading list that follows is intended as an introduction to Africa.
Most of these titles can be obtained in inexpensive paperback editions.

General Collections and Handbooks

Wilfred Cartey and Martin Kilson, eds., *The Africa Reader*, Vintage, 1971.
Vol. I: Colonial Africa; Vol. 2: Independent Africa. An intelligent collection of essays and historical writings, most of them by Africans, dealing
with political and social problems of the past century.

Colin Legum, ed., *Africa Handbook*, Penguin, 1969. A comprehensive review of essential African political and economic data with special essays
on cultural, religious and other subjects.

John Paden and Edward J. Soja, eds., *The African Experience*, Vol. I:
Essays, Northwestern University Press, 1970. A massive, scholarly but
inexpensive collection of essays on African history, society and culture.

History

J. Desmond Clark, *The Pre-History of Africa*, Praeger, 1970. An authoritative survey of what is known about man's origins in Africa, to 1,000 BC.

Roland Oliver and J. D. Fage, *A Short History of Africa*, Penguin, 1970. A
concise introduction from pre-history to modern times.

Basil Davidson, *The African Past*, Penguin, 1966. Well-selected documents
with intelligent commentary on African history.

Religion, Culture and Society

Basil Davidson, *The African Genius*, Little-Brown, 1969. An absorbing,
sympathetic interpretation of African culture and its roots.

John S. Mbiti, *African Religions and Philosophy*, Doubleday Anchor, 1970.
Traditional and modern beliefs described by an African theologian.

Colin Turnbull, *The Lonely African*, Doubleday-Anchor, 1963. The first-
person story of Africans caught in social change, told by an anthropologist.

P. C. Lloyd, *Africa in Social Change*, Penguin, 1969. An introduction to Africa's current problems and the attitudes of its elites toward them.

Jacques Maquet, *Africanity, the Cultural Unity of Black Africa* (trans. Joan Rayfield), Oxford, 1972. A distinguished anthropologist's interpretation of cultural growth throughout the continent.

Art and Music

Frank Willett, *African Art*, Praeger, 1971. Recent, comprehensive, sensible, scholarly introduction to a most exciting subject; paperback.

Ulli Beier, *Contemporary Art in Africa*, Praeger, 1968. Authoritative critical survey of modern painting, sculpture and architecture in Africa, written by a patron-authority.

Miriam Makeba, *The World of African Song*, Random House-Quadrangle, 1969. The great South African singer discusses music's importance.

John Storm Roberts, *Black Music of Two Worlds*, Praeger, 1972. An authoritative survey of traditional and city music in Africa, the US and Latin America.

Geography, Politics, Economics

William A. Hance, *The Geography of Modern Africa*, Columbia University Press, 1964. Massive and authoritative survey of Africa's natural and human resources.

Paul Fordham, *The Geography of African Affairs*, Penguin, 1968. Succinct, thorough, sensible, inexpensive introduction to the continent.

Frantz Fanon, *The Wretched of the Earth*, Grove Press, 1963. Classic study of domination and revolution by Martiniquan psychiatrist engaged in the Algerian war of liberation.

Immanuel Wallerstein, *Africa, the Politics of Unity*, Random House-Vintage, 1967. Readable account of political milestones in recent African development.

Literature

Ezekiel Mphahlele, ed., *African Writing Today*, Penguin, 1967. One of the best collections of modern Africa's prose and poetry, with strong political tonalities, by one of its leading writers.

Gerald Moore and Ulli Beier, eds., *Modern Poetry from Africa*, Penguin, 1968. A judicious sampling of African poets, including translations.

Nature and Wildlife

Archie Carr, *The Land and Wildlife of Africa*, Time-Life, 1964.

Bernhard and Michael Grzimek, *Serengeti Shall Not Die*, Fontana, 1960. Passionate account of efforts to save Africa's greatest aggregate of wildlife.

Louis S. B. Leakey, *Animals of East Africa*, National Geographic, 1969.
J. G. Williams and R. Fennessy, *Birds of Africa*, Collins, 1966. The most accessible of many expert descriptions of African birdlife.

Periodicals

Africa (London), political and economic monthly.
Africa Report (New York), general information on Africa, bimonthly.
Africa Today (Denver), political quarterly.
African Arts (UCLA), cultural quarterly with color photos.
African Development (London), business and economic monthly.
Jeune Afrique (Paris), general information weekly in French.
Journal of Modern African Studies (England), academic quarterly.
Transition (Ghana), cultural and intellectual articles, bimonthly.
West Africa (London), West African political and economic coverage, twice a month.

AFRICAN ART COLLECTIONS IN AMERICAN MUSEUMS

Each of the following museums has a permanent collection of African art consisting of at least 100 pieces. Asterisks designate collections not regularly displayed but which, in most cases, can be seen by appointment.

Alabama: George Washington Carver Museum, Tuskegee Institute (360 pieces). *Arizona:* Heard Museum of Anthropology and Primitive Art,* Phoenix (100); Arizona State Museum,* University of Arizona, Tucson (400). *California:* Robert H. Lowie Museum of Anthropology,* University of California at Berkeley (905); Long Beach Museum of Art* (190); Museum of Ethnic Arts,* University of California at Los Angeles (10,000). *Connecticut:* Peabody Museum of Natural History,* Yale University (1,900). *District of Columbia:* Museum of African Art (3,000). *Illinois:* Dusable Museum of African-American History, Chicago (300); Field Museum of Natural History, Chicago (17,000); Illinois State Museum,* Springfield (100). *Indiana:* Indiana Fine Arts Museum,* Bloomington (700); Indiana University Museum, Bloomington (2,500). *Massachusetts:* Peabody Museum of Archaeology and Ethnology, Cambridge (25,000); Peabody Museum of Salem (3,000). *Michigan:* Museum of Anthropology,* Ann Arbor (300+); Detroit Institute of Arts (500); Michigan State University Museum, East Lansing (444); Oakland University Art Gallery,* Rochester (267). *Missouri:* City Art Museum of St. Louis (200). *Nebraska:* Joslyn Art Museum, Omaha (150). *New Jersey:* Newark Museum (1,000); Museum of Natural History,* Princeton University (200+). *New York:* Brooklyn Children's Museum* (400); Brooklyn Museum (2,000); Buffalo Museum of Science (750); Ithaca College Museum of Art* (190); American Museum of Natural History, New York (26,000); Museum of Primitive

Art,* New York (600); Rochester Museum* (200). *Ohio:* Cincinnati Art Museum (several hundred); Cleveland Museum of Art (200+). *Pennsylvania:* Museum of the Philadelphia Civic Center (2,000); University of Pennsylvania Museum, Philadelphia (10,000); Carnegie Museum, Pittsburgh (1,500). *Tennessee:* Carl van Vechten Gallery of Fine Arts, Fisk University, Nashville (350). *Texas:* Texas Memorial Museum, Austin (150); Dallas Museum of Fine Arts (224). *Virginia:* College Museum, Hampton Institute (950). *Washington:* Seattle Art Museum (150). *Wisconsin:* Logan Museum of Anthropology,* Beloit College (300); Milwaukee Public Museum (580).

V

CONVERSION TABLES

Distance: Kilometers—Miles

km	miles or km	miles
1.609	1	0.621
3.218	2	1.242
4.827	3	1.864
6.437	4	2.485
8.046	5	3.107
16.093	10	6.214
40.232	25	15.535
80.465	50	31.070
160.930	100	62.136
804.650	500	310.680

Temperature

Centigrade	Fahrenheit
− 5	+ 23
0	+ 32
+ 5	+ 41
+10	+ 50
+20	+ 68
+30	+ 86
+36.9	+ 98.4
+40	+104
+50	+122

Weight: Kilograms—Pounds

kg	lb. or kg	lb
0.453	1	2.205
0.907	2	4.409
1.360	3	6.614
1.814	4	8.818
2.268	5	11.023
4.535	10	22.046
9.071	20	44.092
11.339	25	55.116
22.680	50	110.232
45.359	100	220.464

Liquid Capacity

Litres	Pints
0.236	0.5
0.473	1.0
0.946	2.0
1.419	3.0
1.892	4.0

	Gallons
3.785	1.0
7.570	2.0
11.355	3.0
15.140	4.0
18.925	5.0
37.853	10.0

Clothing Sizes

Men's

Suits

American	34	35	36	37	38	39	40	42
British	34	35	36	37	38	39	40	42
Others	34	36	38	40	42	44	46	48

Shirts

American	14½	15	15¼	15¾	16	16½	17	17¼
British	14½	15	15¼	15¾	16	16½	17	17¼
Others	37	38	39	40	41	42	43	44

Shoes

American	8	8½	9½	10½	11	12	12½
British	7½	8	9	10	10½	11½	12
Others	41	42	43	44	45	46	47

Women's

Dresses

American	8	10	12	14	16	18
British	10	12	14	16	18	20
Others	38	40	42	44	46	48

Shoes

American	5	5½	6	6½	7	7½	8	8½
British	3½	4	4½	5	5½	6	6½	7
Others	36	36½	37	37½	38	38½	39	39½

Acknowledgments

We are grateful to the following Africa travelers for their invaluable counsel in the preparation of this book.

Eugene B. Abrams, Wendy Abt, Ted Alexander, Michael Dei Anang, Corinne P. Armstrong, Robert Plant Armstrong, J. H. Asamoah, Pauline H. Baker, Wally Baker, Asgar Barday, Patrick J. Best, Frances Blackwell, Derek Blades, Ben G. Blount, Y. Mpekesa Bongoy, Paul Bory, Brack Brown.

Also, Kent Calder, Barbara Callaway, Mr. and Mrs. Ralph Campbell, John R. Cartwright, Al Castagno, Leo Cefkin, Everett Chard, J. D. F. Colinese, Julien Cornell, Mick D. Cornish, Chester A. Crocker, Daniel J. Crowley, Richard T. Curley, Philip D. Curtin, Fernando Ferreira Da Silva Correia.

Also, John Damis, Ralph K. Davidson, Robert Dean, Marilyn Dexheimer, Gretchen Dihoff, Margarita Dobert, Robert Dodoo, Judy Dollenmayer, Gifford B. Doxsee, David Dunlop, Peter Easton, Fred Eckhard, Joanne and Carl Eicher, Ousmane Elola, M. Esclapon, Aaron Etra.

Also, R. W. Faville, Larry Fellows, Reed Fendrick, Bruce Fetter, Robert I. Fleming, Herbert and Claire Floyd, Philip J. Foster, Charles R. Frank, Jr., John Gedeist, Ann M. Gooch, Joel and Rhona Gregory, C. W. Gusewelle.

Also, David Hapgood, Bernard and Carol Harawa, Lee Haring, James T. Harris, Jr., Jane Banfield Haynes, Molly Hazen, Donald F. Heisel, Jim Hoagland, Mary Kay Hobbs, Allan Hoben, Michael Horowitz, A. J. Hughes, Arthur H. House, Randy Hyman.

Also, Levi L. Igambi, Nancy Iredale, William O. Jones, Cheikh Hamidou Kane, Emma L. Kearse, James King, Alison Kouteh, Clive Lawrence, Victor T. Le Vine, Michael Leapman, Eugene C. Lee, David Lucas, E. Thea Lucas, Edwin Lufte.

Also, David and Nanoo McAdams, Angus McDermid, Alexander MacDonald, Wyatt MacGaffey, Brenda B. Mahoney, Harry Makler, Marjorie and Hal March, Bern Marcowitz, Jim Mittelman, Emmet V. Mittlebeeler, Susanne Mueller, Peter Newman, Ernest S. Nounou, David and Marina Ottaway, Bruce Oudes, Ken Owen.

Also, Eric Pace, Ann and John Paden, R. Pankhurst, Adolphus A. Pater-

954

son, Scott R. Pearson, Betty Plewes, Christian P. Potholm, Henri Razanatseheno, Idrian Resnick, Bryant Robey, Mort Rosenblum, Bernice Rosenthal, Robert Rotberg, Donald Rothchild, Kersi Rustomji.

Also, Paul Saenz, Robert D. H. Sallery, David Saltman, Marc and Sheilah Serfaty, Sayre P. Schatz, Don Shannon, George W. Shepherd, Jr., Don Simpson, Parmeet Singh, William E. Smith, John Spencer, F. Joseph Spieler, Ronald E. Springwater, Harry Stein, David and Ginger Stillman, Norman A. Stillman, Kathy Stone, Herb Straub.

Also, C. R. Taylor, Mustapha Tlilli, Norman Uphoff, Etienne van de Walle, Pierre L. van den Berghe, George J. Volger, W. Dabney Waller, Robert D. Ward, William R. Watson, Susan Wayne, Peter R. Webb, Lyon Weidman, Warren Weinstein, Herb and Kathy Werlin, Gordon Wilson, Jean Kennedy Wolford, Karin and Ed Woltman, John Worrall, Robert M. Wren, Robert Wyatt, Hans Zell.

We also wish to express our deep appreciation to Shelby Allen, Nancy McKeon and Nancy Turck for special assignments and to a gallant corps of editorial and research associates: Ronny Ariessohn, Victor Backus, Linda Colonna, Rhoda Morganthal and Anne Pritchard.

Photographs

Photographs were provided by Louise E. Jefferson, the African-American Institute, United Nations, UNESCO, UNICEF and TAP.

Index

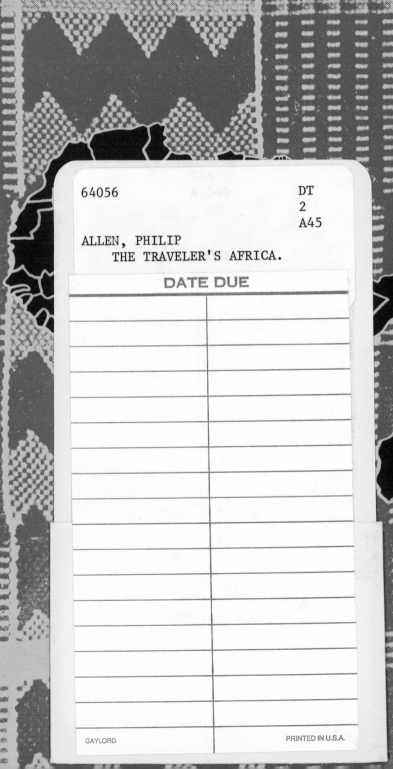

64056   DT
                                         2
                                         A45

ALLEN, PHILIP
     THE TRAVELER'S AFRICA.

DATE DUE